# Writers' & Artists' YEARBOOK 2005

# Writers' & Artists'
# YEARBOOK
# 2005

**Ninety-eighth Edition**

**A directory for writers, artists, playwrights,
writers for film, radio and television,
designers, illustrators and photographers**

**A & C Black · London**

© 2004 A & C Black Publishers Ltd
37 Soho Square, London W1F 0BJ

A CIP catalogue record for this book is available
from the British Library.

ISBN 0-7136-6936-5

Printed in Great Britain by
William Clowes Ltd, Beccles, Suffolk

This edition of *Writers' & Artists' Yearbook* is dedicated to the memory of Giles Gordon, one of the great literary agents of the twentieth century.

# Contents

# Foreword

Maeve Binchy is an award-winning author of several volumes of short stories and novels, including *The Lilac Bus* and *Echoes* (both adapted for television), *Circle of Friends* (adapted for film) and *Scarlet Feather*, which was an international bestseller for six months. Her latest novel, *Quentins*, was a number one bestseller in hardback and when published in paperback went straight to number one in *The Sunday Times* bestsellers list. Maeve Binchy was awarded the Lifetime Achievement Award at the British Book Awards in 1999.

I loved this *Yearbook* 30 years ago when I had written nothing and I love it to this day.

The *Writers' & Artists' Yearbook* is like a magic carpet that would carry the writer anywhere. Into a world filled with amazing magazines about motorcycle maintenance, articles about proofreading advice, about foreign agents, picture research, social security benefits. Things that we might never aspire to at the start of a career. Imagine working out what tax we should expect to pay on our literary earnings, we who had not yet earned one single penny from writing.

The *Yearbook* is like a scaffolding on a building, it sort of suggests that it is half possible to climb up this unreal dream mountain of being a writer. It takes us seriously when our friends laugh their heads off at the notion that we might actually become real writers with real books out there in the shops.

I used to read people's advice too seriously. I thought that established authors must be making it all up. Fancy famous writers being anxious, full of self doubt and weighed down with rejection slips! The very idea of it was ludicrous.

But now I know only too well that we all have to go through a period of apprenticeship and that this *Yearbook* is our trusty guide.

Do I have any of my own rules to share? Of course I do. I was a teacher for eight years and teachers know how to run the world – in fact they *should* be running the world in a fairer society. So of course I have some hints, which if you follow will bring you success. Sit up straight now and listen carefully.

First, write about what you know. I don't know anything about international banking, *haute couture*, espionage or complicated group sex. No point in me writing about any of that. I'd get it wrong. Terribly wrong. But I do know about families and friendships and betrayals, and hopes and ambitions. And I know about Ireland and England and bits of America and bits of Greece and Italy. So I feel safe and comfortable writing about these places.

Second, write as you speak. Not in someone else's accent, but in your own. I speak very fast without much pause for breath. So I write that way too, with not much pause for punctuation. It sounds more natural that way, more authentic somehow. I can always spot a phoney accent in a conversation and it's also easy to see it in writing.

Third, use your eyes as if they were a camera. Swoop around you and try to imprint on your mind what a scene looks like. Suppose you were going to describe a meeting between two people in a shopping mall. Are you sure you know what a shopping mall looks like? Maybe you only half know and therefore will only write a vague misty background to your scene. But if you got into the habit of taking mental photographs you'd do it much better because you will have made the effort to notice things properly and get the atmosphere right.

Fourth, use your ears as a tape recorder, and listen to the way people talk to each other. This will help your dialogue no end. People don't make speeches at each other; they interrupt and half finish sentences. I never hang up on a crossed line as you can hear grand things if you listen carefully. I often follow people to know how their conversation will end. If you look into the middle distance as if you were not the sharpest knife in the drawer they don't seem to notice. The main thing is to not appear too interested, or be seen writing anything down.

Lastly – and this very important – you *have* to send your manuscript to somebody when you've finally written it. Publishers don't come by at dead of night and break into your house and look for it. You have to be brave and let your beloved script out of your hands and give it to someone who might well fling it back at you saying politely that it's rubbish.

This last is the hardest of all, daring to let it go. And that's where the *Writers' & Artists' Yearbook* will be your friend. Turn its pages and you'll see details of publishers listed, *and* agents *and* newspapers *and* magazines. Surely one of them will like us?

The sheer volume of information in the *Yearbook* gives encouragement to the brittle and vulnerable hearts of would-be writers.

**Maeve Binchy**
**March 2004**

# Newspapers and magazines

## Getting started

Of the titles included in the newspapers and magazines section of this *Yearbook*, almost all offer opportunities to the writer. Many publications do not appear in our lists because the market they offer for the freelance writer is either too small or too specialised, or both. To help writers get started, we offer some guidelines to consider before submitting material.

### Study the market
- The importance of studying the market cannot be overemphasised. It is an editor's job to know what readers want, and to see that they get it. Thus, freelance contributions must be tailored to fit a specific market; subject, theme, treatment, length, etc must meet the editor's requirements. This is discussed further in *Writing for newspapers* on page 3 and *Writing for magazines* on page 26.
- Magazine editors frequently complain about the unsuitability of many submissions, so before sending an article or feature, always carefully study the editorial requirements of the magazine – not only for the subjects dealt with but for the approach, treatment, style and length. These comments will be obvious to the practised writer but the beginner can be spared much disappointment by buying copies of magazines and studying their target market in depth.
- For additional information on markets, see the UK volume of *Willings Press Guide*, which is usually available at local reference libraries.

### Check with the editor first
- Before submitting material to any newspaper or magazine it is advisable first to contact the relevant editor. The listings beginning on page 7 give the names of editors for each section of the national newspapers. A quick telephone call or email to a magazine will establish the name of the relevant commissioning editor.
- Most newspapers and many magazines expect copy to be sent by email.
- Editors who accept postal submissions expect them to be well presented: neatly typed, double spaced, with good margins, on A4 paper is the standard to aim at. Always enclose an sae for the return of unsuitable material.
- It is not advisable to send illustrations 'on spec'; check with the editor first. See *Digital imaging for writers* on page 611; listings of *Picture agencies and libraries* start on page 463. For a list of publications which accept cartoons see page 757.

### Explore the overseas market
- The lists of overseas newspapers and magazines in the *Yearbook* contain only a selection of those journals which offer a market for the freelance writer. For fuller listings, refer to *Willings Press Guide Volume 2 International*. The overseas market for stories and articles is small and editors often prefer their

fiction to have a local setting. Some editors require their contributors to be residents of that country.

- Some overseas magazine titles have little space for freelance contributions but many of them will consider outstanding work.
- Proposals or finished articles mailed from the UK overseas (including the Republic of Ireland) should always be accompanied by return postage in the form of International Reply Coupons (IRCs). IRCs can be exchanged in any foreign country for stamps representing the minimum postage payable on a letter sent from one country to another. For further information *tel* (08457) 223344.
- Using an agent to syndicate material written for the overseas market is worth considering. Most agents operate on an international basis and are more aware of current market requirements. Again, return postage should always be included. Listings for *Syndicates, news and press agencies* start on page 121.

## Understand how newspapers and syndicates work
- The larger newspapers and magazines buy many of their stories, and the smaller papers buy general articles, through well-known syndicates. Another avenue for writers is to send printed copies of their stories published at home to an agent for syndication overseas.
- For the supply of news, most of the larger UK and overseas newspapers depend on their own staffs and press agencies. The most important overseas newspapers have permanent representatives in Britain who keep them supplied, not only with news of special interest to the country concerned, but also with regular summaries of British news and with articles on events of particular importance. While many overseas newspapers and magazines have a London office, it is usual for manuscripts from freelance contributors to be submitted to the headquarters' editorial office overseas. Listings of *National newspapers UK and Ireland* start on page 7.

## Payment
- It has always been our aim to obtain and publish the rates of payment offered for contributions by newspapers and magazines. Many publications, however, are reluctant to state a standard rate, since the value of a contribution may be dependent not upon length but upon the standing of the writer or of the information given. Many other periodicals prefer to state 'by negotiation' or 'by arrangement', rather than giving precise payment information.
- A number of magazines will accept and pay for letters to the Editor, brief fillers and gossip paragraphs, as well as puzzles and quizzes. *Magazines by subject area* starting on page 741 provides a rough guide to these markets.

## See also...
- *Regional newspapers UK and Ireland*, page 15
- Newspapers are listed together with magazines for *Australia* (page 108), *Canada* (page 113), *New Zealand* (page 116), *South Africa* (page 117) and *USA* (page 120)

# Writing for newspapers

Richard Keeble outlines the huge scope for freelance journalists writing for newspapers.

Every week more than 160 million newspapers are either sold or given away in Britain. The national mainstream press comprises 10 morning dailies and 10 Sundays. The broadsheets (*Daily Telegraph*, *Financial Times*, *Guardian*, *Independent*, *The Times*) sell around 2.82 million copies daily, the mid-market tabloids (*Daily Mail*, *Daily Express*) 3.35 million, and the red top tabloids (*Daily Star*, *Daily Mirror*, *Sun*) 6.22 million. On Sundays, the broadsheets (*Observer*, *Independent on Sunday*, *Sunday Telegraph and Sunday Times*) sell 2.88 million copies; the *Mail on Sunday* and *Sunday Express* 3.21 million; while the *News of the World*, *Sunday Mirror*, *Sunday People* and *Sunday Sport* sell 7.07 million. At the local level, 37.5 million regional dailies are sold or given away every week, while over six million local paid-for weeklies and 30 million free weeklies are distributed. In addition, there are a vast range of alternative peace-movement, ethnic-minority, religious and leftist newspapers.

Newspapers clearly offer writers an enormous range of opportunities. And freelancing has its definite attractions. As a freelance you can often work from home and so avoid the hassles of office politics and commuting. You can develop a specialist interest. You may have a particular knowledge of wines (built up through attending tasting classes, holidays and reading) and be familiar with some prominent names in the business. Writing reviews and features in this area for the few specialist newspaper sections could well prove financially (and personally) rewarding.

## The freelance challenge

Yet launching into a freelance career is not easy. Many freelances are former full-time staffers who have developed a specialism, sent out linage (freelance copy paid by the line) to nationals and then, through either choice or redundancy, taken the plunge and gone solo or started a small agency. With newspapers increasingly laying off experienced full-time staffers, competition amongst freelances has intensified. And while freelances enjoy certain 'freedoms' not permitted to staff writers, they still cannot avoid the constraints and ethical dilemmas that all journalists face. For instance, you may be very critical of the political and ethical stances of the mainstream press. Thus you may decide to contribute (largely unpaid) to an ethnic-minority, left-wing, religious, peace-movement or environmental newspaper or news magazine and gain your money from other employment. One of the greatest journalists of the last century, George Orwell, committed himself to small-scale, left-wing, literary journals and largely ignored the seductive appeal of Fleet Street. It was his deliberate political choice. Or you may be happy to sell your copy to a Rupert Murdoch-owned newspaper (such as *The Times* or *Sunday Times*). But always be fully aware there are political and ethical implications behind your journalistic decisions.

## Why contacts are crucial

Very few freelances are generalists. They instead develop a specialism (or a discreet range of linked specialisms) and become valuable to editors because of their specialist knowledge, experience and contacts. Thus your major task in launching into a freelance career is to build up a contacts book containing sources' phone numbers, addresses, fax and pager numbers, email and website details. You may have to go to meetings, conferences and press launches, and/or ring up spokespersons of political parties, companies and campaigning bodies. All this takes a lot of time. But from your sources will come ideas for stories, details of events to attend, quotes, and specialist (and hopefully exclusive) information. Many freelances place contact details on a computer database as a back-up while those investigating sensitive issues (such as national security, spying, the arms and drugs trade, share dealings) tend to keep details of important exclusive sources in their heads. Police have been known to raid the homes and computers of journalists involved in sensitive areas and thus every step has to be taken to preserve the anonymity of such contacts.

The skills of interviewing are crucial to all freelances. You normally have to prepare in advance of the meeting and be confident enough in the subject to maintain a flowing interview – while recording accurately at the same time. It's far from easy. You may be tempted to use a tape recorder. But what if it breaks down at the crucial moment? For all interviews you need to make a written note. You may not have the time to learn a shorthand technique such as Teeline (in which 100 words a minute is the industry standard) but you do need to develop your own reliable rapid writing technique.

Get to know the market for your specialist area of interest. Study the different writing styles, the lengths of the sentences and articles in the differing publications. Try to establish, by examining byline patterns, the amount of freelance work accepted and in which particular areas. Analyse the advertising in the publications to get a feel for the intended target readership. Read recent issues carefully to get an idea of the stories covered and, more importantly, not covered. See who are the prominent sources used in stories and those who have been missed or marginalised. Get used to creating files of cuttings. Well-maintained filing cabinets can be invaluable research tools. And when you read documents, journal articles and books, file the notes from these too. But don't become over-reliant on cuttings. Journalists often report inaccurately so checking is usually necessary. Significantly, in its March 1992 report, the Press Complaints Commission (the watchdog promoting an ethical Code of Practice for print journalists) commented: "Cuttings are an essential part of newspaper research but too many journalists now seem to act in the belief that to copy from 10 old stories is better than to write a new one with confirmation by proper fresh enquiry."

## The need for imaginative flair

As a freelance you will have to develop a special journalistic imagination. Ideas will be your lifeblood. A new report highlights a national survey showing students are increasingly going without sleep and as a result their academic work and health are suffering. Do a local follow-up: go to the colleges and universities in your area and interview students, counsellors, lecturers, etc about the issues involved. Better still, take the opposite line and do a feature for the women's section of a Sunday newspaper highlighting career women who need only a few hours sleep a day – and yet still thrive. Or take a major international story such as the dispute between the two nuclear-armed neighbours India and Pakistan. Again think local. Many British cities have Indian and Pakistani communities but their views have been largely ignored. So why not interview people from these countries about the issues? Are they afraid? What do they see as the political factors behind the crisis and what are their solutions? Are there any human interest angles to help humanise the reports? In all these cases you have to move quickly while the issues are still newsworthy.

A lot of starting-up freelances imagine a life sitting at home bashing out on the computer words of wisdom on a range of topics to an admiring public. But it is rare for a freelance career to start in this way. Columnists tend to be experienced journalists, novelists, comedians or other media celebrities and their views are seen by editors to carry authority. As a result they can command substantial salaries. *The Times* columnist Matthew Parris was rumoured to have turned down £300,000 a year to work for the *Independent* while Suzanne Moore was reported to receive £140,000 a year for one column a week for the *Mail on Sunday*. But there are exceptions to this rule. A local newspaper may want to carry an opinionated column from a reader presenting a particular viewpoint – such as that of a youngster, a football fan or an asylum seeker. In this way the paper is striving to make its mark on the local community, with a column aimed at getting people talking – and possibly provoking letters (for or against).

## The rewards of reviewing

Arts reviewing for local papers has its obvious attractions. Most journalists come from humanities backgrounds (resulting in the unfortunate marginalisation of science news in the press) and so there tends to be fierce competition for these posts. Most will be filled by staffers or experienced freelances. But if you have the necessary specialist knowledge, have built up contacts in the area and can write in a lively, original way, you may well find an opening. Reviews serve many functions. They provide basic information: for example, that a play has just opened and can be seen at the theatre indicated. For people who intend to see, read or hear a work (or in the case of broadcasting have already seen or heard it), the review gives an opinion carrying some authority to compare with their own. Yet usually the vast majority of readers will never experience directly the work under review. A concert may have been attended by no more than a hundred people. The review must then exist as a piece of writing in its own right. It must entice the reader through the colour and quality of its prose.

All newspapers have their own house style. This is outlined in a document called the stylebook (occasionally handbook or sheet), though it is increasingly carried onscreen and on the newspaper's website. For instance, you can check out the *Guardian's* stylebook on its website. Stylebooks tend to focus on such elements as spellings (gaol or jail?, Gaddafi or Khadaffi?), punctuation, abbreviations, the use of capitals, titles, Americanisms to avoid, the handling of quotations. Ethical issues, such as the handling of anonymous quotes or how to refer to people with disabilities, can also be covered. Take a close look at your target publications and study their styles. Freelances are not expected to present copy perfectly according to style: sub-editors are on hand to prepare copy for publication. But if your copy shows some awareness of the house style, then the editors will be impressed.

## Some basic requirements

As a freelance you will need internet access on your computer. Most copy is now supplied via email and companies are increasingly supplying press releases through email. You will also need an accountant to advise on tax liabilities, and a pension plan. If you become particularly successful you will have to pay VAT. Most freelances keep in regular touch with their local tax inspector. Remember to log for tax purposes all relevant expenses, such as stationery, office equipment, book and travel expenses. Christopher Browne (in his book *The Journalist's Handbook*, A & C Black, 1999) suggests that beginning freelances should negotiate an overdraft facility of at least £3000 to £4000 with their bank manager after presenting them with a business plan drawn up by an accountant. Membership of the freelance branch of the National Union of Journalists (NUJ) is worth considering. The NUJ, along with local education centres, runs courses for starting-up freelances which can help develop skills and confidence.

Journalism remains a job carrying enormous personal rewards. It is difficult, challenging (politically, ethically, physically) and fun. It requires a formidable range of knowledge and skills. And journalists need to be curious, persistent, imaginative and daring. In the words of Nicholas Tomalin, the *Sunday Times* foreign correspondent killed on the Golan Hights in 1973, journalists should cultivate "rat-like cunning, a plausible manner and a little literary ability". There is a glamorous side to the job, which Hollywood has helped to promote. No wonder the queues for entering the industry are so long.

**Richard Keeble** is Professor of Journalism at Lincoln University. His publications include *The Newspapers Handbook* (Routledge, 3rd edn 2001) and *Ethics for Journalists* (Routledge, 2001).

## Further reading

Randall, David, *The Universal Journalist*, Pluto, 3rd edn 2003

Hicks, Wynford, with Harriett Gilbert and Sally Adams, *Writing for Journalists*, Routledge, 1999

Adams, Sally, *Interviewing for Journalists*, Routledge, 2001

Hicks, Wynford, *English for Journalists*, Routledge, 3rd edn 1998

Pilger, John, *Hidden Agendas*, Vintage, 1998

Peak, Steve (ed), *Media Guide 2004*, Guardian Books in association with Atlantic Books, annually updated

# National newspapers UK and Ireland

## The Business
292 Vauxhall Bridge Road, London SW1V 1DE
*tel* 020-7961 0000 *fax* 020-7961 0101
Sun 50p

Standalone Sunday newspaper for the business and financial community. All aspects of business news with in-depth features ranging from captains of industry to the entrepreneurial and small business sector. Wide economic coverage, IT news, and personal finance features. Length: from 200-word news stories to 2500-word features. Payment: by arrangement.

*Associate Editor* Grant Clelland
*City Editor* Rob Bailhache
*Editor-in-Chief* Andrew Neil
*Political Editor* Fraser Nelson

## Daily Express
Ludgate House, 245 Blackfriars Road, London SE1 9UX
*tel* 0161-228 0789 *fax* 020-7620 1654
Albert House, 17 Bloom Street, Manchester M1 3HZ
*tel* 0161-236 2112
*Editor* Peter Hill
Daily Mon–Fri 35p, Sat 50p
*Supplements* **Saturday, The Sport**

Exclusive news; striking photos. Leader page articles (600 words); facts preferred to opinions. Payment: according to value.

*City Editor* Stephen Kahn
*Diary Editor* Kathryn Spencer
*Environment Editor* John Ingham
*Features Editor* Fergus Kelly
*Foreign Editor* Gabriel Milland
*Literary Editor* Graham Ball
*News Editor* David Leigh
*Political Editor* Patrick O'Flynn
*Sports Editor* Bill Bradshaw
*Women's Editor* Lorna Frame

## Daily Mail
Northcliffe House, 2 Derry Street, London W8 5TT
*tel* 020-7938 6000 *fax* 020-7937 3251
*Editor* Paul Dacre
Daily Mon–Fri 35p, Sat 50p

Highest payment for good, exclusive news. Ideas welcomed for leader page articles (500–800 words). Exclusive news photos always wanted. Founded 1896.
*Supplements* **Weekend**

*City Editor* Alex Brummer
*Diary Editor* Nigel Dempster
*Education Editor* Tony Halpin
*Features Editor* Leaf Kalfayan
*Deputy Foreign Editor* Gerry Hunt
*Health Editor* Victoria Lambert
*Industrial Editor* Darren Behar
*Literary Editor* Jane Mays
*Money Editor* Tony Hazell
*News Editor* Tony Gallagher
*Picture Editor* Paul Silva
*Political Editor* David Hughes
*Showbiz Editor* Nicole Lampert
*Sports Editor* Colin Gibson
*Travel Editor* Mark Edmonds
*Weekend Editor* Heather McGlone

## Daily Mirror
1 Canada Square, Canary Wharf, London E14 5AP
*tel* 020-7293 3000 *fax* 020-7293 3409
*Editor* Richard Wallace
Daily Mon–Sat 35p
*Supplements* **The Look, Mirror Football Mania, The Ticket**

Top payment for exclusive news and news pictures. Freelance articles used, and ideas bought: send synopsis only. 'Unusual' pictures and those giving a new angle on the news are welcomed; also cartoons. Founded 1903.

*Business Editor* Clinton Manning
*Features Editor* Matt Kelly
*Health Editor* Jill Palmer
*Letters Editor* Geraldine Esau
*News Editor* Connor Hanna
*Picture Editor* Ian Down
*Political Editor* Oonagh Blackman
*Sports Editor* Dean Morse

## Daily Record
1 Central Quay, Glasgow G3 8DA
*tel* 0141-309 3000 *fax* 0141-309 3340
*London office* 1 Canada Square, Canary Wharf, London E14 5AP
*tel* 020-7293 3000
*website* www.record-mail.co.uk/rm
*Editor* Bruce Waddell
Daily Mon–Fri 32p, Sat 35p
*Supplements* **Saturday, Living, TV Record, Road Record, Recruitment Record**

Topical articles, from 300–700 words; exclusive stories of Scottish interest and exclusive colour photos.

*Business & Finance Editor* John Peman
*Features Editor* Melanie Harvey
*Health & Science Correspondent* Judith Duffy
*News Editor* Tom Hamilton

*Picture Editor* Stuart Nicol
*Political Editor* Paul Sinclair
*Sports Editor* Alan Thomson

**Saturday**
*Editor* Angela Dewar

Lifestyle magazine and entertainment guide. Reviews, travel features, shopping, personalities. Payment: by arrangement. Illustrations: colour.

## Daily Sport

19 Great Ancoats Street, Manchester M60 4BT
*tel* 0161-236 4466 *fax* 0161-236 4535
*Editor* David Beevers, *Editor-in-Chief* Tony Livesey
Daily Mon–Fri 35p

Factual stories and series. Length: up to 1000 words. Illustrations: b&w and colour photos, cartoons. Payment: £30–£5000. Founded 1988.
*Features & News Editor* Justin Dunn
*Sports Editor* Mark Smith

## Daily Star

Ludgate House, 245 Blackfriars Road, London SE1 9UX
*tel* 020-79288000 *fax* 020-7922 7960
*Editor* Dawn Neesom
Daily Mon–Sat 30p

Hard news exclusives, commanding substantial payment. Major interviews with big-star personalities; short features; series based on people rather than things; picture features. Payment: short features £75–£100; full page £250–£300; double page £400–£600, otherwise by negotiation. Illustrations: line, half-tone. Founded 1978.
*Entertainment Editor* Joe Mott
*Features Editor* Samm Taylor
*News Editor* Kieron Saunders
*Sports Editor* Howard Wheatcroft

## Daily Star Sunday

Express Newspapers, Ludgate House, 245 Blackfriars Road, London SE1 9UX
*tel* 020-7928 8000 *fax* 020-7922 7960
*Editor* Peter Hill
Sun 35p

Opportunities for freelances.

## The Daily Telegraph

1 Canada Square, Canary Wharf, London E14 5DT
*tel* 020-7538 5000 *fax* 020-7538 6242
*websites* www.telegraph.co.uk,
www.sport.telegraph.co.uk,
www.travel.telegraph.co.uk,
www.money.telegraph.co.uk
*Editor* Martin Newland
*Supplements* **Appointments, Arts & Books, Business & Jobs, Gardening, Motoring, Property, Telegraph Magazine, Television & Radio, T2, Weekend, Your Money**

Daily Mon–Fri 45p, Sat 75p

Articles on a wide range of subjects of topical interest considered. Preliminary letter and synopsis required. Length: 700–1000 words. Payment: by arrangement. Founded 1855.
*Arts Editor* Sarah Crompton
*City Editor* Neil Collins
*Education Editor* John Clare
*Environment Editor* Charles Clover
*Fashion Editor* Hilary Alexander
*Features Editor* Richard Preston
*Foreign Editor* Alan Philips
*Health Features Editor* Christine Doyle
*Health News Editor* Celia Hall
*Literary Editor* Kate Summerscale
*Media Correspondent* Tom Leonard
*News Editor* Fiona Baxton
*Picture Editor* Bob Bodman
*Political Editor* George Jones
*Sports Editor* David Welch

**Electronic Telegraph**
*email* et@telegraph.co.uk
*website* www.telegraph.co.uk/
*Editor* Derek Bishton
Daily Free to internet subscribers

Based on *The Daily Telegraph*. Founded 1994.

**Juiced**
*website* www.juiced.com
Weekly Free to internet subscribers

Student magazine.

**Planet**
*website* www.the-planet.co.uk
Free to internet subscribers

Travel writing from *The Daily Telegraph* and *The Sunday Telegraph*.

**Telegraph Magazine**
Free with Sat paper
*Editor* Michelle Lavery

Short profiles (about 1600 words); articles of topical interest. Preliminary study of the magazine essential. Illustrations: all types. Payment: by arrangement. Founded 1964.

## Financial Times

1 Southwark Bridge, London SE1 9HL
*tel* 020-7873 3000 *fax* 020-7873 3076
*website* www.ft.com
*Editor* Andrew Gowers
*Supplements* **Business Books, Companies & Markets, Creative Business, FT Fund Management, FT-IT, How To Spend It, Surveys, Weekend FT, Weekend Money**
Daily Mon–Sat £1

Articles of financial, commercial, industrial and economic interest. Length: 800–1000 words. Payment: by arrangement. Founded 1888.

*Arts Editor* Peter Aspden
*Banking Editor* Charles Pretzlik
*City Editor* Martin Dickson
*Food & Travel Editor* Jill James
*International Affairs Editor* Quentin Peel
*Investment Editor* Philip Coggan
*Lex Editor* George Graham
*Observer Editor* Sunny Tucker
*Political Editor* Brian Groom
*Surveys Editor* Rhys David
*UK Affairs Editor* Roger Blitz
*US edition Editor* Lionel Barber
*Weekend FT Editor* Richard Addis
*World News Editor* Edward Carr

## The Guardian

119 Farringdon Road, London EC1R 3ER
*tel* 020-7278 2332 *fax* 020-7837 2114
164 Deansgate, Manchester M60 2RR
*tel* 0161-832 7200 *fax* 0161-832 5351
*Editor* Alan Rusbridger
Daily Mon–Fri 55p, Sat £1
*Supplements* **Education, Friday Review, G2, The
Guide, Jobs & Money, Life, Literary Review, Media
Guardian, Office Hours, Online, Society, Weekend**

Few articles are taken from outside contributors
except on its feature and specialist pages.
Illustrations: news and features photos. Payment:
from £234.14 per 1000 words; from £75 for
illustrations. Founded 1821.

  *Arts Editor* Charlie English
  *Business Editor* Paul Murphy
  *Economics Editor* Larry Elliott
  *Education Editor* Jeanette Page
  *Fashion Editor* Jess Cartner-Morley
  *Features Editor* Ian Katz
  *Foreign Editor* Harriet Sherwood
  *Home Editor* Ed Pilkington
  *Literary Editor* Claire Armitstead
  *Media Editor* Charlie Burgess
  *News Editor* Andrew Culf
  *Political Editor* Michael White
  *Religious Editor* Stephen Bates
  *Review Editor* Annalena McAfee
  *Science Editor* Tim Radford
  *Sports Editor* Ben Clissitt
  *Travel Editor* Andy Pietrasik
  *Women's Editor* Clare Margetson

### Guardian Unlimited
*website* www.guardian.co.uk
*Editor-in-Chief* Emily Bell

### Weekend
*Editor* Katherine Viner
Free with Sat paper

Features on world affairs, major profiles, food and
drink, home life, the arts, travel, leisure, etc. Also
good reportage on social and political subjects.
Illustrations: b&w photos and line, cartoons.

## The Herald

Scottish Media Newspapers Ltd, 200 Renfield Street,
Glasgow G2 3PR
*tel* 0141-302 7000 *fax* 0141-333 1147
*London office* 3 Waterhouse Square,
138–142 Holborn, London EC1N 2NY
*tel* 020-7882 1060
*website* www.theherald.co.uk
*Editor* Mark Douglas-Home
Daily Mon–Fri 70p, Sat 75p

Articles up to 1000 words. Founded 1783.
  *Arts Editor* Keith Bruce
  *Business Editor* Ian McConnell
  *Diary Editor* Ken Smith
  *Executive Editor* Colin McDiarmid
  *Features Editor* Mark Smith
  *News Editor* Magnus Llewellin
  *Sports Editor* Donald Cowey

## The Independent

Independent House, 191 Marsh Wall,
London E14 9RS
*tel* 020-7005 2000 *fax* 020-7005 2999
*Editor-in-Chief* Simon Kelner
*Supplements* **Business Review, Education, The
Information, Property Supplement, Review, Save
& Spend, Traveller, Weekend Review**
Daily Mon–Fri 60p, Sat £1.10

Occasional freelance contributions; preliminary
letter advisable. Payment: by arrangement. Founded
1986.
  *Arts Editor* David Lister
  *Business & City Editor* Jeremy Warner
  *Education Editor* Richard Garner
  *Environment Editor* Mike McCarthy
  *Features Editor* Adam Leigh
  *Foreign Editor* Leonard Doyle
  *Health Editor* Jeremy Laurance
  *Literary Editor* Boyd Tonkin
  *News Editor* Danny Groom
  *Picture Editor* Lynn Cullen
  *Political Editor* Andrew Grice
  *Sports Editor* Paul Newman

### The Independent Magazine
*Editor* Laurence Earle
Free with Sat paper

Profiles and illustrated articles of topical interest; all
material commissioned. Preliminary study of the
magazine essential. Length: 500–3000 words. Illustrations: cartoons; commissioned colour and b&w
photos. Payment: by arrangement. Founded 1988.

## Independent on Sunday

Independent House, 191 Marsh Wall,
London E14 9RS
*tel* 020-7005 2000 *fax* 020-7005 2999
*Editor* Tristan Davies, *Editor-at-Large* Janet
Street-Porter

*Supplements* **Business, Life Etc, The Sunday Review,
Sportsweek, ABC Magazine, Time Off**
Sun £1.40

News, features and articles. Illustrated, including
cartoons. Payment: by negotiation. Founded 1990.
  *Arts Editor, Life Etc* Marcus Field
  *Business Editor* Jason Nissé
  *Environment Editor* Geoffrey Lean
  *Features Editor, Life Etc* Nick Coleman
  *Foreign Editor* Ray Whitaker
  *News Editor* Robert Mendick
  *Picture Editor* Sophie Batterbury
  *Political Editor* Andy McSmith
  *Sports Editor* Neil Morton

### The Sunday Review

*tel* 020-7293 2000 *fax* 020-7293 2027
*Editor* Andrew Tuck

Original features of general interest with potential for
photographic illustration. Material mostly commissioned. Length: 1000–5000 words. Illustrations:
transparencies. Payment: £150 per 1000 words.

## Ireland on Sunday

Associated Newspapers Ireland Ltd, Embassy
House, Ballsbridge, Dublin 4, Republic of Ireland
*tel* (01) 6375800 *fax* (01) 6375880
*email* news@irelandonsunday.com
*website* www.irelandonsunday.com
*Editor* Paul Drury
Sun €1.80

Mid-market tabloid. Considers unsolicited material.
Length: 2500 words (articles/features), 800 words
(news). Illustrations: cartoons. Payment: by
negotiation. Founded 1997.
  *Features Editor* Aoike Byrne
  *News Editor* Lindsey Fergus
  *Sports Editor* Jack White

## Irish Examiner

1–6 Academy Street, Cork, Republic of Ireland
*tel* (021) 4272722, 4802153 (newsroom)
*fax* (021) 4275477
*email* (department)@examiner.ie
*website* www.examiner.ie
*Editor* Tim Vaughan
Daily Mon–Sat €1.50

Features. Material mostly commissioned. Length: 1000
words. Payment: by arrangement. Founded 1841.
  *Features Editor* Joe Dermody
  *News Editor* John O'Mahony
  *Picture Editor* John Donovan
  *Sports Editor* Tony Leen

## Irish Independent

Independent House, 90 Middle Abbey Street,
Dublin 1, Republic of Ireland
*tel* (01) 7055333 *fax* (01) 8720304/8731787
*Editor* Vincent Doyle

Daily Mon–Sat €1.30

Special articles on topical or general subjects. Length:
700–1000 words. Payment: editor's estimate of value.
  *Business Editor* Richard Curran
  *Diary Editor* Angela Phelan
  *Features Editor* Peter Carvosso
  *News Editor* Philip Molloy
  *Picture Editor* Danny Thornton
  *Political Editor* Gene McKenna
  *Sports Editor* Patrick J. Cunningham

## Irish Times

11–15 D'Olier Street, Dublin 2, Republic of Ireland
*tel* (01) 6792022 *fax* (01) 6719407
*website* www.ireland.com
*Editor* Geraldine Kennedy
Daily Mon–Sat €1.27

Mainly staff-written. Specialist contributions
(800–2000 words) by commission on basis of ideas
submitted. Payment: at editor's valuation.
Illustrations: photos and line drawings.
  *Arts Editor* Deirdre Falvey
  *Features Editor* Sheila Wayman
  *Finance Editor* Barry O'Keeffe
  *Foreign Editor* Peter Murtagh
  *Literary Editor* Caroline Walsh
  *News Editor* John Maher
  *Picture Editor* Peter Thursfield
  *Sports Editor* Malachy Logan

## Mail on Sunday

Northcliffe House, 2 Derry Street,
London W8 5TS
*tel* 020-7938 6000 *fax* 020-7937 3829
*Editor* Peter Wright
Sun £1.20
*Supplements* **Financial Mail on Sunday,
Night & Day, Review, You**

Articles. Payment: by arrangement. Illustrations:
line, half-tone; cartoons. Founded 1982.

  *City Editor* Lisa Buckingham
  *Features Editor* Sian James
  *Literary Editor* Marilyn Warnick
  *News Editor* Sebastian Hamilton
  *Picture Editor* Liz Cocks
  *Political Editor* Simon Walters
  *Sports Editor* Malcolm Vallerius

### Financial Mail on Sunday

*tel* 020-7938 6984
*email* fmos@mailonsunday.co.uk
*website* www.financialmail.co.uk
*Editor* Lisa Buckingham, *Personal Finance Editor*
Jeff Prestridge

City, industry, business, and personal finance. News
stories up to 1500 words. Payment by arrangement.
Full colour illustrations and photography
commissioned.

### Night & Day
*tel* 020-7938 7051 *fax* 020-7937 7488
*Editor* Christena Appleyard

Interviews, entertainment-related features and TV listings. Length: 1000–3000 words. Illustrations: colour photos. Founded 1993.

### Review
*Editor* Jim Gillespie

Investigative journalism, reportage, features, and film, TV, book and theatre reviews.

### You
*Editor* Sue Peart, *Deputy Editor* Catherine Fenton

Women's interest features. Length: 500–2500 words. Payment: by arrangement. Illustrations: full colour and b&w drawings commissioned; also colour photos.

## Morning Star
People's Press Printing Society Ltd,
William Rust House, 52 Beachy Road,
London E3 2NS
*tel* 020-8510 0815 *fax* 020-8986 5694
*email* morsta@geo2.poptel.org.uk
*Editor* John Haylett
Daily Mon–Sat 60p

Newspaper for the labour movement. Articles of general interest. Illustrations: photos, cartoons, drawings. Founded 1930.

    *Arts, Media & Features Editor* Katie Gilmore
    *Diary Editor* Mike Ambrose
    *Financial Editor* Bill Benfield
    *Foreign Editor* Brian Denny
    *Health Editor* Vicky Bryce
    *Industrial & News Editor* Dan Coysh
    *Political Editor* Adrian Roberts
    *Sports Editor* Mark Barber

## News of the World
1 Virginia Street, London E98 1NW
*tel* 020-7782 1000 *fax* 020-7583 9504
*Editor* Andy Coulson
Sun 70p

Uses freelance material. Payment: by negotiation. Founded 1843.

    *Assistant Editor (Features)* Jules Stenson
    *Assistant Editor (News)* Gary Thompson
    *Money Editor* Peter Prendergast
    *Political Editor* Ian Kirby
    *Royal Editor* Clive Goodman
    *Sports Editor* Mike Dunn
    *Travel Editor* Jon Barnsley

### Sunday Magazine
Phase 2, 5th Floor, 1 Virginia Street,
London E1 9BD
*tel* 020-7782 7900 *fax* 020-7782 7474
*Editor* Judy McGuire

## The Observer
119 Farringdon Road, London EC1R 3ER
*tel* 020-7278 2332 *fax* 020-7713 4250
*Editor* Roger Alton
*Supplements* **Business, Cash, Escape, Observer Magazine, Observer Sport Monthly, Observer Food Monthly, Observer Music Monthly, Observer Review, The Observer TV, Sport**
Sun £1.40

Some articles and illustrations commissioned. Payment: by arrangement. Founded 1791.

    *Arts Editor* Jane Ferguson
    *Business Editor* Frank Kane
    *City Editor* Richard Wachman
    *Economics Editor* William Keegan
    *Fashion Editor* Jo Adams
    *Foreign News Editor* Tracy McVeigh
    *Literary Editor* Robert McCrum
    *News Editor* Andy Malone
    *OFM Editor* Nicola Jeal
    *OMM Editor* Caspar Llewellyn Smith
    *OSM Editor* Jason Cowley
    *Picture Editor* Greg Whitmore
    *Political Editor* Kamal Ahmed
    *Review Editor* Louise France
    *Sports Editor* Brian Oliver
    *Travel Editor* Jeannette Hyde

### Observer Magazine
*tel* 020-7713 4175 *fax* 020-7239 9837
*Editor* Allan Jenkins

Commissioned features. Length: 2000–3000 words. Illustrations: first-class colour and b&w photos. Payment: NUJ rates; £150 per illustration.

### The Observer Online
*website* www.observer.co.uk

## The People
1 Canada Square, Canary Wharf, London E14 5AP
*tel* 020-7293 3000 *fax* 020-7293 3517
*website* www.people.co.uk
*Editor* Mark Thomas
*Supplements* **Take it Easy**
Sun 75p

    *Features Editor* Rachael Bletchly
    *Investigations Editor* Nyra Mamhood
    *News Editor* Ian Edmondson
    *Picture Editor* Paula Derry
    *Political Editor* Nigel Nelson
    *Sports Editor* Lee Clayton

Exclusive news and news-feature stories needed. Investigative features, single articles and series considered. Features should be of deep human interest, whether the subject is serious or light-hearted. Very strong sports following. Payment: rates high, even for tips that lead to published news stories.

### Take it Easy
*Editor* Kerry Parnell

## Scotland on Sunday

108 Holyrood Road, Edinburgh EH8 8AS
*tel* 0131-620 8620, 0141-332 6163 *fax* 0131-620 8491
*email* John McLellan
*Supplements* **Spectrum Magazine**
Sun £1

Features on all subjects, not necessarily Scottish.
Payment: varies. Founded 1988.
*News Editor* Peter Laing
*Political Editor* Eddie Barnes

### Spectrum Magazine

*Editor* Lee Randall

## The Scotsman

Barclay House, 108 Holyrood Road,
Edinburgh EH8 8AS
*tel* 0131-620 8620 *fax* 0131-620 8615
*Editor* Iain Martin
Daily Mon–Fri 40p, Sat 55p
*Supplements* **S2, Saturday Magazine**

Considers articles on political, economic and
general themes which add substantially to current
information. Prepared to commission topical and
controversial series from proved authorities. Length:
800–1000 words. Illustrations: outstanding news
pictures, cartoons. Payment: by arrangement.
Founded 1817.
*Arts Editor* Andrew Eaton
*Business Editor* Ian Watson
*Education Editor* Seonag MacKinnon
*Features Editor* Charlotte Ross
*Foreign Editor* Andrew McLeod
*Literary Editor* David Robinson
*News Editor* Gordon Hay
*Political Editor (Westminster)* Fraser Nelson
*Assistant Editor (Politics)* Hamish Macdonell
*Saturday Magazine Editor* Sandra Colamartino
*Sports Editor* Donald Walker
*S2 Editor* Charlotte Ross

## The Star

Independent Star Ltd, Star House, 62A Terenure
Road North, Dublin 6w, Republic of Ireland
*tel* (01) 4901228 *fax* (01) 4902193
*Editor* Gerard Colleran
Daily Mon–Sat €1.10

General articles relating to news and sport, and
features. Length: 1000 words. Illustrations: colour
photos. Payment: by negotiation. Founded 1989.
*News Editor* Michael O'Kane
*Picture Editor* Brian Dowling
*Political Editor* John Downing
*Sports Editor* Eoin Brannigan

## Star Sunday

Independent Star Ltd, Star House, 62A Terenure
Road North, Dublin 6w, Republic of Ireland
*tel* (01) 4901228 *fax* (01) 4902193

*Features Editor* Brian Kelly
*News Editor* Bernard Phelan
*Picture Editor* Brian Kelly
*Sports Editor* Des Dowling

## The Sun

News Group Newspapers Ltd, Virginia Street,
London E1 9XP
*tel* 020-7782 4000 *fax* 020-7488 3253
*Editor* Rebekah Wade
*Supplements* **Super Goals, The TV Mag**
Daily Mon–Fri 28p, Sat 30p

Takes freelance material, including cartoons.
Payment: by negotiation. Founded 1969.
*Business Editor* Ian King
*Features Editor* Sam Carlisle
*Health Editor* Jacqui Thornton
*News Editor* Sue Thompson
*Picture Editor* John Edwards
*Political Editor* Trevor Kavanagh
*Showbiz Editor* Dominic Mohan
*Sports Editor* Ted Chadwick
*Travel Editor* Lisa Bielfeld
*Women's Editor* Sharon Hendry

## The Sunday Business Post

80 Harcourt Street, Dublin 2, Republic of Ireland
*tel* (01) 6026000 *fax* (01) 6796496/6796498
*Editor* Ted Harding
Sun €1.75

Features on financial, economic and political topics;
also lifestyle, media and science articles.
Illustrations: colour and b&w photos, graphics,
cartoons. Payment: by negotiation. Founded 1989.
*Assistant Editor/Property Editor* Gillian Nelis
*Business Editor* Eamon Quinn
*IT Editor* Gavin Daly
*Markets Editor* Michael Murray
*Media Editor* Catherine O'Mahony
*News Director* Fiona Ness
*Political Reporter* Pat Leahy

## Sunday Express

Ludgate House, 245 Blackfriars Road,
London SE1 9UX
*tel* 020-7928 8000 *fax* 020-7620 1653
*Editor* Martin Townsend
Sun £1
*Supplements* **Sunday Express 'S' Magazine,
S:2 Magazine**

Exclusive news stories, photos, personality profiles
and features of controversial or lively interest. Length:
800–1000 words. Payment: top rates. Founded 1918.
*City Editor* David Parsley
*Features Editor* Giulia Rhodes
*Literary Editor* Graham Ball
*News Editor* James Murray
*Political Editor* Tim Shipman
*Sports Editor* Mike Scott

**Sunday Express 'S' Magazine**
*tel* 020-7922 7297
*Editor* Louise Robinson

**S:2 Magazine**
*tel* 020-7922 7025
*Editor* Margaret Hussey

## Sunday Herald
200 Renfield Street, Glasgow G2 3QB
*tel* 0141-302 7800 *fax* 0141-302 7815
*website* www.sundayherald.com
*Editor* Andrew Jaspan
Sun £1
*Supplements* **Business, Review, Seven Days, Sport, Sunday Herald Magazine**

News and stories about Scotland, its characteristics and people. Opportunities for freelances with quality contacts. Founded 1999.
  *Business Editor* Ken Symon
  *Deputy Editor* Richard Walker
  *Features Editor* Charlene Sweeney
  *Magazine Editor* Jane Wright
  *News Editor* David Milne
  *Political Editor* Douglas Fraser
  *Sports Editor* David Dick

## Sunday Independent
Independent House, 90 Middle Abbey Street, Dublin 1, Republic of Ireland
*tel* (01) 7055333 *fax* (01) 7055779
*Editor* Aengus Fanning
Sun £1.20

Special articles. Length: according to subject. Illustrations: topical or general interest, cartoons. Payment: at editor's valuation.
  *Business Editor* Shane Ross
  *Deputy Editors* Anne Harris, Willie Kealy
  *Political Editor* Jody Corcoran
  *Sports Editor* Adhamhnan O'Sullivan

## Sunday Mail
1 Central Quay, Glasgow G3 8DA
*tel* 0141-309 3000 *fax* 0141-309 3582
*London office* 1 Canada Square, Canary Wharf, London E14 5AP
*website* www.record-mail.co.uk/rm
*Editor* Allan Rennie
Sun 70p
*Supplements* **Entertainment, MailSport Monthly, 7-Days**

Exclusive stories and pictures of national and Scottish interest; also cartoons. Payment: above average.
  *Chief Writer* Donna White
  *Features Editor* Susie Cormack
  *Health Editor* Dr Gareth Smith
  *News Editor* Jim Wilson
  *Picture Editor* Andrew Hosie
  *7-Days Editor* Liz Steele

*Showbiz Editor* Billy Sloan
*Sports Editor* George Cheyne

## Sunday Mirror
1 Canada Square, Canary Wharf, London E14 5AP
*tel* 020-7293 3000 *fax* 020-7293 3939
*website* www.sundaymirror.co.uk
*Editor* Tina Weaver
Sun 80p
*Supplements* **M Celebs**

Concentrates on human interest news features, social documentaries, dramatic news and feature photos. Ideas, as well as articles, bought. Payment: high, especially for exclusives. Founded 1963.
  *Associate Editor* Mike Small
  *Associate Editor (News)* Nick Buckley
  *Editor (Features)* Nicki Dawson
  *Editor (Sport)* Craig Tregurtha
  *Picture Editor* Mark Sharp

## Sunday Post
D.C. Thomson & Co. Ltd, 144 Port Dundas Road, Glasgow G4 0HZ
*tel* 0141-332 9933 *fax* 0141-331 1595
Albert Square, Dundee DD1 9QJ
*tel* (01382) 223131 *fax* (01382) 201064
*Editor* David Pollington
Sun 70p

Human interest, topical, domestic and humorous articles, and exclusive news. Payment: on acceptance.

**The Sunday Post Magazine**
*tel* (01382) 223131 *fax* (01382) 201064
*Editor* Jan Gooderham
Monthly Free with paper

General interest articles. Length: 1000–2000 words. Illustrations: colour transparencies. Payment: varies. Founded 1988.

## Sunday Sport
19 Great Ancoats Street, Manchester M60 4BT
*tel* 0161-236 4466 *fax* 0161-236 4535
*email* paul.carter@sportnewspapers.co.uk
*Editor* Paul Carter
Sun 60p
Founded 1986.

## Sunday Telegraph
1 Canada Square, Canary Wharf, London E14 5DT
*tel* 020-7538 5000 *fax* 020-7513 2504
*Editor* Dominic Lawson
Sun £1
*Supplements* **Appointments, City, House and Home, Review, Sport, Sunday Telegraph Magazine, Travel**

Occasional freelance material accepted.
  *Arts Editor* Lucy Tuck
  *City Editor* Robert Peston
  *Comment Editor* Mark Law

*Diary Editor* Tim Walker
*Executive Editor* Con Coughlin
*Foreign Editor* Topaz Amoore
*Literary Editor* Miriam Gross
*News Editor* Richard Ellis
*Picture Editor* Nigel Skelsey
*Political Editor* Patrick Hennessy
*Review Editor* Suzannah Herbert
*Sports Editor* John Ryan
*Travel Editor* Graham Boynton

### Sunday Telegraph Magazine
*tel* 020-7538 7590 *fax* 020-7538 7074
*email* sunmag@telegraph.co.uk
*Editor* Anna Murphy, *Executive Editor* Rebecca Tyrrel
All material is commissioned. Founded 1995.

## The Sunday Times
1 Pennington Street, London E98 1ST
*tel* 020-7782 5000 *fax* 020-7782 5658
*website* www.sunday-times.co.uk
*Editor* John Witherow
Sun £1.40
*Supplements* **Appointments, Doors, Business, Culture, Funday Times, Money, News Review, Rich List, Sport, Style, The Sunday Times Magazine, Travel**

Special articles by authoritative writers on politics, literature, art, drama, music, finance and science, and topical matters. Payment: top rate for exclusive features. Founded 1822.
*Culture Editor* Helen Hawkins
*Economics Editor* David Smith
*Education Correspondent* Judith O'Reilly
*Literary Editor* Caroline Gascoigne
*News Editor* Charles Hymas
*News Review* Vincent Graff
*Chief Political Correspondent* Eben Black
*Sports Editor* Alex Butler
*Travel Editor* Christine Walker

### The Sunday Times Magazine
*tel* 020-7782 7000
*Editor* Robin Morgan

Articles and pictures. Illustrations: colour and b&w photos. Payment: by negotiation.

## The Sunday Times Scotland
Times Newspapers Ltd, 124 Portman Street, Kinning Park, Glasgow G41 1EJ
*tel* 0141-420 5100 *fax* 0141-420 5262
*Editor* Les Snowdon
Free with *The Sunday Times*

News, features and sport. Illustrations: colour photos, cartoons and graphics. Payment: £100 per feature; £50 for illustrations. Founded 1988.

## The Times
1 Pennington Street, London E98 1TT
*tel* 020-7782 5000 *fax* 020-7488 3242
*website* www.the-times.co.uk
*Editor* Robert Thomson
Daily Mon–Fri 50p, Sat 90p
*Supplements* **Bricks & Mortar, Cr me, Football Handbook, The Game, London List, Money, Play, Times 2, Times Law, The Times Magazine, Times Sport, Travel, Weekend**

Outside contributions considered from: experts in subjects of current interest and writers who can make first-hand experience or reflection come readably alive. Phone appropriate section editor. Length: up to 1200 words. Founded 1785.
*Arts Editor* Sarah Vine
*Business/City Editor* Patience Wheatcroft
*Deputy Editor* Ben Preston
*Education Editor* Tony Halpin
*Features Editor* Anne Barrowclough
*Foreign Editor* Bronwen Maddox
*Health Editor* Nigel Hawkes
*Industrial Correspondent* Christine Buckley
*Literary Editor* Erica Wagner
*Media Editor* Ray Snoddy
*News Editor* John Wellman
*Political Editor* Philip Webster
*Saturday Times Editor* Michael Gore
*Science Correspondent* Mark Henderson
*Sports Editor* David Chappell
*Weekend Times Editor* Jane Wheatley

### The Times Magazine
*Editor* Gill Morgan
Free with Sat paper
Features. Illustrated.

## Wales on Sunday
Thomson House, Havelock Street, Cardiff CF10 1XR
*tel* 029-2058 3583 *fax* 029-2058 3725
*Editor* Tim Gordon
Sun 60p

National Sunday newspaper of Wales offering comprehensive news, features and entertainments coverage at the weekend, with a particular focus on events in Wales. Accepts general interest articles, preferably with a Welsh connection. Founded 1989.
*Assistant Editor (Sport)* Nick Rippington
*Deputy Editor* Wayne Davies
*News Editor* Laura Kemp

# Regional newspapers UK and Ireland

Regional newspapers are listed in alphabetical order under region. Some will accept and pay for letters to the editor, brief fillers, and gossip paragraphs, as well as puzzles and quizzes. See also *Writing for newspapers* on page 3.

## BELFAST

### Belfast Telegraph
124–144 Royal Avenue, Belfast BT1 1EB
*tel* 028-9026 4000 *fax* 028-9033 1332, 9055 4540
(news only), 9055 4517 (features), 9055 4508 (sport)
*email* editor@belfasttelegraph.co.uk
*website* www.belfasttelegraph.co.uk
*Editor* Edmund Curran
Daily Mon–Sat 50p

> *Features Editor* John Caruth
> *News Editor* Paul Connolly
> *Picture Editor* Gerry Fitzgerald
> *Sports Editor* John Laverty

Any material relating to Northern Ireland. Payment: by negotiation. Founded 1870.

### Irish News
113–117 Donegall Street, Belfast BT1 2GE
*tel* 028-9032 2226 *fax* 028-9033 7505
*website* www.irishnews.com
*Editor* Noel Doran
Daily Mon–Sat 45p

> *Business Editor* Gary McDonald
> *Features Editor* Joanna Braniff
> *News Editor* Stephen McCaffery
> *Picture Editor* Ann McManus
> *Sports Editor* Thomas Hawkins

Articles of historical and topical interest. Payment: by arrangement. Founded 1855.

### News Letter
46–56 Boucher Crescent, Boucher Road,
Belfast BT12 6QY
*tel* 028-9068 0000 *fax* 028-9066 4412
*email* newsletter@mgn.co.uk
*website* www.newsletter.co.uk
*Editor* Austin Hunter
Daily Mon–Sat 48p

> *Features Editor* Geoff Hill
> *Sports Editor* Brian Millar

Pro-Union. Founded 1737.

### The People
415 Holywood Road, Belfast BT4 2GU
*tel* 028-9056 8000  *fax* 028-9056 8053
4th Floor, Park House, North Circular Road,
Dublin 7, Republic of Ireland
*Editor*  Greg Harkin
Sun 70p

*News Editor* Jason Johnson
*Sports Editor* Alex McGreevy
Northern Ireland edition of *The People*.

### Sunday Life
124 Royal Avenue, Belfast BT1 1EB
*tel* 028-9026 4300 *fax* 028-9055 4507
*email* betty.arnold@belfasttelegraph.co.uk
*Editor* Martin Lindsay
Sun £1

> *Features Editor* Stephanie Bell
> *Deputy Editor and News Editor* Martin Hill
> *Photographic Editor* Darren Kidd
> *Sports Editor* Jim Gracey

Items of interest to Northern Ireland Sunday tabloid readers. Payment: by arrangement. Illustrations: colour and b&w pictures and graphics. Founded 1988.

## CHANNEL ISLANDS

### Guernsey Press and Star
Braye Road, Vale, Guernsey GY1 3BW
*tel* (01481) 240240 *fax* (01481) 240235
*Editor* Richard Digard
Daily Mon–Sat 40p

> *Features Editor* Suzanne Heneghan
> *News Editor* James Falla
> *Sports Editor* Rob Batiste

News and feature articles. Length: 500–700 words. Illustrations: colour and b&w photos. Payment: by negotiation. Founded 1897.

### Jersey Evening Post
PO Box 582, Five Oaks, St Saviour, Jersey JE4 8XQ
*tel* (01534) 611611 *fax* (01534) 611622
*email* editorial@jerseyeveningpost.com
*Editor* Chris Bright
Daily Mon–Sat 40p

> *Features Editor* Elaine Hanning
> *News Editor* Sue le Ruez
> *Picture Editor* Peter Mourant
> *Sports Editor* Ron Felton

News and features with a Channel Islands angle. *Reality* monthly supplement. Length: 1000 words (articles/features), 300 words (news). Illustrations: colour and b&w. Payment: £98 per 1000 words. Founded 1890.

## CORK

### Evening Echo (Cork)
Evening Echo Publications Ltd, 1–6 Academy Street, Cork, Republic of Ireland
*tel* (021) 4272722 *fax* (021) 4802135
*email* firstname.secondname@eecho.ie
*website* eveningecho.ie
*Editor* Maurice Gubbins
Daily Mon–Sat €1.27

>*Deputy Editor* Vincent Kelly
>*Features Editor* John Dolan
>*News Editor* Emma Connolly
>*Picture Editor* Brian Lougheed

Articles, features and news for the area. Illustrations: colour prints.

## DUBLIN

### Evening Herald
90 Middle Abbey Street, Dublin 1, Republic of Ireland
*tel* (01) 7055333
*email* eveningherald@unison.independent.ie
*Editor* Gerard O'Regan
Daily Mon–Sat €1

>*Deputy Editor* Noirin Hegarty
>*Associate Editors* Frank Coghlan, Stephen Rae
>*Assistant Editors* Dave Kenny, Ronan Price, Mark Evans
>*Features Editor* Dave Lawlor
>*Deputy Features Editor* Sile McArdle
>*News Editor* Martin Brennan
>*Assistant News Editor* Bairbre Power
>*Picture Editor* Declan Cahill
>*Sports Editor* David Courtney

Articles. Payment: by arrangement. Illustrations: line, half-tone, cartoons.

### The Sunday Tribune
Tribune Publications plc, 15 Lower Baggot Street, Dublin 2, Republic of Ireland
*tel* (01) 661 5555 *fax* (01) 661 5302
*email* editorial@tribune.ie
*website* www.tribune.ie
*Editor* Matt Cooper
Sun £1

>*Arts Editor* Lise Hand
>*Business Editor* Brian Carey
>*Deputy Editor* Paddy Murray
>*News Editor* Martin Wall
>*Photo Desk* Bea McMunn
>*Sports Editor* Mark Jones
>*Supplements Editor* Ros Dee

Newspaper containing news (inc. foreign), articles, features and photo features. Length: 600–2800

words. Illustrations: colour and b&w photos and cartoons. Payment: £100 per 1000 words; £100 for illustrations. Founded 1980.

## EAST ANGLIA

### Cambridge Evening News
Winship Road, Milton, Cambs. CB4 6PP
*tel* (01223) 434434 *fax* (01223) 434415
*email* newsdesk@cambridge-news.co.uk
*Editor* Colin Grant
Daily Mon–Sat 36p

>*News Editor* John Deex
>*Sports Editor* Chris Gill

The voice of Mid-Anglia – news, views and sport. Illustrations: colour prints, b&w and colour graphics. Payment: by negotiation. Founded 1888.

### East Anglian Daily Times
30 Lower Brook Street, Ipswich, Suffolk IP4 1AN
*tel* (01473) 230023 *fax* (01473) 324871
*Editor* Terry Hunt
Daily Mon–Fri 47p, Sat 55p

>*Features Editor* Julian Ford
>*Head of Photos* Andy Abbott
>*News Editor* Aynsley Davidson
>*Sports Editor* Nick Garnham

Features of East Anglian interest, preferably with pictures. Length: 500 words. Illustrations: colour, b&w. Payment: negotiable; illustrations NUJ rates. Founded 1874.

### Eastern Daily Press
Prospect House, Rouen Road, Norwich NR1 1RE
*tel* (01603) 628311 *fax* (01603) 612930
*London office* House of Commons Press Gallery, House of Commons, London SW1A 0AA
*tel* 020-7219 3384 *fax* 020-7222 3830
*website* www.edp24.co.uk
*Editor* Peter Franzen
Daily Mon–Fri 45p, Sat 55p

Limited market for articles of East Anglian interest not exceeding 900 words. Founded 1870.

### Evening News
Prospect House, Rouen Road, Norwich NR1 1RE
*tel* (01603) 628311 *fax* (01603) 219060
*Editor* David Bourn
Daily Mon–Sat 37p

>*Features Editor* Derek James
>*News Editor* Amanda Patterson
>*Picture Editor* Nolan Lincoln
>*Sports Editor* David Cuffley

Interested in local news-based features. Length: up to 500 words. Payment: NUJ or agreed rates. Founded 1882.

## EAST MIDLANDS

### Burton Mail
Burton Daily Mail Ltd, 65–68 High Street,
Burton on Trent DE14 1LE
*tel* (01283) 512345 *fax* (01283) 515351
*Editor* Paul Hazeldine
Daily Mon–Sat 32p

> *Deputy Editor* Killoran Wills
> *Features Editor* Bill Pritchard
> *News and Picture Editor* Andy Parker
> *Sports Editor* Rex Page

Features, news and articles of interest to Burton and
south Derbyshire readers. Length: 400–500 words.
Illustrations: colour and b&w. Payment: by
negotiation. Founded 1898.

### Chronicle & Echo, Northampton
Northamptonshire Newspapers Ltd, Upper Mounts,
Northampton NN1 3HR
*tel* (01604) 467000 *fax* (01604) 467190
*Editor* Mark Edwards
Daily Mon–Sat 34p

Articles, features and news – mostly commissioned
– of interest to the Northampton area. Length:
varies. Payment: by negotiation. Founded 1931.

### Derby Evening Telegraph
Northcliffe House, Meadow Road, Derby DE1 2DW
*tel* (01332) 291111 *fax* (01322) 253027
*website* www.thisisderbyshire.co.uk
*Editor* Mike Norton
Daily Mon–Sat 30p

> *News Editor* Cheryl Hague
> *News Features Editor* Sarah Newton
> *Picture Editor* Mike Inman
> *Sports Editor* Peter Green

Articles and news of local interest. Payment: by
negotiation.

### The Leicester Mercury
St George Street, Leicester LE1 9FQ
*tel* 0116-251 2512 *fax* 0116-253 0645
*Editor* Nick Carter
Daily Mon–Sat 30p

Occasional articles, features and news; submit ideas
to editor first. Length/payment: by negotiation.
Founded 1874.

### Nottingham Evening Post
Castle Wharf House, Nottingham NG1 7EU
*tel* 0115-948 2000 *fax* 0115-964 4049
*email* newsdesk@nottinghameveningpost.co.uk
*website* www.thisisnottingham.co.uk
*Editor* Graham Glen
Daily Mon–Sat 30p

Material on local issues considered. Founded 1878.

## LONDON

### Evening Standard
Northcliffe House, 2 Derry Street, London W8 5EE
*tel* 020-7938 6000
*website* www.thisislondon.com
*Editor* Veronica Wadley
Daily Mon–Fri 40p

> *Features Editor* Guy Eaton
> *News Editor* Ian Walker
> *Picture Editor* David Ofield
> *Political Editor* Joe Murphy
> *Sports Editor* Simon Greenberg

Articles of general interest considered, 1500 words or
shorter; also news, pictures and ideas. Founded 1827.

#### ES Magazine
*Editor* Mimi Spencer
Weekly Free with paper on Fri

Feature ideas, exclusively about London. Payment:
by negotiation. Illustrations: all types.

#### Homes and Property
*Editor* Janice Morley
Weekly Free with paper on Wed

UK property. Payment: by negotiation.

#### Metrolife
*Editor* Mark Booker
Weekly Free with paper on Thurs

Articles, interviews and features on London life.
Payment: by negotiation.

## NORTH

### Evening Chronicle
Newcastle Chronicle and Journal Ltd, Groat Market,
Newcastle upon Tyne NE1 1ED
*tel* 0191-232 7500 *fax* 0191-232 2256
*Editor* Paul Robertson
Daily Mon–Sat 32p

> *Features Editor* Richard Ord
> *News Editor* Mick Smith
> *Picture Editor* Rod Wilson
> *Sports Editor* Paul New

News, photos and features covering almost every
subject of interest to readers in Tyne and Wear,
Northumberland and Durham. Payment: by prior
arrangement.

### Evening Gazette
Gazette Media Company Ltd, Borough Road,
Middlesbrough TS1 3AZ
*tel* (01642) 245401 *fax* (01642) 232014
*email* editor@eveninggazette.co.uk
*Editor* Steve Dyson
Daily Mon–Sat 30p

News, and topical and lifestyle features. Length: 600–800 words. Illustrations: line, half-tone, colour, graphics, cartoons. Payment: £75 per 1000 words; scale rate or by agreement for illustrations. Founded 1869.

## Hartlepool Mail

Northeast Press Ltd, New Clarence House, Wesley Square, Hartlepool TS24 8BX
*tel* (01429) 239333 *fax* (01429) 869024
*email* mail.news@northeast-press.co.uk
*Editor* Paul Napier
Daily Mon–Sat 32p

> *Deputy Editor* Brian Nuttney
> *News Editor* Peter McCusker
> *Sports Editor* Roy Kelly

Features of local interest. Length: 500 words. Illustrations: colour, b&w photos, line. Payment: by negotiation. Founded 1877.

## The Journal

Groat Market, Newcastle upon Tyne NE1 1ED
*tel* 0191-232 7500 *fax* 0191-261 8869
*email* jnl.newsdesk@ncjmedia.co.uk
*Editor* Brian Aitken
Daily Mon–Sat 35p

> *Features Editor* Jane Hall
> *News Editor* Stephen Rouse
> *Picture Editor* Simon Greener
> *Sports Editor* Kevin Dinsdale

News, sport items and features of topical interest considered. Payment: by arrangement.

## The Northern Echo

Priestgate, Darlington, Co. Durham DL1 1NF
*tel* (01325) 381313 *fax* (01325) 380539
*Editor* Peter Barron
Daily Mon–Sat 35p

> *Features Editor* Jenny Needham
> *News Editor* Nigel Burton
> *Picture Editor* Mike Gibb
> *Sports Editor* Nick Loughlin

Articles of interest to North-East and North Yorkshire; all material commissioned. Preliminary study of newspaper advisable. Length: 800–1000 words. Illustrations: line, half-tone, colour – mostly commissioned. Payment: by negotiation. Founded 1870.

## North-West Evening Mail

Newspaper House, Abbey Road, Barrow-in-Furness, Cumbria LA14 5QS
*tel* (01229) 840150 *fax* (01229) 840164/832141
*Editor* Steve Brauner
Daily Mon–Sat 35p

> *News Editor* Steve Hartley
> *Sports Editor* Leo Clarke

'The Voice of Furness and West Cumbria.' Articles, features and news. Length: 500 words. Illustrations: b&w photos and occasional artwork. Payment: £30 (minimum); £10 for illustrations. Founded 1898.

## The Sunday Sun

Groat Market, Newcastle upon Tyne NE1 1ED
*tel* 0191-201 6158 *fax* 0191-201 6180
*email* scoop.sundaysun@ncjmedia.co.uk
*Editor* Peter Montellier
Sun 65p

Key requirements: immediate topicality and human sidelights on current problems. Particularly welcomed are special features of family appeal and news stories of special interest to the North of England. Length: 200–700 words. Payment: normal lineage rates, or by arrangement. Illustrations: photos. Founded 1919.

## Sunderland Echo

Echo House, Pennywell, Sunderland, Tyne & Wear SR4 9ER
*tel* 0191-501 5800 *fax* 0191-534 5975
*website* www.sunderlandtoday.co.uk
*Editor* Rob Lawson
Daily Mon–Sat 32p

> *Deputy Editor* Paul Larkin
> *Features Editor* Paul Taylor
> *Sports Editor* Neil Watson

Local news, features and articles. Length: 500 words. Illustrations: colour and b&w photos, line, cartoons. Payment: negotiable. Founded 1875.

# NORTH WEST

## The Blackpool Gazette

Blackpool Gazette & Herald Ltd, Avroe House, Avroe Crescent, Blackpool Business Park, Squires Gate, Blackpool FY4 2DP
*tel* (01253) 400888 *fax* (01253) 361870
*email* bpl.editor.al@blackpoolgazette.co.uk
*website* www.blackpoolgazette.co.uk
*Editor* David Helliwell
Daily Mon–Sat 32p

Local news and articles of general interest, with photos if appropriate. Length: varies. Payment: on merit. Founded 1929.

## Bolton Evening News

Newspaper House, Churchgate, Bolton, Lancs. BL1 1DE
*tel* (01204) 522345 *fax* (01204) 365068
*email* ben_editorial@boltoneveningnews.co.uk
*website* www.thisisbolton.co.uk
Daily Mon–Sat 30p

Founded 1867.

## Daily Post

PO Box 48, Old Hall Street, Liverpool L69 3EB
*tel* 0151-227 2000 *fax* 0151-472 2474
*Editor* Jane Wolstenholme
Daily Mon–Sat 32p

*Features Editor* Louise Douglas
*News Editor* Paul Kennedy
*Picture Editor* Steve Shakeshaft
*Sports Editor* Richard Williamson

Articles of general and topical interest to North
West England. No verse or fiction. Payment:
according to value. News and feature illustrations.
Founded 1855.

## Lancashire Evening Post

Oliver's Place, Fulwood, Preston PR2 9ZA
*tel* (01772) 254841 *fax* (01772) 880173
*Editor* Simon Reynolds
Daily Mon–Sat 30p

Topical articles on all subjects. Area of interest
Wigan to Lake District, Lancs, and coast. Length:
600–900 words. Illustrations: colour and b&w
photos, cartoons. Payment: by arrangement.

## Lancashire & Wigan Evening Telegraph

Newspaper House, High Street, Blackburn,
Lancs. BB1 1HT
*tel* (01254) 678678
*website* www.thisislancashire.co.uk
*Editor* Simon Reynolds
Daily Mon–Sat 30p

*News Editor* Andrew Turner
*Picture Editor* Neil Johnson
*Sports Editor* Paul Plunkett

Will consider general interest articles, such as
property, motoring, finance, etc. Payment: by
arrangement. Founded 1886.

## Liverpool Echo

PO Box 48, Old Hall Street, Liverpool L69 3EB
*tel* 0151-227 2000 *fax* 0151-236 4682
*website* www.liverpool.com
*Editor* Mark Dickinson
Daily Mon–Sat 35p

*Acting Head of News* Alison Gow
*Picture Editor* Stephen Shakeshaft
*Sports Editor* John Thompson

Articles of up to 600–800 words of local or topical
interest; also cartoons. Payment: according to merit;
special rates for exceptional material. Connected
with, but independent of, the *Liverpool Daily Post*.
Articles not interchangeable.

## Manchester Evening News

164 Deansgate, Manchester M60 2RD
*tel* 0161-832 7200 (editorial) *fax* 0161-834 3814
*features fax* 0161-839 0968

*website* www.manchesteronline.co.uk
*Editor* Paul Horrocks
Daily Mon–Thurs & Sat 30p, Fri 10p

*Features Editor* Maggie Henfield
*News Editor* Ian Wood
*Picture Editor* John Jeffay
*Sports Editor* Peter Spencer

Feature articles of up to 1000 words, topical or
general interest and illustrated where appropriate,
should be addressed to the Features Editor.
Payment: on acceptance.

## Oldham Chronicle

PO Box 47, Union Street, Oldham, Lancs. OL1 1EQ
*tel* 0161-633 2121 *fax* 0161-627 0905
*email* news@oldham-chronicle.co.uk
*website* www.oldham-chronicle.co.uk
*Editor* Jim Williams
Daily Mon–Fri 32p

News and features on current topics and local
history. Length: 1000 words. Illustrations: colour
and b&w photos and line. Payment: £20–£25 per
1000 words; £16.32–£21.90 for illustrations.
Founded 1854.

# SCOTLAND

## The Courier and Advertiser

D.C. Thomson & Co. Ltd, 80 Kingsway East,
Dundee DD4 8SL
*tel* (01382) 223131 *fax* (01382) 454590
*London office* 185 Fleet Street, London EC4A 2HS
*tel* 020-7400 1030 *fax* 020-7400 1089
*website* www.thecourier.co.uk
Daily Mon–Sat 32p

Founded 1816 and 1801.

## Dundee Evening Telegraph and Post

D.C. Thomson & Co. Ltd, 80 Kingsway East,
Dundee DD4 8SL
*tel* (01382) 223131 *fax* (01382) 454590
*email* general@eveningtelegraph.co.uk
*London office* 185 Fleet Street, London EC4A 2HS
*tel* 020-7400 1030 *fax* 020-7400 1089
*website* www.eveningtelegraph.co.uk
Daily Mon–Fri 28p

## Evening News (Edinburgh)

108 Holyrood Road, Edinburgh EH8 8AS
*tel* 0131-620 8620 *fax* 0131-620 8696
*Editor* Ian Stewart
Daily Mon–Sat 30p

*Features Editor* Gina Davidson
*News Editor* Jim G. Morrison
*Picture Editor* Roger Jonathan
*Sports Editor* Martin Dempster

Features on current affairs, preferably in relation to our circulation area. Women's talking points, local historical articles; subjects of general interest; health and beauty, fashion.

## Evening Express (Aberdeen)

Aberdeen Journals Ltd, PO Box 43, Lang Stracht, Mastrick, Aberdeen AB15 6DF
*tel* (01224) 690222 *fax* (01224) 699575
*Editor* Donald Martin
Daily Mon–Sat 35p

> *Features Editor* Scott Begbie
> *News Editor* Richard Prest
> *Sports Editor* Jim Strachan

Lively evening paper. Illustrations: colour and b&w. Payment: by arrangement.

## Glasgow Evening Times

200 Renfield Street, Glasgow G2 3PR
*tel* 0141-302 7000 *fax* 0141-302 6600
*website* www.eveningtimes.co.uk
*Editor* Charles McGhee
Daily Mon–Sat 32p

Founded 1876.

## Inverness Courier

PO Box 13, 9–11 Bank Lane, Inverness IV1 1QW
*tel* (01463) 233059 *fax* (01463) 243439
*email* editorial@inverness-courier.co.uk
*Editor* Jim Love
2 p.w. Tue 48p, Fri 57p

> *News Editor* Jack Gemmell
> *Sports Editor* David Beck

Articles of Highland interest only. Unsolicited material accepted. Illustrations: colour and b&w photos. Payment: by arrangement. Founded 1817.

## Paisley Daily Express

Scottish and Universal Newspapers Ltd,
14 New Street, Paisley, Renfrewshire PA1 1YA
*tel* 0141-887 7911 *fax* 0141-889 7148
*website* www.insidescotland.co.uk
*Editor* Jonathan Russell
Daily Mon–Sat 35p

> *Sports Editor* Michelle Evans

Articles of Paisley interest only. Considers unsolicited material.

## The Press and Journal

Lang Stracht, Aberdeen AB15 6DF
*tel* (01224) 690222
*email* pj.editor@ajl.co.uk
*website* www.thisisnorthscotland.co.uk
*Editor* Derek Tucker
Daily Mon–Sat 40p

> *Deputy Editor* Richard Neville
> *News Editor* Fiona McWhirr

> *Picture Desk* Joanna Fraser
> *Sports Editor* Alex Martin

Contributions of Scottish interest. Payment: by arrangement. Illustrations: half-tone. Founded 1748.

## The Sun

News International Newspapers, Scotland,
124 Portman Street, Kinning Park, Glasgow G41 1EJ
*tel* 0141-420 5200 *fax* 0141-420 5248
*email* thescottish-sun@the-sun.co.uk
*Editor* Rob Dalton
Daily Mon–Sat 28p

> *Features Editor* David Reynolds
> *News Editor* Alan Muir
> *Picture Editor* Mark Sweeney
> *Sports Editor* Steve Wolstencroft

Scottish edition of *The Sun*. Illustrations: transparencies, colour and b&w prints, colour cartoons. Payment: by arrangement. Founded 1985.

# SOUTH EAST

## The Argus

Argus House, Crowhurst Road, Hollingbury, Brighton SN1 8AR
*tel* (01273) 544544 *fax* (01273) 505703
*email* new@theargus.co.uk
*websites* www.newsquest.co.uk,
www.thisisbrightonandhove.co.uk
*Editor* Simon Bradshaw
Daily Mon–Sat 32p

> *Features Editor* Fraser Addecott
> *News Editor* Rebecca Stephens

Established 1880.

## Evening Echo

Newspaper House, Chester Hall Lane, Basildon, Essex SS14 3BL
*tel* (01268) 522792 *fax* (01268) 469281
*Editor* Martin McNeill
Daily Mon–Fri 32p

> *Features Editor* Sally King
> *News Editor* Chris Hatton
> *Picture Editor* Nick Ansell
> *Sports Editor* Paul Alton

Mostly staff-written. Only interested in local material. Payment: by arrangement. Founded 1969.

## Medway Messenger

Medway Messanger, Medway House, Ginsbury Close, Sir Thomas Longley Road, Medway City Estate, Strood, Kent ME2 2DU
*tel* (01634) 227800 *fax* (01634) 715256
Mon 35p, Fri 45p

> *Senior Editor* Bob Diamond
> *Community Editor* David Jones

*Senior News Editor* Sarah Clark
*Sports Editor* Mike Rees
*Business Editor* Trevor Sturgess

Paper with emphasis on news and sport from the Medway towns. Illustrations:line, half-tone.

## The News, Portsmouth

The News Centre, Hilsea, Portsmouth PO2 9SX
*tel* 023-9266 4488 *fax* 023-92673363
*email* newsdesk@thenews.co.uk
*website* www.thenews.co.uk
*Editor* Mike Gilson
Daily Mon–Sat 34p

> *Features Editor* John Millard
> *News Editor* Colin McNeill
> *Picture Editor* Steve Cutner
> *Sports Editor* Colin Channon

Articles of relevance to southeast Hampshire and West Sussex. Payment by arrangement. Founded 1877.

## Oxford Mail

Newspaper House, Osney Mead, Oxford OX2 0EJ
*tel* (01765) 425262 *fax* (01865) 425557
*email* news@nqo.co.uk
*website* www.newsquest.co.uk
*Editor* Jim McClure
Daily 32p

> *Features Editor* Nick Murray
> *News Editor* John Chipperfield

## Reading Evening Post

8 Tessa Road, Reading, Berks. RG1 8NS
*tel* 0118-918 3000 *fax* 0118-959 9363
*Editor* Andy Murrill
Daily Mon–Fri 25p

> *Features Editor* Kate Magee
> *News Editor* Lucy Rimmer
> *Picture Editor* Steve Templeman
> *Sports Editor* Dave Wright

Topical articles based on current local news. Length: 800–1200 words. Payment: based on lineage rates. Illustrations: half-tone. Founded 1965.

## The Southern Daily Echo

Newspaper House, Test Lane, Redbridge, Southampton SO16 9JX
*tel* 023-8042 4777 *fax* 023-8042 4770
*Editor* Ian Murray
Daily Mon–Sat 35p

> *News Editor* Gordon Sutter
> *Picture Editor* Paul Collins
> *Sports Editor* Simon Carter
> *Supplements Editor* Emma Green

News, articles, features, sport. Length: varies. Illustrations: line, half-tone, colour, cartoons. Payment: NUJ rates. Founded 1888.

## Swindon Evening Advertiser

100 Victoria Road, Old Town, Swindon SN1 3BE
*tel* (01793) 528144 *fax* (01793) 542434
*email* editor@newswilts.co.uk
*website* www.thisiswiltshire.co.uk
*Editor* Simon O'Neill
Daily Mon–Sat 30p

News and information relating to Swindon and Wiltshire only. Considers unsolicited material. Founded 1854.

# SOUTH WEST

## The Bath Chronicle

Bath Newspapers, Windsor House, Windsor Bridge, Bath BA2 3AU
*tel* (01225) 322322 *fax* (01225) 322291
*Editor* David Gledhill
Daily Mon–Fri 35p, Sat 40p

> *Features Editor* Georgette McCready
> *News Editor* Paul Wiltshire
> *Picture Editor* Kevin Bates
> *Sports Editor* Julie Riegal

Welcomes local news and features. Length: 200–500 words. Illustrations: colour photos. Payment: 10p–13p per printed line; £5 per photo. Founded 1760.

## Bristol Evening Post

Temple Way, Bristol BS99 7HD
*tel* 0117-934 3000
*Editor* Mike Lowe
Daily Mon–Sat 35p

> *Features Editor* Bill Davis
> *News Editor* Kevan Blackadder
> *Picture Editor* Shaun Thompson
> *Sports Editor* Chris Bartlett

Takes freelance news and articles. Payment: by arrangement. Founded 1932.

## Daily Echo

Richmond Hill, Bournemouth BH2 6HH
*tel* (01202) 554601 *fax* (01202) 292115
*email* newsdesk@bournemouthecho.co.uk
*website* www.newsquest.co.uk,
www.thisisdorset.co.uk
*Editor* Neal Butterworth
Daily Mon–Sat 32p

> *News Editor* Andy Martin
> *Executive Editor* Peter Tate
> *Features Editor* Kevin Nash

Established 1900.

## Dorset Echo

Newscom, Fleet House, Hampshire Road, Weymouth, Dorset DT4 9XD
*tel* (01305) 830930 *fax* (01305) 830956

*email* newsdesk@dorsetecho.co.uk
*Editor* David Murdock
Daily Mon–Fri 35p, Sat 30p

> *Features Editor* Mike Clarke
> *News Editor* Paul Thomas
> *Picture Editor* Jim Tampin
> *Sports Editor* Paul Baker

News and occasional features (1000–2000 words).
Illustrations: b&w photos. Payment: by negotiation.
Founded 1921.

## Evening Herald

17 Brest Road, Derriford Business Park, Plymouth,
Devon PL6 5AA
*tel* (01752) 765529 *fax* (01752) 765527
*email* news@eveningherald.co.uk
*website* www.thisisplymouth.co.uk
*Editor* Alan Qualtrough
Daily Mon–Sat 32p

Local news, articles and features. Will consider
unsolicited material. Welcomes ideas for articles and
features. Illustrations: colour and b&w prints.

## Express & Echo

Express & Echo Publications Ltd, Heron Road,
Sowton, Exeter, Devon EX2 7NF
*tel* (01392) 442211 *fax* (01392) 442294/442287
*Editor* Steve Hall
Daily Mon–Sat 27p

> *Head of Content* Sue Kemp
> *Picture Editor* James Millar
> *Sports Editor* Richard Davies

Features and news of local interest. Length: 500–800
words (features), up to 400 words (news). Illustrations: colour. Payment: lineage rates; illustrations
negotiable. Founded 1904.

## The Gloucester Citizen

Gloucestershire Newspapers Ltd, St John's Lane,
Gloucester GL1 2AY
*tel* (01452) 424442 *fax* (01452) 420664
*Editor* Ian Mean
Daily Mon–Sat 32p

Local news and features for Gloucester and its
districts. Length: 1000 words (articles/features),
300 words (news). Illustrations: colour. Payment:
negotiable.

## Gloucestershire Echo

Cheltenham Newspaper Co. Ltd, 1 Clarence Parade,
Cheltenham, Glos. GL50 3NY
*tel* (01242) 271900 *fax* (01242) 271803
*email* editor@glosecho.co.uk
*website* www.thisisgloucestershire.co.uk
*Editor* Anita Syvret
Daily Mon–Fri 32p, Sat 35p

Specialist articles with Gloucestershire connections;

no fiction. Material mostly commissioned. Length:
350 words. Payment: £30 per article, negotiable.
Founded 1873.

## Herald Express

Harmsworth House, Barton Hill Road, Torquay,
Devon TQ2 8JN
*tel* (01803) 676000
*website* www.thisissouthdevon.co.uk
*Editor* Brendon Hanrahan
Daily Mon–Sat 30p

## Sunday Independent

Southern Newspapers plc, Burrington Way,
Plymouth PL5 3LN
*tel* (01752) 206600 *fax* (01752) 206164
*Editor* Nikki Rowlands
Sun 65p

News features on West Country topics; features/
articles with a nostalgic theme; short quirky news
briefs (must be original). Length: 600 words (features/
articles), 300 words (news). Illustrations: colour,
b&w. Payment: by arrangement. Founded 1808.

## Western Daily Press

Bristol Evening Post and Press Ltd, Temple Way,
Bristol BS99 7HD
*tel* 0117-934 3000 *fax* 0117-934 3574
*website* www.westpress.co.uk
*Editor* Terry Manners
Daily Mon–Fri 40p, Sat 50p

National, international or West Country topics for
features or news items, from established journalists,
with or without illustrations. Payment: by
negotiation. Founded 1858.

## The Western Morning News

Brest Road, Derriford, Plymouth PL6 5AA
*tel* (01752) 765500 *fax* (01752) 765535
*Editor* Barrie Williams
Daily Mon–Sat 34p

> *News Editor* Laura Snook
> *Picture Editor* Michael Cranmer
> *Sports Editor* Mark Stevens

Articles plus illustrations considered on West
Country subjects. Founded 1860.

# WALES

## South Wales Argus

South Wales Argus Ltd, Cardiff Road, Maesglas,
Newport, Gwent NP20 3QN
*tel* (01633) 777219 *fax* (01633) 777202
*Editor* Gerry Keighley
Daily Mon–Sat 35p

News and features of relevance to Gwent. Length:

500–600 words (features); 350 words (news).
Illustrations: colour prints and transparencies.
Payment: £30 (features), £20 (news) per item;
£20–£25 (photos). Founded 1892.

## South Wales Echo

Thomson House, Havelock Street, Cardiff CF10 1XR
*tel* 029-2058 3622/20223333 *fax* 029-2058 3624
*email* echo.newsdesk@wme.co.uk
*Editor* Alastair Milburn
Daily Mon–Sat 32p

Evening paper: news, sport, features, showbiz, news
features, personality interviews. Length: up to 700
words. Illustrations: photos, cartoons. Payment: by
negotiation. Founded 1884.

## South Wales Evening Post

PO Box 14, Adelaide Street, Swansea SA1 1QT
*tel* (01792) 51000 *fax* (01792) 514697
*email* postbox@swep.co.uk
*website* www.swep.co.uk
*Editor* Spencer Feeney
Daily 33p

> *News Editor* Peter Slee
> *Sports Editor* David Evans

## The Western Mail

Thomson House, Havelock Street, Cardiff CF10 1XR
*tel* 029-2058 3583 *fax* 029-2058 3652
*Editor* Alan Edmunds
Daily Mon–Fri 38p, Sat 50p

Articles of political, industrial, literary or general
and Welsh interest are considered. Illustrations:
topical general news and feature pictures, cartoons.
Payment: according to value; special fees for
exclusive news. Founded 1869.

## WEST MIDLANDS

## Birmingham Evening Mail

PO Box 78, Weaman Street, Birmingham B4 6AY
*tel* 0121-236 3366 *fax* 0121-233 0271
*London office* 1 Canada Square, Canary Wharf,
London E14 5AP
*tel* 020-7293 3000 *fax* 020-7293 3793
*Editor* Roger Borrell
Daily Mon–Sat 32p

> *Deputy Editor* Ray Dunn
> *Features Editor* Alison Handey

Features of topical Midland interest considered.
Length: 400–800 words. Payment: by arrangement.
Founded 1870.

## The Birmingham Post

Weaman Street, Birmingham B4 6AT
*tel* 0121-236 3366 *fax* 0121-625 1105

*London office* 22nd Floor, 1 Canada Square,
Canary Wharf, London E14 5AP
*tel* 020-7293 3455 *fax* 020-7293 3400
*Editor* Fiona Alexander
Daily Mon–Sat 45p

> *Assistant Editor* (Content) Carole Cole
> *Assistant Editor* (Production) Mike Hughes
> *News Editor* Mo Ilyas
> *Picture Editor* Paul Vokes
> *Head of Sport* Fraser Thomson

Authoritative and well-written articles of industrial,
political or general interest are considered,
especially if they have relevance to the Midlands.
Length: up to 1000 words. Payment: by
arrangement.

## Coventry Evening Telegraph

Corporation Street, Coventry CV1 1FP
*tel* 024-7663 3633 *fax* 024-7655 0869
*Editor* Alan Kirby
Daily Mon–Sat 35p

Topical, illustrated articles with a Coventry or
Warwickshire interest. Length: up to 600 words.
Payment: by arrangement.

## Express & Star

Queen Street, Wolverhampton WV1 1ES
*tel* (01902) 313131 *fax* (01902) 319721
*email* general@expressandstar.co.uk
*website* www.westmidlands.com
*London office* Room 110, Temple Chambers,
Temple Avenue, London EC4Y 0DT
*Editor* Warren Wilson
Daily Mon–Sat 30p

> *Head of Features* Jim Walsh
> *Head of News* John Bray
> *Head of Pictures* Tony Adams
> *Sports Editor* Steve Gordos

Founded 1874.

## The Sentinel

Staffordshire Sentinel Newspapers Ltd,
Sentinel House, Etruria, Stoke-on-Trent ST1 5SS
*tel* (01782) 602525 *fax* (01782) 602616
*email* editor@thesentinel.co.uk
*website* www.thisisstaffordshire.co.uk
*Editor* Sean Dooley
Daily Mon–Sat 30p, Sun 35p

> *Features Editor* Julie Stickels
> *Business Correspondent* Stephen Houghton
> *Managing Editor* Roy Coates
> *News Editor* Martin Tideswell
> *Picture Editor* Trevor Slater
> *Sports Editor* Alex Martin

Articles and features of topical interest to the north
Staffordshire/south Cheshire area. Illustrations:
colour and b&w. Payment: by arrangement.
Founded 1873.

## Shropshire Star

Ketley, Telford TF1 5HU
*tel* (01952) 242424 *fax* (01952) 254605
*Editor* Sarah Jane Smith
Daily Mon–Sat 32p

*News Editor* John Simcock
*Picture Editor* Paul Morstatt-Higgs
*Sports Editor* Keith Harrison
*Supplements Dept* Sharon Walters

Evening paper: news and features. No unsolicited material; write to features editor with outline of ideas. Payment: by arrangement. Founded 1964.

## Sunday Mercury

Colmore Circus, Birmingham B4 6AZ
*tel* 0121-234 5567 *fax* 0121-233 0271
*Editor* David Brookes
Sun 60p

*Deptuy Editor* Paul Cole
*Assistant Editor* Tony Larner
*Picture Editor* Adam Fradgley
*Sports Editor* Lee Gibson

News specials or features of Midland interest. Illustrations: colour, b&w, cartoons. Payment: special rates for special matter.

## Worcester Evening News

Berrows House, Hylton Road,
Worcester WR2 5JX
*tel* (01905) 742277 *fax* (01905) 742277
*email* sg@newsquestmidlands.co.uk
*website* www.thisisworcester
*Editor* Stewart Gilbert
Daily Mon–Sat 28p

Local and national news, sport and features. Will consider unsolicited material. Welcomes ideas for articles and features. Length: 800 words (features), 300 words (news). Payment: £50 (features), £35 (news). Illustrations: colour prints.

# YORKSHIRE/HUMBERSIDE

## Evening Courier

PO Box 19, King Cross Street,
Halifax HX1 2SF
*tel* (01422) 260200 *fax* (01422) 260341
*email* editor@halifaxcourier.co.uk
*website* www.halifaxcourier.co.uk
*Editor* John Furbisher
Daily Mon–Sat 33p

*News Editor* John Kenealy
*Sports Editor* Ian Rushworth

Articles of local interest and background to news events. Length: up to 500 words. Illustrations: colour photos. Payment: £25–£40 per article; photos per quality/size used. Founded 1832.

## Evening News

17–23 Aberdeen Walk, Scarborough,
North Yorkshire YO11 1BB
*tel* (01723) 363636 *fax* (01723) 383825
*website* www.scarborougheveningnews.co.uk
*Editor* Ed Asquith

*Deputy Editor* Sue Wilkinson
*News Editor* Neil Pickford
*Sports Editor* Charles Place

## Evening Press

York and County Press, PO Box 29,
76–86 Walmgate, York YO1 9YN
*tel* (01904) 653051 *fax* (01904) 612853
*email* newsdesk@ycp.co.uk
*website* www.thisisyork.co.uk
*Editor* Kevin Booth
Daily Mon–Sat 35p

*Assistant Editors* Chris Buxton, Bill Hearld
*News Editor* Francine Clee
*Picture Editor* Martin Oates
*Sports Editor* Martin Jarred

Articles of North and East Yorkshire interest, humour, personal experience of current affairs. Length: 500–1000 words. Payment: by arrangement. Illustrations: line, half-tone. Founded 1882.

## Grimsby Evening Telegraph

80 Cleethorpe Road, Grimsby,
North East Lincolnshire DN31 3EH
*tel* (01472) 360360 *fax* (01472) 372257
*email* newsdesk@grimsbytelegraph.co.uk
*website* www.thisisgrimsby.co.uk
*Editor* Michelle Lalor
Daily Mon–Sat 27p

*Features Editor* Barrie Farnsworth
*News Editor* David Atkin
*Picture Editor* David Moss
*Sports Editor* Geoff Ford

Considers general interest articles. Illustrations: line, half-tone, colour, cartoons. Payment: by arrangement. Founded 1897.

## The Huddersfield Daily Examiner

Examiner News & Information Services Ltd,
PO Box A26, Queen Street South,
Huddersfield HD1 2TD
*tel* (01484) 430000 *fax* (01484) 437789
*email* editor@examiner.co.uk
*website* www.examiner.co.uk
*Editor* Roy Wright
Daily Mon–Fri 35p

*Features editor* Andrew Flynn
*Picture editor* Neil Atkinson

No contributions required at present. Payment: £10–£15 (short features). Founded 1871.

## Hull Daily Mail

Blundell Corner, Beverley Road, Hull HU3 1XS
*tel* (01482) 327111 *fax* (01482) 584353
*website* www.hulldailymail.co.uk
*Editor* John Meehan
Daily Mon–Sat 30p
  *Features Editor* Jackie Foottit

## The Star

York Street, Sheffield S1 1PU
*tel* 0114-276 7676 *fax* 0114-272 5978
*website* www.sheffweb.co.uk
*Editor* Peter Charlton
Daily Mon–Sat 27p
  *Features Editor* Paul License
  *News Editor* Bob Westerdale
  *Picture Editor* Dennis Lound
  *Sports Editor* Martin Smith

Well-written articles of local character. Length: about 500 words. Payment: by negotiation. Illustrations: topical photos, line drawings, graphics, cartoons. Founded 1887.

## Telegraph & Argus

Hall Ings, Bradford, West Yorkshire BD1 1JR
*tel* (01274) 729511 *fax* (01274) 723634
*email* bradford.editorial@bradford.newsquest.co.uk
*website* www.thisisbradford.co.uk
*Editor* Perry Austin-Clarke
Daily Mon–Sat 32p
  *Assistant Editor (news)* Damian Bates
  *Assistant Editor (sport & pictures)* Simon Waites
  *Features Editor* David Barnett
  *Sports Editor* Blake Richardson

Evening paper: news, articles and features relevant to or about the people of West Yorkshire. Length: up to 1000 words. Illustrations: line, half-tone, colour. Payment: features from £15; line from £5, b&w and colour photos by negotiation. Founded 1868.

## Yorkshire Evening Post

PO Box 168, Wellington Street, Leeds LS1 1RF
*tel* 0113-2432701 *fax* 0113-2388535
*Editor* N.R. Hodgkinson
Daily Mon–Sat 32p
  *Features Editor* Anne Pickles
  *News Editor* Gillian Haworth
  *Picture Editor* Andy Manning
  *Sports Editor* Phil Rostron

News stories and feature articles. Illustrations: colour and b&w, cartoons. Payment: by negotiation. Founded 1890.

## Yorkshire Post

Wellington Street, Leeds LS1 1RF
*tel* 0113-243 2701 *fax* 0113-238 8537
*London office* St Martin's House, 16 St Martin's le Grand, London EC1A 4EN
*tel* 020-7397 8723
*website* www.yorkshireposttoday.co.uk
*Editor* Rachel Campey
Daily Mon–Fri 38p, Sat 50p
  *Acting Features Editor* Eric Roberts
  *Deputy Editor* Duncan Hamilton
  *Picture Editor* Ian Day
  *Sports Editor* Bill Bridge

Authoritative and well-written articles on topical subjects of general, literary or industrial interests. Length: max. 1200 words. Payment: by arrangement. Founded 1754.

# Writing for magazines

Richard Keeble explains the different types of features that magazines run and offers advice to freelance writers on how to approach writing for magazines.

There are well over 9000 mainstream magazines published in Britain – and many hundreds of alternative publications. Research suggests that weekly consumer magazines are read by 39% of adults and monthlies by 48%. Yet while there appears to be an enormous variety of publications, the sector is dominated by just two companies: IPC and EMAP. IPC was sold by Reed Elsevier to Cinven, an investment company, in January 1998 for £860 million and then to AOL Time Warner for £1.3 billion in August 2001. Magazine publishing is clearly big business!

## The differing genres

Freelancing for magazines will normally involve writing features. So it's important from the outset to have a clear idea about the different journalistic genres. Each will have its own writing style, research strategy, tone, and place in the publication. Here is a selection of the genres you might expect to find in a representative range of magazines.

## Hard news

Hard news has the highest status in newspapers and tends to be on the front pages, while magazines may have an opening section carrying hard news. Hard news features usually open with the most striking details and the information given subsequently is generally of lesser importance. Some background details may be needed to make the news intelligible but description, analysis, comment and the subjective 'I' of the reporter are either excluded or included only briefly.

## Soft news

Here the news element is strong and prominent at or near the opening but is treated in a lighter way. Largely based on factual information and quotations, the writing is nonetheless more colourful, with an emphasis on description and comment. The tone, established in the intro (opening) section, may be witty or ironic. The separation of hard and soft news emerged in the second half of the nineteenth century: the first, linked to notions of accuracy, objectivity, neutrality, was used for transmitting information; the second was more an entertainment genre. Magazine opening sections usually adopt this softer approach to news.

## News features

A news feature is usually longer than a straight news story. The news angle is prominent, though not necessarily in the opening section, and quotes again are important. It can contain analysis, comment, descriptions, historical background detail, eye-witness reporting and deeper coverage of the issues and the range of sources.

## Timeless features

These have no specific news angle; the special interest is provided by the subject or sources. For example, such a feature could explore young people's experiences of dealing with sexually transmitted diseases or coming out in terms of sexual orientation.

## Backgrounder/preview/curtain-raiser features

Here the emphasis is not so much on reporting the news as on explaining it, or setting the scene for an event about to happen. For instance, if a major anti-globalisation demonstration is planned for mid-July, that month's magazine (produced well in advance) might carry a feature highlighting the historical background, the arguments of the protestors, the range of voices expected on the march, the hopes of the organisers and the predicted turn-out, and so on. A retrospective is a similar feature looking back on an event.

## Colour features

These concentrate on descriptive, eye-witness reporting, quotations and the build-up of factual details. They need not have a strong news angle. You may visit Highgate cemetery and describe (for a travel or tourist magazine) your experience of walking through it and talking to people. What do they think of Karl Marx, who is buried there?

## Eye-witness news features

These are based on your observations of a newsy event, incorporating such elements as description, conversations, interviews, analysis and comment. You may accompany a rock star for a week as they tour the country and describe the experience for a rock magazine.

## Profiles (sometimes called interviews)

These are portraits in words, usually based on interviews with the subject and sometimes also with their friends, critics, relations, work colleagues.

## Reviews

Reviews include descriptions and assessments of works of art, television programmes, exhibitions, books, theatre shows, CDs, rock gigs and so on.

## Lifestyle features

Lifestyle features include advice columns (such as on health or education matters, gardening or computer problems).

## Comment pieces

If you have an original voice, confidence in your personal writing style and a wide range of interests, then you might well aim to become a columnist. Editorials, on the other hand, reflect the institutional voice of the publication and are rarely written by freelances.

## Getting ideas

You must be immersed in your specialist area, regularly reading and building up cuttings files from the relevant publications, websites, press releases, newsletters of pressure groups, etc. You will need to generate a network of contacts at public events, informal social gatherings, conferences, press launches. And ideas will emerge from conversations with friends and family. Remember your best resources are your own experiences. You have a teenage son who is showing no interest in politics; you could then plan a feature looking at the broader picture, talking to teachers, the youngsters themselves, other parents and political commentators. After 20 years in the same rat-race job you (your family, four dogs and three cats) are quitting to live simply in a remote cottage in Northumbria; so why not write about it?

Developing magazine feature ideas from news reports needs a special imaginative flair. A report from a university media monitoring unit criticises the increasing intrusiveness of the paparazzi photographers. A daily or weekly newspaper (working to relatively short deadlines) will follow up the report, interviewing editors and photographers and placing the current controversy in its historical context. A magazine writer, on the other hand, will have the luxury of a slightly longer deadline – and this throws up opportunities. You could spend a week on the back of a paparazzi's motorbike zooming about the streets of London and describe the experience, the feelings of the photographer and the people they shoot. The feature could involve eye-witness descriptions, dialogue, factual details: as you describe your movements around London so your copy is given extra movement and colour.

## The ethical/political challenge

Always be aware of the ethical/political dilemmas stories can throw up. You are planning a vox pop (a collection of snappy quotes usually accompanied by photographs) about the work of paparazzi photographers: think about the range of people to be shown, in terms of race, gender, age and authority. If someone will speak to you only 'off the record' what do you do? How important is it for your feature to present a balancing range of views? One of your sources is an outspoken racist or sexist: how do you deal with their quotes? And so on.

## The feature package

It's often best to think in terms of producing not just one single article (of say 2500 words) but a package of contrasting features. These will have different lengths and tones and will provide the sub-editor with material for a more interesting layout. Thus the paparazzi package might contain the main eye-witness, participatory feature (1200 words), a background piece outlining the history of the paparazzi and ending with their alleged role in the death of Princess Diana and the ensuing controversy (700 words) and a profile of a prominent photographer who argues strongly for (or against) legislation to restrain intrusive photographers (600 words).

## The structure of the feature
## The opening section

Most features do not start with the traditional five Ws (who, what, where, when, why) and the H (how) of the hard news opening section. The writing can be more flexible – but there is still an urgency needed in the copy to attract the attention of the reader. One of the most popular devices for helping the reader understand a complex event or issue is to begin by focusing on the experience or views of an individual. You are writing a piece about poverty on a bleak housing estate in Manchester, so you focus on the plight of an elderly woman, shivering in her unheated semi and terrified of the yobs who have raided her home three times over the last year and thrown fireworks through her letterbox.

According to the convention in the UK, most news stories don't begin with direct quotations. But features – and in particular profiles – often do. Quotes are useful because they can be colourful, succinct, and convey a lot about the personality of the person quoted. Thus a feature about 'flexpoitation' (as employers are increasingly using flexi-time working arrangements to extend their exploitation of white-collar staff) could begin: 'We all sit in rows now. You log in and log out – even for your 20-minute lunch break. It's more like clocking in at a factory.'

The 'I' of the reporter is only rarely prominent in news intros. But the tone of magazine features (and not just those by regular columnists) can be far more personal, idiosyncratic, even witty. A feature exploring an issue such as fox-hunting, or debt in the developing world, can open with your views; an intro section for a piece about hairdressing can focus on a recent bad experience; and so on. Similarly, while news reports hardly ever begin with a question, features often do. Thus a feature about the boom in ski-ing in the Alps in the New Year could start: 'Have you tried to secure your travel ticket for the Alps yet?'

## The body of the text

While colour, description, opinion, analysis, narrative, quotes, dialogue and historical context may be important in features, they are all still built on the cement of factual or emotional accuracy and a clear sense of structure. Just as in news stories the most important information comes first, with the less important details thereafter, so the body of the feature text is usually intended to expand on an opening section. At the same time, the writing styles of magazine features can be far more colourful. Emotional tones (angry, witty, ironic, condemnatory, adulatory) can vary along with textual rhythms. Indeed, before launching into your writing, as well as planning the structure, it is crucial to identify the emotional core of the piece. Try always to be as authentic as possible (within the constraints of the editorial policy of your target publication).

## The closing section

A hard news story carries information in the order of its news value. The last paragraph is the least important and can be cut without destroying the overall impact. Features can be different, with the final section carrying its own, crucial significance. One feature may explore a range of views or experiences and conclude by passing a comment on them; another may argue a case and come to a conclusion in the final section. The final paragraph may raise a pointed question, contain a striking direct quote, summarise an argument or look ahead to a possible future.

## Pitching ideas

You can choose to write or phone in your idea to a commissioning editor. There is no hard rule here. But even after you have spoken to an editor, they may well want you to spell out the idea by fax, letter or email. Make sure the grammar, spelling, facts, and punctuation in your proposal (as in your copy) are spot on. And don't be tempted to spell out the idea at length. The essential idea should be summarised in one paragraph at most: 'With Martin Scorsese's *Gangs of New York* due to be released in two months, my 1200-word feature will look critically at the way in which Hollywood has represented street gangs in the past.' Don't be vague. Don't say: 'I propose a feature about prostitution in inner cities.' Rather: 'A report published this week has highlighted the rise of prostitution in inner cities. To what extend are students (both male and female) funding their studies through prostitution?'

## Dangers

Publications may steal your ideas and give them to someone else to follow up. And the freelance has absolutely no protection in law against this kind of theft. While written work can be copyrighted, ideas can occur to two people at the same time. One solution is to provide only a bare minimum of background details before the idea is accepted. Personal contact with the commissioning editor also helps create mutual trust and confidence. The best solution is to prove your abilities to the publication with a series of stories, sent on spec or to commission, so they will be concerned not to lose your work to other competitors. Make sure you have a copy of all submitted work. If it is rejected you may want to rework it with some new angles/quotes for a different publication. And be persistent: remember that *Gone with the Wind* was rejected 25 times before it was published.

## Payment

How much should you expect to be paid? Well, the National Union of Journalists draws up a regularly updated list of minimum freelance rates which will give you some idea of what to expect. And remember that if you are a self-employed freelance you own the copyright to your work. This does not mean refusing further use of the material: you can license it, giving permission for a specific use for an agreed fee. Whatever freelancing you end up doing, enjoy the ethical, political, writing challenges. It's not easy but the personal rewards can be substantial. Good luck!

**Richard Keeble** is Professor of Journalism at Lincoln University. He has feelanced for a range of publications including *Tribune, Press Gazette, Peace News*, the *Journalist* and MediaLens.org.

## Further reading

McKay, Jenny, *The Magazines Handbook*, Routledge, 2000
*Willings Press Guide*, Media Information Ltd, annual
Hennessy, Brendan, *Writing Feature Articles*, Focal Press, 3rd edn 1997
Hicks, Wynford, with Harriett Gilbert and Sally Adams, *Writing for Journalists*, Routledge, 1999

# Magazines UK and Ireland

Listings for regional newspapers start on page 15 and listings for national newspapers start on page 7. For quick reference, magazines are listed by subject area starting on page 741.

## Accountancy
40 Bernard Street, London WC1N 1LD
*tel* 020-7833 3291 *fax* 020-7833 2085
*email* postmaster@theabg.demon.co.uk
*website* www.accountancymagazine.com
*Editor* Chris Quick
Monthly £57.50 p.a.

Articles on accounting, taxation, financial, legal and other subjects likely to be of professional interest to accountants in practice or industry, and to top management generally; cartoons. Payment: £140 per page. Founded 1889.

## Accountancy Age
VNU Business Publications, VNU House,
32–34 Broadwick Street, London W1A 2HG
*tel* 020-7316 9236 *fax* 020-7316 9250
*email* accountancy_age@vnu.co.uk
*website* www.accountancyage.com
*Editor* Damian Wild
Weekly £2 (£100 p.a.)

Articles of accounting, financial and business interest. Illustrations: colour photos; freelance assignments commissioned. Payment: by arrangement. Founded 1969.

## Accounting & Business
Association of Chartered Certified Accountants,
10–11 Lincolns Inn Fields, London WC2A 3BP
*tel* 020-7396 5966 *fax* 020-7396 5958
*email* john.prosser@accaglobal.com
*website* www.accaglobal.com
*Editor* John Rogers Prosser
10 p.a. £85 p.a.

Journal of the Association of Chartered Certified Accountants. Accountancy, finance and business topics of relevance to accountants and finance directors. Length: 1300 words. Payment: £150 per 1000 words. Illustrated. Founded 1998.

## Ace Tennis Magazine
Tennis GB, 9–11 North End Road, London W14 8ST
*tel* 020-7605 8000 *fax* 020-7602 2323
*email* nigel.billen@acemag.co.uk
*Editor* Nigel Billen
11 p.a. £2.85

International high profile tennis, including interviews with top players, coaching articles, big tournament reports, health and fitness. Submit synopsis in the first instance. Payment: 20p per word. Founded 1996.

## Active Life
Computer Publishing, 221–223 High Street,
Berkhamstead, Herts. HP4 1AD
*tel* (01442) 289600 *fax* (01442) 879903
*email* activelife@computer-publishing.net
*Editor* Paul Jacques
Monthly £1

Lifestyle advice for the over 50s, including holidays and health, fashion and food, finance and fiction, hobbies and home, personality profiles. Submit ideas in writing. Length: 600–1200 words. Illustrations: colour. Payment: £100 per 1000 words; photos by negotiation. Founded 1989.

## Acumen
6 The Mount, Higher Furzeham, Brixham,
South Devon TQ5 8QY
*tel* (01803) 851098
*Editor* Patricia Oxley
3 p.a. (Jan/May/Sept) £4.50, £12.50 p.a.

Poetry, literary and critical articles, reviews, literary memoirs, etc. Send sae with submissions. Payment: small. Founded 1985.

## Aeroplane Monthly
IPC Magazines Ltd, King's Reach Tower,
Stamford Street, London SE1 9LS
*tel* 020-7261 5849 *fax* 020-7261 5269
*email* aeroplane_monthly@ipcmedia.com
*website* www.aeroplanemonthly.com
*Editor* Michael Oakey
Monthly £3.40

Articles and photos relating to historical aviation. Length: up to 3000 words. Illustrations: line, half-tone, colour, cartoons. Payment: £60 per 1000 words, payable on publication; photos £10–£40; colour £80 per page. Founded 1973.

## Africa: St Patrick's Missions
St Patrick's, Kiltegan, Co. Wicklow,
Republic of Ireland
*tel* (059) 6473600 *fax* (059) 6473622
*email* africa@spms.org
*website* www.spms.org
*Editors* Rev. John Carroll, Rev. Martin Smith
9 p.a. £5 p.a. (€10)

Articles of missionary and topical religious interest. Length: up to 1000 words. Illustrations: line, half-tone, colour.

## Africa Confidential
Blackwell Publishers Ltd, 73 Farringdon Road, London EC1M 3JQ
*tel* 020-7831 3511 *fax* 020-7831 6778
*website* www.africa-confidential.com
*Editor* Patrick Smith
Fortnightly £96 p.a. students, £422 p.a. institutions

News and analysis of political and economic developments in Africa. Unsolicited contributions welcomed, but must be exclusive and not published elsewhere. Length: 1200-word features, 200-word pointers. Payment: from £200 per 1000 words. No illustrations. Founded 1960.

## African Business
IC Publications Ltd, 7 Coldbath Square, London EC1R 4LQ
*tel* 020-7713 7711 *fax* 020-7713 7970
*email* icpubs@africasia.com, a.versi@africasia.com
*Editor* Anver Versi
Monthly £2.50

Articles on business, economic and financial topics of interest to businessmen, ministers, officials concerned with African affairs. Length: 400–750 words; shorter coverage 100–400 words. Illustrations: line, half-tone, cartoons. Payment: £80 per 1000 words; £1 per column cm for illustrations. Founded 1978.

## Agenda
The Wheelwrights, Fletching Street, Mayfield, East Sussex TN20 6TL
*tel* (01435) 872165 *fax* (01435) 872165
*email* agendapoetry@lycos.co.uk
*Editor* Patricia McCarthy, *Assistant Editor* W.S. Milne
Quarterly £26 p.a. (libraries, institutions and overseas: rates on application); £20 OAPs/students

Poetry and criticism. Study the journal before submitting MSS with an sae. Illustrations: half-tone. Payment: variable.

## Air International
Key Publishing Ltd, PO Box 100, Stamford, Lincs. PE9 1XQ
*tel* (01780) 755131 *fax* (01780) 757261
*email* malcolm.english@keypublishing.com
*Editor* Malcolm English
Monthly £3.30

Technical articles on aircraft; features on topical aviation subjects – civil and military. Length: up to 5000 words. Illustrations: colour transparencies/prints, b&w prints/line drawings. Payment: £50 per 1000 words or by negotiation; £20 colour, £10 b&w. Founded 1971.

## Amateur Gardening
IPC Media Ltd, Westover House, West Quay Road, Poole, Dorset BH15 1JG
*tel* (01202) 440840 *fax* (01202) 440860
*email* amateurgardening@ipcmedia.com
*Editor* Tim Rumball
Weekly £1.50

Topical, practical or newsy articles up to 1200 words of interest to keen gardeners. Payment: by arrangement. Illustrations: colour. Founded 1884.

## Amateur Photographer
IPC Magazines Ltd, King's Reach Tower, Stamford Street, London SE1 9LS
*tel* 020-7261 5100 *fax* 020-7261 5404
*email* amateurphotographer@ipcmedia.com
*Editor* Garry Coward-Williams
Weekly £1.99

Editorial submissions are not encouraged. Founded 1884.

## Amateur Stage
Platform Publications Ltd, Hampden House, 2 Weymouth Street, London W1W 5BT
*tel* 020-7636 4343 *fax* 020-7636 2323
*email* cvtheatre@aol.com
*website* www.amdram.org.uk/amstagel.htm
*Editor* Charles Vance
Monthly £2.40

Articles on all aspects of the amateur theatre, preferably practical and factual. Length: 600–2000 words. Illustrations: photos, line drawings. Payment: none. Founded 1946.

## Ambit
17 Priory Gardens, London N6 5QY
*tel* 020-8340 3566
*website* ambitmagazine.co.uk
*Editor* Martin Bax, *Poetry Editors* Henry Graham, Carol-Ann Duffy, *Prose Editors* J.G. Ballard, Geoff Nicholson, *Art Editor* Mike Foreman, *Assistant Editor* Kate Pemberton
Quarterly £6.50 inc. p&p (£25 p.a. UK, £27/€48 Europe, £29/$56 rest of world; £36 p.a., £38/€64 p.a., £40/$73 p.a. institutions)

Poetry, short fiction, art, poetry reviews. New and established writers and artists. Payment: by arrangement. Illustrations: line, half-tone, colour. Founded 1959.

## American Markets Newsletter
175 Westland Drive, Glasgow G14 9JQ
*email* sheila.oconnor@juno.com
*Editor* Sheila O'Connor
6 p.a. £34 p.a. (£63 for 2 years)

Editorial guidelines for US, Canadian and other overseas markets, plus information on press trips, non-fiction/fiction markets and writers' tips. Free syndication for all subscribers. Sample issue £5.95 (payable to S. O'Connor).

## AN Magazine

AN: The Artists Information Company, 1st Floor,
7–15 Pink Lane, Newcastle upon Tyne NE1 5DW
*tel* 0191-241 8000 *fax* 0191-241 8001
*email* edit@anpubs.demon.co.uk
*website* www.a-n.co.uk
*Contact* Editorial Team
Monthly £3.50 (£28 p.a.)

Articles, news and features for visual and applied
artists. Illustrations: transparencies, colour and b&w
photos. Payment: £130 per 1000 words. Founded as
*Artists Newsletter* in 1980.

## Angler's Mail

IPC Media Ltd, King's Reach Tower,
Stamford Street, London SE1 9LS
*tel* 020-7261 5778 *fax* 020-7261 6016
*website* www.ipcmedia.com
*Editor* Tim Knight
Weekly £1.10

News items about coarse and sea fishing. Payment:
by agreement.

## Angling Times

EMAP Active, Bushfield House, Orton Centre,
Peterborough PE2 5UW
*tel* (01733) 232600 *fax* (01733) 465844
*email* richard.lee@emap.com
*Editor* Richard Lee
Weekly £1.20

Articles, pictures, news stories, on all forms of
angling. Illustrations: line, half-tone, colour.
Payment: by arrangement. Founded 1953.

## Animals and You

D.C. Thomson & Co Ltd, Albert Square,
Dundee DD1 9QJ
*tel* (01382) 223131 *fax* (01382) 225511
185 Fleet Street, London EC4A 2HS
*tel* 020-7400 1030 *fax* 020-7400 1089
Monthly (Fri) £1.75

Features, stories and pin-ups for girls who love
animals. Founded 1998.

## Antiques & Art Independent

PO Box 1945, Comely Bank, Edinburgh EH4 1AB
*tel* (07000) 268478
*email* antiquesnews@hotmail.com
*website* www.antiquesnews.co.uk
*Publisher/Editor* Tony Keniston
Quarterly £2

Newspaper for the British antiques and art trade.
News, gossip and controversial personal views on all
aspects of the antiques world welcome. People
stories only. Approach in writing with ideas. Length:
600 words (articles), 200 words (news).
Illustrations: b&w prints. Payment: by negotiation.
Founded 1997.

## Antiques and Collectables

Merricks Media Ltd, Charlotte House,
12 Charlotte Street, Bath BA1 2NE
*tel* (01225) 786800 *fax* (01225) 786801
*email* info@antiques.collectables.co.uk
*website* www.antiques-collectables.co.uk
*Editor* Diana Cambridge
Monthly £2.60

Features on ceramics, furniture, glass, memorabilia,
ephemera, etc aimed at the antiques trade and
general collectors. Includes price guide and news.
Write with idea in the first instance. Length: 1500–
2000 (features). Illustrations: transparencies and
colour prints. Payment £100–£150. Founded 1998.

## Apollo

20 Theobalds Road, London WC1X 8PF
*Editor* Michael Hall
Monthly £8.50

Scholarly articles of about 3000 words on art,
architecture, ceramics, furniture, armour, glass,
sculpture, and any subject connected with art and
collecting. Payment: by arrangement. Illustrations:
half-tone, colour. Founded 1925.

## Aquila

New Leaf Publishing Ltd, PO Box 2518, Eastbourne,
East Sussex BN21 2BB
*tel* (01323) 431313 *fax* (01323) 731136
*email* info@aquila.co.uk
*website* www.aquila.co.uk
*Editor* Jackie Berry
Monthly £35 p.a. (£25 6 months)

Dedicated to encouraging children aged 8–13 to
reason and create, and to develop a caring nature.
Short stories and serials of up to 4 parts. Occasional
features commissioned from writers with specialist
knowledge. Approach in writing with ideas and
sample of writing style, with sae. Length: 700–800
words (features), 1000–1100 words (stories or per
episode of a serial). Illustrations: colour and b&w,
cartoons. Payment: £75 (features); £90 (stories), £80
(per episode). Founded 1993.

## The Architects' Journal

EMAP Business Communications,
151 Rosebery Avenue, London EC1R 4GB
*tel* 020-7505 6700 *fax* 020-7505 6701
*Editor* Isabel Allen
Weekly £1.80 (£78 p.a.)

Articles (mainly technical) on architecture, planning
and building accepted only with prior agreement of
synopsis. Illustrations: photos and drawings.
Payment: by arrangement. Founded 1895.

## Architectural Design

John Wiley & Sons Ltd, 4th Floor, International
House, Ealing Broadway Centre, London W5 5DB

*tel* 020-8326 3800 *fax* 020-8326 3801
*website* www.wiley.co.uk/ad/
*Editor* Helen Castle
6 double issues p.a., £22.50 single issue, £99 p.a.
(£70 p.a. students)

International architectural publication comprising an extensively illustrated thematic profile and magazine back section, *AD Plus*. Uncommissioned articles not accepted. Illustrations: drawings and photos, line (colour preferred). Payment: by arrangement. Founded 1930.

## The Architectural Review

EMAP Construct, 151 Rosebery Avenue,
London EC1R 4GB
*tel* 020-7505 6725 *fax* 020-7505 6701
*email* peter.davey@ebc.emap.com
*website* www.arplus.com/
*Editor* Peter Davey
Monthly £6.95

Articles on architecture and the allied arts. Writers must be thoroughly qualified. Length: up to 3000 words. Payment: by arrangement. Illustrations: photos, drawings, etc. Founded 1896.

## Architecture Today

161 Rosebery Avenue, London EC1R 4QX
*tel* 020-7837 0143 *fax* 020-7837 0155
*Editors* Ian Latham, Mark Swenarton
10 p.a. £4 Free to architects

Mostly commissioned articles and features on today's European architecture. Length: 200–800 words. Illustrations: colour. Payment: by negotiation. Founded 1989.

## Arena

EMAP East, Endeavour House, 189 Shaftesbury Avenue, London WC2H 8JG
*tel* 020-7437 9011
*email* arenamag@emap.com
*Editor* Anthony Noguera
Monthly £3.20

Profiles, articles on a wide range of subjects intelligently treated; art, architecture, politics, sport, business, music, film, design, media, fashion. Length: up to 3000 words. Illustrations: b&w and colour photos. Payment: £300 per 1000 words; varies for illustrations. Founded 1986.

## Art Business Today

The Fine Art Trade Guild,
16–18 Empress Place,
London SW6 1TT
*tel* 020-7381 6616 *fax* 020-7381 2596
*email* abt@fineart.co.uk
*website* www.abtonline.co.uk
*Editor* Mike Sims
5 p.a. £23 p.a.

Distributed to the fine art and framing industry. Covers essential information on new products and technology, market trends and business analysis. Length: 800–1600 words. Illustrations: colour photos, cartoons. Payment: by arrangement. Founded 1905.

## Art Monthly

4th Floor, 28 Charing Cross Road,
London WC2H 0DB
*tel* 020-7240 0389 *fax* 020-7497 0726
*email* info@artmonthly.co.uk
*website* www.artmonthly.co.uk
*Editor* Patricia Bickers
10 p.a. £3.75

Features on modern and contemporary visual artists and art history, art theory and art-related issues; exhibition and book reviews. All material commissioned. Length: 750–1500 words. Illustrations: b&w photos. Payment: features £100–£200; none for photos. Founded 1976.

## The Art Newspaper

70 South Lambeth Road, London SW8 1RL
*tel* 020-7735 3331 *fax* 020-7735 3332
*email* contact@theartnewspaper.com
*website* www.theartnewspaper.com
*Editor* Christina Ruiz
11 p.a. £4.95 (£49 p.a.)

International coverage of visual art, news, politics, law, exhibitions with some feature pages. Length: 200–1000 words. Illustrations: b&w photos. Payment: £120 per 1000 words. Founded 1990.

## Art Review

Art Review Ltd, Hereford House, 23–24 Smithfield Street, London EC1A 9LB
*tel* 020-7236 4880 *fax* 020-7246 3351
*email* info@art-review.co.uk
*website* www.art-review.com
*Editor* Ossian Ward, *Send material to* Hannah Shuckburgh, Assistant Editor
Monthly £4.25

Modern and contemporary art and style features and reviews. Proposals welcome. Payment: from £400 per 1000 words. Illustrations: colour. Founded 1949.

## The Artist

The Artists' Publishing Co. Ltd, Caxton House, 63-65 High Street, Tenterden, Kent TN30 6BD
*tel* (01580) 763673
*Editor* Sally Bulgin
Monthly £2.70

Practical, instructional articles on painting for all amateur and professional artists. Payment: by arrangement. Illustrations: line, half-tone, colour. Founded 1931.

## Artists and Illustrators

The Fitzpatrick Building, 188–194 York Way,
London N7 9QR
*tel* 020-7700 8500 *fax* 020-7700 4985
*email* aim@quarto.com
*website* www.aimag.co.uk
*Editor* James Hobbs
Monthly £2.80

Practical and business articles for amateur and
professional artists. Length: 1000–1500 words.
Illustrations: colour transparencies, high resolution
digital images. Payment: variable. Founded 1986.

## Asian Times

Ethnic Media Group, Unit 2.01, Technology Centre,
65 Whitechapel Road, London E1 1DU
*tel* 020-7650 2000 *fax* 020-7560 2001
*email* asiantimes@ethnicmedia.com
*Editor* Isaac Ham
Weekly 50p

News stories, articles and features of interest to
Britain's Asian community. Founded 1983.

## Astronomy Now

Pole Star Publications, PO Box 175, Tonbridge,
Kent TN10 4ZY
*tel* (01903) 266165 *fax* (01732) 356230
*email* editorial@astronow.cix.co.uk
*website* www.astronomynow.com
*Managing Editor* Steven Young
Monthly £2.95

Aimed at amateur and professional astronomers.
Interested in news items and longer features on
astronomy and some space-related activities.
Writers' guidelines available (send sae). Length:
600–3000 words. Illustrations: line, half-tone,
colour. Payment: 10p per word; from £10 per photo.
Founded 1987.

## Athletics Weekly

Descartes Publishing Ltd, 83 Park Road,
Peterborough PE1 2TN
*tel* (01733) 898440 *fax* (01733) 898441
*email* jason.henderson@athletics-weekly.co.uk
*Editor* Jason Henderson
Weekly £2.25

News and features on track and field athletics, road
running, cross country, fell and race walking.
Material mostly commissioned. Length: 300–1500
words. Illustrations: colour and b&w action and
head/shoulder photos, line. Payment: varies.
Founded 1945.

## Attitude

Northern & Shell Tower, City Harbour,
London E14 9GL
*tel* 020-7308 5090 *fax* 020-7308 5384
*email* attitude@nasnet.co.uk

*Editor* Adam Mattera
Monthly £2.85

Men's style magazine aimed primarily but not
exclusively at gay men. Covers style/fashion,
interviews, reviews, celebrities, humour.
Illustrations: colour transparencies, b&w prints.
Payment: £150 per 1000 words; £100 per full page
illustration. Founded 1994.

## The Author

84 Drayton Gardens, London SW10 9SB
*tel* 020-7373 6642
*Editor* Fanny Blake
Quarterly £12

Organ of the Society of Authors. Commissioned
articles from 1000–2000 words on any subject
connected with the legal, commercial or technical
side of authorship. Little scope for the freelance
writer: preliminary letter advisable. Illustrations:
line, occasional cartoons. Payment: by arrangement.
Founded 1890.

## Auto Express

Dennis Publishing Ltd, 30 Cleveland Street,
London W1T 4JD
*tel* 020-7907 6200 *fax* 020-7907 6234
*email* editorial@autoexpress.co.uk
*website* www.autoexpress.co.uk
*Editor* David Johns
Weekly £1.50

News stories, and general interest features about
drivers as well as cars. Illustrations: colour photos.
Payment: features £350 per 1000 words; photos,
varies. Founded 1988.

## Autocar

Haymarket Publishing Ltd,
60 Waldegrave Road, Teddington,
Middlesex TW11 8LG
*tel* 020-8267 5630 *fax* 020-8267 5759
*email* autocar@haynet.com
*Editor* Steve Sutcliffe
Weekly £2.10

Articles on all aspects of cars, motoring and the
motor industry: general, practical, competition and
technical. Illustrations: line (litho), colour and
electronic (Illustrator). Press day news: Thursday.
Payment: varies; mid-month following publication.
Founded 1895.

## Aviation News

HPC Publishing, Drury Lane, St Leonards-on-Sea,
East Sussex TN38 9BJ
*tel* (01424) 720477 *fax* (01424) 443693/434086
*Editor* Barry C. Wheeler
Monthly £3.40

Covers all aspects of aviation. Many articles
commissioned; will consider competent articles

exploring fresh ground or presenting an individual point of view on technical matters. Illustrated, mainly with photos. Payment: by arrangement.

## B

Attic Futura (UK) Ltd, 16–17 Berners Street, London W1T 3LN
*tel* 020-7664 6470 *fax* 020-7070 3401
*email* letters@bmagazine.co.uk
*Editor* Fran Sheen
Monthly £2.50

Magazine with international flavour for young women aged 18–25. Fashion, beauty, real life stories, topical issues, celebrity features. Contact Catherine McDonnoll in first instance with ideas for articles. Founded 1997.

## Back Street Heroes

19th Floor, 1 Canada Square, Canary Wharf, London E14 5AP
*tel* 020-7772 8300 *fax* 020-7772 8585
*Editor* Stu Garland
Monthly £3.20

Custom motorcycle features plus informed lifestyle pieces. Illustrations: colour, cartoons. Payment: by arrangement. Founded 1983.

## Balance

Diabetes UK, 10 Parkway, London NW1 7AA
*tel* 020-7424 1000 *fax* 020-7424 1081
*email* balance@diabetes.org.uk
*website* www.diabetes.org.uk
*Editor* Martin Cullen
Bi-monthly £2.95

Articles on diabetes and related health and lifestyle issues. Length: 1000–1500 words. Payment: by arrangement. Illustrations: colour. Founded 1935.

## The Banker

Tabernacle Court, 16–28 Tabernacle Court, London EC2 4DD
*tel* 020-7382 8000 *fax* 020-7382 8568
*email* stephen.timewell@ft.com
*Editor-in-Chief* Stephen Timewell
Monthly £215 p.a.

Articles on investment banking and finance, retail banking, banking technology, banking services and systems; bank analysis and top 1000 listings. Illustrations: half-tones and full colour of people, charts, tables, maps, etc. Founded 1926.

## Baptist Times

PO Box 54, 129 Broadway, Didcot, Oxon OX11 8XB
*tel* (01235) 517670 *fax* (01235) 517678
*Editor* Hazel Southam
Weekly 55p

Religious or social affairs, news, features and reviews. Payment: by arrangement. Founded 1855.

## BBC magazines – see page 333

## The Beano

D.C. Thomson & Co. Ltd, Albert Square, Dundee DD1 9QJ
*tel* (01382) 223131 *fax* (01382) 322214
185 Fleet Street, London EC4A 2HS
*tel* 020-7400 1030 *fax* 020-7400 1089
*Editor* Euan Kerr
Weekly 65p

Comic strips for children aged 6–12. Series, 11–22 pictures. Payment: on acceptance.

**Fun Size Beano**
2 p.m. 90p
Founded 1997.

## Bella

H. Bauer Publishing, Academic House, 24–28 Oval Road, London NW1 7DT
*tel* 020-7241 8000 *fax* 020-7241 8056
*Editor* Jayne Marsden *Features Editor* Clare Swatman
Weekly 70p

General interest magazine for women: practical articles on fashion and beauty, health, cooking, home, travel; real life stories, plus fiction up to 1000 words. Payment: by arrangement. Illustrations: line including cartoons, half-tone, colour. Founded 1987.

## Best

The National Magazine Company, 33 Broadwick Street, London W1F 0DQ
*tel* 020-7439 5000 *fax* 020-7312 4176
*Editor* Louise Court, *Fiction Editor* Pat Richardson, *Features Editor* Charlotte Seligman
Weekly 68p

Short stories. No other uncommissioned work accepted, but always willing to look at ideas/outlines. Length: 1000 words for short stories, variable for other work. Illustrations: line, half-tone, colour, cartoons. Payment: by agreement. Founded 1987.

## Best of British

Ian Beacham Publishing, Bank Chambers, 27A Market Place, Market Deeping, Lincs. PE6 8EA
*tel* (01778) 342814 *fax* (01778) 342814
*email* mail@british.fsbusiness.co.uk
*website* www.bestofbritishmag.co.uk
*Editor-in-Chief* Ian Beacham
Monthly £2.95

Nostalgic features about life in the 1930s, 1940s, 1950s and 1960 together with stories celebrating interesting aspects of Britain today. Length: max. 1200 words. Illustrations: colour and b&w.

Payment: from £30 (words); £20 (pictures).
Founded 1994.

## The Big Issue
1–5 Wandsworth Road, London SW8 2LN
*tel* 020-7526 3200
*Editor* Matt Ford
Weekly £1.20

Features, current affairs, reviews, interviews – of
general interest and on social issues. Length: 1000
words (features). No short stories or poetry.
Illustrations: colour and b&w photos and line.
Payment: £160 per 1000 words. Founded 1991.

## The Big Issue Cymru
55 Charles Street, Cardiff CF10 2GD
*tel* 029-2025 5670 *fax* 029-2025 5673
*email* edit@bigissuecymru.fsnet.co.uk
*Editor* Cathryn Scott
Weekly £1.20

The Welsh edition of the *Big Issue*. Content is
relevant to Wales: some articles are taken from the
main London edition but some news features, arts
and music coverage is locally sourced. Considers
unsolicited material. Welcomes ideas for articles and
features. Length: 1000–1500 words (articles/features),
200–400 words (news). Illustrations: colour and
b&w prints and artwork. Payment: 4p per word
(articles/features), 6p per word (news); £40 (cover
photo), £20 for first photo (features) and £10 for all
others used from that commission; £30
(illustrations). Founded 1994.

## The Big Issue in the North
The Big Issue in the North Ltd,
135–141 Oldham Street,
Manchester M4 1LL
*tel* 0161-834 6300 *fax* 0161-819 5000
*Editor* Ato Erzan-Essien
Weekly £1.20

Articles of general interest and on social issues; arts
features and news covering the north of England.
No fiction or poetry, except by the homeless.
Contact the news, arts or deputy editor to discuss
ideas. Length: 1500 words (features/articles),
300–500 (news), 700 (arts features), 350 words
(comment). Payment: £90 per 1000 words. Colour
transparencies, puzzles and quizzes. Founded 1992.

## The Big Issue in Scotland
The Big Issue in Scotland Ltd, 71 Oxford Street,
Glasgow G5 9EP
*tel* 0141-418 7000 *fax* 0141-418 7065
*email* editorial@bigissuescotland.com
*Editor* Claire Bluel, *Send material to* Claire Black,
Deputy Editor
Weekly £1

Features on social issues, human rights, the
environment, injustice, Scotland, medical, health and
crime plus news and arts coverage. Also international
features/news. Length: 1000–2000 words (articles);
500–800 words (news). Illustrations: colour and
b&w. Payment: £100 per 1000 words; £60 per
photo/illustration. Founded 1993.

## The Big Issue South West
5 Brunswick Court, Brunswick Square,
Bristol BS2 8PE
*tel* 0117-908 0091 *fax* 0117-908 0093
*email* editorial@bigissuesouthwest.co.uk
*website* www.bigissuesouthwest.co.uk
*Editor* Cathryn Scott
Weekly £1.20

Social news, general interest features and arts
information for the South West. Considers
unsolicited material. Length: 1200 words
(articles/features), 100–1200 words (news).
Payment: negotiable. Illustrations: colour, payment
negotiable. Founded 1991.

## Bike
EMAP Automotive Ltd, Media House, Lynchwood,
Peterborough PE2 6EA
*tel* (01733) 468000 *fax* (01733) 468196
*email* bike@emap.com
*Editor* Tim Thompson
Monthly £3.50

Motorcycle magazine: interested in articles, features,
news. Length: articles/features 1000–3000 words.
Illustrations: colour and b&w photos. Payment:
£150 per 1000 words; photos per size/position.
Founded 1971.

## Birding World
Sea Lawn, Coast Road, Cley next the Sea, Holt,
Norfolk NR25 7RZ
*tel* (01263) 740913 *fax* (01263) 741014
*email* steve@birdingworld.co.uk
*website* www.birdingworld.co.uk
*Editor* Steve Gantlett
Monthly £43 p.a. (£50 p.a. Europe; £54 p.a. rest of
the world, airmail)

Magazine for keen birdwatchers. Articles and news
stories about mainly European ornithology, with
the emphasis on ground-breaking new material and
identification. Length: up to 3000 words (articles);
up to 1500 words (news). Illustrations: good quality
colour photos of birds. Payment: up to £25 per 500
words; £10–£40 (illustrations). Founded 1987.

## Birdwatch
Solo Publishing Ltd, 3rd Floor, Leroy House,
436 Essex Road, London N1 3QP
*tel* 020-7704 9495 *fax* 020-7704 2767
*website* www.birdwatch.co.uk
*Editor* Dominic Mitchell

Monthly £3.20

Topical articles on all aspects of birds and birding, including conservation, identification, sites and habitats, equipment, overseas expeditions. Length: 700–1500 words. Illustrations: colour slides, b&w photos, colour and b&w line. Payment: from £50 per 1000 words; colour: photos £15–£40, cover £75, line by negotiation; b&w: photos £10, line £10–£40. Founded 1991.

## Bird Watching

EMAP Active Ltd, Bretton Court, Bretton, Peterborough PE3 8DZ
*tel* (01733) 264666 *fax* (01733) 465376
*email* david.cromack@emap.com
*Editor* David Cromack
Monthly £3.20

Broad range of bird-related features and photography, particularly looking at bird behaviour, bird news, reviews and UK birdwatching sites. Limited amount of overseas features. Emphasis on providing accurate information in entertaining ways. Send synopsis first. Length: 1200 words. Illustrations: colour transparencies, bird identification artwork. Payment: by negotiation. Founded 1986.

## Bizarre

Dennis Publishing, Cleveland Street, London W1T 4JD
*tel* 020-7687 7000 *fax* 020-7687 7099
*email* bizarre@ifgmags.com
*website* www.bizarremag.com
*Editor* Alex Godfrey
Monthly £3.10

Features on strange events, adventure, cults, weird people, celebrities, etc. Study the magazine for style before submitting ideas by post or fax. No fiction. Length: 800–2000 words. Payment: £80 per 1000 words. Colour transparencies and prints: £200 per dps, £125 per page. Founded 1997.

## Black Beauty & Hair

Hawker Publications, 2nd Floor, Culvert House, Culvert Road, London SW11 5DH
*tel* 020-7720 2108 *fax* 020-7498 3023
*email* info@blackbeautyandhair.com
*website* www.blackbeautyandhair.com
*Editor* Irene Shelley
Bi-monthly £2.30

Beauty and style articles relating specifically to the black woman; celebrity features. True-life stories and salon features. Length: approx. 1000 words. Illustrations: colour and b&w photos. Payment: £100 per 1000 words; photos £25–£75. Founded 1982.

## Bliss

EMAP Media, Endeavour House, 189 Shaftesbury Avenue, London WC2H 8JG
*tel* 020-7437 9011 *fax* 020-7208 3591
*website* www.blissmag.co.uk
*Editor* Charlotte Crisp
Monthly £1.90

Glamorous young women's glossy magazine. Bright intimate American-style format, with real life stories and reports, beauty, fashion, talent, advice, quizzes. Payment: by arrangement. Founded 1995.

## Blueprint

ETP Ltd, Rosebery House, 41 Springfield Road, Chelmsford CM2 6JJ
*tel* (01245) 491717 *fax* (01245) 499110
*email* ggibson@wilmington.co.uk
*Editor* Vicky Richardson
12 p.a. £3.75

The magazine of modern architecture, design and culture. Interested in articles, features and reviews. Length: up to 2500 words. Illustrations: colour and b&w photos and line. Payment: negotiable. Founded 1983.

## BMA News

British Medical Association, BMA House, Tavistock Square, London WC1H 9JP
*tel* 020-7383 6122 *fax* 020-7383 6566
*Joint Editors* Julia Bell, Caroline Winter-Jones
51 p.a. £73 p.a.

News and features. Length: 700–2000 words (features), 100–300 words (news). Illustrations: transparencies, colour and b&w artwork and cartoons. Payment: by negotiation. Founded 1966.

## Boards

Yachting Press Ltd, 196 Eastern Esplanade, Southend-on-Sea, Essex SS1 3AB
*tel* (01702) 582245 *fax* (01702) 588434
*email* editorial@boards.co.uk
*website* www.boards.co.uk
*Editor* Bill Dawes
Monthly during summer, Bi-monthly during winter £3.30 (10 p.a.)

Articles, photos and reports on all aspects of windsurfing and boardsailing. Payment: by arrangement. Illustrations: line, half-tone, colour, cartoons. Founded 1982.

## The Book Collector

The Collector Ltd, PO Box 12426, London W11 3GW
*tel* 020-7792 3492 *fax* 020-7792 3492
*email* nicolasb@nixnet.clara.co.uk
*Editorial Board* Nicolas Barker (Editor), A. Bell, A. Edwards, J. Fergusson, T. Hofmann, D. McKitterick, Joan Winterkorn

Quarterly £40 p.a. (£43/$68 overseas)

Articles, biographical and bibliographical, on the collection and study of printed books and MSS. Payment: for reviews only. Founded 1952.

## Book and Magazine Collector

Diamond Publishing Ltd, 45 St Mary's Road, London W5 5RQ
*tel* 020-8579 1082 *fax* 020-8566 2024
*Editor* Jono Scott
Monthly £3.20

Articles about collectable authors/publications/subjects. Articles must be bibliographical and include a full bibliography and price guide (no purely biographical features). Approach in writing with ideas. Length: 2000–4000 words. Illustrations: colour and b&w artwork. Payment: £35 per 1000 words. Founded 1984.

## Books Ireland

11 Newgrove Avenue, Dublin 4, Republic of Ireland
*tel* (01) 2692185 *fax* (01) 260 4927
*email* booksi@eircom.net
*Editor* Jeremy Addis, *Features Editor* Shirley Kelly
Monthly (exc. Jan, Jul, Aug) €3.50 (€32 p.a.)

Reviews of Irish-interest and Irish-author books, articles of interest to librarians, booksellers and readers. Length: 800–1400 words. Payment: €80 per 1000 words. Founded 1976.

## The Bookseller

VNU Entertainment Media Ltd, 5th Floor, Endeavour House, 189 Shaftesbury Avenue, London WC2H 8TJ
*tel* 020-7420 6006 *fax* 020-7420 6103
*email* letters.to.editor@bookseller.co.uk
*website* www.thebookseller.com
*Editor* tba
Weekly £175 p.a.

Journal of the UK publishing and bookselling trades. While outside contributions are welcomed, most of the journal's contents are commissioned. Length: about 1000–1500 words. Payment: by arrangement. Founded 1858.

## Bowls International

Key Publishing Ltd, PO Box 100, Stamford, Lincs. PE9 1XQ
*tel* (01780) 755131 *fax* (01780) 757261
*Editor* Melvyn Beck
Monthly £2.80

Sport and news items and features; occasional, bowls-oriented short stories. Illustrations: colour transparencies, b&w photos, occasional line, cartoons. Payment: sport/news approx. 25p per line, features approx. £50 per page; colour £25, b&w £10. Founded 1981.

## Brass Bandworld Magazine

Peak Press Building, Chapel-en-le-Frith, High Peak, Derbyshire SK23 9RQ
*tel* (01298) 812738 *fax* (01298) 815220
*email* editor@brassbandworld.com
*website* www.brassbandworld.com
*Editor* Robert Mulholland
Monthly £3.80

Artlcles, features and news of brass bands internationally. Reviews of concerts and contests, personality profiles, tips, and news from colleges for students, players and audiences. Payment: negotiable. Founded 1981.

## British Birds

The Banks, Mountfield, Robertsbridge, East Sussex TN32 5JY
*tel* (01580) 882039
*email* editor@britishbirds.co.uk
*Editor* Dr Roger Riddington
Monthly £58 p.a. (concessionary rates available)

Publishes major papers on identification, behaviour, conservation, distribution, ecology, movements, status and taxonomy with official reports on: rare breeding birds, scarce migrants and rare birds in Britain. Payment: token. Founded 1907.

## British Chess Magazine

44 Baker Street, London W1U 7RT
*tel* 020-7486 8222  *fax* 020-7486 3355
*email* bcmchess@compuserve.com
*Editor* John Saunders
Monthly £3.25

Authoritative reports and commentary on the UK and overseas chess world. Payment: by arrangement. Founded 1881.

## British Deaf News

7 Empire Court, Albert Street, Redditch, Worcs. B97 4DA
*tel* (01527) 592034, 592044 (text)
*fax* (01527) 592083 *videophone* (01527) 595318
*email* editorial@britishdeafness.com
*website* www.britishdeafnews.com
*Editor* Catya Wheatley
Monthly £1.95, £20 p.a. non-members (£15 p.a. BDA members)

Interviews, features, reviews, articles, news items, letters dealing with deafness. Payment: by arrangement. Illustrations: line, half-tone. Founded 1872.

## British Journalism Review

BJR Publishing Ltd, c/o Sage Publications, 6 Bonhill Street, London EC2A 4PU
*tel* 020-7374 0645 *fax* 020-7374 8741
*email* info@sagepub.co.uk
*Editor* Bill Hagerty
Quarterly £35 p.a. (overseas rates on application)

Comment/criticism/review of matters published by, or of interest to, the media. Length: 1000–3000 words. Illustrations: b&w photos. Payment: by arrangement. Founded 1989.

## The British Journal of Photography

Incisive Photographics Ltd, Incisive Media, Haymarket House, 28–29 Haymarket, London SW1Y
*tel* 020-7484 9700 *fax* 020-7484 9989
*email* bjp.editor@bjphoto.co.uk
*website* www.bjp-online.com
*Editor* Simon Bainbridge
Weekly £1.95

Articles on professional, commercial and press photography, and on the more advanced aspects of amateur, technical, industrial, medical, scientific and colour photography. Illustrations: line, half-tone, colour. Payment: by arrangement. Founded 1854.

## British Medical Journal

BMA House, Tavistock Square, London WC1H 9JR
*tel* 020-7387 4499 *fax* 020-7383 6418
*email* editor@bmj.com
*website* www.bmj.com
*Editor* Richard Smith
Weekly £5

Medical and related articles. Payment: by arrangement. Founded 1840.

## British Philatelic Bulletin

Royal Mail, 148 Old Street, London EC1V 9HQ
*fax* 020-7250 2389
*Editor* J.R. Holman
Monthly £1.10

Articles on any aspect of British philately – stamps, postmarks, postal history; also stamp collecting in general. Length: up to 1500 words (articles); 250 words (news). Payment: £60 per 1000 words. Illustrations: colour. Founded 1963.

## Broadcast

EMAP Media, 33–39 Bowling Green Lane, London EC1R 0DA
*tel* 020-7505 8014 *fax* 020-7505 8050
*Editor* Conor Dignam
Weekly £2.60

News and authoritative articles designed for all concerned with the UK and international TV and radio industry, and with programmes and advertising on TV, radio, video, cable, satellite, digital. Illustrations: colour, b&w, line, cartoons. Payment: by arrangement.

## Brownie

Warners Group Publications plc, Manor Lane, Bourne, Lincs. PE10 9PH
*tel* (01778) 391124

*website* www.girlguiding.org.uk
*Editor* Marion Thompson
Monthly £1.40

Official Magazine of The Guide Association. Short articles for Brownies (girls 7–10 years); fiction with Brownie background (700–800 words); puzzles; 'things to make', etc. Illustrations: colour. Payment: £50 per 1000 words; varies for illustrations.

## Buckinghamshire Countryside

Beaumonde Publications Ltd, PO Box 5, Hitchin, Herts. SG5 1GJ
*tel* (01462) 431237 *fax* (01462) 422015
*email* info@hertscountryside.co.uk
*Editor* Sandra Small
Bi-monthly £1.25

Articles relating to Buckinghamshire. No poetry, puzzles or crosswords. Length: approx. 1000 words. Illustrations: colour transparencies and b&w prints, artwork. Payment: £30 per article. Founded 1995.

## Building

The Builder Group plc, 7th Floor, Anchorage House, 2 Clove Crescent, London E14 2BE
*tel* 020-7560 4000 *fax* 020-7560 4014
*email* adrian_barrick@buildersgroup.co.uk
*Editor* Adrian Barrick
Weekly £2.60

Covers the entire professional, industrial and manufacturing aspects of the building industry. Articles on architecture and techniques at home and abroad considered, also news and photos. Payment: by arrangement. Founded 1842.

## Building Design

CMP Information Ltd, Ludgate House, 245 Blackfriars Road, London SE1 9UY
*tel* 020-7861 6467 *fax* 020-7861 6261
*email* bd@cmpinformation.com
*Editor* Robert Booth
Weekly Controlled circulation

News and features on all aspects of building design. All material commissioned. Length: up to 1500 words. Illustrations: colour and b&w photos, line, cartoons. Payment: £150 per 1000 words; illustrations by negotiation. Founded 1970.

## Built Environment

Alexandrine Press, 1 The Farthings, Marcham, Oxon OX13 6QD
*tel* (01865) 391518 *fax* (01865) 391687
*email* alexandrine@rudkinassociates.co.uk
*Editors* Prof Sir Peter Hall, Prof David Banister
Quarterly £90 p.a.

Articles about architecture, planning and the environment. Preliminary letter advisable. Length: 1000–5000 words. Payment: by arrangement. Illustrations: photos and line.

## The Burlington Magazine
14–16 Duke's Road, London WC1H 9SZ
*tel* 020-7388 1228 *fax* 020-7388 1230
*email* editorial@burlington.org.uk
*Editor* Richard Shone
Monthly £13.20

Deals with the history and criticism of art; book and exhibition reviews; illustrated monthly Calendar section. Potential contributors must have special knowledge of the subjects treated; MSS compiled from works of reference are unacceptable. Length: 500–5000 words. Payment: up to £140. Illustrations: b&w and colour photos. Founded 1903.

## Buses
Ian Allan Publishing Ltd, Riverdene Business Park, Molesey Road, Hersham, Surrey KT12 4RG
*tel* (01932) 266600 *fax* (01932) 266601
*email* alan@millar1.demon.co.uk
*website* www.busesmag.com
*Editor* Alan Millar, PO Box 3759, Glasgow G41 5YN
*tel* 0141-427 6294 *fax* 0141-427 9594
Monthly £3.25

Articles of interest to both road passenger transport operators and bus enthusiasts. Preliminary enquiry essential. Illustrations: colour transparencies, half-tone, line maps. Payment: on application. Founded 1949.

## Business Life
Pegasus House, 37–43 Sackville Street, London W15 3EH
*tel* 020-7925 2544 *fax* 020-7839 4508
*website* www.cedarcom.co.uk
*Editor* Alex Finer
Monthly Free

Inflight magazine for British Airways. Articles and features of interest to the European business traveller. All material commissioned; approach in writing with ideas. Length: 850–2500 words. Illustrations: colour photos and line. Payment: £250 per 1000 words; £100–£400 for illustrations. Founded 1985.

## Business Scotland
Peebles Media Group, Bergius House, Clifton Street, Glasgow G3 7LA
*tel* 0141-567 6000 *fax* 0141-331 1395
*Editor* Graham Lironi
Monthly Controlled circulation

Features, profiles and news items of interest to business and finance in Scotland. Payment: by arrangement. Founded 1947.

## Business Traveller
Perry Publications Ltd, Nestor House, Playhouse Yard, London EC4V 5EX
*tel* 020-7778 0000 *fax* 020-7778 0011
*email* editorial@businesstraveller.com
*website* www.btonline.co.uk
*Editor* Julia Brookes
Monthly £2.90

Articles, features and news on consumer travel aimed at individual frequent international business travellers. Submit ideas with recent clippings and a CV. Length: varies. Illustrations: colour for destinations features; send lists to Deborah Miller, Picture Editor. Payment: on application. Founded 1976.

## Cable Guide
Scorpio Multimedia, 1st Floor, 40 Bernard Street, London WC1N 1LE
*tel* 020-7419 8419 *fax* 020-7419 8400
*website* www.cableguide.co.uk
*Editor* Robin Jarossi
Monthly £3.25 (£30 p.a.)

Features and interviews about programmes featured on cable TV, together with programme listings for cable channels. All material commissioned. Length: up to 1000 words. Illustrations: colour transparencies. Payment: £550 per 1000 words, photo fees negotiable. Founded 1986.

## Cambridgeshire Journal
The Old County School, Northgate Street, Bury St Edmunds, Suffolk IP33 1HP
*email* pippa@acornmagazines.co.uk
*Editor* Pippa Bastin, *Send material to* Pippa Bastin or Alexandra Edoruk
Monthly £2.30

Articles, features and news of interest to Cambridgeshire: history, people, events, natural history and other issues. Also regional lifestyle, i.e. gardens, homes and fashion. Specially commissions most material. Welcomes ideas for articles and features. Length: 1500 words (articles/features), 250 words (news). Payment: £125 (articles/features), none (news). Illustrations: colour transparencies and prints. Founded 1994.

## Camcorder User
WVIP, 53–79 Highgate Road, London NW5 1TW
*tel* 020-7331 1000 *fax* 020-7331 1242
*email* rob.hull@wvip.co.uk
*Editor* Robert Hull
Monthly £3.25

Features on film/video-making techniques, specifically tailored to the amateur enthusiast. Material mostly commissioned. Length: 1000–2500 words. Illustrations: colour and b&w; contact Editor for details. Payment: by arrangement. Founded 1988.

## Campaign
Haymarket Business Publications Ltd, 174 Hammersmith Road, London W6 7JP
*tel* 020-8943 5000

*website* www.brandrepublic.com
*Editor* Caroline Marshall
Weekly £2.65

News and articles covering the whole of the mass communications field, particularly advertising in all its forms, marketing and the media. Features should not exceed 2000 words. News items also welcome. Press day, Wednesday. Payment: by arrangement.

## Camping Magazine

Warner Group Publications, The Maltings, West Street, Bourne, Lincs. PE10 9PH
*tel* (01778) 391116 *fax* (01778) 391116
*Editor* John Lloyd
Monthly £2.80

Covers the spectrum of camping and related activities in all shapes and forms – camping is more than a tent on a site! Lively, anecdotal articles written to guidelines and photos are welcome. Talk to the Editor first. Length: 500–1500 words on average. Illustrations: colour. Payment: by arrangement. Founded 1961.

## Canal & Riverboat

PO Box 618, Norwich NR7 0QT
*tel* (01603) 708930 *fax* (01603) 708934
*email* bluefoxfilms@themag.fsnet.co.uk
*website* www.canalandriverboat.com
*Editor* Chris Cattrall
Monthly £2.70

News, views and articles on UK inland waterways and cruising features, DIY articles and historical features. Length: 1500 words (articles/features), 300 words (news). Payment: £100; £25 (news). Illustrations: colour, plus b&w cartoons. Founded 1978.

## Car

EMAP Automotive Ltd, 3rd Floor, Media House, Lynchwood, Peterborough PE2 6EA
*tel* (01733) 468000 *fax* (01733) 468001
*email* car@emap.com
*Editor* Greg Fountain
Monthly £3.50

Top-grade journalistic features on car driving, car people and cars. Length: 1000–2500 words. Payment: minimum £250 per 1000 words. Illustrations: b&w and colour photos to professional standards. Founded 1962.

## Car Mechanics

Cudham Tithe Barn, Berrys Hill, Cudham, Kent TW16 3AG
*tel* (01959) 541444, 543500 *fax* (01959) 541400
*email* info@kelsey.co.uk
*Editor* Peter Simpson
Monthly £3.10

Practical articles on maintaining, repairing and uprating modern cars for DIY plus the motor trade.

Always interested in finding new talent for our rather specialised market but please study a recent copy before submitting ideas or features. Preliminary letter or phone call outlining feature recommended. Payment: by arrangement. Illustrations: line drawings, colour prints or transparencies. Rarely use words only; please supply text and pictures.

## Caravan Magazine

IPC Country & Leisure Media Ltd, Focus House, Dingwall Avenue, Croydon CR9 2TA
*tel* 020-8774 0600 *fax* 020-8774 0939
*website* www.caravanmagazine.co.uk
*Editor* Steve Rowe
Monthly £2.99

Lively articles based on real experience of touring caravanning, especially if well illustrated by photos. General countryside or motoring material not wanted. Payment: by arrangement. Founded 1933.

## Caribbean Times

Ethnic Media Group, Unit 2, Technology Centre, 65 Whitehchapel Road, London E1 1DU
*tel* 020-7650 2000 *fax* 020-7650 2001
*email* caribbeantimes@hotmail.com
*Editor* Michael Eboda
Weekly 50p

News stories, articles and features of interest to Britain's African–Caribbean community. Founded 1981.

## Carousel – The Guide to Children's Books

The Saturn Centre, 54–76 Bissell Street, Birmingham B5 7HX
*tel* 0121-622 7458 *fax* 0121-666 7526
*email* carousel.guide@virgin.net
*website* www.carousel.guide.co.uk
*Editor* Jenny Blanch
3 p.a. £10.50 p.a. (£15 p.a. Europe; £18 p.a. rest of world)

Reviews of fiction, non-fiction and poetry books for children, plus in-depth articles; profiles of authors and illustrators. Length: 1200 words (articles); 150 words (reviews). Illustrations: colour and b&w. Payment: by arrangement. Founded 1995.

## Cars and Car Conversions

IPC Country & Leisure Media Ltd, Focus House, Dingwall Avenue, Croydon CR9 2TA
*tel* 020-8774 0946 *fax* 020-8774 0935
*email* ccc@ipcmedia.com
*website* www.cccmagazine.com
*Editor* Steve Kirk, *Send material to* Carlin Gerbich, Deputy Editor
Monthly £3.30

Performance car and motorsport articles and features. Specially commissions most material.

Welcomes ideas for articles and features. Illustrations: transparencies, digital images. Founded 1963.

## Caterer & Hotelkeeper

Reed Business Information Ltd, Quadrant House, The Quadrant, Sutton, Surrey SM2 5AS
*tel* 020-8652 8680 *fax* 020-8652 8973/8947
*Editor* Forbes Mutch
Weekly £2

Articles on all aspects of the hotel and catering industries. Length: up to 1500 words. Illustrations: line, half-tone, colour. Payment: by arrangement. Founded 1893.

## The Catholic Herald

Herald House, Lambs Passage, Bunhill Row, London EC1Y 8TQ
*tel* 020-7588 3101 *fax* 020-7256 9728
*email* editorial@catholicherald.co.uk
*website* www.catholicherald.co.uk
*Editor* Luke Coppen
Weekly 80p

Independent newspaper covering national and international affairs from a Catholic/Christian viewpoint as well as church news. Length: articles 600–1200 words. Illustrations: photos of Catholic and Christian interest, cartoons. Payment: by arrangement.

## Catholic Pictorial

Media House, Mann Island, Pier Head, Liverpool L3 1DQ
*tel* 0151-236 2191 *fax* 0151-236 2216
*email* newsdesk@catholicpictorial.co.uk
*website* www.catholicpictorial.co.uk
*Editor* David Mahon
Weekly 60p

News and photo features (maximum 800 words plus illustration) of Merseyside, regional and national Catholic interest only; also cartoons. Has a strongly social editorial and is a trenchant tabloid. Payment: by arrangement. Founded 1961.

## Cat World

Ashdown Publishing, Avalon Court, Star Road, Partridge Green, West Sussex RH13 8RY
*tel* (01403) 711511 *fax* (01403) 711521
*email* editor@catworld.co.uk
*website* www.catworld.co.uk
*Editor* Jo Rothery
Monthly £2.75

Bright, lively articles on any aspect of cat ownership. Articles on breeds of cats and veterinary articles by acknowledged experts only. No unsolicited fiction. All submissions by email or on disk. Illustrations: colour prints, transparencies, TIFFs. Payment: by arrangement. Founded 1981.

## Catholic Times

1st Floor, St James's Buildings, Oxford Street, Manchester M1 6FP
*tel* 0161-236 8856 *fax* 0161-237 5590
*Editor* Kevin Flaherty
Weekly 70p

News (400 words) and news features (800 words) of Catholic interest. Illustrations: colour and b&w photos. Payment: £30–£80; photos £50. Relaunched 1993.

## Cencrastus: Scottish & International Literature, Arts and Affairs

Unit One, Abbeymount Techbase, 2 Easter Road, Edinburgh EH8 8EJ
*tel* 0131-661 5687 *fax* 0131-661 5687
*email* cencrastus1@hotmail.com
*Editor* Raymond Ross, *Managing Editor* Zsvzsanna Varga
Quarterly £2.95 (back copies £2.50); £12 p.a.

Articles, short stories, poetry, reviews. Payment: by arrangement. Illustrations: line, half-tone. Founded 1979.

## Chapman

4 Broughton Place, Edinburgh EH1 3RX
*tel* 0131-557 2207 *fax* 0131-556 9565
*email* chapman-pub@blueyonder.co.uk
*website* www.chapman-pub.co.uk
*Editor* Joy Hendry
3 p.a. £20 p.a.

'Scotland's Quality Literary Magazine.' Poetry, short stories, reviews, criticism, articles on Scottish culture. Illustrations: line, half-tone, cartoons. Payment: £8.00 per page; illustrations by negotiation. Founded 1969.

## Chartered Secretary

16 Park Crescent, London W1B 1AH
*tel* 020-7612 7045 *fax* 020-7612 7034
*email* chartsec@icsa.co.uk
*website* www.charteredsecretary.net
*Editor* Will Booth
Monthly (£67 p.a. post free UK)

Official magazine of The Institute of Chartered Secretaries and Administrators. Practical and topical articles (2000+ words) on law, finance and management affecting company secretaries and other senior administrators in business, not-for-profit sector, local and central government and other institutions in Britain and overseas.

## Chat

IPC Connect Ltd, King's Reach Tower, Stamford Street, London SE1 9LS
*tel* 020-7261 6565 *fax* 020-7261 6534
*website* www.ipcmedia.com
*Editor* June Smith-Sheppard

Weekly 72p

Tabloid weekly for women: 60 word stories, true life features. Payment: by arrangement. Founded 1985.

## Child Education

Scholastic Ltd, Villiers House, Clarendon Avenue, Leamington Spa, Warks. CV32 5PR
*tel* (01926) 887799 *fax* (01926) 883331
*website* www.scholastic.co.uk
*Acting Editor* Michael Ward
Monthly £3.75

For teachers concerned with the education of children aged 4–7. Articles by specialists on practical teaching ideas and methods. Length: 600–1200 words. Payment: by arrangement. Profusely illustrated with photos and artwork; also A1 full colour picture poster. Founded 1924.

## The China Quarterly

School of Oriental and African Studies, Thornhaugh Street, Russell Square, London WC1H 0XG
*tel* 020-7898 4063 *fax* 020-7898 4849
*email* chinaq@soas.ac.uk
*Editor* Dr Julia Strauss
Quarterly £39/$68 p.a. (£80/$135 institutions, £20/$35 students)

Articles on contemporary China. Length: 8000 words approx.

## Choice

1st Floor, 2 King Street,
Peterborough PE1 1LT
*tel* (01733) 555123 *fax* (01733) 427500
*Editor* Norman Wright
Monthly £2.50

Pre- and retirement magazine for 50+ readership. Positive attitude to life – experiences, hobbies, holidays, finance, relationships. If suggesting feature material, include selection of cuttings of previously published work. Payment: by agreement, on publication. Founded 1974.

## Christian Herald

Christian Media Centre, Garcia Estate, Canterbury Road, Worthing,
West Sussex BN13 1EH
*tel* (01903) 821082 *fax* (01903) 821081
*email* news@christianherald.org.uk
features@christianherald.org.uk
*website* www.christianherald.org.uk
Weekly 70p

Evangelical Christian paper with strong emphasis on news and current affairs. Features up to 800 words – profiles, the changing church, Christians, and contemporary culture (e.g. media, TV, music); cartoons. No short stories. Payment: £20–£60, depending on length/pictures used.

## Church of England Newspaper

20–26 Brunswick Place, London N1 6DZ
*tel* 020-7417 5800 *fax* 020-7216 6410
*email* cen@parlicom.com
*website* www.churchnewspaper.com
Weekly 70p

Anglican news and articles relating the Christian faith to everyday life. Evangelical basis; almost exclusively commissioned articles. Study of paper desirable. Length: up to 1000 words. Illustrations: photos, line drawings, cartoons. Payment: c. £40 per 1000 words; photos £22, line by arrangement. Founded 1828.

## Church Times

33 Upper Street, London N1 0PN
*tel* 020-7359 4570 *fax* 020-7226 3073
*email* editor@churchtimes.co.uk
*website* www.churchtimes.co.uk
*Editor* Paul Handley
Weekly 80p

Articles on religious topics are considered. No verse or fiction. Length: up to 1000 words. Illustrations: news photos, sent promptly. Payment: £100 per 1000 words; Periodical Publishers' Association negotiated rates for illustrations. Founded 1863.

## Classic & Sports Car

Haymarket Specialist Motoring Publications Ltd, Somerset House, Somerset Road, Teddington, Middlesex TW11 8RT
*tel* 020-8267 5399 *fax* 020-8267 5318
*Editor* James Elliott
Monthly £3.60

Features on classic cars and sportscars; shows, news and reviews, features and stories. Illustrations: half-tone, colour. Payment: £250 per 1000 words; varies for illustrations. Founded 1982.

## Classic Boat & The Boatman

Focus House, Dingwall Avenue, Croydon CR9 2TA
*tel* 020-8774 0603 *fax* 020-8774 0943
*email* cb@ipcmedia.com
*website* www.classicboat.co.uk
*Editor* Dan Houston
Monthly £3.75

Cruising and technical features, restorations, events, new boat reviews, practical, maritime history; news. Study of magazine essential: read 3–4 back issues and send for contributors' guidelines. Length: 500–2000 words. Illustrations: colour and b&w photos; line drawings of hulls. Payment: £75–£100 per published page. Founded 1987.

## Classic Cars

EMAP Automotive Ltd, Media House, Lynchwood, Peterborough Business Park, Peterborough PE2 6EA
*tel* (01733) 468219 *fax* (01733) 468888

*email* classic.cars@emap.com
*website* www.classiccarsmagazine.co.uk
*Editor* Martyn Moore
Monthly £3.60

Specialist articles on older cars. Length: from 500–4000 words (subject to prior contract). Illustrations: half-tone, colour, cartoons. Payment: by negotiation.

## Classic Stitches

D.C. Thomson & Co. Ltd, 80 Kingsway East, Dundee DD4 8SL
*tel* (01382) 223131 *fax* (01382) 452491
*email* editorial@classicstitches.com
*website* www.classicstitches.com
*Editor* Mrs Bea Neilson
Bi-monthly £3.95

Creative needlework ideas and projects; needlework-based features on designers, collections, work-in-progress and exhibitions. Submissions also welcome for e-mag on website. Length: 1000–1500 words. Illustrations: colour photos, preferably not 35mm. Payment: negotiable. Founded 1994.

## Classical Music

Rhinegold Publishing Ltd, 241 Shaftesbury Avenue, London WC2H 8TF
*tel* 020-7333 1742 *fax* 020-7333 1769
*email* classical.music@rhinegold.co.uk
*website* www.rhinegold.co.uk
*Editor* Keith Clarke
Fortnightly £3.25

News, opinion, features on the classical music business. All material commissioned. Illustrations: colour photos and line; colour covers. Payment: minimum £100 per 1000 words; from £50 for illustrations. Founded 1976.

## Classics

SPL, Berwick House, 8–10 Knoll Rise, Orpington, Kent BR6 0PS
*tel* (01689) 887200 *fax* (01689) 876438
*email* classics@splpublishing.co.uk
*Editor* Tim Morgan
Monthly £3.70

News photos and stories of classic car interest and illustrated features on classic car history, repairs, maintenance and restoration. Study magazine before submitting material. Features must have high level of subject knowledge and technical accuracy. Length: up to 2000 words (features); 200 words (news). Illustrations: colour and b&w. Payment: £120 per 1000 words plus £100 per set of supporting photos (features); £120 per 1000 words plus photos based on £100 per page (news). Founded 1997.

## Climber

Warners Group Publications plc, West Street, Bourne, Lincs. PE10 9PH
*tel* (01778) 391117

*Editor* Bernard Newman
Monthly £3.10

Articles on all aspects of rock climbing/mountaineering in Great Britain and abroad, and on related subjects. Study of magazine essential. Length: 1500–2000 words. Illustrations: colour transparencies. Payment: according to merit. Founded 1962.

## Coin News

Token Publishing Ltd, Orchard House, Duchy Road, Heathpark, Honiton, Devon EX14 1YD
*tel* (01404) 46972 *fax* (01404) 44788
*Editor* John W. Mussell
Monthly £2.95

Articles of high standard on coins, tokens, paper money. Length: up to 2000 words. Payment: by arrangement. Founded 1964.

## Commando

D.C. Thomson & Co. Ltd, Albert Square, Dundee DD1 9QJ
*tel* (01382) 223131 *fax* (01382) 322214
8 p.m. £1

Fictional war stories told in pictures. Scripts: about 135 pictures. Synopsis required as an opener. New writers encouraged; send for details. Payment: on acceptance.

## Commercial Motor

Reed Business Information Ltd, Quadrant House, The Quadrant, Sutton, Surrey SM2 5AS
*tel* 020-8652 3302/3303 *fax* 020-8652 8969
*Editor-in-Chief* Andy Salter
Weekly £1.70

Technical and road transport articles only. Length: up to 1500 words. Payment: varies. Illustrations: drawings and photos. Founded 1905.

## Communicate

BPL Business Media Ltd, Brooklyn House, 22 The Green, West Drayton, Middlesex 4B7 7PQ
*tel* (01895) 421111 *fax* (01895) 431252
*Editor* Joanna Perry
Monthly Controlled circulation

Covers all aspects of telecommunications management: analysis pieces (200–700 words), features (1000–2000 words), case studies (300 words). Some material commissioned. Illustrations: colour photos, line, diagrams. Payment: by arrangement. Founded 1980.

## Community Care

Reed Business Information Ltd, Quadrant House, The Quadrant, Sutton, Surrey SM2 5AS
*tel* 020-8652 4861 *fax* 020-8652 4739
*email* comcare.news@rbi.co.uk
*website* www.communitycare.co.uk

*Editor* Polly Neate
Weekly £1.85

Articles, features and news covering the Social
Services sector.

## Company

National Magazine House, 72 Broadwick Street,
London W1V 2BP
*tel* 020-7439 5000
*email* company.mail@natmags.co.uk
*Editor* Victoria White
Monthly £1.50

Articles on a wide variety of subjects, relevant to
young, independent women. Most articles are
commissioned. Payment: usual magazine rate.
Illustrated. Founded 1978.

## Computer Weekly

Reed Business Information Ltd, Quadrant House,
The Quadrant, Sutton, Surrey SM2 5AS
*tel* 020-8652 3122 *fax* 020-8652 8979
*website* www.computerweekly.com
*Editor* Hooman Bassirian, *News Editor* Mike Simons
Weekly £2.40

Feature articles on IT-related topics for
business/industry users. Length: 1200 words.
Illustrations: b&w and colour photos, line, cartoons.
Payment: £253 per 1000 words; negotiable for
illustrations. Founded 1966.

## Computing

VNU Business Publications, VNU House,
32–34 Broadwick Street, London W1A 2HG
*tel* 020-7316 9158 *fax* 020-7316 9160
*website* www.computing-media.co.uk
*Editor* Colin Barker
Weekly £2.60

Features and news items on corporate procurement
and deployment of IT infrastructure, and on
applications and implications of computers and
telecommunications. Particular sections address the
IT professional career development, and the desktop
computing environment. Length: 1600–2200 words.
Payment: by negotiation. Illustrations: colour
photos, line drawings, cartoons. Founded 1973.

## Condé Nast Traveller

Vogue House, Hanover Square, London W1S 1JU
*tel* 020-7499 9080 *fax* 020-7493 3758
*email* cntraveller@condenast.co.uk
*website* www.cntraveller.co.uk
*Editor* Sarah Miller
Monthly £3.40

Lavishly photographed features on all aspects of
travel, from food and wine to beauty and health.
Illustrations: colour. Payment: by arrangement.
BSME Lifestyle Magazine of the Year, 2000, 2001,
2003. Founded 1997.

## Contemporary

Suite K101, Tower Bridge Business Complex,
100 Clements Road, London SE16 4DG
*tel* 020-7740 1704 *fax* 020-7252 3510
*email* info@contemporary-magazine.com
*website* www.contemporary-magazine.com
*Editors* Roger Tatley, Mark Rappolt
Monthly £5.95

International magazine with extensive coverage of
visual arts, architecture, fashion, film, photography,
books, music, dance and sport. Also includes
interviews, profiles and art news from around the
world. Length: varies. Illustrations: colour
transparencies, hi-res scans. Payment: £100 per 1000
words; none for photos. Founded 1997; relaunched
2002.

## Contemporary Review

Contemporary Review Co. Ltd, PO Box 1242,
Oxford OX1 4FJ
*tel* (01865) 201529 *fax* (01865) 201529
*email* editorial@contemporaryreview.co.uk
*Editor* Dr Richard Mullen
Monthly £3.50

Independent review dealing with questions of the
day, chiefly politics, international affairs, religion,
literature, the arts. Mostly commissioned, but with
limited scope for freelance authors with
authoritative knowledge. TS returned only if sae
enclosed. Intending contributors should study
journal first. Length: 2000–3000 words. No
illustrations. Payment: £5 per page (500 words), 2
complimentary copies. Founded 1866.

## Cosmogirl

National Magazine House, 72 Broadwick Street,
London W1F 9EP
*tel* 020-7439 5081 *fax* 020-7439 5400
*email* cosmogirl.mail@natmags.co.uk
*website* www.cosmogirl.co.uk
*Editor* Celia Duncan, *Send material to* Miranda
Eason
Monthly £2

Little sister to *Cosmopolitan*. Features 'to inspire
teenage girls to be the best they can be'. Specially
commissions most material. Welcomes ideas for
articles and features. Length: 600 words. All
illustrations commissioned. Founded 2001.

## Cosmopolitan

National Magazine House, 72 Broadwick Street,
London W1V 2BP
*tel* 020-7439 5000 *fax* 020-7439 5016
*Editor-in-Chief* Lorraine Candy
Monthly £2.70

Articles. Commissioned material only. Payment: by
arrangement. Illustrated. Founded 1972.

## Country

A & D Media Ltd, Jesses Farm, Snow Hill, Dinton, Nr Salisbury, Wilts. SP3 5HN
*tel* (01722) 716996 *fax* (01722) 716926
*Editor* Geoff Mowday
6 p.a. £2.95 (members only)

Magazine of the Country Gentlemen's Association. News and features covering rural events, countryside, leisure, heritage, homes and gardens. Some outside contributors used. Payment: by arrangement. Founded 1893.

## Country Homes and Interiors

IPC Magazines Ltd, King's Reach Tower, Stamford Street, London SE1 9LS
*tel* 020-7261 6451 *fax* 020-7261 6895
*Editor* Deborah Barker
Monthly £2.80

Articles on property, country homes, interior designs. Illustrations: colour. Payment: from £250 per 1000 words. Founded 1986.

## Country Life

IPC Media Ltd, King's Reach Tower, Stamford Street, London SE1 9LS
*tel* 020-7261 7058 *fax* 020-7261 5139
*Editor* Clive Aslet
Weekly £2.90

Illustrated journal chiefly concerned with British country life, social history, architecture and the fine arts, natural history, agriculture, gardening and sport. Length: about 1000 or 1300 words (articles). Illustrations: mainly colour photos. Payment: according to merit. Founded 1897.

## Country Living

National Magazine House, 72 Broadwick Street, London W1F 9EP
*tel* 020-7439 5000 *fax* 020-7439 5093
*website* www.countryliving.co.uk
*Editor* Susy Smith
Monthly £3

Up-market home-interest magazine with a country lifestyle theme, covering interiors, gardens, crafts, food, wildlife, rural and green issues. Do not send unsolicited material or valuable transparencies. Illustrations: line, half-tone, colour. Payment: by arrangement. Founded 1985.

## Country Quest

7 Aberystwyth Science Park, Aberystwyth, Ceredigion SY23 3AH
*tel* (01970) 615000 *fax* (01970) 624699
*Editor* Erica Jones
Monthly £2

Illustrated articles on matters relating to countryside, history and personalities of Wales and border counties. No fiction. Illustrated work preferred. Length: 1500–2500 words. Payment: by arrangement.

## Country Smallholding

Archant Regional Ltd, Fair Oak Close, Exeter Airport Business Park, Clyst Honiton, Exeter EX5 2UL
*tel* (01392) 888475 *fax* (01392) 888550
*email* editorial@countrysmallholding.com
*website* www.countrysmallholding.com
*Editor* Diane Cowgill
Monthly £2.75

The magazine for smallholders. Practical, how-to articles, and seasonal features, on organic gardening, small-scale poultry and livestock keeping, country crafts, cookery and smallholdings. Approach the Editor in writing with ideas. Length: up to 2000 words. Payment: £40 per 1000 words; photos £10, £50 cover. Founded 1975 as *Home Farm*.

## Country Walking

EMAP Active Ltd, Bretton Court, Bretton, Peterborough PE3 8DZ
*tel* (01733) 264666 *fax* (01733) 282653
*Editor* Jonathan Manning
Monthly £3.10

Features. Length: 1200 words on average. Illustrations: colour transparencies. Payment: by arrangement. Founded 1987.

## The Countryman

Dalesman Publishing Group Ltd, Stable Courtyard, Broughton Hall, Skipton, North Yorks BD23 3AZ
*tel* (01756) 701381
*email* editorial@thecountryman.co.uk
*Editor* Bill Taylor
Monthly £2.20

Every area of rural life. Copy must be trustworthy, well-written, brisk, cogent and light in hand. Articles up to 1200 words. Skilful sketches of life and character from personal knowledge and experience. Dependable natural history based on writer's own observation. Really good matter from old unpublished letters and MSS. Study magazine before submitting material. Illustrations: b&w and colour photos and drawings, but all must be exclusive and out of the ordinary. Payment: min. £70 per 1000 words, usually more, according to merit. Founded 1927.

## Critical Quarterly

*Contributions* Ollie Garrett, School of English, Queen's Building, The Queen's Drive, Exeter EX4 4QH
*website* www.criticalquarterly.co.uk
Quarterly £21 p.a. (£88 p.a. institutions)

Fiction, poems, literary criticism. Length: 2000–5000 words. Study magazine before submitting MSS. Payment: by arrangement. Founded 1959.

## Cumbria and Lake District Magazine

Dalesman Publishing Company Ltd,
Stable Courtyard, Broughton Hall, Skipton,
North Yorkshire BD23 3AE
*tel* (01756) 701381 *fax* (01756) 701326
*email* editorial@dalesman.co.uk
*Editor* Terry Fletcher
Monthly £1.50

Articles of genuine rural interest concerning
Lakeland and Cumbria. Short length preferred.
Illustrations: first-class photos. Payment: according
to merit. Founded 1951.

## Custom Car

Kelsey Publishing Ltd, Cudham Tithe Barn,
Berry's Hill, Cudham, Kent TN16 3AG
*tel* (01959) 541444 *fax* (01959) 541400
*email* cc.mag@kelsey.co.uk
*website* www.kelsey.co.uk/custom
*Editor* Kev Elliott
Monthly £2.95

Customising, drag racing and hot rods. Payment: by
arrangement. Founded 1970.

## Cycle Sport

IPC Leisure & Media Ltd, 5th Floor, Focus House,
9 Dingwall Avenue, Croydon CR9 2TA
*tel* 020-8774 0889 *fax* 020-8774 0952
*email* cycling@ipcmedia.com
*Managing Editor* Robert Garbutt, *Deputy Editor*
Nigel Wynn
Monthly £3.75

Articles and features on European professional
racing. Specially commissions most material but
will consider unsolicited material. Welcomes ideas
for articles and features. Length: 1500–2500 words.
Illustrations: transparencies, colour and b&w
artwork and cartoons, digital images. Payment:
£120 per 1000 words; £50–£150 illustrations.
Founded 1991.

## Cycling Weekly

IPC Music and Sport Ltd, 5th Floor, Focus House,
9 Dingwall Avenue, Croydon CR9 2TA
*tel* 020-8774 0811 *fax* 020-8774 0952
*email* cycling@ipcmedia.com
*Editor* Robert Garbutt
Weekly £2

Racing and technical articles. Illustrations: topical
photos with a cycling interest considered; cartoons.
Length: not exceeding 2000 words. Payment: by
arrangement. Founded 1891.

## Cyphers

3 Selskar Terrace, Ravelagh, Dublin 6,
Republic of Ireland
*tel* (01) 4978866 *fax* (01) 4978866
€12/$25 for 3 issues

Poems, fiction, reviews, translations. Payment: €15
per page. Founded 1975.

## Dairy Farmer

CMP Information Ltd, Sovereign House,
Sovereign Way, Tonbridge, Kent TN9 1RW
*tel* (01732) 377273 *fax* (01732) 377644
*email* phollinshead@cmpinformation.com
*Editor* Peter Hollinshead
Monthly Controlled circulation

In-depth, technical articles on all aspects of dairy
farm management and milk marketing. Length:
normally 800–1400 words with colour photos.
Payment: by arrangement.

## Dalesman

Dalesman Publishing Company Ltd,
Stable Courtyard, Broughton Hall, Skipton,
North Yorkshire BD23 3AE
*tel* (01756) 701381 *fax* (01756) 701326
*email* editorial@dalesman.co.uk
*Editor* Terry Fletcher
Monthly £1.70

Articles and stories of genuine rural interest
concerning Yorkshire (1000–1500 words). Payment:
according to merit. Illustrations: line drawings and
first-class photos preferably featuring people.
Founded 1939.

## Dance Today!

The Dancing Times Ltd, 45–47 Clerkenwell Green,
London EC1R 0EB
*tel* 020-7250 3006 *fax* 020-7253 6679
*email* dancetoday!@dancing-times.co.uk
*website* www.dancing-times.co.uk
*Editor* Sylvia Boerner, *Editorial Adviser* Mary Clarke
Monthly £1.20

Ballroom and social dancing from every aspect,
ranging from competition reports to dance holiday
features and musical reviews. Well-informed
freelance articles are occasionally used, but only
after preliminary arrangements. Payment: by
arrangement. Illustrations: action photos preferred,
b&w or colour. Founded 1956.

## Dancing Times

The Dancing Times Ltd, 45–47 Clerkenwell Green,
London EC1R 0EB
*tel* 020-7250 3006 *fax* 020-7253 6679
*email* dt@dancing-times.co.uk
*website* www.dancing-times.co.uk
*Editor* Mary Clarke, *Editorial Adviser* Ivor Guest
Monthly £2.50

Ballet, contemporary dance and all forms of stage
dancing from general, historical, critical and
technical angles. Well-informed freelance articles
used occasionally, but only after preliminary
arrangements. Payment: by arrangement.

Illustrations: occasional line, action photos preferred; colour welcome. Founded 1910.

## The Dandy

D.C. Thomson & Co. Ltd, Albert Square, Dundee DD1 9QJ
*tel* (01382) 223131 *fax* (01382) 322214
185 Fleet Street, London EC4A 2HS
*tel* 020-7400 1030 *fax* 020-7400 1089
Weekly 65p

Comic strips for children. 10–12 pictures per single page story, 18–20 pictures per 2-page story. Promising artists are encouraged. Payment: on acceptance.

### Funsize Dandy
2 p.m. 90p

## Darts World

World Magazines Ltd, 28 Arrol Road, Beckenham, Kent BR3 4PA
*tel* 020-8650 6580 *fax* 020-8654 4343
*Editor* Tony Wood
Monthly £2.50

Articles and stories with darts theme. Illustrations: half-tone, cartoons. Payment: £40–£50 per 1000 words; illustrations by arrangement. Founded 1972.

## Day by Day

Woolacombe House, 141 Woolacombe Road, London SE3 8QP
*tel* 020-8856 6249
*Editor* Patrick Richards
Monthly £1.20

Articles and news on non-violence and social justice. Reviews of art, books, films, plays, musicals and opera. Cricket reports. Short poems and very occasional short stories in keeping with editorial viewpoint. Payment: £2 per 1000 words. No illustrations required. Founded 1963.

## Decanter

IPC Country & Leisure Media Ltd, 1st Floor, Broadway House, 2–6 Fulham Broadway, London SW6 1AA
*tel* 020-7610 3929 *fax* 020-7381 5282
*email* editorial@decantermagazine.com
*website* www.decanter.com
*Editor* Amy Wislocki
Monthly £3.40

Articles and features on wines, wine travel and food-related topics. Welcomes ideas for articles and features. Length: 1000–1800 words. Illustrations: colour. Payment: £230 per 1000 words. Founded 1975.

## Derbyshire Life and Countryside

Heritage House, Lodge Lane, Derby DE1 3HE
*tel* (01332) 347087/8/9 *fax* (01332) 290688
*email* editorials@hhgroup.co.uk
Monthly £1.75

Articles, preferably illustrated, about Derbyshire life, people and history. Length: up to 800 words. Some short stories set in Derbyshire accepted; no verse. Payment: according to nature and quality of contribution. Illustrations: photos of Derbyshire subjects. Founded 1931.

## Descent

Wild Places Publishing, 51 Timbers Square, Cardiff CF24 3SH
*tel* 029-2048 6557 *fax* 029-2048 6557
*email* descent@wildplaces.co.uk
*website* www.caving.uk.com
*Editor* Chris Howes
Bi-monthly £3.25

Articles, features and news on all aspects of cave and mine sport exploration. Submissions must match magazine style. Length: up to 2000 words (articles/features), up to 1000 words (news). Illustrations: colour and b&w. Payment: on consideration of material based on area filled. Founded 1969.

## The Dickensian

The Dickens Fellowship, Dickens House, 48 Doughty Street, London WC1N 2LX
*Editor* Dr Malcolm Andrews, School of English, Rutherford College, University of Kent, Canterbury, Kent CT2 7NX *fax* (01227) 827001
*email* M.Y.Andrews@ukc.ac.uk
3 p.a. £9.50 p.a. (£12 p.a. institutions; overseas rates on application)

Welcomes articles on all aspects of Dickens' life, works and character. Payment: none. Send contributions (enclose sae if return required) and editorial correspondence to the Editor.

## Director

116 Pall Mall, London SW1Y 5ED
*tel* 020-7766 8950 *fax* 020-7766 8840
*Editor* Joanna Higgins
Monthly £3.25

Authoritative business-related articles. Send synopsis of proposed article and examples of printed work. Length: 500–2000 words. Payment: by arrangement. Illustrations: colour. Founded 1947.

## Dirt Bike Rider

Lancaster & Morecambe Newspapers Ltd, Victoria Street, Morecambe, Lancs. LA4 4AG
*tel* (01524) 32525 *fax* (01524) 842157
*email* sean.lawless@rim.co.uk
*Editor* Sean Lawless
Monthly £2.80

Features, track tests, coverage on all aspects of off-road motor-cycling. Length: up to 2000 words. Illustrations: half-tone, colour, cartoons. Founded 1981.

### Disability Now
6 Market Road, London N7 9PW
*tel* 020-7619 7323 *minicom* 020-7619 7332
*fax* 020-7619 7331
*email* editor@disabilitynow.org.uk
*website* www.disabilitynow.org.uk
*Editor* Mary Wilkinson
Monthly £18 p.a., free to people on income support;
tape version free to people with visual impairment
or severe disability

Newspaper for people with different types of
disability, carers and professionals, and anyone
interested in disability. News and comment on
anything of interest in the disability field: benefits,
services, equipment, jobs, politics, motoring,
holidays, sport, relationships, the arts. All regular
contributors have a disability (unless they are a
parent of someone with a disability). Preliminary
letter or email desirable. Founded 1984.

### Diva
Millivres Prowler Ltd, Spectrum House,
32–34 Gordon House Road, London NW5 1LP
*tel* 020-7424 7400 *fax* 020-7424 7401
*email* edit@divamag.co.uk
*website* www.divamag.com
*Editor* Gillian Rodgerson
Monthly £2.65

Lesbian life and culture: articles, features, news,
short fiction. Length: 1000–2000 words (articles/
features); 300–500 words (news); 1000–2000 words
(short stories). Illustrations: colour and b&w.
Payment: £10 per 100 words; £30–£50 per photo;
£25–£80 per drawing. Founded 1994.

### Diver
55 High Street, Teddington,
Middlesex TW11 8HA
*tel* 020-8943 4288 *fax* 020-8943 4312
*email* enquiries@divermag.co.uk
*website* divernet@www.divernet.com
*Editor* Nigel Eaton
Monthly £3.20

Articles on sub aqua diving and related
developments. Length: 1500–4000 words.
Illustrations: line, half-tone and colour. Payment: by
arrangement. Founded 1953.

### DIY Week
Faversham House Group Ltd, 232A Addington
Road, South Croydon, Surrey CR2 8LE
*tel* 020-8651 7100 *fax* 020-8651 7117
*Editor* Sarah Byrne
Fortnightly

Product and city news, promotions and special
features of recent developments in DIY houseware
and garden retailing. Payment: by arrangement.
Founded 1874.

### Dogs Today
Pet Subjects Ltd, Town Mill, Bagshot Road,
Chobham, Surrey GU24 8BZ
*tel* (01276) 858880 *fax* (01276) 858860
*email* dogs.today@btconnect.com
*Editor* Beverley Cuddy
Monthly £3.50

Study of magazine essential before submitting ideas.
Interested in human interest dog stories, celebrity
interviews, holiday features and anything unusual –
all must be entertaining and informative and
accompanied by illustrations. Length: 800–1200
words. Illustrations: colour, preferably
transparencies or digital, colour cartoons. Payment:
negotiable. Founded 1990.

### Dorset Life – The Dorset Magazine
7 The Leanne, Sandford Lane, Wareham,
Dorset BH20 4DY
*tel* (01929) 551264 *fax* (01929) 552099
*email* dorset.life@virgin.net
*Editor* John Newth
Monthly £2.10

Articles (about 1200 words), photos (colour) and
line drawings with a specifically Dorset theme.
Payment: by arrangement. Founded 1967.

### Drapers
EMAP Communications, 33–39 Bowling Green
Lane, London EC1R 0DA
*tel* 020-7812 3700 *fax* 020-7812 3760
*email* drapers@emap.com
*website* www.drapersrecord.com
*Editor-in-Chief* Eric Musgrave
Weekly £2.75

Business editorial aimed at fashion retailers, large
and small. Payment: by negotiation. Illustrations:
colour and b&w photos. Founded 1887.

### The Dublin Review
PO Box 7948, Dublin 1, Republic of Ireland
*tel/fax* (01) 6788627
*email* brendan_barrington@yahoo.com
*website* www.thedublinreview.com
*Editor* Brendan Barrington
Quarterly £6/€7.50

Essays, criticism, reportage and fiction for the
intelligent general reader. Payment: by arrangement.
Founded 2000.

### Early Music
Oxford University Press, 70 Baker Street,
London W1M 7DN
*tel* 020-7616 5902 *fax* 020-7616 5901
*email* jnl.early-music@oup.co.uk
*website* www.em.oupjournals.org
*Editor* Tess Knighton
Quarterly £10.50 (£46 p.a., institutions £92 p.a.)

Lively, informative and scholarly articles on aspects of medieval, renaissance, baroque and classical music. Payment: £20 per 1000 words. Illustrations: line, half-tone, colour. Founded 1973.

## East Lothian Life

1 Beveridge Row, Belhaven, Dunbar,
East Lothian EH42 1TP
*tel* (01368) 863593 *fax* (01368) 863593
*email* info@east-lothian-life.co.uk
*website* www.east-lothian-life.co.uk
*Editor* Pauline Jaffray
Quarterly £2.50

Articles and features with an East Lothian slant. Length: up to 1000 words. Illustrations: b&w photos, line, cartoons. Payment: negotiable. Founded 1989.

## Eastern Art Report

Eastern Art Publishing Group, PO Box 13666, 27 Wallorton Gardens, London SW14 8WF
*tel* 020-8392 1122 *fax* 020-8392 1422
*email* ear@eapgroup.com
*Managing* Sajid Rizvi, *Send material to* Shirley Rizvi, Executive Editor
Bi-monthly £6 (£30 p.a. individual, £60 p.a. institutions)

Original, well-researched articles on all aspects of the visual arts – Buddhist, Islamic, Judaic, Indian, Chinese and Japanese; reviews. Length of articles: min. 1500 words. Illustrations: colour transparencies, b&w photos; no responsibility accepted for unsolicited material. Payment: by arrangement. Founded 1989.

## Eastern Eye

Ethnic Media Group, Unit 2, 65 Whitechapel Road, London E1 1DU
*tel* 020-7650 2000 *fax* 020-7650 2001
*Editor* Mujibul Islam
Weekly 70p

Articles, features and news of interest to British Asians. Magazine covers music, fashion, film gossip. Freelance material considered. Illustrations: colour. Founded 1989.

## The Ecologist

Unit 18, Chelsea Wharf, 15 Lots Road, London SW10 0QJ
*tel* 020-7351 3578 *fax* 020-7351 3617
*email* belinda@theecologist.org
*Editors* Zac Goldsmith
10 p.a. £3.50

Fully referenced articles on economic, social and environmental affairs from an ecological standpoint. Study magazine first for level and approach. Length: 1000–5000 words. Illustrations: line, half-tone. Payment: by arrangement.

## Economica

STICERD, London School of Economics, Houghton Street, London WC2A 2AE
*tel* 020-7955 7855 *fax* 020-7955 6951
*Editors* Prof F.A. Cowell, Prof Alan Manning, Prof Tore Ellingsen
Quarterly £28 (apply for subscription rates)

Learned journal covering the fields of economics, economic history and statistics. Payment: none. Founded 1921; New Series 1934.

## The Economist

25 St James's Street, London SW1A 1HG
*tel* 020-7830 7000
*website* www.economist.com
*Editor* Bill Emmott
Weekly £2.90

Articles staff-written. Founded 1843.

## The Edge

65 Guinness Buildings, London W6 8BD
*tel* 020-8563 1310
*email* davec@theedge.abelgratis.co.uk
*website* www.theedge.abelgratis.co.uk
*Editor* David Clark
Quarterly £4

Interviews, features, reviews: books, films, music, modern popular culture; imaginative fiction – science fiction, modern urban fiction, horror, etc. Return postage essential. Payment: £30–£300 negotiable.

## Edinburgh Review

220A Buccleugh Place, Edinburgh EH8 9LN
*tel* 0131-651 1415 *fax* 0131-651 1415
*email* Edinburgh.Review@ed.ac.uk
*Editor* Ronald Turnbull
Tri-annual £17 p.a. (individual)

Fiction, poetry, clearly written articles on Scottish and international cultural and philosophical ideas. Payment: by arrangement. Founded 1969.

## Education Journal

17 Park Road, Hampton Hill, Middlesex TW12 1HE
*tel* 020-8979 9473 *fax* 020-8979 9473
*Editor* George Low
Monthly £38 p.a.

Features on policy, management and professional development issues. Major documents and reports gutted down to a brief digest; documents and research listings. Research section combining original reports and updates on research projects. Coverage of parliamentary debates and answers to parliamentary questions, giving statistical data by LEA. Reference section that includes coverage of all circulars, conference reports and opinion column. Length: 1000 words. Illustrations: photos, cartoons. Payment: by arrangement. Founded 1903; relaunched 1996.

## EE Times

CMP Europe Ltd, City Reach, 5 Greenwich View Place, Millharbour, London E14 9NN
*tel* 020-7861 6417 *fax* 020-7861 6253
*email* cedwards@cmp-europe.com
*Editor* Chris Edwards
Weekly £3.25 (£85 p.a.)

News, reviews and features on the electronics industry. Length: 2000 words (features), 200 words (news). Illustrations: colour transparencies, colour and b&w artwork and cartoons. Payment: variable. Founded 1978.

## Electrical Review

Cumulus Business Media, Anne Boleyn House, 9–13 Ewell Road, Cheam, Surrey SM3 8BZ
*tel* 020-8652 8736 *fax* 020-8652 8951
*email* b.evett@cumulusmedia.co.uk
*Managing Editor* Bill Evett
Fortnightly £3.50

Technical and business articles on electrical and control engineering; outside contributions considered. Electrical news welcomed. Illustrations: photos and drawings, cartoons. Payment: according to merit. Founded 1872.

## Electrical Times

Cumulus Business Media, Anne Boleyn House, 9–13 Ewell Road, Cheam, Surrey SM3 8BZ
*tel* 020-8652 8736 *fax* 020-8652 8972
*email* b.evett@cumulusmedia.co.uk
*Managing Editor* Bill Evett
Monthly £3.50

Business and technical articles of interest to contractors and installers in the electrical industries and business services engineers, with illustrations as necessary. Length: 750–1000 words. Payment: negotiable. Illustrations: line, half-tone, colour, cartoons. Founded 1892.

## Elle (UK)

Hachette Filipacchi UK, 16–18 Berners Street, London W1T 3LN
*tel* 020-7150 7000 *fax* 020-7150 7670
*Acting Editor* Laurel Ives
Monthly £2.80

Commissioned material only. Payment: by arrangement. Illustrations: colour. Founded 1985.

## Embroidery

The Embroiderers' Guild, PO Box 42B, East Molesey, Surrey KT8 9BB
*email* jhall@embroiderersguild.com
*website* www.embroiderersguild.com/embroidery
6 p.a. £4.75 (£28.50 p.a.)

Illustrated features on contemporary textile art. Reports on internationally renowned makers. In-depth articles on ethnographic embroidery. Looks inside important collections, and at the history and social history of embroidery. Plus book and exhibition reviews, news and opportunities.

## Empire

Mappin House, 4 Winsley Street, London W1W 8HF
*tel* 020-7436 1515 *fax* 020-7343 8703
*website* www.empireonline.co.uk
*Editor* Colin Kennedy
Monthly £3.30

Guide to film and video: articles, features, news. Length: various. Illustrations: colour and b&w photos. Payment: approx. £300 per 1000 words; varies for illustrations. Founded 1989.

## The Engineer

Centaur Communications Ltd, St Giles House, 50 Poland Street, London W1F 7AX
*tel* 020-7970 4106 *fax* 020-7970 4189
*email* george.coupe@centaur.co.uk
*website* www.e4engineering.com
*Editor* Sean Brierley
50 p.a. Controlled circulation (£118 p.a.)

Features and news on innovation and technology, including profiles, analysis. Length: up to 800 words (news), 1000 words (features). Illustrations: colour transparencies or prints, artwork, line diagrams, graphs. Payment: by negotiation. Founded 1856.

## Engineering

Gillard Welch Ltd, 355 Station Road, Dorridge, Solihull B93 8EY
*tel* (01564) 771772 *fax* (01564) 774776
*Editor* Jonathan Ward
12 p.a. £8

'For innovators in technology, manufacturing and management': features and news. Contributions considered on all aspects of engineering. Illustrations: colour. Founded 1866.

## The English Garden

Romsey Publishing Ltd, Jubilee House, 2 Jubilee Place, London SW3 3TQ
*tel* 020-7751 4800 *fax* 020-7751 4848
*email* theenglishgarden@romseypublishing.com
*Editor* Julia Watson
Monthly £3.20

Features and photography on English gardens, plant genera and garden design. Send written synopsis. Length: 1000 words. Illustrations: colour photos and artwork. Payment: variable. Founded 1997.

## Envoi

44 Rudyard Road, Biddulph Moor, Stoke-on-Trent, Staffs. ST8 7JN
*tel* (01782) 517892
*Editor* Roger Elkin
3 p.a. £15 p.a.

New poetry, including sequences, collaborative works and translations, reviews, articles on modern poets and poetic style; poetry competitions; adjudicator's reports. Sample copy: £3.00. Payment: one complimentary copy. Founded 1957.

## The Erotic Review

30 Cleveland Street, London W1T 4JD
*tel* 020-7907 6404
*email* info@theeroticreview.co.uk
*website* www.theeroticreview.co.uk
*Editor* Rowan Pelling, *Send material to* Susanna Forrest, Assistant Editor
Monthly £3.50

Up-market literary magazine for sensualists and libertines. Length: 1000 words (articles and features), 1000–2000 (short stories). Illustrations: colour and b&w prints, artwork and cartoons. Payment: £50–£75 (articles and features), £50–£75 (short stories); £50 (prints and artwork), £40 (cartoons). Founded 1997.

## ES Magazine – see Evening Standard, page 17

## Esquire

National Magazine House, 72 Broadwick Street, London W1F 9EP
*tel* 020-7439 5000 *fax* 020-7439 5675
*Editor* Simon Tiffin
Monthly £3.40

Quality men's general interest magazine – articles, features. No unsolicited material or short stories. Length: various. Illustrations: colour and b&w photos, line. Payment: by arrangement. Founded 1991.

## Essential Water Garden

Aceville Publications Ltd, 25 Phoenix Court, Hawkins Road, The Hythe, Colchester, Essex CO2 8JY
*tel* (01206) 505977 *fax* (01206) 505985
*email* demelzashea@genie.co.uk
*Editor* Demelza Shea
10 p.a. £2.80

Magazine for owners of all styles and sizes of water gardens, including fish-stocked pools. Practical projects and seasonal solutions. Illustrated step-by-step projects considered; also regular readers' garden feature. Illustrations: colour. Length: approx. 1000 words. Payment: by arrangement. Founded 1998.

## Essentials

IPC Media, King's Reach Tower, Stamford Street, London SE1 9LS
*tel* 020-7261 6970
*Editor* Karen Livermore
Monthly £2.40

Features, plus fashion, health and beauty, cookery. Illustrations: colour. Payment: by negotiation. Founded 1988.

## Essex Life & Countryside

The Mill, Bearwalden Business Park, Wenders Ambo, Saffron Wolden, Essex CB11 49B
*tel* (01799) 544278
*Editor* Robyn Bechelet
Monthly £2.50

Features with Essex emphasis. Length: up to 1200 words. Illustrations: colour photos. Payment: negotiable. Founded 1952.

## Essex Magazine and East Anglian Life

Acorn Magazines Ltd, The Old County School, Northgate Street, Bury St Edmunds, Suffolk IP33 1HP
*tel* (01284) 701190 *fax* (01284) 701680
*Editor* Pippa Bastin
Monthly £2.30

Magazine for residents of Essex and East Anglia covering history, people, places, environment, events, homes and gardens. Considers unsolicited material; no acknowledgement. Welcomes ideas for articles and features. Length: 1500 words features/articles. Illustrations: colour. Payment: £100 per 1500-word feature/article; £50 for front cover image. Founded 1999.

## European Chemical News

Reed Business Information, Quadrant House, The Quadrant, Sutton, Surrey SM2 5AS
*tel* 020-8652 8147 *fax* 020-8652 3375
*email* ecne@rbi.co.uk
*Editor* John Baker
Weekly £374 p.a. Europe (£420 p.a. overseas)

Articles and features concerning business, markets and investments in the chemical industry. Length: 1000–2000 words; news items up to 400 words. Payment: £150–£200 per 1000 words.

## Eventing

IPC Media, Room 2005, King's Reach Tower, Stamford Street, London SE1 9LS
*tel* 020-7261 5388 *fax* 020-7261 5429
*Editor* Amanda Gee
Monthly £3.30

News, articles, features, event reports and opinion pieces – all with bias towards the sport of horse trials. Mostly commissioned, but all ideas welcome. Length: up to 1500 words. Illustrations: colour and b&w, mostly commissioned. Payment: by arrangement. Founded 1984.

## Evergreen

PO Box 52, Cheltenham, Glos. GL50 1YQ
*tel* (01242) 537900 *fax* (01242) 537901
*Editor* Roy Faiers
Quarterly £3.50

Articles about Britain's famous people and infamous characters, its natural beauty, towns and villages, history, traditions, odd customs, legends, folklore, etc; regular articles on old films, songs, radio programmes and variety acts. Length 250–2000 words. Also 'meaningful rather than clever' poetry. Illustrations: colour transparencies. Payment: £15 per 1000 words, £4 poems. Founded 1985.

## Everyday Practical Electronics

Wimborne Publishing Ltd, 408 Wimborne Road East, Ferndown, Dorset BH22 9ND
*tel* (01202) 873872 *fax* (01202) 874562
*email* editorial@epemag.wimborne.co.uk
*website* www.epemag.wimborne.co.uk
*Editor* Mike Kenward
Monthly £3.10

Constructional and theoretical articles aimed at the student and hobbyist. Length: 1000–5500 words. Payment: £55–£90 per 1000 words. Illustrations: line, half-tone. Founded 1971.

## Executive PA

11 Southwark Street, London SE1 1RQ
*tel* 020-7089 5880 *fax* 020-7089 5855
*email* michael@executivepa.net
*Editor* Sara Evans
Quarterly Complimentary

Business to business for working senior secretaries. Length: 700–1400 words. Illustrations: colour. Payment: £140 per 1000 words. Founded 1991.

## Executive Woman

Saleworld Ltd, 2 Chantry Place, Harrow, Middlesex HA3 6NY
*tel* 020-8420 1210 *fax* 020-8420 1691/3
*email* info@execwoman.com
*website* www.execwoman.com
*Editor* Angela Giveon
Bi-monthly £2.50

News and features with a holistic approach to the world of successful working women. Strong business features; articles on management, personnel, networking and mentoring. Length: 500–1000 words. Illustrations: colour and b&w. Payment: £150 per 1000 words; £50–£100. Founded 1987.

## Family Law

21 St Thomas Street, Bristol BS1 6JS
*tel* 0117-923 0600 *fax* 0117-925 0486
*email* familylaw@jordanpublishing.co.uk
*website* www.familylaw.co.uk
*Editors* Elizabeth Walsh, Miles McColl
Monthly £150 p.a.

Articles dealing with all aspects of the law as it affects the family, written from a legal or socio-legal point of view. Length: from 1000 words. Payment: by arrangement. No illustrations. Founded 1971.

## Family Tree Magazine

61 Great Whyte, Ramsey, Huntingdon, Cambs. PE26 1HJ

*tel* (01487) 814050
*email* lesboon@family-tree.co.uk
*website* www.family-tree.co.uk
*Editorial Manager* Sue Fearn
Monthly £2.70 (£27.50 p.a.)

Articles on any genealogically related topics. Payment: £45 per 1000 words. Founded 1984.

## Farmers Weekly

Reed Business Information, Quadrant House, The Quadrant, Sutton, Surrey SM2 5AS
*tel* 020-8652 4911 *fax* 020-8652 4005
*email* farmers.weekly@rbi.co.uk
*website* www.fwi.co.uk
*Editor* Stephen Howe
Weekly £1.75

Articles on agriculture from freelance contributors will be accepted subject to negotiation. Founded 1934.

## Fasttrack

1–3 Frederick's Place, London EC2R 8AB
*tel* 0161-817 3400 *fax* 0161-817 3401
*email* editor@fasttrack-digital.com
*website* www.goldensquare.com
*Editor* Marion Ainge
6 p.a. £15 p.a.

Upbeat magazine targeted mainly at female professional and executive personnel in the 20–40 age group. News and features – success stories, career changes, mentoring, current workplace issues, training opportunities, etc. Founded 1995.

## The Feminist Review

Palgrave Macmillan Ltd, Houndsmill, Basingstoke, Hants RG21 6XS
*tel* (01256) 329242 *fax* (01256) 354018
*email* rsloan@rsa2.demon.co.uk
*website* www.feminist-review.com
*Edited by* a Collective, supported by a group of corresponding editors
3 p.a. £35

The journal's objective is to unite 'research and theory with political practice and contributing to the development of both' together with the exploration and articulation of the socio-economic realities of women's lives. Welcomes contributions from the spectrum of contemporary feminist debate. Empirical work – both qualitative and quantitative – is particularly welcome. In addition, each issue contains some papers which are themed around a specific debate. Founded 1979.

## FHM (For Him Magazine)

EMAP Élan Network, Mappin House, 4 Winsley Street, London W1W 8HF
*tel* 020-7436 1515 *fax* 020-7343 3000
*email* amy.lindsay@fhm.com
*website* www.fhm.com

*Editor* David Davies
Monthly £3.30

Features, fashion, grooming, travel (adventure) and men's interests. Length: 1200–2000 words. Illustrations: colour and b&w photos, line and colour artwork. Payment: by negotiation. Founded 1987.

## The Field

IPC Media Ltd, King's Reach Tower, Stamford Street, London SE1 9LS
*tel* 020-7261 5198 *fax* 020-7261 5358
*website* www.thefield.co.uk
Monthly £3.20

Specific, topical and informed features on the British countryside and country pursuits, including natural history, field sports, gardening and rural conservation. Overseas subjects considered but opportunities for such articles are limited. No fiction or children's material. Articles, length 800–2000 words, by outside contributors considered; also topical 'shorts' of 200–300 words on all countryside matters. Illustrations: colour photos of a high standard. Payment: on merit. Founded 1853.

## Film Review

Visual Imagination Ltd, 9 Blades Court, Deodar Road, London SW15 2NU
*tel* 020-8875 1520 *fax* 020-8875 1588
*email* filmreview@visimag.com
*Editor* Neil Corry
Four weekly £3.30

Features and interviews on mainstream cinema; film and video reviews. No fiction. Length: 1000–3000 words (features), 350 words (reviews). Illustrations: colour and b&w. Payment: £80 per 1000 words; £20 for first image, £10 per additional image. Founded 1950.

## Financial Adviser

FT Finance Ltd, Maple House, 16–28 Tabernacle Court Street, London EC2A 4DD
*tel* 020-7382 8000 *fax* 020-7382 8588
*Editor* Hal Austin
Weekly (£90 p.a.) Free to financial intermediaries working in financial services

Topical personal finance news and features. Length: variable. Payment: by arrangement. Founded 1987.

## Financial Mail on Sunday – see Mail on Sunday, page 10

## Fire

Queensway House, 2 Queensway, Redhill, Surrey RH1 1QS
*tel* (01737) 855431 *fax* (01737) 855418
*Editor* Andrew Lynch
Monthly £6.95 (£61 p.a.)

Articles on firefighting and fire prevention from acknowledged experts only. Length: 600 words. No unsolicited contributions. Illustrations: dramatic firefighting or fire brigade rescue colour photos. Also *Fire International*. Payment: by arrangement. Founded 1908.

## Fishing News

Telephone House, 69–77 Paul Street, London EC2A 4LQ
*tel* 020-7017 4531 *fax* 020-7017 4536
*email* tim.oliver@informa.com
*Editor* Tim Oliver
Weekly £1.10

News and features on all aspects of the commercial fishing industry. Length: up to 1000 words (features), up to 500 words (news). Illustrations: colour and b&w photos. Payment: negotiable. Founded 1913

## The Fix

TTA Press, 5 Martins Lane, Witcham, Ely, Cambs. CB6 2LB
*email* ttapress@aol.com
*website* www.ttapress.com
*Editor* Andy Cox
Bi-monthly 15 p.a. (subscription only)

Reviews of short fiction, in-depth coverage of the world's magazines (both large and small) plus interviews, columns, news and views. Hundreds of markets for writers in every issue. Submissions welcome. Payment: negotiable. Founded 1995.

## Flight International

Reed Business Information Ltd, Quadrant House, The Quadrant, Sutton, Surrey SM2 5AS
*tel* 020-8652 3842 *fax* 020-8652 3840
*email* flight.international@rbi.co.uk
*website* www.flightinternational.com
*Editor* Murdo Morrison
Weekly £2.40

Deals with all branches of aerospace: operational and technical articles, illustrated by photos, engineering cutaway drawings; also news, paragraphs, reports of lectures, etc. News press days: Thurs, Fri. Illustrations: tone, line, colour. Payment: by agreement. Founded 1909.

## Flora International

The Fishing Lodge Studio, 77 Bulbridge Road, Wilton, Salisbury, Wilts. SP2 0LE
*tel* (01722) 743207 *fax* (01722) 743207
*email* floramag@aol.com
*Editor* Maureen Foster
Bi-monthly £2.99

Magazine for flower arrangers and florists. Also features flower-related articles, flower arrangers' gardens and flower-related crafts. Will consider unsolicited material. Welcomes ideas for articles and features. Length: approx. 1000 words (articles/features). Illustrations: transparencies and colour prints, b&w cartoons. Payment: £50 (words), £15 illustrations. Founded 1974.

## Fly-Fishing & Fly-Tying
Rolling River Publications, Aberfeldy Road, Kenmore, Perthshire PH15 2HF
*tel* (01887) 830526 *fax* (01887) 830526
*email* MarkB.ffft@btinternet.com
*website* www.flyfishing-and-flytying.co.uk
*Editor* Mark Bowler
11 p.a. £2.60

Fly-fishing and fly-tying articles, fishery features, limited short stories, fishing travel. Length: 800–2000 words. Illustrations: colour photos. Payment: by arrangement. Founded 1990.

## Focus
Origin Publishing, 14th Floor, Tower House, Fairfax Street, Bristol BS1 3BN
*tel* 0117-927 9009 *fax* 0117-934 9008
*Editor* Paul Parsons
Monthly £3.25

'The magazine of science and discovery.' Articles, features and news with a science-based or technical slant. All material is commissioned. Length: 1000–3000 words (features). Illustrations: colour prints, transparencies and artwork. Payment: £200 per 1000 words; £200 per full-page photo (negotiable). Founded 1992.

## Folio
64–65 North Road, St Andrews, Bristol BS6 5AQ
*tel* 0117-942 8491 *fax* 0117-942 0369
*email* editor@venue.co.uk
*website* www.venue.co.uk
*Editor* Dave Higgitt
Monthly Free

Articles, features, interviews and news on people, places and events with a local connection (Bristol, Bath and Cheltenham area). No short stories or poems. Unsolicited material considered. Length: 600–2000 words (features), variable (news). Illustrations: colour and b&w. Payment: by negotiation. Founded 1994.

## For Women
Fantasy Publications, 4 Selsdon Way, London E14 9GL
*tel* 020-7308 5363
*Fiction Editor* Elizabeth Coldwell
6-weekly £3.50

Women's magazine with erotic emphasis. Features on sex and health; erotic fiction and photos. Erotic fiction welcomed on spec. Fiction guidelines on receipt of sae. Length: 2000–3000 words. Illustrations: colour and b&w photos. Payment: £150 per story. Founded 1992.

## Fortean Times
Box 2409, London NW5 4NP
*tel* 020-7907 6235 *fax* 020-7907 6835
*email* david_sutton@dennis.co.uk
*website* www.forteantimes.com
*Editors* David Sutton
Monthly £3.20

Journal of strange phenomena, experiences, related subjects and philosophies. Articles, features, news, reviews. Length: 500–5000 words; longer by arrangement. Illustrations: colour photos, line and tone art, cartoons. Payment: by negotiation. Founded 1973.

## Fortnight – An Independent Review of Politics and the Arts
11 University Road, Belfast BT7 1NA
*tel* 028-9023 2353/9032 4141 *fax* 028-9023 2650
*email* editor@fortnight.org
*website* www.fortnight.org
*Editor* Malachi O'Doherty
Monthly £2.20

Current affairs analysis, reportage, opinion pieces, cultural criticism, book reviews, poems. Illustrations: line, half-tone, cartoons. Payment: by arrangement. Founded 1970.

## FourFourTwo
Haymarket Leisure Publications Ltd, 38–42 Hampton Road, Teddington TW11 0JE
*tel* 020-8267 5337 *fax* 020-8267 5019
*Editor* Mat Snow
Monthly £3.20

Football magazine with 'adult' approach: interviews, in-depth features, issues pieces, odd and witty material. Length: 2000–3000 words (features), 100–500 words (news/latest score). Illustrations: colour transparencies and artwork, b&w prints. Payment: £200 per 1000 words. Founded 1994.

## FRANCE Magazine
Community Media Ltd, Cumberland House, Oriel Road, Cheltenham, Glos. GL50 1BB
*tel* (01242) 216050 *fax* (01242) 216074
*email* editorial@francemag.com
*website* www.francemag.com
*Editor* Philip Faiers
Bi-monthly £3.99

Informed quality features and articles on the real France, ranging from cuisine to customs to architecture to exploring the hidden France. Length: 800–2000 words. Illustrations: colour transparencies (mounted and captioned). Payment: £100 per 1000 words; £50 per page/pro rata for illustrations. Founded 1989.

## Freelance Market News

Sevendale House, 7 Dale Street, Manchester M1 1JB
*tel* 0161-228 2362 ext. 210 *fax* 0161-228 3533
*email* fmn@writersbureau.com
*Editor* Angela Cox
11 p.a.

Information on UK and overseas publications with editorial content, submission requirements and contact details. News of editorial requirements for writers. Features on the craft of writing, competitions, letters page. Founded 1968.

## Freelance Photographer

Icon Publications Ltd, Maxwell Place,
Maxwell Lane, Kelso, Roxburghshire TD5 7BB
*tel* (01573) 226032 *fax* (01573) 226000
*email* david@maxwellplace.demon.co.uk
*website* www.freelancephotographer.co.uk/photon/
*Editor* David Kilpatrick
6 p.a. £4.95

Illustrated features on professional and craft photography. All material commissioned. Length: 750–2500 words. Illustrations: b&w and colour photos. Payment: £50–£300 per feature, including photos. Founded 1989.

## The Friend

New Premier House, 150 Southampton Row,
London WC1B 5BQ
*tel* 020-7387 7549
*email* editorial@thefriend.org
*website* www.thefriend.org
*Editor* Harry Albright
Weekly £1.30

Material of interest to the Religious Society of Friends and like-minded people; political, social, economic or devotional, considered from outside contributors. Length: up to 1200 words. Illustrations: b&w or colour prints, b&w line drawings. Payment: not usually but will negotiate a small fee with professional writers. Founded 1843.

## Fun Size Beano – see The Beano

## Funsize Dandy – see The Dandy

## The Furrow

St Patrick's College, Maynooth, Co. Kildare,
Republic of Ireland
*tel* (01) 7083741 *fax* (01) 7083908
*email* furrow.office@may.ie
*website* www.thefurrow.ie
*Editor* Rev. Ronan Drury
Monthly €2.30

Religious, pastoral, theological, social articles. Length: up to 3000 words. Payment: average €20 per page (450 words). Illustrations: line, half-tone. Founded 1950.

## The Garden

4th Floor, Churchgate, New Road,
Peterborough PE1 1TT
*tel* (01733) 775775 *fax* (01733) 775819
*email* thegarden@rhs.org.uk
*Editor* Ian Hodgson
Monthly £3.75

Journal of The Royal Horticultural Society. Features of horticultural or botanical interest on a wide range of subjects. Commissioned material only. Length: 1200–2500 words. Illustrations: 35mm or medium format colour transparencies, occasional b&w prints, botanical line drawings; digital images are not accepted for features. Payment: varies. Founded 1866.

## Garden Answers

EMAP Active Ltd, Bretton Court, Bretton,
Peterborough PE3 8DZ
*tel* (01733) 264666 *fax* (01733) 282695
*Editor* Nicola Dela-Croix
Monthly £2.90

Commissioned features and articles on all aspects of gardening. Study of magazine essential. Approach by letter with examples of published work. Length: 750 words. Illustrations: colour transparencies and artwork. Payment: by negotiation. Founded 1982.

## Garden News

EMAP Active Ltd, Bretton Court, Bretton Centre,
Peterborough PE3 8DZ
*tel* (01733) 264666 *fax* (01733) 465990
*email* sarah.page@ecm.emap.com
*Editor* Sarah Page
Weekly £1.20

Up-to-date information on everything to do with plants, growing and gardening. Illustrations: line, colour, cartoons. Payment: by negotiation. Founded 1958.

## Gay Times

Spectrum House, 32–34 Gordon House Road,
London NW5 1LP
*tel* 020-7424 7400 *fax* 020-7424 7401
*email* edit@gaytimes.co.uk
*website* www.gaytimes.co.uk
*Editor* Vicky Powell
Monthly £3.10

Feature articles, full news and review coverage of all aspects of gay and lesbian life. Length: up to 2000 words. Illustrations: colour, line and half-tone, cartoons. Payment: by arrangement. Founded 1972.

## Geographical

Campion Interactive Publishing Ltd, Unit 11,
Pall Mall Deposit, 124–8 Barlby Road,
London W10 6BL
*tel* 020-8960 6400 *fax* 020-8960 6004

*email* magazine@geographical.co.uk
*website* www.geographical.co.uk
*Editor* Nick Smith
Monthly £3.25

Magazine of the Royal Geographical Society. Covers culture, wildlife, environment, science and travel. Illustrations: top quality transparencies, vintage material. Payment: by negotiation. Founded 1935.

## Geographical Journal

Royal Geographical Society (with the Institute of British Geographers), Kensington Gore, London SW7 2AR
*tel* 020-7591 3026 *fax* 020-7591 3001
*email* journals@rgs.org
*Editor* Prof A. Millinglon
4 p.a. £30 (post free), (£81 p.a.)

Papers on all aspects of geography and development of current interest and concern. Large reviews section. Illustrations: photos, maps, diagrams. Founded 1893.

## Geological Magazine

Cambridge University Press, The Edinburgh Building, Shaftesbury Road, Cambridge CB2 2RU
*tel* (01223) 312393
*Editors* Prof I.N. McCave, Dr M.B.Allen, Dr D.M. Pyle, Dr G.E. Budd
Bi-monthly (£276 print, £312 print and online p.a. institutions, £45 p.a. students, US $438 print, $498 print and online USA/Canada/Mexico)

Original articles on all earth science topics containing the results of independent research by experts. Also reviews and notices of current geological literature, correspondence on geological subjects – illustrated. Length: variable. Payment: none. Founded 1864.

## Gibbons Stamp Monthly

Stanley Gibbons Ltd, 7 Parkside, Ringwood, Hants BH24 3SH
*tel* (01425) 472363 *fax* (01425) 470247
*email* hjefferies@stanleygibbons.co.uk
*Editor* Hugh Jefferies
Monthly £2.75 (£33 p.a.)

Articles on philatelic topics. Contact the Editor first. Length: 500–2500 words. Payment: by arrangement, £40 or more per 1000 words. Illustrations: photos, line, stamps or covers.

## Girl About Town Magazine

Independent Magazines, Independent House, 191 Marsh Wall, London E14 9RS
*tel* 020-7005 5000 *fax* 020-7005 5333
*Editor-in-Chief* Bill Williamson
Weekly Free

Articles of general interest to women. Length: about 1100–1500 words. Payment: negotiable.

## Glamour

The Condé Nast Publications Ltd, 6–8 Old Bond Street, London W15 4PH
*tel* 020-7499 9080 *fax* 020-7491 2551
*email* features@glamourmagazine.co.uk
*website* www.glamour.com
*Editor* Jo Elvin, *Features Editor* Miranda Levy
Monthly £1.90

Lifestyle magazine containing fashion, beauty, real life features and celebrity news aimed at women aged 18–34. Feature ideas welcome; approach with brief outline. Length: 500–800 words. Payment: by arrangement. Founded 2001.

## Global

Castle House, 97 High Street, Colchester, Essex CO1 1TH
*tel* (01206) 505921 *fax* (01206) 505929
*email* dom_global@aceville.com
*website* www.globalmagazine.com
*Editor* Dominic Tombs
8 p.a. £2.95

Magazine for people who love to travel. Combines inspirational tales and spectacular images with down-to-earth advice for the novice and seasoned travellers alike. See website for Contributor's Guidelines. Length: 3000 (features). Illustrations: colour transparencies. Payment: £300 (with images) Founded 1998.

## Go Girl Magazine

Egmont Magazines, 184 Drummond Street, London NW1 3HP
*tel* 020-7380 6430
*website* www.egmontmagazines.co.uk
*Editor* Sarah Delmege
13 p.a. £1.60

Magazine for 7–11 year-old girls including fashion, beauty, celebrity news and gossip. Payment: by arrangement. Founded 2003.

## Golf Monthly

IPC Magazines Ltd, King's Reach Tower, Stamford Street, London SE1 9LS
*tel* 020-7261 7237 *fax* 020-7261 7240
*email* golfmonthly@ipcmedia.com
*Editor* Jane Carter
Monthly £3.25

Original articles on golf considered (not reports), golf clinics, handy hints. Illustrations: half-tone, colour, cartoons. Payment: by arrangement. Founded 1911.

## Golf Weekly

EMAP Active Ltd, Bushfield House, Orton Centre, Peterborough PE2 5UW
*tel* (01733) 237111 *fax* (01733) 288025
*email* peter.masters@emap.com

*Editor* Peter Masters
Weekly £2.25

News, tournament reports and articles on golf of interest to golfers. Payment: 15p per word published. Illustrations: photos of golf news and new courses.

## Golf World

EMAP Active Ltd, Bushfield House, Orton Centre, Peterborough PE2 5UW
*tel* (01733) 237111 *fax* (01733) 288025
*Publishing Editor-in-Chief* Dave Clarke
Monthly £3.30

Expert golf instructional articles, 500–3000 words; general interest articles, personality features 500–3000 words. No fiction. No unsolicited material. Payment: by negotiation. Illustrations: line, half-tone, colour, cartoons. Founded 1962.

## Good Housekeeping

National Magazine House, 72 Broadwick Street, London W1F 9EP
*tel* 020-7439 5000 *fax* 020-7439 5616
*website* www.natmags.co.uk
*Editor-in-Chief* Lindsay Nicholson
Monthly £2.80

Articles on topics of interest to intelligent women. No unsolicited features or stories accepted; approach by letter only. Homes, fashion, beauty and food covered by staff writers. Payment: magazine standards. Illustrations: commissioned. Founded 1922.

## GQ

Condé Nast Publications, Vogue House, Hanover Square, London W1S 1JU
*tel* 020-7499 9080 *fax* 020-7495 1679
*website* www.gq/magazine.co.uk
*Editor* Dylan Jones
Monthly £3.20

Style, fashion and general interest magazine for men. Illustrations: b&w and colour photos, line drawings, cartoons. Payment: by arrangement. Founded 1988.

## Granta

2–3 Hanover Yard, Noel Road, London N1 8BE
*tel* 020-7704 9776 *fax* 020-7704 0474
*website* www.granta.com
*Editor* Ian Jack
Quarterly £9.99 (£26.95 p.a.)

Original literary fiction, non-fiction and journalism. Study magazine before submitting work. No poems, essays or reviews. Length: determined by content. Illustrations: photos. Payment: by arrangement. Founded 1889; new series 1979.

## Green Futures

Overseas House, 19–23 Ironmonger Row, London EC1V 3QN
*email* post@greenfutures.org.uk
*website* www.greenfutures.org.uk
*Editor* Martin Wright, *Send material to* Hannah Bullock, Editorial Assistant
Bi-monthly £22 p.a. individuals, £30 p.a. organisations, £38 p.a. businesses (subscription only)

Articles and features on environmental solutions and sustainable futures for people in government, business and higher education. Specially commissions most material. Welcomes ideas for articles and features. Illustrations: high-res digital photos, prints and transparencies. Founded 1996.

## Greetings Today

Lema Publishing, 1 Churchgates Wilderness, Berkhansted, Herts HP4 2AZ
*tel* (01442) 289930 *fax* (01442) 289950
*Publisher-in-Chief* Malcolm Naish, *Editor* Vicky Denton
Monthly £45 p.a. (other rates on application)

Articles, features and news related to the greetings card industry; includes Artists Directory for aspiring artists wishing to attract the eye of publishers. Mainly written in-house; some material taken from outside. Length: varies. Illustrations: line, colour and b&w photos. Payment: by arrangement. Founded 1999; first published 1972.

## The Grocer

William Reed Publishing Ltd, Broadfield Park, Crawley, West Sussex RH11 9RT
*tel* (01293) 613400 *fax* (01293) 610333
*email* grocer.editorial@william-reed.co.uk
*website* www.foodanddrink.co.uk
*Editor* Julian Hunt
Weekly £1.30

Trade journal: articles or news or illustrations of general interest to the grocery and provision trades. Payment: by arrangement. Founded 1861.

## The Grower

Nexus Media Ltd, Nexus House, Azalea Drive, Swanley, Kent BR8 8HU
*tel* (01322) 660070 *fax* (01322) 616324
*email* editor.horticulture@nexusmedia.com
*Editor* Peter Rogers
Weekly £1.35

News and practical articles on commercial horticulture, covering all sectors including fruit, vegetable, salad crop and ornamentals. Founded 1923.

## Guiding Magazine

17–19 Buckingham Palace Road, London SW1W 0PT
*tel* 020-7834 6242 *fax* 020-7828 5791
*website* www.girlguiding.org.uk

*Editor* Wendy Kewley
Monthly £21.60

Official magazine of Girlguiding UK. Articles of interest to women of all ages, with special emphasis on youth work and the Guide Movement. Articles on simple crafts, games and the outdoors especially welcome. Length: up to 600 words. Illustrations: line, half-tone, colour. Payment: £70 per 1000 words.

## H&E Naturist

New Freedom Publications Ltd, Burlington Court, Carlisle Street, Goole, East Yorkshire DN14 5EG
*tel* (01405) 769712 *fax* (01405) 763815
*email* henaturist@btconnect.com
*website* www.healthandefficiency.co.uk
*Editor* Mark Nisbet
Monthly £3.25

Articles on naturist travel, clubs, beaches and naturist lifestyle experiences from the UK, Europe and the world. Length: 700–1500 words. Illustrations: line, colour transparencies and prints featuring naturists in natural settings; also cartoons, humorous fillers and features with naturist themes. Payment: by negotiation but guidelines for contributors and basic payment rates available on request.

## Hairflair

Hairflair Magazines Ltd, Freebournes House, Freebournes Road, Witham, Essex CM8 3US
*tel* (01376) 534557 *fax* (01376) 534546
*Editor* Ruth Page
Bi-monthly £2.60

Hair, beauty, fashion (and related features) for the 16–35 age group. Preliminary letter essential. Length: 800–1000 words. Illustrations: colour and b&w photos. Payment: negotiable. Founded 1985.

## Hampshire – The County Magazine

74 Bedford Place, Southampton SO15 2DF
*tel* 023-8022 3591/8033 3457
Monthly £2

Factual articles concerning all aspects of Hampshire, past and present. Length: 400–1000 words. Payment: by arrangement. Illustrations: mainly colour photos. Founded 1960.

## Harpers & Queen

National Magazine House, 72 Broadwick Street, London W1F 9EP
*tel* 020-7439 5000 *fax* 020-7439 5506
*Editor* Lucy Yeomans
Monthly £3.30

Features, fashion, beauty, art, theatre, films, travel, interior decoration – some commissioned. Illustrations: line and wash, full colour and 2- and 3-colour, and photos. Founded 1929.

## Health & Fitness

Highbury WViP, The Publishing House, 1–3 Highbury Station Road, London N1 1SE
*tel* 020-7226 2222
*email* editorial@hfonline.co.uk
*website* www.hfonline.co.uk
*Editor* Mary Comber
Monthly £2.99

Articles on all aspects of health and fitness. Illustrations: line, half-tone, colour. Payment: by arrangement. Founded 1984.

## Health Club Management

Leisure Media Company Ltd, Portmill House, Portmill Lane, Hitchin, Herts. SG5 1DJ
*tel* (01462) 471920 *fax* (01462) 433909
*email* catherinelarner@leisuremedia.com
*website* www.leisuremedia.co.uk
*Editor* Catherine Larner
Monthly £48 p.a. with *Leisure Management* magazine

Official publication of the Fitness Industry Association. Articles on the operation of health clubs, day spas, fitness and sports centres. Items on consumer issues and lifestyle trends as they affect club management are welcomed. Length: up to 1500 words. Illustrations: colour and b&w photos. Payment: by arrangement. Founded 1995.

## Heat

Emap plc, Endeavour House, 189 Shaftesbury Avenue, London WC2H 8JG
*tel* 020-7437 9011 *fax* 020-7859 8670
*email* heat@emap.com
*Editor* Mark Frith
Weekly £1.50

Features and news on celebrities. Founded 1999.

## Hello!

Wellington House, 69–71 Upper Ground, London SE1 9PQ
*tel* 020-7667 8700 *fax* 020-7667 8716
*Editor* Ronnie Whelan
Weekly £1.85

News-based features – showbusiness, celebrity, royalty; exclusive interviews. Payment: by arrangement. Illustrated. Founded 1988.

## Here's Health

EMAP Esprit, Greater London House, Hampstead Road, London NW1 7EJ
*tel* 020-7347 1893 *fax* 020-7347 1897
*Editor* Sarah Wilson
Monthly £2.60

Articles on how to look and feel great the natural way, eat well, be inspired, and stay fit and healthy. Preliminary letter and clippings essential. Length: 750–1800 words. Payment: on publication. Founded 1956.

## Hertfordshire Countryside

Beaumonde Publications Ltd, PO Box 5, Hitchin, Herts. SG5 1GJ
*tel* (01462) 431237 *fax* (01462) 422015
*email* info@hertscountryside.co.uk
*Editor* Sandra Small
Monthly £1.25

Articles of county interest. No poetry, puzzles or crosswords. Length: approx. 1000 words. Payment: £30 per 1000 words. Illustrations: line, half-tone. Founded 1946.

## Hi-Fi News

IPC Country & Leisure Media Ltd, Focus House, Dingwall Avenue, Croydon CR9 2TA
*tel* 020-8774 0846 *fax* 020-8774 0940
*email* hi-finews@ipcmedia.com
*Editor* Steve Harris
Monthly £3.50

Articles on all aspects of high-quality sound recording and reproduction; also extensive record review section and supporting musical feature articles. Audio matter is essentially technical, but should be presented in a manner suitable for music lovers interested in the nature of sound. Length: 2000–3000 words. Illustrations: line, half-tone. Payment: by arrangement. Founded 1956.

## History Today

20 Old Compton Street,
London W1D 4TW
*tel* 020-7534 8000
*email* admin@historytoday.com
*website* www.admin@historytoday.com
*Editor* Peter Furtado
Monthly £3.80

History in the widest sense – political, economic, social, biography, relating past to present; world history as well as British. Length: 3500 words (articles); 600–1200 words (news/views). Illustrations: prints and original photos. Do not send original material until publication is agreed. Accepts freelance contributions dealing with genuinely new historical and archaeological research. Payment: by arrangement. Send sae for return of MS. Founded 1951.

## Hiya!

3 Drumbrae Avenue, Edinburgh EH12 8TE
*tel* 0131-467 7221 *fax* 0131-467 7223
*email* enquiries@capitalgroup.freeserve.co.uk
*Editor* Janis Sue Smith, *Send material to* Lawrence Service, Editor-in-Chief
Quarterly £2.50

Lifestyle magazine for women aged 23–45 covering health, beauty, fashion, celebrity interviews. Length: 300–1500 words. Payment: negotiable. Founded 1999.

## Home

SPL Publishing Ltd, Berwick House,
8–10 Knoll Rise, Orpington, Kent BR6 0PS
*tel* (01689) 887253 *fax* (01689) 896847
*email* jwooderson@splpublishing.co.uk
*website* www.splpublishing.co.uk
*Editor* Sarah Giles, *Send material to* Kate Sleeman, Features Editor
Monthly £3.20

Home interest magazine for women aged 25–55. Specially commissions most material. Welcomes ideas for articles and features. Founded 1995.

## Home and Family

The Mothers' Union, Mary Sumner House,
24 Tufton Street, London SW1P 3RB
*tel* 020-7222 5533 *fax* 020-7222 1591
*Editor* Jill Worth
Quarterly £1.50

Short articles related to Christian family life. Payment: approx. £70 per 1000 words. Illustrations: colour photos. Founded 1954.

## Home Words

G.J. Palmer & Sons Ltd,
St Mary's Works, St Mary's Plain, Norwich, Norfolk NR3 3BH
*tel* (01603) 612914 *fax* (01603) 624483
*email* admin@scm-canterburypress.co.uk
*Publisher* G.A. Knights, *Editor* Terence Handley MacMath, *Poetry Editor* D.H.W. Grubb
Monthly

Illustrated C of E magazine insert. Articles of popular Christian interest with an Anglican slant (450 words) with relevant photos or illustrations. Payment: by arrangement. Founded 1870.

## Homes and Gardens

IPC Magazines Ltd, King's Reach Tower, Stamford Street, London SE1 9LS
*tel* 020-7261 5000 *fax* 020-7261 6247
*Editor* Deborah Barker
Monthly £3.10

Articles on home interest or design, particularly well-designed British interiors (snapshots should be submitted). Length: articles, 900–1000 words. Illustrations: all types. Payment: generous, but exceptional work required; varies. Founded 1919.

## Homestyle

Essential Publishing, The Tower, Phoenix Square, Colchester, Essex CO4 9PE
*tel* (01206) 796911 *fax* (01206) 796922
*website* www.essentialhomes.com
*Editor* Sally Narraway
Monthly £1.90

Ideas and practical features on home and garden improvements. Merchandise reviews. Length:

2–6 page spreads. Illustrations: colour transparencies, digital images. Payment: by negotiation. Founded 1992.

## Horse & Hound

IPC Media Ltd, King's Reach Tower, Stamford Street, London SE1 9LS
*tel* 020-7261 6315 *fax* 020-7261 5429
*email* jenny_sims@ipcmedia.com
*website* www.horseandhound.co.uk
*Editor* Lucy Higginson
Weekly £1.85

Special articles, news items, photos, on all matters appertaining to equestrian sports. Payment: by negotiation.

## Horse and Rider

Headley House, Headley Road, Grayshott, Surrey GU26 6TU
*tel* (01428) 601020 *fax* (01428) 601030
*email* alison@djmurphy.co.uk
*website* www.horseandridermagazine.co.uk
*Editor* Alison Bridge
Monthly £3.10

Sophisticated magazine covering all forms of equestrian activity at home and abroad. Good writing and technical accuracy essential. Length: 1500–2000 words. Illustrations: photos and drawings, the latter usually commissioned. Payment: by arrangement. Founded 1959.

## Horticulture Week

Haymarket Magazines Ltd, 174 Hammersmith Road, London W6 7JP
*tel* 020-8267 4977
*Editor* Graham Clarke
Weekly £2 (£83 p.a.)

News, technical and business journal for the nursery and garden centre trade, landscape industry and public parks and sports ground staff. Outside contributions considered. No fiction. Length: 500–1500 words. Illustrations: line, half-tone, colour. Payment: by arrangement.

## Hortus

Bryan's Ground, Stapleton, Nr Presteigne, Herefordshire LD8 2LP
*tel* (01544) 260001
*email* all@hortus.co.uk
*website* www.hortus.co.uk
*Editor* David Wheeler
Quarterly £32 p.a. (UK)

Articles on decorative horticulture: plants, gardens, history, design, literature, people; book reviews. Length: 1500–5000 words, longer by arrangement. Illustrations: line, half-tone and wood-engravings. Payment: by arrangement. Founded 1987.

## Hospital Doctor

Reed Healthcare Publishing, Quadrant House, The Quadrant, Sutton, Surrey SM2 5AS
*tel* 020-8652 8745 *fax* 020-8652 8701
*email* hospital.doctor@rbi.co.uk
*Editor* Mike Broad
Weekly Free to 40,000 doctors. (£89 p.a.)

Commissioned features of interest to all grades and specialities of hospital doctors; demand for news tip-offs. Length: features 800–1500 words. Illustrations: colour photos, transparencies, cartoons and commissioned artwork. Payment: £165 per 1000 words, £16 per 100 words (news). Founded c.1977.

## Hot Press

13 Trinity Street, Dublin 2, Republic of Ireland
*tel* (01) 2411500 *fax* (01) 2411539
*email* info@hotpress.ie
*website* www.hotpress.com
*Editor* Niall Stokes
Fortnightly €3.17

High-quality, investigative stories, or punchily written offbeat pieces, of interest to 16–39 year-olds, including politics, music, sport, sex, religion – whatever's happening on the street. Length: varies. Illustrations: colour with some b&w. Payment: by negotiation. Founded 1977.

## Hotdog

Paragon House, St Peter's Road, Bournemouth BH1 2JS
*tel* (01202) 299900 *fax* (01202) 299955
*email* andymc@paragon.co.uk
*website* www.hotdog-magazine.co.uk
*Editor* Andy McDermott
13 p.a. £3.99

In-depth news and features for film fanatics. Specially commissions most material but will consider unsolicited material. Welcomes ideas for articles and features. Length: 1500–3000 words (features), 200–1000 words (news). Payment: 20p per word. Founded 2000.

## Hotel and Catering Review

Jemma Publications Ltd, Marino House, 52 Glasthule Road, Sandycove, Co. Dublin
*tel* (01) 2800000 *fax* (01) 2801818
*email* fcorr@homenet.ie
*Editor* Frank Corr
Monthly IR£22 p.a.

Short news and trade news pieces. Length: approx. 200 words. Features. Payment: £100 per 1000 words. Illustrations: half-tone, cartoons.

## House & Garden

Vogue House, Hanover Square, London W1S 1JU
*tel* 020-7499 9080 *fax* 020-7629 2907

*Editor* Susan Crewe
Monthly £3

Articles (always commissioned), on subjects relating to domestic architecture, interior decorating, furnishing, gardening, household equipment, food and wine.

## House Beautiful

National Magazine Co. Ltd, National Magazine House, 72 Broadwick Street, London W1F 9EP
*tel* 020-7439 5000 *fax* 020-7439 5141
*website* www.housebeautiful.co.uk
*Editor* Kerryn Harper
Monthly £2.60

Specialist 'home' features for the homes of today. Preliminary study of magazine advisable. Payment: according to merit. Illustrated. Founded 1989.

## Housebuilder

56–64 Leonard Street, London EC2A 4JX
*tel* 020-7608 5130
*email* ben.roskrow@house-builder.co.uk
*website* www.house-builder.co.uk
*Editor* Ben Roskrow, *Send material to* Allison Heller
11 p.a. £66 p.a.

Official Journal of the HouseBuilders Federation published in association with the National House-Building Council. Technical articles on design, construction and equipment of dwellings, estate planning and development, and technical aspects of house-building, aimed at those engaged in house and flat construction and the development of housing estates. Preliminary letter advisable. Length: articles from 500 words, preferably with illustrations. Payment: by arrangement. Illustrations: photos, plans, construction details, cartoons.

## HQ Poetry Magazine

39 Exmouth Street, Swindon SN1 3PU
*tel* (01793) 523927
*Editor* Kevin Bailey
3–4 p.a. £2.80 (4 issues £10 p.a. UK, £13 p.a. non-UK)

International in scope, publishes both experimental and traditional work. About one third of the content is devoted to haikuesque and imagistic poetry. Plus review section and articles. Payment: small. Founded 1990.

## i-D Magazine

124 Tabernacle Street, London EC2A 4SA
*tel* 020-7490 9710 *fax* 020-7251 2225
*email* editor@i-Dmagazine.co.uk
*Editor* Avril Mair
Monthly £2.80

International fashion orientated magazine. Includes music, art, design and film. Illustrations: colour and b&w photos. Payment: £100 per 1000 words; photos £50 per page. Founded 1980.

## Ideal Home

IPC Media Ltd, King's Reach Tower, Stamford Street, London SE1 9LS
*tel* 020-7261 5000 *fax* 020-7261 6697
*Editor* Susan Rose
Monthly £2.60

Lifestyle magazine, articles usually commissioned. Contributors advised to study editorial content before submitting material. Payment: according to material. Illustrations: usually commissioned. Founded 1920.

## The Illustrated London News

20 Upper Ground, London SE1 9PF
*tel* 020-7805 5555 *fax* 020-7805 5911
*Editor* Mark Palmer
£2.50

Two special issues published annually: Summer and Christmas. Focuses on London and the UK: culture, the arts, people, dining, fashion, entertainment. All material commissioned but ideas welcome. Founded 1842.

## In Balance Health & Lifestyle Magazine

Pintail Media Ltd, 50 Parkway, Welwyn Garden City, Herts. AL8 6HH
*tel* (01707) 339007
*email* vrb@inbalancemagazine.com
*website* www.inbalancemagazine.com
*Editor* Val Reynolds Brown
Subscription £12 p.a., 2 printed issues p.a. plus weekly update by email newsletter and website updated weekly

Health and lifestyle magazine with therapy listings. Features on alternative therapies and related environmental issues. Ideal platform for unpublished fiction writers. Only commissioned work accepted – welcomes suggestions for features. Founded 1990.

## In Britain

Romsey Publishing Group, Jubilee House, 2 Jubilee Place, London SW3 3TQ
*tel* 020-7751 4800 *fax* 020-7751 4848
*email* inbritain@romseypublishing.com
*website* www.inbritain.co.uk
*Editor* Andrea Spain
Monthly £2.95 (£23.70 p.a. UK/Europe; $33 US)

Upmarket features magazine about places and people in Britain. Very limited freelance material is accepted. Illustrated. Payment: by arrangement. Founded 1930.

## The Independent Magazine – see The
Independent, page 9

## Index on Censorship

Lancaster House, 33 Islington High Street, London N1 9LH
*tel* 020-7278 2313 *fax* 020-7278 1878

*email* judith@indexoncensorship.org
*website* www.indexoncensorship.org
*Editor-in-Chief* Ursula Owen, *Send material to*
Natasha Schmidt, Editorial Co-ordinator
Quarterly £9.50 (£32 p.a.)

Articles up to 3000 words dealing with all aspects of free speech and political censorship. Illustrations: b&w, cartoons. Payment: £75 per 1000 words. Founded 1972.

## Infant Projects

Scholastic Ltd, Villiers House, Clarendon Avenue, Leamington Spa, Warks. CV32 5PR
*tel* (01926) 887799 *fax* (01926) 337322
*Editor* Michael Ward
Bi-monthly £3.75

Practical articles suggesting project activities for teachers of children aged 4–7; material mostly commissioned. Length: 500–1000 words. Illustrations: colour photos and line illustrations, colour posters. Payment: by arrangement. Founded 1978.

## Inspirations For Your Home

SPL Publishing Ltd, Berwick House, 8–10 Knoll Rise, Orpington, Kent BR6 0PS
*tel* (01689) 837200
*Editor* Andrée Frieze
Monthly £2.90

Inspirational features on all aspects of home interest – home design, cookery, decorating, makeovers. Length: 800–1000 words. Payment: by arrangement. Founded 1993.

## InStyle

Time Life International Inc., 5th Floor, Brettenham House, Lancaster Place, London WC2E 7TL
*tel* 020-7322 1510 *fax* 020-7322 1511
*Editor* Dee Nolan, *Features & Fashion Features*
*Director* Louise Chunn
Monthly £3

Fashion, beauty and celebrity lifestyle magazine for style-conscious women aged 25–44. Welcomes ideas for articles and features. Payment: by arrangement. Founded 2001.

## Insurance Age

Informa Group plc, Informa House, 30–32 Mortimer Street, London W1W 7RE
*tel* 020-7017 4129 *fax* 020-7436 8397
*email* jon.guy@informa.com
*website* www.insuranceage.com
*Editor* Jon Guy
Monthly £5

News and features on general insurance and the broker market, personal, commercial, health and Lloyd's of London. Illustrations: transparencies. Payment: by negotiation. Founded 1979.

## Insurance Brokers' Monthly

7 Stourbridge Road, Lye, Stourbridge, West Midlands DY9 7DG
*tel* (01384) 895228 *fax* (01384) 893666
*email* info@brokersmonthly.co.uk
*website* www.brokersmonthly.co.uk
*Editor* Andrew Newman
Monthly £5

Articles of technical and non-technical interest to insurance brokers and others engaged in the insurance industry. Occasional articles of general interest to the City, on finance, etc. Length: 1000–1500 words. Payment: from £40 per 1000 words on last day of month following publication. Authoritative material written under true name and qualification receives highest payment. Illustrations: line and half-tone. Founded 1950.

## InterMedia

International Institute of Communications, 35 Portland Place, London W1B 1AE
*tel* 020-7323 9622 *fax* 020-7323 9623
*email* martin@iicom.org
*Editor* Martin Sims
Bi-monthly £70 p.a. individuals, £150 p.a. library subscription

International journal concerned with policies, events, trends and research in the field of communications, broadcasting, telecommunications and associated issues, particularly cultural and social. Preliminary letter essential. Illustrations: b&w line. Payment: by arrangement. Founded 1970.

## International Affairs

Royal Institute of International Affairs, Chatham House, 10 St James's Square, London SW1Y 4LE
*tel* 020-7957 5700 *fax* 020-7957 5710
*email* ia-ch@riia.org
*website* www.riia.org
*Editor* Caroline Soper
5 p.a. £16 (£50 p.a. individuals, £184 p.a. institutions)

Serious long-term articles on international affairs; approx. 70 books reviewed each issue. Preliminary letter advisable. Article length: average 7000 words. Illustrations: none. Payment: by arrangement. Founded 1922.

## Internet Made Easy

Paragon Publishing, Paragon House, St Peters Road, Bournemouth BH1 2JS
*tel* (01202) 299900 *fax* (01202) 299955
*email* dominicb@paragon.co.uk
*website* www.paragon.co.uk
*Editor* Dominic Brookman
Monthly £3.99

'The easiest guide to using the Net'. Includes practical tutorials on internet software; reviews of websites; net hardware and software; internet news and features. Send paragraph summaries for features to Editor in the first instance. Payment: varies. Founded 1999.

## Interzone

217 Preston Drove, Brighton, East Sussex BN1 6FL
*tel* (01273) 504710
*website* www.sfsite.com/interzone
*Editor* David Pringle
Bimonthly £3.50 (£20 p.a.)

Science fiction and fantasy short stories, articles, interviews and reviews. Read magazine before submitting. Length: 2000–6000 words. Illustrations: line, half-tone, colour. Payment: by arrangement. Founded 1982.

## Investors Chronicle

Tabernacle Court, 16–28 Tabernacle Street, London EC2A 4DD
*Editor* Matthew Vincent
Weekly £3.25

Journal covering investment and personal finance. Occasional outside contributions for surveys are accepted. Payment: by negotiation.

## Ireland of the Welcomes

Fáilte Ireland, Baggot Street Bridge, Dublin 2, Republic of Ireland
*tel* (01) 6024000 *fax* (01) 6024335
*email* iow@faiteireland.ie
*website* www.irelandofthewelcomes.com
*Editor* Letitia Pollard
Bi-monthly €3.17

Articles on cultural, sporting or topographical aspects of Ireland; designed to arouse interest in Irish holidays. Mostly commissioned – preliminary letter advised. No unsolicited MSS. Length: 1200–1800 words. Payment: by arrangement. Illustrations: scenic and topical transparencies, line drawings, some cartoons. Founded 1952.

## Ireland's Own

Channing House, Upper Rowe Street, Wexford, Republic of Ireland
*tel* (053) 40140 *fax* (053) 340191
*email* irelands.own@peoplenews.ie
*Editors* Sean Nolan, Phil Murphy
Weekly €1

Short stories: non-experimental, traditional with an Irish orientation (2000–2500 words); articles of interest to Irish readers at home and abroad (750–1000 words); general and literary articles (750–1000 words). Monthly special bumper editions, each devoted to a particular seasonal topic. Suggestions for new features considered. Payment: varies according to quality and length. Illustrations: photos, cartoons. Founded 1902.

## Irish Farmers Journal

Irish Farm Centre, Bluebell, Dublin 12, Republic of Ireland
*tel* (01) 4199500 *fax* (01) 4520876
*email* editdept@ifj.ie
*website* www.farmersjournal.ie
*Editor* Matthew Dempsey
Weekly €1.90

Readable, technical articles on any aspect of farming. Length: 700–1000 words. Payment: £100–£150 per article. Illustrated. Founded 1948.

## Irish Journal of Medical Science

Royal Academy of Medicine, International House, 20–22 Lower Hatch Street, Dublin 2, Republic of Ireland
*tel* (01) 6623706 *fax* (01) 6611684
*email* journal@rami.ie
*website* www.iformix.com
*Send material to* Mr Thomas N. Walsh
Quarterly €42 (Ireland and EU €156 p.a., non-EU €192 p.a.)

Official Organ of the Royal Academy of Medicine in Ireland. Original contributions in medicine, surgery, midwifery, public health, etc; reviews of professional books, reports of medical societies, etc. Illustrations: line, half-tone, colour.

## Irish Medical Times

24–26 Upper Ormond Quay, Dublin 7, Republic of Ireland
*tel* (01) 8176300 *fax* (01) 8176345
*email* editor@imt.ie
*website* www.imt.ie
*Editor* Aindreas McEntee
Weekly €5.10 (€236 p.a.)

Medical articles, also humorous articles with medical slant. Length: 850–1000 words. Payment: £100 per 1000 words. Illustrations: line, half-tone, colour, cartoons.

## Irish Pages: A Journal of Contemporary Writing

The Linen Hall Library, 17 Donegall Square North, Belfast BT1 5OB
*tel* 028-9064 1644
*email* irishpages@yahoo.co.uk
*website* www.irishpages.org
*Editor* Chris Agee
Biannual £10/€14

Poetry, short fiction, essays, creative non-fiction, memoir, essay reviews, nature writing, translated work, literary journalism, and other autobiographical, historical and scientific writing of literary distinction. Publishes in equal measure writing from Ireland and abroad. Payment: only pays for certain commissions and occasional serial rights. Founded 2002.

## The Irish Post
Thomas Crosbie Holdings Ltd, Cambridge House,
Cambridge Grove, London W6 0LE
*tel* 020-8741 0649 *fax* 020-8741 3382
*email* irishpost@irishpost.co.uk
*website* www.irishpost.co.uk
*Editor* Frank Murphy
Weekly 80p

Coverage of all political, social and sporting events
relevant to the Irish community in the UK. Contains
*Irish I* guide to Irish entertainment countrywide.

## Irish Printer
Jemma Publications Ltd, 52 Glasthule Road,
Sandycove, Co. Dublin, Republic of Ireland
*tel* (01) 2800000 *fax* (01) 2801818
*email* n.tynan@jemma.ie
*Editor* Nigel Tynan
Monthly €60.95 p.a. (€76.18 UK/overseas)

Technical articles and news of interest to the
printing industry. Length: 800–1000 words.
Illustrations: colour and b&w photos. Payment:
€140 per 1000 words; photos £30. Founded 1974.

## Irish Tatler
Smurfit Publications Ltd, 2 Clanwilliam Court,
Lower Mount Street, Dublin 2, Republic of Ireland
*tel* (01) 2405367 *fax* (01) 6619757
*email* feeback@ivenus.com
*website* www.ivenus.com
*Editor* Vanessa Harriss
Monthly €2

General interest women's magazine: beauty,
interiors, fashion, cookery, current affairs, reportage
and celebrity interviews. Length: 2000–4000 words.
In association with ivenus.com. Payment: by
arrangement.

## Jack
Dennis Publishing, Cleveland Street,
London W1T 4JD
*tel* 020-7687 7000 *fax* 020-7687 7099
*email* jack@ifgmags.com,
kimberly.taylorbennett@ifgmags.com
*website* www.jackmagazine.co.uk
*Editor* Michael Hodges, *Send material to* Kimberly
Taylor-Bennett, Editorial Assistant
Monthly £3

'Magazine for intelligent men.' Wide-ranging
content, from humour to sport, from nature to war
to conspiracy theories. Requirements vary. Will
consider unsolicited material. Welcomes ideas for
articles and features. Payment: varies. Founded 2002.

## Jane's Defence Weekly
Sentinel House, 163 Brighton Road, Coulsdon,
Surrey CR5 2YH
*tel* 020-8700 3700 *fax* 020-8763 1007

*website* www.jdw.janes.com
*Editor* Clifford Beal
Weekly £220 p.a. (5-year archive on CD-Rom)

International defence news; military equipment;
budget analysis, industry, military technology,
business, political, defence market intelligence.
Payment: minimum £200 per 1000 words used.
Illustrations: line, half-tone, colour. Founded 1984.

## Jazz Journal International
Jazz Journal Ltd, 3 & 3A Forest Road, Loughton,
Essex IG10 1DR
*tel* 020-8532 0456/0678 *fax* 020-8532 0440
*Publisher/Editor-in-Chief* Eddie Cook
Monthly £3.50

Articles on jazz, record reviews. Telephone or write
before submitting material. Payment: by
arrangement. Illustrations: photos. Founded 1948.

## Jewish Chronicle
25 Furnival Street, London EC4A 1JT
*tel* 020-7415 1500
*Editor* Edward J. Temko
Weekly 60p

Authentic and exclusive news stories and articles of
Jewish interest from 500–1500 words are
considered. Includes a lively arts and leisure section
and regular travel pages. Payment: by arrangement.
Illustrations: of Jewish interest, either topical or
feature. Founded 1841.

## The Jewish Quarterly
92 Dartmouth Road, London NW2 4HA
*tel* 020-8830 5367 (editorial) *fax* 020-8830 5367
*Editor* Matthew Reisz
Quarterly £4.95 (£25 p.a., £35 p.a. Europe, £45 p.a.
overseas)

Articles of Jewish interest, literature, history, music,
politics, poetry, book reviews, fiction. Illustrations:
half-tone. Founded 1953.

## Jewish Telegraph
Telegraph House, 11 Park Hill, Bury Old Road,
Prestwich, Manchester M25 0HH
*tel* 0161-740 9321 *fax* 0161-740 9325
*email* mail@jewishtelegraph.com
*website* www.jewishtelegraph.com
1 Shaftesbury Avenue, Leeds LS8 1DR
*tel* 0113-295 6000 *fax* 0113-295 6006
*email* leeds@jewishtelegraph.com
Harold House, Dunbabin Road, Liverpool L15 6XL
*tel* 0151-475 6666 *fax* 0151-475 2222
*email* liverpool@jewishtelegraph.com
May Terrace, Giffnock, Glasgow G46 6LD
*tel* 0141-621 4422 *fax* 0141-621 4333
*email* glasgow@jewishtelegraph.com
*Editor* Paul Harris
Weekly Manchester 40p, Leeds 35p, Liverpool 35p,
Glasgow 40p

Non-fiction articles of Jewish interest, especially humour. Exclusive Jewish news stories and pictures, international, national and local. Length: 1000–1500 words. Payment: by arrangement. Illustrations: line, half-tone, cartoons. Founded 1950.

## Journal of Alternative and Complementary Medicine

9 Rickett Street, London SW6 1RU
*tel* 020-7385 0012 *fax* 020-7385 4566
*Editor* Graeme Miller
Monthly £2.95 (£33.50 p.a.)

Feature articles (up to 2000 words) and news stories (up to 250 words). Unsolicited material welcome but not eligible for payment unless commissioned. Illustrations: line, half-tone, colour. Payment: by negotiation. Founded 1983.

## Junior Education

Scholastic Ltd, Villiers House, Clarendon Avenue, Leamington Spa, Warks. CV32 5PR
*tel* (01926) 887799 *fax* (01926) 883331
*email* juniored@scholastic.co.uk
*Editor* Tracy Kewley
Monthly £3.75

For teachers of 7–11 year-olds. Articles by specialists on practical teaching ideas, coverage of primary education news; posters; photocopiable material for the classroom. Length: 800–1000 words. Payment: by arrangement. Illustrated with photos and drawings; includes colour poster. Founded 1977.

## Junior Focus

Scholastic Ltd, Villiers House, Clarendon Avenue, Leamington Spa, Warks. CV32 5PR
*tel* (01926) 887799 *fax* (01926) 883331
*email* jfocus@scholastic.co.uk
*Editor* Tracy Kewley
Monthly £3.75

Aimed at teachers of 7–11 year-olds, each issue is based on a theme, closely linked to the National Curriculum. Includes A1 and A3 full-colour posters, 12 pages of photocopiable material and 16 pages of articles. All material commissioned. Length: 800 words. Illustrations: photos and drawings. Payment: £100 per double-page spread; varies for illustrations. Founded 1982.

## Junior Magazine

Beach Magazines & Publishing Ltd,
4 Cromwell Place, London SW7 2JE
*tel* 020-7761 8900 *fax* 020-7761 8901
*email* editorial@juniormagazine.co.uk
*website* www.juniormagazine.co.uk
*Editor* Catherine O'Dolan
Monthly £2.90

Glossy up-market parenting magazine aimed at mothers of children aged 0–8 and reflects the shift in today's society towards older mothers and fathers who have established their careers and homes. Intelligent and insightful features and the best in fashion. Specially commissions most material. Welcomes ideas for articles and features. Payment: £150 per 1000 words (articles/features/short fiction), £300 per feature (colour and b&w photos/artwork). Founded 1998.

## Justice of the Peace

LexisNexis UK, 35 Chancery Lane,
London WC2A 1EL
*tel* 020-7400 2828 *fax* 020-7400 2805
*email* jpn@lexisnexis.co.uk
*Consulting Editor* Adrian Turner, *Send material to* Diana Rose
Weekly £239 p.a.

Professional journal. Articles on magisterial and local government law and associated subjects including family law, criminology, medico-legal matters, penology, police, probation. Information on articles and contributions sent on request. Length: 3000 words. Payment: £200 per feature article or £20 per column (articles). Founded 1837.

## Kent Life

25A Pudding Lane, Maidstone, Kent ME14 1PA
*tel* (01622) 762818 *fax* (01622) 663294
*email* ian.trevett@archant.co.uk,
kate.cowling@kent-life.co.uk
*website* www.kent-life.co.uk
*Editor* Ian Trevett, *Assistant Editor* Kate Cowling
Monthly £2.25

Local lifestyle magazine 'celebrating the best of county life'. Features local people, social events and entertainment and promotes local towns and villages, walks and heritage. Will consider unsolicited material. Welcomes ideas for articles and features. Length: 1000 words (articles/features), 200 words (news), 500 words (short fiction). Illustrations: transparencies, colour and b&w prints, colour artwork. Payment: negotiable.

## Kerrang!

EMAP Performance 2001, PO Box 2930,
London W1A 6DZ
*tel* 020-7436 1515 *fax* 020-7312 8910
*Editor* Ashley Bird
Weekly £1.70

News, reviews and interviews; music with attitude. All material commissioned. Illustrations: colour. Payment: by arrangement. Founded 1981.

## Kids Alive! (The Young Soldier)

The Salvation Army, 101 Newington Causeway,
London SE1 6BN
*tel* 020-7367 4910 *fax* 020-7367 4710
*email* kidsalive@salvationarmy.org.uk

*Editor* Ken Nesbitt
Weekly 50p (£25 p.a. including free membership of
the Kids Alive! Club)

Children's magazine: stories, pictures, cartoon
strips, puzzles, etc; Christian-based with emphasis
on education re addictive substances. Payment: by
arrangement. Illustrations: half-tone, line and
4-colour line, cartoons. Founded 1881.

## Kitchen Garden
12 Orchard Lane, Woodnewton,
Peterborough PE8 5EE
*tel* (01780) 470097 *fax* (01780) 470550
*website* www.kitchengarden.co.uk
*Editor* Andrew Blackford
Monthly £3.10

Magazine for people with a passion for growing
their own vegetables, fruit and herbs. Includes
practical tips and inspirational ideas. Specially
commissions most material. Welcomes ideas for
articles and features. Length: 700–2000 (articles/
features). Illustrations: colour transparencies, prints
and artwork; all commissioned. Payment: varies.
Founded 1997.

## Koi, Ponds & Gardens
Origin Publishing, Tower House, Fairfax Street,
Bristol BS1 3BN
*tel* 0117-927 9009  *fax* 0117-934 9008
*email* hilaryclapham@originpublishing.co.uk
*website* www.koimag.co.uk
*Editor* Hilary Clapham
4-weekly £3.25

A practical and informative guide to the keeping koi
as a hobby, from pond construction to koi health
care. Also includes features on the hobby in Japan.
Length 800–1700 words (articles), 2000–3000 words
(features), 150 words (news). Payment: £80–£170
(articles), £200–£300 (features). Illustrations:
colour.

## The Lady
39–40 Bedford Street,
London WC2E 9ER
*tel* 020-7379 4717 *fax* 020-7836 4620
*website* www.lady.co.uk
*Editor* Arline Usden
Weekly 90p

British and foreign travel, countryside, human-
interest, celebrity interviews, animals, cookery, art
and antiques, historic-interest and commemorative
articles (preliminary letter advisable for articles
dealing with anniversaries). Send proposals for
articles by post. Length: 900–1200 words;
Viewpoint: 500 words. Annual Short Story
Competition in October/November with prize of
£1000 plus. Winning entries printed in magazine.
Payment: by arrangement. Founded 1885.

## Lancashire Magazine
33 Beverley Road, Driffield, Yorkshire YO25 6SD
*tel* (01377) 253232 *fax* (01377) 253232
*Editor* Winston Halstead
Bi-monthly £1.60

Articles about people, life and character of all parts
of Lancashire. Length: 1000 words. Payment:
£35–£40 approx. per published page. Illustrations:
line, half-tone, colour. Founded 1977.

## Lancet
32 Jamestown Road, London NW1 7BY
*tel* 020-7424 4910 *fax* 020-7424 4911
*website* www.thelancet.com
*Editor* Dr Richard Horton
Weekly £5

Research papers, review articles, editorials,
correspondence and commentaries on international
medicine, medical research and policy. Consult the
Editor before submitting material. Founded 1823.

## Land & Liberty
Suite 427, The London Fruit Exchange,
Brushfield Street, London E1 6EL
*tel* 020-7377 8885 *fax* 020-7377 8886
*email* editor@LandandLiberty.org.uk
*website* www.LandandLiberty.org.uk
*Editor* Peter Gibb
Quarterly £3.75 (£15 p.a.)

Explores how common wealth can be used
sustainably as public revenue to enhance and balance
relationships between the individual, the community
and the environment. Articles on land economics,
land taxation, land prices, land speculation as they
relate to housing, the economy, production, politics.
Study of journal essential. Length: up to 3000 words.
Payment: by arrangement. Illustrations: half-tone.
Founded 1894.

## The Lawyer
Centaur Communications Group, 50 Poland Street,
London W1V 4AX
*tel* 020-7970 4614 *fax* 020-7970 4640
*email* lawyer.edit@chiron.co.uk
*website* www.thelawyer.com
*Editor* Catrin Griffiths
Weekly £1.75 (£60 p.a.)

News, articles, features and views relevant to the
legal profession. Length: 600–900 words.
Illustrations: as agreed. Payment: £125–£150 per
1000 words. Founded 1987.

## Legal Week
Global Professional Media Ltd, 99 Charterhouse
Street, London EC1M 6HR
*tel* 020-7566 5600 *fax* 020-7253 8505
*email* jmalpas@gpmuk.com
*website* www.legalweek.net

*Editor* John Malpas
Weekly £2.45

News and features aimed at business lawyers. Length: 750–1000 words (features), 300 words (news). Payment: £150 upwards (features), £75–£100 (news). Considers unsolicited material and welcomes ideas for articles and features. Founded 1999.

**Legal Director**
Monthly

News and features for in-house lawyers.

**Legal IT**
Monthly

News and features for IT decision-makers in the legal industry.

## The Leisure Manager

The Institute of Leisure and Amenity Management, ILAM House, Lower Basildon, Reading, Berks. RG8 9NE
*tel* (01491) 874800 *fax* (01491) 874801
*email* leisuremanager@ilam.co.uk
*website* www.ilam.co.uk
*Editor* Jonathan Ives
Monthly £40 p.a. (£50 p.a. overseas)

Official Journal of The Institute of Leisure and Amenity Management. Articles on amenity, children's play, tourism, leisure, parks, entertainment, recreation and sports management, cultural services. Payment: by arrangement. Illustrations: line, half-tone. Founded 1985.

## Leisure Painter

63–65 High Street, Tenterden, Kent TN30 6BD
*tel* (01580) 763315 *fax* (01580) 765411
*Editor* Jane Stroud
Monthly £2.60

Instructional articles on painting and fine art. Payment: £75 per 1000 words. Illustrations: line, half-tone, colour, original artwork. Founded 1967.

## LGC (Local Government Chronicle)

Greater London House, Hampstead Road, London NW1 7EJ
*tel* 020-7347 1800 *fax* 020-7347 1831
*email* lognews@emap.com
*website* www.lgcnet.com
*Editor* Richard Vize, *Features Editor* Anne Gulland
Weekly £3.45

Aimed at senior managers in local government. Covers politics, management issues, social services, education, regeneration, industrial relations and personnel, plus public sector finance and Scottish and Welsh local government. Length: 1000 words (features). Illustrations: b&w and colour, cartoons. Payment: by arrangement. Founded 1855.

## Life & Work: Editorially Independent Magazine of the Church of Scotland

121 George Street, Edinburgh EH2 4YN
*tel* 0131-225 5722 *fax* 0131-240 2207
*email* magazine@lifeandwork.org
*Editor* Lynne Robertson
Monthly £1.50

Articles not exceeding 1200 words and news; occasional stories. Study the magazine and contact the Editor first. Payment: up to £100 per 1000 words, or by arrangement. Illustrations: photos and line drawings, colour illustrations, cartoons.

## Lincolnshire Life

PO Box 81, Lincoln LN1 1HD
*tel* (01522) 527127 *fax* (01522) 560035
*email* editorial@lincolnshirelife.co.uk
*website* www.lincolnshirelife.co.uk
*Editor* Judy Theobald
Monthly £1.95

Articles and news of county interest. Approach in writing. Length: up to 1600 words. Illustrations: colour photos and line drawings. Payment: varies. Founded 1961.

## The Linguist

The Institute of Linguists, Saxon House, 48 Southwark Street, London SE1 1UN
*tel* 020-7226 2822
*email* linguist@patricia.treasure.co.uk
*website* www.linguistonline.co.uk
*Editor* Pat Treasure
Bi-monthly £7 (£39 p.a.)

Articles of interest to professional linguists in translating, interpreting and teaching fields. Articles usually contributed, but payment by arrangement. All contributors have special knowledge of the subjects with which they deal. Length: 1500–2000 words. Illustrations: line, half-tone.

## The List

The List Ltd, 14 High Street, Edinburgh EH1 1TE
*tel* 0131-558 1191 *fax* 0131-557 8500
*email* editor@list.co.uk
*Editor* Nick Barley
Fortnightly £2.20

Events guide for Glasgow and Edinburgh covering film, theatre, music, clubs, books, city life, art, and TV and video. Considers unsolicited material and welcomes ideas. Length: 200 words (articles), 800 words and above (features). Illustrations: transparencies and colour prints. Payment: £20 (articles), from £60 (features); £25–£50. Founded 1985.

## The Literary Review

44 Lexington Street, London W1F 0LW
*tel* 020-7437 9392 *fax* 020-7734 1844

*Editor* Nancy Sladek
Monthly £3 (£32 p.a.)

Reviews, articles of cultural interest, interviews, profiles, monthly poetry competition. Material mostly commissioned. Length: articles and reviews 800–1500 words. Illustrations: line and b&w photos. Payment: £25 per article; none for illustrations. Founded 1979.

## Loaded

IPC Media Ltd, King's Reach Tower, Stamford Street, London SE1 9LS
*tel* 020-7261 5000 *fax* 020-7261 5557
*email* tammy_butt@ipc.co.uk (features), johnny-cigarettes@ipcmedia.com (handbook)
*website* www.uploaded.com
*Editor* Martin Daubney
Monthly £2.90

Magazine for men aged 18–30. Music, sport, sex, humour, travel, fashion, hard news and popular culture. Address longer features (2000 words) to Features Editor, and shorter items to Handbook Editor. Payment: by arrangement. Founded 1994.

## LOGOS

5 Beechwood Drive, Marlow, Bucks. SL7 2DH
*tel* (01628) 477577 *fax* (01628) 477577
*email* logos-marlow@dial.pipex.com
*Editor* Gordon Graham
Quarterly £45 p.a. (£108 p.a. institutions)

In-depth articles on publishing, librarianship and bookselling with international or interdisciplinary appeal. Length: 3500–7000 words. Payment: 25 offprints/copy of issue. Founded 1990.

## The London Magazine: A Review of Literature and the Arts

32 Addison Grove, London W4 1ER
*tel* 020-8400 5882 *fax* 020-8994 1713
*email* editorial@thelondonmagazine.net
*website* www.thelondonmagazine.net
*Publisher* Christopher Arkell, *Editor* Sebastian Barker
Bi-monthly £6.95 (£32 p.a.)

Poems, stories (2000–5000 words), memoirs, critical articles, features on art, photography, theatre, music, architecture. Sae essential (3 IRCs from abroad). Submissions by email are not accepted except when agreed with the Editor. Payment: by arrangement. Founded 1732.

## London Review of Books

28 Little Russell Street, London WC1A 2HN
*tel* 020-7209 1101 *fax* 020-7209 1102
*email* edit@lrb.co.uk
*Editor* Mary-Kay Wilmers
Fortnightly £2.99

Features, essays, poems. Payment: by arrangement. Founded 1979.

## Lothian Life

Ballencrieff Cottage, Ballencrieff Toll, Bathgate, West Lothian EH48 4LD
*tel* (01506) 632728 *fax* (01506) 635444
*email* editor@lothianlife.co.uk
*website* www.lothianlife.co.uk
*Editor* Susan Coon
Quarterly £2

Articles, profiles etc with a Lothians angle. Length: 800–3000 words. Illustrations: colour and b&w photos, b&w artwork and cartoons. Payment: £20 per 1000 words. Founded 1995.

## MacUser

Dennis Publishing Ltd, 30 Cleveland Street, London W1T 4JD
*tel* 020-7907 6000 *fax* 020-7907 6369
*email* edit@macuser.co.uk
*website* www.macuser.co.uk
*Editor* Nik Rawlinson
Fortnightly £3.50

News, reviews, tutorials and features on Apple Macintosh computer products and topics of interest to their users. Commissioned reviews of products compatible with Mac computers required. Occasional requirement for features relating to Mac-based design and publishing and general computing and internet issues. Ideas welcome. Length: 2000–5000 words (features), approx. 500 words (news), 300–2500 words (reviews). Illustrations: commissioned from Mac-based designers. Payment: £190 per 1000 words; competitive (artwork). Founded 1985.

## Macworld

IDG Communications, 99 Gray's Inn Road, London WC1X 8TY
*tel* 020-7831 9252
*email* editor@macworld.co.uk
*website* www.macworld.co.uk
*Editor* Simon Jary
Every 4 weeks £4.99

All aspects of Apple Macintosh computing, primarily for professional users: industry news, product testing, tips and how-to features. Specially commissions most material. Welcomes ideas for articles and features. Payment: £210 per 1000 words. Digital pictures only. Founded 1989.

## Making Music

VViP Highgate Studios, 53–79 Highgate Road, London NW5 1TW
*tel* 020-7331 1170 *fax* 020-7331 1273
*website* www.makingmusic.co.uk
*Editor* Paul Fowler
Monthly £18 p.a.

Technical, musicianly and instrumental features on rock, pop, blues, dance, world, jazz, soul; little classical. Length: 500–2500 words. Payment: £95 per 1000 words. Illustrations: colour, including cartoons and photos. Founded 1986.

## Management Today

174 Hammersmith Road, London W6 7JP
*tel* 020-8267 4610 *fax* 020-7267 4966
*Editor* Matthew Gwyther
Monthly £40 p.a.

Company profiles and analysis – columns from 1000 words, features up to 3000 words. Payment: £330 per 1000 words. Illustrations: colour transparencies, always commissioned. Founded 1966.

## Marie Claire

European Magazines Ltd, 13th Floor, King's Reach Tower, Stamford Street, London SE1 9LS
*tel* 020-7261 5240 *fax* 020-7261 5277
*email* marieclaire@ipcmedia.com
*Editor* Marie O'Riordan
Monthly £3

Feature articles of interest to today's woman; plus fashion, beauty, health, food, drink and travel. Commissioned material only. Payment: by negotiation. Illustrated in colour. Founded 1988.

## Market Newsletter

Bureau of Freelance Photographers, Focus House, 497 Green Lanes, London N13 4BP
*tel* 020-8882 3315/6 *fax* 020-8886 5174
*email* info@thebfp.com
*website* www.thebfp.com
*Editor* John Tracy
Monthly Private circulation

Current information on markets and editorial requirements of interest to writers and photographers. Founded 1965.

## Marketing Week

St Giles House, 50 Poland Street, London W1F 7AX
*tel* 020-7970 4000 *fax* 020-7970 6721
*website* www.marketing-week.co.uk
*Editor* Stuart Smith
Weekly £2.30

Aimed at marketing management. Accepts occasional features and analysis. Length: 1000–2000 words. Payment: £200 per 1000 words. Founded 1978.

## Maxim

Dennis Publishing Ltd, 30 Cleveland Street, London W1T 4JD
*tel* 020-7907 6410 *fax* 020-7907 6439
*email* editorial.maxim@dennis.co.uk
*website* www.maxim-magazine.co.uk
*Editor* Tom Loxley
Monthly £3.20

Glossy men's lifestyle magazine with news, features and articles. All material is commissioned. Length:

1500–2500 words (features), 150–500 words (news). Illustrations: transparencies. Payment: by negotiation. Founded 1995.

## Mayfair

Paul Raymond Publications, 2 Archer Street, London W1D 7AW
*tel* 020-7292 8000
*email* mayfair@pr-org.co.uk
*website* www.sexclub.co.uk
*Editor* David Spenser
Monthly £2.65

Classic British adult magazine containing features ranging from those on motorbikes and celebrities to those of a more explicit nature, as well as several photo sets. Short stories. Welcomes ideas for articles and features. Length: 1200–1500 words. Illustrations: colour, cartoons. Payment: negotiable. Founded 1965.

## Medal News

Token Publishing Ltd, Orchard House, Duchy Road, Heathpark, Honiton, Devon EX14 1YD
*tel* (01404) 46972 *fax* (01404) 44788
*email* info@tokenpublishing.com
*website* www.tokenpublishing.com
*Editor* John Mussell
10 p.a. £2.95

Well-researched articles on military history with a bias towards medals. Length: up to 2000 words. Illustrations: b&w preferred. Payment: £25 per 1000 words; none for illustrations. Founded 1989.

## Media Week

Quantum Business Media Ltd, Quantum House, 19 Scarbrook Road, Croydon CR9 1LX
*tel* 020-8565 4317 *fax* 020-8565 4394
*email* mweeked@mediaweek.co.uk
*Editor* Tim Burrowes
Weekly £1.85

News and analysis of UK advertising media industry. Illustrations: full colour and b&w. Founded 1985.

## Men Only

2 Archer Street, London W1V 8JJ
*tel* 020-7292 8000 *fax* 020-7734 5030
*Publisher* Paul Raymond, *Editor* Nat Saunders
Monthly £2.60

High-quality glamour photography; explicit sex stories (no erotic fiction); male interest features – sport, humour, entertainment, hedonism! Proposals welcome. Payment: by arrangement. Founded 1971.

## Men's Health

Rodale Press Ltd, 7–10 Chandos Street, London W1M 0AD
*tel* 020-7291 6000 *fax* 020-7291 6053
*website* www.menshealth.co.uk
*Editor* Morgan Rees

10 p.a. £3.20

Active pursuits, grooming, fitness, fashion, sex, career and general men's interest issues. Length 1000–4000 words. Ideas welcome. No unsolicited MSS. Payment: by arrangement. Founded 1994.

## Methodist Recorder

122 Golden Lane, London EC1Y 0TL
*tel* 020-7251 8414
*email* editorial@methodistrecorder.co.uk
*website* www.methodistrecorder.co.uk
*Managing Editor* Moira Sleight
Weekly 72p

Methodist newspaper; ecumenically involved. Limited opportunities for freelance contributors. Preliminary letter advised. Founded 1861.

## Military Modelling

Highbury Leisure Publishing Ltd, Berwick House, 8–10 Knoll Rise, Orpington, Kent BR8 0PS
*tel* (01689) 899200 *fax* (01689) 899240
*Editor* Ken Jones
Monthly £2.99

Articles on military modelling. Length: up to 2000 words. Payment: by arrangement. Illustrations: line, half-tone, colour.

## Minor Monthly

Poundbury Publishing Ltd, Peverill Avenue East, Poundbury, Dorchester, Dorset DT1 3WE
*tel* (01305) 756397 *fax* (01305) 756395
*email* brian@poundbury.co.uk
*website* www.minormonthly.com
*Editor* Brian J. Elliott
Monthly £2.40

Magazine for the Morris Minor owner and enthusiast: news, features, profiles and workshops. Specially commissions most material but will consider unsolicited material. Length: 1000 words. Illustrations: colour prints. Payment: negotiable. Founded 1995.

## Mixmag

EMAP plc, Mappin House, 4 Winsley Street, London W1N 8HF
*tel* 020-7436 1515 *fax* 020-7312 8977
*email* mixmag@emap.com
*website* www.mixmag.net
*Editor* Viv Crask
Monthly £3.85

Dance music and clubbing magazine. Considers unsolicited material. Length: 300–1000 words (articles), 2500–3000 (features). Payment: £200 per 1000 words. Illustrations: colour, b&w. Founded 1984.

## Mizz

IPC Magazines Ltd, King's Reach Tower, Stamford Street, London SE1 9LS
*tel* 020-7261 6319 *fax* 020-7261 6032

*email* mizz@ipcmedia.com
*website* www.ipcmedia.com
*Editor* Sharon Christal
Fortnightly £1.50

Articles on any subject of interest to girls aged 10–14. Approach in writing. Payment: by arrangement. Illustrated. Founded 1985.

## Model Boats

Highbury Leisure Publishing Services Ltd, Berwick House, 8–10 Knoll Rise, Orpington, Kent BR6 0PS
*tel* (01689) 899200 *fax* (01689) 899240
*Editor* John L. Cundell *tel* (01525) 382847
12 p.a. £2.99

Articles, drawings, plans, sketches of model boats. Payment: £25 per page; plans £100. Illustrations: line, half-tone. Founded 1964.

## Model Engineer

Nexus Special Interests Ltd, Nexus House, Azalea Drive, Swanley, Kent BR8 8HU
*tel* (01322) 660070 *fax* (01322) 667633
*Editor* Mike Chrisp
Fortnightly £2.30

Detailed description of the construction of models, small workshop equipment, machine tools and small electrical and mechanical devices; articles on small power engineering, mechanics, electricity, workshop methods, clocks and experiments. Payment: up to £40 per page. Illustrations: line, half-tone, colour. Founded 1898.

## Modern Language Review

Modern Humanities Research Association, c/o Maney Publishing, Hudson Road, Leeds LS9 7DL
Quarterly Price on application

Articles and reviews of a scholarly or specialist character on English, Romance, Germanic and Slavonic languages and literatures. Payment: none, but offprints are given. Founded 1905.

## Modern Painters

3rd Floor, 52 Bermondsey Street, London SE1 3UD
*tel* 020-7407 9246 *fax* 020-7407 9242
*email* info@modernpainters.co.uk
*website* www.modernpainters.co.uk
*Editor* Karen Wright
Quarterly £5.99

Journal of modern and contemporary fine arts and architecture – commissioned articles and features; also interviews. Length: 1000–2500 words. Payment: £100 per 1000 words. Illustrated. Founded 1986.

## Modern Woman Nationwide

Meath Chronicle Ltd, Market Square, Navan, Co. Meath, Republic of Ireland
*tel* (046) 79600 *fax* (046) 23565

*Editor* Margot Davis
Monthly €63 cents

Articles and features on a wide range of subjects of interest to women over the age of 18 (e.g. politics, religion, health, social, personal, sexuality and sex). Length: 200–1000 words. Illustrations: colour photos, line drawings and cartoons. Payment: NUJ rates. Founded 1984.

## Mojo

EMAP Metro, Mappin House, 4 Winsley Street, London W1W 8HF
*tel* 020-7436 1515 *fax* 020-7312 8296
*email* mojo@emap.com
*website* www.mojo4music.com
*Editor* Paul Trynka
Monthly £3.80

Serious rock music magazine: interviews, news and reviews of books, live shows and albums. Length: up to 10,000 words. Illustrations: colour and b&w photos, colour caricatures. Payment: £250 per 1000 words; £200–£400 illustrations. Founded 1993.

## MoneyMarketing

Centaur Communications, St Giles House, 50 Poland Street, London W1T 3QN
*tel* 020-7970 4000 *fax* 020-7943 8097
*Editor* John Lappin
Weekly £1.95

News, features, surveys and viewpoints. Length: features from 900 words. Illustrations: b&w photos, colour and b&w line. Payment: by arrangement. Founded 1985.

## Moneywise

RD Publications Ltd, 11 Westferry Circus, Canary Wharf, London E14 4HE
*tel* 020-7715 8465 *fax* 020-7715 8725
*website* www.moneywise.co.uk
*Editor* Ben Livesey, *Send story ideas to* Sarah Das, Senior Editor
Monthly £3.50

Financial and consumer interest features, articles and news stories. No unsolicited MSS. Length: 1500–2000 words. Illustrations: willing to see designers, illustrators and photographers for fresh new ideas. Payment: by arrangement. Founded 1990.

## More

EMAP Élan, Endeavour House, 189 Shaftesbury Avenue, London WC2H 8JG
*tel* 020-7208 3165 *fax* 020-7208 3595
*Editor* Alison Hall
Fortnightly £1.60

Celebrities, fun, gossip and features, how-to articles aimed at young women. Study of magazine essential. Length: 900–1100 words. Illustrated. Founded 1988.

## Mother & Baby

EMAP Esprit, Greater London House, Hampstead Road, London NW1 7EJ
*tel* 020-7347 1869
*website* www.motherandbaby.co.uk
*Editor* Dani Zur
Monthly £1.99

Features and practical information including pregnancy and birth and babycare advice. Expert attribution plus real-life stories. Length: 1000–1500 words. Payment: by negotiation. Illustrated. Founded 1956.

## Motor Boat and Yachting

IPC Media Ltd, King's Reach Tower, Stamford Street, London SE1 9LS
*tel* 020-7261 5333 *fax* 020-7261 5419
*email* mby@ipcmedia.com
*website* www.mby.com
*Editor* Tom Isitt
Monthly £3.60

General interest as well as specialist motor boating material welcomed. Features up to 2000 words considered on all sea-going aspects. Payment: varies. Illustrations: photos (mostly colour and transparencies preferred). Founded 1904.

## Motor Boats Monthly

IPC Magazines Ltd, King's Reach Tower, Stamford Street, London SE1 9LS
*tel* 020-7261 7256 *fax* 020-7261 7900
*email* mbm@ipcmedia.com
*website* www.mbmclub.com
*Editor* Hugo Andreae
Monthly £3.50

News on motorboating in the UK and Europe, cruising features practical guides and anecdotal stories. Mostly commissioned – send synopsis to the Editor. Length: news up to 200 words, features up to 4000 words. Illustrations: colour transparencies. Payment: by arrangement. Founded 1987.

## Motor Caravan Magazine

IPC Country & Leisure, Focus House, Dingwall Avenue, Croydon CR9 2TA
*tel* 020-8774 0752 *fax* 020-8774 0939
*email* simon_collis@ipcmedia.com
*website* www.motorcaravanmagazine.co.uk
*Editor* Simon Collis
Monthly £2.95

Practical features, touring features (home and abroad), motorhome tests. Length: up to 1500 words. Payment: £60 per page. Founded 1985.

## Motor Cycle News

EMAP Active Ltd, Media House, Peterborough Business Park, Lynchwood, Peterborough PE2 6EA
*tel* (01733) 468000 *fax* (01733) 468028

*email* mcn@emap.com
*website* www.motorcyclenews.com
*Editor* Marc Potter
Weekly £1.60

Features (up to 1000 words), photos and news stories of interest to motorcyclists. Founded 1955.

## Motorcaravan Motorhome Monthly (MMM)

PO Box 88, Tiverton, Devon EX16 7ZN
*email* mmmeditor@warnersgroup.co.uk
*website* www.mmmonline.co.uk
*Editor* Mike Jago
Monthly £2.95

Articles including motorcaravan travel, owner reports and DIY. Length: up to 2500 words. Payment: by arrangement. Illustrations: line, half-tone, colour prints and transparencies. Founded 1966 as *Motor Caravan and Camping*.

## Ms London

Independent Magazines, Independent House, 191 Marsh Wall, London E14 9RS
*tel* 020-7005 5000 *fax* 020-7005 5333
*Editor-in-Chief* Bill Williamson
Weekly Free

Features and lifestyle pieces of interest to young professional working women with a contemporary London bias. All material commissioned. Length: 800–1400 words. Illustrations: no unsolicited illustrations; enquire first. Payment: by negotiation. Founded 1968.

## Mslexia

PO Box 656, Newcastle upon Tyne NE99 1PZ
*tel* 0191-261 6656 *fax* 0191-261 6636
*email* postbag@mslexia.demon.co.uk
*website* www.mslexia.co.uk
*Editor* Debbie Taylor, *Send material to* Melanie Ashby
4 p.a. £18.75 p.a.

Magazine for women writers which combines features and advice about writing, with new fiction and poetry by women. Considers unsolicited material. Length: up to 3000 words (short stories), articles/features by negotiation, up to 6 poems. Illustrations: mono art, photos, colour transparencies. Payment: by negotiation. Founded 1998.

## Muscle & Fitness

Weider Publishing, 10 Windsor Court, Clarence Drive, Harrogate, North Yorkshire HG1 2PE
*tel* (01423) 504516 *fax* (01423) 561494
*website* www.muscle-fitness-europe.com
*Editor* Chris Lund
Monthly £3.40

A guide to muscle development and general health and fitness. Founded 1988.

## Music Teacher

Rhinegold Publishing Ltd, 241 Shaftesbury Avenue, London WC2H 8TF
*tel* 020-7333 1747 *fax* 020-7333 1769
*email* music.teacher@rhinegold.co.uk
*website* www.rhinegold.co.uk
*Editor* Lucien Jenkins
Monthly £3.75

Information and articles for both school and private music teachers, including reviews of books, music, CD-Roms, videos and other music–education resources. Articles and illustrations must both have a teacher, as well as a musical, interest. Length: articles 1000–2000 words. Payment: £120 per 1000 words. Founded 1908.

## Music Week

CMPi, 7th Floor, Ludgate House, 245 Blackfriars Road, London SE1 9UR
*tel* 020-7921 8348
*email* martin@musicweek.com
*Executive Editor* Martin Talbot
Weekly £4 (£195 p.a.)

News and features on all aspects of producing, manufacturing, marketing and retailing music. Payment: by negotiation. Founded 1959.

## Musical Opinion

2 Princes Road, St Leonards-on-Sea, East Sussex TN37 6EL
*tel* (01424) 715167 *fax* (01424) 712214
*email* musicalopinion2@aol.com
*Editor* Denby Richards
Bi-monthly £5 (£28 p.a.)

Suggestions for contributions of musical interest, scholastic, educational, anniversaries and ethnic. Dance, video, CD, opera, festival, book, music reviews. All editorial matter must be commissioned. Payment: on publication. Illustrations: colour photos. Founded 1877.

## Musical Times

22 Gibson Square, London N1 0RD
*Editor* Antony Bye
4 p.a. For subscription rates *tel* (01442) 879097

Musical articles, reviews, 500–6000 words. All material commissioned; no unsolicited material. Illustrations: music. Founded 1844.

## My Weekly

D.C. Thomson & Co. Ltd, 80 Kingsway East, Dundee DD4 8SL
*tel* (01382) 223131 *fax* (01382) 452491
*email* myweekly@dcthomson.co.uk
185 Fleet Street, London EC4A 2HS
*tel* 020-7400 1030 *fax* 020-7400 1089
*Editor* H.G. Watson
Weekly 63p

Short complete stories of 1000–2500 words with humorous, romantic or strong emotional themes. Articles on all subjects of women's interest. Contributions should appeal to women everywhere. Payment: on acceptance. Illustrations: colour and b&w. Founded 1910.

## My Weekly Story Collection
D.C. Thomson & Co. Ltd, Albert Square, Dundee DD1 9QJ
*tel* (01382) 223131 *fax* (01382) 322214
185 Fleet Street, London EC4A 2HS
*tel* 020-7400 1030 *fax* 020-7400 1089
*Editor* Dorothy Hunter
4 p.m. £1

25,000–30,000-word romantic stories aimed at the adult market. Payment: on acceptance; competitive for the market. No illustrations.

## The National Trust Magazine
The National Trust,
36 Queen Anne's Gate,
London SW1H 9AS
*tel* 020-7222 9251 *fax* 020-7222 5097
*website* www.nationaltrust.org.uk
*Editor* Gaynor Aaltonen
3 p.a. Free to members

News and features on the conservation of historic houses, coasts and countryside in the UK. No unsolicited articles. Length: 1000 words (features), 200 words (news). Illustrations: colour transparencies and artwork. Payment: by arrangement; picture library rates. Founded 1969.

## Natural World
EMAP Active Ltd, Bushfield House,
Orton Centre, Peterborough PE2 5UW
*tel* (01733) 237111 *fax* (01733) 465658
*Editor* Trevor Lawson
3 p.a. Free to members

National magazine of the Wildlife Trusts. Short articles on the work of the UK's 47 wildlife trusts. Unsolicited MSS not accepted. Length: up to 1200 words. Payment: by arrangement. Illustrations: line, colour. Founded 1981.

## Naturalist
The University,
Bradford BD7 1DP
*tel* (01274) 234212 *fax* (01274) 234231
*email* m.r.d.seaward@bradford.ac.uk
*Editor* Prof M.R.D. Seaward MSc, PhD, DSc
Quarterly £20 p.a.

Original papers on all kinds of British natural history subjects, including various aspects of geology, archaeology and environmental science. Length: immaterial. Illustrations: photos and line drawings. Payment: none. Founded 1875.

## Nature
Macmillan Magazines Ltd, The Macmillan Building,
4 Crinan Street, London N1 9XW
*tel* 020-7833 4000 *fax* 020-7843 4596
*email* nature@nature.com
*website* www.nature.com/nature
*Editor* Philip Campbell
Weekly £10

Devoted to scientific matters and to their bearing upon public affairs. All contributors of articles have specialised knowledge of the subjects with which they deal. Illustrations: line, half-tone. Founded 1869.

## Nautical Magazine
4–10 Darnley Street, Glasgow G41 2SD
*tel* 0141-429 1234 *fax* 0141-420 1694
*email* info@skipper.co.uk
*website* www.skipper.co.uk
*Editor* L. Ingram-Brown
Monthly £29.40 p.a. (£33 p.a. overseas)

Articles relating to nautical and shipping profession, from 1500–2000 words; also translations. Payment: by arrangement. No illustrations. Founded 1832.

## Needlecraft
Future Publishing Ltd, 30 Monmouth Street,
Bath BA1 2BW
*tel* (01225) 442244 *fax* (01225) 732398
*email* debora.bradley@futurenet.co.uk
*Editor* Debora Bradley
Monthly £3.20

Mainly project-based stitching designs with step-by-step instructions. Features with tight stitching focus (e.g. technique, personality). Length: 1000 words. Illustrated. Payment: £150–£200. Founded 1991.

## .net The Internet Magazine
Future Publishing Ltd, Beaufort Court,
30 Monmouth Street, Bath BA1 2BW
*tel* (01225) 442244 *fax* (01225) 732291
*email* netmag@futurenet.co.uk
*website* www.netmag.co.uk
*Editor* Paul Douglas
Monthly CD edition £4.49

Articles, features and news on the internet. Length: 1000–3000 words. Payment: negotiable. Illustrations: colour. Founded 1994.

## New Beacon
RNIB, 105 Judd Street, London WC1H 9NE
*email* beacon@rnib.org.uk
*Editor* Ann Lee
Monthly £2.40

Articles on all aspects of living with sight loss. Published in clear print, braille, disk, tape editions and email. Length: from 500 words. Payment: by arrangement. Illustrations: high-res jpeg (disk only). Founded 1930; as *Beacon* 1917.

## New Humanist

1 Gower Street, London WC1E 6HD
*tel* 020-7436 1151
*email* editor@newhumanist.org.uk
*website* www.newhumanist.org.uk
*Editor* Frank Jordans
Bimonthly £2.50

Articles on current affairs, philosophy, science, literature and humanism. Length: 500–1500 words. Illustrations: b&w photos. Payment: nominal. Founded 1885.

## New Impact

Anser House of Marlow, Courtyard Offices, 140 Oxford Road, Marlow, Bucks. SL7 2NT
*tel* (01628) 481581 *fax* (01628) 475570
*Managing Editor* Elaine Sihera
5 p.a. £48 p.a. business; £35 p.a. individual; £20 p.a. colleges, min. 2 subscriptions

'Promoting enterprise, training and diversity.'
Articles, features and news on any aspect of training, business and women's issues to suit a multicultural audience; also profiles of personalities, short stories. Length: 900–1000 words. Illustrations: b&w photos if related to profiles. Payment: none. Founded 1993.

## New Internationalist

55 Rectory Road, Oxford OX4 1BW
*tel* (01865) 728181 *fax* (01865) 793152
*email* ni@newint.org
*website* www.newint.org
*Editors* Vanessa Baird, Katharine Ainger, David Ransom
Monthly £2.95 (£28.85 p.a.)

World issues, ranging from food to feminism to peace – examines one subject each month. Length: up to 2000 words. Illustrations: line, half-tone, colour, cartoons. Payment: £80 per 1000 words. Founded 1973.

## New Law Journal

LexisNexis UK, Halsbury House, 35 Chancery Lane, London WC2A 1EL
*tel* 020-7400 2500 *fax* 020-7400 2583
*email* newlaw.journal@lexisnexis.co.uk
*website* newlaw.journal@lexisnexis.co.uk
*Editor* Jane Maynard, *Assistant Editor* Elizabeth Davidson
48 p.a. £4.95

Articles and news on all aspects of the legal profession. Length: up to 2000 words. Payment: by arrangement.

## New Musical Express (NME)

IPC Magazines Ltd, 25th Floor, King's Reach Tower, Stamford Street, London SE1 9LS
*tel* 020-7261 5000 *fax* 020-7261 5185
*Editor* Conor McNicholas, *Deputy Editor* Alex Needham, *Features Editor* Malik Meer

Weekly £1.50

Authoritative articles and news stories on the world's rock and movie personalities. Length: by arrangement. Preliminary letter or phone call desirable. Payment: by arrangement. Illustrations: action photos with strong news angle of recording personalities, cartoons.

## New Scientist

RBI Ltd, 151 Wardour Street, London W1F 8WE
*tel* 020-8652 3500 *fax* 020-7331 2777
*email* enquiries@newscientist.com
*website* www.NewScientist.com
*Editor* Jeremy Webb
Weekly £2.20

Authoritative articles of topical importance on all aspects of science and technology. Intending contributors should study recent copies of the magazine and initially send only a 200-word synopsis of their idea. NB: Does not publish non-peer reviewed theories, poems or crosswords. Payment: varies but average £300 per 1000 words. Illustrations: all styles, cartoons; contact art dept.

## New Statesman

3rd Floor, 52 Grosvenor Gardens, London SW1W 0AU
*tel* 020-7700 3444 *fax* 020-7259 0181
*email* info@newstatesman.co.uk
*Editor* Peter Wilby
Weekly £2.50

Interested in news, reportage and analysis of current political and social issues at home and overseas, plus book reviews, general articles and coverage of the arts, environment and science seen from the perspective of the British Left but written in a stylish, witty and unpredictable way. Length: strictly according to the value of the piece. Illustrations: commissioned for specific articles, though artists' samples considered for future reference; occasional cartoons. Payment: by agreement. Founded 1913.

## New Theatre Quarterly

Oldstairs, Kingsdown, Deal, Kent CT14 8ES
*email* simontrussler@btinternet.com
*Editors* Clive Barker, Simon Trussler, Maria Shevtsova
Quarterly £20 (£32 p.a.)

Articles, interviews, documentation, reference material covering all aspects of live theatre. An informed, factual and serious approach essential. Preliminary discussion and synopsis desirable. Payment: by arrangement. Illustrations: line, half-tone. Founded 1985; as *Theatre Quarterly* 1971.

## New Welsh Review

PO Box 170, Aberystwyth, Ceredigion SY23 1WZ
*tel* (01970) 626230
*email* nwr@welshnet.co.uk

*Editor* Francesca Rhydderch
Quarterly £5.40 (£20 p.a., £38 2 yrs)

Literary – critical articles, short stories, poems, book reviews, interviews and profiles. Especially, but not exclusively, concerned with Welsh writing in English. Theatre in Wales section. Length: up to 3000 words (articles). Illustrations: colour. Payment: £50 per 1000 words (articles); £25 per poem, £75 per short story, £40 per review, £60 per illustration. Founded 1988.

## New Woman

EMAP Élan, Endeavour House, 189 Shaftesbury Avenue, London WC2H 8JG
*tel* 020-7437 9011 *fax* 020-7208 3585
*email* lizzi.hosking@hotmail.com
*website* www.newwoman.co.uk
*Editor* Sara Cremer
Monthly £2.60

Features up to 2000 words. Occasionally accepts unsolicited articles; enclose sae for return. No fiction. Payment: at or above NUJ rates. Illustrated. Founded 1988.

## The New Writer

PO Box 60, Cranbrook, Kent TN17 2ZR
*tel* (01580) 212626 *fax* (01580) 212041
*email* editor@thenewwriter.com
*website* www.thenewwriter.com
*Editor* Suzanne Ruthven *Publisher* Merric Davidson
6 p.a. £3.95

Features, short stories from guest writers and from subscribers, poems, news and reviews. Seeks forward-looking articles on all aspects of the written word that demonstrate the writer's grasp of contemporary writing and current editorial/publishing policies. Length: approx. 1000 words (articles), longer pieces considered; 1000–2000 words (features). Payment: £20 per 1000 words (articles), £10 (stories), £3 (poems). Founded 1996.

## The Newspaper

Young Media Ltd, PO Box 121, Tonbridge, Kent TN12 5ZR
*tel* (01622) 871297 *fax* (01622) 871927
*email* editor@thenewspaper.org.uk
*website* www.thenewspaper.org.uk
*Editor* Jenny MacDonald
6 p.a. Free

Newspaper aimed at 8–14 year-old schoolchildren for use as part of the National Curriculum. Contains similar columns as in any national daily newspaper. Length: 800–1000 words for features and short stories (non-fiction). Payment: £250 per item. Illustrations: colour. Founded 1999.

**Night and Day** – see Mail on Sunday, page 10

## Now

IPC Media Ltd, King's Reach Tower, Stamford Street, London SE1 9LS
*tel* 020-7261 7366 *fax* 020-7261 6789
*Editor* Jane Ennis
Weekly £1.10

Showbiz magazine of celebrity gossip, news, fashion, health and cookery. Most articles are commissioned or are written by in-house writers. Founded 1996.

## Nursery Education

Scholastic Ltd, Villiers House, Clarendon Avenue, Leamington Spa, Warks. CV32 5PR
*tel* (01926) 887799 *fax* (01926) 883331
*email* earlyyears@scholastic.co.uk
*website* www.scholastic.co.uk
*Editor* Susan Sodhi
Monthly £3.75

Practical theme-based activities for educators working with 3–5 year-olds. All ideas based on the Early Learning Goals. Material mostly commissioned.Length: 500–1000 words. Illustrations: colour and b&w; colour posters. Payment: by arrangement. Founded 1997.

## Nursery World

Admiral House, 66–68 East Smithfield, London E1W 1BX
*tel* 020-7782 3120
*Editor* Liz Roberts
Weekly £1.30

For all grades of primary school, nursery and child care staff, nannies, foster parents and all concerned with the care of expectant mothers, babies and young children. Authoritative and informative articles, 800 or 1300 words, and photos, on all aspects of child welfare and early education, from 0–8 years, in the UK. Practical ideas, policy news and career advice. No short stories. Payment: by arrangement. Illustrations: line, half-tone, colour.

## Nursing Times

EMAP Healthcare, Greater London House, Hampstead Road, London NW1 7EJ
*tel* 020-7874 0500 *fax* 020-7874 0505
*Editor* Rachel Downey
Weekly £1.10

Articles of clinical interest, nursing education and nursing policy. Illustrated articles not longer than 2000 words. Contributions from other than health professionals sometimes accepted. Press day: Monday. Illustrations: photos, line, cartoons. Payment: NUJ rates; by arrangement for illustrations. Founded 1905.

**Observer Magazine** – see The Observer, page 11

## Office Secretary (OS Magazine)
Peebles Media Group, 1st Floor, 63 High Street, Witney, Oxon OX28 6HS
*tel* (01993) 775545 *fax* (01993) 778884
*email* paul.ormond@peeblesmedia.com
*website* www.peeblesmedia.com
*Editor* Louise Hackett
Bi-monthly £20 p.a.

Serious features on anything of interest to senior secretaries and executive PAs. No unsolicited MSS; ideas only. Illustrations: colour transparencies and prints. Payment: by negotiation. Founded 1986.

## Official UK Playstation Magazine
Future Publishing UK, 30 Monmouth Street, Bath BA1 2BW
*tel* (01225) 442244 *fax* (01225) 732285
*website* www.futurenet.co.uk
*Editor* Richard Keith
13 p.a. £4.99

Non-technical magazine for the Playstation owner. Payment: by arrangement. Founded 1995.

## OK!
Northern & Shell plc, Ludgate House, 245 Blackfriars Road, London SE1 9UX
*tel* 020-7928 8000 *fax* 020-7579 4607
*Editor* Nic McCarthy
Weekly £2

Exclusive celebrity interviews and photographs. Submit ideas in writing. Length: 1000 words. Illustrations: colour. Payment: £150–£250,000 per feature. Founded 1993.

## The Oldie
65 Newman Street, London W1T 3EG
*tel* 020-7436 8801 *fax* 020-7436 8804
*email* theoldie@theoldie.co.uk
*website* www.theoldie.co.uk
*Editor* Richard Ingrams
Monthly £2.95

General interest magazine reflecting attitudes of older people but aimed at a wider audience. Welcomes features (800–2000 words) on all subjects. Enclose sae for reply/return of MSS. No poetry. Illustrations: welcomes b&w and colour cartoons. Payment: approx. £80–£100 per 1000 words; minimum £50 for cartoons. Founded 1992.

## ontheedge
Greenshires Group Ltd, PO Box 21, Buxton, Derbyshire SK17 9BR
*tel* (01298) 72801 *fax* (01298) 72801
*email* ote@globalnet.co.uk
*website* www.ontheedgemag.co.uk
*Editor* Neil Pearsons
10 p.a. £2.99

Climbing magazine covering mainly British rock climbing. Features all aspects of climbing worldwide from bouldering to mountaineering. Contact Editor to discuss requirements. Founded 1987.

## Opera
36 Black Lion Lane, London W6 9BE
*tel* 020-8563 8893 *fax* 020-8563 8635
*email* editor@operamag.clara.co.uk
*website* www.opera.co.uk
*Editor* John Allison
13 p.a. £3.70

Articles on general subjects appertaining to opera; reviews; criticisms. Length: up to 2000 words. Payment: by arrangement. Illustrations: photos.

## Opera Now
241 Shaftesbury Avenue, London WC2H 8TF
*tel* 020-7333 1740 *fax* 020-7333 1769
*email* opera.now@rhinegold.co.uk
*website* www.rhinegold.co.uk
*Editor* Ashutosh Khandekar
Bi-monthly £4.95

Articles, news, reviews on opera. All material commissioned only. Length: 150–1500 words. Illustrations: colour and b&w photos, line, cartoons. Payment: £120 per 1000 words. Founded 1989.

## Orbis
17 Greenhow Avenue, West Kirby, Wirral CH48 5EL
*tel* 0151-625 1446
*email* carolebaldock@hotmail.com
*Editor* Carole Baldock
Quarterly £4, £15 p.a.; £5/€9/$9, €32/$32 overseas

Poetry, prose (1000 words), news, reviews, views, letters. Up to 4 poems by post; via email, overseas only, up to 2 in body (no attachments). Enclose sae/2 IRCs with all correspondence. Payment: £50 for featured writer. £50 Readers' Award: for piece(s) receiving the most votes (4 winners submitted to Forward Poetry Prize, Single Poem Category); £50 split between 4 (or more) runners-up. Founded 1968.

## Organic Gardening
Sandvoe, North Roe, Shetland ZE2 9RY
*tel* (01806) 533319
*email* organic.gardening@virgin.net
*Editor* Gaby Bartai Bevan
Monthly £2.65

Articles on all aspects of gardening by experienced organic gardeners. Unsolicited material welcome. Length: 600–2000 words. Illustrations: digital images, transparencies, colour photos, line drawings, cartoons. Payment: by arrangement. Founded 1988.

## Other Poetry
29 Western Hill, Durham DH1 4RL
*tel* 0191-386 4058
*website* www.otherpoetry.com
*Editors* Michael Standen (managing), Crista Ermiya,
Peter Bennet, James Roderick Burns
3 p.a. £4.50 (£13/$30 p.a.)

Poetry. Submit up to 6 poems with sae. Payment: £5
per poem. Founded 1979.

## Our Dogs
Oxford Road Station Approach, Manchester M60 1SX
*tel* 0870 731 6500 *fax* 0870 731 6501
*Editor* William Moores
Weekly £1.80

Articles and news on the breeding and showing of
pedigree dogs. Illustrations: b&w photos. Payment:
by negotiation; £10 per photo. Founded 1895.

## Outposts Poetry Quarterly
22 Whitewell Road, Frome, Somerset BA11 4EL
*tel* (01373) 466653 *fax* (01373) 466653
*Editor* Roland John, *Founder* Howard Sergeant MBE,
*Send material to* M. Pargitter
Quarterly £4 (£14 p.a.)

Poems, essays and critical articles on poets and their
work; poetry competitions. Payment: by
arrangement. Founded 1943.

## Oxford Poetry
Magdalen College, Oxford OX1 4AU
*email* editors@oxfordpoetry.co.uk
*website* www.oxfordpoetry.co.uk
*Editors* Kelly Grovier, Carmen Bogan, Sarah Hesketh
(business & subscriptions)
3 p.a. £3 (£9 p.a.)

Previously unpublished poems and translations,
both unsolicited and commissioned; interviews,
articles and reviews. Payment: none. Founded 1910;
refounded 1983.

## Park Home & Holiday Caravan
Focus House, Dingwall Avenue, Croydon CR9 2TA
*tel* 020-8774 0600 *fax* 020-8774 0939
*email* phhc@ipcmedia.com
*Editor* Anne Webb
Monthly £2.60

Informative articles on residential mobile homes
(park homes) and holiday static caravans – personal
experience articles, site features, news items. No
preliminary letter. Payment: by arrangement.
Illustrations: line, half-tone, colour transparencies,
digital images, cartoons. Founded 1960.

## PC Advisor
IDG Communications Ltd, 5th Floor,
85 Tottenham Court Road, London W1T 4TQ
*tel* 020-7291 5920 *fax* 020-7580 1935

*email* pcadvisor_letters@idg.com
*website* www.pcadvisor.co.uk
*Editor* Andrew Charlesworth
Monthly CD edition £2.99, DVD edition £4.99

Aimed at PC-proficient individuals who are looking
for IT solutions that will enhance their productivity
at work and at home. Includes information on the
latest hardware and software and advice on how to
use PCs to maximum effect. Features are
commissioned; unsolicited material may be
considered. Length: 1500–3000 words (features).
Illustrations: colour artwork. Payment: £200 per 1000
words; artwork £200 (A5), £300 (A4). Founded 1995.

## PC Answers
Future Publishing Ltd, 30 Monmouth Street,
Bath BA1 2BW
*tel* (01225) 442244 *fax* (01225) 732295
*email* pcanswers@futurenet.co.uk
*website* www.pcanswers.co.uk
*Editor* Nick Peers
13 p.a. £4.99

Reviews, news and practical/how-to features for
home PC users, excluding games. Length: 2500
words (features). Illustrations: colour. Payment: by
negotiation. Founded 1991.

## PCS View
Public and Commercial Services Union,
160 Falcon Road, London SW11 2LN
*tel* 020-7924 2727 *fax* 020-7924 1847
*email* editor@pcs.org.uk
*website* www.pcs.org.uk
*Editor* Sharon Breen
10 p.a. Free to members

Well-written articles on civil service, trade union
and general subjects considered. Send ideas for
consideration before submitting full article. Length:
600 words. Also photos and humorous drawings of
interest to civil servants. Illustrations: line, half-
tone. Payment: NUJ rates.

## Peace News
5 Caledonian Road, London N1 9DX
*tel* 020-7278 3344 *fax* 020-7278 0444
*email* editorial@peacenews.info
*website* www.peacenews.info
*Submit material to* The Editor
Quarterly £2.50

Political articles based on nonviolence in every
aspect of human life. Illustrations: line, half-tone.
No payment. Founded 1936.

## Peninsular Magazine
Cherrybite Publications, Linden Cottage,
45 Burton Road, Little Neston, Cheshire CH64 4AE
*tel* 0151-353 0967
*email* helicon@globalnet.co.uk

*website* www.cherrybite.co.uk
*Editor* Shelagh Nugent
Quarterly £3.50

Short story magazine: essential to read a current issue before sending MSS. Regular competitions with prizes. Length: up to 4000 words. Payment: £5 per 1000 words. Founded 1996.

## Pensions World

LexisNexis UK, Tolley House,
2 Addiscombe Road,
Croydon CR9 5AF
*tel* 020-8686 9141 *fax* 020-8212 1970
*email* stephanie.hawthorne@lexisnexis.co.uk
*website* www.pensionsworld.co.uk
*Editor* Stephanie Hawthorne
Monthly £84 p.a.

Specialist articles on pensions, investment and law. No unsolicited articles; all material is commissioned. Length: 1500 words. Payment: by negotiation. Founded 1972.

## People Management

Personnel Publications Ltd, 1 Benjamin Street,
London EC1M 5EA
*tel* 020-7296 4200 *fax* 020-7296 4215
*email* editorial@peoplemanagement.co.uk
*website* www.peoplemanagement.co.uk
*Editor* Steve Crabb
Fortnightly £5 (£88 p.a.)

Journal of the Chartered Institute of Personnel and Development. News items and feature articles on recruitment and selection, training and development; pay and performance management; industrial psychology; employee relations; employment law; working practices and new practical ideas in personnel management in industry and commerce. Length: up to 2500 words. Payment: by arrangement. Illustrations: contact art editor.

## People's Friend

D.C. Thomson & Co. Ltd,
80 Kingsway East,
Dundee DD4 8SL
*tel* (01382) 223131 *fax* (01382) 452491
185 Fleet Street, London EC4A 2HS
*tel* 020-7400 1030 *fax* 020-7400 1089
*Send material to* The Editor
Weekly 60p

Fiction magazine for women of all ages. Includes personal and home interests, especially knitting and cookery. Serials (60,000–70,000 words) and complete stories (1500–3000 words) of strong romantic and emotional appeal. Considers stories for children. No preliminary letter required. Illustrations: colour and b&w. Payment: on acceptance. Founded 1869.

## People's Friend Story Collection

D.C. Thomson & Co. Ltd, 2 Albert Square,
Dundee DD1 9QJ
*tel* (01382) 223131 *fax* (01382) 322214
185 Fleet Street, London EC4A 2HS
*tel* 020-7400 1030 *fax* 020-7400 1089
*Editor* Shirley Blair
2 p.m. £1.20

50,000–55,000-word family and romantic stories aimed at 30+ age group. Payment: by arrangement. No illustrations.

## Perfect Home

Brooklands Group Ltd, Medway House,
Lower Road, Forest Row, East sussex RH18 5HE
*tel* (01342) 828700 *fax* (01342) 828701
*email* zena.alli@fox-publishing.com
*Editor* Ann Wallace
Monthly £2.75

Home-related features: readers' homes, makeovers, DIY, product testing/reviews, gardening. Length: 800–1000 words. Payment: by merit. Illustrated. Founded 1992.

## Period Living & Traditional Homes

EMAP East, Mappin House, 4 Winsley Street,
London W1W 8HF
*tel* 020-7343 8775 *fax* 020-7343 8710
*email* period.living@emap.com
*Editor* Sharon Parsons
Monthly £2.95

Articles and features on decoration, furnishings, renovation of period homes; gardens, crafts, decorating in a period style. Illustrated. Payment: varies, according to work required. Founded 1990.

## Personal Computer World

VNU House, 32–34 Broadwick Street,
London W1A 2HG
*tel* 020-7316 9000 *fax* 020-7316 9313
*email* dylan_armbrust@pcw.co.uk
*website* www.pcw.co.uk
*Editor* Dylan Armbrust
Monthly £3.25

Articles about computers, reviews, features and how-to advice. Length: 800–5000 words. Payment: from £150 per 1000 words. Illustrations: line, half-tone, colour. Founded 1978.

## Personal Finance

Charterhouse Communications, Arnold House,
36–41 Holywell Lane, London EC2A 3SF
*tel* 020-7827 5454 *fax* 020-7827 0567
*email* martin.fagan@charterhouse-communications.co.uk
*Editor* Martin Fagan
Monthly £2.75

Articles and features on savings and investment,

general family finance, of interest both to new investors and financially aware readers. All material commissioned: submit ideas in writing to the editor in first instance. Illustrations: colour and b&w photos, colour line drawings. Payment: £200 per 1000 words; illustrations by negotiation. Founded 1994.

## The Photographer

The British Institute of Professional Photography, Fox Talbot House, 2 Amwell End, Ware, Herts. SG12 9HN
*tel* (01920) 487268 *fax* (01920) 487056
*website* www.bipp.com
*Editor* Steve Bavister
Monthly £3.95

Journal of the BIPP covering conventional and digital imaging and images. Authoritative reviews, news, views and high-quality photographs.

## Picture Postcard Monthly

15 Debdale Lane, Keyworth, Nottingham NG12 5HT
*tel* 0115-937 4079 *fax* 0115-937 6197
*email* reflections@argonet.co.uk
*website* www.postcardcollecting.co.uk
*Editor* Brian Lund
Monthly £2.40 (£29 p.a.)

Articles, news and features for collectors of old or modern picture postcards. Length: 500–2000 words. Illustrations: colour and b&w. Payment: £27 per 1000 words; 50p per print. Founded 1978.

## Pig Farming

United Business Media International, Sovereign House, Sovereign Way, Tonbridge, Kent TN9 1RW
*tel* 020-8309 7000 *fax* (01732) 377128
*Editor* Roger Abbott
Monthly £28 p.a.

Practical, well-illustrated articles on all aspects of pig meat production required, particularly those dealing with new ideas in pig management, feeding, housing, health and hygiene, product innovation and marketing. Length: 800–1200 words. Payment: by arrangement. Illustrations: line, half-tone, colour.

## Pilot

The Mill, Bearwalden Business Park, Wendens Ambo, Essex CB11 4GB
*tel* 01799 544200 *fax* 01799 544201
*email* dave.calderwell@pilotweb.co.uk
*website* www.pilotweb.co.uk
*Editor-in-chief* David Calderwell, *Deputy Editor* Nick Bloom
Monthly £3.40

Feature articles on general aviation, private and business flying. Photographs, Illustrations and cartoons. Payment: £125–£1000 per article on acceptance; £25 per photo. Founded 1968.

## The Pink Paper

2nd Floor, Medius House, 63–69 New Oxford Street, London WC1A 1DN
*tel* 020-7845 4300
*email* editorial @pinkpaper.com
*website* www.pinkpaper.com
*Editor* Tris Reid-Smith
Weekly Free

National news magazine for lesbians and gay men. Features (500–1000 words) and news (100–500 words) plus lifestyle section (features 350–1000 words) on any gay-related subject. Illustrations: b&w photos and line plus colour 'scene' photos. Payment: £40–£90 for words; £30–£60 for illustrations. Founded 1987.

## Planet

PO Box 44, Aberystwyth, Ceredigion SY23 3ZZ
*tel* (01970) 611255 *fax* (01970) 611197
*email* planet.enquiries@planetmagazine.org.uk
*website* www.planetmagazine.org.uk
*Editor* John Barnie
6 p.a. £3.25 (£15 p.a.)

Short stories, poems, topical articles on Welsh current affairs, politics, the environment and society. New literature in English. Length of articles: 1000–3500 words. Payment: £50 per 1000 words for prose; £30 minimum per poem. Illustrations: line, half-tone, cartoons. Founded 1970–9; relaunched 1985.

## PN Review

Carcanet Press Ltd, 4th Floor, Conavon Court, 12 Blackfriars Street, Manchester M3 5BQ
*tel* 0161-834 8730 *fax* 0161-832 0084
*email* pnr@carcanet.u-net.com
*website* www.carcanet.co.uk
*Editor* Michael Schmidt
6 p.a. £4.99 (£29.50 p.a.)

Poems, essays, reviews, translations. Submissions by post only. Payment: by arrangement. Founded 1973.

## Poetry Ireland Review/Éigse Éireann

120 St Stephen's Green, Dublin 2, Republic of Ireland
*tel* (01) 478 9974 *fax* (01) 478 0205
*email* poetry@iol.ie
*Editor* Peter Sirr
*Director* Joseph Woods
Quarterly €7.99 (€30.50/$52 p.a.)

Poetry. Features and articles by arrangement. Payment: €32 per contribution or one year's subscription; €51 reviews. Founded 1981.

## Poetry Life

1 Blue Ball Corner, Water Lane, Winchester, Hants SO23 0ER
*tel* (018962) 842621

*website* www.breespace.virgin.net/poetry.life/
*Editor* Adrian Bishop
3 p.a. £6.50

Contemporary poetry plus articles and news.
Payment: negotiable. Founed 1994.

## Poetry London
1A Jewel Road, London E17 4QU
*tel* 020-8521 0776 *fax* 020-8521 0776
*email* editors@poetrylondon.co.uk
*website* www.poetrylondon.co.uk
*Editors* Pascale Petit, Scott Verner, Martha Kapos,
*Send material to* Andre Harris, Business Manager
3 p.a. £11 p.a.

Poems of the highest standard, articles/reviews on
any aspect of modern poetry. Comprehensive
listings of poetry events and resources. Contributors
must be knowledgeable about contemporary poetry.
Payment: £20 minimum. Founded 1988.

## Poetry Nottingham
11 Orkney Close, Stewson Fields, Derby DE24 3LW
*Editor* Adrian Buckner
Quarterly £2.75 (£10 p.a. UK, £17 p.a. overseas)

Poems; reviews; articles. Payment: complimentary
copy. Founded 1946.

## Poetry Review
22 Betterton Street, London WC2H 9BX
*tel* 020-7420 9880 *fax* 020-7240 4818
*email* poetryreview@poetrysociety.org.uk
*website* www.poetrysociety.org.uk
*Editors* Robert Potts, David Herd
Quarterly £30 p.a. (£40 p.a. institutions, schools and
libraries)

Poems, features and reviews; also cartoons. Send no
more than 6 poems with sae. Preliminary study of
magazine essential. Payment: £40 per poem.

## Poetry Wales
38–40 Nolton Street, Bridgend CF31 3BN
*tel* (01656) 663018 *fax* (01656) 649226
*email* poetrywales@seren-books.com
*website* www.seren-books.com
www.poetrywales.co.uk
*Editor* Robert Minhinnick, *Reviews Editor* Amy Wack
Quarterly £4 (£16 p.a.)

Poetry, criticism and commentary from Wales and
around the world. Payment: by arrangement.
Founded 1965.

## Police Journal
Vathek Publishing, 5 Millennium Court,
Derby Road, Douglas, Isle of Man IM2 3EW
*tel* (01624) 863256 *fax* (01624) 863254
*email* mlw@vathek.com
*Publisher* Mairwen Lloyd-Williams
Quarterly £76 p.a.

Articles of technical or professional interest to the
Police Service throughout the world. Payment:
none. Illustrations: line drawings. Founded 1928.

## Police Review
Jane's Information Group, Sentinel House,
163 Brighton Road, Coulsdon CR5 2YH
*tel* 020-8276 4701 *fax* 020-7287 4765
*Editor* Catriona Marchant
Weekly £1.75

News and features of interest to the police and legal
professions. Length: 200–1500 words. Illustrations:
colour photos, line, cartoons. Payment: NUJ rates.
Founded 1893.

## The Political Quarterly
Blackwell Publishing, 9600 Garsington Road,
Oxford OX4 2DQ
*tel* (01865) 776868
*website* www.blackwellpublishing.com
*Editors* Tony Wright MP, Prof Andrew Gamble,
*Literary Editor* Prof Donald Sassoon
*Assistant Editor* Gillian Bromley, 3 Fernhill Close,
Kidlington, Oxford OX5 1BB
4 p.a. (£135 p.a. institutions, £23 p.a. individuals)

Topical aspects of national and international politics
and public administration; takes a progressive, but
not a party, point of view. Send articles to Assistant
Editor. Length: average 5000 words. Payment: about
£100 per article. Founded 1930.

## Pony Magazine
Headley House, Headley Road, Grayshott,
Surrey, Surrey GU26 6TU
*tel* (01428) 601020 *fax* (01428) 601030
*Editor* Janet Rising
Monthly £2.10

Lively articles and short stories with a horsey theme
aimed at readers aged 8–16 . Technical accuracy and
young, fresh writing essential. Length: up to 800
words. Payment: by arrangement. Illustrations:
drawings (commissioned), photos, cartoons.
Founded 1949.

## Popular Crafts
Highbury Leisure, Berwick House, 8–10 Knoll Rise,
Orpington, Kent BR6 0PS
*tel* (01689) 899200 *fax* (01689) 899240
*email* debbie.moss@nexusmedia.com
*website* www.popularcrafts.com
*Editor* Debbie Moss
Monthly £3.10

Covers all kinds of crafts. Projects with full
instructions, profiles and successes of craftspeople,
news on craft group activities, readers' homes,
celebrity interviews, general craft-related articles.
Welcomes written outlines of ideas. Payment: by
arrangement. Illustrated.

## Post Magazine & Insurance Week

Incisive Media plc, Haymarket House,
28–29 Haymarket, London SW1Y 4RX
*tel* 020-7484 9700 *fax* 020-7484 9990
*email* postmag@incisivemedia.com
*website* www.postmag.co.uk
www.insurancewindow.net
*Editor* Jonathan Swift
Weekly £3.95 (£195 p.a.)

Commissioned specialist articles on topics of interest to insurance professionals; news, especially from overseas stringers. Illustrations: colour photos and illustrations, colour and b&w cartoons, line drawings. Payment: £200 per 1000 words; photos £30–£120, cartoons/line by negotiation. Founded 1840.

## Poultry World

Quadrant House, The Quadrant, Sutton,
Surrey SM2 5AS
*tel* 020-8652 4020 *fax* 020-8652 4042
*email* poultry.world@rbi.co.uk
*Editor* Graham Cruikshank
Monthly £2.50

Articles on poultry breeding, production, marketing and packaging. News of international poultry interest. Payment: by arrangement. Illustrations: photos, line.

## Practical Boat Owner

Westover House, West Quay Road, Poole,
Dorset BH15 1JG
*tel* (01202) 440820
*email* pbo@ipcmedia.com
*website* www.pbo.co.uk
*Editor* Sarah Norbury
Monthly £3.20

Sailing magazine that also covers motorboats. Hints, tips and practical articles for cruising skippers – power and sail. Send synopsis first. Payment: by negotiation. Illustrations: photos or drawings. Founded 1967.

## Practical Caravan

Haymarket Magazines Ltd, 60 Waldegrave Road,
Teddington, Middlesex TW11 8LG
*tel* 020-8267 5629 *fax* 020-8267 5725
*email* practical.caravan@haynet.com
*website* www.practicalcaravan.com
*Editor* Alex Newby
Monthly £3.25

Caravan-related travelogues, caravan site reviews; travel writing for existing regular series; technical and DIY matters. Illustrations: colour. Payment negotiable. Founded 1967.

## Practical Fishkeeping

EMAP Active Ltd, Bretton Court, Bretton,
Peterborough PE3 8DZ
*tel* (01733) 264666
*website* www.practicalfishkeeping.co.uk
*Editor* Karen Youngs
Monthly £2.95

Practical fishkeeping in tropical and coldwater aquaria and ponds. Heavy emphasis on inspiration and involvement. Good colour photography always needed, and used. No verse or humour, no personal biographical accounts of fishkeeping unless practical. Payment: by worth. Founded 1966.

## Practical Householder

WVIP, Highgate Studios, 53–79 Highgate Road,
London NW5 1TW
*tel* 020-7331 1138 *fax* 020-7331 1269
*Editor* John McGowan
Monthly £2.15

Articles about 1500 words in length, about practical matters concerning home improvement. Payment: according to subject. Illustrations: line, half-tone. Founded 1955.

## Practical Internet

Paragon Publishing Ltd, Paragon House,
St Peter's Road, Bournemouth BH1 2JS
*tel* (01202) 299900 *fax* (01202) 299955
*website* www.paragon.co.uk
*Editor* Thomas Watson
13 p.a. £4.99

Provides help with getting online and faster, simpler and cheaper internet services, including buying advice, tutorials, jargon-free help, cost-effective solutions and CD-Roms. Payment: by arrangement. Founded 2002.

## Practical Parenting

IPC Media Ltd, King's Reach Tower,
Stamford Street, London SE1 9LS
*tel* 020-7261 5058 *fax* 020-7261 6542
*Editor* Sara Pates
Monthly £2.40

Articles on parenting, baby and childcare, health, psychology, education, children's activities, personal birth/parenting experiences. Send synopsis, with sae. Illustrations: commissioned only; colour: photos, line. Payment: by agreement. Founded 1987.

## Practical Photography

EMAP Active Ltd, Bretton Court, Bretton,
Peterborough PE3 8DZ
*tel* (01733) 264666 *fax* (01733) 465246
*email* practical.photography@emap.com
*Associate Editor* Andrew James
Monthly £3.10

Aimed at anyone who seeks to take excellent quality pictures. Excellent potential for freelance pictures: must be first rate – technically and pictorially – and have some relevance to photographic technique. Freelance ideas for words welcome (the more unusual ideas stand the greatest chance of success). Send synopsis of feature ideas in the first instance. Payment: negotiable but typically £80 per page and £120 per 1000 words. Founded 1959.

## Practical Wireless

PW Publishing Ltd, Arrowsmith Court, Station Approach, Broadstone, Dorset BH18 8PW
*tel* (0870) 2247810 *fax* (0870) 2247850
*email* rob@pwpublishing.ltd.uk
*Editor* Rob Mannion G3XFD
Monthly £2.85

Articles on the practical and theoretical aspects of amateur radio and communications. Constructional projects. Write or email for advice and author's guide. Illustrations: in b&w and colour; photos, line drawings and wash half-tone for offset litho. Payment: by arrangement. Founded 1932.

## Practical Woodworking

Highbury Leisure Publishing Ltd, Berwick House, 8–10 Knoll Rise, Orpington, Kent BR6 0PS
*tel* (01689) 899200 *fax* (01689) 899240
*email* mchisholm@highburyleisure.co.uk
*Editor* Mark Chisholm
Monthly £2.99

Articles of a practical nature covering any aspect of woodworking, including woodworking projects, tools, joints or timber technology. Payment: £75 per published page. Illustrated.

## The Practising Midwife

54 Siward Road, Bromley BR2 9JZ
*tel* 020-8466 1037
*email* prac.mid@ntlworld.com
*Editor* Jennifer Hall, *Managing Editor* Vivienne Riddoch
Monthly £35 p.a.

Disseminates research-based material to a wide professional audience. Research and review papers, viewpoints and news items pertaining to midwifery, maternity care, women's health and neonatal health with both a national and an international perspective. All articles submitted are anonymously reviewed by at least 2 external acknowledged experts. Length: 1000–2000 words (articles); 150–400 words (news); up to 1000 words (viewpoints). Illustrations: colour transparencies and artwork. Payment: by arrangement. Founded 1991.

## The Practitioner

CMP Information Ltd, City Reach, 5 Greenwich View Place, Millharbour, London E14 9NN
*tel* 020-7861 6478 *fax* 020-7861 6544
*email* gmatkin@cmpinformation.com
*Editor* Gavin Atkin
Monthly £12.60 (£82.50 p.a. UK, $194.25 p.a. overseas)

Articles of interest to GPs and vocational registrars, and others in the medical profession. Payment: approx. £200 per 1500 words. Founded 1868.

## Prediction

IPC Country & Leisure, Focus House, Dingwall Avenue, Croydon CR9 2TA
*tel* 020-8774 0600 *fax* 020-8774 0939
*Editor* Tania Ahsan
Monthly £2.95

Articles on astrology and all esoteric subjects. Length: up to 2000 words. Payment: by arrangement. Illustrations: large-format colour transparencies or photos. Founded 1936.

## Pregnancy

Highbury Entertainment, 53–79 Highgate Road, London NW5 17W
*tel* 020-7331 1000 *fax* 020-7331 1108
*email* pregnancy@wvip.co.uk
*Editor* Hannah Rand
6 p.a. £2.99

Articles, features and news on health, lifestyle and labour for expectant parents. Payment £150 per 1000 words. Illustrations: b&w and colour. Founded 1997.

## Press Gazette

Quantum Business Media Ltd, Quantum House, 19 Scarbrook Road, Croydon CR9 1LX
*tel* 020-8565 4374 *fax* 020-8565 4395
*Editor* Ian Reeves
Weekly £2.40

News and features of interest to journalists and others working in the media. Length: 1200 words (features), 300 words (news). Payment: approx. £230 (features), news stories negotiable. Founded 1965.

## Pretext

Pen & Inc Press, School of English and American Studies, University of East Anglia, Norwich NR4 7TJ
*tel* (01603) 592783 *fax* (01603) 507728
*email* info@penandinc.co.uk
*website* www.penandinc.co.uk
*Managing Editor* Katri Skala
3 p.a. £7.99

Literary magazine: fiction, non-fiction and poetry. New and established writers. Length: max. 6000 words. Payment: small. Founded 1999.

## Pride

Hamilton House, 55 Battersea Bridge Road, London SW11 3AX
*tel* 020-7228 3110 *fax* 020-7228 3130
*Managing Editor* Delali Damanka
Monthly £2.30

Lifestyle magazine incorporating fashion and beauty, travel, food and entertaining articles for the young woman of colour. Length: 1000–3000 words. Illustrations: colour photos and drawings. Payment: £100 per 1000 words. Founded 1993; relaunched 1997, 1998.

## Priests & People
The Tablet Publishing Co Ltd, 1 King Street Cloisters, Clifton Walk, London W6 0QZ
*Publisher* Ignatius Kusiak
Monthly £2.50
Journal of pastoral theology especially for parish ministers and for Christians of English-speaking countries. Illustrations: occasional b&w photos. Length and payment by arrangement.

## Prima
National Magazine Company, 72 Broadwick Street, London W1F 9EP
*tel* 020-7439 5000 *fax* 020-7312 4100
*Editor* Maire Fahey
Monthly £2
Articles on fashion, home, crafts, health and beauty, cookery; features. Founded 1986.

## Prima Baby
National Magazine Co Ltd, 72 Broadwick Street, London W1F 9EP
*tel* 020-7312 3852 *fax* 020-7312 3744
*email* prima.baby@natmags.co.uk
*Editor* Julie Goodwin
Monthly £1.95
Magazine for women covering all aspects of pregnancy and childbirth and life with children aged up to 3 years; plus health, fashion. Length: up to 1500 words. Illustrations: colour transparencies. Payment: by arrangement. Founded 1994.

## Printing World
CMP Information, Sovereign House, Sovereign Way, Tonbridge, Kent TN9 1RW
*tel* (01732) 377391 *fax* (01732) 377552
*Editor* Gareth Ward
Weekly £2.75 (£94.50 p.a., overseas £142 p.a.)
Commercial, technical, financial and labour news covering all aspects of the printing industry in the UK and abroad. Outside contributions. Payment: by arrangement. Illustrations: line, half-tone, colour, cartoons. Founded 1878.

## Private Eye
6 Carlisle Street, London W1V 5RG
*tel* 020-7437 4017 *fax* 020-7437 0705
*email* strobes@private-eye.co.uk
*website* www.private-eye.co.uk
*Editor* Ian Hislop
Fortnightly £1.30
Satire. Payment: by arrangement. Illustrations: b&w, line, cartoons. Founded 1961.

## Professional Nurse
EMAP Healthcare Ltd, Greater London House, Hampstead Road, London NW1 7EJ
*tel* 020-7874 0384 *fax* 020-7874 0386
*email* pn@emap.com
*Editor* Carolyn Scott
Monthly £39 p.a.
Articles of interest to the senior nurse. Length: articles: 1500–2000 words; letters: 250–500 words. Payment: by arrangement. Illustrations: commissioned. Founded 1985.

## Professional Photographer
Archant Specialist Ltd, The Mill, Bearwalden Business Park, Wendens Ambo, Saffron Walden, Essex CB11 4GB
*tel* (01799) 544246 *fax* (01799) 544201
*Editor* Steve Hynes
Monthly £3.10
Articles on professional photography, including technical articles, photographer profiles and coverage of issues affecting the industry. Length: 1000–2000 words. Illustrations: colour and b&w prints and transparencies, or digital files; diagrams if appropriate. Payment: from £200. Founded 1961.

## Prospect
Prospect Publishing Ltd, 2 Bloomsbury Place, London WC1A 2QA
*tel* 020-7255 1281 *fax* 020-7255 1279
*email* editorial@prospect-magazine.co.uk
*website* www.prospect-magazine.co.uk
*Editor* David Goodhart
Monthly £3.99
Political and cultural monthly magazine. Essays, features, special reports, reviews, short stories, opinions/analysis. Length: 3000–6000 words (essays, special reports, short stories), 1000 words (opinions). Illustrations: colour and b&w. Payment: by negotiation. Founded 1995.

## PR Week
Haymarket Marketing Publications, 174 Hammersmith Road, London W6 7JP
*tel* 020-8267 4520 *fax* 020-8267 4509
*Editor* Kate Nicholas
Weekly Controlled circulation; £1.85 (£72 p.a.)
News and features on public relations. Length: approx. 800–3000 words. Payment: £185 per 1000 words. Illustrations: colour and b&w. Founded 1984.

## Publishing News
39 Store Street, London WC1E 7DS
*tel* 020-7692 2900
*website* www.publishingnews.co.uk
*Editor* Liz Thomson, *Managing Editor* Rodney Burbeck, *Deputy Editor* Roger Tagholm
Weekly £2

Articles and news items on the book publishing and bookselling industry. Payment: £120 per 1000 words.

## Pulse

CMP Information Ltd, Ludgate House, 245 Blackfriars Road, London SE1 9UY
*tel* 020-7921 8102 *fax* 020-7921 8132
*email* pulse@cmpinformation.com
*Editor* Phil Johnson
Weekly £141.25 p.a.

Articles and photos of direct interest to GPs. Purely clinical material can only be accepted from medically qualified authors. Length: 600–1200 words. Payment: £150 average. Illustrations: b&w and colour photos. Founded 1959.

## Q Magazine

EMAP Performance, Mappin House, 4 Winsley Street, London W1W 8HF
*tel* 020-7436 1515 *fax* 020-7312 8247
*email* q@ecm.emap.com
*website* www.q4music.com
*Editor* Paul Rees
Monthly £3.40

Glossy modern guide to more than just rock music. All material commissioned. Length: 1200–2500 words. Illustrations: colour and b&w photos. Payment: £185 per 1000 words; illustrations by arrangement. Founded 1986.

## QWF

PO Box 1768, Rugby CV21 4ZA
*tel* (01788) 334302
*email* jo@qwfmagazine.co.uk
*website* www.qwfmagazine.co.uk
*Editor* Jo Good, *Send material to* Sally Zigmond, Assistant Editor, 18 Warwick Crescent, Harrogate, North Yorkshire HG2 8JA
Bi-monthly £4.20 (£25 p.a.)

Thought-provoking short stories by female writers (no traditional romances, domestic crises or mainstream fiction) and articles of general interest. Study magazine first. Length: up to 4000 words. Payment: £5 (articles), £10 (short stories). Annual short story competition (up to 5000 words) in any style or genre, on any theme; first prize: £200. Founded 1994.

## RA Magazine

Royal Academy of Arts, Burlington House, Piccadilly, London W1J 0BD
*tel* 020-7300 5820 *fax* 020-7300 5881
*email* ramagazine@royalacademy.org.uk
*website* www.royalacademy.org.uk
*Editor* Sarah Greenberg
Quarterly £4.50

Visual arts and culture articles relating to the Royal Academy of Arts and the wider British and international arts scene. Length:150–1800 words. Illustrations: consult the Editor. Payment: average £250 per 1000 words; illustrations by negotiation. Founded 1983.

## Racing Post

Trinity Mirror, Floor 23, One Canada Square, Canary Wharf, London E14 5AP
*tel* 020-7293 3291 *fax* 020-7293 3758
*email* editor@racingpost.co.uk
*website* www.racingpost.co.uk
*Editor* Chris Smith
Mon–Fri €1.20, Sat, Sun €1.40

News on horseracing, greyhound racing and sports betting. Founded 1986.

## Radio Control Models and Electronics

Nexus Special Interests Ltd, Nexus House, Azalea Drive, Swanley, Kent BR8 8HU
*tel* (01322) 660070 *fax* (01322) 667633
*Editor* Graham Ashby
Monthly £2.85

Well-illustrated articles on topics related to radio control. Payment: £45 per published page. Illustrations: line, half-tone. Founded 1960.

## Radio Times

BBC Worldwide Ltd, 80 Wood Lane, London W12 0TT
*tel* 020-8433 3400 *fax* 020-8433 3160
*email* radio.times@bbc.co.uk
*website* www.radiotimes.com
*Editor* Gill Hudson
Weekly 90p

Articles that preview the week's programmes on British TV and radio. All articles are specially commissioned – ideas and synopses are welcomed but not unsolicited MSS. Length: 600–2500 words. Payment: by arrangement. Illustrations: mostly in colour; photos, graphic designs or drawings.

## Rail

EMAP Active Publications, Bretton Court, Bretton, Peterborough PE3 8DZ
*tel* (01733) 264666 *fax* (01733) 282720
*email* rail@emap.com
*Managing Editor* Nigel Harris
Fortnightly £2.40

News and in-depth features on current UK railway operations. Length: 2000–3000 words (features), 250–400 words (news). Illustrations: colour and b&w photos and artwork. Payment: £75 per 1000 words; £20 per photo except cover (£70). Founded 1981.

## Railway Gazette International

Reed Business Information, Quadrant House, The Quadrant, Sutton, Surrey SM2 5AS
*tel* 020-8652 8608 *fax* 020-8652 3738

*website* www.railwaygazette.com
*Editor* Murray Hughes
Monthly £72 p.a.

Deals with management, engineering, operation and finance of railways worldwide. Articles of practical interest on these subjects are considered and paid for if accepted. Illustrated articles, of 1000–2000 words, are preferred. A preliminary letter is required.

## Railway Magazine
IPC Media Ltd, King's Reach Tower, Stamford Street, London SE1 9LS
*tel* 020-7261 5821 *fax* 020-7261 5269
*Editor* Nick Pigott
Monthly £3.05

Illustrated magazine dealing with all railway subjects; no fiction or verse. Articles from 1500–2000 words accompanied by photos. Preliminary letter desirable. Payment: by arrangement. Illustrations: colour transparencies, half-tone and line. Founded 1897.

## Reader's Digest
The Reader's Digest Association Ltd, 11 Westferry Circus, Canary Wharf, London E14 4HE
*tel* 020-7715 8000
*email* excerpts@readersdigest.co.uk
*website* www.readersdigest.co.uk
*Editor-in-Chief* Katherine Walker
Monthly £2.95

Original anecdotes – £100 for up to 150 words – are required for humorous features. Booklet 'Writing for Reader's Digest' available £4.50 post free.

## Real
H. Bauer Publishing, Academic House, 24–28 Oval Road, London NW1 7DT
*tel* 020-7241 8392 *fax* 020-7241 8090
*email* real.life@bauer.co.uk
*Editor* Sian Rees, *Commissioning Editor* Kate Thompson
Fortnightly £1

Fashion, beauty, health issues and lifestyle features for women aged 25–40 and real life celebrity profiles. Will consider unsolicited material. Approach Commissioning Editor with ideas and outlines. Payment: by arrangement. Founded 2001.

## Reality
Redemptorist Publications, Orwell Road, Rathgar, Dublin 6, Republic of Ireland
*tel* (01) 4922488 *fax* (01) 4922654
*email* info@redemptoristpublications.com
*website* www.redemptoristpublications.com
*Editor* Rev. Gerry Moloney CSSR
Monthly €1.25

Illustrated magazine for Christian living. Illustrated articles on all aspects of modern life, including family, youth, religion, leisure. Length: 1000–1500

words. Payment: by arrangement; average £50 per 1000 words. Founded 1936.

## Record Collector
Unit 101, Wales Farm Road, London W3 6UG
*tel* (0870) 732 8080 *fax* (0870) 732 6060
*email* alan.lewis@dpgmags.co.uk
*website* www.recordcollectormag.com
*Editor* Alan Lewis
Monthly £3.40

Covers all areas of music, with the focus on collectable releases and the reissues market. Specially commissions most material but will consider unsolicited material. Welcomes ideas for articles and features. Length: 2000 (articles/features), 200 (news). Illustrations: transparencies, colour and b&w prints, scans of rare records; all commissioned. Payment: negotiable. Founded 1980.

## Red
Hachette Filipacchi UK Ltd, 64 North Row, London W1K 7LL
*tel* 020-7150 7000 *fax* 020-7150 7685
*Editor* Trish Halpin, *Send material to* Andrea Childs, Assistant Editor
Monthly £3

High-quality articles on topics of interest to women aged 28–40: humour, memoirs, interviews and well-researched investigative features. Approach with ideas in writing in the first instance. Length: 1500 words upwards. Illustrations: transparencies. Payment: NUJ rates. Founded 1998.

## Red Pepper
Socialist Newspaper (Publications) Ltd, 1B Waterlow Road, London N19 5NJ
*email* redpepper@redpepper.org.uk
*website* www.redpepper.org.uk
*Editor* Hilary Wainwright, *Send material to* David Castle, Deputy Editor
Monthly £1.95

Independent radical magazine: news and features on politics, culture and everyday life of interest to the left and greens. Material mostly commissioned. Length: news/news features 200–800 words, other features 800–2000 words. Illustrations: b&w photos, cartoons, graphics. Payment: for investigations, otherwise only exceptionally. Founded 1994.

## Reform
(published by United Reform Church)
86 Tavistock Place, London WC1H 9RT
*tel* 020-7916 8630 *fax* 020-7916 2021 (FAO 'Reform')
*email* reform@urc.org.uk
*Editor* David Lawrence
Monthly £1.40 (£12 p.a.)

Articles of religious or social comment. Length: 600–1000 words. Illustrations: line, half-tone, colour, cartoons. Payment: by arrangement. Founded 1972.

## Report

ATL, 7 Northumberland Street, London WC2N 5RD
*tel* 020-7782 1517 *fax* 020-7925 0529
*email* info@atl.org.uk
*website* www.askatl.org.uk
*Editor* Heather Pinnell
10 p.a. £2.50 (£15 p.a. UK; £27 p.a. overseas)

The magazine from the Association of Teachers and Lecturers (ATL). Features, articles, comment, news about nursery, primary, secondary and further education. Payment: minimum £120 per 1000 words.

## Restaurant Magazine

3rd Floor, 9 Carnaby Street, London W1F 9PE
*tel* 020-7434 9190 *fax* 020-7434 4517
*email* editorial@restaurantmagazine.co.uk
*Editor* Chris Maillard
Bi-weekly £1.95

Articles, features and news on the restaurant trade. Specially commissions most material. Welcomes ideas for articles and features. Illustrations: colour transparencies, prints and artwork. Payment: variable. Founded 2001.

## Retail Week

EMAP Retail, 33–39 Bowling Green Lane, London EC1R 0DA
*tel* 020-7520 1500 *fax* 020-7520 1752
*Editor* Neill Denny
Weekly Controlled circulation (£105 p.a.)

Features and news stories on all aspects of retail management. Length: up to 1000 words. Illustrations: colour photos. Payment: by arrangement. Founded 1988.

## Review – see Mail on Sunday, page 11

## The Rialto

PO Box 309, Aylsham, Norwich NR11 6LN
*website* www.therialto.co.uk
*Editor* Michael Mackmin
3 p.a. £4.25 (£12 p.a., £9 p.a. low income)

For poets and poetry. Sae essential. Payment: by arrangement. Founded 1984.

## Right Start

McMillan-Scott plc, 10 Savoy Street, London WC2E 7HR
*tel* 020-7878 2338 *fax* 020-7379 6261
*Editor* Lynette Lowthian
Bi-monthly £2.10

Features on all aspects of preschool and infant education, child health and behaviour. No unsolicited MSS. Length: 800–1500 words. Illustrations: colour photos, line. Payment: varies. Founded 1989.

## Royal National Institute of the Blind

PO Box 173, Peterborough, Cambs. PE2 6WS
*tel* (0845) 7023153 *fax* (01733) 375001
*email* cservices@rnib.org.uk
*website* www.rnib.org.uk/wesupply/magazine/welcome.htm
*textphone* (0845) 7585691 *helpline* (0845) 7669999

Published by the Royal National Institute of the Blind, the following titles are available via email, on floppy disk and in braille, unless otherwise stated. *3FM* (email and braille), *Absolutely Boys, Absolutely Girls, Access IT, After Hours* (braille), *Aphra, BBC On Air, Big Print newspaper* (large print only), *Blast Off!* (children's magazine; disk and braille), *Braille at Bedtime* (braille), *Broadcast Times* (email and disk), *Broadcast Times* (email and disk), *Busy Solicitor's Digest* (disk and braille), *Channels of Blessing* (disk and braille), *Chess Magazine* (braille), *Christmas Cracker* (disk and braille), *Christmas Radio Guide* (email and braille), *Christmas Television Guide* (email and braille), *Compute IT, Contention, Conundrum, Cricket Fixtures, Daily Bread* (disk and braille), *E-Access Bulletin* (email only), *Eye Contact* (print, email, disk, cassette tape), *Football Fixtures, Good Vibrations, Money Matters, Music Magazine* (disk and braille), *New Beacon* (print, email, disk, cassette tape, braille), *New Literature on Sight Problems* (print, email, disk, cassette tape, braille), *Journal of Physiotherapy, Physiotherapy* (disk, cassette tape, braille), *Physiotherapy Frontline* (cassette tape), *Physiotherapists' Quarterly* (braille, email), *Piano Tuners' Quarterly* (large print, email, disk, cassette tape, braille), *Progress, Proms Guide, Radio Guide* (email and braille), *Ready, Steady, Read* (for new readers of braille in braille only), *Rhetoric, Scientific Enquiry* (disk and braille), *Shaping Up, Shop Window, Shop Window Christmas Guide, Short Stories, Slugs & Snails* (for teenage boys; disk and braille), *Soundings* (cassette tape and web), *SP* (disc and braille), *Sugar & Spice* (for teenage girls; disk and braille), *Tape Medical Bulletin* (cassette tape), *Television Guide* (email and braille), *Theological Times* (disk, cassette tape, braille, email), *Upbeat, You & Your Child, Visability* (print, email, disk, cassette tape), *Vision* (clear print, email, disk, cassette tape, braille), *Welcome to a world of...* (email, disk, web, cassette tape, braille).

## Rugby World

IPC Media Ltd, Kings Reach Tower, Stamford Street, London SE1 9LS
*tel* 020-7261 6830 *fax* 020-7261 5419
*email* Paul_Morgan@ipcmedia.com
*Editor* Paul Morgan
Monthly £3.10

Features and exclusive news stories on rugby. Length: approx. 1200 words. Illustrations: colour photos, cartoons. Payment: £120. Founded 1960.

## Runner's World

Rodale Ltd, 7–10 Chandos Street, London W1M 0AD
*tel* 020-7291 6000 *fax* 020-7291 6080
*email* rwedit@rodale.co.uk
*website* www.runnersworld.co.uk
*Editor* Steven Seaton
Monthly £3.40

Articles on jogging, running, health and fitness.
Payment: by arrangement. Illustrations: line, half-
tone, colour. Founded 1979.

## Running Fitness

Kelsey Publishing Ltd, Arcade Chambers,
Westgate Arcade, Peterborough PE1 1PY
*tel* (01733) 347559 *fax* (01733) 352749
*email* paul.larkins@kelsey.co.uk
*Editor* Paul Larkins
Monthly £3

Practical articles on all aspects of running lifestyle,
especially road running training and events, and
advice on health, fitness and injury. Illustrations:
colour photos, cartoons. Payment: by negotiation.
Founded 1985.

## RUSI Journal

Whitehall, London SW1A 2ET
*tel* 020-7930 5854 *fax* 020-7321 0943
*email* journal@rusi.org
*website* www.rusi.org
*Editor* Dr Terence McNamee
Bi-monthly £7.50

Journal of the Royal United Services Institute for
Defence Studies. Articles on international security,
the military sciences, defence technology and
procurement, and military history; also book
reviews and correspondence. Length: 3000–3500
words. Illustrations: b&w photos, colour
transparencies, maps and diagrams. Payment:
£12.50 per printed page upon publication.

## S:2 Magazine – see Sunday Express, page 13

## Safety Education

Royal Society for the Prevention of Accidents,
Edgbaston Park, 353 Bristol Road,
Birmingham B5 7ST
*tel* 0121-248 2000 *fax* 0121-248 2001
*website* www.rospa.org.uk
*Editor* Janice Cave
3 p.a. £10.50 p.a. for members of Safety Education
Department (£12.50 p.a. non-members)

Articles on every aspect of good practice in safety
education including safety of teachers and pupils in
school, and the teaching of road, home, water,
leisure and personal safety by means of established
subjects on the school curriculum. All ages.
Founded as *Child Safety* 1937; became *Safety
Training* 1940; 1966.

## Saga Magazine

Saga Publishing Ltd, The Saga Building,
Enbrook Park, Folkestone,
Kent CT20 3SE
*tel* (01303) 771523 *fax* (01303) 776699
*Editor* Emma Soames
Monthly £16.95 p.a. Subscription only,
*tel* 0800 056 1057

General interest magazine aimed at the intelligent,
literate 50+ reader. Wide range of articles from
human interest, 'real life' stories, intriguing overseas
interest (not travel), some natural history, celebrity
interviews, photographic book extracts – all
relevant to 50+ audience. Articles mostly
commissioned or written in-house, but genuine
exclusives welcome. Illustrations: colour, digital
media; mainly commissioned but top-quality photo
feature suggestions sometimes accepted. Payment:
competitive rate, by negotiation. Founded 1984.

## Sainsbury's Magazine

New Crane Publishing, 20 Upper Ground,
London SE1 9PD
*tel* 020-7633 0266 *fax* 020-7401 9423
*Editor* Sue Robinson
Monthly £1.20

Features: general, food and drink, health, beauty,
homes; all material commissioned. Length: from
1500 words. Illustrations: colour and b&w photos
and line illustrations. Payment: varies; £400 per full
page for illustrations. Founded 1993.

## Satellite Times

Everpage Ltd, The Stables, West Hill Grange,
North Road, Horsforth, Leeds LS18 5HG
*tel* 0113-258 5008 *fax* 0113-258 9745
*email* info@satellitetimes.co.uk
*Editor-in-Chief* Juliet Cross
Monthly £2.30

TV and film personality articles and interviews,
sports articles, music, competitions. Payment: from
£120 per 1000 words. Founded 1988.

## Saturday – see Daily Record, page 8

## The School Librarian

The School Library Association,
Unit 2, Lotmead Business Village,
Lotmead Farm, Wanborough,
Swindon SN4 0UY
*tel* (01793) 791787 *fax* (01793) 791786
*email* info@sla.org.uk
*website* www.sla.org.uk
*Editor* Ray Lonsdale, DILS, University of Wales,
Aberystwyth, Ceredigion SY23 3AS
Quarterly Free to members (£55 p.a.)

Official journal of the School Library Association.
Articles on school library management, use and

skills, and on authors and illustrators, literacy, publishing. Reviews of books, CD-Roms, websites and other library resources from preschool to adult. Length: 1800–3000 words (articles). Payment: by arrangement. Founded 1937.

## Science Progress
Science Reviews, PO Box 314, St Albans, Herts. AL1 4ZG
*tel* (01727) 847323 *fax* (01727) 847323
*email* scilet@scilet.com
*Editors* Prof David Phillips, Prof Robin Rowbury
Quarterly £195 p.a. ($300 p.a. overseas)

Articles of 6000 words on new scientific developments, written so as to be intelligible to workers in other disciplines. Imperative to submit synopsis before full-length article. Payment: by arrangement. Illustrations: line, half-tone.

## Scientific Computing World
Cambridge Publishers Ltd, 53–54 Sydney Street, Cambridge CB2 3HX
*tel* (01223) 477411 *fax* (01223) 327356
*website* www.scientific-computing.com
*Editor* Dr Tom Wilkie
6 p.a. Free to qualifying subscribers

Features on hardware and software developments for the scientific community, plus news articles and reviews. Length: 800–2000 words. Illustrations: colour transparencies, photos, electronic graphics. Payment: by negotiation. Founded 1994.

## The Scots Magazine
D.C. Thomson & Co. Ltd, 2 Albert Square, Dundee DD1 9QJ
*tel* (01382) 223131 *fax* (01382) 322214
*email* mail@scotsmagazine.com
*website* www.scotsmagazine.com
Monthly £1.45

Articles on all subjects of Scottish interest. Short stories, poetry, but must be Scottish. Illustrations: colour and b&w photos. Articles paid on acceptance: unsolicited material considered. Founded 1739.

## Scottish Book Collector
8 Lauriston Street, Edinburgh EH3 9DJ
*tel* 0131-228 4837
*email* jennie@scottishbookcollector.co.uk
*website* www.scottishbookcollector.co.uk
*Editor* Jennie Renton
Quarterly £3

Articles on book collecting; literary/bibliographical articles, features on writers. Length: 1500–2500 words. Payment: £25 per article. Founded 1987.

## The Scottish Farmer
SMG Magazines Ltd, 200 Renfield Street, Glasgow G2 3PR
*tel* 0141-302 7700 *fax* 0141-302 7799

*Editor* Alasdair Fletcher
Weekly £1.50

Articles on agricultural subjects. Length: 1000–1500 words. Payment: £80 per 1000 words. Illustrations: line, half-tone, colour. Founded 1893.

## Scottish Field
Special Publications, Craigcrook Castle, Craigcrook Road, Edinburgh EH4 3PE
*tel* 0131-312 4550 *fax* 0131-312 4551
*email* editor@scottishfield.co.uk
*Editor* Archie Mackenzie
Monthly £3

Will consider all material with a Scottish link and good photos. Payment: by negotiation. Founded 1903.

## Scottish Home and Country
42 Heriot Row, Edinburgh EH3 6ES
*tel* 0131-225 1724 *fax* 0131-225 8129
*email* magazine@swri.demon.co.uk
*website* www.swri.org.uk
*Editor* Liz Ferguson
Monthly £1

Articles on crafts, cookery, travel, personal experience, rural interest; fashion, health, books. Length: up to 1000 words, preferably illustrated. Illustrations: colour prints/transparencies, b&w, cartoons. Payment: by arrangement. Founded 1924.

## Scottish Memories
Lang Syne Publishers Ltd, Strathclyde Business Centre, 120 Carstairs Street, Glasgow G40 4JD
*tel* 0141-554 9944 *fax* 0141-554 9955
*email* scottish-memories@aol.com
*website* www.scottish-memories.co.uk
*Editor* George Forbes
Monthly £2.50

Features on any aspect of Scottish nostalgia or history, from primeval times to the 1990s. Contact the Editor with an outline in the first instance. Length: 1000 words. Illustrations: colour and b&w. Payment: £70 per 1000 words; £20 per photo. Founded 1993.

## Scouting Magazine
Gilwell House, Gilwell Park, London E4 7QW
*tel* 020-8433 7100 *fax* 020-8433 7103
*Editor* Anna Sorensen
Monthly £2.15

Magazine of the Scout Association. Ideas, news, views, features and programme resources for Leaders and Supporters. Training material, accounts of Scouting events and articles of general interest with Scouting connections. Illustrations: photos – action shots preferred rather than static posed shots for use with articles or as fillers or cover potential, cartoons. Payment: on publication by arrangement.

## Screen International

EMAP Media, 33–39 Bowling Green Lane,
London EC1R 0DA
*tel* 020-7505 8080 *fax* 020-7505 8117
*email* ScreenInternational@compuserve.com
*website* www.screendaily.com
*Editor* Colin Brown
Weekly £2.60 (£135 p.a.)

International news and features on the international
film business. No unsolicited material. Length:
variable. Payment: by arrangement.

## Scuba World

Freestyle Publications Ltd, Alexander House,
Ling Road, Tower Park, Poole, Dorset BH12 4NZ
*tel* (01202) 735090 *fax* (01202) 733969
*email* fraines@freepubs.co.uk
*website* www.freepubs.co.uk
*Editor* Frank Raines
Monthly £3

The official magazine of the Sub-Aqua Association.
Articles, features, news and short stories related to
diving. Unsolicited material welcome. Length:
1300–1400 words (articles/features); 200–300 words
(news); 800 words (short stories); 2000 words
(interviews). Payment: negotiable. Founded 1990.

## Sea Angler

EMAP Active Ltd, Bushfield House, Orton Centre,
Peterborough PE2 5UW
*tel* (01733) 237111 *fax* (01733) 465658
*Editor* Mel Russ
Monthly £2.60

Topical articles on all aspects of sea-fishing around
the British Isles. Payment: by arrangement.
Illustrations: colour. Founded 1973.

## Sea Breezes

Media House, Tromode, Douglas,
Isle of Man IM4 4SB
*tel* (01624) 626018 *fax* (01624) 696573
*Editor* A.C. Douglas
Monthly £2.75

Factual articles on ships and the sea past and
present, preferably illustrated. Length: up to 4000
words. Illustrations: line, half-tone, colour.
Payment: by arrangement. Founded 1919.

## Self Build & Design

151 Station Street, Bruton on Trent,
Staffs. DE14 1BG
*tel* (01283) 742950 *fax* (01283) 742957
*email* ross.stokes@sbdonline.co.uk
*website* www.selfbuildanddesign.com
*Editor* Ross Stokes
Monthly £3.25

Articles on house construction for individual
builders. Welcomes ideas for articles. Payment:

£100–£200 per 1000 words. Illustrations: colour
prints and transparencies.

## Sewing World

Traplet Publications Ltd, Traplet House,
Pendragon Close, Malvern WR14 1GA
*tel* (01684) 588500 *fax* (01684) 594888
*email* sw@traplet.co.uk
*Editor* Wendy Gardiner
Monthly £2.95

'Sewing magazine for sewing machine enthusiasts.'
Articles and step-by-step projects. Length:
1000–1500 words (articles). Illustrations: colour.
Payment: £100 per article including illustrations.
Founded 1995.

## She

National Magazine House, 72 Broadwick Street,
London W1F 9EP
*tel* 020-7439 5000 *fax* 020-7312 3981
*Editor* Terry Tavner, *Send material to* Cayte
Williams, Features Editor
Monthly £2.80

No unsolicited MSS. Ideas with synopses welcome
on subjects ranging from health and relationships
to child care. Payment: NUJ freelance rates.
Illustrations: photos. Founded 1955.

## SHERLOCK

Overdale, 69 Greenhead Road,
Huddersfield HD1 4ER
*tel* (01484) 426957 *fax* (01484) 426957
*email* overdale@btinternet.com
*Editor* David Stuart Davies
6 p.a. £3.95

Articles relating to Sherlock Holmes, crime fiction
and writers. Also short stories. Contact the Editor
with ideas/synopsis in the first instance. Length:
1800 words (articles), 6000–7000 words (short
stories). Payment: by negotiation. Founded 1991.

## Ships Monthly

IPC Country & Leisure (Marine),
222 Branston Road, Burton-on-Trent,
Staffs. DE14 3BT
*tel* (01283) 542721 *fax* (01283) 546436
*Editor* Iain Wakefield
Monthly £2.75 plus 4 enlarged issues (£3.35 each)

Illustrated articles of shipping interest – both
mercantile and naval, preferably of 20th and 21st
century ships. Well-researched, factual material
only. No short stories or poetry. 'Notes for
Contributors' available. Mainly commissioned
material; preliminary letter essential, with sae.
Payment: by arrangement. Illustrations: half-tone
and line, colour transparencies, prints and digital
images on CD with thumbprint contact sheet.
Founded 1966.

## Shoot Monthly

IPC Magazines Ltd, King's Reach Tower,
Stamford Street, London SE1 9LS
*tel* 020-7261 6287 *fax* 020-7261 6019
*Editor* Colin Mitchell
Monthly £2.95

Football magazine for fans of all ages. Features,
profiles of big names in football. Length: 500–2000
words (features). Illustrations: colour transparencies.
Payment: negotiable. Founded 1969.

## Shooting Times and Country Magazine

IPC Magazines Ltd, King's Reach Tower,
Stamford Street, London SE1 9LS
*tel* 020-7261 6180 *fax* 020-7261 7179
*Editor* Julian Murray-Evans
Weekly £1.70

Articles on fieldsports, especially shooting, and on
related natural history and countryside topics.
Unsolicited MSS not encouraged. Length: up to
2000 words. Payment: by arrangement. Illustrations:
photos, drawings, colour transparencies. Founded
1882.

## The Shop: A Magazine of Poetry

Skeagh, Schull, Co. Cork, Republic of Ireland
*email* wakeman@iolfree.ie
*Editors* John and Hilary Wakeman
3 p.a. €19/£15 p.a.

Poems on any subject in any form and occasional
essays on poetry, especially Irish poetry. No
submissions by email. No illustrations required.
Length: 2000–3000 words (essays); any (poems).
Payment: by arrangement. Founded 1999.

## The Short Wave Magazine

Arrowsmith Court, Station Approach, Broadstone,
Dorset BH18 8PW
*tel* (0870) 2247810 *fax* (0870) 2247850
*email* kevin.nice@pwpublishing.ltd.uk
*website* www.pwpublishing.ltd.uk
*Editor* Kevin Nice
Monthly £3.25 (£36 p.a.)

Technical and semi-technical articles, 500–5000
words, on design, construction and operation of
radio receiving equipment. Radio-related photo
features welcome. Payment: £55 per page.
Illustrations: line, half-tone, colour. Founded 1937.

## Shout

D.C. Thomson & Co. Ltd, Albert Square,
Dundee DD1 9QJ
*tel* (01382) 223131 *fax* (01382) 200880
*email* shout@dcthomson.co.uk
185 Fleet Street, London EC4A 2HS
*tel* 020-7400 1030 *fax* 020-7400 1089
*Editor-in-Chief* Jackie Brown
Fortnightly £1.80

Colour gravure magazine for 11–14 year-old girls.
Pop, film and 'soap' features and pin-ups; general
features of teen interest; emotional features, fashion
and beauty advice. Illustrations: colour transparencies. Payment: on acceptance. Founded 1993.

## The Shropshire Magazine

77 Wyle Cop, Shrewsbury, Shrops. SY1 1UT
*tel* (01743) 361979 *fax* (01743) 362128
*Editor* Keith Parker
Monthly £1.50

Articles on topics related to Shropshire, including
countryside, history, characters, legends, education,
food; also home and garden features. Length: up to
1500 words. Illustrations: colour. Founded 1950.

## Sight and Sound

British Film Institute, 21 Stephen Street,
London W1T 1LN
*tel* 020-7255 1444 *fax* 020-7436 2327
*Editor* Nick James
Monthly £3.25

Topical and critical articles on the cinema of any
country; reviews of every film theatrically released in
the UK; book reviews; reviews of every video
released; regular columns from around the world.
Length: 1000–5000 words. Payment: by arrangement.
Illustrations: relevant photos, cartoons. Founded 1932.

## The Sign

G.J. Palmer & Sons Ltd, St Mary's Works,
St Mary's Plain, Norwich, Norfolk NR3 3BH
*tel* (01603) 615995 *fax* (01603) 624483
*email* terencestalbans@aol.com
*Publisher* G.A. Knights, *Editor* Terence Handley
MacMath, *Poetry Editor* D.H.W. Grubb
Monthly 5p

Leading national insert for C of E parish magazines.
Articles of interest to parishes. Items should bear
the author's name and address; return postage
essential or send by email. Length: up to 450 words,
accompanied by photos/illustrations. Up to 3 poems
(copies, not originals) may be sent for consideration
with sae to D.H.W. Gribb, The Spice Trust,
76A St Mark's Road, Henley-on-Thames, Oxon.
Payment: by arrangement. Founded 1905.

## Ski and Board

The Ski Club of Great Britain, The White House,
57–63 Church Road, London SW19 5SB
*tel* (0845) 4580780 *fax* (0845) 4580781
*email* editor@skiclub.co.uk
*website* www.skiclub.co.uk
*Editor* Arnie Wilson
Monthly (Oct–Jan) £3.25

Articles, features, news, true life stories, ski tips,
equipment reviews, resort reports – all in
connection with skiing and snowboarding.

Welcomes ideas for articles and features. Length: 600–2000 words. Illustrations: colour transparencies, colour and b&w artwork and cartoons. Payment: £200 per 1000 words; £100–£200 per photo/illustration. Founded 1903.

## The Skier and The Snowboarder Magazine

Mountain Marketing Ltd, PO Box 386, Sevenoaks, Kent TN13 1AQ
*tel* (0845) 3108303 *fax* (01732) 779266
*email* skierandsnowboarder@hotmail.com
*Editor* Frank Baldwin
5 p.a. (July-May) £2.95

Ski features, based around a good story. Length: 800–1000 words. Illustrations: colour action ski photos. Payment: by negotiation. Founded 1984.

## Slimmer, Healthier, Fitter

Aceville Publications Ltd, 25 Phoenix Court, Hawkins Road, Colchester CO2 8JY
*tel* (01206) 505972 *fax* (01206) 505985
*email* hmulley@aceville.co.uk
*Editor* Helen Mulley
10 p.a. £2.20

Features on health, nutrition, slimming. Personal weight loss stories. Sae essential. Length: 600 or 1200 words. Payment: by arrangement. Founded 1972.

## Slimming Magazine

EMAP Esprit, Greater London House, Hampstead Road, London NW1 7EJ
*tel* 020-7347 1854 *fax* 020-7347 1863
*Editor* Rashmi Madan
12 p.a. £2.10

Articles on psychology, lifestyle and health related to diet and nutrition. Approach the Features Editor in writing with ideas. Length: 1000–1500 words. Payment: by negotiation. Founded 1969.

## Smallholder

Hook House, Hook Road, Wimblington, March, Cambs. PE15 0QL
*tel* (01354) 741182 *fax* (01354) 741182
*email* liz.smallholder@virgin.net
*website* www.smallholder.co.uk
*Editor* Liz Wright
Monthly £2.90

Articles of relevance to small farmers about livestock and crops, organics, conservation, poultry, equipment. Items relating to the countryside considered. Send for copy. Payment: £40 per 1000 words or by arrangement. Illustrations: line, half-tone, cartoons. Founded 1985.

## Smash Hits

EMAP Performance, Mappin House, 4 Winsley Street, London W1W 8HF
*tel* 020-7312 8718 *fax* 020-7636 5792
*email* letters@smashhits.net
*Editor* Lisa Smosarski
Fortnightly £1.90

News, interviews and posters of pop, TV and film stars. Illustrations: colour photos. Payment: varies.

## Snooker Scene

Cavalier House, 202 Hagley Road, Edgbaston, Birmingham B16 9PQ
*tel* 0121-454 2931 *fax* 0121-452 1822
*email* editor@snookerscene.com
*website* www.snookerscene.com
*Editor* Clive Everton
Monthly £2.50 (£25 p.a.)

News and articles about the snooker and billiards scene for readers with more than a casual interest in the games. Payment: by arrangement. Illustrations: photos. Founded 1971.

## Snoop

BritAsian Media Ltd, 5A High Street, Southall, Middlesex UB1 3HA
*tel* 020-8571 7700 *fax* 020-8571 6006
*email* raj@snooplife.com
*website* www.snooplife.co.uk
*Editor* Raj Kaushal
Monthly £3

Entertainment and lifestyle magazine for second and third generation UK Asians (16–35 year-olds): interviews, music, films, fashion, gossip and gigs. Features and articles by arrangement. Founded 1997.

## Solicitors Journal

Wilmington Business Information Ltd, Paulton House, 8 Shepherdess Walk, London N1 7LB
*tel* 020-7490 0049 *fax* 020-7324 2366
*email* editorial@solicitorsjournal.co.uk
Weekly £194 for 48 issues

Articles, by practising lawyers or specialist journalists, on subjects of practical interest to solicitors. Articles on spec should be sent on disk or by email. Length: up to 1800 words. Payment: by negotiation. Founded 1856.

## The Songwriter

International Songwriters Association, PO Box 46, Limerick City, Republic of Ireland
*tel* (061) 228837
*Editor* James D. Liddane
Monthly

Articles on songwriting and interviews with music publishers and recording company executives. Length: 400–5000 words. Payment: by arrangement. Illustrations: photos. Founded 1967.

## Songwriting and Composing

Sovereign House, 12 Trewartha Road, Praa Sands,
Penzance, Cornwall TR20 9ST
*tel* (01736) 762826 *fax* (01736) 763328
*email* songmag@aol.com
*website* www.songwriters-guild.co.uk
*General Secretary* Carole Jones
Quarterly Free to members

Magazine of the Guild of International Songwriters
and Composers. Short stories, articles, letters relating
to songwriting, publishing, recording and the music
industry. Payment: negotiable upon content £25–£60.
Illustrations: line, half-tone. Founded 1986.

## The Spark Magazine

Blue Sax Publishing Ltd, 86 Colston Street,
Bristol BS1 5BB
*tel* 0117-914 3434 *fax* 0117-914 3444
*email* john@thespark.co.uk
*website* www.thespark.co.uk
*Editor* John Dawson
Quarterly Free

'A free... thinking magazine about positive change
for the West Country.' Features on health, fitness,
the environment, social and community issues.
Welcomes ideas for features and articles. Send A4
envelope for writers' guidelines or see website.
Length: varies. Illustrations: colour cover. Payment:
£6.50 per 100 words. Founded 1993.

## The Spectator

56 Doughty Street, London WC1N 2LL
*tel* 020-7405 1706 *fax* 020-7242-0603
*Editor* Boris Johnson, *Publisher* Kimberly Fortier
Weekly £2.40

Articles on current affairs, politics, the arts; book
reviews. Illustrations: colour and b&w, cartoons.
Payment: on merit. Founded 1828.

## Spectrum Magazine – see Scotland on

Sunday, page 12

## Sport First

20–26 Brunswick Place, London N1 6DZ
*tel* 020-7490 7575 *fax* 020-7490 7666
*email* editorial@sportfirst.com
*website* www.sportfirst.com
*Editor* Chris Mann
Weekly £1

Tabloid Sunday newspaper covering all sports.
Length: 800 words (articles), 300–800 words (news).
No unsolicited contributions. Payment: £150 per
1000 words. Founded 1998.

## Springboard

8 Landrock Road, London N8 9HP
*tel* 020-8340 8356
*email* springboardmag@aol.com

*Editor* Fiona Mallin-Robinson
Quarterly £15 p.a.

Short fiction, poetry and articles on writing,
competition news and markets. Aims to suppport
and encourage writers. Competitions in every issue
(free to subscribers) with winning stories, poems
and articles receiving prize money and publication.
Unsolicited material is accepted but writers should
read at least one issue first. Founded 1990.

## The Squash Player

460 Bath Road, Longford, Middlesex UB7 0EB
*tel* (01753) 775511 *fax* (01753) 775512
*email* editor@squashplayer.co.uk
*Editor* Ian McKenzie
10 p.a. £40 p.a.

Covers all aspects of playing squash. All features are
commissioned – discuss ideas with the Editor.
Length: 1000–1500 words. Illustrations: unusual
photos (e.g. celebrities), cartoons. Payment: £75 per
1000 words; £25–£40 for illustrations. Founded 1971.

## Staffordshire Life Magazine

Staffordshire Newsletter Ltd, The Publishing Centre,
Derby Street, Stafford ST16 2DT
*tel* (01785) 257700 *fax* (01785) 253287
*email* editor@staffordshirelife.co.uk
*Editor* Philip Thurlow-Craig
11 p.a. £1.75

County magazine for Staffordshire. Historical
articles; features on county personalities. No short
stories. Contact the Editor in the first instance.
Length: 500–800 words. Illustrations: colour
transparencies and prints. Founded 1948;
relaunched 1980.

## The Stage

Stage House, 47 Bermondsey Street, London SE1 3XT
*tel* 020-7403 1818 *fax* 020-7357 9287
*email* editor@thestage.co.uk
*website* www.thestage.co.uk
*Editor* Brian Attwood
Weekly £1

Original and interesting articles on professional
stage and broadcasting topics may be sent for the
Editor's consideration. Length: 500–900 words.
Payment: £100 per 1000 words. Founded 1880.

## Stamp Lover

National Philatelic Society, British Philatelic Centre,
107 Charterhouse Street, London EC1M 6PT
*tel* 020-7336 0882
*email* nps@philately.org.uk
*Editor* Michael Furnell
6 p.a. £2

Original articles on stamps and postal history.
Illustrations: line, half-tone. Payment: by
arrangement. Founded 1908.

## Stamp Magazine

IPC Media Ltd, Focus Network, 9 Dingwall Avenue,
Croydon CR9 2TA
*tel* 020-8774 0772 *fax* 020-8774 0939
*Editor* Steve Fairclough
Monthly £2.40

Informative articles and exclusive news items on
stamp collecting and postal history. No preliminary
letter. Payment: by arrangement. Illustrations: line,
half-tone, colour. Founded 1934.

## Stand Magazine

School of English, University of Leeds, Leeds LS2 9JT
*tel* 0113-233 4794 *fax* 0113-233 4791
*email* stand@leeds.ac.uk
*website* www.saturn.vcu.edu/~dlatane/stand
*Managing Editor* Jon Glover
Quarterly £6.50 plus p&p (£25 p.a.)

Poetry, short stories, translations, literary criticism.
Send sae/IRCs for return. Payment: £20 per 1000
words (prose); £20 per poem. Founded 1952.

## Staple

35 Carr Road, Walkley, Sheffield S06 2WY
*Editors* Elizabeth Barrett, Ann Atkinson
3 p.a. £15 p.a. (£20 p.a. overseas)

Poetry, short fiction, articles and reviews. Payment:
£5 per poem, £10 fiction/articles. Founded 1982.

## Starburst

Visual Imagination Ltd, 9 Blades Court,
Deodar Road, London SW15 2NU
*tel* 020-8875 1520 *fax* 020-8875 1588
*email* starburst@vismag.com
*website* www.visimag.com
*Editor* Garry Gillat
Monthly plus 4 specials p.a. £3.65

Features and interviews on all aspects of science
fiction. Length: 2000 words. Illustrations: colour
and b&w photos. Payment: £80 per 1000 words;
£10–£20 per image. Founded 1977.

## Star Trek Monthly

Tital Magazines, Titan House,
144 Southwark Street, London SE1 0UP
*tel* 020-7620 0200 *fax* 020-7803 1803
*Editor* Nick Jones
13 p.a. £3.50

Up-to-date news about every aspect of Star Trek,
including all TV series and films, cast interviews,
behind-the-scenes features and product reviews.
Payment: by arrangement. Founded 1995.

## The Strad

Orpheus Publications, Newsquest Magazines,
330 High Holborn, London WC1V 7QT
*tel* 020-7203 6731 *fax* 020-7203 6736
*email* thestrad@orpheuspublications.com

*website* www.thestrad.com
*Editor* Naomi Sadler
12 p.a. £3.75

Features, news and reviews for string instrument
players, teachers, makers and enthusiasts – both
professional and amateur. Specially commissions
most material but will consider unsolicited material.
Welcomes ideas for articles and features. Length:
1000–2000 (articles/features), 100–150 (news).
Payment: £150–£300 (articles/features), varies for
news. Illustrations: transparencies, colour and b&w
prints and artwork, colour cartoons; all
commissioned. Founded 1890.

## Studies, An Irish quarterly review

35 Lower Leeson Street, Dublin 2,
Republic of Ireland
*tel* (01) 6766785 *fax* (01) 6762984
*email* studies@jesuit.ie
*website* www.studiesirishreview.com
*Editor* Rev. Fergus O'Donoghue SJ
Quarterly €6.35

General review of social comment, literature,
history, the arts. Published by the Irish Jesuits.
Articles written by specialists for the general reader.
Critical book reviews. Preliminary letter. Length:
4000 words. Founded 1912.

## Studio Sound

Miller Freeman Entertainment Ltd,
8 Montague Close, London SE1 9UR
*tel* 020-7940 8500 *fax* 020-7407 7102
*Editor* Tim Goodyer
Monthly £5

Articles on all aspects of professional sound
recording. Technical and operational features on the
functional aspects of sound recording, AV post-
production and broadcast; general features on
studio affairs. Length: widely variable. Payment: by
arrangement. Illustrations: line, half-tone, colour.
Founded 1959.

## Suffolk Norfolk Life

Today Magazines Ltd, The Publishing House,
Station Road, Framlingham, Suffolk IP13 9EE
*tel* (01728) 622030 *fax* (01728) 622031
*email* todaymagazines@btopenworld.com
*website* www.suffolknorfolklife.com
*Editor* William Locks
Monthly £1.50

Articles relevant to Suffolk and Norfolk – current
topics plus historical items, art, leisure, etc.
Considers unsolicited material and welcomes ideas
for articles and features. Length: 900–1000 words.
Illustrations: transparencies, colour and b&w prints,
b&w artwork and cartoons. Payment: £30–£50 per
article. Founded 1989.

## Sugar
Hachette Filipacchi, 64 North Row, London W1K 7LL
*tel* 020-7150 7000 *fax* 020-7150 7001
*Acting Editor* Nick Chalmers
Monthly £2.20

Magazine for young women aged 12–17. Fashion, beauty, entertainment, features. Send synopsis first. Will consider unsolicited material. Interested in real-life stories (1200 words), quizzes. Payment: negotiable. Founded 1994.

## Sunday Express 'S' Magazine – see
Sunday Express, page 13

## Sunday Magazine – see News of the World,
page 11

## The Sunday Post Magazine – see Sunday
Post, page 13

## The Sunday Review – see Independent on
Sunday, page 10

## Sunday Telegraph Magazine – see
Sunday Telegraph, page 14

## The Sunday Times Magazine – see The
Sunday Times, page 14

## Swimming Magazine
Swimming Times Ltd, Harold Fern House, Derby Square, Loughborough LE11 5AL
*tel* (01509) 618766 *fax* (01509) 618768
*Editor* Peter Hassall
Monthly £2 (£22 p.a.)

Official journal of the Amateur Swimming Association and the Institute of Swimming Teachers and Coaches. Reports of major events and championships; news and features on all aspects of swimming including synchronised swimming, diving and water polo, etc; accompanying photos where appropriate; short fiction with a swimming theme. Unsolicited material welcome. Length: 800–1500 words. Payment: by arrangement. Founded 1923.

## The Tablet
1 King Street Cloisters, Clifton Walk, London W6 0QZ
*tel* 020-8748 8484 *fax* 020-8748 1550
*email* thetablet@thetablet.co.uk
*website* www.thetablet.co.uk
*Editor* Catherine Pepinster
Weekly £1.55

The senior Catholic weekly. Religion, philosophy, politics, society, books and arts. International coverage. Freelance work welcomed. Length: 1500 words. Illustrations: cartoons. Payment: by arrangement. Founded 1840.

## Take a Break
H. Bauer Publishing Ltd, Academic House, 24–28 Oval Road, London NW1 7DT
*tel* 020-7241 8000
*website* www.bauer.com
*Editor* John Dale
Weekly 72p

Lively, tabloid women's weekly. True life features, celebrities, health and beauty, family, travel; short stories (up to 1500 words); lots of puzzles. Payment: by arrangement. Illustrated. Founded 1990.

## Take a Break's Take a Puzzle
H. Bauer Publishing, Academic House, 24–28 Oval Road, London NW1 7DT
*tel* 020-7241 8229 *fax* 020-7241 8009
*email* take.puzzle@bauer.co.uk
*website* www.bauer.com
*Editor* Rachel Plumridge
Monthly £1.70

Puzzles. Fresh ideas always welcome. Illustrations: colour transparencies and b&w prints and artwork. Work supplied on Mac-compatible disk preferred. Payment: from £25 per puzzle, £30–£90 for picture puzzles and for illustrations not an integral part of a puzzle. Founded 1991.

## TATE
The Condé Nast Publications Ltd, Vogue House, Hanover Square, London W1S 1JU
*tel* 020-7499 9080 *fax* 020-7460 6406
*email* czamani@condenast.co.uk
*Editor* Robert Violette
Bi-monthly £4

Independent visual arts magazine: features, news, interviews, reviews, previews and opinion pieces. Length: up to 3000 words but always commissioned. Illustrations: colour and b&w photos. Payment: negotiable. Founded 1993; relaunched 2002.

## Tatler
Vogue House, Hanover Square, London W1S 1JU
*tel* 020-7499 9080 *fax* 020-7409 0451
*website* www.tatler.co.uk
*Editor* Geordie Greig
Monthly £3.30

Smart society magazine favouring sharp articles, profiles, fashion and the arts. Illustrations: colour, b&w, but all commissioned. Founded 1709.

## Taxation
2 Addiscombe Road, Croydon, Surrey CR9 5AF
*tel* 020-8686 9141 *fax* 020-8212 1988
*email* taxation@tolley.co.uk
*website* www.taxation.co.uk

*Editor* Malcolm Gunn
Weekly £4.20

Updating and advice concerning UK tax law and practice for accountants and tax experts. Length: 2000 words (articles). Payment £100 per 800 words. Founded 1927.

## The Teacher
National Union of Teachers, Hamilton House, Mabledon Place, London WC1H 9BD
*tel* 020-7380 4708 *fax* 020-7383 7230
*Editor* Mitch Howard
8 p.a. Free to NUT members

Articles, features and news of interest to all those involved in the teaching profession. Length: 750 words. Payment: NUJ rates to NUJ members. Founded 1872.

## Technology Ireland
Enterprise Ireland, Strand Road, Dublin 4, Republic of Ireland
*tel* (01) 206 6337 *fax* (01) 206 6342
*email* tecnology.ireland@enterprise-ireland.com
*website* www.technologyireland.ie
*Editor* Tom Kennedy, Mary Sweetman, Sean Dute
Monthly €48 p.a. (IR£38 p.a. overseas)

Articles, features, reviews, news on current business, innovation and technology. Length: 1500–2000 words. Illustrations: line, half-tone, colour. Founded 1969.

## Telegraph Magazine – see The Daily
Telegraph, page 8

## Television
Reed Business Information Ltd, Quadrant House, The Quadrant, Sutton, Surrey SM2 5AS
*tel* 020-8652 8120 *fax* 020-8652 8956
Monthly £2.80

Articles on the technical aspects of domestic TV and video equipment, especially servicing, long-distance TV, constructional projects, satellite TV, video recording, teletext and viewdata, test equipment, monitors. Payment: by arrangement. Illustrations: photos and line drawings for litho. Founded 1950.

## Tempo
Cambridge University Press, The Edinburgh Building, Shaftesbury Road, Cambridge CB2 2RU
*Editorial address* PO Box 171, Herne Bay, Kent CT6 6WD
*email* macval@compuserve.com
*Editor* Calum MacDonald
Quarterly £4.99 (£20 p.a.)

Authoritative articles on contemporary music. Length: 2000–4000 words. Payment: by arrangement. Illustrations: music type, occasional photographic or musical supplements.

## Tennis World
Umbrella Media, 5 Blythe Mews, Olympia, London W14 0HW
*tel* 020-7605 0000 *fax* 020-7605 0020
*email* charlotte.james@umbrellamedia.com
*Editor* Charlotte James
Monthly £2.50

Tournament reports, topical features, personality profiles, instructional articles. Length: 600–1500 words. Payment: by arrangement. Illustrations: line, half-tone, colour.

## TES Cymru
Sophia House, 28 Cathedral Road, Cardiff CF11 9LJ
*tel* 029-206 60201 *fax* 029-206 60207
*website* www.tes.co.uk
*Editor* Karen Thornton
Weekly £1.20

Education newspaper. Articles on education, about special knowledge or teaching experience and short news items about Welsh educational affairs. Length: up to 800 words (articles). Illustrations: line, half-tone. Payment: by arrangement. Founded May 2004.

## TGO (The Great Outdoors) Magazine
Newsquest, 200 Renfield Street, Glasgow G2 3QB
*tel* 0141-302 7700 *fax* 0141-302 7799
*email* cameron.mcneish@magazines.newsquest.co.uk
*Editor* Cameron McNeish
Monthly £3

Articles on walking or lightweight camping in specific areas, mainly in the UK, preferably illustrated. Length: 700–2000 words. Payment: by arrangement. Illustrations: colour. Please apply for guidelines. Founded 1978.

## that's life!
H. Bauer Publishing Ltd, Academic House, 24–28 Oval Road, London NW1 7DT
*tel* 020-7241 8000 *fax* 020-7241 8008
*Editor* Jo Checkley
Weekly 63p

Dramatic true life stories about women. Length: average 1000 words. Illustrations: colour photos and cartoons. Payment: £750. Founded 1995.

## Therapy Weekly
EMAP Healthcare Ltd, Greater London House, Hampstead Road, London NW1 7EJ
*tel* 020-7874 0360 *fax* 020-7874 0368
*Editor* Steve Bagshaw
Weekly Free to NHS and local authority therapists (£47.50 p.a.)

Articles of interest to chartered physiotherapists, occupational therapists and speech and language therapists. Guidelines to contributors available. Send proposals only initially. Length: up to 1000 words. Illustrations: colour and b&w photos, line, cartoons. Payment: by arrangement. Founded 1974 as *Therapy*.

## The Third Alternative

TTA Press, 5 Martins Lane, Witcham, Ely, Cambs. CB6 2LB
*email* ttapress@aol.com
*website* www.ttapress.com
*Editor* Andy Cox
Bi-monthly £4.50 (£21 for 6 issues)

Extraordinary new fiction: science fiction, fantasy, horror, slipstream. Also interviews with, and profiles of, authors and film-makers. Send sae with all submissions. Considers unsolicited material and welcomes ideas for articles and features. Length: 3000–4000 words (articles and features), short stories unrestricted. Illustrations: send samples and portfolios. Payment: £30 per 1000 words on acceptance. Founded 1994.

## Third Way

St Peter's, Sumner Road, Harrow, Middlesex HA1 4BX
*tel* 020-8423 8494 *fax* 020-8423 5367
*email* editor@thirdway.org.uk
10 p.a. £2.90

Aims to present biblical perspectives on the political, social and cultural issues of the day. Payment: by arrangement on publication. Email submissions preferred. Founded 1977.

## This Caring Business

Martin Miu Walker Lane, Hebden Bridge, West Yorkshire HX7 8SJ
*tel* (01422) 874078 *fax* (01422) 847017
*email* vivshep@aol.com
*Editor* Vivien Shepherd
Monthly £64 p.a.

Specialist contributions relating to the commercial aspects of nursing and residential care, including hospitals. Payment: £100 per 1000 words. Illustrations: line, half-tone. Founded 1985.

## This England

PO Box 52, Cheltenham, Glos. GL50 1YQ
*tel* (01242) 537900
*Editor* Roy Faiers
Quarterly £4.25

Articles on towns, villages, traditions, customs, legends, crafts of England; stories of people. Length: 250–2000 words. Payment: £25 per page and pro rata. Illustrations: line, half-tone, colour. Founded 1968.

## Time Out

Time Out Group Ltd, Universal House, 251 Tottenham Court Road, London W1T 7AB
*tel* 020-7813 3000 *fax* 020-7813 6001

*website* www.timeout.com
*Editor* Laura Lee Davies
Weekly £2.35

Listings magazine for London covering all areas of the arts, plus articles of consumer and news interest. Illustrations: colour and b&w. Payment by negotiation. Founded 1968.

## The Times Educational Supplement

Admiral House, 66-68 East Smithfield, London E1W 1BX
*tel* 020-7782 3000 *fax* 020-7782 3202 (news), 020-7782 3199(features)
*email* friday@tes.co.uk (feature outlines), teacher@tes.co.uk (curriculum-related outlines)
*website* www.tes.co.uk
*Editor* Bob Doe
Weekly £1.20

Education newspaper. Articles on education written with special knowledge or experience; news items; books, arts and equipment reviews. Advisable to check with news or picture editor before submitting. Outlines of feature ideas should be faxed or emailed. Illustrations: suitable photos and drawings of educational interest, cartoons. Payment: standard rates, or by arrangement.

## Times Educational Supplement Scotland

Scott House, 10 South St Andrew Street, Edinburgh EH2 2AZ
*tel* 0131-557 1133 *fax* 0131-558 1155
*Editor* Neil Munro
Weekly £1.20

Education newspaper. Articles on education, preferably 800–1000 words, written with special knowledge or experience. News items about Scottish educational affairs. Illustrations: line, half-tone. Payment: by arrangement. Founded 1965.

## Times Higher Education Supplement

Admiral House, 66–68 East Smithfield, London E1W 1BX
*tel* 020-7782 3000 *fax* 020-7782 3300
*Editor* John O'Leary
Weekly £1.40

Articles on higher education written with special knowledge or experience, or articles dealing with academic topics. Also news items. Illustrations: suitable photos and drawings of educational interest. Payment: by arrangement. Founded 1971.

## The Times Literary Supplement

Admiral House, 66–68 East Smithfield, London E1W 1BX
*tel* 020-7782 3000 *fax* 020-7782 3100
*Editor* Peter Stothard
Weekly £2.40

Will consider poems for publication, literary discoveries and articles, particularly of an opinionated kind, on literary and cultural affairs. Payment: by arrangement.

## The Times Magazine – see The Times, page 14

## Today's Fishkeeper

TRMG Ltd, 1 Forum Place, Winchester Court, Hatfield, Herts. AL10 0RN
*tel* (01707) 273999 *fax* (01707) 276555
*Editor* Derek Lambert
Monthly £3.25

Magazine for both the advanced and novice fishkeeper. A team of experts provides selected items that cover the full spectrum of aquarium and pond life, including fish (tropical, cold water, marine, discus and koi), reptiles and amphibians, plants, products and services. Illustrations: colour photos and diagrams. Payment: phone (01858) 438817 for details. Founded 1924.

## Today's Golfer

EMAP Active Ltd, Bushfield House, Orton Centre, Peterborough PE2 5UW
*tel* (01733) 237111 *fax* (01733) 288014
*Editor* Paul Hamblin
Monthly £3.30

Specialist features and articles on golf instruction, equipment and courses. Founded 1988.

## Today's Pilot

Key Publishing Ltd, PO Box 100, Stamford, Lincs. PE9 1XQ
*tel* (01780) 755131 *fax* (01780) 757261
*email* dave.unwin@keypublishing.com
*website* www.todayspilot.co.uk
*Editor* Dave Unwin
Monthly £3.30

General aviation magazine providing information and inspiration for the recreational aviator. Considers unsolicited material. Submit suggestions or an outline in the first instance. Length: 3000 words (articles/features), 1000 words (news). Illustrations: colour. Payment: negotiable (words); £20 per image. Founded 2000.

## Top of the Pops – see page 333

## Top Santé Health & Beauty

EMAP Elán, Endeavour House, 189 Shaftesbury Avenue, London WC2H 8JG
*tel* 020-7437 9011 *fax* 020-7208 3514
*Editor* Juliette Kellow
Monthly £2.10

Articles, features and news on all aspects of health and beauty. Ideas welcome. No unsolicited features.

Illustrations: colour photos and drawings. Payment: £350 per 1300 words; illustrations by arrangement. Founded 1993.

## Total DVD

Highbury WViP, Unit 601, Highgate Studios, 53–79 Highgate Road, London NW5 1TW
*tel* 020-7331 1000 *fax* 020-7331 1242
*email* chris.jenkins@wvip.co.uk
*website* www.totaldvd.net
*Editor* Chris Jenkins
Monthly £3.99

DVD reviews, home entertainment, equipment reviews, news and features. Length: 800–2500 words (articles/features), 100–500 words (news). Payment: £120 per 1000 words. Illustrations: transparencies or digital. Founded 1999.

## Total Film

99 Baker Street, London W1U 6FP
*tel* 020-7317 2600 *fax* 020-7317 0275
*email* totalfilm@futurenet.co.uk
*Editor* Matt Mueller
Monthly £3

Movie magazine covering all aspects of film. Email ideas before submitting material. Not seeking interviews or reviews. Length: 400 words (news); 1000 words (funny features). Payment: £150 per 1000 words; up to £1500 per picture. Founded 1996.

## Total Off Road

151 Station Road, Burton on Trent, Staffs. DE14 1BG
*tel* (01283) 742950 *fax* (01283) 742957
*email* toreditorial@aol.com
*Editor* Alan Kidd
Monthly £3.25

Features on off-roading: expeditions, competitions, modified vehicles, overseas events. Length 1200–3000 words. Payment: £100 per 1000 words. Illustrations: colour and b&w prints; keen to hear from photographers attending UK/overseas off-road events.

## Traditional Woodworking

151 Station Street, Burton-on-Trent, Staffs. DE14 1BG
*tel* (01283) 742950 *fax* (01283) 742957
*email* enquiries@twonline.co.uk
*Editor* Alison Bell
Monthly £2.85

Articles and features for woodworking hobbyists. Includes projects, news and timber-related articles. Length: 2500 words. Payment: by arrangement.

## Trail

EMAP Active Ltd, Bretton Court, Bretton, Peterborough PE3 8DZ
*tel* (01733) 264666 *fax* (01733) 282653

*email* trail@emap.com
*Editor* Guy Procter
Monthly £3.10

Outdoor activity magazine focusing mainly on high level walking with some scrambling, moutain biking and climbing. Very limited opportunities for freelances.

## Traveller

Wexas Ltd, 45 Brompton Road, London SW3 1DE
*tel* 020-7589 0500 *fax* 020-7581 1357
*email* traveller@wexas.com
*website* www.traveller.org.uk
*Editor* Jonathan Lorie
Quarterly Free to Wexas members; back numbers £3 (£3.50 overseas), payable to Wexas

Adventurous and authentic travel writing. Narrative features describe personal journeys to remarkable places. Unsolicited material considered if prose and pictures are excellent. See website for guidelines. Length: 800 words. Illustrations: transparencies, b&w prints. Payment: £150 per 1000 words; colour £50 (£100 cover). Founded 1970.

## Tribune

9 Arkwright Road, London NW3 6AN
*tel* 020-7433 6410
*email* george@tribpub.demon.co.uk
*Editor* Mark Seddon, *Reviews Editor* Caroline Rees
Weekly £2

Political, literary, with Socialist outlook. Informative articles (about 900 words), news stories (250–300 words). No unsolicited reviews or fiction. Payment: by arrangement. Illustrations: cartoons, photos.

## Trout and Salmon

EMAP Active Ltd, Bushfield House, Orton Centre, Peterborough PE2 5UW
*tel* (01733) 237111 *fax* (01733) 465820
*email* sandy.leventon@emap.com
*Editor* Sandy Leventon
Monthly £2.80

Articles of good quality with strong trout or salmon angling interest. Length: 400–2000 words, accompanied if possible by colour transparencies or good quality colour prints. Payment: by arrangement. Illustrations: line, colour transparencies and prints, cartoons. Founded 1955.

## Truck & Driver

Reed Business Information, Quadrant House, The Quadrant, Sutton, Surrey SM2 5AS
*tel* 020-7652 3682 *fax* 020-7652 8988
*Editor* Dave Young
Monthly £2.10

News, articles on trucks, personalities and features of interest to truck drivers. Words (on disk or electronically) and picture packages preferred.

Length: approx. 2000 words. Illustrations: colour transparencies and artwork, cartoons. Payment: negotiable. Founded 1984.

## Trucking

A & S Publishing, Messenger House, 35 St Michael's Square, Gloucester GL1 1HX
*tel* (01452) 317750 *fax* (01452) 415817
*Editor* Richard Simpson
Monthly £2.20

For truck drivers, owner–drivers and operators: news, articles, features and technical advice. Length: 750–2500 words. Illustrations: mostly 35mm colour transparencies. Payment: by negotiation. Founded 1983.

## The Trumpet

Trumpet Ventures Ltd, Wickham House, 10 Cleveland Way, London E1 4TR
*Editor-in-Chief* Femi Okutubo
Fortnightly

Newspaper for the UK's African population. Founded 1995.

## TV Quick

H. Bauer Publishing Ltd, Academic House, 24–28 Oval Road, London NW1 7DT
*tel* 020-7241 8000 *fax* 020-7241 8066
*website* www.bauer.co.uk
*Editor* Lori Miles, *Deputy Editor* Jon Peake
Weekly 65p

TV listings magazine featuring TV-related material. Payment: by arrangement. Founded 1991.

### TV Choice

*Deputy Editor* Jon Peake
Weekly 40p
Founded 2001.

### The Total TV Guide

*Editor* Lori Miles
Weekly 85p
Founded 2003.

## TVTimes Magazine

IPC Media Ltd, 10th Floor, King's Reach Tower, Stamford Street, London SE1 9LS
*tel* 020-7261 7000 *fax* 020-7261 7777
*Editor* Mike Hollingsworth
Weekly 70p

Features with an affinity to ITV, BBC1, BBC2, Channels 4 and 5, satellite and radio personalities and TV generally. Length: by arrangement. Photos: commissioned only. Payment: by arrangement.

## Ulster Business

Greer Publications, 5B Edgewater Business Park, Edgewater Road, Belfast Harbour Estate, Belfast BT3 9JQ

*tel* 028-9078 3223 *fax* 028-9078 3210
*email* russellcampbell@greenpublications.com
*website* www.ulsterbusiness.com
*Editor* Russell Campbell
Monthly £2.30

Feature-based magazine with general business-related editorial for management level and above. Specially commissions most material but will consider unsolicited material. Welcomes ideas for articles and features. Length: 800 words (articles), 1500 words (features). Payment: £60–£80 (articles), £120 (features). No illustrations required. Founded 1987.

## U magazine

Smurfit Communications, 2 Clanwilliam Court, Lower Mount Street, Dublin 2, Republic of Ireland
*tel* (01) 240 5300 *fax* (01) 661 9757
*email* letters@umagazine.ie
*Editor* Fionnuala McCarthy
Monthly €3.43

Fashion and beauty magazine for 18–25 year-old Irish women, with celebrity interviews, talent profiles, real-life stories, sex and relationship features, plus regular pages on the club scene, movies, music and film. Also travel, interiors, health, food, horoscopes. Material mostly commissioned. Payment: varies. Founded 1978.

## Ulster Grocer

Greer Publications, 5B Edgewater Business Park, Belfast Harbour Estate, Belfast BT3 9JQ
*tel* 028-9078 3200 *fax* 028-9078 3210
*email* kathyj@writenow.prestel.co.uk
*Editor* Kathy Jensen
Monthly Controlled circulation

Topical features (1000–1500 words) on food/grocery retailing and exhibitions; news (200 words) with a Northern Ireland basis. All features commissioned; no speculative articles accepted. Illustrations: colour photos. Payment: features £275, product news £160. Founded 1972.

## Under Five Contact

Pre-school Learning Alliance, 69 Kings Cross Road, London WC1X 9LL
*tel* 020-7833 0991 *fax* 020-7837 4942
*email* editor.u5c@pre-school.org.uk
*Contact* The Editor
10 p.a. £30 p.a.

Articles on the role of adults – especially parents/ preschool workers – in young children's learning and development, including children from all cultures and those with special needs. Length: 750 words. Payment: £60 per article. Founded 1962.

## The Universe

1st Floor, St James's Buildings, Oxford Street, Manchester M1 6FP

*tel* 0161-236 8856 *fax* 0161-236 8530
*Editor* Joe Kelly
Weekly 90p

Catholic Sunday newspaper. News stories, features and photos on all aspects of Catholic life required; also cartoons. Send sae with MSS. Payment: by arrangement. Founded 1860.

## Vanity Fair

The Condé Nast Publications Ltd, Vogue House, Hanover Square, London W1S 1JU
*tel* 020-7499 9080 *fax* 020-7493 1962
*website* www.condenast.co.uk
*London Editor* Graydon Carter
*tel* 020-7221 6228 *fax* 020-7221 6269
Monthly £3.30

Media, glamour and politics for grown-up readers. No unsolicited material. Payment: by arrangement.

## The Vegan

The Vegan Society, Donald Watson House, 7 Battle Road, St Leonards-on-Sea, East Sussex TN37 7AA
*tel* (01424) 448820 *fax* (01424) 717064
*email* editor@vegansociety.com
*website* www.vegansociety.com
*Editor* Rick Savage
Quarterly £2.50

Articles on health, nutrition, cookery, vegan lifestyle, land use, animal rights. Length: approx. 1000 words. Payment: by arrangement. Illustrations: photos, cartoons, line drawings – foods, animals, livestock systems, crops, people, events; colour for cover. Founded 1944.

## Venue

Venue Publishing, 64–65 North Road, Bristol BS6 5AQ
*tel* 0117-942 8491 *fax* 0117-942 0369
*email* editor@venue.co.uk
*website* www.venue.co.uk
*Editor* Dave Higgitt
Weekly £1.20

Listings magazine for Bristol and Bath combining comprehensive entertainment information with local features, profiles and interviews. Length: by agreement. Illustrations: colour. Payment: £8.75 per 100 words. Founded 1982.

## Veterinary Review

John C. Alborough Ltd, Lion Lane, Needham Market, Suffolk IP6 8NT
*tel* (01449) 723800 *fax* (01449) 723801
*email* enquiries@jca.uk.com
*Editor* David Watson
Monthly £60 p.a.

News, articles – both topical and technical – for veterinarians. Payment: negotiable.

### Animal Health News
*Editor* David Watson
Bi-monthly £30 p.a.

News, articles and product listings for the agricultural supply trade.

## Viz
Dennis Publishing, Cleveland Street,
London W1T 4JD
*tel* 020-7687 7000  *fax* 020-7687 7099
*email* viz@viz.co.uk
*website* www.viz.co.uk
*Contact* Editorial Cabinet
10 p.a. £1.95

Cartoons, spoof tabloid articles, spoof advertisements. Illustrations: half-tone, line, cartoons. Payment: £300 per page (cartoons). Founded 1979.

## Vogue
Vogue House, Hanover Square, London W1S 1JU
*tel* 020-7499 9080 *fax* 020-7408 0559
*website* www.vogue.co.uk
*Editor* Alexandra Shulman
Monthly £3.30

Fashion, beauty, health, decorating, art, theatre, films, literature, music, travel, food and wine. Length: articles from 1000 words. Illustrated.

## The Voice
Blue Star House, 8th Floor, 234–244 Stockwell Road, London SW9 9UG
*tel* 020-7737 7377 *fax* 020-7274 8894
*email* newsdesk@the-voice.co.uk
*website* www.voice-online.co.uk
*Group Editor* Deidre Forbes, *News Editor* Andrew Clunis, *Arts & Entertainment Editor* Russell Myrie, *Sports Editor* Rodney Hinds
Weekly 85p

Weekly newspaper for black Britons. Includes news, features, arts, sport and a comprehensive jobs and business section. Illustrations: colour and b&w photos. Open to ideas for news and features on sports, business, community events and the arts. Founded 1982.

### woman2woman
*Editor* Nicole Sylvester
*email* nicole2w@the-voice.co.uk
Last Mon of each month

Glossy women's lifestyle supplement addresssing the needs and aspirations of young black Britons. Includes features on entertainment, health, beauty, fahion, careers and relationships. Illustrations: colour photos.

### Young Voices
*website* www.young-voices.co.uk
*Editor* Emelia Kenlock

Monthly, second Tuesday of each month £1.75

News, features, reviews, showbiz highlights and current affairs for 11–19 year-olds. Founded 2003.

## Walk
The Ramblers' Association, 2nd Floor, Camelford House, 87–90 Albert Embankment, London SE1 7TW
*tel* 020-7339 8500 *fax* 020-7339 8501
*email* ramblers@london.ramblers.org.uk
*website* www.ramblers.org.uk
*Editor* Christopher Sparrow
Quarterly Free to members

Magazine of the Ramblers' Association. Articles on walking, access to countryside and related issues. Material mostly commissioned. Length: about 500 words. Illustrations: colour photos. Payment: by agreement. Founded 1935.

## Wallpaper
IPC Media, Brettenham House, Lancaster Place, London WC2E 7TL
*tel* 020-7322 1177 *fax* 020-7322 1171
*email* contact@wallpaper.com
*website* www.wallpaper.com
*Editor-in-Chief* Jeremy Langmead
10 p.a. £3.60

Interiors, architecture, fashion, entertainment and travel. Payment: by arrangement. Founded 1996.

## Wanderlust
PO Box 1832, Windsor SL4 1YT
*tel* (01753) 620426
*website* www.wanderlust.co.uk
*Editor* Lyn Hughes
Bi-monthly £3.50

Features on independent, adventure and special-interest travel. Send sae or visit website for 'Guidelines for contributors'. Length: up to 2500 words. Illustrations: high-quality colour slides (send stocklist first). Payment: by arrangement. Founded 1993.

## The War Cry
The Salvation Army, 101 Newington Causeway, London SE1 6BN
*tel* 020-7367 4900 *fax* 020-7367 4710
*email* warcry@salvationarmy.org.uk
*website* www.salvationarmy.org/warcry
*Editor* Major Nigel Bovey
Weekly 20p (£26 p.a.)

Voluntary contributions: Christian comment on contemporary issues, human interest stories of personal Christian faith; puzzles. Illustrations: line and photos, cartoons. Founded 1879.

## Water Gardener
TRMG, Winchester Court, 1 Forum Place, Hatfield, Herts. AL10 0RN

tel (01707) 273999 *fax* (01707) 276555
*email* christina@trmg.co.uk
*Editor* Christina Guthrie
Monthly £2.95

Magazine for water gardeners of all levels of expertise. Covers ponds and water features of all sizes; also fish and wildlife. Will consider unsolicited material. Welcomes ideas for articles and features. Length: 1000 words (articles), 1500 words (features) 200 words (news). Illustrations: transparencies and colour prints. Payment: varies.

## Waterways World

Waterways World Ltd, 151 Station Street, Burton-on-Trent, Staffs. DE14 1BG
tel (01283) 742952 *fax* (01283) 742957
*email* hugh.potter@wwonline.co.uk
*Editor* Hugh Potter
Monthly £2.95

Feature articles on all aspects of inland waterways in Britain and abroad, including historical material; factual and technical articles preferred. No short stories or poetry. Send sae for Notes for Contributors. Payment: £42 per 1000 words. Illustrations: colour transparencies or prints, line. Founded 1972.

## Wedding and Home

IPC Magazines Ltd, King's Reach Tower, Stamford Street, London SE1 9LS
tel 020-7261 7471 *fax* 020-7261 7459
*email* weddingandhome@ipcmedia.com
*Editor* Kate Barlow, *Deputy Editor* Andrea Paver
Bi-monthly £4.20

Ideas and inspiration for modern brides. Fashion and beauty, information for grooms, real life weddings, planning advice, gift list ideas and honeymoon features. Unsolicited features not accepted. Founded 1985.

## Weekend – see The Guardian, page 9

## The Weekly News

D.C. Thomson & Co. Ltd, Albert Square, Dundee DD1 9QJ
tel (01382) 223131
137 Chapel Street, Manchester M3 6AA
tel 0161-834 5122
144 Port Dundas Road, Glasgow G4 0HZ
tel 0141-332 9933
185 Fleet Street, London EC4A 2HS
tel 020-7400 1030
*Send material to* Rod Cameron, Deputy Editor
Weekly 55p

Real-life dramas of around 1000 words told in the first person. Non-fiction series with lively themes or about interesting people. Keynote throughout is strong human interest. General interest fiction. Illustrations: cartoons. Payment: on acceptance.

## Weight Watchers Magazine

Castlebar Publishing, PO Box 34044, London N13 4YA
tel 020-8882 2555 *fax* 020-8882 5282
*email* info@weightwatchers.co.uk
*Editor Editor* Pat Kane
8 p.a. £2.30

Features: health, beauty, news, astrology; food-orientated articles; success stories. All material commissioned. Length: up to 3 pages. Illustrations: colour photos and cartoons. Payment: by arrangement.

## What Camcorder

Highbury WViP, 53–79 Highgate Road, London NW5 1TW
tel 020-7331 1000 *fax* 020-7331 1242
*email* jake.williams@wvip.co.uk
*Editor* Jake Williams
Monthly £3.25

Technique articles aimed at the beginner on how to use camcorders and equipment tests of camcorders and accessories. Material mostly commissioned. Length: 1000–1800 words. Illustrations: colour photos, diagrams. Payment: £95 per 1000 words; £70 per page for illustrations. Founded 2000.

## What Car?

Haymarket Motoring Magazines Ltd, 60 Waldegrave Road, Teddington, Middlesex TW11 8LG
tel 020-8267 5688 *fax* 020-8267 5750
*Editor* Rob Aherne
Monthly £3.60

Road tests, buying guide, consumer stories and used car features. No unsolicited material. Illustrations: colour and b&w photos, line drawings. Payment: by negotiation. Founded 1973.

## What Laptop & Handheld PC

Crimson Publishing, 2 Sheen Road, Richmond, Surrey TW9 1AE
tel 020-8875 5600 *fax* 020-8875 5601
*email* letters@whatlaptop.co.uk
*website* www.whatlaptop.co.uk
*Editor* Michael Browne
Monthly £3.99

News, reviews and help for anyone who wants to buy or has bought a laptop or handheld computer. Discuss ideas for features with the Editor in the first instance; welcomes ideas for features. Length: up to 1600 words. Payment: by arrangement. Founded 1999.

## What's on TV

IPC Media Ltd, 10th Floor, King's Reach Tower, Stamford Street, London SE1 9LS
tel 020-7261 7769 *fax* 020-7261 7739
*Editor* Colin Tough
Weekly 45p

Features on TV programmes and personalities. All material commissioned. Length: up to 500 words. Illustrations: colour and b&w photos, cartoons. Payment: by agreement. Founded 1991.

## WI Home and Country
104 New King's Road, London SW6 4LY
tel 020-7731 5777 fax 020-7736 4061
Editor Susan Seager
Monthly £1.70

Journal of the National Federation of Women's Institutes for England and Wales. Publishes material related to the Federation's and members' activities; also considers articles of general interest to women, particularly country women, e.g. craft, environment, humour, health, rural life stories, of 800–1200 words. Illustrations: colour and b&w photos and drawings, cartoons. Payment: by arrangement. Founded 1919.

## Wine
Quest Magazines Ltd, Wilmington Publishing,
6–8 Underwood Street, London N1 7JQ
tel 020-7549 2571 fax 020-7549 8622
email wine@wilmington.co.uk
Editor Catharine Lowe
12 p.a. £3.30

Articles, features and news on new developments in wine and spirits; travelogues, tastings and profiles. Illustrations: colour. Payment: £200 per 1000 words. Founded 1983.

## The Wisden Cricketer
The New Boathouse, 136–142 Bramley Road,
London W10 6SR
tel 020-7565 3080 fax 020-7565 3090
Editors John Stern
Monthly £3.25

Cricket articles of exceptional interest (unsolicited pieces seldom used). Length: up to 3000 words. Payment: by arrangement. Illustrations: half-tone, colour.

## Woman
IPC Media, King's Reach Tower, Stamford Street,
London SE1 9LS
tel 020-7261 5000 fax 020-7261 5997
Editor Carole Russell
Weekly 72p

Human interest stories and practical articles of varying length on all subjects of interest to women. Payment: by arrangement. Illustrations: colour transparencies and photos. Founded 1937.

## Woman Alive
Christian Media Centre Ltd, Garcia Estate,
Canterbury Road, Worthing, West Sussex BN13 1EH
tel (01903) 821082 fax (01903) 821081
email womanalive@christianmedia.org.uk

Editor Jackie Stead
Monthly £2.20

Aimed at women aged 25 upwards. Celebrity interviews, topical features, Christian issues, profiles of women in interesting occupations, Christian testimonies and real life stories, fashion, beauty, travel, health, crafts. Unsolicited material should include colour slides or photos. Length: 750–1600 words. Payment £65–£120. Founded 1982.

## Woman and Home
IPC Magazines Ltd, King's Reach Tower,
Stamford Street, London SE1 9LS
tel 020-7261 5000 fax 020-7261 7346
Editorial Director Sue James
Monthly £2.80

Centres on the personal and home interests of the lively minded mature, modern woman. Articles dealing with fashion, beauty, leisure pursuits, gardening, home style; features on topical issues, people and places. Fiction: complete stories from 3000–4500 words in length. Illustrations: commissioned colour photos and sketches. Please note: non-commissioned work is not accepted and regrettably cannot be returned. Founded 1926.

## The Woman Writer
c/o 4 Larch Way, Haywards Heath,
West Sussex RH16 3TY
email swwriters@aol.com
website www.swwj.co.uk
Editor Jennie Lisney
6 p.a. Free to members

Periodical of the Society of Women Writers and Journalists. See under Societies section for further information. Founded 1894.

## Woman's Own
IPC Connect Ltd, King's Reach Tower,
Stamford Street, London SE1 9LS
tel 020-7261 5000
Editor Elsa McAlonan
Weekly 74p

Modern women's magazine aimed at the 20–35 age group. No unsolicited features or fiction. Illustrations: colour and b&w: interior decorating and furnishing, fashion. Address work to relevant department editor. Payment: by arrangement.

## Woman's Way
Smurfit Communications, 2 Clanwilliam Court,
Lower Mount Street, Dublin 2, Republic of Ireland
tel (01) 240 5300 fax (01) 662 2979
email ltaylor@smurfit-comms.ie
Editor Lucy Taylor
Weekly €1.30

Human interest, personality interviews, features on fashion, beauty, celebrities and investigations, short

stories. Length: 1800 words. Payment: approx.
€65–€130. Founded 1963.

## Woman's Weekly

IPC Media Ltd, King's Reach Tower,
Stamford Street, London SE1 9LS
*tel* (0870) 4445000 *fax* 020-7261 6322
*Editor* Gilly Sinclair
Weekly 68p

Lively, family-interest magazine. One fiction serial,
averaging 4000 words each instalment, of general
emotional interest, and several short stories of
1000–2500 words of general emotional interest.
Celebrity and strong human interest features,
health, finance and consumer features, plus beauty,
diet and travel; also inspirational and entertaining
personal stories. Payment: by arrangement.
Illustrations: full colour fiction illustrations, small
sketches and photos. Founded 1911.

## Woman's Weekly Fiction Special

IPC Media Ltd, King's Reach, Stamford Street,
London SE1 9LS
*tel* (0870) 4445000 *fax* 020-7261 6322
*Editor* Olwen Rice
Bi-monthly £1.50

At least 24 stories each issue of 1000–5,000 words of
varied emotional interest, including romance,
humour and mystery. Payment: by arrangement.
Illustrations: full colour. Founded 1998.

## Women's Health

Highbury Lifestyle, 1–3 Highbury Station Road,
London N1 1SE
*tel* 020-7226 2222 *fax* 020-7288 7579
*email* tracey.smith@highburywv.com
*Editor* Tracey Smith
Monthly £2.60

Lifestyle magazine for women covering a wide range
of issues from food and fitness to health and beauty,
including alternative therapies and fashion. Length:
900–1400 words. Payment: by negotiation. Founded
1998.

## The Woodworker

Highbury Leisure, Berwick House, 8–10 Knoll Rise,
Orpington, Kent BR6 0PS
*tel* (01689) 899207
*Editor* Mark Ramuz
Monthly £2.99

For the craft and professional woodworker. Practical
illustrated articles on cabinet work, carpentry, wood
polishing, wood turning, wood carving, rural crafts,
craft history, antique and period furniture; also
wooden toys and models, musical instruments;
timber procurement, conditioning, seasoning; tool,
machinery and equipment reviews. Payment: by
arrangement. Illustrations: line drawings and photos.

## The Word

Divine Word Missionaries, 3 Pembroke Road,
Dublin 4, Republic of Ireland
*tel* (01) 6606646 *fax* (01) 6606646
*email* editor@theword.ie
*Editor* Garry O'Sullivan
Monthly €1

General interest magazine with religious emphasis.
Illustrated articles up to 2000 words and good
picture features. Payment: by arrangement. Illustrations: photos and large colour transparencies.
Founded 1936.

## Workbox Magazine

Ebony Media Ltd, PO Box 25, Liskeard,
Cornwall PL14 6XX
*tel* (01579) 340100 *fax* (01579) 340400
*email* workbox@ebony.co.uk
*website* www.ebony.co.uk/workbox
*Editor* Victor Briggs
Bi-monthly £2.25

Features, of any length, on all aspects of
needlecrafts. No 'how-to' articles. Send sae with
enquiries and submissions. Illustrations: good
colour transparencies. Payment: by agreement.
Founded 1984.

## World Fishing

Nexus Media Ltd, Nexus House, Azalea Drive,
Swanley, Kent BR8 8HU
*tel* (01322) 667633 *fax* (01322) 616324
*Editor* Pilar Santamarcia
Monthly £56 p.a.

International journal of commercial fishing.
Technical and management emphasis on catching,
processing and marketing of fish and related
products; fishery operations and vessels covered
worldwide. Length: 500–1500 words. Payment: by
arrangement. Illustrations: photos and diagrams for
litho reproduction. Founded 1952.

## World Soccer

IPC Media Ltd, King's Reach Tower,
Stamford Street, London SE1 9LS
*tel* 020-7261 5737 *fax* 020-7261 7474
*Editor* Gavin Hamilton
Monthly £2.90

Articles, features, news concerning football, its
personalities and worldwide development. Length:
600–2000 words. Payment: by arrangement.
Founded 1960.

## The World of Interiors

The Condé Nast Publications Ltd, Vogue House,
Hanover Square, London W1S 1JU
*tel* 020-7499 9080 *fax* 020-7493 4013
*email* interiors@condenast.co.uk
*website* www.worldofinteriors.co.uk

*Editor* Rupert Thomas
Monthly £3.80

All material commissioned: send synopsis/visual reference for article ideas. Length: 1000–1500 words. Illustrations: colour photos. Payment: £500 per 1000 words; photos £125 per page. Founded 1981.

## World's Children

Save the Children, 17 Grove Lane, London SE5 8RD
*tel* 020-7703 5400 *fax* 020-7708 2508
*email* publications@scfuk.org.uk
*website* www.savethechildren.org.uk
*Contact* Frances Ellery (Head of Publications)
Quarterly Sent free to regular donors

Magazine of Save the Children. Articles on child welfare and rights, related to Save the Children's work overseas and in the UK. No unsolicited features. Illustrations: colour and b&w photos. Founded 1920.

## The World Today

The Royal Institute of International Affairs, Chatham House, 10 St James's Square, London SW1Y 4LE
*tel* 020-7957 5712 *fax* 020-7957 5710
*email* wt@riia.org
*website* www.theworldtoday.org
*Editor* Graham Walker, *Send material to* Michelle Mannion, Assistant Editor
Monthly £2.50

Analysis of international issues and current events by journalists, diplomats, politicians and academics. Length: 1600–2300 words. Payment: nominal. Founded 1945.

## Writers' Forum

Writers' International Ltd, PO Box 3229, Bournemouth BH1 1ZS
*website* www.writers-forum.com
*Publisher* John Jenkins
10 p.a. £3 (£28 p.a., £40 Europe)

Welcomes articles on any aspect of the craft and business of writing. Length: 800–2000 words. Payment: by arrangement. Poetry and short story competitions in each issue. Founded 1993.

## Writers' News

1st Floor, Victoria House, 143–145 The Headrow, Leeds LS1 5RL
*tel* 0113-200 2929 *fax* 0113-200 2928
*website* www.writersnews.co.uk
*Editor* Derek Hudson
Monthly £44.90 p.a. (£39.90 p.a. CC/DD)

News, competitions and articles on all aspects of writing. Length: 400–1500 words. Illustrations: colour, line, half-tone. Payment: by arrangement. Founded 1989.

## Writing Magazine

1st Floor, Victoria House, 143–145 The Headrow, Leeds LS1 5RL
*tel* 0113-200 2929 *fax* 0113-200 2928
*website* www.writersnews.co.uk
*Editor* Derek Hudson
Bi-monthly £3.20 (free to *Writers' News* subscribers)

Articles on all aspects of writing. Length: 400–1500 words. Illustrations: full colour, line, half-tone. Payment: by arrangement. Founded 1992.

## Yachting Monthly

IPC Media Ltd, Room 2215, King's Reach Tower, Stamford Street, London SE1 9LS
*tel* 020-7261 6040 *fax* 020-7261 7555
*Editor* Paul Gelder
Monthly £3.30

Articles on all aspects of seamanship, navigation, the handling of sailing craft, and their design, construction and equipment. Well-written narrative accounts of cruises in yachts. Length: up to 2250 words (articles), up to 2500 words (narratives). Illustrations: colour transparencies and prints, cartoons. Payment: quoted on acceptance. Founded 1906.

## Yachting World

IPC Media Ltd, Room 2332, King's Reach Tower, Stamford Street, London SE1 9LS
*tel* 020-7261 6800 *fax* 020-7261 6818
*email* yachting_world@ipc.media.com
*website* www.yachtingworld.com
*Editor* Andrew Bray
Monthly £3.60

Practical articles of an original nature, dealing with sailing and boats. Length: 1500–2000 words. Payment: varies. Illustrations: colour transparencies, drawings, cartoons. Founded 1894.

## Yoga & Health

SDB Marketing, PO Box 16969, London E1W 1FY
*tel* 020-7480 5456 *fax* 020-7480 5456
*website* www.yogaandhealthmag.com
*Editor* Jane Sill
Monthly £2.50

Payment: by arrangement. Founded 1993.

## Yorkshire Ridings Magazine

33 Beverley Road, Driffield, Yorkshire YO25 6SD
*tel* (01377) 253232 *fax* (01377) 253232
*Editor* Winston Halstead
Bi-monthly £1.40

Articles exclusively about people, life and character of the 3 Ridings of Yorkshire. Length: up to 1000 words. Payment: approx. £35–£40 per published page. Illustrations: colour, b&w photos; prints preferred. Founded 1964.

**You** – see Mail on Sunday, page 11

## Young People Now

Haymarket Publishing Ltd, 174 Hammersmith
Road, London W6 7JP
*tel* 020-8267 4707 *fax* 0116-285 3775
*email* ypn.editorial@haynet.com
*website* www.ypnmagazine.com
*Editor* Steve Barrett
Weekly £1.75

Informative articles, highlighting issues of concern
to all those who work with young people, including
youth workers, probation and social services,
Connexions Service, teachers and volunteers.
Guidelines for contributors available on request.
Founded 1989.

## Young Writer

Glebe House, Weobley, Herefordshire HR4 8SD
*tel* (01544) 318901 *fax* (01544) 318901
*email* editor@youngwriter.org
*website* www.youngwriter.org
*Editor* Kate Jones
3 p.a. £3.50 (£10 for 3 issues)

Specialist magazine for young writers under 18
years: ideas for them and writing by them. Includes
interviews by children with famous writers, fiction
and non-fiction pieces, poetry; also explores words
and grammar, issues related to writing (e.g.
dyslexia), plus competitions with prizes. Length: 750
or 1500 words (features), up to 400 words (news),
750 words (short stories – unless specified
otherwise in a competition), poetry of any length.
Illustrations: colour – drawings by children,
snapshots to accompany features. Payment: most
children's material is published without payment;
£25–£100 (features); £15 (cover cartoon). Free
inspection copy. Founded 1995.

## Your Cat Magazine

BPG (Stamford) Ltd, Roebuck House,
33 Broad Street, Stamford, Lincs. PE9 1RB
*tel* (01780) 766199 *fax* (01780) 766416
*email* s.parslow@bournepublishinggroup.co.uk
*Editor* Sue Parslow
Monthly £2.75

Practical advice on the care of cats and kittens,
general interest items and news on cats, and true life
tales and fiction. Length: 800–1500 words (articles),
200–300 (news), up to 1000 (short stories).
Illustrations: colour transparencies and prints.
Payment: £80 per 1000 words. Founded 1994.

## Your Dog Magazine

BPG (Stamford) Ltd, Roebuck House,
33 Broad Street, Stamford, Lincs. PE9 1RB
*tel* (01780) 766199 *fax* (01780) 766416
*email* swright@bourneppublishinggroup.co.uk

*Editor* Sarah Wright
Monthly £2.95

Articles and information of interest to dog lovers;
features on all aspects of pet dogs. Length: approx.
1500 words. Illustrations: colour transparencies,
prints and line drawings. Payment: £80 per 1000
words. Founded 1994.

## Your Horse

Emap Active, Bretton Court, Bretton,
Peterborough PE3 8DZ
*tel* (01733) 264666 *fax* (01733) 465100
*email* amanda.stevenson@emap.com
*Editor* Natasha Simmonds
Every 4 weeks £2.75

Practical horse care and riding advice for the leisure
rider and horse owner. Send feature ideas with
examples of previous published writing. Specially
commissions most material. Welcomes ideas for
articles and features. Length: 1500 words. Payment:
£120 per 1000 words. Founded 1983.

## Yours

EMAP Esprit Ltd, Bretton Court,
Peterborough PE3 8DZ
*tel* (01733) 264666 *fax* (01733) 465266
*Editor* Valery McConnell
Monthly £1.20

Features and news about and/or of interest to the
over-50s age group, including nostalgia and short
stories. Study of magazine essential; approach in
writing in the first instance. Length: articles up to
1000 words, short stories up to 1800 words. Illustrations: preferably colour transparencies/prints but
will consider good b&w prints/line drawings,
cartoons. Payment: at the Editor's discretion or by
agreement. Founded 1973.

## Zest

National Magazine House, 72 Broadwick Street,
London W1F 9EP
*tel* 020-7439 5000 *fax* 020-7312 3750
*email* zest.mail@natmags.co.uk
*Editor* Alison Pylkkanen, *Send material to* Susie
Whalley, Feature Editor
Monthly £2.80

Health and beauty magazine. Commissioned
material only: health, fitness and beauty, features,
news and shorts. Length: 50–2000 words.
Illustrations: colour and b&w photos and line.
Payment: by arrangement. Founded 1994.

# Newspapers and magazines overseas

Listings are given for newspapers and magazines in Australia (below), Canada (page 113), New Zealand (page 116) and South Africa (page 117). For information on submitting material to the USA, see page 120. Newspapers are listed under the towns in which they are published.

## AUSTRALIA

### (Adelaide) Advertiser
121 King William Street, Adelaide, SA 5000
*tel* (08) 8206 2000 *fax* (08) 8206 3669
*London office* PO Box 481, 1 Virginia Street,
London E1 9BD
*tel* 020-7702 1355 *fax* 020-7702 1384
*Editor* Mel Mansell
Daily Mon–Fri 90c, Sat $1.30

Descriptive and news background material, 400–800 words, preferably with pictures; also cartoons. Founded 1858.

### (Adelaide) Sunday Mail
121 King William Street, Adelaide, SA 5000
*postal address* GPO Box 339, Adelaide, SA 5001
*tel* (08) 8206 2000 *fax* (08) 8206 3646
*website* www.sundaymail.com.au
*Editor* Phillip Gardner
Sun $1.60

Founded 1912.

### Aircraft & Aerospace Asia Pacific
GPO Box 606, Sydney 2001
*tel* (02) 9213 8267 *fax* (02) 9281 2750
*email* dougnancarrow@yaffa.com.au
*website* www.yaffa.com.au
*Editor* Doug Nancarrow
10 p.a.

Aviation business magazine for industry professionals focusing on Asia Pacific. Welcomes ideas for features. Length: 800–2000 words (features). Payment: on application. Illustrations: digital images only. Founded 1981.

### AQ – Journal of Contemporary Analysis
Australian Institute of Political Science,
PO Box 145, Balmain, NSW 2041
*tel* (02) 9810 5642 *fax* (02) 9810 2406
*website* www.aips.net.au
6 p.a. $60.50 p.a. individuals/schools, $104.50 p.a. organisations ($120 overseas)

Peer-reviewed articles for the informed non-specialist on politics, law, economics, social issues, etc. Length: 3500 words preferred. Payment: none. Founded 1929.

### Art and Australia
Art and Australia Pty Ltd. 11 Cecil Street,
Paddington NSW 2021
*tel* (02) 9331 4455 *fax* (02) 9331 4577
*email* info@artandaustralia.com.au
*website* www.artandaustralia.com.au
*Editor* Claire Armstrong
Quarterly A$17.50, A$108 p.a.

Articles with a contemporary perspective on Australia's traditional and current art, and on international art of Australian relevance, plus exhibition and book reviews. Length: 2000–3000 words (articles), 600–1200 words (reviews). Payment: $250 per 1000 words. Illustrations: colour transparencies. Founded 1916 as *Art in Australia*.

### Art Monthly Australia
GPO Box 804, Canberra, ACT 2601
*tel* (02) 6125 3988 *fax* (02) 6125 9794
*email* art.monthly@anu.edu.au
*website* www.artmonthly.org.au
*Editor* Deborah Clark
10 p.a. March–Dec $6.00

Contemporary visual arts: reviews, commentary, news and book reviews. Specially commissions most material but will consider unsolicited material. Welcomes ideas for articles and features. Length: negotiable. Payment: $200 per 1000 words.

### Australian Bookseller & Publisher
Thorpe-Bowker, Building C3, 85 Turner Street,
Port Melbourne, Victoria 3207
*tel* (03) 8645 0300 *fax* (03) 8645 0333
*email* bookseller.publisher@thorpe.com.au
*website* www.thorpe.com.au
*Editor* Rose Michael
Monthly $95 p.a. ($110 p.a. NZ/Asia; $150 p.a. USA/Canada; $140 p.a. UK/Europe)

Founded 1921.

### The Australian Financial Review
GPO Box 506, Sydney, NSW 2001
*tel* (02) 9282 2512 *fax* (02) 9282 3137
*Editor* Glenn Burge
*London office* 1 Bath Street, London EC1V 9LB
*tel* 020-7688 2777 *fax* 020-7688 3499
*New York office* Suite 1720, 317 Madison Avenue, New York, NY 10017

*tel* 212-398-9494
Daily Mon–Fri $2.20

Investment business and economic news and reviews; government and politics, production, banking, commercial, and Stock Exchange statistics; company analysis. General features in Friday *Weekend Review* supplement.

## Australian Flying

Yaffa Publishing Group, 17–21 Bellevue Street, Surry Hills, NSW 2010
*tel* (02) 9281 2333 *fax* (02) 9281 2750
*email* shelleyross@yaffa.com.au
*Editor* Shelley Ross
6 p.a. $6.25

Covers the Australian aviation industry, from light aircraft to airliners. Payment: by arrangement.

## Australian Geographic

PO Box 321, Terrey Hills, NSW 2084
*tel* (02) 9473 6777 *fax* (02) 9473 6701
*website* www.australiangeographic.com.au
*Managing Editor* Terri Cowley
Quarterly $49.50 p.a.

Articles and features about Australia, particularly life, technology and wildlife in remote parts of the country. Material mostly commissioned. Length: articles, 300–800 words, features, 2000–3000 words. Illustrations: all commissioned. Payment: from $500 per 1000 words; illustrations by negotiation. Founded 1986.

## Australian Home Beautiful

Private Bag 9700, North Sydney, NSW 2059
*tel* (02) 9464 3218 *fax* (02) 9464 3263
*email* homebeaut@pacpubs.com.au
*Editor* Andrea Jones
Monthly $5.90

Interior decoration, furnishing, gardening, cookery, etc. Unsolicited MSS not accepted. Founded 1925.

## Australian Journal of Politics and History

School of Political Science and International Studies and the Department of History, University of Queensland, St Lucia, Queensland 4067
*tel* (07) 3365 3163 *fax* (07) 3365 1388
*email* i.ward@mailbox.uq.edu.au
*Editor* Ian Ward and Andrew Bonnell
4 p.a. $66/£38 p.a. individuals; $144/£110 institutions

Australian, European, Asian, Pacific and international articles. Special feature: regular surveys of Australian Foreign Policy and State and Commonwealth politics. Length: 8000 words max. Illustrations: line, only when necessary. Payment: none.

## Australian Photography

Yaffa Publishing Group, 17–21 Bellevue Street, Surry Hills, NSW 2010
*tel* (02) 9281 2333 *fax* (02) 9281 2750
*email* robertkeeley@yaffa.com.au
*Editor* Robert Keeley
*London office* 2 Milford Road, London W13 9HZ
*tel* 020-8579 4836
*Contact* Robert Logan
Monthly $5.95

Illustrated articles: picture-taking techniques, technical. Length: 1200–2500 words with colour and/or b&w prints or slides. Payment: $80 per page. Founded 1950.

## Australian Powerboat

Yaffa Publishing Group, GPO Box 606, Sydney, NSW 2001
*tel* (02) 9281 2333 *fax* (02) 9281 2750
*Editor* Graham Lloyd
*London office* 2 Milford Road, London W13 9HZ
*tel* 020-8579 4836
*Contact* Robert Logan
Bi-monthly $5.20

Articles and news on boats and boating, racing, water skiing and products. Length: 1500 words (articles), 200 words (news). Illustrations: colour (transparencies preferred). Payment: $100 per 1000 words; from $30. Founded 1976.

## The Australian Women's Weekly

Australian Consolidated Press Ltd, 54 Park Street, Sydney, NSW 1028
*postal address* GPO Box 4178, Sydney, NSW 1028
*tel* (02) 9282 8000 *fax* (02) 9267 4459
*email* dthomas@acp.com.au
*Editor* Deborah Thomas
Monthly $5.20

Fiction and features. Length: fiction 1000–5000 words; features 1000–4000 words plus colour or b&w photos. Payment: according to length and merit. Fiction illustrations: sketches by own artists and freelances.

## The Big Issue Australia

GPO Box 4911VV, Melbourne, Victoria 3001
*tel* (03) 9663 4522
*email* editor@bigissue.org.au
*Editor* Martin Hughes
Fortnightly $3

Profiles and features of general interest and on social issues and entertainment, arts reviews. No fiction. Length: 1000–2500 words (features), up to 900 words (news), 200 words (reviews). Payment: 15c per word (features), $30 (reviews). Colour and b&w cartoons (approx. $100); photos $150–$200. Founded 1996.

## (Brisbane) The Courier-Mail

Queensland Newspapers Pty Ltd, Campbell Street,
Bowen Hills, Brisbane, Queensland 4006
*tel* (07) 3666 8000 *fax* (07) 3666 6696
*email* cmletters@qnp.newsltd.com.au
*website* www.news.com.au
*Editor-in-Chief* C. Mitchell
Daily $1

## (Brisbane) The Sunday Mail

Queensland Newspapers Pty Ltd, PO Box 130,
Campbell Street, Bowen Hills, Brisbane,
Queensland 4006
*tel* 300 30 40 20 *fax* (07) 3666 6787
*email* smletters@qnp.newsltd.com.au
*Editor* Michael Prain
Sun $1.60 inc. GST

Anything of general interest. Length: up to 1500
words. Illustrations: line, photos, b&w and colour,
cartoons. Rejected MSS returned if postage
enclosed.

## The Bulletin

GPO Box 3957, Sydney, NSW 1028
*tel* (02) 9282 8227  *fax* (02) 9267 4359
*email* bulletin@acp.com.au
*website* www.bulletin.ninemsn.com.au
*Editor* Garry Linnezi
Weekly $5.50

'Australia's most quoted news magazine'. News, features
and comment on current issues. Length: 1000–2000
words (articles), 1000–2000 words (features), 500–2000
(news). Payment: by negotiation. Founded 1880.

## Camera

Horwitz Publications Pty Ltd, 55 Chandos Street,
St Leonards, NSW 2065
*tel* (02) 9901 6100 *fax* (02) 9901 6198
*email* paulb@horwitz.com.au
*Editor* Paul Burrows
Monthly $6.50

Magazine for amateur photographers and digital
imaging enthusiasts covering techniques, test
reports, new products. Considers unsolicited
material. Welcomes ideas for articles and features.
Length: 750–1500 words (features/articles).
Illustrations: colour prints and transparencies.
Payment: $300–$500. Founded 1979.

## Cordite Poetry Review

PO BOx 14022, City Mail Processing Centre,
Melbourne 8000
*email* cordite@cordite.org.au
*website* www.cordite.org.au
*Editor* David Prater
4 p.a. Free

Publishes on the internet poetry by new and
emerging Australian authors, alongside feature

articles, reviews, news and gossip items, audio
poetry and special competitions. Also welcomes
material from overseas writers. Length: 100–3000
words (articles and features). Payment: $50–$100.
Illustrations: colour and b&w. Founded 1997.

## Dolly

GPO Box 5201, Sydney, NSW 2001
*tel* (02) 9282 8437 *fax* (02) 9267 4911
*website* www.ninemsn.com.au/dolly
*Editor* Virginia Knight
Monthly $4.60

Features on teen fashion, health and beauty,
personalities, music, social issues and how to cope
with growing up, etc. Length: not less than 1000
words. Illustrations: colour, b&w, line, cartoons.
Payment: by arrangement. Founded 1970.

## EA Today Magazine

PO Box 199, Alexandria, NSW 1435
*tel* (02) 9353 0620 *fax* (02) 9353 0613
*email* electaus@fpc.com.au
*website* www.electronicsaustralia.com.au
*Editor* Graham Cattley
Monthly $6.95

Articles on technical TV and radio, hi-fi, popular
electronics. Length: up to 2000 words. Payment: by
arrangement. Illustrations: line, half-tone, cartoons.

## Harper's Bazaar

ACP Publishing Pty Ltd, 54 Park Street, Sydney,
NSW 2000
*tel* (02) 9282 8703 *fax* (02) 9267 4456
*email* bazaar@acp.com.au
*Editor* Alison Veness-McGourty
10 p.a. $7.50

Fashion, health and beauty, celebrity news, plus
features. Length: 3000 words. Illustrations: colour
and b&w photos. Founded 1998.

## HQ Magazine

35–51 Mitchell Street, McMahons Point, NSW 2060
*tel* (02) 9464 2604 *fax* (02) 9464 3504
*email* hq@pacpubs.com.au
*Editor* Ms Alex Craig
Bi-monthly $7.95

General interest features and profiles for a literate
readership. Length: 1500–5000 words. Illustrations:
colour and b&w photos. Payment: by negotiation.
Founded 1989.

## (Launceston) Examiner

Box 99, PO Launceston, Tasmania 7250
*tel* (03) 633 67111 *fax* (03) 633 47328
*Editor* Rod Scott
Daily $1

Accepts freelance material. Payment: by
arrangement.

## Meanjin

Meanjin Company Ltd, 131 Barry Street, Carlton,
Victoria 3054
*tel* (03) 8344 6950 *fax* (03) 9347 2550
*email* meanjin@unimelb.edu.au
*website* www.meanjin.unimelb.edu.au
*Editor* Dr Ian Britain
Quarterly $19.95

Cultural commentary, fiction, poetry, essays and
discussion of contemporary issues, e.g. biography,
drugs, travel. See website for submission guidelines.
Payment: $50 per poetry item, min. $100 prose.
Founded 1941.

## (Melbourne) Age

The Age Company Ltd, 250 Spencer Street,
Melbourne, Victoria 3000
*tel* (03) 9600 4211 *fax* (03) 9601 2412
*London office* 1 Bath Street, London EC1V 9LB
*tel* 020-7688 2777 *fax* 020-7688 3499
*Editor-in-Chief* Michael Gawenda, *Deputy Editor*
Simon Mann
Daily Mon–Fri $1.10, Sat $1.90, Sun $1.50

Independent liberal morning daily; room
occasionally for outside matter. *Good Weekend* and
*Sunday Life* (illustrated weekend magazines);
*Insight; A2* (includes literary reviews). Accepts
occasional freelance material.

## (Melbourne) Herald Sun

HWT Tower, 40 City Road, Southbank, Victoria 3006
*tel* (03) 9292 1686 *fax* (03) 9292 2112
*Editor* Peter Blunden
*Send material to* Darrell Richardson, Syndications
Manager
Daily Mon–Fri $1, Sat $1.20, Sun $1.50

Accepts freelance articles, preferably with
illustrations. Length: up to 750 words. Illustrations:
half-tone, line, cartoons. Payment: on merit.

## (Melbourne) Sunday Herald Sun

HWT Tower, 40 City Road, Southbank, Victoria 3006
*tel* (03) 9292 2000 *fax* (03) 9292 2080
*Editor* Alan Howe
Weekly $1.50

Accepts freelance articles, preferably with
illustrations. Length: up to 2000 words.
Illustrations: colour. Payment: on merit.

## New Woman

Level 6, 187 Thomas Street, Haymarket, NSW 2000
*tel* (02) 9581 9400 *fax* (02) 9211 9540
*Editor* Sue Wheeler
Monthly $5.95

Irreverent and humorous style of magazine for the
single, professional woman aged 25–35. Includes
celebrity gossip, fashion, beauty, sex and relationships, and entertainment reviews. Founded 1989.

## NW Magazine

54 Park Street, Sydney, NSW 2000
*tel* (02) 9282 8285 *fax* (02) 9264 6005
*Editor* Louisa Hatfield
Weekly $3.50

News and features on celebrities, food, new
products, fashion and astrology. Illustrated.
Payment: by negotiation. Founded 1993.

## Overland

PO Box 14428, Melbourne, Victoria 8001
*tel* (03) 9688 4163 *fax* (03) 9687 7614
*email* overland@vu.edu.au
*Editors* Nathan Hollier, Kath Wilson
Quarterly US$60 p.a. or Aus $42 p.a

Literary and cultural. Australian material preferred.
Payment: by arrangement. Illustrations: line, half-
tone, cartoons.

## People Magazine

GPO Box 2860, Sydney, NSW 2000
*tel* (02) 9288 9648 *fax* (02) 9283 6179
*Editor* Tom Foster
Weekly $3.30

National weekly news-pictorial. Mainly celebrity
stories. Photos depicting exciting happenings,
glamour, show business, unusual occupations, rites,
customs. Payment: $300 per page, text and photos.

## (Perth) The Sunday Times

34–40 Stirling Street, Perth, Western Australia 6000
*tel* (08) 9326 8476 *fax* (08) 9226 8316
*Editor* Brett McCarthy
Sun $1.30

Topical articles to 800 words. Payment: on
acceptance. Founded 1897.

## (Perth) The West Australian

50 Hasler Road, Osborne Park,
Western Australia 6017
*tel* (08) 9482 3111 *fax* (08) 9482 3452
*website* www.thewest.com.au
*Editor* Brian Rogers
Daily Mon–Fri 88c, Sat $1.60

Articles and sketches about people and events in
Australia and abroad. Length: 300–700 words.
Payment: Award rates or better. Illustrations: line,
half-tone. Founded 1833.

## Quadrant

437 Darling Street, Balmain, NSW 2041
*postal address* PO Box 82, Balmain, NSW 2041
*tel* (02) 9818 1155 *fax* (02) 9818 1422
*email* quadrnt@ozemail.com.au
*Editor* P.P. McGuinness
*Literary Editor* Les Murray
Monthly $6.50

Articles, short stories, verse, etc. Prose length: 2000–5000 words. Payment: min. $90 articles/stories, $60 reviews, $40 poems; illustrations by arrangement.

## Reader's Digest (Australia)
PO Box 4353, Sydney, NSW 2001
*tel* (02) 9690 6111 *fax* (02) 9690 6211
*Editor-in-Chief* Thomas Moore
Monthly $5.79 (inc. GST)

Articles on Australian subjects by commission only. No unsolicited MSS accepted. Length: 2500–5000 words. Payment: up to $6000 per article; brief filler paragraphs, $50–$250. Illustrations: half-tone, colour.

## Rock
Wild Publications Pty Ltd, PO Box 415, Prahran, Victoria 3181
*tel* (03) 9826 8482 *fax* (03) 9826 3787
*email* rock@wild.com.au
*website* www.rock.com.au
*Editor* Chris Baxter
Quarterly $8.99

Australian rockclimbing and mountaineering articles, features and news. See website for guidelines to contibutions. Length: 2000 words (articles/features), 200 words (news). Illustrations: colour transparencies. Payment: $85 per page (words and pictures). Founded 1978.

## The Sun-Herald
GPO Box 506, Sydney, NSW 2001
*tel* (02) 9282 2822 *fax* (02) 9282 2151
*London office* John Fairfax (UK) Ltd, 1 Bath Street, London EC1V 9LB
*tel* 020-7688 2777 *fax* 020-7688 3499
*Editor* Philip McLean
Weekly $1.50

Topical articles to 1000 words; news plus sections on current affairs, entertainment, finance, sport and travel. Payment: by arrangement.

## (Sydney) The Daily Telegraph
News Ltd, 2 Holt Street, Surry Hills, NSW 2010
*tel* (02) 9288 3000 *fax* (02) 9288 3311
*Editor-in-Chief* Col Allan
Daily Mon–Fri 90c, Sat $1.20

Modern feature articles and series of Australian or world interest. Length: 1000–2000 words. Payment: according to merit/length.

## The Sydney Morning Herald
PO Box 506, Sydney, NSW 2001
*tel* (02) 9282 2858
*London office* 1 Bath Street, London EC1V 9LB
*tel* 020-7688 2777 *fax* 020-7688 3499
*Editor* Phil Scott
Daily $1.10

Saturday edition has pages of literary criticism and also magazine articles, plus glossy colour magazine. Topical articles 600–4000 words. Payment: varies, but minimum $100 per 1000 words. Illustrations: all types. Founded 1831.

## (Sydney) The Sunday Telegraph
News Ltd, 2 Holt Street, Surry Hills, Sydney, NSW 2010
*tel* (02) 9288 3000 *fax* (02) 9288 3311
*Editor* Jeni Cooper
Weekly $1.60

News and features. Illustrations: transparencies. Payment: varies. Founded 1935.

## Traveltalk West Coast
PO Box 329, North Beach, Western Australia 6920
*tel* (08) 9240 3888 *fax* (08) 9240 2796
*email* jane@traveltalk.biz
*website* www.traveltalk.biz
*Editor* Jane Hammond Foster
Quarterly $3.95

Travel news and features focusing on Western Australia and popular destinations, in Australia and international, servied by direct flights from Perth. Prefers to receive a list of ideas and sample of material initially. Length: 600 words (articles), 1200–1800 words (features), 150–450 words (news). Payment: 40 cents per printed word. Founded 2002.

## Vive
125–127 Little Eveleigh Street, Redfern, NSW 2016
*tel* (02) 9318 0500 *fax* (02) 9318 1140
*email* vive@pol.net.au
*Editor* Angie Buttrose
Bi-monthly $7.95

A business/lifestyle publication aimed at successful executive women. Content includes business profiles, career-related features, travel, food, beauty, working mothers. Specially commissions most material. Welcomes ideas for articles and features via email. Do not send unsolicited material. Length: 1500–2000 words (articles/features). Payment: 65c per word. Illustrations: transparencies, colour and b&w prints and artwork; all commissioned. Founded 1996.

## Vogue Australia
180 Bourke Road, Alexandria NSW 2015
*postal address* PO Box 199, Alexandria NSW 2015
*tel* (02) 9353 6666 *fax* (02) 9353 6600
*Editor* Kirstie Clements
Monthly $7.50

Articles and features on fashion, beauty, health, business, people and the arts of interest to the modern woman of style and high spending power. Ideas welcome. Length: from 1000 words. Illustrations: colour and b&w. Founded 1959.

## Wild

Wild Publications Pty Ltd, PO Box 415, Prahran,
Victoria 3181
*tel* (03) 9826 8482 *fax* (03) 9826 3787
*email* wild@wild.com.au
*website* www.wild.com.au
*Editor* Chris Baxter
4 p.a. $7.99

'Australia's wilderness adventure magazine.'
Illustrated articles of first-hand experiences of the
Australian wilderness, plus book and track reviews,
product tests. See website for guidelines for
contributors. Length: 2500 words (articles), 200
words (news). Colour transparencies. Payment:
$125 per published page. Founded 1981.

## Woman's Day

54–58 Park Street, Sydney, NSW 2000
*tel* (02) 9282 8000 *fax* (02) 9267 4360
*Editor-in-Chief* Alana House
Weekly $3.60

National women's magazine; news, show business,
fiction, fashion, general articles, cookery, home
economy, health, beauty.

# CANADA

## The Beaver: Canada's History Magazine

Canada's National History Society, Suite 478,
167 Lombard Avenue, Winnipeg, Manitoba R3B 0T6
*tel* 204-988-9300 *fax* 204-988-9309
*website* www.thebeaver.ca
*Editor* Annalee Greenberg
Bi-monthly $29.95 p.a. ($37.95 USA, $44.95 p.a.
elsewhere)

Articles on Canadian history. Length: 1500–3000
words, with illustrations. Payment: on acceptance.
Illustrations: b&w and colour archival photos or
drawings. Founded 1920.

## C international contemporary art

PO Box 5, Station B, Toronto, Ontario M5T 2T2
*tel* 416-539-9495 *fax* 416-539-9903
*email* general@cmagazine.com
Quarterly US$8.25

Arts and artists' projects, features, reviews. Accepts
submissions. Length: features (varies), reviews (500
words). Illustrations: transparencies, photos. Payment:
$250–$500 features, $100 reviews. Founded 1972.

## Canadian Literature

University of British Columbia, Buchanan E158,
1866 Main Mall, Vancouver, BC V6T 1Z1
*tel* 604-882-2780 *fax* 604-822-5504
*Editor* E.M. Kröller
4 p.a. $45 p.a. individual; $60 p.a. institutions
(outside Canada add $20 postage)

Articles on Canadian writers and writing in English
and French. No fiction. Length: up to 5000 words.
Payment: none. Founded 1959.

## Canadian Theatre Review (CTR)

Drama Program, University of Guelph, Guelph,
Ontario N1G 2W1
*Contact* Editorial Committee
Quarterly $10.50 ($35 p.a.)

Feature and review articles on Canadian theatre
aimed at theatre professionals, academics and
general audience; book and play reviews. Send MSS
accompanied by PC compatible disk. Length:
2000–3000 words. Illustrations: b&w. Payment:
$200–$275 (features/articles), $75 (book/play
reviews). Founded 1974.

## Canadian Writer's Journal

PO Box 5180, New Liskeard, Ontario P0J 1P0
*tel* 705-647-5424 *fax* 705-647-8366
*email* cwj@cwj.ca
*website* www.cwj.ca
*Editor* Deborah Ranchuk
Bi-monthly $35 p.a.

News on markets and articles on writers' aspirations
for dedicated apprentice and professional Canadian
writers. Considers unsolicited material. Founded
1984.

## Chatelaine

One Mount Pleasant Road, Toronto,
Ontario M4Y 2Y5
*tel* 416-764-1888
*Editor* Rona Maynard
Monthly $2.99

Women's interest articles; Canadian angle preferred.
Payment: on acceptance; from $1000.

## The Dalhousie Review

Dalhousie University, Halifax, Nova Scotia B3H 4R2
*tel* 902-494-2541 *fax* 902-494-3561
*email* Dalhousie.Review@dal.ca
*website* www.dal.ca/~dalrev/
*Editor* Robert Martin
3 p.a. ($32.10 p.a., $85.60 for 3 years; ($40/$100
outside Canada)

Articles on history, literature, political science,
philosophy, sociology, popular culture, fine arts;
short fiction; verse; book reviews. Usually not more
than 3 stories and 10–12 poems in any one issue.
Length: prose, up to 5000 words; verse, less than 40
words. Contributors receive 2 copies of issue and 10
offprints of their work.

## Descant

PO Box 314, Station P, Toronto, Ontario M5S 2S8
*tel* 416-593-2557 *fax* 416-593-9362
*email* descant@web.net

*website* descant.on.ca
*Editor* Karen Mulhallen
Quarterly $15

Literary magazine: short fiction, poetry and essays, previously unpublished. Payment: $100 (articles and fiction) on publication. Illustrations: b&w. Founded 1970.

## Equinox

11450 Albert-Hudon Blvd, Montreal,
QC H1G 3J9
*tel* 514-327-4464 *fax* 514-327-0514
*email* eqxmag@globetrotter.net
*Editor* Martin Silverstone
Bi-monthly ($22.95 p.a. Canada; Can.$29 p.a. USA; Can.$35 elsewhere)

Magazine of discovery in science, human cultures, technology and geography. Accepts articles on hard science topics (length: 250–350 words); welcomes queries (2–3-page outline) for specific assignments. No phone queries please. Illustrations: colour transparencies. Payment: by arrangement. Founded 1982.

## The Fiddlehead

Campus House, 11 Garland Court,
UNB PO Box 4400, Frederiction,
NB E3B 5A3
*tel* 506-453-3501
*email* fid@nbnet.nb.ca
*website* www.lib.unb.ca/texts/fiddlehead
*Editor* Ross Leckie
Quarterly US$10 (US$25 p.a.)

Reviews, poetry, short stories. Payment: approx. $20 per printed page. Founded 1945.

## (Hamilton) The Spectator

44 Frid Street, Hamilton, Ontario L8N 3G3
*tel* 905-526-3333
*website* www.hamiltonspectator.com
*Publisher* Ms Jagoda S. Pike
Daily Mon–Fri 75c Sat $1.75

Articles of general interest, political analysis and background; interviews, stories of Canadians abroad. Length: 800 words maximum. Payment: rate varies. Founded 1846.

## Inuit Art Quarterly

2081 Merivale Road, Ottawa, Ontario K2G 1G9
*tel* 613-224-8189 *fax* 613-224-2907
*email* iaq@inuitart.org
*website* www.inuitart.org
*Editor* Marybelle Mitchell
Quarterly $6.25

Features, original research, artists' perspectives, news. Freelance contributors are expected to have a thorough knowledge of the arts. Length: varies. Illustrations: colour and b&w photos and line. Payment: by arrangement. Founded 1985.

## Journal of Canadian Studies

Trent University, Peterborough, Ontario K9J 7B8
*tel* 705-748-1279 *fax* 705-748-1110
*email* jcs_rec@trentu.ca
*Editors* Stephen Bocking, Jill Smith
Quarterly US$50 p.a. (US$60 p.a. institutions)

Major academic review of Canadian studies. Articles of general as well as scholarly interest on history, politics, literature, society, arts. Length: 7000–10,000 words.

## The Malahat Review

University of Victoria, PO Box 1700 STN CSC,
Victoria, BC V8W 2Y2
*tel* 250-721-8524
*email* malahat@uvic.ca (queries only)
*website* www.malahatreview.com
*Editor* John Barton
Quarterly $35 p.a. ($40 p.a. overseas)

Short stories, poetry, short plays, reviews. Payment: $30 per magazine page. Illustrations: half-tone. Founded 1967.

## Neo-opsis Science Fiction Magazine

4129 Carey Road, Victoria, BC V8Z 4G5
*tel* 250-881-8893
*email* neoopsis@shaw
*website* www.neo-opsis.ca
*Editor* Karl Johanson
Quarterly £6.95

Science fiction short stories, articles, opinion columns and reviews. Considers unsolicited material. Length: up to 4000 words (articles), up to 6000 words (short stories). Illustrations: b&w cartoons. Payment: 2.5 cents per word with max. of $125 for short stories; $30 per cartoon. Founded 2003.

## Performing Arts & Entertainment in Canada (PA&E)

104 Glenrose Avenue, Toronto, Ontario M4T 1K8
*tel* 416-484-4534 *fax* 416-484-6214
*Editor* Sarah Hood, *Send material to* George Hencz
Quarterly $8 p.a. ($14 p.a. elsewhere)

Feature articles on Canadian theatre, music, dance and film artists and organisations; technical articles on scenery, lighting, make-up, costumes, etc. Length: 600–1200 words. Payment: $150–$175, one month after publication. Illustrations: b&w photos, colour slides. Founded 1961.

## Photo Life

1 Dundas Street West, Suite 2500, PO Box 84,
Toronto, Ontario M5G 1Z3
*tel* 800-905-7468 *fax* 800-664-2739
*email* editor@photolife.com
*website* www.photolife.com
*Editors* Anita Dammer, Darwin Wiggett
6 p.a. $4.50 Can., US$3.95

Covers all aspects of photography of interest to amateur and professional photographers. Length: 800–1500 words. Illustrations: colour and b&w photos. Payment: by arrangement. Founded 1976.

## Queen's Quarterly

Queen's University, Kingston, Ontario K7L 3N6
*tel* 613-533-2667 *fax* 613-533-6822
*email* qquarter@post.queensu.ca
*website* www.info.queensu.ca/quarterly
*Editor* Dr Boris Castel
Quarterly $6.50 ($20 p.a.; $40 p.a. institutions)

A multidisciplinary scholarly journal aimed at the general educated reader – articles, short stories and poems. Length: 2500–3500 words (articles), 2000 (stories). Payment: by negotiation. Founded 1893.

## Quill & Quire

70 The Esplanade, Suite 210, Toronto,
Ontario M5E 1R2
*tel* 416-360-0044 *fax* 416-955-0794
*email* info@quillandquire.com
*Editor* Scott Anderson
12 p.a. $59.95 p.a. (outside Canada $95p.a.)

Articles of interest about the Canadian book trade. Payment: from $100. Illustrations: line, half-tone. Subscription includes Canadian Publishers Directory (2 p.a.). Founded 1935.

## Reader's Digest (Canada)

1100 René Levesque Blvd. W, Montreal,
Quebec H3B 5H5
*tel* 514-940-0751
*Editor* Murray Lewis
Monthly $3.25

Original articles on all subjects of broad general appeal, thoroughly researched and professionally written. Outline or query only. Length: 3000 words approx. Payment: from $2700. Also previously published material. Illustrations: line, half-tone, colour.

## (Toronto) The Globe and Mail

444 Front Street West, Toronto, Ontario M5V 2S9
*Publisher* Phillip Crawley, *Editor-in-Chief* Edward Greenspon
Daily 60c

Unsolicited material considered. Payment: by arrangement. Founded 1844.

## Toronto Life

59 Front Street East, Toronto, Ontario M5E 1B3
*tel* 416-364-3333 *fax* 416-861-1169
*website* www.torontolife.com
*Editor* John Macfarlane
Monthly $3.95

Articles, profiles on Toronto and Torontonians. Illustrations: line, half-tone, colour. Founded 1966.

## Toronto Star

One Yonge Street, Toronto, Ontario M5E 1E6
*tel* 416-367-2000
*website* www.thestar.com
*London office* Level 4A, PO Box 495, Virginia Street, London E1 9XY
*tel* 020-7833 0791
Daily Mon–Fri 30c, Sat $1, Sun 75c

Features, life, world/national politics. Payment: by arrangement. Founded 1892.

## (Vancouver) Province

200 Granville Street, Suite 1, Vancouver,
BC V6C 3N3
*tel* 604-605-2063 *fax* 604-606-2720
*Editor-in-Chief* Vivienne Sosnowski
Daily Mon–Fri 70c, Sun $1.40

Founded 1898.

## Vancouver Sun

200 Granville Street, Vancouver, BC V6C 3N3
*tel* 604-605-2180 *fax* 604-605-2323
*email* intouch@png.canwest.com
*website* www.vancouversun.com
*London office* Canwest News, 8 Heath Mansions, Hampstead Grove, London NW3 6SL
*tel* 020-7435 5103
*Editor-in-Chief* Patricia Graham
Daily Mon–Thu 75c; Fri, Sat $1.40

*Mix* arts magazine. Travel, Op-Ed pieces considered. Payment: by arrangement.

## Wascana Review of Contemporary Poetry & Short Fiction

c/o English Department, University of Regina, Regina, Sask. S4S 0A2
*tel* 306-585-4302 *fax* 306-585-4827
*website* www.uregina.ca./wrhome.htm
*Editor* Michael Trussler
Bi-annual $10 p.a. ($12 p.a. outside Canada)

Criticism, short stories, poetry, reviews. Manuscripts from freelance writers welcome. Length: prose, not more than 6000 words; verse, up to 100 lines. Payment: $3 per page for prose; $10 per printed page for verse; $3 per page for reviews. Contributors also receive 2 free copies and a year's subscription. Founded 1966.

## Winnipeg Free Press

1355 Mountain Avenue, Winnipeg, MB R2X 3B6
*tel* 204-697-7000 *fax* 204-697-7412
*website* www.winnipegfreepress.com
*Editor* Nicholas Hirst
Daily Mon–Fri 25c, Sat $1.25, Sun 35c

Some freelance articles. Payment: $100. Founded 1872.

# NEW ZEALAND

## (Auckland) New Zealand Herald
PO Box 32, Auckland
*tel* (09) 379 5050 *fax* (09) 373 6421
*email* editor@herald.co.nz
*website* www.nzherald.co.nz
*Editor* Tim Murphy *Editor-in-Chief* Gavin Ellis
Daily Mon–Fri $1.20, weekend $2.50

Topical and informative articles 800–1100 words.
Payment: minimum $150–$300. Illustrations:
colour negatives or prints. Founded 1863.

## (Auckland) Sunday News
PO Box 1327, Auckland
*tel* (09) 302 1300 *fax* (09) 358 3003
*email* editor@sunday-news.co.nz
*Editor* Clive Nelson
Sun $1.10

News, sport and showbiz, especially with NZ interest.
Illustrations: colour and b&w photos. Founded 1963.

## (Auckland) Sunday Star-Times
PO Box 1409, Auckland
*tel* (09) 302 1300 *fax* (09) 309 0258
*email* feedback@star-times.co.nz
*Editor* Cale Brett
Sun $1.80

## (Christchurch) The Press
Private Bag 4722, Christchurch
*tel* (03) 379 0940 *fax* (03) 364 8238
*email* editorial@press.co.nz
*Editor* Paul Thompson
Daily Mon–Fri 90c, Sat $1.50

Articles of general interest not more than 800
words. Illustrations: photos and line drawings,
cartoons. Payment: by arrangement.

## (Dunedin) Otago Daily Times
PO Box 181, Dunedin
*tel* (03) 477 4760 *fax* (03) 474 7422
*email* odt.editor@alliedpress.co.nz
*website* www.odt.co.nz
*Editor* R.L. Charteris
Daily 80c, Sat/Sun $1.20

Any articles of general interest up to 1000 words,
but preference is given to NZ writers. Topical
illustrations and personalities. Payment: current NZ
rates. Founded 1861.

## Hawke's Bay Today
PO Box 180, Karamu Road North, Hastings
*tel* (06) 878 5155 *fax* (06) 876 0655
*Editor* L. Pierard
Daily 70c

Limited requirements. Payment: $50 upwards for
articles, $15 upwards for photos.

## (Invercargill) The Southland Times
PO Box 805, Invercargill
*tel* (03) 218 1909 *fax* (03) 214 9905
*email* editor@stl.co.nz
*website* www.press.co.nz
*Editor* F.L. Tulett
Daily Mon–Fri 70c, Sat 80c

Articles of up to 800 words on topics of Southland
interest. Payment: by arrangement. Illustrations:
line, half-tone, colour, cartoons. Founded 1862.

## Management Magazine
Profile Publishing, PO Box 5544, Auckland
*tel* (09) 630 8940 *fax* (09) 630 1046
*email* editor@management.co.nz
*Editor* Reg Birchfield
Monthly $6.95

Articles on the practice of management skills and
techniques, individual and company profiles,
coverage of organisational leadership and
management trends and topics. A NZ/Australian
angle or application preferred. Length: 2000 words.
Payment: by arrangement; minimum 30c per word.
Illustrations: photos, line drawings.

## The Nelson Mail
PO Box 244, 15 Bridge Street, Nelson
*tel* (03) 548 7079 *fax* (03) 546 2802
*email* nml@nelsonmail.co.nz
*Editor* Bill Moore
Daily 70c

Features, articles on NZ subjects. Length: 500–1000
words. Payment: up to $100 per 1000 words.
Illustrations: half-tone, colour.

## (New Plymouth) The Daily News
PO Box 444, Currie Street, New Plymouth
*tel* (06) 758 0559 *fax* (06) 758 6849
*email* editor@tnl.co.nz
*Editor* Lance G. Butcher
Daily 90c

Articles preferably with a Taranaki connection.
Payment: by negotiation. Illustrations: half-tone,
cartoons. Founded 1857.

## New Zealand Woman's Day
Private Bag 92512, Auckland
*tel* (09) 308 2718 *fax* (09) 357 0978
*Editor* Louise Wright
Weekly $3.25

Celebrity interviews, exclusive news stories, short
stories, gossip. Length: 1000 words. Illustrations:
colour transparencies; payment according to use.
Payment: by arrangement. Founded 1989.

## New Zealand Woman's Weekly
PO Box 90–119 AMC, Auckland 1
*tel* (09) 360 3820 *fax* (09) 360 3829

*email*  editor@nzww.co.nz
*Editor*  Rowan Dixon
Weekly $3.25

Articles and features of general interest to women aged 30+ and their families: celebrities, news, health, food, fashion, DIY and home improvement, short stories. Considers unsolicited material and welcomes ideas for features and articles. Length: 800–2000 words (features/articles), 500–1500 (fiction). Illustrations: colour. Founded 1932.

## NZ House & Garden

PO Box 6341, Wellesley Street, Auckland
*tel*  (09) 353 1010 *fax* (09) 353 1020
*Editor*  Kate Coughlan
Monthly $8.95

Upmarket magazine that celebrates New Zealand's most interesting houses and beautiful gardens. Inspiration for food and entertaining, and a resource for decor. Considers unsolicited material. Welcomes ideas for articles and features. Length: 500–800 words. Payment: $400. Illustrations: colour transparencies. Founded 1994.

## She

Private Bag 92512, Wellesley Street, Auckland 1036
*tel*  (09) 308 2735 *fax* (09) 302 0667
*email*  she@acpnz.co.nz
*Editor*  Leonie Barlow
Monthly $6.20

Lifestyle magazine for women aged 25–40. Length: 1000–2000 words (features and profiles). Illustrations: colour. Payment: negotiable. Founded 1996.

## Straight Furrow

Rural Press, PO Box 4233, Auckland
*tel*  (09) 376 9786 *fax* (09) 376 9780
*Editor*  Susan Topless

Fortnightly News and features of interest to the farming/rural sector with emphasis on agri-political issues. Length: 500 words news, 1000 words features. Illustrations: colour and b&w photos. Payment: 30c per published word; $15 per published photo. Founded 1933.

## Takahe

Takahe Collective Trust, PO Box 13335, Christchurch 8001
*tel*  (03) 359 8133
3 p.a. $25 for 4 issues ($35 international)

Quality short fiction and poetry by both new and established writers. Payment: approx. $30 per issue. Founded 1989.

## The Timaru Herald

PO Box 46, Bank Street, Timaru
*tel*  (03) 684 4129 *fax* (03) 688 1042
*email*  editor@timaruherald.co.nz

*Editor* D.H. Wood
Daily 65c

Topical articles. Payment: by arrangement. Illustrations: colour or b&w prints.

## (Wellington) The Dominion Post

PO Box 3740, 40 Boulcott Street, Wellington
*tel*  (04) 474 0000 *fax* (04) 474 0350, (04) 474 0185 (editor)
*email*  editor@dompost.co.nz
*website*  www.stuff.co.nz
*Editor*  Tim Pankhurst
Daily Mon–Fri $1, Sat $1.50

General topical articles, 600 words. Payment: NZ current rates or by arrangement. News illustrations, cartoons. Founded 2002 with the merger of *The Dominion* and *The Evening Post*.

## Your Home and Garden

Australian Consolidated Press (New Zealand) Ltd, Private Bag 92512, Wellesley Street, Auckland
*tel*  (09) 308 2700 *fax* (09) 377 6725
*Editor*  Claire McCall
Monthly $6.20

Advice, ideas and projects for homeowners – interiors and gardens. Length: 1000 words. Illustrations: good quality colour transparencies. Payment: 35c per word/ $75 per transparency. Founded 1991.

# SOUTH AFRICA

## Bona

Caxton Magazines, PO Box 32083, Mobeni 4060, KwaZulu-Natal
*tel*  (031) 910-5745
*website*  bona@dbn.caxton.co.za
Monthly R6.95

Articles on human drama, sport, music, medical, social and consumer issues of interest to black people. Length: up to 2000 words. Payment: by arrangement. Illustrations: colour prints, occasionally cartoons.

## (Cape Town) Cape Times

Newspaper House, 4th Floor, 122 St George's Mall, Cape Town 8001
*postal address* PO Box 11, Cape Town 8000
*tel*  (021) 488-4911 *fax*  (021) 488 4744
*website*  www.iol.co.za
*Editor*  Chris Whitfield
Daily R3.80

Contributions must be suitable for a daily newspaper and must not exceed 800 words. Illustrations: photos of outstanding South African interest. Founded 1876.

## Car

PO Box 180, Howard Place 7450
*tel* (021) 530-3153 *fax* (021) 532-2698
*email* car@rsp.co.za
*website* www.cartoday.com
*Editor* John Wright
Monthly R16.95

New car announcements with photos and colour features of motoring interest. Payment: by arrangement. Illustrations: colour, cartoons. Founded 1957.

## Daily Dispatch

Dispatch Media (Pty) Ltd, 35 Caxton Street,
East London 5201
*postal address* PO Box 131, East London 5200
*tel* (043) 702-2000 *fax* (043) 743 5155
*email* eledit@iafrica.com
*website* www.dispatch.co.za
*Editor* Gavin Stewart
Daily Mon–Sat R2.30

Newspaper for the Eastern Cape region. Features of general interest, especially successful development projects in developing countries. Contributions welcome. Illustrations: colour and b&w photographs, artwork, cartoons; provides research facility for a fee to authors and publications. Length: approx. 1000 words (features). Payment: R500; R100 photographs. Founded 1872.

## (Durban) The Mercury

Independent Newspapers KwaZulu-Natal Ltd,
PO Box 47549, Durban 4000
*tel* (031) 308-2258 *fax* (031) 308-2306
*Editor* D. Canning
Daily Mon–Fri R3.60

Serious background news and inside details of world events. Length: 700–900 words. Illustrations: photos of general interest. Founded 1852.

## Fairlady

Media24 Magazines, 40 Heerengracht, 9th Floor,
Naspers Building, Cape Town 8000
*tel* (021) 406-2204 *fax* (021) 406-2930
*email* flmag@fairlady.com
*website* www.fairlady.com
*Editor* Ann Donald
Bi-weekly R11.45

Magazine for women in their 30s covering beauty, fashion, food and interior design. Includes 8 features per issue for which it seeks topical stories written to style. Considers unsolicited material. Length: about 1800 words. Illustrations: colour and b&w prints, colour artwork. Payment: R1.50 per word; R250 per photo, approx. R500 per illustration. Founded 1965.

## Farmer's Weekly

Caxton Magazines, PO Box 1797, Pinegowie,
Johannesburg 2123
*tel* (011) 889-0836
*email* farmersweekly@caxton.co.za
*Editor* Chris Burgess
Weekly R7.95

Articles, generally illustrated, up to 1000 words, on all aspects of practical farming and research with particular reference to conditions in Southern Africa. Includes women's section which accepts suitable, illustrated articles. Illustrations: line, half-tone, colour, cartoons. Payment: according to merit.

## Femina Magazine

Associated Magazines, Box 3647, Cape Town 8000
*tel* (021) 464-6200 *fax* (021) 461-2501
*email* femina@assocmags.co.za
*Editor* Clare O'Donoghue
Monthly R19.95

For busy young professionals, often with families. Humour, personalities, real-life drama, medical breakthroughs, popular science, news-breaking stories and human interest. Payment: by arrangement.

## Garden and Home

Caxton Magazines, PO Box 32083, Mobeni 4060
*tel* (031) 910-5713
*Editor* Les Abercrombie
Monthly R18.95

Well-illustrated articles on gardening suitable for southern hemisphere. Articles for home section on furnishings, decor ideas, food. Payment: by arrangement. Illustrations: half-tone, colour, cartoons.

## Independent Newspapers Gauteng

PO Box 1014, Johannesburg 2000
*tel* (011) 633-9111 *fax* (011) 836-8398
*website* www.iol.co.za

> *Johannesburg* **The Star** Daily R2.40
> **Saturday Star** R3.20
> **Sunday Independent** R6
> *Pretoria* **Pretoria News** Daily R2.50

Accepts articles of general and South African interest; also cartoons. Payment: in accordance with an editor's assessment.

## Independent Newspapers Kwa-Zulu Natal Ltd

18 Osborne Street, Greyville, Durban 4023
*tel* (031) 308-2400 *fax* (031) 308-2427
*website* www.iol.co.za

> *Durban* **Daily News** R2.40
> **Ilanga** Bi-weekly R1.40
> **The Mercury** Daily R3.20
> **The Post** Bi-weekly R3.40
> **Independent on Saturday** R3.20

Accepts articles of general and South African interest; also cartoons. Payment: in accordance with an editor's assessment.

## Independent Newspapers (South Africa) Ltd

PO Box 56, Cape Town 8000
*tel* (021) 488-4911 *fax* (021) 488-4762
*website* www.iol.co.za

> Cape Town **Argus** Daily R2.70
> **Saturday Argus** R5.60
> **Sunday Argus** R5.60
> **Cape Times** Daily R3.10

Accepts articles of general and South African interest; also cartoons. Payment: in accordance with an editor's assessment.

## (Johannesburg) Sunday Times

PO Box 1742, Saxonwold 2132
*tel* (011) 280-5102 *fax* (011) 280-5111
*email* suntimes@sundaytimes.co.za
*Editor* M.Makhavya
Sun R6

Illustrated articles of political or human interest, from a South African angle if possible. Maximum 1000 words long and 2–3 photos. Shorter essays, stories and articles of a light nature from 500–750 words. Payment: average rate £100 a column. Illustrations: colour and b&w photos, line drawings.

## Living and Loving

CTP Caxton Magazines, 4th Floor,
Caxton House, 368 Jan Smuts Avenue,
Craighall Park, Johannesburg
*postal address* PO Box 218 Parklands 2121
*tel* (011) 889 0600 *fax* (011) 889 0668
*website* www.living-loving.co.za
*Editor* Fiona Wayman
Monthly R13.95

Parenting magazine: from pregnancy to preschool. Articles about behaviour and development in the first 7 years of life. First-person parenting experiences – pregnancy and the growing child. Medical news/breakthroughs of interest to parents worldwide. Payment: by merit, on acceptance and publication. Founded 1970.

## Sailing

PO Box 1849, Westville 3630
*tel* (031) 709 6087 *fax* (021) 709 6143
*email* sailing@iafrica.com
*website* www. sailing.co.za
*Editor* Richard Crockett
Monthly

Articles and features on the safety of dinghy, cruising, keelboat and racing sailors. Welcomes ideas for articles and features. Will consider unsolicited material. Illustrations: colour.

## Southern Cross

PO Box 2372, Cape Town 8000
*tel* (021) 465-5007 *fax* (021) 465-3850
*email* scross@global.co.za
*website* www.thesoutherncross.co.za
*Editor* Gunther Simmermacher
Weekly R4

National English-language Catholic weekly. Catholic news reports, world and South African. Length: 550-word articles. Illustrations: photos of Catholic interest from freelance contributors. Payment: 14c per word; illustrations R28

## The Witness

Box 362, Pietermaritzburg, KwaZulu-Natal 3201
*tel* (033) 355-1111 *fax* (033) 355-1122
*email* features@witness.co.za
*Editor* J.H. Conyngham
Daily R3

Accepts topical articles. All material should be submitted direct to the Editor in Pietermaritzburg. Length: 500–1000 words. Payment: average of R400 per 1000 words. Founded 1846.

## Woman's Value

Media 24, PO Box 1802, Cape Town 8000
*tel* (021) 406-2205 *fax* (021) 406-2929
*email* tleroux@womansvalue.com
*website* www.womansvalue.com
*Editor* Terena le Roux
Monthly R13.95

Features on beauty, food, finance, knitting, needlecraft, crafts, home and garden, health and parenting; short stories. 600-word accounts of experiences published on the 'My own story' page. Length: up to 1400 words (features/stories). Payment: R1.30 per word. Colour transparencies.

## World Airnews

PO Box 35082, Northway, Durban 4065
*tel* (031) 564-1319 *fax* (031) 563-7115
*Editor* Tom Chalmers
Monthly £36 p.a.

Aviation news and features with an African angle. Payment: by negotiation.

## Your Family

PO Box 473016, Parklands 2121, Gauteng
*tel* (011) 889-0749
*Editor* Patti Garlick
Monthly R10.95

Cookery, knitting, crochet and homecrafts. Family drama, happy ending. Payment: by arrangement. Illustrations: continuous tone, colour and line, cartoons.

# USA

The *Yearbook* does not contain a detailed list of US magazines and journals. The Overseas volume of *Willings Press Guide* is the most useful general reference guide to US publications, available in most reference libraries. For readers with a particular interest in the US market, the publications listed here will be helpful (please make payments to the US in US funds).

When submitting material to US journals, include a covering letter, together with return postage in the form of International Reply Coupons (IRC). IRCs can be exchanged in any foreign country for stamps representing the minimum postage payable on a letter sent from one country to another. Make it clear what rights are being offered for sale as some editors like to purchase MSS outright, thus securing world copyright, i.e. the traditional British market as well as the US market. Send the MSS direct to the US office of the journal and not to any London office.

In many cases it is best to send a preliminary letter giving a rough outline of your article or story (enclose IRCs for a reply). Most magazines will send a leaflet giving guidance to authors.

## American Markets Newsletter

175 Westland Drive, Glasgow G14 9JQ
*email* sheila.oconnor@juno.com
*Editor* Sheila O'Connor
6 p.a. £34 p.a. (£63 for 2 years)

Editorial guidelines for US, Canadian and other overseas markets, plus information on press trips, non-fiction/fiction markets and writers' tips. Free syndication. Sample issue £5.95 (payable to S. O'Connor).

## Willings Press Guide

Waymaker Ltd, Chess House, 34 Germain Street, Chesham, Bucks. HP5 1SJ
*tel* 0870-7360010 (UK), (1494) 797225 (int.)
*fax* 0870-7360011 (UK), (1494) 797224
*email* willings@waymaker.co.uk
*website* www.willingspress.com
£265 2-volume set; or £180 UK volume, £190 international volume

Two volumes contain details of over 50,000 newspapers, broadcasters, periodicals and special interest titles in the UK and internationally. Usually available at local reference libraries or direct from the publisher. Also available as an online product.

## The Writer

Kalmbach Publishing Co., 21027 Crossroads Circle, PO Box 1612, Waukesha, WI 53187
*tel* 262-796-8776  *fax* 262-798-6468
*website* www.writermag.com
Monthly $29 p.a. ($39 p.a. Canada and foreign)

Contains articles of instruction on all writing fields, lists of markets for MSS and special features of interest to freelance writers everywhere. The Writer Books also publishes books on writing fiction, non-fiction, poetry, articles, plays, etc.

## Writer's Digest

Writer's Digest, 4700 E. Galbraith Road, Cincinannati, OH 45236
*tel* 513-531-2690  *fax* 513-531-2902
*email* writersdigest@fwpubs.com
*website* www.writersdigest.com
($36 plus $10 surface post, $75 airmail)

Monthly magazine for writers who want to write better and sell more; aims to inform, instruct and inspire the freelance and fiction writer.

## Writer's Digest Books

(address above)

Also publishes annually *Novel & Short Story Writer's Market, Children's Writer's & Illustrator's Market, Poet's Market, Photographer's Market, Artist's & Graphic Designer's Market, Guide to Literary Agents* and many other books on creating and selling writing and illustrations.

## The Writer's Handbook

The Writer Books, Kalmbach Publishing Co., 21027 Crossroads Circle, PO Box 1612, Waukesha, WI 53187-1612
*tel* 262-796-8776  *fax* 262-798-6468
*website* www.kalmbach.com
$29.95 plus $5.50 shipping & handling; $7.50 s&h plus 7% GST Canada; $10.50 s&h foreign

Compilation of 50+ articles on writing for publication, many by recognised authors and editors. List of 3000+ markets for the sale of MSS (fiction, non-fiction, poetry, drama, greeting cards), plus lists of US literary agents, writers' organisations, literary contests and writing conferences.

## Writer's Market

Writer's Digest Books (address above)
*website* www.writersmarket.com
($27.99 plus $4 p&p)

An annual guidebook giving editorial requirements and other details of over 4000 US markets for freelance writing. Also available on website.

# Syndicates, news and press agencies

Before submitting material, you are strongly advised to make preliminary enquiries and to ascertain terms of work. Strictly speaking, syndication is the selling and reselling of previously published work although some news and press agencies handle original material.

## Academic File Information Services

Eastern Art Publishing Group, PO Box 13666, 27 Wallorton Gardens, London SW14 8WF
*tel* 020-8392 1122 *fax* 020-8392 1422
*email* afis@eapgroup.com
*website* www.eapgroup.com
*Managing Editor* Sajid Rizvi, *Executive Editor* Shirley Rizvi

Feature and photo syndication with special reference to the developing world and immigrant communities in the West. Founded 1985.

## Advance Features

Stubbs Wood Cottage, Hammerwood, East Grinstead, West Sussex RH19 3QE
*tel* (01342) 850480 *fax* (01342) 850480
*email* advancefeatures@aol.com
*website* www.advancefeatures.uk.com
*Managing Editor* Peter Norman

Crosswords: daily, weekly and theme; general puzzles. Daily and weekly cartoons for the regional, national and overseas press (not single cartoons).

## AFX News Ltd

Finsbury Tower, 103–105 Bunhill Row, London EC1Y 8TN
*tel* 020-7422 4800 *fax* 020-7422 4994
*email* info@afxnews.com
*website* www.afxnews.com
*Managing Director* Stefan Ploghaus, *Director of Marking, Sales & New Business* Jean-Philippe Cunniet

Provides real-time financial news to the international banking and investor community. Has 13 bureaus in major European financial centres. News services available in English, French, German, Dutch, Italian and Spanish covering local and international markets. Wholly owned subsidiary of Agence France Presse (AFP). Founded 1990.

## Agencia Efe

299 Oxford Street, London W1C 2DZ
*tel* 020-7493 7313 *fax* 020-7493 7314
*email* efelondon@btclick.com
*website* www.efe.es
*Director* Fernando Pajares

Spain's international news agency specialising in news writing about Spain and Latin America.

## Alpha incorporating London News Service

63 Gee Street, London EC1V 3RS
*tel* 020-7336 0632 *fax* 020-7253 8419
*Managing Director* Ray Blumire

Worldwide syndication of features and photos.

## The Associated Press Ltd

(News Department), The Associated Press House, 12 Norwich Street, London EC4A 1BP
*tel* 020-7353 1515 *fax* 020-7353 8118
*website* www.apweb.com

Supplies international news to the UK media and collects UK material for the USA.

## Australian Associated Press

12 Norwich Street, London EC4A 1QJ
*tel* 020-7353 0153 *fax* 020-7583 3563
*website* www.aap.com.au

News service to the Australian, New Zealand and Pacific Island press, radio and TV. Founded 1935.

## Neil Bradley Puzzles

Linden House, 73 Upper Marehay, Ripley, Derbyshire DE5 8JF
*tel* (01773) 741500 *fax* (01773) 741555
*email* bradcart@aol.com
*Director* Neil Bradley

Supplies visual puzzles to national and regional press; emphasis placed on variety and topicality with work based on current media listings. Work supplied on disk or prints to Mac or PC. Daily single frame and strip cartoons. Contact for free booklet and disk demo. Founded 1981.

## Brainwarp

PO Box 51, Newton-le-Willows, Merseyside WA3 3NZ
*tel* (01942) 271817
*email* trixie@brainwarp.com
*website* www.brainwarp.com
*Partners* Trixie Roberts, Tony Roberts

Supplies original crosswords, brainteasers, wordsearches, quizzes and word games to editors for the printed page. Commission: standard fees for syndicated work; customised work negotiable. Founded 1987.

## Bulls Presstjänst AB

Tulegatan 39, Box 6519, S-11383 Stockholm, Sweden
*tel* (08) 55520600 *fax* (08) 55520665
*email* kontakt@bulls.se
*website* www.bulls.se

**Bulls Pressedienst GmbH**
Eysseneckstrasse 50, D-60322 Frankfurt am Main, Germany
*tel* (069) 959 270 *fax* (069) 959 27111
*email* sales@bullspress.de

**Bulls Pressetjeneste A/S**
Ebbells Gate 3, N-0183 Oslo, Norway
*tel* 22 98 26 60 *fax* 22 20 49 78
*email* bullsosl@online.no

**Bulls Pressetjeneste**
Ostbanegade 9, 1th, DK-2100 Copenhagen, Denmark
*tel* 35 38 90 99 *fax* 35 38 25 16
*email* kjartan@bulls.dk

**Oy Fennopress AB – a Bulls company**
Arabianranta 6, FIN-00560, Helsinki, Finland
*tel* (09) 612 96 50 *fax* (09) 656 092
*email* ilkka@bullspress.fi

**Bulls Press**
ul. Chocimska 28, Pokoj 509, 00-791 Warsawa, Poland
*tel* (22) 845 90 10 *fax* (22) 845 90 11
*email* krzysztof@bulls.com.pl

**Bulls Press**
Narva MNT 7D, EE 10117 Tallin, Estonia
*tel* (372) 66 96 737 *fax* (372) 66 01 313
*email* bulls@delfi.ee

*Market* newspapers, magazines, weeklies and advertising agencies in Sweden, Denmark, Norway, Finland, Iceland, Poland, The Baltic States, Germany, Austria and German-speaking Switzerland.
*Syndicates* human interest picture stories; topical and well-illustrated background articles and series; photographic features dealing with science, people, personalities, glamour; genre pictures for advertising; condensations and serialisations of best-selling fiction and non-fiction; cartoons, comic strips, film and TV rights, merchandising and newspaper graphics online.

## The Canadian Press

Associated Press House, 12 Norwich Street, London EC4A 1QE
*tel* 020-7353 6355 *fax* 020-7583 4238
*website* www.cp.org
*Chief Correspondent* Kevin Ward

London Bureau of the national news agency of Canada. Founded 1919.

## Celebritext

223 Broomwood Road, London SW11 6JX
*tel/fax* 020-7350 2555
*email* info@celebritext.com
*website* www.celebritext.com
*Contact* Lee Howard

Specialises in music, film and TV celebrity interviews. Commission: 50%. Founded 2000.

## Central Press Features

Temple Way, Bristol BS99 7HD
*tel* 0117-934 3600 *fax* 0117-934 3642
*email* mail@central-press.co.uk
*website* www.central-press.co.uk
*Editor* Dominic Moody

Supplies features, cartoons, crosswords, horoscopes and graphics strips to newspapers, magazines and other publications (including internet sites) in 50 countries. Included in over 100 daily and weekly services are columns of international interest on health and beauty, medicine, employment, sports, house and home, motoring, computers, film and video, children's features, gardening, celebrity profiles, food and drink, finance and law. Also runs a parliamentary service as well as supplying editorial material for advertising features.

## Central Press Lobby

Room 12, Press Gallery, House of Commons, London SW1A OAA
*tel* 020-7219 5287
*email* mail@central-press.co.uk
*website* www.central-press.co.uk

Parliamentary reporting for regional press, TV, trade magazines and websites.

## Children's Express UK

Exmouth House, 3–11 Pine Street, London EC1R OJH
*tel* 020-7833 2577 *fax* 020-7278 7722
*email* enquiries@childrensexpress.btinternet.com
*website* www.childrens-express.org
*Chief Executive* Christopher Wyld, *Chairman* Stephanie Williams

Offers young people aged 8–18 the opportunity to write on issues of importance to them, for newspapers, radio and TV. It operates after school and at weekends. Founded 1995.

## Copyline Scotland

17 Queensgate, Inverness IVI IDF
*tel* (01463) 710695 *fax* (01463) 713695
*email* copylinescotland@aol.com
*Directors* David Love, Maureen Long, Neil MacPhail, Alistair Munro

Copywriting, writing press releases, covering news events for national and local media. Founded 1988.

## J.W. Crabtree and Son

Cheapside Chambers, 43 Cheapside, Bradford BD1 4HP
*tel* (01274) 732937 (office), (01535) 655288 (home)
*fax* (01274) 732937

News and sport. Founded 1919.

## Daily & Sunday Telegraph Syndication
The Telegraph Group Ltd, 1 Canada Square,
Canary Wharf, London E14 5DT
*tel* 020-7538 7505 *fax* 020-7538 7319
*email* syndicat@telegraph.co.uk
*website* www.syndication.telegraph.co.uk

News, features, photography; worldwide
distribution and representation.

## Environmental & Occupational Health Research Foundation
Penrose House, 56 Birtles Road, Whirley,
Cheshire SK10 3JQ
*tel* (01625) 615323 *fax* (01625) 615323
*email* eorhfl@aol.com
*Managing Editor* Peggy Bentham

Undertakes individual commissions and syndicates
articles to diverse science and technology journals
and general consumer media. Peer reviewed and
accredited contributors from academia and
professional institutions.

## Euro-Digest Features
34A Compton Avenue, Brighton BN1 3PS
*tel* (01273) 233615 *fax* (01273) 203622
*Directors* Edward Whitehead, Andrew C.F. Whitehead,
Kirsty Tranter

Represents European press. Human interest and
travel features. Occasional news items. Particularly
interested in material from Scotland, Northern
Ireland and Wales. Commission: by arrangement,
according to subject, etc.

## Europa-Press
Sveavägen 47, 2nd Floor, Box 6410, S-113 82,
Stockholm
*tel* 8-34 94 35 *fax* 8-34 80 79
*email* tord@europapress.se
*Managing Director* Tord Steinsvik

Market: newspapers, magazines, weeklies and
websites in Sweden, Denmark, Norway, Finland, and
the Baltic states. Syndicates high-quality features of
international appeal such as topical articles, photo
features – b&w and colour, women's features, short
stories, serial novels, non-fiction stories and serials
with strong human interest, comic strips.

## Europress Features (UK)
18 St Chads Road, Didsbury,
Nr Manchester M20 9WH
*tel* 0161-445 2945
*email* freddy_12_gb@hotmail.com

Representation of newspapers and magazines in
Europe, Australia, United States. Syndication of top-
flight features with exclusive illustrations – human
interest stories – showbusiness personalities.
30–35% commission on sales of material
successfully accepted; 40% on exclusive illustrations.

## Express Enterprises
Ludgate House, 245 Blackfriars Road,
London SE1 9UX
*tel* 020-7922 7903 *fax* 020-7922 7871

Text and pictures from all Express titles. Archive
from 1900. Numerous strips and political cartoons.
Material handled worldwide for freelance
journalists.

## First Features Syndicate
39 High Street, Battle, Sussex TN33 0EE
*tel* (01424) 870877
*email* first.features@dial.pipex.com
*website* www.first-features.co.uk

All types of feature material.

## Gemini News Service
9 White Lion Street, London N1 9PD
*tel* 020-7278 1111 *fax* 020-7278 0345
*email* gemini@panoslondon.org.uk
*website* www.gemininewsservice.com
*Editor* Dipankar De Sarkar

Network of freelance contributors and specialist
writers all over the world. Specialists in news
features of international, topical and development
interest. Preferred length 800–1200 words.

## Graphic Syndication
4 Reyntiens View, Odiham, Hants RG29 1AF
*tel* (01256) 703004
*email* sensible@screaming.net
*Manager* M. Flanagan

Cartoon strips and single frames supplied to
newspapers and magazines in Britain and overseas.
Terms: 50%. Founded 1981.

## Guardian/Observer News Services
119 Farringdon Road, London EC1R 3ER
*tel* 020-7278 2332

International syndication services of news and
features from *The Guardian* and *The Observer*.

## Hayters Teamwork
Image House, Station Road, London N17 9LR
*tel* 020-8808 3300 *fax* 020-8808 1122
*email* sport@haytersteamwork.com
*website* www.hayters.com
*Managing Director* Nick Callow, *Chief Executive*
Gerry Cox

Sports news, features and data supplied to all
branches of the media. Commission: negotiable
according to merit. Founded 1955.

## India-International News Service
*Head office* Jute House, 12 India Exchange Place,
Kolkata 700001, India
*tel* 22209563

*Proprietor* Eur Ing H. Kothari BSc, DWP(Lond), FIMechE, FIE, FVI, FInstD(Lond), FRAS, FRSA

'Calcutta Letters' and Air Mail news service from Calcutta. Specialists in industrial and technical news.

## INS (International News Service) and Irish News Service

*UK office* 7 King's Avenue, Minnis Bay, Birchington-on-Sea, East Kent CT7 9QL
*tel* (01843) 845022
*Editor and Managing Director* Barry J. Hardy PC,
*Photo Editor* Jan Vanek, *Secretary* K.T. Byrne

News, sport, book and magazine reviews (please forward copies), TV, radio, photographic department; also equipment for TV films, etc.

## International Fashion Press Agency

Penrose House, Birtles Road, Whirley, Cheshire SK10 3JQ
*tel* (01625) 615323 *fax* (01625) 615323
*email* ifpressagy@aol.com
*Directors* P. Bentham (managing), P. Dyson, L.C. Mottershead, L.B. Fell

Monitors and photographs international fashion collections and developments in textile and fashion industry. Specialist writers on health, fitness, beauty and personalities. Undertakes individual commissioned features. Supplies syndicated columns/pages to press, radio and TV (NUJ staff writers and photographers).

## International Press Agency (Pty) Ltd

Sunrise House, 56 Morningside, Ndabeni 7405, South Africa
*tel* (021) 531 1926 *fax* (021) 531 8789
*email* inpra@iafrica.com
*Manager* Mrs T. Temple
*UK office* 12 Marion Court,
134–142 Tooting High Street, London SW17 0RU
*tel* 020-8767 4828
*Managing Editor* Mrs U.A. Barnett PhD

South African agents for many leading British, American and continental press firms for the syndication of comic strips, cartoons, jokes, feature articles, short stories, serials, press photos for the South African market. Founded 1934.

## Joker Feature Service (JFS)

PO Box 253, 6040 AG, Roermond, The Netherlands
*tel* (0475) 337338 *fax* (0475) 315663
*email* info@jfs.nl
*Managing Director* Ruud Kerstens

Feature articles, serial rights, tests, cartoons, comic strips and illustrations, puzzles. Handles TV features, books, internet sites; also production for merchandising.

## Knight Features

20 Crescent Grove, London SW4 7AH
*tel* 020-7622 1467 *fax* 020-7622 1522
*email* peter@knightfeatures.co.uk
*website* www.knightfeatures.co.uk
*Director* Peter Knight, *Associates* Gaby Martin, Andrew Knight, Samantha Ferris

Worldwide selling of strip cartoons and major features and serialisations. Exclusive agent in UK and Republic of Ireland for United Feature Syndicate and Newspaper Enterprise Association of New York. Founded 1985.

## London at Large

Zenith House, 155 Curtain Road, London EC2A 3QY
*tel* 020-7613 2299 *fax* 020-7613 3822
*email* newsbreaks@londonatlarge.com
*website* www.londonatlarge.com
*Directors* Chris Parkinson, Marie Ahsun

Forward planner serving the media: lists press contacts for parties, celebrities, launches, premieres, music, film, video and book releases. Founded 1985.

## London News Service – see Alpha
incorporating London News Service

## Maharaja Features Pvt. Ltd

5–226 Sion Road East, Bombay 400022, India
*tel* 22-4097951 *fax* 22-4097801
*email* mahafeat@bom2.vsnl.net.in
*website* www.welcomeindia.com/maharaja
*Editor* Mrs R. Ravi, *Managing Editor* K.R.N. Swamy

Syndicates feature and pictorial material, of interest to Asian readers, to newspapers and magazines in India, UK and abroad. Specialists in well-researched articles on India by eminent authorities for publication in prestige journals throughout the world. Also topical features 1000–1500 words. Illustrations: b&w prints and colour transparencies.

## Mirrorpix

22nd Floor, 1 Canada Square, Canary Wharf, London E14 5AP
*tel* 020-7293 3700 *fax* 020-7293 2712
*email* desk@mirrorpix.com
*website* www.mirrorpix.com
*Contact* Sales Desk

Images of the past 100 years by photographers of the *Daily Mirror* and her sister titles which document both the light and dark sides of British life: people, places, events and movements.

## National Association of Press Agencies (NAPA)

41 Lansdowne Crescent, Leamington Spa, Warks. CV32 4PR
*tel* (01926) 424181 *fax* (01926) 424760

*website* www.napa.org.uk

*Directors* Denis Cassidy, Chris Johnson, Barrie Tracey

NAPA is a network of independent, established and experienced press agencies serving newspapers, magazines, TV and radio networks. Founded 1983.

## National Sports Reporting

10 Elmete Grange, Menston, Ilkley,
West Yorkshire LS29 6LA
*tel* (01943) 884228
*email* 100654.463@compuserve.com

*Editor* Christopher Harte, *Managers* Michael Latham (Northern Region), David Fox (South West Region), Diana Harding (South East Region), Dave Hammond (Scotland)

News and reporting service for sporting events. Research facilities for radio and TV, particularly sports documentaries. Commission: NUJ rates. Founded 1994.

## New Blitz Literary & TV Agency

Via di Panico 67, 00186 Rome, Italy
*postal address* CP 30047–00193, Rome 47, Italy
*tel* (06) 686 4859 *fax* (06) 686 4859
*email* blitzgacs@inwind.it
*Manager* Giovanni A.S. Congiu

Syndicates worldwide: cartoons, comic strips, humorous books with drawings, feature and pictorial material, topical, environment, travel. Average rates of commission 60/40%, monthly report of sales, payment 60 days after the date of monthly report.

## Newsflash Scotland Press & Picture Agency

Viewfield Chambers, Viewfield Place,
Stirling FK8 1NQ
*tel* (01786) 477310 *fax* (01786) 446145
*email* news@nflash.co.uk
*website* www.newsflashscotland.com
*Director* Frank Gilbridge

News, features and picture agency. Also accepts PR commissions and any other related work. Founded 1993.

## Chandra S. Perera

Cinetra Worldwide Createch (PVT) Ltd,
437 Pethiyagoda, Kelaniya-11600, Sri Lanka
*tel* 94-11-2911885 *fax* 94-11-2911885/2674737/
2674738 ATTN Chandra Perera
*email* cinetraww@dialogsl.net comsvc01@slt.lk
ATTN Chandra Perera

Press and TV news, news films on Sri Lanka and Maldives, colour and b&w photo news and features, photographic and film coverages, screenplays and scripts for TV and films, press clippings. Broadcasting, TV and newspapers; journalistic features, news, broadcasting and TV interviews.

## Pixfeatures

5 Latimer Road, Barnet, Herts. EN5 5NU
*tel* 020-8449 9946 *fax* 020-8441 2725
*Contact* Peter Wickman
*Spanish office tel* 00349 6642 6972
*mobile* (00346) 16129742
*Contact* Roy Wickman

News agency and picture library. Specialises in selling Spanish pictures and features to British and European press.

## The Press Association

292 Vauxhall Bridge Road, London SW1V 1AE
*tel* 020-7963 7000 *fax* 020-7963 7192
*website* www.pa.press.net
*Chief Executive/Editor-in-Chief* Paul Potts,
*Managing Director* Steven Brown

*PA News* Fast and accurate news, photography and information to print, broadcast and electronic media in the UK and Ireland.

*PA Sport* In-depth coverage of national and regional sports, transmitting a huge range of stories, results, pictures and updates every day.

*PA Listings* Page- and screen-ready information from daily guides to 7-day supplements on sports results, TV and radio listings, arts and entertainment, financial and weather listings tailored to suit requirements.

*PA Digital* Top quality content including news and sport for a wide range of multimedia customers.

*PA WeatherCentre* Continuously updated information on present and future weather conditions; consultancy services for media and industry. Founded 1868.

## Press Features Syndicate

9 Paradise Close, Eastbourne, East Sussex BN20 8BT
*tel* (01323) 728760
*Editor* Harry Gresty

Specialises in photo-features, both b&w and colour. Seeks human interest, oddity, glamour, pin-ups, scientific, medical, etc material suitable for marketing through own branches in London, San Francisco, Paris, Hamburg, Milan, Stockholm, Amsterdam (for Benelux), Helsinki.

## Press Gang News

137 Endlesham Road, London SW12 8JN
*tel* 020-8673 4229 020-8673 7778 *fax* 020-8673 3205
*email* mail@pressgangnews.co.uk,
mail@press-gang.fsnet.co.uk
*website* www.pressgangnews.co.uk
*Partners* Mark Christy, Sarah Christy

National news, features and photographic news agency. Seeks good journalists and photographers; considers material from freelance journalists. Keen to receive stories, press releases, etc from individual members of the public and from organisations, etc. Founded 1996.

## The Puzzle House

Ivy Cottage, Battlesea Green, Stradbroke,
Suffolk IP21 5NE
*tel* (01379) 384656 *fax* (01379) 384656
*email* puzzlehouse@btinternet.com
*website* www.thepuzzlehouse.co.uk
*Partners* Roy Preston and Sue Preston

Supply original crosswords, quizzes and puzzles of all types. Commissions taken on any topic, with all age ranges catered for. Wide range of puzzles available for one-off usage. Founded 1988.

## Rann Communication

Level 1, 18–20 Grenfell Street, Adelaide, SA 5000, Australia
*postal address* GPO Box 958, Adelaide, SA 5000, Australia
*tel* (08) 8211 7771 *fax* (08) 8212 2272
*email* chrisrann@rann.com.au
*Proprietor* C.F. Rann

Full range of professional PR, press releases, special newsletters, commercial and political intelligence, media monitoring. Welcomes approaches from organisations requiring PR representation or press release distribution. Founded 1982.

## Reuters Group plc

85 Fleet Street, London EC4P 4AJ
*tel* 020-7250 1122
*email* editor@reuters.com
*website* ww.reuters.com

Global provider of news and financial information. One of the world's biggest agencies. Founded 1851.

## Sirius Media Services

100 Bridge Street, Stowmarket, Suffolk IP14 1BS
*tel* (01449) 674218
*email* mail@siriusmedia.co.uk
*website* www.siriusmedia.co.uk

Crosswords, puzzles and quizzes, plus horoscopes and TV features.

## Solo Syndication Ltd

17–18 Haywards Place, London EC1R 0EQ
*tel* 020-7566 0360 *fax* 020-7566 0388
*Contact* Nick York

Worldwide syndication of newspaper features, photos, cartoons, strips and book serialisations. Agency represents the international syndication of Associated Newspapers (*Daily Mail, Mail on Sunday, Evening Standard*).

## Southern News Service

Exchange House, Hindhead, Surrey GU26 6AA
*tel* (01428) 607330 *fax* (01428) 606351
*email* denis@cassidyandleigh.com
*Partners* Denis Cassidy and Donald Leigh

News stories, features and court coverage. Full picture service, digital and ISDN. Public relations words and pictures. Founded 1960.

## UK Features

38 The Woodlands, Esher, Surrey KT10 8DB
*tel* 020-8398 5676 *fax* 020-8398 9051
*email* robincorry@ukfeatures.com
*Proprietor* Robin Corry

Human interest and general features. Payment: £150–£250 for an early tip-off. Founded 1979.

## United Press UK Ltd

Prince Consort House, 27–29 Albert Embankment, London SE1 7TJ
*tel* 020-7820 4183 (editorial), 020-7820 4180 (admin) *fax* 020-7820 4190
*email* www.upi.com

## Universal Pictorial Press & Agency

29–31 Saffron Hill, London EC1N 8SW
*tel* 020-7421 6000 *fax* 020-7421 6006
*email* ctaylor@uppa.co.uk
*Managing Director* Charles Taylor

Photographic news agency and picture library: the UK's leading archive for British and international personalities from 1944 to present. Digital archive from 1994. Founded 1929.

## Visual Humour

5 Greymouth Close, Stockton-on-Tees TS18 5LF
*tel* (01642) 581847 *fax* (01642) 581847
*email* peterdodsworth@btclick.com
*website* enquiries@businesscartoons.co.uk
*Contact* Peter Dodsworth

Daily and weekly humorous cartoon strips; also single panel cartoon features (not gag cartoons) for possible syndication in the UK and abroad. Picture puzzles also considered. Submit photocopy samples only initially, with sae. Founded 1984.

# Books
## Getting started

To help authors get started with writing we offer some guidelines to consider before submitting material to a publisher. Notes from successful authors in fiction (Joanna Trollope), non-fiction (Simon Winchester) and children's publishing (J.K. Rowling) start on page 237.

There is more competition to get published that ever before. Hundreds of manuscripts (or typescripts) of would-be books land on the desks of publishers and literary agents every day. Both publishers and literary agents acknowledge that potential authors have to be really dedicated (or perhaps very lucky) in order to get their work published. So how can you give yourself the best chance of success? The following seven pointers will give you a head start to get your material noticed by a publisher.

### 1. Agent or publisher?
- First decide whether to approach an agent or to go it alone and submit your material direct to a publisher. Many publishers, particularly of fiction, will only consider material submitted through a literary agent. See *The role of the literary agent* on page 393, *How to get an agent* on page 397 and *Publishing agreements* on page 285 for some of the pros and cons of each approach.
- Whether you choose to approach an agent or a publisher, your work will be subjected to rigorous commercial assessment.

### 2. Choose the right publisher or agent
- Study the entries in this *Yearbook*, examine publishers' lists of publications and websites, and look in the relevant sections in libraries and bookshops for the names of publishers which might be interested in seeing your material.
- A list of literary agents starts on page 400.
- Listings of publishers' names and addresses start on page 135.
- A list of *Publishers of fiction*, by fiction genre, is on page 749.
- The market for children's books is considered in *Writing and the children's book market* on page 247. The list of *Children's book publishers and packagers* on page 752 includes publishers of poetry for children and teenage fiction. A list of *Literary agents for children's books* is on page 756.
- Publishers which consider poetry for adults are listed on page 755. See also *Getting poetry published* on page 299 and *Poetry organisations* on page 305.
- The electronic book market is in its infancy and has no set standards or provision but holds potential for some authors. See *E-publishing* on page 581.
- Authors are strongly advised not to pay for the publication of their work. A reputable publishing house will undertake publication at its own expense, except possibly for works of an academic nature. See *Doing it on your own* on page 255 for an introduction to self publishing and *Vanity publishing* on page 282.

### 3. Prepare your material well

- Presentation is important. For example, no editor will read a handwritten manuscript. If your material is submitted in the most appropriate format a publisher will be more inclined to give attention to it. See *Dos and don'ts on approaching a publisher* on page 130.
- Many publishers' websites give guidance for new writers.
- It is understandable that writers, in their eagerness to show their work to others in the hope of getting it published as soon as possible, will send their manuscript in a raw state. Do not send your manuscript to a publisher until it is *ready* to be seen as it could ruin your chances. Be confident that your work is as good as it can be.

### 4. Approach the publisher in the way they prefer

- Submit your work to the right person within the publishing company or literary agency. Ring or email first to find out who is the best person to receive your work. If the listing in this *Yearbook* does not specify, also ask whether they want a synopsis and sample chapters or the complete manuscript. Many publishers' websites give guidance on how to submit material.
- Never send your only copy of the manuscript. Whilst every reasonable care will be taken of material in a publisher's possession, responsibility cannot be accepted if material is lost or damaged.
- Always include an sae with enough postage for the return of your material. (Send International Reply Coupons if you are writing from outside the country or if you are submitting material from the UK to the Republic of Ireland; for further information *tel* (08457) 223344.)

### 5. Write a convincing letter

- Compose your preliminary letter with care. Writers have been known to send out such letters in duplicated form, an approach unlikely to stimulate a publisher's interest. See *Dos and don'ts on approaching a publisher* on page 130.
- When submitting a manuscript to a publisher, it is a good idea to let them know that you know (and admire!) what they already publish. You can then make your case about where your submission will fit in their list. Let them know that you mean business and have researched the marketplace. See *Understanding the publishing process* on page 232.
- What is the unique selling point of the material you are submitting for publication? You may have an original authorial 'voice', or you may have come up with an amazingly brilliant idea for a series. If, after checking out the marketplace, you think you have something truly original to offer, then believe in yourself and be convincing when you offer it around.

### 6. Get out and network

- Writing can be a lonely business – don't work in a vacuum. Talk to others of your discipline at literature festivals, conferences and book groups; find out if there are any writer groups in your area. Consider doing a course – see *Creative writing courses* on page 634.

- Go to a festival and be inspired! There are many literature festivals held throughout the year (see *Literature festivals* on page 573) which new and well-known authors appear at. You may be able to hear an author you admire speak, and even meet them afterwards.

## 7. Don't give up!

- Editors receive hundreds of manuscripts every day. For a publisher, there are many factors that have to be taken into consideration when evaluating these submissions, the most important of which is 'Will it sell?'
- Be prepared to wait for a decision on your work. Editors and agents are both very busy people so be patient when waiting for a response. Don't pester them too soon.
- Publishing is a big business and it is ever more competitive. Even after an editor has read your work, there are many other people involved before a manuscript is acquired for publication. People from the sales, marketing, publicity, rights and other departments all have to be convinced that the book is right for their list and will sell.
- The harsh reality of submitting a manuscript to a publisher is that you have to be prepared for rejection. But all successful authors have received rejections from a publisher at some time so you are in good company.
- Have patience, persevere. Good luck!

### Publishers' contracts

Following a publishing company's firm interest in a MS, a publisher's contract is drawn up between the author and the publisher (see *Publishing agreements* on page 285). If the author is not entirely happy with the contract presented to them or wishes to take advice, he/she could ask their literary agent, the Society of Authors or the Writers' Guild of Great Britain to check the contract on their behalf – providing the author has an agent and/or is a member of those organisations. Otherwise, the author can either check it for himself (for guidance, see *An Author's Guide to Publishing* and *Understanding Publishers' Contracts*, both books by Michael Legat; see page 289), or seek advice from a solicitor. Before consulting a solicitor, make sure that they are familiar with publishing agreements and can give informed advice. Many local firms have little or no experience of such work and their opinion can often be of limited value and the cost may outweigh any possible gains. See *Editorial, literary and production services* for practitioners who undertake these legal services.

## See also ...

- Book publishers in *Australia* (page 197); in *Canada* (page 200); in *New Zealand* (page 204); in *South Africa* (page 206); and in the *USA* (page 207)
- *Ghostwriting*, page 242
- *Top one hundred chart of 2003 paperback fastsellers*, page 274
- *Book packagers*, page 225
- *The writer's toolkit*, page 599

# Dos and don'ts on approaching a publisher

You want the book you've written to be published. So how do you set about it? Where will you send the typescript? Probably to a publisher, but to which one? Michael Legat offers guidelines on how to proceed.

## Finding a publisher

Do your market research in public libraries and bookshops, and especially in *Writers' and Artists' Yearbook*, to find out which publishers bring out the kind of book you have written. While looking at the *Yearbook* entries, note which publishers are willing to consider books submitted to them directly, rather than through an agent, and which require a letter of enquiry first. Incidentally, if you are hoping to interest an agent, they almost all want an enquiry letter first.

## Enquiry letters

An enquiry letter should be business-like. Don't grovel ('it would be an honour to be published by so distinguished a firm'), don't make jokes ('my

```
                    10 Any Street, Any Town,
                                  Any County

Messrs Dickens and Thackray,
83 Demy Street,
London WC45 9BM              12th March

Dear Sirs,

May I please send for your consider-
ation the novel I have written.

Yours sincerely,

L. Hopeful
```

This letter is far too brief. It gives no information about the kind of novel the author wishes to submit, nor of its length, it doesn't include a sae, and it doesn't even reveal the writer's sex. And since the writer doesn't use a question mark and has misspelt 'Thackeray', it's a good bet that the book will need meticulous and time-consuming copy-editing.

Mum says it's smashing, but maybe you'll think she's prejudiced'), don't be aggressive ('I have chosen you to publish my book, kindly send me your terms by return'). It is a good idea to write to whichever editor in the publishing house is responsible for books of the kind you have written (a phone call will provide this information – but take care to get the right title and spelling of the editor's name). Enclose a stamped addressed envelope. Look at the examples of the two poor enquiry letters followed by a good one on page 133.

You may have noticed that none of the letters refers to sending a disk or email. Such submissions may well become standard in a few years' time, but that stage has not yet been reached. However, once a book has been accepted, the publisher will certainly want a copy of the book on disk if it is available.

## Presentation

Assuming that a publishing firm agrees to look at your book, the editor will expect to see a well-presented typescript (sometimes called a manuscript, abbreviated to MS). Here are some dos and don'ts about its appearance.

Use a typewriter or a word processor, or get a secretarial service to translate your handwriting on to a disk. Don't expect a publisher to read a handwritten script, even if you have a fine Italian hand.

Choose a good quality white A4 paper (preferably not continuous listing paper, or if you must use it, at least separate the pages and remove the perforated edges). Whatever paper you use don't type on both sides, and don't use single spacing (which publishers abhor, and usually refuse to read) – one side of the paper only and double spacing is the rule. And do leave a good margin, at least 3cm, all around the text, using the same margins throughout, so as to have the same number of lines on each page (except at the beginning and end of chapters). Double spacing and good margins allow space for your last-minute corrections to the typescript, for any copy-editor's amendments, and for instructions to the printer. And, not least in importance, a typescript in that style is much easier to read.

Always begin chapters on a new page. Justify on the left hand side only. Don't use blank lines between paragraphs (in the style of most typed letters nowadays), but indent the first line of each paragraph a few spaces. Blank lines should be used only to indicate a change of subject, or time, or scene, or viewpoint.

Be consistent in your choice of variant spellings, capitalisation, use of subheadings, etc. Make up your mind whether you are going to use -ise or -ize suffixes, for example, and whether, if 'village hall' appears in your text, you will type 'village hall' or 'Village Hall'.

For plays, use capitals for character names and underline stage directions or print them in italics. Use single spacing for dialogue, but leave a blank line between one character's speech and that of the next character to speak.

Poetry should be typed in exactly the way that the poem would appear in a printed version, using single or double spacing and various indentations as the poet wishes.

## Organising the pages

Number the pages (or 'folios', as publishers like to call them) straight through from beginning to end. Don't start each chapter at folio 1. If you need to include an extra folio after, say, folio 27, call it folio 27a and write at the foot of folio 27: 'Folio 27a follows'. Then write at the foot of 27a: 'Folio 28 follows'. Obviously, if you want to insert more than one page, you would use '27a', '27b', '27c', and so on. Some writers like to use part of the book's title as well as the folio number: 'Harry 27', for example, but this is not essential.

Create a title page for the book, showing the title and your name or pseudonym. Add your name and address in the bottom right hand corner, and also type it on the last folio of the typescript, in case the first folio becomes detached. You can also add a word count, if you wish (if using the word-counting facility on your word processor, round the figure up or down to the nearest thousand or five thousand). If you want to include a list of your previously published books, a dedication, a quotation, a list of contents or of illustrations, an assertion of your moral rights, or any similar material, use a separate page for each item. Leave these pages unnumbered or use small roman figures – i, ii, iii, etc – so that the first folio to have

```
                    12 Any Street, Any Town,
                                  Any County

Messrs Dickens and Thackeray,
83 Demy Street,
London WC45 9BM              14th March

Dear Sirs,

May I please send you the novel I
have written, which I want to get
published? It's called Wendy Chiltern.
That's the name of the heroine. I am
a 76-year-old grandmother, but all my
friends say that I am very young for
my age and I can certainly claim to
be 'with it'. I belong to the
Townswomen's Guild, and I do a lot of
work at the local Church, and I play
Bridge regularly, so you can tell my
mind's still as sharp as ever.

I have been writing ever since I was
a little girl, without trying to get
anything published, but my friends
have persuaded me to try my luck with
this book. One of them said it was
better than anything by Jackie Collins.
Any publisher would jump at it, she
said. They are all so enthusiastic,
that I just had to 'have a go'…

The book is 57 pages long. It is
properly typed, and all the spelling
mistakes have been corrected. I
should tell you that I am aware that
the novel has some faults. It is just
a little slow to get started, but
once you're into it I am sure you
won't be able to put it down.

If your reply is favourable, I shall
bring the typescript to your office
and perhaps you could spare me a few
minutes to talk about it.

Yours sincerely,

Louise Hopeless (Mrs)
```

This letter is far too long, and includes masses of irrelevant information about the author. The fact that the lady's friends said they liked the book is no recommendation – what else are they going to say to their friend? And no editor is going to be tempted by a slow beginning, however honest it may be for the author to point it out. The book is almost certainly typed in single spacing with minuscule margins, and even so will be a long way short of book-length. And publishers do not spend time interviewing would-be authors – the lady should leave the typescript at reception, and let it speak for itself.

an Arabic number will be the first page of your text.

When fastening the typescript together, don't use pins (which scratch), paperclips (which pick up other papers from a busy editor's desk), or staples (which make it difficult to read). Don't ever fasten the pages together in one solid lump, and it's best to avoid ring binders too. Don't use plastic folders – they are slippery and can very easily cascade off a pile on the editor's desk (which won't please the editor). Almost all publishers prefer to handle each folio separately, so put the typescript into a wallet-type folder, or more than one if necessary. Put the title of the book and your name and address on the outside of the folder.

If illustrations form a large part of your book and you expect to provide them yourself they should be included with the typescript, and equally a selection should accompany a synopsis and specimen chapters. Send copies rather than originals. If your book is for children don't complete all the illustrations until the publisher has decided on the size of the book and the number of illustrations. If you have a friend who wants to supply illustrations for your book, do make sure that they will be up to publishing standard before you accept the offer. You may put off a children's publisher by suggesting an illustrator – they like to choose.

## Waiting for a decision

Many publishers take what seems to be an unconscionable time to give a verdict on typescripts submitted to them. However, a decision whether or not to publish may not be easy, and several readings and consultations with other departments in the publishing house often have to take place before the editor can be sure of the answer. If you have heard nothing after two months, send a polite letter of enquiry; if you get no response, ask for your typescript back, and try another publisher.

Don't expect to be given reasons for rejection. Publishers do not have time to spend on books and authors which they are not going to publish. However, if the rejection letter contains any compliments on your work, you can take them at face value – publishers tend not to encourage authors unless they mean it.

## Copyright material

Copyright exists as soon as you (or anyone else) records anything original to you on paper or film or disk. If you want to quote or otherwise use any material which is someone else's copyright, even if it is a short extract, you will have to get permission to do so, and possibly pay a fee. This applies not only to the text of a book, but also to letters and photographs, the copyright of which belongs to the letter-writer and photographer respectively. You must always give full acknowledgement to the source of the material. Use copyright material without such clearance and acknowledgement, and you are guilty of plagiarism – and another name for plagiarism is stealing. There are some circumstances in which you may use small amounts of text under a rule called 'Fair Dealing'. If your book has been accepted for publication, the publisher will be able to give you advice on the matter. (See also articles on copyright starting on page 669.)

---

14 Any Street, Any Town,
Any County

Ms Ann Clarke,
Messrs Dickens and Thackeray,
83 Demy Street,
London WC45 9BM            16th March

Dear Ms Clarke,

May I please send you my novel, My Son, my Son, for your kind consideration? It is approximately 87,000 words in length and is a contemporary story, telling of the devastating effect on the marriage of the central characters when their 17-year-old son announces that he is gay. It is aimed at the same market as that of Joanna Trollope, although my characters might be described as a little further down the class scale.

I have written a number of articles which have been published not only in my local newspaper, but in a couple of cases in 'The Lady', and once in 'The Observer'. This is my first work of fiction, but I have two other novels with similar backgrounds in mind.

I enclose a sae and look forward to hearing from you. Perhaps you will let me know whether you would prefer to see a synopsis and specimen chapters, or the entire book.

Yours sincerely,

Lucilla Possible

A good enquiry letter. The writer has (we can presume) found out to whom to address the letter, and how the lady spells her name. The letter is brief, but gives a clear picture of what the novel is about, and suggests its possible market, telling the publisher all that is necessary at this stage. It makes the two points that the writer has had some success with her work (do always include such details, provided that they are for professional publications), and that she intends to write other books. It also asks about the possibility of sending a synopsis and specimen chapters rather than the complete book, and that is in fact the way in which most publishers nowadays like to see new material (especially for non-fiction books, but also for novels). Of course, no enquiry letter, however satisfactory, can guarantee a favourable response, but at least with this one no editorial hackles should rise.

## Proofs

When your book is accepted by a publisher you may be asked to do further work on it, and a copy-editor will probably check the typescript line by line and word by word. As the author you should see the final copy before it goes to the printer, and this is almost your last chance to make any changes, whether they are simply the correction of literals or are more extensive than that.

At a later stage you will be sent proofs from the printer, which you will have to read with great care. Any errors which the printer has made are corrected without charge, but if you alter anything else, the publisher will have to pay for the changes and will be entitled to pass on to you any costs which exceed 10–15% of the cost of composition (i.e. the setting of the book in type). That sounds as though it gives you a lot of leeway, but alterations at proof stage are hugely expensive, so avoid them if you possibly can.

Michael Legat became a full-time writer after a long and successful publishing career. He is the author of a number of highly regarded books on publishing and writing.

## See also...

- *Getting started*, page 127
- *Notes from a successful fiction author*, page 237
- *Notes from a successful non-fiction author*, page 239
- *Notes from a successful children's author*, page 241
- *Writing and the children's book market*, page 247
- *Understanding the publishing process*, page 232
- *Publishing agreements*, page 285
- *The role of a literary agent*, page 393
- *How to get an agent*, page 397
- *Copyright questions*, page 669
- *UK copyright law*, page 672

# Book publishers UK and Ireland

*Member of the Publishers Association or Scottish Publishers Association
†Member of the Irish Book Publishers' Association

## AA Publishing
Automobile Association and Business Services,
Fanum House, Basingstoke, Hants. RG21 4EA
*tel* (01256) 491538 *fax* (01256) 322575
*website* www.theAA.com
*Directors* Stephen Mesquita (managing), C. Austin-
Smith (editorial), Robert Firth (production),
Martin Lay (cartography), T.A. Lee (sales)

Travel, atlases, maps, leisure interests, including
Essential Guides, Spiral Guides, City Packs and
Explorer Travel Guides. Founded 1979.

## Abacus – see Time Warner Books UK

## ABC-Clio
26 Beaumont Street, Oxford OX1 2NP
*email* salesuk@abc-clio.com
*website* www.abc-clio.com
*Senior Acquisitions Editor* Simon Mason

General and academic reference: print and electronic
encyclopedias in history, mythology, literature,
ethnic studies; bibliography. Publishes *The Clio
Montessori Series*, and CD-Rom and web versions of
abstracting services in American studies and history.
Branch of ABC-CLIO Inc. Founded 1971.

## Absolute Classics – see Oberon Books

## Absolute Press
Scarborough House, 29 James Street West,
Bath BA1 2BT
*tel* (01225) 316013 *fax* (01225) 445836
*email* sales@absolutepress.co.uk
*website* www.absolutepress.co.uk
*Publisher* Jon Croft, *Directors* Amanda Bennett
(sales), Meg Avent (editorial), Matt Inwood (Art)

General list: cookery, food-related topics, wine,
lifestyle, popular culture, travel. No fiction. *Outlines*
series of monographs on gay and lesbian artists. No
unsolicited MSS. Founded 1979.

## Academic Press – see Elsevier Ltd

## Academy Editions – acquired by Wiley Europe Ltd

## Academy of Light Ltd
Unit Ic, Delta Centre, Mount Pleasant, Wembly,
Middlesex HA0 1UX

*tel* 020-8795 2695 *fax* 020-8903 3748
*email* yubraj@academyoflight.co.uk
*website* www.academyoflight.co.uk
*Managing Director & Chief Editor* Dr Yubraj Sharma,
*Marketing & Financial Director* Mrs Mita Shah

Spirituality and alternative medicine; children's.
Founded 2000.

## Access Press – see HarperCollins Publishers

## Ace Books – see Age Concern Books

## Acorn Editions – see James Clarke & Co. Ltd

## Actinic Press – see Cressrelles Publishing Co. Ltd

## Addison-Wesley – see Pearson Education

## Adlard Coles Nautical – see A & C Black Publishers Ltd

## Age Concern Books
Age Concern England, 1268 London Road,
London SW16 4ER
*tel* 020-8765 7200 *fax* 020-8765 7211
*email* books@ace.org.uk
*Publisher* Richard Holloway

Health and care, advice, finance, gerontology.
Founded 1973.

## Airlife Publishing – see The Crowood Press

## Aladdin/Watts – see The Watts Publishing Group Ltd

## Ian Allan Publishing Ltd
Riverdene Business Park, Molesey Road, Hersham,
Surrey KT12 4RG
*tel* (01932) 266600 *fax* (01932) 266601
*email* info@ianallanpub.co.uk
*website* www.ianallanpublishing.com
*Publishing Manager* Peter Waller

Transport: railways, aircraft, shipping, road; naval
and military history; reference books and
magazines; sport and cycling guides; no fiction.

### Classic Publications (imprint)
Transport, aviation.

**Midland Publishing (imprint)**
Transport: railways, aviation; naval and military history.

**Oxford Publishing Company (imprint)**
Transport: railways, road.

## J.A. Allen
Clerkenwell House, 45–47 Clerkenwell Green, London EC1R 0HT
*tel* 020-7251 2661 *fax* 020-7490 4958
*email* allen@halebooks.com
*Publisher* Caroline Burt

Horse and equestrianism including bloodstock breeding, racing, polo, dressage, horse care, carriage driving, breeds, veterinary and farriery. Books usually commissioned but willing to consider any serious, specialist TSS on the horse and related subjects. Imprint of **Robert Hale Ltd**. Founded 1926.

## George Allen & Unwin Publishers –
acquired by HarperCollins Publishers

## Allen Lane – see Penguin Group (UK)

## W.H. Allen – acquired by Virgin Books Ltd

## Allison & Busby Ltd
Bon Marché Centre, 241–251 Ferndale Road, London SW9 8BJ
*tel* 020-7738 7888 *fax* 020-7733 4244
*email* all@allisonandbusby.co.uk
*website* www.allisonandbusby.com
*Publishing Director* David Shelley, *Editor* Debbie Hatfield, *Press Officer* Nemah Kamar

Literary fiction, crime fiction. Biography and history with a literary theme. Writers' Guides. New proposals accepted (send synopsis and sample pages initially) but sae essential. See website for guidelines.

## Allyn & Bacon – see Pearson Education

## The Alpha Press – see Sussex Academic Press

## Amber Lane Press Ltd
Church Street, Charlbury, Oxon OX7 3PR
*tel* (01608) 810024 *fax* (01608) 810024
*email* info@amberlanepress.co.uk
*Chairman* Brian Clark, *Director/Managing Editor* Judith Scott

Plays, theatre, music. Founded 1978.

## AN The Artists Information Company
1st Floor, 7–15 Pink Lane,
Newcastle upon Tyne NE1 5DW
*tel* 0191-241 8000 *fax* 0191-241 8001
*email* edit@anpubs.demon.co.uk
*website* www.anweb.co.uk

*AN Editor* Gillian Nicol

Provides information, advice and critical debate on contemporary visual arts practice through *AN magazine* (monthly), its website, and a programme of artists' training and professional development for Northern England. Founded 1980.

## Andersen Press Ltd*
20 Vauxhall Bridge Road, London SW1V 2SA
*tel* 020-7840 8703 (editorial) *fax* 020-7233 6263
*email* andersenpress@randomhouse.co.uk
*website* www.andersenpress.co.uk
*Managing Director/Publisher* Klaus Flugge, *Directors* Philip Durrance, Joëlle Flugge (company secretary), Janice Thomson (editorial)

Children's books: picture books, junior and teenage fiction (send synopsis and first 3 chapters with sae); no short stories or poetry. International co-productions. Founded 1976.

## Andromeda Children's Books – see Pinwheel Ltd

## The Angels' Share – see Neil Wilson Publishing Ltd

## Anness Publishing
88–89 Blackfriars Road, London SE1 8HA
*tel* 020-7401 2077 *fax* 020-7633 9499
*Managing Director* Paul Anness, *Publisher* Joanna Lorenz

Practical illustrated books on lifestyle, cookery, crafts, gardening, Mind, Body & Spirit, health and children's non-fiction. Founded 1989.

### Aquamarine (hardback imprint)
Lifestyle, cookery, crafts and gardening.

### Hermes House (imprint)
Illustrated promotional books on practical subjects.

### Lorenz Books (hardback imprint)
Lifestyle, cookery, crafts, gardening, Mind, Body & Spirit, health and children's non-fiction.

### Southwater (paperback imprint)
Lifestyle, cookery, crafts, gardening, Mind, Body & Spirit, health and children's non-fiction.

## Antique Collectors' Club Ltd
Sandy Lane, Old Martlesham, Woodbridge, Suffolk IP12 4SD
*tel* (01394) 389950 *fax* (01394) 389999
*email* sales@antique-acc.com
*website* www.antique-acc.com
*Managing Director* Diana Steel

Fine art, antiques, gardening and garden history, architecture. Founded 1966.

## Anvil Books/The Children's Press[†]
45 Palmerston Road, Dublin 6, Republic of Ireland
*tel* (01) 4973628 *fax* (01) 4968263
*Directors* Rena Dardis (managing), Margaret Dardis
(editorial)

Anvil: Irish history and biography. Only considers
MSS by Irish-based authors and of Irish interest.
Send synopsis with IRCs (no UK stamps);
unsolicited MSS not returned. Children's Press:
adventure, fiction, ages 9–14. Founded 1964.

## Anvil Press Poetry
Neptune House, 70 Royal Hill, London SE10 8RF
*tel* 020-8469 3033 *fax* 020-8469 3363
*email* anvil@anvilpresspoetry.com
*website* www.anvilpresspoetry.com
*Director* Peter Jay

Poetry. Submissions only with sae. Founded 1968.

## Apple Press – see Quarto Publishing plc/
Quintet Publishing Ltd on page 230

## Appletree Press Ltd[†]
14 Howard Street South, Belfast BT7 1AP
*tel* 028-9024 3074 *fax* 028-9024 6756
*email* reception@appletree.ie
*website* www.appletree.ie
*Director* John Murphy

Gift books, biography, cookery, guidebooks, history,
Irish interest, literary criticism, music, photographic,
social studies, sport, travel. Founded 1974.

## Aquamarine – see Anness Publishing

## Arc Publications
Nanholme Mill, Shaw Wood Road, Todmorden,
Lancs. OL14 6DA
*tel* (01706) 812338 *fax* (01706) 818948
*Partners* Rosemary Jones, Tony Ward (general
editor), Angela Jarman, *Associate Editors* John
Kinsella (international), Jean Boase-Beier
(translation), Jo Shapcott (UK)

Poetry. At present we are not accepting new MSS.

## Arcadia Books Ltd
15–16 Nassau Street, London W1W 7AB
*tel* 020-7436 9898 *fax* 020-7436 9898
*email* info@arcadiabooks.co.uk
*website* www.arcadiabooks.co.uk
*Managing Director* Gary Pulsifer, *Publishing Director*
Daniela de Groote

Original paperback fiction, fiction in translation,
autobiography, biography, travel, gender studies, gay
books. Submissions via literary agents only. *Sunday
Times* Small Publisher of the Year 2002/03. Founded
1996.

## Architectural Press – see Elsevier Ltd

## Arcturus – see W. Foulsham & Co. Ltd

## Edward Arnold – now part of Hodder Arnold
– see Hodder Headline Ltd

## Arrow Books Ltd – see Random House
Group Ltd

## Ashgate Publishing Ltd
Gower House, Croft Road, Aldershot,
Hants GU11 3HR
*tel* (01252) 331551 *fax* (01252) 344405
*email* info@ashgatepub.co.uk
*website* www.ashgate.com
*Chairman* Nigel Farrow, *Managing Director and Social
Sciences Publishing Director* Sarah Davies, *Managing
Director and Humanities Publishing Director* Rachel
Lynch, *President Ashgate US* Barbara Church
*Humanities* Ann Donahue (Literary Studies,
19th–20th centuries), Erika Gaffney (Literary
Studies to 18th century; Women and Gender
Studies), Heidi May (Music), Paul Coulam
(Philosophy), Sarah Lloyd (Theology and Religious
Studies), Thomas Gray (History), John Smedley
(Publishing Director, Variorum imprint; History)
*Social Sciences* Alison Kirk (Law), Brendan George
(Academic Business; Economics; Development
Studies), Caroline Wintersgill and Mary Savigar
(Sociology; Social Policy; Social Work), John
Hindley and Guy Loft (Aviation), Kirstin Howgate
(International Relations; Politics),Suzie Duke
(Human Geography; Planning and Design), John
Irwin (Library Reference Publishing)

Publishes a wide range of academic research in the
social sciences and humanities, professional practice
publications in the management of business and
public services, and illustrated books on art,
architecture and design. Founded 1967.

### Gower (imprint)
*website* www.gowerpub.com
*Publishing Director and Commissioning Editor*
Jonathan Norman

Business, management and training.

### Lund Humphries (imprint)
*website* www.lundhumphries.com
*Publishing Director* Lucy Myers, *Commissioning
Editor* Jonathan Jones

Art and architectural history.

### Variorum (imprint)
*Publishing Director* John Smedley

History.

## Ashmolean Museum Publications
Beaumont Street, Oxford OX1 2PH
*tel* (01865) 278010 *fax* (01865) 278018
*website* www.ashmol.ox.ac.uk

*Contact* Susan Moss

Fine and applied art of Europe and Asia, archaeology, history, numismatics. No unsolicited MSS. Photographic archive. Museum founded 1683.

## Aslib (The Association for Information Management)

Temple Chambers, 3–7 Temple Avenue, London EC4Y 0HP
*tel* 020-7583 8900 *fax* 020-7583 8401
*website* www.aslib.com

For books contact Taylor & Francis (01235) 828600; for journals contact Emerald (01206) 796351; for *Managing Information* magazine contact Graham Coult (editor) 020-7583 8900, or see website: www.managinginformation.com

## Aspect Guides – see Bloomsbury Publishing Plc

## Atlantic Books

Ormond House, 26–27 Boswell Street, London WC1N 3JZ
*tel* 020-7269 1610 *fax* 020-7430 0916
*email* enquiries@groveatlantic.co.uk
*Managing Director/Publisher* Toby Mundy

Literary fiction, history, current affairs, biography, politics, reference, autobiography; *The Guardian* and *The Observer* books. No unsolicited submissions. Wholly owned subsidiary of **Grove/Atlantic Inc.,** New York. Founded 2000.

## Atlantic Europe Publishing Co. Ltd

Greys Court Farm, Greys Court, Henley-on-Thames, Oxon RG9 4PG
*tel* (01491) 628188 *fax* (01491) 628189
*email* info@atlanticeurope.com
*website* www.atlanticeurope.com, www.curriculumvisions.com
*Directors* Dr B.J. Knapp, D.L.R. McCrae

Children's colour illustrated information books, co-editions and primary school class books: science, geography, technology, mathematics, history, religious education. No MSS accepted by post; submit by email only with no attachments. Founded 1990.

## Atom – see Time Warner Books UK

## Attic Press – see Cork University Press

## Aureus Publishing Ltd

Castle Court, Castle-upon-Alun, St Bride's Major, Vale of Glamorgan CF32 0TN
*tel* (01656) 880033 *fax* (01656) 880033
*email* info@aureus.co.uk
*website* www.aureus.co.uk
*Director* Meuryn Hughes

Rock and pop, autobiography, sport, aviation, religion; also music. Founded 1993.

## Aurum Press Ltd

25 Bedford Avenue, London WC1B 3AT
*tel* 020-7637 3225 *fax* 020-7580 2469
*email* firstname.surname@aurumpress.co.uk
*website* www.aurumpress.co.uk
*Directors* Bill McCreadie (managing), Piers Burnett (editorial), Graham Eames (sales), Sheila Murphy (non-executive), Khalil Abu-Shawareb (non-executive)

General, illustrated and non-illustrated adult non-fiction: biography and memoirs, military, visual arts, film, sport, travel, fashion, home interest. Imprints: Argentum (photography), Jacqui Small (lifestyle). Founded 1977.

## Award Publications Ltd

1st Floor, 27 Longford Street, London NW1 3DZ
*tel* 020-7388 7800 *fax* 020-7388 7887
*Managing Director* Ron Wilkinson

Children's books: full colour picture story books; early learning, information and activity books. No unsolicited material. Founded 1954.

## Azure Books – see Society for Promoting Christian Knowledge

## Bernard Babani (publishing) Ltd

The Grampians, Shepherds Bush Road, London W6 7NF
*tel* 020-7603 2581/7296 *fax* 020-7603 8203
*Director* M.H. Babani

Practical handbooks on radio, electronics , computing.

## Duncan Baird Publishers

6th Floor, Castle House, 75–76 Wells Street, London W1T 3QH
*tel* 020-7323 2229 *fax* 020-7580 5692
*Directors* Duncan Baird (managing), Bob Saxton (editorial), Roger Walton (art), Alex Mitchell (international sales), Ryan Tring (financial)

Non-fiction, illustrated reference. Founded 1992.

## Balliere Tindall – see Elsevier Ltd (Health Sciences)

## Bantam – see Transworld Publishers

## Bantam Press – see Transworld Publishers

## Barefoot Books Ltd

124 Walcot Street, Bath BA1 5BG
*tel* (01225) 322400 *fax* (01225) 322499
*email* info@barefootbooks.co.uk
*website* www.barefootbooks.co.uk
*Publisher* Tessa Strickland

Children's picture books and audiobooks: myth, legend, fairytale. No unsolicited MSS. Founded 1993.

**Barrie & Jenkins** – former imprint of
Random House Group Ltd

**Bartholomew** – see HarperCollins Publishers

**B.T. Batsford** – see Chrysalis Books Group

## BBC Audiobooks Ltd*
St James House, The Square, Lower Bristol Road,
Bath BA2 3BH
*tel* (01225) 878000 *fax* (01225) 310777
*website* www.bbcaudiobooks.com
*Directors* Paul Dempsey (managing), Jan Paterson
(publishing), Rachel Stammers (marketing)

Large print books and complete and unabridged
audiobooks: general fiction, crime, romance,
mystery/thrillers, westerns, non-fiction. Does not
publish original books. Imprints: Chivers Large
Print, Chivers Audio Books, Black Dagger Crime,
Windsor Large Print, Galaxy Children's Large Print.
Formed in 2002 from the amalgamation of Chivers
Press, Cover To Cover and BBC Radio Collection.

**BBC Worldwide Ltd** – see page 333

**Belair** – see Folens Publishers

**Belitha Press** – see Chrysalis Children's Books

**Bell & Hyman Ltd** – acquired by
HarperCollins Publishers

**David Bennett Books** – see Chrysalis
Children's Books

## Berg Publishers
1st Floor, Angel Court, 81 St Clements Street,
Oxford OX4 1AW
*tel* (01865) 245104 *fax* (01865) 791165
*email* enquiry@bergpublishers.com
*Managing Director* Kathryn Earle

Social anthropology, cultural studies, sport, dress
and fashion studies, European studies, politics,
history. Founded 1983.

## Berkswell Publishing Co. Ltd
PO Box 420, Warminster, Wilts. BA12 9XB
*tel* (01985) 840189 *fax* (01985) 840243
*email* churchwardens@btinternet.com
*Directors* J.N.G. Stidolph, S.A. Abbott

Books of local interest, field sports, church
administration. Ideas and MSS welcome.

**Berlin Verlag** – see Bloomsbury Publishing Plc

**Berlitz Publishing** – see Insight Guides/
Berlitz Publishing

## BFI Publishing
British Film Institute, 21 Stephen Street,
London W1P 2LN
*tel* 020-7255 1444 *fax* 020-7636 2516
*website* www.bfi.org.uk
*Head of Publishing* Jonathan Tilston

Film and media studies; general books on films and
directors. Founded 1982.

**Big Fish** – see Chrysalis Children's Books

**Clive Bingley Ltd** – see Facet Publishing

**BIOS Scientific Publishers** – see Taylor
and Francis Books Ltd

## Birlinn Ltd*
West Newington House, 10 Newington Road,
Edinburgh EH9 1QS
*tel* 0131-668 4371 *fax* 0131-668 4466
*email* info@birlinn.co.uk
*website* www.birlinn.co.uk
*Directors* Hugh Andrew, Hubert Andrew, Neville
Moir, Ronnie Shanks

Scottish history, local interest/history, Scottish
humour, guides, military, adventure, history,
archaeology, vernacular architecture, sport, general
non-fiction. Imprints: John Donald, Polygon.
Founded 1992.

**Polygon (imprint)**
New international and Scottish fiction, poetry, short
stories, popular Scottish and international general
interest. No unsolicited poetry accepted.

**Birnbaum** – see HarperCollins Publishers

## A & C Black Publishers Ltd*
37 Soho Square, London W1D 3QZ
*tel* 020-7758 0200 *fax* 020-7758 0222
*email* enquiries@acblack.com
*website* www.acblack.com
*Chairman* Nigel Newton, *Managing Director* Jill
Coleman, *Directors* Colin Adams, Charles Black,
Sarah Fecher (children's books), Oscar Heini
(production), Paul Langridge (rights), Janet
Murphy (Adlard Coles Nautical), Kathy Rooney,
Terry Rouelett (distribution), David Wightman
(sales), Jonathan Glasspool (reference)

Children's and educational books (including music)
for 3–15 year-olds (preliminary enquiry appreciated
– fiction guidelines available on request); ceramics,
art and craft, drama, ornithology, reference (*Who's
Who, Whitaker's Almanack*), sport, theatre, books
for writers. Subsidiary of Bloomsbury Publishing
plc. Founded 1807.

**Adlard Coles Nautical (imprint)**
Nautical.

**Andrew Brodie (imprint)**
Children's, educational.

**Christopher Helm (imprint)**
Ornithology.

**The Herbert Press (imprint)**
Visual arts.

**Pica Press (imprint)**
Ornithology.

**T & AD Poyser (imprint)**
Ornithology, natural history.

**Thomas Reed (imprint)**
Nautical.

**Reed Nautical Almanac (imprint)**
Navigation and port information.

## Black Ace Books

PO Box 6557, Forfar DD8 2YS
*tel* (01307) 465096 *fax* (01307) 465494
*website* www.blackacebooks.com
*Publisher* Hunter Steele, *Art, Publicity and Sales* Boo
Wood

Fiction, Scottish and general; new editions of
outstanding recent fiction. Some biography, history,
psychology and philosophy. No submissions
without first visiting website for latest list details
and requirements. Imprints: Black Ace Books, Black
Ace Paperbacks. Founded 1991.

## BlackAmber Books Ltd

3 Queen Square, London WC1N 3AU
*tel* 020-7278 2488 *fax* 020-7278 8864
*email* info@blackamber.com
*website* www.blackamber.com
*Publisher* Rosemarie Hudson

Literary fiction and non-fiction and works in
translation by Europe's multicultural authors, in
particluar Black and Asian.
  For novel submissions send one-page synopsis
together with first 3 chapters and sae; for non-
fiction, send a detailed outline with some
accompanying material plus a one-page CV and sae.
Founded 1998.

## Black & White Publishing Ltd*

99 Giles Street, Edinburgh EH6 6BZ
*tel* 0131-625 4500  *fax* 0131-625 4501
*email* mail@blackandwhitepublishing.com
*website* www.blackandwhitepublishing.com
*Directors* Campbell Brown (managing), Alison
McBride

Non-fiction: humour biography, crime, sport,
cookery, general. Fiction: classic Scottish,
contemporary, crime. Founded 1990.

## Black Lace – see Virgin Books Ltd

## Blackstaff Press Ltd[†]

4C Heron Wharf, Sydenham Business Park,
Belfast BT3 9LE
*tel* 028-9045 5006 *fax* 028-9046 6237
*email* info@blackstaffpress.com
*website* www.blackstaffpress.com
*Managing Editor* Patsy Horton

Educational books for primary school children. Also
adult fiction, poetry, biography, history, sport,
politics, natural history, humour. Founded 1971.

## Blackstone Press Ltd – acquired by Oxford University Press

## Black Swan – see see Transworld Publishers

## Blackwater Press – see Folens Publishers

## Blackwell Publishing Ltd*

9600 Garsington Road, Oxford OX4 2DQ
*tel* (01865) 776868 *fax* (01865) 714591
*website* www.blackwellpublishing.com
*Also at* 108 Cowley Road, Oxford OX4 1JF
*email* (01865) 791100  *fax* (01865) 791347
*website* www.blackwellpublishing.com
*Chairman* Nigel Blackwell, *President* Robert
Campbell, *Chief Executive* René Olivieri

Books and journals in medicine, veterinary medicine,
dentistry, nursing and allied health, science
(particularly biology, chemistry and geology), social
sciences, business and humanities. Journals are
delivered online through Blackwell Synergy. Formed
by merging Blackwell Science (founded 1939) and
Blackwell Publishers (founded 1922).

**BMJ Books (imprint)**
Medicine, self-help, alternative medicine.

## Blake Publishing

3 Bramber Court, 2 Bramber Road, London W14 9PB
*tel* 020-7381 0666 *fax* 020-7381 6868
*email* words@blake.co.uk

Popular non-fiction, including biographies and true
crime. No unsolicited fiction. Founded 1991.

## John Blake Publishing Ltd

3 Bramber Court, 2 Bramber Road, London W14 9PB
*tel* 020-7381 0666 *fax* 020-7381 6868
*email* words@blake.co.uk

Popular non-fiction, including biographies, true
crime, food and drink, health. No unsolicited
fiction. Acquired Metro Publishing Ltd 2001.

## Bloodaxe Books Ltd

Highgreen, Tarset, Northumberland NE48 1RP
*tel* (01434) 240500 *fax* (01434) 240505
*email* editor@bloodaxebooks.demon.co.uk
*website* www.bloodaxebooks.com
*Directors* Neil Astley, Simon Thirsk

Poetry, literary criticism. No submissions from new authors this year. Founded 1978.

## Bloomsbury Publishing Plc*

38 Soho Square, London W1D 3HB
*tel* 020-7494 2111 *fax* 020-7434 0151
*website* www.bloomsburymagazine.com
*Chairman and Chief Executive* Nigel Newton,
*Directors* Liz Calder (publishing), Alexandra Pringle (publishing), Kathleen Farrar (international), Karen Rinaldi (Bloomsbury USA), Kathy Rooney (reference), David Ward (sales), Minna Fry (marketing), Katie Collins (publicity), Ruth Logan (rights), Penny Edwards (production), Arzu Tahsin (paperbacks), Sarah Odedina (children's), Colin Adams (finance), Will Webb (design), Jill Coleman

Fiction, biography, illustrated, reference, travel, children's, trade paperbacks and mass market paperbacks. Founded 1986.

### Aspect Guides (imprint)
*email* info@aspectguides.com
*website* www.aspectguides.com

Travel guides including the *French Entrée* series, *Everybody's Guides*, *Access Guides*, *Before You Go*.

### Berlin Verlag (imprint)
*Editorial Director* Dorothee Grisebach

Harback fiction and non-fiction.

### Peter Collin (imprint)
*email* info@petercollin.com
*website* www.petercollin.com

Specialised dictionaries covering many subjects – from business to computing, medicine to tourism, law to banking. Bilingual language dictionaries in various subjects and languages.

## BMJ Books – see Blackwell Publishing Ltd

## Boatswain Press Ltd – now Nautical Data Ltd

## Bodley Head Children's Books – see
Random House Group Ltd

## Booth-Clibborn Editions

12 Percy Street, London W1T 1DW
*tel* 020-7637 4255 *fax* 020-7637 4251
*email* info@booth-clibborn.com
*website* www.booth-clibborn.com

Illustrated books on art, popular culture, graphic design, photography. Founded 1974.

## Bounty – see Octopus Publishing Group

## Bowker

3rd Floor, Farringdon House, Wood Street,
East Grinstead, West Sussex RH19 IU2
*tel* (01342) 310450 *fax* (01342) 310486
*email* vales@bowker.co.uk

*website* www.bowker.co.uk
*Managing Director* Doug McMillan

Print and electronic publishers of bibliographies and serials databases, trade and reference directories and library and information titles. Part of the Cambridge Information Group.

## Boxtree – see Macmillan Publishers Ltd

## Marion Boyars Publishers Ltd

24 Lacy Road, London SW15 1NL
*tel* 020-8788 9522 *fax* 020-8789 8122
*email* catheryn@marionboyars.com
*website* www.marionboyars.co.uk
*Directors* Catheryn Kilgarriff, Rebecca Gillieron (editorial)

Literary fiction, film, memoirs, travel, cultural studies, jazz, music. Will only consider fiction submitted through an agent. Founded 1975.

## Boydell & Brewer Ltd

PO Box 9, Woodbridge, Suffolk IP12 3DF

Medieval studies, history, literature, archaeology, art history. No unsolicited MSS. Founded 1969.

## Bradt Travel Guides Ltd

19 High Street, Chalfont St Peter, Bucks SL9 9QE
*tel* (01753) 893444 *fax* (01753) 892333
*email* info@bradt-travelguides.com
*website* www.bradt-travelguides.com
*Managing Director* Hilary Bradt

Guides for the adventurous traveller who seeks off-beat places and 'the dreamer who would like to travel there but never will'.

## Brandon/Mount Eagle Publications

Cooleen, Dingle, Co. Kerry, Republic of Ireland
*tel* (353) 66 9151463 *fax* (353) 66 9151234
*Publisher* Steve MacDonogh

Fiction, biography and current affairs. No unsolicited MSS.

## Brassey's (UK) Ltd – now Brassey's Conway
Putnam– see Chrysalis Books Group

## Nicholas Brealey Publishing

3–5 Spafield Street, London EC1R 4QB
*tel* 020-7239 0360 *fax* 020-7239 0370
*email* rights@nbrealey-books.com
*website* www.nbrealey-books.com
*Managing Director* Nicholas Brealey

Business, intelligent self-help, popular psychology, cross-cultural studies, travel writing. Founded 1992.

## Breedon Books Publishing Co. Ltd

Breedon House, 3 The Parker Centre,
Mansfield Road, Derby DE21 4SZ
*tel* (01332) 384235 *fax* (01332) 292755

*email* submissions@breedonpublishing.co.uk
*Directors* Steve Caron (Managing Director), Jane
Caron (Finance Director), Anton Rippon (chairman
and editorial), Patricia Rippon, Graham Hales
(production)

Football, sport, local history, archive photography,
heritage. No fiction. Unsolicited MSS welcome.
Preliminary letter essential. Founded 1981.

## Breese Books Ltd
10 Hanover Crescent, Brighton BN2 9SB
*tel* (01273) 687555
*email* martin@HanoverCrescent.com
*website* www.sherlockholmes.co.uk
*Publisher* Martin Breese

Conjuring books, Sherlock Holmes pastiches and
*Breese's Guide to Modern First Editions*. All work is
commissioned and unsolicited submissions are not
required. Founded 1980.

## Brilliant Publications*
1 Church View, Sparrow Hall Farm, Edlesborough,
Dunstable LU6 2ES
*tel* (01525) 229720 *fax* (01525) 229725
*email* editorial@brilliantpublications.co.uk
*website* www.brilliantpublications.co.uk
*Managing Director* Priscilla Hannaford

Resource books for teachers and others concerned
with the education of 0–13 year-olds. All areas of
the curriculum published. Study catalogue or visit
website before sending proposal. Founded 1993.

## The British Library (Publications)*
Publishing Office, The British Library,
96 Euston Road, London NW1 2DB
*tel* 020-7412 7704 *fax* 020-7412 7768
*email* blpublications@bl.uk
*website* www.bl.uk
*Managers* David Way (publishing), Lara Speicher
(managing editor), Catherine Britton (sales and
marketing)

Book arts, bibliography, music, maps, oriental,
manuscript studies, history, literature, facsimiles,
audiovisual, multimedia CD-Rom. Founded 1973.

## British Museum Company Ltd*
46 Bloomsbury Street, London WC1B 3QQ
*tel* 020-7323 1234 *fax* 020-7436 7315
*website* www.britishmuseumcompany.co.uk
*Managing Director* Andrew Thatcher, *Director of
Publishing* Alasdair MacLeod

General and specialised adult and children's books
on art history, archaeology, numismatics, history,
oriental art and archaeology, horology, ethnography.
Division of The British Museum Company Ltd.

## Brockhampton Press – see Caxton
Publishing Group

## Andrew Brodie – see A & C Black Publishers
Ltd

## Brown, Son & Ferguson, Ltd*
4–10 Darnley Street, Glasgow G41 2SD
*tel* 0141-429 1234 (24 hours) *fax* 0141-420 1694
*email* info@skipper.co.uk
*website* www.skipper.co.uk
*Editorial Director* L. Ingram-Brown

Nautical books, plays. Founded 1860.

## Brunner-Routledge – see Psychology Press
Ltd

## Bryntirion Press
Bryntirion, Bridgend CF31 4DX
*tel* (01656) 655886 *fax* (01656) 665919
*email* office@emw.org.uk
*website* www.emw.org.uk
*Press Manager* Huw Kinsey

Theology and religion (in English and Welsh).
Founded 1955.

## Bullfinch Publishing – see Time Warner
Books UK

## Burns & Oates – see The Continuum
International Publishing Group Ltd

## Buster Books – see Michael O'Mara Books Ltd

## Butterworths – see LexisNexis UK

## Butterworth-Heinemann – see Elsevier Ltd

## Cadogan Guides
Network House, 1 Ariel Way, London W12 7SL
*tel* 020-8740 2050 *fax* 020-8740 2059
*email* info@cadoganguides.co.uk
*website* www.cadoganguides.com
*Managing Editor* Natalie Pomier

Travel guides and travel literature. Founded 1982.

## Calder Publications Ltd
51 The Cut, London SE1 8LF
*tel* 020-7633 0599 *fax* 020-7928 5930
*email* info@calderpublications.com
*website* www.calderpublications.com
*Directors* John Calder, Toby Fenton

European, international and British fiction and
plays, art, literary, music and social criticism,
biography and autobiography, essays, humanities
and social sciences, European classics. No
unsolicited MSS. Inquiry letters must include an
sae. Series include: *English National Opera Guides,
Scottish Library, New Writing and Writers, Opera
Library, Historical Perspectives, Thought Bites.*

## Calmann & King Ltd – see Laurence King Publishing Ltd

## Cambridge University Press*

The Edinburgh Building, Shaftesbury Road, Cambridge CB2 2RU
*tel* (01223) 325892 *fax* (01223) 325891 (UK and Ireland), *tel* (01223) 312393 *fax* (01223) 315052 (for Continental Europe, Middle East, North Africa & South Asia)
*email* information@cambridge.org
*website* www.cambridge.org
*Chief Executive of the Press* Stephen R.R. Bourne, *Publishing Division Directors* Andrew Brown (Adademic), Andrew Gilfillan (Educational), Colin Hayes (ELT), Conrad Guettler (Journals), Michael Holdsworth (Business), Ian Brodie (Distribution), James Berry (Financial), Nicholas Reckert (International)

Anthropology and archaeology, art and architecture, astronomy, biological sciences, classical studies, computer science, dictionaries, earth sciences, economics, educational (primary, secondary, tertiary), e-learning products, engineering, film, English language teaching, history, language and literature, law, mathematics, medical sciences, music, philosophy, physical sciences, politics, psychology, reference, technology, social sciences, theology, religion. Journals (humanities, social sciences, STM). The Bible and Prayer Book. Founded 1534.

## Cameron & Hollis

PO Box 1, Moffat, Dumfriesshire DG10 9SU
*tel* (01683) 220808 *fax* (01683) 220012
*email* editorial@cameronbooks.co.uk
*website* www.cameronbooks.co.uk
*Directors* Ian A. Cameron, Jill Hollis

Modern art, decorative art, collecting and film (serious critical works only). Founded 1976.

## Campbell Books – see Macmillan Publishers Ltd

## Canongate Books Ltd*

14 High Street, Edinburgh EH1 1TE
*tel* 0131-557 5111 *fax* 0131-557 5211
*email* info@canongate.co.uk
*website* www.canongate.net
*Publisher* Jamie Byng, *Directors* David Graham (managing), Kathleen Anderson (financial), Caroline Graham (production)

Adult general non-fiction and fiction: literary fiction, translated fiction, music, travel, mountaineering, history and biography. No unsolicited MSS. Founded 1973.

### Canongate Classics (imprint)
*Senior Editor* Rory Watson

Reprint series of key works of Scottish literature ranging from fiction to poetry, to biography, philosophy and travel.

## Canopus Publishing Ltd

27 Queen Square, Bristol BS1 4ND
*tel* 0117-922 6660
*email* robin@canopusbooks.com
*website* www.canopusbooks.com
*Director* Robin Rees

Popular science and astronomy. Founded 1999.

## Canterbury Press Norwich*

St Mary's Works, St Mary's Plain, Norwich NR3 3BH
*tel* (01603) 612914 *fax* (01603) 624483
*email* admin@scm-canterburypress.co.uk
*website* www.scm-canterburypress.co.uk
*Publisher* Christine Smith

Religious doctrine, theology, liturgy, general interest, reference, diaries, guide books, biographies, histories and associated topics, hymn books. Division of SCM–Canterbury Press Ltd, a subsidiary of Hymns Ancient & Modern Ltd.

## Jonathan Cape – see Random House Group Ltd

## Jonathan Cape Children's Books – see Random House Group Ltd

## Carcanet Press Ltd

4th Floor, Alliance House, 28–34 Cross Street, Manchester M2 7AQ
*tel* 0161-834 8730 *fax* 0161-832 0084
*email* pnr@carcanet.u-net.com
*website* www.carcanet.co.uk
*Director* Michael Schmidt

Poetry, *Fyfield* series, Oxford Poets, translations. Founded 1969.

## Carlton Publishing Group

20 Mortimer Street, London W1T 3JW
*tel* 020-7612 0400 *fax* 020-7612 0401
*email* enquiries@carltonbooks.co.uk
*Managing Director* Jonathan Goodman, *Editorial Director* Piers Murray Hill

No unsolicited MSS; synopses and ideas welcome. Imprints: Carlton Books, André Deutsch, Granada Media, Manchester United Books, Prion Books. Owned by ITV plc. Founded 1992.

### André Deutsch (division)
Autobiography, biography, history, current affairs, humour, drink, the arts.

### Carlton Books (division)
Illustrated leisure and entertainment books aimed at the mass market: TV tie-ins, health and

wellbeing, popular science, design, history, music, sport, puzzles.

**Prion Books (division)**
Humour, drink.

**Frank Cass** – see Taylor and Francis Books Ltd

**Cassell Illustrated** – see Octopus Publishing Group

**Cassell Military** – see Weidenfeld & Nicolson

**Cassell Reference** – see Weidenfeld & Nicolson

**Kyle Cathie Ltd**
122 Arlington Road, London NW1 7HP
*tel* 020-7692 7215 *fax* 020-7692 7260
*email* general.enquiries@kyle-cathie.com
*website* www.kylecathie.com
*Publisher and Managing Director* Kyle Cathie

Health, beauty, food and drink, gardening, reference, style, design, Mind, Body & Spirit. Founded 1990.

**Catholic Truth Society**
40–46 Harleyford Road, London SE11 5AY
*tel* 020-7640 0042 *fax* 020-7640 0046
*email* editorial@cts-online.org.uk
*website* www.cts-online.org.uk
*Chairman* Most Rev. Peter Smith DCL,LLB, *General Secretary* Fergal Martin LLB, LLM

General books of Roman Catholic and Christian interest, bibles, prayer books, RE, and booklets of doctrinal, historical, devotional or social interest. MSS of 11,000–15,000 words with up to 6 illustrations considered for publication as pamphlets. Founded 1868.

**Cat's Whiskers** – see The Watts Publishing Group Ltd

**Cavendish Publishing Ltd\***
The Glass House, Wharton Street, London WC1X 9PX
*tel* 020-7278 8000 *fax* 020-7278 8080
*email* info@cavendishpublishing.com
*website* www.cavendishpublishing.com
*Executive Chairman* Sonny Leong, *Managing Director* Jeremy Stein, *Marketing Director* Ruth Phillips, *Managing Editor* Jon Lloyd

A wide range of legal and medico–legal books and journals. Imprints: Birkbeck Law Press, Glass House Press, UCL Press. Founded 1990.

**Caxton Publishing Group**
20 Bloomsbury Street, London WC1B 3QA
*tel* 020-7636 7171 *fax* 020-7636 1922
*Directors* John Maxwell (managing), Jack Cooper (deputy managing)

Reprints, promotional books, remainders. Imprints: Caxton Editions, Brockhampton Press, Knight Paperbacks.

**CBD Research Ltd**
15 Wickham Road, Beckenham, Kent BR3 5JS
*tel* 020-8650 7745 *fax* 020-8650 0768
*email* cbd@cbdresearch.com
*website* www.cbdresearch.com
*Directors* S.P.A. Henderson, A.J.W. Henderson

Directories, reference books, bibliographies, guides to business and statistical information. Founded 1961.

**Chancery House Press (imprint)**
Unusual non-fiction/reference works. Preliminary letter and synopsis with return postage essential.

**Centaur Press** – acquired by Open Gate Press

**Century** – see Random House Group Ltd

**Cescent Books** – imprint of The Mercat Press

**Chambers Harrap Publishers Ltd\***
7 Hopetoun Crescent, Edinburgh EH7 4AY
*tel* 0131-556 5929 *fax* 0131-556 5313
*email* admin@chambersharrap.co.uk
*Managing Director* Maurice Shepherd, *Publishing Manager* Patrick White

English language and bilingual dictionaries, reference, word games. No unsolicited MSS. Write enclosing CV and synopsis.

**Chancery House Press** – see CBD Research Ltd

**Channel 4 Books** – see Transworld Publishers

**Chapman Publishing**
4 Broughton Place, Edinburgh EH1 3RX
*tel* 0131-557 2207 *fax* 0131-556 9565
*email* chapman-pub@blueyonder.co.uk
*website* www.chapman-pub.co.uk
*Editor* Joy Hendry

Poetry and drama: *Chapman New Writing Series*. Also the *Chapman Wild Women Series*. Founded 1970.

**Paul Chapman Publishing Ltd**
1 Oliver's Yard, 55 City Road, London EC1Y ISP
*tel* 020-7324 8500 *fax* 020-7324 8600
*website* www.paulchapmanpublishing.co.uk
*Consultant* P.R. Chapman, *Commissioning Editor* Marianne Lagrange

Education. Subsidiary of **SAGE Publications Ltd**.

## Chartered Institute of Personnel and Development

CIPD House, Camp Road, London SW19 4UX
*tel* 020-8263 3382 *fax* 020-8263 3850
*email* publish@cipd.co.uk
*website* www.cipd.co.uk/publications
*Publishing Manager* Sarah Brown

Personnel management, training and development.

## Chatto & Windus – see Random House Group Ltd

## Cherrytree Books – see Zero to Ten Ltd

## The Chicken House*

2 Palmer Street, Frome, Somerset BA11 1DS
*tel* (01373) 454488 *fax* (01373) 454499
*email* chickenhouse@doublecluck.com
*website* www.doublecluck.com
*Managing Director & Publisher* Barry Cunningham,
*Deputy Managing Director* Rachel Hickman,
*Publishing Director* David Riley, *Creative Director*
Elinor Bagenal

Fiction and non-fiction for age 7+, picture books.

## Child's Play (International) Ltd

Ashworth Road, Bridgemead, Swindon,
Wilts. SN5 7YD
*tel* (01793) 616286 *fax* (01793) 512795
*email* allday@childs-play.com
*website* www.childs-play.com
*Chairman* Adriana Twinn, *Publisher* Neil Burden

Children's educational books: board, picture,
activity and play books; fiction and non-fiction.
Founded 1972.

## Chivers Press – see BBC Audiobooks Ltd

## Christian Education*

1020 Bristol Road, Selly Oak, Birmingham B29 6LB
*tel* 0121-472 4242 *fax* 0121-472 7575
*email* enquiries@christianeducation.org.uk
*website* www.christianeducation.org.uk

Publications and services for teachers of RE
including *RE today* magazine, curriculum booklets,
training material for children and youth workers in
the Church. Worship resources for use in primary
schools. Christian drama and musicals, Activity
Club material and Bible reading resources.

## Chrysalis Books Group

The Chrysalis Building, Bramley Road,
London W10 6SP
*tel* 020-7314 1400 *fax* 020-7221 6455
*website* www.chrysalisbooks.co.uk
*Chairman* Marcus Leaver, *Publishing Director – Trade*
Polly Powell, *Director of Publications* Roger Higgins

Part of Chrysalis Group plc.

## B.T. Batsford (imprint)

*email* batsford@chrysalisbooks.co.uk
*website* www.batsford.com
*Associate Publisher* Tina Persaud

Chess and bridge, art techniques, film, fashion and
costume, practical craft, gardening, embroidery,
lace, woodwork.

## Brassey's Conway Putnam

*Editorial* John Lee, *Associate Publisher* Kate Oldfield

Highly illustrated reference books on naval and
maritime, aviation and military subjects, Mind,
Body & Spirit.

## Collins & Brown (imprint)

*Directors* Kate Cowen (associate), Frank Chambers
(international rights), Richard Samson (UK sales
and marketing)

Lifestyle and interiors, gardening, photography,
practical arts, health and beauty, hobbies and crafts,
natural history, history, ancient civilisation and
general interest.

## Paper Tiger (imprint)

*Commissioning Editor* Chris Stone

Science fiction and fantasy art.

## Pavilion Books Ltd (imprint)

*Contact* Kate Oldfield

Cookery, gardening, travel, humour, sport,
photography, art.

## Robson Books (imprint)

*Publisher* Jeremy Robson

General non-fiction, biography, music, humour,
sport. Unsolicited MSS discouraged; ideas with
synopses welcome with sae.

## Salamander (imprint)

*Publishing Director* Jo Messham

Cookery, crafts, military, natural history, music,
gardening, hobbies, transport, sports.

## Chrysalis Children's Books

The Chrysalis Building, Bramley Road,
London W10 6SP
*tel* 020-7221 2213 *fax* 020-7314 1598
*email* childrens@chrysalisbooks.co.uk
*website* www.chrysalisbooks.co.uk
*Publisher* Sarah Fabiny

Titles range from illustrated educational books
covering all areas of the curriculum to reference and
information books for the home and school. Lively
information and story books for the under 5 age
group; lavishly illustrated, high-quality picture
books for older children; educational guides for
parents; interactive non-fiction and novelty books.
Imprints: Belitha Press, David Bennett Books, Big
Fish, Learning World, Pavilion Children's Books, Zig
Zag. Founded 2003.

**Churchill Livingstone** – see Elsevier Ltd
(Health Sciences)

**Cicerone Press**
2 Police Square, Milnthorpe, Cumbria LA7 7PY
*tel* (01539) 562069 *fax* (01539) 563417
*email* info@cicerone.co.uk
*website* www.cicerone.co.uk
*Managing Director* Jonathan Williams

Guidebooks: walking, trekking, mountaineering, climbing, cycling, etc in Britain, Europe, and worldwide.

**Cico Books**
32 Great Sutton Street, London EC1V 0NB
*tel* 020-7253 7960 *fax* 020-7253 7967
*email* mail@cicobooks.co.uk
*Directors* Mark Collins (managing), Lucinda Richards (publishing)

Lifestyle and interiors and Mind, Body & Spirit. Founded 1999.

**Cima Books** – now Cico Books

**Cisco Press** – see Pearson Education

**Clarendon Press** – former imprint of Oxford University Press

**James Clarke & Co. Ltd***
PO Box 60, Cambridge CB1 2NT
*tel* (01223) 350865 *fax* (01223) 366951
*email* publishing@lutterworth.com
*website* www.lutterworth.com
*Managing Director* Adrian Brink

Theology, academic, reference books. Founded 1859.

**Acorn Editions (imprint)**
Sponsored books.

**Lutterworth Press (subsidiary)**
The arts, biography, children's books (fiction, non-fiction, picture, rewards), educational, environmental, general, history, leisure, philosophy, science, sociology, theology and religion.

**Patrick Hardy Books (imprint)**
Children's fiction.

**T&T Clark** – see The Continuum International Publishing Group Ltd

**Classic Publications** – see Ian Allan Publishing Ltd

**Cló Iar-Chonnachta Teo.†**
Indreabhán, Conamara, Co. Galway, Republic of Ireland
*tel* (091) 593307 *fax* (091) 593362

*email* cic@iol.ie
*website* www.cic.ie
*Director* Micheál Ó Conghaile, *General Manager* Deirdre O'Toole

Irish-language – novels, short stories, plays, poetry, songs, history; cassettes (writers reading from their works in Irish and English). Promotes the translation of contemporary Irish fiction and poetry into other languages. Founded 1985.

**CMP Information Ltd**
Riverbank House, Angel Lane, Tonbridge, Kent TN9 1SE
*tel* (01732) 377591 *fax* (01732) 368324
*email* orders@cmpinformation.com
*website* www.cmpdata.co.uk

Directories for business and industry, including *Benn's Media* and *The Knowledge*, guides for the media and film and TV markets respectively. Subsidiary of United Business Media.

**Co & Bear Productions***
565 Fulham Road, London SW6 1ES
*tel* 020-7385 0888 *fax* 020-7385 0101
*email* info@cobear.co.uk
*Publisher* Beatrice Vincenzini

High-quality illustrated books on lifestyle, photography, art. Imprints: Scriptum Editions, Cartago. Founded 1996.

**Peter Collin** – see Bloomsbury Publishing Plc

**Collins** – see HarperCollins Publishers

**Collins & Brown** – see Chrysalis Books Group

**Collins Crime** – see HarperCollins Publishers

**Collins Dictionaries/COBUILD** – see HarperCollins Publishers

**Collins Gem** – see HarperCollins Publishers

**Collins Jet** – see HarperCollins Publishers

**Collins New Naturalist Library** – see HarperCollins Publishers

**Collins Picture Books** – see HarperCollins Publishers

**Collins Teacher** – see HarperCollins Publishers

**Collins/Times Maps and Atlases** – see HarperCollins Publishers

**Collins Willow** – see HarperCollins Publishers

## Colourpoint Books*

Colourpoint House, Jubilee Business Park,
21 Jubilee Road, Newtownards, Co. Down,
Northern Ireland BT23 4YH
*tel* (028) 9182 0505 *fax* (028) 9182 1900
*email* info@colourpoint.co.uk
*website* www.colourpoint.co.uk
*Directors* Sheila Johnston (commissioning editor),
Norman Johnston (transport editor), Malcolm
Johnston, Wesley Johnston, *Administrator* Michelle
Chambers, *Sales Manager* Lawrence Greer

Educational textbooks; transport – shipping,
aviation, buses, road and railways; religion; Irish
and general interest. Initial approach in writing
please, with full details of proposal and sample
chapters. Include return postage. Founded 1993.

## The Columba Press†

55A Spruce Avenue, Stillorgan Industrial Park,
Blackrock, Co. Dublin, Republic of Ireland
*tel* (1) 2942556 *fax* (1) 2942564
*email* info@columba.ie
*website* www.columba.ie
*Publisher and Managing Director* Seán O'Boyle

Religion (Roman Catholic and Anglican) including
pastoral handbooks, spirituality, theology, liturgy
and prayer; counselling and self-help. Founded
1985.

### Currach Press (imprint)
General non-fiction.

## Conran Octopus – see Octopus Publishing Group

## Constable & Robinson Ltd*

3 The Lanchesters, 162 Fulham Palace Road,
London W6 9ER
*tel* 020-8741 3663 *fax* 020-8748 7562
*email* enquiries@constablerobinson.com
*website* www.constablerobinson.com
*Managing Director* Nick Robinson, *Directors* Jan
Chamier, Nova Jayne Heath, Adrian Andrews

Unsolicited sample chapters, synopses and ideas
welcome with return postage. Do not send MSS; no
email submissions. Founded 1890 (Constable); 1983
(Robinson).

### Constable (imprint)
*Editorial Director* Dan Hind

Biography, fiction, general and military history,
travel and endurance, climbing, landscape
photography, psychology.

### Robinson (imprint: paperbacks)
Crime fiction, *The Daily Telegraph* health books, the
Mammoth series, psychology, true crime, military
history, current affairs.

## Constable Publishers – see Constable & Robinson Ltd

## Consumers' Association – see Which? Ltd

## The Continuum International Publishing Group Ltd

The Tower Building, 11 York Road, London SE1 7NX
*tel* 020-7922 0880 *fax* 020-7922 0881
*email* info@continuumbooks.com
*website* www.continuumbooks.com
*Chairman & Ceo* Philip J. Sturrock, *Directors* Robin
Baird-Smith (publishing: religious and general),
Philip Law (editorial: academic, religious, biblical
studies and theology), Anthony Haynes (editorial:
professional and philosophy), Janet Joyce
(publishing: journals and humanities), Frank Roney
(finance), Ed Suthon (sales and marketing), Benn
Linfield (publishing services)

Serious non-fiction, academic and professional,
including scholarly monographs and educational
texts and reference works in history, politics and
social thought; literature, criticism, performing arts;
religion and spirituality; education, psychology,
women's studies, business. Imprints: Continuum,
Burns & Oates, T&T Clark, Handsel Press,
Thoemmes Press, Mowbray: Moorehouse, Sheffield
Academic Press.

## Conway Maritime Press – now Brassey's

### Conway Putnam – see Chrysalis Books Group

## Thomas Cook Publishing

PO Box 227, Units 19–21, The Thomas Cook
Business Park, Peterborough PE3 8XX
*tel* (01733) 416477 *fax* (01733) 416688
*email* publishing-sales@thomascook.com
*website* www.thomascookpublishing.com
*Managing Director* Donald Greig

Travel guides, rail maps and timetables. Founded
1875.

## Corgi – see Transworld Publishers

## Corgi Children's Books – see Random House Group Ltd

## Cork University Press†

Crawford Business Park, Crosses Green, Cork,
Republic of Ireland
*tel* (021) 4902980 *fax* (021) 4315329
*email* corkunip@ucc.ie
*website* www.corkuniversitypress.com
*Publisher* Mike Collins

Irish literature, history, cultural studies, medieval
studies, English literature, musicology, poetry,
translations. Founded 1925.

**Attic Press (imprint)**
*tel* (021) 4321725
*email* corkunip@ucc.ie

Books by and about women in the areas of social and political comment, women's studies, reference guides and handbooks.

**Coronet** – see Hodder Headline Ltd

**Corvo Books Ltd\***
64 Duncan Terrace, London N1 8AG
*tel* 020-7288 0651
*email* editor@corvobooks.com
*website* www.corvobooks.com
*Publisher* Scott McDonald, *Editor* Julia Rochester

Specialises in personal histories with an international flavour: memor, history, travel, philosophy. Welcomes submissions of previously unpublished, full-length works of non-fiction which use a strong personal voice (or voices) to document historical or contemporary events in any part of the world. Submit the first 3 chapters (or approx. 30pp) and include a sae for its return. Founded 2002.

**Council for British Archaeology**
Bowes Morrell House, 111 Walmgate,
York YO1 9WA
*tel* (01904) 671417 *fax* (01904) 671384
*email* info@britarch.ac.uk
*website* www.britarch.ac.uk
*Director* George Lambrick, *Publications Officer* Jane Thorniley-Walker

British archaeology – academic; practical handbooks; general interest archaeology. Founded 1944.

**Countryside Books**
2 Highfield Avenue, Newbury, Berks. RG14 5DS
*tel* (01635) 43816 *fax* (01635) 551004
*website* www.countrysidebooks.co.uk
*Partners* Nicholas Battle, Suzanne Battle

Books of local or regional interest, usually on a county basis: walking, outdoor activities, local history; also genealogy, aviation. Founded 1976.

**Countrywise Press Ltd** – see Barry Rose
Law Publishers Ltd

**Cover to Cover** – see BBC Audiobooks Ltd

**CRC Press** – see Taylor and Francis Books Ltd

**Crescent Books** – see The Mercat Press

**Crescent Moon Publishing**
PO Box 393, Maidstone, Kent ME14 5XU
*tel* (01622) 729593
*email* cresmopub@yahoo.co.uk
*website* www.crescentmoon.org.uk

*Director* Jeremy Robinson, *Editors* C. Hughes, B.D. Barnacle

Literature, poetry, arts, cultural studies, media, cinema, feminism. Submit sample chapters or 6 poems plus sae, not complete MSS. Founded 1988.

**Cressrelles Publishing Co. Ltd**
10 Station Road Industrial Estate, Colwall, Malvern, Herefordshire WR13 6RN
*tel* (01684) 540154 *fax* (01684) 540154
*email* simonsmith@cressrelles4drama.fsbusiness.co.uk
*Directors* Leslie Smith, Simon Smith

General publishing. Founded 1973.

**Actinic Press (imprint)**
Chiropody.

**J. Garnet Miller (imprint)**
Plays and theatre textbooks.

**Kenyon-Deane (imprint)**
Plays and drama textbooks for amateur dramatic societies. Plays for women.

**Crown House Publishing Ltd**
Crown Buildings, Bancyfelin,
Carmarthen SA33 5ND
*tel* (01267) 211345 *fax* (01267) 211882
*email* books@crownhouse.co.uk
*website* www.crownhouse.co.uk
*Chairman* Martin Roberts, *Directors* David Bowman (managing director), Glenys Roberts, David Bowman, Karen Bowman, Caroline Lenton

Publishes titles in the areas of psychotherapy, education, business training and development, Mind, Body & Spirit. Aim to demystify the latest psychological advances, particularly in the fields of Accelerated Learning, Neuro-Linguistic Programming (NLP) and Hypnosis. Crown House provide professional therapists, consultants and trainers with books detailing the latest cutting edge developments in their fields. Founded 1998.

**The Crowood Press**
The Stable Block, Ramsbury, Marlborough,
Wilts. SN8 2HR
*tel* (01672) 520320 *fax* (01672) 520280
*email* enquiries@crowood.com
*website* www.crowood.com
*Directors* John Dennis (chairman), Ken Hathaway (managing)

Sport, motoring, aviation, military, climbing, walking, fishing, country sports, farming, natural history, gardening, DIY, crafts, dogs, equestrian, games. Founded 1982.

**Airlife Publishing (imprint)**
Aviation, technical and general, military, military history.

**Benjamin Cummings** – see Pearson
Education

**Currach Press** – see The Columba Press

**Current Science Group**
34–42 Cleveland Street, London W1T 4LB
*tel* 020-7323 0323 *fax* 020-7580 1938
*email* csg@cursci.co.uk
*website* www.current-science-group.com
*Chairman* Vitek Tracz

Biological sciences, medicine, pharmaceutical
science, internet communities, electronic publishing.

**James Currey Ltd**
73 Botley Road, Oxford OX2 0BS
*tel* (01865) 244111 *fax* (01865) 246454
*Directors* James Currey, Prof Wendy James FBA,
Dr Douglas H. Johnson, Keith Sambrook

Academic studies of Africa, Caribbean, Third World:
history, anthropology, archaeology, economics,
agriculture, politics, literary criticism, sociology.

**Curzon Press Ltd** – now RoutledgeCurzon –
see Taylor and Francis Books Ltd

**Dalesman Publishing Co. Ltd**
Stable Courtyard, Broughton Hall, Skipton,
North Yorkshire BD23 3AE
*tel* (01756) 701381 *fax* (01756) 701326
*email* editorial@dalesman.co.uk
*Chairman* T.J. Benn, *Chief Executive* C.G. Benn,
*Managing Director* R. Flanagan

Countryside books and magazines covering the
North of England. Founded 1939.

**Terence Dalton Ltd**
Water Street, Lavenham, Sudbury,
Suffolk CO10 9RN
*tel* (01787) 249289 *fax* (01787) 248267
*Directors* T.A.J. Dalton, E.H. Whitehair

Non-fiction.

**C.W. Daniel** – see Random House Group Ltd

**Darton, Longman & Todd Ltd\***
1 Spencer Court, 140–142 Wandsworth High Street,
London SW18 4JJ
*tel* 020-8875 0155 *fax* 020-8875 0133
*email* editorial@darton-longman-todd.co.uk
*Editorial Director* Brendan Walsh

Religious books and bibles, including the following
themes: bible study, spirituality, prayer and
meditation, anthologies, daily readings, healing,
counselling and pastoral care, bereavement,
personal growth, mission, political, environmental
and social issues, biography/autobiography,
theological and historical studies. Founded 1959.

**Darwen Finlayson Ltd** – see Phillimore &
Co. Ltd

**David & Charles Children's Books** – see
Pinwheel Ltd

**David & Charles Ltd**
Brunel House, Newton Abbot,
Devon TQ12 4PU
*tel* (01626) 323200 *fax* (01626) 323319
*Acting Managing Director* Budge Wallis, *Publishing
Director* Sara Domville

High-quality illustrated non-fiction specialising in
military history, crafts, hobbies, art techniques,
gardening, natural history, equestrian, DIY,
photography. Founded 1960.

**Christopher Davies Publishers Ltd**
PO Box 403, Swansea SA1 4YF
*tel* (01792) 648825 *fax* (01792) 648825
*email* editor@cdaviesbookswales.com
*website* www.cdaviesbookswales.com
*Directors* Christopher Talfan Davies (editorial),
D.M. Davies

History, leisure, sport and general books of Welsh
interest only, *Triskele Books.* Founded 1949.

**Dean** – see Egmont Books

**Dedalus Ltd**
24 St Judith's Lane, Sawtry, Cambs. PE28 5XE
*tel* (01487) 832382
*email* info@dedalusbooks.com
*website* www.dedalusbooks.com
*Chairman* Juri Gabriel, *Directors* Eric Lane
(managing), Robert Irwin (editorial), Lindsay
Thomas (marketing), Mike Mitchell (translations)

Original fiction in English and in translation;
Dedalus European Classics, Dedalus concept books.
Founded 1983.

**Giles de la Mare Publishers Ltd**
PO Box 25351, London NW5 1ZT
*tel* 020-7485 2533 *fax* 020-7485 2534
*email* gilesdelamare@dial.pipex.com
*website* www.gilesdelamare.co.uk
*Chairman* Giles de la Mare

Non-fiction: art, architecture, biography, history,
music, travel. Telephone before submitting MSS.
Founded 1995.

**Dekker Publishing** – see Taylor and Francis
Books Ltd

**André Deutsch** – see Carlton Publishing
Group

## diehard
91–93 Main Street, Callander FK17 8BQ
*tel* (01877) 339449
*website* www.poetryscotland.co.uk
*Directors* Ian William King (managing), Sally Evans (marketing)

Scottish poetry. Founded 1993.

## Digital Press – see Elsevier Ltd

## Discovery Walking Guides Ltd
10 Tennyson Close, Dallington,
Northampton NN5 7HJ
*tel* (01604) 244869 *fax* (01604) 752576
*website* www.walking.demon.co.uk
*Chairman* Rosamund C. Brawn

'Walk!' and '34/35 Walks' walking guide books to European destinations. 'Tour & Trail Super-Durable' large scale maps for outdoor adventures. 'Drive' touring maps. GPS The Easy Way. Digital 'Personal Navigator Files' for GPS users. Project proposals welcomed from technologically proficient walking writers who can work to our 'No Compromise' research standards. Founded 1994.

## Dorling Kindersley – see Penguin Group (UK)

## Doubleday Children's Books – see Random House Group Ltd

## Doubleday (UK) – see Transworld Publishers

## The Dovecote Press Ltd
Stanbridge, Wimborne Minster,
Dorset BH21 4JD
*tel* (01258) 840549 *fax* (01258) 840958
*email* online@dovecotepress.com
*website* www.dovecotepress.com
*Editorial Director* David Burnett

Books of local interest: *County in Colour* series, natural history, architecture, history. Founded 1974.

## Dref Wen
28 Church Road, Whitchurch,
Cardiff CF14 2EA
*tel* 029-2061 7860 *fax* 029-2061 0507
*Directors* Roger Boore, Anne Boore, Gwilym Boore, Alun Boore

Original Welsh language novels for children and adult learners. Original, adaptations and translations of foreign and English language full-colour picture story books for children. Educational material for primary/secondary schoolchildren in Wales and England. Founded 1970.

## Dryden Press – see Elsevier Ltd (Health Sciences)

## Dublar Scripts
204 Mercer Way, Romsey, Hants SO51 7QJ
*tel* (01794) 501377 *fax* (01794) 502538
*email* scripts@dublar.freeserve.co.uk
*website* www.dublar.co.uk
*Managing Director* Robert Heather

Pantomimes. Imprint: Sleepy Hollow Pantomimes. Founded 1994.

## Gerald Duckworth & Co. Ltd
1st Floor, 90–93 Cowcross Street, London EC1M 6BF
*tel* 020-7434 4242 *fax* 020-7434 4420
*email* info@duckworth-publishers.co.uk
*website* www.ducknet.co.uk
*Directors* Peter Mayer (chairman), Gillian Hawkins (managing), Deborah Blake (editorial)

General trade publishers with a strong academic division (no fiction). Imprints: Bristol Classical Press. Founded 1898.

## Dunedin Academic Press*
Hudson House, 8 Albany Street, Edinburgh EH1 3QB
*tel* 0131-473 2397 *fax* (01250) 870920
*email* mail@dunedinacademicpress.co.uk
*website* www.dunedinacademicpress.co.uk
*Director* Anthony Kinahan

All types of academic books and books of Scottish interest. Founded 2000.

## Martin Dunitz – see Taylor and Francis Books Ltd

## Earthscan Publications Ltd
8–12 Camden High Street, London NW1 0JH
*tel* 020-7387 8558 *fax* 020-7387 8998
*email* earthinfo@earthscan.co.uk
*website* www.earthscan.co.uk
*Publishing Director* Jonathan Sinclair Wilson,
*Managing Editor* Frances MacDermott

Academic, agriculture, biology, zoology, economics, geography, geology, business, politics, travel. Owned by James & James (Science Publishers) Ltd.

## Ebury Press – see Random House Group Ltd

## Eden – see Transworld Publishers

## Edinburgh University Press*
22 George Square, Edinburgh EH8 9LF
*tel* 0131-650 4218 *fax* 0131-662 0053
www.eup.ed.ac.uk
*Chairman* Tim Rix, *Managing Director* Timothy Wright, *Editorial Director* Ms Jackie Jones

Academic publishers of scholarly books and journals: African studies, media and cultural studies, Islamic studies, geography, history, law, linguistics, literary studies, philosophy, politics, Scottish studies, American studies, religious studies, sociology, classical and ancient history. Trade: Scottish language, literature and culture, Scottish history and politics.

## Éditions Aubrey Walter

27 Old Gloucester Street, London WC1 3XX
*email* aubrey@gmppubs.co.uk
*Publisher* Aubrey Walter

Visual work by gay artists and photographers, usually in the form of a monograph showcasing one artist's work. Work may be submitted on disk, email, transparency, photocopy or photograph.

## The Educational Company of Ireland†

Ballymount Road, Walkinstown, Dublin 12, Republic of Ireland
*tel* (01) 4500611 *fax* (01) 4500993
*email* info@edco.ie
*website* www.edco.ie
*Executive Directors* Frank Maguire (chief executive), R. McLoughlin, *Financial Controller* A. Harrold, *Sales and Marketing Manager* M. Harford-Hughes, *Publisher* Frank Fahy

Educational: all subjects in English or Irish language. Trading unit of Smurfit Ireland Ltd. Founded 1910.

## Educational Explorers

PO Box 3391, Winnersh, Wokingham RG41 5ZD
*tel* 0118-978 9680 *fax* 0118-978 2335
*email* explorers@cuisenaire.co.uk
*website* www.cuisenaire.co.uk
*Directors* M.J. Hollyfield, D.M. Gattegno

Educational, mathematics: *Numbers in colour with Cuisenaire Rods*, languages: *The Silent Way*, literacy, reading: *Words in Colour*; educational films. No unsolicited material. Founded 1962.

## Egmont Books*

239 Kensington High Street, London W8 6SA
*tel* 020-7761 3500 *fax* 020-7761 3510
*email* firstname.surname@ecb.egmont.com
*website* www.egmont.co.uk
*Interim Managing Director* Robert McMenemy, *Publishing Director* David Riley

Children's books: picture books, fiction (ages 4–16), illustrated non-fiction, licensed character list. Publishes under Egmont and Dean.

## Element – now Thorsons/Element, see HarperCollins Publishers

## Edward Elgar Publishing Ltd

Glensanda House, Montpellier Parade, Cheltenham, Glos. GL50 1UA
*tel* (01242) 226934 *fax* (01242) 262111
*email* info@e-elgar.co.uk
*website* www.e-elgar.co.uk
*Managing Director* Edward Elgar

Economics and other social sciences. Founded 1986.

## Elliot Right Way Books

Kingswood Buildings, Brighton Road, Lower Kingswood, Tadworth, Surrey KT20 6TD
*tel* (01737) 832202 *fax* (01737) 830311
*email* info@right-way.co.uk
*website* www.right-way.co.uk
*Managing Directors* Clive Elliot, Malcolm Elliot

Independent publishers of practical non-fiction 'how to' paperbacks. The low-price *Right Way* and *Right Way Plus* series include games, pastimes, horses, pets, motoring, sport, health, business, public speaking and jokes, financial and legal, cookery and etiquette. Similar subjects are covered in the *Clarion* series of large-format paperbacks, sold in supermarkets and bargain bookshops. No freelance proofreaders or editors required. Founded 1946.

## Aidan Ellis Publishing

Whinfield, Herbert Road, Salcombe, Devon TQ8 8HN
*tel* (01548) 842755 *fax* (01548) 844356
*email* mail@aidanellispublishing.co.uk
*website* www.aepub.demon.co.uk
*Publisher* Aidan Ellis

Non-fiction: gardening, maritime, biography, general. Founded 1971.

## ELM Publications and Training

Seaton House, Kings Ripton, Huntingdon, Cambs. PE28 2NJ
*tel* (01487) 773254
*email* elm@elm-training.co.uk
*website* www.elm-training.co.uk
*Managing Director* Sheila Ritchie

Business and management development books, packs and resources; training materials and training courses; some e-learning materials. Actively seeking good tested management development materials, telephone in the first instance please, no MSS. Founded 1977.

## Elsevier Ltd*

The Boulevard, Langford Lane, Kidlington, Oxford OX5 1GB
*tel* (01865) 843000 *fax* (01865) 843010
*website* www.elsevier.com
*Ceo* Gavin Howe, *Ceo Science & Technology (Books & Journals)* Arie Jongejan, *Ceo Health Sciences Division (Books & Journals)* Brian Nairn

Academic and professional reference books; scientific, technical and medical books, journals, CD-Roms and magazines. No unsolicited MSS, but synopses and project proposals welcome. Imprints: Academic Press, Architectural Press, Bailliere Tindall, Butterworth-Heinemann, Churchill Livingstone, Digital Press, Elsevier, Elsevier Advanced Technology, Focal Press, Gulf Professional Press, JAI, Made Simple Books, Morgan Kauffman,

Mosby, Newnes, North-Holland, Pergamon, W.B. Saunders. Division of Reed Elsevier, Amsterdam.

### Elsevier Ltd (Butterworth Heinemann)
Linacre House, Jordan Hill, Oxford OX2 8DP
*tel* (01865) 310366 *fax* (01865) 314541
*website* www.bh.com
*Managing Director* Philip Shaw (Science and Technology Books)

Books and electronic products across business, technical, for students and professionals.

### Elsevier Ltd (Health Sciences)*
32 Jamestown Road, London NW1 7BY
*tel* 020-7424 4200 *fax* 020-7483 2293
*websites* www.elsevier.com, www.elsevierhealth.com
*Managing Director, Health Sciences Europe* Dominic Vaughan

Scientific, technical and medical books and journals. No unsolicited MSS but synopses and project proposals welcome. Imprints: Bailliere Tindall, Churchill Livingstone, Elsevier, Mosby, Pergamon, W.B. Saunders.

### Encyclopaedia Britannica (UK) Ltd
2nd Floor, Unity Wharf, Mill Street, London SE1 2BH
*tel* 020-7500 7800 *fax* 020-7500 7878
*email* enquiries@britannica.co.uk
*website* www.britannica.co.uk
*Managing Director* Leah Mansoor, *Sales & Marketing Director* Jane Helps

### Enitharmon Press
26B Caversham Road, London NW5 2DU
*tel* 020-7482 5967 *fax* 020-7284 1787
*email* books@enitharmon.co.uk
*website* www.enitharmon.co.uk
*Director* Stephen Stuart-Smith

Poetry, literary criticism, fiction, translations, artists' books. No unsolicited MSS. No freelance editors or proofreaders required. Founded 1967.

### Epworth Press
c/o Methodist Publishing House, 4 John Wesley Road, Peterborough PE4 6ZP
*tel* (01733) 325002 *fax* (01733) 384180
*Commissioning Editor* Dr Natalie Watson

Religion, theology, church history, worship, Bible commentaries.

### Estates – see HarperCollins Publishers

### Euromonitor plc
60–61 Britton Street, London EC1M 5UX
*tel* 020-7251 8024 *fax* 020-7608 3149
*email* info@euromonitor.com
*website* www.euromonitor.com
*Directors* T.J. Fenwick (managing), R.N. Senior (chairman)

Business and commercial reference, marketing information, European and International Surveys, directories. Founded 1972.

### Europa Publications Ltd
Haynes House, 21 John Street, London WC1N 2BP
*tel* 020-7583 9855 *fax* 020-7842 2249
*email* sales@europapublications.co.uk
*Directors* R. Horton (managing), P. Kelly (editorial), *General Manager* J.G. North

Directories, international relations, reference, yearbooks. Part of **Taylor and Francis Books Ltd**.

### Evangelical Press of Wales – see Bryntirion Press

### Evans Brothers Ltd*
2A Portman Mansions, Chiltern Street, London W1V 6NR
*tel* 020-7487 0920 *fax* 020-7487 0921
*email* sales@evansbooks.co.uk
*website* www.evansbooks.co.uk
*Directors* Stephen Pawley (managing), Brian D. Jones (international publishing), A.O. Ojora (Nigeria), *UK Publisher* Su Swallow, *Children's Publisher* Anna McQuinn

Educational books, particularly preschool, school library and teachers' books for the UK, primary and secondary for Africa, the Caribbean and Brazil. Part of the Evans Publishing Group. Founded 1908.

### Everyman – see The Orion Publishing Group Ltd

### Everyman's Library
Northburgh House, 10 Northburgh Street, London EC1V 0AT
*tel* 020-7566 6350 *fax* 020-7490 3708
*Publisher* David Campbell

*Everyman's Library* (clothbound reprints of the classics); *Everyman's Library Children's Classics*; *Everyman's Library Pocket Poets*; *Everyman Guides*; *Everyman City Guides*; *Everyman City Map Guides*; *Everyman Chess*. No unsolicited submissions. An imprint of **Alfred A. Knopf**.

### The Exeter Press
Reed Hall, Streatham Drive, Exeter, Devon EX4 4QR
*tel* (01392) 263066 *fax* (01392) 263064
*email* uep@exeter.ac.uk
*website* www.ex.ac.uk/uep/
*Publishers/Directors* Simon Baker, Anna Henderson

Academic and scholarly books on history, local history (Exeter and the South West), archaeology, classical studies, English literature, film history, performance studies, medieval studies, linguistics, modern languages, European studies, maritime studies. Founded 1958.

## Exley Publications Ltd
16 Chalk Hill, Watford, Herts. WD19 4BG
*tel* (01923) 250505 *fax* (01923) 818733/249795
*Directors* Dalton Exley, Helen Exley (editorial),
Lincoln Exley, Richard Exley

Popular colour giftbooks for an international
market. No unsolicited MSS. Founded 1976.

## Expert Books – see Transworld Publishers

## Faber & Faber Ltd*
3 Queen Square, London WC1N 3AU
*tel* 020-7465 0045 *fax* 020-7465 0034
*website* www.faber.co.uk
*Chief Executive* Stephen Page, *Finance Director*
David Tebbutt, *Editor in Chief* Jon Riley, *Sales
Director* Will Atkinson, *Publicity Director* Rachel
Alexander, *Marketing Director* Noel Murphy,
*Production Director* Nigel Marsh, *Rights Director*
Camilla Smallwood, *Children's Director* Suzy Jenvy

High-quality general fiction and non-fiction,
children's fiction and non-fiction, drama, film,
music, poetry. Unsolicited submissions accepted for
poetry only. For information on poetry submission
procedure ring 020-7465 0189, or consult website.

## Fabian Society
11 Dartmouth Street, London SW1H 9BN
*tel* 020-7227 4900 *fax* 020-7976 7153
*email* info@fabian-society.org.uk
*website* www.fabian-society.org.uk
*General Secretary* Sunder Katwala

Current affairs, political thought, economics,
education, environment, foreign affairs, social
policy. Also controls NCLC Publishing Society Ltd.
Founded 1884.

## Facet Publishing*
7 Ridgmount Street, London WC1E 7AE
*tel* 020-7255 0590 *fax* 020-7255 0591
*email* info@facetpublishing.co.uk
*website* www.facetpublishing.co.uk
*Managing Director* Janet Liebster

Library and information science, information
technology, reference works, directories,
bibliographies.

### Clive Bingley Ltd (imprint)
Library and information science, reference works.

### Library Association Publishing (imprint)
Library and information science, information
technology, reference works, directories,
bibliographies.

## C.J. Fallon†
Lucan Road, Palmerstown, Dublin 20,
Republic of Ireland
*tel* (01) 6166400 *fax* (01) 6166499

*email* editorial@cjfallon.ie
*Executive Directors* H.J. McNicholas (managing),
P. Tolan (financial), N. White (editorial)
Educational text books. Founded 1927.

## Falmer Press – now RoutledgeFalmer, see Taylor and Francis Books Ltd

## Fernhurst Books
Duke's Path, High Street, Arundel,
West Sussex BN18 9AJ
*tel* (01903) 882277 *fax* (01903) 882715
*email* sales@fernhurstbooks.co.uk
*website* www.fernhurstbooks.co.uk
*Publisher* Tim Davison

Sailing, watersports. Founded 1979.

## David Fickling Books – see Random House Group Ltd

## Financial Times Prentice Hall – see Pearson Education

## First and Best in Education Ltd
Earlstrees Court, Earlstrees Road, Corby,
Northants. NN17 4HH
*tel* (01536) 399004 *fax* (01536) 399012
*email* info@firstandbest.co.uk
*website* www.firstandbest.co.uk
*Contact* Anne Cockburn (editor)

Education-related books (no fiction). Currently
actively recruiting new writers for schools; ideas
welcome. Sae must accompany submissions.
Founded 1992.

## Fitzroy-Dearborn – see Taylor and Francis Books Ltd

## Five Star – see Serpent's Tail

## Flambard Press
Stable Cottage, East Fourstones, Hexham,
Northumberland NE47 5DX
*tel* (01434) 674360 *fax* (01434) 674178
*website* www.flambardpress.co.uk
*Managing Editor* Peter Lewis, *Deputy Editor*
Margaret Lewis

Poetry and literary fiction. Only hard-copy
submissions with sae considered. Preliminary letter
required. No phone calls. Founded 1990.

## Flame – see Hodder Headline Ltd

## Flame Tree Publishing
Crabtree Hall, Crabtree Lane, London SW6 6TY
*tel* 020-7386 4700 *fax* 020-7386 4701
*email* info@flametreepublishing.com

*website* www.flametreepublishing.com
*Managing Director* Frances Bodiam,
*Publisher/Creative Director* Nick Wells

Music, reference, art, cookery, education. Part of The
Foundry Creative Media Company Ltd. Founded 1992.

## Flicks Books

29 Bradford Road, Trowbridge, Wilts. BA14 9AN
*tel* (01225) 767728
*email* flicks.books@dial.pipex.com
*Partners* Matthew Stevens (publisher), Aletta Stevens

Cinema, TV, related media. Founded 1986.

## Floris Books*

15 Harrison Gardens, Edinburgh EH11 1SH
*tel* 0131-337 2372 *fax* 0131-347 9919
*email* floris@florisbooks.co.uk
*website* www.florisbooks.co.uk
*Editors* Christopher Moore, Gale Winskill, *Children's
Editor* Gale Winskill

Religion, science, Celtic studies, craft; children's
books: picture and board books, activity books.
Founded 1978.

## Flyleaf Press†

4 Spencer Villas, Glenageary, Co. Dublin,
Republic of Ireland
*tel* (02) 845906
*email* flyleaf@indigo.ie
*website* www.flyleaf.ie
*Managing Editor* James Ryan

Irish family history. Founded 1988.

## Focal Press – see Elsevier Ltd

## Fodor Guides – see Random House Group Ltd

## Folens Publishers*

Apex Business Centre, Boscombe Road,
Dunstable LU5 4RL
*tel* (0870) 609 1237 *fax* (0870) 609 1236
*email* folens@folens.com
*website* www.folens.com
*Managing Director* Malcolm Watson, *Publishing
Manager* Peter Burton, *Primary Publisher* Zoe Nichols

Primary and secondary educational books, learn-at-
home books. Imprints: Folens, Belair. Founded
1987.

## Folens Publishers

Hibernian Industrial Estate, Greenhills Road,
Tallaght, Dublin 24, Republic of Ireland
*tel* (01) 4137200 *fax* (01) 4137282
*website* www.folens.ie
*Chairman* Dirk Folens, *Managing Director* John
O'Connor

Educational (primary, secondary, comprehensive,
technical, in English and Irish). Founded 1956.

## Blackwater Press (imprint)†

General non-fiction, Irish interest, children's fiction.
Founded 1993.

## Fontana Press – former imprint of HarperCollins Publishers

## Footprint Handbooks

6 Riverside Court, Lower Bristol Road, Bath BA2 3DZ
*tel* (01225) 469141 *fax* (01225) 469461
*website* www.footprintbooks.com
*Directors* Patrick Dawson (managing), Debbie
Wylde (sales), *Managing Editor* Sophie Blacksell

Travel guides.

## Foulsham – see W. Foulsham & Co. Ltd

## W. Foulsham & Co. Ltd

The Publishing House, Bennetts Close, Slough,
Berks. SL1 5AP
*tel* (01753) 526769 *fax* (01753) 535003
*Managing Director* B.A.R. Belasco, *Editorial Director*
W. Hobson

Life issues. General know-how, cookery, health and
alternative therapies, hobbies and games, gardening,
sport, travel guides, DIY, collectibles, popular new
age. Imprints: Arcturus, Foulsham, Quantum.
Founded 1819.

### Arcturus (imprint)

Units 26–27, Bickels Yard, 151–153 Bermondsey
Street, London SE1 3HA

Military, art and drawing, popular psychology.

### Quantum (imprint)

Mind, Body & Spirit, popular philosophy and
practical psychology.

## Foundery Press – see Methodist Publishing House

## Four Courts Press†

7 Malpas Street, Dublin 8, Republic of Ireland
*tel* (01) 4534668 *fax* (01) 4534672
*email* info@four-courts-press.ie
*website* www.four-courts-press.ie
*Managing Director* Michael Adams

Academic books in the humanities, especially
history, Celtic and medieval studies, art, theology.
Founded 1970.

## Fourth Estate – see HarperCollins Publishers

## Framework Press Educational Publishers Ltd

Heinemann, Halley Court, Jordan Hill,
Oxford OX2 8EJ
*tel* (01865) 314194 *fax* (01865) 314116

*email* nigel.kelly@repp.co.uk
*Publisher* Nigel Kelly

School management, professional development, raising attainment, PSHE and Citizenship. Founded 1983.

## Free Association Books

57 Warren Street, London W1T 5NR
*tel* 020-7388 3182 *fax* 020-8906 0006
*email* info@fabooks.com
*website* www.fabooks.com
*Publisher and Managing Director* T.E. Brown

Social sciences, psychoanalysis, psychotherapy, counselling, cultural studies, social welfare, addiction studies, child and adolescent studies. Also contemporary fiction, including works in translation. No poetry, science fiction or fantasy. Founded 1984.

## W.H. Freeman

Palgrave Publishers Ltd, Houndmills, Basingstoke, Hants RG21 6XS
*tel* (01256) 332807 *fax* (01256) 330688

Science, medicine, economics, psychology, archaeology.

## Free Press – see Simon & Schuster

## Samuel French Ltd*

52 Fitzroy Street, London W1T 5JR
*tel* 020-7387 9373 *fax* 020-7387 2161
*email* theatre@samuelfrench-london.co.uk
*website* www.samuelfrench-london.co.uk
*Directors* Charles R. Van Nostrand (chairman, USA), Vivien Goodwin (managing), Amanda Smith, Paul Taylor

Publishers of plays and agents for the collection of royalties. Founded 1830.

## FT Law & Tax – incorporated into Sweet & Maxwell

## FT Prentice Hall – see Pearson Education

## David Fulton Publishers Ltd*

Chiswick Centre, 414 Chiswick High Road, London W4 5TF
*tel* 020-8996 3610 *fax* 020-8996 3622
*email* mail@fultonpublishers.co.uk, helen.fairlie@fultonpublishers.co.uk, nina.stibbe@fultonpublishers.co.uk
*website* www.fultonpublishers.co.uk
*Chairman* David Fulton, *Publishing Director* Christopher Glennie, *Marketing Director* Rachael Robertson, *Publisher* Helen Fairlie, *Commissioning Editor* Nine Stibbe

Initial and continuing teacher education (special needs, primary and secondary), educational management and psychology. Unsolicited MSS not

returned. Part of Granada Learning Ltd. Founded 1987.

## Gaia Books Ltd – see Octopus Publishing Group

## Gairm Publications

29 Waterloo Street, Glasgow G2 6BZ
*tel* 0141-221 1971 *fax* 0141-221 1971
*Editorial Director* Derick Thomson

(Gaelic and Gaelic-related only) dictionaries, language books, novels, poetry, music, children's books, quarterly magazine, *Gairm*. Founded 1952.

## The Gallery Press

Loughcrew, Oldcastle, Co. Meath, Republic of Ireland
*tel* (049) 8541779 *fax* (049) 8541779
*email* gallery@indigo.ie
*website* www.gallerypress.com
*Editor/Publisher* Peter Fallon

Poetry, drama, occasionally fiction, by Irish authors only at this time. Founded 1970.

## Garland Science – see Taylor and Francis Books Ltd

## J. Garnet Miller – see Cressrelles Publishing Co. Ltd

## Garnet Publishing Ltd

8 Southern Court, South Street, Reading RG1 4QS
*tel* (01189) 597847 *fax* (01189) 597356
*email* enquiries@garnetpublishing.co.uk
*Editorial Manager* Emma G. Hawker

Art, architecture, photography, fiction, religious studies, travel and general, mainly on Middle and Far East, and Islam. Founded 1991.

**Ithaca Press (imprint)**
Post-graduate academic works, especially on the Middle East.

**South Street Press (imprint)**
Non-fiction, including *Behind the Headlines* series.

## Gateway Books – see Gill & Macmillan Ltd

## The Gay Men's Press

PO Box 3220, Brighton BN2 5AU
*tel* (01273) 672823 *fax* 01273) 672159
*email* peterburton@easicom.com
*Commissioning Editor* Peter Burton

Gay-related issues: primarily fiction from literary to popular; limited non-fiction.

## Geddes & Grosset*

David Dale House, New Lanark ML11 9DJ
*tel* (01555) 665000 *fax* (01555) 665694

*email* info@gandg.sol.co.uk
*Publishers* Ron Grosset, Mike Miller

Popular reference, children's non-fiction and activity books. Founded 1988.

## Geographia – now Bartholomew, see HarperCollins Publishers

## Stanley Gibbons Publications

5 Parkside, Christchurch Road, Ringwood, Hants BH24 3SH
*tel* (01425) 472363 *fax* (01425) 470247
*email* info@stangib.demon.co.uk
*website* www.stanleygibbons.com
*Director* Richard Purkis, *Editor* Hugh Jefferies

Philatelic handbooks, stamp catalogues and albums, *Gibbons Stamp Monthly*. Founded 1856.

## Robert Gibson & Sons Glasgow Ltd – see Hodder Gibson

## Gill & Macmillan Ltd†

Hume Avenue, Park West, Dublin 12, Republic of Ireland
*tel* (01) 500 9500 *fax* (01) 500 9599
*website* www.gillmacmillan.ie

Biography or memoirs, educational (secondary, university), history, literature, cookery, current affairs, guidebooks, popular fiction. Founded 1968.

### Gateway Books (imprint)
Spirituality, ecology, metaphysics and alternative science.

### Newleaf (imprint)
Mind, Body & Spirit, popular psychology, self-help, health and healing, lifestyle.

### Tivoli (imprint)
Popular fiction.

## Ginn & Co. – see Harcourt Education Ltd

## Mary Glasgow – former imprint of Nelson Thornes Ltd

## Godsfield Press – see Octopus Publishing Group

## The Goldsmith Press

Newbridge, Co. Kildare, Republic of Ireland
*tel* (045) 433613 *fax* (045) 434648
*email* de@iol.ie
*website* www.irishpoems.com
*Directors* V. Abbott, D. Egan, *Secretary* B. Ennis

Literature, art, Irish interest, poetry. Unsolicited MSS not returned. Founded 1972.

## Gollancz – see The Orion Publishing Group Ltd

## Victor Gollancz Ltd – now incorporated into The Orion Publishing Group Ltd

## Gomer Press

Llandysul, Ceredigion SA44 4QL
*tel* (01559) 362371 *fax* (01559) 363758
*email* gwasg@gomer.co.uk
*website* www.gomer.co.uk
*Directors* Jonathan Lewis, John H. Lewis, *Editors* Mairwen Prys Jones, Bethan Mair, Gordon Jones, Ceri Wyn Jones

Literature and non-fiction with a Welsh background or relevance: biography, history, aspects of Welsh culture, children's books. No unsolicited MSS; preliminary enquiry essential. Founded 1892.

## Government Supplies Agency†

Publications Division, Office of Public Works, 51 St Stephen's Green, Dublin 2, Republic of Ireland
*tel* (01) 6476000 *fax* (01) 6476843

Irish government publications.

## Gower – see Ashgate Publishing Ltd

## Graham & Whiteside Ltd

High Holborn House, 50–51 Bedford Row, London WC1R 4LR
*tel* 020-7067 2500 *fax* 020-7067 2600
*email* sales@major-co-data.com
*Directors* A.M.W. Graham, R.M. Whiteside, P.L. Murphy

Directories for international business and professional markets. Founded 1995.

## Granada Media – see Carlton Publishing Group

## Granta Publications

2–3 Hanover Yard, Noel Road, London N1 8BE
*tel* 020-7704 9776 *fax* 020-7354 3469
*website* www.granta.com
*Editorial Director* George Miller, *Senior Editor* Sara Holloway, *Magazine Editor* Ian Jack

Literary fiction, memoir, political non-fiction, travel, history, etc. Founded 1982.

## Green Books

Foxhole, Dartington, Totnes, Devon TQ9 6EB
*tel* (01803) 863260 *fax* (01803) 863843
*email* edit@greenbooks.co.uk
*website* www.greenbooks.co.uk
*Publisher* John Elford

Environment (practical and philosophical). No fiction or children's books. No MSS; submit synopsis with covering letter, preferably by email. Founded 1987.

**Green Print** – see Merlin Press Ltd

## Greenhill Books/Lionel Leventhal Ltd

Park House, 1 Russell Gardens, London NW11 9NN
*tel* 020-8458 6314 *fax* 020-8905 5245
*email* info@greenhillbooks.com
*website* www.greenhillbooks.com
*Managing Director* Lionel Leventhal, *Deputy Managing Director* Mark Wray

Military history. Founded 1984.

## Gresham Books Ltd

46 Victoria Road, Oxford OX2 7QD
*tel* (01865) 513582 *fax* (01865) 512718
*email* info@gresham-books.co.uk
*website* www.gresham-books.co.uk
*Chief Executive* Paul Lewis

Hymn books, Prayer books, Service books, school histories.

## Grub Street Publishing

4 Rainham Close, London SW11 6SS
*tel* 020-7924 3966/738 1008 *fax* 020-7738 1009
*email* post@grubstreet.co.uk
*website* www.grubstreet.co.uk
*Principals* John B. Davies, Anne Dolamore

Adult non-fiction: military, aviation history, cookery, wine. Founded 1992.

## Guild of Master Craftsman Publications Ltd

166 High Street, Lewes, East Sussex BN7 1XU
*tel* (01273) 477374 *fax* (01273) 478606
*Joint Managing Directors* Jennifer Phillips, Jonathan Phillips

Practical, illustrated crafts, including photography, needlecrafts, dolls' houses, woodworking and other leisure and hobby subjects. Founded 1979.

## Guinness World Records

338 Euston Road, London NW1 3BD
*tel* 020-7891 4567 *fax* 020-7891 4501

*Guinness World Records, British Hit Singles, Guinness World Records* TV shows. A HIT Entertainment company. Founded 1954.

## Gulf Professional Press – see Elsevier Ltd

## Gullane Children's Books – see Pinwheel Ltd

## Gwasg Bryntirion Press – see Bryntirion Press

## Gwasg y Dref Wen – see Dref Wen

## Hachette Illustrated – see Octopus Publishing Group

## Peter Halban Publishers Ltd

22 Golden Square, London W1F 9JW
*tel* 020-7437 9300 *fax* 020-7437 9512
*email* books@halbanpublishers.com
*website* www.halbanpublishers.com
*Directors* Martine Halban, Peter Halban

General fiction and non-fiction; history and biography; Jewish subjects and Middle East. No unsolicited MSS considered; preliminary letter essential. Founded 1986.

## Haldane Mason Ltd

PO Box 34196, London NW10 3YB
*tel* 020-8459 2131 *fax* 020-8728 1216
*email* info@haldanemason.com
*Directors* Sydney Francism (editorial), Ron Samuels (art)

Illustrated general non-fiction: children's, cookery, alternative health, box sets. Opportunities for freelances. Founded 1995.

## Robert Hale Ltd

Clerkenwell House, 45–47 Clerkenwell Green, London EC1R 0HT
*tel* 020-7251 2661 *fax* 020-7490 4958
*email* enquire@halebooks.com
*website* www.halebooks.com
*Directors* John Hale (managing and editorial), Robert Kynaston (financial), Martin Kendall (marketing)

Adult general non-fiction and fiction. Founded 1936.

## Hambledon and London

102 Gloucester Avenue, London NW1 8HX
*tel* 020-7586 0817 *fax* 020-7586 9970
*email* office@hambledon.co.uk
*website* www.hambledon.co.uk
*Managing Director* Martin Sheppard, *Commissioning Director* Tony Morris

History. Winner of *The Sunday Times* Small Publisher of the Year Award 2001–2. Founded in 1980 as Hambledon Press.

## Hamish Hamilton – see Penguin Group (UK)

## Hamlyn – see Octopus Publishing Group

## Handsel Press – see The Continuum International Publishing Group Ltd

## Harcourt Education Ltd*

Halley Court, Jordan Hill, Oxford OX2 8EJ
*tel* (01865) 310533 *fax* (01865) 314641
*email* uk.schools@harcourteducation.co.uk
*website* www.harcourteducation.co.uk
*Chief Executive* John Philbin

Division of Reed Elsevier (UK) Ltd.

**Ginn & Co. (imprint)**
*fax* (01865) 314189
*Managing Director* Paul Shuter

Textbook/other educational resources for primary schools.

**Heinemann Educational (imprint)**
*website* www.heinemann.co.uk
*Publishing Director* Ravi Mirchandani

Textbooks, literature and other educational resources for all levels.

**Rigby Heinemann (imprint)**
*website* www.myprimary.co.uk
*fax* (01865) 314189
*Managing Director* Paul Shuter

Textbook/educational resources for primary schools.

**Harcourt Publishers Ltd** – see Elsevier Ltd (Health Sciences)

**Patrick Hardy Books** – see James Clarke & Co. Ltd

**Harlequin Mills & Boon Ltd\***
Eton House, 18–24 Paradise Road, Richmond, Surrey TW9 1SR
*tel* 020-8288 2800 *fax* 020-8388 2899
*Directors* Pamela Laycock (managing), Stuart Barber (financial and IS), Angela Meredith (production and operations), Ian Roberts (retail sales), Alison Byrne (retail marketing), Karin Stoecker (overseas editorial), Liz Patrick (direct marketing), Jackie McGee (human resources),
Founded 1908.

**Historical™ (imprint)**
*Senior Editor* L. Fildew
Romance fiction.

**Medical™ (imprint)**
*Senior Editor* S. Hodgson
Romance fiction.

**Mira Books® (imprint)**
*Senior Editor* Samantha Bell
Women's fiction.

**Modern Romance™ (imprint)**
*Senior Editor* Tessa Shapcott
Contemporary romance fiction.

**Red Dress Ink™ (imprint)**
*Senior Editor* Samantha Bell
Contemporary women's fiction with energy and attitude.

**Silhouette® (imprint)**
*Editorial Manager* L. Stonehouse
Popular romantic women's fiction.

**Tender Romance™ (imprint)**
*Associate Senior Editor* Bryony Green
Contemporary romance fiction in paperback and hardback.

**HarperCollins Audio** – see HarperCollins Publishers

**HarperCollins Entertainment** – see HarperCollins Publishers

**HarperCollins Publishers\***
77–85 Fulham Palace Road, London W6 8JB
*tel* 020-8741 7070 *fax* 020-8307 4440
*email* firstname.surname@harpercollins.co.uk
*website* www.harpercollins.co.uk
*Ceo/Publisher* Victoria Barnsley

All fiction and trade non-fiction must be submitted through an agent. Unsolicited submissions should be made in the form of a typewritten synopsis. Founded 1819.

**HarperCollins General Books (division)**
*Managing Director* Amanda Ridout

**HarperFiction (division)**
*Publisher* Lynne Drew

**Collins Crime (imprint)**
*Publishing Director* Julia Wisdom

**HarperCollins (imprint)**
General trade fiction and women's fiction.

**Harper Perennial (imprint)**
*Publisher* Louise Tucker
Paperback fiction and non-fiction.

**HarperPress (division)**
*Managing Director/Publisher* Caroline Michel, *Associate Publisher/Editor-in-Chief* Christopher Potter, *Associate Publishing Director* Nicky Eaton

**Fourth Estate (imprint)**
*Publishing Director* NickPearson
Current affairs, literature, popular culture, fiction, humour, politics, science, popular reference.

**HarperCollins (imprint)**
*Publishing Director* Michael Fishwick
General trade non-fiction.

**HarperEntertainment (division)**
*Managing Director/Publisher* Trevor Dolby

**HarperCollins Entertainment (imprint)**
Media-related books from film companions to autobiographies and TV tie-ins.

**Collins Willow (imprint)**
*Publishing Director* Michael Doggart
Sport.

## HarperCollins Audio (imprint)
*Publishing Director* Rosalie George

Selection of fiction and non-fiction recordings of adult and children's titles by famous name readers.

## Estates
*Publishing Director* David Brawn

Authors include Agatha Christie, J.R.R. Tolkien, C.S. Lewis. Imprint: Tolkien.

## Thorsons/Element (division and imprint)
*Managing Director* Belinda Budge, *Publishing Director* Wanda Whiteley

Mind, Body & Spirit.

## HarperCollins Children's (division)
*website* www.harpercollinschildrensbooks.co.uk
*Managing Director* Sally Gritten, *Publishing Directors* Gillie Russell (fiction), Venetia Davie (properties), Sue Buswell (picture books), *Design Director* Sophie Stericker

Quality picture books and book and tape sets for under 7s; fiction for age 6 up to young adult. Imprints: Lions, Collins Picture Books, Collins Jet, Collins Teacher.

## Collins (division)
*Managing Director* Thomas Webster, *Publishing Director, Collins Reference* Sarah Bailey

Reference, including encyclopedias, guides and handbooks, phrase books and manuals on popular reference, art instruction, illustrated, cookery and wine, crafts, DIY, gardening, military, natural history, pet care, Scottish, pastimes. Imprints: Collins, Collins Gem, Collins New Naturalist Library, Jane's, Times Books.

## Collins/Times Maps and Atlases (division and imprint)
*Publishing Directors* Juliet Lawler (international titles), Mike Cottingham (UK titles)

Maps, atlases, street plans and leisure guides. Imprints: Access Press, Bartholomew, Birnbaum, Nicholson.

## Collins Dictionaries/COBUILD (division and imprint)
*Publishing Director* Lorna Sinclair Knight

Bilingual and English dictionaries, English dictionaries for foreign learners.

## Collins Education (division)
*website* www.collinseducation.com
*Managing Director* Jim Green, *Director of Educational Publishing* Paul Cherry, *Publishing Manager, Primary Literacy* Jill Cornish, *Publishing Manager, Maths, Science & ICT* Melanie Hoffman, *Publishing Manager, Secondary English & Drama* Isabelle Zahar, *Publishing Manager, Secondary Humanities, Social Science and Vocational* Thomas Allain Chapman

Books, CD-Roms and online material for UK schools and colleges. Commissioned material only.

## Letterland (imprint)
Home learning titles from preschool to further education.

## Harrap – see Chambers Harrap Publishers Ltd

## Harvill Secker Press – see Random House Group Ltd

## Haus Publishing Ltd
26 Cadogan Court, Draycott Avenue, London SW3 3BX
*tel* 020-7584 6738 *fax* 020-7584 9501
*email* haus@dircon.co.uk
*website* www.life-and-times.co.uk
*Publisher* Barbara Schwepike, *Editorial Director* Robert Pritchard

The Life & Times series of affordable and accessible illustrated biographies. Founded 2002.

## Haynes Publishing
Sparkford, Yeovil, Somerset BA22 7JJ
*tel* (01963) 440635 *fax* (01963) 440001
*website* www.haynes.co.uk
*Directors* J.H. Haynes (chairman), J. Haynes (managing), D.J. Hermelin, M. Minter, M.J. Hughes, G.R. Cook, J. Bunkham, M. Webb

Car and motorcycle service and repair manuals, car handbooks/servicing guides; DIY books for the home; car, motorcycle, motorsport and leisure activities.

## Haynes Motor Trade Division (imprint)
*Editorial Director* Matthew Minter

Car and motorcycle service and repair manuals and technical data books.

## Haynes Special Interest Publishing Division (imprint)
*Editorial Director* Mark Hughes

Cars, motorcycles, motorsport, related biographies, practical maintenance and renovation.

## Headland Publications
*Editorial office* Ty Coch, Galltegfa, Llanfwrog, Ruthin, Denbighshire LL15 2AR
*and* 38 York Avenue, West Kirby, Wirral CH48 3JF
*Director and Editor* Gladys Mary Coles

Poetry, anthologies of poetry and prose. No unsolicited MSS. Founded 1970.

## Headline – see Hodder Headline Ltd

## Headline Book Publishing Ltd – see Hodder Headline Ltd

**Headway** – see Hodder Headline Ltd

**William Heinemann** – see Random House Group Ltd

**Heinemann Educational** – see Harcourt Education Ltd

## Heinemann English Language Teaching
– now Macmillan Heinemann English Language Teaching

**Christopher Helm** – see A & C Black Publishers Ltd

**The Herbert Press** – see A & C Black Publishers Ltd

**Hermes House** – see Anness Publishing

## Nick Hern Books Ltd
The Glasshouse, 49A Goldhawk Road, London W12 8QP
*tel* 020-8749 4953 *fax* 020-8735 0250
*email* info@nickhernbooks.demon.co.uk
*website* www.nickhernbooks.co.uk
*Publisher* Nick Hern

Theatre, professionally produced plays, screenplays. Initial letter required. Founded 1988.

## Hesperus Press Ltd
4 Rickett Street, London SW6 1RU
*tel* 020-7610 3331  020-7610 3217
*email* info@hesperuspress.com
*website* www.hesperuspress.com
*Managing Director/Publisher* Alessandro Gallenzi

Fiction and poetry by Classical authors in English and in translation. Founded 2001.

## Highbury Nexus Special Interests Ltd
Nexus House, Azalea Drive, Swanley, Kent BR8 8HU
*tel* (01322) 660070 *fax* (01322) 616319
*Publisher* Dawn Frosdick-Hopley

Modelling, model engineering, woodworking, aviation, military, boats, crafts.

## Hilmarton Manor Press
Calne, Wilts. SN11 8SB
*tel* (01249) 760208 *fax* (01249) 760379
*email* mailorder@hilmartonpress.co.uk
*website* www.hilmartonpress.co.uk
*Editorial Director* Charles Baile de Laperriere

Fine art, antiques, visual arts, wine, *Who's Who in Art*. Founded 1964.

**Hippo** – see Scholastic Children's Books

## Hippopotamus Press
22 Whitewell Road, Frome, Somerset BA11 4EL
*tel* (01373) 466653 *fax* (01373) 466653
*Editors* Roland John, Anna Martin

Poetry, essays, criticism. Publishes *Outposts Poetry Quarterly*. Poetry submissions from new writers welcome. Founded 1974.

**Historical™** – see Harlequin Mills & Boon Ltd

## Hobsons Publishing plc
Challenger House, 42 Adler Street, London E1 1EE
*tel* 020-7958 5000 *fax* 020-7958 5001
*website* www.hobsons.com
*Chairman* Martin Morgan, *Directors* Chris Letcher (managing), Frances Halliwell, David Harrington, Tanja Kuveljic

Database publisher of educational and careers information under licence to CRAC (Careers Research and Advisory Centre). Founded 1974.

**Hodder & Stoughton** – see Hodder Headline Ltd

**Hodder Children's Books** – see Hodder Headline Ltd

**Hodder Christian** – see Hodder Headline Ltd

## Hodder Gibson
2A Christie Street, Paisley PA1 1NB
*tel* 0141-848 1609 *fax* 0141-889 6315
*email* hoddergibson@hodder.co.uk
*website* www.hodderheadline.co.uk
www.madaboutbooks.com
*Managing Director* John Mitchell

Educational books specifically for Scotland. No unsolicited MSS. Formed by an amalgamation of Robert Gibson & Sons (Glasgow) and the Scottish branch of Hodder & Stoughton Educational. Part of the Hodder Headline Group.

## Hodder Headline Ltd*
338 Euston Road, London NW1 3BH
*tel* 020-7873 6000 *fax* 020-7873 6024
*Chairman* Richard Handover, *Group Chief Executive* Tim Hely Hutchinson, *Directors* Martin Neild (managing, Headline), Jamie Hodder-Williams (managing, Hodder & Stoughton General), Charles Nettleton (managing, Hodder & Stoughton Religious and Hodder Children's Books), Malcolm Edwards (managing, Australia and New Zealand), Philip Walters (managing, Hodder Arnold), Colin Fairbain (finance), David Kewley (interim managing, Bookpoint), Mary Tapissier (group personnel/training/admin)

Founded 1986.

**Headline Book Publishing Ltd (division)**
*Managing Director* Martin Neild, *Publishing Directors* Jane Morpeth (fiction), Heather Holden-Brown (non-fiction)

Publishes under Headline and Review. Commercial and literary fiction (hardback and paperback), and popular non-fiction including autobiography, biography, food and wine, gardening, history, popular science, sport, TV tie-ins.

**Hodder Children's Books (division)**
*Managing Director* Charles Nettleton, *Publishing Directors* Anne McNeil (fiction and picture books), Anne Clark (non-fiction and Wayland)

Publishes under Hodder Children's Books (picture books, fiction and non-fiction) and Hodder Wayland (illustrated non-fiction and reference).

**Hodder Arnold (division)**
*Directors* Philip Walters (managing), Elisabeth Tribe (schools publishing), Katie Roden (consumer education), Georgina Bentliff (health sciences), Mary Attree (journals and reference books), Alyssum Ross (production & design), Catherine Newman (sales & marketing)

Publishes under Hodder & Stoughton Educational, Teach Yourself, Headway. Textbooks for the primary, secondary, tertiary and further education sectors and for self-improvement. Academic and professional books and journals.

**Hodder & Stoughton General (division)**
*Managing Director* Jamie Hodder-Williams, *Publisher* Nick Sawyers, *Non-fiction* Rowena Webb, *Sceptre* Carole Welch, *Fiction* Carolyn Mays, *Audio* Rupert Lancaster, *Submissions Editor* Betty Schwartz

Publishes under Hodder & Stoughton, Coronet, Flame, New English Library, Sceptre, Lir, Mobius. Commercial and literary fiction; biography, autobiography, history, self-help, humour, Mind, Body & Spirit, travel and other general interest non-fiction; audio. Send unsolicited MSS to the Submissions Editor.

**Hodder & Stoughton Religious (division)**
*Managing Director* Charles Nettleton, *Publishing Director* Judith Longman

Publishes under New International Version of the Bible, Hodder Christian Books, Help Yourself, Bibles. Christian books, biography, self-help, gift, health.

**Hodder Wayland** – see Hodder Headline Ltd

**Hogarth Press** – former imprint of Random House Group Ltd

## Hollis Publishing Ltd
Harlequin House, 7 High Street, Teddington, Middlesex TW11 8EL

*tel* 020-8977 7711 *fax* 020-8977 1133
*email* gary@hollis-pr.co.uk
*website* www.hollis-pr.co.uk
*Managing Director* Gary Zabel

Publications include *Hollis PR Annual, Hollis Sponsorship Yearbook, Advertisers Annual, Marketing Handbook*, Hollis Europe, *A.S.K. Hollis* (Directory of Associations) and *SHOWCASE* (International Music Business Guide), Hollis *Media Guide, Sponsorship Newsletter, Sponsorship Showcase.*

**Holt Rinehard & Winston** – see Elsevier Ltd (Health Sciences)

## Honno Ltd (Welsh Women's Press)
Honno Editorial Office, c/o Canolfan Merched y Wawr, Vulcan Street, Aberystwyth, Ceredigion SY23 1JB
*tel* (01970) 623150 *fax* (01970) 623150
*email* post@honno.co.uk
*website* www.honno.co.uk
Publishing Manager: Lindsay Ashford

Literature written by women in Wales or with a Welsh connection. All subjects considered – fiction, non-fiction, poetry, autobiographies. Honno is a community co-operative. Founded 1986.

## Hopscotch Educational Publishing Ltd*
Unit 2, 56 Pickwick Road, Corsham, Wilts. SN13 9BX
*tel* (01249) 701701 *fax* (01249) 701987
*email* sales@hopscotchbooks.com
*website* www.hopscotchbooks.com
*Editorial Director* Margot O'Keeffe, *Creative Director* Frances Mackay

National Curriculum teaching resources for primary schools. All subjects at all levels. Recent successes include *Accelerated Learning in the Literacy Hour* and *Problem Solving.* Founded 1997.

## House of Lochar*
Isle of Colonsay, Argyll PA61 7YR
*tel* (01951) 200232 *fax* (01951) 200232
*email* lochar@colonsay.org.uk
*website* www.houseoflochar.com
*Managing Director* Georgina Hobhouse, *Editorial Director* Kevin Byrne

Scottish history, transport, Scottish literature. Founded 1995.

## How To Books Ltd
3 Newtec Place, Magdalen Road, Oxford OX4 1RE
*tel* (01865) 793806 *fax* (01865) 248780
*email* info@howtobooks.co.uk
*website* www.howtobooks.co.uk
*Publisher and Managing Director* Giles Lewis, *Editorial Director* Nikki Read

Reference. Practical books that inspire. Subjects covered include small business and self-employment, business, management, career development, living and working abroad, property, lifestyle, personal transformation, study skills and student guides, creative writing. Book proposals welcome. Founded 1991.

## Hugo's Language Books – see Penguin Group (UK)

## Hunt & Thorpe – now incorporated into John Hunt Publishing Ltd

## John Hunt Publishing Ltd

46A West Street, New Alresford, Hants SO24 9AU
*tel* (01962) 736880 *fax* (01962) 736881
*email* john@johnhunt-publishing.com
*Director* John Hunt

Children's and adult religious, full colour books for the international market. MSS welcome; send sae. Founded 1989.

**O-Books (imprint)**
Global spirituality and Mind, body & Spirit.

## C. Hurst & Co. (Publishers) Ltd

38 King Street, London WC2E 8JZ
*tel* 020-7240 2666, (night) 020-7624 8713
*fax* 020-7240 2667
*email* hurst@atlas.co.uk
*website* www.hurstpub.co.uk
*Directors* Christopher Hurst, Michael Dwyer

Scholarly 'area studies' covering contemporary history, politics, sociology and religion of Europe, former USSR, Middle East, Asia and Africa. Founded 1967.

## Hutchinson – see Random House Group Ltd

## Hutchinson Children's Books – see Random House Group Ltd

## Icon Books Ltd*

Grange Road, Duxford, Cambridge CB2 4QF
*tel* (01763) 208008  *fax* (01763) 208080
*email* info@iconbooks.co.uk
*website* www.iconbooks.co.uk
*Directors* Peter Pugh (managing), Jeremy Cox (creative), Simon Flynn (marketing)

Non fiction: *Introducing* series, literature, history, philosophy, politics, psychology, sociology, cultural studies, religion, science, current affairs, computers, women, anthropology, humour, music, cinema, linguistics, economics. Founded 1991.

## ICSA Publishing Ltd

16 Park Crescent, London W1B 1AH
*tel* 020-7612 7020 *fax* 020-7612 7034
*email* icsa.pub@icsa.co.uk

*website* www.icsapublishing.co.uk
*Joint Managing Directors* Clare Grist Taylor, Susan Richards

Publishing company of the Institute of Chartered Secretaries and Administrators. Professional business information for the corporate, public and not-for-profit sectors in a range of formats. Founded 1981.

## Ilex

The Old Candlemakers, West Street, Lewes, East Sussex BN7 2NZ
*tel* (01273) 487440 *fax* (01273) 487441
*email* surname@ilex-press.com
*website* www.ilex-press.com
*Directors* Sophie Collins (managing), Steve Luck (editorial), Alastair Campbell

Digital photography, digital graphic design, digital art and imaging, digital video and audio, web design. Founded 2003.

## Independent Music Press/IMP Fiction

PO Box 14691, London SE1 2ZA
*tel* (01440) 788561  *fax* (01440) 788562
*email* info@impbooks.com
*website* www.impbooks.com
*Music Editor* Martin Roach, *Fiction Editor* Kaye Roach

Music: biography, youth culture/street style/subcultures. Fiction: general (no sci-fi, horror, chick lit or crime). Submissions via literary agents only. Founded 1992 (Music), 1998 (IMP).

## In Pinn – see Neil Wilson Publishing Ltd

## Insight Guides/Berlitz Publishing

58 Borough High Street, London SE1 1XF
*tel* 020-7403 0284 *fax* 020-7403 0290
*website* www.insightguides.com
*Managing Director* Jeremy Westwood

Travel, language and related multimedia. Founded 1970.

## Institute of Physics Publishing

Dirac House, Temple Back, Bristol BS1 6BE
*tel* 0117-929 7481 *fax* 0117-930 1186
*website* www.bookmarkphysics.iop.org
*Editorial Manager* John Navas

Monographs, graduate texts, conference proceedings, undergraduate texts and reference works in physics and physics-related science and technology.

## Institute of Public Administration†

Vergemount Hall, Clonskeagh, Dublin 6, Republic of Ireland
*tel* (01) 2403600 *fax* (01) 2698644
*email* dmcdonagh@ipa.ie
*website* www.ipa.ie
*Publisher* Declan McDonagh

Government, economics, politics, law, public management, social policy and administrative history. Founded 1957.

## Inter-Varsity Press
38 De Montfort Street, Leicester LE1 7GP
*tel* 0116-255 1754 *fax* 0116-254 2044
*email* ivp@uccf.org.uk
*website* www.ivpbooks.com
*Managing Editor* S. Carter

Theology and religion.

## Irish Academic Press Ltd
44 Northumberland Road, Ballsbridge, Dublin 4, Republic of Ireland
*tel* (01) 6688244 *fax* (01) 6601610
*email* info@iap.ie
*website* www.iap.ie
*Directors* Stewart Cass, Frank Cass, Michael Philip Zaidner, *Administrator* Rachel Milotte

Scholarly books especially in 19th and 20th century history, literature, heritage and culture. Imprints: Irish University Press, Irish Academic Press. Founded 1974.

## IRS/Eclipse – see LexisNexis UK

## The Islamic Foundation
Markfield Conference Centre, Ratby Lane, Markfield, Leics. LE67 9SY
*tel* (01530) 244944 *fax* (01530) 244946
*Director General* Dr Manazir Ahsan, *Deputy Director* Chowdhury Mueen-Uddin

Books on Islam for adults and children. Founded 1973.

## Ithaca Press – see Garnet Publishing Ltd

## The Ivy Press Ltd
The Old Candlemakers, West Street, Lewes, East Sussex BN7 2NZ
*tel* (01273) 487440 *fax* (01273) 487441
*email* surname@ivypress.com
*website* www.ivypress.com
*Directors* Sophie Collins (managing), Peter Bridgewater (creative), Jenny Manstead (rights)

Design, art, lifestyle, health, Mind, Body & Spirit, DIY, house and garden. Founded 1997.

## JAI – see Elsevier Ltd

## Arthur James Ltd – incorporated into John Hunt Publishing Ltd

## Jane's – see HarperCollins Publishers

## Jane's Information Group
163 Brighton Road, Coulsdon, Surrey CR5 2YH
*tel* 020-8700 3700 *fax* 020-8763 1005

*website* www.janes.com
*Managing Director* Alfred Rolington

Professional publishers in hardcopy and electronic multimedia of military, aviation, naval, defence, reference, police, geo-political. Consumer books in association with **HarperCollins Publishers**.

## Jarrold Publishing
Whitefriars, Norwich NR3 1JR
*tel* (01603) 763300 *fax* (01603) 662748
*Directors* Margot Russell-King (managing), David Loombe (finance), Steve Plackett (supply chain gift and stationery)

UK tourism and heritage guide books and souvenirs, calendars, diaries and gift stationery. Unsolicited MSS, synopses and ideas welcome but approach in writing before submitting to Marketing Department.

## Jordan Publishing Ltd
21 St Thomas Street, Bristol BS1 6JS
*tel* 0117-923 0600 *fax* 0117-925 0486
*website* www.jordanpublishing.co.uk
*Managing Director* Caroline Vandridge-Ames

Law and business administration. Also specialist Family Law imprint (including the *Family Law Journal*). Books, looseleaf services, serials, CD-Roms and online.

## Michael Joseph – see Penguin Group (UK)

## Journeyman Press – see Pluto Press

## Karnak House
300 Westbourne Park Road, London W11 1EH
*tel* 020-7243 3620 *fax* 020-7243 3620
*email* karnakhouse@aol.com
*website* www.karnakhouse.co.uk
*Directors* Amon Saba Saakana (managing), Seheri Sujai (art)

Specialists in African/Caribbean studies worldwide: anthropology, education, Egyptology, fiction, history, language, linguistics, literary criticism, music, philosophy, prehistory. Founded 1979.

## The Kenilworth Press Ltd
Addington, Buckingham MK18 2JR
*tel* (0129 671) 5101 *fax* (0129 671) 5148
*email* mail@kenilworthpress.co.uk
*website* www.kenilworthpress.co.uk
*Directors* David Blunt, Deirdre Blunt

Equestrian, including official publications for the British Horse Society. Founded 1989. Incorporates Threshold Books; founded 1970.

## Kenyon-Deane – see Cressrelles Publishing Co. Ltd

## Kingfisher Publications plc

New Penderel House, 283–288 High Holborn,
London WC1V 7HZ
*tel* 020-7903 9999 *fax* 020-7242 4979
*email* sales@kingfisherpub.co.uk
*website* www.kingfisher.com
*Directors* Nancy Grant (managing), John Richards
(deputy managing), Géraud de Durand (finance),
Catherine Potter (UK sales)

### Kingfisher (imprint)

*Non-fiction Publishing Director* Gill Denton, *Fiction
Publishing Director* Anne Marie Ryan

Children's books. Non-fiction: activity books,
encyclopedias, general history, religion, language,
mathematics, nature, science and technology. Also
fiction, poetry and humour, picture books, board
books. No unsolicited MSS or synopses considered.

## Laurence King Publishing Ltd*

71 Great Russell Street, London WC1B 3BP
*tel* 020-7430 8850 *fax* 020-7430 8880
*email* enquiries@laurenceking.co.uk
*website* www.laurenceking.co.uk
*Directors* Robin Hyman (chairman), Laurence King
(managing), Lesley Ripley Greenfield (editorial:
college and fine arts), Philip Cooper (editorial:
architecture and design), Judith Rasmussen
(production), John Stoddart (financial)

Illustrated books on art, architecture, design,
graphic design, film and photography. Founded
1976.

## Kingscourt – see McGraw-Hill Education

## Jessica Kingsley Publishers*

116 Pentonville Road, London N1 9JB
*tel* 020-7833 2307 *fax* 020-7837 2917
*email* post@jkp.com
*website* www.jkp.com
*Directors* Jessica Kingsley (managing), Amy
Lankester-Owen (editorial)

Psychology, psychiatry, arts therapies, social work,
special needs (especially autism and Asperger
Syndrome), education, law, practical theology.
Founded 1987.

## Kluwer Academic/Plenum Publishers*

Suite 52, Alpha House, 100 Borough High Street,
London SE1 1LB
*tel* 020-7863 3318 *fax* 020-7863 3314
*website* www.wkap.nl
*Publishing Director* Dr Ken Derham, *Senior
Publishing Editors* Joanna Lawrence, Emma Roberts

Academic: biology and zoology, chemistry,
computer science, educational textbooks, business
management, medical, maths, psychology, science
and technical, sociology, anthropology. Founded
1966.

## Charles Knight – see LexisNexis UK

## Knight Paperbacks – see Caxton Publishing Group

## Knockabout Comics

10 Acklam Road, London W10 5QZ
*tel* 020-8969 2945 *fax* 020-8968 7614
*email* knockcomic@aol.com
*website* www.knockabout.com
*Editors* Tony Bennett, Carol Bennett

Humorous and satirical graphic novels for an adult
readership. Founded 1975.

## Kogan Page Ltd*

120 Pentonville Road, London N1 9JN
*tel* 020-7278 0433 *fax* 020-7837 6348
*website* www.kogan.page.co.uk
*Managing Director* Philip Kogan, *Directors* Pauline
Goodwin (editorial), Peter Chadwick (production
and editorial), Gordon Watts (financial), Julie
McNair (sales)

Education, training, business and management,
human resource management, transport and
distribution, marketing, sales, advertising and PR,
finance and accounting, directories, small business,
careers and vocational, personal finance,
international business. Founded 1967.

### Kogan Page Science Ltd (subsidiary)

Engineering science, physics, chemistry, structural
engineering, communication science, materials
science.

### Penton Press (imprint)

Engineering science, materials science, surface
technology, information systems and networks.

## Ladybird – see Penguin Group (UK)

## Kudos Books – see Top That! Publishing plc

## Lawrence & Wishart Ltd

99A Wallis Road, London E9 5LN
*tel* 020-8533 2506 *fax* 020-8533 7369
*email* lw@lwbooks.demon.co.uk
*website* www.lwbooks.co.uk
*Directors* S. Davison (editorial), J. Rodrigues,
B. Kirsch, M. Seaton, J. Rutherford, A. Greenaway,
G. Andrews

Cultural studies, current affairs, history, socialism
and Marxism, political philosophy, politics, popular
culture.

## Lennard Publishing

Windmill Cottage, Mackerye End, Harpenden,
Herts. AL5 5DR
*tel* (01582) 715866
*email* stephenson@lennardqap.co.uk

*Directors* K.A.A. Stephenson, R.H. Stephenson

Sponsored books, special commissions. No unsolicited MSS. Division of Lennard Associates Ltd.

## Letterland – see HarperCollins Publishers

## Letts Educational*
Chiswick Centre, 414 Chiswick High Road, London W4 5TF
*tel* 020-8996 3333 *fax* 020-8742 8390
*email* mail@lettsed.co.uk
*website* www.lettsed.co.uk
*Directors* Stephen Baker (managing), Wayne Davies (publishing), Andrew Thraves (publishing), Helen Jacobs (publishing), Lee Warren (finance)

Accountancy and taxation; children's; computer science; economics; educational and textbooks; industry, business and management; mathematics and statistics; vocational training and careers; homework and revision books. Associate and subsidiary companies: Granada Learning, nferNelson, Black Cat, Granada Media, Semerc. Founded 1979.

## Lewis Masonic
Riverdene Business Park, Molesey Road, Hersham, Surrey KT12 4RG
*tel* (01932) 266600 *fax* (01932) 266601

Masonic books; *Masonic Square Magazine*. Founded 1870.

## LexisNexis UK
Halsbury House, 35 Chancery Lane, London WC2A 1EL
*tel* 020-7400 2500 *fax* 020-7400 2842
*email* customer.services@lexisnexis.co.uk
*website* www.lexisnexis.co.uk
Division of Reed Elsevier (UK) Ltd. Founded 1974.

### Butterworths (imprint)
Legal and tax and accountancy books, journals, looseleaf and electronic services.

### IRS/Eclipse (imprint)
Company and employment law.

### Charles Knight (imprint)
Looseleaf legal works and periodicals on local government law, construction law and technical subjects.

### Tolley (imprint)
Law, taxation, accountancy, business.

## John Libbey & Co. Ltd
PO Box 276, Eastleigh SO50 5YS
*tel* (01342) 315440 *fax* (023) 8065 0259
*email* johnlibbey@aol.com
*Director* John Libbey

Film/cinema, animation. Founded 1979.

## Library Association Publishing – see Facet Publishing

## Libris Ltd
26 Lady Margaret Road, London NW5 2XL
*tel* 020-7482 2390 *fax* 020-7485 2730
*email* libris@onetel.net.uk
*website* www.librislondon.co.uk
*Directors* Nicholas Jacobs, S.A. Kitzinger

Literature, literary biography, German studies, bilingual poetry. Founded 1986.

## The Lilliput Press Ltd[†]
62–63 Sitric Road, Dublin 7, Republic of Ireland
*tel* (01) 6711647 *fax* (01) 6711233
*email* info@lilliputpress.ie
*website* www.lilliputpress.ie
*Managing Director* Antony T. Farrell

General and Irish literature: essays, memoir, biography/autobiography, fiction, criticism; Irish history; philosophy; Joyceana contemporary culture; nature and environment. Founded 1984.

## Frances Lincoln Ltd
4 Torriano Mews, Torriano Avenue, London NW5 2RZ
*tel* 020-7284 4009 *fax* 020-7485 0490
*email* reception@frances-lincoln.com
*website* www.frances-lincoln.com
*Directors* John Nicoll (managing), Anne Fraser (editorial, adult books), Janetta Otter-Barry (editorial, children's books)

Illustrated, international co-editions: gardening, architecture, environment, interiors, art, gift, children's books. Founded 1977.

## Lion Hudson plc*
Mayfield House, 256 Banbury Road, Oxford OX2 7DH
*tel* (01865) 302750 *fax* (01865) 302757
*email* enquiries@lionhudson.com
*website* www.lionhudson.com
*Directors* Paul Clifford (managing & editorial), Denis Cole, Tony Wales, John O'Nions, Roy McCloughry, Nick Jones, Stephen Price, Rodney Shepherd

Reference, paperbacks, illustrated children's books, educational, gift books, religion and theology; all reflecting a Christian position. No adult fiction. Send preliminary letter before submitting MSS. Founded 1971.

## Lions – see HarperCollins Publishers

## Lir – see Hodder Headline Ltd

## Little, Brown – see Time Warner Books UK

**Little Tiger Press** – see Magi Publications

## Liverpool University Press
4 Cambridge Street, Liverpool L69 7ZU
*tel* 0151-794 2233 *fax* 0151-794 2235
*email* robblo@liv.ac.uk
*website* www.liverpool-unipress.co.uk
*Publisher* Robin Bloxsidge

Academic and scholarly books in a range of disciplines. Special interests: art history, European and American literature, science fiction criticism, all fields of history, sociology. New series established include *Liverpool Latin American Studies* and *Studies in Social and Political Thought*. Founded 1899.

**Livewire** – see The Women's Press

## Logaston Press
Little Logaston, Logaston, Woonton, Almeley, Herefordshire HR3 6QH
*tel* (01544) 327344
*email* logastonp@aol.com
*website* www.logastonpress.co.uk
*Proprietor* Andy Johnson

History, social history, archaeology and guides to rural west Midlands and central and south Wales. Founded 1985.

## Lonely Planet Publications
72–82 Rosebery Avenue, London EC1R 4RW
*tel* 020-7841 9000 *fax* 020-7841 9001
*email* go@lonelyplanet.co.uk
*website* www.lonelyplanet.com
*Directors* Tony Wheeler, Maureen Wheeler, *Acting UK Manager* Louise Rice

Country and regional guidebooks, city guides, *Best Of* citybreak guides, city maps, phrasebooks, walking guides, diving and snorkelling guides, pictorial books, health guides, food guides, cycling guides, wildlife guides, first-time travel guides, classic overland routes, and travel photography. Also digital travel guides (*CitySync*), a commercial slide library (Lonely Planet Images) and a TV company. London office established 1991.

**Longman** – see Pearson Education

**Lorenz Books** – see Anness Publishing

**Lund Humphries** – see Ashgate Publishing Ltd

**Lutterworth Press** – see James Clarke & Co. Ltd

## Macdonald Young Books – now Hodder
Children's Books – see Hodder Headline Ltd

## McGraw-Hill Education*
20 Canada Square, Canary Wharf, London E14 5LH
*tel* 020-7176 7000
*email* emea_queries@mcgraw-hill.com
McGraw-Hill House, Shoppenhangers Road, Maidenhead, Berks. SL6 2QL
*tel* (01628) 502500 *fax* (01628) 635895
*website* www.mcgraw-hill.co.uk
*Directors* Simon Allen (managing – EMEA), Alan Martin (operations), Rupert Mitchell (professional, Northern Europe), Murray St Leger (higher education sales & marketing, Northern and Central Europe), Melissa Rosati (higher education, editorial)

Higher education: business, economics, computing, maths, humanities, social sciences, world languages. Professional: business, medical, computing, science, technical, medical, general reference.

**Kingscourt (imprint)**
McGraw-Hill House, Shoppenhangers Road, Maidenhead, Berks. SL6 2QL
*tel* (01628) 502500 *fax* (01628) 635895
*website* www.kingscourt.co.uk

Primary and secondary education.

**Open University Press (imprint)**
Celtic Court, 22 Ballmoor, Buckingham MK18 1XW
*tel* (01280) 823388 *fax* (01280) 823233
*email* enquiries@openup.co.uk
*website* www.openup.co.uk

Social sciences.

**Osborne (imprint)**
Science, engineering, maths, computer science.

## Macmillan Children's Books Ltd – see
Macmillan Publishers Ltd

## Macmillan Education Ltd – see Macmillan
Publishers Ltd

## Macmillan Heinemann English Language Teaching – see Macmillan
Publishers Ltd

## Macmillan Publishers Ltd*
The Macmillan Building, 4 Crinan Street, London N1 9XW
*tel* 020-7833 4000 *fax* 020-7843 4640
*website* www.macmillan.co.uk
*Chief Executive* Richard Charkin, *Directors* M. Barnard, C.J. Paterson, G.R.U. Todd, D. North, Dr A. Thomas, D.J.G. Knight

**Macmillan Children's Books Ltd (division)**
20 New Wharf Road, London N1 9RR
*tel* 020-7014 6000 *fax* 020-7014 6001
*website* www.panmacmillan.com
*Managing Director & Publisher* Kate Wilson,

*Publishing Director, Fiction* Sarah Davies, *Publishing Director, Picture Books* Suzanne Carnell, *Publishing Director, Campbell Books* Camilla Reid

Publishes under Macmillan Children's Books, Campbell Books, Young Picador. Picture books, fiction, poetry, non-fiction, early learning, pop-up, novelty, board books. No unsolicited material.

### Pan Macmillan (division)
20 New Wharf Road, London N1 9RR
*tel* 020-7014 6000 *fax* 020-7014 6001
*Managing Director* David North, *Editorial Directors* Imogen Taylor (fiction), Peter Lavery (TOR (UK) and thrillers), Georgina Morley (non-fiction), *Publisher, Non-fiction* Richard Milner, *Publishing Manager (Macmillan Audio* Alison Muirden, *Publishing Director (Macmillan, Pan and Picador)* Maria Rejt

Novels, crime, science fiction, fantasy and horror. Autobiography, biography, business, gift books, health and beauty, history, humour, natural history, travel, philosophy, politics and world affairs, psychology, theatre and film, gardening and cookery, encyclopedias. Publishes under **Boxtree**, Macmillan, **Pan**, **Picador**, **Sidgwick & Jackson**. Founded 1843.

### Boxtree (imprint)
*Senior Editor* Ingrid Connell, *Editor* Natalie Jerome

TV and film tie-ins; illustrated and general non-fiction; mass market paperbacks linked to TV, film, rock and sporting events; humour.

### Pan (imprint)
*Publisher* Peter Lavery

Fiction: novels, crime, science fiction, fantasy and horror. Non-fiction: sports, theatre and film, travel, gardening and cookery, encyclopedias, general. Founded 1947.

### Picador (imprint)
*Publishing Director* Andrew Kidd

Literary international fiction and non-fiction, poetry. Founded 1972.

### Sidgwick & Jackson (imprint)
*Publisher* Ingrid Connell

Military and war, music, pop and rock. MSS, synopses and ideas welcome. Send to submissions editor, with return postage. Founded 1908.

### Macmillan Education Ltd (division)
Macmillan Oxford, Between Towns Road, Oxford OX4 3PP
*tel* (01865) 405700 *fax* (01865) 405701
*website* www.macmillaneducation.com
*Chairman* Christopher Paterson, *Managing Director* Christopher Harrison, *Publishing Directors* Sue Bale, Alison Hubert, *Finance Director* Paul Emmett, *Production Director* John Peacock, *IT Director* Ian Johnstone

English language teaching materials. School and college textbooks and materials in all subjects for international markets.

### Macmillan Heinemann English Language Teaching
Macmillan Oxford, Between Towns Road, Oxford OX4 3PP
*tel* (01865) 405700 *fax* (01865) 405701
*Chairman* Christopher Paterson, *Managing Director* Christopher Harrison, *Director, ELT Publishing* Sue Bale

English language teaching materials.

### Palgrave Macmillan Ltd (division)
*Managing Director* Dominic Knight, *Publishing Directors* Frances Arnold (College), Sam Burridge (Scholarly and Reference), David Bull (Journals), *Sales and Marketing Directors* Margaret Hewinson, Garrett Kiely, *Operations Director* John Peacock, *Finance Director* Richard Hartgill

Textbooks, monographs and journals in academic and professional subjects.

## Made Simple Books – see Elsevier Ltd

## Magi Publications
1 The Coda Centre, 189 Munster Road, London SW6 6AW
*tel* 020-7385 6333 *fax* 020-7385 7333
*website* www.littletigerpress.com
*Publisher* Monty Bhatia, *Editors* Jude Evans

### Little Tiger Press (imprint)
*email* info@littletiger.co.uk

Quality children's picture books, novelty books, board books, pop-up books and activity books for preschool age to 10 year-olds. New material will be considered from authors and illustrators; see website for guidelines. Founded 1987.

## Mainstream Publishing Co. (Edinburgh) Ltd*
7 Albany Street, Edinburgh EH1 3UG
*tel* 0131-557 2959 *fax* 0131-556 8720
*email* enquiries@mainstreampublishing.com
*website* www.mainstreampublishing.com
*Directors* Bill Campbell, Peter MacKenzie, Fiona Brownlee (marketing), Sharon Atherton (publicity), Ray Cowie (sales), Neil Graham (production), Ailsa Bathgate (editorial)

Biography, autobiography, art, photography, sport, health, guidebooks, humour, literature, current affairs, history, politics. Founded 1978.

### Mainstream Sport (imprint)
Sport.

## Mammoth – former imprint of Egmont Books

## Management Books 2000 Ltd

Forge House, Limes Road, Kemble, Cirencester, Glos. GL7 6AD
*tel* (01285) 771441 *fax* (01285) 771055
*email* M.B.2000@virgin.net
*website* www.mb2000.com
*Directors* N. Dale-Harris, R. Hartman, *Publisher* James Alexander

Practical books for working managers and business professionals: management, business and lifeskills, and sponsored titles. Unsolicited MSS, synopses and ideas for books welcome.

## Manchester United Books – see Carlton Publishing Group

## Manchester University Press*

Oxford Road, Manchester M13 9NR
*tel* 0161-275 2310 *fax* 0161-274 3346
*email* mup@man.ac.uk
*website* www.manchesteruniversitypress.co.uk
*Chief Executive* David Rodgers, *Head of Editorial* Matthew Frost

Works of academic scholarship: literary criticism, cultural studies, media studies, art history, design, architecture, history, politics, economics, international law, modern language texts. Textbooks and monographs. Founded 1904.

## Mandrake of Oxford

PO Box 250, Oxford OX1 1AP
*tel* (01865) 243671
*email* mandrake@mandrake.uk.net
*website* www.mandrake.uk.net
*Directors* Mogg Morgan, Kym Morgan

Occult and bizarre. Founded 1986.

## Manson Publishing Ltd*

73 Corringham Road, London NW11 7DL
*tel* 020-8905 5150 *fax* 020-8201 9233
*email* manson@mansonpublishing.com
*website* www.mansonpublishing.com
*Managing Director* Michael Manson

Medical, scientific, veterinary. Founded 1992.

## Mantra

5 Alexandra Grove, London N12 8NU
*tel* 020-8445 5123 *fax* 020-8446 7745
*email* sales@mantrapublishing.com
*website* www.mantralingua.com
*Managing Director* M. Chatterji

Children's multicultural picture books; multilingual friezes/posters; dual language books/cassettes; South Asian literature/teenage fiction; CD-Roms and videos. Founded 1984.

## Marino Books – see The Mercier Press

## Marshall Pickering – former imprint of HarperCollins Publishers

## Martin Books – see Simon & Schuster

## Kenneth Mason Publications Ltd

The Book Barn, Westbourne, Hants PO10 8RS
*tel* (01243) 377977 *fax* (01243) 379136
*Directors* Kenneth Mason (chairman), Piers Mason (managing), Michael Mason, Anthea Mason

Nautical, slimming, health, fitness; technical journals. Founded 1958.

## Kevin Mayhew Ltd

Buxhall, Stowmarket, Suffolk IP14 3BW
*tel* (01449) 737978 *fax* (01449) 737834
*email* info@kevinmayhewltd.com
*website* www.kevinmayhewltd.com
*Directors* Kevin Mayhew (chairman), Gordon Carter (managing) Ray Gilbert (purchasing), Kevin Whomes (production)

Christianity: prayer and spirituality, pastoral care, preaching, liturgy worship, children's, youth work, drama, instant art. Music: hymns, organ and choral, contemporary worship, piano and instrumental. Contact Editorial Dept before sending MSS/synopses. Founded 1976.

## Meadowside Children's Books

185 Fleet Street, London EC4A 2HS
*tel* 020-7400 1061 *fax* 020-7400 1037
*email* info@meadowsidebooks.com
*website* www.meadowsidebooks.com
*Publisher* Simon Rosenheim, *Art Director* Mark Mills

Picture books, board books, novelty books, pop-up books and sticker books. Founded 2003.

## Medical™ – see Harlequin Mills & Boon Ltd

## Mentor Books†

43 Furze Road, Sandyford Industrial Estate, Dublin 18, Republic of Ireland
*tel* (353) 1 295 2112 *fax* (353) 1 295 2114
*email* all@mentorbooks.ie
*website* www.mentorbooks.ie
*Managing Director* Daniel McCarthy, *Managing Editor* Claire Haugh

General: fiction, non-fiction, children's, guidebooks, biographies, history. Educational (secondary): languages, history, geography, business, maths, science. No unsolicited MSS. Founded 1980.

## The Mercat Press

10 Coates Crescent, Edinburgh EH3 7AL
*tel* 0131-225 5324 *fax* 0131-226 6632
*email* enquiries@mercatpress.com
*website* www.mercatpress.com

*Managing Editors* Seán Costello, Tom Johnstone
Scottish books of general and academic interest. No
new poetry. Founded 1970.

**Crescent Books (imprint)**
Fiction.

## The Mercier Press[†]
Douglas Village, Cork, Republic of Ireland
*tel* (021) 4899858 *fax* (021) 4899887
*email* books@mercierpress.ie
*website* www.mercierpress.ie
*Directors* G. Eaton (chairman), J.F. Spillane
(managing), M.P. Feehan

Irish literature, folklore, history, politics, humour,
education, theology, law, current affairs, health,
mind and spirit, general non-fiction, children's.
Imprint: Marino Books. Founded 1944.

## Merehurst Ltd – see Murdoch Books UK Ltd

## Merlin Press Ltd
PO Box 30705, London WC2E 8QD
*tel* 020-7836 3020 *fax* 020-7497 0309
*email* info@merlinpress.co.uk
*website* www.merlinpress.co.uk
*Managing Director* Anthony Zurbrugg

Radical history and social studies. Letters/synopses
only.

**Green Print (imprint)**
Green politics and the environment.

## Merrell Publishers Ltd
42 Southwark Street, London SE1 1UN
*tel* 020-7403 2047 *fax* 020-7407 1333
*email* mail@merrellpublishers.com
*website* www.merrellpublishers.com
*Publisher* Hugh Merrell, *Editorial Director* Julian
Honer, *Sales & Marketing Director* Emilie Amos

High-quality illustrated books on all aspects of
visual culture, including art, architecture,
photography and design.

## Methodist Publishing House
4 John Wesley Road, Werrington,
Peterborough PE4 6ZP
*tel* (01733) 325002 *fax* (01733) 384180
*email* sales@mph.org.uk
*Chief Executive* Martin Stone

Hymn and service books, general religious titles,
church supplies. Founded 1773.

**Foundery Press (imprint)**
Ecumenical titles.

## Methuen Academic – incorporated into Routledge, see Taylor and Francis Books Ltd

## Methuen Children's Books – former imprint of Egmont Books

## Methuen Publishing Ltd
215 Vauxhall Bridge Road, London SW1V 1EJ
*tel* 020-7798 1600 *fax* 020-7828 2098
*Managing Director* Peter Tummons, *Publishing
Director* Max Eilenberg, *Sales Manager* Haydn Jones,
*Publicity Manager* Margot Weale

Literary fiction and non-fiction: biography,
autobiography, travel, history, sport, drama,
humour, film, performing arts, plays. No unsolicited
MSS.

## Metro Publishing Ltd – see John Blake Publishing Ltd

## Michelin Travel Publications
Hannay House, 39 Clarendon Road, Watford,
Herts. WD17 1JA
*tel* (01923) 205240 *fax* (01923) 205241
*website* www.viamichelin.com
*Head of Travel Publications* J. Lewis

Tourist guides, maps and atlases, hotel and
restaurant guides.

## Midland Publishing – see Ian Allan Publishing Ltd

## Milestone Publications
62 Murray Road, Horndean, Waterlooville PO8 9JL
*tel* (023) 9259 7440 *fax* (023) 9259 1975
*email* info@gosschinaclub.co.uk
*website* www.gosscrestedchina.co.uk
*Managing Director* Lynda J. Pine

Goss & Crested heraldic china, antique porcelain.
Publishing and bookselling division of Goss &
Crested China Club. Founded 1967.

## Miller's – see Octopus Publishing Group

## Mills & Boon® – see Harlequin Mills & Boon Ltd

## Mira Books® – see Harlequin Mills & Boon Ltd

## Mitchell Beazley – see Octopus Publishing Group

## Mobius – see Hodder Headline Ltd

## Modern Romance™ – see Harlequin Mills & Boon Ltd

## Mojo Books – former imprint of Canongate Books Ltd

## Monarch Books

Concorde House, Grenville Place, London NW7 3SA
*tel* 020-8959 3668 *fax* 020-8959 3678
*email* tonyc@angushudson.com
*website* www.angushudson.com
*Editorial Director* Tony Collins

Christian books: issues of faith and society;
leadership, mission, evangelism. Submit synopsis/
2 sample chapters only with return postage.

## Morgan Kauffman – see Elsevier Ltd

## Morrigan Book Company

Killala, Co. Mayo, Republic of Ireland
*tel* (096) 32555 *fax* (096) 32555
*email* morriganbooks@online.ie
*Publisher* Gerry Kennedy, *Administrator* Hilary
Kennedy, *Editor* Gillian Brennan

Non-fiction: general Irish interest, biography, history,
local history, folklore and mythology. Founded 1979.

## Mosby – see Elsevier Ltd (Health Sciences)

## Mount Eagle Publications Ltd – see Brandon/Mount Eagle Publications

## Mowbray: Morehouse – see The Continuum International Publishing Group Ltd

## MQ Publications Ltd

12 The Ivories, 6–8 Northampton Street,
London N1 2HY
*tel* 020-7359 2244 *fax* 020-7359 1616
*email* mail@mqpublications.com
*website* www.mqpublications.com
*Ceo* Zaro Weil

Lifestyle, Mind, Body & Spirit, inspirational,
photography, cookery, popular culture, biography,
gift books. Founded 1993.

## Murdoch Books UK Ltd

Erico House, 6th Floor North, 93–99 Upper
Richmond Road, London SW15 2TG
*tel* 020-8785 5995 *fax* 020-8785 5985
*Ceo* Juliet Rogers, *Publisher* Kay Scarlett
Non-fiction: homes and interiors, gardening,
cookery, craft, cake decorating, DIY.

## John Murray (Publishers) Ltd*

338 Euston Road, London NW1 3BH
*tel* 020-7873 6000 *fax* 020-7873 6446
*Managing Director* Roland Philipps, *Non-fiction*
Gordon Wise, *Fiction* Anya Serota

General: biography and autobiography, letters and
diaries, travel, exploration, general history, fiction.
No unsolicited MSS without preliminary letter.
Founded 1768; acquired by **Hodder Headline Ltd**
2002.

## National Christian Education Council – see Christian Education

## The National Trust

36 Queen Anne's Gate, London SW1H 9AS
*tel* 020-7222 9251 *fax* 020-7222 5097
*Publisher* Margaret Willes

History, cookery, architecture, gardening,
guidebooks, children's non-fiction. No unsolicited
MSS. Founded 1895.

## The Natural History Museum Publishing Division

Cromwell Road, London SW7 5BD
*tel* 020-7942 5336 *fax* 020-7942 5010
*email* publishing@nhm.ac.uk
*website* www.nhm.ac.uk/publishing

Natural sciences; entomology, botany, geology,
mineralogy, palaeontology, zoology, history of
natural history. Founded 1881.

## Nautical Books – now Adlard Coles Nautical – see A & C Black Publishers Ltd

## Nautical Data Ltd

The Book Barn, Westbourne, Hants PO10 8RS
*tel* (01243) 377977 *fax* (01243) 379136
*Directors* Piers Mason, Michael Benson-Colpi

Yachting titles, nautical almanacs.

## NCVO Publications

Regent's Wharf, 8 All Saints Street, London N1 9RL
*tel* 020-7713 6161 *fax* 020-7713 6300
*email* ncvo@ncvo-vol.org.uk
*website* www.ncvo-vol.org.uk
*Head of Publications* tbc

Imprint of the National Council for Voluntary
Organisations. Practical guides, reference books,
directories and policy studies on voluntary sector
concerns including management, employment,
trustee development and finance. No unsolicited
MSS accepted.

## Neate Publishing*

33 Downside Road, Winchester SO22 5LT
*tel* (01962) 841479 *fax* (01962) 841743
*email* sales@neatepublishing.co.uk
*website* www.neatepublishing.co.uk
*Directors* Bobbie Neate (managing), Ann Langran,
Maggie Threadingham

Non-fiction books, CDs and posters for primary
children. Founded 1999.

## Thomas Nelson Ltd – see Nelson Thornes Ltd

## Nelson Thornes Ltd*

Delta Place, 27 Bath Road, Cheltenham,
Glos. GL53 7TH
*tel* (01242) 267100 *fax* (01242) 221914
*email* name@nelsonthornes.com
*website* www.nelsonthornes.com
*Directors* Fred Grainger (managing), David Vincent,
Adrian Ford

Print and electronic publishers for the educational
market: primary, secondary, further education,
professional. Part of the Wolters Kluwer Group of
Companies.

## New Beacon Books

76 Stroud Green Road, London N4 3EN
*tel* 020-7272 4889 *fax* 020-7281 4662
*Directors* John La Rose, Sarah White, Michael La
Rose, Janice Durham

Small specialist publishers: general non-fiction,
fiction, poetry, critical writings, concerning the
Caribbean, Africa, African–America and Black
Britain. No unsolicited MSS. Founded 1966.

## New Cavendish Books

3 Denbigh Road, London W11 2SJ
*tel* 020-7229 6765 *fax* 020-7792 0027
*email* sales@cavbooks.demon.co.uk
*website* www.newcavendishbooks.co.uk

Specialist books for the collector; art reference, Thai
guidebooks. Founded 1973.

**River Books (associate imprint)**
The art and architecture of Southeast Asia.

## New English Library – see Hodder Headline Ltd

## New Holland Publishers (UK) Ltd

Garfield House, 86 Edgware Road, London W2 2EA
*tel* 020-7724 7773 *fax* 020-7258 1293
*email* postmaster@nhpub.co.uk
*website* www.newhollandpublishers.com
*Managing Director* John Beaufoy

Illustrated non-fiction books on natural history,
sports and hobbies, animals and pets, travel
pictorial, travel maps and guides, reference,
gardening, health and fitness, practical art, DIY,
food and drink, outdoor pursuits, craft, humour,
gift books. New proposals accepted (send CV and
synopsis and sample chapters in first instance; sae
essential).

## New Island Books†

2 Brookside, Dundrum Road, Dundrum, Dublin 14,
Republic of Ireland
*tel* (01) 2986867/2989937 *fax* (01) 2982783
*email* staff@newisland.ie
*Directors* Edwin Higel (managing), Fergal Stanley

Fiction, poetry, drama, humour, biography, current
affairs. Founded 1992.

## Newleaf – see Gill & Macmillan Ltd

## Newnes – see Elsevier Ltd

## New Playwrights' Network

10 Station Road Industrial Estate, Colwall,
Nr Malvern, Herefordshire WR13 6RN
*tel* (01684) 540154 *fax* (01684) 540154
*email* simonsmith@cressrelles4drama.fsbusiness.co.uk
*Publishing Director* Leslie Smith

General plays for the amateur, one-act and full
length.

## New Rider – see Pearson Education

## New Theatre Publications/ The Playwright Co-operative

2 Hereford Close, Warrington, Cheshire WA1 4HR
*tel* (0845) 331 3513
*email* i.hornby@ntworld.com
*website* www.plays4theatre.com
*Directors* Paul Beard, Ian Hornby

Plays for the professional and amateur stage.
Submissions encouraged. Founded 1987.

## Nexus – see Virgin Books Ltd

## nferNelson Publishing Co. Ltd*

The Chiswick Centre, 414 Chiswick High Road,
London W4 5TF
*tel* (0845) 6021937 *fax* 020-8996 3660
*email* information@nfer-nelson.co.uk
*website* www.nfer-nelson.co.uk
*General Manager* Tim Cornford

Testing and assessment services for education and
health care, including literacy, numeracy, thinking
skills, ability, learning support and online testing.
Founded 1981.

## Nia – see The X Press

## Nicholson – see HarperCollins Publishers

## Nielsen Book

Endeavour House, 189 Shaftesbury Avenue,
London WC2H 8TJ
*tel* 020-7420 6000 *fax* 020-7836 2909
*President* Jonathan Nowell
*Editorial office* 89–95 Queensway, Stevenage,
Herts. SG1 1EA
*tel* (01438) 44100 *fax* (01438) 745578
*Editorial Manager* Linda Mitchell

Reference including *The Bookseller*, *Whitaker's Books
in Print* and other book trade directories. Nielsen
Book incorporates the following businesses: Nielsen

BookData (comprehensive bibliographic data for books and other published media; see separate entry), Nielsen BookNet (the transaction services allowing the supply chain to trade online and send business messages), and Nielsen BookScan (the international sales data monitoring and analysis service for the English language book industry worldwide). The 3 companies allow the book industry to use market intelligence wisely to promote, support and increase sales of their books worldwide. A VNU business.

## Nightingale Press

6 The Old Dairy, Melcombe Road, Bath BA2 3LR
*tel* (01225) 478444 *fax* (01225) 478440
*email* sales@manning-partnership.co.uk
*website* www.manning-partnership.co.uk
*Directors* Garry Manning (managing), Roger Hibbert (sales)

Self-help, humour, health, lifestyle and relationships. Owned by the Manning Partnership Ltd. Founded 1997.

## James Nisbet & Co. Ltd

Pirton Court, Hitchin, Herts. SG5 3QA
*tel* (01462) 713444 *fax* (01462) 713444
*Directors* Miss E.M. Mackenzie-Wood, Mrs A.A.C. Bierrum

Business management. Founded 1810.

## NMSI

Science Museum, Exhibition Road, London SW7 2DD
*tel* 020-7942 4361 *fax* 020-7942 4362
*email* publicat@nmsi.ac.uk
*website* www.nmsi.ac.uk/publications
*Publications Manager* Ela Ginalska

History of science and technology, public understanding of science, history of photography, railway history, museum guides.

## Northcote House Publishers Ltd

Horndon House, Horndon, Tavistock, Devon PL19 9NQ
*tel* (01822) 810066 *fax* (01822) 810034
*email* northcote.house@virgin.net
*website* www.northcotehouse.com
*Directors* B.R.W. Hulme, A.V. Hulme (secretary)

Education and education management, educational dance and drama, literary criticism (*Writers and their Work*). Founded 1985.

## North-Holland – see Elsevier Ltd

## W.W. Norton & Company

Castle House, 75–76 Wells Street, London W1T 3QT
*tel* 020-7323 1579 *fax* 020-7436 4553
*Managing Director* Alan Cameron

English and American literature, economics, music, psychology, science. Founded 1980.

## NWP – see Neil Wilson Publishing Ltd

## O-Books – see John Hunt Publishing Ltd

## Oak Tree Press

19 Rutland Street, Cork, Republic of Ireland
*tel* (021) 431 3855 *fax* (021) 431 3496
*email* info@oaktreepress.com
*website* www.oaktreepress.com
*Directors* Brian O'Kane, Rita O'Kane

Business management, enterprise, accountancy and finance, law. Special emphasis on titles for small buisness owner/managers. Founded 1991.

## Oberon Books

521 Caledonian Road, London N7 9RH
*tel* 020-7607 3637 *fax* 020-7607 3629
*email* oberon.books@btinternet.com
*website* www.oberonbooks.com
*Managing Director* Charles Glanville, *Publisher* James Hogan, *Editor* Stephen Watson

New and classic play texts, programme texts and general theatre and performing arts books. Founded 1986.

## The O'Brien Press Ltd

20 Victoria Road, Rathgar, Dublin 6, Republic of Ireland
*tel* (01) 492 3333 *fax* (01) 492 2777
*email* books@obrien.ie
*website* www.obrien.ie
*Directors* Michael O'Brien, Ide ní Laoghaire, Ivan O'Brien

Adult: biography, politics, local history, true crime, sport, humour, refernce. Children's: fiction for all ages; illustrated fiction series – *Solos* (age 3+), *Pandas* (age 5+), *Flyers* (age 6+) and *Red Flag* (8+); substantial novels (10+) – contemporary, historical, fantasy. No poetry, adult fiction or academic. Unsolicited MSS (sample chapters only), synopses and ideas for books welcome – submissions will not be returned. Founded 1974.

## The Octagon Press Ltd

PO Box 227, London N6 4EW
*tel* 020-8348 9392 *fax* 020-8341 5971
*email* octagon@schredds.demon.co.uk
*website* www.octagonpress.com
*Managing Director* George R. Schrager

Psychology, philosophy, Eastern religion. All books published are commissioned works so unsolicited MSS not accepted. Founded 1972.

## Octopus Publishing Group

2–4 Heron Quays, London E14 4JP
*tel* 020-7531 8400 *fax* 020-7531 8650
*email* firstname.lastname@octopus-publishing.co.uk
*website* www.octopus-publishing.co.uk
*Chief Executive* Derek Freeman, *Executive Directors* Laura Bamford, Helen Barlow

### Bounty (imprint)

*tel* 020-7531 8601 *fax* 020-7531 8607
*email* bountybooksinfo-bp@bountybooks.co.uk
*Publisher/Managing Director* Alison Goff

Promotional publishing, adult books.

### Cassell Illustrated (imprint)

*tel* 020-7531 8400 *fax* 020-7531 8650
*email* info-ci@cassell-illustrated.co.uk
*website* www.cassell-illustrated.co.uk
*Directors* Alison Goff (publishing and managing), Gabrielle Mander (publishing)

Illustrated books for the international market specialising in gardening, history and heritage, health and humour.

### Conran Octopus (imprint)

*tel* 020-7531 8628 *fax* 020-7531 8627
*email* info-co@conran-octopus.co.uk
*website* www.conran-octopus.co.uk
*Publishing Director* Lorraine Dickie

Quality illustrated books, particularly lifestyle, cookery, gardening.

### Gaia Books (imprint)

*Publisher* Alison Goff

Illustrated reference books on ecology, natural living, health and the mind.

### Godsfield Press (imprint)

*email* enquiries@godsfieldpress.com
*website* www.godsfieldpress.com
*Publisher* Alison Goff

Highly illustrated books for adults in the area of Mind, Body & Spirit with an emphasis on practical application and personal spiritual awareness.

### Hachette Illustrated (imprint)

*tel* 020-7531 8602 *fax* 020-7531 8607
*website* www.hachette-illustrated.co.uk
*Sales & Publishing Director* Rebecca de Rafael

Illustrated reference.

### Hamlyn (imprint)

*tel* 020-7531 8573 *fax* 020-7537 0514
*email* info-ho@hamlyn.co.uk
*website* www.hamlyn.co.uk
*Publisher/Managing Director* Alison Goff

Popular illustrated non-fiction, particularly cookery, health, parenting, home and garden, sport, reference.

### Miller's (imprint)

The Cellars, High Street, Tenterden, Kent TN30 6BN
*tel* (01580) 766411 *fax* (01580) 766100
*email* firstname.lastname@millers.uk.com
*Publisher/Managing Director* Jane Aspden

Quality illustrated books on antiques and collectables.

### Mitchell Beazley (imprint)

*tel* 020-7531 8400 *fax* 020-7531 8650
*email* info-mb@mitchell-beazley.co.uk
*Publisher/Managing Director* Jane Aspden

Quality illustrated books, particularly antiques, gardening, craft and interiors, wine.

### Philip's (imprint)

*tel* 020-7531 8459 *fax* 020-7531 8460
*email* george.philip@philips-maps.co.uk
*website* www.philips-maps.co.uk
*Publisher/Managing Director* John Gaisford

Atlases, maps, astronomy, encyclopedias, globes.

## Oldcastle Books Ltd

18 Coleswood Road, Harpenden, Herts. AL5 1EP
*tel* (01582) 761264 *fax* (01582) 761264
*email* ion@noexit.co.uk
*websites* www.noexit.co.uk,
www.pocketessentials.com, www.highstakes.com
*Director* Ion Mills

Imprints: No Exit Press (crime fiction), High Stakes (gambling), Pocket Essentials (reference guides). Founded 1985.

## The Oleander Press

16 Orchard Street, Cambridge CB1 1JT
*tel* (01223) 357768
*website* www.oleanderpress.com
*Managing Director* Dr Jeremy Toner

Travel, language, literature, Libya, Arabia and Middle East, Cambridgeshire, history, humour, reference, classics. Preliminary letter required before submitting MSS; please send sae for reply. Founded 1960.

## Michael O'Mara Books Ltd

9 Lion Yard, Tremadoc Road, London SW4 7NQ
*tel* 020-7720 8643 *fax* 020-7627 8953
*website* www.mombooks.com
*Chairman* Michael O'Mara, *Managing Director* Lesley O'Mara, *Commissioning Editorial Director* Lindsay Davies

General non-fiction: biography, humour, history, ancient history, anthologies and royal books. Founded 1985.

### Buster Books (imprint)

Novelty and picture books for young children.

## Omnibus Press/Music Sales Ltd

8–9 Frith Street, London W1D 3JB
*tel* 020-7434 0066 *fax* 020-7734 9718
*email* music@musicsales.co.uk

*Chief Editor* Chris Charlesworth
Rock music biographies, books about music.

## On Stream Publications Ltd
Currabaha, Cloghroe, Blarney, Co. Cork,
Republic of Ireland
*tel* (353) 21-4385798 *fax* (353) 21-4385798
*email* info@onstream.ie
*website* www.onstream.ie
*Owner* Rosalind Crowley

Cookery, wine, travel, human interest non-fiction,
local history, academic and practical books.

## Oneworld Publications
185 Banbury Road, Oxford OX2 7AR
*tel* (01865) 310597 *fax* (01865) 310598
*email* info@oneworld-publications.com
*website* www.oneworld-publications.com
*Directors* Juliet Mabey (publisher), Novin Doostdar
(publisher), Helen Coward (managing)

Religion, world religions, inter-religious dialogue,
Islamic studies, philosophy, history, psychology, self-
help, popular science. Founded 1984.

## Onlywomen Press Ltd
40 St Lawrence Terrace, London W10 5ST
*tel* 020-8354 0796 *fax* 020-8960 2817
*email* onlywomenpress@aol.com
*website* www.onlywomenpress.com
*Managing Director* Lilian Mohin

Lesbian feminist: theory, fiction, poetry, crime
fiction and cultural criticism. Founded 1974.

## Open Books Publishing Ltd
Willow Cottage, Cudworth, Nr Ilminster,
Somerset TA19 0PS
*tel* (01460) 52565 *fax* (01460) 52565
*email* patrickta@aol.com
*Directors* P. Taylor (managing), C. Taylor

Gardening. Founded 1974.

## Open Gate Press*
51 Achilles Road, London NW6 1DZ
*tel* 020-7431 4391 *fax* 020-7431 5129
*email* books@opengatepress.co.uk
*website* www.opengatepress.co.uk
*Directors* Jeannie Cohen, Elisabeth Petersdorff,
George Frankl, Sandra Lovell

Psychoanalysis, philosophy, social sciences, religion,
animal welfare, the environment. Founded 1988.

## Open University Press – see McGraw-Hill
Education

## Orbit – see Time Warner Books UK

## Orchard Books – see The Watts Publishing
Group Ltd

## The Orion Publishing Group Ltd*
Orion House, 5 Upper St Martin's Lane,
London WC2H 9EA
*tel* 020-7240 3444 *fax* 020-7240 4822
*website* www.orionbooks.co.uk
*Directors* Jean-Louis Lisimachio (chairman), Peter
Roche (chief executive)

No unsolicited MSS; approach in writing in first
instance. Founded 1992.

### Orion Paperbacks (division)
*Managing Director* Susan Lamb

Mass market fiction and non-fiction under
**Everyman**, **Orion** and **Phoenix** imprints.

### Orion Trade (division)
*Directors* Malcolm Edwards (managing), Jane Wood
(publishing), Ian Marshall

Hardcover fiction (popular fiction in all categories),
non-fiction and audio.

### Gollancz (imprint)
*Contact* Simon Spanton, Jo Fletcher

Science fiction and fantasy.

### Orion Children's Books (division)
*Publisher* Fiona Kennedy

Fiction for younger and older readers, picture
books.

### Weidenfeld & Nicolson
See page 194.

## Osborne – see McGraw-Hill Education

## Osprey Publishing Ltd*
Elms Court, Chapel Way, Botley, Oxford OX2 9LP
*tel* (01865) 727022 *fax* (01865) 727017/727019
*email* info@ospreypublishing.com
*website* www.ospreypublishing.com
*Managing Director* William Shepherd, *Finance
Director* Sarah Lough, *Operations Director* Rebecca
Stuart, *Director, American Operations* Bill Corsa

Illustrated history of war and warfare, and military
aviation. Founded 1969.

## Peter Owen Ltd
73 Kenway Road, London SW5 0RE
*tel* 020-7373 5628/370 6093 *fax* 020-7373 6760
*email* admin@peterowen.com
*website* www.peterowen.com
*Directors* Peter L. Owen (managing), Antonia Owen
(editorial)

Art, belles-lettres, biography and memoir, literary
fiction, general non-fiction, history, theatre and
entertainment. No highly illustrated books. Do not
send fiction without first speaking to the Editorial
Dept unless it is by an established novelist. First
novels rarely published.

## Oxford Publishing Company – see Ian Allan Publishing Ltd

## Oxford University Press*
Great Clarendon Street, Oxford OX2 6DP
*tel* (01865) 556767 *fax* (01865) 556646
*email* enquiry@oup.com
*website* www.oup.com
*Ceo* Henry Reece, *Group Finance Director* Roger Boning, *Academic Division Managing Director* Tim Barton, *UK Children's Educational Division Managing Director* Kate Harris, *ELT Division Managing Director* Peter Marshall, *Publishing Director Journals* Martin Richardson *UK Personnel Director* John Williams, *Sales Director* Tim Mahar

Anthropology, archaeology, architecture, art, belles-lettres, bibles, bibliography, children's books (fiction, non-fiction, picture), commerce, current affairs, dictionaries, drama, economics, educational (infants, primary, secondary, technical, university), English language teaching, electronic publishing, essays, foreign language learning, general history, hymn and service books, journals, law, maps and atlases, medical, music, oriental, philosophy, political economy, prayer books, reference, science, sociology, theology and religion; educational software; *Grove Dictionaries of Music & Art*. Trade paperbacks published under the imprint of Oxford Paperbacks. Founded 1478.

## Palgrave Macmillan Ltd – see Macmillan Publishers Ltd

## Pan Macmillan – see Macmillan Publishers Ltd

## Pandora Press – see Rivers Oram Press

## Paper Tiger – see Chrysalis Books Group

## Parthenon Press – see Taylor and Francis Books Ltd

## Paternoster
PO Box 300, Carlisle, Cumbria CA3 0QS
*tel* (01228) 512512 *fax* (01228) 593388
*email* info@paternoster-publishing.com
*Publisher* Mark Finnie

Biblical studies, Christian theology, ethics, history, mission. Imprints: Paternoster Press, Authentic Lifestyle, Partnership, Regnum, Rutherford House, Challenge, Paternoster Periodicals, SP Media.

## Pavilion Books Ltd – see Chrysalis Books Group

## Pavilion Children's Books – see Chrysalis Children's Books

## Pavilion Publishing (Brighton) Ltd
The Ironworks, Cheapside, Brighton BN1 4GD
*tel* (01273) 623222 *fax* (01273) 625526
*email* info@pavpub.com
*website* www.pavpub.com
*Directors* Chris Parker, Julie Gibson, Loretta Harrison

Health and social care training resources in a variety of fields including learning disability, mental health, community care management, older people, looked-after young people, community justice, drugs, supported housing. Founded 1987.

## Payback Press – former imprint of Canongate Books Ltd

## Peachpit Press – see Pearson Education

## Pearson Education*
Edinburgh Gate, Harlow, Essex CM20 2JE
*tel* (01279) 623623 *fax* (01279) 414130
*email* firstname.lastname@pearsoned-ema.com
*website* www.pearsoned.co.uk
*President, Pearson Education Ltd* Rod Bristow

Materials for school pupils, students and practitioners globally.

## Addison-Wesley (imprint)
Technical.

## Allyn & Bacon (imprint)
Higher education, humanities, social sciences.

## Cisco Press (imprint)
Cisco-systems authorised publisher. Material for networking students and professionals.

## Benjamin Cummings (imprint)
Higher education, science.

## FT Prentice Hall (imprint)
Business for higher education and professional.

## Longman (imprint)
Education for higher education, schools, ELT.

## New Rider (imprint)
Graphics and design.

## Peachpit Press (imprint)
Internet and general computing.

## Penguin Longman (imprint)
ELT.

## QUE Publishing (imprint)
Computing.

## SAMS Publishing (imprint)
Professional computing.

## York Notes (imprint)
Literature guides for students.

## Pen & Inc Press

Pen & Inc Press, School of English and American Studies, University of East Anglia, Norwich NR4 7TJ
*tel* (01603) 592783 *fax* (01603) 507728
*email* info@penandinc.co.uk
*website* www.penandinc.co.uk
*Managing Editor* Katri Skala

Literary fiction, non-fiction, poetry. Founded 1999.

## Pen & Sword Books Ltd

47 Church Street, Barnsley, South Yorkshire S70 2AS
*tel* (01226) 734222 *fax* (01226) 734438
*email* charles@pen-and-sword.co.uk
*website* www.pen-and-sword.co.uk
*Managing Director* Charles Hewitt, *Publishing Manager* Henry Wilson, *Commissioning Editors* Peter Coles, Rupert Harding

Military history, aviation history, naval and maritime, general history, local history. Imprints: Leo Cooper, Pen & Sword Military Classics, Pen & Sword Aviation, Pen & Sword Naval & Maritime.

### Wharncliffe* (imprint)
Local history.

## Penguin Group (UK)*

80 Strand, London WC2R 0RL
*tel* 020-7010 3000 *fax* 020-7010 6060
*website* www.penguin.co.uk
*Ceo* Anthony Forbes Watson, *Managing Directors* Helen Fraser (Penguin), Andrew Welham (Dorling Kindersley)

Owned by Pearson plc.

### Penguin General Books (division)
*Managing Director* Tom Weldon, *Publishing Directors* Tony Lacey (Penguin), Juliet Annan (Viking/Penguin), Simon Prosser (Hamish Hamilton/Penguin), Louise Moore (Michael Joseph/Penguin)

No unsolicited MSS or synopses.

### Hamish Hamilton (imprint)
Fiction, belles-lettres, biography and memoirs, current affairs, history, literature, politics, travel. No unsolicited MSS or synopses.

### Michael Joseph (imprint)
Biography and memoirs, current affairs, fiction, history, humour, travel, health, spirituality and relationships, sports, general leisure, illustrated books. No unsolicited MSS or synopses.

### Penguin (imprint)
Adult paperback books – wide range of fiction, non-fiction, TV and film tie-ins. No unsolicited MSS or synopses.

### Viking (imprint)
*Associate Publisher* Paul Slovak

Fiction and general non-fiction for adults. Founded 1925.

### Penguin Press (division)
*Managing Director* Stefan McGrath, *Publishing Directors* Stuart Proffitt, Nigel Wilcockson, Simon Winder

Serious adult non-fiction, reference, specialist and classics. Imprint: Allen Lane. Series: Penguin Classics, Penguin Modern Classics. No unsolicited MSS or synopses.

### Puffin (division)
*Managing Director* Francesca Dow, *Publishing Directors* Rebecca McNally (fiction), Mandy Suhr (picture books)

Children's paperback and hardback books: wide range of picture books, board books and novelties; fiction; non-fiction and popular culture. No unsolicited MSS or synopses.

### Warne (division)
*websites* www.funwithspot.com, www.flowerfairies.com, www.peterrabbit.com
*Managing Director* Sally Floyer, *Publishing Director* Stephanie Barton

Specialises in preschool illustrated developmental books for 0–6, non-fiction 0–8; licensed brands; children's classic publishing and merchandising properties. No unsolicited MSS.

### Ladybird (division)
*website* www.ladybird.co.uk
*Managing Director* Sally Floyer

### Dorling Kindersley (division)
*Managing Director* Andrew Welham, *Publisher* Christopher Davis, *Adult Publisher* John Roberts, *Children's Publisher* Miriam Farbry, *DK Designs* Sophie Mitchell

Illustrated non-fiction for adults and children: gardening, medical, travel, food and drink, Mind, Body & Spirit, history, reference, pregnancy and childcare, antiques, preschool, 5–8, 8+.

### Hugo's Language Books (imprint)
Hugo's language books and courses.

### Rough Guides (imprint)
345 Hudson Street, New York, NY 10014
*tel* 212-414-3635 *fax* 212-414-3352
*email* mail@roughguides.com
*website* www.roughguides.com
*Publisher* Martin Dunford

Trade paperbacks, travel guides, phrasebooks, music reference, music CDs and internet reference. Founded 1982.

## Penguin Longman – see Pearson Education

## Penton Press – see Kogan Page Ltd

## Pergamon – see Elsevier Ltd

## Persephone Books

59 Lamb's Conduit Street, London WC1N 3NB
*tel* 020-7242 9292 *fax* 020 7242 9272
*email* sales@persephonebooks.co.uk
*website* www.persephonebooks.co.uk
*Managing Director* Nicola Beauman

Reprints of forgotten classics by 20th century women writers with prefaces by contemporary writers. Founded 1999.

## Peterloo Poets

The Old Chapel, Sand Lane, Calstock,
Cornwall PL18 9QX
*tel* (01822) 833473 *fax* (01822) 833989
*email* poets@peterloo.fsnet.co.uk
*website* www.peterloopoets.co.uk
*Publishing Director* Harry Chambers, *Trustees* Brian Perman, David Selzer, Rose Taw, *Honorary President* Charles Causley CBE

Poetry. Founded 1976.

## Phaidon Press Ltd

Regent's Wharf, All Saints Street,
London N1 9PA
*tel* 020-7843 1000 *fax* 020-7843 1010
*website* www.phaidon.com
*Chairman/Publisher* Richard Schlagman, *Managing Director* Andrew Price, *Deputy Publisher* Amanda Renshaw, *Directors* Frances Johnson, Nigel Watts-Morgan, James Booth-Clibborn, Karen Stein

Quality books on the visual arts, including fine art and art history, architecture, design, decorative arts, photography, music, fashion, film.

## Philip's – see Octopus Publishing Group

## Phillimore & Co. Ltd

Shopwyke Manor Barn, Chichester,
West Sussex PO20 2BG
*tel* (01243) 787636 *fax* (01243) 787639
*email* bookshop@phillimore.co.uk
*website* www.phillimore.co.uk
*Directors* Philip Harris JP (chairman), Noel Osborne MA, FSA (managing), Hilary Clifford Brown (marketing), Nicola Willmot (production)

Local and family history; architectural history, archaeology, genealogy and heraldry; also *Darwen County History* series and *History from the Sources* series. Founded 1897.

## Phoenix House – see Weidenfeld & Nicolson

## Piatkus Books

5 Windmill Street, London W1T 2JA
*tel* 020-7631 0710 *fax* 020-7436 7137
*email* info@piatkus.co.uk
*website* www.piatkus.co.uk
*Managing Director* Judy Piatkus, *Deputy Managing*

*Director* Philip Cotterell (marketing), *Non-fiction Editorial Director* Gill Bailey

Fiction, biography, history, sport, memoirs, self-help, health, Mind, Body & Spirit, business, careers, women's interest, how-to and practical, popular psychology, cookery, parenting and childcare, paranormal. Imprints: Piatkus, Portrait. Founded 1979.

## Pica Press – see A & C Black Publishers Ltd

## Picador – see Macmillan Publishers Ltd

## Piccadilly Press

5 Castle Road, London NW1 8PR
*tel* 020-7267 4492 *fax* 020-7267 4493
*email* books@piccadillypress.co.uk
*website* www.piccadillypress.co.uk
*Managing Director & Publisher* Brenda Gardner

Early picture books, parental advice trade paperbacks, trade paperback teenage non-fiction and humorous teenage fiction. Founded 1983.

## Pimlico – see Random House Group Ltd

## Pinwheel Ltd

Winchester House, 259–269 Old Marylebone Road,
London NW1 5XJ
*tel* 020-7616 7200 *fax* 020-7616 7201
*email* angela.brooksbank@pinwheel.co.uk
shaheen.bilgrami@pinwheel.co.uk
*website* www.pinwheel.co.uk
*Managing Director* Andrew Flatt

Children's non-fiction, picture books and novelty titles. Unsolicited MSS will not be returned.

### Andromeda Children's Books (imprint)
*Publishing/Creative Director* Linda Cole
Illustrated non-fiction for children aged 3–12 years old.

### Gullane Children's Books (imprint)
*Creative Director* Paula Burgess
Picture books for children aged 0–8 years old.

### Pinwheel Children's Books (imprint)
*Publishing/Creative Director* Linda Cole
Cloth and novelty books for children aged 0–5 years old.

## Pipers' Ash Ltd

Pipers' Ash, Church Road, Christian Malford,
Chippenham, Wilts. SN15 4BW
*tel* (01249) 720563 *fax* (0870) 0568916
*email* pipersash@supamasu.com
*website* www.supamasu.com
*Editorial Director* Alfred Tyson

Poetry, contemporary short stories, science fiction stories; short novels, biographies, plays, philosophy, translations, children's, general non-fiction. New authors with talent and potential encouraged. Founded 1976.

## Pitkin Unichrome Ltd – see Jarrold Publishing

## Pitman Publishing – now FT Prentice Hall, see Pearson Education

## The Playwrights Publishing Company
70 Nottingham Road, Burton Joyce, Notts. NG14 5AL
*tel* 0115-931 3356
*email* playwrightspublishingco@yahoo.co.uk
*website* www.geocities.com/playwrightspublishingco
*Proprietor* Liz Breeze, *Consultant* Tony Breeze

One-act and full-length drama published on the internet: serious work and comedies, for mixed cast, all women or schools. Reading fee unless professionally produced; sae required. Founded 1990.

## Plexus Publishing Ltd
55A Clapham Common Southside,
London SW4 9BX
*tel* 020-7622 2440 *fax* 020-7622 2441
*email* plexus@plexusuk.demon.co.uk
*website* www.plexusbooks.com
*Directors* Terence Porter (managing), Sandra Wake
(editorial)

Film, music, biography, popular culture, fashion. Imprint: Eel Pie. Founded 1973.

## Pluto Press
345 Archway Road, London N6 5AA
*tel* 020-8348 2724 *fax* 020-8348 9133
*email* pluto@plutobooks.com
*website* www.plutobooks.com
*Directors* Roger van Zwanenberg (managing), Anne Beech (editorial), *Head of Sales* Simon Liebesny, *Head of Marketing* Melanie Patrick

Politics, international anthropology development, media, cultural, economics, history, Irish studies, Black studies, Islamic studies, Middle East, Women's studies. Imprint: Journeyman Press. Founded 1968.

## Pocket Books – see Simon & Schuster

## Point – see Scholastic Children's Books

## The Policy Press
University of Bristol, 4th Floor, Beacon House,
Queen's Road, Bristol BS8 1QU
*tel* 0117-331 4054 *fax* 0117-331 4093
*email* tpp-info@bristol.ac.uk
*website* www.policypress.org.uk
*Publishing Director* Alison Shaw, *Editorial and Production Manager* Dawn Louise Rushen, *Marketing and Sales Manager* Julia Mortimer

Social science publisher, specialising in social and public policy, social work and social welfare. Founded 1996.

## Policy Studies Institute (PSI)
100 Park Village East, London NW1 3SR
*tel* 020-7468 0468 *fax* 020-7388 0914
*email* webstie@psi.org.uk

Economic, cultural, social and environmental policy, political institutions, social sciences.

## Polity Press
65 Bridge Street, Cambridge CB2 1UR
*tel* (01223) 324315 *fax* (01223) 461385
*website* www.polity.co.uk
*Directors* Anthony Giddens, David Held, John Thompson

Social and political theory, politics, sociology, history, media and cultural studies, philosophy, literary theory, feminism, human geography, anthropology. Founded 1983.

## Polygon – see Birlinn Ltd

## Poolbeg Group Services Ltd
123 Grange Hill, Baldoyle, Dublin 13,
Republic of Ireland
*tel* (01) 8321477 *fax* (01) 8321430
*email* poolbeg@poolbeg.com
*website* www.poolbeg.com
*Directors* Kieran Devlin (managing), Paula Campbell (publisher)

Popular fiction, non-fiction, current affairs. Imprint: Poolbeg. Founded 1976.

## Portland Press Ltd
59 Portland Place, London W1B 1QW
*tel* 020-7580 5530 *fax* 020-7323 1136
*email* editorial@portlandpress.com
*website* www.portlandpress.com
*Directors* Rhonda C. Oliver (managing), Chris J. Finch (finance), John Day (IT), Adam Marshall (marketing)

Biochemistry and molecular life science books for graduate, post-graduate and research students. Illustrated science books for children: *Making Sense of Science* series. Founded 1990.

## T & AD Poyser – see A & C Black Publishers Ltd

## Prentice Hall – now FT Prentice Hall, see Pearson Education

## Mathew Price Ltd
The Old Glove Factory, Bristol Road, Sherborne,
Dorset DT9 4HP
*tel* (01935) 816010 *fax* (01935) 816310
*email* mathewp@mathewprice.com
*Chairman* Mathew Price

Illustrated fiction and non-fiction children's books for all ages for the UK and international market. Specialist in flap, pop-up, paper-engineered titles as well as conventional books. Founded 1983.

## Princeton University Press – Europe
3 Market Place, Woodstock, Oxon OX20 1SY
*tel* (01993) 814500 *fax* (01993) 814504
*email* admin@pupress.co.uk
*website* www.pup.princeton.edu
*Publishing Director – Europe* Richard Baggaley

Economics, finance, philosophy and political theory. Part of **Princeton University Press**, USA. European office founded 1999.

## Prion Books – see Carlton Publishing Group

## Profile Books Ltd
58A Hatton Garden, London EC1N 8LX
*tel* 020-7404 3001 *fax* 020-7404 3003
*email* info@profilebooks.co.uk
*website* www.profilebooks.co.uk
*Publisher and Managing Director* Andrew Franklin, *Editorial Director* Stephen Brough

General non-fiction: current affairs, politics, social sciences, history, psychology, business, management. Also publishes in association with *The Economist* and the *London Review of Books*. No unsolicited MSS; phone or send preliminary letter. Founded 1996.

## ProQuest Information and Learning*
The Quorum, Barnwell Road, Cambridge CB5 8SW
*tel* (01223) 215512 *fax* (01223) 215513
*email* info@proquest.co.uk
*website* www.proquest.co.uk
*Executive Directors* Steven Hall (Senior Vice-President & General Manager), Simon Beale (Vice-President, sales & marketing), Julie Carroll-Davis (Vice-President, publishing), Ian McEwan (Vice-President, finance), Stephen Pocock (Vice-President, production), Sarah Rowland (HR Manager), John Taylor (Vice-President, technology & development)

Provider of newspapers, periodicals, literature, dissertations, reference and archival information to educational institutions, libraries and businesses around the world in microform and electronic format. Not a print publisher. Founded 1973.

## Psychology Press Ltd*
27 Church Road, Hove, East Sussex BN3 2FA
*tel* (01273) 207411 *fax* (01273) 205612
*email* info@psypress.co.uk
*website* www.psypress.co.uk

Psychology textbooks and monographs. Part of **Taylor and Francis Books Ltd**.

### Brunner-Routledge (imprint)
*website* www.brunner-routledge.co.uk

Clinical psychology and psychiatry.

## Puffin – see Penguin Group (UK)

## Pushkin Press
12 Chester Terrace, London NW1 4ND
*tel* 020-7266 9136
*email* sasha@pushkinpress.com
*Owner* Melissa Ulfane

Continental European literature in translation. Founded 1997.

## Putnam Aeronautical Books – now Brassey's Conway Putnam – see Chrysalis Books Group

## Quadrille Publishing
5th Floor, Alhambra House, 27–31 Charing Cross Road, London WC2H 0LS
*tel* 020-7839 7117 *fax* 020-7839 7118
*Directors* Alison Cathie (managing), Jane O'Shea and Anne Furniss (editorial), Helen Lewis (art), David Kemp (commercial), Vincent Smith (production)

Illustrated non-fiction: cookery, craft, health and medical, gardening, interiors, magic. Founded 1994.

## Quantum – see W. Foulsham & Co. Ltd

## Quartet Books Ltd
27 Goodge Street, London W1T 2LD
*tel* 020-7636 3992 *fax* 020-7637 1866
*email* quartetbooks@easynet.co.uk
*Chairman* N.I. Attallah, *Managing Director* Jeremy Beale, *Publishing Director* Stella Kane

General fiction and non-fiction, foreign literature in translation, classical music, jazz, contemporary music, biography. Member of the Namara Group. Founded 1972.

## Queen Anne Press
Windmill Cottage, Mackerye End, Harpenden, Herts. AL5 5DR
*tel* (01582) 715866
*email* stephenson@lennardqap.co.uk
*Directors* K.A.A. Stephenson, R.H. Stephenson

Sporting yearbooks, sponsored titles and special commissions. No unsolicited MSS. Division of Lennard Associates Ltd.

## QUE Publishing – see Pearson Education

## Quiller Publishing Ltd
Wykey House, Wykey, Shrewsbury, Shrops. SY4 1JA
*tel* (01939) 261616 *fax* (01939) 261606
*email* info@quillerbooks.com
*website* www.swanhillbooks.com
*Managing Director* Andrew Johnston

### Quiller Press (imprint)
Specialises in sponsored books and publications

sold through non-book trade channels as well as bookshops: architecture, biography, business and industry, collecting, cookery, DIY, gardening, guidebooks, humour, reference, sports, travel, wines and spirits.

**The Sportsman's Press (imprint)**
All country subjects and general sports including fishing, fencing, shooting, equestrian and gunmaking; wildlife art.

**Swan Hill Press (imprint)**
Country and field sports activities, including fishing, cookery, shooting, falconry, equestrian, gundog training, natural history.

## Radcliffe Medical Press Ltd
18 Marcham Road, Abingdon, Oxon OX14 1AA
*tel* (01235) 528820 *fax* (01235) 528830
*email* contact.us@radcliffemed.com
*website* www.radcliffe-oxford.com
*Directors* Andrew Bax (managing), Gill Nineham (editorial), Margaret McKeown (financial), Gregory Moxon (marketing)

Primary care, child health, palliative care, nursing, pharmacy, dentistry, healthcare organisation and management. Founded 1987.

## Ragged Bears Publishing Ltd
Unit 14A, Bennett's Field Trading Estate, Southgate Road, Wincanton, Somerset BA9 9DT
*tel* (01963) 824184 *fax* (01963) 31147
*email* info@raggedbears.co.uk
*website* www.raggedbears.co.uk
*Managing Director* Henrietta Stickland, *Submissions Editor* Barbara Lamb

Preschool and primary age picture and novelty books. Takes very few unsolicited ideas as the list is small. Send sae for return of MSS; do not send original artwork. Imprints: Ragged Bears, Spindlewood. Founded 1994.

## Random House Audio Books – see
Random House Group Ltd

## Random House Business Books – see
Random House Group Ltd

## Random House Children's Books – see
Random House Group Ltd

## Random House Group Ltd*
20 Vauxhall Bridge Road, London SW1V 2SA
*tel* 020-7840 8400 *fax* 020-7233 8791
*website* www.randomhouse.co.uk
*Chairman/Ceo* Gail Rebuck, *Directors* Simon Master (deputy chairman), Ian Hudson (managing), Larry Finlay (managing, Transworld), Mark Gardiner (finance), Brian Davies (managing director, overseas

operations), Alfred Willmann (group bibliographic), Clare Harington (group communications), Philippa Dickinson (children's)
Subsidiary of Bertelsmann AG.

**Arrow Books Ltd (imprint)**
*tel* 020-7840 8518 *fax* 020-7821 7387
*Publishing Director* Kate Elton
Fiction, non-fiction, romance, humour, film tie-ins.

**Jonathan Cape (imprint)**
*tel* 020-7840 8576 *fax* 020-7233 6117
*Directors* Dan Franklin (managing), Robin Robertson, Rebecca Linsley (publicity)
Biography and memoirs, current affairs, drama, fiction, history, poetry, travel. Imprint: Yellow Jersey Press (sport).

**Century (imprint)**
*tel* 020-7840 8554 *fax* 020-7233 6127
*Directors* Richard Cable (managing), Mark Booth (publishing), Oliver Johnson (editorial), Charlotte Bush (publicity)
Fiction, biography, autobiography, general non-fiction.

**Chatto & Windus (imprint)**
*tel* 020-7840 8522 *fax* 020-7233 6123
*Directors* Alison Samuel (publishing), Penny Hoare, Tasja Dorkofikis (publicity)
Art, belles-lettres, biography and memoirs, current affairs, drama, essays, fiction, history, poetry, politics, philosophy, translations, travel, hardbacks and paperbacks. No unsolicited MSS.

**C.W. Daniel (imprint of Ebury Division)**
Homeopathy, mysticism, metaphysical, astrology. Incorporates Health Science Press, L.N. Fowler & Co Ltd and Neville Spearman Publishers.

**Ebury Press (imprint of Ebury Division)**
*tel* 020-7840 8400 *fax* 020-7840 8406
*Directors* Fiona MacIntyre (publisher), Jake Lingwood (senior publishing), Hannah MacDonald (publishing), Carey Smith (illustrated books)
General non-fiction, autobiography, popular history, sport, travel writing, popular science, humour, film and TV tie-ins, music, travel guides, reference, cookery, lifestyle, health and beauty.

**Fodor Guides (imprint of Ebury Press)**
Worldwide annual travel guides.

**Harvill Secker Press (imprint)**
*Publisher* Geoff Mulligan
English-language and world literature in translation (literary fiction, non-fiction and some narrative thrillers); monographs in the fields of ethnography, art, horticulture and natural history. Unsolicited MSS only accepted with sae.

## Hutchinson (imprint)
*tel* 020-7840 8564 *fax* 020-7233 6127
*Directors* Sue Freestone (publishing), Anthony Whittome, Paul Sidey (editorial), Sarah Whale (publicity)

Fiction and non-fiction: biography, memoirs, thrillers, crime, general history, politics, travel, adventure.

## Pimlico (imprint)
*tel* 020-7840 8630 *fax* 020-7233 6117
*Publishing Director* Will Sulkin

History, biography, literature.

## Vintage (imprint)
*tel* 020-7840 8400
*Publisher* Rachel Cugnoni, *Associate Publishing Director* Will Sulkin

Quality fiction and non-fiction.

## William Heinemann (imprint)
*tel* 020-7840 8400 *fax* 020-7233 6127
*Directors* Ravi Mirchandani, Andy McKillop (publishing), Cassie Chadderton (publicity)

Fiction and general non-fiction: crime, thrillers, women's fiction, literary fiction, translations, history, biography, science. No unsolicited MSS and synopses considered.

## Random House Audio Books
*tel* 020-7840 8419 *fax* 020-7233 6127
*Editor* Georgia Marnham

## Random House Business Books
*tel* 020-7840 8550 *fax* 020-7840 6127
*Publishing Director* Clare Smith

Business strategy and management, personal and career development, businessand general finance.

## Rider (imprint of Ebury Division)
*tel* 020-7840 8400 *fax* 020-7840 8406
*Publishing Director* Fiona MacIntyre, *Publishing Director* Judith Kendra

Buddhism, spirituality and personal development, healing, travel, ancient wisdom, paranormal, divination.

## Secker and Warburg (imprint)
*tel* 020-7840 8649 *fax* 020-7233 6117
*Directors* Geoff Mulligan (editorial), Tasja Dorkofikis (publicity)

Literary fiction, general non-fiction. No unsolicited MSS/synopses.

## Vermillion (imprint of Ebury Division)
*tel* 020-7840 8400 *fax* 020-7840 8406
*Directors* Fiona MacIntyre (publisher), Amanda Hemmings (editorial)

Personal development, relationships, parenting, pregnancy and childcare, health, diet and fitness, sex, beauty.

## Random House Children's Books (division)
61–63 Uxbridge Road, London W5 5SA
*tel* 020-8579 2652 *fax* 020-8579 5479
*Managing Director* Philippa Dickinson, *Publishing Director – Fiction* Annie Eaton, *Publishing Director – Picture Books* Caroline Roberts, *Publisher – Doubleday Picture Books* Penny Walker, *Senior Commissioning Editor – Fiction* Alex Antscherl, *Senior Commissioning Editor – Picture Books* Natascha Biebow, *Commissioning Editor – Jonathan Cape Picture Books* Helen Mackenzie-Smith, *Associate Publisher – Jonathan Cape Picture Books* Ian Craig, *Associate Publisher – Jonathan Cape Fiction* Delia Huddy, *Publisher – Jonathan Cape* Tom Maschler, *Publicity Director* Clare Hall-Craggs

Publishes picture books, fiction, poetry, non-fiction and audio cassettes under Bodley Head Children's Books, Corgi Children's Books, Doubleday Children's Books, Hutchinson Children's Books, Jonathan Cape Children's Books, Red Fox Children's Books, David Fickling Books.

## David Fickling Books (imprint)
31 Beaumont Street, Oxford OX1 2NP
*tel* (01865) 339000 *fax* (01865) 339009
*email* dfickling@randomhouse.co.uk
*website* davidficklingbooks.co.uk
*Publisher* David Fickling, *Editor* Bella Pearson

Quality children's fiction and picture books.

## Transworld Publishers (division)
See page 191.

# Ransom Publishing Ltd
Rose Cottage, Howe Hill, Watlington, Oxon OX49 5HB
*tel* (01491) 613711 *fax* (01491) 613733
*email* ransom@ransompublishing.co.uk
*website* www.ransom.co.uk
*Directors* Jenny Ertle (managing), Steve Rickard (creative)

Books for preschool and primary literacy including special needs. Range of digital content from preschool to secondary for literacy, numeracy, science and goegraphy. Founded 1995.

# The Reader's Digest Association Ltd
11 Westferry Circus, Canary Wharf, London E14 4HE
*tel* 020-7715 8000 *fax* 020-7715 8600
*Managing Director* A.T. Lynam-Smith, *Editorial Directors* Katherine Walker (magazine), Cortina Butler (books)

Monthly magazine, condensed and series books; also DIY, computers, puzzles, gardening, medical, handicrafts, law, touring guides, encyclopedias, dictionaries, nature, folklore, atlases, cookery, music; videos.

## Reaktion Books
77–79 Farringdon Road, London EC1M 3JU
*tel* 020-7404 9930 *fax* 020-7404 9931
*email* info@reaktionbooks.co.uk
*website* www.reaktionbooks.co.uk
*Editorial Director* Michael R. Leaman

Art history, design, architecture, history, cultural studies, film studies, Asian studies, travel writing, photography. Founded 1985.

## Rebel Inc. – former imprint of Canongate Books Ltd

## Red Dress Ink™ – see Harlequin Mills & Boon Ltd

## Red Fox Children's Books – see Random House Group Ltd

## Thomas Reed – see A & C Black Publishers Ltd

## Reed Books – now Octopus Publishing Group

## RBI Search
Windsor Court, East Grinstead House, Wood Street, East Grinstead, West Sussex RH19 1XA
*tel* (01342) 326972 *fax* (01342) 335612
*email* information@reedinfo.co.uk
*website* www.reedbusiness.com
*Managing Director* Jerry Gosney

Directories, online and hard copy, covering industrial, financial, travel and media sectors, including *Kelly's, Kompass, The Bankers' Almanac, SSISearch, Gazzetters.com* and *Kemps*. Part of Reed Elsevier plc. Founded 1983.

## William Reed Directories
Broadfield Park, Crawley, West Sussex RH11 9RT
*tel* (01293) 610488 *fax* (01293) 610310
*email* directories@william-reed.co.uk
*website* www.william-reed.co.uk
*Director* Mark de Lange, *Content Manager* Daniel Verrells, *Sales Manager* Helen Chater

Publishers of leading business-to-business directories and reports, including *The Grocer Directory of Buyers and Retailers* and *The Grocer Directory of Manufacturers and Suppliers.*

## Reed Educational and Professional Publishing Ltd – see Harcourt Education Ltd

## Religious and Moral Education Press (RMEP)*
St Mary's Works, St Mary's Plain, Norwich NR3 3BH
*tel* (01603) 612914 *fax* (01603) 624483
*email* admin@scm-canterburypress.co.uk
*website* www.scm-canterburypress.co.uk

*Ceo* Gordon Knights, *Editorial Director* Mary Mears

Books for primary and secondary school pupils, college students, and teachers on religious, moral, personal and social education. Division of SCM–Canterbury Press Ltd, a subsidiary of Hymns Ancient & Modern Ltd.

## Review – see Hodder Headline Ltd

## Reynolds & Hearn Ltd
61A Priory Road, Kew, Richmond, Surrey TW9 3DH
*tel* 020-8940 5198 *fax* 020-8940 7679
*email* richardreynolds@btconnect.com
*website* www.rhbooks.com
*Directors* Richard Reynolds (managing), Marcus Hearn (editorial), David O'Leary, Geoffrey Wolfson

Film, TV, music, entertainment, media. Founded 1999.

## Rider – see Random House Group Ltd

## Rigby Heinemann – see Harcourt Education Ltd

## River Books – see New Cavendish Books

## Rivers Oram Press
144 Hemingford Road, London N1 1DE
*tel* 020-7607 0823 *fax* 020-7609 2776
*email* ro@riversoram.demon.co.uk
*Directors* Elizabeth Rivers Fidlon (managing), Anthony Harris

Non-ficton: social and political science, current affairs, social history, gender studies, sexual politics, cultural studies and photography. Founded 1991.

**Pandora Press (imprint)**
*Managing Editor* Caroline Lazar

Feminist press. General non-fiction: biography, arts, media, health, current affairs, reference and sexual politics.

## Robinson – see Constable & Robinson Ltd

## Robson Books – see Chrysalis Books Group

## George Ronald
46 High Street, Kidlington, Oxon OX5 2DN
*tel* (01235) 529137 *fax* (01235) 529137
*email* sales@grpubl.demon.co.uk
*website* www.grbooks.com
*Managers* W. Momen, E. Leith

Religion, specialising in the Baha'i Faith. Founded 1939.

## Barry Rose Law Publishers Ltd
Little London, Chichester, West Sussex PO19 1PG
*tel* (01243) 775552 *fax* (01243) 779278
*email* books@barry-rose-law.co.uk

Law, local government, police, legal history. Founded 1972.

**Countrywise Press Ltd**
Reprints in paperback of hardcover books from Barry Rose; some non-law titles.

## Rough Guides – see Penguin Group (UK)

## Roundhouse Publishing Ltd
Millstone, Limers Lane, Northam,
North Devon EX39 2RG
*tel* (01237) 474474 *fax* (01237) 474774
*email* roundhouse.group@ukgateway.net
*website* www.roundhouse.net
*Publisher* Alan T. Goodworth

Film, cinema, and performing arts; reference books. No unsolicited MSS. Founded 1991.

## Route
PO Box 167, Pontefract, West Yorkshire WF8 4WW
*tel* (01977) 797695
*email* info@route-online.com
*websites* www.route-online.com,
www.id-publishing.com
*Contact* Ian Daley

Contemporary fiction (novels and short stories) and performance poetry, with a commitment to new writing. Unsolicited MSS discouraged. Visit the website for current guidelines. Ring or write for a free catalogue. Imprint of ID Publishing.

## Routledge – see Taylor and Francis Books Ltd

## RoutledgeCurzon – see Taylor and Francis Books Ltd

## RoutledgeFalmer – see Taylor and Francis Books Ltd

## Royal Collection Enterprises
St James's Palace, London SW1A 1JR
*tel* 020-7024 5584   *fax* 020-7839 8168
*website* www.royal.gov.uk
*Publisher* Jacky Colliss Harvey, *Editor* Marie Leahy

Subjects from within the Royal Collection. Founded 1993.

## Royal National Institute of the Blind
PO Box 173, Peterborough, Cambs. PE2 6WS
*tel* (0845) 7023153 *fax* (01733) 371555
*email* cservices@rnib.org.uk
*website* www.rnib.org.uk
*textphone* (0845) 7585691

Magazines, catalogues and books for blind and partially sighted people, to support daily living, leisure, learning and employment reading needs. Produced in braille, audio, large/legible print, disk

and email. For complete list of magazines see page 88. Founded 1868.

## Ryland Peters & Small
Kirkman House, 12–14 Whitfield Street,
London W1T 2RP
*tel* 020-7436 9090 *fax* 020-7436 9790
*email* info@rps.co.uk
*website* www.rylandpeters.com
*Directors* David Peters (managing), Alison Starling (publishing), Gabriella Le Grazie (art), Joanna Everard (rights), Meryl Silbert (production)

High-quality illustrated books on food and drink, lifestyle, interior design, Mind, Body & Spirit, gardening. Founded 1995.

## SAGE Publications Ltd*
1 Oliver's Yard, 55 City Road, London EC1Y ISP
*tel* 020-7324 8500 *fax* 020-7324 8600
*email* info@sagepub.co.uk
*website* www.sagepub.co.uk
*Directors* Stephen Barr (managing), Katharine Jackson, Ziyad Marar, Richard Fidczuk, Michael Melody (USA), Sara Miller McCune (USA), Paul R. Chapman

Social sciences, behavioural sciences, humanities, STM, software. Founded 1971.

## Saint Andrew Press*
121 George Street, Edinburgh EH2 4YN
*tel* 0131-240 2253 *fax* 0131-220 3113
*email* standrewpress@cofscotland.org.uk
*website* www.standrewpress.com
*Head of Publishing* Ann Crawford

Publishing house of the Church of Scotland: publishes books that explore Christianity, spirituality, faith and ethical and moral issues, as well as more general works of fiction and non-fiction; children's.

## St Pauls
St Pauls Publishing, 187 Battersea Bridge Road,
London SW11 3AS
*tel* 020-7978 4300 *fax* 020-7978 4370
*email* editions@stpauls.org.uk
*website* www.stpauls.ie

Theology, ethics, spirituality, biography, education, general books of Roman Catholic and Christian interest. Founded 1948.

## Salamander – see Chrysalis Books Group

## Salariya Book Company Ltd
Book House, 25 Marlborough Place,
Brighton BN1 1UB
*tel* (01273) 603306 *fax* (01273) 693857
*email* salariya@salariya.com
*website* www.salariya.com

*Director* David Salariya

Children's non-fiction. Imprint: Book House. Founded 1989.

## SAMS Publishing – see Pearson Education

## W.B. Saunders – see Elsevier Ltd (Health Sciences)

## S.B. Publications

c/o 19 Grove Road, Seaford, East Sussex BN25 1TP
*tel* (01323) 893498 *fax* (01323) 893860
*email* sbpublications@tiscali.co.uk
*website* www.sbpublications.co.uk
*Proprietor* Lindsay Woods

Local history, local themes (e.g. walking books, guides), maritime history, transport, specific themes. Founded 1987.

## Scala Publishers

Northburgh House, Northburgh Street,
London EC1V 0AT
*tel* 020-7490 9900 *fax* 020-7336 6870
*email* info@scalapublishers.com
*Chairman* David Campbell, *Directors* Henry Channon, Jan Baily, Antony White, *Director of Museum Publications* Jennifer Wright

Art, architecture, guides to museums and art galleries, antiques. Founded 1992.

## Sceptre – see Hodder Headline Ltd

## Schofield & Sims Ltd

Dogley Mill, Fenay Bridge,
Huddersfield HD8 0NQ
*tel* (01484) 607080 *fax* (01484) 606815
*email* sales@schofieldandsims.co.uk
*Chairman* C.N. Platts

Educational: nursery, infants, primary; posters. Founded 1901.

## Scholastic Ltd*

Villiers House, Clarendon Avenue, Leamington Spa, Warks. CV32 5PR
*tel* (01926) 887799 *fax* (01926) 883331
*website* www.scholastic.co.uk
*Directors* M.R. Robinson (USA), R.M. Spaulding (USA), D.J. Walsh (USA)

### Children's Division

See **Scholastic Children's Books**.

### Direct Marketing

*Managing Director, Book Fair Division & Book Club Division* Miles Stevens-Hoare, *Managing Director, Trade Sales and Marketing* Gavin Lang, *Rights Director* Caroline Hill-Trevor

Children's book clubs and school book fairs.

### Educational Division

*Publishing Director* Anne Peel

Publishers of books for teachers (*Bright Ideas* and other series), primary classroom resources and magazines for teachers (*Child Education, Junior Education* and others). Founded 1964.

## Scholastic Children's Books*

Commonwealth House, 1–19 New Oxford Street,
London WC1A 1NU
*tel* 020-7421 9000 *fax* 020-7421 9001
*email* publicity@scholastic.co.uk
*Publisher* Richard Scrivener

Activity books, novelty books, picture books, fiction for 5–12 year-olds, teenage fiction, series fiction and film/TV tie-ins. Imprints include Hippo, Point, Scholastic Fiction, Scholastic Non-fiction, Scholastic Press. Will consider unsolicited submissions: Send synopsis and sample chapter only. Imprint of **Scholastic Ltd**.

## Scholastic Fiction – see Scholastic Children's Books

## Scholastic Non-fiction – see Scholastic Children's Books

## Scholastic Press – see Scholastic Children's Books

## Science Museum Publications – see NMSI

## SCM Press–Canterbury Press Ltd*

9–17 St Albans Place, London N1 0NX
*tel* 020-7359 8033 *fax* 020-7359 0049
*email* admin@scm-canterburypress.co.uk
*website* www.scm-canterburypress.co.uk
*Publishing Director* Christine Smith

Theological books with special emphasis on text and reference books and contemporary theology for both students and clergy. Founded 1929.

## SCP Publishers Ltd*

Unit 6, Newbattle Abbey Business Annexe,
Newbattle Road, Dalkeith EH22 3LJ
*email* info@scottishbooks.com
*website* www.scottishbooks.com
*Directors* Brian Pugh, Avril Gray

Unsolicited MSS not accepted; send letter, telephone or email before sending material. Founded 1992.

## Scottish Children's Press

*tel* 0131-660 4757 *fax* 0131-660 4666

Scottish fiction, Scottish non-fiction and Scots language, children's writing. Unsolicited MSS not accepted; send letter, telephone or email before sending material. Founded 1992.

**Scottish Cultural Press**
*tel* 0131-660 6366 *fax* 0131-660 4666
'Scottish books for anyone interested in Scotland.'
Literature, poetry, history, archaeology, biography
and environmental history.

**Scribner** – see Simon & Schuster

**Scripture Union**
207–209 Queensway, Bletchley, Milton Keynes,
Bucks. MK2 2EB
*tel* (01908) 856000 *fax* (01908) 856111
*email* postmaster@scriptureunion.org.uk
*website* www.scriptureunion.org.uk
*Publishing Director* Malcolm Hall

Christian books and Bible reading materials for
people of all ages; educational and worship
resources for churches; children's fiction and non-
fiction; adult non-fiction. Founded 1867.

**Seafarer Books**
102 Redwald Road, Rendlesham, Woodbridge,
Suffolk IP12 2TE
*tel* (01394) 420789
*email* info@seafarerbooks.com
*website* www.seafarerbooks.com
*Commissioning Editor* Patricia Eve

Books on traditional sailing, mainly narrative.

**Search Press Ltd**
Wellwood, North Farm Road, Tunbridge Wells,
Kent TN2 3DR
*tel* (01892) 510850 *fax* (01892) 515903
*email* searchpress@searchpress.com
*Directors* Martin de la Bédoyère (managing),
Rosalind Dace (editorial)

Arts, crafts, leisure, gardening. Founded 1970.

**Secker and Warburg** – see Random House
Group Ltd

**Seren**
First Floor, 38–40 Nolton Street,
Bridgend CF31 3BN
*tel* (01656) 663018 *fax* (01656) 649226
*email* seren@seren-books.com
*Director* Mick Felton

Poetry, fiction, drama, history, film, literary criticism,
biography, art – mostly with relevance to Wales.
Founded 1981.

**Serpent's Tail**
4 Blackstock Mews, London N4 2BT
*tel* 020-7354 1949 *fax* 020-7704 6467
*email* info@serpentstail.com
*website* www.serpentstail.com
*Director* Peter Ayrton

Fiction and non-fiction in paperback; literary and
non-mainstream work, and work in translation. No
unsolicited MSS. Imprint: Five Star. Founded 1986.

**Seven Dials** – see Weidenfeld & Nicolson

**Severn House Publishers**
9–15 High Street, Sutton,
Surrey SM1 1DF
*tel* 020-8770 3930 *fax* 020-8770 3850
*email* editorial@severnhouse.com
*website* www.severnhouse.com
*Chairman* Edwin Buckhalter, *Publishing Director*
Amanda Stewart

Hardcover adult fiction for the library market:
romances, crime, thrillers, detective, adventure, war,
science fiction. No unsolicited MSS.

**Sheffield Academic Press** – see The
Continuum International Publishing Group Ltd

**Sheldon Press** – see Society for Promoting
Christian Knowledge

**Sheldrake Press**
188 Cavendish Road, London SW12 0DA
*tel* 020-8675 1767 *fax* 020-8675 7736
*email* mail@sheldrakepress.demon.co.uk
*website* www.sheldrakepress.demon.co.uk
*Publisher* J.S. Rigge

History, travel, architecture, cookery, music;
stationery. Founded 1979.

**Shepheard-Walwyn (Publishers) Ltd**
Suite 604, 50 Westminster Bridge Road,
London SE1 7QY
*tel* 020-7721 7666 *fax* 020-7721 7667
*email* books@shepheard-walwyn.co.uk
*website* www.shepheard-walwyn.co.uk
*Directors* A.R.A. Werner, M.M. Werner

History, biography, political economy, perennial
philosophy; illustrated gift books; Scottish interest.
Founded 1971.

**Shire Publications Ltd**
Cromwell House, Church Street, Princes
Risborough, Bucks. HP27 9AA
*tel* (01844) 344301 *fax* (01844) 347080
*email* shire@shirebooks.co.uk
*website* www.shirebooks.co.uk
*Director* J.W. Rotheroe

*Discovering* paperbacks, Shire Albums, Shire
Archaeology, Shire Natural History, Shire
Ethnography, Shire Egyptology, Shire Garden
History. Founded 1962.

## Short Books Ltd
15 Highbury Terrace, London N5 1UP
*tel* 020-7226 1607 *fax* 020-7226 4169
*email* mark@shortbooks.biz
*website* www.theshortbookco.com
*Editorial Directors* Rebecca Nicolson, Aurea Carpenter

Non-fiction, mainly biography and journalism. Also biographies of famous people from the past for children. All prospective authors will be informed by email of how their proposal has been received. MSS will not be returned. Founded 2000.

## Sidgwick & Jackson – see Macmillan
**Publishers Ltd**

## Sigma Press
5 Alton Road, Wilmslow, Cheshire SK9 5DY
*tel* (01625) 531035 *fax* (01625) 531035
*email* info@sigmapress.co.uk
*website* www.sigmapress.co.uk
*Partners* Graham Beech, Diana Beech

Leisure: country walking, cycling, regional heritage, ecology, sport, folklore; biographies. Founded 1979.

## Silhouette® – see Harlequin Mills & Boon Ltd

## Simon & Schuster*
Africa House, 64–78 Kingsway, London WC2B 6AH
*tel* 020-7316 1900 *fax* 020-7316 0331/2
*website* www.simonsays.co.uk
*Directors* Ian Chapman (managing), Suzanne Baboneau (publishing), Caroline Proud (sales and marketing), Diane Spivey (rights), Ingrid Selberg (children's publishing)

Commercial and literary fiction; general and serious non-fiction; children's. No unsolicited MSS. Founded 1986.

### Free Press (imprint)
*Publisher* Andrew Gordon

Serious adult non-fiction: history, biography, current affairs, science.

### Martin Books (imprint)
*Director* Janet Copleston

Mass market non-fiction.

### Pocket Books (imprint)
Science fiction and fantasy, mass-market fiction and non-fiction paperbacks.

### Scribner (imprint)
*Publishers* Tim Binding, Ben Ball

Literary fiction and non-fiction.

### Simon & Schuster Audioworks
Fiction, non-fiction and business.

### Simon & Schuster Children's Publishing
Fiction and non-fiction.

## Skoob Russell Square
10 Brunswick Centre, off Bernard Street, London WC1N 1AE
*tel* 020-7278 8760 *fax* 020-7278 3137
*email* books@skoob.com
*website* www.skoob.com
*Editorial* M. Lovell

Literary guides, cultural studies, oriental literature. No unsolicited material. Founded 1979.

## Smith Gryphon Ltd – see Blake Publishing

## Colin Smythe Ltd*
PO Box 6, Gerrards Cross, Bucks. SL9 8XA
*tel* (01753) 886000 *fax* (01753) 886469
*website* www.colinsmythe.co.uk
*Directors* Colin Smythe (managing and editorial), Peter Bander van Duren, A. Norman Jeffares, Ann Saddlemyer, Leslie Hayward

Biography, phaleristics, heraldry, Irish literature and literary criticism, folklore, crafts and history. Founded 1966.

## Society for Promoting Christian Knowledge*
Holy Trinity Church, Marylebone Road, London NW1 4DU
*tel* 020-7643 0382 *fax* 020-7643 0391
*email* publishing@spck.org.uk
*Director of Publishing* Simon Kingston

Founded 1698.

### Azure Books (imprint)
*Editor* Alison Barr

Biography and letters, personal growth and relationships, history, humour, spirituality, travel.

### Sheldon Press (imprint)
*Editorial Director* Joanna Moriarty

Popular medicine, health, self-help, psychology.

### SPCK (imprint)
*Editorial Director* Joanna Moriarty

Theology and academic, liturgy, prayer, spirituality, biblical studies, educational resources, mission, gospel and culture.

## Society of Genealogists Enterprises Ltd
14 Charterhouse Buildings, Goswell Road, London EC1M 7BA
*tel* 020-7251 8799 *fax* 020-7250 1800
*email* sales@sog.org.uk
*website* www.sog.org.uk
*Chief Executive* June Perrin

Local and family history books, fiche, disks, CDs, software and magazines plus extensive library facilities.

**South Street Press** – see Garnet Publishing Ltd

**Southwater** – see Anness Publishing

**Souvenir Press Ltd**
43 Great Russell Street, London WC1B 3PD
*tel* 020-7580 9307/8
*Managing Director* Ernest Hecht

Archaeology, biography and memoirs, educational (secondary, technical), general, humour, practical handbooks, psychiatry, psychology, sociology, sports, games and hobbies, travel, supernatural, parapsychology, illustrated books. No unsolicited fiction or children's books; initial enquiry by telephone essential for non-fiction.

**SPCK** – see Society for Promoting Christian Knowledge

**Spellmount Ltd**
The Village Cottage, Staplehurst,
Kent TN12 0BJ
*tel* (01580) 893730 *fax* (01580) 893731
*email* enquiries@spellmount.com
*website* www.spellmount.com
*Proprietor* Jamie A.G. Wilson

Ancients, 15th through to 20th century history/ military history. Send sae with submissions. Founded 1984.

**Spindlewood** – see Ragged Bears Publishing Ltd

**Spon Press** – see Taylor and Francis Books Ltd

**Sportsbooks Ltd**
PO Box 422, Cheltenham, Glos. GL50 2JR
*tel* (01242) 256755 *fax* (0870) 0750 888
*email* randall@sportsbooks.ltd.uk
*website* www.sportsbooks.ltd.uk
*Directors* Randall Northam, Veronica Northam
Sport.

**The Sportsman's Press** – see Quiller Publishing Ltd

**Springer-Verlag London Ltd**
Sweetapple House, Catteshall Road, Godalming,
Surrey GU7 3DJ
*tel* (01483) 418800 *fax* (01483) 415151
*email* postmaster@svl.co.uk
*website* www.springer.co.uk
*Managing Director* John Watson, *Executive Directors* D. Goetz, R. Gebauer

Medicine, computing, engineering, astronomy, mathematics. Founded 1972.

**Stacey International**
128 Kensington Church Street, London W8 4BH
*tel* 020-7221 7166 *fax* 020-7792 9288
*email* enquiries@stacey-international.co.uk
*website* stacey-international.co.uk
*Chairman* Tom Stacey, *Managing Director* Max Scott

Illustrated non-fiction, encyclopedic books on regions and countries, Islamic and Arab subjects, world affairs, children's books, art, travel, belles-lettres. Founded 1973.

**Stainer & Bell Ltd**
PO Box 110, Victoria House, 23 Gruneisen Road,
London N3 1DZ
*tel* 020-8343 3303 *fax* 020-8343 3024
*email* post@stainer.co.uk
*website* www.stainer.co.uk
*Directors* Keith Wakefield (joint managing), Carol Wakefield (joint managing and secretary), Peter Braley, Antony Kearns, Andrew Pratt, Nicholas Williams

Books on music, religious communication. Founded 1907.

**Harold Starke Publishers Ltd**
Pixey Green, Stadbroke, Eye, Suffolk IP21 5NG
*tel* (01379) 388334 *fax* (01379) 388335
*Directors* Naomi Galinski (editorial)
Specialist, scientific, medical, reference.

**Stationery Office (Ireland)** – see Government Supplies Agency

**Stenlake Publishing Ltd**
54–58 Mill Square, Catrine Ayrshire KA5 6RD
*tel* (01290) 552233 *fax* (01290) 551122
*email* sales@stenlake.co.uk
*website* www.stenlake.co.uk
*Managing Director* Richard Stenlake, *Managing Editor* Oliver van Helden

Local history, railways, transport, aviation, canals and mining. Approx 330 titles in print. List covers Wales, Scotland, England, Northern Ireland, Isle of Man and Republic of Ireland. Founded 1997.

**Patrick Stephens Ltd** – see Sutton Publishing Ltd

**Stride Publications**
11 Sylvan Road, Exeter, Devon EX4 6EW
*email* editor@stridebooks.co.uk
*website* www.stridebooks.co.uk
*Managing Editor* Rupert M. Loydell

Poetry, literary experimental and prose poetry fiction, contemporary music and visual arts, interviews. No submissions are currently being sought. Founded 1980.

## Summersdale Publishers Ltd
46 West Street, Chichester, West Sussex PO19 1RP
*tel* (01243) 771107 *fax* (01243) 786300
*email* info@summersdale.com,
sadie@summersdale.com
*website* www.summersdale.com
*Directors* Alistair Williams, Stewart Ferris,
*Commissioning Editor* Sadie Mayne

Commercial non-fiction, particularly travel, martial arts, biography, history and gift books. No poetry or children's literature. Founded 1990.

## Sunflower Books
12 Kendrick Mews, London SW7 3HG
*tel* 020-7589 1862 *fax* 020-7589 1862
*email* mail@sunflowerbooks.co.uk
*website* www.sunflowerbooks.co.uk
*Editorial Director* P.A. Underwood

Travel guidebooks.

## Sussex Academic Press
PO Box 2950, Brighton BN2 5SP
*tel* (01273) 699533 *fax* (01273) 621262
*email* edit@sussex-academic.co.uk
*website* www.sussex-academic.co.uk
*Editorial Director* Anthony Grahame

Theology and religion, British history and Middle East studies. Founded 1994.

### The Alpha Press (imprint)
Religion, history, sport.

## Sutton Publishing Ltd
Phoenix Mill, Thrupp, Stroud, Glos. GL5 2BU
*tel* (01453) 731114 *fax* (01453) 731117
*email* publishing@sutton-publishing.co.uk
*website* www.suttonpublishing.co.uk
*Managing Director* Jeremy Yates-Round, *Editorial* Jaqueline Mitchell (biography), Christopher Feeney (general history), Jonathan Falconer (military), Simon Fletcher (local history)

General academic and specialist publishers of high-quality illustrated books: history, military, biography, archaeology, heritage. Owned by Haynes Publishing. Founded 1978.

### Patrick Stephens Ltd (imprint)
Aviation, maritime and military. New titles and new editions now published under Sutton imprint.

## Swan Hill Press – see Quiller Publishing Ltd

## Swedenborg Society
20–21 Bloomsbury Way, London WC1A 2TH
*tel* 020-7405 7986 *fax* 020-7831 5848
*email* swed.soc@netmatters.co.uk
*website* www.swedenborg.co.uk

The Writings of Swedenborg, biographies and studies of Swedenbourg.

## Sweet & Maxwell*
100 Avenue Road, London NW3 3PF
*tel* 020-7393 7000 *fax* 020-7393 7010
*Directors* Wendy Beecham (managing), Jim Glover, Aris Kassimatis, Hilary Lambert, Wendy Newman, Martin Redfern, Jackie Rhodes

Law. Part of Thomson Legal & Regulatory (Europe) Ltd. Founded 1799; incorporated 1889.

## Take That Ltd
PO Box 200, Harrogate, North Yorkshire HG1 2YR
*tel* (01423) 507545 *fax* (01423) 526035
*email* sales@takethat.co.uk
*website* www.takethat.co.uk
*Managing Director* Chris Brown

Internet/computing, business, finance, gambling. Send sae with synopsis/samples. Founded 1986.

## Tamarind Ltd
PO Box 52, Northwood, Middlesex HA6 1UN
*tel* 020-8866 8808 *fax* 020-8866 5627
*email* info@tamarindbooks.co.uk
*website* www.tamarindbooks.co.uk
*Managing Director* Verna Wilkins

Multicultural children's picture books and posters. All books give a high positive profile to black children. Unsolicited material welcome with return postage. Founded 1987.

## Tango Books Ltd
3D West Point, 36–37 Warple Way, London W3 0RG
*tel* 020-8996 9970 *fax* 020-8996 9977
*email* sales@tangobooks.co.uk
*Directors* Sheri Safran, David Fielder

Children's novelty books, including pop-up, touch-and-feel and cloth books.

## Tarquin Publications
Stradbroke, Diss, Norfolk IP21 5JP
*tel* (01379) 384218 *fax* (01379) 384289
*email* tarquin-books.demon.co.uk
*website* www.tarquin-books.demon.co.uk
*Partners* Gerald Jenkins, Margaret Jenkins

Mathematics and mathematical models; paper cutting, paper engineering and pop-up books for intelligent children. No unsolicited MSS; send suggestion or synopsis in first instance. Founded 1970.

## Tate Publishing
The Lodge, Millbank, London SW1P 4RG
*tel* 020-7887 8869/70 *fax* 020-7887 8878
*email* tgpl@tate.org.uk
*website* www.tate.org.uk
*Chief Executive* Celia Clear, *Publishing Director* Roger Thorp, *Operations Director* Tahir Hussain, *Production Manager* Sophie Lawrence, *Head of Licensing* Jo Matthews, *Head of Products* Rosey Blackmore

Publishers for Tate in London, Liverpool and St Ives. Exhibition catalogues, art books (contemporary, modern and from 1500 if British) and diaries, posters, etc. Also product development, picture library and licensing. Division of Tate Enterprises Ltd. Founded 1995.

## Tauris Academic Studies – see I.B.Tauris & Co. Ltd

## I.B.Tauris & Co. Ltd
6 Salem Road, London W2 4BU
*tel* 020-7243 1225 *fax* 020-7243 1226
*email* mail@ibtauris.com
*website* www.ibtauris.com
*Chairman/Publisher* Iradj Bagherzade, *Managing Director* Jonathan McDonnell

History, biography, politics, international relations, current affairs, Middle East, religion, cultural and media studies, film, art, archaeology, travel guides. Founded 1983.

### Tauris Academic Studies (imprint)
Academic monographs on history, political science and social sciences.

### Tauris Parke Books (imprint)
Illustrated books on architecture, design, photography, cultural history and travel.

### Tauris Parke Paperbacks (imprint)
Non-fiction trade paperbacks: biography, history, travel, cinema, art, cultural history.

## Taylor and Francis Books Ltd*
11 New Fetter Lane, London EC4P 4EE
*tel* 020-7583 9855 *fax* 020-7842 2298
*Moving Sept 04 to* 4 Park Road, Milton Park, Abingdon, Oxon OX14 4RN
*tel* (01235) 828600 *fax* (01235) 828000
*email* info@tandf.co.uk
*websites* www.tandf.co.uk, www.tfinforma.com
*Managing Director, Taylor & Francis Books Ltd* Roger Horton

Taylor and Francis Group plc merged with Informa Group plc in May 2004 to form T&F Informa plc.

### BIOS Scientific Publishers (imprint)
*website* www.bios.co.uk
Bioscience textbooks.

### Frank Cass (imprint)
*email* info@frankcass.com
*website* www.frankcass.com
History, economic and social history, military and strategic studies, politics, international affairs, development studies, African studies, Middle East studies, sports studies, law, business management and academic journals in all of these fields.

### CRC Press (imprint)
*website* www.crcpress.com
Engineering and science books.

### Dekker Publishing (imprint)
Engineering, science and medical.

### Martin Dunitz (imprint)
Medical books.

### Europa Publications Ltd (imprint)
See page 152.

### Fitzroy-Dearborn (imprint)
Reference and academic encyclopedias and handbooks.

### Garland Science (imprint)
*website* www.garlandscience.com
Science textbooks and scholarly works.

### Parthenon Press (imprint)
Medical books.

### Psychology Press Ltd
See page 179.

### Routledge (imprint)
*website* www.routledge.com
Addiction, anthropology, archaeology, Asian studies, business, classical studies, counselling, criminology, development and environment, dictionaries, economics, education, geography, health, history, Japanese studies, library science, language, linguistics, literary criticism, media and culture, nursing, performance studies, philosophy, politics, psychiatry, psychology, reference, social administration, social studies/sociology, women's studies.

### RoutledgeCurzon (imprint)
*website* www.routledgecurzon.com
Academic/scholarly books in the social sciences, particularly Asian studies.

### RoutledgeFalmer (imprint)
*website* www.routledgefalmer.com
Education books.

### Spon Press (imprint)
*website* www.sponpress.com
Architecture, civil engineering, construction, leisure and recreation management, sports science.

### Taylor & Francis (imprint)
*website* www.tandf.co.uk/books
Educational (university), science: physics, mathematics, chemistry, electronics, natural history, pharmacology and drug metabolism, toxicology, technology, history of science, ergonomics, production engineering, remote sensing, geographic information systems.

## Teach Yourself – see Hodder Headline Ltd

## Telegraph Books

Telegraph Group Ltd, 1 Canada Square,
Canary Wharf, London E14 5DT
*tel* 020-7538 6826 *fax* 020-7538 6064
*Publisher* Morven Knowles

Personal finance, crosswords, sport, humour,
cookery, health, general, gardening, history – usually
by *Telegraph* journalists and contributors, and co-
published with major publishing houses. Founded
1920.

## Tempus Publishing Group Ltd

The Mill, Brimscombe Port, Stroud, Glos. GL5 2QG
*tel* (01453) 883300 *fax* (01453) 883233
*Directors* Richard Joseph (chief executive), Geoff
Holmes (operations, USA), Chris McLaren
(managing director UK), Paul Raffle (chief
operating officer), Mike Walton (special projects)

Local and national history throughout the British
Isles; USA (Arcadia Publishing Inc.); modern;
mediaeval; archaeology; sport; industrial and
transport history. Founded 1993.

## Tender Romance™ – see Harlequin Mills & Boon Ltd

## Thames & Hudson Ltd*

181A High Holborn, London WC1V 7QX
*tel* 020-7845 5000 *fax* 020-7845 5050
*email* sales@thameshudson.co.uk
*website* www.thamesandhudson.com
*Directors* T. Neurath (managing), E. Bates, C. Kaine,
C. Ferguson, J. Camplin, P. Hughes, S. Baron,
B. Meek, P. Meades, J. Neurath, T. Evans, T. Naylor,
N. Stangos, N. Palfreyman

Illustrated non-fiction for an international
audience, especially art, architecture, graphic design,
garden and landscape design, archaeology, cultural
history, historical reference, fashion, photography,
ethnic arts, mythology and religion.

## Thames Publishing

c/o William Elkin Music Services, Station Road
Industrial Estate, Salhouse, Norwich NR13 6NS
*tel* (01603) 721302 *fax* (01603) 721801
*email* sales@elkinmusic.co.uk
*website* www.elkinmusic.co.uk
*Publishing Manager* Richard Elkin

Books about music (not pop), particularly British
composers and musicians. Preliminary letter
essential. Founded 1970.

## D.C. Thomson & Co. Ltd – Publications

2 Albert Square, Dundee DD1 9QJ
*London office* 185 Fleet Street, London EC4A 2HS
Publishers of newspapers and periodicals. Children's

books (annuals), based on weekly magazine
characters; fiction. For fiction guidelines, send a
large sae to Central Fiction Dept.

## Thomson Round Hall

43 Fitzwilliam Place, Dublin 2,
Republic of Ireland
*tel* (01) 6625301 *fax* (01) 6625302
*email* info@roundhall.ie
*Director and General Manager* Elanor McGarry

Law. Part of Thomson Legal & Regulatory (Europe)
Ltd.

## Stanley Thornes (Publishers) Ltd – see Nelson Thornes Ltd

## Thorsons/Element – see HarperCollins Publishers

## Time Warner Books UK*

Brettenham House, Lancaster Place,
London WC2E 7EN
*tel* 020-7911 8000 *fax* 020-7911 8100
*Chief Executive* David Young, *Directors* Ursula
Mackenzie (publisher), Barbara Boote (editorial),
Richard Beswick (editorial), Alan Samson
(editorial), Peter Cotton (art), Richard Kitson
(sales), Nigel Batt (financial), Terry Jackson
(marketing), Stephen Roberts (commercial)

Hardback and paperback fiction and general non-
fiction. No unsolicited MSS. Founded 1988.

### Abacus (division)
*Editorial Director* Richard Beswick

Trade paperbacks.

### Atom (division)
*website* www.atombooks.co.uk
*Editorial Director* Tim Holman, *Editor* Darren Nash

Teen fiction.

### Orbit (imprint)
*Editorial Director* Tim Holman

Science fiction and fantasy.

### Bullfinch Publishing (division)
*Editorial Director* Barbara Boote

General non-fiction.

### Little, Brown (division)
*Editorial Director* Richard Beswick

General books: politics, biography, crime fiction,
general fiction).

### Virago (division)
*Publisher* Lennie Goodings

Fiction, including Modern Classics Series,
biography, autobiography and general non-fiction
which highlight all aspects of women's lives.

**Warner (division)**
*Editorial Directors* Barbara Boote, Alan Samson, Hilary Hale

Paperbacks: original fiction and non-fiction; reprints.

**X Libris (imprint)**
*Editor* Sarah Shrubb

Erotic fiction for women.

**Times Books** – see HarperCollins Publishers

**Titan Books**
144 Southwark Street, London SE1 0UP
*tel* 020-7620 0200 *fax* 020-7620 0032
*email* editorial@titanemail.com
*website* www.titanbooks.com
*Publisher and Managing Director* Nick Landau, *Editorial Director* Katy Wild

Graphic novels, including *Simpsons* and *Batman*, featuring comic strip material; film and TV tie-ins and cinema reference books, including *Star Wars* and *Star Trek*. No fiction or children's proposals, no email submissions and no unsolicited material without preliminary letter please; send large sae or email for current author guidelines. Division of Titan Publishing Group Ltd. Founded 1981.

**Tivoli** – see Gill & Macmillan Ltd

**Tolkien** – see HarperCollins Publishers

**Tolley** – see LexisNexis UK

**Top That! Publishing plc**
Marine House, Tide Mill Way, Woodbridge, Suffolk IP12 1AP
*tel* (01394) 386651 *fax* (01394) 386011
*email* lorraine@topthatpublishing.com
*website* www.topthatpublishing.com
*Directors* Barrie Henderson (managing), Simon Couchman (creative), Dave Greggor (sales), Mike Kudar (production)

Children's information and novelty books. Founded 1998.

**Kudos Books (imprint)**
Adult gift books, humour. Founded 1999.

**TownHouse, Dublin†**
Trinity House, Charleston Road, Ranelagh, Dublin 6, Republic of Ireland
*tel* (01) 4972399 *fax* (01) 4970927
*email* books@townhouse.ie
*website* www.townhouse.ie
*Directors* Treasa Coady, Jim Coady

General illustrated non-fiction, popular and literary fiction, art, archaeology and biography. Imprints: TownHouse, Simon and Schuster/TownHouse, Pocket/TownHouse, Scribner/TownHouse. Founded 1981.

**Transworld Publishers\***
61–63 Uxbridge Road, London W5 5SA
*tel* 020-8579 2652 *fax* 020-8579 5479
*email* info@transworld-publishers.co.uk
*website* www.booksattransworld.co.uk
*Managing Director* Larry Finlay, *Publisher* Patrick Janson-Smith, *Deputy Publisher* Bill Scott-Kerr, *Senior Publishing Director* Francesca Liversidge

Division of **Random House Group Ltd**; subsidiary of Bertelsmann AG. No unsolicited MSS accepted.

**Bantam (imprint)**
*Senior Publishing Director* Francesca Liversidge

Paperback general fiction and non-fiction, Mind, Body & Spirit, self-help, travel.

**Bantam Press (imprint)**
*Publishing Director* Sally Gaminara

Fiction, general, cookery, business, crime, health and diet, history, humour, military, music, paranormal, self-help, science, travel and adventure, biography and autobiography.

**Black Swan (imprint)**
*Deputy Publisher* Bill Scott-Kerr

Paperback quality fiction.

**Channel 4 Books (imprint)**
*Publisher* Douglas Young

TV tie-ins.

**Corgi (imprint)**
*Deputy Publisher* Bill Scott-Kerr

Paperback general fiction and non-fiction.

**Doubleday (UK) (imprint)**
*Publishing Director* Marianne Velmans

Literary fiction and non-fiction.

**Eden (imprint)**
*Managing Editor* Katrina Whone

Environmental: the Eden Project.

**Expert Books (imprint)**
*Co-ordinator* Gareth Pottle

Gardening and DIY.

**Treehouse Children's Books**
2nd Floor Offices, Old Brewhouse, Lower Charlton Trading Estate, Shepton Mallet, Somerset BA4 5QE
*tel* (01749) 330529 *fax* (01749) 330544
*email* richard.powell4@virgin.net
*Editorial Director* Richard Powell

Preschool children's books and novelty books. Imprint of Emma Treehouse Ltd. Founded 1989.

**Trentham Books Ltd**
Westview House, 734 London Road, Oakhill, Stoke-on-Trent, Staffs. ST4 5NP
*tel* (01782) 745567 *fax* (01782) 745553

*email* tb@trentham.books.co.uk
*website* www.trentham-books.co.uk
*Editorial office* 28 Hillside Gardens, London N6 5ST
*email* 020-8348 2174
*Directors* Dr Gillian Klein (editorial), Barbara
Wiggins (executive)

Education (including specialist fields – multi-ethnic
issues, equal opportunities, bullying, design and
technology, early years), social policy, sociology of
education, European education, women's studies.
Does not publish books for use by parents or
children, or fiction, biography, reminiscences and
poetry. Founded 1978.

## Trotman & Company Ltd
2 The Green, Richmond, Surrey TW9 1PL
*tel* 020-8486 1150 *fax* 020-8486 1161
*website* www.trotmanpublishing.co.uk
*Managing Director* Toby Trotman, *Editorial Director*
Mina Patria, *Commissioning Editor* Rachel Lockhart

Independent advice and guidance on careers and
higher education. Founded 1970.

## TSO (The Stationery Office)*
*Head office* St Crispins, Duke Street,
Norwich NR3 1PD
*tel* (0870) 6005522 *fax* (0870) 6005533
*website* www.tso.co.uk
*Chief Executive* Tim Hailstone, *Coo* Fred Perkins,
*Commercial Director* Peter Miller, *Sales & Marketing
Director* J. Hook

Publishing and information management services:
business, current affairs, directories, general,
pharmaceutical, professional, reference, National
Curriculum, Learning to Drive.

## Ulric Publishing
PO Box 55, Church Stretton, Shrops. SY6 6WR
*tel* (01694) 781354 *fax* (01694) 781372
*email* books@ulric-publishing.com
*website* www.ulric-publishing.com
*Directors* Ulric Woodhams, Elizabeth Follows

Military and political history – World War Two;
automobilia – classic cars; travel – unique
adventures. No unsolicited MSS. Founded 1992.

## University College Dublin Press†
Newman House, 86 St Stephen's Green, Dublin 2,
Republic of Ireland
*tel* (01) 716 7397 *fax* (01) 716 7211
*email* ucdpress@ucd.ie
*website* www.ucdpress.ie
*Executive Editor* Barbara Mennell

Irish studies, history and politics, literary studies.

## Merlin Unwin Books
Palmers House, 7 Corve Street, Ludlow,
Shrops. SY8 1DB

*tel* (01584) 877456 *fax* (01584) 877457
*email* books@merlinunwin.co.uk
*website* www.countrybooksdirect.com
*Proprietor* Merlin Unwin

Countryside, country cooking and fieldsports
books. Founded 1990.

## Unwin Hyman Ltd – acquired by
**HarperCollins Publishers**

## Usborne Publishing Ltd
Usborne House, 83–85 Saffron Hill,
London EC1N 8RT
*tel* 020-7430 2800 *fax* 020-7430 1562
*email* mail@usborne.co.uk
*website* www.usborne.com
*Directors* Peter Usborne, Jenny Tyler (editorial),
Robert Jones, Keith Ball, David Harte, Lorna Hunt

Children's books: reference, practical, computers,
craft, natural history, science, languages, history,
geography, preschool, fiction. Founded 1973.

## V&A Publications
160 Brompton Road, London SW3 1HW
*tel* 020-7942 2966 *fax* 020-7942 2977
*email* vapubs.info@vam.ac.uk
*website* www.vandashop.co.uk/books
*Head of Publications* Mary Butler

Popular and scholarly books on fine and decorative
arts, architecture, contemporary design, fashion and
photography. Founded 1980.

## Vallentine Mitchell
Crown House, 47 Chase Side, London N14 5BP
*tel* 020-8920 2100 *fax* 020-8447 8548
*email* info@vmbooks.com
*website* www.vmbooks.com
*Directors* Frank Cass (chairman), Stewart Cass,
A.E. Cass, H.J. Osen, Hon. C.V. Callman,
M.P. Zaidner

Jewish history, Jewish thought, Judaism, Holocaust
studies.

## Variorum – see Ashgate Publishing Ltd

## Vega – now incorporated into Brassey's
**Conway Putnam, see Chrysalis Books Group**

## Veritas Publications†
Veritas House, 7–8 Lower Abbey Street, Dublin 1,
Republic of Ireland
*tel* (01) 8788177 *fax* (01) 8786507
*email* publications@veritas.ie
*website* www.veritas.ie

Liturgical and Church resources, religious school
books for primary and post-primary levels,
biographies, academic studies, and general books on
religious, moral and social issues.

**Vermilion** – see Random House Group Ltd

## Verso Ltd
6 Meard Street, London W1F 0EG
*tel* 020-7437 3546 *fax* 020-7734 0059
*email* verso@verso.co.uk
*Directors* Guy Bentham (Managing Director), Gavin Everall (sales and marketing), Robin Blackburn, Tariq Ali, Perry Anderson

Politics, sociology, economics, history, philosophy, cultural studies. Founded 1970.

## Viking – see Penguin Group (UK)

## Vintage – see Random House Group Ltd

## Virago – see Time Warner Books UK

## Virgin Books Ltd
Thames Wharf Studios, Rainville Road, London W6 9HA
*tel* 020-7386 3300 *fax* 020-7386 3360
*website* www.virgin.com/books
*Directors* K.T. Forster (managing), Sir Richard Branson, *Management* Carolyn Thorne (editorial director, illustrated), James Parker (rights), Jamie Moore (marketing), Becke Parker (publicity), Ray Mudie (sales)

### Black Lace (imprint)
*Senior Editor* Kerri Sharp

Erotic fiction by women for women.

### Nexus (imprint)
*Editor* Paul Copperwaite

Erotic fiction.

### Virgin (imprint)
*Editorial* Carolyn Thorne (general), Vanessa Daubney (sport), Stuart Slater (music), Kirstie Addis (general), Barbara Phelan (general)

Popular culture: entertainment, showbiz, arts, film and TV, music, humour, biography and autobiography, popular reference, true crime, sport, travel.

## Virtue Books Ltd
Edward House, Tenter Street, Rotherham S60 1LB
*tel* (01709) 365005 *fax* (01709) 829982
*email* info@virtue.co.uk
*website* www.virtue.co.uk
*Directors* Peter E. Russum, Margaret H. Russum

Books for the professional chef: catering and drink.

## The Vital Spark – see Neil Wilson Publishing Ltd

## VNR – see Wiley Europe Ltd

## University of Wales Press
10 Columbus Walk, Brigantine Place, Cardiff CF10 4UP
*tel* 029-2049 6899 *fax* 029-2049 6108
*email* press@press.wales.ac.uk
*website* www.wales.ac.uk/press
*Director* Ashley Drake

Academic and educational (Welsh and English). Publishers of *Welsh History Review, Studia Celtica, Llên Cymru, Efrydiau Athronyddol, Contemporary Wales, Welsh Journal of Education, Journal of Celtic Linguistics, Alt-J (Association for Learning Technology Journal), Kantian Review.* Founded 1922.

## Walker Books Ltd
87 Vauxhall Walk, London SE11 5HJ
*tel* 020-7793 0909 *fax* 020-7587 1123
*email* mail@walker.co.uk
*website* www.walkerbooks.co.uk
*Directors* David Heatherwick, David Lloyd, Karen Lotz, Roger Alexander (non-executive), Michel Blake, Sarah Foster, Harold G. Gould OBE (non-executive), Mike McGrath, Henryk Wesolowski, Jane Winterbotham, *Company Secretary* Barley Moss

Children's: picture books, non-fiction and novelty titles; junior and teenage fiction. Founded 1980.

## Wallflower Press
4th Floor, 26 Shacklewell Lane, London E8 2EZ
*tel* 020-7690 0115 *fax* 020-7690 4333
*email* info@wallflowerpress.co.uk
*website* www.wallflowerpress.co.uk
*Editorial Director* Yoram Allon, *Technical Director* Howard Seal

The moving image: cinema, TV, screen arts – academic and popular. Founded 1999.

## Warburg Institute
University of London, Woburn Square, London WC1H 0AB
*tel* 020-7862 8949 *fax* 020-7862 8955
*email* warburg@sas.ac.uk
*website* www.sas.ac.uk/warburg/

Cultural and intellectual history, with special reference to the history of the classical tradition.

## Ward Lock – former imprint of Weidenfeld & Nicolson

## Ward Lock Educational Co. Ltd
BIC Ling Kee House, 1 Christopher Road, East Grinstead, West Sussex RH19 3BT
*tel* (01342) 318980 *fax* (01342) 410980
*email* wle@lingkee.com
*website* www.wardlockeducational.com
*Directors* Au Bak Ling (chairman, Hong Kong),

Au King Kwok (Hong Kong), Au Wai Kwok (Hong Kong), Albert Kw Au (Hong Kong), *General Manager* Penny Kitchenham

Primary and secondary pupil materials, Kent Mathematics Project: *KMP BASIC* and *KMP Main* series covering Reception to GCSE, *Reading Workshops*, *Take Part* series and *Take Part* starters, teachers' books, music books, *Target* series for the National Curriculum: *Target Science* and *Target Geography*, religious education. Founded 1952.

## Warne – see Penguin Group (UK)

## Warner – see Time Warner Books UK

## Warner/Chappell Plays Ltd – see Josef Weinberger Plays Ltd

## Franklin Watts – see The Watts Publishing Group Ltd

## The Watts Publishing Group Ltd*
96 Leonard Street, London EC2A 4XD
*tel* 020-7739 2929 *fax* 020-7739 2318
*email* gm@wattspub.co.uk
*website* www.wattspublishing.co.uk
*Directors* Marlene Johnson (managing), Philippa Stewart (publishing, Franklin Watts), Ann-Janine Murtagh (publishing, Orchard Books), Clare Somerville (sales & marketing), Alan Lee (production), Zosia Knopp (rights)

### Cat's Whiskers (imprint)
*Publishing Director* Philippa Stewart
Children's picture books.

### Franklin Watts (division)
*Publishing Director* Philippa Stewart
Children's illustrated non-fiction, reference, education. Imprint: Aladdin/Watts.

### Orchard Books (division)
*Publishing Director* Ann-Janine Murtagh
Children's picture books, fiction, poetry, novelty books, board books.

## Wayland – now Hodder Wayland, see Hodder Headline Ltd

## Websters International Publishers Ltd
2nd Floor, Axe & Bottle Court,
70 Newcomen Street, London SE1 1YT
*tel* 020-7940 4700 *fax* 020-7940 4701
*websites* www.websters.co.uk, www.ozclarke.com
*Chairman and Publisher* Adrian Webster, *Managing Director* Jean-Luc Barbanneau, *Publishing Director* Susannah Webster

Wine, food, travel, health. Founded 1983.

## Weidenfeld & Nicolson
Orion House, 5 Upper St Martin's Lane,
London WC2H 9EA
*tel* 020-7240 3444 *fax* 020-7240 4823
*Managing Director* Adrian Bourne, *Publisher* Alan Samson, *Publishing Director* Ian Drury

Biography and autobiography, current affairs, history, travel, fiction, literary fiction, military history and militaria.

### Weidenfeld & Nicolson Illustrated
*Editor-in-Chief* Michael Dover

Quality illustrated non-fiction: gardening, cookery, wine, art and design, health and lifestyle, history, popular culture, archaeology, British heritage, literature, fashion, architecture, natural history, sport and adventure.

### Cassell Military (imprint)
*Publishing Director* Ian Drury
Military history and militaria.

### Cassell Reference (imprint)
*Publishing Director* Richard Milbank

Language and general interest reference, including Mrs Beeton, the *Brewer's* series and Jonothan Green's *Dictionary of Slang* and in association with Peter Crawley: *Master Bridge Series*.

### Phoenix House (imprint)
*Publishing Director* Ben Buchan
Contemporary fiction.

### Seven Dials (imprint)
*Managing Editor* Nic Cheetham

Quality illustrated paperbacks: food and drink, gardening, heritage, history, lifestyle, art.

## Josef Weinberger Plays Ltd
12–14 Mortimer Street, London W1T 3JJ
*tel* 020-7580 2827 *fax* 020-7436 9016
*email* general.info@jwmail.co.uk
*website* www.josef-weinberger.com

Stage plays only, in both acting and trade editions. Preliminary letter essential.

## Welsh Academic Press
PO Box 733, Cardiff CF14 2YX
*tel* 029-2056 0343 *fax* 029-2056 1931
*email* post@welsh-academic-press.com
*website* www.welsh-academic-press.com
*Managing Director* Ashley Drake

History, politics, biography, Celtic studies. Founded 1994.

## Wharncliffe – see Pen & Sword Books Ltd

## Which? Ltd
2 Marylebone Road, London NW1 4DF
*tel* 020-7770 7000 *fax* 020-7770 7660

*email* books@which.net
*Deputy Director* Kim Lavely, *Head of Which? Books*
Robert Gray

Part of Consumers' Association. Founded 1957.

### Which? Books (imprint)

Restaurant, hotel and wine guides, medicine, law
and personal finance for the layman, careers – all
branded *Which? Books*.

## J. Whitaker & Sons Ltd – see Nielsen Book

## Whittet Books Ltd

Hill Farm, Stonham Road, Cotton, Stowmarket,
Suffolk IP14 4RQ
*tel* (01449) 781877 *fax* (01449) 781898
*email* annabel@whittet.dircon.co.uk
*website* www.whittetbooks.com
*Directors* Annabel Whittet, John Whittet

Natural history, countryside, horticulture, poultry,
livestock, pets, horses. Founded 1976.

## Whurr Publishers Ltd*

19B Compton Terrace, London N1 2UN
*tel* 020-7359 5979 *fax* 020-7226 5290
*email* info@whurr.co.uk
*Director* Anne Bassett

Disorders of human communication, medicine,
psychology, psychiatry, psychotherapy, occupational
therapy, physiotherapy, nursing, for professional
markets only. Founded 1987.

## Wiley Europe Ltd*

The Atrium, Southern Gate, Chichester,
West Sussex PO19 8SQ
*tel* (01243) 779777 *fax* (01243) 775878
*email* europe@wiley.co.uk
*website* www.wileyeurope.com
*Managing Director/Senior Vice President* J.H. Jarvis,
*Director, STM Publishing* M. Davis, *Senior Vice
President, P&T Publishing* S. Smith

Physics, chemistry, mathematics, statistics,
engineering, architecture, computer science,
biology, medicine, earth science, psychology,
business, economics, finance. Imprints: Betty
Crocker, Bible, Capstone, CliffsNotes, Current
Protocols, Ernst & Sohn, ExpressExec, For
Dummies, Frommer's, Howell Book House,
Interscience, Jossey–Bass, J.K. Lasser, Pfeiffer, Red
Hat Press, Scripta Technica, The Unofficial Guide,
Visual, Webster's New World, Wiley Academy,
Wiley–Interscience, Wiley–Liss, ValuSource,
WILEY–VCH, VNR.

## Philip Wilson Publishers Ltd

7 Deane House, 27 Greenwood Place,
London NW5 1LB
*tel* 020-7284 3088 *fax* 020-7284 3099
*email* pwilson@philip-wilson.co.uk
*website* www.philip-wilson.co.uk
*Chairman* P. Wilson, *Director* S. Prohaska, *Managing
Editor* C. Venables, *Production Manager* N. Turpin

Fine and applied art, collecting, museums. Founded
1975.

## Neil Wilson Publishing Ltd*

303 The Pentagon Centre, 36 Washington Street,
Glasgow G3 8AZ
*tel* 0141-221 1117 *fax* 0141-221 5363
*email* info@nwp.co.uk
*website* www.nwp.co.uk, www.angelshare.co.uk,
www.vitalspark.co.uk, www.theinpinn.co.uk
*Managing Director* Neil Wilson

Scottish interest and humour, whiskey and drink-
related (leisure, reference, history, memoir), travel,
hillwalking and climbing. Imprints include The
Angels' Share, 11:19, In Pinn, NWP, The Vital Spark.

### 11:9 (imprint)

*tel* 0141-204 1109
*website* www.11-9.co.uk

Scottish Arts Council/National Lottery-funded
project to bring new Scottish fiction writing to the
marketplace.

## The Windrush Press

Windrush House, Adlestrop, Moreton-in-Marsh,
Glos. GL56 0YN
*tel* (01608) 658758 *fax* (01608) 659345
*email* victoriama.huxley@btinternet.com
*website* www.windrushpress.com
*Managing Director* Geoffrey Smith, *Publishing
Director* Victoria Huxley

History, biography, *The Traveller's History* series,
ancient mysteries. Publishes in association with the
Orion Group. Founded 1987.

## Wizard – see Icon Books Ltd

## Wolters Kluwer (UK) Ltd

145 London Road, Kingston-upon-Thames,
Surrey KT2 6SR
*tel* (0870) 2415719 *fax* 020-8247 1184
*email* info@croner.cch.co.uk
*websites* www.croner.cch.co.uk, www.cch.co.uk

Law, taxation, finance, insurance, looseleaf and
online information services. Founded 1948.

## The Women's Press

Top Floor, 27 Goodge Street, London W1P 2LD
*tel* 020-7580 7806 *fax* 020-7637 1866
*website* www.the-womens-press.com
*Acting Managing Director* Stella Kane

Books by women in the areas of literary and crime
fiction, biography and autobiography, health,
culture, politics, handbooks, literary criticism,
psychology and self-help, the arts. Founded 1978.

**Livewire (imprint)**
Books for teenagers and young women.

## Wooden Books
The Walkmill, Cascob, Presteigne, Powys LD8 2NT
*website* www.woodenbooks.com
*Directors* John Martineau (managing), Anthony
Brandt (secretary), Michael Glickman (overseas)

Magic, mathematics, ancient sciences, esoteric.
Illustrators and cartoonists needed. Founded 1996.

## Woodhead Publishing Ltd
Abington Hall, Abington, Cambridge CB1 6AH
*tel* (01223) 891358 *fax* (01223) 893694
*email* wp@woodhead-publishing.com
*website* www.woodhead-publishing.com
*Managing Director* Martin Woodhead

Engineering, materials, welding, textiles,
commodities, food science and technology,
environmental science. Founded 1989.

## Wordsworth Editions Ltd
8B East Street, Ware, Herts. SG12 9HJ
*tel* (01920) 465167 *fax* (01920) 462267
*email* enquiries@wordsworth-editions.com
*website* www.wordsworth.editions.com
*Directors* Michael Trayler (managing), Helen Trayler
(operations), Dennis Hart (sales)

Reprints of classic books: literary, children's,
exploration, military; myth, legend and folklore;
poetry; reference. Founded 1987.

## X Libris – see Time Warner Books UK

## The X Press
PO Box 25694, London N17 6FP
*tel* 020-8801 2100 *fax* 020-8885 1322
*email* vibes@xpress.co.uk
*website* www.xpress.co.uk
*Editorial Director* Dotun Adebayo, *Marketing
Director* Steve Pope

Black interest popular novels, particularly reflecting
contemporary ethnic experiences. *Black Classics*
series: reprints of classic novels by black writers.
Founded 1992.

**Nia (imprint)**
Literary black fiction.

## Y Lolfa Cyf.
Talybont, Ceredigion SY24 5AP
*tel* (01970) 832304 *fax* (01970) 832782
*email* ylolfa@ylolfa.com
*website* www.ylolfa.com
*Director* Garmon Gruffudd, *Editor* Lefi Gruffudd

Welsh-language popular fiction and non-fiction,
music, children's books; Welsh-language tutors;
Welsh politics in English and a range of Welsh-
interest books for the tourist market. Founded 1967.

## Yale University Press London*
47 Bedford Square, London WC1B 3DP
*tel* 020-7079 4900 *fax* 020-7079 4901
*email* firstname.lastname@yaleup.co.uk
*website* www.yaleup.co.uk
*Managing Director* Robert Baldock

Art, architecture, history, economics, political
science, religion, philosophy, history of science,
biography, current affairs and music. Founded
1961.

## Yellow Jersey Press – see Random House Group Ltd

## York Notes – see Pearson Education

## Young Picador – see Macmillan Publishers Ltd

## Zed Books Ltd
7 Cynthia Street, London N1 9JF
*tel* 020-7837 4014 (general) *fax* 020-7833 3960
*email* zed@zedbooks.demon.co.uk
*website* www.zedbooks.co.uk
*Editors* Robert Molteno, Anna Hardman

Social sciences on international issues; women's
studies, politics, development and environmental
studies; area studies (Africa, Asia, Caribbean, Latin
America, Middle East and the Pacific). Founded
1976.

## Zero to Ten Ltd*
2A Portman Mansions, Chiltern Street,
London W1U 6NR
*tel* 020-7487 0920 *fax* 020-7487 0921
*email* sales@evansbrothers.co.uk
*Publishing Director* Su Swallow

Non-fiction for children aged 0–10: board books,
toddler books, first story books, etc. Part of the
Evans Publishing Group. Founded 1997.

**Cherrytree Books (imprint)**
*UK Publisher* Su Swallow

Children's non-fiction illustrated books mainly for
schools and libraries.

## Zig Zag – see Chrysalis Children's Books

## Zoë Books Ltd
15 Worthy Lane, Winchester, Hants SO23 7AB
*tel* (01962) 851318
*email* enquiries@zoebooks.co.uk
*website* www.zoebooks.co.uk
*Directors* Imogen Dawson (managing/publishing),
C.W. Dawson, J.T. Dawson

Children's information books for the school and
library markets in the UK; specialists in co-editions
for world markets. No unsolicited MSS. No
opportunities for freelances. Founded 1990.

# Book publishers overseas

Listings are given for book publishers in Australia (below), Canada (page 200), New Zealand (page 204), South Africa (page 206) and the USA (page 207).

## AUSTRALIA
*Member of the Australian Publishers Association*

### Access Press
54 Railway Parade, Bassendean,
Western Australia 6054
*postal address* PO Box 446, Bassendean,
Western Australia 6054
*fax* (08) 9379 3188
*website* (08) 9379 3199
*Managing Editor* Helen Weller

Australiana, poetry, history, general. Commissioned works and privately financed books published and distributed. Founded 1974.

### Allen & Unwin Pty Ltd*
83 Alexander Street, Crows Nest, NSW 2065
*postal address* PO Box 8500, St Leonards, NSW 1590
*tel* (02) 8425 0100 *fax* (02) 9906 2218
*email* info@allenandunwin.com
*website* www.allenandunwin.com
*Directors* Patrick Gallagher (managing), Paul Donovan (sales), Peter Eichhorn (finance)

General trade, including fiction and children's books, academic, especially social science and history.

### Michelle Anderson Publishing Pty Ltd*
PO Box 6032, Chapel Street North, South Yarra 3141
*tel* (03) 9826 9028 *fax* (03) 9826 8552
*email* mapubl@bigpond.net.au
*website* www.michelleandersonpublishing.com
*Directors* Michelle Anderson, M. Slamen

General health and mind/body, children's.

### The Australian Council for Educational Research
19 Prospect Hill Road, Private Bag 55, Camberwell, Victoria 3124
*tel* (03) 9277 5555 *fax* (03) 9277 5500
*email* info@acer.edu.au
*website* www.acerpress.com.au

Range of books and kits: for teachers, trainee teachers, parents, psychologists, counsellors, students of education, researchers.

### Blackwell Publishing Asia Pty Ltd
550 Swanston Street, Carlton South, Victoria 3053
*tel* (03) 8359 1100 *fax* (03) 8359 1120
*email* info@blackwellpublishing.com
*website* www.blackwellpublishingasia.com
*Group President* Mark Robertson

Medical, healthcare, life, earth sciences, professional.

### Books & Writers Network Pty Ltd*
PO Box W76, Watsons Bay, NSW 2030
*tel* (02) 9337 6844 *fax* (02) 9337 6822
*website* www.booksandwriters.net.au
*Director* Pat Woolley

Offers short and long run printing, design, editing, layout, promotion, and a new on-line bookshop for self published books. Founded 1974.

### Cambridge University Press Australian Branch*
477 Williamstown Road, Port Melbourne, Victoria 3207
*tel* (03) 8671 1411 *fax* (03) 9676 9955
*email* info@cambridge.edu.au
*website* www.cambridge.edu.au
*Executive Director* Sandra McComb

Academic, educational, reference, English as a second language.

### Dominie Pty Ltd
Drama Department, 8 Cross Street, Brookvale, NSW 2100
*tel* (02) 9905 0201 *fax* (02) 9905 4945
*email* kate@dominie.com.au
*website* www.dominie.com.au

Australian representatives of publishers of plays and agents for the collection of royalties for Samuel French Ltd, Hanbury Plays and Samuel French Inc., The Society of Authors, Bakers Plays of Boston, Nick Hern Books, Pioneer Drama and Dramatic Publishing.

### Elsevier Australia*
30–52 Smidmore Street, Marrickville, NSW 2204
*tel* (02) 9517 8999 *fax* (02) 9550 6007
*Managing Director* W. Fergus Hall

Science, medical and technical books. Imprints: Academic Press, Architectural Press, Butterworth-Heinemann, Cell Press, Churchill Livingstone, Elsevier Science, Engineering Information, Excerpta Medica, The Lancet, MD Consult, MDL, Mosby, North-Holland, Pergamon, Science Direct, Saunders, PDxMD. Established 1972.

**Elsevier Education (division)**
*Managing Director & Children's Publisher* David O'Brien

Curriculum-based textbooks and classroom resources for the states of Australia and across all syllabus areas from kindergarten to Year 12. Imprints: Rigby, Heinemann, CIS, Barrie Publishing, Heinemann Library. Founded 1982.

**Samuel French Ltd** – see Dominie Pty Ltd

## HarperCollins Publishers (Australia) Pty Limited Group*
25–31 Ryde Road, Pymble, NSW 2073
*postal address* PO Box 321, Pymble, NSW 2073
*tel* (02) 9952 5000 *fax* (02) 9952 5555
*Managing Director* Brian Murray, *Children's Publisher* Lisa Berryman

Literary fiction and non-fiction, popular fiction, children's, reference, biography, autobiography, current affairs, sport, lifestyle, health/self-help, humour, true crime, travel, Australiana, history, business, gift/stationery, religion.

## Hill of Content Publishing Co. Pty Ltd – see Michelle Anderson Publishing Pty Ltd

## Hodder Headline Australia Pty Ltd*
Level 17, 207 Kent Street, Sydney, NSW 2000
*tel* (02) 8248 0800 *fax* (02) 2848 0810
*email* auspub@hha.com.au
*website* www.hha.com.au
*Directors* Malcolm Edwards (managing), Lisa Highton, Mary Drum, David Cocking

General, children's. No unsolicited MSS.

## Kangaroo Press – see Simon & Schuster (Australia) Pty Ltd

## Lawbook Co.
PO Box 3502, Rozelle, NSW 2039
*tel* (02) 8587 7000 *fax* (02) 8587 7100
*email* service@thomson.com.au
*website* www.lawbookco.com.au

Law.

## LexisNexis Butterworths Australia*
Tower 2, 475–495 Victoria Avenue, Chatswood, NSW 2067
*postal address* Level 9, Locked Bag 2222, Chatswood Delivery Centre, Chatswood, NSW 2067
*tel* (02) 9422 2222 *fax* (02) 9422 2444
*website* www.butterworths.com.au
*Managing Director* Murray Hamilton, *Editorial/Deputy Managing Director* J. Broadfoot

Legal, tax and commercial.

## Lonely Planet Publications*
Corner Maribyrnong and Parker Streets, Footscray 3011, Victoria
*tel* (03) 8379 8000 *fax* (03) 8379 8111
*email* talk2us@lonelyplanet.com.au
*website* www.lonelyplanet.com.au

Travel guidebooks, phrasebooks, travel literature, pictorial books, city maps; diving and snorkelling, walking, health, restaurant, pre-departure guidebooks, world food, condensed pocket guides. Offices in London, Paris and Oakland, USA. Founded 1973.

## Lothian Books*
132 Albert Road, South Melbourne, Victoria 3205
*tel* 613-9694-4900 *fax* 613-9645-0705
*email* books@lothian.com.au
*website* www.lothian.com.au
*Directors* Peter Lothian (managing), Bruce Hilliard (sales & marketing), *Children's Publisher* Helen Chamberlain

Juvenile, health, gardening, reference, Australian history, business, sport, biography, New Age, humour, Buddhism.

## Macmillan Education Australia Pty Ltd*
*Melbourne office* Locked Bag 1, Prahran, Victoria 3181
*tel* (03) 9825 1025 *fax* (03) 9825 1010
*email* mea@macmillan.com.au
*Sydney office* Level 2, St Martin's Tower, 31 Market Street, Sydney, NSW 2000
*tel* (02) 9285 9200 *fax* (02) 9285 9290
*email* measyd@macmillan.com.au
*Directors* Richard Charkin (chief executive – UK), Ross Gibb (executive chairman), Shane Armstrong (managing), Peter Huntley (sales), Sandra Iversen (primary publishing), Rex Parry (secondary publishing), George Smith (production), *Company Secretary/Financial Controller* Terry White, *Children's Publisher* Sandra Iverson

Educational books.

## Melbourne University Publishing*
268 Drummond Street, Carlton, Victoria 3053
*postal address* PO Box 1167, Carlton South, Victoria 3053
*tel* (03) 9342 0300 *fax* (03) 9342 0399
*email* mup-info@unimelb.edu.au
*website* www.mup.com.au
*Ceo/Publisher* Louise Adler

Academic, scholastic and cultural; educational textbooks and books of reference. Imprint: Miegunyah Press. Founded 1922.

## National Archives of Australia*
PO Box 7423, Canberra Business Centre, ACT 2610
*tel* (02) 6212-3603 *fax* (02) 6213-3914

*email* angelam@naa.gov.au
*website* www.naa.gov.au
*Assistant Director-General, Public & Reader Services*
Maggie Shapley, *Director, Publishing & Personal
Records* Gabrielle Hyslop, *Publications Manager*
Angela McAdam

Australia history (post Federation), genealogy,
reference. Founded 1944; publishing books since
1989.

## NCELTR Publishing*
Macquarie University, NSW 2109
*tel* (02) 9850-7673 *fax* (02) 9850 6055
*email* louise.melou@mq.edu.au
*website* www.ncecltr.mq.edu.au/publications
*Publishing Manager* Louise Melou, *Executive
Director* DeniseMurray

English language materials for teaching and
learning and for the adult migrant English area.
Founded 1990.

## Pan Macmillan Australia Pty Ltd*
Level 18, 31 Market Street, Sydney, NSW 2000
*tel* (02) 9285 9100 *fax* (02) 9285 9190
*email* pansyd@macmillan.com.au
*website* www.macmillan.com.au
*Directors* Ross Gibb (chairman), James Fraser
(publishing), Roxarne Burns (publishing), Siv Toigo
(finance), Peter Phillips (sales), Jeannine Fowler
(publicity and marketing)

Commercial and literary fiction; children's fiction,
non-fiction and character products; non-fiction;
sport.

## Penguin Group (Australia)*
250 Camberwell Road, Camberwell, Victoria 3124
*postal address* PO Box 701, Hawthorn, Victoria 3122
*tel* (03) 9811 2400 *fax* (03) 9811 2620
*website* www.penguin.com.au
*Managing Director* Gabrielle Coyne, *Publishing
Director* Robert Sessions

Fiction, general non-fiction, current affairs,
sociology, economics, environmental, travel guides,
anthropology, politics, children's, health, cookery,
gardening, pictorial and general books relating to
Australia. Imprints: Penguin Books, Viking.
Founded 1946.

## University of Queensland Press*
PO Box 6042, St Lucia, Queensland 4067
*tel* (07) 3365 2127 *fax* (07) 3365 7579
*email* uqp@uqp.uq.edu.au
*website* www.uqp.uq.edu.au
*General Manager* Greg Bain

Scholarly works, tertiary texts, indigenous
Australian writing, Australian fiction, young adult
fiction, poetry, history, general interest. Founded
1948.

## Random House Australia Pty Ltd*
20 Alfred Street, Milsons Point, NSW 2061
*tel* (02) 9954 9966 *fax* (02) 9954 4562
*email* random@randomhouse.com.au
*website* www.randomhouse.com.au
*Managing Director* Margaret Seale, *Head of
Publishing, Random House* Jane Palfreyman, *Head of
Publishing, Bantam Doubleday* Fiona Henderson,
*Children's Publisher* Lindsay Knight, *Illustrated
Publisher* Steve Barnett, *Sales & Marketing Director*
Carol Davidson, *Commercial Manager* Daren Chan,
*Rights & Permissions Manager* Nerrilee Weir

General fiction and non-fiction; children's,
illustrated. MSS submissions – for Random House
and Transworld Publishing, unsolicited non-fiction
accepted, unbound in hard copy addressed to
Submissions Editor. Fiction submissions are only
accepted from previously published authors, or
authors represented by an agent or accompanied by
a report from an accredited assessment service.
Imprints: Arrow, Avon, Ballantine, Bantam, Black
Swan, Broadway, Century, Chatto & Windus, Corgi,
Crown, Dell, Doubleday, Ebury, Fodor, Heinemann,
Hutchinson, Jonathan Cape, Knopf, Mammoth UK,
Minerva, Pantheon, Pavilion, Pimlico, Random
House, Red Fox, Rider, Vermillion, Vintage, Virgin.
Agencies: BBC Worldwide. Subsidiary of
Bertelsmann AG.

## Scholastic Australia Pty Ltd*
PO Box 579, Gosford, NSW 2250
*tel* (02) 4328 3555 *fax* (02) 4323 3827
*website* www.scholastic.com.au
*Managing Director* Ken Jolly, *Children's Publishers*
Ken Jolly, Andrew Berkhut

Children's fiction/non-fiction; educational materials
for elementary schools, teacher reference. Founded
1968.

## Simon & Schuster (Australia) Pty Ltd*
20 Barcoo Street, East Roseville, NSW 2069
*postal address* PO Box 507, East Roseville,
NSW 2069
*tel* (02) 9415 9900 *fax* (02) 9417 4292
*website* www.simonsays.com.au
*Managing Director/Publisher* Jon Attenborough

General non-fiction including anthropology, child
care, hobbies, house and home, how-to, craft,
biography, motivation, management, outdoor
recreation, sport, travel. Imprints: Simon & Schuster
Australia, Kangaroo Press. Founded 1987.

## Thomson Learning Australia*
102 Dodds Street, Southbank, Victoria 3006
*tel* (03) 9685 4111 *fax* (03) 9685 4199
*email* customerservice@thomsonlearning.com.au
*website* www.thomsonlearning.com.au

Educational books.

## Transworld Publishers (Aust) Pty Ltd –

merged with Random House Australia Pty Ltd

## UNSW Press*

University of New South Wales, UNSW Sydney
NSW 2052
*tel* (02) 9664 0900 *fax* (02) 9664 5420
*email* info.press@unsw.edu.au
*website* www.unswpress.com.au
*Managing Director* Dr Robin Derricourt, *Publishing Manager* John Elliot

Environmental studies, ecology, botany, education, sociology, cultural studies, politics, history; general reference; tertiary textbooks. Founded 1962.

## Viking – see Penguin Group (Australia)

## University of Western Australia Press*

UWA, 35 Stirling Hwy, Crawley 6009,
Western Australia
*tel* (618) 6488 3670 *fax* (618) 6488 1027
*email* uwap@cyllene.uwa.edu.au
*website* www.uwapress.uwa.edu.au
*Director* Dr Jenny Gregory

Natural history, history, maritime history, critical studies, women's studies, general non-fiction, contemporary issues, children's picture books, young fiction. Imprints: Cygnet Books, Staples, UWA Press. Founded 1954.

## Weldon Owen Pty Ltd

59 Victoria Street, McMahons Point, Sydney,
NSW 2060
*tel* (02) 9963 9555 *fax* (02) 9929-8352

Illustrated reference, lifestyle and education. Founded 1992.

## John Wiley & Sons Australia Ltd

33 Park Road, Milton, Queensland 4064
*tel* (07) 3859 9755 *fax* (07) 3859 9715
*email* brisbane@johnwiley.com.au
*website* www.johnwiley.com.au
*Managing Director* P. Donoughue

Educational, technical, atlases, professional, reference, trade. Imprints: John Wiley & Sons, Jacaranda, Wright Books. Founded 1954.

# CANADA

*\*Member of the Canadian Publishers' Council*
*†Member of the Association of Canadian Publishers*

## Annick Press Ltd†

15 Patricia Avenue, Toronto, Ontario M2M 1H9
*tel* 416-221-4802 *fax* 416-221-8400
*email* annick@annickpress.com
*website* www.annickpress.com
*Co-editors* Rick Wilks, Colleen MacMillan

Preschool to young adult fiction and non-fiction. Founded 1975.

## Butterworths Canada Ltd – see Lexis Nexis Canada Inc.

## The Charlton Press

PO Box 820, Station Willowdale B, North York,
Ontario M2K 2R1
*tel* 416-488-1418 *fax* 416-488-4656
*email* chpress@charltonpress.com
*website* www.charltonpress.com
*President* W.K. Cross

Collectibles, Numismatics, Sportscard price catalogues. Founded 1952.

## Doubleday Canada*

1 Toronto Street, Suite 300, Toronto,
Ontario M5C 2V6
*tel* 416-364-4449 *fax* 416-957-1587
*website* www.randomhouse.ca
*Chairman* John Neale, *Publisher* Maya Mavjee

General trade non-fiction: current affairs, politics; fiction; children's illustrated. Division of **Random House of Canada Ltd**. Founded 1942.

## Douglas & McIntyre Ltd†

2323 Quebec Street, Suite 201, Vancouver,
BC V5T 4S7
*tel* 604-254-7191 *fax* 604-254-9099
*email* dm@douglas-mcintyre.com

General list, including Greystone Books imprint: Canadian biography, art and architecture, natural history, history, native studies, Canadian fiction. No unsolicited MSS. Founded 1964.

## Dundurn Press†

8 Market Street, Suite 200, Toronto, ON M5E 1M6
*tel* 416-214-5544 *fax* 416-214-5556
*email* info@dundurn.com
*website* www.dundurn.com
*Directors* J. Kirk Howard (President), Beth Bruder (Vic-President, sales), Tony Hawke (editorial)

Serious non-fiction, scholarship, history, biography, art. Part of the Dundurn Group. Founded 1973.

**Boardwalk Books (imprint)**
Young adult fiction.

**Castle Street Mysteries (imprint)**
Mystery fiction.

**Hounslow Press (imprint)**
Popular non-fiction.

**Simon & Pierre Publishing (imprint)**
Theatre, drama, fiction, translations.

## ECW Press Ltd†
2120 Queen Street E, Suite 200, Toronto,
Ontario M4E 1E2
*tel* 416-694-3348 *fax* 416-698-9906
*email* info@ecwpress.com
*website* www.ecwpress.com
*President* Jack David

Popular culture, sports, humour, general trade
books, biographies, guidebooks. Founded 1979.

## Fitzhenry & Whiteside Ltd†
195 Allstate Parkway, Markham, Ontario L3R 4T8
*tel* 905-477-9700 *fax* 905-477-9179
*email* godwit@fitzhenry.ca
*tel* 1-800-387-9776 (toll free)  *fax* 1-800-260-9777
(toll free)
*Director* Sharon Fitzhenry, *Children's Publisher* Gail
Winskill

Trade, educational, children's books. Founded 1966.

## Gage Learning Corporation
164 Commander Boulevard, Toronto,
Ontario M1S 3C7
*tel* 416-293-8141 *fax* 416-293-9009
*website* www.gagelearning.com
*President* Chris Besse

Elementary and secondary school textbooks;
professional and reference materials. Founded 1844.

## Gold Eagle Books – see Harlequin
**Enterprises Ltd**

## Harcourt Canada Ltd*
55 Horner Avenue, Toronto, Ontario M8Z 4X6
*tel* 416-255-4491 *fax* 416-255-4046
*email* firstname_lastname@harcourt.com
*website* www.harcourtcanada.com
*President* Wendy Cochran

Educational materials from K–Grade 12, testing and
assessment. Imprints: Harcourt Religion (formerly
Brown-ROA), Harcourt Brace & Company, Holt,
Rinehart and Winston, MeadowBrook Press, The
Psychological Corporation, Therapy Skill Builders/
Communications Skill Builders. Founded 1922.

## Harlequin Enterprises Ltd*
225 Duncan Mill Road, Don Mills,
Ontario M3B 3K9
*tel* 416-445-5860 *fax* 416-445-8655
*website* www.eharlequin.com

*President & Publisher* Donna Hayes, *Vice President,
Editorial* Isabel Swift

Women's fiction, romance, action adventure,
mystery. Founded 1949.

**Gold Eagle Books (imprint)**
*Editorial Director* Randall Toye

Series action adventure fiction.

**Harlequin Books (imprint)**
*Editorial Director* Tara Gavin

Contemporary and historical romance fiction in
series.

**HQN Books (imprint)**
*Editorial Director* Dianne Maggy
Romantic single-title fiction, comtemporary and
historical.

**Luna Books (imprint)**
*Editorial Director* Dianne Moggy
Romantic fantasy.

**Mira Books (imprint)**
*Editorial Director* Dianne Moggy
Women's fiction: contemporary and historical
dramas, family sagas, romantic suspense and
relationship novels.

**Red Dress Ink (imprint)**
*Editorial Director* Tara Gavin

Women's fiction for the 20-somethings.

**Silhouette Books (imprint)**
*Editorial Director* Tara Gavin

Contemporary romance fiction in series.

**Steeple Hill (imprint)**
*Editorial Director* Tara Gavin

Contemporary inspirational romantic fiction in
series and single title.

**Worldwide Mystery (imprint)**
*Editorial Director* Randall Toye

Contemporary mystery fiction. Reprints only.

## HarperCollins Publishers Ltd*
2 Bloor Street East, 20th Floor, Toronto,
Ontario M4W 1A8
*tel* 416-975-9334 *fax* 416-975-9884
*website* www.harpercanada.com
*President* David Kent

Publishers of literary fiction and non-fiction,
history, politics, biography, spiritual and children's
books. Founded 1989.

## HQN Books – see Harlequin Enterprises Ltd

## Irwin Publishing Ltd
325 Humber College Blvd, Toronto,
Ontario M9W 7C3

*tel* 416-798-0424 *fax* 416-798-1384
*email* irwin@irwin-pub.com
*President* Brian O'Donnell, *Chairman* Jack Stoddart

Educational books at the elementary, high school and college levels.

## Key Porter Books Ltd†
70 The Esplanade, 3rd Floor, Toronto,
Ontario M5E 1R2
*tel* 416-862-7777 *fax* 416-862-2304
*email* aporter@keyporter.com
*website* www.keyporter.com
*Publisher/Ceo* Anna Porter, *President* Diane Davy,
*Children's* Joe Darrell

Fiction, nature, history, Canadian politics, conservation, humour, biography, autobiography, health, children's books. Founded 1981.

## Kids Can Press Ltd†
29 Birch Avenue, Toronto, Ontario M4V 1E2
*tel* 416-925-5437 *fax* 416-960-5437
*email* info@kidscan.com
*Publisher* Valerie Hussey, Karen Boersma

Juvenile/young adult books.

## Knopf Canada – see Random House of
Canada Ltd

## LexisNexis Canada Inc.
75 Clegg Road, Markham, Ontario L6G 1A1
*tel* 905-479-2665 *fax* 905-479-2826
*email* info@lexisnexis.ca

Law and accountancy. Division of Reed Elsevier plc.

## Lone Pine Publishing
10145–81 Avenue, Edmonton, Alberta T6E 1W9
*tel* 780-433-9333 *fax* 780-433-9646
*website* www.lonepinepublishing.com
*Chairman* Grant Kennedy, *Manager* Shane Kennedy

Natural history, outdoor recreation and wildlife guidebooks, gardening, popular history. Founded 1980.

## Luna Books – see Harlequin Enterprises Ltd

## McClelland & Stewart Ltd†
481 University Avenue, Suite 900, Toronto,
Ontario M5G 2E9
*tel* 416-598-1114 *fax* 416-598-7764
*website* www.mcclelland.com
*Chairman* Avie Bennett, *President/Publisher* Douglas M. Gibson

General. Founded 1906.

## McGill-Queen's University Press†
3430 McTavish Street, Montreal, Quebec H3A 1X9
*tel* 514-398-3750 *fax* 514-398-4333

*email* mqup@mqup.ca
*website* www.mqup.ca
Queen's University, Kingston, Ontario K7L 3N6
*tel* 613-533-2155 *fax* 613-533-6822
*email* mqup@qucdn.queensu.ca

Academic, non-fiction, poetry. Founded 1969.

## McGraw-Hill Ryerson Ltd*
300 Water Street, Whitby, Ontario L1N 9B6
*tel* 905-430-5000 *fax* 905-430-5020
*website* www.mcgrawhill.ca

Educational and trade books.

## Mira Books – see Harlequin Enterprises Ltd

## Napoleon Publishing/Rendez Vous Press*†
178 Willowdale Avenue, Suite 201, Toronto,
Ontario M2N 4Y8
*tel* 416-730-9052 *fax* 416-730-8096
*email* napoleon.publishing@transmedia95.com
*website* www.napoleonpublishing.com
*Publisher* Sylvia McConnell, *Editor* Allister Thompson

Children's books and adult fiction. Founded 1990.

## Nelson*
1120 Birchmount Road, Scarbourgh,
Ontario M1K 5G4
*tel* 416-752-9100 *fax* 416-752-9646
*President/Ceo* George W. Bergquist, *Senior Vice President, Finance/Cfo* Lesley Gouldie, *Senior Vice President, School* Greg Pilon, *Vice President, Higher Education* Ron Kelly, *Vice President, Media Services* Susan Cline, *Vice President, Operations* Ed Berman, *Vice President, Human Resources* Marlene Nyilassy, *Editorial Director, Higher Education* Evelyn Veitch, *Director of Publishing, School* David Steele, *Director of Marketing, Higher Education* James Rozsa, *Director of Sales, School* James Reeve, *Director of Information Systems & Technology* Bruce Sharron

Educational publishing: school (K–12), college and university, career education, measurement and guidance, professional and reference, ESL titles. Founded 1914.

## NeWest Press*†
201–8540–10A Street, Edmonton, AB T6G 1E6
*tel* 780-432-9427 *fax* 780-433-3179
*email* wfo@newestpress.com
*website* www.newestpress.com
*Directors* Doug Barbour (President), Don Kerr (Vic-President), Jon Faulds (Secretary), Donna Weis (Treasurer)

Fiction, drama and poetry, and regional non-fiction with a western Canadian focus. Founded 1977.

**Oberon Press**
400–350 Sparks Street, Suite 400, Ottawa,
Ontario K1R 7S8
*tel* 613-238-3275 *fax* 613-238-3275
*website* www3.sympatico.ca.oberon
General.

**Oxford University Press, Canada\***
70 Wynford Drive, Don Mills, Ontario M3C 1J9
*tel* 416-441-2941 *fax* 416-444-0427
*website* www.oup.com/ca
*President* Joanna Gertler
General, educational and academic.

**Pearson Education Canada\***
26 Prince Andrew Place, Toronto,
Ontario M3C 2T8
*tel* 416-447-5101 *fax* 416-443-0948
*website* www.pearsoned.ca
*President* Tony Vander Woude
Academic, technical, educational, children's and
adult, trade.

**Penguin Books Canada Ltd\***
10 Alcorn Avenue, Suite 300, Toronto,
Ontario M4V 3B2
*tel* 416-925-2249 *fax* 416-925-0068
*website* www.penguin.ca
*President* Ed Carson
Literary fiction, memoir, non-fiction (history,
business, current events). Founded 1974.

**Pippin Publishing Corporation**
Suite 232, 85 Ellesmere Road, Toronto,
Ontario M1R 4B9
*tel* 416-510-2918 *fax* 416-510-3359
*email* jld@pippinpub.com
*website* www.pippinpub.com
*President/Editorial Director* Jonathan Lovat Dickson
ESL/EFL, teacher reference, adult basic education,
school texts (all subjects), general trade (non-
fiction).

**Random House of Canada Ltd\***
One Toronto Street, Suite 300, Toronto,
Ontario M5C 2V6
*tel* 416-364 4449 *fax* 416-364-6863
*website* www.randomhouse.com
*Chairman* John Neale
Imprints: Canada, Doubleday Canada, Knopf
Canada, Random House Canada, Seal Books,
Vintage Canada. Subsidiary of Bertelsmann AG.
Founded 1944.

**Red Dress Ink** – see Harlequin Enterprises
Ltd

**Ronsdale Press**[†]
3350 West 21st Avenue, Vancouver, BC V6S 1G7
*tel* 604-738-4688 *fax* 604-731-4548
*email* ronhatch@pinc.com
*website* www.rondalepress.com
*Director* Ronald B. Hatch
Canadian literature: fiction, poetry, biography,
books of ideas. Founded 1988.

**Silhouette Books** – see Harlequin
Enterprises Ltd

**Steeple Hill** – see Harlequin Enterprises Ltd

**Thompson Educational Publishing\***[†]
200–206 Ripley Avenue, Toronto, Ontario M6S 3N9
*tel* 416-766-2763 *fax* 416-766-0398
*email* publisher@thompsonbooks.com
*website* www.thompsonbooks.com
*President* Keith Thompson, *Vice-President* Faye
Thompson
Social sciences. Founded 1989.

**University of Toronto Press Inc.**[†]
10 St Mary Street, Suite 700, Toronto,
Ontario M4Y 2W8
*tel* 416-978-2239 *fax* 416-978-4738
*email* publishing@utpress.utoronto.ca
*website* www.utpress.utoronto.ca
*President/Publisher* George L. Meadows
Founded 1907.

**Tundra Books Inc.**[†]
481 University Avenue, Suite 900, Toronto,
Ontario M5G 2E9
*tel* 416-598-4786 *fax* 416-598-0247
*website* www.tundrabooks.com
*Children's Publisher* Kathy Lowinger
High-quality children's picture books.

**Women's Press\***
180 Bloor Street West, Suite 801, Toronto,
Ontario M5S 2V6
*tel* 416-929-2774 *fax* 416-929-1926
*email* info@cspi.org
*website* www.womenspress.ca
*President & Publisher* Dr Jack Wayne, *Managing
Editor* Althea Prince PhD
The ideas and experiences of women: fiction,
creative non-fiction, children's books, plays,
biography, autobiography, memoirs, poetry. Owned
by Canadian Scholars' Press. Founded 1987.

**Worldwide Mystery** – see Harlequin
Enterprises Ltd

## NEW ZEALAND
*Member of the New Zealand Book Publishers' Association*

### Auckland University Press*
University of Auckland, Private Bag 92019, Auckland
*tel* (09) 373-7528 *fax* (09) 373-7465
*email* aup@auckland.ac.nz
*website* www.auckland.ac.nz/aup
*Director* Elizabeth Caffin

NZ history, NZ poetry, Maori and Pacific studies, politics, sociology, literary criticism, art history, biography, media studies, women's studies. Founded 1966.

### David Bateman Ltd*
30 Tarndale Grove, Bush Road, Albany, Auckland
*postal address* PO Box 100242, North Shore Mail Centre, Auckland 1330
*tel* (09) 415-7664 *fax* (09) 415-8892
*email* bateman@bateman.co.nz
*website* www.bateman.co.nz
*Chairman/Publisher* David L. Bateman, *Directors* Janet Bateman, Paul Bateman (joint managing), Paul Parkinson (joint managing)

Natural history, gardening, encyclopedias, sport, art, cookery, historical, juvenile, travel, motoring, maritime history, business, art, lifestyle. Founded 1979.

### Bush Press Communications Ltd
4 Bayview Road, Hauraki Corner, Takapuna
*postal address* PO Box 33–029, Takapuna, Auckland 1309
*fax* (09) 486-2667
*email* bush.press@clear.net.nz
*website* (09) 486-2667
*Governing Director/Publisher* Gordon Ell ONZM

NZ non-fiction, particularly outdoor, nature, travel, architecture, crafts, Maori, popular history; children's non-fiction. Founded 1979.

### The Caxton Press
113 Victoria Street, Christchurch
*postal address* PO Box 25–088, Christchurch
*tel* (03) 366-8516 *fax* (03) 365-7840
*Director* E.B. Bascand

Local history, tourist pictorial, Celtic spirituality, parent guide, book designers and printers.

### Dunmore Press Ltd*
PO Box 5115, Palmerston North
*tel* (06) 358-7169 *fax* (06) 357-9242
*email* books@dunmore.co.nz
*website* www.dunmore.co.nz
*Directors* Murray Gatenby, Sharmian Firth

Education, history, sociology, business studies, general non-fiction. Founded 1970.

### Godwit Publishing Ltd – acquired by Random House New Zealand Ltd

### Halcyon Publishing Ltd
PO Box 360, Auckland 1015
*tel* (09) 489 5337 *fax* (09) 489 5218
*email* info@halcyonpublishing.co.nz
*website* Managing Director/Publisher Graham Gurr, Editorial Director Antony Entwistle

Hunting, shooting, fishing, outdoor interests. Founded 1982.

### HarperCollins Publishers (New Zealand) Ltd
3 View Road, Glenfield, Auckland
*tel* (09) 443-9400 *fax* (09) 443-9403
*website* www.harpercollins.co.nz
*Managing Director* Tony Fisk, *Children's Publisher* Lorain Day

General literature, non-fiction, reference, children's.

### Hodder Moa Beckett Publishers Ltd
PO Box 100–749, North Shore Mail Centre, Auckland 1330
*tel* (09) 478-1000 *fax* (09) 478-1010
*email* admin@hoddermoa.co.nz
*Managing Director* Kevin Chapman, *Editorial Director* Warren Adler

Sport, gardening, cooking, travel, atlases, general.

### Learning Media Ltd*
Level 3, State Services Commission Building, 100 Molesworth Street, PO Box 3293, Wellington 6001
*tel* (4) 472-5522 *fax* (4) 472 6444
*email* info@learningmedia.co.nz
*website* www.learningmedia.com, www.learningmedia.co.nz

Educational books, websites and CD-Roms for New Zealand and international markets. Texts in English, Maori and 6 Pacific languages. Founded 1993.

### LexisNexis NZ Ltd*
205–207 Victoria Street, Wellington 1
*postal address* PO Box 472, Wellington 1
*tel* (04) 385-1479 *fax* (04) 385-1598
*email* Russell.Gray@lexisnexis.co.nz
*website* www.lexisnexis.co.nz
*Managing Director* Russell Gray

Law, business, academic.

### Mallinson Rendel Publishers Ltd
Level 5, 15 Courtenay Place, PO Box 9409, Wellington
*tel* (04) 802-5012 *fax* (04) 802-5013
*email* publisher@mallinsonrendel.co.nz
*Director* Ann Mallinson

Children's books. Founded 1980.

## Nelson Price Milburn Ltd
1 Te Puni Street, Petone
*postal address* PO Box 38–945, Wellington Mail
Centre, Wellington
*tel* (04) 568-7179 *fax* (04) 568-2115
*email* jacqui.rivera@thomson.com

Children's fiction, primary school texts, especially
school readers and maths, secondary educational.

## New Zealand Council for Educational Research*
Box 3237, Education House, 178–182 Willis Street,
Wellington 1
*tel* (04) 384-7939 *fax* (04) 384-7933
*email* info@nzcer.org.nz
*website* www.nzcer.org.nz
*Director* Robyn Baker, *Publisher* Bev Webber

Education, including educational policy and
institutions, early childhood education, educational
achievement tests, Maori education, curriculum and
assessment, etc. Founded 1934.

## University of Otago Press
University of Otago, PO Box 56, Dunedin
*tel* (03) 479-8807 *fax* (03) 479-8385
*email* university.press@otago.ac.nz
*Managing Editor* Wendy Harrex

Student texts and scholarly works in many
disciplines and general books, including Maori and
women's studies, natural history and environmental
studies, health and fiction. Also publishes journals
including *Landfall* and the *Women's Studies Journal*.
Founded 1958.

## Pearson Education New Zealand Ltd*
Private Bag 102908, North Shore Mail Centre,
Glenfield, Auckland 10
*tel* (09) 444-4968 *fax* (09) 444-4957
*email* firstname.lastname@pearsoned.co.nz
*Managing Director* Rosemary Stagg

New Zealand educational books.

## Random House New Zealand Ltd
Private Bag 102950, North Shore Mail Centre,
Auckland 10
*tel* (09) 444-7197 *fax* (09) 444-7524
*Managing Director* M. Moynahan

Fiction, general non-fiction, gardening, cooking,
art, business, health. Subsidiary of Bertelsmann AG.
Founded 1977.

## Reed Publishing (New Zealand) Ltd*
39 Rawene Road, PO Box 34901, Birkenhead,
Auckland 10
*tel* (09) 480 4950 *fax* (09) 480-4999
*Chairman* John Philbin, *Managing Director* Alan
Smith, *Publishing Manager* Peter Janssen

NZ literature, specialist and general titles, primary,
secondary and tertiary textbooks. Imprints: BBC,
Egmont, Brimax, Butterworth-Heinemann, CIS
Heinemann, Conran, Philip's, Ginn UK,
Heinemann Australia, Heinemann NZ, Heinemann
UK, Heinemann USA, Huia Jasons, Kyle Cathie,
Longacre, Mammoth, Mitchell Beazley, Quadrille,
Reed NZ, Rigby Australia, Rigby USA, Virgin
Publishing.

## RSVP Publishing Company*
PO Box 47166, Ponsonby, Auckland
*tel* (09) 372-3480 *fax* (09) 372 8480
*email* rsvppub@iconz.co.nz
*website* www.rsvp-publishing.co.nz
*Managing Director/Publisher* Stephen Picard

Fiction, metaphysical, children's. Founded 1990.

## Scholastic New Zealand Ltd*
21 Lady Ruby Drive, East Tamaki, Auckland
*postal address* Private Bag 94407, Greenmount,
Auckland
*tel* (09) 274-8112 *fax* (09) 274-8114
*email* publishing@scholastic.co.nz
*website* www.scholastic.co.nz
*General Manager* David Peagram, *Publishing
Manager* Christine Dale

Children's books. Founded 1962.

## Shortland Publications
10 Cawley Street, Ellerslie, Auckland 5
*Submissions* Louise Williams, Shortland
Publications, Private Bag 11904, Ellerslie,
Auckland 5
*tel* (09) 526-6200 *fax* (09) 526-4499
*email* Louise_Williams@mcgraw-hill.com

International primary reading market: potential
authors should familiarise themselves with
Shortland products. Currently seeking submissions
for emergent/early and fluency reading material
(8–24pp) and short fiction (ages 9–12) – MSS up to
1500 words long. All submissions should cater for
an international market; include sae. Founded 1984.

## Tandem Press*
PO Box 34272, Birkenhead, Auckland
*tel* (09) 480-1452 *fax* (09) 480-1455
*email* customers@tandempress.co.nz
*Joint Managing Directors* Robert M. Ross
(publishing), Helen E. Benton (sales & marketing)

Self-help, health, business, food and wine, New
Zealand interest, fiction. Founded 1990.

## Victoria University Press*
Victoria University of Wellington, PO Box 600,
Wellington
*tel* (04) 463-6580 *fax* (04) 463-6581
*email* victoria-press@vuw.ac.nz

*website* www.vuw.ac.nz/vup
*Publisher* Fergus Barrowman

Academic, scholarly books on NZ history, sociology, law; Maori language; fiction, plays, poetry. Founded 1974.

## Viking Sevenseas NZ Ltd
201A Rosetta Road, Raumati
*tel* (04) 902-8240 *fax* (04) 902-8240
*email* vikings@paradise.net.nz
*Managing Director* M.B. Riley

Natural history books on New Zealand only.

## SOUTH AFRICA
*\*Member of the Publishers' Association of South Africa*

## Ad Donker (Pty) Ltd – see Jonathan Ball
Publishers (Pty) Ltd

## Jonathan Ball Publishers (Pty) Ltd*
10–14 Watkins Street, Denver Ext. 4, Johannesburg
*postal address* Box 33977, Jeppestown 2043
*tel* (011) 622-2900 *fax* (011) 622-7610
*Publisher* Francine Blum

**Ad Donker (imprint)**
Africana, literature, history, academic.

**Jonathan Ball (imprint)**
General publications, reference books, South African business, history, politics.

**Delta Books (imprint)**
General South African trade non-fiction.

## Cambridge University Press**
Dock House, Portswood Ridge, Victoria & Alfred Waterfront, Cape Town 8001
*tel* (021) 419-8414
*email* information@cup.co.za
*website* www.cambridge.org
*Director* Hanri Pieterse

African Branch of CUP, responsible for sub-Saharan Africa and English-speaking Caribbean. Publishes distance learning material and textbooks for various African countries, as well as primary reading materials in 28 local African languages.

## Clever Books Pty Ltd*
PO Box 13816, Hatfield, Pretoria 0028
*tel* (012) 3423263 *fax* (012) 4302376
*email* mmcd@cleverbooks.co.za
*General Manager* Michael McDermott

Educational titles for the RSA market. Founded 1981.

## Delta Books – see Jonathan Ball Publishers
(Pty) Ltd

## Galago Publishing (Pty) Ltd
PO Box 1645, Alberton 1450
*tel* (11) 907 2029 *fax* (11) 869 0890
*email* lemur@mweb.co.za
*website* www.galago.co.za
*Managing Director* Fan Stiff, *Publisher* Peter Stiff

Southern African interest: military, political, hunting. Founded 1981.

## Jacklin Enterprises (Pty) Ltd
PO Box 521, Parklands 2121
*tel* (011) 265-4200 *fax* (011) 314-2984
*email* mjacklin@jacklin.co.za
*Managing Director* M.A.C. Jacklin

Children's fiction and non-fiction; Afrikaans large print books. Subjects include aviation, natural history, romance, general science, technology and transportation. Imprints: Mike Jacklin, Kennis Onbeperk, Daan Retief.

## Juta & Company Ltd*
PO Box 14373, Landsdown 7779, Cape Town
*tel* (021) 797-5101 *fax* (021) 762-0248
*email* books@juta.co.za
*website* www.juta.co.za
*Ceo* Rory Wilson

School, academic, professional, law and electronic. Founded 1853.

## University of KwaZulu-Natal Press*
Private Bag X01, Scottsville, 3209 KwaZulu-Natal
*tel* (2733) 260 5226 *fax* (2733) 260 5801
*email* books@ukzn.ac.za
*website* www.ukzn.ac.za
*Publisher* Glenn Cowley

Southern African social, political, economic and military history, gender, natural sciences, African poetry and literature, genealogy, education, biography. Founded 1948.

## Maskew Miller Longman (Pty) Ltd*
Howard Drive, Pinelands 7405, Cape Town
*postal address* PO Box 396, Cape Town 8000
*tel* (021) 531-7750 *fax* (021) 531-4877
*email* administrator@mml.co.za
*website* www.mml.co.za

Educational and general publishers.

## Oxford University Press Southern Africa*
Vasco Boulevard, N1 City, Goodwood, Cape Town 7460
*postal address* PO Box 12119, N1 City, Cape Town 7463
*tel* (021) 595-4400 *fax* (021) 595-4430
*email* oxford.za@oup.com.za
*website* www.oup.com.za
*Managing Director* Kate McCallum

## David Philip Publishers (Pty) Ltd
PO Box 23408, Claremont 7735, Western Cape
*tel* (21) 6744-136 *fax* (21) 6743-358
*email* information@dpp.co.za
*website* www.dpp.co.za
*Managing & Marketing Director* Bridget Impey,
*Publishing Director* Russell Martin, *Non-executive
Directors* David Philip, Marie Philip, Wilmot James,
G.J. Gerwel, Njabulo Ndebele, Steve Kromberg, Alec
Davis, Mike Tissong, Mike Siluma, Zwelakhe Sisulu

Academic, history, social sciences, politics,
biography, belles-lettres, reference books, fiction,
cartoons, educationa. Founded 1971.

## Ravan Press
PO Box 145, Roundburg, Johannesburg 2125
(011) 789 7653 *fax* (011) 789 7636

South African studies: history, politics, social
studies; fiction, literature, biography. Founded 1972.

## Shuter and Shooter Publishers (Pty) Ltd*
230 Church Street, Pietermaritzburg 3201,
KwaZulu-Natal
*postal address* PO Box 109, Pietermaritzburg 3200,
KwaZulu-Natal
*fax* (033) 3946-830/3948-881
*email* www.shuter.co.zadryder@shuter.co.za
*website* (033) 3427-419
*Publishing Director* D.F. Ryder

Primary and secondary educational, science,
biology, history, maths, geography, English,
Afrikaans, biblical studies, music, teacher training,
agriculture, accounting, early childhood,
dictionaries, African languages. Founded 1925.

## Struik Publishers (Pty) Ltd
Cornelius Struik House, 80 McKenzie Street,
Cape Town 8001
*tel* (021) 462-4360 *fax* (021) 462-4379
*email* admin@struik.co.za
*Managing Director* Dick Wilkins

General illustrated non-fiction. Division of New
Holland Publishing (Pty) Ltd. Founded 1962.

## Unisa Press
PO Box 392, Pretoria 0003
*tel* (012) 429-3316 *fax* (012) 429-3221
*email* unisa-press@unisa.ac.za
*website* www.unisa.ac.za/dept/press/index.html
*Head* Phoebe Van Der Walt

Theology and all academic disciplines. Publishers of
University of South Africa. Imprint: UNISA.
Founded 1957.

## Van Schaik Publishers
PO Box 12681, Hatfield, Pretoria 0028
*tel* (012) 342-2765 *fax* (012) 430-3563
*email* vanschaik@vanschaiknet.com

*website* www.vanschaiknet.com
Publishers of school books in English, Afrikaans
and African languages. Specialists in textbooks and
books for the corporate market. Founded 1914.

## Witwatersrand University Press*
PO Wits, Johannesburg 2050
*tel* (011) 484-5910 *fax* (011) 484-5971
*email* klippv@wup.wits.ac.za
*website* www.witspress.wits.ac.za

## Zebra Press
80 McKenzie Street Gardens, Cape Town 8001
*postal address* PO Box 1144, Cape Town 8000
*tel* (021) 462-4360 *fax* (021) 462-4379
*email* moniquev@zebrapress.co.za
*website* www.zebrapress.co.za

Business, contemporary, humour. Imprint of Struik
Publishers. Division of New Holland Publishing
(South Africa) (Pty) Ltd, a member of Johnnic
Publishing Ltd.

# USA
*\*Member of the Association of American Publishers Inc.*

## Abbeville Press
116 West 23rd Street, Suite 500, New York,
NY 10011
*tel* 646-375-2039 *fax* 646-375-2040
*website* www.abbeville.com
*Publisher/President* Robert Abrams

Art and illustrated books. Founded 1977.

## Abingdon Press
PO Box 801, Nashville, TN 37202-0801
*tel* 615-749-6290 *fax* 615-749-6056
*website* www.abingdon.org
*Senior Vice President, Publishing* Harriett Jane Olson

General interest, professional, academic and reference
– primarily directed to the religious market.

## Harry N. Abrams Inc.
100 Fifth Avenue, New York, NY 10011
*tel* 212-206-7715 *fax* 212-645-8437
*website* www.abramsbooks.com
*Ceo/President* Steve Parr

Art and architecture, photography, natural sciences,
performing arts, children's books. No fiction.

## The University of Alabama Press
Box 870380, Tuscaloosa, AL 35487
*tel* 205-348-5180 *fax* 205-348-9201
*Director* Daniel J.J. Ross, *Managing Editor* Suzette
Griffith

American and Southern history, African–American
studies, religion, rhetoric and communication,

Judaic studies, literary criticism, anthropology and archaeology. Founded 1945.

## Applause Theatre and Cinema Book Publishers
151 West 46th Street, 8th Floor, New York, NY 10036
*tel* 212-575-9265 *fax* 646-562-5852
*website* www.applausepub.com
*Ceo* Michael Messina

Performing arts. Founded 1980.

## Arcade Publishing
141 Fifth Avenue, New York, NY 10010
*tel* 212-475-2633 *fax* 212-353-8148
*email* arcadeinfo@arcadepub.com
*website* www.arcadepub.com
*President/Editor-in-Chief* Richard Seaver,
*Publisher/Marketing Director* Jeannette Seaver,
*General Manager/Executive Editor* Cal Barksdale,
*Editors* Darcy Falkenhagen, Savannah Ashawr,
*Publicity* Casey Ebro

General trade, including adult hard cover and paperbacks. No unsolicited MSS.

## The University of Arkansas Press
The University of Arkansas, McIlroy House, 201 Ozark Avenue, Fayetteville, AR 72701
*tel* 479-575-3246 *fax* 479-575-6044
*email* uapress@cavern.uark.edu
*Director* Lawrence J. Malley

History, humanities, literary criticism, Middle East studies, African–American studies, poetry. Founded 1980.

## Atlantic Monthly Press – see Grove/Atlantic Inc.

## Avery – see The Putnam Publishing Group

## Avon Books – see HarperCollins Publishers

## Walter H. Baker Company
PO Box 699222, Quincy, MA 02269
*tel* 617-745-0805 *fax* 617-745-9891
*website* www.bakersplays.com
*President* Charles Van Nostrand, *General Manager* Kurt Gombar, *UK Agent* Samuel French Ltd

Plays and books on the theatre. Also agents for plays. Founded 1845.

## The Ballantine Publishing Group
1540 Broadway, New York, NY 10036
*tel* 212-782-9000 *fax* 212-302-7985
*website* www.randomhouse.com
*President/Publisher* Gina Centrello

Trade and mass-market general fiction, science fiction and non-fiction. Imprints: Ballantine Books, Ballantine Wellspring, Del Rey, Fawcett, Ivy, Library of Contemporary Thought, One World. Division of **Random House Inc**.

## Bantam Dell Publishing Group
1540 Broadway, New York, NY 10036
*tel* 212-782-9000 *fax* 212-302-7985
*website* www.randomhouse.com/bantamdell
*President/Publisher* Irwyn Applebaum

General fiction and non-fiction. Imprints: Bantam Hardcover, Bantam Mass Market, Bantam Trade Paperback, Crimeline, Delacorte Press, Dell, Delta, Dial Press, Domain, DTP, Fanfare, Island, Spectra. Division of **Random House Inc.**

## Barron's Educational Series Inc.
250 Wireless Boulevard, Hauppage, NY 11788
*tel* 631-434-3311 *fax* 631-434-3723
*website* www.barronseduc.com
*Chairman/Ceo* Manuel H. Barron,
*President/Publisher* Ellen Sibley

Test preparation, juvenile, cookbooks, Mind, Body & Spirit, crafts, business, pets, gardening, family and health, art, study guides, school guides. Founded 1941.

## Beacon Press
25 Beacon Street, Boston, MA 02108
*tel* 617-742-2110 *fax* 617-723-3097
*website* www.beacon.org
*Director* Helene Atwan

General non-fiction in fields of religion, ethics, philosophy, current affairs, gender studies, environmental concerns, African–American studies, anthropology and women's studies, nature.

## Berkley Books – see Berkley Publishing Group

## Berkley Publishing Group
375 Hudson Street, New York, NY 10014
*tel* 212-366-2000 *fax* 212-366-2666
*email* online@penguinputnam.com
*website* www.penguinputnam.com
*President, Mass Market Paperbacks* Leslie Gelbman

Fiction and general non-fiction. Imprints: Ace Books, Berkley Books, Boulevard, Diamond Books, HP Books, Jam, Jove, Perigee, Prime Crime, Riverhead Books (trade paperback). Division of **Penguin Putnam Inc.** Founded 1954.

### Berkley Books (imprint)
*President and Publisher* Leslie Gelbman

Fiction and general non-fiction for adults. Imprints: Ace Books, Berkley Books, Boulevard Books, Diamond Books, Jam, Jove, Prime Crime. Founded 1954.

### HP Books (imprint)
*Editorial Director, Automotive* Michael Lutfy

Non-fiction trade paperbacks. Founded 1964.

**Perigee Books (imprint)**
*Vice President/Publisher* John Duff

Non-fiction paperbacks: psychology, spirituality, reference, etc. Founded 1980.

**Riverhead Books (Trade Paperback)**
*Editor* Christopher Knutsen

Fiction and general non-fiction for adults. Founded 1995.

## Bloomsbury USA

Suite 300, 175 Fifth Avenue, New York,
NY 10010
*tel* 212-674-5151 *fax* 212-780-0115
*website* www.bloomsburyusa.com
*Publisher and Editorial Director, Adult Books* Karen Rinaldi, *Deputy Editorial Director, Adult Books* Colin Dickerman, *Executive Editor* Gillian Blake, *Editorial Director, Children's Books* Victoria Wells Arms, *Director of Marketing and Publicity (Children's)* Kate Kubert

Literary fiction, general non-fiction and children's. Branch of **Bloomsbury UK**. Founded 1998.

**BlueHen** – see The Putnam Publishing Group

## R.R. Bowker*

630 Central Avenue, New Providence, NJ 07974
*tel* 908-286-1090 *fax* 908-219-0098
*email* info@bowker.com
*website* www.bowker.com
*President* Michael Cairns

Bibliographies and reference tools for the book trade and literary and library worlds, available in hardcopy, on microfiche, online and CD-Rom. Reference books for music, art, business, computer industry, cable industry and information industry. Division of Cambridge Information Group.

## Boyds Mills Press

815 Church Street, Honesdale, PA 18431
*tel* 570-253-1164 *fax* 570-253-0179
*email* contact@boydsmillspress.com
*website* www.boydsmillspress.com
*President* Clay Winters, *Publisher* Kent L. Brown Jr, *Editorial Director* Larry Rosler, *Art Director* Tim Gillner

Fiction, non-fiction, and poetry trade books for children. Founded 1991.

## Burford Books

PO Box 388, Short Hills, NJ 07078
*tel* 973-258-0960 *fax* 973-258-0113
*email* info@burfordbooks.com
*website* www.burfordbooks.com
*President* Peter Burford

Outdoor activities: golf, sports, fitness, nature, travel. Founded 1997.

## Cambridge University Press*

40 West 20th Street, New York, NY 10011
*tel* 212-924-3900 *fax* 212-691-3239
*website* www.cambridge.org
*Director* Richard L. Ziemacki

## Candlewick Press

2067 Massachusetts Avenue, Cambridge, MA 02140
*tel* 617-661-3330 *fax* 617-661-0565
*website* www.candlewick.com
*Editorial Director/Associate Publisher* Liz Bicknell, *Executive Editor* Mary Lee Donovan, *Editorial Director (novelty)* Joan Powers, *Editor-at-Large* Amy Ehrlich

Children's books 6 months–14 years: board books, picture books, novels, non-fiction, novelty books. Submit material through a literary agent. Subsidiary of **Walker Books Ltd**, UK. Founded 1991.

## Carroll & Graf Publishers Inc.

245 West 17th Street, 11th Floor, New York, NY 10011
*tel* 646-375-2570 *fax* 646-375-2571
*website* www.carrollandgraf.com
*President/Publisher* Herman Graf, *Subrights* Martine Ballen, *Foreign Rights* Lena Dixon

Mystery and crime, popular fiction, history, biography, literature, literary fiction. Founded 1983.

## University of Chicago Press*

1427 East 60th Street, Chicago, IL 60637
*tel* 773-702-7700 *fax* 773-702-2705
*website* www.press.uchicago.edu
*Director* Paula Barker Duffy

Scholarly books and monographs (humanities, social sciences and sciences) general trade books, reference books, and 43 scholarly journals.

## Chronicle Books

85 Second Street, 6th Floor, San Francisco, CA 94105
*tel* 415-537-4200 *fax* 415-537-4460
*email* frontdesk@chroniclebooks.com
*website* www.chroniclebooks.com
*Chairman and Ceo* Nion McEvoy, *Publisher* Jack Jensen, *Associate Publishers* Christine Carswell, Debra Laude, Victoria Rock

Cooking, art, fiction, general, children's, gift, new media, gardening, regional, nature. Founded 1967.

## Coffee House Press

27 N 4th Street, Suite 400, Minneapolis, MN 55401
*tel* 612-338-0125 *fax* 612-338-4004
*UK Representation* Nancy Green Madia
*tel* 212-864-0425 *fax* 212-316-2121
*website* www.coffeehousepress.com
*Publisher* Allan Kornblum

Literary fiction and poetry; collectors' editions. Founded 1984.

## Columbia University Press*

61 West 62nd Street, New York, NY 10023
*tel* 212-459-0600 *fax* 212-459-3678
*website* www.columbia.edu/cu/cup
*UK office* 1 Oldlands Way, Bognor Regis, West
Sussex PO22 9SA
*tel* (01243) 842165 *fax* (01243) 842167
*Editorial Director* Jennifer Crewe

General reference works in print and electronic
formats, translations and serious non-fiction of
more general interest.

## Concordia Publishing House

3558 S Jefferson Avenue, St Louis, MO 63118
*tel* 314-268-1000 *fax* 314-268-1329
*website* www.cph.com
*President* Paul T. McCain

Religious books, Lutheran perspective. Few
freelance MSS accepted; query first. Founded 1869.

## Contemporary Books

130 East Randolph Street, Suite 900, Chicago,
IL 60601
*tel* 312-233-6520 *fax* 312-233-7570
*Vice President* Philip Ruppel

Non-fiction. Imprints: Contemporary Books, Lowell
House, Passport Books, VGM Career Books.
Division of the McGraw-Hill Companies.

## The Continuum International Publishing Group Inc.

370 Lexington Avenue, New York, NY 10017-6503
*tel* 212-953-5858 *fax* 212-953-5944
*email* contin@tiac.net
*website* www.continuum-books.com
*Chairman/Publisher* Philip Sturrock

General non-fiction, education, literature,
psychology, politics, sociology, literary criticism,
religious studies. Founded 1999.

## Cornell University Press*

Sage House, 512 East State Street, Ithaca, NY 14850
*tel* 607-277-2338 *fax* 607-277-2374
*email* cupressinfo@cornell.edu
*website* www.cornellpress.cornell.edu
*Director* John G. Ackerman

Scholarly books. Founded 1869.

## Council Oak Books

1615 S. Baltimore Avenue, Suite 3, Tulsa, OK 74119
*tel* 918-587-6454 *fax* 918-583-4995
*email* jclark@counciloakbooks.com
*website* www.counciloakbooks.com
*Publishing Director* Melissa Lilly, *Editor-in-Chief*
Paulette Millichap

Non-fiction: native American, multicultural, life
skills, life accounts, Earth awareness, meditation.
Founded 1984.

## The Countryman Press

PO Box 748, Rte 12N, Mount Tom Building,
Woodstock, VT 05091
*tel* 802-457-4826 *fax* 802-457-1678
*email* countrymanpress@wwnorton.com
*website* www.countrymanpress.com
*Editorial Director* Kermit Hummel

Outdoor recreation guides for anglers, hikers,
cyclists, canoeists and kayakers, US travel guides,
New England non-fiction, how-to books, country
living books, books on nature and the environment,
classic reprints and general non-fiction. No
unsolicited MSS. Division of **W.W. Norton & Co.
Inc.** Founded 1973.

## Crown Publishing Group

299 Park Avenue, New York, NY 10170
*tel* 212-572-2408 *fax* 212-940-7408
*President/Publisher* Jenny Frost

General fiction, non-fiction, illustrated books.
Imprints: Bell Tower, Clarkson Potter, Crown
Publishers Inc., Harmony Books, Three Rivers Press.
Division of **Random House Inc.**

## DAW Books Inc.

375 Hudson Street, 3rd Floor, New York, NY 10014
*tel* 212-366-2096 *fax* 212-366-2090
*email* daw@penguinputnam.com
*website* www.dawbooks.com
*Publishers* Elizabeth R. Wollheim, Sheila E. Gilbert

Science fiction, fantasy, horror, mainstream thrillers:
originals and reprints. Imprints: DAW/Fantasy,
DAW/Fiction, DAW/Science Fiction. Affiliate of
**Penguin Putnam Inc.** Founded 1971.

## Dial Books for Young Readers – see

**Penguin Putnam Books for Young Readers**

## Doubleday Broadway Publishing Group

1540 Broadway, New York, NY 10036
*tel* 212-782-9000 *fax* 212-302-7985
*website* www.randomhouse.com
*President/Publisher* Stephen Rubin

General fiction and non-fiction. Imprints: Anchor
Bible Dictionary, Anchor Bible Reference Library,
Currency, Doubleday, Doubleday Bible
Commentary, Doubleday/Galilee,
Doubleday/Image, Nan A. Talese, The New
Jerusalem Bible. Division of **Random House Inc.**

## Dover Publications Inc.

31 East 2nd Street, Mineola, NY 11501
*tel* 516-294-7000 *fax* 516-742-5049
*website* www.doverpublications.com
*President, Dover Publications* Clarence Strawbridge,
*Vice-President, Editorial* Paul Negri

Art, architecture, antiques, crafts, juvenile, food,
history, folklore, literary classics, mystery, language,

music, math and science, nature, design and ready-to-use art. Founded 1941.

## Dutton
375 Hudson Street, New York, NY 10014
*tel* 212-366-2000 *fax* 212-366-2666
*email* online@penguinputnam.com
*website* www.penguinputnam.com
*Vice President/Editor-in-Chief* Brian Tart

Fiction and general non-fiction for adults. Imprint: Dutton. Division of **Penguin Putman Inc.**

## Dutton Children's Books – see Penguin Putnam Books for Young Readers

## Facts On File Inc.
132 West 31st Street, 17th Floor, New York, NY 10001-2006
*tel* 212-967 8800 *fax* 212-967 9196
*President* Mark McDonnell, *Editorial Director* Laurie E. Likoff

General reference books and services for colleges, libraries, schools and general public. Founded 1940.

## Family Tree – see Writer's Digest Books

## Farrar, Straus and Giroux Inc.
19 Union Square West, New York, NY 10003
*tel* 212-741-6900 *fax* 212-741-6973
*website* www.fsgbooks.com
*President/Publisher* Jonathan Galassi, *Editor-in-Chief* John Glusman

General publishers. Founded 1945.

## Fodor's Travel Publications – see Random House Inc.

## Four Walls Eight Windows*
39 West 14th Street, Room 503, New York, NY 10011
*tel* 212-206-8965 *fax* 212-206-8799
*email* edit@4w8w.com
*website* www.4w8w.com
*Publisher* John Oakes

Fiction, history, current affairs, biography, environment, health. No unsolicited submissions accepted. Founded 1987.

## Samuel French Inc.
45 West 25th Street, New York, NY 10010
*tel* 212-206-8990 *fax* 212-206-1429

Play publishers and authors' representatives (dramatic).

## Getty Publications*
1200 Getty Center Drive, Suite 500, Los Angeles, CA 90049-1682
*tel* 310-440-7365 *fax* 310-440-7758
*email* pubsinfo@getty.edu

*website* www.getty.edu/bookstore
*Publisher* Christopher Hudson, *General Manager* Kara Kirk, *Editor-in-Chief* Mark Greenberg

Art, art history, architecture, classical art and archaeology, conservation. Founded 1958.

## David R. Godine, Publisher Inc.
9 Hamilton Place, Boston, MA 02108
*tel* 617-451-9600 *fax* 617-350-0250
*email* info@godine.com
*website* www.godine.com
*President* David R. Godine

Fiction, photography, poetry, art, biography, children's, essays, history, typography, architecture, nature and gardening, music, cooking, words and writing, and mysteries. No unsolicited MSS. Founded 1970.

## Greenwillow Books – see HarperCollins Publishers

## Grosset & Dunlap – see Penguin Putnam Books for Young Readers

## Grove/Atlantic Inc.*
841 Broadway, New York, NY 10003-4793
*tel* 212-614-7850 *fax* 212-614-7886
*Publisher* Morgan Entrekin

MSS of permanent interest, fiction, biography, autobiography, history, current affairs, social science, belles-lettres, natural history. Imprints: Atlantic Monthly Press, Grove Press.

## Harcourt Trade Publishers*
525 B Street, Suite 1900, San Diego, CA 92101
*tel* 619-231-6616 *fax* 619-699-6320
*website* www.harcourt.com
*President/Publisher, Adult Books* Dan Farley, *Vice President/Publisher, Children's Books* Louise Pelan

Fiction and non-fiction (history, biography, etc) for readers of all ages. Imprints: Harcourt (hardcover books), Harvest Books (paperbacks) and Harcourt Children's Books. Division of Harcourt Inc.

## HarperCollins Publishers*
10 East 53rd Street, New York, NY 10022
*tel* 212-207-7000 *fax* 212-207-7145
*website* www.harpercollins.com
*HarperCollins SanFrancisco* 1160 Battery Street, San Francisco, CA 94111
*tel* 415-477-4400 *fax* 415-477-4444
*President/Ceo* Jane Friedman

Fiction, history, biography, poetry, science, travel, cookbooks, juvenile, educational, business, technical and religious. No unsolicited material; all submissions must come through a literary agent. Founded 1817.

**HarperCollins General Books Group (division)**
*President/Publisher* Cathy Hemming

**HarperInformation (division)**
Imprints: HarperBusiness, HarperResource, Access, William Morrow Cookbooks.

**HarperSanFrancisco (division)**
Imprint: HarperSanFrancisco.

**HarperTrade (division)**
Imprints: HarperCollins, Perennial, Cliff Street Books, Ecco, Quill, Amistad, HarperAudio, Large Print Editions, Rayo, Fourth Estate, ReganBooks and PerfectBound (e-books).

**Morrow/Avon (division)**
Imprints: William Morrow, Avon, HarperTorch, Eos, HarperEntertainment.

**HarperCollins Children's Books Group**
1350 6th Avenue, New York, NY 10019
*tel* 212-261-6500
*website* www.harperchildrens.com
*President/Publisher* Susan Katz

Imprints: Greenwillow Books, Joanna Cotler Books, Laura Geringer Books, HarperCollins Children's Books, HarperFestival, HarperTrophy, Avon, HarperTempest.

**Harvard University Press***
79 Garden Street, Cambridge, MA 02138-1499
*tel* 617-495 2600 *fax* 617-495-5898
*website* www.hup.harvard.edu
*Director* William P. Sisler, *Editor-in-Chief/ Assistant Director* Aida D. Donald

History, philosophy, literary criticism, politics, economics, sociology, music, science, classics, social sciences, behavioural sciences, law.

**Hastings House/Daytrips Publishers**
2601 Wells Avenue, Suite 161, Fern Park, FL 32730
*tel* 407-339-3600 *fax* 407-339-5900
*email* housebks@aol.com
*website* www.HastingsHouseBooks.com
*Publisher* Peter Leers

Travel.

**Hill and Wang**
19 Union Square West, New York, NY 10003
*tel* 212-741-6900 *fax* 212-633-9385
*website* www.fsgbooks.com
*Publisher*s Thomas Lebin, Elisabeth Sifton

General non-fiction, history, public affairs. Division of **Farrar, Straus and Giroux**. Founded 1956.

**Hippocrene Books Inc.**
171 Madison Avenue, New York, NY 10016
*tel* 212-685-4371 *fax* 212-779-9338
*email* orders@hippocrenebooks.com

*website* www.hippocrenebooks.com
*President/Editorial Director* George Blagowidow

Foreign language books, international cookbooks, foreign language dictionaries, love poetry, travel, military history, Polonia, general trade. Founded 1971.

**Holiday House**
425 Madison Avenue, New York, NY 10017
*tel* 212-688-0085
*President* John Briggs, *Vice-President/Editor-in-Chief* Regina Griffin

General children's books. Send query letter before submitting MSS. Always include sae. No multiple submissions. Founded 1935.

**Henry Holt and Company LLC***
115 West 18th Street, New York, NY 10011
*tel* 212-886-9200 *fax* 212-633-0748
*website* www.henryholt.com
*President/Publisher* John Sterling

History, biography, nature, science, self-help, novels, mysteries; books for young readers; trade paperback line, computer books. Founded 1866.

**The Johns Hopkins University Press***
2715 North Charles Street, Baltimore, MD 21218-4319
*tel* 410-516-6921 *fax* 410-516-6968
*Director* James D. Jordan

History, literary criticism, classics, politics, environmental studies, biology, medical genetics, consumer health, religion, physics, astronomy, mathematics, education. Founded 1878.

**Houghton Mifflin Company***
222 Berkeley Street, Boston, MA 02116
*tel* 617-351-5000

Fiction and non-fiction – cookbooks, history, political science, biography, nature (Peterson Guides), and gardening guides; reference, both adult and juvenile. No unsolicited MSS. Imprints: Mariner (original and reprint paperbacks); Houghton Mifflin Children's Books; American Heritage® Dictionaries. Founded 1832.

**HP Books** – see Berkley Publishing Group

**Hyperion***
77 West 66 Street, New York, NY 10023-6298
*tel* 212-456-0100 *fax* 212-456-0157
*website* www.hyperionbooks.com
*President* Robert Miller, *Vice-President/Publisher* Ellen Archer, *Vice-President/Publisher (Hyperion Books for Children)* Lisa Holton

General fiction and non-fiction, children's books. Division of Buena Vista Publishing, formerly Disney Book Publishing Inc. Founded 1990.

## University of Illinois Press*

1325 South Oak Street, Champaign, IL 61820
*tel* 217-333-0950 *fax* 217-244-8082
*Director* Willis G. Regier

American studies (history, music, literature, religion), working-class and ethnic studies, communications, regional studies, architecture, philosophy and women's studies. Founded 1918.

## Indiana University Press

601 North Morton Street, Bloomington, IN 47404-3797
*tel* 812-855-8817 *fax* 812-855-8507
*email* iupress@indiana.edu
*website* www.indiana.edu/~iupress
*Director* Peter-John Leone

African studies, Russian and East European studies, music, history, women's studies, Jewish studies, African–American studies, film, folklore, philosophy, medical ethics, archaeology, anthropology, paleontology. Reference and high level trade books. Founded 1950.

## International Marine Publishing

PO Box 220, Camden, Maine 04843
*tel* 207-236-4837 *fax* 207-236-6314
*email* nancy_dowling@mcgraw-hill.com
*website* www.internationalmarine.com
www.raggedmountainpress.com
*Editorial Director* Jonathan F. Eaton

Imprints: International Marine (boats, boating and sailing); Ragged Mountain Press (sport, adventure/travel, natural history). Division of the McGraw-Hill Companies. Founded 1992.

## University Press of Kansas

2501 West 15th Street, Lawrence, KS 66049-3905
*tel* 785-864-4154 *fax* 785-864-4586
*email* upress@ku.edu
*website* www.kansaspress.ku.edu
*Director* Fred Woodward, *Editor-in-Chief* Michael Briggs, *Senior Production Editor* Melinda Wirkus, *Assistant Director/Marketing Manager* Susan K. Schott

American history (political, social, cultural, environmental), military history, American political thought, American presidency studies, law and constitutional history, political science. Founded 1946.

## Knopf Publishing Group*

299 Park Avenue, New York, NY 10171
*tel* 212-572-2600 *fax* 212-572-8700
*website* www.randomhouse.com/knopf
*President* Sonny Mehta

General literature, fiction, belles-lettres, sociology, politics, history, nature, science, etc. Imprints: Alfred A. Knopf Inc., Anchor, Everyman's Library, Pantheon Books, Schocken Books, Vintage Books. Division of **Random House Inc.**

## Krause Publications

700 East State Street, Iola, WI 54990-0001
*tel* 715-445-2214 *fax* 715-445-4087
*email* info@Krause.com
*website* www.Krause.com
*Acquisitions Editors* Julie Stephani (sewing/crafts), Donald Gulbrandsen (transportation/firearms/outdoors), Paul Kennedy (antiques/collectibles)

Antiques and collectibles: coins, stamps, automobiles, toys, trains, firearms, comics, records; sewing and crafts, ceramics, outdoors, hunting.

## Little, Brown & Company

1271 Avenue of the Americas, New York, NY 10020
*tel* 212-522-8700 *fax* 212-522-7997
*website* www.twbookmark.com
*Chief Executive* Larry Kirshbaum

General literature, fiction, non-fiction, biography, history, trade paperbacks, children's. Art and photography books under the Bulfinch Press imprint. Imprint of AOL Time Warner Book Group.

## Llewellyn Publications

PO Box 64383, St Paul, MN 55164-0383
*email* info@llewellyn.com
*website* www.llewellyn.com
*President* Carl Llewellyn Weschcke, *Vice President* Gabriel Weschcke

New Age, occult, astrology, magic. Founded 1901.

## The Lyons Press

246 Goose Lane, Guilford, CT 06437
*tel* 203-458-4500
*President/Publisher* Tony Lyons

Outdoor sport, natural history, sports, art, general fiction and non-fiction. Founded 1978.

## McGraw-Hill*

2 Penn Plaza, New York, NY 10121
*tel* 212-512-2000
*website* www.books.mcgraw-hill.com
*Group Vice-President* Theodore Nardin

Professional and reference: engineering, scientific, business, architecture, encyclopedias; college textbooks; high school and vocational textbooks: business, secretarial, career; trade books; training materials for industry. Division of The McGraw-Hill Companies.

## McPherson & Company

PO Box 1126, Kingston, NY 12402
*tel* 845-331-5807 *fax* 845-331-5807
*email* bmcpher@ulster.net
*website* www.mcphersonco.com

*Publisher* Bruce R. McPherson

Literary fiction; non-fiction: art criticism, writings by artists, film-making, etc; occasional general titles (e.g. anthropology). No poetry. No unsolicited MSS; query first. Distributed in UK by Central Books, London. Founded 1974.

## The University of Massachusetts Press
PO Box 429, Amherst, MA 01004-0429
*tel* 413-545-2217 *fax* 413-545-1226
*website* www.umass.edu/umpress
*Director* Bruce G. Wilcox

Scholarly books and works of general interest: American studies and history, black and ethnic studies, women's studies, cultural criticism, architecture and environmental design, literary criticism, poetry, fiction, philosophy, political science, sociology, books of regional interest. Founded 1964.

## Merrell Publishers Ltd
49 West 24th Street, 8th Floor, New York, NY 10010
*tel* 212-929-8344 *fax* 212-929-8346
*email* info@merrellpublishersusa.com
*website* www.merrellpublishers.com
*US Director* Joan Brookbank

High-quality illustrated books on all aspects of visual culture, including art, architecture, photography and design.

## The University of Michigan Press
839 Greene Street, PO Box 1104, Ann Arbor, MI 48106-1104
*tel* 734-764-4388 *fax* 734-615-1540
*email* um.press@umich.edu
*website* www.press.umich.edu/
*Director* Philip Pochoda, *Assistant Director* Mary Erwin, *Executive Editor* LeAnn Fields, *Managing Editor* Christina Milton

Scholarly and general interest works in literary and cultural theory, classics, history, theatre, women's studies, political science, law, American history, American studies, anthropology, economics, jazz; textbooks in English as a second language; regional trade titles. Founded 1930.

## Microsoft Press*
One Microsoft Way, Redmond, WA 98052-6399
*tel* 425-882-8080 *fax* 425-936-7329
*website* www.microsoft.com
*Publisher* Don Falley, *Editorial Director* Kim Fields

Computer books. Division of Microsoft Corp. Founded 1983.

## Milkweed Editions
1011 Washington Avenue South, Suite 300, Minneapolis, MN 55415
*tel* 612-332-3192 *fax* 612-215-2550
*websites* www.milkweed.org, www.worldashome.org

*Editor* Emile Buchwold

Fiction, poetry, essays, the natural world, children's novels (ages 8–14). Founded 1979.

## University of Missouri Press
2910 LeMone Boulevard, Columbia, MO 65201
*tel* 573-882-7641 *fax* 573-884-4498
*website* www.system.missouri.edu/upress
*Director/Editor-in-Chief* Beverly Jarrett, *Acquisitions Editor* Clair Willcox

American and European history, African American studies, American, British and Latin American literary criticism, journalism, political philosophy, art history, regional studies; short fiction. Founded 1958.

## The MIT Press*
5 Cambridge Center, Cambridge, MA 02142-1493
*tel* 617-253-5646 *fax* 617-258-6779
*website* mitpress.mit.edu
*Director* Frank Urbanowski, *Editor-in-Chief* Laurence Cohen

Architecture, art and design, cognitive sciences, neuroscience, linguistics, computer science and artificial intelligence, economics and finance, philosophy, environment and ecology, natural history. Founded 1961.

## Morehouse Publishing Co.
PO Box 1321, Harrisburg, PA 17105
*tel* 717-541-8130 *fax* 717-541-8136
*email* morehouse@morehousegroup.com
*website* www.morehousegroup.com
*President* Kenneth Quigley, *Publisher* Debra Farrington

Religious books, spirituality, children's.

## William Morrow – see HarperCollins Publishers

## The Naiad Press Inc.
PO Box 10543, Tallahassee, FL 32302
*tel* 850-539-5965 *fax* 850-539-9731
*website* www.naiadpress.com
*Ceo* Barbara Grier

Lesbian fiction; non-fiction: bibliographies, biographies, essays. Founded 1973.

## NAL
375 Hudson Street, New York, NY 10014
*tel* 212-366-2000 *fax* 212-366-2666
*email* online@penguinputnam.com
*website* www.penguinputnam.com
*Vice President/Publisher* Kara Welch

Fiction and general non-fiction. Imprints: Mentor, Meridian, New American Library, Onyx, Roc, Signet, Signet Classics, Topaz. Division of **Penguin Putnam Inc.** Founded 1948

## Thomas Nelson Publisher
501 Nelson Place, Nashville, TN 37214-1000
*tel* 615-889-9000 *fax* 615-391-5225
*email* publicity@thomasnelson.com
*website* www.thomasnelson.com
*Executive Vice President, Thomas Nelson Publishing Group* Lee Gessner

Bibles, religious, non-fiction and fiction general trade books. Founded 1798.

## University of New Mexico Press
1720 Lomas Boulevard NE, Albuquerque,
NM 87131-1591
*tel* 505-277-2346 *fax* 505-277-3350
*email* unmpress@unm.edu
*website* www.unmpress.com
*Director* Luther Wilson

Western history, anthropology and archaeology, Latin American studies, photography, multicultural literature, poetry. Founded 1929.

## The University of North Carolina Press*
116 South Boundary Street, Chapel Hill, NC 27514
*tel* 919-966-3561 *fax* 919-966-3829
*website* www.uncpress.unc.ed
*Director* Kate Douglas Torrey

American history, American studies, Southern studies, European history, women's studies, Latin American studies, political science, anthropology and folklore, classics, regional trade. Founded 1922.

## North Light Books – see Writer's Digest Books

## W.W. Norton & Company Inc.
500 Fifth Avenue, New York, NY 10110
*tel* 212-354-5500 *fax* 212-869-0856
*website* www.wwnorton.com

General fiction and non-fiction, music, boating, psychiatry, economics, family therapy, social work, reprints, college texts, science.

## University of Oklahoma Press
1005 Asp Avenue, Norman, OK 73019-6051
*tel* 405-325-2000 *fax* 405-325-4000
*Director* John N. Drayton

American West, American Indians, Mesoamerica, classics, natural history, political science. Founded 1928.

## Orchard Books
555 Broadway, New York, NY 10012
*tel* 212-343-6782 *fax* 212-343-4890
*website* www.scholastic.com
*Editorial Director* Ken Geist

Books for children and young adults; picture books, fiction. Imprint of **Scholastic Inc.** Founded 1987.

## The Overlook Press*
141 Wooster Street, New York, New York 10012
*tel* 212-673-2210 *fax* 212-673-2296
*website* www.overlookpress.com
*President and Publisher* Peter Mayer, *Associate Publisher* Tracy Carns

Non-fiction, fiction, children's books.

## Oxford University Press Inc.*
198 Madison Avenue, New York, NY 10016
*tel* 212-726-6000 *fax* 212-726-6455
*website* www.oup-usa.org
*President* Laura Brown

Scholarly, professional, reference, bibles, college textbooks, religion, medical, music.

## Pantheon Books – imprint of Knopf Publishing Group

## Paragon House Publishers
440 Park Avenue South, 13th Floor, New York,
NY 10016, USA
*tel* (212) 629 9773 *fax* (212) 629 9751
*email* rby@paragonhouse.com
*website* www.paragonhouse.com
*Executive Director* Gordon L. Anderson

Textbooks in philosophy and religion; general non-fiction. Member of the **Continuum International Publishing Group Inc.**

## Peachtree Publishers Ltd
1700 Chattahoochee Avenue, Atlanta,
GA 30318-2112
*tel* 404-876-8761 *fax* 404-875-2578
*email* hello@peachtree-online.com
*website* www.peachtree-online.com
*President and Publisher* Margaret Quinlin, *Editorial Director* Kathy Landwehr

Children's picture books, novels and non-fiction books. Adult non-fiction subjects include self-help, parenting, education, health, regional guides. No adult fiction.

For children's books, send complete MSS; for all others, send query letter with 3 sample chapters and table of contents to Helen Harriss with sase for response and/or return of material. Founded 1977.

## Pelican Publishing Company*
PO Box 3110, Gretna, LA 70054
*tel* 504-368-1175 *fax* 504-368-1195
*email* editorial@pelicanpub.com
*websites* www.pelicanpub.com, www.epelican.com
*Publisher/President* Milburn Calhoun

Art and architecture, cookbooks, travel, history, business, children's. Founded 1926.

## Penguin AudioBooks – see Viking Penguin

**Penguin Books** – see Viking Penguin

## Penguin Putnam Books for Young Readers*

345 Hudson Street, New York, NY 10014
*tel* 212-366-2000 *fax* 212-366-2666
*email* online@penguinputnam.com
*website* www.penguinputnam.com
*President* Douglas Whiteman

Children's: picture books, board and novelty books, young adult novels, mass merchandise products. Imprints: Dial Books for Young Readers, Dutton Children's Books, Dutton Interactive, Phyllis Fogelman Books, Grosset & Dunlap, PaperStar, Philomel, Planet Dexter, Platt & Munk, Playskool, Price Stern Sloan, PSS, Puffin Books, G.P. Putnam's Sons, Viking Children's Books, Frederick Warne. Division of **Penguin Putnam Inc.** Founded 1997.

### Dial Books for Young Readers (imprint)
*fax* 212-414-3394
*President/Publisher* Nancy Paulsen, *Editorial Director* Laura Hornik, *Vice President/Publisher, Phyllis Fogelman Books* Phyllis Fogelman

Children's fiction and non-fiction, picture books, board books, interactive books, novels.

### Dutton Children's Books (imprint)
*tel* 212-366 2792  *fax* 212-243-6002
*President/Publisher* Stephanie Lurie, *Editorial Director, Dutton Children's Trade* Donna Brooks

Picture books, young adult novels, non-fiction photographic books. Founded 1852.

### Grosset & Dunlap (imprint)
*President/Publisher, Grosset & Dunlap* Debra Dorfman

Children's: picture books, activity books, fiction and non-fiction. Imprints: Grosset & Dunlap, Platt & Munk, Somerville House USA, Planet Dexter. Founded 1898.

### Price Stern Sloan (imprint)
*Vice President/Publisher* Jon Anderson

Children's books: novelty/lift-flaps, activity books, middle-grade fiction, middle-grade and YA non-fiction, cutting-edge graphic readers, picture books, books plus. Imprints: Crazy Games, Doodle Art, Planet Dexter, Serendipity, Troubador Press, Wee Sing. Founded 1963.

### Puffin Books (imprint)
*President & Publisher* Tracy Tang

Children's paperbacks. Founded 1935.

### G.P. Putnam's Sons (imprint)
*President/Publisher* Nancy Paulsen

Children's hardcover and paperback books. Imprints: G.P. Putnam's Sons, Philomel Books, PaperStar. Founded 1838.

### Viking Children's Books (imprint)
*President* Regina Hayes
Fiction, non-fiction, picture books. Founded 1925.

### Frederick Warne (imprint)
Original publisher of Beatrix Potter's *Tales of Peter Rabbit*. Founded 1865.

## Penguin Putnam Inc.*

375 Hudson Street, New York, NY 10014
*tel* 212-366-2000 *fax* 212-366-2666
*email* online@penguinputnam.com
*website* www.penguinputnam.com
*President, The Penguin Group* David Wan, *Chairman* John McKinson, *Ceo* David Shanks

Publisher of consumer books in both hardcover and paperback for adults and children; also produces maps, calendars, audiobooks and mass merchandise products. Adult imprints: Ace, Ace/Putnam, Allen Lane The Penguin Press, Avery, Berkley Books, BlueHen, Boulevard, DAW, Dutton, Grosset/Putnam, HP Books, Jove, Mentor, Meridian, Onyx, Penguin, Penguin Classics, Penguin Compass, Perigee, Plume, Prime Crime, Price Stern Sloan Inc., Putnam, G.P. Putnam's Sons, Riverhead Books, Roc, Signet, Signet Classics, Jeremy P. Tarcher, Topaz, Viking, Viking Compass, Viking Studio, Marian Wood Books. Children's imprints: Dial Books for Young Readers, Dutton Children's Books, Grosset & Dunlap, PaperStar, Philomel Books, Planet Dexter, Price Stern Sloan Inc., Puffin, G.P. Putnam's Sons, Viking Children's Books, Wee Sing, Frederick Warne. Divisions: **Berkley Publishing Group, Dutton, Plume, NAL, Penguin Putnam Books for Young Readers, The Putnam Publishing Group, Viking Penguin.**

## Penn State University Press
820 North University Drive, USB1, Suite C, University Park, PA 16802
*tel* 814-865-1327 *fax* 814-863-1408
*website* www.psupress.org
*Editor-in-Chief* Peter Potter

Art history, literary criticism, religious studies, philosophy, political science, sociology, history, Russian and East European studies, Latin American studies and medieval studies. Founded 1956.

## University of Pennsylvania Press*
4200 Pine Street, Philadelphia, PA 19104-4011
*tel* 215-898-6261 *fax* 215-898-0404
*website* www.upenn.edu/pennpress
*Director* Eric Halpern

American and European history, anthropology, art, architecture, business, cultural studies, ancient studies, human rights, literature, health, Pennsylvania regional studies. Founded 1890.

**Perigee Books** – see Berkley Publishing Group

## The Permanent Press and Second Chance Press
4170 Noyac Road, Sag Harbor, NY 11963
*tel* 631-725-1101 *fax* 631-725-8215
*website* www.thepermanentpress.com
*Directors* Martin Shepard, Judith Shepard
Quality fiction. Founded 1978.

## Plume
375 Hudson Street, New York, NY 10014
*tel* 212-366-2000 *fax* 212-366-2666
*email* online@penguinputnam.com
*website* www.penguinputnam.com
*Publisher* Kathryn Court, *President* Clare Ferraro,
*Editor-in-Chief* Trena Keating

Fiction and general non-fiction for adults. Division of **Penguin Putnam Inc.**

## Pocket Books*
1230 Avenue of the Americas, New York, NY 10020
*tel* 212-698-7000 *fax* 212-698-7007
*website* www.simonsays.com
*President/Publisher* Judith M. Curr, *Vice President/Editorial Director* Emily Bestler

General fiction and non-fiction, trade hardcovers and paperbacks, mass market paperbacks. Imprints: Archway Paperbacks, Minstrel Books. Division of Simon & Schuster Adult Publishing Group. Founded 1939.

## Popular Woodworking – see Writer's Digest Books

## Price Stern Sloan – see Penguin Putnam Books for Young Readers

## Princeton University Press*
Princeton, NJ 08540
*postal address* 41 William Street, Princeton, NJ 08540
*tel* 609-258-4900 *fax* 609-258-6305
*website* www.pup.princeton.edu
*Director* Walter Lippincott, *Editor-in-Chief* Sam Elworthy

Scholarly and scientific books on all subjects. Founded 1905.

## Puffin Books – see Penguin Putnam Books for Young Readers

## The Putnam Publishing Group
375 Hudson Street, New York, NY 10014
*tel* 212-366-2000 *fax* 212-366-2643
*email* online@penguinputnam.com
*website* www.penguinputnam.com

General trade books for adults; books on cassette. Imprints: Avery, BlueHen, G.P. Putnam's Sons, Riverhead Books, Jeremy P. Tarcher, Tarcher/Penguin, Putnam Berkley Audio, Marian Wood Books. Division of **Penguin Putnam Inc.**

## G.P. Putnam's Sons (adult) – see The Putnam Publishing Group

## G.P. Putnam's Sons (children's) – see Penguin Putnam Books for Young Readers

## Rand McNally
PO Box 7600, Chicago, IL 60680
*tel* 847-329-2178
*Chairman* John Macomber, *President/Ceo* Norman E. Wells, Jr

Maps, guides, atlases, educational publications, globes and children's geographical titles and atlases in print and electronic formats.

## Random House Inc.*
1540 Broadway, New York, NY 10019
*tel* 212-782-9000 *fax* 212-302-7985
299 Park Avenue, New York, NY 10170
*and* 280 Park Avenue, New York, NY 10017
*tel* 212-572-2600 *fax* 212-572-8700
*website* www.randomhouse.com
*Chairman/Ceo* Peter Olson, *President/Coo* Erik Engstrom

General fiction and non-fiction, children's books. Subsidiary of Bertelsmann AG.

### Random House Audio Publishing Group (division)
*President* Jenny Frost

BDD Audio Publishing, Random House Audio Publishing.

### Random House Children's Media Group (division)
*President & Publisher* Craig W. Virden

Imprints: Children's Publishing (Crown Books for Young Readers, CTW Publishing, Delacorte Press, Disney Books, Doubleday Books for Young Readers, Dragonfly Books, First Choice Chapter Books, Golden Books for Young Readers, Knopf Books for Young Readers, Knopf Paperbacks, Laurel-Leaf, Picture Yearling, Random House Children's Publishing, Skylark, Starfire, Yearling Books); Children's Media.

### Random House Diversified Publishing Group (division)
*President* Jenny Frost

Random House Large Print Publishing; Random House Value Publishing (Children's Classics, Crescent Books, Derrydale, Gramercy Books, Testament Books, Wings Books).

**The Random House Information Group (division)**
*President* Bonnie Ammer

Imprints: Fodor's Travel Publications, Living Language, Princeton Review, Random House Reference, Random House Puzzles and Games.

**Random House Trade Publishing Group (division)**
*President/Editor-in-Chief* Ann Godoff

Imprints: Random House Adult Trade Books, The Modern Library, Villard Books.

## Riverhead Books (Hardcover) – see The Putnam Publishing Group

## Riverhead Books (Trade Paperback) – see Berkley Publishing Group

## Rizzoli International Publications Inc.
300 Park Avenue South, New York, NY 10010
*tel* 212-387-3400 *fax* 212-387-3535
*Publisher* Marta Hallett

Art, architecture, photography, fashion, gardening, design, gift books, cookbooks. Founded 1976.

## Rodale Book Group
400 South 10th Street, Emmaus, PA 18098
*tel* 610-967-5171 *fax* 610-967-8961
*Executive Editor, Rodale General Books* Stephanie Tade, *Editor-in-Chief, Women's Health Books* Tami Booth, *Executive Editor, Home Arts* Ellen Phillips, *Executive Editor, Lifestyle Books* Margot Schupf, *Executive Editor, Men's Health/Sports & Fitness Books* Jeremy Katz, *Senior Editor, Parenting Books* Lou Cinquino

General health, women's health, men's health, senior health, alternative health, fitness, healthy cooking, gardening, pets, spirituality/inspiration, trade health, biography, memoir, current affairs, science, parenting, organics, lifestyle, self-help, how-to, home arts. Founded 1932.

## Rough Guides – see Viking Penguin

## Routledge
270 Madison Avenue, New York, NY 10016
*tel* 212-216-7800 *fax* 212-563-7854
*website* www.routledge-ny.com
*Vice President and Publisher* Mary MacInnes, *Vice President and Publishing Director, Humanities* William P. Germano, *Publishing Director, Reference* Sylvia K. Miller

Music, history, psychology and psychiatry, politics, women's studies, education, sociology, urban studies, religion, lesbian and gay studies, film, media, literary and cultural studies, reference. Subsidiary of Taylor & Francis Books Inc.

## Running Press Book Publishers
125 South 22nd Street, Philadelphia, PA 19103-4399
*tel* 215-567-5080 *fax* 215-568 2919
*President* Stuart Teacher, *Publisher* Carlo DeVito, *Design Director* Bill Jones, *Production Director* Peter Horodowich, *Editorial Director* Jennifer Worick

Art, craft/how-to, general non-fiction, children's books. Imprints: Courage Books, Running Press Miniature Editions. Founded 1972.

## Rutgers University Press
100 Joyce Kilmer Avenue, Piscataway, NJ 08854-8099
*tel* 732-445-7762 *fax* 732-445-7039
*website* www.rutgerspress.rutgers.edu
*Directors* Marlie Wasserman, *Editor-in-Chief* Leslie Mitchner

Women's studies, anthropology, film and media studies, sociology, public health, popular science, cultural studies, literature, religion, history of medicine, Asian–American studies, African–American studies, American history, American studies, art history, regional titles. Founded 1936.

## St Martin's Press Inc.*
175 Fifth Avenue, New York, NY 10010
*tel* 212-674-5151 *fax* 212-420-9314
*website* www.stmartins.com
*President* John Sargent

Trade, reference, college.

## Schocken Books – imprint of Knopf Publishing Group

## Scholastic Inc.*
557 Broadway, New York, NY 10012
*tel* 212-343-6100 *fax* 212-343-6930
*website* www.scholastic.com
*Chairman/President/Ceo* Richard Robinson, *Executive Vice President, Book Group* Barbara Marcus, *Executive Vice President, Scholastic Entertainment* Deborah Forte, *Executive Vice President, Educational Publishing* Julie McGee

Innovative textbooks, magazines, technology and teacher materials for use in both school and the home. Scholastic is a global children's publishing and media company with a corporate mission to instill the love of reading and learning for lifelong pleasure in all children. Founded 1920.

## Scribner – imprint of Simon & Schuster Adult Publishing Group

## Sheridan House Inc.*
145 Palisade Street, Dobbs Ferry, NY 10522
*tel* 914-693-2410 *fax* 914-693-0776
*email* info@sheridanhouse.com

*website* www.sheridanhouse.com
*President* Lothar Simon

Sailing, nautical, travel. Founded 1940.

## Simon & Schuster Adult Publishing Group*

1230 Avenue of the Americas, New York, NY 10020
*tel* 212-698-7000 *fax* 212-698-7007
*President/Publisher* Carolyn K. Reidy

General fiction and non-fiction. Imprints: Fireside, The Free Press, Kaplan, MTV®, PB Press, Pocket Books, Scribner, Scribner Paperback Fiction, S&S Libros en Espanol, Simon & Schuster, S&S Source, Sonnet, Star Trek®, Touchstone, Wall Street Journal Books, Washington Square Press VHI®. Division of Simon & Schuster. Founded 1924.

## Simon & Schuster Children's Publishing Division*

1230 Avenue of the Americas, New York, NY 10020
*tel* 212-698-7200 *fax* 212-698-2793
*President* Kristina Peterson

Preschool to young adult, fiction and non-fiction, trade, library and mass market. Imprints: Aladdin Paperbacks, Atheneum Books for Young Readers, Little Simon, Margaret K. McElderry Books, Simon & Schuster Books for Young Readers, Simon Spotlight. Division of Simon & Schuster. Founded 1924.

## Soho Press Inc.

853 Broadway, New York, NY 10003
*tel* 212-260-1900 *fax* 212-260-1902
*email* soho@sohopress.com
*website* www.sohopress.com
*Publisher* Juris Jurjevics, *Associate Publisher* Laura Hruska

Literary fiction, commercial fiction, mystery, thrillers, travel, memoir, general non-fiction. Founded 1986.

## Stackpole Books

5067 Ritter Road, Mechanicsburg, PA 17055-6921
*tel* 717-796-0411 *fax* 717-796-0412
*email* sales@stackpolebooks.com
*website* www.stackpolebooks.com
*Directors* David Detweiler (chairman), David Ritter (president), Judith Schnell (editorial)

Nature, outdoor sports, Pennsylvania, crafts and hobbies, history, military history. Founded 1930.

## Stanford University Press*

Palo Alto, CA 94304-1124
*tel* 650-723-9434 *fax* 650-725-3457
*website* www.sup.org
*Director* Geoffrey Burn

Scholarly non-fiction, college text, professional.

## Strawberry Hill Press

21 Isis Street, Apt 102, San Francisco, CA 94103-4365
*President* Jean-Louis Brindamour PhD, *Executive Vice-President/Art Director* Ku Fu-Sheng, *Treasurer* Edward E. Serres

Health, self-help, cookbooks, philosophy, religion, history, drama, science and technology, biography, mystery, Third World. No unsolicited MSS; preliminary letter and return postage essential. Founded 1973.

## Jeremy P. Tarcher – see The Putnam Publishing Group

## University of Tennessee Press*

110 Conference Center Building, Knoxville, TN 37996-4108
*tel* 865-974-3321 *fax* 865-974-3724
*email* danforth@utk.edu
*website* www.utpress.org
*Director* Jennifer Siler

American studies: African–American studies, Appalachian studies, history, religion, literature, historical archaeology, folklore, vernacular architecture, material culture. Founded 1940.

## Ten Speed Press

PO Box 7123, Berkeley, CA 94707
*tel* 510-559-1600 *fax* 510-524-1052
*email* order@tenspeed.com
*website* www.tenspeed.com
*President* Philip Wood, *Publisher and Vice President* Kirsty Melville

Career/business, cooking, practical non-fiction, health, women's interest, self-help, children's. Founded 1971.

## University of Texas Press*

PO Box 7819, Austin, TX 78713-7819
*tel* 512-471-7233 *fax* 512-232-7178
*email* utpress@uts.cc.utexas.edu
*website* www.utexas.edu/utpress/
*Director* Joanna Hitchcock, *Assistant Director and Editor-in-Chief* Theresa May, *Assistant Director and Financial Officer* Joyce Lewandowski, *Assistant Director and Design/Production Manager* David Cavazos

Scholarly non-fiction: anthropology, classics and the Ancient World, conservation and the environment, film and media studies, geography, Latin American and Latino studies, Middle Eastern studies, natural history, ornithology, Texas and Western studies. Founded 1950.

## Theatre Arts Books

29 West 35th Street, New York, NY 10001
*tel* 212-216-7877

*Publishing Director* William Germano

Theatre, performance, dance and allied books –
acting techniques, voice, movement, costume, etc; a
few plays. Imprint of **Routledge**.

## Tor Books
175 Fifth Avenue, 14th Floor, New York, NY 10010
*tel* 212-388-0100 *fax* 212-388-0191

Fiction: general, historical, western, suspense,
mystery, horror, science fiction, fantasy, humour,
juvenile, classics (English language); non-fiction:
adult and juvenile. Affiliate of Holtzbrinck
Publishers. Founded 1980.

## Tuttle Publishing/Periplus Editions
153 Milk Street, Boston, MA 02109
*tel* 617-951-4080 *fax* 617-951-4045
*website* www.tuttlepublishing.com
Periplus Editions, 5 Little Road 08–01,
Singapore 536983
*tel* 65-280-3320 *fax* 65-280-6290
*Ceo* Eric Oey, *Publishing Director* Ed Walters

Asian art, culture, cooking, gardening, Eastern
philosophy, martial arts, health. Founded 1948.

## Van Nostrand Reinhold – acquired by John
Wiley & Sons Inc.

## Viking – see Viking Penguin

## Viking Children's Books – see Penguin
Putnam Books for Young Readers

## Viking Penguin
375 Hudson Street, New York, NY 10014
*tel* 212-366-2000 *fax* 212-366-2666
*email* online@penguinputnam.com
*website* www.penguinputnam.com
*Chairman* Susan Petersen Kennedy, *President* Clare
Ferraro

Fiction and general non-fiction for adults. Imprints:
Stephen Greene Press, Pelham, Penguin Books,
Penguin Classics, Penguin Compass, Rough Guides,
Viking, Viking Compass, Penguin AudioBooks,
Allen Lane The Penguin Press. Division of **Penguin
Putnam Inc.** Founded 1975.

### Penguin AudioBooks (imprint)
*Senior Editor* David Highfill

Imprints: Penguin AudioBooks, Penguin
HighBridge Audio. Founded 1990.

### Penguin Books (imprint)
*President/Publisher* Kathryn Court

Fiction and general non-fiction for adults.
Imprints: Penguin, Penguin Classics, Penguin
Compass, Penguin 20th Century Classics. Founded
1935.

### Rough Guides (imprint)
345 Hudson Street, New York, NY 10014
*tel* 212-414-3635 *fax* 212-414-3352
*email* mail@roughguides.com
*website* www.roughguides.com
*Publisher* Martin Dunford

Trade paperbacks, travel guides, phrasebooks, music
reference, music CDs and internet reference.
Founded 1982.

### Viking (imprint)
*Associate Publisher* Paul Slovak

Fiction and general non-fiction for adults. Founded
1925.

## Walker & Co.
104 Fifth Avenue, New York, NY 10011
*tel* 212-727-8300 *fax* 212-727-0984
*websites* www.walkerbooks.com,
www.walkeryoungreaders.com
*Publisher* George Gibson, *Mystery* Michael Seidman,
*Juvenile* Emily Easton

General publishers, biography, popular science,
health, business, mystery, history, juveniles.
Founded 1960.

## Warner Books Inc.
1271 Avenue of the Americas, New York, NY 10020
*tel* 212-522-7200 *fax* 212-522-7991
*website* www.twbookmark.com
*Ceo* Laurence K. Kirshbaum,
*President/Coo/Publisher* Maureen Mahon Egen

Paperback originals and reprints, fiction and non-
fiction, trade paperbacks and hardcover books,
audio books, gift books. Subsidiary of AOL Time
Warner Book Group. Founded 1961.

## University of Washington Press
PO Box 50096, Seattle, WA 98145-5096
*tel* 206-543-4050 *fax* 206-543-3932
*website* www.washington.edu/uwpress.com
*Director* Patrick Soden

Anthropology, Asian–American studies, Asian
studies, art and art history, aviation history,
environmental studies, forest history, Jewish studies,
literary criticism, marine sciences, Middle East
studies, music, regional studies, including history
and culture of the Pacific Northwest and Alaska,
Native American studies, resource management and
public policy, Russian and East European studies,
Scandinavian studies. Founded 1909.

## WaterBrook Press
2375 Telstar Drive, Suite 160, Colorado Springs,
CO 80920
*tel* 719-590-4999 *fax* 719-590-8977
*website* www.waterbrookpress.com
*President* Stephen Cobb

Broad range of Christian fiction and non-fiction. Imprint: Shaw Books. Division of **Random House Inc.**

## Watson-Guptill Publications

770 Broadway, New York, NY 10003
*tel* 646-654-5000 *fax* 646-654-5487
*email* info@watsonguptill.com
*website* www.watsonguptill.com
*Director of Sales & Marketing* Charles Whang, *Senior Acquisitions Editors* Candy Raney, Bob Nirkind, Victoria Craven, Joy Aquilino

Art, crafts, how-to, comic/cartooning, photography, performing arts, architecture and interior design, graphic design, music, entertainment, writing, reference, children's. Imprints: Amphoto Books, Back Stage Books, Billboard Books, Watson-Guptill, Whitney Library of Design. Founded 1937.

## Franklin Watts

90 Sherman Turnpike, Danbury, CT 06816
*tel* 203-797-3500 *fax* 203-797-6986

School and library books for grades K–12.

## Westminster John Knox Press

100 Witherspoon Street, Louisville, KY 40202-1396
*tel* 502-569-5052 *fax* 502-569-8308
*email* wjk@presbypub.com
*website* www.wjkbooks.com
*President & Publisher* David Perkins

Religious, academic, reference, general.

## John Wiley & Sons Inc.*

111 River Street, Hoboken, NJ 07030
*tel* 201-748-6000 *fax* 201-748-6088
*email* info@wiley.com
*website* www.wiley.com
*President/Ceo* William J. Pesce

Specialises in scientific and technical books and journals, textbooks and educational materials for colleges and universities, as well as professional and consumer books and subscription services. Subjects include business, computer science, electronics, engineering, environmental studies, reference books, science, social sciences, multimedia, and trade paperbacks. Founded 1807.

## Marian Wood Books – see The Putnam Publishing Group

## Writer's Digest Books

4700 E. Galbraith Road, Cincinnati, OH 45236
*tel* 513-531-2690 *fax* 513-891-7185

Market Directories, books for writers, photographers and songwriters.

### Family Tree (imprint)
Genealogy.

### North Light Books (imprint)
Fine art, decorative art, crafts, graphic arts instruction books.

### Popular Woodworking (imprint)
How-to in home building, remodelling, woodworking, home organisation.

## Yale University Press*

302 Temple Street, New Haven, CT 06511
*postal address* PO Box 209040, New Haven, CT 06520
*tel* 203-432-0960 *fax* 203-432-0948/2394
*email* firstname.lastname@yale.edu
*website* www.yale.edu/yup
*Director* John E. Donatich

Scholarly books and art books.

# Audio publishers

Many of the audio publishers listed below are also publishers of books.

## Abbey Home Entertainment plc
435–437 Edgware Road, London W2 1TH
*tel* 020-7563 3910  *fax* 020-7563 3911
*Contact* Anne Miles

Specialises in the acquisition, production and distribution of quality audio/visual entertainment for children. Bestselling children's spoken word and music titles are available on CD and cassette in the Tempo range including *Postman Pat*, *Watership Down*, *Michael Rosen*, *Baby Bright*, *Wide Eye*, *SuperTed* and *Fun Song Factory*.

## Backbone Productions Ltd
PO Box 28409, London N19 4WX
*tel* 020-7281 0445  *fax* 020-7561 0105
*email* office@copingwithgrowing.com
*website* www.copingwithgrowing.com
*Managing Director* Edward Harris

Therapeutic resources for children.

## Barefoot Books Ltd
124 Walcot Street, Bath BA1 5BG
*tel* (01225) 322400  *fax* (01225) 322499
*email* info@barefootbooks.co.uk
*website* www.barefootbooks.co.uk
*Publisher* Tessa Stickland, *UK Editor* Natasha Carr

Narrative unabridged audiobooks, spoken and sung. Established 1993.

## Barrington Stoke
Sandeman House, Trunk's Close, 55 High Street, Edinburgh EH1 1SR
*tel* 0131-557 2020  *fax* 0131-557 6060
*email* anna.gibbons@barringtonstoke.co.uk
*website* www.barringtonstoke.co.uk
*Chairman* David Croom, *Managing Director* Sonia Raphael, *Editorial Manager* Anna Gibbons

Cassette tapes accompanied by 2 books: *Virtual Friends* and *Virtual Friends Again* by Mary Hoffman, *Problems with a Python* and *Living with Vampires* by Jeremy Strong, *Tod in Biker City* and *Bicycle Blues* by Anthony Masters, *Hat Trick* and *Ghost for Sale* by Terry Deary. Founded 1998.

## BBC Audiobooks Ltd
St James House, The Square, Lower Bristol Road, Bath BA2 3BH
*tel* (01225) 878000  *fax* (01225) 310771
*website* www.bbcaudiobooks.com
*Managing Director* Paul Dempsey, *Publishing Director* Jan Paterson, *Marketing Director* Rachel Stammers, *Finance Director* Mike Bowen, *Commissioning Editor* Kate Walsh

Spoken word entertainment that can be enjoyed at convenience. Imprints include BBC Radio Collection, Cover to Cover Classics, BBC Cover to Cover, BBC Word for Word, Chivers Audiobooks, Chivers Children's Audiobooks. Formed in 2002 from the amalgamation of Chivers Press, Cover To Cover and BBC Radio Collection.

## Bloomsbury Publishing Plc
38 Soho Square, London W1D 3HB
*tel* 020-7494 2111  *fax* 020-7734 8656
*website* www.bloomsbury.com
*Contact* Arzu Tahsin, Paperback Publishing Director

A broad selection of literary fiction and non-fiction; selected children's fiction and picture book packages.

## Bolinda Publishing
2 Ivanhoe Road, London SE5 8DH
*tel* 020-773 1088
*email* bolinda@marisa.fsbusines.co.uk
*website* www.bolinda.com
*UK Publisher* Marisa McGreevy

CDs and cassettes of children's, teenage and adult fiction titles. UK-based teenage list launched in 2002 with titles including *Troy* by Adele Geras (shortlisted for the Carnegie Medal and the Whitbread Book Awards) and *Thursday's Child* by Sonya Hartnett (winner of *The Guardian* Children's Fiction Prize). UK-based children's and adult lists to be launched in 2004. Publishes 18 titles a year and has 150 titles available. Based in Melbourne, Australia; established in the UK in 2002.

## Cló Iar-Chonnachta Teo.
Indreabhán, Conamara, Co. Galway, Republic of Ireland
*tel* (091) 593307 *fax* (091) 593362
*email* cic@iol.ie
*website* www.cic.ie
*Ceo* Micheál Ó Conghaile, *General Manager* Deirdre O'Toole

Predominantly Irish-language or bilingual poetry with accompanying CD of poet reading his work. Established 1985.

## CSA Word
6A Archway Mews, London SW15 2PE
*tel* 020-8871 0220  *fax* 020-8877 0712
*email* info@csaword.co.uk

website www.csaword.co.uk
Managing Director Clive Stanhope, Audio Director Victoria Williams

CDs and cassettes of classic children's literature such as Just William, Billy Bunter and Black Beauty; also current literary authors. Publishes 3 titles a year and has 20 titles available. Founded 1991.

## 57 Productions
57 Effingham Road, London SE12 8NT
tel/fax 020-8463 0866
email paul@57productions.com
website www.57productions.com
Director Paul Beasley

An agency and production company specialising in the spoken word, especially poetry in a contemporary and multicultural context. Represents and publishes a wide range of writers and performers, including Jean 'Binta' Breeze, Lemn Sissay, John Cooper Clarke, Adrian Mitchell and Benjamin Zephaniah. Established 1992.

## HarperCollins Audio
77–85 Fulham Palace Road, London W6 8JB
tel 020-8741 7070 fax 020-8307 4517
website www.harpercollins.co.uk
Publishing Director Rosalie George

Publishers of a wide range of genres including fiction, non-fiction, poetry, Classics, Shakespeare, comedy, personal development and children's. All works are read by famous actors. Established 1990.

## Hodder Headline Audiobooks
338 Euston Road, London NW1 3BH
tel 020-7873 6000 fax 020-7873 6024
email rupert.lancaster@hodder.co.uk
Publisher Rupert Lancaster, Publicity Lucy Dixon

Publishes outstanding authors from within the Hodder Headline group and from elsewhere. The list is made up of quality non-fiction; fiction, from John le Carré to Louis de Bernieres to Ardal O'Hanlon; WHSmith's Classic Collection; self-help titles from authors such as Susan Jeffers and Richard Carlson; religious titles; children's (i.e. the highly acclaimed dramatised Winnie the Pooh); sporting autobiographies including Alex Ferguson, Brian Moore and Dickie Bird; comedy titles such as Wallace & Gromit and the Magic Roundabout Adventures, bestselling collaborations with Classic FM; Derek Jacobi's acclaimed readings of the Brother Cadfael mysteries, and C.S. Forester's Hornblower novels read by Ioan Gruffudd. Founded 1994.

## Macmillan Audio Books
20 New Wharf Road, London N1 9RR
tel 020-7014 6000 fax 020-7014 6001
email a.muirden@macmillan.co.uk
website www.panmacmillan.co.uk

Audio Publisher Alison Muirden, Editorial Co-ordinator Zoe Howes

Adult fiction, non-fiction and autobiography, and children's. Voted Audio Publisher of the Year 2003 at the Spoken Word Awards. Established 1995.

## Naxos AudioBooks
18 High Street, Welwyn, Herts. AL6 9EQ
tel (01438) 717808 fax (01438) 717809
email naxos_audiobooks@compuserve.com
website www.naxosaudiobooks.com
Managing Director Nicolas Soames

Classic literature, modern fiction, non-fiction, drama and poetry on CD and cassette. Also junior classics and classical music. Founded 1994.

## The Orion Publishing Group Ltd
5 Upper St Martin's Lane, London WC2H 9EA
tel 020-7520 4425 fax 020-7379 6158
email pandora.white@orionbooks.co.uk
Audio Manager Pandora White

Adult and children's fiction. Established 1998.

## Penguin Audiobooks
Penguin Books Ltd, 80 Strand, London WC2R 0RL
tel 020-7010 3000 fax 020-7010 6695
email audio@penguin.co.uk
website www.penguin.co.uk/audio
Audio Publisher Jeremy Ettinghausen

The Audiobooks list reflects the diversity of the Penguin book range, including classic and contemporary fiction and non-fiction, autobiography, poetry, drama and, in Puffin Audiobooks, the best of contemporary and classic literature for younger listeners. Authors include Nick Hornby, Sue Townsend, Seamus Heaney, Roald Dahl and Eoin Colfer. Readings are by talented and recognisable actors. Over 500 titles are now available. Founded 1993.

## Random House Audio
The Random House Group Ltd, 20 Vauxhall Bridge Road, London SW1V 2SA
tel 020-7840 8400 fax 020-7834 2509
email gmarnham@randomhouse.co.uk
website www.randomhouse.co.uk
Managing Editor Richard Cable, Audiobooks Editor Georgia Marnham, Audiobooks Assistant Louisa Gibbs

Fiction, non-fiction and self-help. Authors include John Grisham, Kathy Reichs, Andy McNab, Chris Ryan, Robert Harris, Mark Haddon. Established 1991.

## Red Audio
7–14 Green Park, Sutton on the Forest, York YO61 1ET
tel (01347) 810055 fax (01347) 812705

*email* pam.reed@theredgroup.co.uk
*website* www.redaudio.biz
*Ceo & Editor* Steve Parks, *Head of Production* Pam Reed

CDs and cassettes of business topics such as marketing, start-ups, management and motivation. Publishes approx. 3 titles a year and has 8 titles available. Part of Red Studios UK Ltd. Founded 2001.

## Rickshaw Productions

Suite 125, 99 Warwick Street, Leamington Spa, Warks. CV32 4RB
*tel* (0780) 355 3214
*email* rickprod@aol.com
*website* www.rickshawaudiobooks.co.uk
*Executive Producer* Lindsay Fairgrieve

Specialises in unpublished authors of any nationality and genre. Publishes approx. 2–4 titles each year and has 10 available.

*Submission details* Welcomes submissions by post only from unpublished authors which have been professionally edited and typed, with a one-page synopsis, 2 sample chapters and an sae to cover the cost of return postage by Recorded Delivery. Currently looking especially for short stories and novellas but nothing salacious. Established 1998.

## Simon & Schuster Audioworks

Simon & Schuster, Africa House, 64–78 Kingsway, London WC2B 6AH
*tel* 020-7316 1900 *fax* 020-7316 0331/2
*email* editorial.enquiries@simonandschuster.co.uk
*website* www.simonsays.co.uk
*Publisher* Jonathan Atkins, *Audio Manager* Rumana Haider

Fiction and non-fiction audiobooks. Fiction authors include Jackie Collins, Alan Titchmarsh and Kathy Lette. Non-fiction authors include Stephen Corey, Anthony Robbins, Robin Cook and Stephen Ambrose. Established 1997.

## SmartPass Ltd

15 Park Road, Rottingdean, Brighton BN2 7HL
*tel* (01273) 300742
*email* info@smartpass.co.uk
*website* www.smartpass.co.uk, www.spaudiobooks.com
*Managing Director* Phil Viner, *Creative Director* Jools Viner

Dramatised English literature texts and discussion for secondary schools.

## ThorsonsAudio

77–85 Fulham Palace Road, London W6 8JB
*tel* 020-8307 4706 *fax* 020-8307-4788 (editorial)
*tel* 020-8307 4563 *fax* 020-8307 4199 (publicity)
*email* carole.tonkinson@harpercollins.co.uk (editorial), megan.slyfield@harpercollins.co.uk (publicity)
*Editor* Carole Tonkinson, *Publicity* Megan Slyfield

Thorsons is the health, mind, body and spirit list at HarperCollins (see *Book publishers UK and Ireland*). ThorsonsAudio acquisitions are independent of the Thorsons book business, allowing the label to publish audio versions of not only in-house bestsellers and prize winners, from John Gray's *Men Are from Mars, Women Are from Venus* to Paulo Coelho's *The Alchemist*, but also bestselling titles from other publishers' lists, such as *Emotional Intelligence* by Daniel Goleman. Imprint of **HarperCollins Publishers**.

## Time Warner AudioBooks

Brettenham House, Lancaster Place, London WC2E 7EN
*tel* 020-7911 8044 *fax* 020-7911 8109 (editorial)
*tel* 020-7911 8057 *fax* 020-7911 8102 (publicity)
*email* sarah.shrub@twbg.co.uk, cecilia.duraes@twbg.co.uk
*Editor* Sarah Shrubb, *Publicity* Cecilia Duraes

The AudioBooks list includes abridged titles from Time Warner Books' bestselling authors Alexander McCall Smith, Mitch Albom and David Sedaris. In 2004 the audio list was set to publish around 20 titles, including new fiction from Anita Shreve and Peter Mayle, further tales from Alexander McCall Smith, and Mark Billingham's detective series featuring D.I. Tom Thorne. Readings are by talented and recognisable actors including Tim Pigott-Smith and Andjoa Andoh. Launched 2003.

## Walker Books Ltd

87 Vauxhall Walk, London SE11 5HJ
*tel* 020-7793 0909 *fax* 020-7587 1123
*Publisher* Loraine Taylor

Walker Books publishes high-quality books for children of all ages (see *Book publishers UK and Ireland*). Walker audiobooks include bestselling fiction titles such as the Alex Rider series, *Judy Moody* and *Confessions of a Teenage Drama Queen*. For younger children, the *Listen and Join In* audio range comprises entertaining story-based activities based on favourite picture books, including *We're Going on a Bear Hunt, Guess How Much I Love You* and *Can't You Sleep Little Bear?*

# Book packagers

Many modern illustrated books are created by book packagers, whose special skills are in the areas of book design and graphic content. In-house editors match up the expertise of specialist writers, artists and photographers who usually work on a freelance basis.

**act-two ltd** – now John Brown Junior

## Aetos Ltd
69 Warminster Road, Bathampton,
Bath & NE Somerset BA2 6RU
*tel* (01225) 425745 *fax* (01225) 444966
*email* ron@aetos.co.uk
*General Manager* Athina Adams-Florou, *Publishing Manager* Ron Adams

Full packaging/production service, from original concept to delivery of film or finished copies. Specialises in illustrated educational and general interest books. Publishers' commissions undertaken. Opportunities for freelances.

## Aladdin Books Ltd
28 Percy Street, London W1P 0LD
*tel* 020-7323 3319 *fax* 020-7323 4829
*email* aladdin@dircon.co.uk
*Directors* Charles Nicholas, Bibby Whittaker

Full design and book packaging facility specialising in children's non-fiction and reference. Founded 1980.

## The Albion Press Ltd
Spring Hill, Idbury, Oxon OX7 6RU
*tel* (01993) 831094 *fax* (01993) 831982
*Directors* Emma Bradford (managing), Neil Philip (editorial)

Produces quality integrated illustrated titles from the idea to the printed copy. Specialises in children's books. Publishers' commissions undertaken. No unsolicited MSS. Founded 1984.

## Alphabet & Image Ltd
Marston House, Marston Magna, Yeovil,
Somerset BA22 8DH
*tel* (01935) 851331 *fax* (01935) 851372
*Directors* Anthony Birks-Hay, Leslie Birks-Hay

Complete editorial, picture research, photographic, design and production service for illustrated books on ceramics, fine art, horticulture, architecture, history, etc. Imprint: Marston House. Founded 1972.

## Amber Books Ltd
Bradley's Close, 74–77 White Lion Street,
London N1 9PF
*tel* 020-7520 7600 *fax* 020-7520 7606/7607
*email* enquiries@amberbooks.co.uk
*website* www.amberbooks.co.uk
*Managing Director* Stasz Gnych, *Deputy Managing Director* Sara Ballard, *Publishing Manager* Charles Catton, *Head of Production* Peter Thompson, *Design Manager* Mark Batley

Illustrated non-fiction. Subject areas include military, aviation, transport, crime, general reference and maritime. Opportunities for freelances. Imprints: Brown Books Ltd. Founded 1989.

## Andromeda Oxford Ltd
Kimber House, 1 Kimber Road, Abingdon,
Oxon OX14 1SG
*tel* (01235) 55029611
*email* mail@andromeda.co.uk
*website* www.andromeda.co.uk
*Directors* David Holyoak (managing), Graham Bateman (publishing), Clive Sparling (production), Simon Matthews (finance), Christopher Collier (sales), Linda Cole (creative)

Produces for the international market adult and junior reference books: history, natural history, geography, science, art. Also children's information and activity books. Founded 1986.

## Nicola Baxter
PO Box 215, The Brew House, Framingham Earl Road, Yelverton, Norwich NR14 7UR
*tel* (01508) 491111 *fax* (01508) 491100
*email* nb@nicolabaxter.com
*website* www.nicolabaxter.com
*Manager, Commissioning Editor, Author* Nicola Baxter

Full packaging service for children's books, from concept to film or any part of the process in between. Produces both fiction and non-fiction titles in a wide range of formats, from board books to encyclopedias and also novelty books. Opportunities for freelances. Founded 1990.

## BCS Publishing Ltd
2nd Floor, Temple Court, 109 Oxford Road, Cowley, Oxford OX4 2ER
*tel* (01865) 770099 *fax* (01865) 770050
*email* bcs-publishing@dsl.pipex.com
*Managing and Art Director* Steve McCurdy

Specialises in the preparation of illustrated non-fiction; provides a full creative, design, editorial and production service. Opportunities for freelances. Commissioned work undertaken.

## Bender Richardson White

PO Box 266, Uxbridge, Middlesex UB9 5NX
*tel* (01895) 832444 *fax* (01895) 835213
*email* brw@brw.co.uk
*Directors* Lionel Bender (editorial), Kim Richardson
(sales & production), Ben White (design)

Specialises in children's natural history, science and
family information. Opportunities for freelances.
Founded 1990.

## BLA Publishing Ltd

BIC Ling Kee House, 1 Christopher Road,
East Grinstead, West Sussex RH19 3BT
*tel* (01342) 318980 *fax* (01342) 410980
*Directors* Au Bak Ling (chairman, Hong Kong),
Albert Kw Au (Hong Kong)

High-quality illustrated reference books,
particularly science dictionaries and encyclopedias,
for the international market. Founded 1981.

## The Book Guild Ltd

Temple House, 25 High Street, Lewes,
East Sussex BN7 2LU
*tel* (01273) 472534 *fax* (01273) 476472
*email* info@bookguild.co.uk
*website* www.bookguild.co.uk
*Directors* G.M. Nissen CBE (chairman), Carol Biss
(managing), Anthony Nissen, Jane Nissen, David
Ross, Paul White (financial), Janet Wrench
(production)

Offers a range of publishing options: a
comprehensive package for authors incorporating
editorial, design, production, marketing, publicity
and distribution; editorial and production only for
authors requiring private editions; or a complete
service for companies and organisations requiring
books for internal or promotional purposes – from
brief to finished book. Founded 1982.

## Book Packaging and Marketing

1 Church Street, Blakesley, Towcester,
Northants. NN12 8RA
*tel* (01327) 861300 *fax* (01327) 861300
*Proprietor* Martin F. Marix Evans

Illustrated general and informational non-fiction
and reference for adults, especially military history,
travel, countryside. Product development and
project management; editorial and marketing
consultancy. Very limited opportunities for
freelances. Founded 1990.

## Breslich & Foss Ltd

2A Union Court, 20–22 Union Road, London SW4 6JP
*tel* 020-7819 3990 *fax* 020-7819 3998
*Directors* Paula G. Breslich, K.B. Dunning

Books produced from MS to bound copy stage from
in-house ideas. Specialising in crafts, interiors, health,
children's classics and fairy tales. Founded 1978.

## Bridgewater Book Company

The Old Candlemakers, West Street, Lewes,
East Sussex BN7 2NZ
*tel* (01273) 403120 *fax* (01273) 487441
*email* (surname)@bridgewaterbooks.co.uk
*website* www.bridgewaterbooks.co.uk
*Directors* Terry Jeavons (managing), Peter
Bridgewater, Jenny Manstead

Provides full editorial, design (and where required,
production) service to develop ideas owned by its
publishing clients. Specialises in building entire lists
of illustrated books in all subject areas; developing
individual titles; designing jackets/covers; producing
sales material; rebranding. Opportunities for
freelances. Part of the Ivy Publishing Group.

## John Brown Junior

The New Boathouse, 136–142 Bramley Road,
London W10 6SR
*tel* 020-7565 3000 *fax* 020-7565 3060
*email* info@jbjunior.com
*website* www.jbjunior.com
*Directors* Andrew Jarvis (managing), Sara Lynn
(creative)

Creative development and packaging of children's
products including books, magazines, partworks,
CD-Roms and websites.

## The Brown Reference Group Plc

8 Chapel Place, Rivington Street,
London EC2A 3DQ
*tel* 020-7920 7500 *fax* 020-7920 7501
*email* info@brownreference.com
*website* www.brownreference.com
*Managing Director* Sharon Hutton, *Children's
Publisher* Anne O'Daly

Book, partwork and continuity set packaging services
for trade, promotional and international publishers.
Opportunities for freelances. Founded 1989.

## Brown Wells & Jacobs Ltd

Foresters Hall, 25–27 Westow Street, London SE19 3RY
*tel* 020-8771 5115 *fax* 020-8771 9994
*email* graham@popking.demon.co.uk
*website* www.bwj.org
*Director* Graham Brown

Design, editorial, illustration and production of
high-quality non-fiction illustrated children's
books. Specialities include pop-up and novelty
books. Opportunities for freelances. Founded 1979.

## Cambridge Language Services Ltd

Greystones, Allendale, Northumberland NE47 9PX
*tel* (01434) 683200 *fax* (01434) 683200
*email* paul@oakleaf.demon.co.uk
*Managing Director* Paul Procter

Suppliers to publishers, societies and other
organisations of customised database management

systems, with advanced retrieval mechanisms, and electronic publishing systems for the preparation of dictionaries, reference books, encyclopedias, catalogues, journals, archives. PC (windows) based. Founded 1982.

## Cambridge Publishing Management Ltd
149B Histon Road, Cambridge CB4 3JD
*tel* (01223) 367288 *fax* (01223) 368237
*email* initial.surname@cambridgepm.co.uk
*website* www.cambridgepm.co.uk
*Managing Director* Jackie Dobbyne, *Publishing Director* Julia Morris

Creative editorial and book production company specialising in complete project management of education, ELT, travel and illustrated non-fiction titles, from MS to delivery of final files on disk. Opportunities for freelances. Founded 1999.

## Cameron & Hollis
PO Box 1, Moffat, Dumfriesshire DG10 9SU
*tel* (01683) 220808 *fax* (01683) 220012
*email* editorial@cameronbooks.co.uk
*website* www.cameronbooks.co.uk
*Directors* Ian A. Cameron, Jill Hollis

Illustrated non-fiction: fine arts (including environmental and land art), film, the decorative arts, crafts, architecture, design, antiques, collecting. Founded 1976.

### Edition
Design, editing, typesetting, production work from concept to finished book for galleries, museums, institutions and other publishers. Founded 1976.

## Canopus Publishing Ltd
27 Queen Square, Bristol BS1 4ND
*tel* 0117-922 6660 *fax* 0117-922 6660
*email* robin@canopusbooks.com
*website* www.canopusbooks.com
*Director* Robin Rees

Highly illustrated popular science and astronomy titles for international markets. Founded 1999.

## Carroll & Brown Ltd
20 Lonsdale Road, London NW6 6RD
*tel* 020-7372 0900 *fax* 020-7372 0460
*email* mail@carrollandbrown.co.uk
*Directors* Amy Carroll (managing), Denise Brown (creative)

Editorial and design through to final film and printing of cookery, health, craft, Mind, Body & Spirit, and lifestyle titles. Opportunities for freelances. Founded 1989.

## Cowley Robinson Publishing Ltd
8 Belmont, Bath BA1 5DZ
*tel* (01225) 339999 *fax* (01225) 339995
*website* www.cowleyrobinson.com

*Directors* Lee Robinson (chairman), Stewart Cowley (publishing), Rob Kendrew (production)

Children's international co-editions. Novelty format creation. Licence and character publishing developments. Information and early learning. Founded 1998.

## Design Eye Ltd
4th Floor, The Fitzpatrick Building,
188–194 York Way, London N7 9QP
*tel* 020-7700 7654 *fax* 020-7700 3890
*Managing Director* Jeffrey Nobbs

Packager and publisher of interactive kit books for adults and children: arts and crafts, science, history and fiction. Opportunities for freelances. Member of the Quarto Group. Founded 1988.

## Diagram Visual Information Ltd
195 Kentish Town Road, London NW5 2JU
*tel* 020-7482 3633 *fax* 020-7482 4932
*email* diagramvis@aol.com
*Director* Bruce Robertson

Research, writing, design and illustration of reference books, supplied as film or disk. Opportunities for freelances. Founded 1967.

## Eddison Sadd Editions Ltd
St Chad's House, 148 King's Cross Road,
London WC1X 9DH
*tel* 020-7837 1968 *fax* 020-7837 2025
*email* reception@eddisonsadd.co.uk
*Directors* Nick Eddison, Ian Jackson, David Owen, Elaine Partington, Susan Cole

Illustrated non-fiction books and kits for the international co-edition market. Broad, popular list with emphasis on Mind, Body & Spirit and complementary health. Founded 1982.

## Elm Grove Books Ltd
Elm Grove, Henstridge,
Somerset BA8 0TQ
*tel* (01963) 362498 *fax* (01963) 362982
*email* elmgrovebooks@aol.com
*Directors* Hugh Elwes, Susie Elwes

Packager of children's books. Opportunities for freelances. Founded 1993.

## Endeavour London Ltd
813 Fulham Road, London SW6 5H6
*tel* 020-7348 7262 *fax* 020-7348 7260
*email* endeavourlondon@btopenworld.com
*website* www.endeavourgroupuk.com
*Directors* Charles Merollo (managing),
Sam Hudson (editorial), Franciska Pira (production)

Packager specialising in illustrated books on history, travel and topography. Founded 1996.

## First Rank Publishing

51 Cuckfield Road, Hurstpierpoint, Hassocks,
West Sussex BN6 9RR
*tel* (01273) 834680 *fax* (01273) 831629
*email* byronajacobs@aol.com
*Proprietor* Byron Jacobs

Packager and publisher of sports, games and leisure
books. No unsolicited MSS but ideas and synopses
welcome. Payment usually fees. Also provides
editorial, production and typesetting services.
Founded 1996.

## Focus Publishing

Focus Publishing (Sevenoaks) Ltd,
11A St Botolph's Road, Sevenoaks,
Kent TN13 3AJ
*tel* (01732) 742456 *fax* (01732) 743381
*email* info@focus-publishing.co.uk
*website* www.focus-publishing.co.uk
*Directors* Guy Croton, Caroline Watson

Illustrated non-fiction: gardening, wine and food,
sex and health, sport, aviation, DIY and crafts,
transport. Opportunities for freelances. Founded
1997.

## Graham-Cameron Publishing & Illustration

The Studio, 23 Holt Road, Sheringham,
Norfolk NR26 8NB
*tel* (01263) 821333 *fax* (01263) 821334
*email* forename@graham-cameron.com
*website* www.graham-cameron-illustration.com
*and* 59 Redvers Road, Brighton BN2 4BF
*tel* (01273) 385890
*Directors* Mike Graham-Cameron (managing),
Helen Graham-Cameron (art), Duncan
Graham-Cameron (marketing)

Educational and children's books; information
publications; sponsored publications. Illustration
agency with 37 artists. Do not send unsolicited
MSS. Founded 1984.

## Haldane Mason Ltd

PO Box 34196, London NW10 3YB
*tel* 020-8459 2131 *fax* 020-8728 1216
*email* info@haldane.masoncom
*Directors* Ron Samuel, Sydney Francis

Packager of books on alternative health and
children's non-fiction. Opportunities for freelances.
Founded 1995.

## Hardlines Ltd

Park Street, Charlbury, Oxon OX7 3PS
*tel* (01608) 811255 *fax* (01608) 811442
*email* info@hardlines.co.uk
*website* www.hardlines.co.uk
*Managing Director* R. Hickey, *Directors* P. Wilkinson,
G. Walker

Primary, secondary academic education (geography,
science, modern languages) and co-editions (travel
guides, gardening, cookery). Multimedia (CD-Rom
programming and animations). Opportunities for
freelances. Founded 1985.

## Hart McLeod Ltd

14 Greenside, Waterbeach, Cambridge CB5 9HP
*tel* (01223) 861495 *fax* (01223) 862902
*email* inhouse@hartmcleod.co.uk
*website* www.hartmcleod.co.uk
*Directors* Graham Hart, Chris McLeod

Primarily educational and general non-fiction with
particular experience of revision books, school texts,
ELT. Opportunities for freelances. Founded 1985.

## The Ivy Press Ltd

The Old Candlemakers, West Street, Lewes,
East Sussex BN7 2NZ
*tel* (01273) 487440 *fax* (01273) 487441
*email* surname@ivypress.co.uk
*Directors* Peter Bridgewater, Jenny Manstead, Terry
Jeavons, Sophie Collins

Packagers of illustrated trade books on art, lifestyle,
popular culture, design, health and Mind, Body &
Spirit. Opportunities for authors and freelances.
Founded 1995.

## Lennard Books

Windmill Cottage, Mackerye End, Harpenden,
Herts. AL5 5DR
*tel* (01582) 715866
*email* stephenson@lennardqap.co.uk
*Directors* K.A.A. Stephenson, R.H. Stephenson

Commissioned projects only. Division of Lennard
Associates Ltd.

## Lexus Ltd

60 Brook Street, Glasgow G40 2AB
*tel* 0141-556 0440 *fax* 0141-556 2202
*email* peterterrell@lexusforlanguages.co.uk
*website* www.lexusforlanguages.co.uk
*Director* P.M. Terrell

Reference book publishing (especially bilingual
dictionaries) as contractor, packager, consultant;
translation. Founded 1980.

## Lionheart Books – now incorporated into Bender Richardson White

## Lion Hudson International Co-Editions

Concorde House, Grenville Place,
London NW7 3SA
*tel* 020-8959 3668 *fax* 020-8959 3678
*email* coed@angushudson.com
*website* www.angushudson.com
*Managing Director* Nicholas Jones

Adult and children's Christian books including

international co-editions. Publishing imprints: Candle Books, Monarch Books. Founded 1971 as Angus Hudson; merged with Lion Publishing in 2004.

## Little People Books
The Home of BookBod, Knighton, Radnorshire LD7 1UP
*tel* (01547) 520925
*email* lpb@btclick.com
*website* www.geocities.com/fruitwrappers/magikory.html
*Directors* Grant Jessé (production and managing), Helen Wallis (rights and finance)

Packager of audio, children's educational and textbooks, digital publications, water environment. Parent company: Grant Jessé UK.

## Market House Books Ltd
2 Market House, Market Square, Aylesbury, Bucks. HP20 1TN
*tel* (01296) 484911 *fax* (01296) 437073
*email* books@mhbref.com
*website* www.mhbref.com
*Directors* Dr Alan Isaacs, Dr John Daintith, P.C. Sapsed

Compilation of dictionaries, encyclopedias, and reference books. Founded 1970.

## Marshall Cavendish Partworks Ltd
119 Wardour Street, London W1F 0UW
*tel* 020-7734 6710 *fax* 020-7734 6221
*website* www.marshallcavendish.co.uk
*Group Editor* Rebecca Fry

Cookery, crafts, gardening, do-it-yourself, history, children's interests, general illustrated non-fiction. Founded 1969.

## Marshall Editions Ltd
The Old Brewery, 6 Blundell Street, London N7 9BH
*tel* 020-7700 6700 *fax* 020-7700 4191
*email* info@marshalleditions.com
*Publisher* Hilary Arnold

Highly illustrated non-fiction for adults and children, including history, health, gardening, home design, pets, natural history, popular science.

## Monkey Puzzle Media Ltd
Gissing's Farm, Fressingfield, Eye, Suffolk IP21 5SH
*tel* (01379) 588044 *fax* (01379) 588055
*email* rgc@ndirect.co.uk
*Director* Roger Goddard-Coote

High-quality illustrated children's and adult non-fiction for trade, institutional and mass markets worldwide. Publishers' commissions undertaken. Founded 1998.

## Myriad Editions
6–7 Old Steine, Brighton BN1 1EJ
*tel* (01273) 606700 *fax* (01273) 606708
*email* candida@myriadeditions.com
*website* www.myriadeditions.com
*Directors* Candida Lacey (managing), Paul Jeremy, Corinne Pearlman

Provides print and online solutions for presenting world and national data in visual and accessible forms. Specialises in politics, sustainable development, health issues, economic and social trends. Founded 1993.

## Orpheus Books Ltd
2 Church Green, Witney, Oxon OX28 4AW
*tel* (01993) 774949 *fax* (01993) 700330
*email* info@orpheusbooks.com
*website* www.orpheusbooks.com
*Executive Director* Nicholas Harris (editorial, design and marketing)

Children's illustrated non-fiction/reference. Opportunities for freelance artists. Founded 1993.

## Paragon Publishing
4 North Street, Rothersthorpe, Northants NN7 3JB
*tel* (01604) 832149
*email* mark.webb@tesco.net
*website* www.eteacher.uk.com
*Proprietor* Mark Webb

Packagers of non-fiction books: architecture and design, educational and textbooks, electronic (academic and professional), languages and linguistics, sports and games.

## Playne Books Ltd
Park Court Barn, Trefin, Haverfordwest, Pembrokeshire SA62 5AU
*tel* (01348) 837073 *fax* (01348) 837063
*email* playne.books@virgin.net
*Design and Production* David Playne, *Editor* Gill Davies

Specialises in highly illustrated adult non-fiction and books for very young children. All stages of production undertaken from initial concept (editorial, design and manufacture) to delivery of completed books. Include sae for return of work. Founded 1987.

## Tony Potter Publishing Ltd
1 Stairbridge Court, Bolney Grange Business Park, Stairbridge Lane, Bolney, West Sussex RH17 5PA
*tel* (01444) 232889 *fax* (01444) 232142
*email* sheilamortimer@zoo.co.uk
*website* www.tonypotter.com
*Directors* Tony Potter (managing), Christine Potter, Sheila Mortimer

Creates custom children's book and own brand innovative paper-based products for children and adults. Also creates high-quality children's titles as a packager and occasionally publishes under its own imprint: Tony Potter Publishing. Opportunities for freelance designers. Founded 1997.

## Quantum Publishing
6 Blundell Street, London N7 8BH
*tel* 020-7700 6700 *fax* 020-7700 4191
*email* quantum@quarto.com
*website* www.quarto.com
*Publisher* Isabel Leao

Packager of a wide range of non-fiction titles. Part of the Quarto Group. Founded 1995.

## Quarto Children's Books Ltd
3rd Floor, The Fitzpatrick Building, 188–194 York Way, London N7 9QP
*tel* 020-7607 3322 *fax* 020-7700 2951
*Editorial Director* Beck Ward, *Managing Director* Clyde Hunter

Highly illustrated children's non-fiction and fiction books.

### Apple Press (imprint)
Leisure, domestic and craft pursuits; cookery, gardening, sport, transport, children's.

## Quarto Publishing plc/Quintet Publishing Ltd
The Old Brewery, 6 Blundell Street, London N7 9BH
*tel* 020-7700 6700 *fax* 020-7700 4191
*Publisher (Quarto)* Piers Spence, *Publisher (Quintet)* Ian Costello-Cortes, *Directors* L.F. Orbach, R.J. Morley, M.J. Mousley

International co-editions. Founded 1976/1984.

## Savitri Books Ltd
25 Lisle Lane, Ely, Cambridgeshire CB7 4AS
*tel* (01353) 654327 *fax* (01353) 654327
*email* munni@savitribooks.demon.co.uk
*Director* Mrinalini S. Srivastava

Packaging, publishing, design, production. Founded 1983.

## Studio Cactus Ltd
13 Southgate Street, Winchester, Hants SO23 9DZ
*tel* (01962) 878600 *fax* (01962) 859278
*email* mail@studiocactus.co.uk
*website* www.studiocactus.co.uk
*Editorial Director* Damien Moore, *Art Director* Amanda Lunn

High-quality illustrated non-fiction books for the international market. Undertakes book packaging/production service, from initial concept to delivery of final electronic files. Opportunities for freelances. Founded 1998.

## Tangerine Designs Ltd
2 High Street, Freshford, Bath BA2 7WE
*tel* (01225) 722382 *fax* (01225) 722856
*email* tangerinedesigns@aol.com
*Managing Director* Christine Swift

Packagers and co-edition publishers of children's books including novelty books and licensed titles. New licensed character properties available in 2004. Submissions only accepted if sae is enclosed. Founded 2000.

## The Templar Company plc
Pippbrook Mill, London Road, Dorking, Surrey RH4 1JE
*tel* (01306) 876361 *fax* (01306) 889097
*email* info@templar.co.uk
*website* www.templar.co.uk
*Directors* Amanda Wood, Ruth Huddleston, Elaine Hunt

Children's gift, novelty, picture and illustrated information books; most titles aimed at international co-edition market. Established links with major co-publishers in USA, Australia and throughout Europe. Imprints: Templar Publishing, Amazing Baby.

## Toucan Books Ltd
3rd Floor, 89 Charterhouse Street, London EC1M 6HR
*tel* 020-7250 3388 *fax* 020-7250 3123
*Directors* Robert Sackville West, Ellen Dupont

International co-editions; editorial, design and production services. Founded 1985.

## Emma Treehouse Ltd
Little Orchard House, Mill Lane, Beckington, Somerset BA11 6SN
*tel* (01373) 831215 *fax* (01373) 831216
*email* info@emmatreehouse.com
*website* www.emmatreehouse.com
*Directors* David Bailey, Richard Powell (creative & editorial)

Specialist creator of novelty books for children aged 0–7: bath books, books with a sound concept, cloth books, novelty books, flap books, touch-and-feel books. Packager and co-edition publisher with international recognition for its innovative and often unique concepts. The company has produced over 25 million books, translated into 33 different languages. Opportunities for freelance artists. Founded 1992

## Tucker Slingsby Ltd
Roebuck House, 288 Upper Richmond Road West, London SW14 7JG
*tel* 020-8876 6310 *fax* 020-8876 4104
*email* firstname@tuckerslingsby.co.uk
*Directors* Janet Slingsby, Del Tucker

Packager specialising in highly illustrated books and magazines. Creation, editorial and design to disk, film or finished copy of children's books, magazines and general interest adult titles. Commissioned work undertaken. Opportunities for freelances and picture book artists. Founded 1992.

## Ventura Publishing Ltd

80 Strand, London WC2R 0RL
*tel* 020-7010 3000 *fax* 020-7010 6707
*email* funwithspot@penguin.co.uk
*website* www.funwithspot.com
*Managing Director* Sally Floyer

Specialises in production of the *Spot* books by Eric Hill.

## Wordwright Books

8 St Johns Road, Saxmundham, Suffolk IP17 1BE
*tel* (01728) 604204 *fax* (01728) 604029
*email* wordwright@clara.co.uk
*Director* Charles Perkins

Full packaging/production service – from concept to delivery of film or finished copies. Produces illustrated non-fiction. Also assesses and prepares MSS for the US market. Publishes a small general fiction list. Founded 1987.

## Working Partners Ltd

1 Albion Place, London W6 0QT
*tel* 020-8748 7477 *fax* 020-8748 7450
*email* enquiries@workingpartnersltd.co.uk
*website* www.workingpartnersltd.co.uk
*Chairman* Ben Baglio, *Managing Director* Chris Snowdon, *Creative Director* Rod Ritchie, *Editorial Director* Deborah Smith

Children's and young adult fiction – series, trilogies, single titles. Founded 1995.

# Understanding the publishing process

To anyone who has never worked in publishing the way in which a manuscript is turned into a book can seem like magic but in reality, the process is fairly straightforward. However, no two publishing houses (big or small) do things quite alike and the real magic comes in the way that the different departments work together to give every book the best possible chance of success. Bill Swainson explains the process.

For the purposes of this article I have assumed a medium-sized publishing house, big enough to have a fairly clear division of roles – in smaller houses these roles frequently overlap – and I talk mainly about original publishing.

To begin at the beginning. Communication is everything in publishing and while more and more business is done by email, publishers still receive the majority of their submissions by post. So, the post-room staff, the computer wizards, the office management team, the receptionist who answers the telephone or welcomes visitors, all play a vital part in the process of making books. But it is the managing director who is the 'fat controller' of a company, and who draws all the threads together and gives the company its direction and drive.

### Editorial

Every editorial department has a similar staff structure: commissioning editors (sometimes called acquiring editors) who take on a book and become its champion in the company, copy-editors (sometimes called desk editors) who do the close work on the manuscript, and editorial assistants who support them.

Every publishing company acquires their books from similar sources: literary agents and scouts, other publishers throughout the world, a direct commission from editor to author and, very occasionally, by unsolicited proposal (known unceremoniously in the business as the 'slush pile'). The in-house process goes something like this: the commissioning editor will make a case for a book's acceptance at an 'acquisitions meeting' which is attended by all the other departments directly involved in publishing the book, including sales, marketing, publicity and rights. Lively discussions follow and final decisions are determined from a mixture of commercial good sense (estimated sales figures, likely production costs and an author's track record) and taste – and every company's and every editor's taste is different.

Shortly after acquisition, an 'advance information' sheet is drafted by the commissioning editor. This is the earliest attempt to harness the excitement that led to the book being signed, and it contains all the basic information needed by the rest of the company, including the title, ISBN, format, extent (length), price, rights holder, sales points, short blurb and biographical note. It is the first of many pieces of 'copy' that will be written about the book, and will be used as the template for all others, such as a catalogue entry, jacket blurb or press release.

It is now that the journey of the book really begins, with the finishing line some 10–12 months away. As soon as it arrives in the editorial department the manuscript will receive a 'structural edit'. This involves looking at the book as a whole, everything from its structure and narrative pacing to characterisation and general style, and in the case of non-fiction, looking at illustrations, appendices, bibliography, notes and index. The actual copy-editing usually only takes place when all of the main structural editorial decisions have been made. While commissioning editors may see certain titles through from beginning to end, it is more likely that they'll pass them to their editorial team to manage, while still keeping a watching brief on every aspect of publication. It is at this stage that the more detailed work begins.

The copy-edit is another filtering process done with a very fine mesh net, designed to catch all the errors and inconsistencies in the text, from spelling and punctuation to facts, figures and tics of style. In some publishing houses this is work is done onscreen, but surprisingly many editors prefer to work direct on the typescript because it is easier to spot changes and see where decisions have been made along the way. Once the copy-edit has been completed, the author will be asked to answer any queries that may have arisen. When the commissioning editor, copy-editor and author are happy that the marked-up typescript is in the best possible shape, it is sent to the production department for design and typesetting.

From now on the book will shuttle between the editorial and production departments in the form of proofs, usually in three separate stages. First proofs are read by the author and a proofreader. This is the author's last chance to make any cuts or additions as amendments after this stage become tricky and expensive to implement. Both sets of amendments are then collated and sent to the production department to be made into second proofs. (An index will be compiled at this stage.) Second proofs, or 'revises', are checked against the collated first proofs and any last-minute queries are attended to. They are then returned to the production department to be made into 'final' proofs. Final proofs are, in a perfect publishing world, what the name implies. They are checked against the second proofs, the index (if there is one) is proofread, the prelim pages double-checked and when all is present and correct – the text is ready for press.

## Design

The design department's work on a new book begins usually 10 months in advance of the publication date. Hardback jackets and the paperback covers are publishing's main selling tool. People say you can't judge a book by its cover, but because most (if not all) buying decisions are made by the trade's buyers before the book is printed – up until that time the cover *is* the book. It's what makes the buyer believe in a book enough to order it, and it's one of the most important things that makes a browsing customer pick up a book in the bookshop and pay for it at the till.

Design also produces all other sales material that the marketing department decides it needs to make a good job of the 'sell in', including catalogues, order forms, 'blads' (illustrated sales material), 'samplers' (booklets containing tantalising extracts), posters, book proofs (bound reading proofs) and advertisements.

Most companies try to develop a distinctive look for their books and it's the design department that creates it.

## Production

The production department handles all aspects of book production including text design, although some of the very big companies have a separate department for this. The production department style (or format) the copy-edited typescript by drafting a brief known as a 'type specification' or 'spec'. The spec may be designed specifically for a unique book, or if the book is part of a series, the series spec will be used to give the books the same look and feel. The typescript is then usually despatched to an out-of-house typesetter, although some companies do typesetting in-house, to be made to page proofs. Meanwhile, the production manager (working with the commissioning editor) will choose the binding materials and any embellishments, such as headband, coloured or printed endpapers, or marker ribbon. The print run is also decided (based on advance sales and track record) and an order is placed with the printer.

Most publishing companies use only a few printers, negotiating the best possible rate per book depending on the volume of work they agree to place with the printer. A key role of the production department is to buy print at a rate that allows each tightly budgeted book to make money, and equally important (especially when a book takes off) to manage the supply of reprints so that the publisher's warehouse is never short of stock.

## Sales

'Selling in' in the home market (Britain and Ireland) is done by a team of sales representatives. The reps visit bookshops in their designated area and try to achieve the set sales targets for each book. The number of copies sold pre-publication is known as the subscription sale, or 'sub'.

Selling books effectively to bookshops, both chains and independents and nowadays to supermarkets and other retailers, takes time and careful planning. The British and Irish book trade has developed in such a way that the sales cycle has extended to cover the best part of a year. Even though the actual business of selling may not begin in earnest until eight or nine months prior to publication, the work of preparing sales material begins up to a year ahead. It can, however, be achieved in a shorter time frame and this allows a degree of flexibility for the publisher in case of a crisis or to take advantage of prime opportunities, such as issuing instant books on a burning topic of the day.

Many sales are also made in-house by phone, email and fax and, nowadays, the internet. Many publishers have their own websites and provide customers with the opportunity to buy their books either directly or by a link to another bookselling website. Book clubs still remain an important market for publishers, but they are having a tough time of it in the face of stiff competition from the internet and supermarket sales.

Export sales are achieved using teams of international agents and reps run from in-house by the export sales department. While the bigger companies tend to have their own teams and the smaller companies use freelance agencies and reps, all face a different range of challenges to the home sales team. Here format, discount, royalty rates, shipping, and exchange rates are the key components. The margins are much tighter and it requires a lot of skill and *chutzpah* to generate significant sales and then to maintain a successful international prescence.

## Marketing

It could be said that the marketing department is the engine room of the sales department. It's responsible for preparing all the sales material (catalogues, blads, samplers, etc) used by the sales team to persuade others in the book trade to buy the company's books. Marketing also works alongside the sales department in dealing directly with the big bookshops on special promotions ('Book of the Month', '3 for 2', etc) that are now such a common feature of the larger chains.

This department also prepares the advertising for the trade, such as the post-publication press advertising that, along with reviews and other publicity, persuades customers into the shops to buy a particular book. It also organises the company sales conferences where the new season's publishing is for the first time presented to the sales reps and overseas agents. It's an exciting time and stimulates many of the best ideas on how to sell the new books.

## Publicity

As the marketing department works to sell books with the emphasis on the 'sell in', the publicity department works with the author and the media on 'free' publicity with the emphasis on the 'sell through'. This covers reviews, features, author interviews, bookshop readings and signings, festival appearances, book tours and radio and television interviews and so on.

For each author and their book, the publicity department devises a campaign that will play to the book's or the author's strengths. For instance, best use will be made of written features or radio interviews for authors who are shy in public, just as full advantage will be made of public appearances for those authors who thrive on the thrill of showmanship. In short, the publicist's careful work (which like much of publishing is a mixture of inspiration and enthusiasm on the one hand and efficient planning and flexibility on the other) is designed to get the best results for each individual author and book.

## Rights

It is the aim of the rights department to make the best use of all the rights that were acquired when the contract was first negotiated between publisher and author or the author's agent.

While literary agents are understandably keen to handle foreign and serial rights, many publishing houses have well-developed rights departments with good contacts and are also well placed to sell the rights of a book. Selling rights is very varied and includes anything from requests for film or television rights, translation rights to other countries, or serial rights to a newspaper, to smaller permission requests to reprint a poem or an extract. All are opportunities to promote the book and earn additional income for author and publisher, and at the time of first publication the rights, sales, marketing and publicity departments all work closely together.

Book fairs are key venues for the sale of foreign rights. At the Frankfurt Book

Fair in October and at the London Book Fair in March, publishers and agents from all participating countries meet to form a rights 'bazaar'. Here, editors have the opportunity to hear about and buy new books from publishing houses all over the world. Occasionally rights are sold on the spot, but more commonly the acquisition process is completed later.

## Paperbacks

Paperbacks are published approximately a year after the original publication. Paperback publishing is a key part of publishing today but is a quite different skill to hardback publishing, and is in many respects all about marketing. Efforts are made to identify and broaden the likely market (readership) for a book, making sure that the cover and presentation will appeal to a wide audience, and being ingenious about positioning an author's books in the marketplace where they can be best seen, bought and read. The means used vary from in-store promotions and advertising campaigns to author-led publicity and renewed press coverage in the paperback round-ups. But the energy that drives this inspired and careful work of reinvention comes from the paperback publisher's vision and passion for the book, author and the list as a whole.

## Accounts

Finally, every successful business needs a good finance department. Most publishing houses split the work into two areas – purchase ledger and royalties. Purchase ledger deals with all incoming invoices associated with the company's business. The royalties department deals exclusively with author advances (payable on acquisition, and on delivery or publication of a book) and with keeping account of the different royalty percentages payable on book sales, serial deals, film rights, permissions, etc. This is done so both author and agent can see that an accurate record has been kept against the day when the book earns back its advance (the point at which the royalties earned equal the advance paid) and the author starts earning additional income.

## A special business

This has been a potted breakdown of the inner workings of a medium-sized company. Publishing is a business, and commercial considerations will be apparent in every department, but it is a very special kind of business, one which frequently breaks many of the accepted business rules and often seems to make no sense at all – just think of the hundreds of different lines, formats, price points and discounts. At times it shouldn't work – but somehow, miraculously, it does.

**Bill Swainson** has worked for small, medium and large publishers since 1976 and is currently a Senior Commissioning Editor at Bloomsbury Publishing Plc. He is the editor of *The Encarta Book of Quotations* (Bloomsbury 2000).

## See also...
- *Year-in-view of the publishing industry*, page 268
- *Book distribution*, page 264
- *Helping to market your book*, page 260
- *Who owns whom in publishing*, page 272
- *The role of the literary agent*, 393

# Notes from a successful fiction author

Joanna Trollope shares her experiences of writing success.

I once said to a journalist – rather crossly – that it had only taken me 20 years to be an overnight success. This was in 1993, with my first number one (the paperback of *The Rector's Wife*) and the accompanying media assumption that I had come from nowhere to somewhere at meteoric speed.

People do, of course. Rare, rare people do, but most of us are trudging for years across the creative plateau, honing our skills and cajoling our sinking hearts and *hoping*. I wrote my first published book when my younger daughter was three. When *The Rector's Wife* appeared, she was almost 23, and there'd been 10 books in the interim. Hardly *Bridget Jones*. Scarcely *White Teeth*.

But, on reflection, the long haul suited me. I learned about structure and dialogue and pace and characterisation at my own pace. I might have started with a readership so small it was almost invisible to the naked eye, but it grew, and it grew steadily in a manner that made it feel reliable, as is the case with long-term friendships. It also meant that when success came, it was absolutely lovely, no doubt about that, but there was no question of it turning my middle-aged head.

When I wrote my first published book – a historical novel called *Eliza Stanhope* set around the battle of Waterloo – the publishing climate was very different to how it is now. Many of the great publishing individuals were still alive, agents were a scarcer breed and writing was not seen as a way to becoming instantly, absurdly rich (and, in my view, never should be). I sent my manuscript – poorly typed on thin paper – off to Hamish Hamilton in a brown paper parcel. It was politely returned. I sent it – heart definitely in sink – to Hutchinson. They wrote back – a letter I still have – and invited me, like a job interview, to 'come and discuss my future'.

Even if the rest is history, it is not easy or simple history. There weren't any great dramas, to be sure, no cupboards stuffed with rejection slips, no pulped copies (that came later), but what there was instead was a simply enormous amount of perseverance. I don't want to sound too austere, but I find I rather believe in perseverance when it comes to writing. As V.S. Pritchett once said, most people write better if they *practise*.

And I have to say that I am still practising. I think it very unlikely that I will ever feel I have got it right, and I would be uneasy if that feeling went away. After all, only a very few geniuses – Sophocles, Shakespeare – could claim to be prophets or inventors. Most writers are translators or interpreters of the human condition, but no more. A hefty dose of humility in writing seems to me both seemly and healthy.

Readers, after all, are no fools. Readers may not have a writer's gift of the arrangement of events and people and language, but they know about life and humanity all right. They may even know much more about both than the writer. So not only must they never be forgotten, but they must never be underestimated or patronised either.

Which is one of the reasons, in my case, why I research my novels. For the readers' sake, as well as my own, I have to be as accurate as possible about, say, being the child of a broken home, or the widow of a suicide, or a mistress or an adopted man in his thirties. So, once I've decided upon the theme of a novel (and those can have brewed in my brain for years or be triggered by a chance remark overheard on a bus) I go and talk to people who are in the situation that I am exploring. And I have to say that in all the years of working this way, no one has ever turned me down, and everyone has exceeded my expectations.

This habit has had an unlooked-for advantage. During all the years I've been writing, the business of promotion has grown and grown, and fiction is notoriously difficult to talk about in any medium. But the research gives me – and journalists – subject matter which is, to my relief, honourably relevant but, at the same time, miles away from the inexplicable private, frequently uncomfortable place where writing actually goes on. 'Tell me,' people say, not actually understanding what they are asking, 'Tell me how you write'. Pass.

**Joanna Trollope** is the author of 12 contemporary novels, as well as a number of historical novels published under the name of Caroline Harvey, and a study of women in the British Empire called *Britannia's Daughters*. She divides her time between London and the Cotswolds.

# Notes from a successful non-fiction author

Simon Winchester shares his experiences of writing success.

The research is all done, the reading is complete. Files have been pored over, archives have been plundered. Those Who Know have been consulted. That Which Was Unknown has been explained and one fondly prays, made clear. I am, in consequence, or so I hope, now fully steeped in facts and awash with understanding. The book I have been planning for so very long is at last all in the forefront of my mind – structure, content, tone, pace and rhythm are all there. What now remains is simply – would that it were *simply* – to write it: 100,000 words, says the contract, due in just 100 days.

I live on a farm in the Berkshire Hills of western Massachusetts, and I have a small and ancient wooden barn, 100 yards or so from the main house. I have furnished it with books and a long desk on which are a variety of computers and two typewriters, one manual, the other electric. The farm is where I live. The barn is where I work. Each morning, well before the sun is up, I leave the comforts of the farm and enter this spartan, bookish little universe, and shut the allurements of domesticity behind me for the day. For a 100 days, in fact: for a 100 identical days of a solitary, writerly routine that, for me at least, is the only way I know to get a book properly and fully written.

Inside the barn I tend to follow an unvarying routine. First, as the dawn breaks, I spend two hours looking back over what I wrote the day before: I examine it with what I hope is a sharp and critical eye, checking it for infelicities of language, impropriety of grammar, expanding the inexact, refining the imprecise, making as certain as I can the minutiae of fact and detail. Only when I feel satisfied (never smug) that what I have on the screen represents as good a first draft as I can offer do I press the *print* button on the keyboard, and a few pages of A4 slither into the out-tray. Once that task is done I leave the barn and walk through the early sunlight back to the house for breakfast. I read the papers, drink enough coffee to kick-start both mind and body, and, at nine exactly, I head back again, this time to write for real.

I have a word counter at the top left of my computer screen. Purists may object, but my newspaper days have left me with deadline commitment, and this is the way that I like to work. Whenever I begin a book I set the counter with the start date, the number of words I have to write, the contract date and a very simple calculation – the number of words needed each day to meet the deadline. One hundred days, 100,000 words: 1000 words each day is the initial goal. But things change: the writing life is imperfect, however noble the intentions. Some days are good and maybe I'll write 1500 words, while others are much less satisfactory and, for a variety of reasons, I may write virtually nothing. So the following day's necessary word total will rise and fall depending on the achievement of the day before. It is that figure my system obliges me to set the night before that I'll see on my screen when I arrive in the cold dark before dawn: 1245 words needed today, with 68 more days before the deadline? So be it.

I sit down, arrange my thoughts and hammer away without stopping for the next six hours – each day from nine in the morning until three in the afternoon. This is the solitary pleasure of writing – total concentration, pure lexical heaven. I write on, oblivious to everything around me. Except that I do know when I have done my six hours – because by the time the mid-afternoon is upon me, the sun will have shifted to the window in front of my desk, and in wintertime I have to suffer an uncomfortable hour or so of the sunset's glare. This gives me a perfect excuse to end this second stage of the day and to go off to do something quite different: a run along my country road, usually, followed by tea. By then it is six or so, the sun has fully set and the glare has been replaced by twilight glow. Then I return, for the day's third and final phase: planning for the next day.

I go back to my desk and arrange the papers, books and thoughts that I think I need for the next day's writing. Then I close down the computers – having been sure, of course, to have made the necessary calculations and set the counter to tell me how many words are due on the morrow – and walk back to the house. For a while I try to forget about the book (though I never can). I have dinner, go to a movie, have friends round – and am in bed, invariably, by midnight.

The next day it begins all over again. As before, I spend the first two hours of the morning looking back over what I have written in those six sunlit hours of the day before. As soon as I have tinkered and tweaked, I press *print*. I stack the A4 sheets neatly on the pile from the preceding day. Millimetre by millimetre, day by day, the pile grows taller and thicker, looking ever more substantial. In the first week it has the look and feel of a newspaper essay; after 10 days or so, a magazine article; by a month, it's an outline, then chapter, a monograph, a dissertation – until finally, on one heaven-sent morning, I pick up the pile of paper and it has heft, weight and substance. And then it all changes.

The dream has been made solid. The former featherweight piece of ephemera has been transformed by time into a work-in-progress, a book-in-the-making. After a precisely calculated number of sunrises and sunsets, after yet more walks between barn and farmhouse, after setting and resetting the counter a score of times, and after hours spent reviewing and re-doing and printing and piling and collating and collecting – there, suddenly, is a finished product.

The pile of printed paper and digital confection of finished text will now be placed in the hands of the publishers, who by mysterious dint of designing, printing, binding and jacketing, will in due course turn it into a full-fledged book. *My* new book. After 100 days it is ready to be offered to the world. As for its fate – well, there lies ahead of it what will seem a lifetime of hoping – hoping that it will be lucky, do well and be loved by all. The wish and the prayer of any new parent, who has taken time and care to bring a newborn into the world. But that, of course, is another story. This is just the writing. What follows next is the reading, and that is much less exact of a science.

**Simon Winchester** is the author of some 20 books including *The Surgeon of Crowthorne, The Map that Changed the World, Krakatoa* and *The Meaning of Everything*. He worked as a foreign correspondent for *The Guardian* and *The Sunday Times* for 30 years before turning to full-time writing. He is currently working on a book on the 1906 earthquake and fire in San Francisco.

# Notes from a successful children's author

J.K. Rowling shares her experiences of writing success.

I can remember writing *Harry Potter and the Philosopher's Stone* in a café in Oporto. I was employed as a teacher at the language institute three doors along the road at the time, and this café was a kind of unofficial staffroom. My friend and colleague joined me at my table. When I realised I was no longer alone I hastily shuffled worksheets over my notebook, but not before Paul had seen exactly what I was doing. 'Writing a novel, eh?' he asked wearily, as though he had seen this sort of behaviour in foolish young teachers only too often before. '*Writers' & Artists' Yearbook*, that's what you need,' he said. 'Lists all the publishers and … stuff' he advised before ordering a lager and starting to talk about the previous night's episode of *The Simpsons*.

I had almost no knowledge of the practical aspects of getting published; I knew nobody in the publishing world, I didn't even know anybody who knew anybody. It had never occurred to me that assistance might be available in book form.

Nearly three years later and a long way from Oporto, I had almost finished *Harry Potter and the Philosopher's Stone*. I felt oddly as though I was setting out on a blind date as I took a copy of the *Writers' & Artists' Yearbook* from the shelf in Edinburgh's Central Library. Paul had been right and the *Yearbook* answered my every question, and after I had read and re-read the invaluable advice on preparing a manuscript, and noted the time-lapse between sending said manuscript and trying to get information back from the publisher, I made two lists: one of publishers, the other of agents.

The first agent on my list sent my sample three chapters and synopsis back by return of post. The first two publishers took slightly longer to return them, but the 'no' was just as firm. Oddly, these rejections didn't upset me much. I was braced to be turned down by the entire list, and in any case, these were real rejection letters – even real writers had got them. And then the second agent, who was high on the list purely because I like his name, wrote back with the most magical words I have ever read: 'We would be pleased to read the balance of your manuscript on an exclusive basis…'

**J.K. Rowling** is the best-selling author of the Harry Potter series (Bloomsbury). Her first novel, *Harry Potter and the Philosopher's Stone*, was the winner of the 1997 Nestlé Smarties Gold Prize and her most recent book *Harry Potter and the Goblet of Fire* (2003) broke all records for the number of books sold on the first day of publication. In 1999 she was BA Author of the Year.

# Ghostwriting

It is possible for an unknown writer to make a living as a full-time ghostwriter.
Andrew Crofts shares some of his secrets on how to do it.

## Why do it?

The greatest problem facing any professional writer is finding a steady supply of ideas and subjects so dazzlingly certain to appeal to the book-buying public that publishers are eager to buy. Not only are saleable ideas in short supply, it also takes an inordinate amount of time to research a new subject deeply enough to be able to sell it successfully. You might spend months researching a subject from a number of different sources and still be unable to find a buyer.

One answer is to collaborate with other people who lack writing skills and experience but have good stories to tell, either as fiction or non-fiction, or possess all the necessary information to create a book.

These people can be found in a number of places. They might be celebrities, who would impress publishers because of their notoriety, or ordinary people who have undergone extraordinary experiences. Alternatively, they might be experts in subjects that the public want to know more about.

It's much easier for publishers to market books by celebrities or established experts than those by unknown writers. Apart from a handful of literary stars, few people buy books because of the authors' names, and the media have a limited amount of space in which to write about them. But if you write the autobiography of a soap star, controversial politician or sporting hero, the resulting book will be widely written and talked about in the media. While the author is spending several weeks being whistled around all day from breakfast television to late night television, the ghost can stay comfortably at home and get on with their next project.

The speed with which you can gather the information for a ghosted book means that you can produce far more publishable material in the course of a year than if you were researching each book in order to write them under your own name. Publishers are also willing to pay higher advances because they can see how they will market the book once it is written. Ghosting makes it quite possible for an unknown writer to make a good full-time living as an author. It also provides you with broad writing experience and helps you to build contacts in the publishing industry to whom you can then sell other projects of your own.

Of all the advantages that ghosting offers, however, the greatest must be the opportunities that ghosts get to meet people of interest. It's a licence to ask the sort of impertinent questions that you truly want to know the answers to, and to be allowed inside some of the most extraordinary stories.

Ghosting a book for someone is like being paid to be educated by the best teachers in the world. Imagine, for instance, being asked to ghost *The Origin of the Species* for Darwin, or *The Decline and Fall of the Roman Empire* for Gibbon; being paid to learn everything that is in their heads and then turning their thoughts, words and notes into book form. Could there be a better form of education?

## How to start

The first step could be to approach people you would like to ghost for and offer your services. That might mean your favourite celebrities, who you could write to care of their agents or television companies. It might be people you have read about in the press and who you think have stories that could be developed into books. It's usually possible to find some way of getting a letter or email to them.

A more practical first step, however, might be to approach people who you come across in everyday life and who have an expertise that you think would be popular with a wider audience. If you've been on a course, for instance, find out if the trainer has thought of turning their message into book form. Would a garage mechanic who's good at explaining why your car isn't working be able to supply the material for a book on car maintenance? What about your doctor doing a book on healthcare for a specialist sector of the market? The options are endless.

Anyone who has access to a captive marketplace, like training companies or public speakers, has a ready-made market for books. There are companies who might want to produce books by their chief executives for distribution to employees as well as to the outside world and public relations departments who would relish the idea of getting their clients' messages to wider audiences.

If you're already a writer in another field, approach your existing contacts. A show business journalist, for instance, has access to actors and singers. A sports writer can approach sportspeople they've interviewed in the past. People will nearly always prefer to work with a ghost they already know and trust and feel they have a rapport with, than with a stranger.

At the same time as approaching potential authors, you should also be letting the publishing world know that you're available to work as a ghost. Write to the literary agents and publishers listed in this *Yearbook* to let them know what your experience is and how they can contact you. They will often have clients who they know are not capable of doing their own writing.

## How to sell projects

It's unusual for any publisher to buy a book idea without seeing a synopsis and some sample material. Once you're experienced you will sometimes be able to charge for writing synopses, but at the beginning it's probably wise to offer to do it for free in order to get projects off the ground.

A synopsis must be a hard-selling document that gives the publisher all the reasons why they should commission the book. It might be worth preparing a one- or two-page version first in order to catch their attention and then a longer document (between 5000 and 10,000 words usually suffices) in order to get the message across. It must give the publishers confidence that the book will be written to a high standard and delivered on time. It must be something that their sales teams can immediately see how to sell. Give a brief biography of the author and demonstrate how promotable they will be.

Involve a literary agent, firstly because most publishers don't like dealing directly with authors and secondly because the agent can handle all the money side of the relationship, removing potential conflicts between the author and ghost.

Whenever possible, have one good agent representing both parties in the arrangement. The agent's prime interest will then be in getting the book well published, not in encouraging the ghost and the author to fight one another for larger shares of the resulting royalties. The agent can also act as a conciliatory go-between should the relationship between author and ghost break down.

## Who pays the ghost?

How the ghost gets paid will depend largely on how speculative the project is and on the wishes of the author. It might be that the author is sufficiently confident of the book's success to suggest paying the ghost a fee. How much that fee will be depends on what the author can afford, what they are willing to pay and what the ghost is willing to do the job for. In other words, it's open for negotiation.

If the project already has a publisher and there is no speculative work involved, then it may be that the publisher will suggest a fee. Then there will be little or no room for negotiation. Any writer starting out should accept any book that is offered, even if the money is low, simply in order to build up a track record.

Where there is no publisher involved at the outset, and the author has no money, then suggest splitting all the proceeds 50/50, which includes advances, royalties and foreign rights sales, serialisation fees and payments for film and television rights.

If the author is a celebrity and it's obvious the book will make a large amount of money the ghost might have to accept a lower percentage, or a percentage that will become lower once he or she has received a pre-agreed amount; e.g. the proceeds might be split 50/50 until the ghost has received £50,000, at which stage his or her share might then drop to 40%, and might then drop again at £100,000.

It would be unwise to write an entire book unless some money has been forthcoming, either from a publisher or from the author, but there are cases where even this risk is worth taking. With fiction it is nearly always necessary to write the whole book before any publisher will make an offer, making it a highly risky business. Go into it with your eyes open, knowing that it is closer to buying a lottery ticket than earning a living.

## What skills does a ghost need?

Ghosts must suppress their own egos completely when working on an autobiography – a good discipline for any writer. You're fulfilling a similar function to a barrister in court, using your skills to plead the case of your client. Authors need ghosts who will not challenge them, but will simply listen to what they have to say and understand why they did what they did. If the ghost wishes to be critical of the subject then they must step back and create an objective biography, not an autobiography.

It is essential for the ghost to make the subject feel completely comfortable in his or her company. If they think the ghost is going to criticise them, judge them or argue with them they will not relax, open up or talk honestly. It's not the ghost's job to try to make them change their opinions about anything or anyone, but rather to encourage them to tell their story in the most interesting and coherent way possible. The ghost must be able to coax them off their hobbyhorses and persuade them to answer all the questions that the eventual readers are likely to ask. The author must not sound bitter. Part of the ghost's job is to ensure that the author remains attractive and interesting to the reader.

Once the voice is on tape the ghost then has to create what amounts to an 80,000-word monologue, just as a playwright might do, staying completely in the author's character at all times, using the sort of vocabulary the author would use and expressing the same views, ideas and prejudices.

It's important that a ghost is interested in the subject; otherwise the project will become unbearable. Imagine spending that much time talking to someone who bores you, and then having to go away and write it out all over again.

A ghost must also be able to see the structure of a book from early on in the process. He or she then needs to be able to guide the subject into providing the right material, keeping them on track and clearing up any inconsistencies in the telling of the tale.

## The ghosting process

Sometimes the author has already produced some written material that can provide the bulk of the background. More often the ghost will have a clean slate to work from.

How many hours of taping will be required depends on how succinct the author can be persuaded to be and how quickly the ghost can master the subject. I find that 10–20 hours of useful taping is generally enough to produce a strong first draft. For autobiographies it's important to get them to tell you the story chronologically, so that you know what they have and have not experienced at each stage of the tale. The sequence can always be changed for dramatic effect once the actual writing commences.

It is usually preferable to interview them on their own home ground, where they will be at their most relaxed and least guarded. You will also get a better idea of what their lives are like.

The first draft should be shown to no one until the author has okayed it. They have final veto on what should and shouldn't be in the final draft. Only if they're confident that they have the final say will they be completely open and honest with you. The ghost can advise and warn, but the author has the last word. (Once given the power to make changes they nearly always decide they can't actually think of a better way of putting things and leave the manuscript virtually untouched). If there is arguing to be done, let it be done by the agent and the publisher.

A ghost must expect no glory. Enjoy the experience of the researching and the writing and of being paid to do pleasant work. Sometimes your name will get mentioned on the cover of a book and sometimes it will appear only on the flyleaf. Sometimes you will get a mention in the acknowledgements and sometimes you will not appear at all. You may get billed as 'co-author', but it is more likely to say 'By Big Shot with Joe Bloggs' or 'as told to Joe Bloggs'. It's always useful to have your name there but it can never be allowed to become a problem if it disappears.

## Why publishers use ghosts

Publishers like to use ghostwriters because they know they will be able to rely on them as professionals. They want to know that the book will arrive on time in a publishable form, conforming as nearly as possible to the synopsis or the brief.

Frequently the authors of the books are busy people and hard to get hold of. Sometimes they are temperamental. The publishers consequently rely on the ghosts to act as go-betweens and to make the process of publication as smooth as possible.

The ghost is also the subject's best friend in the publishing business. During the long months when the agent is trying to sell the project and the phone doesn't ring, he or she will assure them that this is perfectly normal and doesn't mean they will never find a publisher. When the publisher wants to change the title or favours a cover in the subject's least favourite colour, the ghost will again have to be there to assure them that it will all be okay on the night. Then, when the book comes out and the subject can't find it on the front table in any of their local book shops, the ghost will have to explain the economics of the business to them and try to dissuade them from ringing the publisher and ranting and raving.

Ghosting is an endlessly varied, interesting and rewarding job – relish every opportunity you are given to practice it.

**Andrew Crofts** was described in the *Independent* as 'the king of modern ghosts'. He has published over 40 ghosted books and has even written a novel, *Maisie's Amazing Maids* (Stratus Books 2001) with a ghostwriter as the central character. He is also the author of *The Freelance Writer's Handbook – How to make money and enjoy life* (Piatkus 2002).

# Writing and the children's book market

Over 10,000 new children's titles are published in the UK every year. Chris Kloet suggests how a potential author can best ensure that their work is published.

Children's book publishing can be difficult for the first-time writer to break into. It is a diverse, overcrowded market, with many thousands of titles currently in print, available both in the UK and from elsewhere via the internet. Children's publishers tend to fill their lists with commissioned books by writers they publish regularly, so they may lack space or be reluctant to take a risk with an untried author. This is a selective, highly competitive, market-led business. Since every new book is expected to meet its projected sales target, your writing must demonstrate solid sales potential, as well as strength and originality, if it is to stand a chance of being published.

Is your work right for today's market? Literary tastes and fashions change. Publishers cater to children whose reading is now almost certainly different from that of your own childhood. In the present electronic media-driven age, few want cosy tales about fairies and bunnies, jolly talking cars or magic teapots. Nor anything remotely imitative. Editors choose original, lively material – something witty, innovative and pacey. They look for polished writing with a fresh, contemporary voice that speaks directly and engages today's critical, media-savvy young readers, who are often easily bored.

Develop a sense of the market so that you can judge the potential for your work. Read widely and critically across the children's book spectrum for an overview, especially noting recent titles. Visit dedicated children's books websites, such as Achuka. As you read, pay attention to the different categories, series, genres and publishers' imprints. This will help you to pinpoint likely publishers. Before submitting your typescript, ensure that your targeted publisher currently publishes in your particular form or genre. Request catalogues from their marketing department; check out their website. Consult the publisher's entry under *Book publishers UK and Ireland* (see page 135). Many publishing houses now stipulate 'No unsolicited MSS or synopses'. Don't spend your time and postage sending work to them; choose instead a publisher who accepts unsolicited work.

You might consider approaching a literary agent who knows market trends, publishers' lists and the faces behind them. Most editors regard agents as filters and may prefer submissions from them, knowing that a preliminary critical eye has been cast over them.

## Picture books

Books for babies and toddlers are often board books and novelties. Unless you are also a professional illustrator (see *Illustrating for children's books*, page 251) they present few opportunities for a writer. Picture books are aimed at children aged between two and five or six, and are usually 32 pages long, giving 12–14 double-page spreads, and illustrated in colour.

Although a story written for this format should be simple, it must be

| Publisher | Series name | Length | Age group | Comments |
|---|---|---|---|---|
| Andersen Press | Tigers | 3000–5000 words 64 pages | 6–9 | B&w illustrations throughout |
| A & C Black | Black Cats | 12,000–14,000 words 96 pages | 10–12 | Short novels; b&w illustrations |
| | Chameleons | 1200 words 48 pages | 5–7 | Colour illustrations throughout |
| Bloomsbury | Young Fiction | 2500 words 64 pages | 5–7 | B&w illustrations throughout |
| | Middle Fiction | 6000 words 64 pages | 7–9 | B&w illustrations throughout |
| Collins Children's Books | Roaring Good Reads | 2000–8000 words | 7–9 | B&w illustrations throughout |
| | Collins Voyager | 20,000 words+ | 9–14 | Fantasy |
| | Collins Flamingo | 30,000–60,000 words | 13–16 | Contemporary fiction |
| Egmont Books | Blue Bananas | 1000 words 48 pages | 5+ | Colour illustrations |
| | Red Bananas | 2000 words 48 pages | 6+ | Colour illustrations |
| | Yellow Bananas | 3000 words 48 pages | 7+ | Colour illustrations |
| | Go Bananas | 1000–3000 words 48 pages | 5–7 | Curriculum-based strand |
| Franklin Watts | Leapfrog | 180 words 32 pages | 4–6 | Colour illustrations throughout |
| | Hopscotch | 350–400 words 32 pages | 5–7 | Colour illustrations throughout |
| Hodder Children's Books | Bite | 35,000+ words | 12+ | Contemporary fiction |
| | Silver | 35,000+ words | 10+ | Fantasy and science fiction |
| | Signature | 35,000+ words | 11+ | Literary fiction |
| Kingfisher | I Am Reading | 1200 words 48 pages | 5–7 | Colour illustrations throughout |
| Orchard Books | Crunchies | 1000–1500 words | 5–7 | B&w line illustrations |
| | Colour Crunchies | 1000–1500 words | 5–7 | Colour illustrations |
| | Super Crunchies | 5000 words | 7–9 | B&w line illustrations |
| | Orchard Storybooks | 7000–15,000 | 8–11 | B&w line illustrations |
| | Red Apples | 20,000–25,000 words | 9–11 | |
| | Black Apples | 30,000–40,000 words | 12+ | |
| Penguin Group | Colour Young Puffin | 1000–2500 words 32–64 pages | 5–8 | Colour illustrations |
| | Young Puffin | 8000–10,000 words 96–128 pages | 7–9 | B&w line illustrations |
| Scholastic Children's Books | Young Hippo | 3500–10,000 words 64–96 pages | 6–9 | B&w illustrations throughout |
| | Hippo | 15,000–25,000 words | 8–12 | |
| | Point | 30,000 words | 12+ | |
| Walker Books | Sprinters | 2000 words | 6–8 | B&w illustrations throughout |
| | Junior fiction | 15,000–25,000 words | 8–12 | |
| | Teenage fiction | 25,000–40,000 words | 12+ | |

structured, with a compelling beginning, middle and end. The theme should interest and be appropriate for the age and experience of its audience. As the text is likely to be reread, it should possess a satisfying rhythm (but beware of rhymes). Ideally, it should be fewer than 1000 words (and could be much shorter), must offer scope for illustration and, finally, it needs strong international appeal. Reproducing full-colour artwork is costly and the originating publisher must be confident of achieving co-productions with publishers overseas, to keep unit costs down. It has to be said: it is a tough field.

Submit a picture book text typed either on single-sided A4 sheets, showing page breaks, or as a series of numbered pages, each with its own text. Do not go into details about illustrations, but simply note anything that is not obvious from the text that needs to be included in the pictures.

## Younger fiction

This area of publishing presents opportunities for the new writer. It covers stories written for the post-picture book stage, when children are reading their first whole novels. Texts vary in length and complexity, depending on the age and fluency of the reader, but tend to be between 1000 and 6000 words long.

Publishers bring out titles under the umbrella of various series, each targeted at a particular level of reading experience and competency. Categories are: beginning or first readers, developing or newly confident, confident, and fluent readers. Note that these are not the same as reading schemes published for the schools market and do not require such a restricted vocabulary. Stories for the bottom end of the age range are usually short, straight-through narratives illustrated throughout in colour, whereas those for older children are broken down into chapters and may be illustrated in black and white. The table on page 248 lists publishers' requirements for some currently published series. Check that your material is correct in terms of length and interest level when approaching a publisher with a submission for a series.

## Genre fiction

Genre fiction is usually published in paperback series and titles are sometimes the work of a single author, but might also be novels from several authors writing in a similar vein. Some fiction aimed at teenagers is published in genre series although it is much less popular than in recent years.

## General fiction

Many novels for children aged 9–12 are published, not in series, but as 'standalone' titles, each judged on its own merits. The scope for different types of stories is wide – adventure stories, fantasies, historical novels, science fiction, ghost and horror stories, humour, and stories of everyday life. Generally, their length is 20,000–40,000 words. This is a rough guide and is by no means fixed. For example, J.K. Rowling's phenomenally successful *Harry Potter* novels weigh in at between 300–750 closely printed pages, and publishers now seem more willing to publish longer texts, particularly fantasies, which are often published as hefty trilogies.

Perhaps more than in other areas of juvenile fiction, the individual editor's tastes will play a significant part in the publishing decision, i.e they want authors' work which *they* like. They, and their sales and marketing departments, also need to feel confident of a new writer's ability to go on to write further books for their lists – nobody is keen to invest in an author who is just a one-book wonder.

When submitting your work it is probably best to send the entire typescript (see *Dos and don'ts on approaching a publisher*, page 130). Although some people advise sending in a synopsis with the first three chapters, a prospective publisher will need to see whether you can sustain a reader's interest to the end of the book.

## Teenage fiction
As noted earlier, some of the published output for teenaged readers is published in series. Increasingly, publishers are targeting this area of the market with edgy, hard-hitting novels about contemporary teenagers, which they publish as standalone titles. There is also a current vogue for 'young adult' novels that have a crossover appeal to an adult readership. This is particularly true of certain types of historical fiction by writers such as Jamila Gavin, Adele Geras and Kevin Crossley-Holland, and of several fantasy writers. For example, Philip Pullman's *The Amber Spyglass* was the first children's book to be the overall winner of the Whitbread Book of the Year award.

## Non-fiction
The last few years have seen fundamental and striking changes in the type of information books published for the young. Hitherto the province, by and large, of specialist publishers catering for the educational market, the field has now broadened to encompass an astonishing range of presentations and formats which are attractive to the young reader. Although the illustrated text book approach still has its place in schools, increasingly, children are wooed into learning about many topics via entertaining and accessible paperback series such as the *Horrible Histories* published by Scholastic, and a host of similar series from other publishers. In writing for this market, it goes without saying that you must research your subject thoroughly and be able to put it across clearly, with an engaging style. Familiarise yourself with the relevant parts of the National Curriculum. Check out the various series and ask the publishers for any guidelines. You will be well advised to check that there is a market for your book before you actually write it, as researching a subject can be both time consuming and costly. Submit a proposal to your targeted publisher, outlining the subject matter and the level of treatment, and your ideas about the audience for your book.

**Chris Kloet** worked as Children's Publisher (1984–97) at Victor Gollancz Ltd, and is now Editor-at-Large at Walker Books. She has written and reviewed children's books and has lectured widely on the subject.

## Further reading
*Children's Writers' & Artists' Yearbook 2005*, A & C Black, 2005

## See also...
- *Notes from a successful children's author*, page 241
- *Children's book publishers and packagers*, page 752
- *Literary agents for children's books*, page 756

# Illustrating for children's books

The world of children's publishing is big business. The huge range of books published each year all carry artwork – lots of it. Maggie Mundy offers guidance for people who are at the start of their career in illustrating for children's books.

## The portfolio

Your portfolio should reflect the best of you and your work, and should speak for itself. Keep its content simple – if too many styles are included, for instance, your work will not leave a lasting impression.

Include some artwork other than those carried out for college projects, e.g. an illustration from a timeless classic to show your abilities, and something modern which reflects your own taste and the area in which you wish to work.

If your strength is for black and white illustration, include pieces with and without tone and with or without a wash. Some publishers want line and tone and some want only line. As cross hatching and stippling can add a lot of extra time to an illustration deadline, it might be advisable to leave out these samples. If you can, include a selection of humour as it can be used effectively in educational books and elsewhere. It is best not to sign and date your work: some artworks can stand the test of time and still look good after a year or two, but if it looks dated … so is the illustrator!

An A3 portfolio is probably the ideal size. Place your best piece of artwork on the opening page and your next best piece on the last page. See *Freelancing for beginners* on page 433 for further information on portfolio presentation.

## Looking at the market

Start by looking thoroughly at what is being published today for children. Take your studies to branches of big retail chains, some independent bookshops, as well as your local library (a helpful librarian should be able to tell you which are the most borrowed books). Absorb the picture books, explore the novelty books, look at the variety of colour covers, and note the range of black line illustrations inside books for children and teenagers. Make a list of the publishers you think may be able to use your particular style.

By making these investigations you will gain an insight into not only the current trends and styles but also the much favoured, oft-published classic children's literature. Most importantly, it will help you identify your market.

In books for a young age range every picture must tell the story – some books have no text and the illustrations say it all. Artwork should be uncluttered, shapes clear, and colour bright. If this does not appeal to you, go up a year or two and note the extra details that are added to the artwork (which still tells the story). Children now need to see more than just clear shapes: they need extra details added to the scene – e.g. a quirky spider hanging around, or a mouse under the bed.

Children are your most critical audience: never think that you can get away with 'any old thing'. Indeed, at the Bologna Book Fair it is a panel of children which judges what they consider to be the best picture book.

## Current trends

Innovative publishers are always on the lookout for something new in illustration styles: something completely different from the tried and tested. More and more they are turning to European and overseas illustrators, often sourced from the Bologna Book Fair exhibitions and illustrators catalogue.

Always strive to improve on your work. Don't be afraid to try out something different and to work it up into acceptable examples. Above all, don't get left behind.

## Making approaches for work

With your portfolio arranged and your target audience in mind, compile a list of publishing houses, packagers and magazines which you think may be suitable for your work.

An agent should know exactly where to place your work, and this may be the easier option (see below). However, you may wish to market yourself by making and going to appointments until you crack your first job.

Alternatively, you could make up a simple broadsheet comprising a black and white and two or three colour illustrations, together with your contact details, and have it colour photocopied or printed. Another inexpensive option is to have your own CDs made up and to send them instead. Send a copy to either the Art Director, the Creative Director or the Senior Commissioning Editor (for picture books) of each potential client on your list. Try to find out the name of the person you would like to see your work. Wait at least a week and then follow up your mailing with a phone call to ask if someone would like to see your portfolio.

Also consider investing in your own website which you can easily update yourself (see *Setting up a website*, page 586).

## Know your capabilities

Know your strengths, but be even more aware of your weaknesses. You will gain far more respect if you admit to not being able to draw something particularly well than by going ahead and producing an embarrassing piece of artwork and having it rejected. You will be remembered for your professional honesty and that client may well try to give you a job where you can use your expertise.

Publishers need to know that you can turn out imaginative, creative artwork while closely following a text or brief, and be able to meet their deadline. It may take an illustrator three weeks to prepare roughs for 32 pages, three weeks to finish the artwork, plus a week to make any corrections. In addition, time has to be allowed for the roughs to be returned. On this basis, how many books can an illustrator realistically take on? Scheduling is of paramount importance (see below).

You will need to become familiar with 'publishing speak' – terms such as gutters, full bleed, holding line, overlays, vignettes, tps, etc. If you don't know the meaning of a term, ask – after all, if you have only recently left college you will not be expected to know all the jargon.

In the course of your work you will have to deal with such issues as contracts, copyright, royalties, public lending rights, rejection fees, etc. The Association of Illustrators, which exists to give help to illustrators in all areas, is well worth joining.

## Organising your workload

When you have reached the stage when you have jobs coming through on a fairly regular basis, organise a comprehensive schedule for yourself so you do not overburden yourself with work. Include on it when roughs have to be submitted, how much work you can fit in while waiting for their approval, the deadline for the artwork, and so on. A wall chart can be helpful for this but another system may work better for you. It is totally unacceptable to deliver artwork late. If you think that you might run over time with your work, let your client know in advance as it may be possible to reach a new agreement for delivery.

## Payment

There are two ways in which an illustrator may be paid for a commission for a book: a flat fee on receipt and acceptance of the artwork, or by an advance against a royalty of future sales. The advance offered could be less than a flat fee but it may result in higher earnings overall. If the book sells well, the illustrator will receive royalty payments twice a year for as long the book is in print.

You need to know from the outset how you are going to be paid. If it is by a flat fee, you may be given an artwork order with a number to be quoted when you invoice. Always read through orders to make sure you understand the terms and conditions. If you haven't been paid within 30 days, send a statement to remind the client, or make a quick phone call to ask when you can expect to receive payment.

With a royalty offer, a contract will be drawn up and this must be checked carefully. One of the clauses will state the breakdown of how and when you will be paid.

Once you have illustrated your first book you should register with the Public Lending Right Office (see page 296) so that you can receive a yearly payment on all UK library borrowings. You will need to cooperate with the author regarding percentages before submitting your own form. The PLR office will give you a reference number, and you then submit details to them of each book you illustrate. It mounts up and is a nice little earner!

## Agents

The role of the agent is to represent the illustrator to the best of their ability and to the illustrator's best advantage. A good agent knows the marketplace and will promote illustrators' work where it will count. An agent may ask you to do one or two sample pieces to strengthen your portfolio, giving them a better chance of securing work for you.

Generally speaking, agents will look after you, your work schedules, payments, contracts, royalties, copyright issues, and try to ensure you have a regular flow of work which you not only enjoy but will stretch your talents to taking on bigger and better jobs. Without exposing your weaknesses, check that you have adequate time in which to do a job and that you are paid a fair rate for the work.

Some illustrators manage well without an agent, and having one is not necessarily a pathway to fame and fortune. Choose carefully: you need to both like and trust the agent and vice versa.

Agents' charges range from 25% to 30%. Find out from the outset how much a prospective agent will charge.

## Finally

Do not be downhearted if progress is at first slow. Everyone starts by serving an apprenticeship, and it is a great opportunity to learn, absorb and soak up as much of the business as possible. Ask questions, get all the advice you can, and use what you learn to improve your craft and thereby your chances of landing a job. Publishers are always on the lookout for fresh talent and new ideas, and one day your talent will be the one they want.

**Maggie Mundy** has been representing illustrators for children's books since 1983. Her agency represents 25 European and British illustrators for children's books.

## Further reading
*Children's Writers' & Artists' Yearbook 2005*, A & C Black, 2005

## See also...
- *Children's book publishers and packagers,* page 752
- *Literary agents for children's books,* page 756
- *Art agents and commercial art studios,* page 440

# Doing it on your own

Reasons for self-publishing are varied. Many highly respected comtemporary and past authors have published their own works. Peter Finch introduces the concept and outlines the implications of such an undertaking.

## Why bother?

You've tried all the usual channels and been turned down; your work is uncommercial, specialised, technical, out of fashion; you are concerned with art while everyone else is obsessed with cash; you need a book out quickly; you want to take up small publishing as a hobby; you've heard that publishers make a lot of money out of their authors and you'd like a slice – all reason enough. But be sure you understand what you are doing before you begin.

## But isn't this cheating? It can't be real publishing – where is the critical judgement? Publishing is a respectable activity carried out by firms of specialists. Writers of any ability never get involved.

But they do. Start self-publishing and you'll be in good historical company: Horace Walpole, Balzac, Walt Whitman, Virginia Woolf, Gertrude Stein, John Galsworthy, Rudyard Kipling, Beatrix Potter, Lord Byron, Thomas Paine, Mark Twain, Upton Sinclair, W.H. Davies, Zane Grey, Ezra Pound, D.H. Lawrence, William Carlos Williams, Alexander Pope, Robbie Burns, James Joyce, Anaïs Nin and Lawrence Stern. All these at some time in their careers dabbled in doing it themselves. William Blake did nothing else. He even made his own ink, handprinted his pages and got Mrs Blake to sew on the covers.

## But today it's different?

Not necessarily. This is not vanity publishing we're talking about although if all you want to do is produce a pamphlet of poems to give away to friends then self-publishing will be the cheapest way. Doing it yourself today can be a valid form of business enterprise. Being twice shortlisted for major literary prizes sharpened Timothy Mo's acumen. Turning his back on mass-market paperbacks, he published *Brownout on Breadfruit Boulevard* on his own. Billy Hopkin's Headline bestseller of Lancashire life, *High Hopes*, began as a self-published title. Susan Hill self-produced her short stories, *Listening to the Orchestra*, and as an example to us all Jill Paton Walsh's self-published *Knowledge of Angels* was shortlisted for the Booker Prize.

## Can anyone do it?

Certainly. If you are a writer then a fair number of the required qualities will already be in hand. The more able and practical you are then the cheaper the process will be. The utterly inept will need to pay others to help them, but it will still be self-publishing in the end.

## Where do I start?

With research. Read up on the subject. Make sure you know what the parts of a book are. Terms like *verso*, *recto*, font, typeface and point size all have to lose their mystery. You will not need to become an expert but you will need a certain familiarity. Don't rush. Learn.

### What about ISBN numbers?

International Standard Book Numbers – a standard bibliographic code, individual to each book published, are used by booksellers and librarians alike. They are issued by the Standard Book Numbering Agency at a cost of £75 plus VAT for ten. Self-publishers may balk at this apparently inordinate expense but the ISBN is the device used by the trade to track titles and if you are serious about your book should be regarded as essential. The Agency issues a free information pack; see *FAQs about ISBNs* on page 290.

### Next?

Put your book together – be it the typed pages of your novel, your selected poems or your story of how it was sailing round the world – and see how large a volume it will make. If you have no real idea of what your book should look like, go to your local bookshop and hunt out a few contemporary examples of volumes produced in a style you would like to emulate. Take your typescript and your examples round to a number of local printers and ask for a quote.

### How much?

It depends. How long is a piece of string? Unit cost is important: the larger the number of copies you have printed the less each will cost. Print too many and the total bill will be enormous. Printing has gone through a revolution in recent years. The arrival of POD (Printing on Demand) and other digital technologies have reduced costs and made short runs economic. But books are still not cheap.

### Can I make it cost less?

Yes. Do some of the work yourself. If you want to publish poems and you are prepared to use a text set by a word processor, you will make a considerable saving. Many word processing programs have publishing facilities which will enhance the look of your text. Could you accept home production, run the pages off on an office photocopier, then staple the sheets? Editions made this way can be very presentable.

For longer texts keyed in on a word processor, savings can be made by supplying the work as a digital file directly to a printer. They can import your text into their program without the need for any rekeying. But be prepared to shop around.

Home binding, if your abilities lie in that direction, can save a fair bit. What it all comes down to is the standard of production you want and indeed at whom your book is aimed. Books for the commercial marketplace need to look like their fellows; specialist publications can afford to be more eccentric.

### Who decides how it looks?

You do. No one should ever ask a printer simply to produce a book. You should plan the design of your publication with as much care as you would a house extension. Spend as much time and money as you can on the cover. It is the part of the book your buyer will see first. If you're stuck, employ a book designer.

#### How many copies should I produce?

Poetry books sell about 300 copies, new novels sometimes manage 1000, literary paperbacks 10,000, mass-market blockbusters over a million. But that is generally where there is a sales team and whole distribution organisation behind the book. Do not, on the one hand, end up with a prohibitively high unit cost by ordering too few copies. One hundred of anything is usually a waste of time. On the other hand can you really sell 3000? Will shops buy in dozens? They will probably only want twos and threes. Take care. Research your market first.

#### How do I sell it?

With all your might. This is perhaps the hardest part of publishing. It is certainly as time consuming as both the writing of the work and the printing of it put together. To succeed here you need a certain flair and you should definitely not be of a retiring nature. If you intend selling through the trade (and even if you don't you are bound to come into contact with bookshop orders at some stage), your costing must be correct and worked out in advance. Shops will want at least 35% (with national chains asking for even more) of the selling price as discount. You'll need about the same again to cover your distribution, promotion and other overheads, leaving the final third to cover production costs and any profit you may wish to make. Multiply your unit production cost by at least four. Commerical publishers often multiply by as much as nine.

Do not expect the trade to pay your carriage costs. Your terms should be 35% post free on everything bar single copy orders. Penalise these by reducing your discount to 25%. Some shops will suggest that you sell copies to them on sale or return. This means that they only pay you for what they sell and then only after they've sold it. This is a common practice with certain categories of publications and often the only way to get independent books into certain shops; but from the self-publisher's point of view it should be avoided if at all possible. Cash in hand is best but expect to have your invoices paid by cheque at a later date. Buy a duplicate pad in order to keep track of what's going on. Phone the shops you

## Low print run printers

Start by asking a few local printers for quotes. It is also worth trying:

### Able Publishing
13 Station Road, Knebworth, Herts SG3 6AP
*tel* (01438) 814316  *fax* (01438) 815232
*email* fp@ablepublishing.co.uk
*website* www.ablepublishing.co.uk

### Biddles Ltd – Short Run Printing
24 Rollesby Road, Hardwick Industrial Estate, King's Lynn, Norfolk PE30 4LS
*tel* (01553) 764728  *fax* (01553) 764633
*email* enquiries@biddles.co.uk
*website* www.biddles.co.uk

### The Better Book Company
Warblington Lodge, The Gardens, Warblington, Havant, Hants PO9 2XH
*tel* 023-9248 1160  *fax* 023-9249 2819
*email* editors@better-book.co.uk
*website* www. better-book.co.uk

### Antony Rowe Ltd
Bumper's Farm, Chippenham, Wilts. SN14 6LH
*tel* (01249) 659705  *fax* (01249) 445535
*email* sales@antonyrowe.co.uk
*website* www.antonyrowe.co.uk

have decided should take your book or turn up in person and ask to see the buyer. Letters and sample copies sent by post will get ignored. Get a freelance distributor to handle all of this for you if you can. But expect to be disappointed. Independent book representatives willing to take on a one-off title are as rare as hen's teeth. If you can contract one they will want another 12% or so commission on top of the shops' discount – but expect to have to go it alone.

### What about promotion?

A vital aspect often overlooked by beginners. Send out as many review copies as you can, all accompanied by slips quoting selling price and name and address of the publisher. Never admit to being that person yourself. Invent a name: it will give your operation a professional feel. Ring up newspapers and local radio stations ostensibly to check that your copy has arrived but really to see if they are prepared to give your book space. Buying advertising space rarely pays for itself but good local promotion with 100% effort will generate dividends.

### What about depositing copies at the British Library?

Under the Copyright Acts the British Library, the Bodleian Library, Oxford, the University Library, Cambridge, the National Library of Scotland, the Library of Trinity College Dublin and the National Library of Wales are all entitled to a free copy of your book which must be sent to them within one month of publication. One copy should go direct to the Legal Deposit Office at the British Library, Boston Spa, Wetherby, West Yorkshire LS23 7BY. The other libraries use an agent, Carryl M. Allardice, Agent for the Copyright Libraries, 100 Euston Street, London NW1 2HQ (*email* cma@cla.ac.uk). Contact her directly to find out how many copies she requires.

### What if I can't manage all this myself?

You can employ others to do it for you. If you are a novelist and you opt for a package covering everything, it could set you back more than £10,000. A number of publishers and associations advertise such services in writers' journals and in the Sunday classifieds. 'Authors. Publish with us.' is a typical ploy. They will do a competent job for you, certainly, but you will still end up having to do the bulk of the selling yourself. It is a costly route, fraught with difficulty. Do the job on your own if you possibly can.

### And what if it goes wrong?

Put all the unsolds under the bed or give them away. It has happened to lots of us. Even the big companies who are experienced at these things have their regular flops. It was an adventure and you did get your book published. On the other hand you may be so successful that you'll be at the London Book Fair selling the film rights and wondering if you've reprinted enough.

### Can the internet help?

The web has yet to take the place of traditional print. However, a good number of authors are setting up their own home pages. From these they advertise themselves and their works, and offer downloadable samples and, in some cases, their complete books. No one has yet made a fortune here and the number of 'hits' some sites claim to get are questionable. Nonetheless, this method of self-promotion comes highly recommended. Self-publishers, if they are not already familiar with the internet, should get on board now. *The Internet: A Writer's Guide* (see further reading) is a good place to start; see also *Setting up a website* on page 586.

Currently, the internet is thick with operators offering to promote or publish work electronically. These range from companies which post sample chapters and then charge readers a fee for the complete work to professional e-book developers who offer books fully formatted for use on hand-held PDAs (Personal Digital Assistants) and other devices (see *E-publishing*, page 581). The jury is still out on where this flux of technological change is going, but if you'd like to test the waters, visit Jane Dorner's site at www.internetwriter.co.uk or consult *Electronic Publishing: The Definitive Guide* by Karen Wiesner.

**Peter Finch** runs Academi, the Welsh National Literature Promotion Agency and Society of Writers. He is a poet, former bookseller and small publisher and author of the *How to Publish Yourself*. His website contains further advice for self-publishers (www.peterfinch.co.uk).

## Further reading

Baverstock, Alison, *Marketing Your Book: An Author's Guide*, A & C Black, 2001

Coleman, Vernon, *How to Publish Your Own Book*, Blue Books, 1999

Dawes, John (ed.), *The Best of Write to Publish!*, John Dawes Publications, 2002

Domanski, Peter and Irvine, Philip, *A Practical Guide to Publishing Books Using Your PC*, Domanski-Irvine Books, 1997

Dorner, Jane, *The Internet: A Writer's Guide*, A & C Black, 2nd edn, 2001

Finch, Peter, *How to Publish Yourself*, Allison & Busby, 4th edn, 2000

Judd, Karen, *Copyediting*, Robert Hale, 2002

Poynter, Dan, *The Self-Publishing Manual: How to Write, Print and Sell Your Own Book*, Para Publishing, 2003

Ross, Tom and Marilyn, *The Complete Guide to Self-Publishing*, Writer's Digest Books, 4th edn, 2002

Shum, F.P. *Publish It Yourself*, Trafford, 2003

Wiesner, Karen, *Electronic Publishing: The Definitive Guide,* Hard Shell Word Factory, 2003

Woll, Thomas, *Publishing for Profit*, Kogan Page, 2000

# Helping to market your book

Authors can enhance their publisher's efforts to sell their book and in this article
Alison Baverstock offers guidance on how they can help. The information is also
relevant to self publishers.

Having a book accepted for publication is immensely satisfying – all the more so
if in the process you have amassed a thick pile of rejection letters spanning
several years. At this stage, some authors decide that, having committed
themselves to work with a professional publishing house, this is the end of their
involvement in the process. They will move on thankfully to the writing of their
next book.

Once you have delivered your manuscript, and it has been accepted for
publication, a publisher should handle all aspects of your book's subsequent
development, from copy-editing and production to promotion and distribution.
But there is a sound pragmatism in remaining vigilant. When it comes to the
marketing of your book, there is a huge amount that you can do to help it sell.

## The challenging marketplace
Each year in Britain alone, over 120,000 books get published or come out in new
editions. All compete for the attention of the same review editors, the same stock
buyers in bookshops, and the largely static number of regular book-buying
members of the general public. It follows that anything an author can do to help
'position' the book, to make it sound different, or just more interesting than
those it competes with, will be a huge advantage.

The marketing of books is not usually an area of high spending and there are
many reasons why. Books are cheap (a novel costs about the same as a cinema
ticket, and much less than a round of drinks), the publishers' profit margins are
low, booksellers claim a percentage of the purchase price as discount (35–50%),
and books sell in relatively small quantities (a mass market novel selling 15,000
copies may be considered a 'bestseller' – compare that with the sales figures for
CDs or computer games). Your publisher will probably try to make maximum
use of (free) publicity to stimulate demand using low-cost marketing
techniques. They are far more likely to arrange for the insertion of a simple
leaflet as a loose insert in a relevant publication, or organise a specific mailing to
members of a relevant society, than book television or billboard advertising.
Your assistance in helping them reach the market could be most important.

## Examine your resources
Think in detail about what resources you have at your disposal that would help
make your book sell, and tell your publisher. Most houses send out an Authors'
Publicity Form about six months before publication, asking you for details of
your book and how you feel it can best be marketed. Whilst the house will
probably not be able to fulfil all your ambitions (mass market advertising is not
possible for every book), they will be particularly interested in your contacts. For

example, were you at school with someone who is now a features writer on *The Times*? Even if you have not spoken since, they may still remember your name. Do your children attend the same school as a contact on your local paper? Do you belong to a society or professional organisation that produces a newsletter for members, organises a conference or regular dining club? All these communication channels provide opportunities for publishers to send information on your book to potential purchasers.

Even greater things may be achieved if you set up the arrangements yourself. Can you arrange for an editorial mention of your book in a society journal (which will carry more weight than an advertisement) or organise for your publisher to take advertising space at a reduced rate? Remember that the less it costs your publishing house to reach each potential customer, the more of the market they will be able to cover out of their planned budgetary spend.

### Offer a peg to your publisher

In trying to stimulate demand for a book, publishers try to achieve publicity (or coverage in the media) at the time of publication. The most usual way of getting this is for the in-house publicist to write a press release about you and your book and send this out to journalists in the hope that they will be interested enough to write about you, or even better decide to interview you.

Your publishing house will need 'pegs' on which to hang stories about you and your book, and it is helpful if you volunteer these rather than waiting to be asked. So, think back over your career and life in general. What is interesting about you? Are there any stories that arise out of the research for the book; incidents that give a flavour of the book and you as a writer?

Try to look at your life as others might see it; events or capabilities you take for granted might greatly interest other people. For example, novelist Catherine Jones is married to a former soldier, and has moved house 15 times in 20 years. In that time she has produced three children and has had appointments with over 40 different classroom teachers. She speaks about her life in a very matter of fact way, but when she wrote her first novel, *Army Wives* (Piatkus), the media were quite fascinated by a world they clearly knew nothing about. They found military jargon particularly compelling, and this proved a wonderful (and headline-producing) peg on which to promote her book.

### Make yourself available

For a mass market title, any publicity that can be achieved will need to be orchestrated at the time of publication. By this time the publisher will hopefully have persuaded booksellers to take stock and the books will be in the shops. If the publicity is successful, but peaks before the books are available to buy, you have entirely missed the boat. If there is no publicity on publication, and no consequent demand, the bookseller has the right to return the books to the publisher and receive a credit note. And in these circumstances it will be *extremely* difficult to persuade them to restock the title having been let down once.

Timing is therefore absolutely crucial, so make yourself available at the time of publication (this is not the time to take your well-earned break). Remember too that, unless you are a very big star, each different newspaper or programme approached will consider its own requirements exclusively, and will not be interested in your own personal scheduling. Not all journalists work every day, and even if they do they like to decide on their own priorities. If you ask for an interview to be rescheduled, it may be dropped completely.

Don't assume that only coverage in the national media is worth having and turn your nose up at local radio and newspapers; they can reach a very wide audience and be particularly effective in prompting sales. You may be able to extend the amount of time and space you get by suggesting a competition or reader/listener offer. Local journalists usually have a much friendlier approach than those who work on the nationals, so if you are a novice to the publicity process this can be a much easier start, and an opportunity to build your confidence.

## Contributing text for marketing

At several stages in the production process your publisher may request your input. You may be asked to provide text for the book jacket or for an author profile, to check information that will be included in the publisher's annual catalogue, or to provide biographical information for their website.

Think in detail about the words you have been asked for, who will read them and in what circumstances, and then craft what you write accordingly. For example, the text on a fiction book jacket (or 'blurb') should not retell the story or give away the plot; rather it should send signals that convey atmosphere, whet the appetite of the reader and show what kind of book they can expect. The potential customer is likely to be reading the blurb in a hurry, perhaps whilst standing in a bookshop being jostled by other shoppers, so it is best to keep it brief.

A non-fiction blurb should establish what the book will do for the reader and what your qualifications are for writing it. Again, keep the details short. The key factor is relevance – what have you done, and what are you qualified to do, that is relevant to the publication in hand?

For both categories of book a third party recommendation will help enormously as this provides objective proof of what a book is like and how useful it is. When books have come out as hardbacks, then extracts from the review coverage can be used on the paperback edition. For previously unpublished authors, a relevant quotation is very helpful instead. Do you know anyone established in the appropriate field who could provide an endorsement for what you have written? Can you contact them and ask them to help? The endorsement does not have to be from someone famous, just someone relevant. For example, a children's book endorsed as a gripping read by a 10-year-old child, or an educational text endorsed by a student who had just passed her exams could both be effective.

You may be asked to check your details in a publisher's catalogue. Bear in mind that your entry will sit alongside everything else they publish, so it must be factual and clear, and not 'knock' other titles on their list.

If you are asked to write website copy, be sure to look at the relevant site before you draft something. Think about the context in which your material will be seen and read (by whom, how often and for how long) and use this information as the basis for writing.

## Marketing after publication

Although most of the effort in marketing your book will inevitably occur at the time of publication (because next month's schedule will bring forward further titles that need the marketing department's attention), there is a great deal of opportunity to carry on selling your book afterwards.

So, if you are asked to speak at a conference or run a training course, ask if your book can be included in the package available to delegates, either as part of the overall price or at a reduced rate. Ask the publishing house for simple flyers (leaflets) on your book which you can hand out on suitable occasions. Then ask the organisers to put a copy inside the delegate pack, on every seat, or in a pile at the back of the hall (or preferably all three!).

Give your publishing house the details of speaking engagements or conferences at which they could usefully mount a display of all their titles (your own included). Even though they published your book, you cannot reasonably expect them to be specialists in every specific field you know intimately, so give them *all* the details they need. For a conference this would include the full title (not just the initials you refer to it by), the organiser's address and contact numbers (not the chairperson's address to which you should send associated papers), the precise dates and times, and any associated deadlines (e.g. stand bookings placed before a certain date may be cheaper). Finally, try to plan ahead rather than passing on key details at the last minute (this is one of publishers' most common complaints about authors!).

When authors get together they will moan about their publishers. But if that energy is channelled into helping promote the books, everyone benefits!

After 10 years in publishing **Alison Baverstock** set up her own marketing consultancy, specialising in running campaigns for the book trade and training publishers to market more effectively. She is a well-established speaker on the book business and has written widely on how to market books. She is the author of *Marketing Your Book: An Author's Guide* (A & C Black 2001) and *How to Market Books* (Kogan Page 2000). She may be contacted at alison.baverstock@btopenworld.com

# Book distribution

Despite the large number of bookshops in the UK, a published book is not guaranteed a place in one of them. Mike Petty charts the journey a book may take from publisher to bookshop and offers reasons why so many books don't reach the high street.

"Why aren't my books in the shops?" The *cri de coeur* is a familiar one (not just from authors, I might add – their editors are prone to similar gripes). There has been an explosion in bookshop numbers in the last decade or so: as of December 2003 there were over 120 Ottakar's branches as opposed to nine in 1992, 61 Borders/Books Etc as against 10 Books Etc, and 204 Waterstone's branches as against 178 Waterstone's/Dillon's. Over the same period WHSmith began to take their claim to be Britain's largest booksellers reasonably seriously. I doubt, however, whether the majority of writers would feel that their lot has improved accordingly; according to a KPMG report in 1998, a mere 3% of titles accounted for 50% of the volume of retail sales.

The mechanics of book distribution are, in outline, simple enough. Anywhere between six and three months before publication all books are subscribed either by sales management or reps to customers, whether individual shops, the head office teams of the chains, or wholesalers. ('Customers' in publisher-speak are people who sell books, not people who buy them from bookshops.) The salespeople will have been primed by their editorial and marketing colleagues as to the qualities and saleability (in theory) of each title, and will be wielding at the very least a jacket and an information sheet bearing the salient details. The customer, if sufficiently impressed by the presentation and the author's sales history, if any, will order a quantity ranging from one to many thousands, plus associated paraphernalia such as dumpbins, posters, etc and these will be delivered in time for publication.

(A publication date, by the way, has very little significance these days, except of course for the author, especially if there is a party or a dinner in the offing. Otherwise it is largely a matter of administrative convenience for publishers and booksellers since, unless specifically asked not to for some reason to do with newsworthiness, bookshops will place stock on sale as soon as they receive it. Books hanging around in stockrooms do not earn money.)

## Distribution centres

A modern book distribution centre is a vast, echoing place, its offices full of the clatter of computer operators, its warehouse area crammed with racks carrying pallets of books stacked up to a hundred feet high, while the air is filled with the sound of forklift trucks and transistor radios. Littlehampton Book Services (LBS), a typical large distribution centre, handles Canongate, Serpent's Tail, Aurum, Watts, Kyle Cathie and Atlantic among others, as well as owners Orion, whose imprints include Weidenfeld and Nicolson, Gollancz and several paperback lists.

The figures are astounding. According to Bridget Radnedge, Publishing Services Director at LBS, the warehouse contains about 25,000 different titles at any one time (out of a database of around 150,000 titles), which translates to somewhere between 25 and 28 million books. Seven to eight thousand separate orders are received per week and are turned round in an average of 3–4 days. In 2002, 34.8 million books were despatched, an average of 650,000 a week. 'Goods In' sees anything up to 400 pallets a day (including 3.6 million returns in 2002), delivered by 20 or so trucks. LBS operates 24 hours a day, though the small hours are reserved for housekeeping chores such as replenishing the forward picking racks, where new and fast-moving titles are stored for easy despatch. These figures will be duplicated at the other half a dozen or so vast distribution centres round the country – and LBS are currently operating at 85% of capacity.

But the mechanics of book distribution do not always work as smoothly as they should. In spite of the best efforts of publishers, warehouses, transport firms, wholesalers and booksellers, the process is best thought of as an obstacle race. The winners will appear in the shops in decent quantities – and, in an ideal world reappear there – while the losers will fall at one of quite a few hurdles along the way.

Small- and medium-size publishers, unable to afford the serious expense of their own warehouses, sign up with one or other of the big boys. In its three warehouses The Book Service (TBS, formerly known as Tiptree Book Services) handles all the Random House and Transworld imprints and dozens of others besides, including Time Warner, Egmont, Virgin, Lonely Planet, Piatkus, Taschen and the AA. A recent recruit is Faber & Faber, who until recently had their own warehouse. If these larger businesses get into trouble, the knock-on effects for their clients can be serious. The changeover to a new computer system is a frequent and apparently inevitable cause for complaint, as is a tendency to overstretch resources in the pursuit of margin. LBS celebrated winning the British Book Award for Distributor of the Year back in January 1998 by expanding their client list. By Christmas of that year their systems were seriously overloaded, they were operating from four sites, and there was talk of books left out in the rain because there was no space under cover. The year ended in a welter of recriminations and threatened lawsuits. Martin Evans, an experienced logistics troubleshooter, was brought in to sort things out, which he did most effectively. But the after-effects, in the shape of compensation claims, lingered for Orion and their French owners Hachette for some time.

## Centralised ordering and promotions

The increasing centralisation of ordering is another obstacle. In rare cases as much as 90% of a book's UK subscription can go to perhaps a dozen key accounts, leaving the balance to be fought over by the on-the-road sales force which traditionally has been the main means of communication with individual bookshops. While in most cases the percentage will be lower than this, there is no doubt that in recent years – and in particular since the collapse of the Net Book Agreement – the balance has shifted significantly towards centralised buying. By 'key accounts' is meant wholesalers (the biggest are THE, Gardners and Bertrams); specialised wholesalers such as Thomas Cork and Aspen who supply supermarkets, motorways and airports; WHSmith; supermarkets who are not otherwise supplied; and – increasingly – the online booksellers. Many of these, such as Blackwell's, Foyles and WHSmith, have their terrestrial counterparts, while others, most notably Amazon, do not. Between centralisation of ordering on the one hand, and increased penetration of the independents by wholesalers on the other, the future for reps is not rosy.

Chains such as Waterstone's are also centralising promotions, leading to the homogenisation of high street bookselling. The range of stock that used to be one of the glories of Waterstone's in particular has inevitably suffered. Promotions such as '3 for 2' or BOGOF (Buy One Get One Free), which are such a common feature in all the chains, arguably get more copies of fewer titles into the hands of more people, but at some cost, one suspects, to the publishers' margins and the authors' royalty accounts. Supermarkets take the process a stage further; if you are one of the few (largely high-profile) authors stocked by the likes of Tesco and Asda you can take pleasure in the expansion – at least in theory – of your readership, but you are entitled to ask whether even your publisher is making any money, let alone you yourself. At the time of writing, Thomas Cork, one of the leading supermarket suppliers, is in deep financial trouble, leading to calls for a re-examination of supermarkets' role in the bookselling business.

## Publishers

Of course not all the obstacles to literary success lie along the supply chain; some can be laid at the door of the publishers themselves. It is self-evident that booksellers will be disinclined to give a book much shelf space if they feel that the publishers aren't putting any promotion behind it. The higher the advance, the more will be spent on promotion, and the more customers – retailers, wholesalers, library suppliers, etc – will be disposed to give that book adequate display.

Decisions are taken as a book makes its stately way through the publication process – at acquisition meetings, marketing meetings, sales meetings – which can affect its ultimate profile in the marketplace. The author can achieve sudden fame – or notoriety – in another field, for instance, or someone powerful and influential will read a proof and pronounce favourably on it. This sort of thing can provide a boost to the morale of the people whose job it is to sell and market books, and this 'buzz' is passed on to the customers and ultimately to the public. As an editor I would often reflect ruefully on the fact that my enthusiastic advocacy in-house seemed to carry less weight than three lines in the *Bookseller* from paperback pundit Sarah Broadhurst, happy though I was to find her agreeing with me.

On the other hand, it can happen that, for no reason that anybody can put their finger on, a book seems to wither on the vine in the months between acquisition and publication. (Failure to come up with a jacket that anybody likes can be a reason.) 'Surely we didn't really think we were going to sell that many,' someone will say, the print run will be cut (to the accompaniment of outraged bleats from its editor), and the book's chances of making any kind of showing in the marketplace cut accordingly.

And, of course, there are returns, which like the poor are always with us. As the old joke has it: publishers don't sell books, they merely lend them to booksellers. One of the insoluble paradoxes that afflict the book trade is that if a publisher *does* put some energy into selling a book into the trade, an avalanche of returns can be its only reward. "The fact has always remained that an unsaleable book is an unsaleable book no matter how it is dressed up; and it is better not to have it in the supply chain at all, getting in the way of books that do have a market," said Peter Kilborn of Book Industry Communication, an organisation set up by the Publishers Association, Booksellers Association and Library Association (now called CILIP, the Chartered Institute of Library and Information Professionals) and the British Library, and charged *inter alia* with finding a solution to the returns problem. Kilborn's rather Darwinian view is not the whole truth, of course – an unsaleable book is not necessarily a bad book, as any author will tell you. In fact you could make a case for saying that if a book is good enough it will sooner or later be remaindered. But until the problem is solved, a decent showing in a bookshop is only a temporary phenomenon; if the books do not sell quickly enough they will be on their way back to the warehouse in months if not weeks.

### Too many books?

So what can the poor author do? While it is certainly the responsibility of publishers to make sure that their products are to be found in bookshops (and far too many books are not so much published as simply made available should anybody happen to want them), it has at least become more possible for authors to make a difference. Online booksellers, while no more immune to cock-ups than their terrestrial counterparts, have made a huge difference to the sheer *availability* of books; the access they offer to writers and their public is absolutely unprecedented. The fact that selling books has been in the forefront of the internet revolution suggests that there is a close correlation between internet users and bookbuyers, and they are out there to be blandished and cajoled. Any author who has a website should make a point of linking to Amazon, or one of the other online booksellers, at the very least. The upcoming print-on-demand revolution means (in theory, at least) that no book need ever go out of print.

"Why isn't my book in the shops?" Everybody seems to agree that too many books are published, though nobody seems disposed to do anything about it, least of all publishers and writers. (Writers may not be incurable optimists, but publishers are.) If your book isn't in the shops, it may simply be that either you or your publisher has failed to differentiate it sufficiently from all the other books in its field, whatever it might be. The odds are not, sadly, on your side. Then again, it's a book trade fact of life that everybody complains; authors complain about publishers and agents, booksellers complain about publishers, publishers complain about absolutely everybody. Yet year after year new discoveries are made, reputations are made, even fortunes are made occasionally. Nothing seems to put writers off writing, including, I trust, the foregoing!

**Mike Petty** was formerly Editorial Director at Picador, Chatto & Windus, Abacus, Bloomsbury and Victor Gollancz. He now runs the publication programme for the Eden Project. An earlier version of this article appeared in *The Author*, the magazine of the Society of Authors.

# Year-in-view of the publishing industry

The face of the publishing industry has changed markedly in recent years. Nicholas Clee summarises the most significant developments that have taken place.

The book publishing industry should have more reasons to be cheerful than for many years. Thanks to the varied contributions of people such as J.K. Rowling, Philip Pullman, David Beckham, former royal butler Paul Burrell, and the BBC's Big Read campaign, books are constantly in the news. The bestsellers are more spectacular than ever. In 2003, J.K. Rowling's fifth Harry Potter novel, *Harry Potter and the Order of the Phoenix*, smashed all records by selling 1.7 million copies in a single day. Potter is of course a one-off, a freak by all previous measurements; but other hardbacks are regularly achieving sales that were uncommon a few years ago. Chart-topping paperbacks, too, are selling in unprecedented numbers. There are more ways than ever for books to reach buyers: through bookshops, supermarkets, newsagents, motorway service stations, garden centres, and gift shops; over the internet; 'off the page' to readers responding to newspaper reviews; through book clubs; through companies that set up displays of books in factories and offices.

However, publishers are not celebrating these successes with the gusto one might expect. Talk to them, and you come away with a sense, if not of crisis, then at least of unease. They describe battles to achieve every sale, books returned unsold in increasing quantities, declining backlist sales, and dismal performances by titles that fail to be selected for retailers' promotions. As high discounts and promotional expenditure erode their margins, a number of public and private companies are falling short of the targets that their owners expect them to reach.

These phenomena have their roots in the 1980s. That decade saw the beginning of a consolidation that has left us with seven conglomerates and a few independents dominating fiction publishing; and it saw the rise of the bookselling chains, as Waterstone's and Dillons (the latter now absorbed into the former) rose to challenge the dominance of W.H. Smith, and as Ottakar's and the Borders/Books Etc group followed them.

## The demise of the Net Book Agreement

For a while, these companies grew by acquisition, or by opening more shops. But there came a time when they had to grow by selling more books; and that was difficult, because the book market was 'mature'. There was one way, though, in which they thought they might be able to expand the market – by using discounts. Hitherto, they had operated according to the terms of the Net Book Agreement (NBA), under which publishers set prices that retailers could not cut. In 1995, the NBA went; publishers introduced recommended retail prices in place of net ones, and the discount wars began.

The new era in book retailing is not the one that the publishers who abandoned the NBA envisaged. They thought that selective discounting would make particular promotions more attractive: special offers on the Booker Prize shortlist, perhaps, or on themed backlist titles, with perhaps a bit of price cutting to lure buyers towards the latest commercial blockbuster. But price cutting has become much more pervasive than that. As I write, there are five novels in the original fiction top 10 with r.r.p.s of £17.99, and they are on sale in bookshops at an average selling price of £12.60. Most of the top 10 paperbacks are being sold at an average £2 off their r.r.p.s of £6.99 or £7.99. You can buy bestselling non-fiction hardbacks with £20 cover prices for about £12.

The revokers of the NBA underestimated three factors: the extent to which supermarkets would become interested in selling books; the saturation of the market by high street booksellers; and the growth in influence of bestseller charts and other sales data.

## The big squeeze

Supermarkets have always sold books. But they became a great deal more interested in them once price constraints had gone. Tesco and Asda led the way, buying up substantial quantities of lead titles, in hardback and paperback, to sell at loss-leading prices – a strategy they could afford much more easily than could specialist bookshops, because customers in supermarkets bought a great many other goods. As supermarkets increased their share of sales of bestselling titles, they gained power to negotiate heftier discounts as well.

Supermarkets are not booksellers: they sell only a tiny proportion of the titles that even a small bookshop will carry. Nevertheless, they have had a powerful effect on the book market. W.H. Smith is a mass-market retailer: it cannot afford to be seen not to offer value for money. So it has had to compete with the price cuts that the supermarkets offer. Waterstone's, the largest bookseller in the UK and with an estate of about 200 branches to maintain, needs to project itself as the place to go for every kind of book you might want, from college texts to the latest John Grisham. So it does not want to be seen to offer uncompetitive prices either. Many people who visit Waterstone's will also have access to a branch of another chain – Ottakar's, perhaps, or Borders, or Books Etc. (Borders, the US chain, has stores under its own name in the UK and also owns the Books Etc chain.) So they, too, must compete. Then there is the internet, where Amazon.com and Amazon.co.uk have always used discounting as a way of attracting customers. The result of all this activity is that independent booksellers, who do not have the clout of the chains, have largely abandoned trying to sell titles that will be on offer elsewhere at prices they cannot match.

There are only so many bestsellers to go round. The big booksellers all need to get healthy market shares on these titles that will sell in high volumes, and that might attract other business too. They know that their customers have plenty of choice about where to shop; as a result, they must offer competitive prices. In the windows of the bookselling chains, you can see continuous three-for-two and other price-cutting promotions.

## Bestseller lists

Coinciding with these developments has been the production of increasingly sophisticated bestseller lists. Until the mid-1990s, the charts that appeared in national newspapers and the trade press reflected survey results from a panel of retailers. Then a firm called BookTrack – now Nielsen BookScan – began monitoring data recorded at point of sale, and now has records of books sold in more than 90% of book retail outlets. BookScan data is used by publishers and booksellers as an industry standard for monitoring their performances, and its charts appear on the books pages of most broadsheet newspapers.

All these factors – supermarket sales of books, aggressive discounting, and the growing influence of bestseller lists – have conspired to lift sales of bestselling titles to unprecedented levels. The result has been a shift in power to those who can dictate whether publishers get these bestsellers: the big retailers, and authors and agents with attractive titles to sell.

Publishers find themselves squeezed from two sides. The big houses need bestsellers, and face intense competition from their rivals to secure them; therefore they find themselves paying advances that reflect not only what the sales of a book will be, but also what the strategic importance is of that book to the company. Then they have to get that book to the top of the bestseller lists – or else the author, disillusioned, will move elsewhere. So they have to give away big discounts to the retailers that can achieve those sales. The supermarkets are in a particularly powerful position. They can dictate whether a book goes to number one or not; but, as they are not stockholding bookshops, they do not have to take everything. If one publisher does not give them what they ask for, they go elsewhere. Supermarket discounts stand at present at about 65%.

If a book does not become the focus of these attentions, it is hard to sell. Publishers are increasingly cautious about taking on books that are not in some way promotable – a word that has come either to signify that authors are good looking or have a story to tell, or that the bookshops will want to include them in a price-cutting campaign. New authors that fit these categories are as welcome as ever. Authors who have failed to achieve significant sales after several books can expect to be dropped; and even those who have done well but not eye-catchingly so might find it hard to retain publishers' interest, as might those who have written books that are modest or hard to classify.

However, it would be wrong to infer from these trends that the book industry today is uniquely exclusive. True, there is a larger gap than ever between the bestsellers and the rest, and fashion holds sway. But it has always been the case that only a tiny proportion of writers has achieved success, while the rest have fallen by the wayside; and, while we always think of contemporary fashion as particularly callous in what it discards, it operates no differently from fashions of the past – recall the novelist Barbara Pym's long exile from publication in the 1960 and 70s.

## Good news for independents

No trend is unaccompanied by some contrary movement. As the big bookselling chains have added more and more shops to their estates, the best independent bookshops have been able to offer the more friendly, individual service that many book lovers prefer. As the big book publishers have consolidated, smaller, independent houses have seized opportunities to take on titles that the conglomerates, thinking big, have overlooked. Consolidation has in some respects worked to the independents' advantage, not only throwing up these titles but also offering them easier routes to market. Big publishers, saving costs, have made use increasingly of freelance design, production, editorial and publicity services; the proliferation of these services has helped smaller houses to produce books to higher standards. Literary editors, other journalists and prize judges may find that the big publishers sate their attention; so they are more likely to look for refreshment and variety elsewhere.

Several recent publishing events seem particularly associated with these trends. In 2002, *Life of Pi* by Yann Martel, published by the small Edinburgh house Canongate, won the Man Booker Prize for Fiction. The novel went on to become one of the bestselling paperbacks of 2003; no one has suggested that one of the big London houses might have sold even more copies. Confirming the impression that the famous names in the field are far from establishing a monopoly of the best fiction, the 2003 Booker judges included on their longlist several titles from small, regional publishers, and one, Clare Morrall's *Astonishing Splashes of Colour* (Tindal Street Press), on their shortlist.

Alexander McCall Smith may have needed a big publisher, Time Warner, to lift his sales into the hundreds of thousands; but it was another small Edinburgh publisher, Polygon, that established him, and succeeded in getting the support from Waterstone's that set him on his way. At Christmas 2003, the number one bestseller came from the independent house Profile Books, and took the unlikely form of a survey of punctuation – it was *Eats, Shoots & Leaves* by Lynne Truss.

## Children's publishing

Another reason to be cheerful is the astonishing surge of interest in children's books. Until Harry Potter came along, children's lists were the poor relations at publishing companies and in the media. But not only did Harry make a lot of money, he also showed that the best children's writing can appeal across age ranges. Philip Pullman confirmed that point, and received recognition for the achievement when his novel *The Amber Spyglass* became the first children's book to receive the Whitbread Book of the Year award. Publishers began paying substantial sums to authors they felt could follow in Rowling's and Pullman's footsteps, and children's authors found themselves receiving media attention that had previously been very rare. Whether sales of children's books, Rowling's apart, have increased over the past few years is open to dispute. What is certain though is that the challenge of getting children to read has taken its proper place high on publishers' agendas.

In the immediate future, consolidation among the big publishers and booksellers will continue – the market is not big enough for all of them. They are very good at what they do; but what they do is not the last word in publishing and bookselling. For many authors, finding alternative routes to readers will become a more common and more rewarding option.

**Nicholas Clee** is editor of *The Bookseller*. He has been a judge of the Booker Prize, the Encore Award and Granta's Best of Young British Novelists. He writes a weekly column on publishing and bookselling for *The Guardian*.

# Who owns whom in publishing

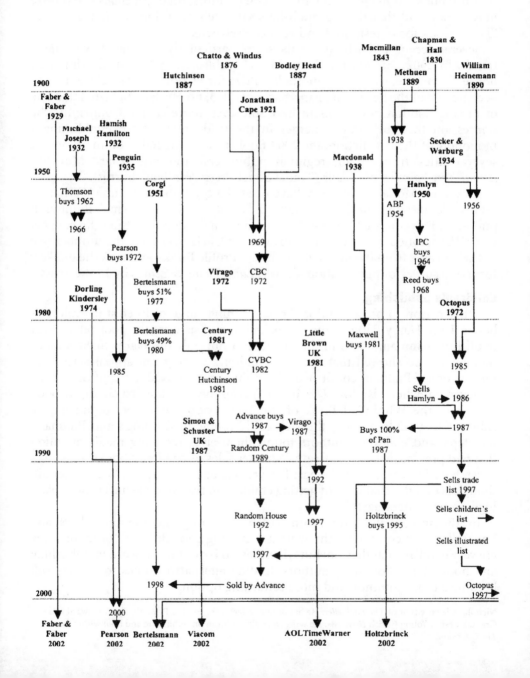

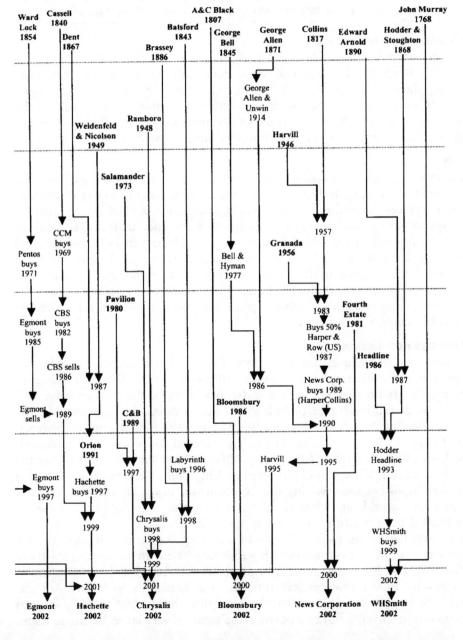

Ward Lock 1854
Cassell 1840
Dent 1867
Brassey 1886
Batsford 1843
A&C Black 1807
George Bell 1845
George Allen 1871
Collins 1817
Edward Arnold 1890
Hodder & Stoughton 1868
John Murray 1768

George Allen & Unwin 1914

Weidenfeld & Nicolson 1949
Ramboro 1948
Harvill 1946

Salamander 1973

CCM buys 1969

Pentos buys 1971

Bell & Hyman 1977
Granada 1956

Pavilion 1980

CBS buys 1982

Egmont buys 1985

CBS sells 1986

1957

1983
Buys 50% Harper & Row (US) 1987

Fourth Estate 1981

Headline 1986

1987

1987

Egmont sells 1989

1989

News Corp. buys 1989 (HarperCollins)

1986

Bloomsbury 1986

C&B 1989

Orion 1991

1990

Labyrinth buys 1996

Harvill 1995

1995

Hodder Headline 1993

Egmont buys 1997

Hachette buys 1997

1997

Chrysalis buys 1998

1998

WHSmith buys 1999

1999

1999

2001

2001

2000

2000

2002

**Egmont 2002**
**Hachette 2002**
**Chrysalis 2002**
**Bloomsbury 2002**
**News Corporation 2002**
**WHSmith 2002**

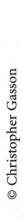

© Christopher Gasson

# Top one hundred chart of 2003 paperback fastsellers

Every year since 1979 Alex Hamilton has compiled for *The Guardian* a chart of the 100 topselling paperbacks published for the first time during that year by British publishers. For readers new to it he describes its terms of reference, and sets the context.

## Bestsellers and fastsellers

A distinction must be made between 'bestsellers' and the term used here – 'fastsellers'. Bestsellers have the real commercial pedigree. Sometimes they make a strong showing in the fastseller lane, but among bestselling authors are hundreds whose books began slowly and only over many years vindicate the faith of the original publisher. D.H. Lawrence and George Orwell are two whose sales in their lifetimes were modest, but posthumous interest spectacular.

## Poetry

While serious poets never repeat Lord Byron's triumph in becoming a bestseller and 'famous overnight', and the only two works with short lines in two decades of fastsellers were collections of comic verse, a poet such as Eliot, not to mention Shakespeare and Chaucer, will eventually rack up sales in millions. And an outside event, such as the Nobel Prize for Seamus Heaney in 1995, produces an immediate harvest. In 1998, the year when the Oxford University Press announced the closure of its poetry section to save money, the late Poet Laureate, Ted Hughes, with the last book of his life, *Birthday Letters*, headed the hardcover selling lists with 145,000 copies, and won every award for which the book could qualify.

## Fiction and non-fiction

The staple of publishing has long been Bibles, classic authors, cookbooks, dictionaries and other reference books. Although fiction dominates counter sales and library borrowings, the top individual titles for the 20th century, with figures over 20 million copies, include most of these categories. For example, *The Guinness Book of Records*, over many editions, passed 85 million copies. However, gross figures of 50–300 million copies are claimed for worldwide hardcover, paperback and translation editions of prolific authors such as Agatha Christie, Alistair MacLean, Mickey Spillane, Stephen King, John Grisham and Catherine Cookson. In all her long writing life Cookson was never off the lists, and her running Transworld sale when she died in 1998 was 53.5 million, with seven unpublished titles to come. (The last appeared in 2003.)

The fastseller list on pages 276–9 is limited to paperbacks that appeared for the first time in that year from British publishers. These are defined in the trade as 'frontlist', and those that remain in print become 'backlist'. It is tempting to enter backlist titles revived as screen tie-ins (e.g. Keneally's *Schindler's Ark* and Harris's *Silence of the Lambs* that both tripled their sales, to 800,000 and 1,580,000 respectively), but except when the figure is very large, I exclude them.

In 2002 the publishers of *Lord of the Rings* (1954/65) made a vast harvest of 12 million copies of Tolkien titles.

## Looking at the figures

From 1979 until the 1990s recession there were always between 102 and 125 titles that passed the 100,000 mark, a figure conveniently round for those who make comparisons – but the figure now rises steadily: this year there were 199. The expansion results partly from fierce and widespread competitive discounting by chain booksellers, supermarket drive, and the bestsellers focus of many high street bookshops. Ubiquitous 'top 10' charts reinforce the successes (of the frontlist, that is; the backlist tends to suffer, a matter of growing concern to publishers and 'mid-list' authors).

A distortion for the few titles published at the end of the year looks likely, but actually it rarely makes much difference. Electronic stock control enables booksellers to match ordering to demand. The significant sale of new paperbacks, particularly by established authors, takes place within a few weeks of their appearance, although a few (sometimes called 'sleepers') do enter the magic circle of bestsellers: *Captain Corelli's Mandolin* by Louis de Bernières went on to sell two million copies after achieving only 60,000 in its first year.

## The authors

Over 20 years, the lists indicate conservative attitudes among buyers. Fewer than 10% of authors generally come from outside the Anglo–American axis (which divides this year 55–35). Few appear in the top 25 who have not appeared somewhere on the list in previous years. (2003 provides four exceptions: the books by Alice Sebold, Yann Martel, Allison Pearson and Alexander McCall Smith.) Once established on it, authors have only to turn in a regular supply of similar works to stay there. However, like typecast actors, they may find too late that they are captives of the market. One author trapped in his own formula was thriller writer Peter Cheyney, who gave his publisher a book unlike his others and was told to bury it, lest it confuse his loyal following.

Leading figures of the 1980s were Wilbur Smith (more than 25 novels past the million, 30 million sales), Stephen King (25 million), Dick Francis (19 million), Barbara Taylor Bradford, Len Deighton, Catherine Cookson, Jeffrey Archer, Danielle Steel and Victoria Holt. To these (minus Holt, who died) the 1990s added regular front-runners in John Grisham and Maeve Binchy, with Patricia Cornwell and Jilly Cooper as top 10 reliables. J.K. Rowling is the outstanding newcomer of this decade, but Ian Rankin and possibly Ian McEwan have also fixed themselves in top positions. With the Cookson file closed, King and Steel are the only two to have figured in every list since 1979. Such authors' names are like a brand. While only seven of 2000 titles were volumes of short stories, two had sales over 750,000, because they were by Frederick Forsyth and Jeffrey Archer, and two reached 500,000 (Archer and Rosamund Pilcher). This year there is one by Ian Rankin.

More than half the buyers of books have always been women but for most of the 1980s hardly more than a quarter of the authors were. In the 1990s their

| No. | Title | Genre | Author | Imprint |
|-----|-------|-------|--------|---------|
| 1 | Dr Atkins' New Diet Revolution | Diet | Robert Atkins (US) | Vermilion |
| 2 | The Summons | Thriller | John Grisham (US) | Arrow |
| 3 | Quentins | Novel | Maeve Binchy (Ire.) | Orion |
| 4 | The Lovely Bones | Novel | Alice Sebold (US) | Picador |
| 5 | Life of Pi | Novel | Yann Martel (Fr. Can.) | Canongate |
| 6 | Angels | Chicklit | Marian Keyes (Ire.) | Penguin |
| 7 | Can You Keep a Secret | Chicklit | Sophie Kinsella (Br.) | Black Swan |
| 8 | Man and Wife | Novel | Tony Parsons (Br.) | HarperCollins |
| 9 | I Don't Know How She Does It | Novel | Allison Pearson (Br.) | Vintage |
| 10 | No.1 Ladies' Detective Agency | Novel | Alexander McCall Smith (Br.) | Abacus |
| 11 | Pandora | Women's lit. | Jilly Cooper (Br.) | Corgi |
| 12 | Just Between Us | Novel | Cathy Kelly (Ire.) | HarperCollins |
| 13 | Girl from the South | Novel | Joanna Trollope (Br.) | Black Swan |
| 14 | Four Blind Mice | Thriller | James Patterson (US) | Headline |
| 15 | Red Rabbit | Thriller | Tom Clancy (US) | Penguin |
| 16 | Coastliners | Novel | Joanne Harris (Br.) | Black Swan |
| 17 | High Society | Novel | Ben Elton (Br.) | Black Swan |
| 18 | 2nd Chance | Thriller | James Patterson (US) | Headline |
| 19 | Lost Light | Thriller | Michael Connelly (US) | Orion |
| 20 | The Beach House | Thriller | James Patterson (US) | Headline |
| 21 | The Cottage | Women's lit. | Danielle Steel (US) | Corgi |
| 22 | Chasing the Dime | Thriller | Michael Connelly (US) | Orion |
| 23 | Into Temptation | Saga | Penny Vincenzi (Br.) | Orion |
| 24 | Grave Secrets | Thriller | Kathy Reichs (US) | Arrow |
| 25 | Fox Evil | Crime | Minette Walters (Br.) | Pan |
| 26 | Night Watch | Fantasy | Terry Pratchett (Br.) | Corgi |
| 27 | Gone for Good | Thriller | Harlan Coben (US) | Orion |
| 28 | Maura's Game | Crime | Martina Cole (Br.) | Headline |
| 29 | The Shelters of Stone | Fantasy | Jean M. Auel (US) | Coronet |
| 30 | Beggars Banquet | S/stories | Ian Rankin (Br.) | Orion |
| 31 | Answered Prayers | Romance | Danielle Steel (US) | Corgi |
| 32 | Prey | Thriller | Michael Crichton (US) | HarperCollins |
| 33 | Beachcomber | Romance | Josephine Cox (Br.) | HarperCollins |
| 34 | Sunset in St Tropez | Women's lit. | Danielle Steel (US) | Corgi |
| 35 | A Married Man | Chicklit | Catherine Alliott (Br.) | Headline |
| 36 | The Janson Directive | Thriller | Robert Ludlum (US) | Orion |
| 37 | Portrait of a Killer | True crime | Patricial Cornwell (US) | Time Warner |
| 38 | The Little Friend | Novel | Donna Tartt (US) | Bloomsbury |
| 39 | Babes in the Wood | Crime | Ruth Rendell (Br.) | Arrow |
| 40 | Sons of Fortune | Novel | Jeffrey Archer (Br.) | Pan |
| 41 | Keane: The Autobiography | Autobiog. | Keane & Dunphy (Ire.) | Penguin |
| 42 | Bad Boy Jack | Saga | Josephine Cox (Br.) | Headline |
| 43 | Everything's Eventual | Horrors | Stephen King (US) | NEL |
| 44 | Dr Atkins' Diet Carb Counter | Diet | Robert Atkins (US) | Vermilion |
| 45 | Hornet Flight | Thriller | Ken Follett (Br.) | Pan |
| 46 | From a Buick 8 | Horror | Stephen King (US) | NEL |
| 47 | Finding Nemo: Book of the Film | Juvenile | Disney (US) | Ladybird |
| 48 | Dr Atkins' New Diet Cookbook | Diet | Robert Atkins (US) | Vermilion |
| 49 | Liberation Day | Thriller | Andy McNab (Br.) | Corgi |
| 50 | Darkest Fear | Thriller | Harlan Coben (US) | Orion |

| RRP | Month | Home | Export | Total | Gross | No. |
|---|---|---|---|---|---|---|
| £7.99 | Jan | 1,117,999 | 27,714 | 1,145,713 | £9,154,247 | 1 |
| £6.99 | Jan | 783,189 | 319,089 | 1,102,278 | £7,704,923 | 2 |
| £6.99 | Apr | 531,121 | 378,292 | 909,413 | £6,356,797 | 3 |
| £7.99 | Jun | 713,090 | 84,446 | 797,536 | £6,372,313 | 4 |
| £7.99 | May | 659,401 | 116,098 | 775,499 | £6,196,237 | 5 |
| £6.99 | Apr | 480,768 | 145,743 | 626,511 | £4,379,312 | 6 |
| £6.99 | Mar | 507,521 | 56,121 | 563,642 | £3,939,858 | 7 |
| £6.99 | May | 460,554 | 89,601 | 550,155 | £3,845,583 | 8 |
| £6.99 | May | 437,823 | 75,377 | 513,200 | £3,587,268 | 9 |
| £6.99 | June | 448,225 | 59,130 | 507,355 | £3,546,411 | 10 |
| £6.99 | Jun | 381,364 | 72,666 | 454,030 | £3,173,670 | 11 |
| £6.99 | July | 335,996 | 114,130 | 450,126 | £3,146,381 | 12 |
| £6.99 | Feb | 394,607 | 48,846 | 443,453 | £3,099,736 | 13 |
| £6.99 | Sept | 353,255 | 87,180 | 440,435 | £3,078,641 | 14 |
| £7.99 | June | 273,532 | 146,043 | 419,575 | £3,352,404 | 15 |
| £6.99 | Jan | 349,706 | 59,722 | 409,428 | £2,861,902 | 16 |
| £6.99 | July | 352,125 | 56,118 | 408,243 | £2,853,619 | 17 |
| £6.99 | Jan | 328,485 | 70,178 | 398,663 | £2,786,654 | 18 |
| £6.99 | Nov | 247,980 | 133,845 | 381,825 | £2,668,957 | 19 |
| £6.99 | Apr | 314,676 | 66,548 | 381,224 | £2,664,756 | 20 |
| £6.99 | Mar | 315,094 | 63,778 | 378,872 | £2,648,315 | 21 |
| £6.99 | June | 248,244 | 129,807 | 378,051 | £2,642,576 | 22 |
| £6.99 | May | 255,866 | 121,594 | 377,460 | £2,638,445 | 23 |
| £6.99 | Mar | 283,248 | 82,666 | 365,914 | £2,557,739 | 24 |
| £6.99 | Aug | 252,159 | 112,371 | 364,530 | £2,548,065 | 25 |
| £6.99 | Oct | 263,076 | 81,551 | 344,627 | £2,408,943 | 26 |
| £6.99 | Jan | 243,119 | 96,608 | 339,727 | £2,374,692 | 27 |
| £6.99 | Apr | 292,158 | 40,759 | 332,917 | £2,327,090 | 28 |
| £7.99 | May | 230,027 | 95,728 | 325,755 | £2,602,782 | 29 |
| £6.99 | Mar | 220,512 | 101,624 | 322,136 | £2,251,731 | 30 |
| £6.99 | Nov | 261,448 | 59,525 | 320,973 | £2,243,601 | 31 |
| £6.99 | Aug | 210,115 | 110,149 | 320,264 | £2,238,645 | 32 |
| £6.99 | Oct | 281,369 | 35,458 | 316,827 | £2,214,621 | 33 |
| £5.99 | Aug | 260,011 | 53,223 | 313,234 | £1,876,272 | 34 |
| £6.99 | July | 288,669 | 20,332 | 309,001 | £2,159,917 | 35 |
| £6.99 | Aug | 158,636 | 150,111 | 308,747 | £2,158,142 | 36 |
| £6.99 | Sept | 241,390 | 66,030 | 307,420 | £2,148,866 | 37 |
| £7.99 | Oct | 254,656 | 52,635 | 307,291 | £2,455,255 | 38 |
| £6.99 | July | 231,694 | 68,811 | 300,505 | £2,100,530 | 39 |
| £6.99 | Nov | 146,997 | 144,428 | 291,425 | £2,037,061 | 40 |
| £7.99 | July | 269,758 | 12,445 | 282,203 | £2,254,802 | 41 |
| £6.99 | Feb | 256,848 | 25,103 | 281,951 | £1,970,837 | 42 |
| £6.99 | Mar | 224,688 | 55,183 | 279,871 | £1,956,298 | 43 |
| £3.99 | Jan | 249,770 | 28,327 | 278,097 | £1,109,607 | 44 |
| £6.99 | May | 157,441 | 108,628 | 266,069 | £1,859,822 | 45 |
| £6.99 | June | 207,738 | 57,819 | 265,557 | £1,856,243 | 46 |
| £2.50 | Sept | 249,984 | 12,670 | 262,654 | £656,635 | 47 |
| £6.99 | Jan | 237,622 | 23,723 | 261,345 | £1,826,802 | 48 |
| £6.99 | Nov | 222,284 | 37,427 | 259,711 | £1,815,380 | 49 |
| £6.99 | July | 187,798 | 67,074 | 254,872 | £1,781,555 | 50 |

| No. | Title | Genre | Author | Imprint |
|---|---|---|---|---|
| 51 | Deadly Embrace | Novel | Jackie Collins (Br.) | Pocket |
| 52 | Beyond Nab End | Autobiog. | William Woodruff (Br.) | Abacus |
| 53 | The Murder Book | Thriller | Jonathan Kellerman (US) | Headline |
| 54 | Till We Meet Again | Saga | Lesley Pearse (Br.) | Penguin |
| 55 | Land of Fire | Thriller | Chris Ryan (Br.) | Arrow |
| 56 | Spies | Novel | Michael Frayn (Br.) | Faber |
| 57 | Kisscut | Crime | Karin Slaughter (US) | Arrow |
| 58 | Shadowmancer | Juvenile | G.P. Taylor (Br.) | Faber |
| 59 | Tears of the Giraffe | Novel | Alexander McCall Smith (Br.) | Abacus |
| 60 | Road to McCarthy | Travel | Pete McCarthy (US) | Sceptre |
| 61 | The Kindness of Strangers | Autobiog. | Kate Adie (Br.) | Headline |
| 62 | Fingersmith | Novel | Sarah Waters (Br.) | Virago |
| 63 | Grail Quest Vagabond | Hist. novel | Bernard Cornwell (Br.) | HarperCollins |
| 64 | Three Weeks in Paris | Women's lit. | Barbara Taylor Bradford (Br.) | HarperCollins |
| 65 | The Autograph Man | Novel | Zadie Smith (Br.) | Penguin |
| 66 | Unless | Novel | Carol Shields (Can.) | 4th Estate |
| 67 | Nadia Knows Best | Chicklit | Jill Mansell (Br.) | Headline |
| 68 | Serious | Autobiog. | John McEnroe (US) | Time Warner |
| 69 | Best of Friends | Novel | Cathy Kelly (Ire.) | HarperCollins |
| 70 | Last Temptation | Crime | Val McDermid (Br.) | HarperCollins |
| 71 | Dead Air | Novel | Iain Banks (Br.) | Abacus |
| 72 | Spellbound | Chicklit | Jane Green (Br.) | Penguin |
| 73 | Samuel Pepys | Biography | Claire Tomalin (Br.) | Penguin |
| 74 | Essential Spike Milligan | Biography | Alexander Games (Br.) | 4th Estate |
| 75 | Dr Atkins for Life | Diet | Robert Atkins (Br.) | Macmillan |
| 76 | He's Got to Go | Chicklit | Sheila O'Flanagan (Ire.) | Headline |
| 77 | A Wing and a Prayer | Saga | Lyn Andrews (Br.) | Headline |
| 78 | Porno | Novel | Irvine Welsh (Br.) | Vintage |
| 79 | Daddy's Little Girl | Crime | Mary Higgins Clark (US) | Pocket |
| 80 | Hidden Talents | Novel | Erica James (Br.) | Orion |
| 81 | Stone Monkey | Thriller | Jeffery Deaver (US) | Coronet |
| 82 | Bravemouth | Biography | Pamela Stephenson (NZ) | Headline |
| 83 | Dying to Tell | Thriller | Robert Goddard (Br.) | Corgi |
| 84 | Vernon God Little | Novel | D.B.C. Pierre (Br.) | Faber |
| 85 | Scaredy Cat | Thriller | Mark Billingham (Br.) | Time Warner |
| 86 | Secrets | Juvenile | Jacqueline Wilson (Br.) | Corgi Yearling |
| 87 | The Gangs of New York | Reportage | Herbert Asbury (US) | Arrow |
| 88 | Without Fail | Thriller | Lee Child (US) | Bantam |
| 89 | First Light | Memoir | Geoffrey Wellum (Br.) | Penguin |
| 90 | The Other Woman's Shoes | Chicklit | Adele Parks (Br.) | Penguin |
| 91 | By the Light of the Moon | Thriller | Dean Koontz (US) | Headline |
| 92 | Lucky Man | Autobiog. | Michael J. Fox (US) | Ebury |
| 93 | Number Ten | Novel | Sue Townsend (Br.) | Penguin |
| 94 | Bride Stripped Bare | Novel | Anon (Aust.) | 4th Estate |
| 95 | Sahara | Travel | Michael Palin (Br.) | Phoenix |
| 96 | Wind Off the Sea | Women's lit. | Charlotte Bingham (Br.) | Bantam |
| 97 | The Good Wife | Novel | Elizabeth Buchan (Br.) | Penguin |
| 98 | Hiding from the Light | Spooky | Barbara Erskine (Br.) | HarperCollins |
| 99 | The Nanny | Novel | Melissa Nathan (Br.) | Arrow |
| 100 | Death's Jest-Book | Crime | Reginald Hill (Br.) | HarperCollins |

| RRP | Month | Home | Export | Total | Gross | No. |
|---|---|---|---|---|---|---|
| £6.99 | May | 210,648 | 40,058 | 250,706 | £1,752,435 | 51 |
| £6.99 | Jan | 248,731 | 2,897 | 251,628 | £1,758,880 | 52 |
| £6.99 | May | 207,609 | 43,838 | 251,447 | £1,757,615 | 53 |
| £6.99 | Mar | 225,933 | 21,242 | 247,175 | £1,727,753 | 54 |
| £6.99 | Jun | 206,758 | 36,940 | 243,698 | £1,703,449 | 55 |
| £6.99 | Jan | 226,234 | 16,876 | 243,110 | £1,699,339 | 56 |
| £6.99 | Sept | 211,544 | 30,988 | 242,532 | £1,695,299 | 57 |
| £5.99 | Jun | 217,217 | 21,218 | 238,435 | £1,428,226 | 58 |
| £6.99 | Aug | 198,577 | 38,054 | 236,631 | £1,654,051 | 59 |
| £6.99 | Mar | 210,849 | 22,424 | 233,273 | £1,630,578 | 60 |
| £7.99 | Jun | 215,990 | 17,218 | 233,208 | £1,863,332 | 61 |
| £7.99 | Feb | 189,644 | 42,090 | 231,734 | £1,851,555 | 62 |
| £6.99 | Jun | 187,806 | 41,349 | 229,155 | £1,601,793 | 63 |
| £6.99 | Mar | 114,632 | 112,056 | 226,688 | £1,584,549 | 64 |
| £7.99 | May | 175,354 | 50,293 | 225,647 | £1,802,920 | 65 |
| £6.99 | Mar | 190,505 | 34,579 | 225,084 | £1,573,337 | 66 |
| £5.99 | Aug | 207,943 | 16,089 | 224,032 | £1,341,952 | 67 |
| £6.99 | June | 195,165 | 28,758 | 223,923 | £1,565,222 | 68 |
| £10.99 | Oct | 123,490 | 95,223 | 218,713 | £2,403,656 | 69 |
| £6.99 | Feb | 170,076 | 45,143 | 215,219 | £1,504,381 | 70 |
| £7.99 | July | 183,930 | 28,367 | 212,297 | £1,696,253 | 71 |
| £6.99 | Dec | 181,157 | 29,436 | 210,593 | £1,472,045 | 72 |
| £8.99 | July | 194,371 | 15,944 | 210,315 | £1,890,732 | 73 |
| £8.99 | Jun | 208,143 | 1,972 | 210,115 | £1,888,934 | 74 |
| £10.99 | Mar | 176,291 | 31,873 | 208,164 | £2,287,722 | 75 |
| £5.99 | May | 175,835 | 28,486 | 204,321 | £1,223,883 | 76 |
| £5.99 | Mar | 191,859 | 11,437 | 203,296 | £1,217,743 | 77 |
| £6.99 | July | 159,548 | 42,455 | 202,003 | £1,412,001 | 78 |
| £6.99 | March | 159,632 | 39,621 | 199,253 | £1,392,778 | 79 |
| £5.99 | June | 158,257 | 41,130 | 199,387 | £1,194,328 | 80 |
| £6.99 | Apr | 152,373 | 46,641 | 199,014 | £1,391,108 | 81 |
| £12.99 | Oct | 10,278 | 187,505 | 197,783 | £2,569,201 | 82 |
| £6.99 | Dec 02 | 158,673 | 38,611 | 197,284 | £1,379,015 | 83 |
| £10.99 | Jan | 137,833 | 57,984 | 195,817 | £2,152,029 | 84 |
| £6.99 | May | 162,206 | 32,075 | 194,281 | £1,358,024 | 85 |
| £4.99 | Mar | 173,864 | 19,297 | 193,161 | £963,873 | 86 |
| £7.99 | Jan | 153,143 | 38,975 | 192,118 | £1,535,023 | 87 |
| £6.99 | April | 144,321 | 46,658 | 190,979 | £1,334,943 | 88 |
| £7.99 | May | 187,928 | 2,846 | 190,774 | £1,524,284 | 89 |
| £6.99 | Aug | 170,990 | 18,681 | 189,671 | £1,325,800 | 90 |
| £6.99 | Aug | 151,320 | 37,402 | 188,722 | £1,319,167 | 91 |
| £6.99 | Jan | 151,069 | 36,673 | 187,742 | £1,312,317 | 92 |
| £6.99 | Sept | 152,561 | 35,114 | 187,675 | £1,311,848 | 93 |
| £9.99 | July | 0 | 186,038 | 186,038 | £1,858,520 | 94 |
| £7.99 | Sept | 145,164 | 38,600 | 183,764 | £1,468,274 | 95 |
| £5.99 | Feb | 156,252 | 27,454 | 183,706 | £1,100,399 | 96 |
| £6.99 | May | 167,952 | 13,389 | 181,341 | £1,267,574 | 97 |
| £6.99 | Apr | 158,998 | 21,455 | 180,453 | £1,261,366 | 98 |
| £5.99 | Apr | 156,152 | 23,622 | 179,774 | £1,076,846 | 99 |
| £6.99 | Mar | 145,303 | 33,403 | 178,706 | £1,249,155 | 100 |

presence gradually increased, and in 2000 they at last achieved parity, to reach 53% in 2001 – mysteriously falling back the next year to 41%, but reasserting themselves again in 2003.

## Genres

More than 80 of the top 100 paperback fastsellers are always fiction. Regular elements of the non-fiction remainder have dealt in diets, horoscopes, jokes, showbiz lives and, latterly, history. Cookery books, being basically tools in daily use, are essentially hardcover bestsellers (with more than seven million in four years for Jamie Oliver's cookbooks). Of fiction, genres fill most slots, particularly thrillers (23 this year), crime, horror, family sagas and a mixed bag of romances. The 'chicklit' fashion for humorous accounts of young women's urban experience, sharing flats, holding a job, finding a man, is evolving into 'mumlit' – and in due course perhaps 'nanlit'. The chicklit pioneer, *Bridget Jones's Diary*, has now passed four million.

Though there is a lesser vogue for 'ladlit', there is no longer an obvious category of the 'men's fiction', once supplied by authors such as Mickey Spillane and Harold Robbins (world sales reached 130 million in his 1970s heyday). Currently the heroics of SAS men, typified by Andy McNab, are the substitute. In the 1970s and early 1980s, with authors such as Russell Braddon and Sven Hassel, hot war outsold sex. But the balloon of the cold war spy story, inflated by Ian Fleming and crewed by Len Deighton, John le Carré, *et al*, fell with the Berlin Wall. Much depends on the policies of the White House and the Kremlin, and the aftermath of recent terrorist action. An interesting development is the arrival of polemics on global issues, typified by the books of Naomi Klein, Eric Schlosser and Michael Moore, whose wicked political reportage attracts young men, the social group least often seen in bookshops.

Science fantasy does better than experimental science fiction. Westerns never figured, despite the fame of Zane Grey, Louis L'Amour and J.T. Edson. Contrary to widespread opinion, erotica has never made publishers an opulent living. Imprints dedicated to soft porn must be content with sales around 25,000, and their living is made more precarious by free material on the internet. Comic books, on the edge of being non-books, and collections of cartoonists of genius, appear *passim*, and quickly fade. Travellers' tales had no significant presence until the American Bill Bryson's flattering farewell journey around Britain sold more copies in one year (1996) than any other travelogue had in 20. But newcomer Pete McCarthy has the best mileage since, followed by Chris Stewart, with the distinction of an imprint specially created for his books, and the travelogues of Michael Palin derived from his televised expeditions.

## Heavyweight to juvenile

Literary authors such as Ian McEwan, John Irving and Jonathan Franzen were never common on the list. However, in recent years the Booker Prize has brought winners in (witness Peter Carey, and Arundati Roy in 1998, the highest to date, and the two most recent laureates, Yann Martel and D.B.C. Pierre). When it works, this award seems to establish books rather than authors, and not all winners reappear. Still, the potential of non-category fiction is evinced by Humberto Eco's *The Name of the Rose*, Tom Wolfe's *The Bonfire of the Vanities*, Salman Rushdie's *Midnight's Children*, and Zadie Smith's first novel *White Teeth*, all well over half a million copies.

The phenomenon at the century's end was a series by J.K. Rowling about a schoolboy wizard called Harry Potter. With five of seven Potter titles published, (and the hero morphing into puberty) they sell more than 50,000 a week in Britain alone. The latest sold 1.6 million hardcover copies on publication day, and had more than doubled that number within six months. Together with Philip Pullman's award-winning trilogy, *His Dark Materials*, they have boosted the status of children's book publishing and the Potter total claimed for 40 countries is upwards of 100 million. Rowling quickly became as popular with children as the late Roald Dahl and Terry Pratchett, who is equally at home on the wilder shores of technology, and whose 48 titles with Transworld sell some 1,850,000 copies a year. Mention must also be made of American horror writer R.L. Stine, claiming worldwide sales of 220 million for 60 children's books.

### The year 2003

The new element for the trade in recent years has been freedom from retail price maintenance and widespread discounting on top hardcover titles. For a few, surprisingly high figures are reported. (Thus, Harris's grotesque thriller *Hannibal* sold 800,000 copies, and Sir Alex Ferguson's *Managing My Life* 600,000). The topselling hardcovers of 2003 continued in the vein of celebrity memoirs, by such as footballer David Beckham (nearing a million), the Royal Butler (750,000 in USA, 540,000 in Britain) and England Rugby Captain Martin Johnson (approx 400,000). Paperbacks are less affected, but perhaps 20% should be deducted from the aggregate money gross shown. The most common price point has stayed on £6.99, though few customers will have paid full price.

In a market with a surplus of books (125,000 new titles emerge every year) the fastsellers' performance seems still the most stable element. The total number of units has risen from 30,247,358 to 31,545,669, but more than a million down on 2001. (The first 25 titles account for 13.5 million books and £97.4 million.) Export, which 40 years ago made up nearly half the total, has dwindled to a low of 20%. In a mature market worth about £1.8 billion, these 100 paperbacks represent a total gross of £226,863,468, but my guess is that, like last year, between £25 million and £30 million were given away in discounts on them alone. You can hear the pips squeaking, not to mention the authors.

**Alex Hamilton** is a journalist and award-winning travel writer, and the author of several novels and volumes of short stories.

### See also...

# Vanity publishing

Mainstream publishers invest their own money in the entire publishing process. In contrast, vanity publishers require an up-front payment. Johnathon Clifford highlights the perils of vanity publishing.

My research into vanity publishing began in 1990 when a 12-year old girl wrote to me in my position as founder and Senior Trustee of the National Poetry Foundation, saying she had found a publisher willing to publish her poetry. I telephoned the 'publisher' under the guise of an aspiring author, and this call was all it took for them to agree to publish my poetry. Their offer was 100 copies of a 38-page book for a fee of £1900, with no need for them to see my poetry first.

## Definition of vanity publishing

'Vanity publishing, also self-styled (often inaccurately) as 'subsidy', 'joint-venture', 'shared-responsibility' or even 'self' publishing, is a service whereby authors are charged to have their work published. Vanity publishers generally offer to publish a book for a specific fee, or offer to include short stories, poems or other literary or artistic material in an anthology, which the authors are then invited to buy.'

– Advertising Standards Authority definition of vanity publishing, 1997

Since then, I have written *Vanity Press & The Proper Poetry Publishers*, a book based on my extensive feedback from vanity companies, assisted the Advertising Standards Authority and collaborated in the making of television and radio programmes. In 1999, I was invited to the House of Lords to talk about the problem of vanity publishing and the need for a change in the law to stop 'rogue traders' in the publishing world. Despite receiving letters of support from 58 MPs, a change to the existing law has yet to be implemented. As a consequence, I set up an 'awareness campaign' consisting of a website and a free advice pack in an effort to protect aspiring authors. The pack, apart from highlighting the business practices of vanity publishers, gives advice on finding a mainstream publisher, internet publishing, the market for short stories and self-publishing. To date, I have sent copies to almost 23,000 individual authors worldwide.

### The perils of vanity publishing

'Vanity publisher' is a phrase I coined in the early 1960s when two American companies were advertising widely in the British press offering to publish poems for £9 and £12 per poem, respectively. Since then the term has also come to mean 'any company that charges a client to publish a book'.

Mainstream publishers invest in the promotion of a book and make their profit from the sale of copies of the book. Vanity publishers, on the other hand, make money from up-front charges. One of the main drawbacks of being published by a vanity publisher is its lack of credibility within the industry. The majority of booksellers and library suppliers are loath to handle vanity books and few reviewers are willing to consider a book published in this way. The Business Unit Director of one of the UK's biggest booksellers wrote: 'We do not buy from vanity publishers except in exceptional circumstances. Their books are, with one or two exceptions, badly produced, over-priced, have poor, uncompetitive jackets and usually have no marketing support.'

I have amassed an extensive collection of documentation from authors who have approached some of the 60-plus vanity publishers operating in the UK. It consists of vanity publishers' initial promotional letters, subsequent written promises, the contracts and letters of complaint from the author, and the vanity publishers' response to those complaints. In recent years, court judgements have found that some vanity publishers are guilty of 'gross misrepresentation of the services they offer' and, as a result, some have been successfully sued and some forced into 'voluntary' liquidation – often only to swiftly reappear under different names.

## How vanity publishers operate

Mainstream publishers never advertise for authors and almost never charge a client, whether known or unknown. Vanity publishers place advertisements wherever they possibly can inviting authors to submit manuscripts. Almost without exception, when authors submit work the vanity publisher will reply that they would like to publish the book but that, as an unknown, the author will have to pay towards the cost. Vanity publishers may tell the author they are very selective in the authors they accept and praise the work, but this is false flattery. I have not been able to find one person during the last 12 years, anywhere in the world, who has been turned down by a vanity publisher – however poorly written their book is. The vanity publisher may state that this is the way many famous authors in the past set out. This is untrue: not one of the quoted 'famous authors' started their writing career by paying a vanity publisher. The BBC programme *Southern Eye* reported that many authors had been sent exactly the same 'glowing report', whatever the subject or quality of their book.

Vanity publishers have charged aspiring authors anything from £1800 up to (in one recorded instance) £20,000 for publishing their book. Many authors have borrowed thousands of pounds on the strength of promised 'returning royalties', as authors are often led to believe that the vanity publisher's marketing department will sell their book for them and that they will recoup their outlay via this service. In December 1997, *Private Eye* ran an article about three authors, one of whom had paid £2400 and the other two £1800 each to a vanity publisher, on the basis that their books would command a 'high level of royalties'. These royalties amounted to £16.35, £21.28 and £47.30 respectively. When the authors complained they each received a threatening letter from the vanity publisher's solicitor. The same company's business practices was a topic featured on the BBC programme *Watchdog* in November 2002.

Some vanity publishers are now asking their clients to pay a 'subvention'. The standard dictionary definition of the word subvention is 'a grant, aid or subsidy paid by a government to an educational institution', so the term is meaningless when used in the context of vanity publishing. The bottom line, however the request for payment is worded, is that the author will bear the full cost of publishing the book. Not a share of, or a subsidy towards, but all the costs and a profit margin on top.

Few vanity publishers quote for a fixed number of copies, leaving the author with little idea what they have paid for. Vanity publishers may simply keep manuscripts 'on file' and only print-on-demand, making it difficult to deliver copies quickly enough to the outlets who *do* order them. There are also companies who propose that once book sales have reached a certain 'target' figure, the client's outlay will be refunded. The number of copies required to be sold is always well in excess of a realistic target.

Some companies claim that part of the service they offer is to send copies of your book to Whitakers, the Copyright Receipt Office and the British Library. In fact, this is a legal requirement for all UK publishers. Other companies claim a 'special' relationship which enables them to supply information on your book to particular outlets on the internet. But Amazon.co.uk, the biggest internet bookseller, does not support this and writes: 'Books are listed on Amazon.co.uk's website in a number of ways – we take feeds from BookData and Whitakers (who automatically update these details on our website) as well as from several wholesalers'.

Authors choosing to vanity publish should be aware that as soon as their last instalment has been paid, the vanity publisher has made maximum profit and does not need to sell a single copy of the author's book.

### Self-publishing

Another way for an author to see their book in print is to self-publish. For self-publishing an author independently funds publication, employing professionals to undertake elements of the process which they cannot do. Most authors are unable to design text pages or covers themselves and will need experts to print the book and (if required) market and promote it. Self-publishing is particularly suited to authors wanting only a few copies.

Since self-publishing has become more widespread, some vanity publishers have misleadingly passed themselves off as self-publishers. However, there is little any vanity publisher can do that the author cannot do better. True self-publishing gives the author much greater control over the production and dissemination of the book. If authors choose to self-publish they should view the whole process, not as money invested to make a return, but as money spent on a pleasurable hobby which will hopefully have been an enjoyable experience.

### Finally...

Aspiring authors should be careful not to be taken in by the promises of some vanity publishers which have so often proved false. The legal phrase 'Caveat Emptor' (Buyer Beware) here becomes 'Caveat Scriptor' – 'Author Beware!'

**Johnathon Clifford** may be contacted on *tel* (01329) 822218 or at johnathon@vanitypublishing.info

# Publishing agreements

Publisher's agreements are not a standard form. Before signing one, the author must check it carefully, taking nothing for granted. Michael Legat navigates the reader through this complex document.

Any author, presented with so complex a document as a publisher's agreement, should read it carefully before signing, making sure that every clause is understood, and not taking anything for granted. Bear in mind that there is no such thing as a standard form. A given publisher's 'standard' contract may not only differ substantially from those of other publishers, but will often vary from author to author and from book to book. Don't be fooled into believing that it is a standard form because it appears to have been printed – most agreements are individually produced on a word processor to give exactly that effect.

## A fair and reasonable agreement

You should be able to rely on your agent, if you have one, to check the agreement for you, or – if you are a member – you can get it vetted by the Society of Authors or the Writers' Guild of Great Britain. But if you are on your own, you must either go to one of the solicitors who specialise in publishing business (probably expensive) or Do It Yourself. In the latter case it will help to compare the contract you have been offered, clause by clause, with a typical Minimum Terms Agreement such as those printed in my own books, *An Author's Guide to Publishing* and *Understanding Publishers' Contracts*.

## Minimum Terms Agreement

The Minimum Terms Agreement (MTA), developed jointly by the Society of Authors and the Writers' Guild, is signed by a publisher on the one hand and the Society and the Guild on the other. It is not an agreement between a publisher and an individual author. It commits the publisher to offering his or her authors terms which are at least as good as those in the MTA. The intention is that only members of the Society and the Guild should be eligible for this special treatment, but in practice publishers who sign the agreement tend to offer its terms to all their authors. There is no standard MTA, and most signatory publishers have insisted on certain variations in the agreement; nevertheless, the more important basic principles have always been accepted. It must be pointed out that the MTA does not usually apply to:

- books in which illustrations take up 40% or more of the space;
- specialist works on the visual arts in which illustrations fill 25% or more of the space;
- books involving three or more participants in royalties; or
- technical books, manuals and reference books.

Since its origins in 1980, comparatively few publishers have signed a Minimum Terms Agreement, although the signatories include several major publishing houses. Some publishers have refused, claiming to treat their authors quite well enough already, while others say that each author and each book is so different that standard terms cannot be laid down. Nonetheless, the MTA has been a resounding success. Almost all non-signatory publishers have adopted some or all of its provisions, and even in the case of the excluded books mentioned above, the terms have tended to improve. All authors can now argue, from a position of some strength, that their own agreements should meet the MTA's standards.

### The provisions of the MTA

The MTA is a royalty agreement (usually the most satisfactory form for an author), and it lays down the minimum acceptable royalties on sales, and the levels at which the rate should rise. These royalties are expressed as percentages of the book's retail price but can easily be adjusted to apply to royalties based on price received, a system to which a number of publishers are changing, increasing the percentages so that the author's earnings are not adversely affected. The MTA also covers the size of the advance (calculated in accordance with the expected initial print quantity and retail price), and recommended splits between publisher and author of moneys from the sale of subsidiary rights (including US and translation rights).

However, the MTA is not by any means concerned solely with money, but with fairness to the author in all clauses of a publishing agreement, special attention being paid to provisions designed to make the author/publisher relationship more of a partnership than it has often been in the past. While recognising the publisher's right to take final decisions on such matters as print quantity, publication date, retail price, jacket or cover design, wording of the blurb, promotion and publicity, and remaindering, the MTA insists that the author has a right to consultation (which should not be an empty formality but should mean that serious consideration is given to his or her views), in all such cases. Also the author's approval must be sought for the sale of any subsidiary rights.

### Some essential clauses

Any publisher's agreement you sign should contain, in addition to acceptable financial terms, clauses covering:

● **Rights licensed.** A clear definition of which rights you are licensing to the publisher. The publisher will normally require volume rights but the agreement must specify whether such rights will apply in all languages (or perhaps only in English) and throughout the world (or only in an agreed list of territories). The duration of the publisher's licence should be spelt out; commonly this is for the period of copyright (currently the author's lifetime plus 70 years), although some publishers now accept a shorter term. A list of those subsidiary rights of which control is granted to the publisher must be included (make sure that the splits of moneys earned from these rights are in accordance with, or approximate reasonably to, those in the MTA, especially in the currently growing area of merchandising).

● **Publication date.** Commitment by the publisher to publication of the book by a specific date (usually within a year or 18 months from the delivery of the typescript). Avoid signing an agreement which is vague on this point, saying, for instance, only that the book will be published 'within a reasonable period'.

- **Copyright**. Confirmation that in all copies of the book the publisher will print a copyright notice in the author's name and a statement that the author has asserted his or her 'Right of Paternity' (the right to be identified as the author in future exploitation of the material in any form), and that a similar commitment will be required from any subsidiary licensee.
- **Fees and permissions**. Clarification, if the book is to include a professionally prepared index or material the copyright of which does not belong to the author, of whether the author or the publisher will be responsible for the fees (or if costs are to be shared, in what proportions) and the clearance of permissions.
- **Acceptable accounting procedures**. Most publishers divide the year into two six-month periods, accounting to the author, and paying any sums due, three months after the end of each period. Look askance at any less frequent accounting or longer delay after the royalty period. The publisher should also agree to pay the author the due share of any subsidiary moneys promptly on receipt, provided that the advance on the book has been earned.
- **Termination**. A clear definition of the various conditions under which the agreement shall be terminated, with reversion of rights to the author.

## Clauses to question

You can question anything in a publisher's agreement before you sign it. Provided that you do so politely and are not just being difficult, the publisher should be prepared to answer every query, to explain, and where possible to meet your objections. Most publishing contracts are not designed to exploit the author unfairly, but you should watch out for:
- **Rights assigned elsewhere**. It is unwise to accept a clause which allows the publisher to assign the rights in your book to another firm or person without your approval.
- **Non-publication**. The contract for a commissioned book often includes wording which alludes to the publisher's acceptance of the work, implying that there is no obligation to publish it if he or she deems it unacceptable. It may be understandable that the publisher wants an escape route in case the author turns in an inferior work, but he or she should be obliged to justify the rejection, and to give the author an opportunity to revise the work to bring it up to standard. If, having accepted the book, the publisher then wishes to cancel the contract prior to publication, the author can usually expect to receive financial compensation, which should be non-returnable even if the book is subsequently placed with another publisher. However, this point is not normally covered in a publishing agreement.
- **Sole publisher**. Some agreements prohibit the author from writing similar material for any other publisher. This may clearly affect the author's earning ability.
- **Editing consultation**. Don't agree to the publisher's right to edit your work without any requirement for him or her to obtain your approval of any changes made.
- **Royalty rate**. While it is normal practice for an agreement to allow the

publisher to pay a lower royalty on books which are sold at high trade discounts, such sales are more frequently made nowadays than in the past, and it is essential to make sure the royalty rate on high discount sales is not unfairly low.

● **Future books**. The Society of Authors and the Writers' Guild are both generally opposed to clauses giving the publisher the right to publish the author's next work, feeling that this privilege should be earned by the publisher's handling of the earlier book. If you accept an option clause, at least make sure that it leaves all terms for a future book to be agreed.

### Electronic and other multimedia rights

The importance of electronic, digital and other multimedia rights, which already require a carefully worded clause in a contract, is likely to increase in years to come, when the only form of publication for a book may be on the internet or whatever may replace it as technology develops. In the meantime publishers, on the one hand, and literary agents and authors' organisations on the other, are in dispute about these rights, including other rights as yet unknown.

The two main issues are concerned with control of the rights and with royalties. Should these rights remain in the direct control of the author (possibly negotiating through an agent) or, as publishers maintain, be regarded as a part of volume rights, and therefore licensed to the publisher? If the publisher controls the rights, should the author receive a royalty of 15% or thereabouts on the publisher's receipts from sales of these rights, or at least 50% of the income, as the Society of Authors and the Association of Authors' Agents insist is fair? Until some agreement has been reached on these and other matters, it is advisable for authors to seek advice on suitable wording of the relevant clause from a literary agent or the Society of Authors or any other established body representing writers.

### Joint and multiple authorship

In the case of joint authorship (a work so written that the individual contributions of the authors cannot be readily separated), the first written agreement should be between the authors themselves, setting out the proportions in which any moneys earned by the book will be split, specifying how the authors' responsibilities are to be shared, and especially laying down the procedure to be adopted should the authors ever find themselves in dispute. The terms of any publishing agreement which they sign (each author having an identical copy) should reflect their joint understanding. The total earnings should not be less than would be paid were the book by a single author, and the authors should have normal rights of consultation.

In the case of multiple authorship (when the work of each contributor can be clearly separated), each author is likely to have an individual contract, and may not be aware of what terms are offered to the others involved. Because of the possibility of disagreement between the authors, the publisher will probably offer little in the way of consultation. All the individual author can do is to ensure that the agreement appears to be fair in relation to the amount of work contributed, and that the author's responsibilities indicated by the contract refer only to his or her work.

## Outright sale

As a general rule no author should agree to surrender his or her copyright to the publisher, although this may be unavoidable in the case of a book with many contributors, such as an encyclopedia. Even then, give up your copyright with great reluctance and only after an adequate explanation from the publisher of why you should (and probably a substantial financial inducement, including, if possible, provision for the payment of a further fee each time the book is reprinted). The agreement itself will probably be no more than a brief and unequivocal letter.

## Subsidies and vanity publishing

Few commercial publishers will be interested in publishing your book on a subsidy basis (i.e. with a contribution from you towards costs), unless perhaps it is of a serious, highly specialised nature, such as an academic monograph, when a publisher who is well established within that particular field will certainly behave with probity and offer a fair contract. Vanity publishers, on the other hand, will accept your book with enthusiasm, ask for 'a small contribution to production costs' (which turns out to be a very substantial sum, not a penny of which you are likely to see again), and will fail to achieve any sales for your book apart from the copies which you yourself buy. If you want to put your own money into the publication of your book, try self-publishing (see page 255) – you will be far better off than going to a vanity house. How do you tell which are the vanity publishers? That's easy – they're the ones who put advertisements in the papers saying things like, 'Authors Wanted!'. Regular publishers don't need to do that.

**Michael Legat** became a full-time writer after a long and successful publishing career. He is the author of a number of highly regarded books on publishing and writing.

## Further reading

Clark, Charles (ed.), *Publishing Agreements: A Book of Precedents*, Butterworths Tolley, 6th edn, 2002

Flint, Michael F., *A User's Guide to Copyright*, Butterworths, 5th edn, 2000

Legat, Michael, *An Author's Guide to Publishing*, Robert Hale, 3rd edn revised, 1998

Legat, Michael, *Understanding Publishers' Contracts*, Robert Hale, 2nd edn revised, 2002

Unwin, Sir Stanley, *The Truth About Publishing*, HarperCollins, 8th edn, 1976, o.p.

# FAQs about ISBNs

The Standard Book Numbering Agency receives a large number of enquiries about the ISBN system. The most frequently asked questions are answered here.

### What is an ISBN?

An ISBN (International Standard Book Number) is a 10-digit product number used by publishers, booksellers and libraries for ordering, listing and stock control purposes. It enables them to identify a specific edition of a specific title in a specific format from a particular publisher. The 10 digits are always divided into four parts, separated by spaces or hyphens. The four parts can be of varying length and are as follows:

- Group Identifier – Identifies a national, geographic or language grouping of publishers. It tells you which of these groupings the publisher belongs to (not the language of the book).
- Publisher Prefix – Identifies a specific publisher or imprint.
- Title Number – Identifies a specific edition of a specific title in a specific format.
- Check Digit – This is always and only the final digit which mathematically validates the rest of the number. It is calculated using a Modulus 11 system with weights 10–2.

### Do all books need to have an ISBN?

There is no legal requirement for an ISBN and it conveys no form of legal or copyright protection. It is a product number.

### What can be gained from using an ISBN?

If you wish to sell your publication through major bookselling chains, or internet booksellers, they will require you to have an ISBN to assist their internal processing and ordering systems. The ISBN also provides access to Bibliographic Databases such as Whitaker BookBank, which are organised using ISBNs as references. These databases are used by the book trade and libraries to provide information for customers. The ISBN therefore provides access to additional marketing tools which could help sales of your product.

### Where can we get an ISBN?

ISBN prefixes are assigned to publishers in the country in which the publisher is based by the national agency for that country. In the UK and Republic of Ireland this agency is the Standard Book Numbering Agency Ltd. The Agency introduces new publishers to the system, assigns prefixes to new and existing publishers and deals with any queries or problems in using the system. The Standard Book Numbering Agency Ltd was the first ISBN Agency in the world. Publishers based elsewhere will not be able to get numbers from the UK Agency but should contact them for details of the relevant Agency.

### Who is eligible for ISBNs?

Any publisher which is publishing a qualifying product for general sale or distribution to the market is eligible (see 'Which products do not qualify for ISBNs?').

### What is a publisher?

It is sometimes difficult to decide who the publisher is and who their agent may be, but the publisher is generally the person or body which takes the financial risk in making a product available. For example, if a product went on sale and sold no copies at all, the publisher is usually the person or body which loses money. If you get paid anyway, you are likely to be a designer, printer, author or consultant of some kind.

### How long does it take to get an ISBN?

In the UK the Standard service time is 10 working days. There is also a Fast Track service, which is a three-working day processing period.

### How much does it cost to get an ISBN?

In the UK there is a registration fee which is payable by all new publishers. The fees are £60 plus VAT for the Standard service and £96 plus VAT for the Fast Track service. A publisher prefix unique to you will be provided and allows for 10 ISBNs. Larger allocations are available where appropriate.

ISBNs are only available in blocks. The smallest block is 10 numbers. It is not possible to obtain a single ISBN.

### Which products do not qualify for ISBNs?

Calendars; diaries; greetings cards, videos for entertainment; documentaries on video/ CD-Rom; computer games; computer application programs; items which are available to a restricted group of people, e.g. a history of a golf club which is only for sale to members, or an educational course book only available to those registered as students on the course.

### Can I turn my ISBN into a barcode?

Where a product carries a barcode and an ISBN, the barcode is derived from the ISBN and includes the Bookland Prefix (978). The barcode also contains a check digit which is derived by a different calculation method from that used for ISBNs. Further information about barcoding for books is available on the Book Industry Communication website (www.bic.org.uk).

## Contact details

### ISBN Agency

3rd Floor, Midas House, 62 Goldsworth Road, Woking GU21 6LQ
*tel* (0870) 777 8712 *fax* (0870) 777 8714
*email* isbn@nielsenbookdata.co.uk
*website* www.whitaker.co.uk/isbn.htm

### What is an ISSN?

An International Standard Serial Number is the numbering system for journals, magazines, periodicals, newspapers and newsletters. It is administered by the British Library (*tel* (01937) 546959).

# Public Lending Right

Under the PLR system, payment is made from public funds to authors (writers, translators, illustrators and some editors/compilers) whose books are lent out from public libraries. Payment is made once a year, and the amount authors receive is proportionate to the number of times (established from a sample) that their books were borrowed during the previous year (July to June).

## The legislation

PLR was created, and its principles established, by the Public Lending Right Act 1979 (HMSO, 30p). The Act required the rules for the administration of PLR to be laid down by a scheme. That was done in the Public Lending Right Scheme 1982 (HMSO, £2.95), which includes details of transfer (assignment), transmission after death, renunciation, trusteeship, bankruptcy, etc. Amending orders made in 1983, 1984, 1988, 1989 and 1990 were consolidated in December 1990 (SI 2360, £3.90). Some further amendments affecting author eligibility came into effect in December 1991 (SI 2618, £1), July 1997 (SI 1576, £1.10), December 1999 (SI 420, £1) and July 2000 (SI 933, £1.50).

## How the system works

From the applications he receives, the Registrar of PLR compiles a register of authors and books which is held on computer. A representative sample of book issues is recorded, consisting of all loans from selected public libraries. This is then multiplied in proportion to total library lending to produce, for each book, an estimate of its total annual loans throughout the country. Each year the computer compares the register with the estimated loans to discover how many loans are credited to each registered book for the calculation of PLR payments. The computer does this using code numbers – in most cases the ISBN printed in the book.

Parliament allocates a sum each year (£7,200,000 for 2003–4) for PLR. This Fund pays the administrative costs of PLR and reimburses local authorities for recording loans in the sample libraries. The remaining money is then divided by the total registered loan figure in order to work out how much can be paid for each estimated loan of a registered book.

## Limits on payments

**Bottom limit**. If all the registered interests in an author's books score so few loans that they would earn less than £5 in a year, no payment is due.

**Top limit**. If the books of one registered author score so high that the author's PLR earnings for the year would exceed £6000, then only £6000 is paid. No author can earn more than £6000 in PLR in any one year.

Money that is not paid out because of these limits belongs to the Fund and increases the amounts paid that year to other authors.

## The sample

The basic sample represents only public libraries (no academic, school, private or commercial libraries are included) and only loans made over the counter (not

## Summary of the 21st year's results

**Registration: authors.** When registration closed for the 21st year (30 June 2003) the number of shares in books registered was 366,565 for 36,362 authors and assignees.

**Eligible loans.** Of the 377 million estimated loans from UK libraries, 169 million belong to books on the PLR register. The loans credited to registered books – 45% of all library borrowings – qualify for payment. The remaining 55% of loans relate to books that are ineligible for various reasons, to books written by dead or foreign authors, and to books that have simply not been applied for.

**Money and payments.** PLR's administrative costs are deducted from the fund allocated to the Registrar annually by Parliament. Operating the Scheme this year cost £812,000, representing some 11.3% of the PLR fund. The Rate per Loan for 2003–4 increased to 4.85 pence and was calculated to distribute all the £6,400,000 available. The total of PLR distribution and costs is therefore the full £7.2 million which the Government provided in 2003–4.

The numbers of authors in various payment categories are as follows:

|         |                  |              |
|---------|------------------|--------------|
| *354    | payments at      | £5000–6000   |
| 350     | payments between | £2500–4999.99 |
| 767     | payments between | £1000–2499.99 |
| 910     | payments between | £500–999.99  |
| 3,875   | payments between | £100–499.99  |
| 12,507  | payments between | £5–99.99     |
| 18,763  | TOTAL            |              |

* includes 280 authors where the maximum threshold applied.

consultations of books on library premises). It follows that only those books which are loaned from public libraries can earn PLR and make an application worthwhile.

The sample consists of the entire loans records for a year from libraries in more than 30 public library authorities spread through England, Scotland, Wales and Northern Ireland. Sample loans represent around 20% of the national total. Several computerised sampling points in an authority contribute loans data ('multi-site' sampling). This change has been introduced gradually, and began in July 1991. The aim has been to increase the sample without any significant increase in costs. In order to counteract sampling error, libraries in the sample change every two to three years. Loans are totalled every 12 months for the period 1 July to 30 June.

An author's entitlement to PLR depends, under the 1979 Act, on the loans accrued by his or her books in the sample. This figure is averaged up to produce first regional and then finally national estimated loans.

### ISBNs

PLR depends on the use of code numbers to identify books lent and to correlate loans with entries on the register so that payment can be made. The system uses the International Standard Book Number (ISBN), which is required for all new registrations. Different editions (e.g. 1st, 2nd, hardcover, paperback, large print) of the same book have different ISBNs.

## Authorship

In the PLR system the author of a book is the writer, illustrator, translator, compiler, editor or reviser. Authors must be named on the book's title page, or be able to prove authorship by some other means (e.g. receipt of royalties). The ownership of copyright has no bearing on PLR eligibility.

**Co-authorship/illustrators**. In the PLR system the authors of a book are those writers, translators, editors, compilers and illustrators as defined above. Authors must apply for registration before their books can earn PLR. This can now be done online through the PLR website. There is no restriction on the number of authors who can register shares in any one book as long as they satisfy the eligibility criteria.

**Writers and/or illustrators**. At least one must be eligible and they must jointly agree what share of PLR each will take. This agreement is necessary even if one or two are ineligible or do not wish to register for PLR. Share sizes should be based on contribution. The eligible authors will receive the share(s) specified in the application. PLR can be any whole percentage. Detailed advice is available from the PLR office.

**Translators**. Translators may apply, without reference to other authors, for a 30% fixed share (to be divided equally between joint translators).

**Editors and compilers**. An editor or compiler may apply, either with others or without reference to them, to register a 20% share. Unless in receipt of royalties an editor must have written at least 10% of the book's content or more than 10 pages of text in addition to normal editorial work. The share of joint editors/compilers is 20% in total to be divided equally. An application from an editor or compiler to register a greater percentage share must be accompanied by supporting documentary evidence of actual contribution.

**Dead or missing co-authors**. Where it is impossible to agree shares with a co-author because that person is dead or untraceable, then the surviving co-author or co-authors may submit an application without the dead or missing co-author but must name the co-author and provide supporting evidence as to why that co-author has not agreed shares. The living co-author(s) will then be able to register a share in the book which will be 20% for the illustrator (or illustrators)

## Most borrowed children's authors

1. Jacqueline Wilson
2. Mick Inkpen
3. R.L. Stine
4. Janet & Allan Ahlberg
5. Lucy Daniels
6. Roald Dahl
7. Enid Blyton
8. Nick Butterworth
9. Eric Hill
10. Dick King-Smith
11. Terry Deary
12. Martin Waddell
13. J.K. Rowling
14. Lucy Cousins
15. Shirley Hughes
16. Sally Grindley
17. David McKee
18. Debi Gliori
19. Jenny Dale
20. Colin McNaughton

These two lists are of the most borrowed authors in UK public libraries. They are based on PLR sample loans in the period July 2002–June 2003. They include all writers, both registered and unregistered, but not illustrators where the book has a separate writer. Writing names are used; pseudonyms have not been combined.

## Most borrowed authors (adult fiction)

1. Danielle Steel
2. Josephine Cox
3. Catherine Cookson
4. Agatha Christie
5. Audrey Howard
6. Jack Higgins
7. James Patterson
8. John Grisham
9. Dick Francis
10. Ian Rankin
11. Ruth Rendell
12. Lynda M. Andrews
13. Emma Blair
14. Mary Higgins Clark
15. Joan Jonker
16. Bernard Cornwell
17. Patricia Cornwell
18. Maeve Binchy
19. Anne Perry
20. Barbara Taylor Bradford

and the residual percentage for the writer (or writers). If this percentage is to be divided between more than one writer or illustrator, then this will be in equal shares unless some other apportionment is requested and agreed by the Registrar.

The PLR Office keeps a file of missing authors (mostly illustrators) to help locate co-authors. Help is also available from publishers, the writers' organisations, and the Association of Illustrators.

**Life and death**. Authors can only be registered for PLR during their lifetime. However, for authors so registered, books can later be registered if first published within one year before their death or 10 years afterwards. New versions of titles registered by the author can be registered posthumously.

**Residential qualifications**. With effect from 1 July 2000, PLR is open to authors living in the European Economic Area (i.e. EU member states plus Norway, Liechtenstein and Iceland). A resident in these countries (for PLR purposes) has his or her only or principal home there. The United Kingdom does not include the Channel Islands or the Isle of Man.

### Eligible books

In the PLR system each separate edition of a book is registered and treated as a separate book. A book is eligible for PLR registration provided that:
- it has an eligible author (or co-author);
- it is printed and bound (paperbacks counting as bound);
- copies of it have been put on sale (i.e. it is not a free handout and it has already been published);
- it is not a newspaper, magazine, journal or periodical;
- the authorship is personal (i.e. not a company or association) and the book is not crown copyright;
- it is not wholly or mainly a musical score;
- it has an ISBN.

### Notification and payment

Every registered author receives from the Registrar an annual statement of estimated loans for each book and the PLR due.

## Sampling arrangements

To help minimise the unfairnesses that arise inevitably from a sampling system, the Scheme specifies the eight regions within which authorities and sampling points have to be designated and includes libraries of varying size. Part of the sample drops out by rotation each year to allow fresh libraries to be included. The following library authorities have been designated for the year beginning 1 July 2004 (all are multi-site authorities):

- London – Harrow, Kingston upon Thames, Bexley, Brent;
- Metropolitan Boroughs – Bolton, North Tyneside, Coventry, The Wirral, Leeds;
- Counties: Northern – Nottinghamshire/Nottingham, Derbyshire/Derby, Lancashire, Northumberland;
- Counties: South West – Hampshire, Worcestershire, Devon, Stoke on Trent;
- Counties: South East – Bedfordshire/Luton, Kent, Milton Keynes/Bucks, West Sussex, Windsor and Maidenhead;
- Scotland – Orkney, Dundee, South Lanarkshire, Fife;
- Northern Ireland – all five Education and Library Boards;
- Wales – Carmarthenshire, Pembrokeshire, Conwy.

Participating local authorities are reimbursed on an actual cost basis for additional expenditure incurred in providing loans data to the PLR Office. The extra PLR work mostly consists of modifications to computer programs to accumulate loans data in the local authority computer and to transmit the data to the PLR Office at Stockton-on-Tees.

## Reciprocal arrangements

Reciprocal PLR arrangements now exist with the German and Dutch PLR schemes. Authors can apply for German and Dutch PLR through the Authors' Licensing and Collecting Society. (Further information on PLR schemes internationally and recent developments within the EC towards wider recognition of PLR is available from the PLR Office or on the international PLR website.)

---

### Further information

**Public Lending Right**

PLR Office, Richard House, Sorbonne Close, Stockton-on-Tees TS17 6DA
*tel* (01642) 604699 *fax* (01642) 615641
*websites* www.plr.uk.com, www.plrinternational.com
*Contact* The Registrar

Application forms, information, publications and a copy of its *Annual Report* are all obtainable from the PLR Office. See website for further information on eligibility for PLR, loans statistics and forthcoming developments.

**PLR Advisory Committee**

Advises the Secretary of State for Culture, Media and Sport and the Registrar on the operation of the PLR scheme.

# Book clubs

## Artists' Choice
Artists' Choice Ltd, PO Box 3, Huntingdon,
Cambs. PE28 0QX
*tel* (01832) 710201 *fax* (01832) 710488
*websites* www.artists-choice.co.uk,
www.acaward.com
Quarterly.

## Baker Books
Manfield Park, Cranleigh, Surrey GU6 8NU
*tel* (01483) 267888 *fax* (01483) 267409
*email* bakerbooks@dial.pipex.com
*website* www.bakerbooks.co.uk
School book clubs for children aged 3–13. Operates
in the UK and reaches English medium schools
overseas.

## BCA
Greater London House, Hampstead Road,
London NW1 7TZ
*tel* 020-7760 6500 *fax* 020-7760 6901
*websites* www.bol.com, www.booksdirect.co.uk
Ancient & Medieval History Book Club, Arts Guild,
Book Club of Ireland, Books for Children,
Computer Book Club, English Book Club, Escape
(The Fiction Club), Fantasy & SF Book Club, The
History Guild, Home Software World, Just Good
Books, Mango, Military and Aviation Book Society,
Mind Body & Spirit, The Mystery & Thriller Club,
QPD (Quality Paperbacks Direct), The Railway
Book Club, The Softback Preview, Taste (A Fresh
Approach to Food), World Books.

## Bibliophile
5 Thomas Road, London E14 7BN
*tel* 020-7515 9222 *fax* 020-7538 4115
*email* order@bibliophilebooks.com
*website* www.bibliophilebooks.com
*Secretary* Annie Quigley
To promote value-for-money reading. Upmarket
literature and classical music on CD available from
mail order catalogue (10 p.a.). Over 3000 titles
covering art and fiction to travel, history and
children's books. Founded 1978.

## The Book People Ltd
Catteshall Manor, Catteshall Lane, Godalming,
Surrey GU7 1UU
*tel* (01483) 861144 *fax* (01483) 861256
*website* www.thebookpeople.co.uk
Popular general fiction and non-fiction, including
children's and travel. Monthly.

## Cygnus Book Club
PO Box 15, Llandeilo, Carmarthenshire SA19 6YX
*tel* (01550) 777977/777701 *fax* (01550) 777569
*email* enquiries@cygnus-books.co.uk
*website* www.cygnus-books.co.uk
Includes psychology and self-help, diet, health and
exercise, world religions, new economics and
education, green issues, mythology, spirituality.
Monthly.

## The Folio Society
44 Eagle Street, London WC1R 4FS
*tel* 020-7400 4222 *fax* 020-7400 4242
*website* www.foliosoc.co.uk
Fine editions of classic literature.

## Letterbox Library
71-73 Allen Road, London N16 8RY
*tel* 020-7503 4801 *fax* 020-7503 4800
*email* info@letterboxlibrary.com
*website* www.letterboxlibrary.com
Multicultural and non-sexist children's books.

## The Poetry Book Society
Book House, 45 East Hill, London SW18 2QZ
*tel* 020-8870 8403. *fax* 020-8870 0865
*email* info@poetrybooks.co.uk
*website* www.poetrybooks.co.uk
*Chair* Daisy Goodwin, *Director* Chris Holifield
This unique book club for readers of poetry was
founded in 1953 by T.S. Eliot, and is funded by the
Arts Council England. Every quarter, selectors
choose one outstanding publication (the PBS
Choice), and recommend 4 other titles. Members
can receive some or all of these books free and are
also offered substantial discounts on other poetry
books. The Poetry Book Society also administers
the T.S. Eliot Prize (see page 553), produces the
quarterly membership magazine, the *Bulletin*, and
has an education service providing teaching
materials for primary and secondary schools. Write
for details.

## Readers' Union Ltd
Brunel House, Forde Close, Newton Abbot,
Devon TQ12 4PU
*tel* (01626) 323200 *fax* (01626) 323318
Includes Country Sports Book Society, The Craft
Club, Craftsman Book Society, Equestrian Book
Society, Gardeners Book Society, Needlecrafts with
Cross Stitch Book Society, Photographic Book
Society.

## Red House

PO Box 142, Bangor LL57 4ZP
*tel* (0870) 1919980  *fax* (0870) 6077720
*email* enquiries@redhouse.co.uk
*website* www.redhouse.co.uk

The children's arm of the UK's largest supplier of
cut-price books, The Book People. Red House
specialises in providing a huge selection of books to
children at competitive prices through a catalogue
and their website. It is not a book club as there is no
commitment to buy every month. Sponsors of the
Red House Children's Book Award.

## Writers' Bookshelf

PO Box 168, Wellington Street, Leeds LS1 1RF
*tel* 0113-238 8333 *fax* 0113-238 8330
*email* janet.davison@writersnews.co.uk

Books for writers.

# Poetry

## Getting poetry published

Michael Schmidt examines the challenges for poets who wish to see their work published.

Start with this axiom: you have not come here to make money.

I write as a publisher who has spent over 30 years not making money out of poetry, and as a quondam poet whose rewards were never material, either. Money may be a consequence, but only in a few cases, usually obtained in the form of grants and bursaries, when a career is well beyond the point at which an article such as this is of interest.

In the old days, right up through the 1950s, there was a popular tradition of verse writing: people kept commonplace books for friends to write lines in when visiting. Or folk composed ballads, Christmas poems, dialect eclogues, limericks. Verse was part of social engagement. It took itself seriously in formal terms but made no pretence of being 'art'. There was a level of competence in making conventional verses, sometimes beyond English, in Latin or Greek, and most people could tell a good piece of verse from a bad one. Jane Austen's family was given to playful versing. In second-hand bookshops you find tomes with verse inscriptions. Like weekend painters, verse writers expressed themselves clearly and skilfully, bringing direct, strictly occasional pleasure to another person or a group. The ambition to Get Published At All Costs had not set in. Now it has; it has been endemic for three decades. The social space for verse has almost vanished, and with it the popular versifying skills. Such a loss has consequences. Dr Johnson in *The Life of Savage* reflects that 'negligence and irregularity, long continued, will make knowledge useless, wit ridiculous, and genius contemptible'. The creative writing culture of reception nowadays seems to be defined less as readership or audience, more as 'market'. Is this change regrettable? Yes. Has it brought any benefits? To the art of poetry, to poetry readership, very few.

Even today, weekend painters know their work will never hang in the Tate; amateur musicians (singers, instrumentalists, composers) content themselves with making music as an end in itself. But the occasional versifier is a dying breed, like the red squirrel, replaced by the interloping grey who, a year into writing, submits work to a dozen editors at once, declaring it to be original, relevant, topical. In the twinkling of an eye these strident creatures absorb, without troubling to learn names, the art of Chaucer, Spenser, Milton, Cowper, Dickinson, Walcott, Rich. Their opinion of modern poetry is low. But then they do not base their opinion on a very large sample. They will have heard of the market leaders and remember some of the poetry read at school.

As an editor at a small publishing house I receive over 2000 full manuscripts a year (and many more submissions for *PN Review*). Telephone calls, letters and emails ask what kind of poetry we publish, whether we publish poetry at all, or how much it will cost to have poems printed. Few poets submitting are aware of the editorial contents of a poetry publisher's list, despite websites and other resources offering this information. Many have read, perhaps in this volume, which publishers have a poetry list and try, without doing a smidgen of research. Without reading. Few seem aware of how large a shoal of wannabe poets surrounds the little flotilla of publishers, editors and other validators. Poetry becomes a means to an end, not an end in itself: to be a poet, go for prizes, give readings and all the peripheral rewards which in the end poison and parch the individual spring, assuming it has more than illusory water in it.

## Publishing in book form

An article of this kind usually proffers advice: how to present a manuscript, how to address an editor, what to expect from a contract, etc. I'd rather try to give writers who believe they have a body of publishable work a realistic sense of the chance of publication, and a realistic preparation for its aftermath, assuming the first goal is achieved. Better to counsel realism than foster illusion.

First, the chances of book publication. More than 1000 new books of verse are published each year, but few are marketed or sold and fewer still reviewed. A list like the one I edit, with 40 poetry titles a year, accommodates at most two or three first collections. Other substantial poetry publishers go for a year or five without adding new names to their lists. Few first collections sell over 1000 copies. Indeed, some may sell fewer than 300. The book trade has become resistant to all but the market leaders in poetry; few independent presses get their poets even into some of the leading chains.

The ecology of poetry publishing, as distinct from that of standard trade publishing, is based more and more narrowly on events. A poet can publish his or her own work, paying a printer to do the job and selling at readings. But then, who is going to invite a self-published poet to read? A poet can go to one of the vanity presses and pay a more substantial sum for the promise of exposure. Again, such publication capitalises on illusion and, as the title proclaims, vanity (see *Vanity publishing*, page 282).

There *are* new opportunities which can be valuable. Any poet is free to post work on the web, in both text and voice form, inviting response. It's quite cheap to do so and response is almost immediate. There are electronic magazines as well. In a sense, the withering away of the poetry book trade is a harbinger of the wider impact of the web. Unfortunately, the web is not discriminating and it is hard to know how a critical take on work self-published on the web will develop. At every stage, it seems to me, poets are tempted to succumb, in their eagerness for publication, to acts of desperation. Publish and be damned! Luck would be a fine thing. There is not even a sufficient audience to damn new work on the web. The question must be, how to publish and be sufficiently visible to *be* damned, or welcomed, as the case may be. But we are getting ahead of ourselves: the first question must be the quality of the work and the motive of the writer.

Before looking for a publisher, writers of verse (as of anything else) should interrogate themselves. *Why* do I want to be published in book form? Is it mere whim or is my work genuinely original? The only way you can answer these questions is by wide reading, not only of contemporaries but also of poets from the past. To be able to judge your art, you must understand it, as you would any other. What makes my work original? In a few instances subject matter in itself can be sufficiently interesting to justify a book, but this is rare: it has more to do with the accidents of birth and upbringing than with any choices a poet might make. Originality is expressed in diction, prosody and form. It need not be dazzling. Edward Thomas recognised Robert Frost's originality, reviewing *North of Boston* in 1914: 'This is one of the most revolutionary books of modern times, but one of the quietest and least aggressive. It speaks, and it is poetry.'

A poet who sets out to get published without understanding in depth the art practised, and the nature of the work intended for publication, is on a hiding to very little. Chances are that such a poet will make decisions that ensure the poetry remains unread.

Ask, before you solicit editorial judgment, to whom your poetry is likely to appeal: To friends and family? The local community (is it in dialect, locally relevant in some way)? To a religious group? Is your work sufficiently distinctive to appeal beyond those groups from which your identity is derived?

### Seeking critical appraisal

If a spouse, relation, teacher or friend, commends your verse, it will be gratifying, but how informed are they, and is their response to you as writer or to the writing? Is it courtesy or real validation? Kind Sir John Betjeman used to write a note to anyone who sent him poems saying 'you show potential' or 'talent'. Thousands of poets thus commended would take his endorsement and include it for the next 20 years with each magazine and volume submission. The commendation of a kind writer is, alas, not worth the paper it is written on. If an established writer believes in your work, he or she will make it a mission to send your work to an editor.

It is important to get a critical purchase on your work, not to overestimate it. Some poets accept that their level is, say, among small magazines; they are content to exist there in a community of similarly committed writers. They do not try for the 'better magazines', knowing they haven't a chance of getting in. They may blame those magazines as elitist and cliquish and no doubt some of them are, but elites and cliques that are permeable to quality. Finding one's level is an early stage in establishing peace of mind: always to aim too high and so to invite rebuff finally undermines self-respect.

Never ask an editor for comments and criticisms unless you are willing to take them. I am often been asked for 'a serious appraisal'. When work seems genuinely interesting I offer detailed advice, and often receive back angry letters or defences of work I have risked commenting upon. A poem works or fails to work; no amount of argufying can convert an experienced reader. I may come to understand more clearly what the intention of a poem *was*, and therefore better to understand how far short it has fallen.

## Magazines, the internet and broadcasting

Most editors advise new writers to seek publication in magazines first. This is mixed advice. It assumes the poet writes 'filler' poems, the fast food that can be served up in a weekly journal. If you are published in magazines the editor does not respect, it may diminish his or her respect for your work. It is crucial, especially if you are not prolific, to try for publication in places where (a) the work will be widely read and (b) publication will increase your visibility. The *Times Literary Supplement* and *London Review of Books* have a curious and unpredictable taste; several specialised journals are worth trying, *Poetry Review, London Magazine, Stand, Poetry London, The North* and *PN Review* among them. It is crucial to subscribe to journals you find congenial, read them regularly and get a sense of the wider world of contemporary publication. Among foreign magazines worth close attention are *Parnassus, Raritan* and *Salt*.

Publication in web magazines can be satisfying; it can also be dangerous for your copyright (the work slips out of your control), and few editors of my acquaintance credit the web as a place to look for poems. Remember that a poem first published on the web is unlikely to be published in a reputable magazine.

Broadcasting is as unpredictable a medium of dissemination as the web. There are slots for various kinds of poetry on radio: dramatic, lyric, etc. Look at the broadcasting schedules, familiarise yourself with the poetry programmes and producers, locally and nationally. On many networks a broadcast poem is heard by quite a large, if not a discriminating or informed, audience. Editors have been known to track down poems heard in broadcast, especially in the poet's own voice if that poet is a good performer.

### The importance of market research

Where should you do your market research for a book publisher? In your personal library of modern poetry books (you ought to have one, with books by favourite authors from a variety of imprints). Most publishers have editorial priorities which are more or less coherent, expressed in anthologies or in the general choice offered. The chief imprints are Faber, Picador, Penguin, Cape and Chatto among larger players, and Arc, Anvil, Bloodaxe, Carcanet, Enitharmon and Seren among the independents. Many other valuable outlets exist. The Poetry Book Society

## Poetry magazines

### The North
The Poetry Business, The Studio, Byram Arcade, Westgate, Huddersfield HD1 1ND

### Parnassus: Poetry in Review
205 West 89th Street, No 8F, New York, NY 10024, USA
*tel* 212-362-3492 *fax* 212-875-0148
*email* parnew@aol.com
No submissions are accepted by email.

### Raritan Literary Magazine
Rutgers – The State University of New Jersey, 31 Mine Street, New Brunswick, NJ 08903, USA
*tel* 732-932-7887 *fax* 732-932-7855

### Salt Literary Magazine
PO Box 202, Applecross, Western Australia 6153
*email* jvk20@hermes.cam.ac.uk
*Editor* John Kinsella

Details for the other magazines mentioned in the article may be found in either *Magazines UK and Ireland* starting on page 31 or *Poetry organisations*, which follows this article.

makes a convenient selection and has useful catalogues, but trusting a book club's choices is no safer for the poetry than for the fiction lover. Always read *beyond*.

In approaching journal editors or publishers it is important to indicate that you know who they are, and why you have chosen them over others. A brief letter is sufficient. If you practise multiple submissions, warn the editors to whom you write. Some editors follow a geological time-scale in replying. If you have not had a reply in six weeks, feel free to send your work elsewhere, but should the first editor accept it in the end, you must immediately withdraw it from other editors.

Success is slow: a hundred rejections may precede an acceptance. Or acceptance may never quite come. If it doesn't, how do you deal with failure? Many wannabe poets who cannot get visibly published develop a strategy of blame. It is not, they insist, the quality of the work that deprives them of readership, it is the cabals that control the avenues of transmission. Jonathan Swift knew this:

If on Parnassus' top you sit,
You rarely bite, are always bit:
Each poet of inferior size
On you shall rail and criticise ...

Other poets study 'the market' and try to follow the latest fashion. Runt-Raines, runt-Muldoons and Motions, have given way to runt-Duffys and Armitages. Aping success can seem to work: in my late 'teens, when the *New Statesman* had rejected me several times, I wrote a poem in what I took to be the style of Ted Walker, a poet popular with the magazine's poetry editor. Sure enough, my verse was accepted. I had the same experience with *Poetry Now* on radio. The editor loved what he called 'the macabre' and I delivered precisely that. Such poems, cynically composed, had a short half-life. Imitation is part of any serious apprenticeship, but publishing unacknowledged imitations, especially if they are written not to develop skills but to achieve publication, is a form of failure.

### Dealing with success

Assuming the Muses of publication smile, how do you deal with success? Success can be failure postponed. A book is edited, designed, published, and then falls into a black hole of neglect. A book is published and receives negative reviews. A book is published, receives good reviews, but fails to sell. A book is published, receives good reviews, sells, but the next book does less well and there is a future of diminishing returns. The judge at the pearly gates will declare, 'It is the sort of verse which was modern in its time'.

Real success is rare and has little to do with the strategies outlined here. No poet living in the UK at this time makes a living solely from writing poems. Most write and teach, or write and perform, or have a day job, or write in other genres (novels, radio and television plays, journalism) as well as poetry. Assuming the poetry is good and/or well received, there will be invitations to perform. Fees vary from about £100 to £1000, depending on the occasion and the venue. A poet who is a good performer will read once or twice a week for a period of time and sell more books than a poet who cannot perform convincingly, even if the latter's poems are better. Indeed some apparently substantial reputations are based on performance skills rather than on the quality of the poetry.

Real success is judged less by the marketplace, more by a culture of reception which gradually grows alert to new work and explores it. It may be, if the work you are writing is original and challenging, that you will have to develop your own means of transmission on paper (a magazine, a pamphlet or book publishing house) or on the web. As long as the vehicles you create exist to serve not only your own work, but poetry more widely, whether the writing of fellow radicals or neglected texts from the past that helped shape your perspectives and formal approaches. The creation of such vehicles means that you retain control of production and dissemination; eventually the endeavour, particular and general, is acknowledged, the work read. You are in dialogue with readers.

The endorsement of an Establishment consisting of the larger publishers, specialist lists, journals and the academy, is not a guarantee of quality. What is a guarantee is a readership which will go out of its way to get hold of your work – a poem in a magazine, a pamphlet, an e-poem, a book – and will invest time and creative energy in reading you and taking bearings from what you propose.

It would be churlish of me not to mention that many poets spend their time and resources on entering competitions, and competitions are a way (the three or four major ones) of making yourself briefly visible. A competition-winning poem is not 'news that stays news', as Pound said poetry ought to be, but mere news. Mere news with money attached: not to be sneezed at. There is also the matter of fees and advances. For a 24-line poem published in a journal, payment will vary from £30 to £500, depending on the outlet. The advance for a book of poems, especially a first collection, will vary from £300 to £3000, with the occasional mad exception.

In negotiating a publishing contract, it is worth remembering that the greatest value your poems will have in the long term for you, as for your publisher, is unlikely to be the book sales. What will matter in the end, assuming your work becomes established, is the subsidiary rights: anthology, quotation, broadcasting, electronic, translation. Several poetic estates live handsomely on subsidiary rights income. For three decades I have been publishing William Carlos Williams' poetry.

So much depends
upon

a red wheel
barrow...

Eight simple lines have earned Williams' estate, and his publisher, between £27 and £35 per week over that period.

**Michael Schmidt** is editor of *PN Review* and director of Carcanet Press.

# Poetry organisations

Poetry is one of the easiest writing art forms to begin with, though the hardest to excel at or earn any money from. Many organisations offer advice, information and resources to writers and readers at all levels, and as many as possible are included here. Jules Mann, Director of the Poetry Society, lists below the organisations which can help poets take their poetry further.

## Where to get involved

### The Poetry Society
22 Betterton Street, London WC2H 9BX
*tel* 020-7420 9880 *fax* 020-7240 4818
*email* info@poetrysociety.org.uk
*website* www.poetrysociety.org.uk

The Poetry Society was set up to help poetry and poets thrive in Britain and is a registered charity funded by the Arts Council England. The Society offers advice and information to all, with a more comprehensive level of information available to members. Membership is open to anyone interested in poetry and includes 4 issues each of the magazine *Poetry Review* and the newsletter *Poetry News*. The Society's website offers an excellent interactive regional guide to poetry organisations, venues, publishers and bookshops around the UK through its Poetry Landmarks of Britain section.

The Society also publishes education resources (see later); promotes National Poetry Day; runs a critical service called Poetry Prescription (£50 for 100 lines – 20% discount to members); provides an education advisory and training service, school membership, youth membership and a thriving website. A range of events and readings take place at the Poetry Café and the Poetry Studio at the Society's headquarters in Covent Garden.

Competitions run by the Society include the National Poetry Competition, the largest open poetry competition in Britain each year with a first prize of £5000, the biannual Corneliu M. Popescu Prize for European Poetry Translation and the Foyle Young Poets of the Year Award. Membership: £35 full, £25 concessions. Founded 1909.

### Poetry Ireland
120 St Stephen's Green, Dublin 2,
Republic of Ireland
*tel* (01) 478 9974 *fax* (0) 478 0205
*email* poetry@iol.ie
*website* www.poetryireland.ie

Poetry Ireland is the national organisation dedicated to developing, supporting and promoting poetry throughout Ireland. It is a resource and information point for any member of the public with an interest in poetry and works towards creating opportunities for poets working or living in Ireland. It is grant-aided by both the Northern and Southern Arts Councils of Ireland and is a resource centre with the Austin Clarke Library of over 10,000 titles. It publishes the quarterly magazine *Poetry Ireland Review* and the bi-monthly newsletter *Poetry Ireland News*. Poetry Ireland organises readings in Dublin and nationally, and runs a Writers-in-Schools Scheme.

### The Poetry Book Society
Book House, 45 East Hill, London SW18 2QZ
*tel* 020-8870 8403 *fax* 020-8870 0865
*email* info@poetrybooks.co.uk
*website* www.poetrybooks.co.uk
*Chair* Daisy Goodwin, *Director* Chris Holifield

This unique book club for readers of poetry was founded in 1953 by T.S. Eliot, and is funded by the Arts Council England. Every quarter, selectors choose one outstanding publication (the PBS Choice), and recommend 4 other titles. Members can receive some or all of these books free and are also offered substantial discounts on other poetry books. The Poetry Book Society also administers the T.S. Eliot Prize (see page 553), produces the quarterly membership magazine, the *Bulletin*, and has an education service providing teaching materials for primary and secondary schools. Write for details.

### The British Haiku Society
Lenacre Ford, Woolhope, Hereford HR1 4RF
Secretary David Walker
*tel* (01432) 860328
*email* davidawalker@btinternet.com
*website* www.britishhaikusociety.org

The Society runs the prestigious annual James W. Hackett International Haiku Award, the Nobuyuki Yuasa Annual International Award for Haibun and the bienniel Sasakawa Prize worth £2500 for original contributions in the field of haikai. It is active in promoting the teaching of haiku in schools and colleges, and is able to provide readers, course/workshop leaders and speakers for poetry groups, etc. It has created a haiku teaching/learning kit for schools. Write for membership details. Founded 1990.

## Survivors Poetry

Diorama Arts Centre, 34 Osnaburgh Street,
London NW1 3ND
*tel* 020-7916 5317 *fax* 020-7916 0830
*email* survivor@survivorspoetry.org.uk

Survivors Poetry provides poetry workshops,
performances, readings, publishing, networking and
training for survivors of mental distress in London
and the UK. Survivors Poetry is funded by the Arts
Council England and was founded in 1991 by
4 poets who have had first-hand experience of the
mental health system. It works in partnership with
local and national arts, mental health, community,
statutory and disability organisations. Its outreach
project has established a network of 30 writers'
groups in the UK.

## Where to get information

Your local library should have information about
the local poetry scene. Many libraries are actively
involved in promoting poetry as well as having
modern poetry available for loan. Local librarians
promote writing activities with, for example,
projects like Poetry on Loan and Poetry Places
information points in West Midlands Libraries.

## The Poetry Library

Level 5, Royal Festival Hall, London SE1 8XX
*tel* 020-7921 0943/0664 *fax* 020-7921 0939
*email* poetrylibrary@rfh.org.uk
*website* www.poetrylibrary.org.uk

The principal roles of the Poetry Library are to
collect and preserve all poetry published in the UK
since about 1912 and to act as a public lending
library. The Library also keeps a wide range of
international poetry. It has 2 copies of each title
available and a collection of about 40,000 titles in
English and English translation. The Library also
provides an education service (see page 308).

Founded in 1953 by the Arts Council, the Library
runs an active information service, which includes a
unique noticeboard for lost quotations, and tracing
authors and publishers from extracts of poems.
Current awareness lists are available for magazines,
publishers, competitions, bookshops, groups and
workshops, evening classes and festivals on receipt
of a large sae. The Library also stocks a full range of
British poetry magazines as well as a selection from
abroad. When visiting the Library, look out for the
Voice Box, a performance space for literature; a
programme is available from 020-7921 0906. Open
11am–8pm Tuesday to Sunday. Membership: free
with proof of identity and current address.

## The Northern Poetry Library

County Library, The Willows, Morpeth,
Northumberland NE61 1TA
*tel* (01670) 534514 (poetry enquiries)
*tel* (01670) 534524 (poetry dept)

The Northern Poetry Library has over 14,000 titles
and magazines covering poetry published since
1945. For information about epic through to classic
poetry, a full text database is available of all poetry
from 600–1900. A postal lending service is available
to members, who pay for return postage.
Membership is free to anyone living in the areas of
Tyne and Wear, Durham, Northumberland,
Cumbria and Cleveland. Founded 1968.

## The Scottish Poetry Library

5 Crichton's Close, Canongate,
Edinburgh EH8 8DT
*tel* 0131-557 2876 *fax* 0131-557 8393
*email* inquiries@spl.org.uk
*website* www.spl.org.uk

The Scottish Poetry Library is run along similar
lines to the Poetry Library in London. It specialises
in 20th century poetry written in Scotland, in Scots,
Gaelic and English. It also collects some pre-20th-
century poetry and contemporary poetry from all
over the world. Information and advice is given, and
visits by individuals, groups and schools are
welcome. Borrowing is free of charge and there is a
membership scheme (£20 p.a.), which includes use
of the members' reading room and a regular
newsletter. It has branches in libraries and arts
centres throughout Scotland and also runs a library
touring service. Readings and exhibitions are
regularly organised, particularly during the
Edinburgh Festival. Founded 1984.

## Arts Council England

*website* www.artscouncil.org.uk
Arts Council England has 9 regional offices and
local literature officers can provide information on
local poetry groups, workshops and societies (see
page 502). Some give grant aid to local publishers
and magazines and help fund festivals, literature
projects and readings, and some run critical
services.

## The internet

You can get many links with good internet poetry
magazines through the following:

## The Poetry Kit

*website* www.poetrykit.org

## The Poetry Society of America

*website* www.poetrysociety.org

# Where to get poetry books

See the Poetry Book Society on page 305. The Poetry Library provides a list of bookshops which stock poetry. For second-hand mail order poetry books try:

## The Poetry Bookshop

The Ice House, Brook Street,
Hay-on-Wye HR3 5BQ
*tel* (01497) 821812

## Peter Riley

27 Sturton Street, Cambridge CB1 2QG
*tel* (01223) 576422
*email* priley@dircon.co.uk

# Where to celebrate poetry

Festival information should be available from Arts Council England offices (see page 502). See also *Literature festivals* on page 573

## The British Council

Information Officer, Literature Dept,
The British Council, 11 Portland Place,
London W1N 4EJ
*tel* 020-7930 8466 *fax* 020-7389 3199
*website* www.britishcouncil.org/arts/literature

Send a large sae or visit the website for a list of forthcoming festivals.

# Where to perform

In London, Express Excess and Vice Verso are 2 of the liveliest venues and they regularly feature the best performers, while Poetry Unplugged at the Poetry Café is famous for its weekly open mike nights (Tuesdays 7.30pm). Other performance venues listed below have readings. For up-to-date information, read *Time Out* and *What's On in London*).

For venues outside London, check local listings, ask at libraries and Arts Council England offices, and visit the Landmarks of Britain section of the Poetry Society's website (www.poetrysociety.org.uk).

## Apples and Snakes Performance Poetry

Battersea Arts Centre, Lavender Hill,
London SW11
*tel* 020-7223 2223

## Coffee House Poetry

Troubadour Coffee House, 265 Old Brompton Road,
London SW5
*tel* 020-7370 1434

## Express Excess

The Enterprise, 2 Haverstock Hill, London NW3
*tel* 020-7485 2659

## Poetry Café

22 Betterton Street, London WC2
*tel* 020-7420 9888

## Vice Verso

Bread and Roses, 68 Clapham Manor Street,
London SW4
*tel* 020-8341 6085

## Voice Box

Level 5, Royal Festival Hall, London SE1
*tel* 020-7960 4242

# Competitions

There are now hundreds of competitions to enter and as the prizes increase, the highest being £5000 (first prize in the National Poetry Competition and the Arvon Foundation International Poetry Competition), so does the prestige associated with winning such competitions.

To decide which competitions are worth entering, make sure you know who the judges are and think twice before paying large sums for an anthology of 'winning' poems which will only be read by entrants wanting to see their own work in print. The Poetry Library publishes a list of competitions each month (available free on receipt of a large sae). See also *Getting poetry published* on page 299 and *Prizes and awards* on page 546.

Literary prizes are given annually to published poets and as such are non-competitive. An A–Z guide to literary prizes can be found on the Booktrust website (www.booktrust.org.uk).

# Where to write poetry

## The Arvon Foundation

**Lumb Bank – The Ted Hughes Arvon Centre**
Hebden Bridge, West Yorkshire HX7 6DF
*tel* (01422) 843714 *fax* (01422) 843714
*website* www.arvonfoundation.org
**The Arvon Foundation at Totleigh Barton**
Sheepwash, Beaworthy, Devon EX21 5NS
*tel* (01409) 231338 fax (01409) 231144
**The Arvon Foundation at Moniack Mhor**
Teavarren, Kiltarlity, Beauly,
Inverness-shire IV4 7HT
*tel* (01463) 741675 *fax* (01463) 741733
**The Hurst – The John Osborne Arvon Centre**
Clunton, Craven Arms, Shrops. SY7 0JA
*tel* (01588) 640658 *fax* (01588) 640509
*email* hurst@arvonfoundation.org

The Arvon Foundation's 4 centres run 5-day residential courses throughout the year to anyone over the age of 16, providing the opportunity to live and work with professional writers. Writing genres explored include poetry, narrative, drama, writing for children, song writing and the performing arts. Bursaries are available to those receiving benefits. Founded in 1968.

## The Poetry School
1a Jewel Road, London E17 4QU
*tel/fax* 020-8223 0401 *tel* 020-8985 0090
*email* thepoetryschool@phonecoop.coop
*website* www.poetryschool.com

Using London venues, the Poetry School offers a core programme of tuition in reading and writing poetry. It provides a forum to share experience, develop skills and extend appreciation of both traditional and innovative aspects of poetry.

## The Poet's House/Teach na hÉigse
Clonbarra, Falcarragh, County Donegal, Republic of Ireland
*tel* (074) 65470 *fax* (074) 65471
*email* phouse@iol.ie

The Poet's House runs 3 10-day poetry courses in July and August. An MA degree in creative writing is validated by Lancaster University, and the Irish Language Faculty includes Cathal O'Searcaigh. The poetry faculty comprises 30 writers, including Paul Durcan and John Montagu.

## Ty Newydd
Taliesin Trust, Ty Newydd, Llanystumdwy, Criccieth, Gwynedd LL52 0LW
*tel* (01766) 522811 *fax* (01766) 523095
*email* post@tynewydd.org
*website* www.tynewydd.org

Ty Newydd runs week-long writing courses encompassing a wide variety of genres, including poetry, and caters for all levels, from beginners to published poets. All the courses are tutored by published writers. Writing retreats are also available.

## Groups on the internet
It is worth searching for discussion groups and chat rooms on the internet. There are plenty of them; John Kinsella's is highly recommended, which is junk mail-resistant and highly informative:

## John Kinsella's
*email* poetryetc@jiscmail.ac.uk

## The Poetry Kit
*website* www.poetrykit.org/wkshops2.htm

## Local groups
Local groups vary enormously so it is worth shopping around to find one that suits your poetry. Up-to-date information can be obtained from Arts Council England regional offfices (see page 502).

The Poetry Library publishes a list of groups for the Greater London area which will be sent out on receipt of a large sae.

# Help for young poets and teachers

## National Association of Writers in Education (NAWE)
PO Box 1, Sheriff Hutton, York YO60 7YU
*tel/fax* (01653) 618429
*email* paul@nawe.co.uk
*website* www.nawe.co.uk
NAWE is a national organisation, which aims to widen the scope of writing in education, and coordinate activities between writers, teachers and funding bodies. It publishes the magazine *Writing in Education* and is author of a writers' database which can identify writers who fit the given criteria (e.g. speaks several languages, works well with special needs, etc) for schools, colleges and the community. Publishes *Reading the Applause: Reflections on Performance Poetry by Various Artists*. Write for membership details.

## The Poetry Library
Children's Section, Royal Festival Hall, London SE1 8XX
*tel* 020-7921 0664
*website* www.poetrylibrary.org.uk

For young poets, the Poetry Library has about 4000 books incorporating the SIGNAL Collection of Children's Poetry. It also has a multimedia children's section, from which cassettes and videos are available to engage children's interest in poetry.

The Poetry Library has an education service for teachers and writing groups. Its information file covers all aspects of poetry in education. There is a separate collection of books and materials for teachers and poets who work with children in schools, and teachers may join a special membership scheme to borrow books for the classroom.

## Poetry Society Education
The Poetry Society, 22 Betterton Street, London WC2H 9BX
*tel* 020-7420 9894 *fax* 020-7240 4818
*email* education@poetrysociety.org.uk
*website* www.poetrysociety.org.uk

For over 30 years the Poetry Society has been introducing poets into classrooms, providing teachers' resources and producing colourful, accessible publications for pupils. A publication celebrating National Poetry Day is sent free to schools, giving an insight into the best of contemporary poetry.

Schools membership (£50 secondary, £30 primary)

offers publications, training opportunities for teachers and poets, a free subscription to *Poems on the Underground* and a consultancy service giving advice on working with poets in the classroom. *Poetryclass*, an INSET training project funded by the DfES, employs poets to train teachers at primary and secondary level. People aged 11–18 can join the Society and receive poetry books and posters, quarterly copies of *Poetry News*, and a Young Writer's Pack giving advice on developing writing skills.

Poetry Society publications for schools include *The Poetry Book for Primary Schools* and *Jumpstart Poetry in the Secondary School*, a young poets pack and posters for school Key Stage 1 to GCSE requirements. A full catalogue of poetry resources, details of youth membership, the Foyle Young Poets of the Year Award, school membership and education residencies are available from the Education Department.

## Young poetry competitions

Children's competitions are included in the competition list provided by the Poetry Library (free on receipt of a large sae).

## Foyle Young Poets of the Year Award

The Poetry Society, 22 Betterton Street, London WC2H 9BX
*tel* 020-7420 9894 *fax* 020-7240 4818
*email* education@poetrysociety.org.uk
*website* www.poetrysociety.org.uk

Free entry for 11–18 year-olds with unique prizes.

## Christopher Tower Poetry Prize

Tower Poetry, Christ Church, Oxford OX1 1DP
*tel/fax* (01865) 286591
*email* info@towerpoetry.org.uk
*website* www.towerpoetry.org.uk/prize/index.html

An annual poetry competition from Christ Church, Oxford, open to 16–18 year-olds in UK schools and colleges. The poems should be no longer than 48 lines, on a different chosen theme each year. Prizes: £1500 (1st), prize £750 (2nd), £500 (3rd). Every winner also receives a prize for their school. Highly commended entries each receive £200.

## Further reading

Baldwin, Michael, *The Way to Write Poetry*, Hamish Hamilton, 1982, o.p.

Chisholm, Alison, *The Craft of Writing Poetry*, Allison & Busby, 1997, repr. 2001

Chisholm, Alison, *A Practical Poetry Course*, Allison & Busby, 1997

Corti, Doris, *Writing Poetry*, Writers News Library of Writing/Thomas & Lochar, 1994

Fairfax, John, and John Moat, *The Way to Write*, Elm Tree Books, 2nd edn revised, 1998

Finch, Peter, *How to Publish Your Poetry*, Allison & Busby, 2nd edn, 1998

Forbes, Peter, *Scanning the Century*, Penguin Books, 2000

Hamilton, Ian, *The Oxford Companion to Twentieth Century Poetry in English*, OUP, 1996

Hyland, Paul, *Getting into Poetry*, Bloodaxe, 2nd edn, 1997

Livingstone, Dinah, *Poetry Handbook for Readers and Writers*, Macmillan, 1992

O'Brien, Sean, *The Firebox*, Picador, 1998

*Reading the Applause: Reflections on Performance Poetry by Various Artists*, NAWE, 1999

Riggs, Thomas (ed.), *Contemporary Poets*, St James Press, 7th edn, 2000

Roberts, Philip Davies, *How Poetry Works*, Penguin Books, 2nd edn, 2000

Sansom, Peter, *Writing Poems*, Bloodaxe, 1994, reprinted 1997

Sweeney Matthew, and John Williams, *Teach Yourself Writing Poetry*, Hodder and Stoughton, 2003

Whitworth, John, *Writing Poetry*, A & C Black, 2001

## USA

Breen, Nancy, *Poet's Market*, Writer's Digest Books, USA, 2004 (due Aug 2003)

Fulton, Len, *Directory of Poetry Publishers*, Dustbooks, USA, 19th edn, 2003–4

Fulton, Len, *The International Directory of Little Magazines and Small Presses*, Dustbooks, USA, 39th edn, 2003–4

Preminger, Alex, *New Princeton Encyclopedia of Poetry and Poetics*, Princeton University Press, 3rd edn, 1993

### See also...

- *Publishers of poetry*, page 755
- *Getting poetry published*, page 299

# Television, film and radio

## Adaptations from books

Although every writer wants to create their own work and find their own voice, adaptation is a good way both to generate income and to learn about how to write for other formats. It can also be a chance for a writer to raise their profile, with a successful adaptation sometimes leading to an original commission. Kate Sinclair explains.

Although every writer wants to create their own work and find their own voice, adaptation is a good way both to generate income and to learn about the disciplines of different media: how to write for other formats.

Writers may be approached to adapt their own work from one medium to another during their career. For example, John Mortimer originally wrote *A Voyage Round My Father* for the radio and later adapted it for stage, film and finally, for television. There are also opportunities for both writers and directors to adapt someone else's work from one performance medium to another or from a novel to any of the above.

Every year classic novels are made into adaptations for all media. These may be for the theatre, such as Helen Edmundson's version of *War and Peace* (Shared Experience/RNT), or for radio such as *Rob Roy* (the Classic Serial, Radio 4). Television carries dramatisations like *The Forsyte Saga* (ITV) or *Daniel Deronda* (BBC), and film features screenplays such as Terence Davies' version of Edith Wharton's *The House of Mirth*. Although these are usually costly to produce, involving large casts and – particularly in the visual media – the considerable expense of recreating the period in which they were written, they command loyal audiences and seem to be in steady demand. These classic projects also generate significant income both from DVD/video sales and from sales to overseas companies and networks. Some adapters are as well known as writers who concentrate on their own work. For example, Andrew Davis has become almost a household name for his television dramatisations of *Pride and Prejudice, The Way of the World* and, most recently, *Dr Zhivago*.

Producers in radio, television and film are also in regular contact with publishers and literary agents to keep abreast of contemporary novels which may work well in another format. I currently work as the Books Executive for Film Four to find books, both fiction and non-fiction, which may become television dramas or feature films. The BBC also employs someone in this capacity to identify suitable material for their Serials and Film Departments. Both radio producers and film companies are also sent potential books by the publicity departments of publishing houses. Writers may also make direct approaches to producers and commissioners with material that they feel they can successfully transcribe for that particular medium.

There is clearly, then, a market for adaptations of all types, with the added stimulus to the adapter of exploring technically how another writer writes – their use of language, the way they structure a narrative, their characterisation. There is the opportunity to learn from the skill and subtlety of great writers and there is the challenge of finding ways to transport a story from one form to another, with all the creative possibilities that this presents.

## What to adapt, and why?

Just because a narrative works in one format doesn't guarantee that it will in another. Form and story are often inextricably bound together. Something works as a radio play precisely because it appeals to a listening audience and is able to exploit the possibilities of sound. A novel may have a reflective subject, or concentrate on a character's inner thoughts, and not on external action. While this may be fine for reading quietly alone, it could leave a theatre, television or film audience bored and longing for something to happen.

There are some stories, however, which seem to work in almost any media and which have almost become universal (though different treatments bring out diverse aspects of the original). For example, Henry James's *The Turn of the Screw* was written as a novella. It subsequently became a much-performed opera, with a libretto by Myfanwy Piper and music by Benjamin Britten; an acclaimed film, re-titled *The Innocents* with the screenplay by John Mortimer; and a recent television adaptation for ITV by Nick Dear. What makes a narrative like this transmute so successfully?

At the most simplistic level it must be dramatic. Radio, television and film, like the theatre, need drama to hold their audiences. Aristotle's premise that 'all drama is action', and should have protagonists whom we identify with, antagonists who oppose them, and the reversals, climaxes and resolutions which typify a dramatic structure. This is not necessarily the case for a novel; it is easy to be seduced by a tale that has personal resonance or beautiful language and forget the basic template which has, after all, worked for thousands of years. Reminding yourself of this when considering the suitability of any material for adaptation could spare you a rejection or a great deal of later reworking.

## Knowing the media

The other important consideration is a detailed knowledge of the final medium. The adapter needs to understand why that particular story is specifically suited to it and ideally have experience of writing for that form, as well as an awareness of the current market for the project. It is vital to know precisely what is currently being produced and by whom. Staff and policies change very quickly, so the more up-to-date your research is, the better your chance of creating a successful adaptation and being able to get it accepted.

If you are adapting for the theatre, how often do you go and when was the last time you saw a production that wasn't originally written for the stage? As well as observing how successful it was, both artistically and in box office terms, would you know whether that company or theatre regularly programmes adaptations, and if so, what sort? Do they, like Shared Experience, have a reputation primarily for classics, or do they, like the Loft at the Royal National Theatre, or The Royal

Exchange, Manchester, produce versions of contemporary novels? Are you sufficiently aware of the tastes of the current artistic director and the identity of the theatre to know whether to send your project to the Royal Shakespeare Company, the West Yorkshire Playhouse or Southwark Playhouse? This is not necessarily just a question of scale or level, but more a reflection of contemporary trends and the specific policy of each of these institutions. Whilst the overall remit of a theatre or company may remain the same – if they are funded to produce only new plays, it is unlikely that this will alter – individual personnel and fashions will change regularly and it is important to keep in touch.

## Television and radio

The same holds true for all the other media and, if anything, is even more important in radio and television. All of the broadcast media are now subject to the rigorous demands of ratings, which in turn make for extremely precise scheduling. Programmes have strong identities, and conversations with producers and commissioners will inevitably involve a discussion of which slot a project is suited to and what has recently been shown or broadcast. Up-to-the-minute knowledge of the work being produced by a company or broadcaster is therefore essential.

For example, BBC Radio 3's *Wire* is specifically for new work by contemporary writers and therefore isn't suitable for a classic adaptation of a novel. Radio 4 produces the Classic Serial on Sunday afternoons and *Women's Hour* has a regular serialisation slot that can be contemporary or classic and is often an adapted novel. Biographies or autobiographies are also frequently abridged and read on Radio 4 at 9.45am on weekdays. For a detailed knowledge of this output there can be no substitute for studying the *Radio Times*, seeing what is programmed, and listening to what gets produced in which slots. Being able to envisage the eventual destination for a chosen adaptation helps you to choose the right project and place it successfully.

In television this process of research is more complex. As well as strong competition between the BBC and the larger independent broadcasters (ITV, Channel 4, Carlton, Granada, etc) to secure an audience, there is also considerable rivalry between the hundreds of independent production companies to receive commissions. The ratings war means that scheduling is paramount and big dramatic adaptations are often programmed at exactly the same time on BBC 2 and ITV. Familiarity with the output of each channel is crucial when suggesting projects for adaptation, either to a commissioner or a production company. Again, watching dramatisations and noting what format they are in, who is producing them, and when they are being broadcast, is all part of the job.

As a general rule it is helpful to know that both adaptations and writing commissioned directly for television, tend to be divided into several basic categories (not including soaps). Single dramas are usually high profile, broadcast at peak times and are about two hours long. Series consist of a number of weekly parts shown over several weeks (3, 4, 6, 8 and 10 are all common), each part lasting anywhere between 30 and 60 minutes; there has also recently been a trend for fewer 90-minute-long episodes. Finally there are two-part dramas or event pieces which take place on consecutive nights with each part between one and two hours long. The percentage of adaptations will generally be lower than newly commissioned drama, although this is entirely dependent upon the type of slot and the broadcaster. For example, the BBC has approximately double the budget per hour for drama that Channel 4 has, and produces many more dramatisations of classic novels. Likewise, ITV has currently been producing regular serialisations of classics and single adaptations in association with HSBC. Channel 4, when it commissions adaptations, tends to focus on cutting-edge contemporary novels, such as *White Teeth* by Zadie Smith, adapted by Simon Burke. And there are of course always exceptions to all these trends, which is why it is necessary to be an aware and regular viewer.

If you want to adapt for film, the nature of what will work and when, seems to be more open-ended, though it is of course important to go regularly to the cinema and know what has been produced recently. This may be to do with the nature of distribution – the fact that most films are on in a number of cinemas for several weeks – and the time it takes to make a film – often years between the initial idea and eventual screening. However, you still need to keep up-to-date with who is producing what and when. It is worth noting though that there is a strong relationship between books and film. At the current time approximately half of the projects in development at Film Four are based on book adaptations.

## The rights

Once you have selected your material and medium, it is vital to establish who has the rights to the original and whether these are available for negotiation. Sometimes this involves a bit of detective work. If the writer is dead, it is necessary to find out whether there is an estate and if the work is still subject to copyright.

Copyright law is extremely complex. In the UK it has altered from 50 to 70 years, so some texts that were out of copyright have gone back in again (for further information see *UK copyright law*, page 672). This varies, however, around the world so it is essential therefore that you seek expert advice concerning the current rules of copyright for any potential project, depending on the country of origin.

It is usually possible to begin the search for the copyright holder and source of rights from the imprint page of the novel, play, film script, etc. If this information is not given, try the publisher, the Society of Authors or the Writers' Guild.

In the case of a living writer, you will need to establish who their literary agent is – if they have one – and contact them to see if adaptation is possible and how much it will cost. The scale of costs will depend upon the medium. Rights for a stage adaptation are often separate from film or television options. If a book or play has already been optioned, this means that it is probably not available for a period of at least 12–18 months. Should the purchaser of the option choose not to renew, or fail to produce the adaptation within the required timescale, rights may become available again. Many agreements include an extension clause for a further fixed time period, however, and this is particularly common in film as the end-product is rarely produced within 18 months.

Large film companies, particularly in Hollywood, will often buy the rights to a book or script outright, sometimes for a substantial sum. The proposed version may never get made but legally the original will not be available for adaptation by anyone else. If the writer or material is famous enough, or if they have a good agent, a time limit will be part of the original agreement. Complete buy-outs are less common in the UK.

The cost of acquiring rights varies significantly with the scale of the project, the profile of the writer and the intended medium. Usually an initial payment will be needed to secure the rights for a fixed period, followed by the same amount again, should an extension be necessary. In addition, there is nearly always some form of royalty for the original writer or estate in the form of a percentage of the overall profits of the final production, film, or broadcast. This will normally have a 'bottom ceiling' – a minimum amount or reserve – which must be paid whether or not the final work is financially successful. With television, film or radio, there may be a further payment for repeats and in the theatre the rate may well alter if the production transfers. Sometimes, with a low-budget production such as a fringe show or short film, a writer or estate will waive any initial rights fee and only expect a royalty.

Legalities aside, time spent forming a relationship with the writer of the original, or whoever manages their estate, has other another much more important function, a creative one, that of getting closer to the source material.

## How to adapt

I don't believe it is possible to lay down a set of rules for adapting, any more than one could invent a meaningful template for creative writing. The only observation I can offer, therefore, is personal and a reflection of my own taste.

When I recommend or commission an adaptation, either to direct in the theatre, or for television and film, my first requirement is that something in the original story has hooked me and I want to see the original given another life and another audience. I have to be able to imagine that it has the potential to work dramatically in a different format and can often already see or hear fragments of it.

At this stage I ask myself a lot of questions about the material. Why should it be done in another medium? How is it possible to achieve this particular part of the narrative, this character, this tone, this sequence of action, in a way that is different but still truthful, a sort of creative equivalent, like a metaphor. For me, it is all about thinking laterally and being enthused about the new possibilities another form will generate from the original, or vice versa.

This process generally leads me back to the source, be it book, film or play, in order to dig over everything about it and its writer. As well as looking at other adaptations to see what parts of the original have been enhanced or cut, I like to meet and talk to the writer. If they are no longer alive I try to find out about them from books and/or people who knew them. I want to know what interested them; what were they thinking when they were writing; even what they looked at every day. If possible, I like to go and visit the places they have written about or the place in which they wrote. This process of total immersion helps me to get under the skin of the original.

While this is entirely personal, it raises an interesting question which I believe any adapter needs to answer for themselves. How closely do you wish to replicate the original material and how much do you intend to depart from it? Choosing not to stick closely to the source may be the most creative decision you make but you must understand why you are doing it and what the effect will be. After all, two different trains of thought, styles and imaginations need to be fused together for this transformation to be complete and it is important that the balance between them works. I once spoke to a writer who was commissioned to adapt a well-known myth for Hollywood. Several drafts later, when he had been asked to alter all the key elements of the story to the point where it was unrecognisable, he decided to quit. It was the right decision and the film was a flop.

While respect for the writer and the source material is fundamental, there are of course lots of examples where enormous lateral and creative changes have been made to make a story work to optimum effect in its new medium. What matters ultimately is the integrity of the final product. At its best, it is like a marriage of two minds, celebrating the talents of both writer and adapter in an equally creative partnership.

Kate Sinclair is the Books Executive for Film Four. She has also worked as a director in theatre and radio.

## Successful collaborations

Here is an entirely subjective list of my personal favourites among recent successful collaborations, by way of example.

### Film

*Trainspotting* (Irvine Welsh, screenplay John Hodges)
*Persuasion* (Jane Austen, screenplay Nick Dear)

### Television

*The Way of the World* (Anthony Trollope, adaptation Andrew Davies)
*The Forsyte Saga* (John Galsworthy, adaptation Stephen Mallatratt)
*Brideshead Revisited* (Evelyn Waugh, adaptation John Mortimer)
*The Buddha of Suburbia* (Hanif Kureshi, adaptation Roger Michell and Hanif Kureshi)
*Longitude* ( Dava Sobel, adaptation Charles Sturridge)

### Theatre

*The Mill on the Floss* (George Eliot, adaptation Helen Edmundson)
*Nana* (Emile Zola, adaptation Pam Gems)
*The Magic Toyshop* (Angela Carter, adaptation Bryony Lavery)

### Radio

*The Old Curiosity Shop* (Charles Dickens, adaptation Mike Walker)

# Writing for television

Writing for television can be an extremely rewarding career. Anji Loman Field says anyone with the right aptitude and attitude can succeed, and here she gives sound advice for the potential screenwriter.

## The markets

There are various openings for new writers in television, but apart from competitions and special projects these are hardly ever advertised. The BBC's latest information on opportunities for new writers can be found at www.bbc.co.uk/writersroom. The openings fall into four categories:

## Single drama

There are fewer slots nowadays for the single play – a 30- or even 60-minute one-off drama is highly unlikely to find a market. Occasionally broadcasters will gather single plays together under a collective banner but it's best to think of individual projects as either standalone television films, two-parters or even four-parters. It's always worth asking television companies for their guidelines on single drama and film. Channel 4 is currently commissioning 30-minute dramas from new writers via its Independent Film & Video department.

## Series and serials

Although it has been known for a new writer to sell an original series or serial, it is a relatively rare occurrence. Writers with a track record of writing for existing strands are far more likely to be taken seriously. Long-running soaps like *EastEnders*, *Emmerdale* and *Family Affairs* are often in the market for new writers, but check first. If the door is open, a good 'calling card script' is usually the way in. Submit an original piece of work in a similar genre that is at least an hour long and shows your ability to create believable characters, write sparkling dialogue and tell a compelling story. You may be invited to try out for one of these long-running shows.

## Dramatisations/adaptations

A new writer is extremely unlikely to be commissioned to adapt or dramatise someone else's work for television. However, if there's something you really want to adapt and you can afford to take out an 'option' on the rights (or already own them, if it is your own novel or play) then write the script on spec. If you have a good script and can show that you own the rights, you could succeed.

## Situation comedy

This is the one area where production companies and broadcasters are desperate for new talent, and there are often competitions open to new writers. If you are a good comedy writer and market your work well, you will undoubtedly succeed (see 'Writing situation comedy' below).

## Aptitude and attitude

The first prerequisite in writing for television is that you enjoy the medium, and actually watch the kinds of shows that you would be interested in writing for. A cynical approach will always show through. And before sitting down to write that first television script, arm yourself with the appropriate skills by examining the medium as a whole.

- **Tape the kind of show you'd like to write for and analyse it**. How many scenes are there? What length are they? How much of the story happens 'off camera'? Knowing the answers to these questions will help you to understand the grammar of screen, and enable you to write a more professional script.
- **Study the structure of story telling**. There are plenty of books on the subject, and although it is never a good idea to follow structural paradigms to the letter, absorb as much information as possible so that the essential 'rules' on character, motivation and plot filter through into your writing.
- **Read scripts**. Some are published in book form, but a huge variety of scripts are also available from specialist book shops such as Offstage (*tel* 020-7485 4996), the Screenwriter's Store (*tel* 020-8469 2244) and the internet.
- **If you want to write sitcom, see as many live recordings of shows as possible**. This enables you to understand the techniques involved in television production, and particularly the physical constraints imposed by the studio. Free tickets for sitcom recordings are usually available – phone the broadcasters for information.
- **Be realistic**. Don't make your first project too ambitious in terms of screen time, locations or special effects. If you can 'contain the action' and make your first script affordable to shoot, it is far more likely to be taken seriously.

## Learning the craft

Even the most successful and experienced screenwriters say they never stop learning. Some have been lucky enough to learn the skill of writing for the screen in a subliminal way. For example, Lynda La Plante (*Prime Suspect*) was an actress with plenty of opportunity for studying scripts and production techniques before she turned her hand to writing; John Sullivan (*Only Fools and Horses*) worked in the props department at the BBC on countless sitcoms, and used to take the scripts home to study. But there are other ways to learn. Script workshops are particularly useful.

There are many courses and workshops available. These range from small self-help groups, where writers give each other feedback on their work, to full- and part-time Screenwriting MA courses at universities (e.g. in London, Sheffield, Leicester, Bournemouth, Manchester and Leeds). Evening classes are springing up in local colleges, and there are even script workshops on the internet. Workshops can help in the following ways:

- **Discipline**. The hardest thing most writers ever have to do is sit down and face that blank screen or page. Joining a script workshop – where you *have* to deliver an outline or a treatment, or the next 20 pages of your script by a certain date – provides the push that so many writers need.

- **Feedback**. Reading and giving feedback on other people's work helps you to focus on getting your own script right. It is also good to get used to the idea of showing your own work to others and getting their feedback. Television writing is generally a collaborative process and writers need to be pleasant to work with, and receptive to ideas. Knowing when to argue a point and when to concede are crucial skills which can be developed in good writing workshops.

- **Rewriting**. Learn to Love the Rewrite. It is such a major achievement to get to the end of a first draft that it is all too easy to rush to the post box and send it off to several production companies at once. *Four Weddings and a Funeral*, a Channel 4-funded project, went through 17 rewrites before finally reaching the screen. So before you post your masterpiece:

- Leave it to 'settle' for a few days and do something completely different – allow your head to clear completely. Then re-read the script from beginning to end – from as objective a viewpoint as possible – and make necessary changes.

- Get feedback so that you're sure your script is ready to send. Be warned: knowing how to read and analyse a script properly is a particular skill. Unless they are equipped in this area, *never* ask your friends or relations to read your script. Their comments could either lull you into a false sense of security or destroy your confidence for ever. Feedback from other writers in your workshop group is best. There are some organisations (including the Screenwriters' Workshop) which offer a professional script feedback service for a moderate fee.

## Writing situation comedy

Situation comedy writing is the most lucrative area of television, and deservedly so. Have you ever tried making an audience laugh several times a minute for 25 minutes for at least six weeks running, and maybe (in the case of *Last of the Summer Wine*) for 20 long years?

Despite its name, sitcom is less about situation and much more about character. It is better to start with funny and engaging characters in mind and then (if it isn't part and parcel of the character) find the perfect situation in which to place them than it is to begin with the premise 'nobody's ever set a sitcom in a nuclear power station before'. It is not the setting that makes the audience laugh, it is the characters.

A good exercise in seeing if you can write funny material is to write an episode of an existing sitcom. If *Fawlty Towers* is your all-time favourite, study a few episodes and then try your own. It will never get made, but you'll learn a lot in the process – and sample scripts like this are often useful as calling card scripts. Some of the broadcast companies issue guidelines on writing situation comedy – phone their comedy departments for information.

## Competitions

Broadcasters occasionally run writing competitions or 'new writing initiatives'. Check their websites – and general screenwriters' websites – for up-to-date information. Also, watch out for annual awards run by organisations such as PAWS (People's Awareness of Science, *tel* 020-8214 1543), the BBC Talent (www.bbc.co.uk/talent), and the Orange Prize for Screenwriting (*tel* (07970)

111999 www.orangeprize.com). Details can be found in the trade press and via relevant websites and screenwriting organisations. See also *Prizes and awards* on page 546.

## Breaking in
### Do you need an agent?

Many new writers are keen to get an agent before they attempt to sell anything, but this can be an arduous process and there are few agents prepared to take on a completely untried writer.

The best way to get an agent is to first get an offer of a deal on a project. Most *bona fide* production companies and broadcasters will happily recommend a selection of agents to writers they want to do business with. If you can phone an agent and say 'so-and-so wants to option/ commission my project and has recommended you as an agent' s/he is far more likely to be interested. And at that point you can pick and choose the agent who is right for you, rather than going with the first one to say "yes".

### Selling yourself

Once you are sure you have a good script, where do you send it? If you've done your homework, you will already

### Euroscript
Suffolk House, 1–8 Whitfield Place, London W1T 5JU
*tel/fax* 020-7387 5880
*email* info@euroscript.co.uk
*website* www.euroscript.co.uk

A script development organisation aiming to place great screenplays at the heart of the industry. Originally funded by the European Union's Media II programme, the service is now worldwide. Professional development support is provided for screenwriters, producers and production companies through consultancy, Film Story Competition (deadlines: 30 April and 31 October each year) and international workshops.

### Film London
20 Euston Centre, Regents Place, London NW1 3JH
*tel* 020-7387 8787  *fax* 020-7387 8788
*website* www.filmlondon.org.uk

Offers grants that enable writers, producers and directors to make their projects. Consult website or send sae for further information.

### National Association of Television Program Executives (NATPE)
452 Oakleigh Road North, London N20 0RZ
*tel* 020-8361 3793  *fax* 020-8368 3824
*website* www.natpe.org
*Contact* Pam Smithard

Non-profit TV programming and content association dedicated to the continued growth and success of the global TV marketplace. Year-round activities include the annual conference and exhibition, which reaches tens of thousands of key decisionmakers in virtually every sector of the TV industry.

know which channel is the most likely to be interested. But sometimes it is better to send to an independent production company rather than directly to a broadcaster, so do a bit more research. Check out the companies that are making the kind of show you've written and approach them first.

A preliminary letter or phone call can save you time and money because some smaller companies simply don't have the resources to read unsolicited material. If you feel that a certain production company is absolutely right for your project, write a letter giving a brief synopsis of the project and asking if they will read the script. If they agree, your script will join the 'solicited' pile. And if it fits the bill, they may even pick it up and develop it. But don't expect overnight results. It can sometimes take many months before scripts are even read by small and/or busy companies.

Sending your script directly to a broadcaster can lead to a commission, but unless you target a particular producer whose work you admire you will

### PACT (Producers Alliance for Cinema and Television)

45 Mortimer Street, London W1W 8HJ
*tel* 020-7331 6000 *fax* 020-7331 6700
*email* enquiries@pact.co.uk
*website* www.pact.co.uk

Serves the feature film and independent TV production sector. The *PACT Directory* lists contacts in all areas (£30 to non-members). (See also page 529.)

### Arts Council England regional offices

Many regional offices offer grants that enable writers, producers and directors to make their projects (see page 502).

### The Screenwriters' Workshop

(formerly London Screenwriters' Workshop)
Suffolk House, 1–8 Whitfield Place, London W1T 5JU
*tel/fax* 020-7387 5511
*email* screenoffice@tiscali.co.uk
*website* www.lsw.org.uk

Runs regular courses, workshops and events. Educational charity. (See also page 536.)

### The Spotlight

7 Leicester Place, London WC2H 7RJ
*tel* 020-7437 7631 *fax* 020-7437 7631
*email* info@splotlightcd.com
*website* www.splotlightcd.com
Publishes a book called *Contacts*, which contains useful information and contact addresses.

### The Writers' Guild of Great Britain

15 Britannia Street, London WC1X 9JN
*tel* 020-7833 0777 *fax* 020-7833 4777
*email* admin@writersguild.org.uk
*website* www.writersguild.org.uk

Trade union-affiliated organisation for professional writers. Negotiates rates for TV drama with the BBC and the ITV Network Centre. (See also page 498.)

probably have less control over who you work with.

### Being 'discovered'

If you can get your work 'rehearse-read' by actors in front of an audience it will help your writing, and may even lead to discovery. Many script readings are attended by development executives from television and production companies and there are many stories of individuals being picked up from such projects. TAPS (Television Arts Performance Showcase) (*tel* (01932) 592151), Player–Playwrights (*tel* 020-8883 0371) and the Screenwriters' Workshop, all organise rehearsed readings.

### Development hell

This is the place between finding someone who wants to produce your script and waiting for the 'suits' at the television companies to give the final go-ahead for the project. In the meantime you will have been paid, perhaps just an option fee, or maybe a commission fee for a script or two. Either way, *never put all your eggs in one development basket*. Aim eventually to have several projects bubbling under for every one that comes to the boil.

A realistic optimism is required for this game. Don't believe anything wonderful will happen until you actually have that signed contract in front of you. In the meantime keep writing, keep marketing and, if you possibly can, keep making contacts in the industry. If you're good at schmoozing, go to as many industry events as possible and make new contacts. If you can send a script to a producer with a covering letter saying 'I heard your talk the other day…' you will immediately arouse interest.

### Coping with rejection

The standard rejection letter is the worst part of this business. When it is accompanied by your returned script – looking decidedly un-read – it is very easy to become disillusioned. The trick is this: change your mental attitude to the point where if you don't receive at least one rejection letter in the post every day, you feel rejected! So long as you are absolutely sure that your work is good, keep sending it out. Sooner or later you'll get a nicer, more personalised rejection letter, and then eventually perhaps even a cup of tea with the producer...

## Selling ideas

Completely new writers do occasionally sell ideas but are much more likely to sell the idea alone, i.e. the 'format rights', and will probably end up not writing the script. If you have a great calling card script or two, or have had a few episodes of something produced, your ideas will be taken much more seriously. At this stage you might well sell a project on the basis of a short outline or synopsis, and be paid to write the script(s).

All scripts must be typed and properly formatted if they are to be taken seriously. If you dread the practical aspects of getting your script onto the page it might be worth investing in a screenwriting software program for your computer. They take the pain out of screenwriting by auto-formatting and numbering the pages and scenes, thus enabling you to move scenes around and restructure your script with ease. Such facilities allow writers to concentrate wholly on the creative process and can therefore be quite liberating, even for those who type well. Contact the Screenwriters' Store for details and advice.

## Summary

Writing for television is not generally something that can be taken up as a hobby. It may look easy but huge amounts of work and commitment are required in order to succeed. If that doesn't put you off, and it is what you really want to do, then go for it. And good luck!

**Anji Loman Field** worked as a television producer for several years before turning to writing. She has since written drama, comedy drama and animation for film, television and radio, and has taught writing at the Screenwriters' Workshop, the Royal College of Art and the London Institute.

## Further reading

Friedmann, Julian, *How to Make Money Scriptwriting*, Intellect Books, 2000
Kelsey, Gerald, *Writing for Television*, A & C Black, 3rd edn, 1999
Seger, Linda, *Making a Good Script Great*, Samuel French Inc. (pbk), 1994
Vogler, Christopher, *The Writer's Journey*, Pan, 2nd revised edn, (pbk), 1999
Wolfe, Ronald, *Writing Comedy*, Robert Hale, 2003

# Writing drama for radio

Writing drama for radio allows a freedom which none of the other performing arts can give. Lee Hall guides the radio drama writer to submit a script which will be both well received and merit production.

With upwards of 300 hours of radio drama commissioned each year, radio is an insatiable medium and, therefore, one which is constantly seeking new blood. It is no surprise to find that many of our most eminent dramatists, such as Pinter and Stoppard, did important radio work early in their careers.

Although the centrality of radio has been eclipsed somewhat by television and fringe theatre, it continues to launch new writers, and its products often find popular recognition in other media (for example, the film version of Anthony Mingella's *Truly Madly Deeply*). Because radio is often cited as the discoverer and springboard of so many talents, this should not obscure the fact that many writers make a living primarily out of their radio writing and the work itself is massively popular, with plays regularly getting audiences of over 500,000 people.

For the dramatist, the medium offers a variety of work which is difficult to find anywhere else: serials, dramatisations, new commissions of various lengths (from a couple of minutes to several hours), musicals, soap operas, adaptations of the classics, as well as a real enthusiasm to examine new forms.

Because it is no more expensive to be in the Hindu Kush than to be in a laundrette in Deptford, the scope of the world is only limited by the imagination of the writer. However, though radio drama in the 'Fifties and 'Sixties was an important conduit for absurdism, there is a perceived notion that radio drama on the BBC is domestic, Home Counties and endlessly trotting out psychological trauma in a rather naturalistic fashion. This is not a fair assessment of the true range of work presented. The BBC itself is anxious to challenge this idea and as the face of broadcasting changes, there is a conscious move to attract new audiences with new kinds of work.

## Get to know the form

Listen to as many plays as possible, read plays that are in print, and try to analyse what works, what doesn't and why. This may seem obvious, but it is easy to fall back on your preconceived notions of what radio plays are. The more you hear other people's successes and failures, the more tools you will have to discriminate when it comes to your own work.

Plays on radio tend to fit into specific time slots: 30, 60, 75, 90 minutes, and each slot will have a different feel – an afternoon play will be targeted at a different audience from one at 10.30pm.

A radio play will be chosen on artistic grounds but nevertheless a writer should be familiar with the market. This should not be seen as an invitation merely to copy forms or to try to make your play 'fit', but an opportunity to gain some sense of what the producers are dealing with. Producers are looking for new and fresh voices, ones which are unique, open new areas or challenge certain preconceptions. This is not to suggest you should be wilfully idiosyncratic but to be aware that it is the individuality of your 'voice' that people will notice.

Write what you feel strongly about, in the way that most attracts you. It should be bold, personal, entertaining, challenging and stimulating. Radio has the scope to explore drama that wouldn't get produced in theatres or on television, so treat it as the most radical forum for new writing. How many times have you listened to the radio with the sense that you've heard it all before? Never feel limited by what exists but be aware how your voice can enrich the possibilities of the future.

## Who to approach

Opportunities for writing for radio in the UK are dominated by the BBC. Whilst there are increasing opportunities with independent stations, BBC Radio Drama overwhelms the field. Its output is huge. The variety of the work – from soaps to the classics – makes it the true national repertory for drama in its broadest sense. However, the BBC is increasingly commissioning productions from independent producers, so you can:

● send your unsolicited script to the BBC WritersRoom (formerly the New Writing Initiative; see page 332) where it will be assessed by a reader. If they find it of interest they will put you in contact with a suitable producer.

● approach a producer directly. This may be a producer at the BBC or at an independent company (see page 348). Both will give a personal response based on their own taste, rather than an institutional one.

Producers have a broad role: they find new writers, develop projects, edit the script, cast the actors, record and edit the play, and even write up the blurb for the *Radio Times*. Because of this intense involvement, the producer needs to have a strong personal interest in the writer or writing when they take on a project.

The system of commissioning programmes at the BBC is such that staff producers or independent production companies offer projects to commissioning editors to decide upon. Thus, a writer must be linked to a producer in the first instance to either get their play produced or get a commission for a new piece of work. Therefore, going direct to a producer can be a convenient short cut, but it requires more preparation.

## Approaching a producer

Discovering and developing the work of new writers is only a small part of a producer's responsibilities, so be selective. Do your homework – there is little point in sending your sci-fi series to a producer who exclusively produces one-off period comedies.

To help decide which producer will be the most receptive to your work, become familiar with the work of each producer you are intersted in and the type of writers they work with. Use the *Radio Times* to help with your research and listen to as many of their plays as possible. It is well worth the effort in order to be sure to send your play to the right person. If you can quote the reasons why you've chosen them in particular, it can only help to get a congenial reception. It will also give you confidence in their response, as the comments – good or bad – will be from someone you respect.

## Submitting your work

Don't stuff your manuscript into an envelope as soon as you've written 'The End'. You owe it to yourself to get the script into the best possible state before anyone sees it. First impressions matter and time spent refining will pay dividends in attracting attention.

Ask a person you trust to give you some feedback. Try to edit the work yourself, cutting things that don't work and spending time revising and reinventing anything which you think could be better. Make sure that what you send is the best you can possibly do.

Producers have mountains of scripts to read. The more bulky your tome the less enthusiastically it will be received. (It's better to send a sparkling 10-page sample than your whole 300-page masterpiece.) Try to make the first scene excellent. The more you can surprise, engage or delight in the first few pages, the more chance the rest will be carefully read. The adage that a reader can tell whether a play is any good after the first three pages might be wholly inaccurate but it reflects a cynicism versed by the practice of script reading. The reader will probably approach your script with the expectation that it is unsuitable, and part of getting noticed is jolting them out of their complacency.

Have your script presentably typed. Make sure your letter of introduction is well informed and shows that you haven't just picked a name at random. Do not send it to more than one producer at a time, as this is considered bad etiquette. And don't expect an instantaneous response – it may take a couple of months before you receive a reply. Don't be afraid of calling up if they keep you waiting for an unreasonable length of time, but don't badger people as this will inevitably be counterproductive.

## Finally

Don't be discouraged by rejection and *don't* assume that because one person has rejected your script that it is no good. It is all a question of taste. Use the criticism positively to help your work, not as a personal attack.

Lee Hall has written several plays for BBC Radio, including the award-winning *Spoonface Steinberg*, which he has since adapted for TV and theatre. His translations of theatre plays include Brecht's *Mr Puntilla and His Man Matti* and *Mother Courage*, and Goldoni's *The Servant with Two Masters*. His play *Cooking with Elvis* was nominated for an Olivier Award for Best New Comedy, and his screenplay for *Billy Elliot* was Oscar nominated.

# Digital broadcasting

Digital broadcasting is expanding rapidly. David Teather introduces this new media and looks at the implications for writers.

Digital broadcasting offers choice from hundreds of channels and the chance to offer interactive services to viewers. As many as 10 digital services are able to occupy the frequency previously occupied by one analogue service. Picture quality is far sharper using digital transmission.

Interactive services are so far only being used for e-commerce – for instance, Sky's television shopping and banking service Open. But a number of broadcasters are beginning to explore different ways of using the services for entertainment. In its coverage of Wimbledon, for instance, the BBC used the Sky Digital service to allow viewers to choose which court they wanted to watch. Ultimately, viewers will be able to link straight from a programme to associated websites, merchandising or online discussion points covering issues raised in a show. Digital transmission costs are also much lower which makes it more commercially viable for niche channels to exist.

## The story so far

The first company to launch digital services was Sky which now has more than 7 million digital subscribers. Its customer numbers for pay-TV stations had plateaued, but are now rising again as a result of digital broadcasting.

Of the cable companies, Telewest began its digital services at the end of 1999 and NTL (which now owns Cable & Wireless) started in mid 2000. The plug was pulled on ITV Digital, a joint venture between Carlton Communications and Granada which enabled digital services to be sent via traditional roof-top aerials, in April 2002. It has been replaced by Freeview, a joint venture between the BBC, BSkyB and Crown Castle, which offers around 30 channels. The service is free as the name suggests and is being received by around 3 million homes. Former ITV Digital subscribers can receive it through their existing set top boxes, while new viewers simply need to buy a box or own a digital television set.

The uptake of digital services was given a huge boost when the fierce competition for subscribers led Sky to scrap the £200 charge for the set-top boxes needed to unscramble the digital signal.

The government is aiming to switch off analogue and would like to do so before 2010. By that time, digital set-top boxes should have been replaced by television sets able to receive digital signals – but sales so far have been slow. The switch-off date for analogue is highly political because it will cause an inevitable outcry when old sets become useless.

## Free-to-air channels

There are a number of free-to-air channels. The BBC has controversially set up a number of new channels: BBC3, aimed at the youth market; BBC4, an arts-based channel; and BBC News 24 which – as the name suggests – screens news

24 hours a day. Rival companies such as Sky have argued that the licence fee should not be used to prop up stations like News 24 in a commercial marketplace. During the day, BBC3 and BBC4 run two children's channels, Cbeebies, for a preschool audience and CBBC for older children. The BBC has committed around £300 million to digital services: BBC3 has the biggest budget of £53 million, BBC4 has a budget of £32 million and the

## The technical explanation

The BBC offers this definition: 'Digital Broadcasting is transmission by converting sound and picture into binary digits – a series of ones and noughts. Digital signals are more robust than analogue signals and can occupy parts of the spectrum unavailable to analogue. A process of compression also allows many digital services within the space taken by one analogue service.'

children's channels have a combined budget of £20 million. UK History, a documentary-based channel is also available on Freeview. Each of the channels is a mixture of repeats from other mainstream channels and new commissions.

ITV Network's ITV2 also shows catch-up episodes of programmes like *Coronation Street*, as well trumpeting a large number of US imports. All of the existing five free-to-air channels are also available in digital format. Other channels on Freeview include Sky News, QVC and Full On Entertainment.

### Video-on-demand

The next step in the digital revolution is video-on-demand. A number of companies are offering services, including the cable companies and Kingston Communications, which runs a joint venture over telephone wires with BSkyB in Hull. Users are able to download films or television programmes at will, and fast forward, pause and rewind them. Programme-makers like the BBC have already sold packages to some of the video-on-demand firms and writers need to consider the implications for the potential sell-on of copyright.

Video-on-demand could become widespread with the advent of a technology called ADSL (Asymmetrical Digital Subscriber Line), which upgrades existing copper telephone wires for high bandwidth use such as pay-TV without the need to dig up roads. ADSL is becoming more widely available on BT's networks. A ban on broadcasting being carried over BT's lines has now been lifted but costs are still prohibitively high.

Digital technology in the next few years will enable video-quality film to be sent over mobile phone networks. The mobile phone industry has the networks in place and is beginning to sell the necessary handsets after many delays.

### New channels, new opportunities?

The explosion of new channels may suggest that there will be an equally huge demand for new writing talent to help fill the extra airtime. Through a joint venture with Flextech Television, the BBC has six pay-TV channels, including UK Gold, UK Play and UK Drama. The evidence so far, however, is that money is being spent largely on three things: sports rights, movies and US imports. Most original programming on pay-TV channels is very low budget and is far more likely to be a cookery or pop music show than original drama.

Unfortunately, rather than playing to their own strengths, the BBC and ITV appear to be drawn into competing with the entertainment channels at their level. 'Once upon a time the BBC set the standards of quality and everyone else had to try and compete,' says one writer. 'That doesn't happen any more. Now the BBC competes with the others for crap.'

The level of competition among broadcasters now also means that where original drama is being commissioned it is often low budget. In fact, many writers believe that in the short term digital technology has not opened opportunities at all and see the future as pretty bleak. Management gurus, though, maintain that 'content is king' and that those broadcasters who triumph will be the ones who produce the most compelling programming.

## Copyrights

The Writers' Guild notes a recent case where a writer saw a 30 year-old show he had penned being repeated again and again on a pay-TV channel and demanded to know why he wasn't being paid. It turned out that he had signed his rights away in 1972.

If the explosion of channels made possible by digital technology isn't leading to a wave of new commissioning then writers could at least hope for healthier repeat fees. The culture of broadcasters forcing writers to sign away their rights for a lump sum so that they can show a programme whenever they like is becoming increasingly prevalent. The usual royalty is 5.6% of the sale price, which gives the owner the right to show the programme a set number of times over a given period.

Broadcasters blame the need to sell to the US market programmes which are unencumbered by copyright issues. When selling work, writers should remember how many more times, potentially, a programme will appear on air because of the growth in distribution platforms, and therefore at least try to protect their rights. The rapid changes in technology has also led writers' unions to recommend that contracts over the shortest space of time possible are agreed.

## Original programming

There are at last some encouraging signs, however, led by Channel 4 and followed by Sky. Channel 4 has long supported new writing talent through its backing of British film and has found its own pay-TV distribution outlet with FilmFour.

Sky One has a total budget of around £90 million but its efforts in original programming have met with mixed results – probably the most successful has been the football drama *Dream Team*. However, Sky's original programming has largely been forced upon it as the cost of acquiring top US content has soared due to increased competition – the reason why it lost the rights to show *Friends* and *ER*, two of Sky One's biggest ratings pullers, to Channel 4. Channel 4 is commissioning original programming for its digital entertainment channel, E4.

Sky attempted to launch its own film business, Sky Pictures, but abandoned the project after its first few films met with tepid reviews and box office sales. NTL, Britain's largest cable company, has dipped its toe into original programming but like its rival, Telewest, is in a precarious financial position and more in cost-cutting than commissioning mode.

## Digital radio

The attributes of digital radio are similar to those of television. It was supposed to be the next revolution, but it has yet to catch on. The growth of stations is still in its infancy. In London, for instance, there will be three so-called 'multiplexes' of eight stations awarded to various consortia of existing radio groups. Interactive services will be on offer with the most obvious for radio including up-to-date traffic or weather reports displayed on a digital monitor on request. Digital radio could also lead to music or programming on demand similar to that of digital television programming.

A number of stations are now being broadcast in both digital and analogue as well as a growing number in digital alone. The BBC has launched five new radio stations, including one devoted to the spoken word, BBC7. So far, though, the industry has been held back by the prohibitive cost of hardware – the radios currently cost around £300.

**David Teather** is at *The Guardian*.

# Inside the BBC

Helen Weinstein has compiled an introduction for writers who want to break into the BBC.
For more information visit the BBC website: www.bbc.co.uk

## The BBC structure

Major restructuring introduced by the former Director-General Greg Dyke resulted in the creation of 5 programming divisions:

- Radio & Music
- Drama, Entertainment & CBBC (Children)
- Factual & Learning
- Sport
- News

To find out about the commissioning process visit www.bbc.co.uk/commissioning/

A New Media division is developing the BBC's interactive TV and radio online activities.

If you wish to submit an unsolicited idea to the BBC you need to team up with a BBC Production department who will help you develop that idea into a fully formulated proposal which would be ready for the BBC to consider. If it is an idea of local interest then contact your Regional BBC network. If it is your first submission then take a look at the BBC Talent website: www.bbc.co.uk/talent

Writers who want to pitch an idea for radio or TV can contact an independent production company who can take the idea through the same commissioning route as an in-house producer. The best way of getting in touch with an independent production company is to do some research about the companies who produce the type of programmes you have an idea for. Many of these companies are members of PACT (Producers Alliance for Cinema and Television, see page 529), which represents the independent sector and its website gives detailed information on independents: www.pact.co.uk

To submit a programme idea directly to the BBC programme division, send it to the head of department or editor. You will either be put in contact with the Development Producer in that department or your idea will be submitted to a relevant producer for review.

Alternatively, to find in-house BBC producers to contact with a specific programme idea a good route is to select a programme that is of a similar genre to your idea, and then to contact the producer directly by finding their name through the listings in the *Radio Times*.

*website* www.bbc.co.uk
*Director-General* Mark Thompson
*Deputy Director-General* Mark Byford
*Director, Television* Jana Bennett
*Director, Sport* Peter Salmon

*Director of New Media & Technology* Ashley Highfield
*Controller, BBC One* Lorraine Heggessy
*Controller, BBC Two* Roly Keating
*Controller, BBC Three* Stuart Murphy
*Controller, BBC Four* Janice Hadlow
*Controller, CBBC* Dorothy Prior

## Radio & Music

BBC Broadcasting House, Portland Place, London W1A 1AA
*tel* 020-7580 4468

BBC Radio & Music provides speech and music programmes for the 5 national networks (Radio 1, Radio 2, Radio 3, Radio 4 and Radio Five Live) and to 5 digital stations (1Xtra, 6Music, BBC7, Five Live Sports Extra and The Asian Network). Programmes are made by Factual & Learning, Radio Drama and Radio Entertainment. And the division also supplies most of the production of the Television Classical Music Unit and the World Service. All BBC national radio stations are available on CAB digital radio, digital TV and via the internet.

*Director, BBC Radio & Music* Jenny Abramsky
*Controller, Radio One and 1Xtra* Andy Parfitt
*Controller, Radio Two and 6Music* Lesley Douglas
*Controller, Radio Three* Roger Wright
*Controller, Radio Four and BBC7* Helen Boaden
*Controller, Radio Five Live and Sports Extra* Bob Shennan
*Head of Programmes, 6Music* Ric Blaxill
*Head of Programmes, BBC7* Mary Kalemkerian
*Head of Asian Network* Vijay Sharma

## Radio Drama

*Head of Radio Drama* Gordon House
*Editor, Birmingham Drama & The Archers* Vanessa Whitburn

## Radio Entertainment

*Editor, Radio Entertainment* John Pidgeon

## Radio Factual & Learning

*Controller, Radio & Music Factual, London* Graham Ellis
*Editor, Bristol* Clare McGinn
*Editor, Bristol Natural History Unit* Julian Hector
*Editor, Birmingham* Andrew Thorman
*Head of Specialist Music and Compliance 2* Dave Barber
*Editor, Manchester* Ian Bent

## Radio News
*Head of Radio News* Steve Mitchell
*Executive Editor, Radio Current Affairs* Gwyneth Williams

## Radio Sport
*Head of Radio* Gordon Turnbull
*Editor* Gill Pulsford

## Drama, Entertainment & CBBC
*Director* Alan Yentob

## Drama
BBC Television Centre, Centre House,
Wood Lane, London W12 7SB
*tel* 020-8743 8000
Drama has departments in London, Birmingham and Manchester and produces a broad range of plays, serials, series and readings for TV, film, BBC Radio 3, BBC Radio 4 and BBC World Service.

Note that drama and comedy proposals must be in the form of a fully written script. Drama scripts for single plays and comedy scripts should be sent to the BBC WritersRoom (see below).

Drama scripts for series should be sent with an A4 sae to:
Serena Cullen, Head of Development,
BBC Drama Series, Room D414, BBC Centre House, 56 Wood Lane, London W12 7SB

## Drama Development in the North
BBC New Broadcasting House, Oxford Road,
Manchester M60 ISJ
*tel* 0161-200 2020
BBC Broadcasting Centre, Pebble Mill Road,
Birmingham B5 7QQ
*tel* 0121-432 8888

The Manchester team also operates radio drama workshops, primarily for writers in the North of England. For further information, send an sae requesting their guidelines.

The Birmingham radio team reads the unsolicited scripts for writers in the Midlands, East Anglia, and South West, but does not have a formal new writing department.

*Controller, Drama Commissioning* Jane Tranter
*Controller, Continuing Drama Series* Mal Young
*Head of Drama Serials* Laura Mackie
*Senior Executive Producer Drama Serials* Hilary Salmon
*Head of Casting, Drama Series* Jane Deitch
*Head of Radio Drama, Bush House* Gordon House
*Executive Producer, Radio Drama, Birmingham* Vanessa Whitburn
*Executive Producer, Radio Drama, Manchester* Sue Roberts
*Head of Films & Single Drama* David Thompson
*Head of Development Films* Tracey Scoffield

*Head of Development Television Series* Serena Cullen
*Head of Development Television Serials* Sarah Brown
*Head of Independents, Drama* Gareth Neame
*Head of Interactive Drama and Entertainment* Sophie Walpole
*Head of Fiction Lab* Richard Fell

## Entertainment
BBC Television Centre, Wood Lane,
London W12 7RJ
*tel* 020-8743 8000
*website* www.bbc.co.uk/entertainment

The BBC provides a wide range of entertainment programming and has dedicated teams who will review unsolicited ideas from the public. Entertainment formats such as quiz and game shows should be pitched to:
Format Entertainment Development Team,
Room 4032, BBC Television Centre, Wood Lane,
London W12 7RJ

Factual entertainment ideas should be sent to the Factual Entertainment Development Office next door at Room 4021.

Comedy and sitcom scripts should be sent with an A4 sae to:
BBC Radio Entertainment (Scripts), Room 5411,
BBC Broadcasting House, Portland Place,
London W1A 1AA

*Head of Entertainment Group* Wayne Garvie
*Head of Comedy* Sophie Clarke-Jervoise
*Head of Comedy, Entertainment* Jon Plowman
*Editor, Comedy Entertainment* Kenton Allen
*Creative Head, Entertainment Events* Bea Ballard
*Editor, Mainstream Entertainment* Kevin Bishop
*Editor, Comedy Entertainment* Jo Sargent
*Creative Head, Format Entertainment* Richard Hopkins
*Editor, Light Entertainment* Martin Scott
*Creative Head, Factual Entertainment* David Mortimer
*Editor, Radio Entertainment* John Pidgeon
*Executive Editor, Music Entertainment* Andi Peters
*Creative Head, Music Entertainment* Mark Cooper
*Editor, Archive Programmes* Caroline Wright

## Entertainment & Features, Manchester
BBC New Broadcasting House, PO Box 27,
Oxford Road, Manchester M60 ISJ
*tel* 0161-200 2020
A network TV department responsible for a wide range of factual, entertainment and music programming. The department is also committed to spotting new comedy talent in the North West.

*Managing Editor* Helen Bullough
*Executive Producers* Caroline Roberts, Robin Ashbrook, Ricky Kelehar, Sumi Connock, Mario Dubois

## CBBC (Children)

BBC Television Centre, Wood Lane,
London W12 7RJ
*tel* 020-8743 8000

There are opportunities for new writers in this
highly competitive area. Unsolicited programme
proposals from individual writers and independent
production companies are passed to the relevant
genre head. The CBBC department is searching for
new writing and screen presenting talent, across the
CBBC output. CBBC prefer treatments of
programme ideas to be sent via email. Presenter
enquiries need to send a showreel of approximately
3 minutes on VHS.
CBBC Treatments & Scripts,
Development Executive, CBBC Creates,
Room E1200, East Tower, BBC Television Centre,
Wood Lane, London W12 7RJ
*email* amanda.gabbitas@bbc.co.uk

*Controller, CBBC* Dorothy Prior
*Head of Entertainment* Anne Gilchrist
*Head of Drama* Elaine Sperber
*Head of On-Air* Paul Smith
*Head of Education* Sue Nott
*Head of CBBC News & Factual Programmes* Roy
  Milani
*Head of Pre-School* Clare Elstow
*Head of Acquisitions* Michael Carrington
*Development Executive* Amanda Gabbitas

## BBC WritersRoom

1 Mortimer Street, London WIT 3JA
*tel* 020-7765 2703
*website* www.bbc.co.uk/writersroom
Unsolicited scripts for TV drama and narrative
comedy, films, single plays and radio drama and
comedy are coordinated by BBC WritersRoom. The
department produces *Writers' Guidelines*, a detailed
information pack which includes advice on how to
write radio and TV scripts, current trends, available
markets, contacts, free audience opportunities and
further reading. To receive one, send an A4 first
class sae to the address above. Since competition is
fierce, writers are strongly advised to read the
guidelines before submitting scripts, one at a time.
Do not send scripts by email, only printouts by post
to the New Writing Co-ordinator. All writers
submitting scripts are considered for the initiative's
highly targeted writing schemes and workshops.
The website offers further advice, interviews, and
free downloadable scripts and formatting templates.
The BBC also offers regional access competitions
for writers. Contact BBC Talent for information:
www.bbc.co.uk/talent

*Creative Director, New Writing* Kate Rowland
*New Writing Co-ordinator* Jessica Dromgoole

## Factual & Learning

*Director* John Willis

## Documentaries and Contemporary Factual, London

BBC White City, 201 Wood Lane,
London W12 7TS
*tel* 020-8752 5252

Produces a wide range of TV documentary,
consumer affairs, leisure and lifestyle programming.

*Controller* Anne Morrison
*Commissioner* Tom Archer
*Deputy Controller* Donna Taberer

## Contemporary Factual, Birmingham

BBC, The Mailbox, Royal Mail Street,
Birmingham B1 1LX
*tel* 0121-432 8888
*Head of Documentaries & Contemporary Factual*
  Tessa Finch

## Contemporary Factual, Bristol

BBC Broadcasting House, White Ladies Road,
Bristol BS8 2LR
*tel* 0117-973 2211
*Head of Documentaries & Contemporary Factual*
  Mark Hill

## Specialist Factual

BBC White City, 201 Wood Lane, London W12 7TS
*tel* 020-8752 5252

Produces TV programming in specialist genres: arts,
history, science, etc.

*Controller* Keith Scholey
*Commissioner* Emma Swain

## Natural History Unit

BBC Broadcasting House, White Ladies Road,
Bristol BS8 2LR
*tel* 0117- 973 2211
*Head of Natural History Unit* Neil Nightingale
*Editor, Natural History Radio* Julian Hector

## Religion & Ethics

BBC New Broadcasting House, PO Box 27,
Oxford Road, Manchester M60 1SJ
*tel* 0161-200 2020
*Head of Religion and Ethics* Alan Bookbinder
*Executive Producer, Radio* David Coomes

## Learning & Interactive

BBC White City, 201 Wood Lane, London W12 7TS
*tel* 020-8752 5252

This is a new unit that commissions and produces a
broad range of online and interactive factual
output. This department is actively looking for new
writers.

*Controller* Liz Cleaver
*Creative Director, Learning* Nick Ware
*Controller, Children's Education* Frank Flynn

## Sport
BBC Television Centre, Wood Lane,
London W12 7RJ
*tel* 020-8743 8000

Multimedia coverage of a wide range of sports in the UK and worldwide.

*Director, Sport* Peter Salmon
*Head of Programmes & Planning* Pat Younge
*Head of General Sport* Barbara Slater
*Head of Major Events* Dave Gordon
*Head of Football and Boxing* Niall Sloane
*Director of Sports Rights and Finance* Dominic Coles
*Head of Radio* Gordon Turnbull
*Head of Sports News, Development & Interactive*
  Andrew Thompson

## News
BBC Television Centre, Wood Lane,
London W12 7RJ
*tel* 020-8743 8000

BBC News is the biggest news organisation in the world with over 2500 journalists, 45 bureaus worldwide and 15 networks and services across TV, radio and new media.

*Director, News* Richard Sambrook
*Deputy Director, News* Mark Damazer
*Head of TV News* Roger Mosey
*Head of Radio News* Steve Mitchell
*Head of Radio Current Affairs* Gwyneth Williams
*Head of News Production Facilities* Peter Coles
*Head of Newsgathering* Adrian Van Klaveren
*Head of Political Programmes* Fran Unsworth
*Head of Current Affairs & Business* Peter Horrocks
*Chief Operating Officer* Peter Phillips
*Divisional Manager* Claire Paul
*Head of New Media Interactive* Richard Deverell
*Head of Strategy News* Alix Pryde
*Head of Communications* Janie Ironside Wood

## World Service
Bush House, PO Box 76, The Strand,
London WC2B 4PH
*tel* 020-7557 2941 *fax* 020-7557 1912
*email* worldservice.press@bbc.co.uk
*website* www.bbc.co.uk/worldservice

BBC World Service provides radio services in English and 42 other languages, via short wave and in an increasing number of cities around the world on FM and MW. The English service is available 24 hours a day in real audio on the internet. Classic contemporary drama, novels, short stories, soap operas and poetry are all a feature of its English service, plus a wide range of arts, documentaries, education, features, music, religious affairs, science,

sports and youth programmes. In addition, BBC World Service provides on-the-spot-coverage of world news, giving a global perspective on international events.

*Acting Director* Nigel Chapman
*Director, English Network* Phil Harding

## BBC Worldwide
Woodlands, 80 Wood Lane, London W12 0TT
*tel* 020-8433 2000 *fax* 020-8749 0538
*website* www.bbcworldwide.com

BBC Worldwide Limited is the commercial consumer arm, and a wholly owned subsidiary of the BBC. The company was formed in 1994 to develop a coordinated approach to the BBC's commercial activities: TV channels, publishing, product licensing, internet and interactive. BBC Worldwide exists to maximise the value of the BBC's assets for the benefit of the licence payer, and re-invest in to BBC programming.

*Chief Executive* Rupert Gavin

## Audio tapes, CDs and books
BBC Audiobooks, St James House, The Square,
Lower Bristol Road, Bath BA2 3SB
*tel* (01225) 335336 *fax* (01225) 31077
*website* www.bbcaudiobooks.com

Every year around 200 audio tapes and CDs of BBC radio and TV programmes are released, mainly of comedy, readings and dramatised serials. Over 1000 titles are on CD and tape. The department welcomes writers to pitch ideas for new products.

*Publishing Director, BBC Audiobooks* Jan Paterson
  Ideas for books that would extend audience enjoyment of a BBC Radio or TV programme should be pitched with a short synopsis to:

*Commissioning Editor, Factual* Shirley Patton
*Commissioning Editors, Lifestyle* Vivien Bowler &
  Nicky Copeland

## Magazines
Freelance contributions are regularly used by BBC Worldwide magazines, but the use of unsolicited material is rare as the editorial links closely to BBC programme content. Ideas for articles that clearly fit the remit of a magazine should be pitched via a short written summary to the Editor.

*Radio Times* Gill Hudson
*BBC Gardeners' World* Adam Pasco
*BBC Easy Gardening* Ceri Thomas
*Gardens Illustrated* Clare Foster
*BBC Good Food* Gillian Carter
*BBC Easy Food* Sara Buenfeld
*BBC Good Homes* Lisa Allen
*BBC History* Greg Neale. Published by Origin
  Publishing
*BBC Homes & Antiques* Mary Carroll

*BBC Music* Helen Wallace. Published by Origin Publishing

*BBC Parenting* Susie Boone

*eve* Jane Bruton

*Olive* Christine Hayes

*Songs of Praise* Liz Vercoe

*BBC Top Gear* Michael Harvey

*What to Wear* Sara Manning

*BBC Wildlife* Sophie Stafford. Published by Origin Publishing (a wholly owned subsidiary of BBC Magazines), 14th Floor, Tower House, Fairfax Street, Bristol BS1 3BN

All ideas for BBC children's and teenage magazines should be send to the magazine concerned (*BBC Toybox, Teletubbies, Bob the Builder, Tweenies, Noddy, BBC Learning is Fun, It's HOT, Girl Talk, Top of the Pops*).

## Nations and Regions

BBC Media Centre, 201 Wood Lane, London W12 7TQ

*tel* 020-8743 8000

BBC Nations and Regions is responsible for around three-quarters of all the BBC's domestic output – a total of about 7000 hours of TV and over 250,000 hours of radio programming a year. BBC Northern Ireland, BBC Scotland and BBC Wales produce a growing number of programmes for the national networks, as well as providing comprehensive services for viewers and listeners in their own nations. The BBC's English Regions are responsible for 12 TV regional news and current affairs services across England; for 40 BBC local radio stations and 42 local *Where I Live* websites with their emphasis on news and information for their local communities.

*Director, Nations and Regions* Pat Loughrey

### BBC Northern Ireland

BBC Broadcasting House, Ormeau Avenue, Belfast BT2 8HQ

*tel* 028-9033 8000

*website* www.bbc.co.uk/ni

BBC Northern Ireland produces a broad spectrum of radio and TV programmes, both for the BBC's national networks and for the home audience. Output includes news and current affairs, documentaries, education, entertainment, sport, music, religion and ethics and programmes in, and relating to, Irish and Ulster Scots. It also has a thriving drama department which produces material for network radio and TV, including serials, single dramas and readings.

In addition to making network radio programmes for Radios 1, 2, 3, 4, 5 Live, BBC7 and BBC World Service, BBC Northern Ireland also makes programmes for local audiences on BBC Radio Ulster and BBC Radio Foyle.

*Controller, BBC Northern Ireland* Anna Carragher

*Head of Broadcasting* Peter Johnston

*Head of Programme Production* Mike Edgar

*Head of News & Current Affairs* Andrew Colman

*Head of Creative Development* Bruce Batten

*Head of Drama* Patrick Spence

*Head of Interactive Services & Learning* Kieran Hegarty

*Editor, Radio* Susan Lovell

*Editor, Radio Foyle* Ana Leddy

### BBC Radio Ulster

BBC Broadcasting House, Ormeau Avenue, Belfast BT2 8HQ

*tel* 028-9033 8000

### BBC Radio Foyle

8 Northland Road, Londonderry BT48 7JD

*tel* 028-7126 2244

### BBC Scotland

BBC Broadcasting House, Queen Margaret Drive, Glasgow G12 8DG

*tel* 0141-339 8844

*website* www.bbc.co.uk/scotland

BBC Scotland is the most varied production centre outside London, providing BBC TV and radio networks and BBC World Service with pivotal drama, comedy, entertainment, children's, leisure, documentaries, religion, education, arts, music, news, current affairs and political coverage. *End of Story* and *Writing Scotland* are recent factual TV series which invited writers to directly contribute their material. Internet development is also a key element of production activity. Its drama department, along with Scottish Screen (see page 536), is responsible for the highly successful initiative, *Tartan Shorts*, which promotes film-making in the nation and provides a platform for emerging Scottish creative talent, including actors, writers, directors and producers. On the back of this, Scottish Screen again teamed up with BBC Scotland alongside BBC Films and ContentFilm plc to launch the new low-budget film scheme, *Fast Forward Features*, to enable film-makers to move from short film-making into mainstream movies.

In addition to making network output, BBC Scotland transmits more than 950 hours of TV programming per year on BBC 1 Scotland and BBC 2 Scotland, including the Scottish soap, *River City*. BBC Radio Scotland is the country's only national radio station, and is on air 18 hours per day, every day, with local programmes also broadcast on Radio Scotland's FM frequency in the Northern Isles, and there are daily bulletins for listeners in the Highlands, Grampian, Borders, and the southwest. BBC Radio nan Gaidheal provides a Gaelic service on a separate FM frequency for around 65 hours a week.

*Controller, BBC Scotland* Ken MacQuarrie
*Controller, Network Development, Nations & Regions*
  Colin Cameron
*Head of News & Current Affairs* Blair Jenkins
*Head of Drama* Barbara McKissack
*Commissioning Editor* Ewan Angus
*Head of Radio Scotland* Maggie Cunningham
*Head of Radio Drama* Patrick Rayner
*Head of Gaelic* Donalda MacKinnon
*Head of Radio Scotland* Maggie Cunningham
*Head of Radio Drama* Patrick Rayner
*Editor, Radio nan Gaidheal* Donalda MacKinnon

## BBC Radio Scotland
BBC Broadcasting House, Queen Margaret Drive,
Glasgow G12 8DG
*tel* 0141-339 8844

## BBC Radio nan Gaidheal
Rosebank, Church Street, Stornoway,
Isle of Lewis HS1 2LS
*tel* (01851) 705000

## BBC Alba, Craoladh nan Gaidheal
7 Culduthel Road, Inverness IV2A 4AD
*tel* (01463) 720720

## BBC Radio Orkney
Castle Street, Kirkwall, Orkney KW15 1DF
*tel* (0141) 339884

## BBC Radio Shetland
Pitt Lane, Lerwick, Shetland ZE1 0DW
*tel* (01595) 694747

## BBC Wales
BBC Broadcasting House, Llandaff,
Cardiff CF5 2YQ
*tel* 029-2032 2000
*website* www.bbc.co.uk/wales

BBC Wales provides a wide range of services in
Welsh and in English, on radio, TV and online. This
includes more than 20 hours a week of programmes
on BBC 1 Wales and BBC 2 Wales, and the digital
service BBC 2W. Regular output includes the
flagship news programme *Wales Today*, the current
affairs strand *Week In Week Out*, and live rugby on
*Scrum V*. A further 10 hours a week are shown in
the Welsh-language channel S4C, including the
news programme *Newyddion*, the nightly soap
opera *Pobol y Cwm* plus a range of programmes for
schools. Its 2 radio stations – BBC Radio Wales,
broadcasting in English, and BBC Radio Cymru,
broadcasting in Welsh – each provide 20 hours a
day of news, entertainment, music and sports
output. Political coverage on all services has
expanded following the creation of the National
Assembly for Wales. BBC Wales also produces
popular drama-documentaries, education and
music programmes for audiences throughout the
UK, including the biennial BBC Singer of the World
in Cardiff competition, accompanied by the BBC
National Orchestra of Wales.

*Controller, BBC Wales* Menna Richards
*Head of Programmes (English)* Clare Hudson
*Head of Programmes (Welsh)* Keith Jones
*Head of Marketing & Communications* Huw Roberts
*Head of News & Current Affairs* Mark O'Callaghan
*Head of Drama* Julie Gardner
*Head of Sport* Nigel Walker
*Head of Factual* Adrian Davies
*Head of Arts* Paul Islwyn Thomas
*Head of Music* David Jackson
*Music Director, BBC National Orchestra of Wales*
  David Murray
*Editor, Radio Cymru* Aled Glynne Davies
*Editor, Radio Wales* Julie Barton

## BBC Radio Cymru (Welsh Language)
BBC Broadcasting House, Llandaff,
Cardiff CF5 2YQ
*tel* 029-2032 2000

## BBC Radio Wales (English Language)
BBC Broadcasting House, Llandaff,
Cardiff CF5 2YQ
*tel* 029-2032 2000

**Helen Weinstein** is a documentary maker. She works as a producer, presenter and researcher in BBC Radio
and TV and specialises in history programmes. Last year Helen won The Sony Gold Radio News Award for
Radio 4's investigative history series *Document: The Day They Made It Rain*.

# BBC regional television and local radio

The BBC's English Regions are responsible for 12 TV regional news and current affairs services across England, and for 40 BBC local radio stations providing news and information for their local communities.

## BBC English Regions (TV and radio)
BBC Birmingham, The Mailbox, Royal Mail Street,
Birmingham B1 1XL
*tel* 0121-567 6767
*Controller, English Regions* Andy Griffee
*Chief Assistant* Laura Ellis
*Head of Programming* Craig Henderson
*Head of New Services* John Allen
*Head of Sport* Charles Runcie
*Development Editor (Radio)* Chris Van Schaick

## BBC East
The Forum, Millennium Place, Norwich NR2 1BH
*tel* (01603) 618331
*Head of Regional and Local Programmes* Tim
   Bishop

## BBC Radio Cambridgeshire
PO Box 96, 104 Hills Road, Cambridge CB2 1LD
*tel* (01223) 259696
*email* cambs@bbc.co.uk

## BBC Essex
PO Box 765, 198 New London Road,
Chelmsford CM2 9XB
*tel* (01245) 616000
*email* essex@bbc.co.uk

## BBC Radio Norfolk
The Forum, Millennium Place, Norwich NR2 1BH
*tel* (01603) 617411
*email* radionorfolk@bbc.co.uk

## BBC Radio Northampton
Broadcasting House, Abington Street,
Northampton NN1 2BH
*tel* (01604) 239100
*email* radionorthampton@bbc.co.uk

## BBC Radio Suffolk
Broadcasting House, St Matthew's Street,
Ipswich IP1 3EP
*tel* (01473) 250000
*email* radiosuffolk@bbc.co.uk

## BBC Three Counties Radio
PO Box 3CR, Hastings Street, Luton LU1 5XL
*tel* (01582) 637400
*email* 3cr@bbc.co.uk

## BBC East Midlands
London Road, Nottingham NG2 4UU
*tel* 0115-955 0500
*Head of Regional and Local Programmes* Alison Ford

## BBC Radio Derby
PO Box 104.5, Derby DE1 3HL
*tel* (01332) 361111
*email* radio.derby@bbc.co.uk

## BBC Radio Leicester
Epic House, Charles Street, Leicester LE1 3SH
*tel* 0116-251 6688
*email* radioleicester@bbc.co.uk

## BBC Radio Lincolnshire
Radio Buildings, PO Box 219, Newport,
Lincoln LN1 3XY
*tel* (01522) 511411
*email* radio.lincolnshire@bbc.co.uk

## BBC Radio Nottingham
London Road, Nottingham NG2 4UU
*tel* 0115-955 0500
*email* radio.nottingham@bbc.co.uk

## BBC Yorks & East Lincs
Queens Court, Queens Gardens, Hull HU1 3NP
*tel* (01482) 323232
*Head of Regional and Local Programmes* Helen
   Thomas

## BBC Radio Humberside
Queens Court, Queens Gardens, Hull HU1 3NP
*tel* (01482) 323232
*email* radio.humberside@bbc.co.uk

## BBC London
35C Marylebone High Street, London W1A 6FL
*tel* 020-7224 2424
*Executive Editor* Michael MacFarlane

## BBC London 94.9
PO Box 94.9, Marylebone High Street,
London W1A 6FL
*tel* 020-7224 2424
*email* yourlondon@bbc.co.uk

## BBC North East and Cumbria
Broadcasting Centre, Barrack Road,
Newcastle upon Tyne NE99 2NE
*tel* 0191-232 1313
*Head of Regional and Local Programmes* Wendy Pilmer

## BBC Radio Cleveland
Broadcasting House, PO Box 95FM, Newport Road,
Middlesbrough TS1 5DG
*tel* (01642) 225211
*email* radio.cleveland@bbc.co.uk

## BBC Radio Cumbria
Annetwell Street, Carlisle CA3 8BB
*tel* (01228) 592444
*email* radio.cumbria@bbc.co.uk

## BBC Radio Newcastle
Broadcasting Centre, Barrack Road,
Newcastle-Upon-Tyne NE99 1RN
*tel* 0191-232 4141
*email* radio.newcastle@bbc.co.uk

## BBC North West
New Broadcasting House, Oxford Road,
Manchester M60 1SJ
*tel* 0161-200 2000
*Head of Regional and Local Programmes* Martin
  Brooks

## BBC Manchester
PO Box 27, Oxford Road, Manchester M60 1SJ
*tel* 0161-200 2000
*email* manchester.online@bbc.co.uk

## BBC Radio Lancashire
26 Darwen Street, Blackburn, Lancs. BB2 2EA
*tel* (01254) 262411
*email* radio.lancashire@bbc.co.uk

## BBC Radio Merseyside
55 Paradise Street, Liverpool L1 3BP
*tel* 0151-708 5500
*email* radio.merseyside@bbc.co.uk

## BBC South
Broadcasting House, Havelock Road,
Southampton SO14 7PW
*tel* 023-8022 6201
*Head of Regional and Local Programmes* Eve Turner

## BBC Radio Berkshire
PO Box 104.4, Reading, Berks. RG4 8FH
*tel* 0118-946 4200
*email* berkshire.online@bbc.co.uk

## BBC Radio Oxford
269 Banbury Road, Oxford OX2 7DW
*tel* (08459) 311444
*email* radio.oxford@bbc.co.uk

## BBC Radio Solent
Broadcasting House, Havelock Road,
Southampton SO14 7PW
*tel* 023-8063 1311
*email* radio.solent@bbc.co.uk

## BBC South East
The Great Hall, Mount Pleasant Road,
Tunbridge Wells, Kent TN1 1QQ
*tel* (01892) 670000
*Head of Regional and Local Programmes* Leo Devine

## BBC Radio Kent
The Great Hall, Mount Pleasant Road,
Tunbridge Wells, Kent TN1 1QQ
*tel* (01892) 670000
*email* radio.kent@bbc.co.uk

## BBC Southern Counties Radio
Broadcasting Centre, Guildford GU2 7AP
*tel* (01483) 306306
*email* southern.counties.radio@bbc.co.uk

## BBC South West
Broadcasting House, Seymour Road,
Mannamead, Plymouth PL3 5BD
*tel* (01752) 229201
*Head of Regional and Local Programmes* John Lilley

## BBC Radio Cornwall
Phoenix Wharf, Truro, Cornwall TR1 1UA
*tel* (01872) 275421
*email* radio.cornwall@bbc.co.uk

## BBC Radio Devon
Broadcasting House, Seymour Road, Mannamead,
Plymouth PL3 5YQ
*tel* (01752) 260323
*email* radio.devon@bbc.co.uk

## BBC Radio Guernsey
Bulwer Avenue, St Sampsons, Guernsey GY2 4LA
*tel* (01481) 200600
*email* radio.guernsey@bbc.co.uk

## BBC Radio Jersey
18 Parade Road, St Helier, Jersey JE2 3PL
*tel* (01534) 870000
*email* jersey@bbc.co.uk

## BBC West

Broadcasting House, Whiteladies Road,
Bristol BS8 2LR
*tel* 0117-973 2211
*Head of Regional and Local Programmes* Andrew
Wilson

## BBC Radio Bristol

PO Box 194, Bristol BS99 7QT
*tel* 0117-974 1111
*email* radio.bristol@bbc.co.uk

## BBC Radio Gloucestershire

London Road, Gloucester GL1 1SW
*tel* (01452) 308585
*email* radio.gloucestershire@bbc.co.uk

## BBC Radio Somerset Sound

14–15 Paul Street, Taunton, Somerset TA1 4DA
*tel* (01823) 252437
*email* somerset@bbc.co.uk

## BBC Radio Swindon

PO Box 1234, Swindon SN1 3RW
*tel* (01793) 513626
*email* radio.swindon@bbc.co.uk

## BBC Wiltshire

Broadcasting House, 56–58 Prospect Place,
Swindon SN1 3RW
*tel* (01793) 513626
*email* wiltshire@bbc.co.uk

## BBC West Midlands

The Mailbox, Royal Mail Street,
Birmingham B1 1XL
*tel* 0121-567 6767
*Head of Regional and Local Programmes* David
Holdsworth

## BBC Hereford & Worcester

Hylton Road, Worcester WR2 5WW
*tel* (01905) 748485
*email* bbchw@bbc.co.uk

## BBC Radio Shropshire

2–4 Boscobel Drive, Shrewsbury SY1 3TT
*tel* (01743) 248484
*email* radio.shropshire@bbc.co.uk

## BBC Radio Stoke

Cheapside, Hanley, Stoke-on-Trent ST1 1JJ
*tel* (01782) 208080
*email* radio.stoke@bbc.co.uk

## BBC WM (Birmingham)

PO Box 206, Birmingham, B5 7SD
*tel* (08453) 009956
*email* bbcwm@bbc.co.uk

## BBC Coventry & Warwickshire

Holt Court, 1 Greyfriars Road, Coventry CV1 2WR
*tel* (02476) 860086
*email* coventry@bbc.co.uk, warwickshire@bbc.co.uk

## BBC Yorkshire

Broadcasting Centre, Woodhouse Lane,
Leeds LS2 9PX
*tel* 0113-244 1188
*Head of Regional and Local Programmes* Tamsin O'Brien

## BBC Radio Leeds

Broadcasting Centre, Woodhouse Lane,
Leeds LS2 9PN
*tel* 0113-244 2131
*email* radio.leeds@bbc.co.uk

## BBC Radio Sheffield

54 Shoreham Street, Sheffield S1 4RS
*tel* 0114-273 1177
*email* radio.sheffield@bbc.co.uk

## BBC Radio York

20 Bootham Row, York YO3 7BR
*tel* (01904) 641351
*email* northyorkshire.radio@bbc.co.uk

## BBC North Yorkshire

20 Bootham Row, York YO3 7BR
*tel* (01904) 540314
*email* northyorkshire@bbc.co.uk

## BBC South Yorkshire

54 Shoreham Street, Sheffield S1 4RS
*tel* 0114-273 1177
*email* south.yorkshire@bbc.co.uk

# BBC broadcasting rights and terms

Contributors are advised to check latest details of fees with the BBC.

## Rights and terms – television
### Specially written material

Fees for submitted material are paid on acceptance. For commissioned material, half the fee is paid on commissioning and half on acceptance as being suitable for television. All fees are subject to negotiation above the minima.

In November 2002 a new TV script agreement was introduced. It replaced the old BBC/Guild script agreement for dramatic scripts of 15 minutes and over. The terms were agreed with the PMA and the Writers' Guild. The most significant changes are:

- On First Day of Principal Photography an advance payment of either 15% or 115% of script fee will be made against:
  - (a) repeats/commercial exploitation: 100% of script fee plus/or
  - (b) 5-year licence of Public Service use (excluding BBC1 and BBC2): 15%

(a) only applies to scripts commissioned for BBC1 or BBC2 (but excludes long-running series; (b) applies to BBC1 and BBC2 commissions and also scripts for BBC3 and BBC4 and long-running series on BBC1 and BBC2. Rates for BBC4 may be up to 50% less than those quoted below for specially written material.

- Rates for one performance of a 60-minute original television play are a minimum of £7045 for a play written by a beginner and a 'going rate' of £8806 for an established writer, or *pro rata* for shorter or longer timings.
- Fees for a 50-minute episode in a series during the same period are a minimum of £5304 for a beginner and a 'going rate' of £6630 for an established writer.
- Fees for a 50-minute dramatisation are a minimum of £3813 for a beginner and a 'going rate' of £4766 for an established writer.
- Fees for a 50-minute adaptation of an existing stage play or other dramatic work are a minimum of £2321 for a beginner and a 'going rate' of £2901 for an established writer.

### Specially written light entertainment sketch material

- The rates for sketch material range from £50 per minute for beginners with a 'going rate' of £70 for established writers.
- The fee for a quickie or news item is half the amount of the writer's per minute rate.
- Fees for submitted material are payable on acceptance and for commissioned material half on signature and half on acceptance.

### Published material

- Prose works: £21.98 per minute.
- Poems: £25.52 per half minute.

## Stage plays and source material for television
- Fees for stage plays and source novels are negotiable.

## Rights and terms – radio
### Specially written material
Fees are assessed on the basis of the type of material, its length, the author's status and experience in writing for radio. Fees for submitted material are paid on acceptance. For commissioned material, half the fee is paid on commissioning and half on acceptance as being suitable for broadcasting.
- Rates for specially written radio dramas in English (other than educational programmes) are £48.09 a minute for beginners and a 'going rate' of £73.20 a minute for established writers. This rate covers two broadcasts.

### Specially written short stories
- Fees range from £148 for 15 minutes.

## Published material
### Domestic radio
- Dramatic works: £14.52 per minute.
- Prose works: £14.52 per minute.
- Prose works required for dramatisation: £11.32 per minute.
- Poems: £14.52 per half minute.

### World Service Radio (English)
- Dramatic works: £7.27 per minute for broadcasts within a seven-day period.
- Prose works: £7.27 per minute for broadcasts within a seven-day period.
- Prose works required for dramatisation: £5.67 per minute for broadcasts within a seven-day period.
- Poems: £7.27 per half minute for broadcasts within a seven-day period.
- Foreign Language Services are approximately one-fifth of the rate for English Language Services.

## Television and radio
### Repeats in BBC programmes
- Further proportionate fees are payable for repeats.

## Use abroad of recordings of BBC programmes
If the BBC sends abroad recordings of its programmes for use by overseas broadcasting organisations on their own networks or stations, further payments accrue to the author, usually in the form of additional percentages of the basic fee paid for the initial performance or a royalty based on the percentage of the distributors' receipts. This can apply to both sound and television programmes.

## Value Added Tax
There is a self-billing system for VAT which covers radio, World Service and television for programmes made in London.

## Talks for television

Contributors to talks will be offered the standard television talks contract which provides the BBC certain rights to broadcast the material in a complete, abridged and/or translated manner, and which provides for the payment of further fees for additional usage of the material whether by television, domestic radio or external broadcasting. The contract also covers the assignment of material and limited publication rights. Alternatively, a contract taking in all standard rights may be negotiated. Fees are arranged by the contract authorities in London and the Regions.

## Talks for radio

Contributors to talks for domestic radio and World Service broadcasting may be offered either:

● the standard talks contract which takes rights and provides for residual payments, as does the television standard contract; or

● an STC (Short Talks Contract) which takes all rights except print publication rights where the airtime of the contribution does not exceed five minutes and which has set fees or disturbance money payable; or

● an NFC (No Fee Contract) where no payment is made which provides an acknowledgement that a contribution may be used by the BBC.

# Independent national television

## Channel 5 Broadcasting Ltd
22 Long Acre, London WC2E 9LY
*tel* 020-7550 5555, (08457) 050505 (comments)
*fax* 020-7550 5554
*email* leatherp@five.tv.co.uk (press office)
*website* www.five.tv.co.uk
*Director of Programmes* Kevin Lygo

The fifth and last national 'free-to-air' terrestrial 24-hour TV channel. Commissions a wide range of programmes to suit all tastes. Established 1997.

## Channel 4 Television Corporation
124 Horseferry Road, London SW1P 2TX
*tel* 020-7396 4444, 020-7306 8333 (viewer enquiries), 020-7396 4444 (E4 and FilmFour information) *fax* 020-7306 8347
*website* www.channel4.com
*Director of Programmes* Kevin Lygo

Commissions and purchases programmes for broadcast during the whole week throughout the UK (except Wales). Also broadcasts subscription film channel FilmFour and digital entertainment channel E4.

## GMTV
London Television Centre, Upper Ground, London SE1 9TT
*tel* 020-7827 7000 *fax* 020-7827 7001
*email* talk2us@gmtv.co.uk
*website* www.gmtv.co.uk
*Director of Programmes* Peter McHugh

GMTV1 is ITV's national breakfast TV service, 6.00–9.25am, 7 days a week. GMTV2 is GMTV's digital, satellite and cable channel shown on ITV2 daily 6.00–9.25am.

## ITN (Independent Television News Ltd)
200 Gray's Inn Road, London WC1X 8XZ
*tel* 020-7833 3000, 020-7430 4700 (press offfice)
*fax* 020-7430 4868
*email* editor@itn.co.uk, viewer.liaison@itn.co.uk (comments)

*website* www.itn.co.uk
*ITV News Editor* David Mannion, *Channel 4 News Editor* Jim Gray, *Five News Editor* Gary Rogers, *ITN Radio Editor* Nicholas Wheeler

Provides the national news programmes for ITV, Channel 4 and Channel 5. Owned by Carlton Communications, Daily Mail, Granada, Reuters, United Business Media.

## ITV Network Ltd/ITV Association
200 Gray's Inn Road, London WC1X 8HF
*tel* 020-7843 8000 *fax* 020-7843 8158
*email* info@itv.com
*website* www.itv.co.uk
*Managing Director (Granada)* Mick Desmond, *Managing Director (Carlton)* Clive Jones, *Director of Programmes* Nigel Pickard

Comprises 16 independent regional TV licensees, broadcasting across 15 regions of the UK. Commissions and schedules its own programmes and from independent production companies, shown across the ITV network. The ITV terrestrial channel is ITV1.

## The Office of Communications (Ofcom)
– see page 664

## S4C
Parc Ty Glas, Llanishen, Cardiff CF14 5DU
*tel* 029-20747444 *fax* 029-20754444
*email* s4c@s4c.co.uk
*website* www.s4c.co.uk
*Chief Executive* Huw Jones, *Director of Programmes* Iona Jones

The Welsh Fourth Channel. S4C's analogue service broadcasts 32 hours per week in Welsh: 22 hours are commissioned from independent producers and 10 hours are produced by the BBC. Most of Channel 4's output is rescheduled to complete this service. S4C's digital service broadcasts 12 hours per day in Welsh.

# Independent regional television

It is advisable to check before submitting any ideas/material – in all cases, scripts are preferred to synopses. Programmes should be planned with natural breaks for the insertion of advertisements. These companies also provide some programmes for Channel 4.

## Anglia Television Ltd

Anglia House, Norwich NR1 3JG
*tel* (01603) 615151 *fax* (01603) 631032
*email* angliatv@angliatv.com
*website* www.angliatv.com
*Head of Programmes* Neil Thompson

Provides programmes for the East of England, daytime discussion programmes, documentaries and factual programmes for UK and international broadcasters. Launched 1959.

## Border Television Ltd

The Television Centre, Carlisle CA1 3NT
*tel* (01228) 25101  *fax* (01228) 541384
*website* www.border-tv.com
*Controller of Programmes* Neil Robinson

Provides programmes for, Cumbria, the Borders and the Isle of Man, during the whole week. Ideas for programmes, but not drama programmes, are considered from outside sources. Suggestions should be sent to Neil Robinson, Controller of Programmes. Launched 1961.

## Carlton Television, Central

Gas Street, Birmingham B1 2JT
*tel* 0121-643 9898 *fax* 0121-643 4897
*website* www.carlton.tv.co.uk/central
*Head of Programmes* Duncan Rycroft

Provides ITV programmes for the East, West and South Midlands 7 days a week.

## Carlton Television, London

101 St Martin's Lane, London WC2N 4AZ
*tel* 020-7240 4000 *fax* 020-7240 4171
*website* www.carlton.tv.co.uk.london
*Head of Programmes* Emma Barker

Provides ITV programmes for London and the South East from Monday to Friday.

## Carlton Television, West Country

Langage Science Park, Plymouth PL7 5BQ
*tel* (01752) 333333 *fax* (01752) 333444
*website* www.carlton.com/westcountry
*Head of Programmes* Jane McCloskey

ITV franchise holder that provides programmes for South West England throughout the week. In-house production mainly news, regional current affairs and topical features; other regional features commissioned from independent producers.

## Channel Television

The Television Centre, La Pouquelaye Road, St Helier, Jersey JE1 3ZD
*tel* (01534) 816816 *fax* (01534) 816817
Television House, St Sampson's, Guernsey GY2 4LA
*tel* (01481) 241888 *fax* (01481) 241889
*email* broadcast@channeltv.co.uk
*website* www.channeltv.co.uk
*Director of Programmes* Karen Rankine

Channel Television, the smallest ITV broadcaster, produces 5.5 hours of local programmes each week relating to Channel Islands news, events and current affairs. Launched 1962.

## Grampian Television plc

Queens Cross, Aberdeen AB5 4XJ
*tel* (01224) 848848 *fax* (01224) 848800
Harbour Chambers, Dock Street, Dundee DD1 3HW
*tel* (01382) 591000 *fax* (01382) 591010
23-25 Huntly Street, Inverness IV3 5PR
*tel* (01463) 242624
*website* www.grampiantv.com
*Head of Programmes* Derrick Thomson

Provides programmes for North Scotland during the whole week. Launched 1961.

## Granada Television Ltd

Granada Television Centre, Quay Street, Manchester M60 9EA
*tel* 0161-832 7211  *fax* 0161-953 0283
Upper Ground, London SE1 9LT
*tel* 020-7620 1620
*website* www.granadatv.com
*Director of Programmes* John Whiston

The ITV franchise holder for the North West of England. Produces programmes across a broad range for both its region and the ITV Network. Writers are advised to make their approach through agents who would have some knowledge of Granada's current requirements. Launched 1956.

## HTV Wales/Cymru

HTV Wales, The Television Centre, Culverhouse Cross, Cardiff CF5 6XJ
*tel* 029-2059 0590  *fax* 029-2059 7183
*email* public.relations@htv-wales.co.uk
*website* www.htvwales.com

Provides programmes for Wales during the whole week. Produces programmes for home and international sales.

## HTV West

The Television Centre, Bristol BS4 3HG
*tel* 0117-9722 722 *fax* 0117-972 2400
*email* presspr@htv-west.co.uk
*website* www.htv-west.com
*Director of Programmes* Jane McCloskey

Provides programmes for the West of England
during the whole week. Produces programmes for
home and international sales.

## London Weekend Television (LWT)

The London Television Centre, London SE1 9LT
*tel* 020-7620 1620
*website* www.lwt.co.uk
*Production Director* Claire Poyser

Broadcasts to Greater London and much of the
Home Counties area from Friday 5.15pm to
Monday 6.00am (excluding 6.00–9.25am on
Sat/Sun). Launched 1968.

## Meridian Broadcasting

Television Centre, Southampton, Hants SO14 0PZ
*tel* 023-8022 2555 *fax* 023-8033 5050
*website* www.meridiantv.com
*Programmes Controller* Mark Southgate

The ITV franchise holder for the South and South
East. Broadcasts local news to 3 separate sub-
regions, provides a wide range of quality award-
winning regional programmes, and makes a
significant contribution to the ITV networks and
other channels.

## Scottish Television Ltd

200 Renfield Street, Glasgow G2 3PR
*tel* 0141-300 3000 *fax* 0141-300 3580
*website* www.scottishtv.co.uk
*Managing Director* Sandy Ross

Wholly owned subsidiary of Scottish Media Group,
making drama and other programmes for the ITV

network. Scottish Television Ltd also includes
Ginger Television.
• Material (STV): ideas and formats for long-form
series with or without a Scottish flavour. Approach
Controller of Drama, Eric Coulter.
• Material (Ginger): produces compelling
programmes for groups of all ages. Contact:
Elizabeth Partuka.

## Tyne Tees Television Ltd

The Television Centre, City Road,
Newcastle upon Tyne NE1 2AL
*tel* 0191-261 0181 *fax* 0191-261 2302
*email* tyne.tees@granadamedia.com
*website* www.tynetees.tv.co.uk
*Programme Controller* Graeme Thomson

Serving North East England and North Yorkshire
7 days a week, 24 hours a day.

## Ulster Television (UTV)

Ormeau Road, Belfast, Northern Ireland BT7 1EB
*tel* 028-9032 8122 *fax* 028-9024 6695
*email* info@u.tv.co.uk
*website* www.u.tv.co.uk
*Director of TV* Alan Bremner

Provides programmes for Northern Ireland.
Launched 1959.

## Yorkshire Television Ltd

The Television Centre, Kirkstall Road,
Leeds LS3 1JS
*tel* 0113-243 8283 *fax* 0113-244 5107
*website* www.yorkshiretv.com
*Head of Programmes* Clare Morrow

Yorkshire Television is a Network Company which
produces many programmes for the ITV Network
and the Yorkshire area 7 days a week. Material
preferred submitted through agents. Launched 1968.

# Digital, satellite and cable television

Digital broadcasting has dramatically increased the number and reception quality of television channels. Approximately 50% of UK homes now have digital television. The UK's main digital suppliers are listed below. Details of **multichannel television** can be obtained from Ofcom (www.ofcom.org.uk), and a selection is listed below. **Teletext** is written pages of information (news, weather, holidays, sport, television, entertainment). The two main teletext services are Ceefax on the BBC and Teletext on ITV, Channel 4 and Channel 5. There are teletext services available via the digital format but they are not listed here.

## Freeview

DTV Services Ltd, Broadcast Centre (BC3 D5), 201 Wood Lane, London W12 7TP
*tel* (0870) 8809980
*website* www.freeview.co.uk

Free digital service run by 3 shareholders the BBC, Crown Castle International and BskyB.

## NTL Group

NTL House, Bartley Wood Business Park, Hook, Hants RG27 9UP
*tel* (01256) 752000 *fax* (01256) 752100
*website* www.ntl.com

The UK's top cable TV provider.

## Sky Digital

BskyB, Grant Way, Isleworth, Middlesex TW7 5QD
*tel* (0870) 240 3000
*website* www.sky.com

The UK's number one digital satellite provider, with over 5 million subscribers. Sky premium channels include: Sky Cinema, Sky Moviemax, Sky News, Sky One, Sky Premier, Sky Sports 1–3, Sky Sports extra, Sky Sports News, Sky Travel.

## Telewest Communications

Unit 1, Genesis Business Park, Albert Drive, Woking, Surrey GU21 5RW
*tel* (01483) 750900
*website* www.telewest.co.uk

The UK's second largest cable provider.

## Multichannel television

### BBC Four

Room 6239, Television Centre, Wood Lane, London W12 7RJ
*tel* 020-8576 3193
*website* www.bbc.co.uk/bbcfour

Entertainment and documentary.

### BBC News 24

Television Centre, Wood Lane, London W12 7RJ
*tel* 020-8743 8000
*website* www.bbc.co.uk/bbcnews24

News and weather.

### BBC Three

Television Centre, Wood Lane, London W12 7RJ
*tel* 020-8743 8000
*website* www.bbc.co.uk/bbcthree

Entertainment.

### BBC World

Television Centre, Wood Lane, London W12 7RJ
*tel* 020-8443 8000
*email* bbcworld@bbc.co.uk
*website* www.bbcworld.com

News and information.

### Challenge

Flextech Television, 160 Great Portland Street, London W1W 5QA
*tel* 020-7299 5000
*website* www.challengetv.co.uk

Game and quizz shows.

### CNBC Europe

10 Fleet Place, London EC4M 7QS
*tel* 020-7653 9300
*website* www.cnbceurope.com

Business.

### CNN

Turner Broadcasting System Europe Ltd, Turner House, 16 Great Marlborough Street, London W1F 7HS

*tel* 020-7693 0942
*website* www.edition.cnn.com
News.

## Discovery Channel
160 Great Portland Street, London W1W 5QA
*tel* 020-7462 3600
*website* www.discoverychannel.co.uk
Documentaries.

## E4
124 Horseferry Road, London SW1P 2TX
*tel* 020-7396 4444
*website* www.channel4.com/e4
Entertainment.

## Eurosport
Lacon House, 84 Theobalds Road, London WC1X 8RW
*tel* 020-7468 7777
*website* www.eurosport.co.uk
Sports.

## FilmFour
124 Horseferry Road, London SW1P 2TX
*tel* 020-7396 4444
*website* www.filmfour.com
Feature films.

## God Digital
Crown House, Borough Road, Sunderland SR1 1HW
*tel* 0191-568 0800
*website* www.god.tv
Religion.

## The History Channel
Grant Way, Isleworth, Middlesex TW7 5QD
*tel* 020-7705 3000
*website* www.thehistorychannel.co.uk
Historical documentaries.

## ITN News
200 Grays Inn Road, London WC1X 8XZ
*tel* 020-7833 3000
*website* www.itv.com/news
News.

## ITV2
200 Grays Inn Road, London WC1X 8HF
*tel* 020-7843 8000
*website* www.itv.com/itv2
Entertainment.

## Living
160 Great Portland Street, London W1W 5QA
*tel* 020-7299 5000
*website* www.livingtv.co.uk
Daytime magazine.

## MTV2
17–29 Hawley Crescent, London NWE1 8TT
*tel* 020-7284 6348
*website* www.mtv2europe.co.uk
Music videos.

## MTV Networks Europe
180 Oxford Street, London W1D 1DS
*tel* 020-7284 7777
*website* www.mtv-europe.com
Music video channels.

## Paramount Comedy
3–5 Rathbone Place, London W1T 1HJ
*tel* 020-7478 5300
*website* www.paramountcomedy.co.uk
American sit-coms.

## QVC
Marco Polo House, 346 Queenstown Road, Chelsea Bridge, London SW8 4NQ
*tel* 020-7705 5600
*website* www.qvcuk.com
Shopping.

## Sci-Fi
Universal Studios Networks Ltd, PO Box 4276, London W1A 7YE
*tel* 020-7535 3517
*website* www.ukscifi.com

## Sky Movies Premier (x5)
Grant Way, Isleworth, Middlesex TW7 5QD
*tel* 020-7705 3000
*website* www.skymovies.com
Films.

## Sky News
Grant Way, Isleworth, Middlesex TW7 5QD
*tel* 020-7705 3000
*website* www.skynews.co.uk

## Sky One
Grant Way, Isleworth, Middlesex TW7 5QD
*tel* 020-7705 3000
*website* www.skyone.co.uk
Entertainment.

## Sky Sports 1,2,3, Extra
Grant Way, Isleworth, Middlesex TW7 5QD
*tel* 020-7705 3000
*website* www.skysports.com
Sports.

## TMF The Music Factory
17–29 Hawley Crescent, London NW1 8TT
*tel* 020-7284 6348
Music videos.

## Travel Channel
66 Newman Street, London W1T 3EQ
*tel* 020-7636 5401
*website* www.travelchannel.co.uk
Travel information.

## Trouble
160 Great Portland Street, London W1W 5QA
*tel* 020-7299 5000
*website* www.trouble.co.uk
Teenage ntertainment.

## UK Food
UKTV, 2nd Floor, Flextech Building,
160 Great Portland Street, London W1W 5QA
*tel* 020-7765 1974
*email* ukfood@bbc.co.uk
Food programmes.

## UK Gold
UKTV, 2nd Floor, Flextech Building,
160 Great Portland Street, London W1W 5QA
*tel* 020-7765 0440
*email* ukgold@bbc.co.uk
Classic British programmes.

## UK Style
UKTV, 2nd Floor, Flextech Building,
160 Great Portland Street, London W1W 5QA
*tel* 020-7765 1974
*website* www.ukstyle.tv
Lifestyle.

## VH1
17–29 Hawley Crescent, London NW1 8TT
*tel* 020-7284 6348
*website* www.vh1.co.uk
Current music videos.

## VH1 Classic
Zee TV, 64 Newman Street, London NW1 8TT
*tel* 020-7284 6348
*website* www.vh1.co.uk
Classic music videos.

## Teletext

## Ceefax
Room 7540, BBC Television Centre, Wood Lane,
London W12 7RJ
*tel* 020-8576 1801
*email* ceefax@bbc.co.uk
*Editor* Paul Brannan
Provides service on BBC

## Data Broadcasting International
Allen House, Station Road, Egham,
Surrey TW20 9NT
*tel* (01784) 471515
*website* www.databroadcasting.co.uk
*Managing Director* Peter Mason

## SimpleActive
Allen House, Station Road, Egham,
Surrey TW20 9NT
*tel* (01784) 477711
*website* www.databroadcasting.co.uk

## Teletext Ltd
101 Farm Lane, London SW6 1QJ
*tel* 020-7386 5000
*email* dutyed@teletext.co.uk
*website* www.teletext.co.uk
*Editorial Director* John Sage
Provides service on ITV, Channel 4 and S4C.

# Television and film producers

Jean McConnell advises on submitting a screenplay for consideration.

The recommended approach for placing material is through a recognised literary agent (see page 400). Most film companies have a story department to which material can be sent for consideration by its editors. If you choose to submit material direct, first check with the company to make sure it is worth your while. Many of the feature films these days are based on already bestselling books. However, there are some companies, particularly those with a television outlet, which will sometimes accept unsolicited material if it seems to be exceptionally original.

When a writer submits material direct to a company, some of the larger ones – usually those based in the United States – may request that a Release Form be signed before they are prepared to read it. This document is ostensibly designed to absolve the company from any charge of plagiarism if they should be working on a similar idea and also to limit their liability in the event of any legal action. Writers must make up their own minds whether they wish to sign this but, in principle, it is not recommended.

There are a number of independent companies making films specifically for television presentation and some of these are included in the list below.

**Jean McConnell** is a founder member of the Writers' Guild of Great Britain. She has written screenplays, radio and stage plays, and books. She is a member of the Crime Writers' Association and the Society of Women Writers and Journalists.

## Aardman Animations

Gas Ferry Road, Bristol BS1 6UN
*tel* 0117-984 8485 *fax* 0117-984 8486
*email* mail@aardman.com
*website* www.aardman.com
*Head, Script Development* Mike Cooper, *Development Executive (Shorts & Series)* Helen Brunsdon

Specialists in model animation. No unsolicited treatments. Founded 1972.

## Absolutely Productions

Craven House 226, 121 Kingsway, London WC2B 6PA
*tel* 020-7930 3113 *fax* 020-7930 4114
*email* info@absolutely-uk.com
*website* www.absolutely-uk.com
*Contact* Miles Bullough

Drama and comedy screenplays for cinema and TV, and TV entertainment programmes. Unsolicited scripts are not accepted. Founded 1989.

## Anglo-Fortunato Films Ltd

170 Popes Lane, London W5 4NJ
*tel* 020-8932 7676  *fax* 020-8932 7491
*Contact* Luciano Celentino, Managing Director

Action comedy and psychological thriller screenplays for cinema and TV. Will only accept material if submitted through an agent. Founded 1972.

## British Lion

Pinewood Studios, Iver, Bucks. SL0 0NH
*tel* (01753) 651700 *fax* (01753) 656844
*website* www.britishlionfilms.com
*Contact* Peter Snell

Screenplays and treatments for cinema. No unsolicited material. Founded 1927.

## Brook Lapping Productions Ltd

6 Anglers Lane, London NW5 3DG
*tel* 020-7428 3100 *fax* 020-7284 0626
*website* www.brooklapping.com
*Directors* Anne Lapping, Brian Lapping, Norma Percy, Alex Connock, Sam Cash

TV documentaries and current affairs.

## Carlton Television Productions

35–38 Portman Square, London W1H 0NU
*tel* 020-7486 6688 *fax* 020-7486 1132
*Director of Programmes* Steve Hewlett

Comprises Carlton Television Productions, Planet 24 and Action Time and makes programmes for all UK major broadcasters (ITV, BBC, Channel 4, Channel 5 and Sky) and regional programmes for Carlton Central, Carlton London and Carlton Westcountry. Drama department encourages the submission of scripts and outlines through an agent.

## Catalyst Film and Television International Ltd
Brook Green Studios, 186 Shepherds Bush Road, London W6 7NL
*tel* 020-7603 7030 *fax* 020-7603 9519
*Contact* Head of Drama Development

Screenplays/novels for adaptation for film and TV. Will only consider material submitted through an agent or publisher. Founded 1991.

## Celador Productions Ltd
39 Long Acre, London WC2E 9LG
*tel* 020-7240 8101 *fax* 020-7845 9541

Unsolicited scripts are not accepted.

## Celtic Films
22 Grafton Street, London W1S 4EX
*tel* 020-7409 2080 *fax* 020-7409 2383
*email* info@celticfilms.co.uk
*website* www.celticfilms.co.uk
*Contact* Rebecca Torman

Feature films and high-end drama for cinema and TV. Welcomes new scripts.

## Chatsworth Television Ltd
97–99 Dean Street, London W1D 3TE
*tel* 020-7734 4302 *fax* 020-7437 3301
*email* television@chatsworth-tv.co.uk
*website* www.chatsworth-tv.co.uk
*Managing Director* Malcolm Heyworth

Entertainment, factual and drama. Sister companies in TV distribution and licensing. Founded 1980.

## Children's Film and Television Foundation Ltd
Elstree Film and Television Studios, Borehamwood, Herts. WD6 1JG
*tel* 020-8953 0844 *fax* 020-8207 0860
*email* annahome@cftf.onyxnet.co.uk
*Chief Executive* Anna Home

Development and co-production of films for children and the family, both for the theatric market and TV. Will consider screenplays for cinema. Founded 1951.

## Chrysalis Group
Chrysalis Building, Bramley Road, London W10 6SP
*tel* 020-7221 2213

Light entertainment, documentaries, drama, sports.

## Collingwood O'Hare Entertainment
10–14 Crown Street, London W3 8SB
*tel* 020-8993 3666 *fax* 020-8993 9595
*email* info@crownstreet.co.uk
*Contact* Helen Stroud, Head of Development

Children's animation series for TV for ages 0–8, e.g. *Yoko! Jakamoko! Toto!*. Will only consider material submitted via an agent. Founded 1988.

## The Comedy Unit
Glasgow TV & Film Studios, The Media Park, Craigmont Street, Glasgow G20 9BT
*tel* 0141-305 666 *fax* 0141-305 6600
*email* general@comedyunit.co.uk
*Contact* Niall Clark, Script Editor

Develops and produces a wide range of high-quality scripted and broken comedy series, as well as entertainment and factual entertainment programmes. New comedy writing is encouraged, as are entertainment and factual entertainment programme ideas or formats. Submit material by post or email. Response time approx. one month. Founded 1996.

## Company Pictures
Suffolk House, 1–8 Whitfield Place, London W1T 5JU
*tel* 020-7380 3900 *fax* 020-7380 1166
*email* enquiries@companypictures.co.uk
*Contact* George Faber, Charles Pattinson, Max Massenbach

Screenplays for TV drama and feature films. All material should be submitted through an agent. Founded 1997.

## Convergence Productions
10–14 Crown Street, London W3 8SB
*tel* 020-8993 3666 *fax* 020-8993 9595
*email* info@crownstreet.co.uk
*Contact* Helen Stroud, Head of Development

Documentary series, and drama films and series (Convergence). Limited development capacity – generates own ideas/projects. Prefers material to be submitted through an agent. Founded 1988.

## Cosgrove Hall Films Ltd
8 Albany Road, Chorlton-Cum-Hardy, Manchester M21 0AW
*tel* 0161-882 2500 *fax* 0161-882 2555
*email* animation@chf.co.uk
*Contact* Nicola Davies, Assistant Script Editor

Screenplays for cinema and TV for animation (drawn, model or CGI) or a 'live action'/animation mix. Series material especially welcome, preschool to adult. Founded 1976.

## Crosshands Ltd/ACP Television
Crosshands, Coreley, Ludlow, Shrops. SY8 3AR
*tel* (01584) 890893 *fax* (01584) 890893
*email* mail@acptv.com
*Contact* Richard Uridge

Radio and TV documentaries.

## Cutting Edge
27 Erpington Road, London SW15 1BE
*tel* 020-8780 1476 *fax* 020-8780 0102

Documentaries, current affairs. No unsolicited material.

## The Walt Disney Company Ltd
3 Queen Caroline Street, London W6 9PE
tel 020-8222 1000 fax 020-8222 2795

Screenplays not accepted by London office. Must be submitted by an agent to The Walt Disney Studios in Burbank, California.

## Diverse Productions
Gorleston Street, London W14 8AX
tel 020-7603 4567 fax 020-7603 2148
website www.diverse.co.uk

Documentaries, science, business history, travel, the arts, music, entertainment, children's.

## Ecosse Films Ltd
Brigade House, 8 Parsons Green, London SW6 4TN
tel 020-7371 0290 fax 020-7736 3436
website www.ecossefilms.com

High-quality films and dramas for cinema and TV. Material is considered only if it is submitted through an agent. Founded 1988.

## Endemol
Shepherd's Building Central, Charechrost Way, London W14 0EE
tel (0870) 333 1700 fax (0870) 333 1800

Entertainment, documentary, drama, children's arts, news, current affairs, religion.

## Fairwater Films Ltd
68 Vista Rise, Llandaff, Cardiff CF5 2SD
tel 029-2057 8488 fax 029-2057 8488
email tbarnes@netcomuk.co.uk
Managing Director Tony Barnes

Animation for cinema and TV; live action entertainment. All material should be submitted through an agent. Founded 1982.

## Feelgood Fiction Ltd
49 Goldhawk Road, London W12 8QP
tel 020-8746 2535 fax 020-8740 6177
email feelgood@feelgoodfiction.co.uk
Managing Director Philip Clarke, Drama Producer Laurence Bowen

Film and TV drama.

## The First Film Company Ltd
38 Great Windmill Street, London W1D 7LU
tel 020-7439 1640 fax 020-7437 2062
Producers Roger Randall-Cutler, Robert Cheek

Screenplays for cinema. All material should be submitted through an agent. Founded 1984.

## Focus Films Ltd
The Rotunda Studios, rear of 116–118 Finchley Road, London NW3 5HT
tel 020-7435 9004 fax 020-7431 3562
email focus@pupix.demon.co.uk

Contact Lucinda Van Rie
Screenplays for cinema. Will only consider material submitted through an agent. Founded 1982.

## Mark Forstater Productions Ltd
27 Lonsdale Road, London NW6 6RA
tel 020-7624 1123 fax 020-7624 1124
Contact Rosie Homan

Film and TV production. No unsolicited scripts.

## Front Page Films
507 Riverbank House, 1 Putney Bridge Approach, London SW6 3JD
Contact Script Editor

Screenplays for cinema. Founded 1985.

## Gaia Communictions
Sanctuary House, 35 Harding Avenue, Eastbourne, East Sussex BN22 8PL
tel (01323) 727183 fax (01323) 734809
email production@gaiacommunications.co.uk
website www.gaiacommunications.co.uk
Directors Robert Armstrong, Loni von Grüner

Specialises in Southeast regional documentary programmes, particularly historical and tourist. Founded 1987.

## Noel Gay Television
Shepperton Studios, Studios Road, Shepperton, Middlesex TW17 0QD
tel (01932) 592569 fax (01932) 592172
Contact Lesley McKirdy

Treatments for TV; entertainment, comedy and drama. Founded 1987.

## The Good Film Company
The Studio, 5–6 Eton Garages, Lambolle Place, London NW3 4PE
tel 020-7794 6222 fax 020-7794 4651
website www.goodfilms.co.uk

Commercials. No unsolicited material.

## Greenwich Village Productions
14 Greenwich Church Street, London SE10 9BJ
tel 020-8853 5100 fax 020-8293 3001
email info@greenwichvillage.tv
website www.greenwichvillage.tv
Creative Director John Taylor

Drama, short films, arts documentaries and features. Unsolicited scripts only via agents.

## Hartswood Films
Twickenham Studios, The Barons, St Margaret's, Twickenham, Middlesex TW1 2AW
tel 020-8607 8736 fax 020-8607 8744
Producers Beryl Vertue, Sue Vertue, Elaine Cameron

Screenplays for cinema and TV; comedy and drama. No unsolicited material. Founded 1981.

## Hat Trick Productions Ltd
10 Livonia Street, London W1F 8AF
*tel* 020-7434 2451 *fax* 020-7287 9791
*website* www.hattrick.com
*Contact* Denise O'Donoghue

Situation and drama comedy series and light entertainment shows. Founded 1986.

## The Jim Henson Company
30 Oval Road, London NW1 7DE
*tel* 020-7428 4000 *fax* 020-7428 4001
*website* www.henson.com
*President, Jim Henson Television Europe* Angus Fletcher, *Director of Development, Jim Henson Television* Sophie Finston, *International Development Co-ordinator* Clare Lewis

Screenplays for cinema and TV; fantasy, family and children's programmes – usually involving puppetry or animatronics. All material should be submitted through an agent. Founded 1979.

## Mike Hopwood Productions Ltd
Winton House, Stoke Road, Stoke-on-Trent ST4 2RW
*tel* (01782) 848800 *fax* (01782) 749447
*Contact* Development Executive

Screenplays for cinema; drama and factual TV programmes. No unsolicited material. Founded 1991.

## Icon Films
4 West End, Somerset Street, Bristol BS2 8NE
*tel* 0117-924 8535 *fax* 0117-924 0386
*website* www.iconfilms.co.uk

Film and TV documentaries. Welcomes new material.

## Ignition Films Ltd
1 Wickham Court, Bristol BS16 1DQ
*tel* 0117-958 3087 *fax* 0117-965 7674
*email* ignition@blueyonder.co.uk
*website* www.ignition.pwp.blueyonder.co.uk
*Contact* Alison Sterling

Screenplays for cinema and TV. Material only accepted through agents. Founded 1999.

## Illuminations
19–20 Rheidol Mews, Rheidol Terrace, London N1 8NU
*tel* 020-7288 8400 *fax* 020-7359 1151
*email* linda@illumin.co.uk
*website* www.illumin.co.uk
*Contact* Linda Zuck

Cultural documentaries, arts and entertainment for broadcast TV. Founded 1982.

## Lion Television
191 Askew Road, London W12 9AX
*tel* 020-8735 4000

Light entertainment, documentaries, drama, children's, the arts, news/current affairs, religion.

## Little Bird Company Ltd
9 Grafton Mews, London W1P 5LG
*tel* 020-7380 3980 *fax* 020-7380 3981
*email* firstname@littlebird.co.uk
*Contact* N. Mirza

Screenplays for cinema and TV. No unsolicited material. Founded 1982.

## Little Dancer Ltd
Avonway, 3 Naseby Road, London SE19 3JJ
*tel* 020-8653 9343
*email* Littdan99@cs.com
*Producer* Robert Smith

Screenplays for cinema and TV; drama. Founded 1992.

## LWT and United Productions
London TV Centre, Upper Ground, London SE1 9LT
*tel* 020-7620 1620
*Controller of Drama* Michele Buck

Producers of TV and film. Founded 1996.

## Malone Gill Productions Ltd
27 Campden Hill Road, London W8 7DX
*tel* 020-7937 0557 *fax* 020-7376 1727
*email* malonegill@aol.com
*Contact* Georgina Denison

TV programmes. Founded 1978.

## Maya Vision International Ltd
43 New Oxford Street, London WC1A 1BH
*tel* 020-7836 1113 *fax* 020-7836 5169
*email* info@mayavisionint.com
*website* www.mayavisionint.com
*Producer/Director* Rebecca Dobbs

Features, TV dramas and documentaries. No unsolicited scripts. Founded 1982.

## MBC
43 Whitfield Street, London W1P 6TG
*tel* 020-7258 6800

Entertainment, documentaries, current affairs.

## Monogram Productions Ltd
45–49 Mortimer Street, London W1W 8HX
*tel* 020-7470 0035
*Managing Director* Eileen Quinn

Screenplays for cinema and TV; drama series and serials only. All material should be submitted through an agent. Founded 1997; merged with Scottish Independent Wark Clements 2001.

## MW Entertainments
48 Dean Street, London W1D 5BF
*tel* 020-7734 7707 *fax* 020-7734 7727
*email* mw@michaelwhite.co.uk

Screenplays for cinema. Treatments and synopses only. Founded 1963.

## Oxford Scientific Films
Lower Road, Long Hanborough, Oxon OX8 8LL
*tel* (01993) 881881 *fax* (01993) 882808
*website* www.osf.uk.com

Natural history and science documentaries.
Welcomes new material.

## Pathé Pictures
14–17 Kenthouse, Market Place, London W1W 8AR
*tel* 020-7323 5151 *fax* 020-7631 3568

Feature film production company. Will consider
proposals submitted via an agent or production
company.

## Pearson
1 Stephen Street, London W1F 1PJ
*tel* 020-7691 6000 *fax* 020-7691 6100

Light entertainment, drama and children's TV
programmes.

## Penumbra Productions Ltd
80 Brondesbury Road, London NW6 6RX
*tel* 020-7328 4550 *fax* 020-7328 3844
*email* nazpenumbra@aol.com
*Contact* H.O. Nazareth

Contemporary social-issue drama and docs for
feature films and TV; non-broadcast videos to
commissions. Send synopsis only, not scripts,
preferably by email. Founded 1981.

## Picture Palace Films Ltd
13 Egbert Street, London NW1 8LJ
*tel* 020-7586 8763 *fax* 020-7586 9048
*email* info@picturepalace.com
*website* www.picturepalace.com
*Contact* Malcolm Craddock

Screenplays for cinema and TV; low budget films;
TV drama series. Material only considered if
submitted through an agent. Founded 1971.

## Planet 24 Productions Ltd
35–38 Portman Square, London W1H 0NU
*tel* 020-7486 6268 *fax* 020-7612 0679
*website* www.planet24.com
*Managing Director* Ed Forsdick

Light entertainment, factual entertainment, music,
features and computer animation. Wholly owned
subsidiary of Carlton Communications Plc.

## Portobello Pictures Ltd
PO Box 31579, London W11 3YA
*tel* 020-7379 5566 *fax* 020-7379 5599
*Contact* Eric Abraham

Screenplays for cinema. Founded 1987.

## Praxis Films Ltd
PO Box 290, Market Rasen, Lincs. LN3 6BB
*tel* (01472) 399976 *fax* (01472) 399976

*email* info@praxisfilms.com
*website* www.praxisfilms.com
*Contact* Lori Wheeler, Head of Development

Documentaries, news, current affairs, all factual
genres for TV. No drama/movies. Proposals via
website preferred. Founded 1985.

## Prospect Pictures
13 Wandsworth Plain, London SW18 1ET
*tel* 020-7636 1234

Documentaries, light entertainment.

## RDF Television
The Gloucester Building, Kensington Village,
Avonmore Road, London W14 8RF
*tel* 020-7013 4000 *fax* 020-7013 4001

Light entertainment, documentary, drama, arts,
news, current affairs, religion.

## September Films Ltd
Glen House, 22 Glenthorne Road, London W6 0NG
*tel* 020-8563 9393 *fax* 020-8741 7214
*email* september@septemberfilms.com
*website* www.septemberfilms.com
*Head of Production* Elaine Day, *Head of Drama and
Film Development* Nadine Mellor

Factual entertainment and documentary specialists
expanding further into TV drama and film.
Founded 1993.

## SH Production
Green Dene Cottage, Honeysuckle Bottom,
East Horsley, Surrey KT24 5TD
*tel* (01483) 281792 *fax* (01483) 281792
*Contact* Robert Symes

Broadcast and non-broadcast commercial material,
English and German voiceovers for films, video
production. Founded 1988.

## Specific Films
25 Rathbone Street, London W1T 1NQ
*tel* 020-7580 7476 *fax* 020-7494 2676
*email* info@specificfilms.com
*Contact* Michael Hamlyn

Feature-length films.

## Spice Factory UK Ltd
81 The Promenade, Peacehaven, East Sussex BN10 8LS
*tel* (01273) 585275 *fax* (01273) 585304
*email* script@spicefactory.co.uk
*Contact* Lucy Shuttleworth, Head of Development

Feature film production company. No unsolicited
submissions. Founded 1995.

## Sunset & Vine Productions
30 Sackville Street, London W1X 1DB
*tel* 020-7478 7300

Documentaries, sports, entertainment.

## Talisman Films Ltd
5 Addison Place, London W11 4RJ
*tel* 020-7603 7474 *fax* 020-7602 7422
*email* email@talismanfilms.com
*Contact* Richard Jackson

Screenplays for cinema and TV. Material only considered if submitted through an agent. Single page treatments accepted. Founded 1991.

## TalkBack Productions
20–21 Newman Street, London W1T 1PG
*tel* 020-7861 8000 *fax* 020-7861 8001

TV situation comedies and comedy dramas, features, straight drama. Send unsolicited material to PA to Managing Director; material through an agent to Peter Fincham. Founded 1981.

## Tiger Aspect Productions
*Drama* and *Tiger Aspect Pictures* 5 Soho Square, London W1V 5DE
*tel* 020-7434 0672 *fax* 020-7544 1665
*Comedy* 7 Soho Street, London W1D 3DQ
*tel* 020-7434 0700 *fax* 020-7434 1798
*email* general@tigeraspect.co.uk
*website* www.tigeraspect.co.uk

TV drama, comedy and sitcoms. All material should be submitted through an agent. Founded 1993.

## Transworld International
Axis Centre, Burlington Lane, London W1D 3DQ
*tel* 020-8233 5300
*website* www.imgworld.com

Major sporting events, e.g. Wimbledon and The Olympics.

## Twentieth Century Fox Productions Ltd
Twentieth Century House, 31–32 Soho Square, London W1D 3AP
*tel* 020-7437 7766 *fax* 020-7434 2170

Will not consider unsolicited material.

## Twenty Twenty Television
20 Kentish Town Road, London NW1 9NX
*tel* 020-7284 2020 *fax* 020-7284 1810
*email* mail@twentytwenty.tv
*Executive Producer* Claudia Milne

Current affairs, documentaries, science and educational programmes, drama. Founded 1982.

## Twofour Productions Ltd
Quay West Studios, Old Newnham,
Plymouth PL7 5BH
*tel* (01752) 333900 *fax* (01752) 344224
*email* enq@twofour.co.uk
*website* www.twofour.co.uk
*Contact* Melanie Leach, Development Dept

Factual, factual entertainment, leisure and lifestyle, and children's TV programmes. Founded 1987.

## Upfront Television Ltd
39–41 New Oxford Street, London WC1A 1BN
*tel* 020-7836 7702/3 *fax* 020-7836 7701
*email* upfront@btinternet.com
*website* www.celebritiesworldwide.com
*Contact* Richard Brecker, Joint Managing Director

Consultants for production companies producing chat shows, documentaries and award ceremonies. Books celebrities for high-profile shows and events around the world. Founded 1991.

## Wall to Wall Television
8–9 Spring Place, London NW5 3ER
*tel* 020-7485 7424

Documentaries, drama, the arts.

## Warner Bros. Productions Ltd
Warner House, 98 Theobald's Road,
London WC1X 8WB
*tel* 020-7984 5000

Screenplays for cinema. Submit material via an agent.

## Warner Sisters Film & TV Ltd
The Cottage, Pall Mall Deposit, 124 Barlby Road, London W10 6BL
*tel* 020-8960 3550 *fax* 020-8960 3880

Screenplays for cinema and TV; TV programmes. All material should be submitted through an agent.

## Working Title Films
*Films* 76 Oxford Street, London W1D 1BS
*tel* 020-7307 3000 *fax* 020-7307 3003
*website* www.workingtitlefilms.com
*Chairmen* Tim Bevan and Eric Fellner,
*Head of Development* Debra Hayward (films)
*TV* 77 Shaftesbury Avenue, London W1V 8HQ
*tel* 020-7494 4001 *fax* 020-7255 8600
*Head of Television* Simon Wright
*WT2* 76 Oxford Street, London W1D 1BS
*Head of Development* Natascha Wharton

Screenplays for films; TV drama and comedy; low budget films (WT2).

## World Productions Ltd
Eagle House, 50 Marshall Street, London W1F 9BQ
*tel* 020-7734 3536 *fax* 020-7758 7000
*email* firstname@world-productions.com
*website* www.world-productions.com
*Contact* Office Manager

Screenplays for TV; TV drama series and serials; feature films.

## Zenith Entertainment Ltd
43–45 Dorset Street, London W1U 7NA
*tel* 020-7224 2440 *fax* 020-7224 3194
*email* general@zenith-entertainment.co.uk

Screenplays for cinema; TV drama. No unsolicited scripts.

# Independent national radio

UK domestic radio services are broadcast across three wavebands: FM (or VHF), medium wave and long wave. A number of radio stations are now being broadcast in both analogue and digital (see page 368).

## Classic FM
7 Swallow Place, London W1B 2AG
*tel* 020-7343 9000 *fax* 020-7344 2703
*email* enquiries@classicfm.co.uk
*website* www.classicfm.com
*Managing Director* Roger Lewis

The UK's only 100% classical music radio station; national and international news. Launched 1992.

## Commercial Radio Companies Association (CRCA)
77 Shaftesbury Avenue, London W1D 5DU
*tel* 020-7306 2603 *fax* 020-7470 0062
*email* info@crca.co.uk
*website* www.crca.co.uk

CRCA is the trade body for UK commercial radio representing commercial radio to Government, the Radio Authority (see below), copyright societies and other organisations concerned with radio. CRCA is a source of advice to members and acts as a clearing house for radio information.

CRCA runs the Radio Advertising Clearance Centre. It jointly owns Radio Joint Audience Research Ltd (RAJAR) with the BBC and JICRIT Ltd (an electronic means of buying, selling and accounting for radio advertisements) with the IPA.

CRCA is a founder member of the Association of European Radios (AER), which lobbies European institutions on behalf of commercial radio.

## Digital One Ltd
20 Southampton Street, London WC2E 7QH
*tel* 020-7288 4600
*email* info@digitalone.co.uk
*website* www.ukdigitalradio.com

Commercial digital radio multiplex operator. Founded 1999.

## IRN (Independent Radio News)
6th Floor, 200 Gray's Inn Road, London WC1X 8XZ
*tel* 020-7430 4090 *fax* 020-7430 4092
*email* news@irn.co.uk
*website* www.irn.co.uk

National news provider to all UK commercial radio stations, including live news bulletins, sport and financial news, and coverage of the House of Commons.

## Oneword
Landseer House, 19 Charing Cross Road, London WC2H 0ES
*tel* 020-7976 3030 *fax* 020-7930 9460
*email* info@oneword.co.uk
*website* www.oneword.co.uk
*Managing Director* Ben Budworth, *Programme Manager* Christina Captieux

The first commercial national radio station to be exclusively dedicated to the transmission of books, plays, comedy and discussion. Broadcasts 7 days a week on Sky (channel 877), Freeview (channel 85), NTL (channel 893), DAB digital radio and streams live on the internet. Founded 2000.

## The Radio Authority – now The Office of Communications (Ofcom) – see page 664

## TalkSPORT
18 Hatfields, London SE1 8DJ
*tel* 020-7959 7800 *fax* 020-7959 7874
*website* www.talksport.net
*Chief Executive* Kelvin Mackenzie, *Programme Director* Mike Parry

Sports commentary, comments and coverage. Launched 1995.

## TEAMtalk252/Atlantic 252
78 Wellington Street, Leeds LS1 2EQ
*tel* 0870-128 3333
*website* www.teamtalk.com

Broadcast from Southern Ireland but with two-thirds of its audience in the UK. Formerly called Atlantic 252. Founded 1989.

## Virgin 1215
1 Golden Square, London W1F 9DJ
*tel* 020-7434 1215 *fax* 020-7434 1197
*email* reception@virginradio.co.uk
*website* www.virginradio.co.uk
*Chief Executive* John Pearson, *Programme Director* Paul Jackson

Rock and contemporary music. Available on digital, analogue and the internet. Launched in 1993.

# Independent local radio

Refer to the Office of Communications (www.ofcom.org.uk) for more details.

*Stations offering some/occasional opportunities for creative input from local writers. Check with the station before submitting material.

## ENGLAND

### Alton/Haslemere
Delta FM 102, 65 Weyhill, Haslemere,
Surrey GU27 1HN
*tel* (01428) 651971 *fax* (01428) 658971
*email* studio@deltaradio.co.uk
*website* www.deltaradio.co.uk

### Aylesbury
Mix 96, Friars Square Studios, 11 Bourbon Street,
Aylesbury, Bucks. HP20 2PZ
*tel* (01296) 399396 *fax* (01296) 398988
*email* mix@mix96.co.uk
*website* www.mix96.co.uk

### Barnstaple
Lantern FM, Unit 2B, Lauder Lane, Barnstaple,
Devon EX31 3TA
*tel* (01271) 340340 *fax* (01271) 340345
*website* www.koko.com

### Basingstoke
107.6 Kestrel FM, 2nd Floor, Paddington House,
The Walks Shopping Centre, Basingstoke RG21 7LJ
*tel* (01256) 694000 *fax* (01256) 694111
*website* www.kestrelfm.com

### Bassetlaw
Trax FM, PO Box 444, Worksop, Notts. S80 1GP
*tel* (01909) 500611 *fax* (01909) 500445
*website* www.traxfm.co.uk

### Bath
Bath FM, Station House, Ashley Avenue,
Lower Weston, Bath BA1 3DS
*tel* (01225) 471571 *fax* (01225) 471681
*email* studio@bath.fom
*website* www.bath.fm

### Bedford
96.9 Chiltern FM, 55 Goldington Road,
Bedford MK40 3LT
*tel* (01234) 272400 *fax* (01234) 325137
*website* www.koko.com

### Birmingham
96.4 FM BRMB, 9 Brindleyplace, 4 Oozells Square,
Birmingham B1 2DJ
*tel* 0121-245 5000 *fax* 0121-245 5245

*email* info@brmb.co.uk
*website* www.brmb.co.uk

### Birmingham
Galaxy 102.2, 1 The Square, 111 Broad Street,
Birmingham B15 1AS
*tel* 0121-695 0000 *fax* 0121-696 1007
*email* galaxy1022@galaxy.co.uk
*website* www.galaxy1022.co.uk

### Birmingham
Radio XL 1296 AM, KMS House, Bradford Street,
Birmingham B12 0JD
*tel* 0121-753 5353 *fax* 0121-753 3111
*email* arun@radioxl.net
*website* www.radioxl.net

### Birmingham
Capital Gold (1152), 30 Leicester Square,
London WC2H 7LA
*tel* 020-7766 6000 *fax* 020-7766 6393
*email* info@capitalgold.co.uk
*website* www.capitalgold.com

### Blackpool
Radio Wave 96.5, 965 Mowbray Drive, Blackpool,
Lancs. FY3 7JR
*tel* (01253) 304965 *fax* (01253) 301965
*email* any@thewavefm.co.uk
*website* www.thewavefm.co.uk

### Bolton & Bury
Tower FM, The Mill, Brownlow Way,
Bolton BL1 2RA
*tel* (01204) 387000 *fax* (01204) 534065
*website* www.towerfm.co.uk

### Bournemouth
2CR FM *and* Classic Gold 828, 5 Southcote Road,
Bournemouth BH1 3LR
*tel* (01202) 259259 *fax* (01202) 255244
*websites* www.koko.com,
www.classicgolddigital.com

### Bradford
Sunrise FM, Sunrise House, 30 Chapel Street,
Little Germany, Bradford BD1 5DN
*tel* (01274) 735043 *fax* (01274) 728534
*website* www.sunriseradio.fm

### Bradford, Huddersfield & Halifax
Classic Gold 1278/1530 AM *and* The Pulse,
Pennine House, Forster Square, Bradford BD1 5NE
*tel* (01274) 203040 *fax* (01274) 203130
*website* www.pulse.co.uk,
www.classicgolddigital.com

### Bridgwater
BCRfm, Royal Clarence House, York Building,
High Street, Bridgwater, Somerset TA6 4WE
*tel* (01278) 727701 *fax* (01278) 727705
*email* info@bcrfm.co.uk
*website* www.bcrfm.co.uk

### Bridlington
Yorkshire Coast Radio – Bridlington's Best,
PO Box 1024, Harbour Road, Bridlington,
East Yorkshire YO15 2YR
*tel* (01262) 404400 *fax* (01262) 404404
*website* www.yorkshirecoastradio.com

### Brighton
Juice 107, PO Box 107.2, Brighton BN1 1QG
*tel* (01273) 386107 *fax* (01273) 273107
*email* admin@nonstopjuice.com
*website* www.nonstopjuice.com

### Brighton/Eastbourne & Hastings
Southern FM, Radio House, PO Box 2000,
Brighton BN41 2SS
*tel* (01273) 430111 *fax* (01273) 430098
*website* www.southernfm.com

### Brighton/Eastbourne & Hastings
Capital Gold (1323 and 945), 30 Leicester Square,
London WC2H 7LA
*tel* 020-7766 6000 *fax* 020-7766 6393
*email* info@capitalgold.co.uk
*website* www.capitalgold.com

### Bristol
Star 107.3, Bristol Evening Post Building,
Temple Way, Bristol BS99 7HD
*tel* 0117-910 6600 *fax* 0117-925 0941
*website* www.star1073.co.uk

### Bristol & Bath
Classic Gold 1260 AM *and* GWR FM, PO Box 2000,
1 Passage Street, Bristol BS2 0JF
*tel* 0117-984 3200 *fax* 0117-984 5202
*email* reception@classicgold.musicradio.com,
reception@gwrfm.musicradio.com
*websites* www.classicgolddigital.co.uk, www.koko.com

### Burgess Hill & Haywards Heath
Bright 106.4, The Market Place Shopping Centre,
Burgess Hill, West Sussex RH15 9NP
*tel* (01444) 248127 *fax* (01444) 248553
*email* info@bright1064.com
*website* www.bright1064.com

### Burnley
2BR, Imex, Lomeshaye Business Village, Netson,
Lancs BB9 7DR
*tel* (01282) 690000 *fax* (01282) 69001
*website* www.2br.co.uk

### Cambridge
Star 107.9, Radio House, Sturton Street,
Cambridge CB1 2QF
*tel* (01223) 722300 *fax* (01223) 577686
*email* firstname.surname@star1079.co.uk
*website* www.star1079.co.uk

### Cambridge & Newmarket
Q103 FM, Enterprise House, The Vision Park,
Chivers Way, Histon, Cambridge CB4 9WW
*tel* (01223) 235255 *fax* (01223) 235161
*website* www.koko.com

### Carlisle
CFM, PO Box 964, Carlisle CA1 3NG
*tel* (01228) 818964 *fax* (01228) 819444
*email* reception@cfmradio.com
*website* www.cfmradio.com

### Chelmsford
Dream 107.7 FM, 6th Floor, Cater House,
High Street, Chelmsford, Essex CM1 1AL
*tel* (01245) 259400 *fax* (01245) 259558
*website* www.dream107.com

### Cheltenham
Star 107.5 FM, Cheltenham Film Studios, 1st Floor,
West Suite, Arle Court, Matherley Lane,
Cheltenham, Glos. GL51 6PN
*tel* (01242) 699555 *fax* (01242) 699666
*website* www.star1075.co.uk

### Chester
Dee 106.3 Ltd, 2 Chantry Court, Chester CH1 4QN
*tel* (01244) 391000 *fax* (01244) 391010
*email* info@dee1063.com
*website* www.dee1063.com

### Chesterfield
Peak 107 FM, Radio House, Foxwood Road,
Chesterfield S41 9RF
*tel* (01246) 269107 (01246) 269933
*email* info@peak107.com
*website* www.peak107.com

### Chichester, Bognor Regis & Littlehampton
Spirit FM 96.6, Dukes Court, Bognor Road,
Chichester, West Sussex PO19 8FX
*tel* (01243) 773600 *fax* (01243) 786464
*email* info@spiritfm.net
*website* www.spiritfm.net

## Colchester

SGR Colchester, Abbeygate Two, 9 Whitewell Road, Colchester CO2 7DE
*tel* (01206) 575859 *fax* (01206) 216149
*website* www.koko.com

## Cornwall

Pirate FM102·2/8, Carn Brea Studios, Wilson Way, Redruth, Cornwall TR15 3XX
*tel* (01209) 314400 *fax* (01209) 314345
*email* enquiries@piratefm102.co.uk
*website* www.piratefm102.co.uk

## Coventry

Classic Gold 1359 *and* Mercia FM, Hertford Place, Coventry CV1 3TT
*tel* (01203) 868200 *fax* (01203) 868202
*websites* www.classicgolddigital.com,
www.koko.com

## Coventry

Kix 96, Watch Close, Spon Street, Coventry CV1 3LN
*tel* 024-7652 5656 *fax* 024-7655 1744
*website* www.kix.fm

## Darlington

Alpha 103.2, Radio House, 11 Woodland Road, Darlington, Co. Durham DL3 7BJ
*tel* (01325) 255552 *fax* (01325) 255551
*email* mail@alpha1032.net
*website* www.alpha1032.net

## Derby

Ram FM, 35–36 Irongate, Derby DE1 3GA
*tel* (01332) 851100 *fax* (01332) 851199
*website* www.koko.com

## Doncaster

Trax FM, PO Box 444, Doncaster DN4 5GW
*tel* (01302) 341166 *fax* (01302) 326104
*website* www.traxfm.co.uk

## Dover & Folkestone

Neptune Radio, PO Box 1068, Dover CT16 1GB
*tel* (01304) 202505 *fax* (01304) 212717
*website* www.neptuneradio.co.uk

## Eastbourne

107.5 Sovereign Radio, 14 St Mary's Walk, Hailsham, East Sussex BN27 1AF
*tel* (01323) 442700 *fax* (01323) 442866
*email* info@1075sovereignradio.co.uk
*website* www.1075sovereignradio.co.uk

## East of England

Vibe FM, Alpha Business Park, 6–12 White House Road, Ipswich, Suffolk IP31 5LT
*tel* (01473) 467500 *fax* (01473) 467549
*email* information@vibefm.co.uk
*website* www.vibefm.co.uk

## East Lancashire

Asian Sound Radio, Globe House, Southall Street, Manchester M3 1LG
*tel* 0161-288 1000 *fax* 0161-288 9000
*website* www.asiansoundradio.co.uk

## East Midlands

106 Century FM, City Link, Nottingham NG2 4NG
*tel* 0115-910 6100 *fax* 0115-910 6107
*email* info106@centuryfm.com
*website* www.centuryfm.com

## Exeter & Torbay

Classic Gold Digital 666/954 *and* Gemini FM, Hawthorn House, Exeter Business Park, Exeter, Devon EX1 3QS
*tel* (01392) 444444 *fax* (01392) 444433
*websites* www.classicgolddigital.com,
www.koko.com

## Fenland

Star 107.1 *and* 107.5, 5 Church Mews, Wisbech, Cambs. PE13 1HL
*tel* (01945) 464465 *fax* (01945) 464464
*email* mail@star1071.co.uk
*website* www.star1071.co.uk

## Gloucestershire/Cheltenham

Severn Sound *and* Classic Gold 774, Bridge Studios, Eastgate Centre, Gloucester GL1 1SS
*tel* (01452) 313200 *fax* (01452) 313213
*websites* www.classicgolddigital.com,
www.koko.com

## Greater London

Capital Gold (1548), 30 Leicester Square, London WC2H 7LA
*tel* 020-7766 6000 *fax* 020-7766 6393
*email* info@capitalgold.co.uk
*website* www.capitalgold.com

## Greater London

Heart 106·2, The Chrysalis Building, Bramley Road, London W10 6SP
*tel* 020-7468 1062 *fax* 020-7470 1065
*website* www.heart1062.co.uk

## Greater London

Jazz FM 102.2, 26–27 Castlereagh Street, London W1H 5DL
*tel* 020-7706 4100 *fax* 020-7723 9742
*email* info@jazzfm.com
*website* www.jazzfm.com

## Greater London

Kiss 100 FM *and* Magic 105.4 FM, Mappin House, 4 Winsley Street, London W1W 8HF
Magic: *tel* 020-7955 1054  *fax* 020-7312 8189
Kiss: *tel* 020-7975 8100  *fax* 020-7975 8150
*websites* www.kiss100.com, www.magic1054.com

## Greater London

LBC News 1152 AM *and* LBC 97.3 FM, The
Chrysalis Building, Bramley Road, London W10 6SP
*tel* 020-7314 7300 *fax* 020-7314 7322
*websites* www.lbc.co.uk, www.newsdirect.com

## Greater London

95.8 Capital FM, 30 Leicester Square,
London WC2H 7LA
*tel* 020-7766 6000 *fax* 020-7766 6100
*email* info@capitalradio.com
*website* www.capitalfm.com

## Greater London

Premier Christian Radio, 22 Chapter Street,
London SW1P 4NP
*tel* 020-7316 1300 *fax* 020-7233 6706
*email* premier@premier.org.uk
*website* www.premier.org.uk

## Greater London

Spectrum Radio, 4 Ingate Place, London SW8 3NS
*tel* 020-7627 4433 *fax* 020-7627 3409
*email* name@spectrumradio.net
*website* www.spectrumradio.net

## Greater London

Sunrise Radio, Sunrise House, Merrick Road,
Southall, Middlesex UB2 4AU
*tel* 020-8574 6666 *fax* 020-8813 9800
*website* www.sunriseradio.com

## Greater London

Virgin 105.8, 1 Golden Square, London W1F 9DJ
*tel* 020-7434 1215 *fax* 020-7434 1197
*email* reception@virginradio.co.uk
*website* www.virginradio.co.uk

## Greater London

Xfm, 30 Leicester Square, London WC2H 7LA
*tel* 020-7766 6600 *fax* 020-7766 6601
*website* www.xfm.co.uk

## Greater Manchester, Merseyside & South & Central Lancashire

Galaxy 102, 5th Floor, The Triangle, Hanging Ditch,
Manchester M4 3TR
*tel* 0161-279 0300 *fax* 0161-279 0301
*website* www.galaxy102.co.uk

## Great Yarmouth & Lowestoft

103.4 The Beach, PO Box 103.4, Lowestoft,
Suffolk NR32 2TL
*tel* (0845) 3451035 *fax* (0845) 3451036
*website* www.thebeach.co.uk

## Grimsby

Compass FM, 26A Wellengate, Grimsby DN32 0RA
*tel* (01472) 346666 *fax* (01472) 508811

*email* enquiries@compassfm.co.uk
*website* www.compassfm.co.uk

## Guernsey

104.7 Island FM, 12 Westerbrook, St Sampson,
Guernsey GY2 4QQ, Channel Islands
*tel* (01481) 242000 *fax* (01481) 249676
*email* firstname@islandfm.guernsey.net
*website* www.islandfm.guernsey.net

## Guildford

County Sound Radio 1566 AM *and* 96.4 The Eagle,
Dolphin House, North Street, Guildford GU1 4AA
*tel* (01483) 300964 *fax* (01483) 531612
*websites* www.ukrd.co.uk, www.964eagle.co.uk

## Hampshire & Isle of Wight

Capital Gold (1170–1557), 30 Leicester Square,
London WC2H 7LA
*tel* 020-7766 6000 *fax* 020-7766 6393
*email* info@capitalgold.co.uk
*website* www.capitalgold.com

## Harlow

Ten 17, Latton Bush Centre, Southern Way, Harlow,
Essex CM18 7BB
*tel* (01279) 431017 *fax* (01279) 445289
*website* www.koko.com

## Harrogate

97.2 Stray FM, The Hamlet, Hornbeam Park
Avenue, Harrogate HG2 8RE
*tel* (01423) 522972 *fax* (01423) 522922
*website* www.972strayfm.com

## Hastings

107.8 Arrow FM, Priory Meadow Centre, Hastings,
East Sussex TN34 1PJ
*tel* (01424) 461177 *fax* (01424) 422662
*email* info@arrowfm.co.uk
*website* www.arrowfm.co.uk

## Havering

Soul City 107.5 FM, Lambourne House,
7 Western Road, Romford, Essex RM1 3LD
*tel* (0870) 6071075 *fax* (0870) 2403286
*website* www.soulcity1075.com

## Hereford & Worcester

Wyvern FM, 5 Barbourne Terrace, Worcester WR1 3JZ
*tel* (01905) 612212 *fax* (01905) 746637
*website* www.koko.com

## Hereford & Worcester

Classic Gold 954/1530, PO Box 262,
Worcester WR6 5ZE
*tel* (01905) 740600 *fax* (01905) 740608
*and* 18 Broad Street, Hereford HR4 9AP
*tel* (01432) 360246 *fax* (01432) 360247
*website* www.themagicam.com

## Hertford

Hertbeat fm, The Pump House, Knebworth Park,
Herts SG3 6HQ
*tel* (01438) 810900 *fax* (01438) 815100
*email* info@hertbeat.com
*website* www.hertbeat.com

## High Wycombe

Swan FM, PO Box 1170, High Wycombe HP13 6WQ
*tel* (01494) 446611 *fax* (01494) 445400
*website* www.swanfm.co.uk

## Hinckley

Fosseway Radio, PO Box 107, Hinckley,
Leics. LE10 1WR
*tel* (01455) 614151 *fax* (01455) 616888
*email* enquiries@fossewayradio.co.uk
*website* www.fossewayradio.co.uk

## Huddersfield

Home 107.9, The Old Stableblock, Lockwood Park,
Huddersfield HD1 3UR
*tel* (01484) 321107 *fax* (01484) 311107
*email* info@home1079.com
*website* www.home1079.com

## Humberside

Magic 1161 AM *and* 96.9 Viking FM,
The Boathouse, Commercial Road, Hull HU1 2SG
*tel* (01482) 593067 *fax* (01482) 593067
*websites* www.magic1161.co.uk,
www.vikingfm.co.uk

## Ipswich & Bury St Edmunds

SGR-FM *and* Classic Gold Amber (Suffolk),
Alpha Business Park, 6–12 White House Road,
Ipswich IP1 5LT
*tel* (01473) 461000 *fax* (01473) 741200
*websites* www.classicgolddigital.com,
www.koko.com

## Isle of Man

Manx Radio, PO Box 1368, Broadcasting House,
Douglas, Isle of Man IM99 1SW
*tel* (01624) 682600 *fax* (01624) 682604
*email* postbox@manxradio.com
*websites* www.manxradio.com, www.radiott.com

## Isle of Wight

Isle of Wight Radio, Dodnor Park, Newport PO30 5XE
*tel* (01983) 822557 *fax* (01983) 822109
*email* admin@iwradio.co.uk
*website* www.iwradio.co.uk

## Jersey

Channel 103 FM, 6 Tunnell Street, St Helier,
Jersey JE2 4LU, Channel Islands
*tel* (01534) 888103 *fax* (01534) 887799
*website* www.channel103.com

## Kendal & Windermere

Lakeland Radio, Lakeland Food Park, Plum Garths,
Crook Road, Kendal LA8 8QJ
*tel* (01539) 737380 *fax* (01539) 737390
*website* www.lakelandradio.co.uk

## Maidstone, Medway and East Kent

Invicta FM, Radio House, John Wilson Business
Park, Whitstable, Kent CT5 3QX
*tel* (01227) 772004 *fax* (01227) 771560
*email* info@invictaradio.co.uk
*website* www.invictaradio.com

## Kettering, Corby, Wellingborough

Connect FM, Unit 1, Centre 2000, Kettering,
Northants. NN16 8PU
*tel* (01536) 412413 *fax* (01536) 517390
*email* info@connectfm.com
*website* www.connectfm.com

## Kings Lynn

KL.FM 96·7, 18 Blackfriars Street, Kings Lynn,
Norfolk PE30 1NN
*tel* (01553) 772777 *fax* (01553) 766453
*email* admin@klfmradio.co.uk
*website* www.klfm967.co.uk

## Kingston-upon-Thames

107.8 FM Thames, The Old Post Office,
110–112 Tolworth Broadway, Surbiton,
Surrey KT6 7JD
*tel* 020-8288 1300 *fax* 020-8288 1312
*email* info@thamesradio.com
*website* www.thamesradio.com

## Knowsley

KCR 106.7 FM, The Studios, Cables Retail Park,
Prescot, Knowsley L34 5NQ
*tel* 0151-290 1501 *fax* 0151-290 1505
*website* www.kcr fm

## Leeds

96.3 Aire FM *and* Magic 828, 51 Burley Road,
Leeds LS3 1LR
*tel* 0113-283 5500 *fax* 0113-283 5501
*websites* www.radioaire.com, www.magic828.co.uk

## Leicester

Leicester Sound, 6 Dominus Way, Meridian
Business Park, Leicester LE19 1RP
*tel* 0116-256 1300 *fax* 0116-256 1303
*website* www.koko.com

## Leicester

Sabras Radio, Radio House, 63 Melton Road,
Leicester LE4 6PN
*tel* 0116-261 0666 *fax* 0116-266 7776
*email* info@sabrasradio.com
*website* www.sabrasradio.com

## Lincolnshire

Lincs FM, Witham Park, Waterside South,
Lincoln LN5 7JN
*tel* (01522) 549900 *fax* (01522) 549911
*email* enquiries@lincsfm.co.uk
*website* www.lincsfm.co.uk

## Liverpool

Juice 107.6, 27 Fleet Street, Liverpool L1 4AR
*tel* 0151-707 3107 *fax* 0151-707 3109
*email* mail@juiceliverpool.com
*website* www.juice.fm

## Liverpool

Radio City 96·7 *and* Magic 1548,
St Johns Beacon, 1 Houghton Street,
Liverpool L1 1RL
*tel* 0151-472 6800 *fax* 0151-472 6821
*websites* www.radiocity.co.uk, www.magic1548.com

## London (Lewisham)

Fusion 107.3, Astra House, Arklow Road,
London SE14 6EB
*tel* 020-8691 9202 *fax* 020-8469 0033
*website* www.fusion1073.com

## London (North)

London Greek Radio, LGR House, 437 High Road,
London N12 0AP
*tel* 020-8800 8001 *fax* 020-8800 8005
*email* sales@lgr.co.uk
*website* www.lgr.co.uk

## London (North)

London Turkish Radio, 185ʙ High Road,
London N22 6BA
*tel* 020-8881 0606/2020 *fax* 020-8881 5151
*website* www.londonturkishradio.com

## London (North)

Choice 107.1 FM, 291–299 Borough High Street,
London SE1 1JG
*tel* 020-7378 3969 *fax* 020-7378 3911
*email* info@choicefm.com
*website* www.choicefm.com

## Loughborough

107 Oak FM, 7 Waldron Court,
Prince William Road, Loughborough LE11 5GD
*tel* (01509) 211711 *fax* (01509) 246107
*website* www.oak.fm

## Ludlow

Sunshine 855, Unit 11, Burway Trading Estate,
Ludlow, Shrops. SY8 1EN
*tel* (01584) 873795 *fax* (01584) 875900
*email* sunshine855@ukonline.co.uk
*website* www.sunshine855.com

## Luton

97.6 Chiltern FM *and* Classic Gold 792/828
(Bedford & Luton), Chiltern Road, Dunstable,
Beds. LU6 1HQ
*tel* (01582) 676200 *fax* (01582) 676201
*websites* www.koko.com,
www.classicgolddigital.com

## Macclesfield

106.9 Silk FM, Radio House, Bridge Street,
Macclesfield, Cheshire SK11 6DJ
*tel* (01625) 268000 *fax* (01625) 269010
*email* mail@silkfm.com
*website* www.silkfm.com

## Maidstone, Medway & East Kent

Capital Gold (1242 and 603), 30 Leicester Square,
London WC2H 7LA
*tel* 020-7766 6000 *fax* 020-7766 6393
*email* info@capitalgold.co.uk
*website* www.capitalgold.com

## Manchester

Capital Gold (1458), 30 Leicester Square,
London WC2H 7LA
*tel* 020-7766 6000 *fax* 020-7766 6393
*email* info@capitalgold.co.uk
*website* www.capitalgold.com

## Manchester

Key 103 *and* Magic 1152, Castle Quay, Castlefield,
Manchester M5 4PR
*tel* 0161-288 5000 *fax* 0161-288 5071
*websites* www.key103.com,
www.manchestermagic.com

## Mansfield

Mansfield 103.2 FM, The Media Suite, Brunts
Business Centre, Samuel Brunts Way, Mansfield,
Notts. NG18 2AH
*tel* (01623) 646666 *fax* (01623) 660606
*email* info@mansfield103.co.uk

## Milton Keynes

FM 103 Horizon, Broadcast Centre,
Vincent Avenue, Crownhill Industry,
Milton Keynes MK8 0AB
*tel* (01908) 269111 *fax* (01908) 564063
*email* reception@horizon.musicradio
*website* www.koko.com

## Morecambe Bay

The Bay, PO Box 969, St George's Quay,
Lancaster LA1 3LD
*tel* (01524) 848747 *fax* (01524) 848787
*email* information@thebay.fm
*website* www.thebay.fm

## Newbury

Kick FM, The Studios, 42 Bone Lane, Newbury,
Berks. RG14 5SD
*tel* (01635) 841600 *fax* (01635) 841010
*email* mail@kickfm.com
*website* www.kickfm.com

## Northampton

Northants 96 *and* Classic Gold 1557,
19–21 St Edmunds Road, Northampton NN1 5DY
*tel* (01604) 795600 *fax* (01604) 795601
*websites* www.koko.com,
www.classicgolddigital.com

## North East England

Century Radio, Century House, PO Box 100,
Gateshead NE8 2YX
*tel* 0191-477 6666 *fax* 0191-477 5660
*email* info@centuryfm.co.uk
*website* www.centuryfm.co.uk

## North East England

Galaxy 105–106, Kingfisher Way, Silverlink Business
Park, Tyne & Wear NE28 9NX
*tel* 0191-206 8000 *fax* 0191-206 8080
*website* www.galaxy1056.co.uk

## North West England

105.4 Century FM, Laser House, Waterfront Quay,
Salford Quays, Manchester M5 2XW
*tel* 0161-400 0105 *fax* 0161-400 0173
*email* info1054@centuryfm.co.uk
*website* www.centuryfm.co.uk

## North West England

Jazz FM 100.4, 8 Exchange Quay,
Manchester M5 3EJ
*tel* 0161-877 1004 *fax* 0161-877 1005
*email* jazzinfo@jazzfm.com
*website* www.jazzfm.com

## Norwich

Broadland 102 *and* Classic Gold Amber, St George's
Plain, 47–49 Colegate, Norwich NR3 1DB
*tel* (01603) 630621 *fax* (01603) 671175
*websites* www.classicgolddigital.com,
www.koko.com

## Nottingham & Derby

96 Trent FM *and* Classic Gold Gem,
29–31 Castle Gate, Nottingham NG1 7AP
*tel* 0115-952 7000 *fax* 0115-912 9302
*websites* www.classicgolddigital.com,
www.koko.com

## Oldham

96.2 The Revolution, PO Box 962, Oldham OL1 3JF
*tel* 0161-621 6500 *fax* 0161-621 6521
*website* www.revolutiononline.co.uk

## Oxford & Banbury

Fox FM, Brush House, Pony Road, Oxford OX4 2XR
*tel* (01865) 871038 *fax* (01865) 871036
*email* fox@foxfm.co.uk
*website* www.foxfm.co.uk

## Peterborough

Classic Gold 1332 AM *and* 102·7 Hereward FM,
PO Box 225, Queensgate Centre,
Peterborough PE1 1XJ
*tel* (01733) 460460 *fax* (01733) 281445
*websites* www.classicgolddigital.com, www.koko.com

## Peterborough

Lite FM, 2nd Floor, 5 Church Street,
Peterborough PE1 1XB
*tel* (01733) 898106 *fax* (01733) 898107
*website* www.litefm.co.uk

## Plymouth

Classic Gold 1152 *and* 97FM Plymouth Sound,
Earl's Acre, Plymouth PL3 4HX
*tel* (01752) 275600 *fax* (01752) 275605
*websites* www.classicgolddigital.com,
www.koko.com

## Bournemouth & Poole

Fire 107.6 FM, Quadrant Studios, Old Christchurch
Road, Bournemouth BH1 2AD
*tel* (01202) 318100 *fax* (01202) 318110
*website* www.fire1076.com

## Portsmouth

107.4 The Quay, Flagship Studios, PO Box 1074,
Portsmouth PO2 8YG
*tel* (02392) 364141 *fax* (02392) 364151
*website* www.quayradio.com

## Preston & Blackpool

97.4 Rock FM, PO Box 974, Preston, Lancs. PR1 1XS
*tel* (01772) 477700 *fax* (01772) 201917
*website* www.rockfm.co.uk

## Preston & Blackpool

Magic 999, St Paul's Square, Preston, Lancs. PR1 1YE
*tel* (01772) 477700 *fax* (01772) 477701
*website* www.magic999.com

## Reading

New City FM, 8 Tessa Road, Reading RG1 8NS
*tel* 0118-918 3000 *fax* 0118-918 3064
*email* tony.grundy@newcityradio.co.uk

## Reading, Basingstoke & Andover

2–TEN FM *and* Classic Gold 1431/1485,
PO Box 2020, Calcot, Reading RG31 7FG
*tel* 0118-945 4400 *fax* 0118-928 8513
*websites* www.classicgolddigital.com,
www.koko.com

## Reigate & Crawley
102.7 Mercury FM *and* Classic Gold 1521,
The Stanley Centre, Kelvin Way, Crawley,
West Sussex RH10 9SE
*tel* (01293) 519161 *fax* (01293) 560927
*websites* www.classicgolddigital.com,
www.koko.com

## Rugby
107.1 Rugby FM, Suites 4–6, Dunsmore Business
Centre, Spring Street, Rugby CV21 3HH
*tel* (01788) 541100 *fax* (01788) 541070
*website* www.rugbyfm.co.uk

## Rutland & Stamford
Rutland Radio, 40 Melton Road, Oakham,
Rutland LE15 6AY
*tel* (01572) 757868 *fax* (01572) 757744
*email* enquiries@rutlandradio.co.uk
*website* www.rutlandradio.co.uk

## Salisbury
Spire FM, City Hall Studios, Malthouse Lane,
Salisbury, Wilts. SP2 7QQ
*tel* (01722) 416644 *fax* (01722) 416688
*email* admin@spirefm.co.uk
*website* www.spirefm.co.uk

## Scarborough
Yorkshire Coast Radio, PO Box 962, Scarborough,
North Yorkshire YO12 5YX
*tel* (01723) 500962 *fax* (01723) 501050
*email* info@yorkshirecoastradio.com
*website* www.yorkshirecoastradio.com

## Severn Estuary
Vibe 101, Radio House, 1 Passage Street,
Bristol BS2 0JF
*tel* 0117-901 0101 *fax* 0117-984 3204
*website* www.vibe101.co.uk

## Shaftesbury
97.4 Vale FM, Longmead, Shaftesbury SP7 8PL
*tel* (01747) 855711 *fax* (01747) 855722
*website* www.valefm.co.uk

## Slough, Windsor & Maidenhead
Star 106·6, The Observatory Shopping Centre,
Slough, Berks. SL1 1LH
*tel* (01753) 551066 *fax* (01753) 512277
*email* onair@1066starfm.co.uk
*website* www.starfm.co.uk

## Solent area
Wave 105.2 FM, 5 Manor Court,
Barnes Wallis Road, Segensworth East,
Fareham PO15 5TH
*tel* (01489) 481057 *fax* (01489) 481100
*website* www.wave105.com

## Southampton
107.8 SouthCity FM, City Studios, Marsh Lane,
Southampton SO14 3ST
*tel* 023-8022 0020 *fax* 023-8022 0060
*email* info@southcityfm.co.uk
*website* www.southcityfm.co.uk

## South & West Yorkshire
Real Radio, Sterling Court, Capitol Park,
Leeds WF3 1EL
*tel* 0113-238 1114 *fax* 0113-238 1911
*website* www.realradiofm.com

## South-East Staffordshire
Centre FM, 5–6 Aldergate, Tamworth,
Staffs B79 7DJ
*tel* (01827) 318000 *fax* (01827) 318002
*website* www.centre.fm

## Southend & Chelmsford
Classic Gold Breeze *and* Essex FM, Radio House,
Clifftown Road, Southend-on-Sea, Essex SS1 1SX
*tel* (01702) 333711 *fax* (01702) 345224
*websites* www.classicgolddigital.com,
www.koko.com

## Stroud
Star 107 FM, Brunel Mall, London Road, Stroud,
Glos. GL5 2BP
*tel* (01453) 767369 *fax* (01453) 757107
*email* studio@star107.co.uk
*website* www.ukrd.com

## South Hampshire
Capital Gold (1170 and 1557) *and* Ocean FM *and*
103.2 Power FM, Radio House, Whittle Avenue,
Segensworth West, Fareham PO15 5SH
*tel* (01489) 589911 *fax* (01489) 589453
*websites* www.powerfm.com, www.oceanfm.com

## South Hams
South Hams Radio, Unit 1G,
South Hams Business Park, Churchstow,
Kingsbridge, Devon TQ7 3QH
*tel* (01548) 854595 *fax* (01548) 857345
*website* www.koko.com

## Southport
107.9 Dune FM, The Power Station, Victoria Way,
Southport PR8 1RR
*tel* (01704) 502500 *fax* (01704) 502540
*website* www.dunefm.co.uk

## South Yorkshire
Hallam FM *and* Magic AM, Radio House,
900 Herries Road, Sheffield S406 1RH
*tel* 0114-209 1000 *fax* 0114-285 3159
*websites* www.hallamfm.co.uk, www.magicam.co.uk

## Stockport

Imagine FM, Regent House, Heaton Lane,
Stockport SK4 1BX
*tel* 0161-609 1400 *fax* 0161-609 1401
*email* info@imaginefm.net

## Stoke-on-Trent

Signal One *and* Signal 2, Stoke Road,
Stoke-on-Trent ST4 2SR
*tel* (01782) 441300 *fax* (01782) 441301
*websites* www.signal1.co.uk, www.signal2.co.uk

## Stratford upon Avon

FM 102 – The Bear, The Guard House Studios,
Banbury Road, Stratford upon Avon CV37 7HX
*tel* (01789) 262636 *fax* (01789) 263102
*email* info@thebear.co.uk
*website* www.thebear.co.uk

## Sunderland

Sun FM, PO Box 1034, Sunderland SR5 2YL
*tel* 0191-548 1034 *fax* 0191-548 7171
*email* progs@sun-fm.com
*website* www.sun-fm.com

## Swindon

Classic Gold 936/1161, Lime Kiln Lane, Lime Kiln,
Wootton Bassett, Swindon SN4 7EX
*tel* 0117-984 3200 *fax* 0117-984 3202
*website* www.classicgolddigital.com

## Swindon & West Wiltshire

GWR FM 97.2, PO Box 2000, Swindon SN4 7EX
*tel* (01793) 842600 *fax* (01793) 842602
*website* www.koko.com

## Teesside

TFM *and* Magic 1170, Radio House, Yale Crescent,
Thornaby, Stockton-on-Tees TS17 6AA
*tel* (01642) 888222 *fax* (01642) 868288
*websites* www.magic1170.co.uk, www.tfmradio.co.uk

## Telford

107.4 Telford FM, PO Box 1074,
Telford TF3 3WG
*tel* (01952) 280011 *fax* (01952) 280010
*website* www.telfordfm.co.uk

## Tendring

Dream 100 FM, Northgate House, St Peters Street,
Colchester CO1 1HT
*tel* (01206) 764466 *fax* (01206) 715102
*website* www.dream100.com

## Tunbridge Wells & Sevenoaks

KM–FM West Kent, 1 East Street, Tonbridge,
Kent TN9 1AR
*tel* (01732) 369200 *fax* (01732) 369201
*website* www.kentonline.co.uk

## Tyne & Wear

Magic 1152 *and* Metro FM, Longrigg, Swalwell,
Newcastle upon Tyne NE99 1BB
*tel* 0191-420 0971 *fax* 0191-488 8611
*websites* www.metroradio.com, www.magic1152.co.uk

## Wakefield

Ridings FM, PO Box 333, Monckton Road,
Wakefield WF2 7YQ
*tel* (01924) 367177 *fax* (01924) 367133
*email* enquiries@ridingsfm.co.uk
*website* www.ridingsfm.co.uk

## Warminster

107.5 3TR FM, Riverside Studios, Boreham Hill,
Bistopstrow, Warminster BA12 9HQ
*tel* (01985) 211111 *fax* (01985) 211110
*website* www.3trfm.com

## Warrington

107.2 Wire FM, Warrington Business Park,
Long Lane, Warrington WA2 8TX
*tel* (01925) 445545 *fax* (01925) 657705
*email* info@wirefm.com
*website* www.wirefm.com

## Watford & St Albans

Watford's Mercury 96.6, Unit 5, The Metro Centre,
Dwight Road, Watford WD18 9UP
*tel* (01923) 205470 *fax* (01923) 205471
*email* firstname.surname@musicradio.com
*website* www.koko.com

## West Cumbria

CFM, PO Box 964, Carlisle CA1 3NG
*tel* (01228) 818964 *fax* (01228) 819444
*email* reception@cfmradio.com
*website* www.cfmradio.com

## West Midlands

100.7 Heart FM, 1 The Square, 111 Broad Street,
Birmingham B15 1AS
*tel* 0121-695 0000 *fax* 0121-696 1007
*email* heartfm@heartfm.co.uk
*website* www.heartfm.co.uk

## West Midlands

Saga 105.7 FM, 3rd Floor, Crown House,
Beaufort Court, 123 Hagley Road,
Birmingham B16 8LD
*tel* 0121-452 1057 *fax* 0121-452 3222
*website* www.saga1057fm.co.uk

## Weston-Super-Mare

Star 107.7 FM, 11 Beaconsfield Road,
Weston-Super-Mare BS23 1YE
*tel* (01934) 624455 *fax* (01934) 629922
*website* www.star1077.co.uk

## West Somerset

Quay West Radio, Harbour Studios, The Esplanade,
Watchet, Somerset TA23 0AJ
*tel* (01984) 634900 *fax* (01984) 634811
*email* studio@quaywest.fm
*website* www.quaywest.fm

## Weymouth & Dorchester

Wessex FM, Radio House, Trinity Street, Dorchester,
Dorset DT1 1DJ
*tel* (01305) 250333 *fax* (01305) 250052
*website* www.wessexfm.co.uk

## Wigan

102.4 Wish FM, Orrell Lodge, Orrell Road,
Wigan WN5 8HJ
*tel* (01942) 761024 *fax* (01942) 777694
*email* studio@wish_fm.com

## Winchester

Win FM, PO Box 1072, The Brooks,
Winchester SO23 8FT
*tel* (01962) 841071 *fax* (01962) 841079
*website* www.winfm.co.uk

## Wirral

Wirral's Buzz 97.1, Media House, Claughton Road,
Birkenhead CH41 6EY
*tel* 0151-650 1700 *fax* 0151-647 5427
*website* www.koko.com

## Wolverhampton

107.7 The Wolf, 10th Floor, Mander House,
Wolverhampton WV1 3NB
*tel* (01902) 571070 *fax* (01902) 571079
*email* studio@thewolf.co.uk
*website* www.thewolf.co.uk

## Wolverhampton, Shrewsbury & Telford

Beacon FM *and* Classic Gold WABC, 267 Tettenhall
Road, Wolverhampton WV6 0DE
*tel* (01902) 461300 *fax* (01902) 461299
*websites* www.classicgolddigital.com, www.koko.com

## Yeovil & Taunton

Orchard FM, Haygrove House, Taunton TA3 7BT
*tel* (01823) 338448 *fax* (01823) 368318
*website* www.koko.com

## York

Minster FM, PO Box 123, Dunnington,
York YO19 5ZX
*tel* (01904) 488888 *fax* (01904) 481088
*email* general@minsterfm.co.uk
*website* www.minsterfm.com

## Yorkshire

Galaxy 105, Josephs Well, Hanover Walk,
off Park Lane, Leeds LS3 1AB
*tel* 0113-213 0105 *fax* 0113-213 1055
*email* mail@galaxy105.co.uk
*website* www.galaxy105.co.uk

## Yorkshire Dales with Skipton

Fresh Radio, Firth Street, Skipton BD23 2PT
*tel* (01756) 799991 *fax* (01756) 799771
*email* info@freshradio.co.uk
*website* www.freshradio.co.uk

# NORTHERN IRELAND

## Belfast

Citybeat 96.7, 46 Stranmillis Embankment,
Belfast BT9 5FN
*tel* 028-9020 5967 *fax* 028-9020 0023
*email* music@citybeat.co.uk
*website* www.citybeat.co.uk

## Coleraine

Q97.2 Causeway Coast Radio, 24 Cloyfin Road,
Coleraine BT52 2NU
*tel* 028-703 59100 *fax* 028-703 26666
*email* sales@q972.fm
*website* www.q972.fm

## Londonderry

Q102·9 FM, The Riverview Suite,
87 Rossdowney Road, Waterside,
Londonderry BT47 5SU
*tel* 028-7134 4449 *fax* 028-7131 1177
*website* www.q102.fm

## Mid Ulster

Mid 106, 2C Park Avenue, Burn Road,
Cookstown BT80 8AH
*tel* 028-8675 8696 *fax* 028-8676 1550
*website* www.mid106fm.co.uk

## Mid Ulster

Mid FM, 15 Drumanee Road, Bellaghy,
Co. Londonderry BT45 8LE
*tel* 028-9020 5967
*email* midfm@hotmail.com

## Northern Ireland

Cool FM, PO Box 974, Belfast BT1 1RT
*tel* (01247) 817181 *fax* (01247) 814974
*email* music@coolfm.co.uk
*website* www.coolfm.co.uk

## Northern Ireland

Downtown Radio, Newtownards,
Co. Down BT23 4ES
*tel* 028-9181 5555 *fax* 028-9181 8913
*email* programmes@downtown.co.uk
*website* www.downtown.co.uk

## Omagh & Enniskillen

Q101.2 FM Radio West, 42A Market Street, Omagh,
Co. Tyrone BT78 1EH
*tel* 028-8224 5777 *fax* 028-8225 9517
1 Belmore Mews, Enniskillen,
Co. Fermanagh BT74 6AA
*tel* 028-6632 0777 *fax* 028-6632 0676
*email* manager@q101west.fm
*website* www.q101west.fm

## SCOTLAND

### Aberdeen

Northsound One *and* Northsound Two,
45 Kings Gate, Aberdeen AB15 4EL
*tel* (01224) 337000 *fax* (01224) 400003
*email* northsound@srh.co.uk
*websites* www.northsound1.co.uk,
www.northsound2.co.uk

### Arbroath/Carnoustie

RNA FM, Radio North Angus, Arbroath Infirmary,
Rosemount Road, Arbroath, Angus DD11 2AT
*tel* (01241) 879660 *fax* (01241) 439664
*email* info@radionorthangus.co.uk
*website* www.radionorthangus.co.uk

### Ayr

West FM *and* West Sound AM, Radio House,
54A Holmston Road, Ayr KA7 3BE
*tel* (01292) 283662 *fax* (01292) 283665
*websites* www.westfmonline.com,
www west-sound.co.uk

### The Borders

Radio Borders, Tweedside Park, Galashiels TD1 3TD
*tel* (01896) 759444 0845 3457080
*website* www.radioborders.com

### Central Scotland

Beat 106 Ltd, The Four Winds Pavilion,
Pacific Quay, Glasgow G51 1EB
*tel* 0141-566 6106 *fax* 0141-566 6110
*email* info@beat106.com,
programming@radioborders.com
*website* www.beat106.com

### Central Scotland

Real Radio, PO Box 101, Parkway Court,
Glasgow Business Park, Glasgow G69 6GA
*tel* 0141-781 1011 *fax* 0141-781 1112
*email* firstname.surname@realradiofm.com
*website* www.realradio.com

### Dumbarton

Castle Rock FM 103, Pioneer Park Studios, Unit 3,
80 Castlegreen Street, Dumbarton G82 1JB
*tel* (01389) 734422 *fax* (01389) 734380

*email* info@castlerockfm.com
*website* www.castlerockfm.com

### Dumfries & Galloway

South West Sound, Unit 40,
The Loreburne Centre, High Street,
Dumfries DG1 2BD
*tel* (01387) 250999 *fax* (01387) 265629
*email* info@westsound.co.uk
*website* www.westsound.co.uk

### Dundee

Wave 102 FM, 8 South Tay Street,
Dundee DD1 1PA
*tel* (01382) 901000 *fax* (01382) 900999
*email* studio@wave102.co.uk
*website* www.wave102.co.uk

### Dundee/Perth

Tay AM *and* Tay FM, 6 North Isla Street,
Dundee DD3 7JQ
*tel* (01382) 200800 *fax* (01382) 423252
*email* tayam@radiotay.co.uk
*website* www.radiotay.co.uk

### Edinburgh

Forthone *and* Forth 2, Forth House, Forth Street,
Edinburgh EH1 3LE
*tel* 0131-556 9255 *fax* 0131-558 3277
*email* info@forthone.com, info@forth2.com
*websites* www.forthone.com, www.forth2.com

### Fife

Kingdom FM, Haig House, Haig Business Park,
Balgonie Road, Markinch, Fife KY7 6AQ
*tel* (01592) 753753 *fax* (01592) 757788
*email* info@kingdomfm.co.uk
*website* www.kingdomfm.co.uk

### Fort William & Parts of Lochaber

Nevis Radio, Ben Nevis Estate,
Fort William PH33 6PR
*tel* (01397) 700007 *fax* (01397) 701007
*email* studio@nevisradio.co.uk
*website* www.nevisradio.co.uk

### Glasgow

Clyde 1 *and* Clyde 2, Clydebank Business Park,
Clydebank, Glasgow G81 2RX
*tel* 0141-565 2200 *fax* 0141-565 2265
*email* info@clyde1.com, info@clyde2.com
*websites* www.clyde1.com, www.clyde2.com

### Inverness

Moray Firth Radio (MFR), PO Box 271,
Scorguie Place, Inverness IV3 8UJ
*tel* (01463) 224433 *fax* (01463) 243224
*email* mfr@mfr.co.uk
*website* www.mfr.co.uk

## Inverurie

NECR, Town House, Kintore,
Inverurie AB51 0UX
*tel* (01467) 632909 *fax* (01467) 632969
*email* necrradio102.ifmsales@supanet.com
*website* www.necrfm.co.uk

## Kintyre, Islay & Jura

Argyll FM, 27–29 Longrow, Campbelltown,
Argyll PA28 6ER
*tel* (01586) 551800 *fax* (01586) 551888
*email* argyllfm@hotmail.com

## North Lanarkshire

Clan FM, Radio House, Rowantree Avenue,
Newhouse Industrial Estate, Newhouse,
Lanarkshire ML1 5RX
*tel* (01698) 733107 *fax* (01698) 733318
*website* www.clanfm.com

## Oban

Oban FM, 132 George Street, Oban,
Argyll PA34 5NT
*tel* (01631) 570057 *fax* (01631) 570530
*email* obanfmradio@btconnect.com
*website* www.obanfm.tk

## Paisley

96.3 QFM, 65 Sussex Street, Kinning Park,
Glasgow G41 1DX
*tel* 0141-429 9430 *fax* 0141-429 9431
*website* www.Q96.net

## Peterhead

Waves Radio Peterhead, Unit 2, Blackhouse
Industrial Estate, Peterhead AB42 1BW
*tel* (01779) 491012 *fax* (01779) 490802
*email* waves@radiophd.freeserve.co.uk
*website* www.wavesfm.com

## Pitlochry & Aberfeldy

Heartland FM, Atholl Curling Rink, Lower
Oakfield, Pitlochry, Perthshire PH16 5HQ
*tel* (01796) 474040 *fax* (01796) 474007
*email* mailbox@heartlandfm.co.uk
*website* www.heartlandfm.co.uk

## Shetland

SIBC, Market Street, Lerwick, Shetland ZE1 0JN
*tel* (01595) 695299 *fax* (01595) 695696
*email* info@sibc.co.uk
*website* www.sibc.co.uk

## Stirling & Falkirk

Central FM, 201 High Street, Falkirk FK1 1DU
*tel* (01324) 611164 *fax* (01324) 611168
*email* mail@centralfm.co.uk
*website* www.centralfm.co.uk

## Ullapool

Lochbroom FM, Mill Street, Ullapool,
Ross-shire IV26 2UN
*tel* (01854) 613131 *fax* (01854) 613132
*email* radio@lochbroomfm.co.uk
*website* www.lochbroomfm.co.uk

## Western Isles

Isles FM, PO Box 333, Stornoway,
Isle of Lewis HS1 2PU
*tel* (01851) 703333 *fax* (01851) 703322
*email* islesfm@isles.fm
*website* www.isles.fm

# WALES

## Bridgend

Bridge 106.3 FM, Cambria House, Wyndham Street,
Bridgend CF31 1EY
*tel* (01656) 647777 *fax* (01656) 673611
*website* www.bridge.fm

## Caernarfon

Champion 103 FM, Llys y Dderwen, Parc Menai,
Bangor, Gwynedd LL57 4BN
*tel* (01248) 671888 *fax* (01248) 671971
*email* sarah.smithard@musicradio.com
*website* www.champion103.com

## Cardiff & Newport

Red Dragon FM, Atlantic Wharf, Cardiff CF10 4DJ
*tel* 029-2066 2066 *fax* 029-2066 2060
*email* mail@reddragon.co.uk
*website* www.reddragonfm.co.uk

## Cardiff & Newport

Capital Gold (1305–1359), 30 Leicester Square,
London WC2H 7LA
*tel* 020-7766 6000 *fax* 020-7766 6393
*website* www.capitalgold.com

## Ceredigion

Radio Ceredigion, Yr Hen Ysgol Gymraeg, Ffordd
Alexandra, Aberystwyth, Ceredigion SY23 1LF
*tel* (01970) 627999 *fax* (01970) 627206
*email* admin@ceredigionradio.co.uk
*website* www.ceredigionradio.co.uk

## Heads of South Wales Valleys

Valleys Radio, Festival Park, Victoria,
Ebbw Vale NP23 8XW
*tel* (01495) 301116 *fax* (01495) 300710
*email* admin@valleysradio.co.uk
*website* www.valleysradio.co.uk

## Montgomeryshire

Radio Maldwyn, The Studios, The Park, Newtown,
Powys SY16 2NZ

*tel*  (01686) 623555 *fax* (01686) 623666
*email*  radio.maldwyn@ukonline.co.uk
*website*  www.magic756.net

## North Wales Coast
Coast FM, PO Box 963, Bangor LL57 4ZR
*tel*  (01248) 673272 *fax* (01248) 671971
*website*  www.coastfm.co.uk

## Pembrokeshire
Radio Pembrokeshire, 14 Old School Estate,
Station Road, Narberth, Pembrokeshire SA67 7DU
*tel*  (01834) 869384 *fax* (01834) 861524
*website*  www.radiopembrokeshire.com

## South Wales Region
Real Radio, PO Box 6105, Ty-Nant Court,
Cardiff CF15 8YF
*tel*  029-2031 5100 *fax* 029-2031 5150
*email*  info@realradiofm.com
*website*  www.realradiofm.com

## Swansea
Swansea Sound, PO Box 1170, Victoria Road,
Gowerton, Swansea SA4 3AB
*tel*  (01792) 511170 *fax* (01792) 511171
*email*  info@swanseasound.co.uk
*website*  www.swanseasound.co.uk

## Swansea
The Wave 96·4 FM, PO Box 964, Victoria Road,
Gowerton, Swansea SA4 3AB
*tel*  (01792) 511964 *fax* (01792) 511965
*email*  info@thewave.co.uk
*website*  www.thewave.co.uk

## Wrexham & Chester
MFM 103.4 *and* Classic Gold Marcher 1260,
The Studios, Mold Road, Gwersyllt,
Wrexham LL11 4AF
*tel*  (01978) 752202
*websites* www.classicgolddigital.com,
www.mymfm.com

# Digital audio broadcasting

Digital transmission technology has a broadcasting capacity many times bigger than analogue, having many more radio stations.

## National multiplexes

### BBC Radio

Broadcasting House, Portland Place,
London W1A 1AA
*tel* 020-7580 4468
*website* www.bbc.co.uk/radio

Broadcasts network services to the UK, Isle of Man and the Channel Islands. There are also national services in Wales, Scotland and Northern Ireland and 40 local radio stations in England and the Channel Islands. Launched 1995.

### Digital One

7 Swallow place, London SE1 8DJ
*tel* 020-7959 7800
*website* www.ukdigitalradio.com
*Operations Executive* Glyn Jones, *Broadcast Manager* Dawn Banks

Digital radio network with more than 85% UK population coverage. Broadcasts Classic FM, Virgin Radio and TalkSPORT plus other channels unique to digital radio – Planet Rock, Core, Life, Oneword, PrimeTime Radio, The Digizone. Launched 1999.

## Local multiplexes

### Aberdeen and Central Scotland

Switchdigital (Scotland) Ltd, 18 Hatfields,
London SE1 8DJ
*tel* 020-7959 7800 *fax* 020-7959 9009
*email* info@switchdigital.com

Broadcasts 24 hours a day:

Aberdeen
Kiss, Smash Hits!, Waves Radio, NECR, Northsound One and Two, BBC Radio Scotland, BBC Radio nan Gaidheal

Central Scotland
Galaxy, Jazz FM, Beat 106, Real Radio, The Arrow, Heart, Smash Hits!, BBC Radio nan Gaidheal

### Ayr, Dundee & Perth, Edinburgh, Glasgow, Inverness, Northern Ireland

Score Digital, 3 South Avenue,
Clydebank Business Park,
Glasgow G81 2RX
*tel* 0141-565 2347 *fax* 0141-565 2318
*website* www.scoredigital.co.uk

Broadcasts 24 hours a day:

Ayr
West FM, West Sound, 3C, UCA, The Storm, Smash Hits!, BBC radio Scotland, BBC Radio nan Gaidheal

Dundee & Perth
Tay FM, Tay Am, 3C, The Access Channel,  The Storm, Smash Hits!, BBC Radio Scotland, BBC nan Gaidheal

Edinburgh
3C, Kiss, Forth One, Forth 2, Xfm, Sunrise Radio, Saga, BBC Radio Scotland

Glasgow
Clyde 1 and 2, 3C, Sunrise Radio, 96.3 QFM, Xfm, Kiss, Saga Radio, BBC Scotland

Inverness
MFR, 3C, MFR 1107, BBC Radio Scotland, BBC nan Gaidheal

Northern Ireland
Downtown, Cool FM, City Beat 96.7, Q102.9, Classic FM, PrimeTime, 3C, Kiss, BBC Radio Ulster

### Birmingham, Greater London I, Manchester

CE Digital, 30 Leicester Square,
London WC2H 7LA
*tel* 020-7766 6000 *fax* 020-7766 6100

Broadcasts 24 hours a day:

Birmingham
BRMB, Capital Gold, Xfm, Radio XL, Magic, Kiss, Sunrise, BBC Radio WM

Greater London I
Capital FM, Capital Gold, Century, Kiss, Magic, LBC 1152 and 97.3, Xfm, Sunrise Radio, Smash Hits!, Capital Disney

Manchester
Key 103, Magic 1152, Kiss, Capital Gold, Xfm, Asian Sound, BBC GMR

### Bournemouth, Bristol/Bath, Coventry, Exeter and Torbay, Norwich, Peterborough, Southend & Chelmsford, Swindon/West Midlands, Wolverhampton, Shrewsbury, Telford

Now Digital, PO Box 2000, 1 Passage Street,
Bristol BS99 7SN
*tel* 020-7959 7800 *fax* 020-7911 7302
*website* www.now-digital.com

Broadcasts 24 hours a day:

## Bournemouth
2CR FM, Classic Gold, Kiss, Wave 105, Saga, Passion for the Planet, The Storm, SBN, BBC Radio Solent

## Bristol/Bath
GWR FM, Classic Gold, The Storm, Xfm, Kiss, Saga, Passion for the Planet, now.data, SBN, BBC Radio Bristol

## Coventry
Mercia FM, Classic Gold, Kix 96, The Storm, Sunrise, SBN, Kiss, YAAR, BBC Radio Coventry & Warwickshire

## Exeter & Torbay
Gemini FM, Classic Gold, Kiss, The Storm, Passion for the Planet, SBN, BBC Radio Devon

## Norwich
Broadband 102, Vibe, 106.4 The Beach, The Storm, Passion for the Planet, 3C, SBN, AbracaDABra, Smash Hits!

## Peterborough
Hereward FM, Classic Gold, Vibe, 3C, Passion for the Planet, SBN, Smash Hits!, BBC Radio Cambridgeshire

## Southend & Chelmsford
Essex FM, Breeze, Saga, The Storm, Passion for the Planet, TBC, Kiss, SBN, BBC Radio Essex

## Swindon/West Midlands
Swindon only – GWR FM Wilts, Saga, Swindon FM, BBC Radio Swindon
West Wiltshire only – GWR FM Bath, BBC Radio Wiltshire
Both – Kiss, Capital Disney, The Storm, Passion for the Planet, SBN

## Wolverhampton, Shrewsbury, Telford
Beacon FM, Classic Gold, The Storm, Xfm, Sunrise Radio, YAAR, Kiss, SBN, BBC Radio WM, BBC Radio Shropshire (WST)

## Leicester, Nottingham,
Now Digital (East Midland) Ltd, PO Box 2000, 1 Passage Street, Bristol BS99 7SN
*tel* 020-7911 7300 *fax* 020-7911 7302
*website* www.now-digital.com

## Leicester
Leicester Sound, Classic Gold GEM, Galaxy, Capital Disney, Sabras Sound, A Plus, Century 106, BBC Radio Leicester

## Nottingham
106 Trent FM, Classic Gold GEM, 106 Century FM, Saga, Galaxy, Capital Disney, The Storm, A Plus, BBC Radio Nottingham

## Bradford & Huddersfield, Stoke-on-Trent, Swansea
TWG – Emap Digital, 18 Hatfields, London SE1 8DJ

*tel* 020-7959 7800 *fax* 020-7959 9009
*email* info@switchdigital.com
Provides 8 programme services.

## Bradford & Huddersfield
The Pulse, Classic Gold, Sunrise Radio, Smash Hits!, Kiss

## Stoke-on-Trent
Signal 1 and 2, Kiss, Smash Hits!, The Storm, BBC Radio Stoke

## Swansea
The Wave, Swansea Sound, Kiss, Smash Hits!, TBC, BBC Radio Cyrmu, BBC Radio Wales

## Cardiff & Newport, Kent, South Hampshire, Sussex Coast,
Capital Radio Digital, 30 Leicester Square London WC2H 7LA
*tel* 020-7766 6000 *fax* 020-7766 6100

Contemporary hit radio. Broadcasts 24 hours a day:

## Cardiff & Newport
Red Dragon FM, Capital Gold, Century, Xfm, BBC Radio Wales, BBC Radio Cymru

## Kent
Invicta FM, Capital Gold, Kent Digital Extra, Saga Radio, Xfm, Kiss, Swale Sound, Totally Radio, BBC Radio Kent

## South Hampshire
Ocean FM, 103.2 Power FM, Capital Gold, Wave 105.2, Saga, Passion for the Planet, Xfm, SouthCity FM, Southampton Hospital Radio, BBC Radio Solent

## Sussex Coast
Southern FM, Capital Gold, Juice 107.2, Xfm, Saga, Kiss, Gaydar Radio, Spirit FM, Totally Radio, BBC Southern Counties

## Central Lancashire, Humberside, Leeds, Liverpool, South Yorkshire, Teeside, Tyne & Wear
Emap Digital Radio Ltd, Radio House, 900 Herries Road, Sheffield S6 1RH
*tel* 0114-209 1033 *fax* 0114-209 1031
*website* www.emapdigitalradio.com

Broadcasts 24 hours a day:

## Central Lancashire
97.4 Rock FM, Kiss, Magic 999, Classic Gold, Xfm, 3C, Smash Hits!, BBC Radio Lancashire

## Humberside
96.9 Viking FM, Magic 1161, Lincs FM, Classic Gold, Xfm, Smash Hits!, Kiss, BBC Radio Humberside

## Leeds
96.3 Aire FM, Classic Gold, Kiss, Magic 828, Ridings FM, Xfm, Smash Hits!, BBC Radio Leeds

## Liverpool
Radio City 96.7, Magic 1548, Kiss, Classic Gold, Xfm, 3C, Smash Hits!, BBC Radio Merseyside

## South Yorkshire
Hallam FM, Magic, Kiss, Trax FM, Classic Gold, Xfm, Smash Hits!, BBC Radio Sheffield

## Teeside
Classic Gold, Kiss, Magic 1170, 96.6 TFM, Xfm, 3C, Smash Hits!, BBC Radio Cleveland

## Tyne & Wear
Metro FM, Magic 1152, Kiss, 3C, Classic Gold, Xfm, Smash Hits!, BBC Radio Newcastle

## Greater London II
Switchdgital Ltd, 18 Hatfields, Lodnon SE1 8DR
*tel* 020-7959 7800 *fax* 020-7401 9009
*email* info@switchdigital.com
Broadcasts 24 hours a day: Hits, Galaxy, YAAR, The Groove, Travel Now, Hart 106.2 FM, Jazz FM, Saga Radio, Spectrum Radio 558AM, BBC London Live.

## Greater London III
The Digital Radio Group (London) Ltd,
7 Swallow Place, London W1R 7AA
*tel* 020-7911 7300 *fax* 020-7911 7302
*website* www.thedigitalradiogroup.com
Broadcasts 24 hours a day: The Arrow, AbracaDABra, Choice, Liquid, Passion for the Planet, Gaydar Radio, Mean Country, The Storm, Breeze, SBN.

## North East England, North West England, South Wales/Severn Estuary, West Midlands, Yorkshire
MXR, The Chrysalis Building, 13 Bramley Road, London W10 6SP
*tel* 020-7221 2213 *fax* 020-7314 1062
*website* www.getdadigitalradio.com
Broadcasts 24 hours a day:

## North East England
Urban Choice, Heart, The Arrow, Smooth, Digital News Network, Galaxy, Jazz FM, Century FM, Capital Disney

## North West England
Urban Choice, Heart, The Arrow, Smooth, Digital News Network, Galaxy, Jazz FM, Century FM, Capital Disney

## South Wales/Severn Estuary
Urban Choice, Heart, The Arrow, Smooth, Digital News Network, Vibe 101, Jazz FM, Real radio, Capital Disney

## West Midlands
Galaxy, Heart, Saga Radio, Capital Disney, Jazz FM, The Arrow, Smooth, Digital News Network

## Yorkshire
Capital Disney, Urban Choice, Heart, Jazz FM, The Arrow, Smooth, Digital News Network, Galaxy, Real Radio

# Independent radio producers

Many writers approach independent production companies direct and, increasingly, BBC Radio is commissioning independent producers to make programmes.

## All Out Productions
50 Copperas Street, Manchester M4 1H5
0161-834 9955 *fax* 0161-834 6978
*email* mail@allout.co.uk
*website* www.allout.co.uk
*Contact* David Cook

Documentaries and feature programmes. Founded 1994.

## Cork Campus Radio
Level 3, Áras na Mac Léinn, University College Cork, Cork City, Republic of Ireland
*tel* (021) 4902170 *fax* (021) 4903108
*email* radio@ucc.ie
*Contact* Sinéad O'Donnell, Station Manager

Produces dramatic works by new writers; stories of 1800–2000 words from the annual Fallen Leaves Short Story Competition; and the weekly *On the Road* documentary series. Oxygen 2001 SMEDIA Award winner – best student radio station. Founded 1995.

## Crosshands Ltd/ACP Television
Crosshands, Coreley, Ludlow, Shrops. SY8 3AR
*tel* (01584) 890893 *fax* (01584) 890893
*email* mail@acptv.com
*Contact* Richard Uridge

Radio and TV documentaries.

## CSA Word
6A Archway Mews, London SW15 2PE
*tel* 020-8871 0220 *fax* 020-8877 0712
*email* info@csaword.co.uk
*website* www.csaword.co.uk
*Audio Manager* Victoria Williams

Produces readings, plays and features/documentaries. Allow approx. 2 months for response to submissions. Founded 1992.

## Ruth Evans Productions
4 Offlands Cottages, Moulsford, Oxon OX10 9HP
*tel* (01491) 651331
*email* ruthevans@msn.com
*Contact* Ruth Evans

Documentaries and feature programmes for BBC World Service and Radio 4. Founded 2002.

## Fast Forward Productions
22 Fleshmarket Close, Edinburgh EH1 1DY
*tel* 0131-220 0200 *fax* 0131-220 2297
*Producer* Adrian Quine

Aviation. Founded 1994.

## Festival Productions Ltd
11 Old Steine, Brighton BN1 1EJ
*tel* (01273) 669595 *fax* (01273) 669596
*email* post@festivalradio.com
*website* www.festivalradio.com
*Managing Director* Steve Stark

Plays, docs, features and programmes. Founded 1989.

## The Fiction Factory
14 Greenwich Church Street, London SE10 9BJ
*tel* 020-8853 5100 *fax* 020-8293 3001
*email* radio@fictionfactory.co.uk
*website* www.fictionfactory.co.uk
*Creative Director* John Taylor

Plays, dramatisations, readings, documentaries and features mainly for BBC network radio and the World Service. Original radio drama scripts considered if targeted at existing BBC slots. Script reading fee except for submissions from established writers – some student exemptions. No charge for considering programme ideas and outlines. Founded 1993.

## First Writes Theatre Co Ltd
The Old Barn, High Street, Little Eversden, Cambridge CB3 7HE
*tel/fax* (01223) 264129
*email* firstwrites@oldbarn.primex.co.uk
*website* www.first-writes.co.uk
*Director* Richard Blake

Drama for BBC Radio 3 and 4: original plays and adaptations. No unsolicited material. Founded 1991.

## Flannel
21 Berwick Street, London W1F 0PZ
*tel* 020-7287 9277 *fax* 020-7287 7785
*Contact* Kate Haldane

Drama, comedy and features for BBC Radio. Considers comedy narrative, sketch show and panel game ideas. Will only consider material if submitted via an agent. Founded 2002.

## Heavy Entertainment Ltd
Canalot Studios, 222 Kensal Road, London W10 5BN
*tel* 020-8960 9001/2 *fax* 020-8960 9003
*Company Directors* David Roper, Davy Nougarède

Audiobooks, radio documentaries and commercials. Showreels and promotional audio and video. Two studios available for hire. Founded 1992.

## Mike Hopwood Productions Ltd
Winton House, Stoke Road, Stoke-on-Trent ST4 2RW
*tel* (01782) 848800 *fax* (01782) 749447
*Editor* Mike Hopwood

Plays, docs, comedy, soaps, light entertainment. No unsolicited material. Founded 1991.

## Loftus Productions Ltd
2A Aldine Street, London W12 8AN
*tel* 020-8740 4666
*email* ask@loftusproductions.co.uk
*website* www.loftusproductions.co.uk
*Contact* Nigel Acheson

Produces features, documentaries and readings and drama for BBC Radio. Founded 1996.

## Jane Marshall Productions
The Coach House, Westhill Road, Blackdown,
Leamington Spa, Warks. CV32 6RA
*tel* (01926) 831680
*email* jane@jmproductions.freeserve.co.uk

Single voice readings for BBC Radio – abridged published fiction and non-fiction. Founded 1994.

## Mediatracks
93 Columbia Way, Blackburn, Lancs. BB2 7EA
*tel* (01254) 691197 *fax* (01254) 723505
*email* info@mediatracks.co.uk
*Contact* Steve Johnson

Music and general interest docs for BBC local radio network. Founded 1987.

## Pennine Productions LLP
2 Grimeford Lane, Anderton, Chorley, Lancs. PR6 9HL
*tel* (01257) 482559
*email* mike@pennine.biz
*website* www.pennine.biz
*Contact* Mike Hally

Wide range of features for BBC Radio. Book readings for Radio 4 from Autumn 2004. No unsolicited material – phone/email/write first. Founded 2000.

## Penumbra Productions Ltd
80 Brondesbury Road, London NW6 6RX
*tel* 020-7328 4550 *fax* 020-7328 3844
*email* nazpenumbra@aol.com
*Contact* H.O. Nazareth

Drama and documentaries for Radio 3 only. Send synopses by email. Founded 1981.

## Promenade Enterprises
6 Russell Grove, London SW9 6HS
*tel* 020-7582 9354 *fax* 020-7564 3026
*email* info@promenadeproductions.com
*website* www.promenadeproductions.com
*Contact* Nicholas Newton

Drama. Will only consider plays if submitted via an agent. Founded 1998.

## SH Radio
Green Dene Cottage, Honeysuckle Bottom,
East Horsley, Surrey KT24 5TD
*tel* (01483) 283223 *fax* (01483) 281792
*Contact* Robert Symes

Broadcast and non-broadcast commercial material (English and German). Founded 1988.

## Smooth Operations
PO Box 286, Cambridge CB1 7XW
*tel* (01223) 244544 *fax* (01223) 244384
*email* nick@smoothoperations.com
*Contact* Nick Barraclough
6 Millgate, Delph, Oldham OL3 5JG
*tel* (01457) 873752 *fax* (01457) 878500
*email* john@smoothoperations.com
*website* www.smoothoperations.com
*Contact* John Leonard

Music-based docs and series and online content provision for BBC radio. Founded 1992.

## Lou Stein
14A Tavistock Place, London WC1H 9RD
*email* loustein@yahoo.com
*Contact* Lou Stein

Plays for BBC Radio. Founded 2000.

## Testbed Productions
5th Floor, 14–16 Great Portland Street,
London W1W 8QW
*tel* 020-7436 0555 *fax* 020-7436 2800
*email* mail@testbed.co.uk
*website* www.testbed.co.uk
*Directors* Viv Black, Nick Baker

Documentaries, phone-ins and quizzes for BBC Radio. Welcomes ideas for radio quizzes and comedies but not drama scripts. Founded 1992.

## Watershed Partnership Ltd
16 Church Lane, Marple, Stockport SK6 6DE
*email* admin@watershed.uk.com
*Contact* Chris Wallis

Radio readings of serialised fiction and non-fiction and drama. Will consider new plays. Founded 1996.

## Whistledown Productions Ltd
PO Box 36633, London SE1 4NQ
*tel* 020-7922 1120 *fax* 020-7261 0939
*Contact* David Prest, Managing Director

Social, historical and popular culture documentaries as well as authored narratives, biographical features and magazine programmes for BBC network radio. Also syndicated tapes and other work for commercial companies. Founded 1998.

# Television and radio overseas

Opportunities are outlined here for submitting material to television and radio companies in Australia, Canada, Republic of Ireland, New Zealand and South Africa.

## AUSTRALIA

### Australian Broadcasting Corporation (ABC)

Box 9994, Sydney, NSW 2001
*tel* 612-9333-1500 *fax* 612-9333-5305
*email* comments@your.abc.net.au
*website* www.abc.net.au
*Manager for Europe* Australian Broadcasting Corporation, 54 Portland Place, London W1N 4DY

Provides TV, radio and online programmes in a national broadcasting service; operates Radio Australia internationally.

ABC TV restricts its production resources to work closely related to the Australian environment. ABC radio also looks principally to Australian writers for the basis of its drama output. However, ABC radio is interested in reading or auditioning new creative material of a high quality from overseas sources and this may be submitted in script or taped form. No journalistic material is required. Talks on international affairs are commissioned.

### Commercial Radio Australia Ltd

Level 5, 88 Foveaux Street, Surry Hills, NSW 2010
*tel* (02) 9281 6577 *fax* (02) 9281 6599
*email* mail@commercialradio.com.au
*website* www.commercialradio.com.au
*Ceo* Joan Warner

Industry body for commercial radio stations within Australia. See website.

### Federation of Australian Commercial Television Stations (FACTS)

44 Avenue Road, Mosman, NSW 2088
*tel* (02) 9960 2622 *fax* (02) 9969 3520
*Ceo* Julie Flynn

Represents all 48 commercial TV stations.

## CANADA

### Canadian Broadcasting Corporation

250 Lanark Avenue, PO Box 3220, Stn. 'C', Ottawa, Ontario K1Y 1E4
*tel* 613-724-1200
*email* commho@ottawa.cbc.ca
*website* www.cbc.radio-canada.ca

### CTV Inc.

9 Channel Nine Court, Scarborough, Ontario M1S 4B5
*tel* 416-332-5000 *fax* 416-332-6314

## IRELAND

### Broadcasting Commission of Ireland

2–5 Warrington Place, Dublin 2, Republic of Ireland
*tel* (01) 676 0966 *fax* (01) 676 0948
*email* info@bci.ie
*website* www.bci.ie

Under the Irish Broadcasting Act 2001, the name and role of the Independent Radio & Television Commission (IRTC) was changed to the Broadcasting Commission of Ireland. Consequentially, it now has a much expanded remit. In addition to its functions contained in the Radio & Television Act 1988, its new functions include the licensing of new TV services on terrestrial, cable, MMDS and satellite platforms, as well as the development of codes of programming and advertising standards for TV and radio services.

To date, its activities have included the establishment of:
• an independent TV programme service (TV3);
• a national radio service (100-102 Today FM);
• 23 local commercial radio services;
• 2 special interest radio services;
• 14 community/community of interest radio services;
• 7 hospital/institutional radio services;
• approximately 20 short-term special event licences per annum.

It is envisaged that further licences will be granted for both commercial and non-commercial radio stations.

### Radio Telefís Éireann (RTÉ)

Donnybrook, Dublin 4, Republic of Ireland
*tel* (01) 208 3111 *fax* (01) 208 3080
*email* press@rte.ie
*website* www.rte.ie

The Irish national broadcasting service operating radio and TV.

*Television* Ongoing production of an urban drama serial. Currently of interest: drama series for mainstream audiences, serials (preferably contemporary) and situation comedies (preferably set in Ireland or of strong Irish interest), with preferred length of commercial half hour or one hour. Proposals for serials and series suitable for a young adult Network 2 audience, either cutting edge or humorous, which could exploit a low-cost DV production model are of particular interest. Full scripts will not be considered – treatments and series/serial outlines only, except in cases where projects are already part funded. Before submitting material to the Drama or Entertainment departments, authors are advised to write to the department in question to establish initial interest, timing of commissioning rounds, etc.

*Radio* Ongoing production of hour-long dramas each week. Occasional full 2-hour productions and seasons of drama. Short stories (length 13–14 minutes) in Irish or English suitable for broadcasting; plays (running 28 or 58 minutes) are welcome. Guidelines on writing for radio drama are available from the RTÉ Radio Drama Department, Radio Centre, Donnybrook, Dublin 4.

# NEW ZEALAND

## The Radio Network of New Zealand Ltd
Private Bag 92198, Auckland
*tel* (09) 373-0000 *fax* (09) 367-4650
*Ceo* John McElhinney

A radio company controlling a NZ-wide group of commercial radio stations in metropolitan and provincial markets. The station brand groups are Newstalk ZB, Classic Hits, ZM, Easy Listening i, Hauraki, Radio Sports Network, and Community.

## Television New Zealand Ltd
PO Box 3819, Auckland
*tel* (09) 916-7000 *fax* (09) 379-4907
*website* www.tvnz.co.nz
*Chairman* Ross Armstrong, *Ceo* Ian Fraser

A Crown-owned company, TVNZ is charged with operating a commercially successful TV business, acting with social responsibility in the provision of quality services. Of particular importance is the provision of TV programmes which reflect and foster New Zealand's identity and culture, and which are in the overall national interest. TVNZ broadcasts on 2 nationwide channels with a web presence via the organisation's internet portal, nzoom.com

Local and international activities include programme production, outside broadcasting services (through subsidiary company Moving Pictures), multimedia development, merchandising, Teletext, signal distribution and programming supply and transmission consultancy services in Australia, South-East Asia and the Pacific.

# SOUTH AFRICA

## South African Broadcasting Corporation (SABC)
Private Bag X1, Auckland Park 2006
*tel* (011) 714-9111 *fax* (011) 714-3106
*website* www.sabc.co.za

*Television* Operates 6 TV services (4 free-to-air and 2 pay-TV). Three of the free-to-air channels, SABC1, SABC2 and SABC3, accept scripts in English for drama and comedy, either for one-off programmes or series.

*Radio* Operates 19 internal radio networks and one external radio service. The service which makes the greatest use of written material in English is SAFM.

*Drama* One-hour plays of all kinds welcomed. Half-hour plays are occasionally broadcast.

*Short stories* Short stories of all kinds (1500–1800 words) are welcomed.

*Children's programmes* Short stories, plays and serials (maximum 15 minutes) may be submitted.

*Talks* Most are locally commissioned, but outstanding material of particular interest may be submitted (3–10 minutes).

# Theatre

## Writing for the theatre

Writing for the theatre is a competitive market but thoroughly researching this market will improve the chances of your work being accepted. Christopher William Hill offers guidance.

If anybody ever attempts to convince you that writing for the theatre is a soft career option, ignore them and walk away. It is a competitive market and it would be wrong to suggest otherwise. There are many more playwrights than producing theatres. Although the odds are stacked against you, it is still sometimes possible to scrape a living as a playwright. Of course, there are a number of ways in which you can improve the chances of your work being accepted.

### Research your market

It is important to try to understand why a theatre company may produce one play and reject another (due to size of theatre, casting limitations, preferences of the artistic management, etc). Go to the theatre as regularly as possible and read as many plays, contemporary and classic, as you can. In addition, theatre reviews in national and regional newspapers can be extremely useful. *Theatre Record* (fortnightly; *tel* 020-8737 8489, *email* editor@theatrerecord.demon.co.uk *website* www.theatrerecord.com, *Editor and Publisher* Ian Herbert) provides comprehensive press cuttings for West End and regional plays. *The Stage* (weekly), gives informed background to current and forthcoming theatre productions.

The Royal National Theatre and the Theatre Museum in Covent Garden both hold video-taped recordings of many recent London theatre productions. It is only possible to view these recordings on site (subject to appointment) but, again, it is a helpful way of expanding your knowledge of contemporary British theatre.

On a more practical level, many theatres offer writing classes. This is an important way of making contact with a theatre and fellow dramatists. Contrary to popular myth, most writers benefit from time away from their draughty garrets.

A number of 'self-help' books on play writing are available, offering advice on every aspect of writing for the theatre. Each author will have a different approach to his or her work, and it is worth spending time finding a book which is suitable for you. As well as providing practical tips on constructing a script, many books also offer reassurance that all the emotions experienced by a playwright (elation, writer's block, despair, etc) are shared by even the most experienced dramatists.

### Constructing your script

When writing your play it is worth bearing in mind a number of practical considerations. First and foremost, write the play that you want to write and trust in your own view of the world. Be wary of trying to surf dramatic trends. If you are conscious of a trend developing you have almost certainly missed it.

Be conscious of the cost of mounting a production. It usually follows that the more characters you write into a play, the more actors you need to play them. A script requiring more than six actors may seem prohibitive to a theatre company. From time to time writers will submit plays with casts of 18 plus, and whilst an extremely well-established writer may (occasionally, but rarely) get away with this, an unknown playwright stands little or no chance of having his or her script accepted. Character doubling (with actors playing multiple roles) can be a pragmatic way of negotiating the casting hurdle. This is often a matter for discussion between writer, director and producer, prior to production.

Beware the famous theatrical adage 'you got to have a gimmick'. Never let anybody convince you that innovation is a bad thing but try not to innovate just for the sake of it. The best way to get noticed is by writing a good play. Be careful of using cynical marketing ploys in order to sell your work. Plays with a strong regional voice are eagerly received by many theatre companies, but do not attempt to 'regionalise' a play that you have already written in order to pitch it at a specific theatre.

It is easy to forget that the primary objective in the theatre is to entertain. Try to grab the audience's attention as quickly as possible. Many scripts suffer from elaborate 'set-up' before the drama of the play can actually begin. A laborious introduction to character and situation is a guaranteed way of losing your audience (metaphorically and physically).

No matter how tightly plotted a play is, it will always be undermined by poor dialogue. Strangely, many writers are apt to forget that dialogue is written to be spoken. It is often useful to read your work aloud, especially if you are new to play writing. If a line is difficult to read, re-write it. Try not to produce 'interchangeable' dialogue. Each character should have their own distinctive voice, tone, rhythm and thought processes (spoken and unspoken). Check back through the play. How easy is it to distinguish between characters?

Do not overload the script with stage directions. Detailed notes about set design and lighting requirements will often be ignored. Ultimately, it is the job of the director to realise your work on stage and, whilst your input will undoubtedly be canvassed, it is not your responsibility to produce the play. It is the director's job to direct and the designer's job to design. Similarly, actors object to detailed notes in the script, indicating how their lines should be delivered.

### Reviewing your work

Resist the temptation to start editing your play the moment you have finished writing. Apart from missing glaring errors in the script, you can easily lose sight of the essential qualities of the play, and edit simply for the sake of editing. Allow it to sit for a few weeks before doing anything more. It is very easy to find yourself swept along on a tide of euphoria as you finish writing, but this can be delusional.

Viewing your own work with a truly objective eye is always difficult, but it is an ability that can be cultivated with time. It may be easier to accept constructive criticism from someone whose opinion you value, before entrusting your script to the tender mercies of a theatre's literary department. Make any alterations to your script that you consider appropriate. There will rarely be an opportunity to re-submit a rejected script.

## Approaching theatre companies

Once you are satisfied that your script is ready to send out, stop and take stock. Remember, it is not necessary to have an agent in order to send your work to a theatre. Although an agent's relationship with a director or literary manager may result in a faster response to a script, lack of representation should not count against you. Theatre companies are always on the lookout for new talent. However, it is important to bear in mind that a number of opinions about your work will have been formed before the script is even opened.

Many of the initial obstacles you need to overcome are not related to the script itself. Even envelopes and cover letters present problems for the unwary. Never forget that literary managers are sensitive creatures. A script addressed 'dear sir or madam' is an indication that the play is being sent out as a circular, with no specific focus. A bit of research helps avoid this embarrassment. Do not email your script unless a theatre expressly requests that you do this. Even in this technological age, it is still preferable to send a script by post.

Avoid unnecessary script embellishments. A simple cover letter, brief outline of previous work and a clean (white) A4 play text is all that is expected. Fancy binding, photographs, CDs, projected set designs, casting suggestions, etc, will have a strangely dispiriting effect on the script reader. Allow the play to speak for itself. It should go without saying (but unfortunately does not) that all text must be printed in black ink. The use of multi-coloured inks to distinguish between characters will undoubtedly show you up as a novice. Colour blind literary managers will be disinclined to sympathise with you.

You do not need to invest in costly script-formatting software as there is no professionally approved standard for the layout of play texts. A number of software programmes offer script templates; these are also downloadable from the internet. A cursory glance through a handful of contemporary play scripts will reveal the myriad of different page layouts employed by playwrights and publishers. Find the layout that is right for you. Allow wide margins, with space at the head and foot of each page. Secure the script in such a way that pages can be turned easily and make sure that each page is numbered.

## Waiting for a response

Once your script has been delivered into the hands of a theatre company, do be prepared to wait. Many theatres will write to acknowledge receipt of the script. Some theatres will also give an indication of how long it will take them to offer a response. If you have heard nothing after six months it might be worth dropping the theatre a line (if only to retrieve your script), but do take into account the sheer volume of scripts they receive.

When the theatre company finally responds, you are unlikely to be offered in-depth analysis of your work, unless they show an interest in producing the play.

Again, this is due to the vast quantity of unsolicited material they receive. In certain cases, brief comments may be offered. Companies which focus exclusively on new writing may provide more detailed script reports.

Some theatres offer a script-reading service, providing a comprehensive response to the play for a small fee. This can be one of the most effective ways of gaining objective professional advice about your work. Although charging for this feedback may seem mercenary, it is important to remember that script readers are paid very little for their services. Many readers have considerable knowledge of the theatre and their advice can be invaluable to a new writer.

Even if a script is unsuitable, an artistic director or literary manager may still want to meet with the writer. Although this will not necessarily lead to future production, it is an indication that they see you as a writer of promise. This is a good opportunity to forge a relationship with a theatre, and may result in a speedier response to any work you submit in the future. Unless the theatre requests a re-write, a play that is re-written as a result of feedback from the literary department will almost certainly be returned unread.

There is nothing more depressing than the thud of returned play scripts dropping through the letterbox. Choosing a play for production is a subjective process, reflecting the tastes of the literary department and the predilections of the theatre company. Even good plays are rejected. Try not to be disheartened by your first rejection letter. Chances are you will have to endure many more.

Although your play may have been read more than once and discussed at a readers panel meeting, the literary manager's decision is final. There are stories (sadly not apocryphal) of playwrights attempting to employ strong-arm tactics in order to gain production of their work. This is a risky gambit. There is a subtle distinction between single-minded dedication to your work and psychosis. Be careful not to cross this line. Allow a day of mourning for your rejected script, then move on.

## In production

On the other hand, what if a theatre is interested in producing your play? Do not feel pressured into making an immediate decision. It is easy, especially if you have never had your work produced, to succumb to flattery. Bide your time. It is worth considering that many theatres enjoy the kudos of premiering new work, but once your play has had its first production (unless it is a runaway success) other theatres may be reluctant to produce it.

If a theatre expresses an interest in commissioning you or optioning an existing play (offering a fixed term within which to produce your play), it is advisable to seek the professional advice of an agent. However, this can take time, so do not lose heart if an agent is not immediately forthcoming. Most theatres will offer an agreed standard contract, which provides a degree of security for the writer and the theatre. If in doubt, consider taking independent legal advice or contact the Writers' Guild.

Do not despair if you are rejected by an agent. Many agencies are simply too busy with existing clients to take on new writers. An agent may enjoy your work but not feel enthusiastic enough to represent you. It is a question of personal taste. Persevere until you find an agent who is as enthusiastic about your work as you are.

Once a theatre has optioned your work, things can move quickly. Even the largest of theatre companies may discover holes in their programming which need to be filled. Conversely, you may have to wait a considerable period of time before your work can be staged. Either way, in principle you should have the right to agree on a director and designer for your play. In practice this may never happen. Many theatres rely on staff directors, or a pool of tried and tested practitioners. Financial considerations can also be restrictive.

The relationship between the writer and director is, of course, vital to the success of a production. Try not to be precious about your work. Be as objective as possible. Cuts or re-writes will often be suggested, before or during the rehearsal process. This is not an attempt to undermine the writer, but an opportunity to consolidate the script. Of course, if you have any reservations about a script alteration, talk to the director or literary manager about it. Changes to the script cannot be made without your express approval, but do not pull rank just for the sake of it.

Insist on access to the publicity material a theatre produces for your play. It is a contractual obligation and the theatre should honour this. In many cases the marketing department will approach you for blurb (for flyers and press releases). This is the first contact most audience members will have with your play, and you will want to make sure that your work is accurately represented.

Again, if you are unhappy about any aspect of the production, speak to the director. Most problems can be easily rectified if nipped in the bud.

## Selling your script

Although you would be hard pressed to find a playwright who took up the profession for financial gain, money is still a consideration. In the case of a non-commissioned play, the majority of the fee will be paid on signature of the contract, with a final sum payable on acceptance of the play. This gives the producing theatre the opportunity to request any revisions to the script before agreeing to production. A proportion of the fee will be a non-returnable advance against royalties. In most cases the royalty will be 8% of the net box office receipts.

If a theatre commissions a play from scratch, the fee should be paid in the following way: roughly half of the total fee on signature of the contract; a further quarter of the fee on completion of the first draft; the final quarter on acceptance of the script for production. Again, a proportion of the fee will be a non-returnable advance against royalties. As with a non-commissioned play, the royalty will normally be 8% of net box office receipts.

The most difficult thing to predict is when the final sum of the commission fee will arrive. When is a play ready for production? How long is a piece of string? You may well find that you spend anywhere between six and 18 months, even longer, restructuring your play so that it is suitable for production. Only in exceptional cases will the first draft of a script be accepted. Some theatres may never produce the resulting play, although the 'policy' of over-commissioning is perhaps not such a prevalent evil as writers are often led to believe. Of greater concern is the tendency to option a play, then leave the playwright waiting indefinitely for the work to be produced.

A commission does not guarantee production. Once a script has been rejected, all rights revert to the writer, who will then be entitled to offer the script to another company.

Financially, it is important to pace yourself. The commission fee may have to last you a considerable period of time. Tempting though it may be, resist the urge to cash your first cheque and embark on a shopping spree.

Many established writers choose not to write to commission, preferring instead to write a play as and when the muse takes them. For a young or relatively inexperienced writer this may not be the most practical way of keeping body and soul together.

## Playing the field

Even if you have managed to secure the services of an agent, this is no guarantee of work. It is in a playwright's best interests to seek employment as actively as possible.

Nowadays, it would be extremely unusual for a writer's first play to be offered a West End run. A play which proves itself in the regions may be offered a transfer, but this would be the exception, not the rule. However, there are a number of fringe venues in London that may provide an opportunity to see your work staged. This will not necessarily result in overnight success, but it can often bring your work to the attention of reviewers and other theatre companies.

There is also a vibrant theatrical community at work outside London. Regional theatres are keen to foster links with local writers, and this can be a very good way of establishing yourself as a playwright. Many subsidised touring companies may also consider commissioning work, although this will usually be tailored to specific considerations, such as the number of performers in the company, suitability for touring, etc.

Although persistence will not always be rewarded, it is certainly an approach worth trying. If all else fails, turn impresario and produce your own work. Many playwrights have established themselves in this way, forming their own companies and producing plays on the fringe circuit. Without a production a play is little more than a blueprint.

**Christopher William Hill** is a recent recipient of an Arts Council Theatre Writing Bursary and has been writer-in-residence at Plymouth Theatre Royal (Pearson Playwrights' Scheme Bursary). He has worked as a degree lecturer, reader and script editor. His stage plays include *Multiplex, Lam, Song of the Western Men* and *Blood Red, Saffron Yellow*.

# Theatre producers

This list is divided into London theatres (below), provincial theatres (page 384) and touring companies (page 389). See also *Writing for the theatre* on page 375 and *Literary agents for television, film, radio and theatre* on page 756.

There are various types of theatre companies and it is helpful to know what they include. Metropolitan new writing theatre companies are largely London-based theatres which specialise in new writing (Hampstead Theatre, Royal Court, Bush Theatre, Soho Theatre, etc). Regional repertory theatre companies are theatres based in towns and cities across the country which may do new plays as part of their repertoire. Commercial producing managements are unsubsidised profit-making theatre producers who may occasionally be interested in new plays to take on tour or to present in the West End. Small and/or middle-scale touring companies are companies (mostly touring) which may exist to explore or promote specific themes or are geared towards specific kinds of audiences.

Individuals also have a role. Independent theatre practitioners include, for example, actors who may be looking for interesting plays in which to appear. Independent theatre producers include, for example, young directors or producers who are looking for plays to produce at the onset of their career. There are also drama schools and amateur dramatics companies.

## LONDON

### Bush Theatre
Shepherd's Bush Green, London W12 8QD
*tel* 020-7602 3703 *fax* 020-7602 7614
*email* info@bushtheatre.co.uk
*website* www.bushtheatre.co.uk
*Literary Manager* Nicola Wilson

Welcomes unsolicited full-length stage scripts (plus one small and one large sae). Commissions writers, including those at an early stage in their career. Produces 9 premieres a year.

### Michael Codron Plays Ltd
Aldwych Theatre Offices, Aldwych,
London WC2B 4DF
*tel* 020-7240 8291 *fax* 020-7240 8467

### Finborough Theatre
118 Finborough Road, London SW10 9ED
*tel* 020-7244 7439 *fax* 020-7835 1853
*email* admin@finboroughtheatre.co.uk
*website* www.finboroughtheatre.co.uk
*Artistic Director* Neil McPherson

A new writing venue. Also presents revivals of neglected 20th century plays, music theatre and recently has staged UK premieres of foreign work,

particularly from Ireland, the USA and Canada. The theatre building has been recently refurbished. The theatre is also available for hire and the fee is sometimes negotiable to encourage interesting work. Unsolicited scripts can no longer be accepted. Founded 1980.

### Robert Fox Ltd
6 Beauchamp Place, London SW3 1NG
*tel* 020-7584 6855 *fax* 020-7225 1638
*email* rf@robertfoxltd.com

Independent theatre and film production company. Stages productions mainly in the West End and on Broadway. Welcomes scripts from new writers. Founded 1980.

### Hampstead Theatre
Eton Avenue, London NW3 3EU
*tel* 020-7449 4200 *fax* 020-7449 4201
*email* literary@hampsteadtheatre.com
*website* www.hampsteadtheatre.com
*Contact* Literary Manager

The newly opened theatre has been designed with writers in mind. It allows for bold and flexible staging within an intimate auditorium. The artistic policy is the production of the best British and international new plays. All plays are read and discussed, with feedback given to all writers with potential. It usually takes 4 months to respond. Include postage with submissions. No plays accepted by email. For futher details see website.

## Bill Kenwright Ltd
BKL House, 106 Harrow Road,
London W2 1RR
*tel* 020-7446 6200 *fax* 020-7446 6222
*email* info@kenwright.com
*Managing Director* Bill Kenwright, *Deputy Managing Director* Simon Meadon

Commercial producing management presenting revivals and new works for the West End and for touring theatres.

## King's Head Theatre
115 Upper Street, London N1 1QN
*tel* 020-7226 8561 *fax* 020-7226 8507
*website* www.kingsheadtheatre.org
*Contact* Dan Crawford, Artistic Director

Off-West End theatre producing revivals and new works. No unsolicited submissions.

## Lyric Hammersmith
King Street, London W6 0QL
*tel* (08700) 500511 *fax* 020-8741 5965
*email* enquiries@lyric.co.uk
*website* www.lyric.co.uk
*Directors* Simon Mellor, Neil Bartlett

A producing theatre as well as a receiving venue for work by theatre companies, translators, performers and composers. Unsolicited scripts for in-house productions not accepted.

## Moral Support
Studio 2, Greville House, 35 Greville Street,
London EC1N 8TB
*tel* (07958) 418515
*website* www.moralsupportonline.org
*Contact* Zoe Klinger

The company brings together writers, musicians and other freelance practitioners to create new work with the emphasis on producing new writing and performance styles, to be performed in a variety of locations. Its performance technique has been described as 'an utterly original theatrical language'. Available for commissions of new plays, performance and dance. Established 1997.

## The Old Red Lion Theatre
418 St John Street,
London EC1V 4NJ
*tel* 020-7833 3053 *fax* 020-7833 3053
*Artistic Director* Melanie Tait

Interested in contemporary pieces, especially from unproduced writers. No funding: incoming production company pays to rent the theatre. Sae essential with enquiries. Founded 1977.

## Orange Tree Theatre
1 Clarence Street, Richmond, Surrey TW9 2SA
*tel* 020-8940 0141 *fax* 020-8332 0369
*email* admin@orange-tree.demon.co.uk
*website* www.orangetreetheatre.co.uk

Producing venue. New works presented generally come from agents or through writers' groups. The theatre asks that writers contact the theatre first by letter and do not send unsolicited scripts.

## Polka Theatre for Children
240 The Broadway, London SW19 1SB
*tel* 020-8545 8320 *fax* 020-8545 8365
*email* info@polkatheatre.com
*website* www.polkatheatre.com
*Artistic Director* Annie Wood, *Contact* Richard Shannon, Director of New Writing

Exclusively for children between 18 months and 16 years of age, the Main Theatre seats 300 and The Adventure Theatre seats 80. Programmed for 18 months to 2 years in advance. Theatre of new writing, with targeted commissions. Founded 1967.

## The Questors Theatre
Mattock Lane, London W5 5BQ
*tel* 020-8567 0011 *fax* 020-8567 8736
*email* nw@questors.org.uk
*website* www.questors.org.uk
*Theatre Manager* Paul Maurel, *Contact for new work* Evan Rule

Largest community theatre in Europe producing around 20 shows a year, specialising in modern and classical world drama. No unsolicited scripts.

## Really Useful Theatres
Manor House, 21 Soho Square, London W1D 3QP
*tel* 020-7494 5200 *fax* 020-7434 1217
*email* info@rutheatres.com
*website* www.rutheatres.com
*Production Director* Nica Burns

Owns 13 West End theatres: Adelphi, Apollo, Cambridge, Duchess, Garrick, Gielgud, Her Majesty's, London Palladium, Lyric Shaftesbury Avenue, New London, Palace, Queens and Theatre Royal Drury Lane. Now commissions new plays from both established writers and new talent. Founded 1978.

## Royal Court Theatre
Sloane Square, London SW1W 8AS
*tel* 020-7565 5050 *fax* 020-7565 5002
*Literary Manager* Graham Whybrow

New plays.

## Royal National Theatre
South Bank, London SE1 9PX
*tel* 020-7452 3323 *fax* 020-7452 3350
*Literary Manager* Jack Bradley

Limited opportunity for the production of unsolicited material, but submissions welcome. No synopses or treatments. Send to Literary Manager, together with an sae with return postage for the script.

## Royal Shakespeare Company

1 Earlham Street, London WC2H 9LL
*tel* 020-7845 0515 *fax* 020-7845 0505
*website* www.rsc.org.uk
*Artistic Director* Michael Boyd, *Dramaturg* Paul Sirett

The RSC is a classical theatre company based in Stratford-upon-Avon. It has recently transformed itself to create the opportunity for different ensemble companies to work on distinct projects that will open both in Stratford and at various venues in London. The Company also has an annual residency in Newcastle and tours both nationally and internationally.

As well as Shakespeare, English classics and foreign classics in translation, ambitious new plays counterpoint the RSC's repertory, especially those which celebrate language. The Dramaturgy Department is proactive rather than reactive, and seeks out the plays and playwrights it wishes to commission. It will read translations of classic foreign works submitted, or of contemporary works where the original writer and/or translator is known. It is unable to read unsolicited works from less established writers, and can only return scripts if an sae is enclosed with the submission.

## Scamp Film and Theatre Ltd

1st Floor, 26–28 Neal Street, London WC2H 9QQ
*tel* 020-7240 8890 *fax* 020-7240 7099
*email* post@scampltd.com
*Contact* Office Manager

Independent theatre producer of new work and revivals. No unsolicited scripts. Founded 2003.

## Soho Theatre and Writers' Centre

21 Dean Street, London W1D 3NE
*tel* 020-7287 5060 *fax* 020-7287 5061
*email* writers@sohotheatre.com
*website* www.sohotheatre.com
*Artistic Director* Abigail Morris

Always on the look out for new plays and playwrights and welcome unsolicited scripts. These are read by a professional panel who write a detailed critical report. Also offers various levels of workshop facilities, including rehearsed reading and platform performances, for promising playwrights, and in-depth script development with the Artistic Director and Writers' Centre Director. See also the Verity Bargate Award on page 548.

## Tabard Theatre

2 Bath Road, London W4 1LW
*tel* 020-8995 6035 *fax* 020-8994 5985

## TEG Productions

11–15 Betterton Street, London WC2H 9BP
*tel* 020-7379 1066 *fax* 020-7836 9454
*email* teg@plays.demon.co.uk
*Contact* Jeremy Meadow

Produces 2–4 new plays with commercial potential and revivals per year, all with 'star' casting. Welcomes scripts from new writers. Founded 1997.

## Theatre of Comedy Company

Shaftesbury Theatre, 210 Shaftesbury Avenue, London WC2H 8DP
*tel* 020-7379 3345 *fax* 020-7836 8181
*Contact* Executive Producer

Commercial producing management creating a broad range of plays. Welcomes new scripts from writers. Founded 1983.

## Theatre Royal, Stratford East

Gerry Raffles Square, London E15 1BN
*tel* 020-8534 7374 *fax* 020-8534 8381
*website* www.stratfordeast.com
*Artistic Director* Philip Hedley, *Deputy Director* Mr Kerry Michael

Middle-scale producing theatre. Specialises in new writing: currently developing contemporary British musicals. Welcomes new plays that are unproduced, full in length, and which relate to its diverse multicultural, Black and Asian audience.

## The Tricycle Theatre Company

Tricycle Theatre, 269 Kilburn High Road, London NW6 7JR
*tel* 020-7372 6611 *fax* 020-7328 0795
*Contact* Nicolas Kent

Metropolitan new writing theatre company with particular focus on Black and Irish writing. Script-reading service but fee charged for unsolicited scripts.

## Triumph Proscenium Productions Ltd

Suite 4, Waldorf Chambers, 11 Aldwych, London WC2B 4DA
*tel* 020-7343 8800 *fax* 020-7343 8801
*email* dcwtpp@aol.com

## Unicorn Theatre for Children

*Admin offices* St Mark's Studios, Chillingworth Road, London N7 8QJ
*tel* 020-7700 0702 *fax* 020-7700 3870
*email* admin@unicorntheatre.com
*website* www.unicorntheatre.com
*Administrative Director* Christopher Moxon, *Artistic Director* Tony Graham, *Associate Director* Rebecca Gatward, *Literary Manager* Carl Miller, *Associate Artist (Literary)* Charles Way

At the end of 2005 Unicorn will move into its new London home near Tower Bridge, where it will produce a year-round programme of theatre for children aged 4–12, their families and schools. Eight in-house productions of full-length plays with professional casts will be staged across 2 auditoriums alongside visiting companies and education work. Unicorn rarely commissions plays from writers who are new to it, but it is keen to hear from writers who are interested to work with Unicorn in the future. Do not send unsolicited MSS. Send a short statement describing why you would like to write for Unicorn and a CV or a summary of your relevant experience.

## Warehouse Theatre

Dingwall Road, Croydon CR0 2NF
*tel* 020-8681 1257 *fax* 020-8688 6699
*email* info@warehousetheatre.co.uk
*website* www.warehousetheatre.co.uk
*Artistic Director* Ted Craig

South London's new writing theatre. Seats 100. Produces 2–3 in-house plays a year and co-produces with companies which share the commitment to new work. The theatre continues to build upon its tradition of discovering and nurturing new writers: activities include a monthly writers' workshop and the annual International Playwriting Festival (see page 558). Unsolicited scripts are accepted but it is more advisable to submit plays via the Festival. Also hosts a youth theatre workshop, Saturday morning children's theatre and a community outreach programme.

## White Bear Theatre Club

138 Kennington Park Road, London SE11 4DJ
*tel* 020-7793 4193 *fax* 020-7793 9193
*email* mkwbear@hotmail.com
*Contact* Julia Parr

Metropolitan new writing theatre company. Welcomes scripts from new writers. Founded 1990.

## Michael White

48 Dean Street, London W1D 5BF
*tel* 020-7734 7707 *fax* 020-7734 7727

## Young Vic Theatre Company

Chester House, Kennington Park, Brinnen Estate, 1–3 Brixton, London SW9
*tel* 020-7922 8400 *fax* 020-7922 8401
*email* info@youngvic.org
*website* www.youngvic.org
*General Manager* Mark Feakins

Metropolitan producing theatre producing classic plays. Founded 1969.

# Provincial

## Abbey Theatre

26 Lower Abbey Street, Dublin 1,
Republic of Ireland
*tel* (01) 8872200 *fax* (01) 8729177
*Artistic Director* Ben Barnes, *Managing Director* Brian Jackson

Mainly produces plays written by Irish authors or on Irish subjects. Foreign classics are however regularly produced.

## Actual Theatre

25 Hamilton Drive, Glasgow G12 8DN
*tel* 0141-339 0654 *fax* 0141-339 0654
*Artistic Director* Susan C. Triesman

Produces 'difficult and taboo subjects' as well as experimental theatre. Welcomes scripts from new writers. Founded 1980.

## Yvonne Arnaud Theatre Management Ltd

Millbrook, Guildford,
Surrey GU1 3UX
*tel* (01483) 440077 *fax* (01483) 564071
*email* yat@yvonne-arnaud.co.uk
*website* www.yvonne-arnaud.co.uk
*Contact* James Barber

Producing theatre which also receives productions.

## The Belgrade Theatre

Belgrade Square, Coventry CV1 1GS
*tel* 024-7625 6431 *fax* 024-7655 0680
*email* admin@belgrade.co.uk
*website* www.belgrade.co.uk
*Contact* Denise Atcheson

Produces new plays developed in conjunction with Theatre Absolute, through the Writing House.

## Birmingham Repertory Theatre Ltd

Broad Street, Birmingham B1 2EP
*tel* 0121-245 2000 *fax* 0121-245 2100
*email* info@birmingham-rep.co.uk
*website* www.birmingham-rep.co.uk
*Artistic Director* Jonathon Church, *Executive Director* Stuart Rogers, *Associate Director (Literary)* Ben Payne

Aims to provide a platform for the best work from new writers from both within and beyond the West Midlands region. The development, commissioning and production of new writing takes place across the full range of the theatre's programme including: the Main House (capacity 830); the Door (capacity 190 max.), a space dedicated to new work; and its annual Community tours. Unsolicited submissions are welcome principally from the point of view of beginning a relationship with a writer. Priority in such development work is given to writers from the region.

## The Bootleg Theatre Company
23 Burgess Green, Bishopdown, Salisbury,
Wilts. SP1 3EL
*tel* (01722) 421476
*email* colin@bootlegtheatrecompany.fsnet.co.uk
*Contact* Colin Burden

Metropolitan new writing theatre company and
independent theatre practitioner. Stages 2
productions per year. Welcomes scripts from new
writers. Founded 1985.

## Bristol Old Vic
Theatre Royal, King Street,
Bristol BS1 4ED
*tel* 0117-949 3993 *fax* 0117-949 3996
*website* www.bristol-old-vic.co.uk
*Associate Director* Gareth Machin, *Executive Director*
Sarah Smith

Programme includes class plays in the Theatre
Royal (650 seats) and new writing in the New Vic
Studio (150 seats). Plays must have enough popular
appeal to attract an audience of significant size. Will
read and report on unsolicited scripts for a fee of
£25 per script.

Also seeks emerging talent to the Basement, a
profit share venue (50 seats) committed to
producing one-act plays by unproven writers. Will
read plays free of charge but no report can be
provided. New Vic Studio often receives
productions of new plays from visiting companies.

## The Byre Theatre of St Andrews
Abbey Street, St Andrews KY16 9LA
*tel* (01334) 476288 *fax* (01334) 475370
*email* enquiries@byretheatre.com
*website* www.byretheatre.com
*Artistic Director* Stephen Wrentmore

Offers an exciting year-round programme of
contemporary and classic drama, dance, concerts,
comedy and innovative education and community
events. Operates a blend of in-house and touring
productions. Maintains a policy of producing new
and established work. Education programme caters
for all ages with Youth workshops and Haydays (for
50+). Offers support for new writing through the
Byre Writers, a well-established and successful
playwrights group.

## Chester Gateway Theatre Trust Ltd
Hamilton Place, Chester CH1 2BH
*tel* (01244) 318603 *fax* (01244) 317277
*website* www.chestergateway.co.uk
*Chief Executive* Jasmine Hendry

Mid-scale theatre with 2 in-house productions per
year. Also presents a diverse programme of theatre,
dance, comedy and music. The Learning and
Outreach Department undertakes schools drama
tours and workshops.

## Chichester Festival Theatre Ltd
Chichester Festival Theatre, Oaklands Park,
Chichester, West Sussex PO19 4AP
*tel* (01243) 784437 *fax* (01243) 787288
*email* admin@cft.org.uk
*website* www.cft.org.uk
*Artistic Directors* Martin Duncan, Ruth Mackenzie,
Steven Pimlott

Festival Season April–Oct in Festival and Minerva
Theatres together with a year-round education
programme.

## Clwyd Theatr Cymru
Mold, Flintshire CH7 1YA
*tel* (01352) 756331 *fax* (01352) 701558
*email* drama@celtic.co.uk,
william.james@clwyd-theatr-cymru.co.uk
*website* www.clwyd-theatr-cymru.co.uk
*Director* Terry Hands, *Literary Manager* William James

Produces a season of plays each year performed by a
core ensemble, along with tours throughout Wales
(in English and Welsh). Plays are a mix of classics,
revivals, contemporary drama and new writing.
Considers plays by Welsh writers or with Welsh
themes.

## Colchester Mercury Theatre Ltd
Balkerne Gate, Colchester, Essex CO1 1PT
*tel* (01206) 577006 *fax* (01206) 769607
*email* mercury.theatre@virgin.net
*Contact* (Playwrights' Group) Adrian Stokes

Regional repertory theatre presenting works to a
wide audience. Produces some new work, mainly
commissioned. Runs local Playwrights' Group for
adults with a serious commitment to writing plays.

## The Coliseum Theatre
Fairbottom Street, Oldham OL1 3SW
*tel* 0161-624 1731 *fax* 0161-624 5318
*Chief Executive* Kevin Shaw

Interested in new work, particularly plays set in the
North. Contact by letter with scenario initially.

## Contact Theatre Company
Oxford Road, Manchester M15 6JA
*tel* 0161-274 3434 *fax* 0161-274 0640
*email* info@contact-theatre.org.uk
*Artistic Director* John E. McGrath

Interested in working with and for young people
aged 13–30. Send sae for writers' guidelines.

## Derby Playhouse Ltd
Theatre Walk, Eagle Centre, Derby DE1 2NF
*tel* (01332) 363271 *fax* (01332) 547200
*email* admin@derbyplayhouse.co.uk
*website* www.derbyplayhouse.co.uk
*Chief Executive* Karen Hebden, *Creative Producer*
Stephen Edwards

Regional repertory company. Unsolicited scripts: send a letter with synopsis, a resumé of your writing experience and any 10 pages of your script. A review of this material will determine whether a complete copy of the script is required.

## Druid Theatre Company
Druid Theatre, Chapel Lane, Galway, Republic of Ireland
*tel* (091) 568617/568660 *fax* (091) 563109
*email* info@druidtheatre.com
*Artistic Director* Garry Hynes, *Managing Director* Fergal McGrath

Producing company presenting a wide range of national and international plays. Emphasis on new Irish writing.

## The Dukes
Moor Lane, Lancaster LA1 1QE
*tel* (01524) 598505 *fax* (01524) 598519
*Artistic Director* Ian Hastings

## Dundee Repertory Theatre
Tay Square, Dundee DD1 1PB
*tel* (01382) 227684
*website* www.dundeereptheatre.co.uk
*Artistic Director* James Brining

Regional repertory theatre company. Concentrates resources on commissions for contemporary Scottish writers.

## Everyman Theatre
Regent Street, Cheltenham, Glos. GL50 1HQ
*tel* (01242) 512515 *fax* (01242) 224305
*email* admin@everymantheatre.org.uk
*website* www.everymantheatre.org.uk
*Chief Executive* Philip Bernays, *Artistic Director* Sue Colverd

Regional presenting and producing theatre promoting a wide range of plays. Small-scale experimental, youth and educational work encouraged in The Other Space studio theatre. Contact the Artistic Director before submitting material.

## Focus Theatre Company (Scotland)
c/o The Ramshorn Theatre, 98 Ingram Street, Glasgow G1 1ES
*tel* 0141-552 3489 *fax* 0141-553 2036
*email* ramshorn.theatre@strath.ac.uk
*Artistic Director* Susan C. Triesman

Produces women's plays and feminist work. Also holds workshops. Welcomes scripts from new writers. Founded 1982.

## Grand Theatre
Singleton Street, Swansea SA1 3QJ
*tel* (01792) 475242 *fax* (01792) 475379
*email* gary.iles@swansea.gov.uk

*website* www.swanseagrand.co.uk
*General Manager* Gary Iles

Regional receiving theatre.

## Harrogate Theatre
Oxford Street, Harrogate, North Yorkshire HG1 1QF
*tel* (01423) 502710 *fax* (01423) 563205
*website* www.harrogatetheatre.com
*Associate Director* Steve Ansell

Regional repertory theatre and touring company producing both classic and contemporary plays. Scripts welcome from writers within the Yorkshire region; 10-page excerpts from writers outside the Yorkshire region.

## Haymarket Theatre Company
The Haymarket Theatre, Wote Street, Basingstoke, Hants RG21 7NW
*tel* (01256) 323073 *fax* (01256) 357130
*email* info@haymarket.org.uk
*website* www.haymarket.org.uk

Produces up to 8 main house shows a year plus a full and integrated education programme. Interested in co-producing and up to 4 visiting shows. Introduced a 3-year ensemble acting company-in-residence from August 2003. New writing needs to fit the international season theatre. Contact before sending a synopsis.

## Leicester Haymarket Theatre
Belgrave Gate, Leicester LE1 3YQ
*tel* 0116-253 0021 *fax* 0116-251 3310
*email* enquiry@leicesterhaymarkettheatre.org
*website* www.leicesterhaymarkettheatre.org

Regional producing theatre company.

## Library Theatre Company
St Peter's Square, Manchester M2 5PD
*tel* 0161-234 1913 *fax* 0161-228 6481
*email* ltc@libraries.manchester.gov.uk
*website* www.librarytheatre.com
*Contact* Artistic Director

Contemporary drama, classics, plays for children. Aims to produce drama which illuminates the contemporary world. Will consider scripts from new writers. Allow 4 months for response. Founded 1952.

## Liverpool Everyman and Playhouse
Liverpool and Merseyside Theatres Trust Ltd, 13 Hope Street, Liverpool L1 9BH
*tel* 0151-708 3700 *fax* 0151-708 3701
*email* info@everymanplayhouse.com
*website* www.everymanplayhouse.com
*Executive Director* Deborah Aydon, *Artistic Director* Gemma Bodinetz, *General Manager* Tim Brunsden

Produces and presents theatre.

## Liverpool Lunchtime Theatre

Unity Theatre, 1 Hope Place, Liverpool L1 9BG
*tel* 0151-709 4332 *fax* 0151-709 7182
*Contact* Irene Ryan, Administration Manager

New writing development company. Productions and showcases when funding permits. Promising scripts developed to production standard, and links created with other new writing theatres and organisations. Send sae for return of script. Founded 1983.

## Live Theatre

27 Broad Chare, Quayside,
Newcastle upon Tyne NE1 3DF
*tel* 0191-232 1232
*email* info@live.org.uk
*website* www.live.org.uk
*Enquiries* Wendy Barnfather, *Script Submissions* Jeremy Herrin

New writing theatre company and venue. Stages 3–4 productions per year of new writing, comedy, musical-comedy, etc.

## The New Theatre Co

The New Theatre, Temple Bar, 43 East Essex Street, Dublin 2, Republic of Ireland
*tel* (1) 6703361 *fax* (1) 6711943
*email* info@thenewtheatre.com
*website* www.thenewtheatre.com
*Joint Artistic Directors* Anthony Fox, Ronian Wilmot

Innovative theatre producing plays by classic as well as Irish writers whose work deals with issues pertaining to contemporary Irish society. Welcomes scripts from new writers. Founded 1997.

## New Vic Theatre

Etruria Road, Newcastle under Lyme ST5 0JG
*tel* (01782) 717954 *fax* (01782) 712885
*email* admin@newvictheatre.org.uk
*Artistic Director* Gwenda Hughes, *General Manager* Nick Jones

Europe's first purpose built theatre-in-the-round, presenting classics, music theatre, contemporary plays, new plays.

## The New Wolsey Theatre

Civic Drive, Ipswich, Suffolk IP1 2AS
*tel* (01473) 295911 *fax* (01473) 295910
*Chief Executive* Sarah Holmes, *Artistic Director* Peter Rowe, *Artistic Associate, Community & Education* Mary Swan

Mixed economy theatre. New writing and co-productions always condsidered.

## Northcott Theatre

Stocker Road, Exeter, Devon EX4 4QB
*tel* (01392) 223999
*Artistic Director* Ben Crocker

Regional producing theatre company.

## Northern Stage (Theatrical Productions) Ltd

Newcastle Playhouse, Barras Bridge,
Newcastle upon Tyne NE1 1RH
*tel* 0191-232 3366 *fax* 0191-261 8093
*email* info@northernstage.com
*website* www.northernstage.com
*Artistic Director* Alan Lyddiard

The Newcastle Playouse is currently closed and reopening is planned for Autumn 2005 as a European centre for performing arts.

## Nottingham Playhouse

Nottingham Theatre Trust Ltd, Wellington Circus, Nottingham NG1 5AF
*tel* 0115-947 4361 *fax* 0115-947 5759
*website* www.nottinghamplayhouse.co.uk/playhouse
*Chief Executive* Stephanie Sirr, *Artistic Director* Giles Croft

Works closely with communities of Nottingham and Nottinghamshire. Takes 6 months to read unsolicited MSS.

## Nuffield Theatre

University Road, Southampton SO17 1TR
*tel* 023-8031 5500 *fax* 023-8031 5511
*Script Executive* John Burgess

Repertory theatre producing straight plays and musicals, and some small-scale fringe work. Interested in new plays.

## Octagon Theatre

Howell Croft South, Bolton BL1 1SB
*tel* (01204) 529407 *fax* (01204) 556502
*email* info@octagonbolton.co.uk
*website* www.octagonbolton.co.uk
*Executive Director* John Blackmore, *Operations Manager* Lesley Etherington, *Artistic Director* Mark Babych, *Production Manager* Lesley Chenery

Fully flexible professional theatre. Year round programme of own productions and visiting companies.

## The Palace Theatre Watford Ltd

Clarendon Road, Watford, Herts. WD17 1JZ
*tel* (01923) 235455 *fax* (01923) 819664
*Contact* Lawrence Till, Artistic Director

Regional repertory theatre. Produces 8 plays each year, both classic and contemporary drama. Welcomes synopses of new plays before submitting scripts.

## Peacock Theatre

The Abbey Theatre, 26 Lower Abbey Street, Dublin 1, Republic of Ireland
*tel* (01) 8872200 *fax* (01) 8729177
*Artistic Director* Ben Barnes, *Managing Director* Brian Jackson, *Peacock Theatre Director* Ali Curran

Experimental theatre associated with the Abbey Theatre; mostly new writing.

## Perth Theatre Ltd

185 High Street, Perth PH1 5UW
*tel* (01738) 472700 *fax* (01738) 624576
*email* info@perththeatre.co.uk
*website* www.perththeatre.co.uk
*General Manager* Paul Hackett

Combination of 3- and 4-weekly repertoire of plays and musicals, incoming tours, one-night variety events and studio productions.

## Plymouth Theatre Royal

Theatre Royal, Royal Parade, Plymouth PL1 2TR
*tel* (01752) 230340 *fax* (01752) 230499
*website* www.theatreroyal.com
*Chief Executive* Adrian Vinken, *Artistic Director* Simon Stokes

Stages small, middle and large-scale drama and music theatre. Commissions and produces new plays. Unsolicited play scripts with sae are read and responded to. Send one script at a time by post only; no email submissions please.

## Queen's Theatre, Hornchurch

Billet Lane, Hornchurch, Essex RM11 1QT
*tel* (01708) 462362 *fax* (01708) 462363
*email* info@queens-theatre.co.uk
*website* www.queens-theatre.co.uk
*Artistic Director* Bob Carlton

500-seat producing theatre serving outer East London with permanent company of actors/musicians presenting 8 mainhouse and 3 TIE productions each year. Treatments welcome; unsolicited scripts may be returned unread. Queen's Theatre Writer's Group showcases new work Sept–March; contact Education & Outreach Manager for details.

## The Ramshorn Theatre/Strathclyde Theatre Group

98 Ingram Street, Glasgow G1 1ES
*tel* 0141-552 3489 *fax* 0141-553 2036
*email* ramshorn.theatre@strath.ac.uk
*Contact* Susan C. Triesman (Director of Drama, University of Strathclyde)

Develops new writing (including experimental) through Ramshorn New Playwrights Initiative. Founded 1992.

## Royal Exchange Theatre Company Ltd

St Ann's Square, Manchester M2 7DH
*tel* 0161-833 9333 *fax* 0161-832 0881
*website* www.royalexchange.co.uk
*Executive Director* Patricia Weller

Varied programme of major classics, new plays, musicals, contemporary British and European drama; also explores the creative work of diverse cultures.

## Royal Lyceum Theatre Company

Royal Lyceum Theatre, Grindlay Street, Edinburgh EH3 9AX
*tel* 0131-248 4848 *fax* 0131-228 3955
*email* royallyceumtheatre@cableinet.co.uk
*website* www.lyceum.org.uk
*Artistic Director* Mark Thomson

Edinburgh's busiest repertory company, producing an all-year-round programme of classic, contemporary and new drama. Interested in work of Scottish writers.

## Salisbury Playhouse

Malthouse Lane, Salisbury, Wilts. SP2 7RA
*tel* (01722) 320117 *fax* (01722) 421991
*email* info@salisburyplayhouse.com
*Artistic Director* Joanna Read

Regional repertory theatre producing a broad programme of classical and modern plays and new writing.

## Scarborough Theatre Trust Ltd

Stephen Joseph Theatre, Westborough, Scarborough, North Yorkshire YO11 1JW
*tel* (01723) 370540 *fax* (01723) 360506
*email* enquiries@sjt.uk.com
*website* www.sjt.uk.com
*Literary Manager* Laura Harvey

Regional repertory theatre company which produces about 10 plays a year, many of which are premieres. The theatre has an excellent reputation for comedy. Plays should have a strong narrative and a desire to entertain, though nothing too lightweight will be considered. Enclose a sae with all submissions.

## Sheffield Theatres

55 Norfolk Street, Sheffield S401 1DA
*tel* 0114-249 5999 *fax* 0114-249 6003
*Chief Executive* Grahame Morris

Large-scale producing house with distinctive thrust stage; smallish studio; Victorian proscenium arch theatre used mainly for touring productions.

## The Sherman Theatre

Senghennydd Road, Cardiff CF24 4YE
*tel* 029-2064 6901 *fax* 029-2064 6902
*email* admin@shermantheatre.demon.co.uk
*website* www.shermantheatre.co.uk
*General Manager* Margaret Jones
*Contact* Programme Coordinator

Plays mainly for 15–25 age range, plus under 7's Christmas show. Founded 1974.

## Show of Strength Theatre Company Ltd

74 Chessel Street, Bedminster, Bristol BS3 3DN
*tel* 0117-902 0235
*website* www.showofstrength.org.uk

*Artistic Director* Sheila Hannon

Small-scale company committed to producing new and unperformed work. Send sae for return of MSS. Founded 1986.

## Theatre Royal
Windsor, Berks. SL4 1PS
*tel* (01753) 863444 *fax* (01753) 831673
*Executive Producer* Bill Kenwright, *Executive Director* Mark Piper

Regional producing theatre presenting a wide range of productions from classics to new plays.

## Traverse Theatre
10 Cambridge Street, Edinburgh EH1 2ED
*tel* 0131-228 3223 *fax* 0131-229 8443
*email* katherine@traverse.co.uk, neil@traverse.co.uk
*website* www.traverse.co.uk
*International Literary Associate* Katherine Mendelsohn, *Literary Assistant* Neil Coull

Scotland's new writing theatre with a special interest in Scottish writers and writers based in Scotland. Will read unsolicited scripts but an sae must be included for return of script.

## The West Yorkshire Playhouse
Playhouse Square, Quarry Hill, Leeds LS2 7UP
*tel* 0113-213 7800 *fax* 0113-213 7250
*email* mail@wyp.org.uk
*Artistic Director* Ian Brown, *Literary Manager* Alex Chisholm

Twin auditoria complex; community theatre. Has a policy of encouraging new writing from Yorkshire and Humberside region. Send script with an sae for its return to the Literary Manager.

## York Citizens' Theatre Trust Ltd
Theatre Royal, St Leonard's Place, York YO1 7HD
*tel* (01904) 658162 *fax* (01904) 611534
*Chief Executive* Ludo Keston, *Artistic Director* Damian Cruden

Repertory productions, tours.

# Touring companies

## Actors Touring Company
Alford House, Aveline Street, London SE11 5DQ
*tel* 020-7735 8311 *fax* 020-7735 1031
*email* atc@atc-online.com
*website* www.atc-online.com
*Executive Producer* Emma Dunton

Small to medium-scale company producing innovative contemporary work for young audiences.

## Compass Theatre Company
Carver Street Institute, 24 Rockingham Lane, Sheffield S401 4FW
*tel* 0114-275 5328 *fax* 0114-278 6931
*email* info@compasstheatrecompany.com
*website* www.compasstheatrecompany.com
*Artistic Director* Neil Sissons, *General Manager* Craig Dronfield

Touring classical theatre nationwide. Does not produce new plays.

## Eastern Angles
Sir John Mills Theatre, Gatacre Road, Ipswich IP1 2LQ
*tel* (01473) 218202 *fax* (01473) 384999
*email* admin@easternangles.co.uk
*website* www.easternangles.co.uk
*Contact* Ivan Cutting

Touring company producing new work with a regional theme. Stages 3 productions per year. Welcomes scripts from new writers in the East of England region. Founded 1982.

## Graeae Theatre Company
LVS Resource Centre, 356 Holloway Road, London N7 6PA
*tel* 020-7700 2455 *minicom* 020-7700 8184
*fax* 020-7609 7324
*email* info@graeae.org
*website* www.graeae.org
*Executive Producer* Roger Nelson, *Artistic Director* Jenny Sealey, *Administrator* Annette Burghes

Small-scale company. Welcomes scripts from disabled writers. Founded 1980.

## The Hiss & Boo Company Ltd
1 Nyes Hill, Wineham Lane, Bolney, West Sussex RH17 5SD
*tel* (01444) 881707 *fax* (01444) 882057
*email* ian@hissboo.co.uk

Not much scope for new plays, but will consider comedy thrillers/chillers and plays/musicals for children. No unsolicited scripts – telephone first. Plays/synopses will be returned only if accompanied by an sae.

## Hull Truck Theatre Co. Ltd

Hull Truck Theatre, Spring Street, Hull HU2 8RW
*tel* (01482) 224800 *fax* (01482) 581182
*email* admin@hulltruck.co.uk
*website* www.hulltruck.co.uk
*Executive Director* Joanne Gower, *Artistic Director*
John Godber, *Associate Director* Gareth Tudor Price

World-renowned small-cast touring company
presenting popular and accessible theatre.
Commissions up to six new plays each year.
Produces plays in-house at Hull Truck Theatre as
well as touring throughout the year to mid, large
and small scale venues. The venue also hosts Sunday
Comedy Nights and Jazz nights and local amateur
and student companies. Also presents the world
premieres of the plays of John Godber, the
company's Artistic Director.

## The London Bubble

3–5 Elephant Lane, London SE16 4JD
*tel* 020-7237 4434 *fax* 020-7231 2366
*email* admin@londonbubble.org.uk
*website* www.londonbubble.org.uk

## M6 Theatre Company (Studio Theatre)

Hamer C.P. School, Albert Royds Street, Rochdale,
Lancs. OL16 2SU
*tel* (01706) 355898 *fax* (01706) 711700
*email* info@m6theatre.co.uk
*Contact* Jane Milne

Theatre-in-education company providing high
quality theatre for children, young people and
community audiences.

## New Perspectives Theatre Company

The Old Library, Leeming Street, Mansfield,
Notts. NG18 1NG
*tel* (01623) 635225 *fax* (01623) 635240
*email* info@newperspectives.co.uk
*website* www.newperspectives.co.uk
*General Manager* Cathy Leigh, *Artistic Director*
Daniel Buckroyd

A new writing company which commissions 3–4
writers each year and performs small-scale theatre
productions to community and arts venues
nationally.

## NITRO

6 Brewery Road, London N7 9NH
*tel* 020-7609 1331 *fax* 020-7609 1221
*email* info@nitro.co.uk
*website* www.nitro.co.uk
*Artistic Director* Felix Cross, *General Manager* Philip
Bray

Commissions and produces new and innovative
musical theatre writing by black writers, that
expresses the contemporary aspirations, cultures
and issues that concern black people.

## NTC Touring Theatre Company

The Playhouse, Bondgate Without, Alnwick,
Northumberland NE66 1PQ
*tel* (01665) 602586 *fax* (01665) 605837
*email* admin@ntc-touringtheatre.co.uk
*website* www.ntc-touringtheatre.co.uk
*Artistic Director* Gillian Hambleton

Performs a wide cross-section of work: new plays,
extant scripts, classic and modern. Particularly
interested in non-naturalism, physical theatre and
plays with direct relevance to rural audiences.

## Out of Joint

7 Thane Works, Thane Villas, London N7 7PH
*tel* 020-7609 0207 *fax* 020-7609 0203
*email* ojo@outofjoint.co.uk
*website* www.outofjoint.co.uk
*Contact* Max Stafford-Clark

Touring company producing new plays and some
revivals. Welcomes scripts from writers. Founded
1993.

## Oxford Stage Company

12 Mercer Street, London WC2H 9QD
*tel* 020-7438 9940 *fax* 020-7438 9941
*email* info@oxfordstage.co.uk
*website* www.oxfordstage.co.uk
*Contact* Development Producer

A middle-scale touring company presenting 3–4
productions per year: revivals of established
masterpieces, modern classics, and new work.

## Paines Plough

4th Floor, 43 Aldwych, London WC2B 4DN
*tel* 020-7240 4533 *fax* 020-7240 4534
*email* office@painesplough.com
*website* www.painesplough.com
*Artistic Director* Vicky Featherstone, *Associate
Director* John Tiffany, *Literary Associate* Lucy
Morrison

Tours new plays by British writers nationwide. The
company believes that the playwright's voice should
be at the centre of contemporary theatre and works
with new and experienced writers. A programme of
workshops and readings develops new work.
Provides support for commissioned writers to push
themselves, with the aim to produce the most
ambitious and challenging of new theatre writing.
Considers all unsolicited scripts from UK writers –
send sae for return of script.

## Proteus Theatre Company

Queen Mary's College, Cliddesden Road,
Basingstoke, Hants RG21 3HF
*tel* (01256) 354541 *fax* (01256) 356186
*email* info@proteustheatre.com
*website* www.proteustheatre.com
*Artistic Director* Mark Helyar, *Associate Director*

Deborah Wilding, *General Manager* Julie Bladon

Small-scale touring company particularly committed to new writing and new work, education and community collaborations. Produces 3 touring shows per year plus several community projects. Founded 1979.

## Quicksilver National Touring Theatre

4 Enfield Road, London N1 5AZ
*tel* 020-7241 2942 *fax* 020-7254 3119
*email* talktous@quicksilvertheatre.org
*website* www.quicksilvertheatre.org
*Joint Artistic Director/Ceo* Guy Holland, *Joint Artistic Director* Carey English

A professional touring theatre company which brings live theatre to theatres and schools all over the country. Delivers good stories, original music, kaleidoscopic design and poignant, often humorous, new writing to entertain and make children and adults think. Two to three new plays a year for 3–5 year-olds, 7–11 year-olds and 6+ years and families. Founded 1977.

## Real People Theatre Company

37 Curlew Glebe, Dunnington, York YO19 5PQ
*tel/fax* (01904) 488870
*email* sueann@curlew.totalserve.co.uk
*website* www.realpeopletheatre.co.uk
*Contact* Sue Lister, Artistic Director

Women's theatre company. Welcomes scripts from women writers. Founded 1999.

## Red Ladder Theatre Company

3 St Peters Buildings, York Street, Leeds LS9 8AU
*tel* 0113-245 5311 *fax* 0113-245 5351
*email* wendy@redladder.co.uk
*website* www.redladder.co.uk
*Artistic Director* Wendy Harris

Theatre performances for young people (14–25) in youth clubs and small-scale theatre venues. Commissions at least 2 new plays each year. Runs the Asian Theatre School, an annual theatre training programme for young Asians in Yorkshire.

## Red Shift Theatre Company

TRG2 Trowbray House, 108 Weston Street, London SE1 3QB
*tel* 020-7378 9787 *fax* 020-7378 9789
*email* mail@redshifttheatreco.co.uk
*website* www.redshifttheatreco.co.uk
*Artistic Director* Jonathan Holloway

Productions include adaptations, classics, new plays. No commissions planned before 2004.

## 7:84 Theatre Company (Scotland) Ltd

333 Woodlands Road, Glasgow G3 6NG
*tel* 0141-334 6686 *fax* 0141-334 3369
*email* admin@784theatre.com

*website* www.784theatre.com
*Artistic Director* Lorenzo Mele

Presents 2–3 productions per year of political new writing and relevant classical texts. Welcomes scripts from new writers. Founded 1973.

## Shared Experience Theatre

The Soho Laundry, 9 Dufour's Place, London W1F 7SJ
*tel* 020-7434 9248 *fax* 020-7287 8763
*email* admin@sharedexperience.org.uk
*website* www.sharedexperience.org.uk
*Joint Artistic Directors* Nancy Meckler, Polly Teale

Middle-scale touring company presenting 2 productions per year: innovative adaptations or translations of classic texts, and some new writing. Tours nationally and internationally. Founded 1975.

## Snap People's Theatre Trust

29 Raynham Road, Bishop's Stortford, Herts. CM23 5PE
*tel* (01279) 461607 *fax* (01279) 506694
*email* info@snaptheatre.co.uk
*Contact* Gill Bloomfield

Produces theatre for young adults, children and families. Emphasis on new writing. Welcomes scripts from new writers. Founded 1978.

## Solent Peoples Theatre (SPT)

135 St Mary Street, Southampton SO14 1NX
*tel* 023-8063 4381 *fax* 023-8063 5717
*email* solent@solentpeoples.demon.co.uk
*General Manager* Susan Carpenter

SPT has developed its artistic programme through participatory projects, to incorporate a multimedia, cross art form approach to theatre that will offer richer opportunities and experience to both community and company. Works with diverse groups/individuals for whom an integrated approach to the creation/presentation of new work in performance makes that work more exciting, relevant and accessible.

## The Sphinx Theatre Co. Ltd

25 Short Street, London SE1 8LJ
*tel* 020-7401 9993/4 *fax* 020-7401 9995
*Artistic Director* Sue Parrish

Women writers only.

## The Steam Industry

c/o Finborough Theatre, 118 Finborough Road, London SW10 9ED
*tel* 020-7244 7439 *fax* 020-7835 1853
*email* admin@finboroughtheatre.co.uk
*website* www.steamindustry.co.uk
*Artistic Director* Phil Willmott

Produces new writing, radical adaptations of classic

texts and musicals. Unsolicited scripts are no longer accepted. Founded 1994.

## Talawa Theatre Company

3rd Floor, 23–25 Great Sutton Street,
London EC1V 0DN
*tel* 020-7251 6644 *fax* 020-7251 5969
*email* hq@talawa.com
*Artistic Director* Paulette Randall

Scripts from new writers considered. Particularly interested in scripts from black writers and plays portraying a black experience.

## Theatre Absolute

57–61 Corporation Street, Coventry CV1 1GQ
*tel* (02476) 257380 *fax* (02476) 550680
*email* info@theatreabsolute.co.uk
*website* www.theatreabsolute.co.uk
*Contact* Julia Negus

Independent theatre producer of contemporary plays. Stages one premiere and tour over 2-year period. Founded 1992.

## Theatre Centre

Units 7 & 8, Toynbee Workshops,
3 Gunthorpe Street, London E1 7RQ
*tel* 020-7377 0379 *fax* 020-7377 1376
*email* admin@theatre-centre.co.uk
*website* www.theatre-centre.co.uk
*Director* Rosamunde Hutt

New writing company producing and touring nationally and internationally. Professional theatre for young people – schools, arts centres, venues. Founded 1953.

## Theatre Workshop

34 Hamilton Place, Edinburgh EH3 5AX
*tel* 0131-225 7942 *fax* 0131-220 0112
*Contact* Robert Rae

Cutting edge, professional, inclusive theatre company. Plays include new writing/community/children's/disabled. Scripts from new writers considered.

## Tiebreak Theatre Company

Heartsease High School, Marryat Road,
Norwich NR7 9DF
*tel* (01603) 435 209 *fax* (01603) 435 184
*email* info@tiebreak-theatre.com
*website* www.tiebreak-theatre.com
*Contact* Kaja Holloway

Presents 2–3 productions per year of children's and young people's theatre for schools and national venues. Founded 1982.

# Literary agents

## The role of the literary agent

Depending on their perspective, people have very different ideas as to what literary agents actually do. With over three decades of experience behind him, the late Giles Gordon explains here what the role of the literary agent entails.

It occurs to me (and it really hasn't previously although I've been an agent – don't groan – for more than 30 years) that what writers think of as 'the role' of the literary agent is quite different from the actuality.

Having said that, agents work in more various ways than publishers do. Publishers accept manuscripts from writers, whether 'professional' (meaning having published some books) or 'amateur' (as yet unpublished), and make them available to the world, or at least have them printed and bound. With non-fiction, most books will be commissioned after seeing an outline and a few specimen chapters.

I don't believe an agent has 'a role', in that that makes him or her sound pompous or important. The late publisher Colin Haycraft wrote 'The world is a peculiar place, but it has nothing on the world of books. This is largely a fantasy world in which the pecking order goes as follows: if you can't cope with life, write about it; if you can't write, publish; if you can't get a job in publishing, become a literary agent; if you are a failed literary agent – God help you!'

It's funny and a bit unfair but only a bit. It makes the fundamental point that writers are what count and it is they who keep the book trade in business. No author should ever forget this, or fear and quake when confronted with a literary agent or a publisher. We all live off your talent, such as it is.

Most good agents today (and, of course, there are good agents and bad agents) have been publishers, mostly editors; and thus they have at least a working knowledge of what happens in publishers' offices and how a book gets out into the world.

The dilemma is that agents are interested in books, the written word, yet an agency, large or small, is essentially a business and authors should expect it to be that. Would-be published authors frequently say: it doesn't cost you anything to offer my masterpiece (sorry, manuscript) to publishers. Why don't you take a chance? The answer to that is because time is money, and overheads are inevitably involved in offering each and every manuscript to publishers. Including salaries, postage, paper, packaging, internet costs, office rent, electricity, heating and everything else.

A literary agency most emphatically isn't a finishing school for aspiring authors. Our agency Curtis Brown, probably the biggest in the UK, receives hundreds of unsolicited manuscripts each week. Every one is looked at but time, if nothing else, doesn't permit us to provide detailed responses to manuscripts we don't instantly take to, for whatever reason.

In short, literary agents are professional workers whose primary responsibility is to earn a living for themselves and their dependents. Having said that, they have chosen the world of books which would suggest that they enjoy reading, yet ought to be discriminating about it.

As every second person in the world right now seems to be touting a manuscript, agents are finding it seriously difficult to keep up with the reading demanded of them. Even more so perhaps than publishers because, although they don't always admit it, these days editors and publishing houses very much regard agents as the primary sifters of material, of separating the wheat from the chaff.

The agent's real job is to 'represent' the individual authors he or she has elected to act for. An agent or agency ultimately should be judged by the quality of the writers it represents. Although an agent may choose to act for a particular author, it is essentially the author who has selected the agent, or at least decided to place the fate of his or her writing in the agent's hands.

It is therefore important that the author should be satisfied that he or she is both in reliable hands and has as an agent someone with whom they can get on. Easier said than done perhaps, but I always advocate that new authors who have written anything of the slightest interest should shop around and interview three or four agents and then decide with whom they would get on best. If the manuscript is any good, agents should be in competition to represent it

Every agency is different. PFD and Curtis Brown each employs over 50 staff, and has numerous agents, specialising in different areas: books, journalism, film, television, theatre, talent, even 'horse flesh' – by which I mean actors. There are large accounts departments which have the most fundamental responsibilities in an agency, primarily to check all money for clients that comes in, to ensure that the publisher or other payers have accounted accurately, and to get the money to the client as soon as humanly possible. No agency should sit on clients' money for more than a few days at most.

At the other end of the size scale, there are the very many single person agencies. These are often set up by editors previously employed by publishing conglomerates who persuade authors they have worked with to go with them.

The agent, or agency, makes its income entirely as a result of commission on sales of their clients' work. Increasingly, with office and other business overheads spiralling, agencies are having to charge 15% commission on sales in the UK, and 20% on sales to the USA and in translation: the latter percentage is frequently shared with a sub-agent on the ground in the relevant country.

It is a shock to new agents who have had salaried jobs in publishing to realise how hard it is to earn a living income from 10% or 15% of the average publisher's advance. Whereas the larger agencies have specialised departments, the one-person and other smaller agencies have to become master – or mostly mistresses – of the entire field, although some specialised aspects of the work (e.g. translation and film) are often farmed out. Some writers prefer dealing with an agent who does everything, while others prefer so-called experts who sell different aspects of their work. It depends entirely on the relationship between author and agent, and the temperament of both.

Which takes me really to the heart of the matter. However much I admire an author's work, I wouldn't be an effective agent for him or her unless as human beings we get on. One of my colleagues believes that when an agent undertakes to represent an author, that is a contract for life. The agent has a fiduciary and moral commitment to that writer and his or her financial livelihood. I'm of the view that if the relationship turns sour – the author has become impossible or the agent has become useless – it is better to part company.

Yet it must never be forgotten that an agent is in the service of the author (Lopakhin in *The Cherry Orchard* comes to mind). The author employs the agent and makes it possible for the agent to earn his or her living thanks to the primary material the author provides. And this is the case even if, paradoxically, the agent, as very occasionally happens, achieves for the author such good contracts that the author becomes a millionaire.

No two authors want the same thing. Some want money, some want security of different kinds, some just want to be published, some want to be bestsellers, some do it as therapy, some do it because they believe they are geniuses, some do it because they believe it will advance their careers in their day jobs. Some want to write part time, some want to write full time. Thus no two authors make the same demands of their agents and thus it is essential that the agent gets to know the author from the beginning of their relationship and tries to find out what the author requires.

From the would-be published writer's point of view, it is useful to know how a literary agent evolves his or her list. It is said, with apparent paradox, that it is easier for a previously unpublished author to acquire a publisher than an agent. This is literally true in that last year over 130,000 different titles were published in the UK, a mind-boggling 2000-plus different books on average every single week of the year. There may be hundreds of individual agents but no agent can adequately represent more than a certain number of authors.

I – and I only use the example of myself because I know my client list better than any other – currently represent 125 authors. Five or six are internationally known, including a Booker Prize winner and a few that have been on the shortlist and haven't yet won. About half my clients write fiction, half non-fiction.

Almost every time I have taken on a writer before having met him or her, the relationship has not in the long term survived. Publishers can get away with never meeting their authors because they publish *books*, whereas agents represent *human beings*. The author has to believe that the agent is doing the best possible job for him or her which probably, but not invariably, means getting the biggest bucks by way of an advance as that way the publisher will strive strenuously in the marketplace to recoup the initial investment.

Not always though, because if the agent is in a position (i.e. it is a first book, and first books these days are more saleable than subsequent books, or one by a *very famous author*) to demand too much money the publisher may, between signature of the agreement and publication of the book, realise that he or she has been blackmailed, made an ass of, and to cut his or her losses not be prepared to spend more money on promoting a lost cause.

Again I will reiterate that the agent works for and is employed by the author. Some inexperienced writers may believe that publishers employ agents and pay them baksheesh to seduce them into offering them their best books. This is not so. If an agent or agency is to survive, or at least become established, there must be an author or two who makes a considerable income to pay for the overtures and beginners who, down the years, will become the future major earners.

And yet the major earners are not subsidising the new authors. I remember years ago John Fowles telling me that he met someone after *The French Lieutenant's Woman* had been on the US bestseller lists for many months who said she couldn't understand why he continued to use a literary agent as obviously he now made more than a respectable living from his writing. Fowles courteously pointed out that it was precisely because there was now money to be made from his books that he needed an agent to make sure he wasn't exploited.

That is the point. No writer needs a literary agent who cannot sell his or her books. In recent years, sadly and depressingly (but I hope not too cynically), I have declined to represent a number of new writers – mostly novelists but sometimes non-fiction writers because of their favoured subject matter. Much as I have admired their talent I haven't believed I would be able to find or persuade a publisher to take on their work. Ultimately failing to find a good publisher for an author means that the agent has failed the writer.

It doesn't really do for the agent to say 'I still think you have written a work of genius; the publishers are idiots for not realising it'. It is the responsibility of the agent to persuade the publisher of the genius or commercial viability of manuscripts submitted.

Saddest of all, any self-respecting agent can usually tell within 20 or 30 seconds of looking at unsolicited submissions, both the letter of submission and the manuscript, whether the book is any good or not. That is the cruellest stroke of all. And no author when submitting a manuscript to an agent should say that his or her family and friends say that it is better than most books published because they would, wouldn't they?

Most books about how to get published tell authors to submit a synopsis and two or three specimen chapters to an agent. Certainly it is in the interests of the agent that the author should do that but if the author believes in his or her book the entire thing should be sent. It is too easy for an agent to decline an author's submission on the strength of a few chapters. If the agent is hooked from the beginning, he or she should want to read on. If he or she isn't, the manuscript is going to go back to the author.

**Giles Gordon** died on 14 November 2003. He was a very well-respected man, reputed to have single-handedly revolutionised the world of English publishing by being loyal to his clients and placing them in the best publishing houses. His clients included Peter Ackroyd, Sue Townsend, Fay Weldon and Prince Charles. He joined Curtis Brown on 1995; the branch in Scotland where he worked is now closed.

## See also...

- *Dos and don'ts on approaching a publisher*, page 130
- *How to get an agent*, page 397

# How to get an agent

New writers and illustrators wishing to have their work published frequently ask whether it is worth their while finding an agent. Philippa Milnes-Smith demystifies the role of the literary agent.

This article is for all those who are prepared to dedicate themselves to the pursuit of publication. If you are currently experiencing just a vague interest in being a writer or illustrator, stop reading now. You are unlikely to survive the rigorous commercial assessment to which your work will be subjected. If you are a children's writer or illustrator do not think that the process will be any easier. It's just as tough, if not tougher.

### So, what is a literary agent and why would I want one?
You will probably already have noticed that contacts for many publishers are provided in the *Writers' & Artists' Yearbook*. This means that there is nothing to prevent you from pursuing publishers directly yourself. Indeed, if you can answer a confident 'yes' to all the questions below, and have the time and resources to devote to this objective, you probably don't need an agent:
1. Do you have a thorough understanding of the publishing market and its dynamics?
2. Do you know who are the best publishers for your book and why? Can you evaluate the pros and cons of each?
3. Are you financially numerate and confident of being able to negotiate the best commercial deal available in current market conditions?
4. Are you confident of being able to understand fully and negotiate a publishing or other media contract?
5. Do you enjoy the process of selling yourself and your work?
6. Do you want to spend your creative time on these activities?
An agent's job is to deal with all of the above on your behalf. A good agent will do all of these well.

### So, is that is all an agent does?
Agents aren't all the same. Some will provide more editorial and creative support; some will help on longer term career planning; some will be subject specialists; some will involve themselves more on marketing and promotion. Such extras may well be taken into consideration in the commission rates charged.

### I have decided I definitely do want an agent. Where do I begin?
When I left publishing and talked generally to the authors and illustrators I knew, a number of them said it was now more difficult to find an agent than a publisher. Why is this? The answer is a commercial one. An agent will only take someone on if they can see how and why they are going to make money for the client and themselves. To survive, an agent needs to make commission and to do

this they need projects they can sell. An agent also knows that if he/she does not sell a client's work, the relationship isn't going to last long.

### So the agent just thinks about money?

Well, some agents may just think about money. And it might be all you care about. But good agents do also care about the quality of work and the clients they represent. They are professional people who commit themselves to doing the best job they can. They also know that good personal relationships count – and that they help everyone enjoy business more. This means that, if and when you get as far as talking to a prospective agent, you should ask yourself the questions: 'Do I have a good rapport with this person? Do I think we will get along? Do I understand and trust what they are saying?' Follow your instinct – more often than not it will be right.

### So how do I convince an agent that I'm worth taking on?

Start with the basics. Make your approach professional. Make sure you only approach an appropriate agent who deals with the category of book you are writing/illustrating. Phone to check to whom you should send your work and whether there are any particular ways your submission should be made (if it's not clear from the listings in this *Yearbook*). Only submit neat, typed work on single-sided A4 paper. Send a short covering letter with your manuscript explaining what it is, why you wrote it, what the intended audience is and providing any other *relevant* context. Always say if and why you are uniquely placed and qualified to write a particular book. Provide your professional credentials, if any. If you are writing an autobiography, justify why it is of public interest and why your experiences set you apart. Also, provide a CV (again, neat, typed, relevant) and a stamped addressed envelope for the return of your manuscript. Think of the whole thing in the same way as you would a job application, for which you would expect to prepare thoroughly in advance. You might only get one go at making your big sales pitch to an agent. Don't mess it up by being anything less than thorough.

### And if I get to meet an agent?

Treat it like a job interview (although hopefully it will be more relaxed than this). Be prepared to talk about your work and yourself. An agent knows that a prepossessing personality in an author is a great asset for a publisher in terms of publicity and marketing – they will be looking to see how good your inter-personal skills are.

### And if an agent turns my work down? Should I ask them to look again? People say you should not accept rejection.

No means no. Don't pester. It won't make an agent change his/her mind. Instead, move on to the next agency – the agent there might feel more positive. The agents who reject you may be wrong. But the loss is theirs.

**Even if an agent turns my work down, isn't it worth asking for help with my creative direction?**

No. Agents will often provide editorial advice for clients but will not do so for non-clients. Submissions are usually sorted into two piles of 'yes, worth seeing more' and 'rejections'. There is not another pile of 'promising writer but requires further tutoring'. Creative courses and writers' and artists' groups are better options to pursue for teaching and advice (see *Websites for writers*, page 591, *Creative writing courses*, page 634 and *Editorial, literary and production services*, page 643). It is, however, important to practise and develop your creative skills. You wouldn't expect to be able to play football without working at your ball skills or practise as a lawyer without studying to acquire the relevant knowledge. If you are looking to get your work published, you are going to have to compete with professional writers and artists – and those who have spent years working at their craft.

If I haven't put you off yet, it just remains for me to say good luck – and don't forget to buy plenty of stamps, envelopes and A4 paper.

**Philippa Milnes-Smith** is a literary agent and children's specialist at the agency LAW (Lucas Alexander Whitley). She was previously Managing Director of Puffin Books.

## See also...
- *Literary agents for children's books*, page 756
- *Literary agents for television, film, radio and theatre*, page 756

# Literary agents UK and Ireland

*Full member of the Association of Authors' Agents

## A & B Personal Management Ltd

Paurelle House, 91 Regent Street, London W1B 4EL
*tel* 020-7734 6047/8 *fax* 020-7734 6318
*Directors* R.W. Ellis, R. Ellis

Full-length MSS. Scripts for TV, theatre, cinema;
also novels, fiction and non-fiction (home 12.5%,
overseas 15%), performance rights (12.5%). No
unsolicited material: write first before submitting
synopsis. No reading fee for synopsis, plays or
screenplays, but fee charged for full-length MSS.
Return postage required. Founded 1982.

## Sheila Ableman Literary Agency

122 Arlington Road, London NW1 7HP
*tel* 020-7485 3409 *fax* 020-7485 3409
*email* sheila@ableman.freeserve.co.uk
*Contact* Sheila Ableman

Non-fiction including history, science, biography,
autobiography (home 15%, USA/translation 20%).
Specialises in TV tie-ins and ghost writing. No
poetry, children's, cookery, gardening or sport.
Unsolicited MSS welcome. Approach in writing
with publishing history, CV, synopsis, 3 chapters
and sae for return. No reading fee. Founded 2000.

## The Susie Adams Rights Agency

8 Sullivan Road, London SE11 4UH
*tel* 020-7582 6765 *fax* 020-75820 7745
*email* SusieARA@aol.com
*Agent* Susie Adams

Subsidiary rights agent on behalf of packagers,
literary agents and publishers: foreign language and
co-edition rights worldwide, UK serial, book club,
merchandise and other sub rights. No authors.
Founded 1998.

## The Agency (London) Ltd*

24 Pottery Lane, London W11 4LZ
*tel* 020-7727 1346 *fax* 020-7727 9037
*email* info@theagency.co.uk
*Executives* Stephen Durbridge, Leah Schmidt,
Sebastian Born, Julia Kreitman, Bethan Evans,
Hilary Delamere (children's books), Katie Haines,
Ligeia Marsh, Faye Webber, Nick Quinn

Represents writers for theatre, film, TV, radio and
children's book writers and illustrators. Also film
and TV rights in novels and non-fiction. Adult
novels represented only for existing clients.
Commission: 10% unless sub-agents employed
overseas; works in conjunction with agents in USA
and overseas. Strictly no unsolicited material. No
reading fee. Founded 1995.

## Gillon Aitken Associates Ltd*

18–21 Cavaye Place, London SW10 9PT
*tel* 020-7373 8672 *fax* 020-7373 6002
*email* reception@gillonaitken.co.uk
*Contacts* Gillon Aitken, Clare Alexander, Lesley
Shaw (also handles film/TV), *Associated Agents*
Anthony Sheil, Mary Pachnos

Fiction and non-fiction (home 10%, USA 20%,
translation 20%, film/TV 10%). No plays, scripts or
children's fiction unless by existing clients. Send
preliminary letter with half-page synopsis and first
30pp of sample material and adequate return
postage, in the first instance. No reading fee.

*Clients* include Caroline Alexander, John
Banville, Pat Barker, Nicholas Blincoe, Gordon
Burn, John Cornwell, Josephine Cox, Sarah Dunant,
Susan Elderkin, Sebastian Faulks, Helen Fielding,
John Fowles, Germaine Greer, Mark Haddon, Susan
Howatch, Liz Jensen, John Keegan, Pete McCarthy,
V.S. Naipaul, Jonathan Raban, Piers Paul Read,
Michèle Roberts, Nicholas Shakespeare, Gillian
Slovo, Matt Thorne, Colin Thubron, Salley Vickers,
A.N. Wilson, Robert Wilson. Founded 1977.

## Michael Alcock Management*

Clerkenwell House, 45–47 Clerkenwell Green,
London EC1R 0HT
*tel* 020-7837 8137 *fax* 020-7837 8787
*email* alcockmgt@aol.com
*Agents* Michael Alcock, Anna Power

Fiction and non-fiction (home 15%, overseas 20%,
performance rights 15%). General non-fiction,
mainly biography, history, current affairs, health and
lifestyle; literary and commercial fiction. No reading
fee. Send letter, CV including previous writing and
media experience, and synopsis and first 3 chapters
with sae. Overseas associates: **Andrew Nurnberg
Associates**. Division of Johnson & Alcock Ltd.

*Authors* include Tamsin Blanchard, Barbara Currie,
Tom Dixon, Yehudi Gordon, Mark Griffiths, Joanna
Hall, Lisa Hilton, Lynne Robinson, Barnaby Rogerson,
Barry Turner, Lowri Turner. Founded 1997.

## Jacintha Alexander Associates – see
LAW Ltd

## The Ampersand Agency

Ryman's Cottages, Little Tew, Oxon OX7 4JJ
*tel* (01608) 683677 *fax* (01608) 683449
*email* peter@theampersandagency.co.uk
*website* www.theampersandagency.co.uk
*Partners* Peter Buckman, Peter Janson-Smith

Literary and commerical fiction and non-fiction (home 10%, USA 15%, translation 20%). No reading fee. Will suggest revision.

Represents the Georgette Heyer Estate. Founded 2003.

## Darley Anderson Literary, TV and Film Agency*

Estelle House, 11 Eustace Road, London SW6 1JB
*tel* 020-7385 6652 *fax* 020-7386 5571
*email* enquiries@darleyanderson.com
*website* www.darleyanderson.com
*Contacts* Darley Anderson, Lucie Whitehouse (foreign rights), Elizabeth Wright (women's fiction, thrillers and crime), Julia Churchill (non-fiction and children's books), Rosi Bridge (finance)

Commercial fiction and non-fiction; children's fiction; selected scripts for film and TV (home 15%, USA/translation 20%, film/TV/radio 20%). No poetry or academic books.

Special interests (fiction): all types of thrillers, crime/mystery and young male fiction. All types of American and Irish novels. All types of women's fiction. Sagas, chick-lit; contemporary and literary. Also comic fiction.

Special interests (non-fiction): celebrity autobiographies, biographies, sports books, 'true-life' women in jeopardy, revelatory history and science, popular psychology, self improvement, diet, beauty, health, fashion, animals, humour/cartoon, cookery, gardening, inspirational, religious.

Send preliminary letter, synopsis and first 3 chapters. Return postage/sae essential for reply. Disk and emailed submissions cannot be considered.
Overseas associates: APA Talent & Literary Agency (LA/Hollywood), Liza Dawson Literary Agency (New York) and 21 leading foreign agents worldwide.

*Clients* include Liz Allen, Richard Asplin, Anne Baker, Catherine Barry, Paul Carson, Caroline Carver, Cathy Cassidy, Lee Child, Kira Cochrane, Martina Cole, John Connolly, Margaret Dickinson, Rose Doyle, Joan Jonker, Astrid Longhurst, Rani Manicka, Carole Matthews, Lesley Pearse, Lynda Page, Allan Pease, Adrian Plass, Sheila Quigley, Carmen Reid, Mary Ryan, Rebecca Shaw, Peter Sheridan, Kwong Kuen Shan, Linda Taylor, Elizabeth Waite.

## Anubis Literary Agency

6 Birdhaven Close, Lighthorne Heath, Warks. CV35 0BE
*tel* (01926) 642588 *fax* (01926) 642588
*Contacts* Steve Calcutt, Maggie Heavey

Genre fiction: crime, thrillers, horror, science fiction, fantasy (home 15%, USA/translation 20%). No other material considered. Send 50pp, a one-page synopsis and sae (essential). No reading fee. No telephone calls. Works with the **Marsh Agency Ltd** on translation rights.

*Clients* include Lesley Asquith, Anthea Ingham,

Tim Lebbon, Adam Roberts, Steve Savile, Brett A. Savory, Zoe Sharp. Founded 1994.

## Associated Publicity Holdings Ltd

7 Kensington Church Court, London W8 4SP
*tel* 020-7937 5277 *fax* 020-7937 2833
*email* Jonathan.Harris@aph-agent.demon.co.uk
*Managing Director* Jonathan G. Harris

Full-length MSS. Fiction and non-fiction, particularly sport, history, archaeology, biographies, thrillers and crime novels (home 15%, overseas 20%), performance, film and TV rights (15%). Send outline, 2 sample chapters and sae. Works with foreign agencies. No reading fee. Founded 1987.

## Author Literary Agents

53 Talbot Road, London N6 4QX
*tel* 020-8341 0442 *mobile* (07989) 318245
*email* agile@authors.co.uk
*Contact* John Havergal

Send a half–one-page outline, plus first chapter/scene/section only for initial appraisal (home 15%, overseas/ translations 25%). Sae essential for reply. No reading fee. Also thought-through game, toy, animation, picture, graphics and children's concepts, for book and screen (25% + VAT). Founded 1997.

## Don Baker Associates

25 Eley Drive, Rottingdean, East Sussex BN2 7FH
*tel* (01273) 386842 *fax* (01273) 386842
*Directors* Donald Baker, Katy Quayle

Full-length MSS. Fiction, film, TV and theatre scripts (home 12.5%, overseas 15%). Reading fee. Send sae. No unsolicited MSS. Founded 1996.

## Blake Friedmann Literary, TV & Film Agency Ltd*

122 Arlington Road, London NW1 7HP
*tel* 020-7284 0408 *fax* 020-7284 0442
*email* firstname@blakefriedmann.co.uk
*Directors* Carole Blake, Julian Friedmann, Barbara Jones, Conrad Williams, Isobel Dixon

Full-length MSS. Fiction: thrillers, women's novels and literary fiction; non-fiction: investigative books, biography, travel; no poetry or plays (home 15%, overseas 20%). Specialises in film and TV rights; place journalism and short stories for existing clients only. Represented worldwide in 26 markets. Preliminary letter, synopsis and first 2 chapters preferred. No reading fee.

*Authors* include Gilbert Adair, Jane Asher, Edward Carey, Elizabeth Chadwick, Victoria Clayton, Barbara Erskine, Ann Granger, Maeve Haran, Ken Hom, Glenn Meade, Lawrence Norfolk, Gregory Norminton, Joseph O'Connor, Sheila O'Flanagan, Sian Rees, Michael Ridpath, Tim Sebastian, Julian Stockwin. Founded 1977.

## BookBlast Ltd

PO Box 20184, London W10 5AU
*tel* 020-8968 3089 *fax* 020-8932 4087
*website* www.bookblast.com
*Contact* Address material to the Company

Full-length MSS (home 12%, overseas 20%), TV
and radio (15%), film (20%). Fiction and non-
fiction. No scripts, horror, crime, science fiction,
fantasy, poetry, health, cookery, gardening, short
stories, academic articles or children's books. Radio,
TV and film rights sold mainly in works by existing
clients. No reading fee. No unsolicited approaches
at present. No new clients taken on except by
recommendation. Founded 1997.

## The Book Bureau Literary Agency

7 Duncairn Avenue, Bray, Co. Wicklow,
Republic of Ireland
*tel* (01) 276 4996 *fax* (01) 276 4834
*email* thebookbureau@oceanfree.net
*Managing Director* Geraldine Nichol

Full-length MSS (home 10%, USA 15%, translation
20%). Fiction preferred – thrillers, Irish novels,
literary fiction, women's novels and general
commercial. No horror, science fiction, children's or
poetry. Strong editorial support. No reading fee.
Preliminary letter, synopsis and 3 sample chapters.
Return postage essential, iec from UK and abroad.
Works with agents overseas.

## Alan Brodie Representation Ltd

211 Piccadilly, London W1J 9HF
*tel* 020-7917 2871 *fax* 020-7917 2872
*email* info@alanbrodie.com
*website* www.alanbrodie.com
*Directors* Alan Brodie, Sarah McNair, Alison Lee

Specialises in stage plays, radio, TV, film (home
10%, overseas 15%); no prose fiction or general
MSS. Represented in all major countries. No
unsolicited scripts; recommendation from known
professional required.

## Rosemary Bromley Literary Agency

Avington, Winchester, Hants SO21 1DB
*tel* (01962) 779656 *fax* (01962) 779656
*email* rosemarybromley.juvenilia@clara.co.uk

Specialises in biography, travel, leisure, cookery,
health (home 10%, overseas from 15%). No poetry.
No unsolicited MSS. Send full details of work on
offer with return postage. No fax, telephone or
email enquiries. For children's books see **Juvenilia**.

## Jenny Brown Associates

42 The Causeway, Edinburgh EH15 3PZ
*tel* 0131-620 1556
*email* jenny-brown@blueyonder.co.uk
*website* www.jennybrownassociates.com
*Director* Jenny Brown

Literary fiction and non-fiction, women's fiction,
writing from Scotland (home 10%, overseas 20%).
No reading fee. Will suggest revision. Works in
conjunction with the **Marsh Agency**.

*Authors* include Des Dillon, Janet Morgan,
Suhayl Saadi, Diana Hendry, Alex Gray, Laura
Marney, Christopher Whyte, Jennie Erdal, Anne
MacLeod. Founded 2002.

## Felicity Bryan*

2A North Parade, Banbury Road,
Oxford OX2 6LX
*tel* (01865) 513816 *fax* (01865) 310055

Fiction and general non-fiction (home 10%,
overseas 20%). Translation rights handled by
Andrew Nurnberg Associates; works in conjunction
with US agents. No unsolicited submissions.

## Brie Burkeman*

14 Neville Court, Abbey Road,
London NW8 9DD
*tel* (0709) 223 9113/(0870) 199 5002
*fax* (0709) 223 9111/(0870) 199 1029
*email* brie.burkeman@mail.com
*Proprietor* Brie Burkeman

Commercial and literary full-length fiction and
non-fiction. Film and theatre scripts (Home 15%,
Overseas 20%). No academic text, poetry, short
stories, musicals or short films. No reading fee but
return postage essential. Unsolicited email
attachments will be deleted without opening. Also
associated with Serafina Clarke Ltd and
independent film/TV consultant to literary agents.
Founded 2000.

## Campbell Thomson & McLaughlin Ltd*

1 King's Mews, London WC1N 2JA
*tel* 020-7242 0958 *fax* 020-7242 2408
*Directors* John McLaughlin, Charlotte Bruton

Full-length book MSS (home 10%, overseas up to
20% including commission to foreign agent). No
poetry, plays or TV/film scripts, short stories or
children's books. Preliminary letter with sae
essential. No unsolicited synopses or MSS. No
reading fee. USA agents represented: Raines &
Raines, the Fox Chase Agency, Inc. Representatives
in most European countries.

## Capel & Land Ltd*

29 Wardour Street, London W1D 6PS
*tel* 020-7734 2414 *fax* 020-7734 8101
*email* georgina@capelland.co.uk
*Agents* Georgina Capel (literary), Robert Caskie
(film), Anita Land (TV)

Literary and commercial fiction, history, biography;
film and TV (home/overseas 15%). No reading fee;
will suggest revision.

*Clients* include Julie Burchill, Andrew Greig,

Eamonn Holmes, Jean Marsh, Rt Hon. Dr Mo Mowlam, Cristina Odone, Jeremy Paxman, Henry Porter, Andrew Roberts, Simon Sebag Montefiore, Louis Theroux, Lucy Wadham. Founded 1999.

## Casarotto Ramsay & Associates Ltd

National House, 60–66 Wardour Street, London W1V 4ND
*tel* 020-7287 4450 *fax* 020-7287 9128
*email* agents@casarotto.uk.com
*Directors* Jenne Casarotto, Giorgio Casarotto, Tom Erhardt, Tracey Hyde, Sara Pritchard, Mel Kenyon, Charlotte Kelly, Jodi Shields, Chris Cope

MSS – theatre, films, TV, sound broadcasting only (10%). Works in conjunction with agents in USA and other foreign countries. Preliminary letter essential. No reading fee.

*Authors* include Paul Abbott, Alan Ayckbourn, J.G. Ballard, Peter Barnes, Edward Bond, Caryl Churchill, Pam Gems, Christopher Hampton, David Hare, Nick Hornby, Amy Jenkins, Neil Jordan, Frank McGuiness, Phyllis Nagy, Mark Ravenhill, Willy Russell, Martin Sherman, Shawn Slovo, Fay Weldon, Timberlake Wertenbaker, David Wood. Founded 1989.

## Celia Catchpole

56 Gilpin Avenue, London SW14 8QY
*tel* 020-8255 7200 *fax* 020-8288 0653
*website* www.celiacatchpole.co.uk

Specialises as agent for children's writers and illustrators (home 10% writers, 15% illustrators; overseas 20%). No unsolicited MSS. Founded 1996.

## Chapman & Vincent*

The Mount, Sun Hill, Royston, Herts. SG8 9AT
*tel* (01763) 245005 *fax* (01763) 243033
*email* info@chapmanvincent.co.uk
*Directors* Jennifer Chapman, Gilly Vincent

Original non-fiction and (occasionally) quality fiction (home 15%; overseas 20%). No children's, genre fiction or poetry. No reading fee. Clients come mainly from personal recommendation. No phone calls; submissions by post only. Send synopsis and 2 sample chapters with sae.

*Authors* include George Carter, Leslie Geddes-Brown, Sara George, Rowley Leigh.

## Mic Cheetham Literary Agency

11–12 Dover Street, London W1S 4LJ
*tel* 020-7495 2002 *fax* 020-7495 5777
*website* www.miccheetham.com
*Director* Mic Cheetham, *Contact* Simon Kavanagh

General and literary fiction, science fiction, some non-fiction (home/overseas 10–20%); film, TV and radio rights (10–20%); will suggest revision. Works with the **Marsh Agency Ltd** for foreign rights. No unsolicited MSS. No reading fee. Founded 1994.

## Judith Chilcote Agency

8 Wentworth Mansions, Keats Grove, London NW3 2RL
*tel* 020-7794 3717
*email* judybks@aol.com
*Director* Judith Chilcote

Commercial fiction, non-fiction – self-help and health, cookery, celebrity, autobiography and biography, current affairs, TV tie-ins (home 15%, overseas 20–25%). No short stories, science fiction, children's, poetry. Works in conjunction with overseas agents and New York affiliate. No reading fee but preliminary letter with 3 chapters only, CV and sae essential. Founded 1990.

## Teresa Chris Literary Agency

43 Musard Road, London W6 8NR
*tel* 020-7386 0633
*Director* Teresa Chris

All fiction, especially crime, women's commercial, general and literary fiction; all non-fiction, especially biography, history, health, cooking, arts and crafts. No science fiction, horror, fantasy, short stories, poetry, academic books (home 10%, USA 15%, rest 20%). Own US office: Thompson & Chris Literary Agency. No reading fee. No unsolicited MSS. Send introductory letter describing work, first 3 chapters and sae. Founded 1988.

## Christy & Moore Ltd – see Sheil Land Associates Ltd

## Mary Clemmey Literary Agency*

6 Dunollie Road, London NW5 2XP
*tel* 020-7267 1290 *fax* 020-7482 7360

High-quality fiction and non-fiction with an international market (home 10%, overseas 20%, performance rights 15%). No children's books or science fiction. TV, film, radio and theatre scripts from existing clients only. Works in conjunction with US agent. No reading fee. No unsolicited MSS. Approach first by letter with sae. Founded 1992.

## Jonathan Clowes Ltd*

10 Iron Bridge House, Bridge Approach, London NW1 8BD
*tel* 020-7722 7674 *fax* 020-7722 7677
*Directors* Jonathan Clowes, Ann Evans, Lisa Whadcock

Literary and commercial fiction and non-fiction, film, TV, theatre and radio (home 15%, overseas 20%). No reading fee. No unsolicited MSS. Works in association with agents overseas. Founded 1960.

*Clients* include Sir Kingsley Amis Estate, Dr David Bellamy, Bill Dare, Len Deighton, David Harsent, Elizabeth Jane Howard, David Lawrence, Doris Lessing, David Nobbs, Gillian White.

## Elspeth Cochrane Personal Management

14/2 Second Floor, South Bank Commercial Centre,
140 Battersea Park Road, London SW11 4NB
*tel* 020-7622 0314 *fax* 020-7622 5815
*email* info@ecpma.com
*Contact* Elspeth Cochrane

Fiction, non-fiction, biographies, screenplays and
plays (12.5%). No children's fiction. No unsolicited
MSS. Send preliminary letter, synopsis and sae in
first instance. No reading fee.

*Clients* include Alex Jones, Dominic Leyton,
Royce Ryton, F.E.Smith, Robert Tanitch and Greald
Vaughn-Hughes. Founded 1960.

## Rosica Colin Ltd

1 Clareville Grove Mews, London SW7 5AH
*tel* 020-7370 1080 *fax* 020-7244 6441
*Directors* Sylvie Marston, Joanna Marston

All full-length MSS (excluding science fiction and
poetry); also theatre, film and sound broadcasting
(home 10%, overseas 10–20%). No reading fee, but
may take 3–4 months to consider full MSS. Send
synopsis only in first instance, with letter outlining
writing credits and whether MS has been previously
submitted, plus return postage.

*Authors* include Richard Aldington, Simone de
Beauvoir (in UK), Samuel Beckett (publication
rights), Steven Berkoff, Alan Brownjohn, Sandy
Brownjohn, Donald Campbell, Nick Dear, Neil
Donnelly, J.T. Edson, Bernard Farrell, Rainer Werner
Fassbinder (in UK), Jean Genet, Mary Halpin, Franz
Xaver Kroetz, Don McCamphill, Heiner Müller (in
UK), Graham Reid, Botho Strauss (in UK), Anthony
Vivis, Wim Wenders (in UK). Founded 1949.

## Conville & Walsh Ltd*

118–120 Wardour Street, London W1V 3LA
*tel* 020-7287 3030 *fax* 020-7287 4545
*email* firstname@convilleandwalsh.com
*Directors* Clare Conville, Patrick Walsh (book
rights), Sam North (film/TV), Peter Tallack
(popular science)

Literary and commercial fiction plus serious and
narrative non-fiction. Particularly interested in first
novelists plus scientists, historians and journalists.
No reading fee.

*Clients* include Marina Benjamin, John
Burningham, Kate Cann, Helen Castor, Tom
Conran, Michael Cordy, Mike Dash, Prof John
Emsley, Steve Erikson, Katy Gardner, Christopher
Hart, Dermot Healy, James Holland, Tom Holland,
Sebastian Horsley, David Huggins, Guy Kennaway,
Manjit Kumar, P.J. Lynch, Hector Macdonald, Mark
Mason, Prof Arthur Miller, Harland Miller, Joshua
Mowll, Jacqui Murhall, Ruth Padel, D.B.C. Pierre,
Rebbecca Ray, Patrick Redmond, Candace Robb,
Mark Sanderson, Saira Shah, Tahir Shah, Nicky
Singer, Simon Singh, Doran Swade, Dr Richard

Wiseman, Adam Wishart, Isabel Wolff, and the
Estate of Francis Bacon. Founded 2000.

## Jane Conway-Gordon Ltd*

1 Old Compton Street, London W1D 5JA
*tel* 020-7494 0148 *fax* 020-7287 9264

Full length MSS (home 15%, overseas 20%).
Represented in all foreign countries. No reading fee
but preliminary letter and return postage essential.
Founded 1982.

## Coombs Moylett Literary Agency – see

Sfakianos Moylett Literary Agency

## Rupert Crew Ltd*

1A King's Mews, London WC1N 2JA
*tel* 020-7242 8586 *fax* 020-7831 7914
*email* rupertcrew@compuserve.com
*Directors* Doreen Montgomery, Caroline
Montgomery

International representation, handling volume and
subsidiary rights in fiction and non-fiction
properties (home 15%, elsewhere 20%); no plays,
poetry, journalism or short stories. No reading fee,
but preliminary letter and return postage essential.
Also acts independently as publishers' consultants.
Founded 1927 by F. Rupert Crew.

## Curtis Brown Group Ltd*

Haymarket House, 28–29 Haymarket,
London SW1Y 4SP
*tel* 020-7396 6600 *fax* 020-7396 0110
*email* cb@curtisbrown.co.uk
*Group Managing Director* Jonathan Lloyd, *Financial
Director* Mark Collingbourne, *Australia: Managing
Director* Fiona Inglis, *Books London* Jonathan Lloyd,
Anna Davis, Jonny Geller, Hannah Griffiths, Ali
Gunn, Camilla Hornby, Anthea Morton-Saner, Peter
Robinson, Vivienne Schuster, Janice Swanson
(children's), John Saddler

Agents for the negotiation in all markets of novels,
general non-fiction, children's books (home 10%,
overseas 20%) and associated rights (including
multimedia), as well as film, theatre, TV and radio
scripts. Outline for non-fiction and short synopsis
for fiction with 2–3 sample chapters and
autobiographical note. No reading fee. Return
postage essential. Also represents directors,
designers and presenters. Return postage essential.
Founded 1899.

## Judy Daish Associates Ltd

2 St Charles Place, London W10 6EG
*tel* 020-8964 8811 *fax* 020-8964 8966
*Agents* Judy Daish, Sara Stroud, Tracey Elliston

Theatre, film, TV, radio (rates by negotiation). No
unsolicited MSS. No reading fee. Founded 1978.

## Caroline Davidson Literary Agency

5 Queen Anne's Gardens, London W4 1TU
*tel* 020-8995 5768 *fax* 020-8994 2770

Handles novels and non-fiction of high quality, including reference works (12.5%). Send preliminary letter with CV and detailed, well thought-out book proposal/synopsis and/or first 50pp of novel. Large sae with return postage essential. No reading fee. Quick response.

*Authors* include Andrew Dalby, Emma Donoghue, Cindy Engel, Chris Greenhalgh, Paul Hillyard, Tom Jaine, Huon Mallalieu, Linda Sonntag. Founded 1988.

## Merric Davidson Literary Agency

12 Priors Heath, Goudhurst, Kent TN17 2RE
*tel* (01580) 212041 *fax* (01580) 212041
*email* md@mdla.co.uk
*Contact* Merric Davidson

Specialising in contemporary adult fiction (home 10%, overseas 20%). No unsolicited MSS. Preliminary letter with synopsis, author information and sae. No initial reading fee, may suggest revision, subsequent editorial advice by arrangement.

*Authors* include Alys Clare, Francesca Clementis, Murray Davies, Alison Habens, Frankie Park, Simon Scarrow. Founded 1990.

## Felix De Wolfe

Garden Offices, 51 Maida Vale, London W9 1SD
*tel* 020-7289 5770 *fax* 020-7289 5731

Theatre, films, TV, sound broadcasting, fiction (home 10–15%, overseas 20%). No reading fee. Works in conjunction with many foreign agencies.

## DGA

55 Monmouth Street, London WC2H 9DG
*tel* 020-7240 9992 *fax* 020-7395 6110
*email* assistant@davidgodwinassociates.co.uk
*website* www.davidgodwinassociates.co.uk
*Directors* David Godwin, Heather Godwin

Literary fiction and general non-fiction (home 10%, overseas 20%). No reading fee; send sae for return of MSS. Founded 1995.

## Dorian Literary Agency (DLA)*

Upper Thornehill, 27 Church Road, St Marychurch, Torquay, Devon TQ1 4QY
*tel* (01803) 312095 *fax* (01803) 312095
*Proprietor* Dorothy Lumley

General fiction, and specialising in popular fiction For adults: women's fiction, romance, historicals; crime and thrillers; science fiction, fantasy, dark fantasy and horror. Reading only very selectively. No poetry or drama. (Home 10–12.5%, USA 15%, translation 20%). No reading fee. Contact initially by post with 1–3 chapters and brief outline plus return postage/sae. No telephone calls, faxes or

emails. Represents Fedogan & Bremer Publishers (USA) for UK/translation and Ethan Ellenberg Literary Agency (USA).

*Authors* include Gillian Bradshaw, Kate Charles, Brian Lumley, Stephen Jones, Andy Ramic, Rosemary Rowe, Lyndon Stacey. Founded 1986.

## Bryan Drew Ltd

Quadrant House, 80–82 Regent Street, London W1B 5AU
*tel* 020-7437 2293 *fax* 020-7437 0561
*email* bryan@bryandrewltd.com
*Literary Manager* Bryan Drew

Scripts for TV, films and theatre (home 10%, overseas 15%). General fiction, thrillers, biographies, humour (home 10%, overseas 15%). No reading fee. Will suggest revision. Founded 1962.

## Robert Dudley Agency

8 Abbotstone Road, London SW15 1QR
*tel* 020-8788 0938 *fax* 020-8780 3586
*email* rdudley@btinternet.com
*Proprietor* Robert Dudley

Specialises in history, biography, sport, health, management, politics, IT and personal development (home 10%, overseas 15%; film/TV/radio 15%, 20%). No reading fee. Will suggest revision.

*Authors* include Steve Biko, Simon Caulkin, Paul Cornish, Clive Couldwell, Paul Gannon, Eva Kolinsky, David Osler, Tim Phillips, Sol Shulman. Founded 2000.

## Toby Eady Associates Ltd

3rd Floor, 9 Orme Court, London W2 4RL
*tel* 020-7792 0092 *fax* 020-7792 0879
*email* toby@tobyeady.demon.co.uk
jessica@tobyeady.demon.co.uk
*website* www.tobyeadyassociates.co.uk
*Contacts* Toby Eady, Jessica Woollard

Fiction and non-fiction (home 15%, overseas 20%). Special interests: China, Middle East, Africa, India. No film/TV scripts or poetry. Approach by personal recommendation. Overseas associates: **La Nouvelle Agence** (France), Mohrbrooks (Germany), Jan Michael (Holland), The Buckman Agency (Italy, Spain, Portugal and Scandinavia), Joanne Wang (China).

*Clients* include Nada Awar Jarrar, Julia Blackburn, Mark Burnell, John Carey, Robert Carter, Bernard Cornwell, Rana Dasgupta, Fadia Faqir, Kuki Gallmann, Xiaolu Guo, Liu Hong, Natasha Illum Berg, Susan Lewis, Julia Lovell, Robert Macfarlane, Francesca Marciano, Kanan Makiya, Patrick Marnham, Linda Polman, Fiammetta Rocco, Deborah Scroggins, Samia Secageldin, Rachel Seiffert, John Stubbs, Robert Winder, Ann Wroe, Xinran Xue. Estates of Peter Cheyney, Ted Lewis, Mary Wesley. Founded 1968.

## Eddison Pearson Ltd

10 Corinne Road, London N19 5EY
*tel* 020-7700 7763 *fax* 020-7700 7866
*email* info@eddisonpearson.com
*Contact* Clare Pearson

Children's books and scripts, literary fiction and
non-fiction, poetry (home 10%, overseas 15%). No
unsolicited MSS. Enquire by letter enclosing brief
writing sample and sae. Email enquiries welcome
but no email submissions please. No reading fee.
May suggest revision where appropriate.

   *Authors* include Valerie Bloom, Sue Heap, Sally
Lloyd-Jones, Robert Muchamore, Mary Murphy,
Ruth Symes.

## Edwards Fuglewicz*

49 Great Ormond Street, London WC1N 3HZ
*tel* 020-7405 6725 *fax* 020-7405 6726
*Partners* Ros Edwards and Helenka Fuglewicz

Literary and commercial fiction (but no children's
fiction, science fiction, horror or fantasy); non-
fiction: biography, history, popular culture (home
15%, USA/translation 20%). No unsolicited MSS or
email submissions. No reading fee. Founded 1996.

## Faith Evans Associates*

27 Park Avenue North, London N8 7RU
*tel* 020-8340 9920 *fax* 020-8340 9410

Small agency (home 15%, overseas 20%). New
clients by personal recommendation only. Co-
agents in most countries. No phone calls, scripts or
unsolicited MSS.

   *Authors* include Melissa Benn, Shyam Bhatia,
Cherie Booth, Eleanor Bron, Carolyn Cassady,
Caroline Conran, Helen Falconer, Alicia Foster,
Midge Gillies, Ed Glinert, Cate Haste, Jim Kelly,
Helena Kennedy, Seumas Milne, Tom Paulin, Sheila
Rowbotham, Lorna Sage, Rebecca Stott, Harriet
Walter, Elizabeth Wilson, Francesca Weisman.
Founded 1987.

## John Farquharson Ltd – see Curtis Brown

Group Ltd

## Janet Fillingham Associates

52 Lowther Road, London SW13 9NU
*tel* 020-8748 5594 *fax* 020-8748 7374
*email* office@jfillassoc.co.uk
*Director* Janet Fillingham

Film and TV only (home 10%, overseas 15–20%).
Strictly no unsolicited MSS; professional
recommendation required. Founded 1992.

## Film Rights Ltd

Mezzanine, Quadrant House, 80–82 Regent Street,
London W1B 5AU
*tel* 020-7734 9911 *fax* 020-7734 0044

*email* information@filmrights.ltd.uk
*website* www.filmrights.ltd.uk
*Directors* Brendan Davis, Joan Potts

Theatre, films, TV and sound broadcasting (home
10%, overseas 15%). No reading fee. Represented in
USA and abroad. Founded 1932.

## Laurence Fitch Ltd

Mezzanine, Quadrant House, 80–82 Regent Street,
London W1B 5AU
*tel* 020-7734 9911 *fax* 020-7437 0561
*email* information@laurencefitch.com
*website* www.laurencefitch.com
*Directors* F.H.L. Fitch, Joan Potts, Brendan Davis

Theatre, films, TV and sound broadcasting (home
10%, overseas 15%). Also works with several
agencies in USA and in Europe.

   *Authors* include Ray Coony, John Chapman,
Carlo Ardito, John Graham, Edward Taylor, Dawn
Lowe-Watson, Peter Coke, Glyn Robbins, Robin
Hawdon, John Rooney and the Estate of the late
Dodie Smith.

## Jill Foster Ltd

9 Barb Mews, Brook Green, London W6 7PA
*tel* 020-7602 1263 *fax* 020-7602 9336

Theatre, films, TV and sound broadcasting (12.5%).
Particularly interested in film and TV comedy and
drama. No novels or short stories. No reading fee.
Preliminary letter essential. No submissions by
email. Do not send material in the first instance.
Founded 1978.

## Fox & Howard Literary Agency

4 Bramerton Street, London SW3 5JX
*tel* 020-7352 8691 *fax* 020-7352 8691
*Partners* Chelsey Fox, Charlotte Howard

General non-fiction: biography, history and popular
culture, reference, business, mind, body & spirit,
health and fitness (home 15%, overseas 20%). No
reading fee, but preliminary letter and synopsis with
sae essential for response. Founded 1992.

## Fraser & Dunlop Ltd, Fraser & Dunlop Scripts Ltd – see PFD

## Fraser Ross Associates

6 Wellington Place, Edinburgh EH6 7EQ
*tel/fax* 0131-553 2759, 0131-657 4412
*email* lindsey.fraser@tiscali.co.uk,
kjross@tiscali.co.uk
*Partners* Lindsey Fraser, Kathryn Ross

Writing and illustration for children's books, but
not exclusively (home 10%). No reading fee. Will
suggest revision, depending on individual
submission. Founded 2002.

## French's

78 Loudoun Road, London NW8 0NA
*tel* 020-7483 4269 *fax* 020-7722 0754
*Directors* John French, Mark Taylor

All MSS; specialises in novels and screenplays
(home/overseas 10%); theatre, films, TV, radio
(10%). Reading service available, details on
application. Sae must be enclosed with all MSS.

## Futerman, Rose & Associates*

Heston Court Business Park, 19 Camp Road,
London SW19 4UW
*tel* 020-8947 0188 *fax* 020-8605 2162
*email* guy@futermanrose.co.uk
*website* www.futermanrose.co.uk
*Contact* Guy Rose

Scripts for film and TV; commercial fiction and
non-fiction with film potential, biography, show
business (15–20%). No unsolicited MSS, science
fiction or fantasy. Send preliminary letter with a
brief résumé, detailed synopsis and sae. Overseas
associates.

*Clients* include Iain Duncan Smith, Royston Ellis,
Adam Hamdy, Paul Hendy, Russell Warren Howe,
Rev. Joanna Jepson, Sue Lenier, Eric MacInnes, Tony
Prince, Paul Rattigan, Yvonne Ridley, Frederick E.
Smith, Gordon Thomas, Michael Walker, Mark
White, Simon Woodham, Allen Zeleski. Founded
1984.

## Jüri Gabriel

35 Camberwell Grove, London SE5 8JA
*tel* 020-7703 6186 *fax* 020-7703 6186

Quality fiction and non-fiction (i.e. anything that
shows wit and intelligence); radio, TV and film, but
mainly selling these rights in existing works by
existing clients. Full-length MSS (home 10%,
overseas 20%), performance rights (10%); will
suggest revision where appropriate. No short
stories, articles, verse or books for children. No
reading fee; return postage essential. Jüri Gabriel is
the chairman of Dedalus (publishers).

*Authors* include Maurice Caldera, Diana
Constance, Miriam Dunne, Pat Gray, Robert Irwin,
John Lucas, 'David Madsen', Richard Mankiewicz,
David Miller, Andy Oakes, John Outram, Stefan
Szymanski, Dr Terence White, Chris Wilkins, Dr
Robert Youngson.

## Eric Glass Ltd

25 Ladbroke Crescent, London W11 1PS
*tel* 020-7229 9500 *fax* 020-7229 6220
*Director* Janet Glass

Full-length MSS only; also theatre, films, TV, and
sound broadcasting. No unsolicited MSS. Founded
1932.

## David Godwin Associates – see DGA

## Annette Green Authors' Agency*

1 East Cliff Road, Tunbridge Wells, Kent TN4 9AD
*tel* (01892) 514275 *fax* (01892) 518124
*email* annettekgreen@aol.com
*website* www.annettegreenagency.co.uk
*Partners* Annette Green, David Smith

Full-length MSS (home 15%, overseas 20%).
Literary and general fiction and non-fiction,
popular culture, history, science, teenage fiction. No
dramatic scripts, poetry, SF or fantasy. No reading
fee. Preliminary letter, synopsis, sample chapter and
sae essential.

*Authors* include Andrew Baker, Nick Barlay, Julia
Bell, Bill Broady, Meg Cabot, Simon Conway, Terry
Darlington, Fiona Gibson, Justin Hill, Max
Kinnings, Maria McCann, Adam MacQueen, Ian
Marchant, Lembit Opik MP, Prof Charles Pasternak,
Peter Shapiro, Rev. Victor Stock, Elizabeth
Woodcraft. Founded 1998.

## Christine Green Authors' Agent*

6 Whitehorse Mews, Westminster Bridge Road,
London SE1 7QD
*tel* 020-7401 8844 *fax* 020-7401 8860
*website* www.christinegreen.co.uk

Fiction and general non-fiction. Full-length MSS
(home 10%, overseas 20%). Works in conjunction
with agencies in Europe and Scandinavia. No
reading fee, but preliminary letter and return
postage essential. Founded 1984.

## Louise Greenberg Books Ltd*

The End House, Church Crescent, London N3 1BG
*tel* 020-8349 1179 *fax* 020-8343 4559
*email* louisegreenberg@msn.com

Full-length MSS (home10%, overseas 20–25%).
Literary fiction and non-fiction. No reading fee.
Return postage and sae essential. No telephone
enquiries. Founded 1997.

## Greene & Heaton Ltd*

37 Goldhawk Road, London W12 8QQ
*tel* 020-8749 0315 *fax* 020-8749 0318
*website* www.greeneheaton.co.uk
*Contacts* Carol Heaton, Judith Murray, Antony
Topping, Linda Davis (children's)

All types of fiction and non-fiction (home 10–15%,
USA/translation 20%). No original scripts for
theatre, film or TV. Send no more than a brief
covering letter, synopsis and 3 chapters. No reply to
unsolicited submissions without sae and/or return
postage. Overseas associates worldwide.

*Clients* include Mark Barrowcliffe, Bill Bryson,
Jan Dalley, Marcus du Sautoy, Hugh Fearnley-
Whittingstall, Colin Forbes, Michael Frayn, P.D.
James, William Leith, Mary Morrissy, William
Shawcross, Sarah Waters. Founded 1963.

## Gregory & Company Authors' Agents*
3 Barb Mews, London W6 7PA
*tel* 020-7610 4676 *fax* 020-7610 4686
*email* info@gregoryandcompany.co.uk
*website* www.gregoryandcompany.co.uk
*Contacts* Jane Gregory, *Editorial* Broo Doherty,
*Rights* Claire Morris

Fiction and general non-fiction (home 15%,
USA/translation/radio/film/TV 20%). Special
interests (fiction): literary, commercial, women's
fiction, crime, suspense and thrillers. Particularly
interested in books which will also sell to publishers
abroad. No original plays, film or TV scripts (only
published books are sold to film and TV), science
fiction, fantasy, poetry, academic or children's
books. No reading fee. Editorial advice given to own
authors. No unsolicited MSS: send preliminary
letter with CV, synopsis, first 3 chapters and future
writing plans plus return postage. Short
submissions (3pp) by fax or email. Represented
throughout Europe, Asia and USA. Founded 1987.

## David Grossman Literary Agency Ltd
118B Holland Park Avenue, London W11 4UA
*tel* 020-7221 2770 *fax* 020-7221 1445

Full-length MSS (home 10–15%, overseas 20%
including foreign agent's commission), performance
rights (15%). Works in conjunction with agents in
New York, Los Angeles, Europe, Japan. No reading
fee, but preliminary letter required. No submissions
by fax or email. Founded 1976.

## Marianne Gunn O'Connor Literary Agency
Morrison Chambers, Suite 17, 32 Nassau Street,
Dublin 2, Republic of Ireland
*email* mariannegunn@eircom.net
*Contact* Marianne Gunn

Non-commerical and literary fiction, non-fiction –
biography, Mind, Body & Spirit, health, children's
fiction (UK 15%, overseas 20%, film/TV 20%). No
reading fee.
    *Clients* include Patrick McCabe, Naill Williams,
Morag Prunty, Claire Kilroy, Julie Dam, Cecilia
Ahern, Paddy McMahon. Founded 1996.

## The Rod Hall Agency Ltd
3 Charlotte Mews, London W1T 4DZ
*tel* 020-7637 0706 *fax* 020-7637 0807
*email* office@rodhallagency.com
*website* www.rodhallagency.com
*Director* Charlotte Mann

Specialises in writers for stage, screen and radio but
also deals in TV and film rights in novels and non-
fiction (home 10%, overseas 15%). No reading fee.
    *Clients* include Simon Beaufoy, Jeremy Brock,
Dario Fo, Susan Hill, Liz Lochhead, Martin

McDonagh, Andrea Newman, Simon Nye,
Ol Parker, Matthew Parkhill, Lucy Prebble, Richard
Smith, Juliette Towhidi. Founded 1997.

## Margaret Hanbury*
27 Walcot Square, London SE11 4UB
*tel* 020-7735 7680 *fax* 020-7793 0316
*email* maggie@mhanbury.demon.co.uk

Personally run agency specialising in quality fiction
and non-fiction (home 15%, overseas 20%).
    *Authors* include George Alagiah, J.G. Ballard,
Simon Callow, Jordan, Judith Lennox. Founded 1983.

## Antony Harwood Ltd
103 Walton Street, Oxford OX2 6EB
*tel* (01865) 559615  *fax* (01865) 310660
*email* mail@antonyharwood.com
*Contacts* Antony Harwood, James Macdonald
Lockhart

General and genre fiction; general non-fiction
(home 15%, overseas 20%). Will suggest revision.
No reading fee.
    *Authors* include Amanda Craig, Louise Doughty,
Peter F. Hamilton, Alan Hollinghurst, A.L. Kennedy,
Douglas Kennedy, Chris Manby, George Monbiot,
Garth Nix, Tim Parks. Founded 2000.

## A.M. Heath & Co. Ltd*
79 St Martin's Lane, London WC2N 4RE
*tel* 020-7836 4271 *fax* 020-7497 2561
*website* www.amheath.com
*Directors* William Hamilton (managing), Sara
Fisher, Sarah Molloy, Victoria Hobbs

Full-length MSS. Literary and commercial fiction
and non-fiction, children's (home 10–15%, USA
20%, translation 20%), performance rights (15%).
No science fiction, screenplays, poetry or short
stories except for established clients. No reading fee.
Agents in USA and all European countries and Japan.
    *Clients* include Bella Bathurst, Anita Brookner,
Helen Cresswell, Patricia Duncker, Geoff Dyer, Katie
Fforde, Graham Hancock, Tobias Hill, Conn
Iggulden, Hilary Mantel, Maggie O'Farrell, Tim
Pears, Susan Price, Adam Thorpe, Barbara Trapido.
Founded 1919.

## David Higham Associates Ltd*
5–8 Lower John Street, Golden Square,
London W1F 9HA
*tel* 020-7434 5900 *fax* 020-7437 1072
*email* dha@davidhigham.co.uk
*website* www.davidhigham.co.uk
*Managing Director* Anthony Goff, *Books* Veronique
Baxter, Anthony Goff, Bruce Hunter, Jacqueline
Korn, Lizzy Kremer, Caroline Walsh, *Foreign Rights*
Ania Corless, *Film/TV/Theatre* Gemma Hirst, Nicky
Lund, Georgina Ruffhead

Agents for the negotiation of all rights in fiction, general non-fiction, children's fiction and picture books, plays, film and TV scripts (home 15%, USA/translation 20%). Represented in all foreign markets. Preliminary letter and return postage essential. No reading fee. Founded 1935.

## Vanessa Holt Ltd*
59 Crescent Road, Leigh-on-Sea,
Essex SS9 2PF
*tel* (01702) 473787 *fax* (01702) 471890
*email* vanessa@holtlimited.freeserve.co.uk

General adult fiction and non-fiction (home 15%, overseas 20%, TV/film/radio 15%). Works in conjunction with foreign agencies in all markets. No reading fee. No unsolicited MSS; send query letter first with sae. No overseas submissions. Founded 1989.

## Valerie Hoskins Associates
20 Charlotte Street, London W1T 2NA
*tel* 020-7637 4490 *fax* 020-7637 4493
*email* vha@vhassociates.co.uk
*Proprietor* Valerie Hoskins, *Agent* Rebecca Watson

Film, TV and radio; specialises in animation (home 12.5%, overseas max. 20%). No unsolicited MSS; preliminary letter essential. No reading fee, but sae essential. Works in conjunction with US agents.

## Tanja Howarth Literary Agency*
19 New Row, London WC2N 4LA
*tel* 020-7240 5553 *fax* 020-7379 0969
*email* tanja.howarth@btinternet.com

Full-length MSS. General fiction and non-fiction, thrillers, contemporary and historical novels (home 15%, USA/translation 20%). No unsolicited MSS, and no submissions by fax or email. No reading fee. Specialists in handling German translation rights. Represented in the USA by various agents. Founded 1970.

## ICM Books
4–6 Soho Square, London W1D 3PZ
*tel* 020-7432 0800  *fax* 020-7432 0808
*email* ksutton@icmtalent.com
*Contact* Kate Jones, Margaret Halton, Tricia Davey, Elizabeth Iveson, Betsy Robbins

Fiction and non-fiction. No unsolicited MSS; send a query letter, sample chapters and sae first.
   *Authors* include Arthur Miller, Patricia Cornwell, Donna Tartt, Rageh Omaar, Haruki Murakami. Division of **International Creative Management Inc.**

## IMG Literary UK
The Pier House, Strand on the Green,
London W4 3NN
*tel* 020-8233 5000 *fax* 020-8233 5001

*Chairman* Mark H. McCormack, *Agents* Sarah Wooldridge (London), Mark Reiter and Lisa Queen (New York), Fumiko Matsuki (Japan)

Celebrity books, sports-related books, commercial fiction, non-fiction and how-to business books (home 15%, USA 20%, elsewhere 25%). No theatre, children's, academic or poetry. No reading fee.

## The Inspira Group
5 Bradley Road, London EN3 6ES
*tel* 020-8292 5163  *fax* (0870) 139 3057
*email* darin@theinspiragroup.com
*website* www.theinspiragroup.com
*Managing Director* Darin Jewell

Humour, lifestyle, fiction and children's (home 15%, overseas 15%). No reading fee. Will suggest revision. Founded 2001.

## Intercontinental Literary Agency*
33 Bedford Street, London WC2E 9ED
*tel* 020-7379 6611 *fax* 020-7379 6790
*email* ila@ila-agency.co.uk
*Contacts* Nicki Kennedy, Sam Edenborough, Mary Esdaile

Represents translation rights for PFD, London, Harold Matson Company Inc., New York, the Turnbull Agency (John Irving) Inc., and Lucas Alexander Whitley Ltd. Founded 1965.

## International Literary Representation & Management LLC
186 Bickenhall Mansions, Bickenhall Street,
London W1U 6BX
*tel* 020-7224 1748 *fax* 020-7224 1802
*email* info@yesitive.com
*website* www.yesitive.com
*Vice President for Europe* Peter Cox

European office of US agency. Represents authors with major international potential. Commission by agreement. Only considers submissions if guidelines found on website have been followed. No unsolicited MSS. No radio or theatre scripts. No reading fee.
   *Clients* include Martin Bell OBE, Brian Clegg, Brian Cruver, Caris Davis, Senator Orrin Hatch, Barbara Jacobs, Michael J. Nelson, Michelle Paver, Saxon Roach, David Soul. Founded 1993.

## International Scripts
1A Kidbrooke Park Road,
London SE3 0LR
*tel* 020-8319 8666 *fax* 020-8319 0801
*Directors* H.P. Tanner, J. Lawson

Specialises in full-length contemporary and women's fiction, biographies, business and general non-fiction (home 15%, overseas 20%), performance rights (15–20%); no poetry or short stories. Works with overseas agents. Preliminary letter and sae required. An editorial contribution plus return postage may be requested for reading MSS.

*Authors* include Jane Adams, Zita Adamson, Ashleigh Bingham, Simon Clark, Dr James Fleming, June Gadsby, Ed Gorman, Peter Haining, Julie Harris, Robert A. Heinlein, Anna Jacobs, Anne Jones, Richard Laymon, Trevor Lummis, Nick Oldham, Chris Pascoe, Christine Poulson, Mary Ryan, John and Anne Spencer, Janet Woods. Founded 1979.

## Barrie James Literary Agency

Rivendell, Kingsgate Close, Torquay, Devon TQ2 8QA
*tel* (01803) 326617
*email* mail@newauthors.org.uk
*website* www.newauthors.org.uk
*Contact* Barrie James

Internet site for new writers and poets to display their work to publishers.No unsolicited MSS. First contact: send sae or email. Founded 1997.

## Janklow & Nesbit (UK) Ltd

29 Adam & Eve Mews, London W8 6UG
*tel* 020-7376 2733 *fax* 020-7376 2915
*email* queries@janklow.co.uk
*Agents* Tif Loehnis, Claire Paterson

Commercial and literary fiction and non-fiction. No unsolicited MSS. Send informative covering letter and return postage with full outline (non-fiction), synopsis and 3 sample chapters (fiction). US and foreign rights handled by **Janklow & Nesbit Associates** in New York.

## JMLA

The Basement, 94 Goldhurst Terrace, London NW6 3HS
*tel* 020-7372 8422 *fax* 020-7372 8423
*Managing Director* Judy Martin

Non-fiction, biography and jazz and its origins and history, American jazz biographies, art and surrealism (home 15%, overseas 20%). No plays, poetry, cookery, gardening or children's stories. Translation rights handled by the **Marsh Agency Ltd**. No reading fee, but sae required for all unsolicited MSS, together with details of publishing history. Founded 1990.

## Johnson & Alcock*

Clerkenwell House, 45–47 Clerkenwell Green, London EC1R 0HT
*tel* 020-7251 0125 *fax* 020-7251 2172
*email* info@johnsonandalcock.co.uk
*Contacts* Michael Alcock, Andrew Hewson, Anna Power, Merel Reinink

Full-length MSS (home 15%, US and translation 20%). Literary and commercial fiction, children's fiction; general non-fiction including current affairs, biography and memoirs, history, lifestyle, health and personal development. No poetry, screenplays, science fiction, technical or academic material. No unsolicited MSS; approach by letter in the first instance giving details of writing and other media experience, plus synopsis. For fiction send one-page synopsis and first three chapters. Sae esssential for response. No reading fee. Founded 1956.

## Jane Judd Literary Agency*

18 Belitha Villas, London N1 1PD
*tel* 020-7607 0273 *fax* 020-7607 0623

General non-fiction and fiction (home 10%, overseas 20%). Special interests: women's fiction, crime, thrillers, narrative non-fiction. No short stories, film/TV scripts, poetry or plays. No reading fee, but preliminary letter with synopsis, first chapter and sae essential. Works with agents in USA and most foreign countries. Founded 1986.

## Juvenilia

Avington, Winchester, Hants SO21 1DB
*tel* (01962) 779656 *fax* (01962) 779656
*email* juvenilia@clara.co.uk
*Contact* Rosemary Bromley

Full-length MSS for the children's market, fiction and non-fiction (home 10%, overseas from 15%), illustration (10%), performance rights (10%). Short stories only if specifically for picture books, radio or TV. No unsolicited MSS; preliminary letter with sae and full details essential. Postage for acknowledgement and return of material imperative. No fax, telephone or email enquiries. Founded 1973.

## Michelle Kass Associates*

36–38 Glasshouse Street, London W1B 5DL
*tel* 020-7439 1624 *fax* 020-7734 3394
*Proprietor* Michelle Kass

Full-length MSS. Literary fiction and drama scripts for film (home 10%, overseas 15–20%). Will suggest revision where appropriate. Works with agents overseas. No reading fee. Absolutely no unsolicited MSS without a preliminary phone call. Founded 1991.

## Frances Kelly Agency*

111 Clifton Road, Kingston-upon-Thames, Surrey KT2 6PL
*tel* 020-8549 7830 *fax* 020-8547 0051

Full-length MSS. Non-fiction: general and academic, reference and professional books, all subjects (home 10%, overseas 20%), TV, radio (10%). No reading fee, but no unsolicited MSS; preliminary letter with synopsis, CV and return postage essential. Founded 1978.

## Peter Knight Agency

20 Crescent Grove, London SW4 7AH
*tel* 020-7622 1467 *fax* 020-7622 1522
*email* peter@knightfeatures.co.uk
*website* www.knightfeatures.co.uk
*Director* Peter Knight, *Associates* Gaby Martin,
Andrew Knight, Samantha Ferris

Motor sports, cartoon books, business, history and
factual and biographical material. No poetry, science
fiction or cookery. Overseas associates: United Media
(USA), Auspac Media (Australia), Puzzle Company.
No unsolicited MSS. Send letter accompanied by CV
and sae with synopsis of proposed work.

*Clients* include Ralph Barker, Frank Dickens,
John Dodd, Gray Jolliffe, Angus McGill, Chris
Maslanka, Barbara Minto, Lisa Wild. Founded 1985.

## LAW Ltd*

14 Vernon Street, London W14 0RJ
*tel* 020-7471 7900 *fax* 020-7471 7910
*email* firstname@lawagency.co.uk
*Contacts* Mark Lucas, Julian Alexander, Araminta
Whitley, Alice Saunders, Celia Hayley, Lucinda Cook,
Peta Nightingale, Hannah Bellamy, Philippa Milnes-
Smith (children's) Helen Mulligan (children's)

Full-length commercial and literary fiction, non-
fiction and children's books (home 15%, US and
translation 20%). No fantasy (except children's),
plays poetry or textbooks. Film and TV scripts
handled for established clients only. Unsolicited
MSS considered; send brief covering letter, short
synopsis and 2 sample chapters. Sae essential. No
emailed or disk submissions. Overseas associates
worldwide. Founded 1996.

## LBLA (Lorella Belli Literary Agency)

54 Hartford House, 35 Tavistock Crescent,
London W11 1AY
*tel* 020-7727 8547 *fax* (0870) 7874194
*email* info@lorellabelliagency.com
*website* www.lorellabelliagency.com
*Proprietor* Lorella Belli

Fiction and general non-fiction (home 15%,
overseas 20%, dramatic 20%). Particularly
interested in first-time writers, journalists,
international and multicultural writing and books
on Italy. No children's, science fiction, fantasy,
academic, poetry, original scripts. No reading fee.
May suggest revision. Send outline plus 2 chapters
for non-fiction; synopsis and initial 3 chapters for
fiction. Sae essential. Works with overseas and
dramatic associates; represents American and other
foreign agencies.

*Authors* include Sean Bidder, Zoë Brân, Scott
Capurro, Sean Coughlan, Dario Fo, Jacopo Fo, Nino
Filasto, Emily Giffin, Paul Martin, Nisha Minhas,
Rupert Steiner, Marcello Vannucci, Diana Winston.
Founded 2002.

## Cat Ledger Literary Agency*

20–21 Newman Street, London W1T 1PG
*tel* 020-7861 8226 *fax* 020-7861 8001

General non-fiction and fiction but no short stories,
film/TV scripts, poetry or plays (home 10%,
overseas 20%). No reading fee but preliminary
letter, synopsis and sae essential. Represented in all
foreign countries.

## Barbara Levy Literary Agency*

64 Greenhill, Hampstead High Street,
London NW3 5TZ
*tel* 020-7435 9046 *fax* 020-7431 2063
*Director* Barbara Levy, *Associate* John Selby
(solicitor)

Full-length MSS. Fiction and general non-fiction
(home 10%, overseas by arrangement). Film and
TV rights for existing clients only. No reading fee,
but preliminary letter with synopsis and sae
essential. Translation rights handled by the **Marsh
Agency Ltd**; works in conjunction with US agents.
Founded 1986.

## Limelight Management*

33 Newman Street, London W1T 1PY
*tel* 020-7637 2529 *fax* 020-7637 2538
*email* limelight.management@virgin.net
*website* www.limelightmanagement.com
*Directors* Fiona Lindsay, Linda Shanks

Full-length and short MSS. Food, wine, health,
crafts, gardening, interior design (home 15%,
overseas 20%), TV and radio rights (10–20%); will
suggest revision where appropriate. No reading fee.
Founded 1991.

## The Christopher Little Literary Agency*

10 Eel Brook Studios, 125 Moore Park Road,
London SW6 4PS
*tel* 020-7736 4455 *fax* 020-7736 4490
*email* info@christopherlittle.net
*website* www.christopherlittle.net
*Contacts* Christopher Little, Kellee Nunley, Emma
Schlesinger, Neil Blair (Legal)

Commercial and literary full-length fiction and
non-fiction (home 15%; USA, Canada, translation,
audio, motion picture 20%). No poetry, plays,
science fiction, fantasy, textbooks, illustrated
children's or short stories. Film scripts for
established clients only. No reading fee. First contact
– send detailed preliminary letter in the first
instance with synopsis, first 2–3 chapters and sae.
Founded 1979.

*Authors* include Steve Barlow and Steve
Skidmore, Paul Bajoria, Andrew Butcher, Will
Dawes, Janet Gleeson, Carol Hughes, Alastair
MacNeil, Robert Mawson, Haydn Middleton, A.J.
Quinnell, Robert Radcilffe, J.K. Rowling, Darren
Shan, Wladyslaw Szpilman, John Watson.

## London Independent Books

26 Chalcot Crescent, London NW1 8YD
*tel* 020-7706 0486 *fax* 020-7724 3122
*Proprietor* Carolyn Whitaker

Specialises in commercial, fantasy and teenage
fiction, show business, travel. Full-length MSS
(home 15%, overseas 20%). Will suggest revision of
promising MSS. No reading fee.

    *Authors* include Eric Braun, Keith Gray, Tim
Mackintosh-Smith, Glenn Mitchell, Connie Monk,
Richard Morgan, Kevin Rushby, Emma Sinclair,
Chris Wooding. Founded 1971.

## Andrew Lownie Literary Agency*

17 Sutherland Street, London SW1V 4JU
*tel* 020-7828 1274 *fax* 020-7828 7608
*email* lownie@globalnet.co.uk
*website* www.andrewlownie.co.uk
*Director* Andrew Lownie

Full-length MSS. Biography, history, reference,
current affairs, and packaging journalists and
celebrities for the book market (worldwide 15%).
No reading fee; will suggest a revision.

    *Authors* include Theo Aronson, Juliet Barker, the
Joyce Cary Estate, Tom Devine, Peter Evans, David
Fisher, Jonathan Fryer, Laurence Gardner, Timothy
Good, Lawrence James, Robert Jobson, Leo
McKinstry, Julian Maclaren-Ross Estate, Norma
Major, Sir John Mills, Tom Pocock, Nick Pope, Martin
Pugh, John Rae, Richard Rudgley, Desmond Seward,
David Stafford, Andrew Wheatcroft, Alan Whicker;
*The Oxford Classical Dictionary, The Cambridge Guide
to Literature in English*. Founded 1988.

## Lucas Alexander Whitley – see LAW Ltd

## Jennifer Luithlen Agency

88 Holmfield Road, Leicester LE2 1SB
*tel* 0116-273 8863 *fax* 0116-273 5697
*Agents* Jennifer Luithlen, Penny Luithlen

Not looking for new clients. Children's books; adult
fiction: crime, historical, saga (home 10%, overseas
20%), performance rights (15%). Founded 1986.

## Lutyens & Rubinstein*

231 Westbourne Park Road, London W11 1EB
*tel* 020-7792 4855 *fax* 020-7792 4833
*Directors* Sarah Lutyens, Felicity Rubinstein
*Submissions* Susannah Godman

Fiction and non-fiction, commercial and literary
(home 15%, overseas 20%). Send outline/2 sample
chapters and sae. No reading fee. Founded 1993.

## Duncan McAra

28 Beresford Gardens, Edinburgh EH5 3ES
*tel* 0131-552 1558 *fax* 0131-552 1558
*email* duncanmcara@hotmail.com

Literary fiction; non-fiction: art, architecture,
archaeology, biography, military, Scottish, travel
(home 10%, overseas 20%). Preliminary letter with
sae essential. No reading fee. Founded 1988.

## Eunice McMullen Children's Literary Agent Ltd

Low Ibbotsholme Cottage, Off Bridge Lane,
Troutbeck Bridge, Windermere, Cumbria LA23 1HU
*tel* (01539) 448551 *fax* (01539) 442289
*email* eunicemcmullen@totalise.co.uk
*Director* Eunice McMullen

All types of children's books, particularly picture
books (home 10%, overseas 15%). No unsolicited
scripts. Telephone enquiries only. Founded 1992.

    *Authors* include Wayne Anderson, Sam Childs,
Caroline Jane Church, Jason Cockcroft, Ross Collins,
Charles Fuge, Maggie Kneen, David Melling, Angela
McAllister, Angie Sage and Susan Winter. Founded
1992.

## Andrew Mann Ltd*

1 Old Compton Street, London W1D 5JA
*tel* 020-7734 4751 *fax* 020-7287 9264
*email* manuscript@onetel.net.uk
*Contacts* Anne Dewe, Tina Betts, Sacha Elliot

Full-length MSS. Scripts for TV, cinema, radio and
theatre (home 15%, USA and Europe 20%).
Associated with agents worldwide. No reading fee,
but no unsolicited MSS without preliminary
enquiry and sae. Email submissions – synopses only.
Founded 1968.

## Sarah Manson Literary Agent

6 Totnes Walk, London N2 0AD
*tel* 020-8442 0396
*email* submissions@smliteraryagent.com
*Proprietor* Sarah Manson

Specialises exclusively in fiction for children and
young adults (home 10%, overseas 20%). Send
letter, brief author biography, one-page synopsis,
first 3 chapters with sae. Or send brief email
enquiry with no attachment. Founded 2002.

## Marjacq Scripts

34 Devonshire Place, London W1G 6JW
*tel* 020-7935 9499 *fax* 020-7935 9115
*email* enquiries@marjacq.com
*website* www.marjacq.com
*Contact* Philip Patterson (books), Luke Speed
(film/TV)

All full-length MSS (home 10%, overseas 20%),
including commercial and literary fiction and non-
fiction, crime, thrillers, commercial, women's
fiction, children's, science fiction, history, biography,
sport, travel, health. No poetry. Send first 3 chapters
with synopsis. May suggest revision. Film and TV
rights, screenplays, radio plays, documentaries,
screenplays/radio plays: send full script with 1–2

page short synopsis/outline. Strong interest in writer/directors: send show reel with script. Also looking for documentary concepts and will accept propoals from writer/directors. Sae essential for return of submissions.

*Clients* include: Nathalie Abi-Ezzi, Anita Anderson, Paul Arrowsmith, John Connor, Richard Craze, Andrew Ellard, James Follett, Rosie Goodwin, Ros Jay, Claes Johansen, Chris O'Neill, Michael Taylor, Gordon Torburn, R.D. Wingfield and the Estate of George Markstein. Founded 1974.

## The Marsh Agency Ltd*
11–12 Dover Street, London W1S 4LJ
*tel* 020-7399 2800 *fax* 020-7399 2801
*email* enquiries@marsh-agency.co.uk
*website* www.marsh-agency.co.uk
*Director* Paul Marsh

Specialises in selling international rights in English and foreign language writing. Represents UK, USA and Canadian agencies and publishers, and some individual authors. Also UK rights for general fiction and non-fiction. No TV, film, radio, theatre, poetry or children's. Unsolicited submissions (outline and sample chapters) accepted by email. No reading fee. See also **Paterson Marsh Ltd**. Founded 1994.

## Martinez Literary Agency
60 Oakwood Avenue, London N14 6QL
*tel* 020-8886 5829
*Contacts* Françoise Budd, Mary Martinez

Fiction, children's books, arts and crafts, interior design, autobiographies, popular music, sport and memorabilia (home 15%; USA, overseas and translation 20%; performance rights 20%). Not accepting any new writers. Founded 1988.

## Blanche Marvin
21A St John's Wood High Street, London NW8 7NG
*tel* 020-7722 2313 *fax* 020-7722 2313

Full-length MSS (15%), performance rights. No reading fee but return postage essential.
*Authors* include Christopher Bond.

## MBA Literary Agents Ltd*
62 Grafton Way, London W1T 5DW
*tel* 020-7387 2076 *fax* 020-7387 2042
*email* firstname@mbalit.co.uk
*Contacts* Diana Tyler, John Richard Parker, Meg Davis, Laura Longrigg, David Riding

Handles fiction and non-fiction, and TV, film, radio and theatre scripts (home 15%, overseas 20%; theatre, TV, radio 10%; films 10–20%). No unsolicited material. Works in conjunction with agents in most countries. UK representative for **Writers House LLC**, the Donald Maass Agency, the Martha Millard Agency, the **Frances Collin Agency**,

Montreal Contracts/the Rights Agency and the **Jabberwocky Literary Agency**. Founded 1971.

*Children's authors* include David Colbert, Sally Jones, Garvashe Phinn, Christopher Russell, Mimi Thebo.

## William Morris Agency (UK) Ltd*
52–53 Poland Street, London W1F 7LX
*tel* 020-7534 6800 *fax* 020-7534 6900
*website* www.wma.com
*Managing Director* Stephanie Cabot

Worldwide theatrical and literary agency with offices in New York, Beverly Hills, Nashville and Miami. Handles film and TV scripts, TV formats; fiction and general non-fiction (film/TV 10%, UK books 15%, USA books and translation 20%). No unsolicited material; MSS only when preceded by letter. No reading fee. London office founded 1965.

## Laura Morris Literary Agency
21 Highshore Road, London SE15 5AA
*tel* 020-7732 0153 *fax* 020-7732 9022
*email* laura.morris@btinternet.com
*Director* Laura Morris

Literary fiction, film studies, biography, media, cookery, culture/art, humour (home 10%, overseas 20%). No unsolicitied MSS, no children's books.

*Authors* include Peter Cowie, Laurence Marks and Maurice Gran, David Thomson, Brian Turner, Janni Visman. Founded 1998.

## Judith Murdoch Literary Agency*
19 Chalcot Square, London NW1 8YA
*tel* 020-7722 4197

Full-length fiction only, especially accessible literary and commercial women's fiction (home 15%, overseas 20%). No thrillers, science fiction/fantasy, poetry, short stories or children's. Approach by letter, *not* telephone, sending the first 2 chapters and synopsis. Return postage/sae essential. Editorial advice given; no reading fee. Translation rights handled by the **Marsh Agency Ltd**. Founded 1993.

*Clients* include Meg Hutchinson, Lisa Jewell, Pamela Jooste.

## Maggie Noach Literary Agency*
22 Dorville Crescent, London W6 0HJ
*tel* 020-8748 2926 *fax* 020-8748 8057
*email* m-noach@dircon.co.uk

Very few new clients taken on as it is considered vital to give individual attention to each author's work. High-quality full-length fiction; general non-fiction (especially biography, travel, history); children's books (text only) for reading age 8 upwards. Material submitted on an exclusive basis preferred (home 15%, USA/translation generally 20%). No short stories, poetry, plays, screenplays, cookery, gardening, Mind, Body & Spirit, scientific/

academic/specialist non-fiction or any illustrated books. Send a brief description of the book plus 2–3 sample chapters. Return postage essential. Email attachments will not be opened and faxed submissions will not be considered. No reading fee. Founded 1982.

## Andrew Nurnberg Associates Ltd*
Clerkenwell House, 45–47 Clerkenwell Green, London EC1R 0QX
*tel* 020-7417 8800 *fax* 020-7417 8812

Specialises in the sale of translation rights.

## Alexandra Nye, Writers & Agents
Craigower, 6 Kinnoull Avenue, Dunblane, Perthshire FK15 9JB
*tel* (01786) 825114
*Director* Alexandra Nye

Literary fiction, Scottish history, biographies; no poetry or plays (home 10%, overseas 20%, translation 15%). No phone calls please. Preliminary letter with synopsis preferred; sae essential for return. Reading fee for supply of detailed report on MSS. Founded 1991.

## David O'Leary Literary Agency
10 Lansdowne Court, Lansdowne Rise, London W11 2NR
*tel/fax* 020-77229 1623
*email* d.o'leary@virgin.net

Popular and literary fiction and non-fiction. Special interests: Ireland, history, popular science (Fees: home 10%, overseas 20%, performance rights 15%). No reading fee. Write, call or email before submitting MSS. Please enclose sae.
    *Authors* include Alexander Cordell, Daniel O'Brien, Jim Lusby, Derek Malcolm, Ken Russell. Founded 1988.

## Deborah Owen Ltd*
78 Narrow Street, Limehouse, London E14 8BP
*tel* 020-7987 5119/5441 *fax* 020-7538 4004
*Contact* Deborah Owen

Small agency specialising in only two authors: Delia Smith and Amos Oz. No new authors. Founded 1971.

## Mark Paterson & Associates – see
**Paterson Marsh Ltd**

## Paterson Marsh Ltd*
11–12 Dover Street, London W15 4LJ
*tel* 020-7399 2800 *fax* 020-7399 2801
*email* paterson@patersonmarsh.co.uk
*website* www.patersonmarsh.co.uk
*Contacts* Mark Paterson, Stephanie Ebdon

Book-length MSS; general but with special experience in psychoanalysis, psychotherapy, history and education (20% worldwide including sub-agents' commission). No fiction, articles or short stories except for existing clients. No children's books. Preliminary letter with synopsis, sample material and return postage essential.
    *Authors* include Sigmund Freud, Anna Freud, Hugh Brogan, Donald Winnicott, Peter Moss, Sir Arthur Evans, Dorothy Richardson, Hugh Schonfield, Georg Groddeck, Patrick Casement, John Seely. Founded 1955.

## John Pawsey
60 High Street, Tarring, Worthing, West Sussex BN14 7NR
*tel* (01903) 205167 *fax* (01903) 205167

General non-fiction, particularly biography, popular culture and sport; crime, thriller and suspense fiction only (home 12.5%, overseas 25%). No science fiction, fantasy, horror, poetry, short stories, journalism, children's or original film and stage scripts. Preliminary letter and return postage with all correspondence essential. Works in association with agencies in the USA, Europe and the Far East. Will suggest revision if MS sufficiently promising. No reading fee.
    *Authors* include David Ashforth, Jennie Bond, William Fotheringham, Don Hale, Patricia Hall, Elwyn Hartley Edwards, Dr David Lewis, Anne Mustoe and Kathryn Spink. Founded 1981.

## Maggie Pearlstine Associates Ltd*
31 Ashley Gardens, Ambrosden Avenue, London SW1P 1QE
*tel* 020-7828 4212 *fax* 020-7834 5546
*email* post@pearlstine.co.uk

General non-fiction and fiction. Special interests: history, current affairs, biography, health (home 10–12.5%; overseas, journalism and media 20%). Translation rights handled by **Gillon Aitken Associates Ltd**. No children's, poetry, horror, science fiction, short stories or scripts. Seldom takes on new authors. Prospective clients should write an explanatory letter and enclose a sae and the first chapter only. No submissions accepted by fax, email or from abroad. No reading fee.
    *Authors* include John Biffen, Matthew Baylis, Kate Bingham, Menzies Campbell, Robin Cook, Frank Dobson, Kim Fletcher, Roy Hattersley, Charles Kennedy, Mark Leonard, Quentin Letts, Claire Macdonald, Dr Raj Persaud, Prof Lesley Regan, Hugo Rifkind, Winifred Robinson, Jackie Rowley, Henrietta Spencer-Churchill, Prof Alan Stewart, Prof Robert Winston. Founded 1989.

## The Peters Fraser and Dunlop Group Ltd – see PFD

## PFD*

Drury House, 34–43 Russell Street,
London WC2B 5HA
*tel* 020-7344 1000 *fax* 020-7836 9539
*email* postmaster@pfd.co.uk
*website* www.pfd.co.uk
*Joint Chairmen* Anthony Jones and Tim Corrie,
*Managing Director* Anthony Baring, *Books* Caroline
Dawnay, Michael Sissons, Pat Kavanagh, Charles
Walker, Rosemary Canter (children's), Rosemary
Scoular, Robert Kirby, Simon Trewin, James Gill,
*Serial* Pat Kavanagh, Carol Macarthur, *Film/TV* Tim
Corrie, Anthony Jones, Norman North, Charles
Walker, St John Donald, Natasha Galloway, Louisa
Thompson, Jago Irwin, Lynda Mamy, *Actors* Maureen
Vincent, Dallas Smith, Lindy King, Ruth Cooper,
Ruth Young, Lucy Brazier, Kathryn Fleming, Duncan
Hayes, *Theatre* Kenneth Ewing, St John Donald,
Nicki Stoddart, Rosie Cobbe, *Children's* Rosemary
Canter, *New Media* Rosemary Scoular, *Translation
Rights* Intercontinental Literary Agency,
*Documentary/presenters* Sophie Laurimore, Rosemary
Sconlar, *US Illustrators' Representation* Harriet Kasak,
*PFD New York* Zoë Pagnamenta, Mark Reiter

Handles the full range of books including fiction,
children's and non-fiction as well as scripts for film,
theatre, radio and TV, actors and multimedia
projects (home 10%; USA and translation 20%).
Has 75 years of international experience in all
media. Send a full outline for non-fiction and short
synopsis for fiction with 2–3 sample chapters and
autobiographical note. Screenplays/TV scripts
should be addressed to the 'Film & Script Dept'. The
Children's Dept accepts unsolicited written material
in the form of a covering letter, brief plot summary
and 3 chapters of text; submissions from illustrators
are also welcome. Material submitted on an exclusive
basis preferred; in any event it should be disclosed if
material is being submitted to other agencies or
publishers. Return postage essential. No reading fee.
No guaranteed response to submissions by email.
See website for detailed submissions guidelines.

## Murray Pollinger – see David Higham

### Associates Ltd

## Pollinger Ltd*

9 Staple Inn, Holborn, London WC1V 7QH
*tel* 020-7404 0342 *fax* 020-7242 5737
*email* info@pollingerltd.com
*website* www.pollingerltd.com
*Chairman* Paul Woolf, *Managing Director* Lesley
Pollinger, *Rights Manager* Katy Loffman, *Consultants*
Gerald Leigh Pollinger, Joan Deitch

All types of general trade adult and children's
fiction and non-fiction books; intellectual property
developments, illustrators/photographers (home
15%, translation 20%). Overseas, media and

theatrical associates. No unsolicted material.

*Clients* include Derry Brabbs, Michael Coleman,
Teresa Driscoll, Catherine Fisher, Phillip Gross,
Catherine Johnson, Gary Latham, Kelly McKain,
Gary Paulsen, Nicholas Rhea and Sue Welford. Also
the estates of H.E.Bates, Vera Chapman, Louis
Bromfield, Erskine Caldwell, D.H.Lawrence, John
Masters, W.H.Robinson, Eric Frank Russell, Clifford
D. Simak and other notables. Founded 2002.

## Shelley Power Literary Agency Ltd*

13 rue du Pre Saint Gervais, 75019 Paris, France
*tel* 0142 38 36 49 *fax* 0140 40 70 08
*email* shelley.power@wanadoo.fr

General fiction and non-fiction. Full-length MSS
(home 10%, USA and translation 19%). No
children's books, poetry or plays. Works in
conjunction with agents abroad. No reading fee, but
preliminary letter with return postage as from UK
or France essential. No submissions by email. Also
based in the UK. Founded 1976.

## Elizabeth Puttick Literary Agency*

46 Brookfield Mansions, Highgate West Hill,
London N6 6AT
*tel* 020-8340 6383 *fax* 0870 751 8098
*email* agency@puttick.com
*website* www.puttick.com
*Director* Elizabeth Puttick

Full-length MSS (home 15%, overseas 20%).
General non-fiction with special interest in self-
help, mind, body & spirit, health, childcare, cookery,
business, science, biography, history, current affairs,
women's issues, illustrated books, TV and film tie-
ins. No fiction, poetry, screenplays, drama,
children's books. No reading fee. Send preliminary
letter with synopsis; return postage essential.

*Authors* include William Bloom, Robin Bloor,
Nirmála Herzia, Martin Lewis, Emma Restall Orr.
Founded 1995.

## PVA Management Ltd

Hallow Park, Worcester WR2 6PG
*tel* (01905) 640663 *fax* (01905) 641842
*email* pva@pva.co.uk
*Managing Director* Paul Vaughan

Full-length MSS. Non-fiction only (home 15%,
overseas 20%, performance rights 15%). Please send
synopsis and sample chapters with return postage.

## The Lisa Richards Agency

46 Upper Baggot Street, Dublin 4, Republic of Ireland
*tel* (01) 660 3534 *fax* (01) 660 3545
*email* fogrady@eircom.net
*Contact* Faith O'Grady

Fiction and general non-fiction (home 10%, UK
15%, US and translation 20%, Film and TV 15%).
Approach with proposal and sample chapter for

non-fiction, and 3–4 sample chapters and synopsis for fiction (sae essential). Translation rights handled by the **Marsh Agency Ltd**. No reading fee.

*Authors* include June Considine, Judi Curtin, Denise Deegan, Christine Dwyer Hickey, Tara Heavey, Arlene Hunt, Declan Lynch, Roisin Meaney, Pauline McLynn, Sarah O'Brien. Founded 1998.

## Rogers, Coleridge & White Ltd*
20 Powis Mews, London W11 1JN
*tel* 020-7221 3717 *fax* 020-7229 9084
*Directors* Deborah Rogers, Gill Coleridge, Patricia White (USA, children's), David Miller, Laurence Laluyaux, *Consultant* Ann Warnford-Davis

Full-length book MSS, including children's books (home 10%, USA 15%, translation 20%). No unsolicited MSS, and no submissions by fax or email. Founded 1967.

## Elizabeth Roy Literary Agency
White Cottage, Greatford, Nr Stamford, Lincs. PE9 4PR
*tel* (01778) 560672 *fax* (01778) 560672

Children's fiction and non-fiction – writers and illustrators (home 10–15%, overseas 20%). Send preliminary letter, synopsis and sample chapters with names of publishers and agents previously contacted. Return postage essential. No reading fee. Founded 1990.

## Uli Rushby-Smith Literary Agency
72 Plimsoll Road, London N4 2EE
*tel* 020-7354 2718 *fax* 020-7354 2718
*Director* Uli Rushby-Smith

Fiction and non-fiction, literary and commercial (home 15%, USA/foreign 20%). No poetry, plays or film scripts. Send outline, sample chapters (no disks) and return postage. No reading fee. UK representatives of **Curtis Brown Ltd**, New York (children's books) and Penguin Canada, Penguin South Africa, Columbia University Press (USA), Alice Toledo Agency (Netherlands). Founded 1993.

## Saddler Literary Agency
9 Curzon Road, London W5 1NE
*tel* 020-8998 4868 *fax* 020-8998 8851
*Proprietor* John Saddler

Quality fiction and non-fiction (home 10%, overseas 20%). No science fiction or fantasy. No reading fee. Founded 2001.

## Rosemary Sandberg Ltd
6 Bayley Street, London WC1B 3HB
*tel* 020-7304 4110 *fax* 020-7304 4109
*Directors* Rosemary Sandberg, Ed Victor

Children's writers and illustrators, general fiction and non-fiction. Absolutely no unsolicited MSS: client list is full. Founded 1991.

## The Sayle Literary Agency
Bickerton House, 25–27 Bickerton Road, London N19 5JT
*tel* 020-7263 8681 *fax* 020-7561 0529
*Proprietor* Rachel Calder

Fiction: general and crime. Non-fiction: current affairs, social issues, travel, biographies, history (home 15%, USA/translation 20%). No plays, poetry, textbooks, children's, technical, legal or medical books. No unsolicited MSS. No reading fee but preliminary letter and return postage essential. Overseas associates: Dunow & Carlson Agency, Darhansoff, Verrill and Feldman, Anne Edelstein Literary Agency, Sally Wofford-Girand Agency, **New England Publishing Associates**, USA. Translation rights handled by the **Marsh Agency Ltd**. Film and TV rights handled by **Sayle Screen Ltd**.

## Sayle Screen Ltd
11 Jubilee Place, London SW3 3TD
*tel* 020-7823 3883 *fax* 020-7823 3363
*email* info@saylescreen.com
*website* www.saylescreen.com
*Agents* Jane Villiers, Matthew Bates, Toby Moorcrofts

Specialises in scripts for film, TV, theatre and radio (home 10%, overseas 15–20%). No reading fee. Preliminary letter and return postage essential. Represents film and TV rights in fiction and non-fiction for the **Sayle Literary Agency**, **BlackAmber Books Ltd** and **Greene and Heaton Ltd**. Works in conjunction with agents in New York and Los Angeles.

## Richard Scott Simon Ltd – see Sheil Land Associates Ltd

## Sfakianos Moylett Literary Agency
3 Askew Road, London W12 9AA
*tel* 020-8740 0454 *fax* 020-8354 3065
*Contacts* Lisa Moylett, Nathalie Sfakianos

Commercial and literary fiction and non-fiction (home 15%, overseas 15%, film /TV 15%). Fiction: thrillers, crime/mystery; women's literary and contemporary. Non-fiction: biography; history and current affairs. Send synopsis, first 3 chapters and sae (essential). No disk or email submissions. No reading fee. Works with foreign agents.

## The Sharland Organisation Ltd
The Manor House, Manor Street, Raunds, Northants. NN9 6JW
*tel* (01933) 626600 *fax* (01933) 624860
*email* tsoshar@aol.com
*website* www.sharlandorganisation.co.uk
*Directors* Mike Sharland, Alice Sharland

Specialises in film, TV, stage and radio rights throughout the world (home 15%, overseas 20%); also negotiates multimedia, interactive TV deals, speaking engagements and computer game contracts. Preliminary letter and return postage is essential. No reading fee. Works in conjunction with overseas agents. Founded 1988.

## Anthony Sheil

18–21 Cavaye Place, London SW10 9PT
*tel* 020-7373 8672 *fax* 020-7373 6002
*email* anthony@gillonaitken.co.uk
*Proprietor* Anthony Sheil, Mary Pachnos

Quality fiction and non-fiction (home 10%, overseas 20%). No reading fee. Works in conjunction with **Gillon Aitken Associates Ltd**.

*Authors* include Caroline Alexander, John Banville, Josephine Cox, John Fowles, John Keegan, Robert Wilson.

## Sheil Land Associates Ltd*

43 Doughty Street, London WC1N 2LH
*tel* 020-7405 9351 *fax* 020-7831 2127
*email* info@sheilland.co.uk
*Agents UK and US* Sonia Land, Luigi Bonomi, Vivien Green, Amanda Preston, *Film/theatre/TV* John Rush, Roland Baggott, *Foreign* Amelia Cummins, Vanessa Forbes

Full-length general, commercial, quality and literary fiction and non-fiction, including: social politics, history, military history, gardening, thrillers, crime, romance, drama, biography, travel, cookery, humour, UK and foreign estates (home 15%, USA/translation 20%). Also theatre, film, radio and TV scripts. Welcomes approaches from new clients either to start or to develop their careers. Preliminary letter with sae essential. No reading fee. Overseas associates: Georges Borchardt, Inc. (Richard Scott Simon). UK representatives for Farrar, Straus & Giroux, Inc. US film and TV representation: CAA, APA and others.

*Clients* include Peter Ackroyd, Henry Blofeld, Melvyn Bragg, Stephanie Calman, Steven Carroll, Gennaro Contaldo, Catherine Cookson Estate, Anna del Conte, Elizabeth Corley, Seamus Deane, Charlie Dimmock, Alan Drury, Erik Durschmied, Alan Garner, Robert Green, Bonnie Greer, Susan Hill, Richard Holmes, HRH The Prince of Wales, John Humphrys, Mark Irving, Simon Kernick, James Long, Richard Mabey, Colin McDowell, Richard Madeley and Judy Finnigan, Patrick O'Brian Estate, Esther Rantzen, Pam Rhodes, Jean Rhys Estate, Steve Rider, Martin Riley, Colin Schindler, Tom Sharpe, Alan Sillitoe, Martin Stephen, Brian Sykes, Jeffrey Tayler, Rachel de Thame, Alan Titchmarsh, Rose Tremain, Phil Vickery, Tommy Walsh, John Wilsher, Paul Wilson, Chris Woodhead. Founded 1962.

## Caroline Sheldon Literary Agency*

*London office* 71 Hillgate Place, London W8 7SS
*tel* 020-7727 9102
*mailing address for MSS* Thorley Manor Farm, Thorley, Yarmouth, Isle of Wight PO41 0SJ

*tel* (01983) 760205
*Proprietor* Caroline Sheldon

Full-length MSS. General fiction, women's fiction, and children's books (home 10%, overseas 20%). No reading fee. Synopsis and first 3 chapters with large sae in case of return required initially. Founded 1985.

## Jeffrey Simmons

15 Penn House, Mallory Street, London NW8 8SX
*tel* 020-7224 8917 *fax* 020-7224 8918
*email* jas@london-inc.com

Specialises in fiction (no science fiction, horror or fantasy), biography, autobiography, show business, personality books, law, crime, politics, world affairs. Full-length MSS (home from 10%, overseas from 15%). Will suggest revision. No reading fee, but preliminary letter essential.

## Sinclair-Stevenson

3 South Terrace, London SW7 2TB
*tel* 020-7581 2550 *fax* 020-7581 2550
*Directors* Christopher Sinclair-Stevenson, Deborah Sinclair-Stevenson

Full-length MSS (home 10%, USA/translation 20%). General – no children's books. No reading fee; will suggest a revision. Founded 1995.

## Robert Smith Literary Agency Ltd*

12 Bridge Wharf, 156 Caledonian Road, London N1 9UU
*tel* 020-7278 2444 *fax* 020-7833 5680
*email* robertsmith.literaryagency@virgin.net
*Directors* Robert Smith, Anne Smith

Non-fiction: autobiography and biography, health and nutrition, cookery, lifestyle, popular culture, music, TV and film tie-ins, true crime, investigative journalism, illustrated books (home 15%, overseas 20%). No unsolicited MSS. No reading fee. Will suggest revision.

*Authors* include Martin Allen, Carol Clerk, Stewart Evans, Neil and Christine Hamilton, James Haspiel, Roberta Kray, Norman Parker, Nikola Pleasence, Mike Reid, Prof William Rubinstein, Keith Skinner, Douglas Thompson. Founded 1997.

## Abner Stein*

10 Roland Gardens, London SW7 3PH
*tel* 020-7373 0456 *fax* 020-7370 6316
*Contacts* Abner Stein, Arabella Stein

Full-length and short MSS (home 10%, overseas 20%). No reading fee, but no unsolicited MSS; preliminary letter and return postage required.

## Micheline Steinberg Associates

4th floor, 104 Great Portland Street, London W1W 6PE
*tel* 020-7631 1310 *fax* 020-7631 1146
*email* info@steinplays.com

Full-length MSS – theatre, films, TV, radio (home 10%, overseas 15%). Dramatic Associate for **Pollinger Ltd**; works in conjunction with agents in USA and other countries. No reading fee, but preliminary letter essential and return postage with MSS. Founded 1987.

## Rochelle Stevens & Co.
2 Terretts Place, Upper Street, London N1 1QZ
*tel* 020-7359 3900 *fax* 020-7354 5729
*email* info@rochellestevens.com
*Proprietor* Rochelle Stevens, *Associates* Frances Arnold, Lucy Fawcett

Drama scripts for film, TV, theatre and radio (home 10%, overseas 15%). Preliminary letter, CV and sae essential. No reading fee. Founded 1984.

## Shirley Stewart Literary Agency
3rd Floor, 21 Denmark Street, London WC2H 8NA
*tel* 020-7836 4440 *fax* 020-7836 3482
*Director* Shirley Stewart

Specialises in literary fiction and general non-fiction (home 10–15%, overseas 20%). No poetry, plays, film scripts, science fiction, fantasy or children's books. No reading fee. Send preliminary letter, synopsis and first 3 chapters plus return postage. Founded 1993.

## The Susijn Agency
3rd Floor, 64 Great Titchfield Street,
London W1W 7QH
*tel* 020-7580 6341 *fax* 020-7580 8626
*email* info@thesusijnagency.com
*website* www.thesusijnagency.com
*Director* Laura Susijn

Specialises in world rights in English and non-English language literature: literary fiction and general non-fiction (home 15%, overseas 20%, theatre/film/TV/ radio 15%). Send synopsis and 2 sample chapters. No reading fee.

*Authors* include Peter Ackroyd, Uzma Aslam Khan, Gilad Atzman, Robin Baker, Robert Craig, Radhika Jha, Jeffrey Moore, Anita Nair, Karl Shaw, Paul Sussman, Dubravka Ugrešic;, Alex Wheatle, Adam Zameenzad. Founded 1998.

## Talent Media Group t/a ICM
Oxford House, 76 Oxford Street,
London W1D 1BS
*tel* 020-7636 6565 *fax* 020-7323 0101
*email* writers@icmlondon.co.uk
*Directors* Duncan Heath, Susan Rodgers, Lyndsey Posner, Sally Long-Innes, Paul Lyon-Maris, *Literary Agents* Susan Rodgers, Jessica Sykes, Catherine King, Greg Hunt, Hugo Young, Michael McCoy, Duncan Heath, Paul Lyon-Maris

Specialises in scripts for film, theatre, TV, radio (home 10%, overseas 10%).

## The Tennyson Agency
10 Cleveland Avenue, London SW20 9EW
*tel* 020-8543 5939
*email* enquiries@tenagy.co.uk
*website* www.tenagy.co.uk
*Theatre, TV & Film Scripts* Christopher Oxford, *Arts/Humanities* Adam Sheldon

Scripts and related material for theatre, film and TV (home 15%, overseas 20%). No reading fee.

*Clients* include Vivienne Allen, Tony Bagley, Iain Grant, Jonathan Holloway, Julian Howell, Philip Hurd-Wood, Joanna Leigh, Steve Macgregor, John Ryan, Walter Saunders, Diana Ward. Founded 2002.

## J.M. Thurley Management
Archery House, 33 Archery Square, Walmer, Deal, Kent CT14 7JA
*tel* (01304) 371421 *fax* (01304) 371416
*email* JMThurley@aol.com
*Contact* Jon Thurley

Specialises in commercial and literary full-length fiction and commercial work for film and TV. No plays, poetry, short stories, articles or fantasy. No reading fee but preliminary letter and sae essential. Editorial/creative advice provided to clients (home 15%, overseas 20%). Links with leading US and European agents. Founded 1976.

## Lavinia Trevor*
The Glasshouse, 49A Goldhawk Road,
London W12 8QP
*tel* 020-8749 8481 *fax* 020-8749 7377

Fiction and non-fiction, including popular science, for the general reader. No children's books, poetry or science fiction. No reading fee. Brief autobiographical letter, approx. first 50pp and sae. Founded 1993.

## Jane Turnbull*
Barn Cottage, Veryan, Truro TR2 5QA
*tel* (01872) 501317

Fiction and non-fiction (home 10%, USA/translation 20%), performance rights (15%). No science fiction, romantic fiction, children's or short stories. Works in conjunction with **Gillon Aitken Associates Ltd** for translation rights. No reading fee. Preliminary letter and sae essential; no unsolicited MSS. Founded 1986.

## United Authors Ltd
11–15 Betterton Street, London WC2H 9BP
*tel* 020-7470 8886 *fax* 020-7470 8887
*email* editorial@unitedauthors.co.uk

Fiction, non-fiction, children's, biography, travel. Full-length MSS (home 12%, overseas 15%), short MSS (12%/20%), film and radio (15%/20%), TV (15%/15%). Will suggest revision.

*Authors* include Charlotte Bingham, Terence Brady, Sydney Gilliatt, Peter Willet, and the Estate of John Bingham. Founded 1998.

## Ed Victor Ltd*
6 Bayley Street, Bedford Square, London WC1B 3HE
*tel* 020-7304 4100 *fax* 020-7304 4111
*email* sophie@edvictor.com
*Executive Chairman* Ed Victor, *Joint Managing Directors* Sophie Hicks, Margaret Phillips, *Directors* Carol Ryan, Graham C. Greene CBE, Leon Morgan, Hitesh Shah, *Editorial Director* Philippa Harrison

Fiction, non-fiction and children's books (home 15%, USA 15%, children's 10%, translation 20%). No short stories, poetry or film/TV scripts or plays. No reading fee. No unsolicited MSS. No response to submissions by email. Represented in all foreign markets.

*Authors* include Eoin Colfer, Sir Ranulph Fiennes, Frederick Forsyth, A.A. Gill, Josephine Hart, Jack Higgins, Erica Jong, Nigella Lawson, Kathy Lette, Allan Mallinson, Nigel Nicolson, Anne Robinson, and the Estates of Douglas Adams, Raymond Chandler, Dame Iris Murdoch, Sir Stephen Spender, Irving Wallace. Founded 1976.

## Robin Wade Literary Agency
33 Cormorant Lodge, Thomas More Street, London E1W 1AU
*tel* 020-7488 4171 *fax* 020-7488 4172
*email* rw@rwla.com
*website* www.rwla.com
*Director* Robin Wade, *Associate* Jo Kitching

General fiction and non-fiction, but no poetry, plays or short stories (home 10%, overseas 20%). Send descriptive preliminary email. No reading fee. Founded 2001.

## Watson, Little Ltd*
Capo Di Monte, Windmill Hill, London NW3 6RJ
*tel* 020-7431 0770 *fax* 020-7431 7225
*email* enquiries@watsonlittle.com
*Directors* Sheila Watson, Amanda Little, Sugra Zaman

Adult and children's fiction and non-fiction (home 15%, translation 19%, film/video/TV 10%). Fiction: commercial women's, crime and literary. Non-fiction special interests: history, science, popular psychology, self-help, business and general leisure books. No short stories, TV/play/film scripts or poetry. Not interested in exclusively academic writers. Send informative preliminary letter and synopsis with return postage. No unsolicited MSS. No reading fee. Works in conjunction with worldwide agents. Film and TV associates: the **Sharland Organisation Ltd** and Hurley Lowe Management.

## A.P. Watt Ltd*
20 John Street, London WC1N 2DR
*tel* 020-7405 6774 *fax* 020-7831 2154 (books), 020-7430 1952 (drama)
*email* apw@apwatt.co.uk
*website* www.apwatt.co.uk
*Directors* Caradoc King, Linda Shaughnessy, Derek Johns, Georgia Garrett, Nick Harris, Natasha Fairweather, Shelia Crowley

Full-length MSS; dramatic works for all media (home 10%, USA and foreign 20% including commission to foreign agent). No poetry. No reading fee. No unsolicited MSS.

## WCA Licensing
3 Calais Street, London SE5 9LP
*tel* 020-7564 5898 *fax* 020-7564 3501
*email* ecollins@wca.co.uk
*Partners* Elaine Collins, Arabella Woods

Specialises in non-fiction: cookery, lifestyle, gardening, TV tie-ins (home 15%, overseas 20%). No reading fee; will suggest a revision. Founded 1993.

## Josef Weinberger Plays Ltd
12–14 Mortimer Street, London W1T 3JJ
*tel* 020-7580 2827 *fax* 020-7436 9616

Specialises in stage plays. Works in conjunction with overseas agents. No unsolicited MSS; preliminary letter essential. Founded 1938.

## Dinah Wiener Ltd*
12 Cornwall Grove, London W4 2LB
*tel* 020-8994 6011 *fax* 020-8994 6044

Full-length MSS only, fiction and general non-fiction (home 15%, overseas 20%), film and TV in association (15%). No plays, scripts, poetry, short stories or children's books. No reading fee, but preliminary letter and return postage essential.

## Jonathan Williams Literary Agency
Rosney Mews, Upper Glenageary Road, Glenageary, Co. Dublin, Republic of Ireland
*tel* (01) 2803482 *fax* (01) 2803482
*Director* Jonathan Williams

General fiction and non-fiction, preferably by Irish authors (home 10%). Will suggest revision; no reading fee unless a very fast decision is required. Return postage appreciated (no British stamps – please use IRCs). Sub-agents in Germany, Italy, France, Denmark, Japan. Founded 1981.

## Elisabeth Wilson
24 Thornhill Square, London N1 1BQ
*fax* 020-7609 6045

Rights agent and consultant; illustrated books, non-fiction (no children's). No reading fee. Founded 1979.

## The Wylie Agency (UK) Ltd
17 Bedford Square, London WC1B 3JA
*tel* 020-7908 5900 *fax* 020-7908 5901
*President* Andrew Wylie

Literary fiction and non-fiction (home 10%, overseas 20%, USA 15%). No unsolicited MSS; send preliminary letter with 2 sample chapters and sae in first instance. Founded 1996.

# Literary agents overseas

Before submitting material, writers are advised to send a preliminary letter with an sae or IRC (International Reply Coupon) and to ascertain terms. Listings for overseas literary agents other than in the USA start on page 427.

*Member of the Association of Authors' Representatives

## USA

### American Play Company Inc.
19 West 44th Street, Suite 1204, New York, NY 10036
*tel* 212-921-0545 *fax* 212-869-4032
*President* Sheldon Abend

### AMG/Renaissance – see The Firm

### The Axelrod Agency*
49 Main Street, PO Box 357, Chatham, NY 12037
*tel* 518-392-2100 *fax* 518-392-2944
*President* Steven Axelrod

Full-length MSS. Fiction and non-fiction, software (home 15%, overseas 20%), film and TV rights (15%); will suggest revision where appropriate. Works with overseas agents. No reading fee. Founded 1983.

### The Balkin Agency Inc.*
PO Box 222, Amherst, MA 01004
*tel* 413-548-9835 *fax* 413-548-9836
*email* balkin@crocker.com
*Director* Richard Balkin, *European and British Representative* Chandler Crawford Agency USA

Full-length MSS – adult non-fiction only (home 15%, overseas 20%). Query first. May suggest revision. No reading fee.

### Virginia Barber Literary Agency Inc., The Writers Shop – see William Morris Agency Inc.

### Berman, Boals & Flynn Inc.*
208 West 30th Street, Suite 401, New York, NY 10001
*tel* 212-868-1068 *fax* 212-868-1052
*Agents* Judy Boals, Jim Flynn

Dramatic writing only (and only by recommendation).

### Georges Borchardt Inc.*
136 East 57th Street, New York, NY 10022
*tel* 212-753-5785 *fax* 212-838-6518
*Directors* Georges Borchardt, Anne Borchardt

Full-length and short MSS (home/British/performance 15%, translations 20%). Agents in most foreign countries. No unsolicited MSS. No reading fee. Founded 1967.

### Brandt & Hochman Literary Agents Inc.*
1501 Broadway, New York, NY 10036
*tel* 212-840-5760
*British Representative* A.M. Heath & Co. Ltd

Full-length and short MSS (home 15%, overseas 20%), performance rights (15%). No reading fee.

### The Helen Brann Agency Inc.*
94 Curtis Road, Bridgewater, CT 06752
*tel* 860-354-9580 *fax* 860-355-2572

### Carlisle & Company*
121 East 17th Street, New York, NY 10003, USA
*tel* 212-813-1881 *fax* 212-813-9567
*website* www.carlisleco.com
*Directors* Michael V. Carlisle, Emma Parry, Christy D. Fletcher

Narrative non-fiction, science, history, biography, literary fiction (home 15%, overseas 20%). Founded 1998.

### Maria Carvainis Agency Inc.*
1350 Avenue of the Americas, Suite 2905, New York, NY 10019
*tel* 212-245-6365 *fax* 212-245-7196
*President* Maria Carvainis, *Executive Vice President* Frances Kuffel

Adult fiction and non-fiction (home 15%, overseas 20%). Fiction: all categories except science fiction and fantasy, especially literary and mainstream; mystery, thrillers and suspense; historical, Regency, contemporary women's, young adult. Non-fiction: politics and film history, biography and memoir, medicine and women's issues; business, finance, psychology, popular science. Works in conjunction with foreign, TV and movie agents. No reading fee. Query first; no unsolicited MSS. No queries by fax or email.

### Frances Collin Literary Agent*
PO Box 33, Wayne, PA 19087-0033
*tel* 610-254-0555

Full-length MSS (home 15%, overseas 20%, performance rights 20%). Specialisations of interest to UK writers: mysteries, women's fiction, history, biography, science fiction, fantasy. No screenplays. No reading fee. No unsolicited MSS. Letter queries must include sufficient IRCs. Works in conjunction with agents worldwide. Founded 1948; successor to Marie Rodell-Frances Collin Literary Agency.

## Don Congdon Associates Inc.*

156 Fifth Avenue, Suite 625, New York, NY 10010
*tel* 212-645-1229 *fax* 212-727-2688
*email* dca@doncongdon.com
*Agents* Don Congdon, Michael Congdon, Susan Ramer, Cristina Concepcion

Full-length and short MSS. General fiction and non-fiction (home 15%, overseas 19%), performance rights (15%); will sometimes suggest revision. Works with co-agents overseas. No reading fee but no unsolicited MSS – query first with return postage or sase for reply. Does not accept phone calls from querying authors. Founded 1983.

## Richard Curtis Associates Inc.

171 East 74th Street, Floor 2, New York, NY 10021
*tel* 212-772-7363 *fax* 212-772-7393
*website* www.curtisagency.com
*President* Richard Curtis

All types of commercial non-fiction (home 15%, overseas 25%, film/TV 15%). Will suggest revision. No reading fee. Send sase with all queries. Foreign rights handled by Baror International. Founded 1970.

## Curtis Brown Ltd*

10 Astor Place, New York, NY 10003
*tel* 212-473-5400
*Branch office* 1750 Montgomery Street, San Francisco, CA 94111
*tel* 415-954-8566
*President* Peter Ginsberg, *Ceo* Timothy Knowlton
*Contact* Query Department

Fiction and non-fiction, juvenile, film and TV rights. No unsolicited MSS; query first with sase. No reading fee; no handling fees.

## Joan Daves Agency

21 West 26th Street, New York, NY 10010
*tel* 212-685-2663 *fax* 212-685-1781
*Director* Jennifer Lyons, *Assistant* Katie La Storia

One-page query letter (home 15%, overseas 20%, film 15%). No reading fee. Subsidiary of **Writers House LLC**. Founded in 1952 by Joan Daves.

## Sandra Dijkstra Literary Agency*

PMB 515, 1155 Camino Del Mar, Del Mar, CA 92104-2605
*tel* 858-755-3115 *fax* 858-792-2822
*email* sdla@dijikstraagency.com
*President* Sandra Dijkstra

Fiction and non-fiction: narrative, history, business, psychology, science, memoir/biography, contemporary, women's, suspense; selected children's projects (home 15%, overseas 20%).

Works in conjunction with foreign and film agents. All submissions must include synopsis and sase (or IRC). No reading fee. Founded 1981.

## Donadio & Ashworth Inc.*

121 West 27th Street, Suite 704, New York, NY 10001
*tel* 212-691-8077 *fax* 212-633-2837
*Owner* Candida Donadio, *Associates* Edward Hibbert, Neil Olson, Peter Steinberg, Ira Silverberg
Literary fiction and non-fiction.

## Dunham Literary, Inc.*

156 Fifth Avenue, Suite 625, New York, NY 10010-7002
*website* www.dunhamlit.com
*Contact* Jennie Dunham

Literary fiction and non-fiction, alternative spirituality, children's books (home 15%, overseas 20%). No reading fee. Founded 2000.

## Dystel & Goderich Literary Management*

One Union Square West, New York, NY 10003
*tel* 212-627-9100 *fax* 212-627-9313
*website* www.dystel.com
*Contacts* Jane D. Dystel, Miriam Goderich, Stacey Glick, Michael Bourret, Jim McCarthy, Jessica Papin

Full-length and short MSS (home 15%, overseas 19%, film, TV and radio 15%). General fiction and non-fiction: literary and commercial fiction; narrative non-fiction; self-help; cookbooks; parenting; children's books; science fiction/fantasy. No reading fee. Founded 1994.

## Peter Elek Associates/The Content Company, Inc.

5111 JFK Boulevard East, West New York, NJ 07093
*tel* 201-558-0323 *fax* 201-558-0307
*email* info@theliteraryagency.com
*website* www.theliteraryagency.com
*Directors* Peter Elek, Helene W. Elek *Submissions* Lauren Mactas

Full-length fiction/non-fiction. Illustrated adult non-fiction: style, culture, popular history, popular science, current affairs; juvenile picture books (home 15%, overseas 20%), performance rights (20%); will sometimes suggest revision. Works with overseas agents. No reading fee. Experienced in licensing for multimedia, online and off-line. Founded 1979.

## Ann Elmo Agency Inc.*

60 East 42nd Street, New York, NY 10165
*tel* 212-661-2880 *fax* 212-661-2883
*Director* Lettie Lee

Full-length fiction and non-fiction MSS (home 15%, overseas 20%), theatre (15%). Works with foreign agencies. No reading fee. Send query letter only with sase or IRC.

## Diana Finch Literary Agency

116 West 23rd Street, Suite 500, New York, NY 10011
*tel* 646-375-2081 *fax* 212-851-8405
*email* diana.finch@verizon.net
*Owner* Diana Finch

Memoirs, narrative non-fiction, literary fiction
(home 15%, overseas 20%). No reading fee.
Founded 2003.

## The Firm

9465 Wilshire Boulevard, Beverly Hills, CA 90212
*tel* 310-860-8000 *fax* 310-860-8132
*Contacts* Alan Nevins, Irv Schwartz, Michael Prevett

Full-length MSS. Fiction and non-fiction, plays
(home 15%, overseas 20%), film and TV rights
(home 10%, overseas 20%), performance rights. No
unsolicited MSS; query first, submit outline. No
reading fee. Founded 1934.

## ForthWrite Literary Agency & Speaker's Bureau/Keller Media Inc

100 Wilshire Boulevard, Suite 625, Santa Monica,
CA 90401
*tel* 310-394-8940 *fax* 310-394-9857
*email* agent@kellermedia.com
*website* www.kellermedia.com
*Owner* Wendy Keller

We help authors get book deals and speaking
engagements worldwide. Only non-fiction: business,
self-help popular psychology, how-to. Subjects
include: animals, art, horticulture/gardening,
archaeology, European history (especially English),
biography, health (especially homeopathy and
alternative medicines), parenting, coffee table
(illustrated) books, crafts (bobbin lace, handicrafts,
etc), nature, psychology. Send IRC with query.
Response in 8 weeks. Founded 1988.

## The Fox Chase Agency Inc.

Walnut Hill Plaza, Suite 140, 150 South Warner
Road, King of Prussia, PA 19406
*tel* 610-341-9840 *fax* 610-341-9842

## Jeanne Fredericks Literary Agency Inc.*

221 Benedict Hill Road, New Canaan, CT 06840
*tel* 203-972-3011 *fax* 203-972-3011
*email* jfredrks@optonline.net

Quality non-fiction, especially health, science,
women's issues, gardening, antiques and decorative
arts, biography, cookbooks, popular reference,
business, natural history (home 15%, overseas
20%). No reading fee. Query first, enclosing sase.
Member of AAR and Authors Guild. Founded 1997.

## Robert A. Freedman Dramatic Agency Inc.*

1501 Broadway, Suite 2310, New York, NY 10036
*tel* 212-840-5760

Plays, motion picture and TV scripts. Send letter of
enquiry first, with sase. No reading fee.

## Samuel French Inc.*

45 West 25th Street, New York, NY 10010
*tel* 212-206-8990 *fax* 212-206-1429
*President* Charles R. Van Nostrand

Play publishers; authors' representatives. No reading
fee.

## Sarah Jane Freyman Literary Agency

59 West 71st Street, Suite 9B, New York, NY 10023
*tel* 212-362-9277 *fax* 212-501-8240
*email* sjfs@aol.com
*President* Sarah Jane Freymann

Book-length fiction and general non-fiction. Special
interest in serious non-fiction, mainstream
commercial fiction, contemporary women's fiction,
Latino American, Asian American, African American
fiction and non-fiction. Non-fiction: women's issues,
biography, health/fitness, psychology, self-help,
spiritual, natural science, cookbooks, pop culture.
Works in conjunction with **Abner Stein** in London.
No reading fee. Query with sase. Founded 1974.

## Jay Garon-Brooke Associates Inc. – see

Pinder, Lane & Garon-Brooke Associates Ltd

## Gelfman Schneider Literary Agents Inc.*

250 West 57th Street, Suite 2515, New York, NY 10107
*tel* 212-245-1993 *fax* 212-245-8678
*Directors* Jane Gelfman, Deborah Schneider

General adult fiction and non-fiction (home 15%,
overseas 20%). Works in conjunction with **Curtis
Brown**, London. Will suggest revision. No reading
fee but please send sase for return of material.

## Goodman Associates, Literary Agents*

500 West End Avenue, New York, NY 10024
*tel* 212-873-4806
*Partners* Arnold P. Goodman, Elise Simon Goodman

Adult book length fiction and non-fiction (home
15%, overseas 20%). No reading fee. Accept new
clients by referral only. Founded 1976.

## Sanford J. Greenburger Associates Inc.*

55 Fifth Avenue, New York, NY 10003
*tel* 212-206-5600 *fax* 212-463-8718
*website* www.greenburger.com
*Contacts* Heide Lange, Faith Hamlin, Theresa Park,
Elyse Cheney, Daniel Mandel, PeterMcGuigan, Julie
Barker, Matt Bialer

Fiction and non-fiction, film and TV rights. No
unsolicited MSS; query first. No reading fee.

## The Joy Harris Literary Agency Inc.*

156 Fifth Avenue, Suite 617, New York,
NY 10010-7002

*tel* 212-924-6269 *fax* 212-924-6609
*email* gen.office@jhlitagent.com
*President* Joy Harris

## John Hawkins & Associates Inc.*
71 West 23rd Street, Suite 1600, New York, NY 10010
*tel* 212-807-7040 *fax* 212-807-9555
*website* www.jhaliterary.com
*President* John Hawkins, *Vice-President* William
Reiss, *Foreign Rights* Moses Cardona, *Other Agents*
Warren Frazier, Anne Hawkins

Fiction, non-fiction, juvenile. No reading fee.
Founded 1893.

## The Jeff Herman Agency LLC
PO Box 1522, Stockblidge, MA 01262
*tel* 413-298-0077 *fax* 413-298-8188
*email* jeff@jeffherman.com
*website* www.jeffherman.com

Business, reference, popular psychology, computers,
health, spirituality, general non-fiction (home/overseas
15%); will suggest revision where appropriate. Works
with overseas agents. No reading fee. Founded 1986.

## Frederick Hill Bonnie Nadell Inc.
1842 Union Street, San Francisco, CA 94123
*tel* 415-921-2910 *fax* 415-921-2802
*Branch office* 505 North Robertson Blvd,
Los Angeles, CA 90048
*tel* 310-860-9605 *fax* 310-860-9672

Full-length fiction and non-fiction (home 15%,
overseas 20%). Send query letter initially. Works in
conjunction with agents in Scandinavia, France,
Germany, Holland, Japan, Spain. No reading fee.
Founded 1979.

## IMG Literary – see Lisa Queen IMG Literary

## International Creative Management Inc.*
40 West 57th Street, New York, NY 10019
*tel* 212-556-5600 *fax* 212-556-5665
*London office* 4–6 Soho Square, London W1D 3PZ
*tel* 020-7432 0800 *fax* 020-7432 0808

No unsolicited MSS; send query letter.

## Janklow & Nesbit Associates
445 Park Avenue, New York, NY 10022
*tel* 212-421-1700 *fax* 212-980-3671, 212-355 1403
*email* postmaster@janklow.com
*Partners* Morton L. Janklow, Lynn Nesbit, *Senior
Vice President* Anne Sibbald
*Agents* Tina Bennett, Amy Howell, Luke Janklow,
Richard Morris, Eric Simonoff, *Foreign rights* Cullen
Stanley, Dorothy Vincent, Cecile Barendsma, Kate
Schafer

Commercial and literary fiction and non-fiction.
No unsolicited MSS. Works in conjunction with
**Janklow & Nesbit (UK) Ltd.** Founded 1989.

## JCA Literary Agency Inc.*
27 West 20th Street, Suite 1103, New York, NY 10011
*tel* 212-807-0888
*Contacts* Jeff Gerecke, Tony Outhwaite, Peter
Steinberg

Adult fiction and non-fiction. No unsolicited MSS;
query first.

## Barbara S. Kouts, Literary Agent*
PO Box 560, Bellport, NY 11713
*tel* 631-286-1278 *fax* 631-286-1538

Full-length MSS. Fiction and non-fiction, children's
and adult (home 15%, overseas 20%); will suggest
revision. Works with overseas agents. No reading
fee. Send query letter first. Founded 1980.

## The Lazear Agency Inc./Talkback
431 2nd Street, Ste 300, Hudson, WI 54016
*tel* 715-531-0012 *fax* 715-531-0016
*Contacts* Jonathon Lazear, Wendy Lazear, Christi
Cardenas, Julie Mayo

Fiction: full-length MSS; non-fiction: proposals.
Adult fiction and non-fiction; film and TV rights;
foreign language rights; audio, video and electronic
rights (home 15%, overseas 20%). No reading fee.
No unsolicited MSS; 2–3 page query first with sase
for response. No faxed queries. Founded 1984.

**Talkback: A Speaker's Bureau**: book packaging and
select entertainment management.

## The Lescher Agency Inc.*
47 East 19th Street, New York, NY 10003
*tel* 212-529-1790 *fax* 212-529-2716
*email* susanlescher@aol.com
*Director* Susan Lescher

Full-length MSS (home 15%, overseas 25%). No
unsolicited MSS; query first with sase, or email. No
reading fee.

## Ellen Levine Literary Agency Inc. – see
Trident Media Group

## Sterling Lord Literistic Inc.
65 Bleecker Street, New York, NY 10012
*tel* 212-780-6050 *fax* 212-780-6095
*Directors* Sterling Lord, Peter Matson, Philippa
Brophy

Full-length and short MSS (home 15%, overseas
20%), performance rights (15%). Will suggest
revision. No reading fee.

## Margret McBride Literary Agency*
7744 Fay Avenue, Suite 201, La Jolla, CA 92037
*tel* 858-454-1550 *fax* 858-454-2156
*President* Margret McBride

Business, mainstream fiction and non-fiction
(home 15%, overseas 25%). No poetry or children's

books. No reading fee. Submit query letter with sase to Margret McBride. Founded 1981.

## Gerard McCauley Agency Inc.*
PO Box 844, Katonah, NY 10536
*tel* 914-232-5700

Specialises in history, biography, public affairs for the general reader.

## Anita D. McClellan Associates*
50 Stearns Street, Cambridge, MA 02138
*tel* 617-576-6950
*Director* Anita D. McClellan

General fiction and non-fiction. Full-length MSS (home 15%, overseas 20%). Will suggest revision for agency clients. No unsolicited MSS. Send preliminary letter and sase bearing US postage or IRC.

## McIntosh & Otis Inc.*
353 Lexington Avenue, New York, NY 10016
*tel* 212-687-7400 *fax* 212-687-6894
*Adult* Eugene H. Winick, Samuel L. Pinkus, Elizabeth Winick, *Juvenile* Christina Biamonte, Tracey Adams, *Film and TV* Evva Joan Pryor

Adult and juvenile literary fiction and non-fiction, film and TV rights. No unsolicited MSS; query first with outline, sample chapters and sase. No reading fee. Founded 1928.

## Carol Mann Agency*
55 Fifth Avenue, New York, NY 10003
*tel* 212-206-5635 *fax* 212-675-4809
*Associates* Carol Mann, James Fitzgerald, Kim Goldstein, Leyhla Ahuile

Psychology, popular history, biography, pop culture, general non-fiction; fiction (home 15%, overseas 20%). Works in conjunction with foreign agents. No reading fee. Founded 1977.

## Mildred Marmur Associates Ltd*
2005 Palmer Avenue, PMB 127, Larchmont, NY 10538-2469
*tel* 914-834-1170 *fax* 914-834-2840
*email* marmur@westnet.com,
lebowitz@westnet.com
*President* Mildred Marmur, *Associate* Jane Lebowitz

Not taking on any new clients. Founded 1987.

## The Evan Marshall Agency*
Six Tristam Place, Pine Brook, NJ 07058-9445
*tel* 973-882-1122 *fax* 973-882-3099
*email* evanmarshall@thenovelist.com
*website* www.thenovelist.com
*President* Evan Marshall

General fiction (home 15%, overseas 20%). Works in conjunction with overseas agents. Will suggest revision; no reading fee. Founded 1987.

## The Marton Agency Inc.*
1 Union Square West, Suite 612, New York, NY 10003-3303
*tel* 212-255-1908 *fax* 212-691-9061
*email* info@martonagency.com
*Owner* Tonda Marton

Stage plays only.

## Harold Matson Company Inc.*
276 Fifth Avenue, New York, NY 10001
*tel* 212-679-4490 *fax* 212-545-1224

Full-length MSS (home 15%, UK 19%, translation 19%). No unsolicited MSS. No reading fee. Founded 1937.

## Helen Merrill Ltd
295 Lafayette Street, Suite 915, New York, NY 10012

No unsolicited MSS. No books. No phone calls or faxes. Send query letter with professional recommendation and sase or email address.

## William Morris Agency Inc.*
1325 Avenue of the Americas, New York, NY 10019
*tel* 212-586-5100
*Executive VP* Owen Laster, *Senior VPs* Jennifer Rudolph Walsh, Suzanne Gluck, Virginia Barber, Joni Evans, Mel Berger, *Agents* Manie Barron, Jay Mandel, Tracy Fisher, *Foreign Rights Director* Tracy Fisher, *Foreign Rights Coordinator* Shana Kelly, *First Serial and Audio Manager* Karen Gerwin

General fiction and non-fiction (home 15%, overseas 20%, performance rights 15%). Will suggest revision. No reading fee.

## Multimedia Product Development Inc.*
410 South Michigan Avenue, Suite 724, Chicago, IL 60605
*tel* 312-922-3063 *fax* 312-922-1905
*Contacts* Jane Jordan Browne, Danielle Egan-Miller

General fiction and non-fiction (home 15%, overseas 20%, performance rights 15%). Works in conjunction with foreign agents. Will suggest revision; no reading fee. Founded 1971.

## Jean V. Naggar Literary Agency Inc.*
216 East 75th Street, Suite 1E, New York, NY 10021
*tel* 212-794-1082
*President* Jean V. Naggar, *Agents* Alice Tasman, Anne Engel, Jennifer Weltz (rights)

Mainstream commercial and literary fiction (no formula fiction); non-fiction: psychology, science, biography (home 15%, overseas 20%), performance rights (15%). Works in conjunction with foreign agents. No reading fee. Founded 1978.

## New England Publishing Associates Inc.*
PO Box 5, Chester, CT 06412
*tel* 860-345-READ *fax* 860-345-3660
*email* nepa@nepa.com
*website* www.nepa.com
*Contacts* Elizabeth Frost-Knappman, Edward W. Knappman, Ron Formica, Kris Schiavi, Vicki Harlow

Serious non-fiction for the adult market (home 15%, overseas varies), performance rights (varies). Works in conjunction with foreign publishers. No reading fee; will suggest revision – if undertaken. Representatives: Rachel Calder Sayles Literary Agency (London); **Michael Meller Literary Agency** (Germany); A. Mediation Littéraire (France); **ACER Agencia Literaría** (Spain); **Andrew Nurnberg Associates** (Hungary). Dramatic rights: Joel Gotler, IPG.

## Harold Ober Associates Inc.*
425 Madison Avenue, New York, NY 10017
*tel* 212-759-8600 *fax* 212-759-9428
*Directors* Phyllis Westberg, Emma Sweeney, Knox Burger, Alex Smithline, Pamela Malpas

Full-length MSS (home 15%, British 20%, overseas 20%), performance rights (15%). Will suggest revision. No reading fee. Founded 1929.

## Fifi Oscard Agency Inc.
110 W 40th Street, New York, NY 10018
*tel* 212-764-1100 *fax* 212-840-5019
*email* fifioscard@aol.com
*Agents* Fifi Oscard, Peter Sawyer, Carolyn French, Carmen La Via, Kevin McShane

Full-length MSS (home 15%, overseas 20%), theatrical performance rights (10%). Will suggest revision. Works in conjunction with many foreign agencies. No reading fee, but no unsolicited submissions.

## James Peter Associates Inc.
PO Box 358, New Canaan, CT 06340
*tel* 203-972-1070 *fax* 203-972-1759
*email* gene_brissie@msm.com
*Contacts* Bert Holtje, Gene Brissie

Non-fiction, especially history, politics, popular culture, health, psychology, reference, biography (home 15%, overseas 20%). Foreign rights handled by: Bobbe Siegel, 41 West 83rd Street, New York, NY 10024. Will suggest revision. No reading fee. Founded 1971.

## The Pimlico Agency Inc.
PO Box 20447, Cherokee Station, New York, NY 10021
*tel* 212-628-9729 *fax* 212-535-7861
*Contacts* Christopher Shepard, Catherine Brooks, *Directors* Kay McCauley, Kirby McCauley

Adult non-fiction and fiction. No unsolicited MSS.

## Pinder, Lane & Garon-Brooke Associates Ltd*
159 West 53rd Street, Suite 14, New York, NY 10019
*tel* 212-489-0880 *fax* 212-586-9346
*email* pindel@interport.net
*London Representative* Abner Stein

Specialises in fiction and non-fiction: biographies and lifestyle. Writer must be referred by an editor or a client. Will not read unsolicited MSS.

## PMA Literary and Film Management Inc.
Old Chelsea Station, PO Box 1817, New York, NY 10011
*tel* 212-929-1222 *fax* 212-206-0238
*email* pmalitfilm@aol.com
*website* www.pmalitfilm.com
*President* Peter Miller, *Development Associate* Scott Hoffman

Full-length MSS. Specialises in commercial fiction (especially thrillers), true crime, non-fiction (all types), and all books with global publishing and film/TV potential (home 15%, overseas 25%), films, TV (10–20%). Works in conjunction with agents worldwide. Preliminary enquiry with career goals, synopsis and resumé essential. Founded 1976.

## Lisa Queen IMG Literary
825 Seventh Avenue, 9th Floor, New York, NY 10019
*tel* 212-489-5400 *fax* 212-246 1118

Fiction (no science fiction) and non-fiction. Send query letter with sase.

## Helen Rees Literary Agency
376 North Street, Boston, MA 02113-2103
*tel* 617-227 9014 *fax* 617-227 8762
*email* reesliterary@aol.com
*Contact* Joan Mazmanian, *Associates* Ann Collette, Lorin Rees

Business books, self-help, biography, autobiography, political, literary fiction (home 15%). Works with foreign agent. No reading fee. Submit query letter with sase. Founded 1982.

## The Angela Rinaldi Literary Agency*
PO Box 7877, Beverly Hill, CA 90212-7877
*tel* 310-842-7665 *fax* 310-877-3143
*email* amr@rinaldiliterary.com
*President* Angela Rinaldi

Mainstream and literary adult fiction; non-fiction (home 15%, overseas 20%). No reading fee. Founded 1994.

## Rosenstone/Wender*
38 East 29th Street, 10th Floor, New York, NY 10016
*tel* 212-725-9445 *fax* 212-725-9447
*Contacts* Phyllis Wender, Susan Perlman Cohen, Sonia Pabley

Fiction, non-fiction, film and TV rights. No unsolicited MSS; query first. No reading fee.

## Russell & Volkening Inc.*
50 West 29th Street, Suite 7E, New York, NY 10001
*tel* 212-684-6050 *fax* 212-889-3026
*Contact* Timothy Seldes, Kirsten Ringer

General fiction and non-fiction, film and TV rights. No screenplays. No unsolicited MSS; query first with letter and sase. No reading fee.

## Schiavone Literary Agency, Inc.
236 Trails End, West Palm Beach, FL 33413-2135
*tel/fax* 516-966-9294
*email* profschia@aol.com
*President* James Shiavone

Fiction and non-fiction, specialising in celebrity biography and memoirs (home 15%, overseas 20%). No reading fee. Will suggest revision. Founded 1996.

## Susan Schulman Literary & Dramatic Agents Inc.*
454 West 44th Street, New York, NY 10036
*tel* 212-713-1633 *fax* 212-581-8830
*email* schulman@aol.com

Agents for negotiation in all markets (with co-agents) of fiction, general non-fiction, children's books, academic and professional works, and associated subsidiary rights including plays and film (home 15%, UK 7.5%, overseas 20%). No reading fee. Return postage required.

## Scott Meredith Literary Agency LP
1675 Broadway, New York, NY 10019
*tel* 212-698-0785 *fax* 212-977-5997
*website* www.scottmeredith.com
*President* Arthur Klebanoff

General fiction and non-fiction. Founded 1946.

## The Shukat Company Ltd*
340 West 55th Street, Suite 1A, New York, NY 10019
*tel* 212-582-7614 *fax* 212-315-3752
*email* staff@shukat.com
*President* Scott Shukat, *Contacts* Maribel Rivas, Lysna Scriven-Marzani

Theatre, films, TV, radio (15%). No reading fee. No unsolicited material accepted.

## The Spieler Agency
154 West 57th Street, Room 135, New York, NY 10019
*tel* 212-757-4439 *fax* 212-333-2019
*email* spieleragency@spieleragency.com
*Directors* F. Joseph Spieler, Lisa M. Ross, John F. Thornton, Deirdre Mullane

Full- and short-length MSS. History, politics, ecology, business, consumer reference, some fiction (home 15%, overseas 20%). No reading fee. Query first with sample and sase. Founded 1982.

## Philip G. Spitzer Literary Agency*
50 Talmage Farm Lane, East Hampton, NY 11937
*tel* 631-329-3650 *fax* 631-329-3651

General fiction and non-fiction; specialises in mystery/suspense, sports, politics, biography, social issues.

## Roslyn Targ Literary Agency Inc.*
105 West 13th Street, New York, NY 10011
*tel* 212-206-9390 *fax* 212-989-6233
*email* roslyntarg@aol.com

Fiction and non-fiction: query with outline, publication history and CV. Fiction: query with synopsis or outline, and CV and publication history. All submissions require sase. No phone queries. Affiliates in most foreign countries. No reading fee.

## Trident Media Group*
41 Madison Avenue, New York, NY 10010
*tel* 212-899-0620
*website* www.tridentmediagroup.com
*Executive Vice President* Ellen Levine

Full-length MSS: biography, contemporary affairs, women's issues, history, science, literary and commercial fiction (home 15%, overseas 20%); in conjunction with co-agents, theatre, films, TV (15%). Will suggest revision. Works in conjunction with agents in Europe, Japan, Israel, Brazil, Argentina, Australia, Far East. No reading fee; preliminary letter and sase and US postage essential.

## Ralph M. Vicinanza Ltd*
303 West 18th Street, New York, NY 10011
*tel* 212-924-7090
*Contacts* Ralph Vicinanza, Christopher Lotts, Christopher Schelling

Fiction: literary, women's, 'multicultural', popular (especially science fiction, fantasy, thrillers), children's. Non-fiction: history, business, science, biography, popular culture. Foreign rights specialists. New clients by professional recommendation only. No unsolicited MSS.

## Austin Wahl Agency Inc.
1820 North 76th Court, Elmwood Park, IL 60707-3631
*tel* 708-456-2301 *fax* 708-456-2031
*President* Thomas Wahl

Full-length and short MSS (home 15%, overseas 20%), theatre, films, TV (10%). No reading fee; professional writers only. Founded 1935.

## Wallace Literary Agency Inc.
177 East 70th Street, New York, NY 10021
*tel* 212-570-9090 *fax* 212-772-8979
*Director* Lois Wallace

No cookery, humour, how-to; film, TV, theatre for agency clients. Will suggest revision. No unsolicited

MSS; no faxed queries. Will only answer queries with return postage. Founded 1988.

## Watkins/Loomis Agency Inc.
133 East 35th Street, New York, NY 10016
*tel* 212-532-0080 *fax* 212-889-0506
*President* Gloria Loomis, *Contact* Katherine Fausset

Fiction and non-fiction. No unsolicited MSS; query first with sase. No reading fee. Representatives: **Abner Stein** (UK), the **Marsh Agency Ltd** (foreign).

## Wecksler-Incomco
170 West End Avenue, New York, NY 10023
*tel* 212-787-2239 *fax* 212-496-7035
*email* jacinny@aol.com
*President* Sally Wecksler, *Associate* Joann Amparan-Close

Illustrated books, non-fiction, business books, some literary fiction, children's books (home 15%, overseas 20%); will suggest revision where appropriate. No reading fee. No submissions by fax or email: only hard copy will be read. Founded 1971.

## Rhoda Weyr Agency – see Dunham
Literary, Inc.

## Writers House LLC*
21 West 26th Street, New York, NY 10010
*tel* 212-685-2400 *fax* 212-685-1781
*President* Albert Zuckerman, *Executive Vice-President* Amy Berkower

Fiction and non-fiction, including all rights; film and TV rights. No screenplays or software. Write a one-page letter in first instance, saying what's wonderful about your book, what it is about and why you are the best person to write it. No reading fee. Founded 1974.

## The Writers Shop – see William Morris
Agency Inc.

## The Wylie Agency Inc.
250 West 57th Street, Suite 2114, New York, NY 10107
*tel* 212-246-0069 *fax* 212-586-8953
*email* mail@wylieagency.com
*Directors* Andrew Wylie (president), Sarah Chalfant

Literary fiction/non-fiction. No unsolicited MSS accepted. London office: the **Wylie Agency UK Ltd**.

## Mary Yost Associates Inc.
59 East 54th Street, Suite 72, New York, NY 10022
*tel* 212-980-4988 *fax* 212-935-3632
*email* yostbooks59@aol.com

Full-length and short MSS (home and overseas 10%). Works with individual agents in all foreign countries. Will suggest revision. No reading fee. Founded 1958.

# Argentina

## International Editors Co.
Avenida Cabildo 1156, 1426 Buenos Aires
*tel* 54-11-4788-2992 *fax* 54-11-4786-0888

## The Nancy H. Smith Literary Agency
Ayacucho 1867, 2B, Buenos Aires 1112
*tel* (54 11) 4804 5508 *fax* (54 11) 4804 5508
*email* meg@interlink.com.ar
*Contact* Margaret Murray
*London office* 30 Acton Lane, London W4 5ED
*tel* 020-8995 4769 *fax* 020-8747 4012
*email* distobart@aol.com
*Contact* Diana Stobart

No reading fee. Founded 1938.

# Australia

## Bryson Agency Australia Pty Ltd
PO Box 226, Finders Lane PO, Melbourne 8009
*tel* (613) 9620 9100 *fax* (613) 9621 2788
*email* agency@bryson.com.au
*website* www.bryson.com.au
*Contact* Fran Bryson

Represents writers operating in all media: print, film, TV, radio, the stage and electronic derivatives; specialises in representation of book writers. Unsolicited MSS must include sample first chapters (5000 words max.), a synopsis, CV and return postage. Query first before sending.

## Curtis Brown (Australia) Pty Ltd
PO Box 19, Paddington, Sydney, NSW 2021
*tel* (02) 9331 5301/9361 6161 *fax* (02) 9360 3935
*email* info@curtisbrown.com.au
*Agents* Fiona Inglis, Pippa Masson

No reading fee.

## Diversity Management
PO Box 1449, Darlinghurst, Sydney, NSW 1300
*tel* 612-9130-4305 *fax* 612-9365-1426
*email* bill@diversitym.com.au
*website* www.diversitym.com.au
*Director* Bill Tikos

All genres of non-fiction, illustrated books (home/overseas 20%). No reading fee. Founded 2001.

# Brazil

## Agência Literária BMSR
Rua Visconde de Pirajá, 414 s1 1108 Ipanema, 22410-002 Rio de Janeiro, RJ
*tel* (55-21) 2287-6299 *fax* (55-21) 2267-6393
*email* lucia@bmsr.com.br

*website* www.bmsr.com.br
*Contacts* Lucia de Mello e Souza Riff, Lucia Riff,
Laura Riff, João Paulo Riff

Home 10%, overseas 20%. No reading fee. Will
suggest revision. Founded 1991.

## Tassy Barham Associates
23 Elgin Crescent, London W11 2JD
*tel* 020-7229 8667 *fax* 020-7229 8667
*email* t@ssybarham.freeserve.co.uk
*Proprietor* Tassy Barham

Specialises in representing British and US authors,
agents and publishers in Brazil. Founded 1999.

## Karin Schindler and Suely Pedro dos Santos Rights Representatives
Caixa Postal 19051, 04505–970 São Paulo, SP
*tel* 55-11-5041-9177 *fax* 55-11-5041-9077
*email* kschind@terr.com.br
suelypedrosantos@uol.com.br

# Canada

## Acacia House Publishing Services Ltd
51 Acacia Road, Toronto, Ontario M4S 2K6
*tel* 416-484-8356 *fax* 416-484-8356
*email* fhanna.acacia@rogers.com
*Managing Director* Mrs Frances A. Hanna, *Vice
President* Bill Hanna

Literary fiction/non-fiction, quality commercial
fiction, most non-fiction, except business books
(15% English worldwide, 25% translation,
performance 20%). No science fiction, horror or
occult. Works with overseas agents. Query first with
sample of 50pp max. Include return postage. No
reading fee. Founded 1985.

## Authors' Marketing Services Ltd
PO Box 84668, 2336 Bloor Street West,
Toronto M6S 4Z7
*tel* 416-763 8797 *fax* 416-763-1504
*email* authorslhoffman@cs.com
*Director* Larry Hoffman

Adult fiction, biography and autobiography (home
15%, overseas 20%). Reading fee charged for
unpublished writers; will suggest a revision.
Founded 1978.

## The Cooke Agency Inc.
278 Bloor Street East, Suite 305, Toronto,
Ontario M4W 3M4
*tel* 416-406-3390 *fax* 416-406-3389
*email* agents@cookeagency.ca
*President* Dean Cooke

Literary fiction and non-fiction (home 15%,
overseas 20%). British subagent: **Greene & Heaton
Ltd**. Founded 1992.

## Anne McDermid & Associates Ltd
92 Willcocks Street, Toronto, Ontario M5S 1C8
*tel* 416-324 8845 *fax* 416-324 8870
*email* anne@mcdermidagency.com
*website* www.mcdermidagency.com
*Director* Anne McDermid

Literary fiction and non-fiction, and quality
commercial fiction; no children's literature (home
15%, US 15%, overseas 20%). No reading fee.
Founded 1996.

## Bella Pomer Agency Inc.
22 Shallmar Boulevard, PH2, Toronto,
Ontario  M5N 2Z8
*tel* 416-781-8597 *fax* 416-782-4196
*President* Bella Pomer

Not considering new clients. Founded 1978.

## Carolyn Swayze Literary Agency
WRPO Box 39588, White Rock,
British Columbia V4B 5L6
*tel* 604-538-3478
*email* cswaze@direct.ca
*website* www.swayzeagency.com
*Proprietor* Carolyn Swayze

Literary and commercial fiction, some juvenile and
teen books. No romance, SF, poetry, screenplays, or
picture books. Eager to discover lively, thought-
provoking narrative non-fiction, especially in the
fields of science, history, travel, politics, and memoir.

*Submission details* No telephone calls: make
contact either by post or send short queries by
email, providing a brief resumé which describes
who you are. Include publication credits, writing
awards, education and experience relevant to your
book project. Include a one-page synopsis of the
book and – if querying via post – include sase for
the return of your materials. Do not include
original photographs or artwork. Include sase if
acknowledgement of receipt of materials is
required. Will not open unsolicited attachments.
Allow 6 weeks or longer for a reply. Founded 1994.

# Eastern Europe

## Aura-Pont, Theatrical and Literary Agency Ltd
Radlická 99, Prague 5, Czech Republic
*tel* (420) 2 51 55 02 07 *fax* (420) 2 51 55 02 07
*email* aura-pont@aura-pont.cz
*website* www.aura-pont.cz
*Director* Zuzana Jezková

Handles authors' rights in books, theatre, film, TV,
radio, software – both Czech and foreign (home
10%, overseas 15%). Founded 1990.

## DILIA
Krátkého 1, 190 03 Prague 9, Czech Republic
*tel* (420) 2 83 89 15 87 *fax* (420) 2 83 89 35 99
*email* info@dilia.cz
*website* www.dilia.cz
Theatrical and literary agency.

## Lex Copyright
Szemere utca 21, 1054 Budapest, Hungary
*tel* (36) 1 332 9340 *fax* (36) 1 331 6181
*email* lexcopy.bp@mail.datanet.hu
*Director* Dr Gyorgy Tibor Szanto

Specialises in representing American and British authors in Hungary. Founded 1991.

## Lita
Mozartova 9, CS–81530, Bratislava, Slovakia
*tel* (421) 7 313623 *fax* (421) 7 580 2246

Slovak Literary Agency.

## Andrew Nurnberg Associates Prague, s.r.o
Seifertova 81, 130 00 Prague 3, Czech Republic
*tel* (420) 2 22 78 20 41 *fax* (420) 2 22 78 23 08
*email* nurnprg@mbox.vol.cz
*Contacts* Petra Tobisková, Lucie Strakova

## Prava I Prevodi Literary Agency Permissions & Rights Ltd
Yu-Business Centre, Blvd Mihaila Pupina 10B/I, 5th Floor, Suite 4, 11070 Belgrade, Serbia and Montenegro
*tel* (381) 11 3119880 *fax* (381) 11 3119879
*email* ana@pip.co.yu office@pip.co.yu
*Director* Predraq Milenkovic, *Foreign Rights* Ana Milenkovic

Specialises in representing American and British authors in former Eastern Europe (15 languages). Founded 1983.

## France

## Agence Hoffman
77 Boulevard Saint-Michel, 75005 Paris
*tel* (1) 43 26 56 94 *fax* (1) 43 26 34 07
*email* info@agence-hoffman.com

## Agence Michelle Lapautre
6 rue Jean Carriès, 75007 Paris
*tel* (1) 47 34 82 41 *fax* (1) 47 34 00 90
*email* lapautre@club-internet.fr

## Bureau Littéraire International
1 rue Alfred Laurant, F–92100 Boulogne Billancourt
*tel* (1) 46 05 39 11
*Contact* Geneviéve Ulmann

## La Nouvelle Agence
7 rue Corneille, 75006 Paris
*tel* (1) 43 25 85 60 *fax* (1) 43 25 47 98
*email* lnaparis@wanadoo.fr
*Contacts* Mary Kling, Vanessa Kling, Michèle Kanonidis

## Promotion Littéraire
12 rue Pergolèse, 75116 Paris
*tel* (1) 45 00 42 10  *fax* (01) 45 00 10 18
*email* promolit@club-internet.fr
*Director* Mariella Giannetti

Fiction, essays. Founded 1977.

## Germany (see also Switzerland)

## Agence Hoffman
Bechsteinstrasse 2, 80804 Munich
*tel* 089-308 48 07 *fax* 089-308 21 08

## Michael Meller Literary Agency
Sandstrasse 33, 80335 Munich
*tel* (089) 366371 *fax* (089) 366372
*email* info@melleragency.com
*website* www.melleragency.com

Full-length MSS. Fiction and non-fiction, screenplays for films and TV (home 15%, overseas 20%). No reading fee. Founded 1988.

## Thomas Schlück GmbH
Literary Agency, Hinter der Worth 12, 30827 Garbsen
*tel* 05131-497560 *fax* 05131-497589
*email* mail@schlueckagent.com
*website* www.schlueckagent.com

No reading fee.

## India

## Ajanta Books International
1 U.B. Jawahar Nagar, Bungalow Road, Delhi 110007
*tel* 27415016, 23926182 *fax* 91-11-27415016
*email* ajantabi@vsnf.com ajantabi@eth.net
*Proprietor* S. Balwant

Full-length MSS in social sciences and humanities (commission varies according to market – Indian books in Indian and foreign languages, foreign books into Indian languages). Will suggest revision; charges made if agency undertakes revision; reading fee. Founded 1975.

# Israel

## I. Pikarski Ltd Literary Agency

200 Hayarkon Street, PO Box 4006, Tel Aviv 61040
*tel* 03-5270159/5231880 *fax* 03-5270160
*email* gabpikar@inter.net.il
*Director* Ilana Pikarski

General trade publishing and merchandising rights.
Founded 1977.

# Italy

## Agenzia Letteraria Internazionale SRL

Via Valpetrosa 1, 20123 Milano
*tel* (02) 865445, 861572 *fax* (02) 876222
*email* alidmb@tin.it

## Eulama SRL

Via Guido de Ruggiero 28, 00142 Rome
*tel* (06) 540 73 09 *fax* (06) 540 87 72
*email* eulama@tin.it
*Directors* Harald Kahnemann, Karin von Prellwitz,
Norbert von Prellwitz, Pina Ocello von Prellwitz

International licensing agency representing
publishing houses, agents and authors of adult and
children's books worldwide. General and literary
fiction, non-fiction, academic works in humanities.
Promoting Italian, German and Spanish language
authors and publishers worldwide. Reading fee.
Founded 1962.

## Grandi & Associati SRL

Via Caradosso 12, 20123 Milan
*tel* (02) 469 55 41/481 89 62 *fax* (02) 481 95108
*email* agenzia@grandieassociati.it
*website* www.grandieassociati.it
*Directors* Laura Grandi, Stefano Tettamanti

Provides publicity and foreign rights consultation
for publishers and authors as well as sub-agent
services; will suggest revision where appropriate.
Reading fee. Founded 1988.

## ILA (International Literary Agency) USA

I–18010 Terzorio-IM
*tel* (018) 448 4048 *fax* (018) 448 7292
*email* libriggbooks@libero.it

Publishers' and authors' agent, interested only in
series of best-selling and mass market books by
proven, published authors with a track record. Also
interested in published books on antiques and
collectibles. No reading fee. Founded 1969.

## New Blitz Literary & TV Agency

Via di Panico 67, 00186 Rome
*postal address* CP 30047–00193, Rome 47
*tel* (06) 686 4859 *fax* (06) 686 4859
*email* blitzgacs@inwind.it

*Literary Department* Giovanni A.S. Congiu
No reading fee.

## Piergiorgio Nicolazzini Literary Agency

Via GB Moroni 22, Micano 20146
*tel* (02) 487 13365
*email* info@pnla.it
*website* www.pnla.it
*Director* Piergiorgio Nicolazzini

Literary and commerical fiction and non-fiction
(home 10%, overseas 15–20%). No reading fee. Will
suggest revision. Founded 1998.

# Japan

## The English Agency (Japan) Ltd

Sakuragi Building 4F, 6–7–3 Minami Aoyama,
Minato-ku, Tokyo 107-0062
*tel* 03-3406 5385 *fax* 03-3406 5387
*Managing Director* Hamish Macaskill

Handles work by English-language writers living in
Japan; arranges Japanese translations for
internationally established publishers, agents and
authors; arranges Japanese contracts for Japanese
versions of all media. Standard commission: 10%.
Own representatives in New York and London. No
reading fee. Founded 1979.

## Orion Literary Agency

1–7–12–4F Kanda-Jimbocho, Chiyoda-ku,
Tokyo 101
*tel* 03-3295-1405 *fax* 03-3295-4366

# Netherlands

## Auteursbureau Greta Baars-Jelgersma

Villa Beau Rivage, Maasstaete 40, 6585 CB, Mook (L)
*tel* (024) 6963336 *fax* (024) 6963293

Literature; illustrated co-productions, including
children's, art, handicraft, hobby and nature
(home/overseas 20%). Works with overseas agents.
Occasionally charges a reading fee. Founded 1951.

## Internationaal Literatuur Bureau B.V.

Postbus 10014, 1201 DA, Hilversum
*tel* (035) 621 35 00 *fax* (035) 621 57 71
*email* mkohn@planet.nl
*website* www.ilb.nu
*Contacts* Linda Kohn, Brigitte van der Klaauw

# New Zealand

## Glenys Bean Writer's Agent

PO Box 60509, Titirangi, Auckland
*tel* (09) 812 8486 *fax* (09) 812 8188
*email* g.bean@clear.net.nz

Adult and children's fiction, educational, non-fiction, film, TV, radio (10–20%). Send preliminary letter, synopsis and sae. No reading fee. Represented by **Sanford Greenburger Associates Ltd** (USA). Translation/foreign rights: the **Marsh Agency Ltd**. Founded 1989.

## Michael Gifkins & Associates

PO Box 6496, Wellesley Street PO, Auckland 1000
*tel* (09) 523-5032 *fax* (09) 5235033
*email* michale.gifkins@xtra.co.nz
*Director* Michael Gifkins

Literary and popular fiction, fine arts, children's and young adult fiction, substantial non-fiction (non-academic) co-publications (home 15%, overseas 20%). No reading fee. Will suggest revision. Founded 1985.

## Richards Literary Agency

11 Channel View Road, Campbells Bay, Auckland 11
*postal address* PO Box 31–240, Milford, Auckland 9
*tel* (09) 479-5681 *fax* (09) 479-5681
*email* ria.richards@clear.net.nz
*Partners* Ray Richards, Nicki Richards Wallace

Full-length MSS, fiction, non-fiction, adult, juvenile, educational, academic books; films, TV, radio (home 15%, overseas 10–20%). Preliminary letter, synopsis with sae required. No reading fee. Co-agents in London and New York. Founded 1977.

# Portugal

## Ilidio da Fonseca Matos

Avenida Gomes Pereira, 105–3°–B, 1500–328 Lisbon
*tel* (21) 716 2988 *fax* (21) 715 4445
*email* ilidio.matos@oninet.pt

No reading fee.

# Russia

## Prava I Perevody

Bolshaya Bronnaya Street 6A, Moscow 103670
*tel* (095) 203 5280 *fax* (095) 203 0229
*email* prava@aha.ru
*Director* Konstantin Palchikov

Specialises in representing US and British authors in Russia, Latvia, Lithuania, Estonia and Ukraine. Founded 1993.

# Scandinavia

## Bookman Literary Agency

Bastager 3, DK–2950 Vedbaek, Denmark
*tel* (45) 45 89 25 20 *fax* (45) 45 89 25 01
*email* ihl@bookman.dk

Handles rights in Denmark, Sweden, Norway, Finland and Iceland for foreign authors.

## Gösta Dahl & Son, AB

Enhörningsgränd 14, S–167 58 Bromma, Sweden
*tel* 08 25 62 35 *fax* 08 25 62 35

## Leonhardt & Høier Literary Agency aps

Studiestraede 35, DK–1455 Copenhagen K, Denmark
*tel* 33 13 25 23 *fax* 33 13 49 92
*email* anneli@leonhardt-hoier.dk

No reading fee.

## Lennart Sane Agency AB

Holländareplan 9, S–374 34 Karlshamn, Sweden
*tel* 0454 123 56 *fax* 0454 149 20
*email* lennart.sane@teila.com
*Directors* Lennart Sane, Elisabeth Sane, Ulf Töregård

Fiction, non-fiction, children's books. Founded 1969.

## Sane Töregård Agency AB

Holländareplan 9, S–374 34 Karlshamn, Sweden
*tel* (46) 454 12356 *fax* (46) 454 14920
*email* ulf.toregard@sanetoregard.se
*Directors* Lennart Sane, Ulf Töregård

Represents authors, agents and publishers in Scandinavia and Holland for rights in fiction, non-fiction and children's books. Founded 1995.

# South Africa

## Frances Bond Literary Services

14 Gary Inn Crescent, Westville,
Westville North 3630, KwaZulu-Natal
*postal address* PO Box 223, Westville 3630
*tel* (031) 2662007 *fax* (031) 2662007
*email* fbond@mweb.co.za
*Managing Editor* Frances Bond, *Chief Editor* Eileen Molver

Full length MSS. Fiction and non-fiction; juvenile and children's literature. Consultancy service on contracts and copyright. Preliminary phone call or letter and sase required. Reading fee terms on application. Founded 1985.

## Cherokee Literary Agency

3 Blythwood Road, Rondebosch, Cape 7700
*tel* (021) 671 4508

*email* dklee@mweb.co.za
*Director* D.K. Lee

Children's picture books in translation (home 10%). Founded 1988.

## Sandton Literary Agency
PO Box 785799, Sandton 2146
*tel* (011) 4428624
*Directors* J. Victoria Canning, M. Sutherland

Full-length MSS and screenplays; lecture agents. Professional editing. Reading fee for unpublished or self-published writers. Write enclosing sae or phone first. Works in conjunction with Renaissance-Swan Film Agency Inc., Los Angeles, USA. Founded 1982.

# Spain

## ACER Literary Agency
Amor de Dios 1, 28014 Madrid
*tel* 1-369-2061 *fax* 1-369-2052
*Directors* Elizabeth Atkins, Laure Merle d'Aubigné

Represents UK, US, French and German publishers for Spanish and Portuguese translation rights; represents Spanish- and Portuguese-language authors (home/overseas 10%). Will suggest revision where appropriate; £20 reading fee. Founded 1959.

## Agencia Literaria Carmen Balcells S.A.
Diagonal 580, 08021 Barcelona
*tel* 93-200-89-33 *fax* 93-200-70-41
*email* ag-balcells@ag-balcells.com
*Contact* Gloria Gutiérrez

## Mercedes Casanovas Literary Agency
Iradier 24, 08017 Barcelona
*tel* 93-212-47-91 *fax* 93-417-90-37

Literature, non-fiction, children's books (home 10%, overseas 20%). Works with overseas agents. No reading fee. Founded 1980.

## International Editors Co., S.A.
Rambla Catalunya 63, 3°–1a, 08007 Barcelona
*tel* 93-215-88-12 *fax* 93-487-35-83
*email* ieco@internationaleditors.com

## RDC Agencia Literaria SL
C. Fernando VI, No 13–15, Madrid 28004
*tel* 91-308-55-85 *fax* 91-308-56-00
*Director* Raquel de la Concha

Representing foreign fiction, non-fiction, children's books and Spanish authors. No reading fee.

## Lennart Sane Agency AB
Paseo de Mejico 65, Las Cumbres-Elviria,
E–29600 Marbella (Malaga)
*tel* 95-283-41-80 *fax* 95-283-31-96

*email* lennart.sane@telia.com

Fiction, non-fiction, children's books, film and TV scripts. Founded 1965.

## Julio F. Yañez
Agencia Literaria S.L., Via Augusta 139, 6–2a,
08021 Barcelona
*tel* 93-200-71-07, 93-200-54-43 *fax* 93-209-48-65
*email* yanezag@retemazil.es

# Switzerland

## Paul & Peter Fritz AG Literary Agency
Jupiterstrasse 1, CH–8032 Zürich
*postal address* Postfach 1773, CH–8032 Zürich
*tel* 41 44 388 41 40 *fax* 41 44 388 41 30
*email* info@fritzagency.com

Represents authors, agents and publishers in German-language areas. No reading fee.

## Liepman AG
Maienburgweg 23, CH–8044 Zürich
*tel* (044) 261 76 60 *fax* (044) 261 01 24
*email* info@liepmanagency.com
*Contacts* Eva Koralnik, Ruth Weibel

Represents authors, agents and publishers from all over the world for German translation rights, and selected international authors for world rights. No reading fee.

## Mohrbooks AG, Literary Agency
Klosbachstrasse 110, CH–8032 Zürich
*tel* (01) 244 8626 *fax* (01) 244 8627
*email* info@mohrbooks.com
*website* www.mohrbooks.com
*Contacts* Sabine Ibach, Sebastian Ritscher

No reading fee.

## Neue Presse Agentur (NPA)
Haldenstrasse 5, Frauenfeld, CH–8500
*tel* (052) 721 43 74
*Director* René Marti

Looking for occasional contributors to write for German/Swiss papers and magazines in the German language. Founded 1950.

## Niedieck Linder AG
Zollikerstrasse 87, Postbox, CH–8034 Zürich
*tel* (01) 381 65 92 *fax* (01) 381 65 13
*website* www.nlagency.ch

Represents German-language authors and Italian-language authors on the German market as well as major literary estates on a worldwide basis. No reading fee.

# Art and illustration

## Freelancing for beginners

Fig Taylor describes the opportunities open to freelance illustrators and discusses types of fee and how to negotiate one to your best advantage.

Full-time posts for illustrators are extremely rare. Because commissioners' needs tend to change on a regular basis, most artists have little choice but to freelance – offering their skills to a variety of clients in order to make a living.

Illustration is highly competitive and a professional attitude towards targeting, presenting, promoting and delivering your work will be vital to your success. Likewise, a realistic understanding of how the industry works and of your place within it will be key. Without adequate research into your chosen field(s) of interest, you may find yourself approaching inappropriate clients – a frustrating and disheartening experience for both parties and a waste of your time and money.

### Who commissions illustration?
### Magazines and newspapers

Whatever your illustrative ambitions, you are most likely to receive your first commissions from editorial clients. The comparatively modest fees involved allow art editors the freedom to take risks, so many are keen to commission newcomers. Briefs are generally fairly loose though deadlines can be short, particularly where daily and weekly publications are concerned. However, fast turnover also ensures a swift appearance in print, thus reassuring clients in other, more lucrative, spheres of your professional status. Given then that it is possible to use magazines as a springboard, it is essential to research them thoroughly when seeking to identify your own individual market. Collectively, editorial clients accommodate an infinite variety of illustrative styles and techniques. Don't limit your horizons by approaching only the most obvious titles and/or those you would read yourself. Consider also trade and professional journals, free publications and those available on subscription from membership organisations or charities. Seeking out as many potential clients as possible will benefit you in the long term.

### Book publishing

With the exception of non-fiction, where the emphasis is on decorative, specialist and technical illustration, most publishers are predominantly interested in full-colour figurative work for use on covers. Strong, representational work, showing the figure in a narrative context, is invaluable to commissioners of mass market paperback fiction, especially historical romance, science fiction and fantasy – while the recent fashion illustration renaissance has strongly influenced the packaging of contemporary women's fiction. A broader range of styles can be accommodated by those smaller publishers and imprints specialising in literary, upmarket fiction. On the whole, publishing deadlines are civilised and mass market covers particularly well paid.

Children's publishers use a wide variety of styles, covering the gamut from baby books, activity and early learning, through to full-colour picture books, covers for young adults and black and white line illustrations for the 8–11 year-old age group. Author/illustrators are particularly welcomed by picture book publishers – though, whatever your style, you must be able to develop believable characters and sustain them throughout a narrative. See *Illustrating for children's books* on page 251.

### Greeting cards

Many illustrators are interested in providing designs for cards and giftwrap. For specific information on the gift industry which, unlike the areas covered here, works on a speculative basis, see *Winning the greeting card game* on page 445.

## Useful addresses

### Archant Specialist
24A Unit Workshops, 1–13 Adler Street, London E1 1EE
*tel* 020-7247 4959
*email* caroline.roberts@virgin.net
*website* www.grafikmagazine.net
Publishes *Grafik Magazine*.

### Association of Illustrators
81 Leonard Street, London EC2A 4QS
*tel* 020-7613 4328 *fax* 020-7613 4417
*email* info@a-o-illustrators.demon.co.uk
*website* www.theaoi.com

Publishes *Survive – the Illustrators Guide to a Professional Career* and *Rights – the Illustrators Guide to Professional Practice and Images*. See also page 504.

### Boomerang Media Ltd
PO Box 141, Aldershot, Hants GU12 4XX
*tel* (01252) 368368

### BRAD Group
33–39 Bowling Green Lane, London EC1R 0DA
*tel* 020-7505 8000
*website* www.intellangencia.com
Publishes *ALF* (Account List File).

### Centaur Communications
49–50 Poland Street, London W1V 4AX
*tel* 020-7439 4222
*email* patrick.burgoyne@centaur.co.uk
*websites* www.creativereview.co.uk,
www.design-week.co.uk
Publishes *Design Week* and *Creative Review*.

### Design companies

Both designers and their clients (who are largely uncreative and will, ultimately, be footing the bill) will be impressed and reassured by relevant, published work so wait until you're in print before approaching them. Although fees are significantly higher than those in editorial and publishing, this third-party involvement generally results in a more restrictive brief. Deadlines may vary and styles favoured range from conceptual through to realistic, decorative, humorous and technical – with those involved in multimedia and web design favouring illustrators with animation skills.

Magazines such as *Design Week*, *Creative Review* (published by Centaur Communications) and *Grafik Magazine* (published by Archant) will keep you abreast of developments in the design world and help you identify clients' individual areas of expertise. Meanwhile, *The Creative Handbook* (published by Reed Business Information and also available online), carries many listings. Individual contact names are also available at a price from database specialists

**Elfande Ltd**
Surrey House, 31 Church Street, Leatherhead,
Surrey KT22 8EF
*tel* (01372) 220300 *fax* (01372) 220340
*email* mail@contact-uk.com
*website* www.contact-uk.com
Publishes *Contact Illustrators* and *New Talent*.

**File FX**
Unit 11, 83–93 Shepperton Road, London N1 3DF
*tel* 020-7226 6646
*email* info@filefx.co.uk

Specialises in providing creative suppliers with up-
to-date information on commissioning clients in all
spheres.

**Haymarket Business Publications**
22 Bute Gardens, London W6 7HN
*tel* 020-7413 4036
*email* campaign@haynet.com
*website* www.brandreplubic.com
Publishes *Campaign*.

**Reed Business Information**
Windsor Court, East Grinstead House,
Wood Street, East Grinstead,
West Sussex RH19 1XA
*tel* (01342) 332028 *fax* (01342) 332037
*email* chb@reedinfo.co.uk
*website* www.chb.com
Publishes *The Creative Handbook*.

File FX, who can provide creative suppliers with up-to-date information on commissioning clients in all spheres.

## Advertising agencies

As with design, you should ideally be in print before seeking advertising commissions. Fees can be high, deadlines short and clients extremely demanding. A wide range of styles are used and commissions might be incorporated into direct mail or press advertising, featured on hoardings and poster sites or animated for television. Fees will vary, depending on whether a campaign is local or national.

Most agencies employ an art buyer to look at portfolios. A good one will know what each creative team is currently working on and may refer you to specific art directors. Agency listings and client details may be found in *ALF* (Account List File, published by the BRAD Group), while *Creative Review* and the weekly *Campaign* (published by Haymarket Business Publications) carry agency news.

## Portfolio presentation

In general, UK commissioners prefer to see someone with a strong, consistent, recognisable style rather than an unfocused jack-of-all trades type. Thus, when assembling your professional portfolio, try to exclude samples which are, in your own eyes, weak, irrelevant, uncharacteristic or simply unenjoyable to do and focus on your strengths instead. Should you be one of those rare, multi-talented individuals who finds it hard to limit themselves stylistically, try splitting conflicting work into separate portfolios geared towards different kinds of clients.

A lack of formal training need not be a handicap providing your portfolio accurately reflects the needs of the clients you target. Some illustrators find it useful to assemble 'mock-ups' using existing magazine layouts. By responding to the copy and replacing original images with your own illustrations, it is easier to see how your work will look in context. Eventually, as you become established you'll be able to augment these with published pieces.

Ideally, your folder should be of the zip-up, ring-bound variety and never exceed A2 in size as clients usually have little desk space. Complexity of style and diversity of subject matter will dictate how many samples to include but all should be neatly mounted on lightweight paper or card and placed inside protective plastic sleeves. High-quality photographs and laser copies are acceptable to clients but tacky out-of-focus snapshots are not. Also avoid including multiple sketchbooks and life drawings, which are anathema to clients. It will be taken for granted that you know how to draw from observation.

## Interviews and beyond

Making appointments can be hard work but clients take a dim view of spontaneous visits from passing illustrators. Having established the contact name (either from a written source or by asking the company directly), clients are still best approached by letter or telephone call. Many publishing houses are happy to see freelances, though portfolio 'drop-offs' are also quite common. Some clients will automatically take photocopies of your work for reference. However, it's advisable to have some kind of promotional material to leave behind such as a CD, postcard or advertising tearsheet. Always ask an enthusiastic client if they know of others who might be interested in your work. Personal recommendation almost always guarantees an interview.

Cleanliness, punctuality and enthusiasm are more important to clients than how you dress – as is a professional attitude to taking and fulfilling a brief. A thorough understanding of each commission is paramount from the outset. You will need to know your client's requirements regarding roughs; format, size and flexibility of artwork; preferred medium; and whether the artwork is needed in colour or black and white. You will also need to know when the deadline is. Never, under any circumstances agree to undertake a commission unless you are certain you can deliver on time and always work within your limitations. Talent is nothing without reliability.

## Self-promotion

There are many ways an illustrator can ensure their work stays uppermost in the industry's consciousness, some more expensive than others. Images can be emailed, put onto CD or posted on a website. Advertising in prestigious hardback annuals such as Elfande's *Contact Illustrators* and the Association of Illustrators' *Images* – which are distributed free to commissioners – can be effective but doesn't come cheap and, in the case of *Images*, only those professionally selected are permitted to buy pages for their winning entries. A more affordable – albeit one-off – alternative for newcomers is Elfande's softback springboard, *New Talent*, which also benefits from free distribution.

As commissioners increasingly turn to the internet for inspiration, websites are becoming a viable and affordable method of self-promotion (see *Setting up a website*, page 586). Advertisers in *Contact Illustrators* automatically qualify for a web portfolio of 12 images with links back to individual websites. This option is also open to *New Talent* advertisers at a discounted rate. Currently, it is also possible for illustrators to promote their work on the *Contact* website without appearing in either of the Elfande annuals. The Association of Illustrators (AOI) website features an archive of work from recent editions of *Images*. Both members and non-members can pay to appear in a similarly categorised Image File or the site's Directory, providing links and contact details.

Free publicity can be had courtesy of Boomerang Media Ltd, who will print appropriate images to go in postcard advertising racks. Distribution includes cafés, bars, cinemas, health clubs, universities and schools.

## Be organised

Once you are up and running, it is imperative to keep organised records of all your commissions. Contracts can be verbal as well as written, though details – both financial and otherwise – should always be confirmed in writing and duplicated for your files. Likewise, keep corresponding client faxes, letters, emails and order forms. AOI publications *Survive – the Illustrator's Guide to a Professional Career* and *Rights – the Illustrator's Guide to Professional Practice* offer a wealth of practical, legal and ethical information. Subjects covered include contracts, fee negotiation, agents, licences, royalties and copyright issues.

## Money matters

The type of client, the purpose for which you are being commissioned and the usage of your work can all affect the fee you can expect to receive, as can your own professional attitude. Given that it is *extremely* inadvisable to undertake a commission without first agreeing on a fee, you will have to learn to be upfront about funds.

## Licence *v.* copyright

Put simply, according to current EU legislation, copyright is the right to reproduce a piece of work anywhere, *ad infinitum*, for any purpose, for a period ending 70 years after the death of the person who created it. This makes it an extremely valuable commodity.

By law, copyright automatically belongs to you, the creator of your artwork, unless you agree to sell it to another party. In most cases, clients have no need to purchase it, and the recommended alternative is for you to grant them a licence instead, governing the precise usage of the artwork. This is far cheaper from the client's perspective and, should they subsequently decide to use your work for some purpose other than those outlined in your initial agreement, will benefit you too as a separate fee will have to be negotiated. It's also worth noting that even if you were ill-advised enough to sell the copyright, the artwork would still belong to you unless you had also agreed to sell that.

## Rejection and cancellation fees

Most commissioners will not expect you to work for nothing unless you are involved in a speculative pitch, in which case it will be up to you to weigh up the pros and cons of your possible involvement. Assuming you have given a job your best shot – i.e. carried out the client's instructions to the letter – it's customary to receive a rejection fee even if the client doesn't care for the outcome: 25% is customary at developmental/rough stage and 50% at finished artwork stage. (Clear this with the client before you start, as there are exceptions to the rule.) Cancellation fees are paid when a job is terminated through no fault of the artist or, on occasion, even the client. Customary rates in this instance are 25% before rough stage, 33% on delivery of roughs and 100% on delivery of artwork.

## Fixed v. negotiable fees

Editorial and publishing fees are almost always fixed with little, if any, room for haggling and are generally considerably lower than advertising and design fees, which tend to be negotiable. A national full-colour 48-sheet poster advertising Marks & Spencer is likely to pay more than a local black and white press ad plugging a poodle parlour. If, having paid your editorial dues, you find yourself hankering after commissions from the big boys, fee negotiation – confusing and complicated as it can sometimes be – will become a fact of life. However you choose to go about the business of cutting a deal, it will help if you disabuse yourself of the notion that the client is doing you a whopping favour by considering you for the job. Believe it or not, the client *needs* your skills to bring his/her ideas to life. In short, you are worth the money and the client knows it.

## Pricing a commission

Before you can quote on a job, you'll need to know exactly what it entails. For what purpose is the work to be used? Will it be used several times and/or for more than one purpose? Will its use be local or national? For how long is the client intending to use it? Who is the client and how soon do they want the work? Are you up against anyone else (who could possibly undercut you)?

Next, ask the client what the budget is. Believe it or not there's a fair chance they might tell you. Whether they are forthcoming or not, don't feel you have to pluck a figure out of thin air or agree to their offer immediately. Play for time. Tell them you need to review your current workload and that you'll get back to them within a brief, specified period of time. If nothing else, haggling over the phone is less daunting than doing it face to face. If you've had no comparable commissions to date and are an AOI member, check out the going rate by calling them for pricing advice. Failing that, try speaking to a friendly client or a fellow illustrator who's worked on similar jobs.

When you begin negotiating, have in mind a bottom-line price you're prepared to do the job for and always ask for slightly more than your ideal fee as the client will invariably try to beat you down. You may find it useful to break down your asking price in order to explain exactly what it is the client is paying for. How you do this is up to you. Some people find it helpful to work out a daily rate incorporating overheads such as rent, heating, materials, travel and telephone charges, while others prefer to negotiate on a flat fee basis. There are also illustrators who charge extra for something needed yesterday, time spent researching, model hire if applicable and so on. It pays to be flexible, so if your initial quote exceeds the client's budget and you really want the job, tell them you are open to negotiation. If, on the other hand, the job looks suspiciously thankless, stick to your guns. If the client agrees to your exorbitant demands, the job might start to look more appetising.

## Getting paid

Once you've traded terms and conditions, done the job and invoiced the client, you'll then have the unenviable task of getting your hands on your fee. It is customary to send your invoice to the accounts department stating payment within 30 days. It is also customary for them to ignore this entreaty, regardless of the wolf at your door, and pay you when it suits them. Magazines pay promptly, usually within 4–6 weeks; everyone else takes 60–90 days – no matter what.

Be methodical when chasing up your invoice. Send out a statement the moment your 30 days has elapsed and call the accounts department as soon as you like. Take names, note dates and the gist of their feeble excuses. ("It's in the post", "He's in a meeting", "He's on holiday and forgot to sign the cheque before he went"), and keep on chasing. Don't worry about your incessant nagging scuppering your plans of further commissions as these decisions are solely down to the art department, and they think you're a gem. Should payment still not be forthcoming three months down the line, it might be advisable to ask your commissioner to follow things up on your behalf. Chances are they'll be horrified you haven't been paid yet and things will be speedily resolved. In the meantime, you'll have had a good deal of practice talking money, which can only make things easier next time around.

## And finally...

Basic book-keeping – making a simple, legible record of all your financial transactions, both incoming and outgoing – will be crucial to your sanity once the tax inspector starts to loom. It will also make your accountant's job easier, thereby saving you money. If your annual turnover is less than £15,000, it is unnecessary to provide the Inland Revenue with detailed accounts of your earnings. Information regarding your turnover, allowable expenses and net profit may simply be entered on your tax return. Although an accountant is not necessary to this process, many find it advantageous to employ one. The tax system is complicated and dealing with the Inland Revenue can be stressful, intimidating and time consuming. Accountants offer invaluable advice on tax allowances, National Insurance and tax assessments, as well as dealing expertly with the Inland Revenue on your behalf – thereby enabling you to attend to the business of illustrating. See *Income tax* on page 714, *Social security contributions* on page 726 and *Social security benefits* on page 735.

**Fig Taylor** initially began her career as an illustrators' agent in 1983. For 19 years she has been the resident 'portfolio surgeon' at the Association of Illustrators and also operates as a private consultant to non-AOI member artists. In addition, she lectures extensively in Business Awareness to BA and HND illustration students throughout the UK.

# Art agents and commercial art studios

Before submitting work, artists are advised to make preliminary enquiries and to ascertain terms of work. Commission varies but averages 25–30%. The Association of Illustrators (see page 504) provides a valuable service for illustrators, agents and clients.

*Member of the Society of Artists Agents
†Member of the Association of Illustrators

## Academy of Light Ltd
Unit 1c, Delta Centre,
Mount Pleasant, Wembly,
Middlesex HA0 1UX
*tel* 020-8795 2695 *fax* 020-8903 3748
*email* yubraj@academyoflight.co.uk
*website* www.academyoflight.co.uk
*Contact* Dr Yubraj Sharma, Managing Director

Represents 10 artists specialising in spirituality, medicine, caricature and humour and producing illustrations for books, cards, magazines and advertising. Commission: 25%.

## Advocate†
Advocate Gallery, 372 Old York Road,
London SW18 1SP
*tel* (07000) 238622 *fax* 020-8874 7661
*email* mail@advocate-art.com
*website* www.advocate-art.com
*Director* Edward Burns

Represents 110 artists with 6 agents. Recently launched *Devil's Advocate*, representing alternative illustrators. Supplies work to book publishers, design and advertising agencies, greeting card and fine art publishers, ceramic manufacturers and potteries, and supplies editorial illustrations. Also has an original art gallery, a stock library and licensing agency for its art character 'Newton's Law'. Founded as a co-operative in 1996.

## Allied Artists
The Gallery at Richmond,
63 Sheen Road,
Richmond upon Thames TW9 1YJ
*tel* 020-8334 1010 *fax* 020-8334 9900
*email* info@alliedartists.uninev.co.uk,
mary@umbrellapublishing.ca
*websites* www.alliedartists.uninev.co.uk,
www.umbrellapublishing.ca
*Contacts* Gary Mills, Mary Burtenshaw

Represents over 40 artists specialising in highly finished realistic figure illustrations, stylised juvenile illustrations for children's books, and cartoons for magazines, books, plates, prints, cards and advertising. Extensive library of stock illustrations. Commission: 33%. Founded 1998.

## Arena*†
Quantum Artists Ltd, 108 Leonard Street,
London EC2A 4RH
*tel* 020-7613 4040 *fax* 020-7613 1441
*email* info@arenaworks.com
*website* www.arenaworks.com
*Contact* Tamlyn Francis

Represents 35 artists working mostly for book covers, children's books and design groups. Average commission 20%. Founded 1970.

## Artist Partners Ltd*†
14–18 Ham Yard, Great Windmill Street,
London W1D 7DE
*tel* 020-7734 7991 *fax* 020-7287 0371
*email* chris@artistpartners.demon.co.uk
*website* www.artistpartners.com
*Managing Director* Christine Isteed

Represents 40 artists, including specialists in their field, producing artwork in every genre for advertising campaigns, storyboards, children's and adult book covers, newspaper and magazine features and album covers. New artists are only considered if their work is of an exceptionally high standard, in which case submission should be by post only and include an sae. Commission: 30%. Founded 1951.

## The Art Market*†
51 Oxford Drive, London SE1 2FB
*tel* 020-7407 8111 *fax* 020-7407 8222
*email* info@artmarketillustration.com
*website* www.artmarketillustration.com
*Director* Philip Reed

Represents 20 artists creating illustrations for publishing, design and advertising. Founded 1989.

## The Artworks*†
70 Rosaline Road, London SW6 7QT
*tel* 020-7610 1801 *fax* 020-7610 1811
*email* info@theartworksinc.com
*website* www.theartworksinc.com
*Director* Lucy Scherer
*Consultant* Allan Manham

Represents 30 artists. Undertakes artwork for illustrated gift books and children's books. Commission: 20%. Founded 1982.

## Associated Freelance Artists Ltd

124 Elm Park Mansions, Park Walk,
London SW10 0AR
*tel* 020-7352 6890 *fax* 020-7352 8125
*email* pekes.afa@virgin.net
*Directors* Eva Morris, Doug FitzMaurice

Freelance illustrators mainly in children's
educational fields, and some greeting cards.

## Beehive Illustration[†]

42A Cricklade Street, Cirencester, Glos. GL7 1JH
*tel* (01285) 885149 *fax* (01285) 641291
*email* info@beehiveillustration.co.uk
*website* www.beehiveillustration.co.uk
*Contact* Paul Beebee

Represents 60 artists specialising in education and
general children's publishing illustration.
Commission: 25%. Founded 1989.

## Sarah Brown Agency

10 The Avenue, London W13 8PH
*tel* 020-8998 0390 *fax* 020-8843 1175
*email* sbagency@gxn.co.uk
*website* www.sbagency.com
*Contact* Brian Fennelly

Illustrations for publishing and advertising. Sae
essential for unsolicited material. Commission: 25%
UK, 25% USA (flat artwork 33.3%). Founded 1977.

## Central Illustration Agency*[†]

36 Wellington Street, London WC2E 7BD
*tel* 020-7240 8925/836 1106 *fax* 020-7836 1177
*email* c.illustration.a@dial.pipex.com
*website* www.centralillustration.com
*Director* Brian Grimwood, Louisa St Pierre

Represents 70 artists producing illustrations for
design, publishing, animation and advertising.
Commission: 30%. Founded 1983.

## Début Art[†]

30 Tottenham Street, London W1T 4RJ
*tel* 020-7636 1064 *fax* 020-7580 7017
*email* debutart@coningsbygallery.demon.co.uk
*website* www.debutart.com
*Directors* Andrew Coningsby, Samuel Summers Rill,
Kelly Fysh

Represents 60 artists working in mixed media,
digital, photographic 3D and 2D collage and
montage. Commission: 25%. Founded 1985.

## Barry Everitt Associates

23 Mill Road, Stock, Essex CM4 9LJ
*tel* (01284) 828685
*Contact* Barry M. Everitt

Design and art resource specialising in licensing
reproduction rights for greetings cards, fine art
prints, calendars, giftware, etc. Always pleased to see
the work of new and established artists and

illustrators. Colour copies or photographs required
initially with sae for return or reply, but telephone
first for details.

## Ian Fleming Associates*[†]

41 Pumphouse Close, London SE16 7HS
*tel* 020-7064 4666 *fax* 020-7064 4660
*email* fleming1@btclick.com
*website* www.ianflemingart.com
*Directors* Jon Rogers, Cariona Wydmanski

Represents 20 artists who work across the board –
advertising, design and publishing. Commission:
33%. Founded 1971.

## Folio Illustrators' & Designers' Agents*[†]

10 Gate Street, Lincoln's Inn Fields,
London WC2A 3HP
*tel* 020-7242 9562 *fax* 020-7242 1816
*email* all@folioart.co.uk
*website* www.folioart.co.uk

All areas of illustration. Send sae with samples.
Founded 1976.

## Fountainhead

Houldsworth Mill, Houldsworth Street, Reddish,
Stockport, Cheshire SK5 6DA
*tel* 0161-975 6125  *fax* 0161-975 6126
*email* rob@imagebay.com
*Directors* Rob Richardson, Sean Gamble

Represents 20 artists producing illustration, fine art,
photography and decorative images. Produces and
licenses designs/images for use on greeting cards,
giftwrap, paper products, ceramics and textiles.
Commission: 30%. Founded 1994.

## Graham-Cameron Illustration[†]

The Studio, 23 Holt Road, Sheringham,
Norfolk NR26 8NB
*tel* (01263) 821333 *fax* (01263) 821334
*and* Duncan Graham-Cameron, Graham-Cameron
Illustration, 59 Redvers Road, Brighton BN2 4BF
*tel* (01273) 385890
*email* duncan@graham-cameron-illustration.com
*website* www.graham-cameron-illustration.com
*Partners* Mike Graham-Cameron, Helen
Graham-Cameron, Duncan Graham-Cameron

Represents 37 artists. Undertakes all forms of
illustration for publishing and communications.
Specialises in educational, information and
children's books. Send A4 copies of sample
illustrations with sae. No MSS. Founded 1985.

## The Guild of Aviation Artists

Trenchard House, 85 Farnborough Road,
Farnborough, Hants. GU14 6TF
*tel* (01252) 513123 *fax* (01252) 510505
*email* admin@gava.org.uk
*website* www.gava.org.uk

*President* Michael Turner PGAVA, *Secretary* Susan Gardner

Professional body of 500 artists specialising in aviation art in all mediums. The Guild sells, commissions and exhibits members' work. Commission: 25%. Founded 1971.

## John Hodgson Agency
38 Westminster Palace Gardens, Artillery Row, London SW1P 1RR
*tel* 020-7580 3773 *fax* 020-7222 4468

Publishing (children's picture books). Essential to send sae with samples. Commission: 25%. Founded 1965.

## Illustration Ltd*†
2 Brooks Court, Cringle Street, London SW8 5BX
*tel* 020-7720 5202 *fax* 020-7720 5920
*email* team@illustrationweb.com
*website* www.illustrationweb.com
*Contact* Harry Lyon-Smith, Marie-Claire Carver, Vanessa Dell

Represents 150 artists producing illustrations and animation for international advertisers, designers, publishers and editorial clients. Commission: 33.3% or 25%. Founded 1929.

## Image by Design
The Cottage, Pryor House, Preston, Hitchin, Herts. SG4 7UD
*tel* (01462) 422244 *fax* (01462) 422248
*email* enquiries@imagebydesign-licensing.co.uk
*website* www.imagebydesign-licensing.co.uk
*Contact* Lucy Brenham

Quality artwork for all products including prints, greeting cards, stationery, ceramics, etc. Commission: negotiable. Founded 1987.

## The Inkshed*†
98 Columbia Road, London E2 7QB
*tel* 020-7613 2323 *fax* 020-7613 2726
*email* makecontact@inkshed.co.uk
*website* www.inkshed.co.uk
*Partners* Tim Woolgar, Jacqueline Hollister, *Contact* Melanie Grimshaw, Abby Glassfield (agents)

Represents 31 artists who work across the board – advertising, design, publishing, editorial. Commission: 25%. Founded 1985.

## Kathy Jakeman Illustration†
Richmond Business Centre, 23–24 George Street, Richmond, Surrey TW9 1HY
*tel* 020-8973 2000 *fax* (07071) 225 115
*email* kathy@kji.co.uk
*website* www.kji.co.uk

Illustration for publishing – especially children's; also design, editorial and advertising. Do not send samples by email. Commission: 25%. Founded 1990.

## Libba Jones Associates
Hopton Manor, Hopton, Nr Wirksworth, Derbyshire DE4 4DF
*tel* (01629) 540353 *fax* (01629) 540577
*email* ljassociates@easynet.co.uk
*website* www.libbajonesassociates.com
*Contacts* Libba Jones, Ieuan Jones

High-quality artwork and design for china, greetings cards and giftwrap, jigsaw puzzles, calendars, prints, posters, stationery, book illustration, fabric design. Submission of samples required for consideration. Founded 1983.

## David Lewis Illustration Agency
Worlds End Studios, 134 Lots Road, London SW10 0RJ
*tel* 020-7435 7762, *mobile* (07931) 824674
*fax* 020-7435 1945
*email* davidlewis34@hotmail.com
*website* www.davidlewisillustration.com
*Director* David Lewis, *Associate Director* Robin Broadway

Considers all types of illustration for a variety of applications but mostly suitable for book and magazine publishers, design groups, recording companies and corporate institutions. Also offers a comprehensive selection of images suitable for subsidiary rights purposes. Send return postage with samples. Do not send CDs or emails. Commission: 30%. Founded 1974.

## Frances McKay Illustration
14A Ravensdon Street, London SE11 4AR
*tel* 020-7582 2327 *mobile* 07703 344334
*fax* 020-7735 3303
*email* frances@francesmckay.com
*website* www.francesmckay.com
*Proprietor* Frances McKay

Represents 17+ artists for illustration mainly for children's books, magazines and products, greetings cards and stationery. Submit colour copies of recent work or email low-res scans; sae essential for return of all unsolicited samples. Commission: 25%–35%. Founded 1999.

## John Martin & Artists†
12 Haven Court, Hatfield Peverel, Chelmsford, Essex CM3 2SD
*tel* (01245) 380337 *fax* (01245) 382055
*email* bernardjma@aol.com
*website* www.jm-a.co.uk
*Contact* Bernard Bowen-Davies

Represents 25 illustrators, mainly producing artwork for children's fiction/ non-fiction and educational books. Include return postage with submissions. Founded 1956.

## Meiklejohn Illustration*†
5 Risborough Street, London SE1 0HF
*tel* 020-7593 0500 *fax* 020-7593 0501
*email* mjn@mjgrafix.demon.co.uk
*websites* www.theartbook.com,
www.meiklejohn.co.uk
*Contacts* Paula White, Lindsey Bender

All types of illustration.

## N.E. Middleton
Richmond Business Centre, 23–24 George Street,
Richmond, Surrey TW9 1HY
*tel* 020-8973 2000 *fax* (07071) 225 115

Designs for greetings cards, stationery, prints,
calendars and china.

## Maggie Mundy Illustrators' Agency
14 Ravenscourt Park Mansions, Dalling Road,
London W6 0HG
*tel* 020-8748-2391
*email* maggiemundy@compuserve.com

Represents 20 artists in varying styles of illustration
for children's books. The Agency's books are closed.

## NB Illustration†
40 Bowling Green Lane, London EC1R 0NE
*tel* 020-7278 9131 *fax* 020-7278 9121
*email* info@nbillustration.co.uk
*website* www.nbillustration.co.uk
*Directors* Joe Najman, Charlotte Berens, Paul Najman

Represents 20+ artists and will consider all material
for the commercial illustration market. Sae
essential. Commission: 30%. Founded 2000.

## The Organisation*†
The Basement, 69 Caledonian Road, London N1 9BT
*tel* 020-7833 8268 *fax* 020-7833 8269
*email* lorraine@organisart.co.uk
*website* www.organisart.co.uk
*Contact* Lorraine Owen

Various styles of illustration supplied for book work
in adult, children's and educational markets. Also
for print, advertising, packaging and editorial.
Average commission: 30%. Sae essential for
unsolicited samples. Founded 1987.

## Oxford Designers & Illustrators Ltd
Aristotle House, Aristotle Lane, Oxford OX2 6TR
*tel* (01865) 512331 *fax* (01865) 512408
*email* richardcorfield@odi-illustration.co.uk
*website* www.o-d-i.com
*Directors* Peter Lawrence (managing), Richard
Corfield, Andrew King

Studio of 20 illustrators working for publishers,
business and industry. All types of artwork
including science, technical, airbrush, graphic,
medical, biological, botanical, natural history,

figure, cartoon, maps, diagrams, and charts.
Artwork supplied as PDF files or on a CD, Zip
optical disk or ISDN, Mac or PC, with both b&w
and colour proofs. Not an agency. Founded 1968.

## Pennant Inc.*†
16 Littleton Street, London SW18 3SY
*tel* 020-8947 4002 *fax* 020-8946 7667
*email* matt@pennantinc.co.uk
*website* www.pennantinc.co.uk
*Director* Matthew Doyle

Illustrations for publishing, design and advertising.
Samples must be accompanied by an sae.
Commission: 30%. Founded 1992.

## Phosphor Art Ltd*
41 The Pump House, Pump House Close,
London SE16 7HS
*tel* 020-7064 4666 *fax* 020-7064 4660
*email* info@phosphorart.com
*website* www.phosphorart.com
*Directors* Jan Rogers, Catriona Wydmanski

Represents 32 artists producing artwork in current
professional styles. Commission: 33.3%. Founded
1999.

## Pink Barge
13 Wyndham Place, London W1H 2PY
*tel* 020-7486 1053 *fax* 020-7262 1130
*Director* Maggee Barge

Represents 20 artists working in advertising,
publishing and corporate art. Commission: 25%.
Founded 1982.

## Sylvie Poggio Artists Agency†
36 Haslemere Road, London N8 9RB
*tel* 020-8341 2722 *fax* 020-8374 1725
*email* sylviepoggio@blueyonder.co.uk
*website* www.sylviepoggio.com
*Directors* Slyvie Poggio, Bruno Caweat

Represents 35 artists producing illustrations for
publishing and advertising. Commission 25%.
Founded 1992.

## Linda Rogers Associates†
PO Box 330, 163 Half Moon Lane,
London SE24 9WB
*tel* 020-7501 9106 *fax* 020-7501 9175
*email* lr@lindarogers.net
*website* www.lindarogers.net
*Partners* Linda Rogers, Peter Sims, Jess Sims

Represents 65 illustrators and author/illustrators in
all fields of illustration. Specialises in children's
books, educational, information books; adult leisure
books and magazines. Reply only with sae. Artwork
samples only viewed via post, *not* by email.
Commission: 25%. Founded 1973.

## SGA Illustration Agency[†]

18 High Street, Hadleigh, Suffolk IP7 5AP
*tel* (01473) 824083 *fax* (01473) 827846
*email* info@sgadesignart.com
*website* www.sgadesignart.com

Represents over 50 illustrators, mainly working within publishing (early learning through to teenage). Also manages projects from conception to final film. See website for portfolio of illustration samples. Commission: 30%. Founded 1985.

## Specs Art[†]

93 London Road, Cheltenham, Glos. GL52 6HL
*tel* (01242) 515951
*email* roland@specsart.com
*website* www.specsart.com
*Partners* Roland Berry, Stephanie Prosser

High-quality illustration and animation work for advertisers, publishers and all other forms of visual communication. Specialises in licensed character illustration.

## Temple Rogers Artists' Agency

120 Crofton Road, Orpington, Kent BR6 8HZ
*tel* (01689) 826249 *fax* (01689) 896312
*Contact* Patrick Kelleher

Illustrations for children's educational books and magazine illustrations. Commission: by arrangement.

## Vicki Thomas Associates

195 Tollgate Road, London E6 5JY
*tel* 020-7511 5767 *fax* 020-7473 5177
*email* vickithomasassociates@yahoo.co.uk
*website* www.vickithomasassociates.com
*Consultant* Vicki Thomas

Considers the work of illustrators and designers working in greetings and gift industries, and promotes such work to gift, toy, publishing and related industries. Written application and b&w photocopies required. Commission: 30%. Founded 1985.

## Thorogood Illustration Ltd[†]

5 Dryden Street, London WC2E 9NW
*tel* 020-8859 7507, 020-8488 3195
*fax* 020-8333 7677
*email* draw@thorogood.net
*website* www.thorogood.net
*Directors* Doreen Thorogood, Stephen Thorogood

Represents 30 artists for advertising, design, publishing and animation work. Send return postage with samples. Commission: 30%. Founded 1977.

## TWO:Design London Ltd

Studio 20, The Arches, Hartland Road, London NW1 8HR
*tel* 020-7267 1118 *fax* 020-7482 0221
*email* studio@twodesign.net
*website* www.twodesign.net
*Directors* Graham Peake

Art studio providing comprehensive services: design, photography, image creation and manipulation, typesetting, artworking, marketing, point-of-sale material, etc. Specialists in general books, magazines and periodicals. Founded 1997.

## Wildlife Art Ltd[†]

The Lodge, Cargate Lane, Saxlingham Thorpe, Norwich NR15 1TU
*tel* (01508) 471500 *fax* (01508) 470391
*website* www.wildlife-art.co.uk

Illustrations of all things natural, including gardening and food. Clients range from children's/adults' books to design and advertising agencies. Illustrations on all subjects including wildlife, history, children's stories, science and geography, from packaging and adult reference books to children' picture books and magazine series. Sae must be included with work submitted for consideration. Commission: 30%. Founded 1992.

# Winning the greeting card game

The UK population spends £1.2 billion a year on greeting cards yet finding a route into this fiercely competitive industry is not always easy. Jacqueline Brown steers artists through the greeting card maze. fee and how to negotiate one to your best advantage.

The UK greeting card industry leads the world on two counts – design and innovation and per capita send. On average people in the UK send 50 cards a year, 85% of which are bought by women.

But just how do you, as an artist, go about satisfying this voracious appetite of the card-sending public? There are two main options: either to become a greeting card publisher yourself or to supply existing greeting card publishers with your artwork and be paid a fee for doing so.

The idea of setting up your own greeting card publishing company may sound exciting, but this decision should not be taken lightly. Going down this route will involve taking on all the set up and running costs of a publishing company as well as the production, selling and administrative responsibilities. This often leaves little time for you to do what you do best – creating the artwork.

There are estimated to be around 800 greeting card publishers in the UK, ranging in size from one-person operations to multinational corporations, roughly 200 of which are regarded as 'serious' publishers (see page 449). Not all of them accept freelance artwork, but a great many do. Remember, whatever the size of the company, all publishers rely on good designs.

## Finding the right publishers

While some publishers concentrate on producing a certain type of greeting card (e.g. humorous, fine art or juvenile), the majority publish a variety of greeting card ranges. Unfortunately, this makes it more difficult for you as an artist to target the most appropriate potential publishers for your work. There are various ways in which you can research the market, quickly improve your publisher knowledge and, therefore, reduce the amount of wasted correspondence:

● **Go shopping.** Browse the displays in card shops, newsagents and other high street shops, department stores and gift shops. This will not only give you an insight into what is already available but also which publishers

### Some greeting card language

**Own brand/bespoke publishers.** These design specific to a retailer's needs.

**Spring Seasons.** The industry term to describe greeting cards for Valentine's Day, Mother's Day, Easter and Father's Day. Publishers generally launch these ranges all together in June/July.

**Greeting card types.** Traditional; cute or whimsical; contemporary/quirky art; juvenile; handmade or hand-finished; fine art; photographic, humorous.

**Finishes and treatments.** Artists will not be expected to know the production techniques and finishes, but a working knowledge is often an advantage. Some of the most commonly used finishes and treatments include: embossing (raised portion of a design), die-cutting (where the card is cut into a shape or includes an aperture), foiling (metallic film) and flitter (a glitter-like substance).

## Further information

### The Greeting Card Association

United House, North Road, London N7 9DP
tel 020-7619 0396
*email* gca@max-publishing.co.uk
*website* www.greetingcardassociation.org.uk

The UK trade association for greeting card publishers. Its website contains leaflets on freelance designing and writing for greeting cards complete with lists of publishers which accept freelance work.

### Trade fairs

#### Spring & Autumn Fairs Birmingham, NEC

*Contact* TPS *tel* 020-8277 5830
*Takes place* 5–8 Sept 2004, 6–10 Feb 2005,
4–7 Sept 2005

#### Top Drawer, Earls Court

*Contact* Clarion Events *tel* 020-7370 8374
*Takes place* 12–14 Sept 2004, 16–18 Jan 2005,
22–25 May 2005

#### Home and Gift, Harrogate

*Contact* Clarion Events *tel* 020-7370 8374
*Takes place* 17–20 July 2005

### Trade magazines

#### Greetings Today

(formerly Greetings Magazine)
Lema Publishing, Unit No. 1, Queen Mary's Avenue, Watford, Herts. WD18 7JR
*tel* (01923) 250909 *fax* (01923) 250995
*Publisher-in-Chief* Malcolm Naish, *Editor* Vicky Denton
Monthly £45 p.a. (other rates on application)

Articles, features and news related to the greetings card industry. Includes Artists Directory for aspiring artists wishing to attract the eye of publishers. Runs seminars for small publishers and artists.

#### Progressive Greetings Worldwide

Max Publishing, United House, North Road, London N7 9DP
*tel* 020-7700 6740 *fax* 020-7607 6411
12 p.a. (£40 p.a.)

The official magazine of the Greeting Card Association. Provides an insight to the industry, including an up-to-date list of publishers, a new product section and a free showcase for artists and illustrators. Special supplements include *Focus on Art Cards, Focus on Humorous Cards, Focus on Words & Sentiments, Focus on Kids* and *Focus on Giftwrap*.

Hosts The Henries, the greeting card industry awards. The September edition includes details of the finalists in the different categories and the November issue features the winners.

may be interested in your work. Most publishers include their contact details on the backs of the cards.

● **Trade fairs.** There are a number of trade exhibitions held during the year at which publishers exhibit their greeting card ranges to retailers and overseas distributors. By visiting these exhibitions, you will gain a broad overview of the design trends in the industry, as well as the current ranges of individual publishers. Some publishers are willing to meet artists and look through their portfolios on the stand but others are not. If you believe your work could be relevant for them, ask for a contact name and follow it up afterwards. Have a supply of business cards handy, perhaps illustrated with some of your work, to leave with publishers.

### Types of publishers

There are two broad categories of publisher – wholesale and direct-to-retail – each employing a different method of distribution to reach the retailer.

Wholesale publishers distribute their products to the retailer via greeting card wholesalers or cash-and-carry outlets. They work on volume sales and have a rapid turnover of designs, many being used with a variety of different captions. For example, the same floral design may be used for cards for mothers, grandmothers, aunts and sisters. It is therefore usual for the artist to leave a blank space on the design to accommodate the caption. Until recently, wholesale publishers were generally only interested in traditional, cute and juvenile designs, but they now publish across the board, including contemporary and humorous ranges.

Direct-to-retail (DTR) publishers supply retailers via sales agents or reps. Most greeting cards sold through specialist card shops and gift shops are supplied by DTR publishers, which range from multi-national corporations down to small, trendy niche publishing companies. These publishers market series of ranges based on distinctive design themes or characters. Categories of DTR cards include contemporary art/fun, fine art, humour, children's, photographic, traditional and handmade.

## Approaching a publisher

Unfortunately, there is no standard way of approaching and submitting work to a card publisher. The first step is to establish that the publisher you wish to approach accepts work from freelance artists; then find out their requirements for submission and to whom it should be addressed.

It is always better to send several examples of your work to show the breadth of your artistic skills. Some publishers prefer to see finished designs while others are happy with well-presented sketches. Never send originals: instead send photocopies, laser copies or photographs, and include at least one design in colour. Never be tempted to sell similar designs to two publishers – a bad reputation will follow you around.

Some publishers will be looking to purchase individual designs for specific sending occasions while others will be more intent on looking for designs which could be developed to make up a range. Bear in mind that publishers work a long way in advance, e.g. Christmas ranges are launched to the retailers in January. Development of a range may take up to six months prior to launching.

Also remember that cards in retail outlets are rarely displayed in their entirety. Therefore, when designing a card make sure that some of the 'action' appears in the top half.

## When interest is shown

Some publishers respond to submissions from artists immediately while others prefer to deal with them on a monthly basis. A publisher's response may be in the form of a request for more submissions of a specific design style or of a specific character. This speculative development work is usually carried out free of charge. Always meet your deadline (news travels fast in the industry).

A publisher interested in buying your artwork will probably then issue you with a contract. This may cover aspects such as the terms of payment; rights of usage of the design (e.g. is it just for greeting cards or will it include giftwrap and/or stationery?); territory of usage (most publishers want worldwide rights); and ownership of copyright or license period.

There is no set industry standard rate of pay for greeting card artists. Publishers pay artists either on a per design or per range basis in one of the following ways:

- **Flat fee.** A one-off payment is made to the artist for ownership of a design for an unlimited period. The industry standard is around £200–£250 for a single design, and payment on a sliding scale for more than one design.
- **Licensing fee.** The publisher is granted the right to use a piece of artwork for

a specified number of years, after which the full rights revert to the artist. Payment to the artist is approximately £150 upwards per design.

● **Licensing fee** plus royalty. As above plus a royalty payment on each card sold. Artists would generally receive a minimum of £100 for the licensing fee plus 3% of the trade price of each card sold.

● **Advance royalty deal.** A goodwill advance on royalties is paid to the artist. In the case of a range, the artist would receive a goodwill advance of say £500–£1000 plus 5% additional royalty payment once the threshold is reached.

● **Royalty only.** The artist receives regular royalty payments, generally paid quarterly, based on the number of cards sold. Artists should expect a sales report and royalty statement.

The fees stated above should only be regarded as a rough guideline. Fees and advances are generally paid on completion of artwork. Publishers which have worldwide rights pay royalties for sales overseas to artists, although these will be on a pro rata basis to the export trade price.

**Jacqueline Brown** is editor of *Progressive Greetings Worldwide* and general secretary of the Greeting Card Association.

# Card and stationery publishers which accept illustrations and verses

Before submitting work, artists are advised to write giving details of the work they have to offer, and asking for requirements.

*Member of the Greeting Card Association

## Allium Arts*
2066 The Big Peg, 120 Vyse Street,
Birmingham B18 6NF
*tel* 0121-687 1403 *fax* 0121-687 1406
*email* shelley@alliumarts.co.uk
*website* www.alliumarts.co.uk
*Directors* Richard Westley-Smith, Nick Westley-Smith, Ian Winstanley, Shelley Wheatley

Contemporary fine art for high-quality retailers. No verses. Founded 2003.

## Card Connection Ltd*
Park House, South Street, Farnham, Surrey GU9 7QQ
*tel* (01252) 892300 *fax* (01252) 892363
*email* ho@card-connection.co.uk
*website* www.card-connection.co.uk
*Managing Director* Simon Hulme, *Senior Product Manager* Alison Mahoney

Everyday and seasonal designs. Styles include cute, fun, traditional, floral, contemporary, graphic, art, photography. Submit colour copies. Humour designs and jokes. Sentiment verse. Founded 1992.

## Carlton Cards Ltd*
Mill Street East, Dewsbury,
West Yorkshire WF12 9AW
*tel* (01924) 465200
*website* www.carltoncards.co.uk
*Marketing Director* Keith Auty, *Creative Director* Linda Marshall

All types of artwork, any size; submit as colour roughs, colour copies or transparencies. Especially interested in humorous artwork and ideas.

## Caspari Ltd*
9 Shire Hill, Saffron Walden, Essex CB11 3AP
*tel* (01799) 513010 *fax* (01799) 513101
*Managing Director* Keith Entwisle

Traditional fine art/classic images; 5 x 4in transparencies. No verses. Founded 1990.

## Charity Christmas Card Council*
221 St John Street, London EC1V 4LY
*tel* 020-7702 5090 *fax* 020-7702 5092
*email* karnthorsson@charitycards.org

*website* www.charitycards.org

Traditional and contemporary Christmas cards for the corporate market. Submit artwork on CD-Rom or 5 x 4in transparencies. No verses. Charitable not-for-profit organisation. Founded 1966.

## Colneis Marketing Ltd*
York House, 2–4 York Road, Felixstow IP11 7QQ
*tel* (01394) 271668 *fax* (01394) 275114
*email* colneiscards@btopenworld.co.uk
*website* www.colneisgreetingcards.com
*Proprietor* John Botting

Photographs (preferably medium format) and colour artwork of nature and cute images. Considers verses. Founded 1994.

## Colour House Graphics*
58 Matilda Street, London N1 1BG
*tel* 020-7700 7780 *fax* 020-7700 7727
*email* colourhousegraphics@hotmail.com
*Partners* John Ellner and Margaret Ellner

Contemporary styles of painting of subjects relating to people's everyday lives. Particularly interested in sophisticated, loose, graphic styles. No verses. Founded 1990.

## Gallery Five Ltd*
Regent House, 24 Nutford Place, London W1H 5YN
*tel* 020-8741 3891 *fax* 020-8741 4444

Send samples of work FAO 'Gallery Five Art Studio'. Colour photocopies, Mac-formatted zip/CD acceptable, plus sae. Founded 1961.

## Gemma International Ltd*
Linmar House, 6 East Portway, Andover,
Hants. SP10 3LU
*tel* (01264) 388400 *fax* (01264) 366243
*website* www.gemma-international.co.uk
*Directors* L. Rudd-Clarke, M. Rudd-Clarke,
A. Parkin, T. Rudd-Clarke, W. O'Loughlin,
R. Howard, K. Bishop

Cute, contemporary, leading-edge designs for children, teens and young adults, and mainstream adult humour. Considers humorous verses. Founded 1984.

## Gibson Greetings International Ltd

Gibson House, Hortonwood 30, Telford,
Shrops. TF1 7YF
*tel* (01952) 608333 *fax* (01952) 605259
*email* jan_taylor@gibson-greetings.co.uk
*Product Director* Jan Taylor

All everyday and seasonal illustrations: cute,
humorous, juvenile, traditional and contemporary
designs, as well as surface pattern. Greeting card
traditional and humorous verse. Founded 1991.

## Graphic Humour Ltd

4 Britannia House, Point Pleasant, Wallsend,
Tyne & Wear NE28 6HA
*tel* 0191-295 4200 *fax* 0191-295 3916
*email* enquiries@graphic-humour.demon.co.uk
*website* www.graphic-humour.demon.co.uk

Risqué and everyday artwork ideas for greetings
cards; short, humorous copy. Founded 1984.

## Greetings Cards By Noel Tatt Ltd*

t/a Noel Tatt Group, Appledown House, Barton
Business Park, Appledown Way, New Dover Road,
Canterbury, Kent CT1 3TE
*tel* (01227) 811600 *fax* (01227) 811601
*email* mail@noeltatt.co.uk
*Directors* Jarle Tatt, Diane Tatt, Richard Parsons,
Ian Hylands

Greetings cards, giftwrap. Founded 1988.

## The Greetings Factory Ltd

PO Box 662, Watford, Herts. WD17 2ZX
*tel* (01923) 210100 *fax* (01923) 246008
*email* info@hotchpotch.net
*website* www.hotchpotch.net
*Director* Paul Steele

Colour artwork for greetings cards, giftwrap and
social stationery. Considers verses. Founded 1997.

## Hallmark Cards Plc*

Hallmark House, Bingley Road,
West Yorkshire BD9 8SD
*email* 1willi2@hallmark-uk.com
*website* www.hallmark.com
*Submissions* Katy Jones

Illustrations: all subjects considered. Submit colour
copies and/or transparencies but not original
artwork. Ensure that all work is named and includes
an sae. Words: humour only wil be considered.

## Hanson White – UKG Speciality Products

9th Floor, Wettern House, 56 Dingwall Road,
Croydon, Surrey CR0 0XH
*tel* 020-8260 1200 *fax* 020-8260 1213
*email* hannah.turpin@ukgsp.co.uk,
sally.hipkins@ukgsp.co.uk
*Submissions Editors* Hannah Turpin and Sally
Hipkins

Humorous artwork and cartoons for greeting cards,
including Christmas, Valentine's Day, Mother's Day
and Father's Day. Humorous copy lines, punchline
jokes, poems and rhymes; guidelines available.
Founded 1958.

## Jarrold Publishing

(incorporating Pitkin and Unichrome brands)
Whitefriars, Norwich NR3 1JR
*tel* (01603) 763300 *fax* (01603) 662748
*email* publishing@jarrold.co.uk
*website* www.jarrold-publishing.co.uk
*Directors* Margot Russell-King (managing), David
Lombe (finance), Steve Plackett (supply chain gift
and stationery)

UK tourism and heritage guide books and
souvenirs, calendars, diaries and gift stationery.
Unsolicited MSS, synopses and ideas welcome but
approach in writing before submitting to Marketing
Department. Founded 1770.

## Jodds*

PO Box 353, Bicester, Oxon OX27 0GS
*tel* (01869) 278550 *fax* (01869) 278551
*email* design@joddscards.com
*website* www.joddscards.com
*Partners* M. Payne and J.S. Payne

Contemporary art style greetings cards; must give
out a warm feel. Submit colour photocopies with
sae. No verses. Founded 1988.

## Leeds Postcards

4 Granby Road, Leeds LS6 3AS
*email* xtine@leedspostcards.com
*website* www.leedspostcards.com
*Contact* Christine Hankinson

Publisher and distributor of radical postcards for
the wall and post.

## Lima Design*

110 Dunstans Road, London SE22 0HE
*tel/fax* 020-8693 4257
*email* info@limadesign.co.uk
*website* www.limadesign.co.uk
*Proprietor* Lisa Breakwell

Produces contemporary, design-conscious cards, all
hand applied using resisters and capacitors, ribbon,
indoor sparklers, animal-shaped rubber bands,
metallic thread and beads. Founded 2002.

## Ling Design Ltd*

The Old Brewery, Newtown, Bradford on Avon,
Wilts. BA15 1NF
*tel* (01225) 863991 *fax* (01225) 863992
*email* info@lingdesign.co.uk
*website* www.lingdesign.co.uk
*Creative Director* Kirsten Boyd

Artwork for greetings cards and giftwrap.

## Medici*

Grafton House, Hyde Estate Road, London NW9 6JZ
tel 020-8205 2500 fax 020-8205 2552
email sales@medici.co.uk
website www.medici.co.uk
Contact The Art Department

Requirements: full colour or b&w paintings/sketches/etchings/designs suitable for reproduction as greeting cards. Send preliminary letter with brief details of work and colour copies only.

## The Monster Factory*

Unit 207, Welsbach House, 3–9 Broomhill Road,
London SW18 4JQ
tel 020-8875 9988 fax 020-8870 4488
email info@themonsterfactory.com
website www.themonsterfactory.com
Directors Martin Grix, Kate Eagar

Publishers of innovative stationery with a funky, design-led feel. Specialises in handmade ranges, unusual printing techniques and quirky illustration. Will consider original new concepts and fresh artwork styles with bags of character and humour. Do not send original artwork. No verses. Founded 2000.

## The Paper House Group plc*

Waterwells Drive, Gloucester, Glos. GL2 2PH
tel (01452) 888999 fax (01452) 888912
email dewi.morris@paperhouse.co.uk
website www.paperhouse.co.uk
Product Director Chris Wilcox

Specialises in cartoon humour illustration, contemporary art styles and traditional verse design for special occasions and family birthday.

## Paperlink Ltd*

356 Kennington Road, London SE11 4LD
tel 020-7582 8244 fax 020-7587 5212
email info@paperlinkcards.com
website www.paperlinkcards.com
Directors Louise Tighe, Jo Townsend, Tim Porte,
Tim Purcell

Publishers of ranges of humorous and contemporary art greetings cards. Produce products under licence for charities. Founded 1986.

## Paper Studios

4 Britannia House, Point Pleasant, Wallsend,
Tyne and Wear NE28 6HA
tel 0191-295 4200 fax 0191-295 3916
email paperstudios@graphic-humour.demon.co.uk

Traditional, floral and cute designs for greetings cards for all occasions – artwork and 35mm transparencies. Verses considered. Founded 1999.

## Pepperpot

Royston Road, Duxford, Cambridge CB2 4QY
tel (01223) 836825 fax (01223) 833321

Publishing Controller Linda Worsfold

Gift stationery, photo albums, gift cards. Colour illustrations; cute/traditional/floral. Division of Copywrite Designs Ltd.

## Pineapple Park*

58 Wilbury Way, Hitchin, Herts. SG4 0TP
tel (01462) 442021 fax (01462) 440418
email info@pineapplepark.co.uk
website www.pineapplepark.co.uk
Directors Peter M. Cockerline, Sarah M. Parker

Illustrations and photographs for publication as greetings cards. Contemporary, cute, humour: submit artwork or laser copies with sae. Photographic florals always needed. Humour copy/jokes accepted without artwork. Also concepts for ranges. Founded 1993.

## Powell Publishing*

57 Coombe Valley Road, Dover, Kent CT17 0EX
tel (01304) 213999 fax (01304) 240151
email Geraldine@powellprint.co.uk
website www.charitychristmascards.co.uk
Directors B.W. Powell (chairman), T.J. Paulett
(managing)

Greetings card publishers. Interested in Christmas designs for the charity card market. Division of Powell Print Ltd.

## The Publishing House*

PO Box 81, Banbury, Oxon OX16 3YL
tel (01295) 271144 fax (01295) 277403
Directors Naval Phandy, M. Munder

General and also multicultural cards across all faiths. No verses.

## Nigel Quiney Publications Ltd*

Cloudesley House, Shire Hill, Saffron Walden,
Essex CB11 3FB
tel (01799) 520200 fax (01799) 520100
website www.nigelquiney.com
Contact Ms J. Arkinstall, Product & Marketing
Director

Everyday and seasonal greetings cards and giftwrap including fine art, photographic, humour, fun art, contemporary and cute. Submit colour copies, photographs or transparencies: no original artwork.

## Rainbow Cards Ltd*

Kingswood Business Park, Holyhead Road,
Albrighton, Wolverhampton,
West Midlands WV7 3AU
tel (01902) 376000 fax (01902) 376001
email sales@rainbowcards.co.uk
website www.rainbowcards.co.uk

Artwork for humorous and traditional greetings cards. Founded 1976.

## Really Good*
The Old Mast House, The Square, Abingdon,
Oxon OX14 5AR
*tel* (01235) 537888 *fax* (01235) 537779
*website* www.reallygood.uk.com
*Director* David Hicks

Always looking for fun and funny artwork in a
quirky or modern way to publish on cards, stationery
or gifts. Send samples on paper rather than on disk,
etc. Allow plenty of time for review. Founded 1987.

## Felix Rosenstiel's Widow & Son Ltd
Fine Art Publishers, 33–35 Markham Street,
London SW3 3NR
*tel* 020-7352 3551 *fax* 020-7351 5300
*email* sales@felixr.com
*website* www.felixr.com

Invites offers of original oil paintings and strong
watercolours of a professional standard for
reproduction as picture prints for the picture
framing trade. Any type of subject considered; send
photographs of work.

## Royle Publications Ltd – see The Paper
House Group plc

## Santoro Graphics Ltd
Rotunda Point, 11 Hartfield Crescent,
London SW19 3RL
*tel* 020-8781 1100 *fax* 020-8781 1101
*email* enquiries@santorographics.com
*website* www.santorographics.com
*Directors* Lucio Santoro, Meera Santoro (art)

Publishers of innovative and award-winning designs
for greetings cards, giftwrap and gift stationery.
Bold contemporary images with an international
appeal. Subjects covered: quirky and humorous,
whimsical, Fifties, Seventies, futuristic! Styles
include traditional to stylised. Submit samples as
colour photocopies, transparencies or on CD, or via
email as jpgs or pdf files. Founded 1985.

## Second Nature Ltd*
10 Malton Road, London W10 5UP
*tel* 020-8960 0212 *fax* 020-8960 8700
*email* rods@secondnature.co.uk
*website* www.secondnature.co.uk
*Publishing Director* Rod Schragger

Contemporary artwork for greetings cards and
handmade cards; jokes for humorous range; short
modern sentiment; verses. Founded 1981.

## Soul*
Old Mast House, The Square, Abingdon,
Oxon OX14 5AR
*tel* (01235) 537816 *fax* (01235) 537817
*website* www.souluk.com
*Director* David Hicks

Publishers of contemporary, fine and quirky art.
Allow plenty of time for review. Do not send
originals. Sister company of Really Good.

## Noel Tatt Group/Impress Publishing*
Appledown House, Barton Business Park,
Appledown Way, New Dover Road, Canterbury,
Kent CT1 3TE
*tel* (01227) 811600 *fax* (01227) 811601
*email* mail@noeltatt.co.uk
*Director* Jarle Tatt

General everyday cards – broad mix; Christmas.
Will consider verses. Founded 1964.

## Vital Cards Ltd*
PO Box 274, Leatherhead, Surrey KT22 0WL
*tel* (01372) 842753 *fax* (01372) 841051
*email* info@vitalcards.com
*website* www.vitalcards.com
*Managing Director* Peter Galazka

Contemporary art-based designs always considered
for quality greeting card ranges. Submit colour
copies, photographs or CDs. Do not send original
artwork. No verses. Founded 2003.

## Wishing Well Studios Ltd*
Kellet Close, Martland Park, Wigan, Lancs. WN5 0LP
*tel* (01942) 218888 *fax* (01942) 218899
*email* studio@wishingwell2.demon.co.uk
*website* www.wishingwell.co.uk
*Directors* David Evans, Brian Phillips, *Contact* Susie
Riley

Rhyming and prose verse 4–24 lines long; also jokes.
All artwork styles considered. Do not send originals.

## Woodmansterne Publications Ltd*
1 The Boulevard, Blackmoor Lane, Watford,
Herts. WD18 8UW
*tel* (01923) 200600 *fax* (01923) 200601
*email* anne@woodmansterne.co.uk

Greetings cards, wrapping paper, notecards and
social stationery featuring fine and contemporary
art and photography (colour and b&w). Submit
colour copies, photographs or transparencies. No
verses.

## World's Greatest Minds Ltd*
3 Palace Yard Mews, Bath BA1 2NH
*tel* (0870) 770 9802 *fax* (0870) 770 9803
*email* mail@worldsgreatestminds.com
*website* www.worldsgreatestminds.com
*Directors* Paul Baines, Elaine Baines

Quotation cards with illustrated or photographic
contemporary designs. Considers verses. Founded
1994.

# Picture research

## The freelance photographer

Becoming a successful freelance photographer is as much about marketing as photographic talent. Bruce Coleman and Ian Thraves discuss possibilities for the freelance photographer.

Having an outstanding portfolio is one thing, but to receive regular commissions takes a good business head and sound market knowledge. Although working as a professional photographer can be tough, it is undoubtedly one of the most interesting and rewarding ways of earning a living.

### Entering professional photography

A good starting point is to embark on one of the many college courses available, which range from GCSE to degree level, and higher. These form a good foundation, though most teach only the technical aspects of photography and very few cover the basics of running a business. But a good college course will provide students with the opportunity to become familiar with photographic equipment and develop skills without the restrictions and pressures found in the workplace.

In certain fields, such as commercial photography, it is possible to learn the trade as an assistant to an established photographer. A photographer's assistant will undertake many varied tasks, including preparing camera equipment and lighting, building sets, obtaining props and organising locations, as well as general mundane chores. It usually takes only a year or two for an assistant to become a fully competent photographer, having during that time learnt many technical aspects of a particular field of photography and the fundamentals of running a successful business. There is, however, the danger of a long-standing assistant becoming a clone of the photographer worked for, and it is for this reason that some assistants prefer to gain experience with other photographers rather than working for just one for a long period of time. The Association of Photographers can help place an assistant.

However, in other fields of photography, such as photojournalism or wildlife photography, an assistant is not generally required, and photographers in these fields have to learn for themselves as they work.

### Identifying your market

From the outset, identify which markets are most suitable for the kind of subjects you photograph. Study each market carefully and only offer images which suit the client's requirements.

Usually photographers who specialise in a particular field do better than those who generalise. By concentrating on one or two subject areas they become expert at what they do. Those who make a name for themselves are invariably specialists, and it is far easier for the images of, for example, an exceptional fashion photographer or an award-winning wildlife photographer to be remembered than the work of someone who covers a broad range of subjects.

In addition, photographers who produce work with individual style (e.g. by experimenting with camera angles or manipulating images to create unusual effects) are far more likely to make an impact. Alternative images which attract attention and can help sell a product are always sought after. This is especially true of advertising photography, but applies also to other markets such as book and magazine publishers, who are always seeking eye-catching images to use on front covers.

## Promoting yourself

Effective self-promotion tells the market who you are and what service you offer. A first step should be to create an outstanding portfolio of images, tailored to appeal to the targeted market. Photographers targeting a few different markets should create an individual portfolio for each rather than presenting a single general one, including only a few relevant images. A portfolio containing between 10 and 20 images is enough for a potential client to judge a photographer's abilities.

Images should be presented in a format which the client is used to handling. Transparencies (perhaps duplicated to a larger size for easier viewing and general impact) are usually suitable for the editorial markets, but often more general companies prefer to view high-quality prints. Images can also be presented on CD-Rom and, unlike a traditional portfolio, can be left with potential clients to keep and refer to. Any published material (often referred to as 'tearsheets') should also be added to a portfolio. Tearsheets are often presented mounted and laminated in plastic.

Business cards and letterheads should be designed to reflect style and professionalism. Consider using a good graphic designer to design a logo for use on cards, letterheads and any other promotional literature. Many photographers produce postcard-size business cards and include an image as well as their name and logo.

### Professional organisations

**The Association of Photographers**
*Co-Secretary* Gwen Thomas,
81 Leonard Street, London EC2A 4QS
*tel* 020-7739 6669 *fax* 020-7739 8707
*email* general@aophoto.co.uk
*website* www.the-aop.org
See page 504.

**British Institute of Professional Photography**
Fox Talbot House, Amwell End, Ware,
Herts. SG12 9HN
*tel* (01920) 464011
*email* bippware@aol.com
*website* www.bipp.com
See page 510.

**Master Photographers Association**
Jubilee House, 1 Chancery Lane, Darlington,
Co. Durham DL1 5QP
*tel* (01325) 356555 *fax* (01325) 357813
*email* info@mpauk.com
*website* www.mpauk.com
See page 525.

**The Royal Photographic Society**
The Octagon, Milsom Street, Bath BA1 1DN
*tel* (01225) 462841 *fax* (01225) 448688
*email* rps@rps.org
*website* www.rps.org
See page 533.

**BAPLA (British Association of Picture Libraries and Agencies)**
See page 506.

Other than word of mouth, advertising is probably the best way of making your services known to potential clients. For a local market, a business directory such as *Yellow Pages* is a good start. Specialist directories in which photographers can advertise include *The Creative Handbook* and *Contact Photographers* (see page 456).

Cold calling by telephone is probably the most cost-effective and productive way of making contacts, and these should be followed up by an appointment for a personal visit (if possible) in order to show a portfolio of images. This helps to ensure you will not be forgotten.

Most photographers now use the internet as a medium to promote themselves. A cleverly designed website is a stylish and cost-effective way to expose a photographer's portfolio to a global market, as well as being a convenient way for a potential client to view a photographer's work. A personal website address should be added to business stationery and to other forms of advertising together with the usual address and telephone number information.

Creating a website is usually much cheaper than advertising using conventional published print media. However, its design should be carefully composed and is probably best left to a professional website designer (see *Setting up a website*, page 586). Although many images and details about your business can be placed on a website, one limiting factor is the time it can take to download the images due to the size of the files. Unless this is a relatively quick process the viewer may lose patience and cancel access to the site.

A well-organised exhibition of images is a very effective way of bringing your work to the attention of current and potential new clients. Throw a preview party with refreshments for friends, colleagues and specially invited guests from the industry. A show which is well reviewed by critics who write for newspapers and magazines can generate additional interest.

As a photographer's career develops, the budget for self-promotion should increase. Many established photographers will go as far as producing full-colour mailers, posters, and even calendars, which all contain examples of their work.

## Digital photography

Digital photography and image-enhancement and manipulation using computer technology are now widely used in the photographic industry. Since the cost of digital cameras and other hardware can be considerably cheaper than using large quantities of film, many photographers are now using this technology.

There are various levels of quality produced by digital cameras and photographers should consider the requirements of their market prior to investing in expensive hardware which is prone to rapid change and improvement. At the cheaper level (£2000–£5000) the 35mm style digital cameras manufactured by companies such as Nikon and Canon can produce outstanding quality images suitable for many end uses. Cameras like these are now used predominantly for press, PR and general commercial work.

At a higher level, many commercial studio photographers have invested in a 'digital capture back', which is a high-quality chip which can be adapted to fit many of the conventional studio cameras. This system is far more expensive, but is capable of producing file sizes which closely compare in quality to a high-resolution scan from large format film. Thus the images are suitable for any end use, such as top-quality advertisements. Photographers thinking of supplying stock libraries with digital images should realise that it is often this kind of quality which is required, as stock libraries are looking to supply a diverse range of markets, including advertising.

Image-enhancement and manipulation using a computer program such as Adobe Photoshop provides photographers with an on-screen darkroom where the possibilities for creating imaginative images are endless. As well as being useful for retouching purposes and creating photo compositions, it provides the photographer with an opportunity to create more unusual images. It is therefore especially useful for targeting the advertising market, where fantasy images are more important than reality.

## Useful information

### Bureau of Freelance Photographers

Focus House, 497 Green Lanes, London N13 4BP
*tel* 020-8882 3315 *fax* 020-8886 5174
*website* www.thebfp.com
*Chief Executive* John Tracy

Helps the freelance photographer by providing information on markets and a free advisory service. Publishes *Market Newsletter* (monthly). Membership: £45 p.a.

### Directories

### Reed Business Information

Windsor Court, East Grinstead House, Wood Street, East Grinstead, West Sussex RH19 1XA
*tel* (01342) 332034 *fax* (01342) 332037

Publishes *The Creative Handbook*.

### Elfande Ltd

Surrey House, 31 Church Street, Leatherhead, Surrey KT22 8EF
*tel* (01372) 220300 *fax* (01372) 220340
*email* mail@contact-uk.com
*website* www.contact-uk.com

Publishes *Contact Photographers*.

## Using a stock library

As well as undertaking commissions, photographers have the option of selling their images through a photographic stock library or agency. There are many stock libraries in the UK, some specialising in specific subject areas, such as wildlife photography, and others covering general subjects (see *Picture agencies and libraries*, page 463).

Stock libraries are fiercely competitive, all fighting for a share of the market, and it is therefore best to aim to place images with an established name, although competition amongst photographers will be strong. Each stock library has different specific requirements and established markets, so contact them first before making a submission. Some libraries will ask to see a few hundred images from a photographer in order to judge for consistency of quality and saleability. Stock libraries selling images through catalogues or over the internet will often consider an initial submission of just a few images, knowing that it is possible to accumulate significant fees from a small number of outstanding individual images marketed this way.

Images placed with a library remain the property of the photographer and libraries do not normally sell images outright to clients, but lease them for a specific use for a fee, from which commission is deducted. This means that a single image can accumulate many sales over a period of time. The commission rate is usually about 50% of every sale generated by the library. This may sound high, but it should be borne in mind that the library takes on all overheads, marketing costs and other responsibilities involved in the smooth running of a business, allowing the photographer the freedom to spend more time taking pictures.

Photographers should realise, however, that stock photography is a long-term investment and it can take some time for sales to build up to a significant income. Clearly, photographers who supply the right images for the market, and are prolific, are those who do well, and there are a good number of photographers who make their entire living as full-time stock photographers, never having to undertake commissioned work.

## Royalty-free CD companies

Many stock libraries are now marketing royalty-free images on CD-Rom. These companies usually obtain images by purchasing them from photographers for a flat fee or pay royalties to the photographer based on CD sales. Once a CD has been purchased by a client they, in effect, own the images on the CD and are therefore able to reproduce them as many times as they wish, paying no further fees. A typical CD may contain one hundred high-resolution reproduction-quality images in a variety of subject areas, including most specialist subjects.

Although photographers may be tempted to sell images to these companies in order to gain an instant fee, they should be aware that placing images with a traditional stock library can be far more fruitful financially in the long term, since a good image can accumulate very high fees over a period of time and go on selling for many years to come. Furthermore, the photographer always retains the rights to his or her own images.

## Running your own library

Photographers choosing to market their own images or start up their own library have the advantage of retaining a full fee for every picture sale they make. But it is unlikely that an individual photographer could ever match the rates of an established library, or make the same volume of sales per image. However, the internet has opened a new marketing avenue for photographers, who now have the opportunity to sell their images worldwide. Previously, only an established stock library would have been able to do this. Before embarking on establishing a home library, photographers should be aware that the business of marketing images is essentially a desk job which involves a considerable amount of paperwork and time, which could be spent taking pictures.

When setting up a picture library, your first consideration should be whether to build up a library of your own images, or to take on other contributing photographers. Many photographers running their own libraries submit additional images to bigger libraries to increase the odds of making a good income. Often, a photographer's personal library is made up of work rejected by the larger libraries, which are usually only interested in images that will regularly sell and generate a high turnover. However, occasional sales can generate a significant amount of income for the individual. Furthermore, a photographer with a library of specialised subjects stands a good chance of gaining recognition with niche markets, which can be very lucrative if the competition for those particular subjects is low.

If you take on contributing photographers, the responsibility for another's work becomes yours, so it is important to draw up a contract with terms of business for both your contributing photographers and your clients. Loss or damage of images is the most important consideration when sending pictures to clients (most libraries will charge clients a fee of £400–£600 per image for loss or damage of originals). It is often worth checking that a company wishing to receive transparencies does have adequate insurance to cover these fees, which can amount to a considerable figure if a large quantity of images is lost or damaged. On no account should images be sent to companies which refuse to take responsibility for loss or damage, nor to private individuals, unless they are working on a freelance basis for an established company. It should also be clearly stated in your terms that all pictures in the client's possession become the client's responsibility until they are returned and inspected for damage by the library. Many libraries are now taking a safer approach to distributing images by scanning them first and then supplying them as digital files either on CD or direct to clients, usually via ISDN or Broadband. In addition to being a much cheaper way of distributing images, the problem of loss or damage or original material is also eliminated.

Reproduction fees should also be established on a strict basis, bearing in mind that you owe it to your contributing photographers to command fees which are as high as possible when selling the rights to their images. It is also essential that you control how pictures will be used and the amount of exposure they will receive. The fees should be established according to the type of client using the image and how the image itself will be reproduced. Important factors to consider are where the image will appear, to what size it will be reproduced, the size of the print run, and the territorial rights required by the client. Many libraries also apply holding fees in cases where clients hold on to pictures for periods of time longer than a month.

**Bruce Coleman** is Chairman of Bruce Coleman The Natural World and past President of the British Association of Picture Libraries. **Ian Thraves** is a freelance photographer and former picture editor at Bruce Coleman The Natural World (www.thravesphoto.co.uk).

# The picture research revolution

Julian Jackson describes how picture researchers have had to change the way they work since entering the 'digital age'.

Picture researchers find the images you see in books, magazines, on television shows and videos, and now on CD-Roms and the internet. For many years picture research was a relatively static profession. The procedures for contacting picture suppliers didn't change very much. The researcher would phone or fax a supplier with a request then a package of transparencies or prints would arrive in the post. Since entering the 'digital age' this has changed dramatically. Now picture researchers need to learn new skills in addition to the old ones. They need considerable internet search competencies. They also need enough technological knowledge to check that digital files are of sufficient quality for their use, which may be for a much wider variety of media. In an era of rapid technological change they need to keep an eye out for developments such as new file formats or software.

**Courses and training**

**London School of Publishing**
David Game House, 69 Notting Hill Gate, London W11 3JS
*tel* 020-7221 3399 *fax* 020-7243 1730
*email* lsp@easynet.co.uk
*website* www.publishing-school.co.uk
A 10-week evening course suitable for anyone wanting to pursue a career in picture research.

**The Publishing Training Centre at Book House**
45 East Hill, London SW18 2QZ
*tel* 020-8874 2718 *fax* 020-8870 8985
*email* publishing.training@bookhouse.co.uk
*website* www.train4publishing.co.uk
One-day picture research course suitable for those already working in publishing, aimed at those who already have some picture research experience. Also offers Picture Research by Distance Learning, a comprehensive course for home study.

## Traditional picture research

There are two sorts of researchers: freelances, and salaried staff, sometimes called 'in-house' researchers. The way they both approach a job is the same. Generally most picture research assignments follow this pattern:

1. Briefing and creation of picture list.
2. The picture researcher contacts picture libraries, press agencies, photographers, museums, galleries or other picture sources, by phone, fax, email or personal visit.
3. Photography is commissioned, if appropriate.
4. Pictures arrive and are 'booked in'.
5. A preliminary selection is made, usually by the picture researcher, designer and editor working in concert.
6. Rejected pictures are returned to the library.
7. A final selection is made.
8. The picture researcher negotiates the fees, creates a list of contributors to be credited, and checks the proofs.
9. The picture researcher returns all the remaining unused pictures, and those used when they return from the printers or other production organisations.
10. The picture researcher keeps records and sends complementary copies or

'tearsheets' (the page that the supplier's picture was used on) to the various suppliers of the pictures.

This is a broad view of how all picture research assignments work, whether for traditional media such as books, or new media like CD-Roms. In some cases there might already be a fee structure in place so the researcher does not have to do fee negotiation.

## Skills required

Picture researchers need to be organised, diligent, capable of leaps of the imagination when necessary ("I bet there's a museum devoted to shopping bags somewhere!"), and above all *diplomatic*. They need the ability to wheedle images out of sometimes unresponsive people: professional image libraries pride themselves on swift, efficient service, but picture researchers have to deal with museum staff, private collectors, individual photographers, PR people, and the odd complete nutter who just happens to own the rights to *the picture you must have*. Of all the skills necessary, this is the most vital.

A good picture researcher also needs diligence and good organisation.

### Picture Researcher's Handbook
by Hilary and Mary Evans, 7th edn, Pira

No picture researcher should be without this invaluable and comprehensive source of picture libraries worldwide. The book clearly lists where picture libraries are, the subjects they cover and addresses, websites, email addresses, telephone and fax numbers.

### BAPLA Directory
BAPLA, 18 Vine Hill, London EC1R 5DZ
*tel* 020-7713 1780 *fax* 020-7713 1211

Lists all the current members of the British Association of Picture Libraries and Agencies (BAPLA).

### Stock Index
The Publishing Factory, 32 Queensway, London W2 3RX
*tel* 020-7727 4236 *fax* 020-7792 4034
*email* space@creativecityonline.com
*website* www.stock-index-online.com

Supports the leading source books to specialist stock photography libraries. A free online research facility containing catalogues and industry news.

### Picture Research in a Digital Age
by Julian Jackson
*website* www.julianjackson.co.uk/pic_res_dig.htm

This e-book covers digital photography, scanning, searching the internet, and many other important topics to enable researchers to get the best out of the digital age. It is available online, and can be downloaded immediately.

Diligence means keeping tabs on the pictures so they do not get lost. Though theoretically this isn't difficult, with large amounts of material and perhaps over-eager designers who take pictures from the files without telling you, transparencies do get lost. It isn't even necessary to lose the transparency: taking one out of its mount to scan, then losing the mount is often enough to mean hours of searching through delivery notes in order to track down which library it came from.

Though this is not often evident to outsiders, pictures are *valuable*. If a photographer has trekked to the Grand Canyon at dawn, and you lose the original, that picture is gone forever. A £400 replacement fee is not really too much in that particular case but some loss fees are much higher. While the occasional picture may go astray, the more a picture researcher keeps control over the situation, the fewer catastrophes will happen. For example, only give the designers selected images and keep the 'rejects', and note which images they have retained.

## Useful organisations

**The Association of Photographers**
See page 504.

**BAPLA (British Association of Picture Libraries and Agencies)**
See page 506.

**DACS (Design and Artists Copyright Society)**
See page 689.

**The Picture Research Association**
See page 530.

If you are a freelance and working from home there could be significant costs if you lose some pictures, so you need to take a careful look at your house contents insurance to see if that eventuality is covered. Once you deliver material to the client, then their insurance should cover it, but this is a point to note.

### The digital wave

Digitisation of files and the advent of the internet in general has caused a revolution in picture research. Agonised waits for a package of transparencies to arrive from Inner Mongolia are a thing of the past; now pictures can be sent by ISDN in seconds. Commissioning a photographer is streamlined when you can look at his or her portfolio online. Email is particularly convenient for dealing with suppliers in different time zones.

Like the famous 'butterfly' chaos theory, digitisation has caused a tornado which is roaring through the industry. Deadlines are shorter, leaving less time for considered decisions. Unlike transparencies, digital files can be unusable for a variety of invisible factors: for example, bad scanning, wrong resolution, corruption. These problems usually become evident at the last possible moment. Old-style picture researchers would have rejected a bad transparency or print at an early stage so these problems would have been avoided.

In recent years, picture researchers have had to learn powerful computer search skills and develop understandings of many technological concepts. For some this has been a difficult process that has lessened the enjoyment of the job. Unfortunately, one of the spin-offs from digitisation has been that employers may mistakenly believe that a researcher can do his or her job from behind a computer. However, it is estimated that only 3%–5% of the pictures of major collections are currently digitised. The personal visit to a source to find images, and forge a relationship with the people there – often experts in their subject – is still an essential part of the job.

### Old style v. digital

There are advantages and disadvantages to both ways of working. Most picture researchers will continue to handle prints and transparencies in the conventional manner alongside downloading, modifying, and transmitting digital files from their computer.

- One distinct advantage of digital files is that they can be instantly downloaded from the web or sent via ISDN, ADSL or other means.
- Working with digital files means that there are no time-consuming and tedious returns to do.
- Analogue media – prints, negatives and transparencies – can be immediately

assessed for quality. To assess the quality of a digital file, further investigation is required.

● Intricate keywording systems often fail to find pictures which the library holds. Phoning the library's experienced staff may well be a better use of your time than spending hours wrestling with an online search system.

● Sometimes it is hard to keep track of digital files on a computer system, especially if the file name is just a number, as opposed to a descriptive name, such as 'Picture of Paris.jpg'.

● Negotiating fees remains the same. It is what the picture is *used* for, not whether it is analogue or digital, that is the main criterion.

## Picture research now

Picture research has changed. Old-style methods of receiving transparencies in the post and viewing them on a lightbox are still valid, but the speed and convenience of digital files means that online picture research is essential for researchers. Modern researchers need high levels of computer search skills to enable them to find the pictures they want, whether it's by searching the web generally, or accessing the online search systems of picture libraries.

**Julian Jackson** is a writer, internet expert and consultant to the UK picture research industry. He has close links with many companies and organisations within the photographic industry. His website is www.julianjackson.co.uk

# Picture agencies and libraries

As well as supplying images to picture editors, picture researchers and others who use pictures, picture agencies and libraries provide a service to the freelance photographer as one way of selling their work. Most of the agencies and libraries listed in this section take work from other photographers. To find which ones cover specific subjects see page 758.

**\*Member of the British Association of Picture Libraries and Agencies (BAPLA)**

If you want to introduce your work to a library or agency, send samples on CDs or disks, or send tearsheets, duplicates or colour photocopies. Find out if they accept images via email or ISDN. Your work runs the risk of getting lost or damaged whilst in transit so never send unsolicited original material. To find out if agencies operate with analogue or digital files, or both, and which subject areas agencies and libraries cover, see the image/contact database of reputable and accredited libraries and agencies listed at the BAPLA (British Association of Picture Libraries and Agencies) website (www.bapla.org). BAPLA (see page 506) also supports the writer or freelance photographer through its free online job vacancy service – see the website for details.

## See also ...
- *Card and stationery publishers which accept photographs*, page 493
- *Syndicates, news and press agencies*, page 121
- *The freelance photographer*, page 453
- *The picture research revolution*, page 459
- *National newspapers UK and Ireland*, page 7

## AA World Travel Library*
16th Floor, Forum House, Basing View, Basingstoke, Hants. RG21 4EA
*tel* (01256) 491588 *fax* (01256) 492440
*email* travel-images@theaa.com
*Picture Sales Manager* Liz Allen

Approx. 160,000 colour transparencies of worldwide travel images. All images are available in digital format. Part of AA Publishing. Founded 1990.

## A.A. & A. Ancient Art & Architecture Collection*
Suite 1, 1st Floor, 410–420 Rayners Lane, Pinner, Middlesex HA5 5DY
*tel* 020-8429 3131 *fax* 020-8429 4646
*email* library@aaacollection.co.uk
*website* www.aaacollection.com

Specialises in the history of civilisations of the Middle East, Mediterranean countries, Europe, Asia, Americas, from ancient times to recent past, their arts, architecture, beliefs and peoples.

## Abode Interiors Picture Library Ltd*
Albion Court, 1 Pierce Street, Macclesfield, Cheshire SK11 6ER
*tel* (01625) 500070 *fax* (01625) 500910
*email* info@abodepix.co.uk
*website* www.abodepix.co.uk
*Contact* Judi Goodwin

Colour photo library specialising in English and Scottish house interiors of all styles, types and periods. High-quality material only; terms by agreement. Phone before sending material. Founded 1993.

## Academic File News Photos
Eastern Art Publishing Group, PO Box 13666, 27 Wallorton Gardens, London SW14 8WF
*tel* 020-8392 1122 *fax* 020-8392 1422
*email* afis@eapgroup.com
*website* www.eapgroup.com
*Director* Sajid Rizvi

Daily news coverage in UK and general library of arts, cultures, people and places, with special reference to

the Middle East, North Africa and Asia. New
photographers welcomed to cover UK and abroad.
Sample pictures accepted over email. Founded 1985.

## acestock.com*
Satellite House, 2 Salisbury Road, London SW19 4EZ
*tel* 020-8944 9944 *fax* 020-8944 9940
*email* info@acestock.com
*website* www.acestock.com

General library: people, industry, business, travel,
commerce, skies, sport, music and natural history.
Worldwide syndication. Sae for enquiries. Very
selective editing policy. Terms: 50%. Founded 1980.

## Action Plus*
54–58 Tanner Street, London SE1 3PH
*tel* 020-7403 1558 *fax* 020-7403 1526
*email* info@actionplus.co.uk
*website* www.actionplus.co.uk

Specialist sports and action picture library.
Comprehensive collection of creative images,
including all aspects of 130 professional and
amateur sports worldwide. Covers all age groups, all
ethnic groups and all levels of ability. 35mm colour
stock and online digital archive. Terms: 50%.
Founded 1986.

## Lesley and Roy Adkins Picture Library
Ten Acre Wood, Heath Cross, Whitestone,
Exeter EX4 2HW
*tel* (01392) 811357 *fax* (01392) 811435
*email* mail@adkinsarchaeology.com
*website* www.adkinsarchaeology.com

Colour library covering archaeology, ancient history,
history and heritage; prehistoric, Roman, Greek,
Egyptian and medieval sites and monuments;
landscape, countryside, architecture, towns, villages
and religious monuments. Founded 1989.

## Aerofilms*
Aerofilms Ltd, Gate Studios, Station Road,
Borehamwood, Herts. WD6 1EJ
*tel* 020-8207 0666 *fax* 020-8207 5433
*email* library@aerofilms.com

Comprehensive library – over 2.5 million photos
going back to 1919 – of vertical and oblique aerial
photographs of UK; large areas with complete
cover. Founded 1919.

## Air Photo Supply
42 Sunningvale Avenue, Biggin Hill,
Kent TN16 3BX
*tel* (01959) 574872
*email* norman.rivett@virgin.net

Aircraft and associated subjects, Southeast England,
colour and monochrome. No other photographers'
material required. Founded 1963.

## akg-images*
5 Melbray Mews, 158 Hurlingham Road,
London SW6 3NS
*tel* 020-7610 6103 *fax* 020-7610 6125
*email* enquiries@akg-london.co.uk
*website* www.akg-images.co.uk

Principal subjects covered: art, archaeology and
history. Exclusive UK and US representative for the
Archiv für Kunst und Geschichte (AKG) with full
access to the 10 million images held by AKG Berlin.
Also exclusively represents the Erich Lessing Culture
and Fine Art Archives in the UK. Founded 1994.

## Alamy.com*
Unit 6F, Milton Park, Abingdon, Oxon OK14 4RR
*tel* (01235) 844603 *fax* (01235) 844650
*email* memterservices@alamy.com
submissions@alamy.com
*website* www.alamy.com
*Contact* Alexandra Bortkiemiz, Director of
Photography

Over 100,000 digital images of all subjects including
business, lifestyle, travel, abstracts, concepts, still life,
sports, food, wildlife, landscapes, fine art, science,
celebrities, historical, reportage. Photographers must
supply their own scans and keywording, which is
completed online after submission. Scans are
checked for technical quality. For initial approach
register at the website. Image submission guidelines
and Contributor Agreement are both available
online. Correspondence by email is preferred. Terms:
image submission fee (fees are offset against sales).
Non-exclusive contract. Photographer receives up to
90% of sale commission.

## Bryan and Cherry Alexander Photography*
Higher Cottage, Manston, Sturminster Newton,
Dorset DT10 1EZ
*tel* (01258) 473006 *fax* (01258) 473333
*email* alexander@arcticphoto.co.uk
*website* www.arcticphoto.co.uk

Polar regions with emphasis on indigenous peoples
of the North. Landscape and wildlife: Alaska to
Siberia and Antarctica. Founded 1973.

## Allied Artists
5 Fauconberg Road, London W4 3JZ
*tel* 020-8995 5500 *fax* 020-8995 8844
*email* info@alliedartists.ltd.uk
*website* www.alliedartists.ltd.uk
*Contacts* Gary Mills, Mary Burtenshaw

Agency for illustrators specialising in a wide range
of styles for magazines, books, children's books and
advertising. Large colour library. Founded 1983.

## Allsport UK – incorporated into Getty Images

## American History Picture Library
3 Barton Buildings, Bath BA1 2JR
*tel* (01225) 334213 *fax* (01225) 480554

Photographs, engravings, colour transparencies covering the exploration and social, political and military history of North America from 15th to 20th century: conquistadors, civil war, railroads, the Great Depression, advertisements, Prohibition and gangsters, moon landings and space.

## AMIS
26 Kirkcaldy Road, Burntisland, Fife KY3 9HQ
*tel* (01592) 873546 *fax* (01592) 873546
*Proprietor* Hamish Brown MBE, FRSGS

Picture library on Moroccan sites, topography, mountains, travel. Illustration service. Commissions undertaken. No pictures purchased.

## Ancient Egypt Picture Library*
6 Branden Drive, Knutsford, Cheshire WA16 8EJ
*tel* (01565) 633106 *fax* (01565) 633106
*email* BobEgyptPL@aol.com

Images of Egypt, including most of the ancient sites and views of modern Egypt. All photographs (over 30,000 colour transparencies) taken by an Egyptologist, who can also provide full historical/ archaeological information. Founded 1996.

## Andalucía Slide Library
Apto 499, Estepona, Málaga 29680, Spain
*tel* (34) 952-793647 *fax* (34) 952-880138
*email* info@andaluciaslidelibrary.com
*website* www.andaluciaslidelibrary.com
*Contact* Michelle Chaplow

Colour transparencies and digital images covering all aspects of Andalucía and Spain, principally its geography and culture. Also images of Portugal, Madeira, Malta. Commissions undertaken. Founded 1991.

## Andes Press Agency*
26 Padbury Court, London E2 7EH
*tel* 020-7613 5417 *fax* 020-7739 3159
*email* apa@andespressagency.com
*Director* Carlos Reyes

Social, political and economic aspects of Latin America, Africa, Asia, Middle East, Europe and Britain; specialises in Latin America and contemporary world religions. Founded 1983.

## Heather Angel/Natural Visions*
Highways, 6 Vicarage Hill, Farnham, Surrey GU9 8HJ
*tel* (01252) 716700 *fax* (01252) 727464
*email* hangel@naturalvisions.co.uk
*website* www.naturalvisions.co.uk

Colour transparencies (35mm and 2¼in square) with worldwide coverage of natural history and biological subjects including animals, plants, natural habitats (deserts, polar regions, rainforests, wetlands, etc), landscapes, gardens, close-ups and underwater images; also man's impact on the environment – pollution, acid rain, urban wildlife, etc. Large China file including pandas in all seasons. Extensive water file (liquid, solid and vapour). With our new online website (over 16,000 images) we can now send a digital lightbox to authors with an email. We then supply high res. digital files to the publisher. Pictures cannot be supplied *gratis* for personal use.

## Animal Photography*
4 Marylebone Mews, New Cavendish Street, London W1G 8PY
*tel* 020-7935 0503 *fax* 020-7487 3038
*email* thompson@animal-photography.co.uk
*website* www.animal-photography.co.uk

Horses, dogs, cats, small pets, East Africa, Galapagos. Other photographers' work not represented. Founded 1955.

## Aquarius Library*
PO Box 5, Hastings, East Sussex TN34 1HR
*tel* (01424) 721196 *fax* (01424) 717704
*email* aquarius.lib@clara.net
*website* www.aquariuscollection.com
*Contact* David Corkill

Showbusiness specialist library with over one million colour and b&w images: film stills, classic portraiture, candids, archive material to present. New material added every week. Downloadable website of TV & film stills. Division of SPM London Ltd.

## Arcaid Architectural Photography and Picture Library*
Parc House, 25–37 Cowleaze Road, Kingston upon Thames, Surrey KT2 6DZ
*tel* 020-8546 4352 *fax* 020-8541 5230
*email* arcaid@arcaid.co.uk
*websites* www.arcaid.co.uk, www.alamy.com/arcaid

'The built environment' – international collection: architecture, interior design, lifestyle interiors, gardens, travel, museums, historic and contemporary. Terms: 50%.

## Archivio Veneziano – see Venice Picture Library

## Arctic Camera
66 Ashburnham Grove, London SE10 8UJ
*tel* 020-8692 7651 *fax* 020-8692 7651
*email* Derek.Fordham@btinternet.com
*Contact* Derek Fordham

Colour transparencies of all aspects of Arctic life and environment. Founded 1978.

## Ardea Wildlife Pets Environment*
35 Brodrick Road, London SW17 7DX
tel 020-8672 2067 fax 020-8672 8787
email info@ardea.com
website www.ardea.com
Contact Sophie Napier

Specialist worldwide natural history photographic library of animals, birds, plants, fish, insects, reptiles, worldwide scenics and domestic pets.

## Art Sense
1 Town Mead Business Centre, William Morris Way, London SW6 2SZ
tel 020-7751 0007 fax 020-7751 0007
email joefilmbase@btconnect.com
website www.joefilmbase.com

General library: fashion, catwalk, people, business, ideas, art photos, business, traders, travel, dance, concerts, cars, boats, lifestyle, nature, worldwide. Transparencies: 35mm, 6 x 7cm, etc. Founded 1991.

## The Associated Press Ltd*
News Photo Department, The Associated Press House, 12 Norwich Street, London EC4A 1BP
tel 020-7427 4260/4266, 020-7427 4263 (library manager) fax 020-7427 4269
email london_photolibrary@ap.org
website www.apwideworld.com

News, features, sports, 20th century history, personalities.

## Australia Pictures
28 Sheen Common Drive, Richmond, London TW10 5BN
tel 020-7602 1989 fax 020-7602 1989
Contact John Miles

Comprehensive library covering Australia, Aboriginals and their art, indigenous peoples, underwater, Tibet, Peru, Bolivia, Iran, Irian Jaya, Pakistan, Yemen. Founded 1988.

## Aviation Picture Library (Austin J. Brown)*
116 The Avenue, St Stephen's, London W13 8JX
tel 020-8566 7712 mobile (07860) 670073
fax 020-8566 7714
email avpix@aol.com
website www.aviationpictures.com

Worldwide aviation photographic library, including dynamic views of aircraft. Aerial and travel library including Europe, Caribbean, USA, and East and West Africa. Material taken since 1960. Specialising in air-to-air and air-to-ground commissions. Chief photographers for *Flyer* magazine. Founded 1970.

## A-Z Botanical Collection Ltd
192 Goswell Road, London EC1V 7DT
tel 020-7253 0991 fax 020-7253 0992

email sales@azbotanical.com
website www.idspicturedesk.com
Library Manager Johanna Lindsay-MacDougall

Colour transparencies of plant life worldwide, including named gardens, habitats, gardening, still life, romantic seasonal shots, fungi, pests and diseases, etc (6 x 6cm, 35mm, 5 x 4in).

## B. & B. Photographs
Prospect House, Clifford Chambers, Stratford upon Avon CV37 8HX
tel (01789) 298106 fax (01789) 292450
email BandBPhotographs@btinternet.com

35mm/medium format colour library of horticulture (especially pests and diseases) and geography (worldwide), natural history and biological education. Other photographers' work not represented. Founded 1974.

## Bandphoto Agency
29–31 Saffron Hill, London EC1N 8SW
tel 020-7421 6000 fax 020-7421 6006
website www.uppa.co.uk

International news and feature picture service for British and overseas publishers.

## Barnaby's Picture Library – see Mary Evans Picture Library

## Barnardo's Photographic Archive*
Tanners Lane, Barkingside, Ilford, Essex IG6 1QG
tel 020-8498 7345 fax 020-8498 7090
email Stephen.pover@barnados.org.uk
website www.barnardos.org.uk

Extensive collection of b&w and colour images dating from 1874 to the present day covering social history with the emphasis on children and child care. Also 300 films dating from 1905. Founded 1872.

## BBC Natural History Unit Picture Library – see Nature Picture Library

## BBC Photo Library*
B116, Television Centre, Wood Lane, London W12 7RJ
tel 020-8225 7193 fax 020-8576 7020
email research-central@bbc.co.uk
website www.bbcresearchcentral.com
Photo Sales Coordinator Richard Jeffery

A unique collection of 4 million stills dating from 1922 and the earliest days of radio and TV broadcasting. Stills can be researched by name, programme title and subject, and images supplied in print, transparency or digital formats.

## Dr Alan Beaumont
52 Squires Walk, Lowestoft, Suffolk NR32 4LA
tel (01502) 560126

*email* embeaumont@supernet.com

Worldwide collection of monochrome prints and colour transparencies (35mm and 6 x 7cm) of natural history, countryside, windmills and aircraft. Brochure and subject lists available. No other photographers required.

## Stephen Benson Slide Bureau

45 Sugden Road, London SW11 5EB
*tel* 020-7223 8635
*email* info@avintageoccasion.com

World: agriculture, archaeology, architecture, commerce, everyday life, culture, environment, geography, science, tourism. Speciality: South America, the Caribbean, Australasia, Nepal, Turkey, Israel and Egypt. Assignments undertaken.

## bfi Stills, Posters and Designs*

British Film Institute, 21 Stephen Street, London W1T 1LN
*tel* 020-7957 4797 *fax* 020-7323 9260
*email* still.films@bfi.org.uk
*website* www.bfi.org.uk
*Stills, Posters and Designs Manager* Tess Quinn

The world's most comprehensive collection of film and TV images with 7 million photographs and colour transparencies from over 200,000 films and TV programmes. The collection holds on- and off-screen moments, portraits of the world's most famous stars – and those behind the camera who made them famous – in addition to images of studios, cinemas and special events. Visits by appointment. Copyright clearance is the responsibility of the user. Stills archive founded 1948.

## Bird Images

28 Carousel Walk, Sherburn in Elmet, North Yorkshire LS25 6LP
*tel* (01977) 684666 *fax* (01977) 684666
*email* paul@birdvideodvd.com
*Principal* P. Doherty

Specialist in the birds of Britain and Europe, including video footage from Europe and North America. Expert captioning service available. Founded 1989.

## John Birdsall Social Issues Photo Library*

75 Raleigh Street, Nottingham NG7 4DL
*tel* 0115-978 2645 *fax* 0115-978 5546
*email* photos@johnbirdsall.co.uk
*website* www.johnbirdsall.co.uk
*Contact* Anna Grapes

Contemporary social documentary library specialising in model released images of children, youth, older people, health, families, disability, education, housing, work; also Nottingham and surrounding area; Spain, Cuba, India – commissions

and stock pictures. Online catalogue searchable in both English and German. Founded 1980.

## The Anthony Blake Photo Library*

20 Blades Court, Deodar Road, London SW15 2NU
*tel* 020-8877 1123 *fax* 020-8877 9787
*email* info@abpl.co.uk
*website* www.abpl.co.uk

Food and wine images from around the world, including raw ingredients, finished dishes, shops, restaurants, markets, agriculture and viticulture. Commissions undertaken. Contributors welcome. Brochure available.

## John Blake Picture Library – see Stockwave

## Sarah Boait Photography and Picture Library

*tel* (01409) 281354 *fax* (01409) 281354
*email* sarahboait@compuserve.com
*website* www.sarahboait.co.uk

The British Isles, especially the West Country and locations from legend and folklore; also world travel, world religions. No contributors' work accepted.

## Bodleian Library*

Oxford OX1 3BG
*Published slides and filmstrips*
*tel* (01865) 277214/277152 *fax* (01865) 277187
*email* slidesales@bodley.ox.ac.uk
*websites* www.bodley.ox.ac.uk/dept/scwmss/wmss/medieval/browse.htm, www.bodley.ox.ac.uk/dept/scwmss/wmss/medieval/slides/cumulative.htm, www.bodley.ox.ac.uk/dept/scwmss/wmss/Orderforms2002-UK-EU.pdf, www.bodley.ox.ac.uk/dept/scwmss/wmss/Orderforms2002-World.pdf
*Imaging Service*
*tel* (01865) 277215/277061 *fax* (01865) 287127
*email* repro@bodley.ox.ac.uk
*website* www.bodley.ox.ac.uk/dept/imaging

*Published slides and manuscripts:* Library of 32,000 35mm colour transparencies in slides or filmstrips for immediate sale (not hire). There is an iconographical index to the images, which are mostly from medieval manuscripts.

*Imaging Service:* Large format transparencies more suitable for reproduction are available to order, as are copies, photographs and microfilm of any other items from the Bodleian's vast collections.

## Chris Bonington Picture Library*

Badger Hill, Hesket Newmarket, Wigton, Cumbria CA7 8LA
*tel* (016974) 78286 *fax* (016974) 78238
*email* frances@bonington.com
*website* www.bonington.com
*Manager* Frances Daltrey

Mountains and mountaineering, climbers and

climbing in Tibet, Nepal and the Himalayas. Includes the Peter Boardman and Joe Tasker collections.

## BookArt & Architecture Picture Library
1 Woodcock Lodge, Epping Green,
Hertford SG13 8ND
*tel* (01707) 875253 *fax* (01707) 875286
*email* dcsharpd@btopenworld.co.uk

Modern and historic buildings, landscapes, works of named architects in Great Britain, Europe, Scandinavia, North America, India, Southeast Asia, Japan, North and East Africa; modern sculpture. Listed under style, place and personality. CD-Rom/ DVD supplied. Founded 1991.

## Boxing Picture Library
3 Barton Buildings, Bath BA1 2JR
*tel* (01225) 334213 *fax* (01225) 480554

Prints, engravings and photos of famous boxers, boxing personalities and famous fights from 18th century to recent years.

## The Bridgeman Art Library*
17–19 Garway Road, London W2 4PH
*tel* 020-7727 4065 *fax* 020-7792 8509
*email* london@bridgeman.co.uk
*website* www.bridgeman.co.uk

Source of fine art images for publication. Acts as an agent for thousands of museums, galleries and private collections throughout the world. Every subject, era and style represented from cave paintings to pop art and beyond, including many historical events and personalities. Also offers research service and acts as copyright agent to a growing number of artists. Website catalogue and online ordering available. Founded 1972.

## Britain on View*
Image Resource Centre, Thames Tower,
Black's Road, London W6 9EL
*tel* 020-8563 3120 *fax* 020-8563 3130
*email* pmortlock@bta.org.uk
*website* www.britainonview.com
*Contact* Paul Mortlock

Photo library of the British Tourist Authority. British culture, society, events, landscapes, towns and villages, tourist attractions.

## British Library Imaging Services*
96 Euston Road, London NW1 2DB
*tel* 020-7412 7614 *fax* 020-7412 7771
*email* imagesonline@bl.uk
*website* www.bl.uk/imagesonline

Illustrative and historical material from manuscripts, printed books, oriental and Indian items, maps, music and philately. Fully searchable website. New photography undertaken. Founded 1996.

## David Broadbent Birds
*tel/fax* (01594) 531381
*email* info@davidbroadbent.com
*website* www.davidbroadbent.com

Highly stylised and pictorial library of British birds, bird reserves and important wildlife landscapes. Commissions undertaken. New material welcome. Terms: 50%. Founded 1989.

## Hamish Brown, Scottish Photographic
26 Kirkcaldy Road, Burntisland,
Fife KY3 9HQ
*tel/fax* (01592) 873546

Picture library on Scottish sites, topography, mountains, travel. Book illustrations. Commissions undertaken. No pictures purchased.

## Camera Press Ltd*
21 Queen Elizabeth Street, London SE1 2PD
*tel* 020-7378 1300 *fax* 020-7278 5126

B&w prints and colour transparencies including up-to-date coverage of British royalty, portraits of world statesmen, politicians, entertainers, reportage, humour, nature, pop, features. Terms: 50%. Founded 1947.

## CartoonStock*
Unit 2, Lansdown Mews, Bath BA1 5DY
*tel* 01225 789600 01225 789642
*email* admin@cartoonstock.com
*website* www.cartoonstock.com
*Director* Joel Mishon

Library of over 50,000 cartoons and comic illustrations. B&w and colour cartoons by over 250 cartoonists whose work appears in national and overseas newspapers and magazines and other publications. Full database may be searched online. Founded 1998.

## Rev. J. Catling Allen
7 St Barnabas, The Beauchamp Community,
Newland, Malvern WR13 5AX
*tel* (01684) 899390

Library of colour transparencies (35mm) and b&w photos of Bible Lands, including archaeological sites and the religions of Christianity, Islam and Judaism. Medieval abbeys and priories, cathedrals and churches in Britain. Also historic, rural and scenic Britain. (Not an agent or buyer.)

## Celebrity Pictures Ltd*
98 De Beauvoir Road, London N1 4EN
*tel* 020-7275 2700 *fax* 020-7275 2701
*email* info@celebritypictures.co.uk
*website* www.celebritypictures.co.uk
*Marketing Manager* Sarah Eisner

Celebrity studio portraiture: film, music, TV, fashion, sport, men's, the Arts. More than 20,000 colour high-res jpeg scans available. Generous negotiable deals. Office in Los Angeles. Founded 1990s.

## Cephas Picture Library*

Hurst House, 157 Walton Road, East Molesey, Surrey KT8 0DX
*tel* 020-8979 8647 *fax* 020-8224 8095
*email* mickrock@cephas.co.uk
*website* www.cephas.co.uk

Comprehensive library of food and drink photos: wine and vineyards, spirits, beer and cider, food and drink worldwide. Free catalogue available; specialist knowledge.

## Christie's Images*

1 Langley Lane, London SW8 1TJ
*tel* 020-7582 1282  *fax* 020-7582 5632
*email* imageslondon@christies.com
*website* www.christiesimages.com
*Marketing & Development Director* Mark Lynch

One million colour transparencies of fine and decorative art and collectibles from the world's leading auction house. Founded 1992.

## Chrysalis Images

64 Brewery Road, London N7 9NT
*tel* 020-7697 3000 *fax* 020-7697 3001
*email* permissions@chrysalisbooks.co.uk
*Picture Research Team Leader* Zoë Hollermann

General collection including cookery, crafts, history, military, natural history, space, transport and travel. Founded 1996.

## COI Photo Library – see Stockwave

## Michael Cole Camerawork*

The Coach House, 27 The Avenue, Beckenham, Kent BR3 2DP
*tel* 020-8658 6120 *fax* 020-8658 6120
*email* mikecole@dircon.co.uk
*website* www.tennisphotos.com

Probably the largest and most comprehensive tennis library in the world comprising over half a million colour and b&w images. Includes over 50 years of the Wimbledon Championships. Founded 1945.

## Bruce Coleman Inc.

117 East 24th Street, New York, NY 10010-2919, USA
*tel* 212-979-6252 *fax* 212-979-5468
*email* norman@bciusa.com
*website* www.bciusa.com
*President* Norman Owen Tomalin

Specialises in the natural world and travel destinations around it. All subjects required. Traditional colour transparencies and digital stock media.

## Bruce Coleman The Natural World

Chalfont House, Hampden Road, Chalfont St Peter, Bucks. SL9 9RY
*tel* (0870) 4204186 *fax* (0870) 4204187
*email* library@brucecoleman.co.uk
*website* www.brucecoleman.co.uk

Creative images of nature, animals, landscapes, space and wildlife. Catalogues available.

## Collections*

13 Woodberry Crescent, London N10 1PJ
*tel* 020-8883 0083 *fax* 020-8883 9215

The British Isles only: places, people, buildings, industry, leisure; specialist collections on customs, castles, bridges, London, plus an extensive collection on Ireland. Founded 1990.

## Colorific/Getty Images News Services – incorporated into Getty Images

## Dee Conway Ballet & Dance Picture Library*

110 Sussex Way, London N7 6RR
*tel* 020-7272 7845 *fax* 020-7272 7966
*email* library@ddance.co.uk
*website* www.ddance.co.uk
*Proprietor* Dee Conway

Classical ballet, modern dance, flamenco, tango, rock, jive, mime; dance from India, Africa, Russia, China, Japan, Thailand; informal class pictures of dance, music and drama. Colour and b&w images. Founded 1995.

## Thomas Cook Archives

15–16 Coningsby Road, Peterborough PE3 8SB
*tel* (01733) 417350 *fax* (01733) 416255
*email* paul.smith@thomascook.com
*Company Archivist* Paul Smith

History of travel and tourism in the late 19th and early 20th centuries: posters, photos, brochure covers (1851–1960). Founded 1999.

## Corbis*

111 Salusbury Road, London NW6 6RG
*tel* 020-7644 7400 *fax* 020-7644 7401
*email* info@corbis.com
*website* www.corbis.com

Over 2.1 million images available online from a total of 65 million. The images are from professional photographers, museums, cultural institutions and public and private collections worldwide including the Bettmann Archive, Ansel Adams, Lynn Goldsmith, the Turnley Collection and Hulton Deutsch. Covers a wide range of subjects including celebrities and news. Founded 1989.

## Sylvia Cordaiy Photo Library*

45 Rotherstone, Devizes, Wilts. SN10 2DD
*tel* (01380) 728327 *fax* (01380) 728328
*email* info@sylvia-cordaiy.com
*website* www.sylvia-cordaiy.com

Worldwide travel and architecture, global
environmental topics, wildlife and domestic animals,
veterinary, comprehensive UK and London files,
Paul Kaye b&w archive. Terms: 50%. Founded 1990.

## Country Life Picture Library*

King's Reach Tower, Stamford Street, London SE1 9LS
*tel* 020-7261 6337 *fax* 020-7261 6216
*email* camilla_costello@ipcmedia.co.uk
*website* www.clpicturelibrary.co.uk
Library Manager Camilla Costello

Over 120,000 b&w photos and 80,000 colour
transparencies of country houses, historic buildings
and churches in Britain and abroad, as seen on the
pages of *Country Life* magazine since 1897. Also
holds images of some of the world's most beautiful
gardens and landscapes, as well as interior views
showing architectural details, furniture, paintings,
antiques and sculptures, often in their original
settings. Additionally, the library houses images,
mainly in colour, that have featured in *Country Life*
in more recent years, including sporting and social
events, rural and specialist crafts, agriculture,
animals and people. Founded 1897.

## Crafts Council Photostore®*

44A Pentonville Road, London N1 9BY
*tel* 020-7806 2503 *fax* 020-7833 4479
*email* photostore@craftscouncil.org.uk
*website* www.craftscouncil.org.uk/photostore

Comprehensive source of visual material for
contemporary British crafts. Spanning the last 30
years, subject areas cover: jewellery, ceramics,
furniture, glass, woodwork, paperwork,
bookbinding, domestic objects, decorative forms,
lettering, textiles, fashion accessories, basketry,
musical instruments and public art. Images can be
accessed through Photostore, the Craft Council's
interactive database, open during working hours
(no appointment necessary) and through regional
terminals. Founded 1973.

## Peter Cumberlidge Photo Library

Sunways, Slapton, Kingsbridge, Devon TQ7 2PR
*tel* (01548) 580461 *fax* (01548) 580588
*email* info@petercumberlidge.co.uk
*Contact* Jane Cumberlidge

Nautical, travel and coastal colour transparencies
35mm and 6 x 6cm. Specialities: boats, harbours,
marinas, inland waterways. Travel and holiday
subjects in Northern Europe, the Mediterranean,
and New England, USA. No other photographers'
material required. Founded 1982.

## Sue Cunningham Photographic*

56 Chatham Road, Kingston-upon-Thames,
Surrey KT1 3AA
*tel* 020-8541 3024 *fax* 020-8541 5388
*email* pictures@scphotographic.com
*website* www.scphotographic.com

International coverage on many subjects: Latin
America, Africa and Eastern Europe. Also Western
Europe, London (including aerial).

## Das Photo

Chalet le Pin, Domaine de Bellevue 181,
6940 Septon, Belgium
*tel* (32) 86-322426 *fax* (32) 86-322426
Old School House, Llanfilo, Brecon, Powys LD3 0RH
*email* dasphotogb@aol.com

Arab countries, Americas, Europe, Caribbean,
Southeast Asia, Amazon, world festivals,
archaeology, people, biblical, education, schools,
modern languages. Founded 1975.

## Barry Davies

Penddaulwyn Uchaf, Capel Dewi,
Carmarthen SA32 8AG
*mobile* (07870) 663182

Natural history, landscape, Egypt, children, outdoor
activities and general subjects. Formats 35mm,
6 x 6cm, 6 x 7cm, 6 x 17cm, 5 x 4in. Other
photographers' work not accepted. Founded 1983.

## Dennis Davis Photography

9 Great Burrow Rise, Northam, Bideford,
Devon EX39 1TB
*tel* (01237) 475165

Gardens, wild and garden flowers, domestic
livestock including rare breeds and poultry,
agricultural landscapes, architecture – interiors and
exteriors, landscape, coastal, rural life. Commissions
welcomed. No other photographers required.
Founded 1984.

## James Davis Travel Photography

65 Brighton Road, Shoreham, West Sussex BN43 6RE
*tel* (01273) 452252 *fax* (01273) 440116
*email* library@eyeubiquitous.com
*website* www.eyeubiquitous.com
*Proprietor* Paul Seheult

Stock transparency library specialising in worldwide
travel photos.

## Peter Dazeley*

The Studios, 5 Heathmans Road, London SW6 4TJ
*tel* 020-7736 3171 *fax* 020-7371 8876
*email* dazeleyp@aol.com

Extensive golf library dating from 1970. Colour and
b&w coverage of major tournaments, with over
250,000 images of players, courses worldwide, action

shots, portraits, trophies, including miscellaneous images: clubs, balls and teaching shots.

## George A. Dey
Drumcairn, Aberdeen Road, Laurencekirk, Kincardineshire AB30 1AJ
*tel* (01561) 378845

Scottish Highland landscapes, Highland Games, forestry, seabirds, castles of Northeast Scotland, gardens, spring, autumn, winter scenes, veteran cars, North Holland, New Zealand (North Island). Mostly 35mm, some 6 x 6cm. Founded 1986.

## Douglas Dickins Photo Library
2 Wessex Gardens, London NW11 9RT
*tel* 020-8455 6221

Worldwide collection of colour transparencies (mostly 6 x 6cm, some 35mm) and b&w prints (10 x 8in originals), specialising in Asia, particularly India and Indonesia; also USA, Canada, France, Austria and Switzerland, Japan, China, Burma. Founded 1946.

## C.M. Dixon*
The Orchard, Marley Lane, Kingston, Canterbury, Kent CT4 6JH
*tel* (01227) 830075 *fax* (01227) 831135

Europe, Iceland, Jordan, Sri Lanka, Tunisia, Turkey, former USSR. Main subjects include agriculture, ancient art, archaeology, architecture, clouds, geography, geology, history, horses, industry, meteorology, mosaics, mountains, mythology, occupations, people.

## Earth Images Picture Library
Manor Cottages, Burnett, Keynsham, Bristol BS31 2TF
*tel* 0117-986 1144 *fax* 0117-986 1144
*Director* Richard Arthur

Earth from Space (satellite remote sensing); earth science and art-in-science imagery – from cosmic to sub-atomic. Founded 1989.

## Ecoscene*
The Oasts, Headley Lane, Passfield, Liphook, Hants GU30 7RX
*tel* (01428) 751056 *fax* (01428) 751057
*email* sally@ecoscene.com
*website* www.ecoscene.com
*Contact* Sally Morgan

Specialists in environment and wildlife. Subjects include agriculture, conservation, energy, industry, pollution, habitats and habitat loss, sustainability, wildlife; worldwide coverage. Terms: 55% to photographer. Founded 1987.

## Edifice*
14 Doughty Street, London WC1N 2PL
*tel* 020-7242 0740 *fax* 020-7267 3632

*email* info@edificephoto.com
*website* www.edificephoto.com
*Partners* Philippa Lewis, Gillian Darley

Holds approx. 55,000 colour transparencies of architecture worldwide. All images are exteriors, with details as well as general views. Knowledgeable staff. Fully searchable database. Approx. 10% of available material can be seen online. Terms: 50%. Founded 1986.

## Education Photos*
April Cottage, Warners Lane, Albury Heath, Guildford, Surrey GU5 9DE
*tel* (01483) 203846
*email* johnwalmsley@educationphotos.co.uk
*website* www.educationphotos.co.uk
*Proprietor* John Walmsley

Digital photos of education, careers, portraits of ordinary people. Now searchable online. Commissions undertaken. Founded 1987.

## English Heritage Photo Library*
23 Savile Row, London W1S 2ET
*tel* 020-7973 3338/3339 *fax* 020-7973 3027

Wide range of high-quality colour transparencies, ranging from ancient monuments to artefacts, legendary castles to stone circles, elegant interiors to industrial architecture and post-war listed buildings.

## Environmental Investigation Agency*
62–63 Upper Street, London N1 0NY
*tel* 020-7354 7960 *fax* 020-7354 7961
*email* communications@eia-international.org
*website* www.eia-international.org
*Communications & Press Co-ordinator* Ashley Misplon
Specialists in still and moving images of environmental crime, including the illegal trade in endangered species, ozone-depleting substances and illegal logging; also animals in their natural environment. Founded 1984.

## Greg Evans International Photo Library
ICS House, 32 Crossways, Silwood Road, Sunninghill, Ascot, Berks. SL5 0PL
*tel* 020-7636 8238 *fax* 020-7637 1439
*email* greg@gregevans.net
*website* www.gregevans.net

Comprehensive, general colour library with over 300,000 transparencies. Subjects include: abstract, aircraft, arts, animals, beaches, business, children, computers, couples, families, food/restaurant, women, industry, skies, sports (action and leisure), UK scenics, worldwide travel. Visitors welcome; combined commissions undertaken; no search fee. Photographers' submissions welcome. Searchable website. Free brochure/CD-Rom. Founded 1979.

## Mary Evans Picture Library*

59 Tranquil Vale, London SE3 0BS
*tel* 020-8318 0034 *fax* 020-8852 7211
*email* pictures@maryevans.com
*website* www.maryevans.com

Historical archive of illustrations, photographs, prints and ephemera documenting all aspects of the past, from ancient times to the later decades of the 20th century. Subject areas: social and political history, portraits, events, transport, costume, trade and industry, places worldwide and natural history plus specialist material on folklore and paranormal phenomena. Notable acquisitions include the Thomas Fall Collection of historic dog photographs, the Weimar Archive documenting the Third Reich, and Barnaby's Library covering social scenes and events from the thirties to the seventies, MEPL's own material is complemented by many contributors such as Sigmund Freud Copyrights, the Women's Library (women's rights), and the Meledin Collection of 20th century Russian history, and by the work of individual photographers and illustrators such as Roger Mayne and Arthur Rackham. Over 150,000 images searchable online. Brochure on request. Founder member of BAPLA (British Association of Picture Libraries & Agencies). Compilers of thte *Picture Researcher's Handbook* published by Pira International.

## Exile Images*

1 Mill Row, West Hill Road,
Brighton BN1 3SU
*tel* (01273) 208741 *fax* (01273) 382782
*email* pics@exileimages.co.uk
*website* www.exileimages.co.uk
*Contact* Howard Davies

Online photo library with more than 5,000 pictures relating to refugees, conflicts, asylum, UK protests, and third world issues. Picture editiors can download high resolution photography from fully searchable online library. Founded 2000.

## Eyeline Photography

12 Wrights Way, Woolpit, Bury St Edmunds,
Suffolk IP30 9TY
*tel* (01359) 242344
*email* colin@colinjarman.co.uk
*website* www.colinjarman.co.uk

Sailing. Founded 1979.

## FAMOUS Pictures & Features Agency*

13 Harwood Road, London SW6 4QP
*tel* 020-7731 9333 *fax* 020-7731 9330
*email* info@famous.uk.com
*website* www.famous.uk.com

Colour pictures and features library covering music, film and TV personalities. Terms: 50%. Founded 1990.

## Feature-Pix Colour Library – see World Pictures

## Financial Times Pictures

Number One, Southwark Bridge, London SE1 9HL
*tel* 020-7873 3671 *fax* 020-7873 4606
*email* photosynd@ft.com

Colour and b&w library serving the *Financial Times*. Specialises in world business, industry and commerce; world politicians and statespeople; cities and countries; plus many other subjects. Also *FT* maps and graphics. All material available in colour and b&w, print and electronic formats. Library updated daily.

## Fine Art Photographic Library*

Rawlings House, 2A Milner Street, London SW3 2PU
*tel* 020-7589 3127 *fax* 020-7584 1944
*email* info@fineartphotolibrary.com

Holds over 25,000 transparencies of paintings by British and European artists, from Old Masters to contemporary. Free brochure. CD-Rom available. Founded 1980.

## FirePix International*

68 Arkles Lane, Anfield, Liverpool L4 2SP
*tel* 0151-260 0111 *fax* 0151-260 0111
*email* info@firepix.com
*website* www.firepix.com
*Contact* Tony Myers ARPS, GIFireE

Holds 23,000 images of fire and firefighters at work in the UK, USA, Japan and China. Established by photographer Tony Myers after 28 years in service with the British Fire Service. Many images are stored digitally; CD-Rom available. Founded 1995.

## Fogden Wildlife Photographs*

Flat 1, 78 High Street, Perth PH1 5TH
*tel* (01738) 580811 *fax* (01738) 580811
*email* susan.fogden@virgin.net
*website* www.fogdenphotos.com
*Library Manager* Susan Fogden

Wide coverage of natural history, including camouflage, warning coloration, mimicry, breeding strategies, feeding, animal/plant relationships, environmental studies, especially in rainforests and deserts. Founded 1980.

## Christine Foord

155B City Way, Rochester, Kent ME1 2BE
*tel* (01634) 847348 *fax* (01634) 847348

Colour picture library of over 1000 species of wild flowers. Also British insects, garden flowers, pests and diseases, lichen, mosses and cacti.

## Forest Life Picture Library*

Forestry Commission, 231 Corstorphine Road,
Edinburgh EH12 7AT

*Picture Researcher* Neill Campbell
*tel* 0131-314 6411
*email* neill.campbell@forestry.gsi.gov.uk
*Business Manager* Douglas Green
*tel* 0131-314 6200 *fax* 0131-314 6285
*email* douglas.green@forestry.gsi.gov.uk

Tree species, forest and woodland views and management, landscapes, wildlife, flora and fauna, conservation, sport and leisure. Founded 1983.

## Werner Forman Archive*
36 Camden Square, London NW1 9XA
*tel* 020-7267 1034 *fax* 020-7267 6026
*email* wfa@btinternet.com
*website* www.werner-forman-archive.com

Art, architecture, archaeology, history and peoples of ancient, oriental and primitive cultures. Founded 1975.

## Format Photographers – see Panos
Pictures and Photofusion

## Fortean Picture Library*
Henblas, Mwrog Street, Ruthin LL15 1LG
*tel* (01824) 707278 *fax* (01824) 705324
*email* janet.bord@forteanpix.demon.co.uk
*website* www.forteanpix.demon.co.uk

Colour and b&w pictures covering strange phenomena: UFOs, Loch Ness Monster, ghosts, Bigfoot, witchcraft, etc; also antiquities (especially in Britain – prehistoric and Roman sites, castles, churches).

## Fotoccompli – The Picture Library
35 Birch Croft Road, Sutton Coldfield B75 6BP
*tel* 0121-378 1064 *fax* 0121-240 8950
*email* djgriffiths@lineone.net
*website* www.fotoccompli.com

Comprehensive library, ranging from abstracts to zoology, with added specialism of the building and construction industries. Terms: 50%. Minimum retention period: 3 years. Founded 1989.

## Fotomas Index
12 Pickhurst Rise, West Wickham, Kent BR4 0AL
*tel* 020-8776 2772 *fax* 020-8776 2236

Specialises in supplying pre-20th century (mostly pre-Victorian) illustrative material to publishing and academic worlds, and for TV and advertising. Complete production back-up for interior décor, exhibitions and locations.

## Fotosports International
The Barn, Swanbourne, Bucks. MK17 0SL
*tel* (01296) 720773 *fax* (01296) 728181
*email* info@fotosports.com
*website* www.fotosports.com
*Contact* Roger Parker, Partner

250,000 b&w photos and 250,000 colour transparencies of sports: soccer (domestic, foreign, World Cup 1970s to present), tennis majors, Formula One motor racing, American football (inc. Superbowl) 1985–95; some golf, rugby, cricket. Founded 1968.

## Freelance Focus
39 Scotts Garth Close, Tickton, Beverley, East Yorkshire HU17 9RQ
*tel* (01964) 501729 *fax* (01964) 501729
*email* freelancefocus@hull24.com
*Contact* Gary Hicks

UK/international network of photographers. Stock pictures covering most subjects, worldwide, at competitive rates. Assignments undertaken for all types of clients. Founded 1988.

## John Frost Newspapers
22B Rosemary Avenue, Enfield, Middlesex EN2 0SS
*tel* 020-8366 1392/0946 *fax* 020-8366 1379
*email* andrew@johnfrostnewspapers.com
*website* www.johnfrostnewspapers.co.uk

Headline stories from 80,000 British and overseas newspapers and 100,000 press cuttings reporting events since 1850.

## Brian Gadsby Picture Library
17 route des Pyrénées, 65700 Labatut-Riviere, Hautes Pyrénées, France
*tel* (33) 5 62 96 38 44
*email* GadsbyJB@aol.com

Colour transparencies (6 x 4.5cm, 35mm) and b&w prints. Wide range of subjects but emphasis on travel and the environment: UK, Europe (particularly France), Ecuador and Galapagos Islands, Patagonia, Sri Lanka. Natural history: mainly birds and plant life (wild and garden). Large wildfowl file. No other photographers' material required.

## Andrew N. Gagg's Photo Flora*
Town House Two, Fordbank Court, Henwick Road, Worcester WR2 5PF
*tel* (01905) 748515
*email* a.n.gagg@ntlworld.com
*website* www.homepage.ntlworld.com/a.n.gagg/photo/photoflora.html
*Contact* Andrew N. Gagg

Comprehensive collection of British and European wild plants. Travel: Egypt, India, Tibet, China, Nepal, Myanmar, Thailand, Mexico, Vietnam and Cambodia. Founded 1982.

## Galaxy Picture Library*
34 Fennels Way, Flackwell Heath, High Wycombe, Bucks. HP10 9BY
*tel* (01628) 521338 *fax* (01628) 520132
*email* robin@galaxypix.com

*website* www.galaxypix.com
*Contact* Robin Scagell

Astronomy: specialities include the night sky, amateur astronomy, astronomers and observatories. Founded 1992.

## Garden and Wildlife Matters Photographic Library*

Marlham, Henley's Down, Battle,
East Sussex TN33 9BN
*tel* (01424) 830566 *fax* (01424) 830224
*email* gardens@gmpix.com
*website* www.gmpix.com
*Contact* Dr John Feltwell

*Plants 10,000* Over 10,000 scientifically named species and cultivars of garden flowers, wild plants, trees (over 1000 species), grasses, crops, herbs, spices, houseplants, carnivorous plants, climbers (especially Clematis), roses, geraniums and pelargoniums, and pests.

*General gardening* How-to, gardening techniques, garden design and embellishments, cottage gardens, USA designer-gardens, 200 garden portfolios from 16 states in the USA, 100 portfolios from 12 European countries. Founded 1993.

## Garden World Images*

Grange Studio, Woodham Road, Battlesbridge,
Wickford, Essex SS11 7QU
*tel* (01245) 325725 *fax* (01245) 429198
*email* info@gardenworldimages.com
*website* www.gardenworldimages.com
*Partners* Françoise Davis and Lisa Smith

All aspects of horticulture, including large and small gardens, specialist sections on all subjects including trees, fruit, vegetables, herbs, cacti, orchids, grasses, cultivated and wild flowers from all over the world, pests and diseases, action shots. Founded 1951.

## Colin Garratt – see Railways – Milepost 92½

## Genesis Space Photo Library

Greenbanks, Robins Hill, Raleigh, Bideford,
Devon EX39 3PA
*tel* (01237) 471960 *fax* (01237) 472060
*email* tim@spaceport.co.uk
*website* www.spaceport. co.uk
*Contact* Tim Furniss

Specialises in rockets, spacecraft, spacemen, Earth, Moon, planets, stars, galaxies, the Universe. Founded 1990.

## Geo Aerial Photography*

4 Christian Fields, London SW16 3JZ
*tel* 020-8764 6292, 0115-981 9418 *fax* 020-8764 6292, 0115-981 9418
*email* geo-aerial@geo-group.co.uk
*website* www.geo-group.co.uk

*Director* J.F.J. Douglas

Air-to-air and air-to-ground colour library: natural and cultural/man-made landscapes and individual features. Subjects from UK, Scandinavia, Middle East, Asia and Africa. Commissions undertaken. Terms: 50%. Founded 1992.

## GeoScience Features*

6 Orchard Drive, Wye, Kent TN25 5AU
*tel* (01233) 812707 *fax* (01233) 812707
*email* gsf@geoscience.demon.co.uk
*website* www.geoscience.demon.co.uk
*Director* Dr Basil Booth

Colour library (35mm to 5 x 4in). Animals, biology, birds, botany, chemistry, earth science, ecology, environment, geology, geography, habitats, landscapes, macro/micro, peoples, plants, travel, sky, weather, wildlife and zoology; Americas, Africa, Australasia, Europe, India, Southeast Asia. Over a third of a million colour images available as film or high-res digital images. CD-Rom available.

## Geoslides*

4 Christian Fields, London SW16 3JZ
*tel/fax* 020-8764 6292, 0115-981 9418
*email* geoslides@geo-group.co.uk
*website* www.geo-group.co.uk
*Library Director* John Douglas

Broadly based and substantial collections from Africa, Asia, Antarctic, Arctic and sub-Arctic areas, Australia (Blackwood Collection). Worldwide commissions undertaken. Terms: 50% on UK sales. Founded 1968.

## Mark Gerson Photography

3 Regal Lane, Regents Park Road,
London NW1 7TH
*tel* 020-7286 5894 *fax* 020-7267 9246
*email* mark.gerson@virgin.net

Portrait photographs of personalities, mainly literary, in colour and b&w from 1950 to the present. No other photographers' material required.

## Getty Images*

101 Bayham Street, London NW1 0AG
*tel* 0800-376 7977 *fax* 020-7544 3334
*email* sales@gettyimages.co.uk
*website* www.gettyimages.co.uk

Leading imagery company, creating and providing the largest collection of still and moving images to communication professionals – from sports and news photography to archival and contemporary. Collections include: Stone, Taxi, the Image Bank, Photodisc, Hulton Archive, Getty Images News & Sport, Digital Vision, National Geographic, FoodPix, Bridgeman Art Library. See website for futher details.

## John Glover Photography

The Oast Houses, Headley Lane, Passfield,
Hants GU30 7RX
*tel* (01428) 751925 *mobile* (07973) 307078
*fax* (01428) 751191
*email* john@glovphot.demon.co.uk
*website* www.glovphot.demon.co.uk

Gardens and gardening, from overall views of
gardens to plant portraits with Latin names; UK
landscapes including ancient sites, Stonehenge, etc.
Founded 1979.

## Martin and Dorothy Grace

40 Clipstone Avenue, Mapperley,
Nottingham NG3 5JZ
*tel* 0115-920 8248 *fax* 0115-962 6802
*email* graces@lineone.net

General British natural history, specialising in native
trees, shrubs, flowers, ferns, habitats and ecology.
Founded 1984.

## Tim Graham Picture Library*

31 Ferncroft Avenue, London NW3 7PG
*tel* 020-7435 7693 *fax* 020-7431 4312
*email* mail@timgraham.co.uk

Royal Family in this country and on tours;
background pictures on royal homes, staff, hobbies,
sports, cars, etc; English and foreign country scenes;
international Heads of State, VIPs and celebrities.
Founded 1978.

## Angela Hampton – Family Life Picture Library

Holly Tree House, The Street, Walberton, Arundel,
West Sussex BN18 0PH
*tel* (01243) 555952 *fax* (01243) 555952
*website* www.familylifepictures.co.uk
*Proprietor* Angela Hampton

Contemporary lifestyle images including pregnancy,
childbirth, babies and children, parenting,
behaviour, education, medical, holidays, pets,
families, couples, teenagers, women's health, men's
health, retirement. Also domestic and farm animals.
Around 100,000 colour transparencies. Founded
1991.

## Robert Harding World Imagery*

58–59 Great Marlborough Street, London W1F 7JY
*tel* 020-7478 4000 *fax* 020-7478 4161
*email* info@robertharding.com
*website* www.robertharding.com

Picture library with extensive range of subjects,
including rights protected and royalty free, in
particular travel, lifestyle, business and industry,
botany, science and medical. Full e-commerce
website with over 120,000 searchable images. Free
catalogue.

## Harper Horticultural Slide Library

219 Robanna Drive, Seaford, VA 23696, USA
*tel* 757-898-6453 *fax* 757-890-9378
*email* pamharper@mindspring.com

160,000 35mm slides of plants, gardens and native
habitats.

## Jason Hawkes Library

Zoom House, Burghfield Common,
Reading RG7 3DN
*tel* (01189) 832837 *fax* (01189) 832634
*email* library@jasonhawkes.com
*website* www.jasonhawkes.com
*Library Manager* Chris Lacey

Aerial photography of London and Britain; also
Europe, USA and Australia. Online searchable
database of over 8000 images. Founded 1998.

## Heritage & Natural History Photography

37 Plainwood Close, Summersdale, Chichester,
West Sussex PO19 5YB
*tel* (01243) 533822 *fax* (01243) 533822
*Contact* Dr John B. Free

Archaeology, history, agriculture: Arabia, China,
India, Iran, Ireland, Japan, Kenya, Mediterranean
countries, Mexico, Nepal, North America, Oman,
Russia, Thailand, UK. Bees and bee-keeping, insects
and small invertebrates, tropical crops and flowers.

## Historical Features & Photos

Hollyville, Maesycrugiau, Pencader,
Carmarthenshire SA39 9DL
*tel* (01559) 395310
*email* john.norris3@btinternet.com
*website* www.historicalfeatures.com
*Director* John Norris

Approx. 10,000 b&w photos and 80,000 colour
transparencies of historical architecture, including
medieval castles of England and Wales. Also
includes all aspects of historical events, including
recreations with re-enactment groups from Ancient
Greece to modern weaponry. Research also
undertaken for TV and film companies. Founded
1995.

## Pat Hodgson Library & Picture Research Agency

Jasmine Cottage, Spring Grove Road, Richmond,
Surrey TW10 6EH
*tel* 020-8940 5986 *fax* 020-8940 5986
*email* pat.hodgpix@virgin.net

Small collection of b&w historical engravings, book
illustrations, ephemera, etc; some colour and
modern photos. Subjects include history,
Victoriana, ancient civilisations, occult, travel. Text
written and research undertaken on any subject.

## Holt Studios*

The Courtyard, 24 High Street, Hungerford,
Berks. RG17 0NF
*tel* (01488) 683523 *fax* (01488) 683511
*email* library@holt-studios.co.uk
*website* www.holt-studios.co.uk

110,000 pictures on worldwide agriculture,
horticulture, crops and associated pests (and their
predators), diseases and deficiencies, farming people
and practices, livestock, machinery, landscapes,
diverse environments, natural flora and fauna.
Extensive gardens and garden plants collection.
Founded 1981.

## Horizon International

Horizon International Images Ltd, Horizon House,
Route de Picaterre, Alderney, Guernsey GY9 3UP
*tel* (01481) 822587 *fax* (01481) 823880
*email* mail@hrzn.com
*website* www.hrzn.com

Specialist stock library. Images include leisure and
lifestyle, business and industry, science and
medicine, environment and nature, world travel.
Founded 1978.

## Hortipix/PSP Image Library

49 Palmerston Avenue, Goring by Sea,
West Sussex BN12 4RN
*tel* (01903) 503147
*email* enquiries@peterstiles.com
*websites* www.peterstiles.com, www.hortipix.co.uk

Stock image library specialising in pictures of plants,
flowers, watergardening and most horticultural/
gardening subjects. Also pictorial views of the
Channel Islands and UK, tropical marine aquarium
fish and invertebrates. Illustrated garden articles and
commissioned horticultural photography.

## David Hosking

Pages Green House, Wetheringsett, Stowmarket,
Suffolk IP14 5QA
*tel* (01728) 861113 *fax* (01728) 860222
*email* pictures@flpa-images.co.uk
*website* www.flpa-images.co.uk
*Contact* David Hosking FRSP

Natural history subjects, especially birds, worldwide.
Including Eric Hosking's b&w collection.

## Houses & Interiors Photographic Features Agency

192 Goswell Road, London EC1V 7DT
*tel* 020-7253 0991 *fax* 020-7253 0992
*Contact* Anna Gibson

Stylish house interiors and exteriors, people in their
homes and gardens, home dossiers, renovations,
architectural details, interior design, gardens and
houseplants. Also step-by-step photographic
sequences of DIY subjects, fresh and dried flower
arrangements and gardening techniques. Food.
Colour only. Commissions undertaken. Terms:
50%, negotiable. Founded 1985.

## Hulton Archive – see Getty Images

## Huntley Film Archive

191 Wardour Street, London W1F 8ZE
*tel* 020-7287 8000 *fax* 020-7287 8001
*email* films@huntleyarchives.com
*website* www.huntleyarchives.com
*Archivist* Amanda Huntley

Documentary and cinema stills and movies.
Founded 1984.

## Hutchison Picture Library

65 Brighton Road, Shoreham-by-sea,
West Sussex BN43 6RE
*tel* (01273) 440113 *fax* (01273) 440116
*email* library@hutchisonpictures.co.uk
*website* www.hutchisonpictures.co.uk

General colour library; worldwide subjects:
agriculture, the environment, festivals, human
relationships, industry, landscape, peoples, religion,
towns, travel. Founded 1976.

## The Illustrated London News Picture Library*

20 Upper Ground, London SE1 9PF
*tel* 020-7805 5585 *fax* 020-7805 5905
*email* research@ilnpictures.co.uk
*website* www.ilnpictures.co.uk
*Manager* Luci Gosling

Engravings, photos, illustrations in b&w and colour
from 1842 to present day, especially 19th and 20th
century social history, wars, portraits, royalty.
Collection includes the Seaco Picture Library of
transport and travel images.

## The Image Bank – see Getty Images

## Image Diggers

618B Finchley Road, London NW11 7RR
*tel* 020-8455 4564 *fax* 020-8455 4564
*email* ziph@macunlimited.net
*website* www.imagediggers.netfirms.com
*Contact* Neil Hornick

Stills archive covering performing arts, popular
culture, human interest, natural history,
architecture, nautical, children and people, strange
phenomena, etc. Also audio and video for research
purposes, books, and ephemera including
magazines, comic books, sheet music, postcards.
Founded 1980.

## Imagefinder Pte Ltd

228A South Bridge Road, Singapore 058777
*tel* (65) 324 3747 *fax* (65) 324 3748

*email* imagef@mbox4.singnet.com.sg
*Director* Rashidah Hamid

General photo library with strong focus on Asian-related material. Founded 1998.

## Images of Africa Photobank*
11 The Windings, Lichfield, Staffs. WS13 7EX
*tel* (01543) 262898 *fax* (01543) 417154
*email* info@imagesofafrica.co.uk
*website* www.imagesofafrica.co.uk
*Library Manager* Jacquie Shipton, *Proprietor* David Keith Jones FRPS

135,000 images covering 20 African countries: Botswana, Chad, Egypt, Ethiopia, Kenya, Lesotho, Madagascar, Malawi, Morocco, Mozambique, Namibia, Rwanda, South Africa, Swaziland, Tanzania, Uganda, Zaire, Zambia, Zanzibar and Zimbabwe. Specialities: wildlife, people, landscapes, tourism, hotels and lodges, National Parks and Reserves. Terms: 50%. Founded 1983.

## ImageState Pictor Ltd*
Ramillies House, 1–2 Ramillies Street, London W1F 7LN
*tel* 020-7734 7344 *fax* 020-7434 0673
*website* www.imagestate.co.uk
*Office Manager* Julie Chamberlain

Contemporary rights-protected and royalty-free images, footage and music. Subjects include people, business, UK and world travel, industry and sport. Founded 1983.

## Imperial War Museum*
Photograph Archive, Austral Street, London SE11 4SL
*tel* 020-7416 5333/8 *fax* 020-7416 5355
*email* photos@iwm.org.uk
*website* www.iwm.org.uk
www.iwmcollections.org.uk

National archive of over 6 million photos, dealing with conflict in the 20th century involving the armed forces of Britain and the Commonwealth countries. Open by appointment Mon–Fri. Prints made to order. Founded 1917.

## International Press Agency (Pty) Ltd
Sunrise House, 56 Morningside, Ndabeni 7405, South Africa
*tel* (021) 531 1926 *fax* (021) 531 8789
*email* inpra@iafrica.com

Press photos for South African market. Founded 1934.

## The Irish Image Collection*
Ballydowane East, Bunmahon, Kilmacthomas, Co, Waterford, Republic of Ireland
*tel* (51) 292020 *fax* (51) 292020
*email* george@theirishimagecollection.ie
*website* www.theirishimagecollection.ie

Covers all 32 countries in Ireland and features diverse subjects: agriculture, pubs, sport, gardens, megalithic archaeology, tradition, many aspects of Irish life, etc. Fully searchable website.

## Isle of Wight Pictures
60 York Street, Cowes, Isle of Wight PO31 7BS
*tel* (01983) 290366 *mobile* (07768) 877914
*fax* (01983) 290366
*email* patrick@patrickeden.co.uk
*website* www.patrickeden.co.uk
*Proprietor* Patrick Eden

Covers all aspects of the Isle of Wight, including landscape, aerial, industry, agriculture, tourism, Cowes Week, nautical aspects. Over 5000 pictures; any picture not on file can be shot to order. All images available as originals or in digital formats. Founded 1985.

## Japan Archive
9 Victoria Drive, Horsforth, Leeds LS18 4PN
*tel* 0113-258 3244
*email* stephen.turnbull@virgin.net
*website* www.stephenturnbull.com
*Contact* S.R. Turnbull

Japan: modern, daily life, architecture, religion, history, personalities, gardens, natural world; European castles. Founded 1993.

## Jazz Index
26 Fosse Way, London W13 0BZ
*tel* 020-8998 1232 *fax* 020-8998 2880
*email* christianhim@jazzindex.co.uk
*website* www. jazzindex.co.uk

Specialist photo library of jazz, blues and contemporary music. Comprehensive selection of archives material, atmospheric images of performers, portraits, smoky clubs, audiences, instruments. Terms: 50%. Founded 1979.

## J.S. Library International
101A Brondesbury Park, London NW2 5JL
*tel* 020-8451 2668 *fax* 020-8459 0223/8517
*email* js@online24.co.uk
*website* www.jslibrary.com

The J.S. Royal collection, Art collection, Hollywood collection, Celebrity service, particularly authors. Travel, fauna and flora and general pictures. New photographers and material required. Assignments worldwide undertaken. Founded 1979.

## Just Europe
50 Basingfield Road, Thames Ditton, Surrey KT7 0PD
*tel* 020-8398 2468 *fax* 020-8398 2468
*email* justeurope@altavista.com

Europe – major cities, towns, people and customs. Assignments undertaken; background information available; advice/research service. Founded 1989.

## Katz Pictures Ltd*
109 Clifton Street, London EC2A 4LD
*tel* 020-7749 6000 *fax* 020-7749 6001
*email* info@katzpictures.com
*website* www.katzpictures.com

Images of people, world events and travel features.

## Kilmartin House Trust
Kilmartin House, Kilmartin,
Argyll PA31 8RQ
*tel* (01546) 510278 *fax* (01546) 510330
*email* museum@kilmartin.org
*website* www.kilmartin.org
*Contact* D.J. Adams McGilp

Ancient monuments, archaeological sites; artefacts and excavations. Aerial photographs of Mid Argyll. Colour prints and transparencies. Publishers of historical/archaeological works, including fiction. Founded 1994.

## Lakeland Life Picture Library
Langsett, Lyndene Drive, Grange-over-Sands, Cumbria LA11 6QP
*tel* (015395) 33565 (answerphone)
*email* davidwjones@ktdinternet.com
*website* www.lakelandlifepicturelibrary.co.uk

English Lake District: industries, crafts, sports, shows, customs, architecture, people. Also provides colour and b&w, illustrated articles. Not an agency. Catalogue available. Founded 1979.

## Frank Lane Picture Agency Ltd
Pages Green House, Wetheringsett, Stowmarket, Suffolk IP14 5QA
*tel* (01728) 860789 *fax* (01728) 860222
*email* pictures@flpa-images.co.uk
*website* www.flpa-images.co.uk

Natural history, ecology, environment, farming, geography, trees and weather.

## Michael Leach
Brookside, Kinnerley, Oswestry SY10 8DB
*tel* (01691) 682639 *fax* (01691) 682003
*email* mike.leach@lineone.net
*website* www.michael-leach.co.uk

General worldwide wildlife and natural history subjects, with particular emphasis on mammals (especially great apes) and urban wildlife. Comprehensive collection of owls from all over the world. No other photographers required.

## Lebrecht Music and Arts*
58B Carlton Hill, London NW8 0ES
*tel* 020-7625 5341, 020-7372 8233
*fax* 020-7625 5341
*email* pictures@lebrecht.co.uk
*website* www.lebrecht.co.uk
*Director* Elbie Lebrecht

The world's most comprehensive archive of music images from antiquity to the 21st century has expanded to incorporate coverage of ballet, literature, fine art and artists, film stills. UK representative of two large French and German libraries. Founded 1992.

## Dave Lewis Nostalgia Collection
20 The Avenue, Starbeck, Harrogate, North Yorkshire HG1 4QD
*tel* (01423) 888642 *fax* (01423) 888642
*email* lewisattic@ntlworld.com
*website* www.lewisnostalgia.co.uk

A collection of advertising, packaging, points of sale and magazine reference from 1800–1970s. Founded 1995.

## Link Picture Library*
33 Greyhound Road, London W6 8NH
*tel* 020-7381 2261/2433 *fax* 020-7385 6244
*email* lib@linkpicturelibrary.com
*website* www.linkpicturelibrary.com
*Proprietor* Orde Eliason

Specialist archives on Central and Southern Africa, India, China, Southeast Asia and Israel. Commissions accepted. Terms: 50%. Founded 1982.

## Elizabeth Linley Collection
The Elizabeth Linley Studio, 29 Dewlands, Godstone, Surrey RH9 8BS
*tel* (01883) 742702, 742451
*Contact* Audrey I.B. Thomas

Prints, b&w photos and colour transparencies of 18th- and 19th-century artists, portraits, illustrations, theatre, society events, architecture.

## London Metropolitan Archives
40 Northampton Road, London EC1R 0HB
*tel* 020-7332 3820 *minicom* 020-7278 8703
*fax* 020-7833 9136
*email* ask.lma@corpoflondon.gov.uk
*website* www.cityoflondon.gov.uk/lma

Largest local authority record office in the UK, with 32 miles of archives. Nearly 900 years of London history is contained in the records of London government, businesses, charities, hospitals, churches, etc. Collections include books, documents, photographs, maps and drawings. 100,000-volume reference library specialising in London history.

## Lonely Planet Images*
*website* www.lonelyplanetimages.com
*Australasia* 90 Maribrynong Street, Footscray, Victoria 3011
*tel* (03) 8379 8181 *fax* (03) 8379 8182
*email* lpi@lonelyplanet.com.au
*Contact* Ellen Burrows

*Americas* Lonely Planet Images, 150 Linden Street, Oakland, California 94607
*tel* 510-893-8555 *fax* 800-275-8555
*email* lpi@lonelyplanet.com
*Contact* Jain Lemos
*Europe* 72–82 Rosebery Avenue, London EC1R 4RW
*tel* 020-7841 9000 *fax* 020-7841 9001
*email* lpi@lonelyplanet.co.uk
*Contact* Miranda Duffy

Online collection of travel-related images. Searchable website.

## The Billie Love Historical Collection
Reflections, 3 Winton Street, Ryde, Isle of Wight PO33 2BX
*tel* (01983) 812572 *fax* (01983) 616515
*Proprietor* Billie Love

Photos (late 19th century–1930s), engravings, coloured lithographs, covering subjects from earliest times, people, places and events up to the Second World War; also more recent material. Founded 1969.

## Ludvigsen Library
Scoles Gate, Hawkedon, Suffolk IP29 4AU
*tel* (01284) 789246 *fax* (01284) 789246
*email* sam@ludvigsen.com
*Photographic resources* Sam Turner

Specialist automotive and motor racing photo library. Includes much rare and unpublished material from John Dugdale, Edward Eves, Max le Grand, Peter Keen, Karl Ludvigsen, Rodolfo Mailander, Ove Nielsen, Stanley Rosenthall and others. Founded 1984.

## The MacQuitty International Collection*
7 Elm Lodge, River Gardens, Stevenage Road, London SW6 6NZ
*tel* 020-7385 5606 *fax* 020-7385 5606
*email* miranda.macquitty@btinternet.com

300,000 photos covering aspects of life in 70 countries: archaeology, art, buildings, flora and fauna, gardens, museums, people and occupations, scenery, religions, methods of transport, surgery, acupuncture, funeral customs, fishing, farming, dancing, music, crafts, sports, weddings, carnivals, food, drink, jewellery and oriental subjects. Period: 1920 to present day.

## Mander & Mitchenson Theatre Collection*
Jerwood Library of the Performing Arts, King Charles Building, Old Royal Naval College, London SE10 9JF
*tel* 020-8305 4426 *fax* 020-8305 3993
*email* rmangan@tcm.ac.uk

Prints, drawings, photos, programmes, etc, theatre, opera, ballet, music hall, and other allied subjects including composers, playwrights, etc. All periods.

## Marine Wildlife Photo Agency
Vine Villa, Mount Road, Llanfairfechan, North Wales LL33 0DW
*tel* (01248) 681361 *fax* (01248) 681361
*email* info@marinewildlife.co.uk
*website* www.marinewildlife.co.uk
*Proprietor* Paul Kay

35mm and medium format images of UK and Irish (temperate) marine life and associated subjects (coastal services, environmental issues, etc). Subjects range from straight animal/plant portraits through to abstracts; also underwater scenic photos. Digital images and scans available. Founded 1992.

## John Massey Stewart Picture Library
20 Hillway, London N6 6QA
*tel* 020-8341 3544 *fax* 020-8341 5292
*email* jms@gn.apc.org

Large collection Russia/USSR, including topography, people, culture, Siberia, plus Russian and Soviet history, 3000 pre-revolutionary PCs, etc. Also Britain, Europe (including Bulgaria, Poland, Slovenia and Turkey), Alaska, USA, Israel, Sinai desert, etc; and classical composers (portraits, houses, graves, monuments, etc).

## S. & O. Mathews
Little Pitt Place, Brighstone, Isle of Wight P030 4DZ
*tel* (01983) 741098 *fax* (01983) 740592
*email* oliver@mathews-photography.com
*website* www.mathews-photography.com

Gardens, plants and landscapes.

## Chris Mattison
138 Dalewood Road, Sheffield S108 0EF
*tel* 0114-236 4433 *fax* 0114-236 4433
*email* chris.mattison@btinternet.com
*website* www.chris.mattison.btinternet.co.uk

Colour library specialising in reptiles and amphibians; other natural history subjects; habitats and landscapes in Africa, Southeast Asia, South America, USA, Mexico, Mediterranean. Captions or detailed copy supplied if required. No other photographers' material required.

## Bill Meadows Picture Library
11 Begonia Close, St Peters, Worcester WR5 3LZ
*tel* (01905) 350801 *fax* (01905) 350801
*Proprietor* Bill Meadows

Aspects of Great Britain: general scenic including towns and villages; buildings and monuments; agricultural, industrial and building sites; urban scenes and services; misuse of the environment, vandalism, etc; recreational, 'people at play'; natural history subjects. 20,000 b&w photographs and 50,000 (6 x 6cm and 35mm) colour transparencies. Founded 1968.

## Medimage

32 Brooklyn Road, Coventry CV1 4JT
*tel* (01203) 668562 *fax* (01203) 668562
*email* chambersking@ntlworld.com
*Contact* Anthony King

Specialist library of medium format transparencies of subjects in Mediterranean countries and the Czech Republic: agriculture, architecture, crafts, festivals, flora, industry, landscapes, markets, portraits, recreation, seascapes, sport and transport. Commissions undertaken. Other photographers' work not accepted. Founded 1992.

## Merseyside Photo Library*

Suite 6, Egerton House, Tower Road, Birkenhead, Wirral CH41 1FN
*tel* 0151-666 2289 *fax* 0151-650 6976
*email* ron@rja-mpl.com
*website* www.merseysidephotolibrary.com
*Operated by* Ron Jones Associates

Library specialising in images of Liverpool and Merseyside but includes other destinations. Founded 1989.

## Microscopix

Middle Travelly, Beguildy, Nr Knighton, Powys LD7 1UW
*tel* (01547) 510242 *fax* (01547) 510317
*email* semages@microscopix.co.uk
*website* www.microscopix.co.uk

Scientific photo library specialising in scanning electron micrographs and photomicrographs for technical and aesthetic purposes. Commissioned work, both biological and non-biological, undertaken offering a wide variety of applicable microscopical techniques. Founded 1986.

## Military History Picture Library

3 Barton Buildings, Bath BA1 2JR
*tel* (01225) 334213 *fax* (01225) 480554

Prints, engravings, photos, colour transparencies covering all aspects of warfare and uniforms from ancient times to the present.

## Mirrorpix*

One Canada Square, Canary Wharf, London E14 5AP
*tel* 020-7293 3700 *fax* 020-7293 2712
*email* desk@mirrorpix.com
*website* www.mirrorpix.com
*Contact* Sales desk

Images of the past 100 years by photographers of the *Daily Mirror* and her sister titles which document both the light and dark sides of British life: people, places, events and movements.

## Monitor Picture Library*

Monitor Press Features Ltd, The Forge, Roydon, Harlow, Essex CM19 5HH

*tel* (01279) 792700 *fax* (01279) 792600
*email* sales@monitorpicturelibrary.com
*website* www.monitorpicturelibrary.com
*Contact* Eleanore White, Stewart White

UK and international personalities 1850–1994. B&w and colour.

## Motorcycles Unlimited

48 Lemsford Road, St Albans, Herts. AL1 3PR
*tel* (01727) 869001 *fax* (01727) 869014
*email* rolandbrown@motobike.demon.co.uk
*Owner* Roland Brown

Motorbikes of all kinds, from latest roadsters to classics, racers to tourers. Detailed information available on all machines pictured. Founded 1993.

## Motoring Picture Library*

National Motor Museum, Beaulieu, Hants SO42 7ZN
*tel* (01590) 614656 *fax* (01590) 612655
*email* motoring.pictures@beaulieu.co.uk
*websites* www.alamy.com/mpl,
www.heritage-images.com

All aspects of motoring, cars, commercial vehicles, motor cycles, personalities, etc. Illustrations of period scenes and motor sport. Also large library of 5 x 4in and smaller colour transparencies of veteran, vintage and modern cars, commercial vehicles and motorcycles. Over 800,000 images in total.

## Mountain Dynamics

Heathcourt, Morven Way, Monaltrie, Ballater AB35 5SF
*tel* (013397) 55081 *fax* (013397) 55526
*email* gpa@globalnet.co.uk
*Proprietor* Graham P. Adams

Scottish and European mountains – from ground to summits – in panoramic (6 x 17cm), 5 x 4in and medium format. Commissions undertaken. Terms: 50%. Founded 1990.

## Mountain Visions and Faces

25 The Mallards, Langstone, Havant, Hants PO9 1SS
*tel* 023-9247 8441
*email* mtvisions@hotmail.com
*website* www.mountainvisions.co.uk
*Contact* Graham Elson, Roslyn Elson

Colour transparencies of mountaineering, skiing, and tourism in Europe, Africa, Himalayas, Arctic, Far East, South America and Australia. Does not act as agent for other photographers. Founded 1984.

## Museum of London*

London Wall, London EC2Y 5HN
*tel* 020-7814 5605 *fax* 020-7600 1058
*email* lpringle@museumoflondon.org.uk
*website* www.museumoflondon.org.uk
*Picture Library Manager* Lucy Pringle

London history.

**The Mustograph Agency** – see Mary
Evans Picture Library

## The National Archives Image Library*

The National Archives, Ruskin Avenue, Kew,
Surrey TW9 4DU
*tel* 020-8392 5225 *fax* 020-8487 1974
*email* image-library@nationalarchives.gov.uk
*website* www.nationalarchives.gov.uk/imagelibrary

Unique collection of millions of historical
documents on a wide range of formats from 1086
to 1960s. Special collections include: Victorian and
Edwardian advertisements and photographs,
Second World War propaganda, military history,
maps, decorative and technical designs and
medieval illuminations. Founded 1995.

## National Galleries of Scotland Picture Library*

The Dean Gallery, 73 Belford Road,
Edinburgh EH4 3DS
*tel* 0131-624 6258, 0131-624 6260 *fax* 0131-623 7135
*email* picture.library@nationalgalleries.org
*website* www.nationalgalleries.org
*Photographic & Licensing Manager* Deborah Hunter

Fine art from Renaissance to present day. Specialist
subjects include landscape, still life, portraits, genre,
animals and costume.

## National Maritime Museum Picture Library*

National Maritime Museum, Greenwich,
London SE10 9NF
*email* picturelibrary@nmm.ac.uk
*website* www.nmm.ac.uk
*Contact* David Taylor *tel* 020-8312 6631,
Lucy Waitt *tel* 020-8312 6704

Maritime, transport, time and space and historic
photographs.

## National Museums & Galleries of Northern Ireland, Ulster Folk & Transport Museum

153 Bangor Road, Cultra, Holywood,
Co. Down BT18 0EU, Northern Ireland
*tel* 028-9042 8428 *fax* 028-9042 8728
*email* t.kenneth.anderson@talk21.com
*Head of Dept of Photography* T.K. Anderson

Photographs from 1850s to the present day,
including the work of W.A. Green, Rose Shaw and
R.J. Welsh while he was under contract to Harland
and Wolff Ltd. Subjects include Belfast shipbuilding
(80,000 photographs, including 70 original
negatives of the *Titanic*), road and rail transport,
folk life, agriculture and the linen industry. B&w
and colour (35mm, medium and large format).
Founded 1962.

## National Portrait Gallery Picture Library*

St Martin's Place, London WC2H 0HE
*tel* 020-7312 2474 *fax* 020-7312 2464
*email* picturelibrary@npg.org.uk
*website* www.npg.org.uk
*Contact* Tom Morgan

Pictures of brilliant, daring and influential
characters who made British history, are available
for publication. Images can be searched, viewed and
ordered on the website. Copyright clearance is
arranged for all the images supplied.

## Natural Image

24 Newborough Road, Wimborne, Dorset BH21 1RD
*tel* (01202) 849142 *fax* (01202) 848419
*email* bob.gibbons@which.net
*Contact* Dr Bob Gibbons

Colour library covering natural history, habitats,
countryside and gardening (UK and worldwide);
special emphasis on conservation. Commissions
undertaken. Terms: 50%. Founded 1982.

## The Nature and Landscape File

24 Southleigh Crescent, Leeds LS11 5TW
*tel* 0113-2715535 *mobile* (07866) 057823
*Proprietor* Dr Mark Lucock

Natural history subjects and landscapes from
around the world, especially the UK, southern
Europe, North America. Specialises in
photomacrographic images. 30,000 large- and
small-format colour transparencies. Founded 1997.

## Nature Picture Library*

c/o BBC Broadcasting House, Whiteladies Road,
Bristol BS8 2LR
*tel* 0117-9746720 *fax* 0117-9238166
*email* info@naturepl.com
*website* www.naturepl.com

Photographs illustrating all aspects of nature:
mammals, birds, insects, reptiles, marine life, plants,
landscapes, indigenous peoples, environmental
issues and wildlife filming.

## Peter Newark Picture Library

3 Barton Buildings, Bath BA1 2JR
*tel* (01225) 334213 *fax* (01225) 480554

One million pictures: engravings, prints, paintings
and photographs on all aspects of world history
from ancient times to the present.

## New Blitz Literary & TV Agency

Via di Panico 67, 00186 Rome, Italy
*postal address* CP 30047-00193, Rome 47, Italy
*tel* (06) 686 4859 *fax* (06) 686 4859
*email* blitzgacs@inwind.it
*Contact* Giovanni A.S. Congiu

News and general library.

## NHPA Ltd*
57 High Street, Ardingly, West Sussex RH17 6TB
*tel* (01444) 892514 *fax* (01444) 892168
*email* nhpa@nhpa.co.uk
*website* www.nhpa.co.uk

Specialises in high-quality images covering all aspects of the natural world. Represents over 120 leading wildlife and environmental photographers with more than 200,000 pictures on file. Comprehensive coverage of British, European and worldwide nature and wildlife. Includes not only mainstream natural history subjects but rare and exotic species, conservation and environmental images, plus pets, agriculture, plants and marine life. Website holds over 18,000 hi-res images, available for download. *A–Z of Nature* catalogue and brochure available.

## Northern Picture Library – see Stockwave

## Christine Osborne Pictures – see World
Religions Photo Library

## OSF Ltd, Photo Library*
Ground Floor, Network House, Station Yard, Thame OX9 3UH
*tel* (01844) 262370 *fax* (01844) 2623808
*email* enquiries@osf.uk.com
*website* www.osf.uk.com

Specialises in all aspects of the natural world, worldwide. Includes wildlife, underwater, science, landscapes, seascapes, plants, gardens, seasons, environment, country life, natural habitats, weather, space, adventure sports, domestic animals and pets. Film footage also available: natural world, wildlife, global locations, medical, science, time-lapse and special effects.

## PA Photos*
292 Vauxhall Bridge Road, London SW1V 1AE
*tel* 020-7963 7032/34/35 *fax* 020-7963 7066
*email* paphotos.research@pa.press.net
*website* www.paphotos.com

Over 7 million photos dating from the turn of the 20th century, covering news, sport, royalty and showbiz. Library updated daily. Searches undertaken, or customers are welcome to visit.

## PAL (Performing Arts Library)
1st Floor, Production House, 25 Hackney Road, London E2 7NX
*tel* 020-7749 4850 *fax* 020-7749 4858
*email* admin@peformingartslibrary.com
*website* www.performingartslibrary.com

Continually updated specialist image collection covering classical music, opera, theatre, musicals, instruments, festivals, venues, circus, ballet and contemporary dance. Almost one million images from late 19th century onwards.

## Panos Pictures*
Studio 3B, 38 Southwark Street, London SE1 1UN
*tel* 020-7234 0010 *fax* 020-7357 0094
*email* pics@panos.co.uk
*website* www.panos.co.uk

Third World and Eastern European documentary photos focusing on social, political and economic issues with a special emphasis on environment and development. Files on agriculture, conflict, education, energy, environment, family life, festivals, food, health, industry, landscape, people, politics, pollution, refugees, religions, rural life, transport, urban life, water, weather. Terms: 50%. Founded 1986.

## Papilio Natural History & Travel Library
The Oasts, Headley Lane, Liphook, Hants GU30 7RX
*tel* (01428) 751056 *fax* (01428) 751057
*email* library@papiliophotos.com
*website* www.papiliophotos.com
*Contacts* Vicki Coombs (library), Robert Pickett

Worldwide coverage of natural history and travel; commissions undertaken. More than 100,000 images held. Colour catalogue available. Founded 1988.

## Ann and Bury Peerless*
22 King's Avenue, Minnis Bay, Birchington-on-Sea, Kent CT7 9QL
*tel* (01843) 841428 *fax* (01843) 848321

Art, craft (including textiles), archaeology, architecture, dance, iconography, miniature paintings, manuscripts, museum artefacts, social, cultural, agricultural, industrial, historical, political, educational, geographical subjects and travel in India, Pakistan, Bangladesh, Afghanistan, Burma, Cambodia, China, Egypt, Hong Kong, Indonesia (Borobudur, Java), Iran, Israel, Kenya, Libya, Malta, Malaysia, Morocco, Nepal, Russia (Moscow, St Petersburg, Samarkand and Bukhara, Uzbekistan), Sri Lanka, Spain, Sudan, Taiwan, Thailand, Tunisia, Uganda, Vietnam, Zambia and Zimbabwe. Specialist material on historical and world religions: Hinduism, Buddhism, Jainism, Judaism, Christianity, Confucianism, Islam, Sikhism, Taoism, Zoroastrianism (Parsees of India).

## Chandra S. Perera Cinetra
437 Pethiyagoda, Kelaniya–11600, Sri Lanka
*tel* (94) 11-2911885 *fax* (94) 11-2911885, 2674-737
*email* cinetraww@dialogsl.net comsvc01@slt.lk
Cinetra Worldwide Createch (Pvt) Ltd,
437 Pethiyagoda, Kelaniya-11600, Sri Lanka
*tel/fax* (94) 11-2911885, 2674-737, 2674-738
*Managing Director* Chandra S. Perera

B&w and colour library including news, wildlife, religious, social, political, sports, adventure, environmental, forestry, nature and tourism. Photographic and journalistic features on any subject. Founded 1958.

## Photofusion*

17A Electric Lane, London SW9 8LA
*tel* 020-7733 3500 *fax* 020-7738 5509
*email* library@photofusion.org
*website* www.photofusion.org

Covers all aspects of UK contemporary life with an emphasis on social and environment issues. Catalogue available. Photographers available for commission.

## The Photolibrary Wales*

2 Bro-nant, Church Road, Pentyrch,
Cardiff CF15 9QG
*tel* 029-2089 0311 *fax* 029-2089 2650
*email* info@photolibrarywales.com
*website* www.photolibrarywales.com
*Director* Steve Benbow

Comprehensive collection of contemporary images of Wales. Subjects include landscape, lifestyle, current affairs, sport, industry, people. Over 100 photographers represented. Digital files and transmission available. Colour transparencies and b&w prints. Commission: 50%. Founded 1998.

## Photolibrary.com*

81A Endell Street, London WC2H 9AJ
*tel* 020-7836 5591 *fax* 020-7379 4650
*website* www.photolibrary.com

Requires digital material on all subjects. Submit via website.

## Photo Link

126 Quarry Lane, Northfield, Birmingham B31 2QD
*tel* 0121-475 8712 *fax* 0121-604 0480
*email* vines@aviationphotolink.co.uk
*website* www.aviationphotolink.co.uk
*Contact* Mike Vines

Colour and b&w aviation library, covering subjects from 1909 to the present day. Specialises in air-to-air photography. Assignments undertaken. Over 10,000 aviation images from around the world are added every year. Can also research, advise and write aviation stories and press releases. Founded 1990.

## Photo Resources

The Orchard, Marley Lane, Kingston, Canterbury, Kent CT4 6JH
*tel* (01227) 830075 *fax* (01227) 831135

Ancient civilisations, art, archaeology, world religions, myth, and museum objects covering the period from 30,000 BC to AD 1900.

## Pictor International Ltd – see ImageState

Pictor Ltd

## The Picture Company

100 Pondcroft Road, Knebworth, Herts. SG3 6DE
*tel* (01438) 814418 *mobile* (07850) 971491

*fax* (01438) 814418
*email* chrisbonass@hotmail.co.uk
*website* www.flightonfilm.co.uk
*Contact* Chris Bonass

Colour transparencies (2¼ x 2¼in and 35mm) of people and places worldwide. Taken by award-winning film and TV cameraman and largely unseen and unpublished. Also aviation pictures old and new, including air-to-air photography and a unique archive on 16mm film and broadcast videotape. Used by BBC, C4, etc. Assignments undertaken. Founded 1993.

## Picturepoint Ltd – see Topham Picturepoint

## Picturesmiths Ltd

Manor Farm Cottage, Main Road, Curbridge, Witney, Oxon OX29 7NT
*tel* (01993) 771907 *fax* (01993) 706383
*email* roger@picturesmiths.co.uk
*website* www.picturesmiths.co.uk
*Managing Director* Roger M. Smith

Plant photography, from portraits, close-ups and macrophotography to plant associations, colour themes and garden scenes. Colour transparencies. Founded 1997.

## Sylvia Pitcher Photo Library

75 Bristol Road, London E7 8HG
*tel* 020-8552 8308 *fax* 020-8552 8308
*email* SPphotolibrary@aol.com

Musicians: blues, jazz, old-time country and bluegrass, cajun and zydeco, soul and gospel, pop (1960s and 1970s), plus related ephemera. Views and details of the USA: countryside, 'small-town America', shacks, railroads, rural Americana. Archival: early 20th century – mainly cottonfields, riverboats and various cities in the USA. 1960s–1970s: girls (both white and black) and couples. Founded 1968.

## Pixfeatures

5 Latimer Road, Barnet, Herts. EN5 5NU
*tel* 020-8449 9946 *fax* 020-8441 2725
Spanish office, *mobile* 0034-616 129742
*Contact* Peter Wickman

Historical pictures and features covering big news events, royalty, showbiz. Travel (all countries). National newspapers' extensive collection of people in the news to 1970. *Stern* magazine features (before 1985). Spanish scenarios, towns, monuments. Documentary and historical photos. Special collections: Dukes of Windsor and Kent, Kennedys, Beatles, Keeler/Levy, trainrobbers, Second World War/Nazis. Terms: 50%.

## Popperfoto (Paul Popper Ltd)*

The Old Mill, Overstone Farm, Overstone, Northampton NN6 0AB

*tel* (01604) 670670 *fax* (01604) 670635
*email* popperfoto@msn.com
*websites* www.popperfoto.com,
www.thegalleryatpopperfoto.com

Over 14 million images, covering 150 years of photographic history. Unrivalled archival material, world-famous sports library and extensive stock photography. Credit line includes Reuters, Bob Thomas Sports Photography, UPI, AFP and EPA, Acme, INP, Planet, Paul Popper, Exclusive News Agency, Victory Archive, Odhams Periodicals Library, *Illustrated*, Harris Picture Agency, and H.G. Ponting which holds the Scott 1910–12 Antarctic expedition material.

Colour from 1940, b&w from 1870 to present. Major subjects covered worldwide include: events, personalities, wars, royalty, sport, politics, transport, crime, history and social conditions. Popperfoto policy is to make material available, same day, to clients throughout the world. Mac-desk accessible. Researchers welcome by appointment. Free catalogue available.

*POPPERFOTO Online* includes half a million photos with delivery of full resolution images. *The Gallery at POPPERFOTO* features limited edition, hand-printed fine art photographs which can also be ordered online.

### Premaphotos Wildlife*

Amberstone, 1 Kirland Road, Bodmin,
Cornwall PL30 5JQ
*tel* (01208) 78258 *fax* (01208) 72302
*email* pics@premaphotos.co.uk
*website* www.premaphotos.co.uk
*Contact* Dr Rod Preston-Mafham

Library of 35mm transparencies; wide range of natural history subjects from around the world, including camouflage, mimicry, warning coloration, parental care, courtship, mating, flowers, fruits, fungi, habitats (particularly rainforests and deserts), and many more. Specialists in invertebrate behaviour and cacti. Captions and copy can be provided. Founded 1978.

### Press Association Photos – see PA Photos

### Press Features Syndicate

9 Paradise Close, Eastbourne, East Sussex BN20 8BT
*tel* (01323) 728760

For full details see page 125.

### Public Record Office Image Library –
see The National Archives Image Library

### Punch Cartoon Library*

87–135 Brompton Road, London SW1X 7XL
*tel* 020-7225 6710/6793 *fax* 020-7225 6712
*email* punch.library@harrods.com
*website* www.punch.co.uk

Holds over 500,000 cartoons that appeared in Punch magazine from 1841–1992, indexed under subject categories: humour, historical events, politics, fashion, sport, personalities, etc.

### Railways – Milepost 92½*

Milepost 92½, Newton Harcourt, Leics. LE8 9FH
*tel* 0116-259 2068 *fax* 0116-259 3001
*email* contacts@milepost92-half.co.uk
*website* www.milepost92-half.co.uk

Comprehensive library representing all aspects of modern railway operations and scenic pictures from the UK and abroad. Includes Colin Garratt's collection of world steam trains as well as archive b&w photos. Welcomes contributing photographers and also archives, and markets picture collections on behalf of individuals. Founded 1969.

### Raleigh International Picture Library*

Raleigh House, 27 Parson's Green Lane,
London SW6 4HZ
*tel* 020-7371 8585
*email* press@raleigh.org.uk
*website* www.raleighinternational.org
*Contact* Kate Davies

Stock colour images from around the world, especially remote landscapes, people and flora/fauna. Updated from expeditions 11 times a year. Open to researchers by appointment only, Mon–Fri, 9.30am–4.00pm.

### Redferns Music Picture Library*

7 Bramley Road, London W10 6SZ
*tel* 020-7792 9914 *fax* 020-7792 0921
*email* info@redferns.com
*website* www.redferns.com
*Contact* Dede Millar

All styles of music, from 18th century classical composers to current Top 10, plus instruments, crowds, festivals and atmospherics. Brochure available. Pictures can be researched and sent digitally through website.

### Retna Pictures Ltd*

West Complex, Pinewood Studios, Pinewood Road,
Iver Heath, Bucks. SL0 0NH
*tel* (01753) 785450 *fax* (01753) 785451
*email* ukinfo@retna.com
*website* www.retna.com

Two libraries: celebrity (early and contemporary music, films and personalities) and lifestyle (people, family life, work, leisure and food). Founded 1984.

### Retrograph Nostalgia Archive

Number 10, Hanover Crescent,
Brighton BN2 9SB
*tel* (01273) 687554
*email* retropix1@aol.com
*website* www.retrograph.com

Worldwide advertising, packaging, posters, postcards, decorative and fine art illustrations from 1880–1970. Special collections include Victoriana illustrations and scraps (1860–1901), fashion and beauty (1880–1975), RetroTravel Archive: travel and tourism, RetroGourmet Archive: food and drink (1890–1950). Research service and Image Consultancy services; RetroMontages: Victoriana montage design service. Free colour leaflets. Founded 1984.

## Rex Features Ltd*

18 Vine Hill, London EC1R 5DZ
*tel* 020-7278 7294 *fax* 020-7837 4812
*email* rex@rexfeatures.com
*websites* www.rexfeatures.com, www.timepix.com
*Editorial Director* Mike Selby, *Library Sales Manager* Glen Marks

International news and features photo agency and picture library serving more than 30 countries, and representing hundreds of photographers. Covers celebrity, news, human interest, pop and showbiz, etc. UK representative of TimePix, the picture archive of Time Inc. which includes the Mansell Collection, the British archive of historical images. Founded 1953.

## Ritmeyer Archaeological Design

114 Turners Avenue, Hawthorndene, Adelaide, SA 5051, Australia
*tel* (08) 8278 6865
*email* ritmeyer@adam.com.au
*website* www.templemountonline.com
*Contact* Leen and Kathleen Ritmeyer

Colour transparencies of the archaeology of the Holy Land with the emphasis on Jerusalem and the Temple Mount. Architectural reconstruction drawings of ancient sites, such as temples, synagogues, mosques and churches. Special collection of scenes of Jewish temple ritual illustrated on to-scale model of the first century temple in Jerusalem. Drawing commissions undertaken. Founded 1983.

## Ann Ronan Picture Library

c/o Celimage Image Partners Ltd, Cherwell Innovation Centre, Unit 78 Heyford Park, Upper Heyford, Bicester, Oxon OX25 5HD
*tel* (01869) 238377 *fax* (01869) 238378
*email* ann.ronan@heritage-group.org
*website* www.heritage-images.com

Woodcuts, engravings, etc social and political history plus history of science and technology, including military and space, literature and music.

## Roundhouse Ornithology Collection

Mathry Hill House, Mathry, Pembrokeshire SA62 5HB
*tel* (01348) 837008 *fax* (01348) 837008
*email* john@stewartsmith.fsnet.co.uk

*Contact* John Stewart-Smith

Colour library specialising in birds of UK, Europe, Middle East (especially), North Africa, Far East and South America. Founded 1991.

## Royal Collection Enterprises*

Photographic Services, Windsor Castle, Windsor, Berks. SL4 1NJ
*tel* (01753) 868286 *fax* (01753) 620046
*email* photoservices@royalcollection.org.uk
*website* www.royal.gov.uk
*Head of Photographic Services* Miss Shruti Patel

Works of art comprising 10,000 pictures, enamels and miniatures, 20,000 drawings, 10,000 watercolours, 500,000 prints and thousands of pieces of furniture, sculpture, glass, porcelain, arms and armour, textiles and jewellery. Available for hire are a wide range of colour transparencies of items in the collection, including works by Van Dyck, Rembrandt, Holbein and Leonardo da Vinci, as well as b&w prints, for purchase. Orders, which should be as specific as possible, must be received in writing and are always treated as urgent.

## Royal Geographical Society Picture Library*

1 Kensington Gore, London SW7 2AR
*tel* 020-7591 3060 *fax* 020-7591 3061
*email* pictures@rgs.org
*website* www.rgs.org/picturelibrary
*Contact* Picture Library Manager

Worldwide coverage of geography, travel, exploration, expeditions and cultural environment from 1870s to the present. Founded 1830.

## Royalpics – see Stockwave

## The Royal Society for Asian Affairs

2 Belgrave Square, London SW1X 8PJ
*tel* 020-7235 5122 *fax* 020-7259 6771
*email* info@rsaa.org.uk
*website* www.rsaa.org.uk

Library of 19th and 20th century books on Asia, mainly central Asia and archive of original 19th and 20th century b&w photos, glass slides, etc of Asia. Publishes *Asian Affairs* (3 p.a.).

## Royal Society of Chemistry Library and Information Centre

Burlington House, Piccadilly, London W1J 0BA
*tel* 020-7440 3373 *fax* 020-7287 9798
*email* library@rsc.org
*website* www.rsc.org

Covers all aspects of chemistry information. Images collection dating from the 17th century includes prints and photographs of famous chemists, *Vanity Fair* cartoons, scenes, lantern slides of similar subjects and colour photomicrographs of crystal structures. Founded 1841.

## RSPCA Photolibrary*

RSPCA Trading Ltd, Wilberforce Way, Southwater, Horsham, West Sussex RH13 9RS
*tel* 0870-754 0150 *fax* 0870-753 0150
*email* pictures@rspcaphotolibrary.com
*website* www.rspcaphotolibrary.com
*Manager* Andrew Forsyth

A comprehensive collection of natural history pictures representing the work of over 500 photographers, including the Wild Images collection. Its files include wild, domestic and farm animals, birds, marine life, veterinary work, animal welfare and environmental issues and a record of the work of the RSPCA. Founded 1993.

## Dawn Runnals Photographic Library

5 St Marys Terrace, Kenwyn Road, Truro, Cornwall TR1 3SW
*tel* (01872) 279353

General library: land and seascapes, flora and fauna, sport, animals, people, buildings, boats, harbours, miscellaneous section; details of other subjects on application. Other photographers' work not accepted. Sae appreciated with enquiries. Founded 1985.

## Russia and Eastern Images*

Sonning, Cheapside Lane, Denham, Uxbridge, Middlesex UB9 5AE
*tel* (01895) 833508
*email* easteuropix@btinternet.com
*website* www.easteuropix.com
*Library Manager* Mark Wadlow

Architecture, cities, landscapes, people and travel images covering Russia and the former Soviet Union. Excellent background knowledge available and Russian language spoken. Founded 1988.

## Peter Sanders Photography Ltd*

24 Meades Lane, Chesham, Bucks. HP5 1ND
*tel* (01494) 773674, 771372 *fax* (01494) 773674
*email* photos@petersanders.com
*website* www.petersanders.com

Specialises in the world of Islam, its cultures, lifestyles, architecture, landscapes, festivals and industry. Countries covered include: China, Egypt, India, Iran, Kenya, Kosovo, Kuwait, Mali, Mauritania, Morocco, Saudi Arabia, Senegal, Spain, Sudan, Turkey, Turkmenistan, USA and Europe and more. Also other religions. Founded 1987.

## S & G Press Agency Ltd

63 Gee Street, London EC1V 3RS
*tel* 020-7336 0632 *fax* 020-7253 8419

Press photos and vast photo library. Send photos, but negatives preferred.

## Science Photo Library*

327–9 Harrow Road, London W9 3RB
*tel* 020-7432 1100 *fax* 020-7286 8668
*email* info@sciencephoto.com
*website* www.sciencephoto.com

Subjects include the human body, health and medicine, research, genetics, technology and industry, space exploration and astronomy, earth science, satellite imagery, environment, nature and wildlife and the history of science. Over 100,000 images available online. Founded 1979.

## Science & Society Picture Library*

Science Museum, Exhibition Road, London SW7 2DD
*tel* 020-7942 4400 *fax* 020-7942 4401
*email* piclib@nmsi.ac.uk
*website* www.nmsi.ac.uk/piclib

We are currently digitising over 50,000 of the best from the millions of images in our collections. Science & Society has one of the widest ranges of photographs, paintings, prints, posters and objects in the world. The images come from the collections of the National Museum of Science & Industry (NMSI) - which includes the Science Museum, the National Railway Museum and the National Museum of Photography, Film & Television. Our website details the extent of our interests. Images are available as high or low resolution via email or ftp, alternatively transparency or print can be supplied. Founded 1993.

## Scope Features

26 St Cross Street, London EC1N 8UH
*tel* 020-7405 2997 *fax* 020-7831 4549
*email* images@scopefeatues.com
*website* www.scopefeatues.com

Colour images of personalities, particularly TV personalities. Scope Beauty: colour situations/beauty pictures.

## Scotland in Focus Picture Library

Unit 5, Langlee Centre, Marigold Drive, Galashiels, Selkirkshire TD1 2LP
*tel* (01896) 755124 *fax* (01896) 752370
*email* library@scotfocus.sol.co.uk
*website* www.scotfocus.com

Specialist library offering thousands of stock images to illustrate every aspect of Scottish life and work.

**Scottish Wildlife Library**: Environmental and natural history. All Scottish material required on 35mm and upwards, medium format preferred. Photographers must enclose return postage. Terms: 50%. Founded 1988.

## SCR Photo Library

Society for Co-operation in Russian and Soviet Studies, 320 Brixton Road, London SW9 6AB

*tel* 020-7274 2282 *fax* 020-7274 3230
*email* ruslibrary@scrss.org.uk
*website* www.scrss.org.uk

Russian and Soviet life and history. Comprehensive coverage of cultural subjects: art, theatre, folk art, costume, music; agriculture and industry, architecture, armed forces, education, history, places, politics, science, sport. Also material on contemporary life in Russia, the CIS and the Baltic states; posters and theatre props, artistic reference, advice. Research by appointment only. Founded 1924.

## Sealand Aerial Photography Ltd*

Meadows Unit, 51 Stane Street, Halnaker, Chichester, PO18 0NF
*tel* (01243) 781551 *fax* (01243) 781551
*email* info@sealandaerial.co.uk
*website* www.sealandaerial.co.uk

Aerial photo coverage of any subject that can be photographed from the air in the UK. Most stock on 2¼in format colour negative/transparency. Subjects constantly updated from new flying. Founded 1976.

## Mick Sharp Photography

Eithinog, Waun, Penisarwaun, Caernarfon, Gwynedd LL55 3PW
*tel* (01286) 872425 *fax* (01286) 872425
*email* mick.jean@virgin.net

Archaeology, ancient monuments, buildings, churches, countryside, environment, history, landscape, past cultures and topography. Emphasis on British Isles, but material also from other countries. Access to other specialist collections on related subjects. B&w prints from 5 x 4in negatives, and 35mm and 6 x 4.5cm colour transparencies. Founded 1981.

## Shout Picture Library

Mordene House, Merritts Hill, Illogan, Redruth, Cornwall TR16 4DF
*tel* (01209) 210525
*email* john@shoutpictures.com
*website* www.shoutpictures.com
*Contact* John Callan

Specialises in the emergency services: fire, police and ambulance. Also hospital, medical and trauma, education. Contact Library for password to the secure website. Commissions accepted. Founded 1994.

## Brian and Sal Shuel – see Collections

## Sites, Sights and Cities

1 Manchester Court, Moreton-in-Marsh, Glos. GL56 0BY
*tel* (01608) 652829 *fax* (01608) 652829

*email* paul.dev@tesco.net
*Director* Paul Devereux

Ancient monuments, mainly in Britain, Egypt, Greece and USA; city features in UK, Europe and USA; general nature shots. Founded 1990.

## Skishoot – Offshoot*

Hall Place, Upper Woodcott, Whitchurch, Hants RG28 7PY
*tel* (01635) 255527 *fax* (01635) 255528
*email* skishootsnow@aol.com
*website* www.skishoot.co.uk
*Librarians* Jo Crossley, Kate Parker

Library specialising in all aspects of skiing and snowboarding. Also France, all year round. Assignments undertaken. Terms: 50%. Founded 1986.

## Skyscan Photolibrary*

Oak House, Toddington, Cheltenham, Glos. GL54 5BY
*tel* (01242) 621357 *fax* (01242) 621343
*email* info@skyscan.co.uk
*website* www.skyscan.co.uk

Specialist aerial photolibrary now covering air-to-ground, aviation and aerial sports. Contributing photographers work from planes, helicopters, masts, balloons, gliders and other aerial platforms. Images can be placed in-house on an agency basis or retained by the photographer and requested for use on a brokerage basis; both terms: 50%. Founded 1984.

## Snookerimages (Eric Whitehead Photography)

25 Oak Street, Windermere, Cumbria LA23 1EN
*tel* (015394) 48894 *mobile* (07768) 808249
*fax* (015394) 48294
*email* eric@snookerimages.co.uk
*website* www.snookerimages.co.uk
*Contact* Eric Whitehead

Specialist picture library covering the sport of snooker. Over 20,000 images of all the professional players dating from 1984 to the present day: players away from the table in locations throughout the world as well as action images.

## Society for Anglo-Chinese Understanding

Sally & Richard Greenhill Photo Library, 357 Liverpool Road, London N1 1NL
*tel* 020-7607 8549 *fax* 020-7607 7151
*email* sr.greenhill@virgin.net

Colour and b&w prints of China, late 1960s–1989. Founded 1965.

## Society for Co-operation in Russian and Soviet Studies – see SCR Photo Library

## Sotheby's Picture Library*

34–35 New Bond Street, London W1A 2AA
tel 020-7293 5383 fax 020-7293 5062
email piclib.london@sothebys.com
Contact Sue Daly, Researcher

Art and antiques; Cecil Beaton archive of
photographs. Founded 1993.

## Sporting Pictures (UK) Ltd*

7A Lambs Conduit Passage, London WC1R 4RG
tel 020-7405 4500 fax 020-7831 7991
email photos@sportingpictures.com
website www.sportingpictures.com
Director Crispin J. Thruston, Contact Sue Evans

Specialises in sports, sporting events, sportspersons,
amateur sport.

## Steffi Schubert, Wildlife Conservation Collection Photographic Library

Bramble Cottage, Foxhill, St Cross, South Elmham,
Harleston, Norfolk IP20 0NX
tel (01986) 782279 fax (01986) 782279

All aspects of British wildlife and fauna. Founded
1990.

## The Still Moving Picture Company

8 Saxe Coburg Place, Edinburgh EH3 5BR
tel 0131-332 1123 fax 0131-332 9123
email info@stillmovingpictures.com
websites www.stillmovingpictures.com,
www.stilldigital.co.uk

Over 150,000 pictures of Scotland and all things
Scottish; sport (Allsport agent for Scotland). Online
service via 'stilldigital' website. Founded 1991.

## STILL PICTURES The Whole Earth Photo Library*

199 Shooters Hill Road, London SE3 8UL
tel 020-8858 8307 fax 020-8858 2049
email info@stillpictures.com
website www.stillpictures.com
Proprietor Mark Edwards

Specialises in people and the environment; the
Third World; nature; wildlife and habitats. Includes
industry, agriculture, indigenous peoples and
cultures, nature and endangered species. Terms:
50%. Founded 1970.

## Stockwave

Headquarters Aylesbury office
tel (01296) 747878 fax (01296) 748648
email enquiries@stockwave.com
websites www.stockwave.com, www.royalpics.com

Collections encompassing Britain, Europe and the
world. British events (including social calendar),
social/political news, government, politicians,
industrial, tourism, science and technology, defence,
lifestyle, Royal family, film and stage personalities.

**John Blake Picture Library**: General topography of
England, Europe and the rest of the world.
Landscapes, architecture, churches, gardens,
countryside, towns and villages. Horse trials covered
including Badminton and Gatcombe Park.

**COI Photo Library**: Includes many important and
previously unseen images of Britain's government,
political events, interior views of the Houses of
Parliament and 10 Downing Street, etc, British
Royal archives, Festival of Britain, industrial and
manufacturing archives, agriculture, education,
defence.

**Northern Picture Library**: Northern England
scenery; cities of Northern England and Scotland;
architecture and industrial scenes of Northern
England past and present.

**Royalpics**: Dedicated site for Royal pictures from
Stockwave, COI Archives and other major photo
libraries.

## Tony Stone Images – see Getty Images

## Survival Anglia Photo Library – see OSF Ltd, Photo Library

## Sutcliffe Gallery

1 Flowergate, Whitby, North Yorkshire YO21 3BA
tel (01947) 602239 fax (01947) 820287
email photographs@sutcliffe-gallery.fsnet.co.uk
website www.sutcliffe-gallery.co.uk

Collection of 19th century photography, all by
Frank M. Sutcliffe Hon. FRPS (1853–1941), especially
inshore fishing boats and fishing community; also
farming interests. Period covered 1872–1910.

## Syndication International – see Mirrorpix

## Charles Tait Photo Library

Kelton, St Ola, Orkney KW15 1TR
tel (01856) 873738 fax (01856) 875313
email charles.tait@zetnet.co.uk
website www.charles-tait.co.uk

Colour photo library specialising in the Scottish
islands, especially Orkney, Shetland, the Western
Isles (including outliers) and Caithness.
Archaeology, landscapes, seascapes, wildlife, crafts,
industries, events, transport, and sites of interest.
Also mainland Scotland and Hadrian's Wall, plus
France, Venice, Alaska, and New England. Over
100,000 images in formats ranging from 35mm to 5
x 4in, including 70mm panoramic and 6 megapixel
digital. Images available to browse online; high-res
scans on CD and by email. Publisher of postcards,
calendars, guidebooks. Founded 1978.

## The Tank Museum Archive & Reference Library

The Tank Museum, Bovington, Dorset BH20 6JG
*tel* (01929) 405096 *fax* (01929) 462410
*email* librarian@tankmuseum.co.uk
*website* www.tankmuseum.co.uk

International collection, from 1900 to present, of armoured fighting vehicles and military transport, including tanks, armoured cars, personnel carriers, cars, lorries and tractors, First and Second World War Royal Armoured Corps War Diaries and associated documents.

## Telegraph Colour Library – incorporated into Getty Images

## Theatre Museum

National Museum of the Performing Arts,
1E Tavistock Street, London WC2E 7PR
*tel* 020-7943 4700 *fax* 020-7943 4777
*website* www.theatremuseum.org

In addition to extensive public displays on live entertainment and education programme, the Museum has an unrivalled collection of programmes, playbills, prints, photos, videos, texts and press cuttings relating to performers and productions from the 17th century onwards. Available by appointment (book 3 weeks in advance), free of charge through the Study Room. Open Wed–Fri 10.30am–4.30pm. Reprographic services available.

## Tibet Pictures*

28 Sheen Common Drive, Richmond,
Surrey TW10 5BN
*tel* 020-7602 1989 *fax* 020-7602 1989
*Contact* Jonathan Miller

Specialises in the people, architecture, history, religion and politics of Tibet. Also Yemen. Colour and b&w. Founded 1992.

## Topham Picturepoint*

PO Box 33, Edenbridge, Kent TN8 5PB
*tel* (01732) 863939 *fax* (01732) 860215
*email* admin@TopFoto.co.uk
*website* www.TopFoto.co.uk

Eight million contemporary and historical images. Over seven hundred thousand available online. New photographers are not being considered at this stage.

## B.M. Totterdell Photography*

Constable Cottage, Burlings Lane, Knockholt,
Kent TN14 7PE
*tel* (01959) 532001 *fax* (01959) 532001
*email* btrial@btinternet.com

Specialist volleyball library, covering all aspects of the sport. Founded 1989.

## Transworld/Scope – see Scope Features

## Travel Ink Photo & Feature Library*

The Old Coach House, 14 High Street,
Goring-on-Thames, Nr Reading,
Berks. RG8 9AR
*tel* (01491) 873011 *fax* (01491) 875558
*email* info@travel-ink.co.uk
*website* www.travel-ink.co.uk

Travel, tourism, lifestyles and peoples around the world. Comtemporary. Specialist collections of Greece, France, Asia, the UK and the Americas. Images immediately available to order and download from website. Founded 1988.

## Travel Photo International

9 Halsall Green, Wirral CH63 9NA
*tel* 0151-334 2300 *fax* 0151-334 2300

Touristic interest including scenery, towns, monuments, historic buildings, archaeological sites, local people. Specialises in travel brochures and books. Terms: 50%.

## Trevillion Picture Library

75 Jeddo Road, London W12 9ED
*tel* 020-8740 9005 *fax* 020-8740 9088
*email* michael@trevillion.com
*website* www.trevillion.com
*Contact* Michael Trevillion, Managing Director

Specialises in 'art' style photography and inspirational imagery. Also handles the archive of Bruce Chatwin. Founded 1997.

## TRH Pictures*

Bradley's Close, 74–77 White Lion Street,
London N1 9PF
*tel* 020-7520 7647 *fax* 020-7520 7606
*email* trh@trhpictures.co.uk
*website* www.trhpictures.co.uk
*Director* Ted Nevill

Specialises in colour transparencies and b&w photos of the history of civil and military aviation, modern warfare from the American Civil War, transport on land and sea, and the exploration of space. Commission: 50%. Founded 1983.

## Tropix Photo Library*

44 Woodbines Avenue, Kingston upon Thames,
Surrey KT1 2AY
*tel/fax* 020-8546 0823, 0151 625 4576
*email* images@tropix.co.uk
*website* www.tropix.co.uk

All aspects of tropics, sub-tropics and non-tropical developing countries. Plus MerseySlides: photos of Liverpool. Positive, progressive and model-released images. Preliminary enquiry in writing essential, by email. Visit website for full submission guidelines. No unsolicited material. Terms: 50%. Founded 1982.

## True North Picture Source

26 New Road, Hebden Bridge,
West Yorkshire HX7 8EF
*tel* (01422) 845532
*email* john@trunorth.demon.co.uk
*Proprietor* John Morrison

The life and landscape of the North of England. No
other photographers' work required. 30,000
transparencies (35mm and medium format).
Commissions undertaken. Founded 1992.

## Ulster Folk & Transport Museum – see

National Museums & Galleries of Northern
Ireland, Ulster Folk & Transport Museum

## Universal Pictorial Press & Agency (UPPA)*

29–31 Saffron Hill, London EC1N 8SW
*tel* 020-7421 6000 *fax* 020-7421 6006
*email* ctaylor@uppa.co.uk
*website* www.uppa.co.uk

Photo library containing notable Royal, political,
company, academic, legal, diplomatic, church,
military, pop, arts, entertainment and sports
personalities and well-known views and buildings.
Commercial, industrial, corporate and public
relations photo assignments undertaken. Founded
1929.

## V&A Images*

Victoria & Albert Museum, Cromwell Road,
London SW7 2RL
*tel* 020-7942 2483/6/9 *fax* 020-7942 2482
*email* vanda.images@vam.ac.uk
*website* www.vandaimages.com

A vast collection of photographs from the world's
largest museum of decorative and applied arts,
reflecting culture and lifestyle spanning over 1000
years of history to the present time. Digital delivery
or large format transparencies of contemporary and
historical textiles, costumes and fashions, ceramics,
furniture, metalwork, glass, sculpture, toys and
games, design and photographs from around the
world. Unique photos include 1960s fashion by
John French, Harry Hammond's behind-the-scenes
pop idols, Houston Rogers' theatrical world of the
1930s–70s, images of royalty by Lafayette, and
images by Cecil Beaton and 19th century pioneer
photographers. Images from the inexhaustible
shelves of the National Art Library and Library of
Art & Design, and from the Theatre Museum and
Museum of Childhood are readily available.

## Colin Varndell Natural History Photography

The Happy Return, Whitecross, Netherbury,
Bridport, Dorset DT6 5NH

*tel* (01308) 488341
*email* colin_varndell@hotmail.com
*Proprietor* Colin Varndell

UK wildlife and landscape with particular emphasis
on birds, mammals, butterflies, wild flowers and
habitats. 110,000 colour transparencies. Founded
1980.

## Venice Picture Library*

c/o The Bridgeman Art Library,
17–19 Garway Road, London W2 4PH
*tel* 020-7727 4065 *fax* 020-7792 8509
*email* london@bridgeman.co.uk
*website* www.bridgeman.co.uk
*Contact* Jenny Page

Specialises in Venice, covering most aspects of the
city, islands and lagoon, especially architecture and
the environment. Founded 1990.

## John Vickers Theatre Collection

27 Shorrolds Road, London SW6 7TR
*tel* 020-7385 5774

Archives of British theatre and portraits of actors,
writers and musicians by John Vickers from
1938–74.

## Vidocq Photo Library

162 Burwell Meadow, Witney, Oxon OX28 5JJ
*tel* (01993) 778518
*email* vidocq@which.net
*website* www.vidocq/languages.co.uk

Specialist in photographs for language and
educational text books. Detailed coverage of France.
Assignments undertaken. Founded 1983.

## Visions in Golf

The Barn, 6 Woodend Court, Dodworth, Barnsley,
South Yorkshire S75 3UA
*tel* (01226) 286111 *fax* (0870) 831 1941
*email* mark@vigltd.fsnet.co.uk
*Proprietor* Mark Newcombe

Every aspect of worldwide golf, including an archive
dating back to the late 19th century and world-
famous golf courses. Over 350,000 colour
transparencies and 5000 b&w images, the majority
of which are availabe on digital. Commission: 50%.
Founded 1984.

## Christopher Ware Photography

65 Trinity Street, Barry,
South Glamorgan CF62 7EX
*tel* (01446) 420875
*Proprietor* Christopher Ware

Colour and b&w photos of industry and
transport of the southeast Wales area; also civil and
military aircraft. Commissions undertaken.
Founded 1970.

## Simon Warner

Whitestone Farm, Stanbury, Keighley,
West Yorkshire BD22 0JW
*tel* (01535) 644644 *fax* (01535) 644644
*email* photos@simonwarner.co.uk
*website* www.simonwarner.co.uk

Landscape photographer with own stock pictures of
northern England, North Wales and Northwest
Scotland.

## Waterways Photo Library*

39 Manor Court Road, London W7 3EJ
*tel* 020-8840 1659 *fax* 020-8567 0605
*email* watphot39@aol.com
*website* www.waterwaysphotolibrary.com
*Contact* Derek Pratt

British inland waterways; canals, rivers; bridges,
aqueducts, locks and all waterside architectural
features; watersports; waterway holidays, boats,
fishing; town and countryside scenes. No other
photographers' work required. Founded 1976.

## The Weimar Archive – see Mary Evans
Picture Library

## Welfare History Picture Library

Heatherbank Museum of Social Work, Caledonian
University, Cowcaddens Road, Glasgow G4 0BA
*tel* 0141-331 8637 *fax* 0141-331 3005
*email* a.ramage@gcal.ac.uk
*website* www.lib.gcal.ac.uk/heatherbank/

Social history and social work, especially child
welfare, poorhouses, prisons, hospitals, slum
clearance, women's movement, social reformers and
their work. Catalogue on request and on website.
Founded 1975.

## Wellcome Photo Library*

210 Euston Road, London NW1 2BE
020-7611 8348 fax 020-7611 8577
*email* photolib@wellcome.ac.uk
*website* www.medphoto.wellcome.ac.uk
*Library Manager* Catherine Draycott

Leading source of images on the history of
medicine, modern biomedical science and clinical
medicine.

## Richard Welsby Photography

1 Breadalbane Terrace, Edinburgh EH11 2BW
*tel* 0131-337 9975 *fax* 0131-337 9975
*email* richardwelsby@orkney.com
*website* www.richardwelsby.com
*Contact* Richard Welsby

Specialist library of the Orkney Islands: business
and industry, scenics, geology, archaeology and
historic; wide coverage of flowers, plants and other
natural history subjects; aerials. Founded 1984.

## Westcountry Pictures

10 Headon Gardens, Countess Wear, Exeter,
Devon EX2 6LE
*tel* (01392) 426640 *fax* (01392) 209080
*email* peter@cooperphotography.co.uk
*website* www.cooperphotography.co.uk
*Contact* Peter Cooper

All aspects of Devon and Cornwall – culture, places,
industry and leisure. Founded 1989.

## Western Americana Picture Library

3 Barton Buildings, Bath BA1 2JR
*tel* (01225) 334213 *fax* (01225) 480554

Prints, engravings, photos and colour
transparencies on the American West, cowboys,
gunfighters, Indians, including pictures by Frederic
Remington and Charles Russell, etc.

## Roy J. Westlake

West Country Photo Library, 31 Redwood Drive,
Plympton, Plymouth PL7 2FS
*tel* (01752) 336444 *fax* (01752) 336444
*Contact* Roy J. Westlake ARPS

Specialises in all aspects of Devon, Cornwall,
Dorset, Somerset and Wiltshire. Medium format
transparencies of landscapes, seascapes,
architecture, etc. Other photographers' work not
required. Founded 1960.

## Eric Whitehead Photography – see
Snookerimages (Eric Whitehead Photography)

## Wilderness Photographic Library*

*tel* (01524) 272149 *fax* (01524) 272149
*email* wildernessphoto@bt.internet.com
*website* www.photosource.co.uk/wildernessphoto.htm
*Director* John Noble FRGS

Specialist library in mountain and wilderness
regions, especially polar. Associated aspects of
people, places, natural history, geographical
features, exploration and mountaineering,
adventure sports, travel.

## Wildlife Matters Photographic Library

Marlham, Henley's Down, Battle,
East Sussex TN33 9BN
*tel* (01424) 830566 *fax* (01424) 830224
*email* gardens@gmpix.com
*website* www.gmpix.com
*Contact* Dr John Feltwell

Ecology, conservation and environment; habitats
and pollution; agriculture and horticulture; general
natural history, entomology; Mediterranean
wildlife; rainforests (Amazon, Central America,
Costa Rica and Indonesia); aerial pics of
countryside UK, Europe, USA. Founded 1980.

## The Neil Williams Classical Collection
22 Avon, Hockley, Tamworth, Staffs. B77 5QA
*tel* (01827) 286086 *fax* (01827) 286086
*email* neil@classicalcollection.co.uk
*Proprietor* Neil Williams PGC(Mus), BA Hons, Hum

Specialises in classical music ephemera, including portraits of composers, musicians, conductors, opera singers, ballet stars, impresarios, and music-related literary figures. Old and sometimes rare photographs, postcards, antique prints, cigarette cards, stamps, concert programmes, Victorian newspapers, etc. Also modern photographs of composer references such as museums, statues, memorials, etc. Also freelance writer of concert programme notes and CD liner notes.

Other subjects: music in art, musical instruments, manuscripts, concert halls, opera houses and other music venues. Founded 1996.

## David Williams Picture Library*
50 Burlington Avenue, Glasgow G12 0LH
*tel* 0141-339 7823 *fax* 0141-337 3031

Specialises in travel photography; wide coverage of Scotland, Iceland and Spain. Also other European countries and Western USA and Canada. Subjects include: cities, towns, villages, 'tourist haunts', buildings, landscapes and natural features; geology and physical geography of Scotland and Iceland. Commissions undertaken. Catalogue available. Founded 1989.

## Windrush Photos*
99 Noah's Ark, Kemsing, Sevenoaks, Kent TN15 6PD
*tel* (01732) 763486 *fax* (01732) 763285
*email* dt@windrushphotos.demon.co.uk
*email* wwww.windrushphotos.com
*Owner* David Tipling

Worldwide wildlife and landscapes; birds a speciality. Captioning and text services; ornithological consultancy. Photographic and features commissions undertaken. Terms: 50%. Founded 1991.

## Tim Woodcock
59 Stoodham, South Petherton, Somerset TA13 5AS
*tel* (01460) 242788
*email* tim@timwoodcock.co.uk
*website* www.timwoodcock.co.uk

British and Eire landscape, seascape, architecture and heritage; children, parenthood, adults and education; gardens and containers; mountain biking. Location commissions undertaken. Terms: 50%. Founded 1983.

## World Pictures*
25 Gosfield Street, London W1W 6HQ
*tel* 020-7437 2121/436 0440 *fax* 020-7439 1307
*email* worldpictures@btinternet.com

*website* www.worldpictures.co.uk
*Directors* David Brenes, Carlo Irek

Over 600,000 medium and large format colour transparencies aimed at travel and travel-related markets. Extensive coverage of cities, countries and specific resort areas, together with material of an emotive nature, i.e. children, couples and families on holiday, all types of winter and summer sporting activities, motoring abroad, etc. Terms: 50%; major contributing photographers 60%.

## World Religions Photo Library*
53A Crimsworth Road, London SW8 4RJ
*tel* 020-7720 6951 *fax* 020-7720 6951
*email* co@worldreligions.co.uk
*websites* www.worldreligions.co.uk,
www.middleeastpictures.com

Specialist stock on religions from more than 50 countries: major faiths, places of worship, rites of passage, shrines, pilgrimage, sacred foods, culture and ecclesiastical buildings – temples, churches, mosques, etc. Also stocks the developing world: Middle East/Arab States, North Africa, Central Asian Republics, South Asia and Indian Ocean, Southeast Asia, Pacific/Australia. Major files on travel, crafts, agriculture, food, people. Member of the British Guild of Travel Writers. Specialises in illustrated editorial features. Welcomes submissions from photographers covering any of these subjects. The library is managed by Christine Osborne Pictures (also proprietor of Middle East Pictures).

## Murray Wren
3 Hallgate, London SE3 9SG
*tel* 020-8852 7556
*email* murraywren@aol.com

Outdoor nudes. Mostly unposed and natural. Colour, b&w and digital. Also nudist/natural photographs of club, beach and holiday resorts in the Uk and Europe. Associated MSS by arrangement. Historic and erotic art form throughout the ages in b&w only. All material from total library to individual pictures available for outright sale or reproduction fee. Digital images via email or CD possible. No new photographers required.

## The Allan Wright Photo Library
The Stables, Parton, Castle Douglas, Kirkcudbrightshire DG7 3NB
*tel* (016444) 470260 *fax* (016444) 470202
*email* allan@lyricalscotland.com
*website* www.lyricalscotland.com

Source of 'Lyrical Scotland' range of images featuring all of Scotland. Founded 1986.

## Gordon Wright Scottish Photo Library
25 Mayfield Road, Edinburgh EH9 2NQ
*tel* 0131-667 1300 *fax* 0131-667 1300

*email* gordon.wrightII@btopenworld.com
*website* www.scottish-books-photos.co.uk
*Managing Director* Gordon Wright

Specialist library illustrating Scotland: cities, towns and villages; landscapes and landmarks including the Orkney Islands; Scottish nationalism, personalities and writers. 56,000 b&w photos and 11,000 colour transparencies. Founded 1960.

## Yemen Pictures
Flat 2, Auriol Mansions, Edith Road,
London W14 0ST
*tel* 020-7602 1989 *fax* 020-7602 1989
*Contact* John Miles

Specialist colour library of Yemen, covering all aspects of culture, people, architecture, dance, qat and music. Also Africa, Australia, Middle East and Asia. Founded 1995.

## York Archaeological Trust Picture Library
Cromwell House, 13 Ogleforth, York YO1 7FG
*tel* (01904) 663000 *fax* (01904) 663024
*email* ckyriacou@yorkarchaeology.co.uk
*website* www.yorkarchaeology.co.uk
*Picture Librarian* C. Kyriacou

York archaeology covering Romans, Dark Ages, Vikings and Middle Ages; traditional crafts; scenes of York and Yorkshire. Founded 1987.

## Yorkshire Now!
4 Keelham Place, Denholme, Bradford,
West Yorkshire BD13 4HL
*tel* (01274) 831652 *fax* (01274) 831652
*email* rose@xelex.freeserve.co.uk
*Proprietors* Melvyn Strelitze, Rose White

B&w and colour images and videos of towns, cities, industries, etc in Yorkshire. Commissions undertaken. Founded 1998.

## Zoological Society of London*
Regent's Park, London NW1 4RY
*tel* 020-7449 6293 *fax* 020-7586 5743
*email* library@zsl.org
*website* www.zsl.org
*Librarian* Ann Sylph

Archive collection of photographs, paintings and prints, from the 16th century onwards, covering almost all vertebrate animals, many now extinct or rare, plus invertebrates. Founded 1826.

# Card and stationery publishers which accept photographs

Before submitting work, photographers are advised to ascertain requirements, including terms and conditions. Only top quality material should be submitted; inferior work is never accepted. Postage for return of material should be enclosed.

## *Member of the Greeting Card Association

## Britannia Products Ltd
Dawson Lane, Dudley Hill, Bradford,
West Yorkshire BD4 6HW
*tel* (01274) 784200 *fax* (01274) 651218
*Managing Director* Steve McNally

Designs and manufactures greetings cards, giftwrap and calendars. Submit transparencies (5 x 4in). Brands: Fine Art Graphics, Paws for Thought, The Comedy Club, Just Kiddin', Academy, Mother Earth, Animates, Fleurs, Truffles. Division of Hallmark Cards (Holdings) Ltd. Founded 1980.

## Card Connection Ltd*
Park House, South Street, Farnham,
Surrey GU9 7QQ
*tel* (01252) 892300 *fax* (01252) 892363
*email* ho@cardconnection.co.uk
*website* www.card-connection.co.uk

*Managing Director* Adrian Atkinson, *Senior Product and Marketing Manager* Alison Mahoney

Cute, humour, traditional, floral, contemporary, photography. Submit colour copies or 5 x 4in transparencies of originals. Humour and sentimental verse. Founded 1992.

## Caspari Ltd*
9 Shire Hill, Saffron Walden, Essex CB11 3AP
*tel* (01799) 513010 *fax* (01799) 513101
*Managing Director* Keith Entwisle

Traditional fine art/classic images; 5 x 4in transparencies. No verses. Founded 1990.

## Chapter and Verse (International) Ltd
Granta House, 94–96 High Street, Linton,
Cambs. CB1 6JT
*tel* (01223) 891951 *fax* (01223) 894137

*email* sales@chapter-and-verse.sagehost.co.uk
*website* www.chapter-and-verse-stationery.co.uk

Buildings, animals, flowers, scenic, or domestic subjects in series, suitable for greetings cards and postcards. All sizes of transparency. No verses. Founded 1981.

### Colneis Marketing Ltd*
York House, 2–4 York Road, Felixstow IP11 7QQ
*tel* (01394) 271668  *fax* (01394) 275114
*email* colneiscards@btopenworld.co.uk
*website* www.colneisgreetingcards.com
*Proprietor* John Botting

Photographs (preferably medium format) and colour artwork of nature and cute images. Considers verses. Founded 1994.

### Pineapple Park
58 Wilbury Way, Hitchin, Herts. SG4 0TP
*tel* (01462) 442021 *fax* (01462) 440418
*email* info@pineapplepark.co.uk
*website* www.pineapplepark.co.uk
*Directors* Peter M. Cockerline, Sarah H. Parker

Illustrations and photographs for publication as greetings cards. Contemporary, cute, humour: submit artwork or laser copies with sae. Photographic florals always needed. Humour copy/jokes accepted without artwork. Also concepts for ranges. Founded 1993.

### Nigel Quiney Publications Ltd*
Cloudesley House, Shire Hill, Saffron Walden, Essex CB11 3FB
*tel* (01799) 520200 *fax* (01799) 520100
*website* www.nigelquiney.com
*Contact* Ms J. Arkinstall, Product & Marketing Director

Everyday and seasonal greetings cards and giftwrap including fine art, photographic, humour, fun art, contemporary and cute. Submit colour copies, photographs or transparencies: no original artwork.

### J. Salmon Ltd
100 London Road, Sevenoaks, Kent TN13 1BB
*tel* (01732) 452381 *fax* (01732) 450951
*email* enquiries@jsalmon.co.uk

Picture postcards, calendars, greeting cards and local view booklets.

### Santoro Graphics Ltd
Rotunda Point, 11 Hartfield Crescent, London SW19 3RL
*tel* 020-8781 110 *fax* 020-8781 1101
*email* enquiries@santorographics.com
*website* www.santorographics.com
*Directors* L. Santoro, M. Santoro

Publishers of innovative and award-winning designs for greetings cards, giftwrap and gift stationery. Bold contemporary images with an international appeal. Subjects covered: b&w, colour floral, quirky and humorous, whimsical, Fifties, Seventies, futuristic! All formats accepted in both b&w and colour; transparencies ideally 5 x 4in but will accept 35mm. Founded 1985.

### Scandecor Ltd
3 The Ermine Centre, Hurricane Close, Huntingdon, Cambs. PE29 6WY
*tel* (01480) 456395 *fax* (01480) 456269
*email* mail@scandecor-ltd.co.uk
*Managing Director* Derek Shirley

Transparencies all sizes. Founded 1967.

### Noel Tatt Group/Impress Publishing*
Appledown House, Barton Business Park, Appledown Way, New Dover Road, Canterbury, Kent CT1 3TE
*tel* (01227) 811600 *fax* (01227) 811601
*email* mail@noeltatt.co.uk
*Director* Jarle Tatt

General everyday cards – broad mix; Christmas. Will consider verses. Founded 1964.

### Woodmansterne Publications Ltd
1 The Boulevard, Blackmoor Lane, Watford, Herts. WD18 8UW
*tel* (01923) 200600  *fax* (01923) 200601
*email* anne@woodmansterne.co.uk

Greetings cards, wrapping paper, notecards and social stationery featuring fine and contemporary art and photography (colour and b&w). Submit colour copies, photographs or transparencies. No verses.

# Societies, prizes and festivals

## The Society of Authors

The Society of Authors is an independent trade union, representing writers' interests in all aspects of the writing profession, particularly publishing, but also broadcasting, television and films, theatre and translation.

Founded over 100 years ago, the Society now has more than 7500 members. It has a professional staff, responsible to a Management Committee of 12 authors, and a Council (an advisory body meeting twice a year) consisting of 60 eminent writers. There are specialist groups within the Society to serve particular needs: the Academic Writers Group, the Broadcasting Group, the

> 'It does no harm to repeat, as often as you can, "Without me the literary industry would not exist: the publishers, the agents, the sub-agents, the accountants, the libel lawyers, the departments of literature, the professors, the theses, the books of criticism, the reviewers, the book pages – all this vast and proliferating edifice is because of this small, patronised, put-down and underpaid person."'  – *Doris Lessing*

Children's Writers and Illustrators Group, the Educational Writers Group, the Medical Writers Group and the Translators Association (see page 541). There are also groups representing Scotland and the North of England.

### What the Society does for members

Through its permanent staff (including a solicitor), the Society is able to give its members a comprehensive personal and professional service covering the business aspects of authorship, including:

- providing information about agents, publishers, and others concerned with the book trade, journalism, broadcasting and the performing arts;
- advising on negotiations, including the individual vetting of contracts, clause by clause, and assessing their terms both financial and otherwise;
- helping with members' queries, major or minor, over any aspect of the business of writing;
- taking up complaints on behalf of members on any issue concerned with the business of authorship;
- pursuing legal actions for breach of contract, copyright infringement, and the non-payment of royalties and fees, when the risk and cost preclude individual action by a member and issues of general concern to the profession are at stake;
- holding conferences, seminars, meetings and social occasions;
- producing a comprehensive range of publications, free of charge to members, including the Society's quarterly journal, *The Author. Quick Guides* cover many aspects of the profession such as: copyright, publishing contracts,

libel, income tax, VAT, authors' agents, permissions, indexing, and the protection of titles. The Society also publishes occasional papers on subjects such as film agreements, packaged books, revised editions, multimedia, and vanity publishing.

### Further membership benefits

Members have access to:

- the Retirement Benefit Scheme;
- a group Medical Insurance Scheme with BUPA;
- the Pension Fund (which offers discretionary pensions to a number of members);
- the Contingency Fund (which provides financial relief for authors or their dependents in sudden financial difficulties);
- free membership of the Authors' Licensing and Collecting Society (ALCS);
- books and other products at special rates;
- membership of the Royal Over-Seas League at a discount.

The Society frequently secures improved conditions and better returns for members. It is common for members to report that, through the help and facilities offered, they have saved more, and sometimes substantially more, than their annual subscriptions (which are an allowable expense against income tax).

### What the Society does for authors

The Society lobbies Members of Parliament, Ministers and Government Departments on all issues of concern to writers. Recent issues have included the operation and funding of Public Lending Right, the threat of VAT on books, copyright legislation and European Union initiatives. Concessions have also been obtained under various Finance Acts.

The Society litigates in matters of importance to authors. For example, the Society backed Andrew Boyle when he won his appeal against the Inland Revenue's attempt to tax the Whitbread Award.

The Society campaigns for better terms for writers. With the Writers' Guild, it has negotiated 'minimum terms agreements' with many leading publishers. The translators' section of the Society has also drawn up a minimum terms agreement for translators which has been adopted by Faber & Faber, and has been used on an individual basis by a number of other publishers.

## Membership

### The Society of Authors

84 Drayton Gardens, London SW10 9SB
*tel* 020-7373 6642
*email* info@societyofauthors.org
*website* www.societyofauthors.org
*General Secretary* Mark Le Fanu

Membership is open to authors who have had a full-length work published, broadcast or performed commercially in the UK and to those who have had a full-length work accepted for publication, but not yet published; and those who have had occasional items broadcast or performed, or translations, articles, illustrations or short stories published. The owner or administrator of a deceased author's copyrights can become a member on behalf of the author's estate. Writers who have been offered a contract seeking a contribution towards publication costs may apply for one year's associate membership and have the contract vetted.

The annual subscription (which is tax deductible) is £80 (£75 by direct debit after the first year). There is a special rate for partners living at the same address. Authors under 35 not yet earning a significant income from writing, may pay a lower subscription of £56. Authors over 65 may pay at the reduced rate after their first year of membership.

Contact the Society for a membership booklet and copy of *The Author*.

The Society is recognised by the BBC for the purpose of negotiating rates for writers' contributions to radio drama, as well as for the broadcasting of published material. It was instrumental in setting up the ALCS (see page 686), which collects and distributes fees from reprography and other methods whereby copyright material is exploited without direct payment to the originators.

The Society keeps in close touch with the Arts Councils, the Association of Authors' Agents, the British Council, the Institute of Translation and Interpreting, the Department for Culture, Media and Sport, the National Union of Journalists, the Publishers Association and the Writers' Guild of Great Britain.

The Society is a member of the European Writers Congress, the British Copyright Council and the National Book Committee.

## Awards

The Society of Authors administers:

- Travelling Scholarships which give honorary awards;
- four prizes for novels: the Betty Trask Awards, the Encore Award, the McKitterick Prize and the Sagittarius Prize;
- two prizes for a full-length published work: the Somerset Maugham Awards and *The Sunday Times* Young Writer of the Year Award;
- two poetry awards: the Eric Gregory Awards and the Cholmondeley Awards;
- the Tom-Gallon and Olive Cook Awards for short story writers;
- the Authors' Foundation and Kathleen Blundell Trust, which give grants to published authors working on their next book;
- the Richard Imison Award for a writer new to radio drama;
- awards for translations from French, German, Italian, Dutch, Portuguese, Spanish and Swedish into English;
- the Francis Head Bequest for assisting authors who, through physical mishap, are temporarily unable to maintain themselves or their families;
- medical book awards.

# The Writers' Guild of Great Britain

The Writers' Guild of Great Britain is the writers' trade union and is affiliated to the TUC.

The Writers' Guild of Great Britain is the writers' trade union, affiliated to the TUC, and represents writers' interests in film, television, radio, theatre and publishing. Formed in 1959 as the Screenwriters' Guild, the union gradually extended into all areas of freelance writing activity and copyright protection. In 1974, when book authors and stage dramatists became eligible for membership, substantial numbers joined. In June 1997 the Theatre Writers' Union membership unified with that of the Writers' Guild to create a larger, more powerful writers' union.

Apart from necessary dealings with Government and policies on legislative matters affecting writers, the Guild is, by constitution, non-political, has no involvement with any political party, and members pay no political levy.

The Guild employs a permanent secretary and staff and is administered by an Executive Council of 26 members. It has a national and regional/branch structure with committees representing Scotland, Wales, London and the South East, the North West, the North East, the Midlands and the South West of England. The Guild comprises practising professional writers in all media, united in common concern for one another and regulating the conditions under which they work.

## The Writers' Guild and agreements

The Guild's basic function is to negotiate minimum terms in those areas in which its members work. Those agreements form the basis of the individual contracts signed by members. Further details are given below. The Guild also gives individual advice to its members on contracts and other matters which the writer encounters in his or her professional life.

## Television

In 2002 the Guild concluded negotiations with the BBC for a new Television Script Commissioning Agreement. The new terms came into effect on 1 November 2002. A new agreement for television production was also agreed with PACT (Producers Alliance of Cinema and Television) which came into effect on 1 February 2003.

The Guild has national agreements with the BBC, the ITV companies, PACT and TAC (representing Welsh language television producers). These agreements regulate minimum fees and going rates, copyright licence, credits, and general conditions for television plays, series and serials, dramatisations and adaptations. One of the Guild's most important achievements has been the establishment of pension rights for members. The BBC, ITV companies and independent producers pay a pension contribution of between 6% and 8% of the standard writer's fee on the understanding that the Guild member pays between 4% and 6%.

The advent of digital and cable television channels and the creation of the BBC's commercial arm has seen the Guild in constant negotiation. The Guild now has agreements for all of the BBC's digital channels and for its joint venture channels.

In 1997, the Guild negotiated substantial revised terms and conditions for writers who are commissioned by the ITV companies. The new agreement includes a provision for the non-arms length sale of material to digital and cable channels, thus ensuring that writers receive market prices for the use of their material on these new channels.

## Film

In 1985 an important agreement was signed with the two producer organisations: the British Film and Television Producers' Association and the Independent Programme Producers Association (now known as PACT). Since then there has been an industrial agreement covering UK film productions. Pension fund contributions have been negotiated for Guild members in the same way as for the BBC and ITV. The Agreement was renegotiated in February 1992 and negotiations on an updated agreement are in progress.

## Radio

The Guild has a standard agreement for Radio Drama with the BBC, establishing a fee structure which is annually reviewed. In 1985 the BBC agreed to extend the pension scheme already established for television writers to include radio writers. In 1994 a comprehensive revision of the Agreement was undertaken. The Guild negotiated special agreements for Radio 4's *The Archers*, the World Service soap *Westway*, and for the online streaming of BBC Radio services. This agreement was being renegotiated during 2004 to cover digital radio.

## Books

The Guild fought long, hard and successfully for the loans-based Public Lending Right to reimburse authors for books lent in libraries. This is now law and the Guild is constantly in touch with the Registrar of the scheme, which is administered from offices in Stockton-on-Tees. Together with the Society of Authors, the Guild has drawn up a draft Minimum Terms Book Agreement which has been widely circulated amongst publishers. A new model contract is in preparation.

## Theatre

In 1979 the Guild, together with the Theatre Writers' Union, negotiated the first ever industrial agreement for theatre writers. The Theatres National Committee Agreement covers the Royal Shakespeare Company, the National Theatre Company and the English Stage Company.

In June 1986, a new agreement was signed with the Theatrical Management Association, which covers some 95 provincial theatres. In 1993, this agreement was comprehensively revised and included a provision for a year-on-year increase in fees in line with the Retail Price Index.

After many years of negotiation, an agreement was concluded in 1991 between the Guild and the Independent Theatre Council, which represents some 200 of the smaller and fringe theatres as well as educational, touring companies. This agreement was revised in 2002 and the minimum fees are reviewed annually.

## Other activities

The Guild is in touch with Government and national institutions wherever and whenever the interests of writers are in question or are being discussed. It holds cross-party Parliamentary lobbies with Equity and the Musicians Union to ensure that the various art forms they represent are properly cared for.

Working with the Federation of Entertainment Unions, the Guild makes its views known to Government bodies on a broader basis. It keeps in touch with the Arts Councils of Great Britain, Ofcom and other national bodies, and has close working relationships with Equity and the Musicians' Union.

Internationally, the Guild plays a leading role in the International Affiliation of Writers' Guilds, which includes the American Guilds East and West, the Canadian Guilds (French and English), and the Australian and New Zealand Guilds. When it is possible to make common cause, the Guilds act accordingly. The Guild takes a leading role in the European Writers' Congress and the Fédération des Scénaristes d'Europe. The Guild is becoming more involved with matters at European level where the harmonisation of copyright law and the regulation of a converged audiovisual/telecommunications are of immediate interest.

## Membership activities

The Guild in its day-to-day work takes up problems on behalf of individual members, gives advice on contracts, and helps with any problems which affect the lives of its members as professional writers. Members have access to free legal advice and professional contract vetting. Regular Craft Meetings are held by all the Guild's specialist committees. This gives Guild members the opportunity of meeting those who control, work within, or affect the sphere of writing within which they work.

## In conclusion

The writer is an isolated individual in a world in which individual voices are not always heard. The Guild brings together those writers in order to make common cause in respect of the many vitally important matters which are susceptible to influence only from the position of the collective strength which the Guild enjoys.

## Membership

### The Writers' Guild of Great Britain
15 Britannia Street, London WC1X 9JN
*tel* 020-7833 0777 *fax* 020-7833 4777
*email* admin@writersguild.org.uk
*website* www.writersguild.org.uk
*General Secretary* Bernie Corbett

Membership of the Guild is open to all persons entitled to claim a single piece of written work of any length for which payment has been received under written contract in terms not less favourable than those existing in current minimum terms agreements negotiated by the Guild. Candidate membership (£75) is open to all those who are taking their first steps into writing but who have not yet received a contract. The minimum subscription is currently £150, or 1% of an author's income earned from professional writing sources in the previous calendar year, with a cap of £1500. All Full members are automatically members of the Authors Licensing and Collecting Society (ALCS). The Guild is a corporate member of the ALCS and maintains its links through representation on its board.

Members receive the *Writers' Bulletin*, which carries articles, letters and reports written by members, plus an email newsletter every Friday. Other benefits include free entry to the British Library reading rooms, and reduced entry to the National Film Theatre and regional film theatres.

# Societies, associations and clubs

The societies, associations and clubs listed here will be of interest to both writers and artists. They include appreciation societies devoted to specific authors, professional bodies and national institutions. Some also offer prizes and awards (see page 546).

## Academic Writers Group – see The Society of Authors

## Academi (Welsh Academy)

*Main Office* 3rd Floor, Mount Stuart House, Mount Stuart Square, Cardiff CF10 5FQ
*tel* 029-2047 2266 *fax* 029-2049 2930
*email* post@academi.org
*website* www.academi.org
*North West Wales Office* Ty Newydd, Llanystumdwy, Cricieth, Gwynedd LL52 0LW
*tel* (01766) 522817 *fax* (01766) 523095
*email* academi.gog@dial.pipex.com
*South West Wales Office* Dylan Thomas Centre, Somerset Place, Swansea SA1 1RR
*tel* (01792) 463980 *fax* (01792) 463993
*Chief Executive* Peter Finch
*Membership* Associate: £15 p.a. (waged), £7.50 (unwaged)

Academi is the trading name of Yr Academi Gymreig, the Welsh National Literature Promotion Agency and Society of Writers. With funds mostly provided from public sources, it has been constitutionally independent since 1978. It runs courses, competitions (including the Cardiff International Poetry and Book of the Year Competition), conferences, tours by authors, festivals and represents the interests of Welsh writers and Welsh writing both inside Wales and beyond. Its publications include *Taliesin* (3 p.a.), a literary journal in the Welsh language; *A470* (bi-monthly), a literature information magazine; *The Oxford Companion to the Literature of Wales*, *The Welsh Academy English–Welsh Dictionary*, and a variety of translated works.

Academi administers a range of schemes including Writers on Tar, Writers Residencies and Writing Squads for young people. Academi also runs services for writers in Wales such as bursaries, critical advice and mentoring. Founded 1959.

## Alliance of Literary Societies

*Secretary* Rosemary Culley, 22 Belmont Grove, Havant, Hants PO9 3PU
*tel* 023-9247 5855 *fax* (0870) 056 0330
*email* rosemary@sndc.demon.co.uk
*website* www.sndc.demon.co.uk
*Open Book*, Greta, Sandford Avenue, Church Stretton, Shrops. SY6 7AB
*tel* (01694) 722821
*Editor* Thelma Thompson

*Membership* Charge depends on size of society
Membership comprises 100+ affiliated literary societies. Aims to act as a valuable liaison body between member societies as a means of sharing knowledge, skills and expertise, and may also act as a pressure group when necessary. The Alliance can assist in the preservation of buildings, places and objects which have literary associations. Produces 2 newsletters a year, plus a literary magazine *Open Book* and a handbook.

## American Literary Translators Association (ALTA)

c/o University of Texas at Dallas, Box 830688, Richardson, TX 75083-0688, USA
*tel* 972-883-2093 *fax* 972-883-6303
*website* www.literarytranslators.org
*Secretary* Jessie Dickey

A broad-based organisation dedicated to the promotion of literary translation through services to literary translators, forums on the theory and practice of translation, collaboration with the international literary community, and advocacy on behalf of the library translator. Founded 1978.

## American Society of Composers, Authors and Publishers

One Lincoln Plaza, New York, NY 10023, USA
*tel* 212-621-6000 *fax* 212-874 8480
*President and Chairman* Marilyn Bergman

## American Society of Indexers (ASI)

10200 West 44th Avenue, Suite 304, Wheat Ridge, CO 80033, USA
*tel* 303-463-2887 *fax* 303-422-8894
*email* info@asindexing.org
*website* www.asindexing.org

Aims to increase awareness of the value of high-quality indexes and indexing; offer members access to educational resources that enable them to strengthen their indexing performance; keep members up to date on indexing technology; defend and safeguard the professional interests of indexers.

## Artists Association of Ireland

43 Temple Bar, Dublin 2, Republic of Ireland
*tel* (01) 8740529 *fax* (01) 6771585
*email* info@artistsireland.com
*website* www.artistsireland.com
*Contact* Administrator

*Membership* £45 p.a.

Information and advice resource for professional visual artists in Ireland. Publishes *Art Bulletin* (6 p.a.), available on subscription. Founded 1981.

## Arts Club

40 Dover Street, London W1S 4NP
*tel* 020-7499 8581 *fax* 020-7409 0913
*website* www.theartsclub.co.uk
*Club Secretary* Anthony Pitkin

For all those connected with or interested in the arts, literature and science. Founded 1863.

## Arts Council England

14 Great Peter Street, London SW1P 3NQ
*tel* (0845) 300 6200 *textphone* 020-7973 6564
*fax* 020-7973 6590
*email* enquiries@artscouncil.org.uk
*website* www.artscouncil.org.uk
*Chief Executive* Peter Hewitt, *Chair* Prof Christopher Frayling

The national development agency for the arts in England, distributing public money from Government and the National Lottery. Arts Council England's main funding programme is Grants for the Arts, which is open to individuals, arts organisations, national touring companies and other people who use the arts in their work.

Arts Council England has one national and 9 regional offices. It has a single contact telephone and email address for general enquiries (see above). Founded 1946.

### East

Eden House, 48–49 Bateman Street, Cambridge CB2 1LR
*tel* (0845) 300 6200 *textphone* (01223) 306893
*fax* (0870) 242 1271

### East Midlands

St Nicholas Court, 25–27 Castle Gate, Nottingham NG1 7AR
*tel* (0845) 300 6200 *fax* 0115-950 2467

### London

2 Pear Tree Court, London EC1R 0DS
*tel* (0845) 300 6200 *textphone* 020-7608 4101
*fax* 020-7608 4100

### North East

Central Square, Forth Street, Newcastle upon Tyne NE1 3PJ
*tel* (0845) 300 6200 *textphone* 0191-255 8500
*fax* 0191-230 1020

### North West

Manchester House, 22 Bridge Street, Manchester M3 3AB
*tel* (0845) 300 6200 *textphone* 0161-834 9131
*fax* 0161-834 6969

### South East

Sovereign House, Church Street, Brighton BN1 1RA
*tel* (0845) 300 6200 *textphone* (01273) 710659
*fax* (0870) 2421257

### South West

Bradninch Place, Gandy Street, Exeter EX4 3LS
*tel* (0845) 300 6200 *textphone* (01392) 433503
*fax* (01392) 229229

### West Midlands

82 Granville Street, Birmingham B1 2LH
*tel* (0845) 300 6200 *textphone* 0121-643 2815
*fax* 0121-643 7239

### Yorkshire

21 Bond Street, Dewsbury, West Yorkshire WF13 1AX
*tel* (0845) 300 6200 *textphone* (01924) 438585
*fax* (01924) 466522

## The Arts Council/An Chomhairle Ealaíon

Literature Officer, 70 Merrion Square, Dublin 2, Republic of Ireland
*tel* (01) 6180200 *fax* (01) 6761302
*website* www.artscouncil.ie
*Literature Officer* Sinéad MacAodha, *Visual Arts Officer* Oliver Dowling

The national development agency for the arts in Ireland. Founded 1951.

## Arts Council of Northern Ireland

MacNeice House, 77 Malone Road, Belfast BT9 5JW
*tel* 028-9038 5200 *fax* 028-90661715
*website* www.artscouncil-ni.org
*Chief Executive* Roisín McDonough, *Literature Officer* Robbie Meredith, *Visual Arts Officer* Iain Davidson

Promotes and encourages the arts throughout Northern Ireland. Artists in drama, dance, music and jazz, literature, the visual arts, traditional arts and community arts, can apply for support for specific schemes and projects. The value of the grant will be set according to the aims of the application. Applicants must have contributed regularly to the artistic activities of the community, and been resident for at least one year in Northern Ireland.

## The Arts Council of Wales

9 Museum Place, Cardiff CF10 3NX
*tel* 029-2037 6500 *minicom* 029-2039 0027
*fax* 029-2022 1447
*email* info@artswales.org.uk
*website* www.artswales.org.uk
*Chairman* Geraint Talfan Davies, *Chief Executive* Peter Tyndall, *Senior Officer: Dance* Siri Wigdel, *Senior Development Officer for Visual Arts* Emma Geliot, *Senior Development Officer for Crafts* Nathalie Camus, *Senior Officer: Drama* Sandra Wynne, *Senior Officer: Music* Simon Lovell-Jones

National organisation with specific responsibility for the funding and development of the arts in Wales. ACW receives funding from the National Assembly for Wales and also distributes the National Lottery funds in Wales to the arts. From these resources, ACW makes grants to support arts activities and facilities. Some of the funds are allocated in the form of annual revenue grants to full-time arts organisations. It also operates schemes which provide financial and other forms of support for individual activities or projects. ACW undertakes this work in both the English and Welsh languages.

### North Wales Regional Office
36 Princes Drive, Colwyn Bay LL29 8LA
*tel* (01492) 533440 *minicom* (01492) 532288
*fax* (01492) 533677

### Mid and West Wales Regional Office
6 Gardd Llydaw, Jackson Lane,
Carmarthen SA31 1QD
*tel* (01267) 234248 *minicom* (01267) 223469
*fax* (01267) 233084

### South Wales Office
9 Museum Place, Cardiff CF10 3NX
*tel* 029-2037 6525 *minicom* 029-2039 0027
*fax* 029-2022 1447

## Aslib (The Association for Information Management)
Staple Hall, Stone House Court, London EC3A 7PB
*tel* 020-7903 0000 *fax* 020-7903 0011
*email* aslib@aslib.com
*website* www.aslib.com
*Ceo* Roger Bowes

Actively promotes best practice in the management of information resources. It represents its members and lobbies on all aspects of the management of and legislation concerning information at local, national and international levels. Aslib provides consultancy and information services, professional development training, conferences, specialist recruitment, internet products, and publishes primary and secondary journals, conference proceedings, directories and monographs. Founded 1924.

## Association for Scottish Literary Studies (ASLS)
c/o Dept of Scottish History, 9 University Gardens, University of Glasgow G12 8QH
*tel* 0141-330 5309
*email* office@asls.org.uk
*website* www.asls.org.uk
*Hon. President* Alan MacGillivray, *Hon. Secretary* Bill Aitken, *Publishing Manager* Duncan Jones
*Membership* £38 p.a. individulas, £10 UK students, £67 corporate

Promotes the study, teaching and writing of Scottish literature and furthers the study of the languages of Scotland. Publishes annually an edited text of Scottish literature, an anthology of new Scottish writing, a series of academic journals and a Newsletter (2 p.a.). Also publishes *Scotnotes* (comprehensive study guides to major Scottish writers), literary texts and commentary cassettes designed to assist the classroom teacher, and a series of occasional papers. Organises 3 conferences a year. Founded 1970.

## Association of American Correspondents in London (AACL)
*Secretary* Elizabeth Lea, c/o Time Magazine, Brettenham House, Lancaster Place, London WC2E 7TL
*tel* 020-7322 1084 *fax* 020-7322 1230

## Association of American Publishers Inc.
71 Fifth Avenue, New York, NY 10003, USA
*tel* 212-255-0200 *fax* 212-255-7007
*website* www.publishers.org
*President and Ceo* Patricia S. Schroeder
Founded 1970.

## Association of Art Historians (AAH)
70 Cowcross Street, London EC1M 6EJ
*tel* 020-7490 3211 *fax* 020-7490 3277
*email* admin@aah.org.uk
*website* www.aah.org.uk
*Administrator* Claire Davies
*Membership* Various options for personal membership; corporate membership available

Formed to promote the study of art history and ensure wider public recognition of the field. Publishes *Art History* journal, *The Art Book* magazine, *Bulletin* newsletter. Annual conference and book fair in March/April. Founded 1974.

## Association of Assistant Librarians –
see Career Development Group

## The Association of Authors' Agents
20 John Street, London WC1N 2DR
*tel* 020-7405 6774 *fax* 020-7831 2154
*email* aaa@lutyensrubinstein.co.uk
*website* www.agentsassoc.co.uk
*President* Derek Johns, *Vice President* Sara Fisher, *Treasurer* Paul Marsh, *Secretary* Simon Trewin

Maintains a code of professional practice to which all members commit themselves; holds regular meetings to discuss matters of common professional interest; provides a vehicle for representing the view of authors' agents in discussion of matters of common interest with other professional bodies. Founded 1974.

## Association of Authors' Representatives Inc.

PO Box 237201, Ansonia Station, New York, NY 10023, USA
*tel* 212-252-3695
*website* www.aar-online.org

Founded 1991.

## Association of British Science Writers

Wellcome Wolfson Building, 165 Queen's Gate, London SW7 5HE
*tel* (0870) 7703361 *fax* (0870) 7707102
*email* absw@absw.org.uk
*website* www.absw.org.uk
*Chairman* Pallab Ghosh, *Administrator* Barbara Drillsma

Association of science writers, editors, and radio, film and TV producers concerned with the presentation and communication of science, technology and medicine. Aims to improve the standard of science writing and to assist its members in their work.

## Association of Canadian Publishers

161 Eglinton Avenue East, Suite 702, Toronto, Ontario M4P 1J5, Canada
*tel* 416-487-6116 *fax* 416-487-8815
*email* info@canbook.org
*website* www.publishers.ca
*Executive Director* John P. Pelletier

Founded 1976; formerly Independent Publishers Association, 1971.

## Association of Christian Writers

*Administrator* Mrs J.L. Kyriacou, All Saints Vicarage, 43 All Saints Close, Edmonton, London N9 9AT
*tel* 020-8884 4348
*email* admin@christianwriters.org.uk
*Membership* £20 p.a. (£17 DD)

Resigtered charity that aims to see the quality of writing in every area of the media, either overtly Christian or shaped by a Christian perspective, reaching the widest range of people across the UK and beyond. To inspire and equip people to use their talents and skills with integrity to devise, write and market excellent material which comes from a Christian world view. Founded 1971.

## Association of Freelance Editors, Proofreaders and Indexers

*Contact 1* Priscilla O'Connor, 3 The Lawn, Oldtown Mill, Celbridge, Co. Kildare, Republic of Ireland
*tel/fax* (353 01) 601 2846
*email* priscillaoconnor@eircom.net
*Contact 2* Brenda O'Hanlon, 11 Clonard Road, Sandyford, Dublin 16
*tel* (353 01) 295 2194 *fax* (353 01) 295 2300

*email* brenda@ohanlonmediaservices.com
*website* www.publishingireland.com

Provides information to publishers on freelances through a list of members and their qualifications. Also protects the interests of freelances, and provides social contact for isolated workers.

## Association of Freelance Journalists

*President* Martin Scholes, 2 Glen Cottages, Brick Hill Lane, Beverley Glen, Ketley, Telford, Shrops. TF2 6SB
*email* aj_info@yahoo.co.uk
*website* www.afj.home-page.org
*Membership* £30 p.a.

Aims to foster the interests of freelance journalists and news photographers, especially those on a low income, including those working as stringers, local correspondents, writers for specialist fields, etc. Founded 1996.

## The Association of Illustrators

81 Leonard Street, London EC2A 4QS
*tel* 020-7613 4328 *fax* 020-7613 4417
*website* www.theaoi.com
*Contact* Membership Secretary

Exists to support illustrators, promote illustration and encourage professional standards in the industry. Publishes bi-monthly magazine; presents an annual programme of events; annual competition, exhibition and tour of Images – the Best of British Illustration (call for entries: late spring). Founded 1973.

## The Association of Learned and Professional Society Publishers

*Chief Executive* Sally Morris, South House, The Street, Clapham, Worthing, West Sussex BN13 3UU
*tel* (01903) 871 686 *fax* (01903) 871457
*email* chief.exec@alpsp.org
*website* www.alpsp.org
*Membership* Open to not-for-profit publishers and allied organisations

The International trade association for non-profit publishers. Founded 1972.

## The Association of Photographers (AOP)

*Co-Secretary* Gwen Thomas, 81 Leonard Street, London EC2A 4QS
*tel* 020-7739 6669 *fax* 020-7739 8707
*email* general@aophoto.co.uk
*website* www.the-aop.org
*Membership* £250 p.a.

Exists to protect and promote the interests of fashion advertising and editorial photographers. Founded 1968.

## The Jane Austen Society

*Secretary* Maggie Lane, 1 Brookleaze, Sea Mills,
Bristol BS9 2ET
*email* mlane@bgs.bristol.sch.uk
*website* www.janeaustensociety.org.uk
*Membership* £15 p.a. UK, £250 life; £18 overseas,
£300 life

Aims to promote interest in, and enjoyment of, Jane
Austen's novels and letters. Regular publications,
meetings and conferences. Twelve branches in UK.
Founded 1940.

## Australia Council

PO Box 788, Strawberry Hills, NSW 2012, Australia
*located at* 372 Elizabeth Street, Surry Hills,
NSW 2010, Australia
*tel* (02) 9215 9000 *fax* (02) 9215 9111
*email* mail@ozco.gov.au
*website* www.ozco.gov.au
*Chairperson* David Gonski

Provides a broad range of support for the arts in
Australia, embracing music, theatre, literature,
visual arts, crafts, Aboriginal arts, community and
new media arts. It has 8 major Boards: Literature,
Visual Arts/Craft, Music, Theatre, Dance, New
Media, Community Cultural Development, Major
Performing Arts, as well as the Aboriginal and
Torres Strait Islander Arts Board.

The Literature Board's chief objective is to
support the writing of all forms of creative literature
– novels, short stories, poetry, plays and literary
non-fiction. It also assists with the publication of
literary magazines, has a book publishing subsidies
programme, and initiates and supports projects of
many kinds designed to promote Australian
literature both within Australia and abroad.

## Australian Copyright Council

PO Box 1986, Strawberry Hills, NSW 2012,
Australia
*tel* (02) 9318 1788 *fax* (02) 9698 3536
*email* info@copyright.org.au
*website* www.copyright.org.au

An independent non-profit organisation which
aims to assist creators and other copyright owners
to exercise their rights effectively; raise awareness in
the community generally about the importance of
copyright; research and identify areas of copyright
law which are inadequate or unfair; seek changes to
law and practice to enhance the effectiveness and
fairness of copyright; foster cooperation amongst
bodies representing creators and owners of
copyright.

The Council comprises 23 organisations or
associations of owners and creators of copyright
material, including the Australian Society of Authors,
the Australian Writers Guild and the Australian Book
Publishers Association. Founded 1968.

## Australian Library and Information Association

PO Box E441, Kingston, ACT 2604, Australia
*tel* (02) 6215 8222 *fax* (02) 6282 2249
*email* enquiry@alia.org.au
*website* www.alia.org.au
*Executive Director* Jennefer Nicholson

Aims to promote and improve the services of
libraries and other information agencies; to improve
the standard of library and information personnel
and foster their professional interests; to represent
the interests of members to governments, other
organisations and the community; and to
encourage people to contribute to the improvement
of library and information services by supporting
the association.

## Australian Publishers Association (APA)

60/89 Jones Street, Ultimo, NSW 2007, Australia
*tel* (02) 9281 9788 *fax* (02) 9281 1073
*email* apa@publishers.asn.au
*website* www.publishers.asn.au
*Chief Executive* Susan Bridge

## The Australian Society of Authors

PO Box 1566, Strawberry Hills NSW 2012, Australia
*located at* 98 Pitt Street, Redfern NSW 2016
*tel* (02) 9318 0877 *fax* (02) 9318 0530
*email* asa@asauthors.org
*website* www.asauthors.org
*Executive Director* José Borghino

## Australian Writers' Guild (AWG)

8/50 Reservoir Street, Surry Hills, NSW 2010
*tel* (02) 9281 1554 *fax* (02) 9281 4321
*email* admin@awg.com.au
*website* www.awg.com.au

The professional association for all performance
writers, i.e. writers for film, TV, radio, theatre, video
and new media. The AWG is recognised throughout
the industry in Australia as being the voice of
performance writers. Established 1962.

## Authors' Club (at The Arts Club)

40 Dover Street, London W1S 4NP
*tel* 020-7408 5092 *fax* 020-7409 0913
*Secretary* Lucy Jane Tetlow
*Membership* Apply to Secretary

Founded by Sir Walter Besant, the Authors' Club
welcomes as members writers, publishers, critics,
journalists, academics and anyone involved with
literature. Administers the Authors' Club Best First
Novel Award and the Sir Banister Fletcher Award.
Founded 1891.

## Authors' Licensing and Collecting Society Ltd – see page 686

## AXIS

Visual Arts Information Service, Leeds Metropolitan University, 8 Queen Square, Leeds LS2 8AJ
*tel* (0870) 443 0701 *fax* (0870) 443 0703
*AXIS Information Service* (0870) 443 0702
*email* axis@lmu.ac.uk
*website* www.axisartists.org.uk

Provides information on contemporary artists and makers living/working in Britain to national and international clients. The AXIS database features 16,000+ images by over 4000 artists (professionals and recent graduates). The database can be accessed on CD-Rom, online and on the AXIS Information Service line. Printouts of artist CVs, artwork images, and contact details are available to potential buyers, commissioners, exhibitors and collaborators. AXIS receives funding from the Arts Councils of England, Scotland and Wales. Founded 1991.

## BAFTA (The British Academy of Film and Television Arts)

195 Piccadilly, London W1J 9LN
*tel* 020-7734 0022 *fax* 020-7292 5868
*email* reception@bafta.org
*website* www.bafta.org
*Chief Executive* Amanda Berry
*Membership* £195 p.a., £98 (under age 30),
£98 overseas, £88 country

The pre-eminent organisation in the UK for film, TV and interactive entertainment, recognising and promoting the achievement and endeavour of industry practitioners. BAFTA Awards are awarded annually by members to their peers in recognition of their skills and expertise. The Academy's premises provide club facilities with a 200-seat cinema and 40-seat preview theatre. Provides a full and varied programme of industry-related events, masterclasses, seminars and panel discussions, which are open to both members and non-members. Founded 1947.

## BANA (Bath Area Network for Artists)

The Old Malthouse, Comfortable Place,
Upper Bristol Road, Bath BA1 3AJ
*tel* 01225 471714
*email* enquiries@bana-arts.co.uk
*website* www.bana-arts.co.uk
*Membership* £10 p.a.

An artist-led network that aims to raise the profile of arts activity in the Bath area, to establish and strengthen links between artists, artists' groups and art promoters, and advocate for increased investment in local arts activities. BANA was established by artists, for artists, and works through artists to achieve its aims. It is a non-selective network and its membership is made up of artists committed to professional practice. Core activities and services include the BANA website and artists'

database, a newsletter, artist café events and a continuing professional development programme. Founded 1998.

## BAPLA (British Association of Picture Libraries and Agencies)

18 Vine Hill, London EC1R 5DZ
*tel* 020-7713 1780 *fax* 020-7713 1211
*email* enquiries@bapla.org.uk
*website* www.bapla.org
*Chief Executive* Linda Royles

Offers comprehensive information and advice about finding, buying and selling images. Founded 1975.

## The Beckford Society

The Timber Cottage, Crockerton,
Warminster BA12 8AX
*tel* (01985) 213195 *fax* (01985) 213239
*email* sidney.blackmore@btinternet.com
*Membership* £10 p.a. minimum

Aims to promote an interest in the life and works of William Beckford of Fonthill (1760–1844) and his circle. Encourages Beckford studies and scholarship through exhibitions, lectures and publications, including *The Beckford Journal* (annual) and occasional newsletters. Founded 1995.

## Thomas Lovell Beddoes Society

9 Amber Court, Belper, Derbyshire DE56 1HG
*tel* (01773) 828066
*email* john@beddoes.demon.co.uk
*website* www.beddoes.org

Aims to promote an interest in the life and works of Thomas Lovell Beddoes (1803–49). The Society promotes and undertakes Beddoes studies, and disseminates and publishes useful research. Founded 1994.

## The Arnold Bennett Society

*Secretary* Carol Garton, 4 Field End Close,
Trentham, Stoke-on-Trent STA 8DA
*Membership* £9 p.a. individuals, £11 p.a. family
(UK); £11 individuals p.a., £13 family p.a. (outside UK); £5 p.a. (students)

Aims to promote the study and appreciation of the life, works and times not only of Arnold Bennett (1867–1931) himself, but also of other provincial writers with particular relationship to North Staffordshire.

## E.F. Benson: The Tilling Society

5 Friars Bank, Guestling, Hastings,
East Sussex TN35 4EJ
*fax* (01424) 813237
*Secretaries* Cynthia and Tony Reavell
*Membership* £8 p.a., £10 overseas; full starters membership (inc. amalgamations of all back newsletters) £34, overseas £38

Aims to bring together enthusiasts, wherever they may live, for E.F. Benson and his Mapp & Lucia novels. Annual gathering in Rye. Publishes 2 journal-length newsletters a year. Founded 1982.

## The E.F. Benson Society

The Old Coach House, High Street, Rye,
East Sussex TN31 7JF
*tel* (01797) 223114
*Secretary* Allan Downend
*Membership* £7.50 p.a. single, £8.50 2 people at same address, £12.50 overseas

Aims to promote interest in the author E.F. Benson and the Benson family. Arranges annual literary evening, annual outing to Rye (July) and other places of Benson interest, talks on the Bensons and exhibitions. Archive includes the Austin Seckersen Collection, transcriptions of the Benson diaries and letters. Publishes postcards, anthologies of Benson's works, a Benson biography, books on Benson and an annual journal, *The Dodo*. Also sells out-of-print Bensons to members. Founded 1984.

## Bibliographical Society

c/o Institute of English Studies, Room 304,
Senate House, Malet Street, London WC1E 7HU
*tel* 020-7389 2150
*email* secretary@bibsoc.org.uk
*President* David Shaw, *Secretary* Margaret Ford

Acquisition and dissemination of information upon subjects connected with historical bibliography. Founded 1892.

## The Blackpool Art Society

The Studio, Wilkinson Avenue, Blackpool FY3 9HB
*President* Mrs Valerie Anderson
*Hon. Secretary* Eileen Potter, 12 Seventh Avenue, Blackpool FY4 2ED
*tel* (01253) 407541
*email* johneileen@potter965.fsnet.co.uk

Autumn exhibition (members' work only). Studio meetings, practicals, lectures, etc, out-of-door sketching, workshops. Founded 1884.

## Book Publishers Association of New Zealand Inc.

PO Box 36477, Northcote, Auckland 1309,
New Zealand
*tel* (09) 480-2711 *fax* (09) 480-1130
*email* bpanz@copyright.co.nz
*website* www.bpanz.org.nz
*President* Elizabeth Caffin

## Books Across the Sea

The English-Speaking Union of the Commonwealth, Dartmouth House, 37 Charles Street, London W1J 5ED
*tel* 020-7529 1550 *fax* 020-7495 6108

*email* esu@esu.org
*website* www.esu.org
The English Speaking Union of the United States,
144 East 39th Street, New York, NY 10016, USA
*tel* 212-818-1200 *fax* 212-867-4177
*email* info@english-speakingunion.org

World voluntary organisation devoted to the promotion of international understanding and friendship. Exchanges books with its corresponding BAS Committees abroad. The books are selected to reflect the life and culture of each country and the best of its recent publishing and writing. New selections are announced by the bulletin, *The Ambassador Booklist*.

## The Booksellers Association of the United Kingdom & Ireland Ltd

272 Vauxhall Bridge Road, London SW1V 1BA
*tel* 020-7802 0802 *fax* 020-7802 0803
*email* mail@booksellers.org.uk
*Chief Executive* T.E. Godfray

Founded 1895.

## Booktrust

Book House, 45 East Hill, London SW18 2QZ
*tel* 020-8516 2977 *fax* 020-8516 2998
*email* info@booktrust.org.uk
*websites* www.booktrust.org.uk,
www.booktrusted.com
*Membership Booktrusted News* subscription: £25 p.a.
*Chairman* Trevor Glover, *Executive Director* Chris Meade

Booktrust is an independent charity bringing books and people together. It exists to open up the world of books and reading to people of all ages and cultures. Its services and activities include the Book Information Service, a unique specialist information service for all queries on books and reading (business callers are charged at £1.50 per minute on 0906-516 1193, weekdays 10am–1pm). Booktrust administers a number of literary prizes, including the Orange, Commonwealth, Nestlé Smarties and the Booktrust Teenage Prize, and runs a series of reader development projects.

The Children's Literature Team at Booktrust offers advice and information on all aspects of children's reading and books. The 'booktrusted' website is dedicated to children's books and resources for professionals working with young readers, including annotated book lists, information about organisations concerned with children's books, publishers, children's book news and much more. Booktrust also produces a range of publications and resource materials for National Children's Book Week. Subscribers receive 4 issues of *Booktrusted News* and a copy of the *Best Book Guide for Children and Young Adults*. Booktrust also coordinates the national Bookstart (books for babies) programme which gives free advice and books to parents/carers attending their baby's health checks.

## The George Borrow Society
*Hon. Secretary* Ms K.J. Cann, 21 Mulberry Close, Cambridge CB4 2AS
*website* www.clough5.fsnet.co.uk/gb.html
*Membership* £12.50 p.a.

Promotes knowledge of the life and works of George Borrow (1803–81), traveller and author. Publishes *Bulletin* (bi-annual). Founded 1991.

## British Academy
10 Carlton House Terrace, London SW1Y 5AH
*tel* 020-7969 5200 *fax* 020-7969 5300
*email* secretary@britac.ac.uk
*website* www.britac.ac.uk
*President* Viscount Runciman, *Humanities Vice-President* Prof. W.E. Davies, *Social Sciences Vice-President* Prof H.G. Genn, *Treasurer* Prof R.J.P. Kain, *Foreign Secretary* Prof C.N.J. Mann, *Publications Secretary* Dr D.J. McKitterick, *Research Secretary* Prof R.J. Bennett, *Secretary* P.W.H. Brown CBE

The national Academy for the humanities and social sciences: an independent and self-governing fellowship of scholars, elected for distinction and achievement in one or more branches of the academic disciplines that make up the humanities and social sciences. Its primary purpose is to promote research and scholarship in those areas: through research grants and other awards, the sponsorship of a number of research projects and of research institutes overseas; the award of prizes and medals; and the publication both of sponsored lectures and seminar papers and of fundamental texts and research aids prepared under the direction of Academy committees. It also acts as a forum for the discussion of issues of interest and concern to scholars in the humanities and the social sciences, and it provides advice to the Government and other public bodies. Founded 1901.

## British Academy of Composers and Songwriters
British Music House, 25–27 Berners Street, London W1T 3LR
*tel* 020-7636 2929 *fax* 020-7636 2212
*email* info@britishacademy.com
*website* www.britishacademy.com
*Contact* Kizzy Donaldson, Head of Membership

The Academy represents the interests of composers and songwriters across all genres, providing advice on professional and artistic matters. It administers a number of major events, including the annual Ivor Novello Awards and British Compser Awards.

## British American Arts Association (BAAA) – see Centre for Creative Communities (CCC)

## The British Association of Communicators in Business
Suite A, 1st floor, The Auriga Building, Davy Avenue, Knowl Hill, Milton Keynes MK5 8HG
*tel* (0870) 1217606 *fax* (0870) 1217601
*email* enquiries@cib.uk.com
*website* www.cib.uk.com

Aims to be the market leader for those involved in corporate media management and practice by providing professional, authoritative, dynamic, supportive and innovative services. Founded 1949.

## British Association of Journalists
*General Secretary* Steve Turner, 89 Fleet Street, London EC4Y 1DH
*tel* 020-7353 3003 *fax* 020-7353 2310
*Membership* £17.50 per month national newspaper staff, national broadcasting staff and national news agency staff; £10 p.m. other seniors including magazine journalists, PRs, freelances; £7.50 p.m. under age 24

Aims to protect and promote the industrial and professional interests of journalists. Founded 1992.

## British Association of Picture Libraries and Agencies – see BAPLA (British Association of Picture Libraries and Agencies)

## British Centre for Literary Translation
University of East Anglia, Norwich NR4 7TJ
*tel* (01603) 592785 *fax* (01603) 592737
*email* bclt@uea.ac.uk
*website* www.literarytranslation.com
*Coordinator* Catherine Fuller

BCLT is funded by Arts Council England and the Universtiy of East Anglia. It aims to raise the profile of literary translation in the UK through events, publications, activities and research aimed at professional translators, students and the general reader. Activities include the annual NESTA Sebald Lecture in London, Summer School, translator-in-residence scheme funded by the EC Culture 2000 programme and a joint website with the British Council. BCLT coordinates a PhD programme in literary translation and offers units at undergraduate and postgraduate level. It is joint sponsor with BCLT of the John Dryden Translation Prize. Publishes the journals *In Other Words*, *New Books in German* and the anthology *Rearranging the World*. It is a member of the international RECIT literary translation network. Founded 1989.

## The British Copyright Council

Copyright House, 29–33 Berners Street,
London W1T 3AB
*tel* (01986) 788 122 *fax* (01986) 788 847
*email* copyright@bcc2.demon.co.uk
*Vice-Presidents* Geoffrey Adams, Maureen Duffy,
*Chairman* Prof Gerald Dworkin, *Vice Chairmen*
Gwen Thomas, David Lester, Kate Pool, *Secretary*
Janet Ibbotson, *Treasurer* Hugh Jones

Aims to defend and foster the true principles of
creators' copyright and their acceptance throughout
the world, to bring together bodies representing all
who are interested in the protection of such
copyright, and to keep watch on any legal or other
changes which may require an amendment of the
law.

## The British Council

10 Spring Gardens, London SW1A 2BN
*tel* 020-7930 8466 *fax* 020-7839 6347
*website* www.britishcouncil.org
*Chair* Baroness Helena Kennedy QC, *Director-
General* David Green, *Director Literature* Margaret
Meyer, *Director Arts* Sue Harrison

The British Council connects people worldwide
with learning opportunities and creative ideas from
the UK, and builds lasting relationships between the
UK and other countries. It works in 110 countries,
where it has over 180 libraries and information
centres, each catering to the needs of the local
community with print and electronic resources. In
2003–04, 300,000 library members borrowed 7.5
million books and videos. British Council libraries
not only provide information and materials to
users, but also promote the latest UK publications.

Working in close collaboration with book trade
associations, British Council offices organise book
and electronic publishing exhibitions ranging from
small, specialist displays to participation in major
international book fairs. Other projects include
Global Publishing Information, a collection of
online publishing market reports on international
markets compiled in collaboration with the
Publishers Association. It also provides various
resources on its website for those interested in
finding out more about UK publishing.

Details of the British Council's many publications
are available online (www.britishcouncil.org/
publications/index.htm). The British Council is the
agent for the Department for International
Development (DFID) for book aid projects in
developing countries, and is an authority on
teaching English as a second or foreign language. It
also gives advice and information on curriculum,
methodology, materials and testing.

The British Council promotes British literature
overseas through writers' tours, academic visits,
seminars and exhibitions. It publishes *New Writing*,
an annual anthology of unpublished short stories,
poems, extracts from works in progress and essays;
and a series of literary bibliographies, including
*Eyes Wide Open: New Fiction from the UK
1999–2001*, *Hunting Down the Universe: A
Bibliography of Popular Science and Literature*, and
*Teaching Management Principles Using Literature*.
Through its Literature Department, the British
Council provides an overview of UK literature and
a range of online resources on its literature website,
www.britishcouncil.org/arts/literature. This includes
a literary portal (www.literature.britishcouncil.org),
directories of postgraduate and short courses in
literature and creative writing, a directory of literary
conferences, information about UK and
Commonwealth authors on
www.contemporarywriters.com and
www.literarytranslation.com, including translation
workshops. A worldwide online book club and
reading group for adults, teenagers and children
(www.encompassculture.com) was launched in May
2003, and also www.youngtranslators.com for
young European translators.

The Visual Arts Department, part of the British
Council's Arts Group, develops and enlarges
overseas knowledge and appreciation of British
achievement in the fields of painting, sculpture,
printmaking, design, photography, the crafts and
architecture, working closely with the British
Council's overseas offices and with professional
colleagues in the UK and abroad.

Further information about the work of the
British Council is available from Press and Public
Relations at the above address, or from British
Council offices overseas.

## The British Fantasy Society

201 Reddish Road, South Reddish,
Stockport SK5 7HR
*tel* 0161-476 5368 (after 6pm)
*email* faliol@yahoo.com
*website* www.britishfantasysociety.org.uk
*President* Ramsey Campbell, *Secretary* Robert
Parkinson
*Membership* £25 p.a.

For devotees of fantasy, horror and related fields, in
literature, art and the cinema. Publications include
*British Fantasy Newsletter* (quarterly) featuring news
and reviews and several annual booklets, including:
*Dark Horizons*; *Masters of Fantasy* on individual
authors. There is a small-press library and an
annual convention and fantasy awards sponsored by
the Society. Founded 1971.

## British Film Institute (BFI)

21 Stephen Street, London W1T 1LN
*tel* 020-7255 1444
*24-hour BFI Events Line* 0870-240 4050
*fax* 020-7436 0439

*website* www.bfi.org.uk
*Chair* Anthony Minghella CBE, *Acting Director*
Adrian Wootton

The BFI offers opportunities for people to
experience, learn and discover more about the
world of film and moving image culture. It
incorporates the BFI National Library, the magazine
*Sight and Sound* (monthly), the BFI National Film
Theatre, the annual London Film Festival, and the
BFI London IMAX, and provides advice and
support for regional cinemas and film festivals
across the UK. The BFI also undertakes the
preservation of, and promotes access to films, TV
programmes, computer games, museum collections,
stills, posters and designs, and other special
collections. Founded 1933.

## British Guild of Beer Writers
*Secretary* Peter Hayden
*tel* 020-8853-8585
*email* peterhayden@onetel.net.uk
*Membership* £40 p.a

Aims to improve standards in beer writing and at
the same time extend public knowledge of beers
and brewing. The Gold and Silver Tankard Awards
are given annually to writers and broadcasters
judged to have made the most valuable contribution
to this end. Publishes a directory of members with
details of their publications and their particular
areas of interest, which is circulated to the media.
Founded 1988.

## The British Guild of Travel Writers
*Secretariat* Charlotte Copenam, 12 Askew Crescent,
London W12 9DN
*tel* 020-8749-1128
*email* charlotte@virtualnecessities.com
*website* www.bgtw.org

Arranges meetings, discussions and visits for its 220
members (who are all professional travel
journalists) to promote and encourage the public's
interest in travel. Publishes a monthly newsletter
(for members only), website and annual *Yearbook*,
which contain details of members and lists travel
industry PRs and contacts. Annual awards for
journalism (members only) and the travel trade.

## The British Haiku Society
*Secretary* David Walker, Lenacre Ford, Woolhope,
Hereford HR1 4RF
*tel* (01432) 860328
*email* davidwalker@btinternet.com
*website* www.britishhaikusociety.org
*Membership* £25 p.a. UK, £28 Europe, £32 rest of
world, £20 concession/unwaged

Aims to pioneer the appreciation and writing of
haiku, senryu, renku and tanka in the UK and the
rest of Europe, and to establish links with haiku
societies throughout the world. Publishes the

journal *Blithe Spirit*, and a newsletter, *The Brief*, and
holds national events. Administers the biennial
Sasakawa Prize (worth £2500), James W. Hackett
International Award and the Nobuyuki Yuasa
International English Haibun Contest. Founded
1990.

## British Institute of Professional Photography
Fox Talbot House, Amwell End, Ware,
Herts. SG12 9HN
*tel* (01920) 464011
*email* info@bipp.com
*website* www.bipp.com

Exists to represent all who practise photography as
a profession in any field; to improve the quality of
photography; establish recognised examination
qualifications and a high standard of conduct; to
safeguard the interests of the public and the
profession. Admission can be obtained either via
examinations, or by submission of work and other
information to the appropriate examining board.
Fellows, Associates and Licentiates are entitled to
the designation Incorporated Photographer or
Incorporated Photographic Technician. Organises
numerous meetings and conferences in various
parts of the country throughout the year; publishes
*The Photographer* journal (monthly), plus various
pamphlets and leaflets on professional photography.
Founded 1901; incorporated 1921.

## British Interactive Media Association (BIMA)
Briarlea House, Southend Road, Billericay,
Essex CM11 2PR
*tel* (01277) 658107 *fax* (0870) 0517842
*email* info@bima.co.uk
*website* www.bima.co.uk
*Office Administrator* Janice Cable
*Membership* Open to any organisation or individual
with an interest in multimedia. £650 p.a. commercial,
£300 institutional, £35 individual plus VAT

Established to promote a wider understanding of
the benefits of interactive multimedia to industry,
government and education and to provide a regular
forum for the exchange of views amongst members.
Publishes regular newsletters. Founded 1984.

## The British Science Fiction Association Ltd
*Membership Secretary* Estelle Roberts, 97 Sharp
Street, Newland Avenue, Hull HU5 2AE
*email* bsfa@enterprise.net
*President* Arthur C. Clarke

For authors, publishers, booksellers and readers of
science fiction, fantasy and allied genres. Publishes
*Matrix*, an informal magazine of news and
information; *Focus*, an amateur writers' magazine;

*Vector*, a critical magazine and the Orbiter Service, a network of postal writers workshops. Trophies are awarded annually to the winner in each category of the BSFA Awards: best UK-published novel, best UK short story, best UK artwork and best UK non-fiction/anthology. Founded 1958.

## British Society of Comedy Writers
*President* Kenneth Rock, 61 Parry Road, Ashmore Park, Wolverhampton, West Midlands WV11 2PS
*tel* (01902) 722729 *fax* (01902) 722729
*email* info@bscw.co.uk
*website* www.bscw.co.uk
*Membership* £75 p.a. full, £40 p.a. subscriber

Aims to bring together writers and industry representatives in order to develop new projects and ideas. Holds an annual international comedy conference, networking days and workshops to train new writers to professional standards. A script reading service is available. Founded 1999.

## British Society of Miniaturists
*Director* Margaret Simpson, Briargate,
2 The Brambles, Ilkley, West Yorkshire LS29 9DH
*Membership* By selection

'The world's oldest miniature society.' Holds 2 open exhibitions a year. Founded 1895.

## British Society of Painters in Oils, Pastels and Acrylics
Briargate, 2 The Brambles, Ilkley,
West Yorkshire LS29 9DH
*Membership* By selection
*Director* Margaret Simpson

Promotes interest and encourages high quality in the work of painters in these media. Holds 2 open exhibitions a year. Founded 1988.

## British Watercolour Society
*Director* Margaret Simpson, Briargate,
2 The Brambles, Ilkley, West Yorkshire LS29 9DH
*tel* (01943) 609075

Promotes the best in traditional watercolour painting. Holds 2 open exhibitions a year. Founded 1830.

## Broadcasting Entertainment Cinematograph and Theatre Union (BECTU), Writers Section
373–377 Clapham Road, London SW9 9BT
*tel* 020-7346 0900 *fax* 020-7346 0901
*email* info@bectu.org.uk
*website* www.bectu.org.uk
*General Secretary* R. Bolton

Aims to defend the interests of writers in film, TV and radio. By virtue of its industrial strength, the Union is able to help its writer members to secure favourable terms and conditions. In cases of disputes with employers, the Union can intervene in order to ensure an equitable settlement. Its production agreement with PACT lays down minimum terms for writers working in the documentary area. Founded 1991.

## Broadcasting Group – see The Society of Authors, page 495

## The Brontë Society
*Membership Secretary* The Brontë Parsonage Museum, Haworth, Keighley,
West Yorkshire BD22 8DR
*tel* (01535) 642323 *fax* (01535) 647131
*email* bronte@bronte.prestel.co.uk
*website* www.bronte.org.uk

Acquisition, preservation, promotion of the memoirs and literary remains of the Brontë family; exhibitions of MSS and other subjects. Publishes *Brontë Studies* (3 p.a.) and *The Brontë Gazette* (bi-annual). Its Museum is open throughout the year.

## The Browning Society
*Contact* Dr Berry Chevasco, 52 Esmond Road, Bedford Park, London W4 1JQ
*tel* 020-8995 4900
*email* b.chev@virgin.net
*website* www.browningsociety.org
*Membership* £15 p.a.

Aims to widen the appreciation and understanding of the lives and poetry of Robert Browning and Elizabeth Barrett Browning, and other Victorian writers and poets. Founded 1881; refounded 1969.

## The John Buchan Society
*Membership Secretary* Russell Paterson, Limpsfield, 16 Ranfurly Road, Bridge of Weir, Renfrewshire PA11 3EL
*tel* (01505) 613116
*Membership* £10 p.a. full/overseas; other rates on application

Promotes a wider understanding and appreciation of the life and works of John Buchan. Encourages publication of a complete annotated edition of Buchan's works, and supports the John Buchan Centre and Museum at Broughton, Borders. Holds regular meetings and social gatherings; produces a Newsletter and a Journal. Founded 1979.

## Bureau of Freelance Photographers
Focus House, 497 Green Lanes, London N13 4BP
*tel* 020-8882 3315 *fax* 020-8886 5174
*website* www.thebfp.com
*Chief Executive* John Tracy
*Membership* £45 p.a. UK; £60 p.a. overseas

Exists to help the freelance photographer by providing information on markets, and free advisory service. Publishes *Market Newsletter* (monthly). Founded 1965.

## Byron Society (International)

Byron House, 6 Gertrude Street, London SW10 0JN
*tel* 020-7352 5112 *fax* 020-7352 1226
*Hon. Director* Mrs Elma Dangerfield CBE
*Membership* £20 p.a

Aims to promote research into the life and works of Lord Byron by seminars, discussions, lectures and readings. Publishes *The Byron Journal* (annual, £6.50 plus postage). Founded 1971.

## Randolph Caldecott Society

*Secretary* Kenn Oultram, Clatterwick House, Little Leigh, Northwich, Cheshire CW8 4RJ
*tel* (01606) 891303 (office), 781731 (evening)
*Membership* £10–£15 p.a.

Aims to encourage an interest in the life and works of Randolph Caldecott, the Victorian artist, illustrator and sculptor. Meetings held in Chester and London. Liaises with the American Caldecott Society. Founded 1983.

## Cambridge Bibliographical Society

University Library, West Road, Cambridge CB3 9DR
*tel* (01223) 333123 *fax* (01223) 333160
*email* nas1000@cam.ac.uk
*Secretary* Nicholas Smith

To encourage the study of bibliography, including book and MS production, book collecting and the history of libraries. It publishes *Transactions* (annual) and a series of monographs, and arranges a programme of lectures and visits. Founded 1949.

## Canadian Authors Association

PO Box 419, Campbellford, Ontario K0L 1L0, Canada
*tel* 705-653-0323, 866-216-6222 (toll free)
*fax* 705-653-0593
*email* canauth@redden.on.ca
*website* www.CanAuthors.org/national.html
*President* Ishbel Moore, *Administrator* Alec McEachern

## Canadian Magazine Publishers Association

425 Adelaide St.W., Suite 700, Toronto, Ontario M5V 3C1, Canada
*tel* 416-504-0274 *fax* 416-504-0437
*email* cmpainfo@cmpa.ca
*websites* www.cmpa.ca, www.magomania.com
*President* Mark Jamison

Founded 1973.

## Canadian Publishers' Council

250 Merton Street, Suite 203, Toronto, Ontario M4S 1B1, Canada
*tel* 416-322-7011 *fax* 416-322-6999

*email* pubadmin@pubcouncil.ca
*website* www.pubcouncil.ca
*Executive Director* Jacqueline Hushion

## CANSCAIP (Canadian Society of Children's Authors, Illustrators & Performers)

40 Orchard View Boulevard, Suite 101, Toronto, ON M4R 1B9, Canada
*tel* 416-515-1559
*email* office@canscaip.org
*website* www.canscaip.org
*Office Manager* Lena Coakley
*Membership* $75 p.a. Full member (published authors and illustrators), $45 Insitutional Friend, $35 Friend

A non-profit support network for children's artists. Promotes children's literature and performances through Canada and internationally. Founded 1977.

## Career Development Group

c/o CILIP, 7 Ridgmount Street, London WC1E 7AE
*President* Joanna Ball BA, MA, MCLIP, *Secretary* Lorna Robertson BSC, MSC, MCLIP

Publishes bibliographical aids, the journal *Impact*, works on librarianship; and runs educational courses. Founded 1895.

## Careers Writers' Association

*Membership Secretary* Anne Goodman, 16 Caewal Road, Llandaff, Cardiff CF5 2BT
*tel* 029-2056 3444 *fax* 029-2065 8190
*email* anne.goodman5@ntlworld.com
*website* www.careerswriters.co.uk
*Membership* £20 p.a.

Society for established writers on the inter-related topics of education, training and careers. Holds occasional meetings on subjects of interest to members, and circulates details of members to information providers. Founded 1979.

## The Lewis Carroll Society

*Secretary* Alan White, 69 Cromwell Road, Hertford, Herts. SG13 7DP
*email* alanwhite@tesco.net
*website* www.lewiscarrollsociety.org.uk
*Membership* £15 p.a. UK, £18 Europe, £20/$34 elsewhere; special rates for institutions

Aims to promote interest in the life and works of Lewis Carroll (Revd Charles Lutwidge Dodgson) and to encourage research. Activities include regular meetings, exhibitions, and a publishing programme that includes the first annotated, unexpurgated edition of his diaries in 9 volumes, the Society's journal *The Carrollian* (2 p.a.), a newsletter, *Bandersnatch* (quarterly) and the *Lewis Carroll Review* (occasional). Founded 1969.

## Lewis Carroll Society (Daresbury)

*Secretary* Kenn Oultram, Clatterwick House,
Little Leigh, Northwich, Cheshire CW8 4RJ
*tel* (01606) 891303 (office), 781731 (evening)
*Membership* £5 p.a.

Aims to encourage an interest in the life and works
of Lewis Carroll, author of *Alice's Adventures*.
Meetings take place at Carroll's birth village
(Daresbury, Cheshire). Elects an annual 'Alice', who
is available for public engagements. Founded 1970.

## Cartoonists Club of Great Britain

*Secretary* Richard Tomes, 29 Ulverley Crescent,
Olton, Solihull, West Midlands B92 8BJ
*tel* 0121-706 7652
*email* r.tomes@virgin.net
*website* www.ccgb.org.uk
*Membership* Fee on joining: £50; thereafter £35 p.a.

Aims to encourage social contact between members
and endeavours to promote the professional
standing and prestige of cartoonists.

## Centerprise Literature Development Project

Centerprise Trust, 136–138 Kingsland High Street,
London E8 2NS
*tel* 020-7249 6572
*email* sharoncenterlit@care4free.net
*Contact* Eva, Sharon

An advice and resource centre for writers of fiction
and poetry, servicing Central, East and North
London. Runs courses and workshops in creative
writing, organises poetry and book readings,
discussions and debates on literary and relevant
issues, writers' surgeries, and telephone information
on resources for writers in London. Publishes
*Calabash* newsletter for Writers of Black and Asian
origin. Funded by London Arts. See also page 634.
Founded 1995.

## Centre for Creative Communities (CCC)

118 Commercial Street, London E1 6NF
*tel* 020-7247 5385 *fax* 020-7247 5256
*email* info@creativecommunities.org.uk
*website* www.creativecommunities.org.uk
*Director* Jennifer Williams

A non-profit-making organisation working in the
field of arts, education and community
development. Conducts research, organises
conferences, produces a quarterly newsletter and is
part of an international network of arts and
education organisations. Maintains a specialised
arts, education and community development
library. CCC is not a grant-giving organisation.

## The Chartered Institute of Journalists

*General Secretary* Dominic Cooper, 2 Dock Offices,
Surrey Quays Road, London SE16 2XU
*tel* 020-7252 1187 *fax* 020-7232 2302
*email* memberservices@ioj.co.uk
*Membership* £195 p.a. maximum, £97.50 trainees,
£133 affiliate

The senior organisation of the profession, the
Chartered Institute has accumulated funds for the
assistance of members. A Freelance Division links
editors and publishers with freelances and a
Directory is published of freelance writers, with
their specialisations. There are special sections for
broadcasters, motoring correspondents, public
relations practitioners and overseas members.
Occasional contributors to the media may qualify
for election as Affiliates. Founded in 1884;
incorporated by Royal Charter in 1890.

## The Chartered Society of Designers

5 Bermondsey Street, London SE1 3UW
*tel* 020-7357 8088 *fax* 020-7407 9878
*email* csd@csd.org.uk
*website* www.designweb.co.uk/csd
*Director* Brian Lymbery

Works to promote and regulate standards of
competence, professional conduct and integrity,
including representation on government and official
bodies, design education and awards. The services
to members include general information,
publications, guidance on copyright and other
professional issues, access to professional indemnity
insurance, as well as the membership magazine *csd*.
Activities in the regions are included in an extensive
annual programme of events and training courses.

## The Chesterton Society

*Hon. Secretary* Robert Hughes KHS, 11 Lawrence
Leys, Bloxham, Nr Banbury, Oxon OX15 4NU
*tel* (01295) 720869 *mobile* (07789) 752098
*Membership* £12.50 p.a.

Aims to promote interest in the life and work of
G.K. Chesterton and those associated with him or
influenced by his writings. Two lectures a year.
Publishes the *Chesterton Quarterly Review* (4 p.a.).
Founded 1974.

## Children's Book Circle

c/o Rachel Wade, Hodder Children's Books,
338 Euston Road, London NW1 3BH
*tel* 020-7873 6000 *fax* 020-7873 6477
*email* rachel.wade@hodder.co.uk
*Membership Secretary* Nicola Wilkinson,
Egmont Children's Books, 239 Kensington High
Street, London W8 6SA
*tel* 020-7761 3500 *fax* 020-7761 3510
*email* nicola.wilkinson@ukegmont.com
*Membership* £15 p.a. if working inside M25; £12
outside

Provides a discussion forum for anybody involved
with children's books. Meetings are addressed by a

panel of invited speakers and topics focus on current and controversial issues. Holds the annual Patrick Hardy lecture and administers the Eleanor Farjeon Award. Founded 1962.

## Children's Books History Society
*Secretary* Ms Sarah Mahurter, 66 Idmiston Square, Worcester Park, Surrey KT4 7SY
*tel* 020-8830-6084 *fax* 020-8830-6084
*email* sjamahuter@hotmail.com
*Membership* £10 p.a.; apply for overseas rates

Aims 'to promote an appreciation of children's books, and to study their history, bibliography and literary content'. Holds approx. 6 meetings and produces 3 substantial *Newsletters* and an occasional paper per year. The Harvey Darton Award is given biennially for a book that extends knowledge of British children's literature of the past. Founded 1969.

## Children's Books Ireland
17 Lower Camden Street, Dublin 2
*tel/fax* (01) 8725854
*email* info@childrensbooksireland.com
*website* www.children'sbooksireland.com
*Administrative Officer* Liz Marshall
*Membership* €25/£18 p.a. individual, €35/£26 p.a. institution, €45/£40 p.a. overseas, €15/£11 p.a. student

Committed to raising awareness of the value and importance of children's books and to playing a central role in promoting, celebrating and supporting all aspects of children's books. Formed in 1996.

## Children's Writers and Illustrators
**Group** – see The Society of Authors, page 495

## CILIP (Chartered Institute of Library and Information Professionals)
7 Ridgmount Street, London WC1E 7AE
*tel* 020-7255 0500 *textphone* 020-7255 0505
*fax* 020-7255 0501
*email* info@cilip.org.uk
*website* www.cilip.org.uk
*Chief Executive* Bob McKee PhD, FRSA, MCLIP
*Membership* Varies according to income

CILIP was formed on 1 April 2002 following the unification of the Institution of Information Scientists and the Library Association. It is the leading membership body for library and information professionals, with around 23,000 members in the UK and overseas. Its monthly magazine *Update* and fortnightly *Gazette* are distributed free to members. The IIS was originally founded in 1958 and the LA in 1877.

## Circle of Wine Writers
*Administrator* Andrea Warren, 166 Meadvale Road, London W5 1LS

*tel* 020-8930 0181 *fax* (01494) 670200
*email* administrator@winewriters.org
*website* www.winewriters.org
*Membership* By election, £35 p.a.

An association for those engaged in communicating about wines and spirits. Produces *Circle Update* newsletter (5 p.a.), organises tasting sessions as well as a programme of meetings and talks. Founded 1960.

## The John Clare Society
*Hon. Secretary* 9 The Chase, Ely, Cambs. CB6 3DR
*tel* (01353) 668438
*email* moyse.helpston@talk21.com
*website* www.vzone.virgin.net/linda.curry/jclaresociety
*Membership* £10 p.a. UK individual

Promotes a wider appreciation of the life and works of the poet John Clare. Founded 1981.

## Classical Association
*Administrator* Clare Roberts, Senate House, Malet Street, London WC1E 7HU
*tel* 020-7862 8706 *fax* 020-7862 8729
*email* croberts@sas.ac.uk
*website* www.sas.ac.uk/icls/classass

Exists to promote and sustain interest in classical studies, to maintain their rightful position in universities and schools, and to give scholars and teachers opportunities for meeting and discussing their problems.

## CLÉ: The Irish Book Publishers' Association
19 Parnell Square, Dublin 1, Ireland
*tel* (056) 7756 333 *fax* (056) 7756 333
*email* info@publishingireland.com
*website* www.publishingireland.com
*President* Fergal Tobin, *Administrator* Jolly Ronan

## The William Cobbett Society
*Chairman* Molly Townsend, 10 Grenehurst Way, Petersfield, Hants GU31 4AZ
*tel* (01730) 262060
*Membership* £8 p.a.

Aims to make the life and work of William Cobbett better known. Founded 1976.

## The Wilkie Collins Society
*Membership Secretary* Paul Lewis, 4 Ernest Gardens, London W4 3QU
*email* paul@paullewis.co.uk
*website* www.wilkiecollins.org
*Chairman* Andrew Gasson
*Membership* £10 p.a. EU, £18 international

Aims to promote interest in the life and works of Wilkie Collins. Publishes a newsletter, an occasional scholarly journal and reprints of Collins's lesser known works. Founded 1981.

## Comedy Writers Association UK (CWAUK)

*Membership Secretary* Mary Gamon, 12 Erskine Road, Colwyn Bay, Conwy, North Wales LL29 8EV
*email* info@cwauk.co.uk
*website* www.cwauk.co.uk
*Membership* £36 p.a. + one-off £5 registration fee. Open to everyone interested in comedy writing

The largest group of independent comedy writers in the UK with contacts around the world. Holds one-day seminars with invited industry speakers. Provides advice on writing and career development, and monthly newsletter and monthly market information. Founded 1981.

## Comhairle nan Leabhraichean/The Gaelic Books Council

22 Mansfield Street, Glasgow G11 5QP
*tel* 0141-337 6211 *fax* 0141-353 0515
*email* fios@gaelicbooks.net
*website* www.gaelicbooks.net
*Chair* Prof Donald E. Meek

Stimulates Scottish Gaelic publishing by awarding publication grants for new books, commissioning authors and providing editorial services and general assistance to writers and readers. Has its own bookshop of all Gaelic and Gaelic-related books in print and runs a book club; catalogue available. Founded 1968.

## Comics Creators Guild

*Postal address only* 22 St James' Mansions, West End Lane, London NW6 2AA
*website* www.comicscreators.org.uk

Open to all those concerned with, or interested in, professional comics creation. Holds monthly meetings and publishes a newsletter (monthly), a Directory of Members' Work, Submission Guidelines for the major comics publishers, sample scripts for artists, a 'Guide to Contracts' and 'Getting Started in Comics', a beginners' guide to working in the industry, and *Comics Forum* (quarterly), a magazine of art and criticism.

## The Joseph Conrad Society (UK)

*The Conradian*, Dr Allan Simmons, Dept of English, St Mary's College, Twickenham, Middlesex TW1 4SX
*Chairman* Keith Carabine, *President* Philip Conrad, *Secretary* Hugh Epstein, *Editor* Allan Simmons

Maintains close and friendly links with the Conrad family. Activities include an annual international conference; publication of *The Conradian* and a series of pamphlets; and maintenance of a study centre at the Polish Cultural Centre, 238–246 King Street, London W6 0RF. Administers the Juliet McLauchlan Prize: £100 annual award for the winner of an essay competition. Founded 1973.

## Copyright Clearance Center Inc.

222 Rosewood Drive, Danvers, MA 01923, USA
*tel* 978-750-8400 *fax* 978-750-4470
*website* www.copyright.com

## Copyright Council of New Zealand Inc.

PO Box 36477, Northcote, Auckland 1309, New Zealand
*tel* (09) 480-2711 *fax* (09) 480-1130
*Chairman* Terence O'Neill-Joyce, *Secretary* Kathy Sheat

## The Copyright Licensing Agency Ltd –
see page 684

## Crime Writers' Association

*email* secretary@thecwa.co.uk
*website* www.thecwa.co.uk
*Membership* Associate membership open to publishers, journalists, booksellers specialising in crime literature

Full membership open to professional writers of crime novels, short stories, plays for stage, TV and radio, or of other serious works on crime. Publishes *Red Herrings* (monthly), available to members only. Founded 1953.

## The Critics' Circle

*Contact* Catherine Cooper, Administrator, c/o 69 Marylebone Lane, London W1U 2PH
*tel* 020-7224 1410 (office hours)
*President* Charles Osborne, *Hon. General Secretary* Charles Hedges
*Membership* By invitation of the Council

Aims to promote the art of criticism, to uphold its integrity in practice, to foster and safeguard the professional interests of its members, to provide opportunities for social intercourse among them, and to support the advancement of the arts. Such invitations are issued only to persons engaged professionally, regularly and substantially in the writing or broadcasting of criticism of drama, music, films, dance and the visual arts. Founded 1913.

## Cyngor Llyfrau Cymru – see Welsh Books Council/Cyngor Llyfrau Cymru

## Deaf Broadcasting Council

50 Clevedon Road, London SE20 7QQ
*fax* (07970) 150006, 020-8676 0534
*email* pennybes@aol.com
*website* www.deafbroadcastingcouncil.org.uk
*Chair* Penny Beschizza

## Design and Artists Copyright Society –
see page 689

## Dickens Fellowship

The Dickens House, 48 Doughty Street,
London WC1N 2LX
*tel* 020-7405 2127 *fax* 020-7831 5175
*Joint Hon. Secretaries* Dr Tony Williams, Thelma Grove
*Membership* On application

Based in house occupied by Charles Dickens 1837–9.
Publishes *The Dickensian* (3 p.a.). Founded 1902.

## Directory & Database Publishers Association

*Secretary* Rosemary Pettit, PO Box 23034,
London W6 0RJ
*tel* 020-8846 9707
*Membership* £120–£1200 p.a.

Maintains a code of professional practice; aims to
raise the standard and professional status of UK
directory and database publishing and to protect
(and promote) the legal, statutory and common
interests of directory publishers; provides for the
exchange of technical, commercial and management
information between members. Founded 1970.

## Directory of Writers' Circles

39 Lincoln Way, Harlington, Beds. LU5 6NG
*tel* (01525) 873197
*email* diana@writers-circles.com
*website* www.writers-circles.com
*Publisher & Editor* Diana Hayden

Publishes a directory of writers' circles for the UK
and Eire which is updated twice annually.

## 'Sean Dorman' Manuscript Society

Cherry Trees, Crosemere Road, Cockshutt,
Ellesmere, Shropshire SY12 0JP
*tel* (01939) 270293
*Director* Mary Driver

Provides mutual help among writers and aspiring
writers in the UK. By means of circulating MSS
parcels, members receive constructive criticism of
their own work and read and comment on the work
of others. Each 'Circulator' has up to 9 participants
and members' contributions may be in any
medium: short stories, chapters of a novel, poetry,
magazine articles, etc. Send sae for full details and
application form. Founded 1957.

## The Arthur Conan Doyle Society

*Organisers* Christopher and Barbara Roden,
PO Box 1360, Ashcroft, B.C., Canada V0K 1A0
*tel* 250-453-2045 *fax* 250-453-2075
*email* ashtree@ash-tree.bc.ca
*website* www.ash-tree.bc.ca/acdsocy.html
*Membership* £16 p.a. (airmail extra)

Promotes the study of the life and works of Sir
Arthur Conan Doyle. Publishes *ACD* journal (bi-
annual) and occasional reprints of Conan Doyle
material. Occasional conventions. Founded 1989.

## Early English Text Society

Christ Church, Oxford OX1 1DP
*website* www.eets.org.uk
*Hon. Director* Prof John Burrow *Executive Secretary*
R.F.S. Hamer
*Membership* £15 p.a.

Aims to bring unprinted early English literature
within the reach of students in sound texts.
Founded 1864.

## The Eckhart Society

Summa, 22 Tippings Lane, Woodley, Reading,
Berks. RG5 4RX
*tel* 0118-9690118
*email* ashleyyoung@aysumma.demon.co.uk
*website* www.eckhartsociety.org
*Secretary* Ashley Young
*Membership* £16 p.a.; £9 OAPs/students

Aims to promote the understanding and
appreciation of Eckhart's writings and their
importance for Christian thought and practice; to
facilitate scholarly research into Eckhart's life and
works; and to promote the study of Eckhart's
teaching as a contribution to inter-religious
dialogue. Founded 1987.

## Edinburgh Bibliographical Society

c/o National Library of Scotland, George IV Bridge,
Edinburgh EH1 1EW
*tel* 0131-226-4531
*Secretary* Dr W. McDougall, *Treasurer* P. Freshwater
*Membership* £10 p.a., £15 institutions; £5 full-time
students

Encourages bibliographical activity through
organising talks for members, particularly on
bibliographical topics relating to Scotland, and visits
to libraries. Also publishes *Transactions* (generally
every 3 years, free to members) and other
occasional publications. Founded 1890.

## Educational Writers Group – see The Society of Authors, page 495

## The George Eliot Fellowship

*Secretary* Mrs K.M. Adams, 71 Stepping Stones
Road, Coventry CV5 8JT
*tel* 024-7659 2231
*website* www.george-eliot-fellowship.com
*President* Jonathan G. Ouvry
*Membership* £10 p.a.

Promotes an interest in the life and work of George
Eliot (1819–80) and helps to extend her influence;
arranges meetings; produces an annual journal, a
quarterly newsletter and other publications. Awards
the annual George Eliot Fellowship Prize (£250) for
an essay on Eliot's life or work, which must be
previously unpublished and not exceed 2500 words.
Founded 1930.

## English Association

University of Leicester, University Road,
Leicester LE1 7RH
*tel* 0116-252 3982 *fax* 0116-252 2301
*email* engassoc@le.ac.uk
*website* www.le.ac.uk/engassoc/
*Chair* Elaine Treharne, *Chief Executive* Helen Lucas

Aims to further knowledge, understanding and
enjoyment of English literature and the English
language, by working towards a fuller recognition of
English as an essential element in education and in
the community at large; by encouraging the study
of English literature and language by means of
conferences, lectures and publications; and by
fostering the discussion of methods of teaching
English of all kinds.

## English Speaking Board (International) Ltd

26A Princes Street, Southport PR8 1EQ
*tel* (01704) 501730 *fax* (01704) 539637
*email* admin@esbuk.org
*website* www.esbuk.org
*President* Christabel Burniston MBE, *Chairman* Prof
Andrew Trott
*Membership* £25 p.a. individuals, £50 corporate

Aims to foster all activities concerned with oral
communication. Offers assessment qualifications in
practical speaking and listening skills for candidates
at all levels in schools, vocational and business
contexts; also for those with learning difficulties and
those for whom English is an acquired language.
Also provides training courses in teaching and
delivery of oral communication. Offers membership
to all those concerned with the development and
expression of the English language. Members
receive *Speaking English* (2 p.a.); articles are invited
on any special aspect of spoken English.

## The English-Speaking Union

Dartmouth House, 37 Charles Street,
London W1J 5ED
*tel* 020-7529 1550 *fax* 020-7495 6108
*email* esu@esu.org
*website* www.esu.org
*Director-General* Mrs Valerie Mitchell OBE
*Membership* Various categories

Aims to promote international understanding and
human achievement through the widening use of
the English language throughout the world. The
ESU is an educational charity which sponsors
scholarships and exchanges, educational
programmes promoting the effective use of English,
and a wide range of international and cultural
events. Members contribute to its work across the
world. Administers the Marsh Biography Award
(see page 560). See also Books Across the Sea.
Founded 1918.

## European Broadcasting Union

PO Box 45, Ancienne Route 17,
CH–1218 Grand Saconnex (Geneva),
Switzerland
*tel* 41 22 717 2111 *fax* 41 22 747 4000
*email* ebu@ebu.ch
*website* www.ebu.ch
*Secretary-General* Jean Réveillon

The largest professional association of national
broadcasters. Working on behalf of its members in
the European area, the EBU negotiates broadcasting
rights for major sports events; operates the
Eurovision and Euroradio networks; organises
programme exchanges; stimulates and coordinates
co-productions; and provides a full range of other
operational, commercial, technical, legal and
strategic services. Founded 1950.

## Fabian Society

11 Dartmouth Street, London SW1H 9BN
*tel* 020-7227 4900 *fax* 020-7976 7153
*email* info@fabian-society.org.uk
*website* www.fabian-society.org.uk
*General Secretary* Sunder Katwala (Mr)

Current affairs, political thought, economics,
education, environment, foreign affairs, social
policy. Also controls NCLC Publishing Society Ltd.
Founded 1884.

## Federation Against Copyright Theft Ltd (FACT)

7 Victory Business Centre, Worton Road, Isleworth,
Middlesex TW7 6DB
*tel* 020-8568 6646 *fax* 020-8560 6364
*email* investigator@fact-uk.org.uk
*Contact* David Lowe, Director General

Aims to protect the interests of its members and
others against infringement in the UK of copyright
in cinematograph films, TV programmes and all
forms of audiovisual recording. Founded 1982.
   The Copyright Hotline offers advice and
information to anyone who wants to use film,
music or software copyrights. It is part of a
collective initiative by FACT, Federation Against
Software Theft (FAST), Music Publishers
Association (MPA), Mechanical Copyright
Protection Society (MCPS), Performing Right
Society (PRS) and British Music Rights (BMR).

## Federation of British Artists

17 Carlton House Terrace, London SW1Y 5BD
*tel* 020-7930 6844 *fax* 020-7839 7830
*email* info@mallgalleries.com
*website* www.mallgalleries.org.uk

Administers 9 major National Art Societies at the
Mall Galleries, The Mall, London SW1.

### Federation of European Publishers

204 avenue de Tervuren, 1150 Brussels, Belgium
*tel* (2) 770 11 10 *fax* (2) 771 20 71
*email* malemann@fep-fee.be
*website* www.fep-fee.be
*President* Anton C. Hilscher, *Director* Mechthild von Alemann

Represents the interests of European publishers on EU affairs; informs members on the development of EU policies which could affect the publishing industry. Founded 1967.

### The Federation of Indian Publishers

18/1–C Institutional Area, Aruna Asaf Ali Marg (near JNU), New Delhi 110067, India
*tel* 26852263, 26964847 *fax* 26864054
*email* fipl@satyam.net.in

### Federation of Spanish Publishers' Association

Cea Bermúdez, 44–2 Dcha. 28003 Madrid, Spain
*tel* (91) 534 51 95 *fax* (91) 535 26 25
*email* fgee@fge.es
*website* www.federacioneditores.org
*President* Yoldi L'lbeda, *Director* Antonio Avila

### The Federation of Worker Writers and Community Publishers

Burslem School of Art, Queen Street, Stoke-on-Tent ST6 3EJ
*tel* (01782) 822327 *fax* (01782) 822327
*email* thefwwcp@tiscali.co.uk
*website* www.thefwwcp.org.uk
*Membership* £40 p.a. funded groups; £20 unfunded

A network of writers groups and community publishers which promotes working-class writing and publishing. Founded 1976.

### Financial Journalists' Group

Secretary, c/o Association of British Insurers, 51 Gresham Street, London EC2V 7HQ
*tel* 020-7216 7410
*Chairman* Chris Wheal
*Membership* No fee

Aims to give journalists working in the area of, or with an interest in, finance and financial services, a forum to learn more about some of the issues involved, and meet colleagues with similar interests. Founded 1997.

### The Fine Art Trade Guild

16–18 Empress Place, London SW6 1TT
*tel* 020-7381 6616 *fax* 020-7381 2596
*email* info@fineart.co.uk
*website* www.fineart.co.uk
*Managing Director* Rosie Sumner

Promotes the sale of fine art prints and picture framing in the UK and overseas markets; establishes and raises standards amongst members and communicates these to the buying public. The Guild publishes *The Directory* and *Art Business Today*, the trade's longest established magazine, and various specialist books. Founded 1910.

### First Film Foundation

*Director* Jonathan Rawlinson, 9 Bourlet Close, London W1W 7BP
*tel* 020-7580 2111 *fax* 020-7580 2116
*email* info@firstfilm.demon.co.uk
*website* www.firstfilm.co.uk

A charity that exists to help new British writers, producers and directors make their first feature film. Provides a range of unique educational and promotional programmes that give film-makers the contacts, knowledge and experience they need to achieve this goal. Founded 1987.

### FOCAL International Ltd (Federation of Commercial AudioVisual Libraries International Ltd)

Pentax House, South Hill Avenue, South Harrow, Middlesex HA2 0DU
*tel* 020-8423 5853 *fax* 020-8933 4826
*email* info@focalint.org
*website* www.focalint.org
*Commerical Manager* Anne Johnson, *General Manager* Julie Lewis

Founded 1985.

### The Folklore Society

The Warburg Institute, Woburn Square, London WC1E 0AB
*tel* 020-7862 8564
*email* folklore.society@talk21.com
*website* www.folklore-society.com
*Hon. Secretary* Dr Juliette Wood

Collection, recording and study of folklore. Founded 1878.

### Foreign Press Association in London

*Registered Office* 11 Carlton House Terrace, London SW1Y 5AJ
*tel* 020-7930 0445 *fax* 020-7925 0469
*email* secretariat@foreign-press.org.uk
*website* www.foreign-press.org.uk
*President* Catherine Mayes, *General Manager* Bob Jenner
*Membership* Entrance fee: £155; £153 p.a. Full membership open to overseas professional journalists residing in the UK; Associate membership available for British press and freelance journalists

Aims to promote the professional interests of its members. Founded 1888.

## Free Painters & Sculptors

*Registered office* 14 John Street, London WC1N 2EB
*Hon. Secretary* Owen Legg, 152 Hadlow Road,
Tonbridge, Kent TN9 1PB
*Membership Secretary* Joan Jago, 606 Nelson House,
Dolphin Square, London SW1V 3NZ

Promotes group shows 4 times a year in prestigious galleries in London. Sponsors all that is exciting in contemporary art.

## French Publishers' Association

115 Blvd St Germain, 75006 Paris, France
*tel* (1) 44 41 40 50 *fax* (1) 44 41 40 77
*website* www.sne.fr

## The Gaelic Books Council – see Comhairle nan Leabhraichean/The Gaelic Books Council

## Garden Writers Guild

*Administrator* Angela Clarke, c/o Institute of
Horticulture, 14–15 Belgrave Square,
London SW1X 8PS
*tel* 020-7245 6943 *fax* 020-7245 6943
*email* gwg@horticulture.org.uk
*website* www.gardenwriters.co.uk
*Membership* £45 p.a.

Aims to raise the standards of gardening communicators. Administers annual awards to encourage excellence in garden writing, trade and consumer press journalism, TV and radio broadcasting, as well as garden photography. Founded 1991.

## The Gaskell Society

Far Yew Tree House, Over Tabley, Knutsford,
Cheshire WA16 0HN
*tel* (01565) 634668
*email* JoanLeach@aol.com
*website* www.gaskellsociety.users.btopenworld.com
*Hon. Secretary* Mrs Joan Leach
*Membership* £12 p.a., £16 corporate and overseas

Promotes and encourages the study and appreciation of the work and life of Elizabeth Cleghorn Gaskell. Holds regular meetings in Knutsford, London, Manchester and Bath, visits and residential conferences, produces an annual Journal and bi-annual Newsletters. Founded 1985.

## Gay Authors Workshop

Kathryn Byrd, BM Box 5700, London WC1N 3XX
*Membership* £7 p.a., £3 unwaged

Exists to encourage writers who are lesbian, gay or bisexual. Quarterly newsletter. Founded 1978.

## German Publishers' and Booksellers' Association

Postfach 100442, 60004 Frankfurt am Main, Germany
*tel* (069) 13060 *fax* (069) 1306201

*email* info@boev.de
*website* www.boersenverein.de
*General Manager* Dr Harald Heker

## The Ghost Story Society

PO Box 1360, Ashcroft, British Columbia V0K 1A0,
Canada
*tel* 250-453-2045 *fax* 250-453-2075
*email* ashtree@ash-tree.bc.ca
*website* www.ash-tree.bc.ca/GSS.html
*Secretary* Barbara Roden
*Membership* £22/US$35/Can.$40

Provides enthusiasts of the classic ghost story with a forum to discuss and appreciate the genre. Publishes *All Hallows* (3 p.a.) journal which contains news, articles, reviews and approx. 60pp of new fiction. Founded 1989.

## Graphical, Paper & Media Union

Keys House, 63–67 Bromham Road,
Bedford MK40 2AG
*tel* (01234) 351521 *fax* (01234) 270580
*email* general@gpmu.org.uk
*website* www.gpmu.org.uk
*General Secretary* Tony Dubbins

## Graham Greene Birthplace Trust

*Secretary* Ken Sherwood, Rhenigidale, Ivy House
Lane, Berkhamsted, Herts. HP4 2PP
*tel* (01442) 865158
*email* secretary@grahamgreenebt.org
*website* www.grahamgreenebt.org
*Membership* £8 p.a., £20 3 years

Exists to study the works of Graham Greene (1904–91). The Trust promotes the Annual Graham Greene Festival and Graham Greene trails. It publishes a quarterly newsletter, occasional papers, videos and CDs, and maintains a small archive. It administers the Graham Greene Memorial Awards. Special events and exhibitions are being planned to celebrate the centenary of Greene's birth on 2 October 2004. Founded 1997.

## The Greeting Card Association

United House, North Road, London N7 9DP
*tel* 020-7619 0396
*website* www.greetingcardassociation.org.uk
*Administrator* Sharon Little

See website for information on freelance designing and writing for greeting cards. Official magazine: *Progressive Greetings Worldwide*. See page 446.

## Guernsey Arts Council

La Fontaine, Courtil de la Fontaine, Kings Road,
St Peter Port, Guernsey GY1 1QB, CI
*email* tdguernsey@cwgsy.net eales@guernsey.net
*Chairman* Mrs Terry Domrille, *Secretary* Elizabeth
Eales *tel* (01481) 263189

## Guild of Agricultural Journalists
*Hon. General Secretary* Don Gomery,
Isfield Cottage, Church Road, Crowsborough,
East Sussex TN6 1BN
*tel* (01892) 611618 *fax* (01892) 613394
*email* don.gomery@farmingline.com
*website* www.gaj.org.uk
*President* Baroness Byford, *Chairman* Jonathan Page

Established to promote a high standard among
journalists who specialise in agricultural matters
and to assist them to increase their sources of
information and technical knowledge.

## The Guild of Aviation Artists
Trenchard House, 85 Farnborough Road,
Farnborough, Hants. GU14 6TF
*tel* (01252) 513123 *fax* (01252) 510505
*email* admin@gava.org.uk
*website* www.gava.org.uk
*President* Michael Turner PGAvA,
*Secretary/Administrator* Susan Gardner
*Membership* £60 p.a. Full Members (by invitation),
£45 Associates, £25 Friends

Formed to promote aviation art through the
organisation of exhibitions and meetings. Holds
annual open exhibition in July in London; £1000
prize for 'Aviation Painting of the Year'. Quarterly
members' newsletter. Founded 1971.

## Guild of Food Writers
*Administrator* Christina Thomas, 48 Crabtree Lane,
London SW6 6LW
*tel* 020-7610 1180 *fax* 020-7610 0299
*email* gfw@gfw.co.uk
*website* www.gfw.co.uk
*Membership* £70 p.a.

Aims to bring together professional food writers
including journalists, broadcasters and authors, to
print and issue an annual list of members, to extend
the range of members' knowledge and experience
by arranging discussions, tastings and visits, and to
encourage the development of new writers by every
means, including competitions and awards. There
are 7 awards for 2004 and entry is not restricted to
members of the Guild. Founded 1984.

## Guild of Health Writers
*Administrator* Jatinder Dua, 1 Broadmead Close,
Hampton, Middlesex TW12 3RT
*tel* 020-8941 2977 *fax* 020-8941 2977
*email* admin@healthwriters.com
*website* www.healthwriters.com
*Membership* £40 p.a.

Brings together professional journalists dedicated to
providing accurate, broad-based information about
health and related subjects to the public. Publishes a
directory of members. Founded 1995.

## The Guild of International Songwriters & Composers
Sovereign House, 12 Trewartha Road, Praa Sands,
Penzance, Cornwall TR20 9ST
*tel* (01736) 762826 *fax* (01736) 763328
*email* songmag@aol.com
*website* www.songwriters-guild.co.uk
*Secretary* Carole Ann Jones
*Membership* £42 p.a. UK, £50 EU/overseas

Gives advice to members on contractual and
copyright matters; assists with protection of
members rights; assists with analysis of members'
works; international collaboration register free to
members; outlines requirements to record
companies, publishers, artists. Publishes *Songwriting
& Composing* (quarterly).

## The Guild of Motoring Artists
*Administrator* David Purvis, 71 Brook Court,
Watling Street, Radlett, Herts. WD7 7JA
*tel* (01923) 853803
*email* sharon@scott-fairweather.freeserve.co.uk
*website* www.newspress.co.uk/guild
*Membership* £27.50 p.a., £22.50 Associate,
£18 Friend

Aims to promote, publicise and develop motoring
fine art; to build a recognised group of artists
interested in motoring art, holding events and
exchanging ideas and support; to hold motoring art
exhibitions. Founded 1986.

## The Guild of Motoring Writers
*Contact* General Secretary, 30 The Cravens,
Smallfield, Surrey RH6 9QS
*tel* (01342) 843294 *fax* (01342) 844093

Aims to raise the standard of motoring journalism.
For writers, broadcasters, photographers on matters
of motoring, but who are not connected with the
motor industry.

## Guild of Railway Artists
*Chief Executive Officer* F.P. Hodges Hon. GRA,
45 Dickins Road, Warwick CV34 5NS
*tel* (01926) 499246
*email* frank.hodges@tinyworld.co.uk
*website* www.railart.co.uk

Aims to forge a link between artists depicting
railway subjects and to give members a corporate
identity; also stages railway art exhibitions and
members' meetings. Founded 1979.

## Hakluyt Society
c/o The Map Library, The British Library,
96 Euston Road, London NW1 2DB
*tel* (01428) 641850 *fax* (01428) 641933
*email* office@hakluyt.com
*website* www.hakluyt.com

*President* Prof R.C. Bridges, *Hon. Secretary & Series Editor* Prof W.F. Ryan

Publication of original narratives of voyages, travels, naval expeditions, and other geographical records. Founded 1846.

## The Thomas Hardy Society
PO Box 1438, Dorchester, Dorset DT1 1YH
*tel* (01305) 251501 *fax* (01305) 251501
*email* info@hardysociety.org
*website* www.hardysociety.org
*Membership* £18 p.a., £22.50 overseas

Publishes *The Thomas Hardy Journal* (3 p.a.). Biennial conference in Dorchester, 2004. Founded 1967.

## Harleian Society
College of Arms, Queen Victoria Street, London EC4V 4BT
*tel* 020-7236 7728 *fax* 020-7248 6448
*Chairman* J. Brooke-Little CVO, MA, FSA, *Hon. Secretary* T.H.S. Duke, Chester Herald of Arms

Instituted for transcribing, printing and publishing the heraldic visitations of Counties, Parish Registers and any manuscripts relating to genealogy, family history and heraldry. Founded 1869.

## Hesketh Hubbard Art Society
17 Carlton House Terrace, London SW1Y 5BD
*tel* 020-7930 6844 *fax* 020-7839 7830
*website* www.mallgalleries.org.uk
*President* Simon Whittle

Weekly life drawing classes open to all.

## The Hilliard Society of Miniaturists
*The Executive Officer* Pauline Warner, Priory Lodge, 7 Priory Road, Wells, Somerset BA5 1SR
*tel* (01749) 674472 *fax* (01749) 674472
*website* www.art-in-miniature.org
*President* Heather O. Catchpole RMS, PHSF, MASSA, MASF
*Membership* From £25 p.a.

Founded to increase knowledge and promote the art of miniature painting. Annual Exhibition held in June at Wells; seminars; Young People's Awards (11–19 years); Newsletter. Member of the World Federation of Miniaturists. Founded 1982.

## The James Hilton Society
*Hon. Secretary* Dr J.R. Hammond, 49 Beckingthorpe Drive, Bottesford, Nottingham NG13 0DN
*website* www.jameshiltonsociety.co.uk
*Membership* £10 p.a. (£7 concessions)

Aims to promote interest in the life and work of novelist and scriptwriter James Hilton (1900–54). Publishes quarterly newsletter and organises conferences. Founded 2000.

## Historical Novel Society
*Secretary* Richard Lee, Marine Cottage, The Strand, Starcross, Devon EX6 8NY
*tel* (01626) 891962
*email* histnovel@aol.com
*website* www.historicalnovelsociety.com
*Membership* £18 p.a.

Promotes the historical novel via short story competitions, conferences, a society magazine *Solander* (2 p.a.) and reviews (*Historical Novels Review*, quarterly). Membership is open to all and includes eminent novelists. Founded 1997.

## The Sherlock Holmes Society of London
*General enquiries* Heather Owen, 64 Graham Road, London SW19 3SS
*tel* 020-8540 7657 *fax* 020-8540 7657
*email* heatherowen@tiscali.co.uk
*website* www.sherlock-holmes.org.uk
*Membership* R.J. Ellis, 13 Crofton Avenue, Orpington, Kent BR6 8DU
*tel/fax* (01689) 811314
*email* shsl221b@aol.com
*President* A.D. Howlett MA, LLB, *Chairman* Philip Porter
*Membership* £14 p.a. UK/Europe, £18 Far East, US$30.50 USA

Aims to bring together those who have a common interest as readers and students of the literature of Sherlock Holmes, and to encourage the pursuit of knowledge of the public and private lives of Sherlock Holmes and Dr Watson. Membership includes *The Sherlock Holmes Journal* (2 p.a.). Founded 1951.

## Hopkins Society
*Secretary* Oughtrington Rectory, Lymm, Cheshire WA13 9JB
*website* www.hopkinsoc.freeserve.co.uk
*Membership* £7 p.a., £10 outside Europe

Aims to promote and celebrate the work of the poet Gerard Manley Hopkins, to inform members about the latest publications about Hopkins and to support educational projects concerning his work. Annual lecture held in North Wales in the spring; publishes a newsletter (2 p.a.) Founded 1990.

## Horror Writers Association (HWA)
PO Box 50577, Palo Alto, CA 94303, USA
*email* hwa@horror.org
*website* www.horror.org
*UK* Jo Fletcher, 24 Pearl Road, London E17 4QZ
*Membership* $65 p.a. North America, $75/£48 elsewhere

A worldwide organisation of writers and publishing professionals dedicated to promoting the interests of writers of horror and dark fantasy. There are 3 levels of membership: for new writers, established writers and non-writing horror professionals. Founded 1987.

## Housman Society
80 New Road, Bromsgrove, Worcs. B60 2LA
*tel* (01527) 874136
*email* info@housman-society.co.uk
*website* www.housman-society.co.uk
*Chairman* Jim Page
*Membership* £10 p.a.

Aims to foster interest in and promote knowledge of A.E. Housman and his family. Sponsors a lecture at the Guardian Hay Festival. Publishes an annual journal and bi-annual newsletter. Founded 1973.

## Incorporated Society of Musicians
10 Stratford Place, London W1C 1AA
*tel* 020-7629 4413 *fax* 020-7408 1538
*email* membership@ism.org
*website* www.ism.org
*President* Prof John Morehen, *Chief Executive* Neil Hoyle
*Membership* £115 p.a.

Professional body for musicians. Aims to promote the art of music; protect the interests and raise the standards of the musical profession; provide services, support and advice for its members. Publishes *Music Journal* (12 p.a.), a yearbook and 3 Registers of Specialists annually.

## Independent Publishers Guild
PO Box 93, Royston, Herts. SG8 5GH
*tel* (01763) 247014 *fax* (01763) 246293
*Membership* £85 + VAT p.a. Open to new and established publishers and book packagers; supplier membership is available to specialists in fields allied to publishing (but not printers and binders)

Provides an information and contact network for independent publishers. The IPG also voices the concerns of member companies with the book trade. Founded 1962.

## Independent Theatre Council (ITC)
12 The Leather Market, Weston Street, London SE1 3ER
*tel* 020-7403 1727 *fax* 020-7403 1745
*email* admin@itc-arts.org
*website* www.itc-arts.org
*Director* Charlotte Jones
*Membership* Prices vary according to type of membership

ITC is the UK management association for the performing arts. It empowers and supports its diverse membership by providing high-quality management, legal and financial advice; developing tailored arts management training; creating excellent networking opportunities; and representing the sector with a powerful, articulate

voice. ITC is committed to working with a range of partners to promote, develop and support its members. Founded 1974.

## Institute of Designers in Ireland
*Details* Hon. Secretary, 8 Merrion Square, Dublin 2, Republic of Ireland
*tel* (01) 7167885 *fax* (01) 7168736
Membership €171 p.a. full, €57 associate

Irish design profession's representative body, covering every field of design. Founded 1972.

## Institute of Linguists
Saxon House, 48 Southwark Street, London SE1 1UN
*tel* 020-7940 3100 *fax* 020-7940 3101
*email* info@iol.org.uk
*website* www.iol.org.uk

Professional association for translators, interpreters and language tutors with 'Find-a-Linguist' website service. International language examinations run by its Educational Trust. One subsidiary NRPSI Ltd manages the National Register of Public Service Interpreters. Another, Language Services Ltd, offers customised assessments and services.

## The Institute of Translation & Interpreting (ITI)
*Contact* The Secretary, Fortuna House, South Fifth Street, Milton Keynes MK9 2EU
*tel* (01908) 325250 *fax* (01908) 325259
*email* info@iti.org.uk
*website* www.iti.org.uk

A professional association of translators and interpreters which aims to promote the highest standards in translating and interpreting. It has a strong corporate membership and runs professional development courses and conferences, sometimes in conjunction with its language, regional and subject networks. Membership is open to those with a genuine and proven involvement in translation and interpreting of all kinds, but particularly technical and commercial translation. As a full and active member of the International Federation of Translators, it maintains good contacts with translators and interpreters worldwide. ITI's directory of members (online) and its bi-monthly bulletin are available from the Secretariat.

## The International Guild of Artists
Briargate, 2 The Brambles, Ilkley, West Yorkshire LS29 9DH
*Director* Leslie Simpson FRSA

Organises 4 seasonal exhibitions per year for 3 national societies: Society of Miniaturists, British Society of Painters in Oils, Pastels & Acrylics and British Watercolour Society. Promotes these 3 societies in countries outside the British Isles.

## International Publishers Association

3 avenue de Miremont, CH–1206 Geneva,
Switzerland
*tel* (022) 346-30-18 *fax* (022) 347-57-17
*email* secretariat@ipa.vie.org
*President* Pere Vicens, *Secretary-General* Mr Jens
Bammel
Founded 1896.

## International Society of Typographic Designers

*Hon. Secretary* Helen Cornish, Chapelfield Cottage,
Randwick, Stroud, Glos. GL6 6HS
*tel* (01453) 759311 *fax* (01453) 767466
*email* helen.randwick@virgin.net
*Chair* Freda Sack FISTD

Advises and acts on matters of professional and
educational practice, provides a better
understanding of the typographic craft and the
rapidly changing technology in the graphic
industries by lectures, discussions and through the
journal *Typographic*. Students of typography and
graphic design are encouraged to gain membership
of the Society by entering the annual student
assessment project. Founded 1928.

## International Theatre Exchange

c/o Drama Association of Wales, The Old Library,
Singleton Road, Splott, Cardiff CF24 2ET
*tel* 029-2045 2200 *fax* 029-2045 2277
*email* aled.daw@virgin.net
*website* www.aitaiata.org
*Secretariat* Aled Rhys-Jones

Aims to encourage, foster and promote exchanges
of theatre; student, educational, adult, theatre
activities at international level. To organise
international seminars, workshops, courses and
conferences, and to collect and collate information
of all types for national and international
dissemination.

## International Visual Communication Association (IVCA)

19 Pepper Street, Glengall Bridge,
London E14 9RP
*tel* 020-7512 0571 *fax* 020-7512 0591
*email* info@ivca.org
*website* www.ivca.org
*Membership Secretary* Nick Gardiner
*Membership* From £175 p.a.

For those who work in business communication.
Aims to promote the industry and provide a
collective voice; provides a range of services,
publications and events to help existing and
potential users to make the most of what video,
film, multimedia and live events can offer their
business. Founded 1987.

## The Irish Book Publishers' Association –
see CLÉ: The Irish Book Publishers' Association

## The Irish Copyright Licensing Agency

19 Parnell Square, Dublin 1, Republic of Ireland
*tel* (01) 8729202 *fax* (01) 8722035
*email* icla@esatlink.com
*Executive Director* Samantha Holman

Licences schools and other users of copyright
material to photocopy extracts of such material, and
distributes the monies collected to the authors and
publishers whose works have been copied. Founded
1992.

## Irish Playwrights and Screenwriters Guild

Irish Writers' Centre, 19 Parnell Square, Dublin 1,
Republic of Ireland
*tel* (01) 8721302 *fax* (01) 8726282
*email* moffatts@intigo.ie
*Secretary* Sean Moffatt

Represents writers' interests in theatre, radio and
screenwriting. Founded 1969.

## Irish Translators' Association

Irish Writers' Centre, 19 Parnell Square, Dublin 1,
Republic of Ireland
*tel* (01) 8721302 *fax* (01) 8726282
*email* netonnet@iol.ie
*website* www.translatorsassociation.ie
*Hon. Secretary* Annette Schiller
*Membership* p.a. €55 professional, €30 ordinary,
€15 student, €80 corporate

Promotes translation in Ireland, the translation of
Irish authors abroad and the practical training of
translators, and promotes the interests of
translators. Catalogues the works of translators in
areas of Irish interest; secures the awarding of prizes
and bursaries for translators; and maintains a
detailed register of translators. Founded 1986.

## Irish Writers Centre

19 Parnell Square, Dublin 1, Republic of Ireland
*tel* (01) 8721302 *fax* (01) 8726282
*email* info@writerscentre.ie
*website* www.writerscentre.ie
*Director* Cathal McCabe, *Administrator* Katherine
Moore

National organisation for the promotion of writers
and writing in Ireland. It runs an extensive
programme of events at its headquarters; it operates
the Writer in Community Scheme which funds
events throughout Ireland; it runs an education
programme which offers courses and workshops in
writing; it operates an International Writers'
Exchange Programme. See website for further
details. Founded 1991.

## Irish Writers' Union/Comhar na Scríbhneoirí

Irish Writers' Centre, 19 Parnell Square, Dublin 1, Republic of Ireland
*tel* (01) 8721302 *fax* (01) 8726282
*email* info@writerscentre.ie
*website* www.ireland.writers.com
*Chairman* Conor Kostick, *Secretary* Anthony P. Quinn

The Union aims to advance the cause of writing as a profession, to achieve better remuneration and more favourable conditions for writers and to provide a means for the expression of the collective opinion of writers on matters affecting their profession. Founded 1986.

## The Richard Jefferies Society

*Hon. Secretary* Phyllis Treitel, Eidsvoll, Bedwells Heath, Boars Hill, Oxford OX1 5JE
*tel* (01865) 735678
*Membership* £7 p.a. Worldwide membership

Promotes interest in the life, works and associations of the naturalist and novelist, Richard Jefferies; helps to preserve buildings and memorials, and cooperates in the development of a Museum in his birthplace. Arranges regular meetings in Swindon, and occasionally elsewhere; organises outings and displays; publishes a Journal and a Newsletter in the spring and an Annual Report in September. Founded 1950.

## The Johnson Society

Johnson Birthplace Museum, Breadmarket Street, Lichfield, Staffs. WS13 6LG
*tel* (01543) 264972
*email* honlitsec@lichfieldrambler.co.uk
*website* www.lichfieldrambler.co.uk
*Hon. General Secretary* Norma Hooper, *Hon. Literary Secretary* John Dudley

Aims to encourage the study of the life and works of Dr Samuel Johnson; to preserve the memorials, associations, books, manuscripts and letters of Dr Johnson and his contemporaries; and to work with the local council in the preservation of his birthplace.

## Johnson Society of London

*Secretary* Mrs Zandra O'Donnell MA, 255 Baring Road, London SE12 0BQ
*tel* 020-8851 0173
*President* The Viscountess Eccles

Aims to study the life and works of Dr Johnson, and to perpetuate his memory in the city of his adoption. Founded 1928.

## The Sheila Kaye-Smith Society

*Secretary* Christine Hayward, 22 The Cloisters, St John's Road, St Leonards-on-Sea, East Sussex TN37 6JT
*tel* (01424) 422139 *fax* (01424) 883268
*Membership* £6 p.a. single, £9 joint

Aims to stimulate and widen interest in the work of the Sussex writer and novelist, Sheila Kaye-Smith (1887–1956). Produces *The Gleam* (annual) and occasional papers, and organises talks. Founded 1987.

## Keats-Shelley Memorial Association

*Hon. Secretary* David Leigh-Hunt, 1 Satchwell Walk, Leamington Spa, Warks. CV32 4QE
*tel* (01926) 427400 *fax* (01926) 335133
*Chairman* Hon. Mrs H. Cullen
*Membership* £10 p.a. minimum

Owns and supports house in Rome where John Keats died as a museum open to the public, and celebrates the poets Keats, Shelley and Leigh Hunt. Occasional meetings; poetry competitions; annual *Review*, 2 literary awards, and progress reports. Founded 1903.

## Kent and Sussex Poetry Society

*Contact* John Arnold, 39 Rockington Way, Crowborough, East Sussex TN6 2NJ
*tel* (01892) 662781
*Secretary* Joyce Mandel Walter
*email* joyce345@yahoo.co.uk, john@kentandsussexpoetrysociety.org
*website* www.kentandsussexpoetrysociety.org
*President* Laurence Lerner, *Chairman* Clive Eastwood
*Membership* £10 p.a. full, £5 country members/ concessions

Based in Tunbridge Wells, the Society was formed to create a greater interest in poetry. Well-known poets address the Society, a Folio of members' work is produced and a full programme of recitals, discussions, competitions and readings is provided. See page 558 for details of Open Poetry Competition. Founded 1946.

## The Kipling Society

*Hon. Secretary* Jane Keskar, 6 Clifton Road, London W9 1SS
*tel* 020-7286 0194
*email* jane@keskar.fsworld.co.uk
*website* www.kipling.org.uk
*Membership* £22 p.a. (£20 p.a. for standing orders)

Aims to honour and extend the influence of Rudyard Kipling (1865–1936), to assist in the study of his writings, to hold discussion meetings, to publish a quarterly journal, and to maintain a Kipling Library in London and a Kipling Room in The Grange, Rottingdean, near Brighton.

## The Charles Lamb Society

BM Elia, London WC1N 3XX
*website* www.users.ox.ac.uk/~scat1492/clsoc.htm
*Chairman* Nicholas Powell, *Membership Secretary* Cecilia Powell

*Membership* Personal: £12/$28 p.a. (single), £18 (double). Corporate: £18/$42 p.a.

Publishes the academic journal *The Charles Lamb Bulletin* (quarterly). The Society's extensive library of books and MSS by and about Charles Lamb is housed at the Guildhall Library, Aldermanbury, London EC2P 2EJ. Founded 1935.

### The Lancashire Authors' Association

*General Secretary* Eric Holt, 5 Quakerfields, Westhoughton, Bolton BL5 2BJ
*tel* (01942) 791390
*Membership* £10 p.a.

'For writers and lovers of Lancashire literature and history.' Publishes *The Record* (quarterly). Founded 1909.

### The D.H. Lawrence Society

*Secretary* Ron Faulks, 24 Briarwood Avenue, Nottingham NG3 6JQ
*tel* 0115-950 3008
*Membership* £14 UK, £16 Europe, £19 rest of world, UK retired persons and students £12

Aims to bring together people interested in D.H. Lawrence (1885–1930), to encourage study of his work, and to provide information and guides for people visiting Eastwood. Founded 1974.

### The T.E. Lawrence Society

PO Box 728, Oxford OX2 6YP
*website* www.telsociety.org
*Membership* £18 p.a., £23 overseas

Promotes the memory of T.E. Lawrence and furthers knowledge by research into his life; publishes *Journal* (bi-annual) and *Newsletter* (quarterly). Founded 1985.

### League of Canadian Poets

920 Yonge Street, Suite 608, Toronto, Ontario M4W 3C7, Canada
*tel* 416-504-1657 *fax* 416-504 0096
*email* info@poets.ca
*website* www.poets.ca
*Executive Director* Edita Page

Aims to promote the interests of poets and to advance Canadian poetry in Canada and abroad. Administers 3 annual awards; operates the 'Poetry Spoken Here' webstore; runs National Poetry Month; publishes a newsletter and *Poetry Markets for Canadians*, *Who's Who in The League of Canadian Poets*, *Poets in the Classroom* (teaching guide). Promotes and sells members' poetry books. Founded 1966.

### Little Theatre Guild of Great Britain

*Public Relations Officer* Michael Shipley, 121 Darwen Road, Bromley Cross, Bolton BL7 9BG
*tel* (01204) 304103

Aims to promote closer cooperation amongst the little theatres constituting its membership; to act as coordinating and representative body on behalf of the little theatres; to maintain and advance the highest standards in the art of theatre; and to assist in encouraging the establishment of other little theatres. Its yearbook is available to non-members for £5.

### The Marlowe Society

*Newsletter Editor & Webmaster* Roger Hards, Venusmead, 36 Venus Street, Congresbury, Bristol BS49 5EZ
*tel* (01934) 834780
*email* rogerhards@venusmead.go-plus.net
*Membership* £12 p.a., £7 concessions, £15/$26 overseas

Registered charity that aims to extend appreciation and widen recognition of Christopher Marlowe (1564–93) as the foremost poet and dramatist preceding Shakespeare, whose development he influenced. Holds meetings and cultural visits, and issues a bi-annual magazine. Founded 1955.

### The John Masefield Society

*Chairman* Peter J.R. Carter, The Frith, Ledbury, Herefordshire HR8 1LW
*tel* (01531) 633800 *fax* (01531) 631647
*email* petercarter@btinternet.com
*website* www.sas.ac.uk/ies
*Membership* £5 p.a., £10 overseas, £8 family/institution

Aims to stimulate interest in, and public awareness and enjoyment of, the life and works of the poet John Masefield. Holds an annual lecture and other, less formal, readings and gatherings; publishes an annual journal and frequent newsletters. Founded 1992.

### Master Photographers Association

Jubilee House, 1 Chancery Lane, Darlington, Co. Durham DL1 5QP
*tel* (01325) 356555 *fax* (01325) 357813
*email* info@mpauk.com
*website* www.mpa@mpauk.com
*Membership* £115 p.a.

Exists to promote and protect professional photographers. Members qualify for awards of Licentiate, Associate and Fellowship.

### Mechanical-Copyright Protection Society Ltd (MCPS)

Copyright House, 29–33 Berners Street, London W1T 3AB
*tel* 020-7580 5544, 020-8769 4400 *fax* 020-7306 4455, 020-8769 8792
*website* www.mcps.co.uk
*Chief Executive* John Hutchinson

## The Media Society

*Secretary* Peter Dannheisser, 56 Roseneath Road,
London SW11 6AQ
*tel* 020-7223 5631 *fax* 020-7223 5631
*Membership* £35 p.a.

Exists to promote and encourage collective and
independent research into the standards,
performance, organisation and economics of the
media and hold regular discussions, debates, etc on
subjects of topical or special interest and concern to
print and broadcast journalists and others working
in or with the media. Founded 1973.

## Mediawatch-UK

*Director* John C. Beyer, 3 Willow House,
Kennington Road, Ashford, Kent TN24 0NR
*tel* (01233) 633936 *fax* (01233) 633836
*email* info@mediawatchuk.org
*website* www.mediawatchuk.org
*Chairman* John Milton Whatmore
*Membership* £10 p.a.

Aims to encourage viewers and listeners to react
effectively to programme content; to initiate and
stimulate public discussion and parliamentary
debate concerning the effects of broadcasting, and
other mass media, on the individual, the family and
society; to secure – then uphold – effective
legislation to control obscenity and pornography in
the media. Founded 1965.

## Medical Journalists Association

*Hon. Secretary* Sue Lowell, 101 Cambridge Gardens,
London W10 6JE
*tel* 020-8968 1614 *fax* 020-8968 7910
*email* sue4382@aol.com
*Chairman* John Illman
*Membership* £30 p.a.

Aims to improve the quality and practice of health
and medical journalism. Administers major awards
for health and medical journalism and broadcasting.
Publishes The *MJA Directory* and *MJA News*
newsletter. Founded 1966.

## Medical Writers Group – see The Society
of Authors, page 495

## William Morris Society

Kelmscott House, 26 Upper Mall, London W6 9TA
*tel* 020-8741 3735 *fax* 020-8748 5207
*email* william.morris@care4free.net
*website* www.morrissociety.org
*Secretary* Peter Faulkner

Aims to spread knowledge of the life, work and
ideas of William Morris; publishes *Newsletter*
(quarterly) and *Journal* (2 p.a.). Library and
collections open to the public Thurs and Sat,
2–5pm. Founded 1955.

## Music Publishers Association Ltd

3rd Floor, Strandgate, 20 York Buildings,
London WC2N 6JU
*tel* 020-7839 7779 *fax* 020-7839 7776
*email* info@mpaonline.org.uk
*Chief Executive* Sarah Faulder
*Membership* Details on request

Trade organisation representing over 200 UK music
publisher members: promotes and safeguards its
members' interests in copyright, trade and related
matters. Sub-committees and groups deal with
particular interests. Founded 1881.

## National Acrylic Painters' Association (NAPA)

134 Rake Lane, Wallasey, Wirral,
Merseyside CH45 1JW
*tel* 0151-639 2980 *fax* 0151-639 2980
*Membership* The Executive Council,
c/o Alan Edwards, 6 Berwyn Boulevard, Bebington,
Wirral CH63 5LR
*tel* 0151-645 8433
*email* alan.edwards420@ntlworld.com
*websites* www.art-arena.com/napa,
www.watercolor-online.com/napa, www.napa-usa.org
*President* Alwyn Crawshaw, *Director/Founder*
Kenneth J. Hodgson

Promotes interest in, and encourages excellence and
innovation in, the work of painters in acrylic. Holds
an annual exhibition and regional shows: awards are
made. Worldwide membership. Publishes a
newsletter known as the *International NAPA
Newspages*. Founded 1985; American Division
established 1995.

## National Association of Press Agencies

The Administrator, 41 Lansdowne Crescent,
Leamington Spa, Warks. CV32 4PR
*tel* (01926) 424181 *fax* (01926) 424760
*website* www.napa.org.uk
*Membership* £250 p.a.

Trade association representing the interests of the
leading national news and photographic agencies.
Founded 1983.

## National Association of Writers' Groups

*Headquarters* The Arts Centre, Biddick Lane,
Washington, Tyne and Wear NE38 2AB
*Secretary* Diane Wilson, 40 Burstall Hill,
Bridlington, East Yorkshire YO16 7GA
*tel* (01262) 609228 *fax* (01262) 609228
*email* nawg@tesco.net
*website* www.nawg.co.uk
*Membership* £25 p.a. plus £5 registration per group;
£10 Associate individuals

Aims 'to advance the education of the general public
throughout the UK, including the Channel Islands, by

promoting the study and art of writing in all its aspects.' Publishes *Link* bi-monthly magazine. Annual Festival of Writing held in Durham 3–5 Sept 2005. Annual Creative Writing Competition. Founded 1995.

## National Campaign for the Arts (NCA)

Pegasus House, 37–43 Sackville Street, London W1S 3EH
*tel* 020-7333 0375 *fax* 020-7333 0660
*Director* Victoria Todd, *Deputy Director* Anna Leatherdale
*Membership* £50 p.a., £25 unwaged; special rates for organisations

Independent advocacy and lobbying organisation that exists to promote the interests of the arts world in all its diversity. It is funded through membership subscriptions to ensure its independence. Founded 1985.

## National Council for the Training of Journalists (NCTJ)

Latton Bush Centre, Southern Way, Harlow, Essex CM18 7BL
*tel* (01279) 430009 *fax* (01279) 438008
*email* info@nctj.com
*website* www.nctj.com

A registered charity which aims to advance the education and training of trainee journalists, including press photographers. Full-time courses run at 34 colleges/universities in the UK. Distance learning courses also available in newspaper and magazine journalism and sub-editing. Founded 1952.

## National Library for the Blind (NLB)

Far Cromwell Road, Bredbury, Stockport SK6 2SG
*tel* 0161-355 2000 *minicom* 0161-355 2043
*fax* 0161-355 2098
*email* enquiries@nlbuk.org
*website* www.nlb-online.org

The website provides a gateway to library and information services for visually impaired people.

## National Literacy Trust

Swire House, 59 Buckingham Gate, London SW1E 6AJ
*tel* 020-7828 2435 *fax* 020-7931 9986
*email* contact@literacytrust.org.uk
*websites* www.literacytrust.org.uk, www.rif.org.uk, www.readon.org.uk
*Director* Neil McClelland, *PA* Jacky Taylor

Independent registered charity dedicated to building a literate nation in which everyone enjoys the skills, self-esteem and pleasures that literacy can bring. The only organisation concerned with raising literacy standards for all age groups throughout the UK. Maintains an extensive website with literacy news, summaries of key issues, research and examples of practice nationwide; organises an

annual conference, courses and training events; publishes a quarterly magazine, *Literacy Today*, and runs a range of initiatives to turn promising ideas into effective action. Initiatives include the National Reading Campaign, funded by the government; Reading is Fundamental, UK, which provides free books to children; Reading The Game, involving the professional football community; the Talk To Your Baby campaign; and the Literacy and Social Inclusion Project, a partnership with the Basic Skills Agency. Founded 1993.

## National Society for Education in Art and Design

The Gatehouse, Corsham Court, Corsham, Wilts. SN13 0BZ
*tel* (01249) 714825 *fax* (01249) 716138
*website* www.nsead.org
*General Secretary* Dr John Steers NDD, ATC, AE, PhD

The leading national authority concerned with art, craft and design across all phases of education in the UK. Offers the benefits of membership of a professional association, a learned society and a trade union. Has representatives on National and Regional Committees concerned with Art and Design Education. Publishes *Journal of Art and Design Education* (3 p.a.; Blackwells) and *Start* magazine for primary schools. Founded 1888.

## National Society of Painters, Sculptors and Printmakers

*Hon. Secretary* Gwen Spencer, 122 Copse Hill, London SW20 0NL
*tel* 020-8946 7878
*website* www.nationalsociety.co.uk

An annual exhibition at the Atrium Gallery, Whiteleys, Queensway, London W2 (8–21 Nov, 2004). Not an open exhibition but artists are welcome to apply for membership. Newsletter (2 p.a.) for members. Founded 1930.

## National Union of Journalists

*Head Office* Headland House, 308–312 Gray's Inn Road, London WC1X 8DP
*tel* 020-7278 7916 *fax* 020-7837 8143
*email* acorn.house@nuj.org.uk

Trade union for working journalists with 28,000 members and 147 branches throughout the UK and the Republic of Ireland, and in Paris, Brussels, and the Netherlands. It covers the newspaper press, news agencies and broadcasting, the major part of periodical and book publishing, and a number of public relations departments and consultancies, information services and Prestel-Viewdata services. Administers disputes, unemployment, benevolent and provident benefits. Official publications: *The Journalist* (bi-monthly), *Freelance Directory*, *Freelance Fees Guide* and policy pamphlets.

## National Viewers' and Listeners' Association – see Mediawatch-UK

## NCTJ – see National Council for the Training of Journalists (NCTJ)

## The Edith Nesbit Society
21 Churchfields, West Malling, Kent ME19 6RJ
*email* mmccarthy30@hotmail.com
*website* www.the railway-children.co.uk
*Membership* £6 p.a.; £12 organisations/overseas

Aims to promote an interest in the life and works of Edith Nesbit (1858–1924) by means of talks, a regular newsletter and and other publications, and visits to relevant places. Founded 1996.

## New English Art Club
17 Carlton House Terrace, London SW1Y 5BD
*tel* 020-7930 6844 *fax* 020-7839 7830
*website* www.mallgalleries.org.uk
*President* Ken Howard RA

For all those interested in the art of painting, and the promotion of fine arts. Open Annual Exhibition at the Mall Galleries, The Mall, London SW1, open to all working in painting, drawing, pastels and prints.

## New Playwrights Trust – see Writernet

## New Science Fiction Alliance (NSFA)
Chris Reed, BBR, PO Box 625, Sheffield S201 3GY
*website* www.bbr-online.com/catalogue
*Publicity Officer* Chris Reed

The NSFA is committed to supporting the work of new writers and artists by promoting independent and small press publications worldwide. It was founded by a group of independent publishers to give writers the opportunity to explore the small press and find the right market for their material. It offers a mail order service for magazines. Founded 1989.

## Newspaper Press Fund
Dickens House, 35 Wathen Road, Dorking, Surrey RH4 1JY
*tel* (01306) 887511 *fax* (01306) 888212
*Secretary* David Ilott

For the relief of hardship amongst journalists, their widows and dependants. Financial assistance and retirement housing are provided.

## The Newspaper Publishers Association Ltd
34 Southwark Bridge Road, London SE1 9EU
*tel* 020-7207 2200 *fax* 020-7928 2067

## Newspaper Society
Bloomsbury House, 74–77 Great Russell Street, London WC1B 3DA

*tel* 020-7636 7014 *fax* 020-7631 5119
*AdDoc* DX35701 Bloomsbury
*email* ns@newspapersoc.org.uk
*website* www.newspapersoc.org.uk
*Director* David Newell

## New Writing North
2 School Lane, Whickham, Newcastle upon Tyne NE16 4SL
*tel* 0191-488 8580 *fax* 0191-488 8576
*email* mail@newwritingnorth.com
*website* www.newwritingnorth.com
*Director* Claire Malcolm, *Administrator* Silvana Michelini, *Education Director* Anna Summerford

The literature development agency for the North East. Offers advice and support to writers of poetry, prose and plays. See website. Founded 1996.

## New Zealand Writers Guild
PO Box 47886, Ponsonby, Auckland, New Zealand
*tel* (09) 360-1408 *fax* (09) 360-1409
*email* info@nzwritersguild.org.nz
*website* www.nzwritersguild.org.nz
*Membership* NZ$150-$400 full, $99 associate

Aims to represent the interests of New Zealand writers (TV, film, radio and theatre); to establish and improve minimum conditions of work and rates of compensation for writers; to provide professional services for members. Founded 1975.

## Outdoor Writers' Guild
*Secretary* Hazelle Jackson, PO Box 118, Twickenham TW1 2XB
*tel* 020-8538 9468 *fax* 020-8538 9468
*email* info@owg.org.uk
*website* www.owg.org.uk
*Membership* £65 p.a.

Association of the leading practitioners in outdoor media; represents members' interests to representative bodies in the outdoor industry; circulates members with news of media opportunities; provides a forum for members to meet colleagues and others in the outdoor industry. Presents annual literary and photographic awards. Members include writers, journalists, broadcasters, illustrators, photographers, editors and publishers. Founded 1980.

## Wilfred Owen Association
17 Belmont, Shrewsbury SY1 1TE
*website* www.1914-18.co.uk/owen
*Membership* £6 p.a. (£10 overseas), £15 groups/institutions, £4 concessions

Aims to commemorate the life and work of Wilfred Owen, and to encourage and enhance appreciation of his work through visits, public events, a newsletter and journal. Founded 1989.

## Oxford Bibliographical Society
Bodleian Library, Broad Street, Oxford OX1 3BG
*Secretary* Dr Julia Walworth, Merton College, Oxford
*email* treasurer@oxbibsoc.org.uk
*website* www.users.bathspa.ac.uk/oxbibsoc/
*Membership* £20 p.a.

Exists to encourage bibliographical research.
Founded 1922.

## PACT (Producers Alliance for Cinema and Television)
45 Mortimer Street, London W1W 8HJ
*tel* 020-7331 6000 *fax* 020-7331 6700
*email* enquiries@pact.co.uk
*website* www.pact.co.uk
*Chief Executive* John McVay, *Information Manager*
David Alan Mills
*Pact Scotland* 249 West George Street,
Glasgow G2 4QE
*tel* 0141-222 4880 *fax* 0141-222 4881
*email* margaret@pact.co.uk
*Head of Nations & Regions* Margaret Scott

The main trade association for feature film and
independent TV production companies. Represents
the interests of over 1000 production companies
throughout the UK: promotes and protects the
commercial interests of its members; lobbies
government and regulators on their behalf;
negotiates terms of trade with broadcasters; provides
a range of membership services including advice on
business affairs, industrial relations and legal advice;
operates a copyright registration service for
members' proposals and treatments for films and
TV programmes. Its representative office in Glasgow
serves the interests of its regional members.

## The Pastel Society
17 Carlton House Terrace, London SW1Y 5BD
*tel* 020-7930 6844 *fax* 020-7839 7830
*website* www.mallgalleries.org.uk
*President* Moira Huntly

Pastel and drawings in pencil or chalk. Annual
Exhibition open to all artists working in dry media
held at the Mall Galleries, The Mall, London SW1.
Members elected from approved candidates' list.
Founded 1899.

## The Mervyn Peake Society
*Treasurer* Frank Surry, 2 Mount Park Road,
London W5 2RP
*Hon. President* Sebastian Peake, *Chairman* Brian
Sibley
*Membership* £12 p.a. UK and Europe, £5 students,
£16 all other countries

Devoted to recording the life and works of Mervyn
Peake; publishes a journal and newsletter. Founded
1975.

## PEN, International
*International Secretary* Terry Carlbom,
9–10 Charterhouse Buildings, Goswell Road,
London EC1M 7AT
*tel* 020-7253 4308 *fax* 020-7253 5711
*email* intpen@dircon.co.uk
*website* www.internationalpen.org.uk
*International President* Jii Gruša
*Membership* Apply to Centres

A world association of writers. PEN was founded in
1921 by C.A. Dawson Scott under the presidency of
John Galsworthy, to promote friendship and understanding between writers and to defend freedom of
expression within and between all nations.

The initials PEN stand for Poets, Playwrights,
Editors, Essayists, Novelists – but membership is
open to all writers of standing (including
translators), whether men or women, without
distinction of creed or race, who subscribe to these
fundamental principles. PEN takes no part in state
or party politics. The International PEN Writers in
Prison Committee works on behalf of writers
imprisoned for exercising their right to freedom of
expression, a right implicit in the PEN Charter to
which all members subscribe. The International
PEN Translations and Linguistic Rights Committee
strives to promote the translations of works by
writers in the lesser-known languages and to defend
those languages. The Writers for Peace Committee
exists to find ways in which writers can work for
peaceful co-existence in the world. The Women
Writers' Committee works to promote women's
writing and publishing in developing countries. The
Writers in Exile Network helps exiled writers.
International Congresses are held most years. The
70th Congress will be held in Tromsø, Norway.

Membership of any one Centre implies
membership of all Centres; at present 138
autonomous Centres exist throughout the world.

Associate membership is available for writers not
yet eligible for full membership and for persons
connected with literature. The English Centre has a
programme of literary lectures, discussion, dinners
and parties. A yearly Writers' Day is open to the
public as are some literary lectures.

### English PEN Centre
*President* Alastair Niven OBE
*Administrative Director* Susanna Nicklin, Lancaster
House, 33 Islington High Street, London N1 9LH
*tel* 020-7713 0023 *fax* 020-7713 0005
*email* enquiries@englishpen.org
*website* www.englishpen.org

### Scottish PEN Centre
*President* Tessa Ransford OBE, 31 Royal Park Terrace,
Edinburgh EH8 8JA
*email* info@scottishpen.org
*website* www.scottishpen.org

**Irish PEN Centre**
*President* Brian Friel
*Secretary* Christine Dwyer Hickey, Irish Pen Cente,
Dunoon, Old Lucan Road, Palmerstown, Dublin 20,
Republic of Ireland
*tel* (353) 1 623 9133
*email* irishpen@ireland.com

## Performing Right Society Ltd (PRS)
Copyright House, 29–33 Berners Street,
London W1T 3AB
*tel* 020-7580 5544 *fax* 020-7306 4455
*website* www.prs.co.uk
*Chief Executive* John Hutchinson

## Periodical Publishers Association
Queens House, 28 Kingsway, London WC2B 6JR
*tel* 020-7404 4166 *fax* 020-7404 4167
*email* info1@ppa.co.uk
*website* www.ppa.co.uk
*Chief Executive* Ian Locks

## The Personal Managers' Association Ltd
*Liaison Secretary* Angela Adler, 1 Summer Road,
East Molesey, Surrey KT8 9LX
*tel* 020-8398 9796 *fax* 020-8398 9796
*email* aadler@thepma.com

Association of theatrical agents in the theatre, film
and entertainment world generally.

## The Picture Research Association
c/o 1 Willow Court, off Willow Street,
London EC2A 4QB
*tel* 020-7739 8544 *fax* 020-7782 0011
*email* chair@picture-research.org.uk
*website* www.picture-research.org.uk

Professional organisation of picture researchers and
picture editors. Its aims are:
• to promote the recognition of picture research,
management, editing, picture buying and supplying
as a profession requiring particular skills and
knowledge;
• to bring together all those involved in the picture
profession and provide a forum for information
exchange and interaction;
• to encourage publishers, TV and video production
organisations, internet companies, and any other
users of images to use the PRA freelance register and
engage a member of PRA to obtain them, thus
ensuring that professional standards are maintained;
• to advise those specifically wishing to embark on a
profession in the research and supply of pictures for
all types of visual media information, providing
guidelines and standards in so doing.

## Pier Playwrights
PO Box 141, Brighton, East Sussex BN2 1LZ
*tel* (01273) 625132

*email* admin@pierplaywrights.co.uk
*website* www.pierplaywrights.co.uk
*Administrator* Chris Taylor
*Membership* £15 p.a.

Aims to support and encourage writers and their
writing for performance in all its forms. Activities
include a script-reading service (members only),
workshops from visiting professionals, and a
monthly newsletter. Pier Playwrights is a registered
charity supported by the Arts Council and is open
to all dramatic writers in South and South East
England. Founded 1990.

## Player-Playwrights
*Secretary* Peter Thompson, 9 Hillfield Park,
London N10 3QT
*tel* 020-8883 0371
*email* p-p@dial.pipex.com
*Membership* £10 in first year and £6 thereafter (plus
£2 per attendance)

Meets on Monday evenings upstairs at the Horse
and Groom, 128 Great Portland Street, London W1.
The society reads, performs and discusses plays and
scripts submitted by members, with a view to
assisting the writers in improving and marketing
their work. Newcomers and new acting members
are always welcome. Founded 1948.

## The Poetry Book Society
Book House, 45 East Hill, London SW18 2QZ
*tel* 020-8870 8403 *fax* 020-8870 0865
*email* info@poetrybooks.co.uk
*website* www.poetrybooks.co.uk
*Chair* Daisy Goodwin, *Director* Chris Holifield

Foremost in getting books of new poetry to readers
through quarterly selections, special offers, and 300-
strong backlist which it sells at favourable rates to
members. Website features over 1000 post-1950s
poetry books for sale. Publishes *Bulletin* (quarterly)
and runs the annual T.S. Eliot Prize for the best
collection of new poetry. Operates as a charitable
Book Club with annual membership (£10, £32,
£125) open to all. Education resources for
secondary schools and Children's Poetry Bookshelf
for primary schools and libraries. Also plays role in
promoting and stimulating sales of poetry books.

## The Poetry Library – see page 306

## The Poetry Society
22 Betterton Street, London WC2H 9BX
*tel* 020-7420 9880 *fax* 020-7240 4818
*email* info@poetrysociety.org.uk
*website* www.poetrysociety.org.uk
*Subscriptions* Subscriptions and Membership Dept,
Freepost 5410, London WC2H 9BR
*tel* 020-7420 9881 *fax* 020-7240 4818
*Chair* Richard Price, *Director* Jules Mann

*Membership* Open to all; national membership

Aims to help poets and poetry thrive in Britain today. Publishes *Poetry Review* (quarterly) and *Poetry News* (quarterly), has an information and imagination service, runs promotions and educational projects, helps to coordinate National Poetry Day and the annual National Poetry Competition (see page 562). Provides a unique critical service, Poetry Prescription, where poetry of up to 100 lines is appraised by a chosen poet. Runs the Poetry Café at its premises in Covent Garden, which is also a venue for regular and one-off events, and is also available for hire for small readings and seminars (contact Jess York, *tel* 020-7420 9887). Founded 1909.

## The John Polidori Literary Society

*Contact* The Secretary, PO Box 6078, Nottingham NG16 4HX
*Founder/President* Franklin Charles Bishop
*Membership* By invitation only

Promotes and encourages the appreciation of the life and works of Anglo-Italian John William Polidori MD (1795–1821) – novelist, poet, tragedian, philosopher, diarist, essayist, reviewer, traveller and one of the youngest ever students to obtain a medical degree at the age of 19. He introduced into English literature the icon of the vampire portrayed as an aristocratic, handsome seducer both cynical and amoral with his seminal work *The Vampyre – A Tale* (1819). The Society has a programme of republishing Polidori's literary works, including a recently found cache of previously unknown letters. The Society houses a collection of rare letters and memorabilia connected with Polidori. Founded 1990.

## The Beatrix Potter Society

*Secretary* Sidney Blackmore, 9 Broadfields, Harpenden, Herts. AL5 2HJ
*tel* (01582) 769755
*email* beatrixpottersociety@tiscali.co.uk
*website* www.beatrixpottersociety.org.uk
*Membership* £15 p.a. UK, £20 overseas

Promotes the study and appreciation of the life and works of Beatrix Potter as author, artist, diarist, farmer and conservationist. Founded 1980.

## The Powys Society

*Hon. Secretary* Dr Peter J. Foss, 82 Linden Road, Gloucester GL1 5HD
(01452) 304539
*email* pjfoss@supanet.com
*website* www.powys-society.org

Aims to promote the greater public recognition and enjoyment of the writings, thought and contribution to the arts of the Powys family, particularly John Cowper (1872–1963), Theodore (1875–1953) and Llewelyn (1884–1939) Powys, and the many other

family members and their close friends. Publishes an annual scholarly journal (*The Powys Journal*) and 3 newsletters per year, and holds an annual weekend conference in August, as well as other activities. Founded 1967.

## The Press Complaints Commission

*Acting Director* Tim Toulmin, 1 Salisbury Square, London EC4Y 8JB
*tel* 020-7353 1248 *Helpline tel* 020-7353 3732
*fax* 020-7353 8355
*email* pcc@pcc.org.uk
*website* www.pcc.org.uk
*Chairman* Sir Christopher Meyer

Independent body founded to oversee self-regulation of the Press. Deals with complaints by the public about the contents and conduct of British newspapers and magazines and advises editors on journalistic ethics. Complaints must be about the failure of newspapers or magazines to follow the letter or spirit of a Code of Practice, drafted by newspaper and magazine editors, adopted by the industry and supervised by the Commission. Founded 1991.

## The J.B. Priestley Society

*Secretary* Rod Slater, 54 Framingham Road, Sale, Greater Manchester M33 3RJ
*tel* 0161-962 1477 (evening) *fax* 0161-962 7538
*email* rodslater@ukonline.co.uk
*Membership* £10 p.a. single, £15 family, £5 concessions

Aims to widen the knowledge, understanding and appreciation of the published works of J.B. Priestley (1894–1984) and to promote the study of his life and career. Holds lectures and discussions and shows films. Publishes a newsletter and journal. Organises walks to areas with Priestley connections, Annual Priestley Night and other social events. Founded 1997.

## Printmakers Council

Ground Floor Unit, 23 Blue Anchor Lane, London SE16 3UL
*tel* 020-7250 1927 *fax* 020-7250 1927
*President* Stanley Jones, *Chair* Sheila Sloss
*Membership* £60 p.a., £30 students

Artist-led group which aims to promote the use of both traditional and innovative printmaking techniques by: holding exhibitions of prints; providing information on prints and printmaking to both its membership and the public; encouraging cooperation and exchanges between members, other associations and interested individuals. Founded 1965.

## Private Libraries Association

Ravelston, South View Road, Pinner, Middlesex HA5 3YD
*website* www.the-old-school.demon.co.uk/pla.htm

*President* Colin Franklin, *Hon. Editors* David Chambers, Paul W. Nash, *Hon. Secretary* James Brown
*Membership* £25 p.a.

International society of book collectors and private libraries. Publications include *The Private Library* (quarterly), annual *Private Press Books*, and other books on book collecting. Founded 1956.

## The Publishers Association

29B Montague Street, London WC1B 5BW
*tel* 020-7691 9191 *fax* 020-7691 9199
*email* mail@publishers.org.uk
*website* www.publishers.org.uk
*Chief Executive* Ronnie Williams OBE, *Director of International and Trade Divisions (BDCI)* Ian Taylor, *Director of Educational, Academic and Professional Publishing* Graham Taylor

Founded 1896.

## Publishers' Association of South Africa (PASA)

PO Box 15277, Vlaeberg 8018, South Africa
*tel* (021) 726-7677 *fax* (021) 726-1733
*email* pasa@publishsa.co.za
*website* www.publishsa.co.za

## Publishers Licensing Society Ltd (PLS)

37–41 Gower Street, London WC1E 6HH
*tel* 020-7299 7730 *fax* 020-7299 7780
*email* pls@pls.org.uk
*website* www.pls.org.uk
*Chairman* Maurice Long, *Chief Executive* Alicia Wise

PLS has mandates from over 1600 publishers. These non-exclusive licences allow PLS to include those publishers' works as part of the repertoire offered to licensees by CLA. The licences permit photocopying and some digitisation of parts of copyright works. The money collected from these licences is shared between publishers and authors and PLS has responsibility for distributing the publishers' share to the mandating companies. PLS represents the interests of a wide range of publishers from the multinationals to the single-title publisher. Founded 1981.

## Publishers Publicity Circle

*Secretary/Treasurer* Heather White, 65 Airedale Avenue, London W4 2NN
*tel* 020-8994 1881
*email* ppc-@lineone.net
*website* www.publisherspublicitycircle.co.uk

Enables all book publicists to meet and share information regularly. Monthly meetings provide a forum for press journalists, TV and radio researchers and producers to meet publicists collectively. Awards are presented for the best PR campaigns. Monthly newsletter includes recruitment advertising. Founded 1955.

## The Radclyffe International Philosophical Association

BM–RIPhA, Old Gloucester Street, London WC1N 3XX
*email* riphassoc@aol.com
*President* William Mann FRIPhA, *Secretary General* John Khasseyan FRIPhA
*Membership* £30 p.a. (Fellows, Members and Associates)

Aims to dignify those achievements which might otherwise escape formal recognition; to promote the interests and talent of its members; to encourage their good fellowship; and to form a medium for the exchange of ideas between members. Published authors and artists usually enter at Fellowship level. Founded 1955.

## The Radio Academy

5 Market Place, London W1W 8AE
*email* info@radioacademy.org
*website* www.radioacademy.org
*Director* John Bradford

The professional association for those engaged in the UK radio industry with over 2000 individual members and 30 corporate patrons. Organises conferences, seminars, debates, the annual UK Radio Festival and social events for members in all regions of the UK; publishes *Off Air* (quarterly) newsletter and an annual *Yearbook*. Provides administrative support for the Student Radio Association and the Radio Studies Network and organises a series of regional training events for those interested in getting into radio.

## Regional Arts Offices – see Arts Council England

## Ridley Art Society

50 Crowborough Road, London SW17 9QQ
*tel* 020-8682 1212
*email* info@ridleyart.com
*President* Ken Howard RA, *Chairman* dickon

Represents a wide variety of attitudes towards the making of art. In recent years has sought to encourage younger artists. At least one Central London Members' exhibition a year. Founded 1889.

## The Romantic Novelists' Association

*Chairman* Anthea Kenyon, 36 Eastgate, Hallaton, Market Harborough, Leics. LE16 8UB
*tel* (01858) 555602 *fax* (01858) 555026
*website* www.rna-uk.org
*Hon. Secretary* Catherine Jones, 3 Griffin Road, Thame, Oxon OX9 3LB, *tel* 01844 213947

Aims to raise the prestige of Romantic Authorship. Open to romantic and historical novelists. See also page 564.

## Royal Academy of Arts

Piccadilly, London W1J 0BD
*tel* 020-7300 8000 *fax* 020-7300 8001
*website* www.royalacademy.org.uk
*President* Prof Phillip King,
*Keeper* Brendan Neiland RA

Academicians (RA) are elected from the most distinguished artists in the UK. Holds major loan exhibitions throughout the year including the Annual Summer Exhibition (June–Aug). Also runs art schools for 60 postgraduate students in painting and sculpture.

## Royal Birmingham Society of Artists

4 Brook Street, St Paul's, Birmingham B3 1SA
*tel* 0121-236 4353 *fax* 0121-236 4555
*Membership* Friends £22 p.a.

The Society has 2 floors of exhibition space and a craft gallery in the city centre. Members (RBSA) and Associates (ARBSA) are elected annually. Holds 4 Open Exhibitions: 3 all-media exhibitions (Spring, Summer and Winter) – send sae for schedules, available 6 weeks prior to Exhibition. A further Open £1000 First Prize Exhibition is held (June/July) for works in any media. Other substantial money prizes can be won with no preference given to Members and Associates. Also a varying programme of exhibitions throughout the year, including the Autumn Exhibition, open to Members and Associates, and 2 Friends Exhibitions (February and August). Friends of the RBSA are entitled to attend various functions and to submit work for the Annual Exhibitions.

## Royal Institute of Oil Painters

17 Carlton House Terrace, London SW1Y 5BD
*tel* 020-7930 6844 *fax* 020-7839 7830
*website* www.mallgalleries.org.uk
*President* Olwen Tarrant

Promotes and encourages the art of painting in oils. Open Annual Exhibition at the Mall Galleries, The Mall, London SW1.

## Royal Institute of Painters in Water Colours

17 Carlton House Terrace, London SW1Y 5BD
*tel* 020-7930 6844 *fax* 020-7839 7830
*website* www.mallgalleries.org.uk
*President* Ronald Maddox Hon. RWS
*Membership* Elected from approved candidates' list

Promotes the appreciation of watercolour painting in its traditional and contemporary forms, primarily by means of an annual exhibition at the Mall Galleries, The Mall, London SW1 of members' and non-members' work and also by members' exhibitions at selected venues in Britain and abroad. Founded 1831.

## The Royal Literary Fund

3 Johnson's Court, off Fleet Street, London EC4A 3EA
*tel* 020-7353 7150 *fax* 020-7353 1350
*email* egunnrlf@globalnet.co.uk
*website* www.rlf.org.uk
*President* Peter Janson-Smith, *General Secretary* Eileen Gunn

Founded in 1790, the Fund is the oldest charity serving literature, set up to help writers and their families who face hardship. It does not offer grants to writers who can earn their living in other ways, nor does it provide financial support for writing projects. But it sustains authors who have for one reason or another fallen on hard times – illness, family misfortune, or sheer loss of writing form. Applicants must have published work of approved literary merit, which may include important contributions to periodicals. The literary claim of every new applicant must be accepted by the General Committee before the question of need can be considered.

## The Royal Musical Association

*Secretary* Dr Jeffrey Dean, 4 Chandos Road, Chorlton-cum-Hardy, Manchester M21 0ST
*tel* 0161-861 7542 *fax* 0161-861 7543
*email* jeffrey.dean@stingrayoffice.com
*website* www.rma.ac.uk

## The Royal Photographic Society

The Octagon, Milsom Street, Bath BA1 1DN
*tel* (01225) 462841 *fax* (01225) 448688
*email* rps@rps.org
*website* www.rps.org

Open membership organisation which promotes the art and science of photography and electronic imagery. Publishes *The RPS Journal* (monthly) and *Imaging Science Journal* (quarterly). Founded 1853.

## Royal Scottish Academy

The Mound, Edinburgh EH2 2EL
*tel* 0131-225 6671 *fax* 0131-220 6016
*email* info@royalscottishacademy.org
*President* Ian McKenzie Smith OBE, PRSA, *Secretary* Bill Scott RSA, *Treasurer* Isi Metzstein OBE, RSA

Academicians (RSA) and Associates (ARSA) and non-members may exhibit in the Annual Exhibition of Painting, Sculpture and Architecture, held approximately mid April–July; Festival Exhibition Aug–Oct. Royal Scottish Academy Student Exhibition held in March and the Salvesen Scholarship Exhibition in Nov–Dec. Founded 1826.

## The Royal Society

6–9 Carlton House Terrace, London SW1Y 5AG
*tel* 020-7451 2500 *fax* 020-7930 2170
*email* press@royalsoc.ac.uk
*website* www.royalsoc.ac.uk
*President* Lord May of Oxford OM, AC, Kt, PRS,

*Treasurer* Prof David Wallace CBE, DL, FRS, FREng, *Biological Secretary* Prof David Read FRS, *Physical Secretary* Prof Sir John Enderby CBE, FRS, *Foreign Secretary* Prof Dame Julia Higgins DBE, FRS, FREng, *Executive Secretary* Mr S. Cox CVO

## The Royal Society for Asian Affairs
2 Belgrave Square, London SW1X 8PJ
*tel* 020-7235 5122 *fax* 020-7259 6771
*email* info@rsaa.org.uk
*website* www.rsaa.org.uk
*President* The Lord Denman CBE, MC TD, *Chairman of Council* Sir Donald Hawley KCMG, MBE, *Secretary* Norman Cameron MA, BA
*Membership* £55 p.a. London, £45 more than 60 miles from London and overseas, £10 up to age 25

For the study of all Asia past and present; fortnightly lectures, etc; library. Publishes *Asian Affairs* (3 p.a.), free to members. Founded 1901.

## Royal Society for the encouragement of Arts, Manufactures and Commerce (RSA)
8 John Adam Street, London WC2N 6EZ
*tel* 020-7930 5115 *fax* 020-7839 5805
*email* journal@rsa.org.uk
*website* www.theRSA.org
*Chairman of Council* Sir Paul Judge, *Executive Director* Penny Egan, *Commercial Director* Chris Bond, *Fellowship and Information Director* Dr Geoffrey Botting, *Programme Director* Paul Crake, *Director of Finance* Philip Bunt, *Editor, RSA Journal* Morice Mendoza, *Press Officer* Barbara Ormston

With over 20,000 Fellows, the RSA sustains a forum for people from all walks of life to come together to address issues, shape new ideas and stimulate action. It works through projects, award schemes and its lecture programme, the proceedings of which are recorded in *RSA Journal*. Founded 1754.

## Royal Society of British Artists
17 Carlton House Terrace, London SW1Y 5BD
*tel* 020-7930 6844 *fax* 020-7839 7830
*website* www.mallgalleries.org.uk
*President* Cav. Romeo di Girolamo, *Keeper* Alfred Daniels

Incorporated by Royal Charter for the purpose of encouraging the study and practice of the arts of painting, sculpture and architectural designs. Annual Open Exhibition at the Mall Galleries, The Mall, London SW1, open to artists working in any 2- or 3-dimensional medium.

## Royal Society of Literature
Somerset House, Strand, London WC2R 1LA
*tel* 020-7845 4676 *fax* 020-7845 4679
*email* info@rslit.org
*Chairman of Council* Maggie Gee, FRSL, *Secretary* Maggie Fergusson

*Membership* £30 p.a.

For the promotion of literature and encouragement of writers by way of lectures, discussions, readings, and by publications. Administers the Royal Society of Literature Award under the W.H. Heinemann Bequest, the V.S. Pritchett Memorial Prize, the Royal Society of Literature Ondaatje Prize and the Royal Society of Literature/Jerwood Awards. Founded 1820.

## Royal Society of Marine Artists
17 Carlton House Terrace, London SW1Y 5BD
*tel* 020-7930 6844 *fax* 020-7839 7830
*website* www.mallgalleries.org.uk
*President* Bert Wright

Aims to promote and encourage marine painting. Open Annual Exhibition at the Mall Galleries, The Mall, London SW1 for any artists whose main interest is the sea, or tidal waters, or some object essentially connected therewith.

## The Royal Society of Miniature Painters, Sculptors and Gravers
*Executive Secretary* Mrs Pam Henderson, 1 Knapp Cottages, Wyke, Gillingham, Dorset SP8 4NQ
*tel* (01747) 825718; 020-7222 2723 (during exhibitions)
*email* hendersons@dial.pipex.com
*website* www.royal-miniature-society.org.uk
*President* Elisabeth R. Meek, PSWA, HS, FRSA, *Hon. Secretary* Barbara Penketh Simpson
*Membership* By selection and standard of work over a period of years (ARMS associate, RMS full member)

Annual Open Exhibition in June at the Mall Galleries, The Mall, London SW1. Hand in April; schedules available in January (send sae). Applications and enquiries to the Executive Secretary. Founded 1895.

## Royal Society of Painter-Printmakers
Bankside Gallery, 48 Hopton Street, London SE1 9JH
*tel* 020-7928 7521
*email* info@banksidegallery.com
*website* www.banksidegallery.com
*President* Anita Kline PRE
*Membership* Open to British and overseas artists. An election of Associates is held annually; for particulars apply to the Secretary. Friends membership is open to all those interested in artists' original printmaking

Organises workshops and lectures on original printmaking and holds one members' exhibition per year. Founded 1880.

## Royal Society of Portrait Painters
17 Carlton House Terrace, London SW1Y 5BD
*tel* 020-7930 6844 *fax* 020-7839 7830
*President* Andrew Festing

Annual Exhibition at the Mall Galleries, The Mall,

London SW1, of members' work and that of selected non-members. Three high-profile artists' awards are made: the Ondaatje Prize for Portraiture (£10,000), the Carroll Foundation Young Portrait Painters Award (£3000), and the Prince of Wales Award for Portrait Drawing (£2000). Also commissions consultancy service. Founded 1891.

## Royal Television Society

Holborn Hall, 100 Gray's Inn Road, London WC1X 8AL
*tel* 020-7430 1000 *fax* 020-7430 0924
*email* membership@rts.org.uk
*website* www.rts.org.uk
*Chief Executive* Simon Albury, *Membership Services Manager* Deborah Halls
*Membership* £70 p.a.

The Society is a unique, central, independent forum to debate the art, science and politics of TV. Holds awards, conferences, dinners, lectures and workshops. Founded 1927.

## Royal Watercolour Society

Bankside Gallery, 48 Hopton Street, London SE1 9JH
*tel* 020-7928 7521
*email* info@banksidegallery.com
*website* www.banksidegallery.com
*President* Trevor Frankland, PRWS, RE
*Membership* Open to British and overseas artists; election of Associates held annually. Friends membership is open to all those interested in watercolour painting

Arranges lectures on watercolour paintings; organises residential/non-residential courses; holds an open exhibition in the summer. Exhibitions: spring and autumn. Founded 1804.

## Royal West of England Academy

Queens Road, Clifton, Bristol BS8 1PX
*tel* 0117-973 5129 *fax* 0117-923 7874
*website* www.rwa.org.uk
*President* Derek Balmer

An art Academy/gallery whose objectives are to advance the education of the public in the fine arts and in particular to promote the appreciation and practice of the fine arts and to encourage and develop talent in the fine arts. Founded 1844.

## The Ruskin Society

*Hon. Secretary* Dr C.J. Gamble, 49 Hallam Street, London W1W 6JP
*Membership* £10 p.a.

Aims to encourage a wider understanding of John Ruskin (1819–1900) and his contemporaries. Organises lectures and events which seek to explain to the public the nature of Ruskin's theories and to place these in a modern context. Affiliated to the Ruskin Foundation. Founded 1997.

## The Ruskin Society of London

*Membership Secretary* Mrs A. Hardy, 351 Woodstock Road, Oxford OX2 7NX
*tel* (01865) 310987/515962
*Chairman and General Secretary* Miss O.E. Forbes-Madden
*Membership* £10 p.a.

Promotes literary and biographical interest in John Ruskin and his contemporaries. Publishes an annual *Ruskin Gazette*, free to members. Members are also affiliated to other literary societies. Founded 1985.

## SAA (Society for All Artists)

PO Box 50, Newark, Notts. NG23 5GY
*tel* (01949) 844050 *fax* (01949) 844051
*email* inspiration@saa.co.uk
*website* www.saa.co.uk
*Membership* £22.50–£42 p.a. including paintings exhibition insurance and third party public liability, £27.50 overseas

Aims to 'inform, encourage and inspire all who want to paint', from complete beginners to professionals; to promote friendship and companionship amongst fellow artists. Holds meetings and events locally and nationally, organises painting holidays, workshops, local and international exhibitions and competitions, publishes newsletter *Paint* (6 p.a.) and *SAA Home Shopping* catalogue. Founded 1992.

## The Malcolm Saville Society

*Membership Secretary* Richard Griffiths, 78A Windmill Road, Mortimer, Berks. RG7 3RL
*email* mystery@witchend.com
*website* www.witchend.com
*Membership* £7.50 p.a. UK and EU, £12 outside EU

Aims to remember and promote interest in the work of Malcolm Saville (1901–82), children's author. Regular social activities, book search, library, contact directory and magazine (3 p.a.). Founded 1994.

## The Dorothy L. Sayers Society

*Chairman* Christopher J. Dean, Rose Cottage, Malthouse Lane, Hurstpierpoint, West Sussex BN6 9JY
*tel* (01273) 833444 *fax* (01273) 835988
*website* www.sayers.org.uk
*Secretaries* Lenelle Davis, Jasmine Simeone
*Membership* £14 p.a. UK, £16.50 Europe, $28 USA

Aims to promote and encourage the study of the works of Dorothy L. Sayers; to collect archive materials and reminiscences about her and make them available to students and biographers; to hold an annual conference and other meetings; to publish proceedings, pamphlets and a bi-monthly bulletin. Founded 1976.

## Scattered Authors Society

*Secretary* Anne Cassidy, 150 Wanstead Lane, Ilford, Essex IG1 3SG
*email* anne.cassidy4@btopenworld.com

Aims to provide a forum for informal discussion, contact and support for professional writers in children's fiction. Founded 1998.

## Scottish Arts Club

24 Rutland Square, Edinburgh EH1 2BW
*tel* 0131-229 8157 *fax* 0131-229 8887
*email* info@scottishartsclub.co.uk
*website* www.scottishartsclub.co.uk
*Hon. Secretary* Mhairi Kerr *tel* 0131-229 8157
*Membership* £330 p.a. full; reductions available

## Scottish Arts Council

12 Manor Place, Edinburgh EH3 7DD
*tel* 0131-226 6051
*email* help.desk@scottisharts.org.uk
*website* www.scottisharts.org.uk
*Chairman* James Boyle, *Director* Graham Berry, *Head of Literature* Gavin Wallace, *Head of Visual Arts* Amanda Catto

Principal channel for government funding of the arts in Scotland, the Scottish Arts Council is funded by the Scottish Executive. It aims to develop and improve the knowledge, understanding and practice of the arts, and to increase their accessibility throughout Scotland. It offers about 1300 grants a year to artists and arts organisations concerned with the visual arts, drama, dance and mime, literature, music, festivals, and traditional, ethnic and community arts. It is also the distributor of National Lottery funds to the arts in Scotland.

## Scottish Book Trust (SBT)

Sandeman House, 55 High Street, Edinburgh EH1 1SR
*tel* 0131-524 0160 *fax* 0131-524 0161
*email* info@scottishbooktrust.com
*website* www.scottishbooktrust.com

With a particular responsibility towards Scottish writing, SBT exists to promote literature and reading, and aims to reach (and create) a wider reading public than has existed before. It also organises exhibitions, readings and storytellings, administers the Live Literature Scotland Scheme, operates an extensive children's reference library available to everyone and provides a book information service. SBT has a range of publications and advises other relevant art organisations. Founded 1960.

## Scottish Daily Newspaper Society

48 Palmerston Place, Edinburgh EH12 5DE
*tel* 0131-220 4353 *fax* 0131-220 4344
*email* info@sdns.org.uk
*Director* J.B. Raeburn FCIS

## Scottish Newspaper Publishers Association

48 Palmerston Place, Edinburgh EH12 5DE
*tel* 0131-220 4353 *fax* 0131-220 4344
*email* info@snpa.org.uk
*website* www.snpa.org.uk
*Director* J.B. Raeburn FCIS

## Scottish Publishers Association

Scottish Book Centre, 137 Dundee Street, Edinburgh EH11 1BG
*tel* 0131-228 6866 *fax* 0131-228 3220
*email* enquiries@scottishbooks.org
*website* www.scottishbooks.org
*Director* Lorraine Fannin, *Administrator* Carol Lothian, *Member Services Manager* Liz Small, *Information and Development Administrator* Katherine A. Naish

Founded 1973.

## Scottish Screen

2nd Floor, 249 West George Street, Glasgow G2 4QE
*tel* 0141-302 1700 *fax* 0141-302 1711
*email* info@scottishscreen.com
*website* www.scottishscreen.com
*Information Manager* Isabella Edgar

Develops, encourages and promotes every aspect of film, TV and new media in Scotland through script and company development, short film production, distribution of National Lottery film production finance, training, education, exhibition funding, Film Commission Locations support and the Scottish Screen Archive.

## Screenwriters' Workshop

Suffolk House, 1–8 Whitfield Place, London W1T 5JU
*tel* 020-7387 5511
*email* screenoffice@tisali.co.uk
*website* www.lsw.org.uk
*Contact* Administrator
*Membership* £40 p.a.

Forum for contact, information and tuition, the SW helps new and established writers work successfully in the film and TV industry, and organises a continuous programme of activities, events, courses and seminars, all of which are reduced to members and open to non-members at reasonable rates. The SW is the largest screenwriting group in Europe and supports Euroscript, a Media II-funded organisation developing scripts for film and TV throughout the EU. Founded 1983.

## SCRIBO

*Contact* K. & P. Sylvester, Flat 1, 31 Hamilton Road, Bournemouth BH1 4EQ
*Membership* Joining fee: £5 (send sae); no annual subscription

A postal forum for novelists (published and unpublished), SCRIBO aims to give friendly, informed encouragement and help, to discuss all matters of interest to novelists and to offer criticism via MSS folios: crime/thrillers, fantasy/science fiction, mainstream, aga-saga/popular women's fiction, plus literary folios. Founded 1971.

## The Shaw Society

*Secretary* Barbara Smoker, 51 Farmfield Road, Downham, Bromley, Kent BR1 4NF
*tel* 020-8697 3619
*email* anthnyellis@aol.com
*Membership* £15/$30 p.a.

Improvement and diffusion of knowledge of the life and works of Bernard Shaw and his circle. Meetings in London; annual festival at Ayot St Lawrence in July. Publishes *The Shavian*.

## Society for Editors and Proofreaders (SfEP)

*Office* Riverbank House, 1 Putney Bridge Approach, London SW6 3JD
*tel* 020-7736 3278
*email* admin@sfep.org.uk
*website* www.sfep.org.uk

Works to promote high editorial standards and achieve recognition of its members' professional status, through local and national meetings, an annual conference, an email discussion group, a regular newsletter and a programme of reasonably priced workshops/training sessions. These sessions help newcomers to acquire basic skills, enable experienced editors to update their skills or broaden their competence, and also cover aspects of professional practice or business for the self-employed. An annual Directory of members' services is available. The Society supports moves towards recognised standards of training and accreditation for editors and proofreaders and has developed its own Accreditation in Proofreading qualification. It has close links with the Publishing Training Centre and the Society of Indexers, is represented on the BSI Technical Committee dealing with copy preparation and proof correction (BS 5261), and works to foster good relations with all relevant bodies and organisations in the UK and worldwide. Founded 1988.

## The Society for Theatre Research

c/o The Theatre Museum, 1E Tavistock Street, London WC2E 7PR
*email* e.cottis@btinternet.com
*website* www.str.org.uk
*Hon. Secretaries* Eileen Cottis and Frances Dann

Publishes annual volumes and journal (3 p.a.), *Theatre Notebook*, holds lectures and makes annual research grants (current total sum approx. £4000).

Starting in 1998, the Society's 50th anniversary, it awards an annual prize of £400 for the best book published in English on the historical or current practice of the British theatre.

## Society of Artists Agents

21C Montpellier Row, London SE3 0RL
*tel* (07870) 628 709
*email* jennieward@btopenworld.com
*website* www.thesaa.com
*Contact* Jennifer Ward

Formed to promote professionalism in the illustration industry and to forge closer links between clients and artists through an agreed set of guidelines. The Society believes in an ethical approach through proper terms and conditions, thereby protecting the interests of the artists and clients. Founded 1992.

## The Society of Authors – see page 495

## The Society of Botanical Artists

*Executive Secretary* Mrs Pam Henderson, 1 Knapp Cottages, Wyke, Gillingham, Dorset SP8 4NQ
*tel* (01747) 825718
*email* pam@soc-botanical-artists.org
*website* www.soc-botanical-artists.org
*Founder President* Suzanne Lucas FLS, RMS, *Executive Vice President* Margaret Stevens
*Membership* Through selection. £120 p.a.; £20 friend members

Aims to encourage the art of botanical painting. Annual Open Exhibition held in July/August at the Mall Galleries, London SW1. Hand in end June. Entry schedules available from the Executive Secretary from March on receipt of sae. Founded 1985.

## Society of Children's Book Writers and Illustrators (SCBWI)

Flat 3, 124 Norwood Road, London SE24 9AY
*tel* 020-8671 7539
*email* scbwi_bi@hotmail.com
*website* www.wordpool.co.uk/scbwi
*Regional Adviser* Natascha Biebow
*Membership* £44 p.a. plus a one-off fee of £7

An international network for the exchange of knowledge between professional writers, illustrators, editors, publishers, agents, librarians, educators, booksellers and others involved with literature for young people. Sponsors 2 annual conferences on writing and illustrating books and multimedia – in New York (February) and Los Angeles (summer) – as well as dozens of regional conferences and events throughout the world. Publishes a bi-monthly newsletter, *The Bulletin*, and information publications, and awards grants for works in progress. The SCBWI also presents the annual Golden Kite Award for the best fiction and non-fiction books, which is open both to published and unpublished writers and illustrators.

The SCBWI British Isles region meets quarterly for a speaker or workshop event. Also sponsors local critique groups and publishes *Words and Pictures* quarterly newsletter, which includes up-to-date events and marketing information and articles on the craft of children's writing and illustrating in the British Isles. The yearly Writer's Day and Illustrator's Day includes workshops and the opportunity to meet publishing professionals. Founded 1971.

## The Society of Civil and Public Service Writers

*Secretary* Mrs J.M. Lewis, 17 The Green, Corby Glen, Grantham, Lincs. NG33 4NP
*email* joan@lewis.fs.net.co.uk
*Membership* £15 p.a.; Poetry Workshop add £3

Welcomes serving and retired members of the Civil Service, Armed Forces, Post Office and BT, the nursing profession, and other public servants. Members can be aspiring or published writers. Holds annual competitions for short stories, articles and poetry, plus occasional for longer works. Offers email and postal folios for short stories and articles; holds an AGM and occasional meetings; publishes *The Civil Service Author* (quarterly) magazine. Send sae for details. Founded 1935.

## Society of Editors

*Director* Bob Satchwell, University Centre, Granta Place, Mill Lane, Cambridge CB2 1RU
*tel* (01223) 304080 *fax* (01223) 304090
*email* info@societyofeditors.org
*website* www.societyofeditors.org
*Membership* £230 p.a.

Formed from the merger of the Guild of Editors and the Association of British Editors, the Society has more than 450 members in national, regional and local newspapers, magazines, broadcasting, new media, journalism education and media law, campaigning for media freedom. Publishes *Briefing* (monthly). Founded 1999.

## Society of Graphic Fine Art

PO Box 7727, Maldon, Essex CM9 6WW
*website* www.sgfa.org.uk
*President* David Brooke
*Membership* By election

A fine art society. Holds an annual open exhibition of work of high quality with an emphasis on good drawing, whether by pen, pencil (with our without wash), watercolour, pastel or any of the forms of printmaking. Founded 1919.

## Society of Heraldic Arts

46 Reigate Road, Reigate, Surrey RH2 0QN
*tel* (01737) 242945

*website* www.heraldic-arts.com
*Secretary* John Ferguson ARCA, SHA, DFACH, FRSA, FHS
*Membership* £12 p.a. associate, £17 craft

Aims to serve the interests of heraldic artists, craftsmen, designers and writers, to provide a 'shop window' for their work, to obtain commissions on their behalf and to act as a forum for the exchange of information and ideas. Also offers an information service to the public. Candidates for admission as craft members should be artists or craftsmen whose work comprises a substantial element of heraldry and is of a sufficiently high standard to satisfy the requirements of the Society's advisory council. Founded 1987.

## Society of Indexers – see page 614

## The Society of Limners

*Founder/President* Elizabeth Davys Wood MBE, 2 Glentrammon Close, Green Street Green, Orpington, Kent BR6 6DL
*tel* (01689) 851158
*email* dionevenables@clara.net
*Membership* £30 p.a., £15 Friends (open to non-exhibitors); £45, £20 overseas

Aims to promote an interest in miniature painting (in any medium), calligraphy and heraldry and encourage their development to a high standard. New members are elected after the submission of 4 works of acceptable standard and guidelines are provided for new artists. Members receive up to 4 newsletters a year and 2 annual exhibitions are arranged. Founded 1986.

## The Society of Medical Writers

*Chairman* Dr David Brooks, The Barn, Tonacliffe Road, Whitworth, Lancs. OL12 8SJ
*Secretary* Mr Wilfred Hopkins, 633 Liverpool Road, Southport PR8 3NG

Aims to recruit members from all branches of the medical profession, together with all professions allied to medicine, to foster interest in literature and in writing – not solely about medicine but also about art, history, music, theatre, etc. Members are encouraged to write fiction, poetry, plays, book reviews, etc. Publishes *The Writer* (2 p.a.); register of members and their writing interests published electronically each year. Holds an annual conference in which various aspects of literature and writing are explored in a relaxed and informal atmosphere. Founded 2001 as successor to the General Practitioner Writers Association.

## Society of Scribes and Illuminators (SSI)

*Hon. Secretary* 6 Queen Square, London WC1N 3AT
*email* scribe@calligraphyonline.org
*website* www.calligraphyonline.org
*Membership* £28 Lay members; £23 Friends

Aims to advance the crafts of writing and illumination. Holds regular exhibitions, provides opportunities for discussion, demonstration and sharing of research. Founded 1921.

## The Society of Sussex Authors

*Secretary* Michael Legat, Bookends,
Lewes Road, Horsted Keynes, Haywards Heath,
West Sussex RH17 7DP
*tel* (01825) 790755 *fax* (01825) 790755
*email* michael@bookends.claranet.com
*Membership* £10 p.a. Open to writers living in
Sussex who have had at least one book
commercially published or who have worked
extensively in journalism, radio, TV or the theatre

Aims to encourage social contact between members, and to promote interest in literature and authors. Founded 1969.

## Society of Wildlife Artists

17 Carlton House Terrace, London SW1Y 5BD
*tel* 020-7930 6844 *fax* 020-7839 7830
*website* www.mallgalleries.org.uk
*President* Bruce Pearson

Aims to promote and encourage the art of wildlife painting and sculpture. Open Annual Exhibition at the Mall Galleries, The Mall, London SW1, for any artist whose work depicts wildlife subjects (botanical and domestic animals are not admissable).

## The Society of Women Artists

*Executive Secretary* 1 Knapp Cottages, Wyke,
Gillingham, Dorset SP8 4NQ
*tel* (01747) 825718 *fax* (01747) 826835
*email* hendersons@dial.pipex.com
*website* www.society-women-artists.org.uk
*President* Elizabeth Meek RMS, HS, FRSA
*Membership* Election by invitation, based on work
submitted to the exhibition

Founded in 1855 when women were not considered as serious contributors to art and could not compete for professional honours, the Society continues to promote art by women. Receiving day in April for annual open exhibition held in June at Mall Galleries, The Mall, London SW1.

## Society of Women Writers and Journalists

*Secretary* Zoe King, Calvers Farm, Thelveton, Diss,
Norfolk IP21 4NG
*tel* (01379) 740550
*email* zoe@zoeking.com
*Membership* £35 p.a. town, £30 country,
£25 overseas

For women writers: lectures, monthly workshops/speakers; members' postal critique service. Publishes *The Woman Writer* (6 p.a.). Founded 1894.

## Society of Young Publishers

*Contact* The Secretary, c/o The Bookseller,
Endeavour House, 189 Shaftesbury Avenue,
London WC2H 8TJ
*email* thesyp@thesyp.org.uk
*website* www.thesyp.org.uk
*Membership* Open to anyone employed in
publishing or hoping to be soon; Associate
membership available to those over the age of 35

Organises monthly speaker meetings at which senior figures talk on topics of key importance to the industry today, and social and other events. Runs a job database which matches candidates with potential employers. Meetings are held in Central London, usually on the last Wednesday of the month at 6.30pm. Also a branch in Oxford. Founded 1949.

## South African Writers' Circle

*Secretary* Ann Carter, PO Box 115, Hillcrest 3650,
South Africa
*tel* (031) 7655706
*email* brianduc@mweb.co.za
*website* www.sawc.sos.co.za
*Membership* R95 p.a. local, R100 overseas

Aims to help and encourage all writers, new and experienced, in the art of writing. Publishes a monthly *Newsletter*, and runs competitions with prizes for the winners. Founded 1960.

## South & Mid Wales Association of Writers (SAMWAW)

*Secretary* Julian Rosser, c/o IMC Consulting Group,
Denham House, Lambourne Crescent,
Cardiff CF14 5ZW
*tel* 029-2076 1170 *fax* 029-2076 1304
*email* info@imcconsultinggroup.co.uk
*Membership* £10 p.a. single, £15 joint

Aims to encourage the art of writing in all its forms, for both beginners and established writers. Offers a range of courses. Publishes a newsletter and runs competitions, including the Mathew Prichard Award for Short Story Writing (see page 565). Founded 1965.

## Southwest Scriptwriters

*Secretary* John Colborn *tel* 0117-909 5522
*email* southwest_scriptwriters@hotmail.com
*website* www.southwest-scriptwriters.co.uk
*Membership* £5 p.a.

Workshops members' drama scripts for stage, screen, radio and TV with the aim of improving their chances of professional production, meeting at the Bristol Old Vic. Also hosts regular talks by professional dramatists. Presents short annual seasons of script-in-hand performances of members' work at a major Bristol venue. Bi-monthly newsletter. Founded 1994.

## Spoken Word Publishing Association (SWPA)

*Administrator* Zoe Howes, Macmillan Audio Books, 20 New Wharf Road, London N1 9RR
*tel* 020-7014 6041
*website* www.swpa.co.uk
*Membership* £50–£600 p.a. plus VAT

The UK trade association for the spoken word industry, SWPA brings together all those involved – publishers, performers, producers, distributors, retailers, manufacturers. It aims to increase the profile of the spoken word in the media, the retail trade and among the general public, and to provide a forum for discussion. Founded 1994.

## Sports Journalists' Association of Great Britain (SJA)

*Secretary* Trevor Bond, 244 Perry Street, Billericay, Essex CM12 0QP
*tel* (01277) 651708 *fax* (01277) 622890
*email* trevjanbondl@aol.com
*website* www.sportsjournalists.org.uk
*Membership* £23.50 p.a., £11.75 regional

Represents sports journalists across the country and is Britain's voice in international sporting affairs. Offers advice to members covering major events, acts as a consultant to organisers of major sporting events on media requirements. Member of the BOA Press Advisory Committee. Founded 1948.

## The Robert Louis Stevenson Club

*Secretary* Dr Alan Marchbank, 12 Dean Park, Longniddry, East Lothian EH32 0QR
*tel* (01875) 852976 (01875) 853328
*email* alan@amarchbank.freeserve.co.uk
*Membership* £15 p.a., £100 10 years, £180 life

Aims to foster interest in Robert Louis Stevenson's life (1850–94) and works through various events and its newsletter. Founded 1920.

## The Bram Stoker Society

*Hon. Secretary* David Lass, Regent House, Trinity College, Dublin 2, Republic of Ireland
*fax* (01) 6719003 FAO David Lass
*email* dlass@tcd.ie
*websites* www.vampyreempire.com, www.benecke.com/stoker.html
*Hon. Treasurer* Dr Albert Power, 43 Castle Court, Killiney Hill Road, Killiney, Co. Dublin, Republic of Ireland
*Membership* £10 p.a. UK, €10 EU, $20 USA/rest of the world

Aims to promote the study and appreciation of Bram Stoker's (1847–1912) works and his influence in the areas of cinema, theatre and music, as well as his importance in the Gothic horror genre. Publishes an annual Journal and an occasional

Newsletter. Holds regular meetings with the Society's affiliated body, the Bram Stoker Club, in Trinity College, Dublin; and promotes an annual summer school in Clontarf, Dublin, held on a weekend in July. Founded 1980.

## Sussex Playwrights' Club

*Hon. Secretary*, 2 Brunswick Mews, Hove, East Sussex BN3 1HD
*website* www.newventure.org.uk

See 'features' page on website.

## Swedish Publishers' Association

Drottninggaten 97, 2 tr., 113 60 Stockholm, Sweden
*tel* 46-8-736-1940 *fax* 46-8-736-1944
*email* svf@forlagskansli.se
*website* www.forlagskansli.se
*Director* Kristina Ahlinder

Founded 1843.

## The Tennyson Society

*Hon. Secretary* Kathleen Jefferson, Central Library, Free School lane, Lincoln LN2 1EZ
*tel* (01522) 552851 *fax* (01522) 552858
*email* linnet@lincolnshire.gov.uk
*website* www.tennysonsociety.org.uk
*Membership* £8 p.a., £10 family, £15 institutions

Promotes the study and understanding of the life and work of the poet Alfred, Lord Tennyson and supports the Tennyson Research Centre in Lincoln. Holds lectures, visits and seminars; publishes the *Tennyson Research Bulletin* (annual), Monographs and Occasional Papers; tapes/recordings available. Founded 1960.

## Theatre Writers' Union – incorporated into The Writers' Guild of Great Britain, page 498

## Angela Thirkell Society

*Chairman* Mrs I.J. Cox, 32 Murvagh Close, Cheltenham, Glos. GL53 7QY
*tel* (01242) 251604
*email* penny.aldred@ntlworld.com
*website* www.angelathirkellsocitey.com
*Secretary* Mrs P. Aldred, 54 Belmont Park, London SE13 5BN
*tel* 020-8244 9339
*Membership* £10 p.a.
Aims 'to honour the memory of Angela Thirkell (1890–1960) as a writer, and to make her works available to new generations'. Publishes an *Annual Journal*, and encourages Thirkell studies. Founded 1980.

## The Edward Thomas Fellowship

1 Carfax, Undercliff Drive, St Lawrence, Isle of Wight PO38 1XG
*tel* (01983) 853366

*Hon. Secretary* Colin G. Thornton
*Membership* single £7 p.a., joint £10 p.a.

Aims to perpetuate the memory of Edward Thomas, poet and writer, foster an interest in his life and work, to assist in the preservation of places associated with him and to arrange events which extend fellowship amongst his admirers. Founded 1980.

## Dylan Thomas Society of Great Britain
5 Church Park, Mumbles, Swansea SA3 4DE
*tel* (01792) 520080
*Chair* Mrs E. Jenkins
*Membership* £5 p.a. single, £8 p.a. double

Aims to promote an interest in the works of Dylan Thomas (1914–53) and other Anglo–Welsh writers. Founded 1977.

## The Tolkien Society
*Secretary* Sally Kennett, 210 Prestbury Road, Cheltenham, Glos. GL52 3ER
*website* www.tolkiensociety.org
*Membership Secretary* Trevor Reynolds, 65 Wentworth Crescent, Ash Vale, Surrey GU12 5LF
*email* trevor@caerlas.demon.co.uk

## The Translators Association
84 Drayton Gardens, London SW10 9SB
*tel* 020-7373 6642
*email* info@societyofauthors.org
*website* www.societyofauthors.org
*Membership* £80 p.a. (£75 DD), including membership of the Society of Authors

Specialist unit within the membership of the Society of Authors (see page 495), exclusively concerned with the interests and special problems of translators into English whose work is published or performed commercially in Great Britain and English-speaking countries overseas. Members are entitled to general and legal advice on all questions connected with their work, including remuneration and contractual arrangements with publishers, editors, broadcasting organisations. Administers a range of translation prizes. Founded 1958.

## The Trollope Society
9ᴀ North Street, London SW4 0HN
*tel* 020-7720 6789 *fax* 020-978 1815
*email* trolsoc@barset.fsnet.co.uk
*Chairman* Priscilla Hungerford,
*Secretary* Phyllis Eden
*Membership* £24 p.a., £240 life

Has produced the first ever complete edition of the novels of Anthony Trollope. Founded 1987.

## The Turner Society
BCM Box Turner, London WC1N 3XX
*Chairman* Eric Shanes

*Membership* £15 p.a.

Aims to foster a wider appreciation of all facets of Turner's work; to encourage exhibitions of his paintings, drawings and engravings. Publishes *Turner Society News* (3 p.a.). Founded 1975.

## United Society for Christian Literature
Albany House, 67 Sydenham Road, Guildford GU1 3RY
*tel* (01483) 888580 *fax* (01483) 888581
*email* headoffice@feedtheminds.org
*website* www.feedtheminds.org
*Chairman* John Clark

Exists to aid Christian literature principally in the world's poorest countries. Founded 1799.

## Vampire Research Society
*International Secretary* Dennis Crawford, 3–22 Northwood Hall, Hornsey Lane, London N6 5PH
*email* vampireresearchsociety@gothicpress.freeserve.co.uk
*Membership* By invitation

The Society's sole purpose is to study and investigate vampirological phenomena, and publishes its research findings in books and academic reports. Holds the largest archive of vampire-related material in the world, to which membership allows access. Publishes a newsletter. Not affiliated to any other vampire interest group and remains aloof from the wider subculture. Founded 1970.

## Ver Poets
*Organiser/Editor* May Badman, Haycroft, 61–63 Chiswell Green Lane, St Albans, Herts. AL2 3AL
*tel* (01727) 867005
*email* may.badman@virgin.net
*Membership* £12.50 p.a. UK, £15/$30 overseas

Encourages the writing and study of poetry as a part of our culture. Help and advice, assessment and comment on work are available on request. Holds meetings (fortnightly) in St Albans; organises workshops and competitions for members, and produces anthologies of members' work. The annual Open Competition (October) is also open to non-members. Founded 1966.

## Visiting Arts
Bloomsbury House, 74–77 Great Russell Street, London WC1B 3DA
*tel* 020-7291 1600 *fax* 020-7291 1616
*email* information@visitingarts.org.uk
*website* www.visitingarts.org.uk
*Director* Terry Sandell ᴏʙᴇ

Works to ensure high-quality contemporary arts are brought into the UK from countries across the world and to extend the dialogue between UK artists and their overseas counterparts. Visiting Arts

works with UK promoters, curators, managers, etc
to develop the presentation of work from overseas
in the UK. The projects it funds cover a large range
of countries of origin, art forms, and venue sizes
and locations, as Visiting Arts aims to place its
resources strategically to ensure a higher profile to
foreign arts and to extend the opportunities for
audiences across the UK.

Activities include providing advice, information,
training, consultancy, publications, special projects
and project development, and covers the
performing arts, visual, applied and media arts,
crafts, design, literature, film, architecture and some
museum activity.

Visiting Arts is an independent educational
charity funded by the British Council, the Foreign
and Commonwealth Office, the 4 national Arts
Councils of England, Scotland, Wales and Northern
Ireland and the Department for Culture, Media and
Sport. Founded 1977.

## Voice of the Listener & Viewer Ltd (VLV)

101 King's Drive, Gravesend, Kent DA12 5BQ
*tel* (01474) 352835
*Chairman* Jocelyn Hay, *Administrative Secretary*
Linda Forbes

Independent association representing the citizen
and consumer interests in broadcasting and the
interests of listeners and viewers on all broadcasting
issues at UK and European level. Concerned to
maintain the principle of public service plus
independence, quality and diversity in British
broadcasting. Has some 2000 individual members,
nearly 30 charities as corporate members and more
than 50 colleges in academic membership. Holds
frequent public conferences all over UK. Maintains
a panel of speakers. Holds the archives of the
former Broadcasting Research Unit (1980–90),
British Action for Children's Television (BACTV)
1988–94, as well as its own archive. Publishes a
quarterly newsletter and briefings on broadcasting
developments. Presents annual awards for
Excellence in Broadcasting. Founded 1983.

## The Walmsley Society

*Secretary* Fred Lane, April Cottage, 1 Brand Road,
Hampden Park, Eastbourne, East Sussex BN22 9PX
*Membership Secretary* Mrs Elizabeth Buckley,
21 The Crescent, Hipperholm, Halifax,
West Yorkshire HX3 8NQ

Aims to promote and encourage an appreciation of
the literary and artistic heritage left to us by Leo
and J. Ulric Walmsley. Founded 1985.

## Mary Webb Society

*Secretary* Sue Higginbotham, 8 The Knowe,
Willaston, Neston, Cheshire CH64 1TA
*tel* 0151-327 5843

*email* suehigginbotham@yahoo.co.uk
*website* www.marywebb.2ya.com

For devotees of the literature and works of Mary
Webb and of the beautiful Shropshire countryside
of her novels. Publishes a bi-annual Journal,
organises summer schools and other events in
various locations related to Webb's life and works.
Archives, lectures; tours arranged for individuals
and groups. Founded 1972.

## The H.G. Wells Society

*Hon. General Secretary* Steve McLean,
Dept. of English Literature, University of Sheffield,
Shearwood Mount, Shearwood Road,
Sheffield S10 2TD
*website* www.hgwellsusa.50megs.com
*Membership* £16 p.a., £20 corporate

Promotes an active interest in and an appreciation
of the life, work and thought of H.G. Wells.
Publishes *The Wellsian* (annual) and *The Newsletter*
(bi-annual). Founded 1960.

## Welsh Academy – see Academi (Welsh Academy)

## Welsh Books Council/Cyngor Llyfrau Cymru

Castell Brychan, Aberystwyth,
Ceredigion SY23 2JB
*tel* (01970) 624151 *fax* (01970) 625385
*email* castellbrychan@cllc.org.uk
*websites* www.cllc.org.uk, www.gwales.com
*Director* Gwerfyl Pierce Jones

A national body funded directly by the Welsh
Assembly Government which provides a focus for
the publishing industry in Wales. Awards grants for
publishing in Welsh and English. Provides services
to the trade in the fields of editing, design,
marketing and distribution. The Council is a key
enabling institution in the world of books and
provides services and information in this field to all
who are associated with it. Founded 1961.

## The West Country Writers' Association

*Secretary* Judy Joss, High Wotton,
Wotton Lane, Lympstone, Exmouth,
Devon EX8 5AY
*tel* (01395) 222749
*email* judy@josser.freeserve.co.uk
*website* www.westcountrywriters.co.uk
*President* Christopher Fry FRSL DLitt,
*Chair* Dr David Keep
*Membership* Open to published authors, £10 p.a.

Aims to foster love of literature in the West Country
and to give authors an opportunity of meeting to
exchange news and views. Holds Annual Weekend
Congress and Regional Meetings. Newsletter (2 p.a.).

## The Oscar Wilde Society
100 Peacock Street, Gravesend, Kent DA12 1EQ
*tel* (01474) 535 978
*email* vanessaharris@members.vzi.co.uk
*Secretary* Vanessa Harris

Aims to promote knowledge, appreciation and study of the life, personality and works of the writer and wit Oscar Wilde (1854–1900). Activities include meetings, lectures, readings and exhibitions, and visits to associated locations. Members receive a journal, *The Wildean* (2 p.a.), and a newsletter, *Intentions* (6 p.a.). Founded 1990.

## The Henry Williamson Society
*General Secretary* Sue Cumming, 7 Monmouth Road, Dorchester, Dorset DT1 2DE
*tel* (01305) 264092
*email* zseagull@aol.com
*website* www.henrywilliamson.org
*Membership Secretary* Margaret Murphy, 16 Doran Drive, Redhill, Surrey RH1 6AX
*tel* (01737) 763228
*email* mm@misterman.freeserve.co.uk
*Chairman* Margaret White
*Membership* £12 p.a.

Aims to encourage a wider readership and greater understanding of the literary heritage left by Henry Williamson. Two meetings annually; also weekend activities. Publishes an annual journal. Founded 1980.

## Charles Williams Society
*Secretary* Richard Sturch, 35 Broomfield, Stacey Bushes, Milton Keynes MK12 6HA
*email* charles_wms_soc@yahoo.co.uk
*website* www.geocites.com/charles_wms_soc

Aims to promote interest in the life and work of Charles Walter Stansby Williams (1886–1945) and to make his writings more easily available. Founded 1975.

## The P.G. Wodehouse Society (UK)
*Details* Tony Ring, 34 Longfield, Great Missenden, Bucks. HP16 0EG
*tel* (01494) 864848 *fax* (01494) 863048
*email* tring@sauce34.freeserve.co.uk
*website* www.eclipse.co.uk/wodehouse
*Membership* £15 p.a.

Aims to promote enjoyment of P.G. Wodehouse (1881–1975). Publishes *Wooster Sauce* (quarterly) and *By The Way* papers (3 p.a.) which cover diverse subjects of Wodehousean interest. Holds events, entertainments and meetings throughout Britain. Founded 1997.

## Women in Publishing (WiP)
c/o Gill Rowley, 3 Gordon Road, London W5 2AD
*email* info@wipub.org.uk
*website* www.wipub.org.uk
*Membership* £25 p.a.

Promotes the status of women within publishing; encourages networking and mutual support among women; provides a forum for the discussion of ideas, trends and subjects to women in the trade; offers advice on publishing careers; supports and publicises women's achievements and successes. Each year WiP presents 2 awards: the Pandora Award is given in recognition of significant personal contributions to women in publishing, and the New Venture Award is presented to a recent venture which reflects the interests and concerns of women or minority groups in the 21st century. Founded 1979.

## Women Writers Network
*Membership Secretary* Cathy Smith, 23 Prospect Road, London NW2 2JU
*tel* 020-7794 5861
*Membership* £45 p.a.; meetings only: £5 at door

London-based network serving both salaried and independent women writers from all disciplines, and providing a forum for the exchange of information, support and networking opportunities. Holds monthly meetings, workshops and publishes a Newsletter and members' online Directory. Send sae for information. Founded 1985.

## Virginia Woolf Society of Great Britain
*Details* Stuart N. Clarke, Fairhaven, Charnleys Lane, Banks, Southport PR9 8HJ
*tel* (01903) 764655 *fax* (01903) 764655
*email* snclarke@talk21.com
*website* www.orlando.jp.org/vwsgb/
*Membership* £15 p.a., £20 overseas

Acts as a forum for British admirers of Virginia Woolf (1882–1941) to meet, correspond and share their enjoyment of her work. Publishes the *Virginia Woolf Bulletin*. Founded 1998.

## The Wordsworth Trust
Dove Cottage, Grasmere, Cumbria LA22 9SH
*tel* (015394) 35544 *fax* (015394) 35748
*email* enquiries@wordsworth.org.uk
*website* www.wordsworth.org.uk
*Membership* £20 p.a.

To preserve and enhance Dove Cottage, the Collection and the historic environment of Town End for future generations; to give people of all ages the chance to fulfill their creative potential; to develop the education and lifelong learning programmes for the benefit of the widest possible audience. Founded 1891.

## Worshipful Company of Stationers and Newspaper Makers
Stationers' Hall, London EC4M 7DD
*tel* 020-7248 2934 *fax* 020-7489 1975

*Master* C. James G. Benn, *Clerk* Brig. Denzil Sharp AFC

One of the Livery Companies of the City of London. Connected with the printing, publishing, bookselling, newspaper and allied trades. Founded 1557.

## Writernet

Cabin V, Clarendon Buildings, 25 Horsell Road, London N5 1XL
*tel* 020-7609 7474 *fax* 020-7609 7557
*email* writernet@btinternet.com
*website* www.writernet.org.uk
*Executive Director* Jonathan Meth
*Membership* Rates on application

Works with all new writing in all performance contexts. Provides writers for all forms of live and recorded performance – working at any stage of their career – with a range of services which enable them to pursue their careers better. Aims to network writers into and through the industry, principally by providing information, advice, guidance and career development training to meet the requirements of writers and producers alike. Also provides a wide range of producers who employ writers with the opportunity to make more informed choices to meet their needs. Writernet is an innovative interface between the writer and producer. Founded 1985.

## The Writers Advice Centre for Children's Books

The Courtyard Studio, 43A Lesbourne Road, Reigate, Surrey RH2 7JS
*tel* (01737) 242999
*email* WritersAdvice@aol.com
*Director* Cherith Baldry

Editorial and marketing advice to children's writers. Founded 1994.

## Writers' Circles Handbook

*Contact* Jill Dick, Oldacre, Horderns Park Road, Chapel-en-le-Frith, High Peak SK23 9SY
*tel* (01298) 812305
*email* oldacre@bt.internet.com
*website* www.btinternet.com/~oldacre

Handbook for writers' circles with information, articles, and a comprehensive list of all known circles and groups meeting in the UK. Some overseas entries too. Regular free updates available after initial purchase. Cost: £5 post free.

## Writers Guild of America, East Inc. (WGAE)

*Executive Director* Mona Mangan, 555 West 57 Street, Suite 1230, New York, NY 10019, USA
*tel* 212-767-7800
*Membership* 1.5% of covered earnings

Represents writers in screen and TV for collective bargaining. It provides member services including pension and health, as well as educational and professional activities. Founded 1954.

## Writers Guild of America, West Inc. (WGA)

*Executive Director* John McLean, 7000 West 3rd Street, Los Angeles, CA 90048, USA
*tel* 323-951-4000 *fax* 323-782-4800
*website* www.wga.org
*Membership* $2500 initiation, $25 quarterly, 1.5% of income annually

Union representing and servicing 9000 writers in film, broadcast, cable and multimedia industries for purposes of collective bargaining, contract administration and other services, and functions to protect and advance the economic, professional and creative interests of writers. Monthly publication, *Written By*, available by subscription. Founded 1933.

## Writers Guild of Canada

123 Edward Street, Suite 1225, Toronto, Ontario M5G 1E2, Canada
*tel* 416-979-7907 *toll free* 1-800-567-9974
*fax* 416-979-9273
*email* info@wgc.ca
*website* www.wgc.ca
*Executive Director* Maureen Parker
*Membership* $150 p.a. plus 2% of fees earned in the Guild's jurisdiction

Represents over 1700 professional writers of film, TV, animation, radio, documentary and multimedia. Negotiates and administers collective agreements with independent producers as well as the CBC, TVO and NFB. The Guild also publishes *Canadian Screenwriter* magazine.

## The Writers' Guild of Great Britain – see

page 498

## Writers in Oxford

*Membership Secretary* Rob Walters, 18 Paradise Square, Oxford OX1 1TW
*tel* (01865) 208930
*email* rob@satin.co.uk
*Membership* £20 p.a.

Exists to promote valuable discussion and social meetings among all kinds of published writers in and around Oxfordshire. Activities include: topical lunches and dinners, where subjects important to the writer are discussed; showcase evenings; parties. Publishes a regular newsletter, *The Oxford Writer*. Founded 1992.

## The Writers' Union of Canada

90 Richmond Street East, Suite 200, Toronto, Ontario M5C 1P1

*tel* 416-703-8982 *fax* 416-504-9090
*email* info@writersunion.ca
*website* www.writersunion.ca

## Yachting Journalists' Association

*Secretary* Barry Pickthall, Booker's Yard, The Street, Walberton, Arundel, West Sussex BN18 0PF
*tel* (01243) 555561 *fax* (01243) 555562
*email* ppl@mistral.co.uk
*Membership* £40 p.a.

Aims to further the interests of yachting, sail and power, and yachting journalism. Members vote annually for the Yachtsman of the Year, headline title of the British Nautical Awards, and the Young Sailor of the Year Award. Founded 1969.

## The Yorkshire Dialect Society

*Hon. Secretary* Michael Park, 51 Stepney Avenue, Scarborough YO12 5BW
*Membership* £10 p.a.

Aims to encourage interest in: dialect speech, the writing of dialect verse, prose and drama; the publication and circulation of dialect literature; the study of the origins and the history of dialect and kindred subjects. Organises meetings; publishes *Transactions* (annual) and *The Summer Bulletin* free to members; list of other publications on request. Founded 1897.

## Francis Brett Young Society

*Secretary* Mrs J. Hadley, 92 Gower Road, Halesowen, West Midlands B62 9BT
*tel* 0121-422 8969
*website* www.fbysociety.co.uk
*Membership* £7 p.a., £70 p.a. life

Aims to provide opportunities for members to meet, correspond, and to share the enjoyment of the author's works. Publishes a journal (2 p.a.). Founded 1979.

# Prizes and awards

This list provides details of many British prizes, competitions and awards for writers and artists, including grants, bursaries and fellowships, as well as details of major international prizes. See page 764 for a quick reference to its contents.

## J.R. Ackerley Prize for Autobiography

*Information* PEN, Lancaster House, 33 Islington High Street, London N1 9LH
*tel* 020-7713 0023 *fax* 020-7713 0005
*email* enquiries@englishpen.org
*website* www.englishpen.org

An annual prize (£1000 and a silver Dupont pen) given for an outstanding work of literary autobiography written in English and published during the previous year by an author of British nationality or an author who has been a long-term resident in the UK. No submissions please – books are nominated by the judges only. Founded 1982.

## The Alexander Prize

Literary Director, Royal Historical Society, University College London, Gower Street, London WC1E 6BT
*tel* 020-7387 7532 *fax* 020-7387 7532
*email* royalhistsoc@ucl.ac.uk
*website* www.rhs.ac.uk

An annual award of £250 or a silver medal for a paper based on original historical research. Candidates must either be under the age of 35 or be registered for a higher degree now or within the last 3 years. Closing date: 1 November each year.

## The Hans Christian Andersen Awards

*Details* International Board on Books for Young People, Nonnenweg 12, Postfach, CH–4003 Basel, Switzerland
*tel* (61) 272 29 17 *fax* (61) 272 27 57
*email* ibby@ibby.org
*website* www.ibby.org

The Medals are awarded every 2 years to a living author and an illustrator who by the outstanding value of their work are judged to have made a lasting contribution to literature for children and young people.

## Artists' Residencies in Tuscany

*Enquiries* 31 Addison Avenue, London W11 4QS
*email* rmka101@ucl.ac.uk
*website* www.geocities.com/bgomperts/Artists_in_Tuscany.html

Annual bursaries (value up to £2000) provide board, lodging and studio facilities at the Centro Verrocchio in Italy. Also, small grants to support experimental projects on specified themes. Available by competitive application. Open to artists aged 25–45 (UK only). Funded by the Juliet Gomperts Memorial Trust. Closing date: end of January. Send sae for further details.

## The Arts Council/An Chomhairle Ealaíon, Ireland

*Details* The Arts Council/An Chomhairle Ealaíon, 70 Merrion Square, Dublin 2, Republic of Ireland
*tel* (01) 618 0200 *fax* (01) 676 1302
*email* artistsservices@artscouncil.ie
*website* www.artscouncil.ie

Publishes a guide for individuals and organisations to Arts Council bursaries, awards and schemes. It is also available online. This guide is called Supports for Artists.

## Arts Council England

*Details* The Literature Dept, Arts Council England, 14 Great Peter Street, London SW1P 3NQ
*tel* (0845) 300 6200 *textphone* 020-7973 6564
*fax* 020-7973 6590
*email* enquiries@artscouncil.org.uk
*website* www.artscouncil.org.uk

Arts Council England presents national prizes rewarding creative talent in the arts. These are awarded through the Council's flexible funds and are not necessarily open to application: the Children's Award, the David Cohen British Literature Prize, the Independent Foreign Fiction Prize, John Whiting Award, Meyer Whitworth Award and the Raymond Williams Community Publishing Prize. See the separate entries for details.

## Arts Council England, London

Literature Administrator, Arts Council England, London, 2 Pear Tree Court, London EC1R 0DS
*tel* 020-7608 6100 *fax* 020-7608 4100
*website* www.artscouncil.org.uk

Arts Council England, London, is the regional office for the Capital, covering 32 boroughs and the City of London. Grants are available through the 'Grants for the arts' scheme throughout the year to support a variety of literature projects, focusing on:
• live literature
• support for small presses in the publishing of new or under-represented creative writing and, in particular, translation projects; and

• new poetry collections.

Contact Literature Unit for more information or see website for an application form.

## Arts Council England Writers' Awards

The Literature Dept, Arts Council England, 14 Great Peter Street, London SW1P 3NQ
*tel* 020-7973 6442
*email* info.literature@artscouncil.org.uk
*website* www.artscouncil.org.uk

The Arts Council England offers 15 awards annually of £7000 each for writers who need finance for a period of concentrated work on their next book. These Awards are open to writers who have been previously published in book form. Poetry, fiction, autobiography, biography, drama intended for publication, literature for young people, and other creative works are eligible. At least one award will be reserved specifically for a writer of Literature for Young People and the Clarissa Luard Award will be made to a fiction writer under 35 years of age. The Award winners will be determined by a panel of 3 judges, who are themselves writers.

## Arvon Foundation International Poetry Competition

*Details* Arvon Foundation Poetry Competition, 2nd Floor, 42A Buckingham Palace Road, London SW1W 0RE
*tel* 020-7931 7611
*email* lcomps@arvonfoundation.org

A biennial competition for previously unpublished poems written in English. First prize £5000, plus at least £5000 in other cash prizes. Next competition: spring 2006. Founded 1980.

## The Asham Award

*Details* The Administrator, Asham Literary Endowment Trust, c/o Town Hall, High Street, Lewes, East Sussex BN7 2QS

A biennial national short story competition for women writers over the age of 18 and currently resident in the UK who have not previously had a novel or anthology published. Winners receive a cash prize and inclusion in an anthology published by Bloomsbury. Next competition will be launched in October 2005. Send an A5 sae in August for an entry form. Founded 1996.

## The Australian/Vogel Literary Award

PO Box 8500, St Leonards, NSW 1590, Australia
*website* www.allenandunwin.com

An annual award of $20,000 for a chosen unpublished work of fiction, Australian history or biography. Entrants must be under 35 years of age on the closing date and must normally be residents of Australia. The MS must be between 30,000 and 125,000 words and must be an original work entirely by the entrant written in English. It cannot be under consideration to any publisher or award. See website for details. Closing date: 31 May. Founded 1980.

## Authors' Club Awards

*Details* Ann de La Grange, Secretary, Authors' Club, 40 Dover Street, London W1S 4NP
*tel* 020-7499 8581 *fax* 020-7409 0913

### Best First Novel Award

An award of £1000 is presented at a dinner held in the Club, to the author of the most promising first novel published in the UK during each year. Entries (one from each publisher's imprint) are accepted during October and November and must be full-length novels – short stories are not eligible. Instituted by Lawrence Meynell in 1954.

### Sir Banister Fletcher Award for Authors' Club

The late Sir Banister Fletcher, a former President of both the Authors' Club and the Royal Institute of British Architects instituted an annual prize 'for the book on architecture or the arts most deserving'. The award is made on the recommendation of the Professional Literature Committee of RIBA, to whom nominations for eligible titles (i.e. those written by British authors or those resident in the UK and published under a British imprint) should be submitted by the end of May of the year after publication. The prize of £1000 is awarded by the Authors' Club during September. First awarded in 1954.

## The Authors' Contingency Fund

*Details* Awards Secretary, The Society of Authors, 84 Drayton Gardens, London SW10 9SB
*tel* 020-7373 6642 *tel fax* 020-7373 5768
*email* info@societyofauthors.org
*website* www.societyofauthors.org

This fund makes modest grants to published authors who find themselves in sudden financial difficulties. Apply for an information sheet and application form.

## The Authors' Foundation

The Society of Authors, 84 Drayton Gardens, London SW10 9SB
*tel* 020-7373 6642
*email* info@societyofauthors.org
*website* www.societyofauthors.org

Grants are available to novelists, poets and writers of non-fiction who are published authors working on their next book. The aim is to provide funding (in addition to a proper advance) for research, travel or other necessary expenditure. Closing dates: 30 April and 30 September. Send sae for an information sheet. Founded in 1984 to mark the centenary of the Society of Authors.

## The Aventis Prizes for Science Books

*Details* The Royal Society, 6–9 Carlton House
Terrace, London SW1Y 5AG
*tel* 020-7451 2513 *fax* 020-7451 2693
*email* scott.keir@royalsoc.ac.uk
*website* www.aventissciencebookprizes.com

These annual prizes reward books that make science
more accessible to readers of all ages and
backgrounds. Prizes of up to a total of £30,000 are
awarded in 2 categories: General (£10,000) for a
book with a general readership; and Junior (£10,000)
for a book written for people aged under 14. Up to 5
shortlisted authors in each category receive £1000.

Eligible books should be written in English and
their first publication in the UK must have been
between 1 January and 31 December 2004. Seven
copies of each entry should be supplied with a fully
completed entry form. Entries may cover any aspect
of science and technology but educational
textbooks published for professional or specialist
audiences are not eligible. The Prizes are managed
by the Royal Society in cooperation with the
sponsor, Aventis. Founded 1988.

## BA/Book Data Author of the Year

*Details* The Booksellers Association of the UK and
Ireland Ltd, 272 Vauxhall Bridge Road,
London SW1V 1BA
*tel* 020-7802 0802 *fax* 020-7802 0803

This annual award of £1000 is judged by members
of the Booksellers Association (3200 bookshops) in
a postal ballot. Any living, British or Irish published
writer is eligible and the award is given to the
author judged to have had the most impact in the
year. Founded 1993.

## BAFTA (British Academy of Film and Television Arts) Awards

*Chief Executive* Amanda Berry, 195 Piccadilly,
London W1J 9LN
*tel* 020-7734 0022 *fax* 020-7292 5868
*email* reception@bafta.org
*website* www.bafta.org

The pre-eminent organisation in the UK for film,
TV and interactive, recognising and promoting the
achievement and endeavour of industry
practitioners. BAFTA Awards are awarded annually
by members to their peers in recognition of their
skills and expertise. Founded 1947.

## Verity Bargate Award

*Details* Literary Assistant, Soho Theatre *and* Writers'
Centre, 21 Dean Street, London W1D 3NE
*email* writers@sohotheatre.com
*website* www.sohotheatre.com

A biennial award, set up in honour of the
company's co-founder, is made to the writer of a
new and previously unperformed full-length play.

Writers with 3 or more professional productions to
their credit are ineligible. The prize represents an
option to produce the play by Soho Theatre
Company. Next award: 2006.

## The David Berry Prize

Council of the Royal Historical Society, University
College London, Gower Street, London WC1E 6BT
*tel* 020-7387 7532 *fax* 020-7387 7532
*email* royalhistsoc@ucl.ac.uk
*website* www.rhs.ac.uk

Candidates may select any subject dealing with
Scottish history. Value of prize: £250. Closing date:
31 October each year.

## Besterman/McColvin Medals – see The CILIP/Whitaker Reference Awards

## Biscuit International Poetry and Fiction Prizes

*Details* Biscuit International Poetry and Fiction
Prizes, Biscuit Publishing, PO Box 123, Washington,
Newcastle upon Tyne NE37 2YW
*tel/fax* 0191-431 1263
*email* info@biscuitpublishing.com
*website* www.biscuitpublishing.com
*Director* Brian Lister

The outright poetry winner has his/her full
collection published and £1000 advance royalties.
Outright short story winner has his/her novella
(40,000 words) or a short story collection published
and £1000 advance royalties. Write for set of rules.
Closing date: 31 May each year. Founded 2001.

## The Bisto Book of the Year Awards

*Details* The Administrator, Children's Books
Ireland, 17 Lower Camden Street, Dublin 2,
Republic of Ireland
*tel* (01) 872 5854 *fax* (01) 872 5854
*email* info@childrensbooksireland.com,
bistoawards@childrensbooksireland.com

Annual awards open to authors and/or illustrators
who were born in Ireland, or who were living in
Ireland at the time of a book's publication.

### The Bisto Book of the Year Award
An award of €3000 is presented to the overall
winner (text and/or illustration).

### Bisto Merit Awards
A prize fund of €2400 is divided between 3 authors
and/or illustrators.

### Bisto Eilís Dillon Award
An award of €1000 is presented to an author for a
first children's book.

Closing date: 15 January 2005 for work published
between 1 January and 31 December 2004. Founded
1990.

## The Kathleen Blundell Trust

Kathleen Blundell Trust, The Society of Authors,
84 Drayton Gardens, London SW10 9SB
*tel* 020-7373 6642
*email* info@societyofauthors.org
*website* www.societyofauthors.org

Awards are given to published writers under the age
of 40 to assist them with their next book. The
author's work must 'contribute to the greater
understanding of existing social and economic
organisation', but fiction is not excluded. Closing
dates: 30 April and 30 September. Send sae for an
information sheet.

## The Boardman Tasker Prize

*Details* Maggie Body, Pound House, Llangennith,
Swansea SA3 1JQ
*email* margaretbody@lineone.net
*website* www.boardmantasker.co.uk

This annual prize of £2000 is given for a work of
fiction, non-fiction or poetry, the central theme of
which is concerned with the mountain environment.
Authors of any nationality are eligible but the work
must be published or distributed in the UK. Entries
from publishers only. Founded 1983.

## The Man Booker International Prize

Colman Getty PR, Middlesex House,
34–42 Cleveland Street, London W1T 4JE
*tel* 020-7631 2666
*email* pr@colmangettypr.co.uk
*website* www.manbookerinternational.com

A new prize of £60,000 to complement the annual
Man Booker Prize by recognising one writer's
achievement in continued creativity, development
and overall contribution to world fiction. It will be
awarded once every 2 years to a living author who
has published fiction either originally in English, or
generally available in translation in the English
language.
    The Man Booker International Prize will echo
and reinforce the annual Man Booker Prize for
Fiction in that literary excellence will be its sole
focus. The first winner will be announced in mid
2005. Sponsored by the Man Group.

## The Man Booker Prize

Colman Getty PR, Middlesex House,
34–42 Cleveland Street, London W1T 4TE
*tel* 020-7631 2666 *fax* 020-7631 2699
*email* cathryn@colmangettypr.co.uk
*website* www.themanbookerprize.co.uk
*Contact* Cathryn Summerhayes

This annual prize for fiction of £65,000, including
£2500 to each of 6 shortlisted authors, is awarded to
the best novel published each year. It is open to
novels written in English by citizens of the British
Commonwealth and Republic of Ireland and
published for the first time in the UK by a British

publisher, although previous publication of a book
outside the UK does not disqualify it. Entries only
from UK publishers who may each submit not
more than 2 novels with scheduled publication
dates between 1 October of the previous year and
30 September of the current year, but the judges
may also ask for other eligible novels to be
submitted to them. In addition, publishers may
submit eligible titles by authors who have been
shortlisted or won the Booker Prize previously.
Sponsored by the Man Group.

## Booktrust Early Years Awards

*Details* Booktrust, Book House, 45 East Hill,
London SW18 2QZ
*tel* 020-8516 2973 *fax* 020-8516 2978
*email* kate@booktrust.org.uk,
tarryn@booktrust.org.uk
*Contact* Kate Mervyn Jones, Tarryn McKay

The winners of each of 2 categories, Best Picture
Book for Pre-School Children and the Best New
Illustrator Award, will each receive a cheque for
£2000. Closing date: June 2005.

## The Booktrust Teenage Prize

*Details* Booktrust, Book House, 45 East Hill,
London SW18 2QZ
*tel* 020-8516 2986 *fax* 020-8516 2978
*email* hannah@booktrust.org.uk
*Contact* Hannah Rutland

The first annual national book prize to recognise
and celebrate the best in young adult fiction. The
author of the best book for teenagers receives £1500
and is chosen from a shortlist of 6. Eligible books
must be fiction, aimed at teenagers between the ages
of 13 and 16 and written in English by a citizen of
the UK, or an author resident in the UK. The work
must be published between 1 July and 30 June.
Established 2003.

## BP Portrait Award

*Details* National Portrait Gallery, St Martin's Place,
London WC2H 0HE
*tel* 020-7306 0055 *fax* 020-7306 0056
*website* www.npg.org.uk

An annual award to encourage young artists (aged
18–40) to focus upon and develop the theme of
portraiture within their work. 1st prize: £25,000 plus
at the judges' discretion a commission worth £3000 to
be agreed between the NPG and the artist; 2nd prize
£8000; 3rd prize £4000; 4th prize £4000. Closing date:
March/April. A selection of entrants' work is exhibited
at the National Portrait Gallery June–Oct.

## Alfred Bradley Bursary Award

*Details* BBC Radio Drama Department,
BBC North, New Broadcasting House,
Oxford Road, Manchester M60 1SJ
*tel* 0161-244 4052

This biennial bursary of £6000 (over 2 years, plus a full commission for a radio play) is awarded to a writer resident in the North of England who has had a small amount of work published or produced. The scheme also allows for a group of finalists to receive small bursaries and develop ideas for radio drama commissions. Next closing date: November 2004.

## The Branford Boase Award

*Details* The Administrator, 8 Bolderwood Close, Bishopstoke, Eastleigh SO50 5PG
*tel* (01962) 826658 *fax* (01962) 856615
*email* anne@marleyhcl.freeserve.co.uk

An annual award is made to a first-time writer of a full-length children's novel (age 7+) published in the preceding year; the editor is also recognised. Its aim is to encourage new writers for children and to recognise the role of perceptive editors in developing new talent. The Award was set up in memory of the outstanding children's writer Henrietta Branford and the gifted editor and publisher Wendy Boase who both died in 1999. Closing date for nominations: end of March of each year. Founded 2000.

## The Bridport Prize

*Details* Bridport Arts Centre, South Street, Bridport, Dorset DT6 3NR
*tel* (01308) 485064 *fax* (01308) 485120
*email* frances@poorton.demon.co.uk
*website* www.bridportprize.org.uk

Annual prizes are awarded for poetry and short stories – 1st £3000, 2nd £1000, 3rd £500 in both categories. Entries should be in English, original work, typed or clearly written, and never published, read on radio/TV/stage. Winning stories are read by a leading London literary agent, without obligation, and an anthology of winning entries is published each autumn. Send sae for entry form or enter online. Closing date: 30 June each year.

## The British Academy Book Prize

*Details* External Relations, The British Academy, 10 Carlton House Terrace, London SW1Y 5AH
*tel* 020-7969 5200 *fax* 020-7969 5413
*email* m.reade@britac.ac.uk
*website* www.britac.ac.uk

Aims to increase the public appreciation of the humanities and social sciences by celebrating outstanding scholarly works that appeal to the non-specialist. Eligible books must be published in English in the UK; the author may be of any nationality. The award is £2500. Applications from publishers only. Closing date: 11 February 2005.

## British Academy Medals and Prizes

The British Academy, 10 Carlton House Terrace, London SW1Y 5AH
*tel* 020-7969 5200 *fax* 020-7969 5300
*email* secretary@britac.ac.uk
*website* www.britac.ac.uk

A number of medals and prizes are awarded for outstanding work in various fields of the humanities on the recommendation of specialist committees: Burkitt Medal for Biblical Studies; Derek Allen Prize (made annually in turn for musicology, numismatics and Celtic studies); Sir Israel Gollancz Prize (for English studies); Grahame Clark Medal for Prehistoric Archaeology; Kenyon Medal for Classical Studies; Rose Mary Crawshay Prize (for English literature); Serena Medal for Italian Studies; Leverhulme Medal and Prize.

## The British Academy Research Awards

The British Academy, 10 Carlton House Terrace, London SW1Y 5AH
*tel* 020-7969 5200 *fax* 020-7969 5300
*email* secretary@britac.ac.uk
*website* www.britac.ac.uk

These awards are made quarterly to scholars conducting advanced academic research in the humanities and social sciences, and normally resident in the UK. Applications are accepted for travel and maintenance expenses in connection with an approved programme of research. There are also awards for attendance at scholarly conferences overseas; and for postdoctoral fellowships, research readerships and research professorships.

## British Book Awards

*Details* Merric Davidson, PO Box 60, Cranbrook, Kent TN17 2ZR
*tel* (01580) 212041 *fax* (01580) 212041
*email* nibbies@mdla.co.uk
*website* www.britishbookawards.com

Presented annually, major categories include: Author of the Year, Publisher of the Year, Bookseller of the Year, Children's Book of the Year. Founded 1989.

## British Council Grants to Artists Scheme

*Details* Grants to Artists Officer, Visual Arts Dept, British Council, 10 Spring Gardens, London SW1A 2BN
*tel* 020-7389 3045 *fax* 020-7389 3101
*website* www.britishcouncil.org/arts

The Visual Arts Department of the British Council is concerned with the promotion and presentation of UK art overseas. These awards (£100–£2000) are specifically aimed at UK visual artists who have been invited to exhibit their work abroad. It is there to help with the costs of the artists' travel and the transport and packaging of their work. Artists should submit a completed application form, CV, 6 slides of their work and a letter of invitation from the overseas venue before the deadline. The committee meets 3–4 weeks after this to decide on all the applications. Closing dates: 1 Feb, 1 May, 1 Aug, 1 Nov.

## British Fantasy Awards

*Details* Robert Parkinson, Secretary, The British Fantasy Society, 201 Reddish Road, South Reddish, Stockport SK5 7HR
*email* faliol@yahoo.com
*website* www.britishfantasysociety.org.uk

Members of the British Fantasy Society vote annually for the best novel, short fiction, artist, small press and anthology of the preceding year. The awards take the form of a statuette. Closing date for nominations: end May each year. Founded 1972.

## British Press Awards

*Event Manager* Angie Reid, Quantum Business Media, 19 Scarbrook Road, Croydon CR9 1LX
*tel* 020-8565 4392 *fax* 020-8565 4395
*email* angier@qpp.co.uk

Annual awards for British journalism judged by more than 80 respected, influential judges as well as representatives from all the national newspaper groups. Closing date: mid January 2005.

## The Caine Prize for African Writing

*Details* Nick Elam, Administrator, 2 Drayson Mews, London W8 4LY
*tel* 020-7376 0440 *fax* 020-7938 3728
*email* caineprize@jftaylor.com

An annual award of $15,000 for a short story published in English (may be a translation into English) by an African writer in the 5 years before the closing date, and not previously submitted. Indicative length 3000–15,000 words. Submissions only by publishers. Closing date: 31 January each year.

## Cardiff International Poetry Competition

*Details/entry form* Cardiff International Poetry Competition, PO Box 438, Cardiff CF10 5YA
*website* www.academi.org

Eight prizes totalling £7000 are awarded annually for unpublished poetry written in English (prizes: 1st £5000; 2nd £700; 3rd £300; plus 5 prizes of £200). Entry forms may also be downloaded from the website. Closing date: January 2005.

## Carnegie Medal – see The CILIP Carnegie and Kate Greenaway Awards

## The Children's Award

*Details* Charles Hart, Literature Dept, Arts Council England, 14 Great Peter Street, London SW1P 3NQ
*tel* 020-7973 6480
*email* charles.hart@artscouncil.org.uk
*website* www.artscouncil.org.uk

This award of £6000 is for playwrights who write plays of at least 45 minutes long for children up to the age of 12. Plays must have been professionally produced between 1 July 2004 and 30 June 2005.

## The Children's Laureate

*Details* The Administrator, 19 Melrose Court, Calmore, Southampton SO40 2UZ
*tel* 023-8086 8562
*email* childrenslaureate@talkgas.net

A biennial award of £10,000 to honour a writer or illustrator of children's books for a lifetime's achievement. It highlights the importance of children's book creators in developing readers and illustrators of the future. Children's Laureates: Quentin Blake (1999–2001), Anne Fine (2001–3), Michael Morpurgo (2003–5). Founded 1998.

## Cholmondeley Awards

*Administered by* The Society of Authors, 84 Drayton Gardens, London SW10 9SB

These honorary awards are to recognise the achievement and distinction of individual poets. Submissions are not accepted. Total value of awards about £8000. Established by the then Dowager Marchioness of Cholmondeley in 1965.

## The CILIP Carnegie and Kate Greenaway Awards

*email* marketing@cilip.org.uk
*website* www.ckg.org.uk

Recommendations for the following 2 awards are invited from members of CILIP (the Chartered Institute of Library and Information Professionals), who are asked to submit a preliminary list of not more than 2 titles for each award, accompanied by a 50-word appraisal justifying the recommendation of each book. The awards are selected by the Youth Libraries Group of CILIP.

### Carnegie Medal

Awarded annually for an outstanding book for children (fiction or non-fiction) written in English and first published in the UK during the preceding year or co-published elsewhere within a 3-month time lapse.

### Kate Greenaway Medal

Awarded annually for an outstanding illustrated book for children first published in the UK during the preceding year or co-published elsewhere within a 3-month time lapse. Books intended for older as well as younger children are included, and reproduction will be taken into account. The Colin Mears Award (£5000) is awarded annually to the winner of the Kate Greenaway Medal.

## The CILIP/Whitaker Reference Awards

*email* marketing@cilip.org.uk
*website* www.cilip.org.uk

### The Besterman/McColvin Medals

Awarded annually for outstanding works of reference published in the UK during the preceding year. There are 2 categories, one for electronic formats and one for printed works. Recommendations are invited from Members of CILIP (the Chartered Institute of Library and Information Professionals), publishers and others, who are asked to submit a preliminary list of not more than 3 titles via the website. Winners receive a cash prize of £500, a certificate and a prestigious golden medal.

### The Walford Award

Awarded annually to an individual who has made a sustained and continued contribution to the science and art of British bibliography over a period of years. The bibliographer's work can encompass effort in the history, classification and description of printed, written, audiovisual and machine-readable materials. Recommendations may be made for the work of a living person or persons, or for an organisation. The award can be made to a British bibliographer or to a person or organisation working in the UK. The winner receives a cash prize of £500.

### The Wheatley Medal

Awarded annually for an outstanding index published during the preceding year. Printed indexes to any type of publication may be submitted for consideration, providing that the whole work, including the index, or the index alone has originated in the UK. Recommendations for the award are invited from members of CILIP and the Society of Indexers, publishers and others; nominations should be made via the website. The final selection is made by a committee consisting of representatives of the CILIP Cataloguing and Indexing Group and the Society of Indexers.

## Citigroup Photography Prize

*Information* The Photographers' Gallery, 5 Great Newport Street, London WC2H 7HY
*tel* 020-7831 1772 *fax* 020-7836 9704
*website* www.photonet.org.uk

An annual prize of £20,000 is awarded to the individual who is judged to have made the most significant contribution to the medium of photography over the previous year. Anyone who has exhibited or published a substantial body of work in the UK in the year prior to the award is eligible. Runners up are awarded £2000 each. Nominations deadline: August 2005 (provisional). Founded 1996.

## Arthur C. Clarke Award

*email* arthurcclarkeaward@yahoo.co.uk
*website* www.clarkeaward.com

An annual award of £2004 plus engraved bookend is given for the best science fiction novel with first UK publication during the previous calendar year. Titles are submitted by publishers.
Founded 1985.

## The David Cohen British Literature Prize

*Details* The Literature Dept, Arts Council England, 14 Great Peter Street, London SW1P 3NQ
*tel* 020-7973 5325
*website* www.artscouncil.org.uk

This prize marks a lifetime's literary achievement. The winner receives £40,000 plus an additional £12,000 to fund new work. For further information about the prize, including how members of the public can forward their choice of author to be considered for the judges, contact the Literature Dept.

## Commonwealth Writers Prize

*Details* Booktrust, Book House, 45 East Hill, London SW18 2QZ
*tel* 020-8516 2973/2972 *fax* 020-8516 2978
*email* kate@booktrust.org.uk, tarryn@booktrust.org.uk
*Contact* Kate Mervyn-Jones, Tarryn McKay

This annual award is for the best work of fiction in English by a citizen of the Commonwealth published in the year prior to the award. A prize of £10,000 is awarded for overall best book and £3000 is awarded to the overall best first published book. The overall winners are selected from 8 regional winners who each receive £1000 for being regional winners. Sponsored by the Commonwealth Foundation. Established 1987.

## The Thomas Cook Travel Book Award

*Details* Travel Book Award, Thomas Cook Publishing, PO Box 227, Coningsby Road, Peterborough PE3 8SB
*tel* (01733) 417352 *fax* (01733) 416688

This annual award (£10,000) is given to encourage the art of travel writing and to inspire the wish to travel. Travel narrative books (150pp minimum) written in English and published between 1 January and 31 December of the preceding year are eligible. Established in 1980.

## The Duff Cooper Prize

*Details* Artemis Cooper, 54 St Maur Road, London SW6 4DP
*tel* 020-7736 3729 *fax* 020-7731 7638

An annual prize for a literary work in the field of biography, history, politics or poetry published in English or French and submitted by a recognised publisher during the previous 12 months. The prize of £3000 comes from a Trust Fund established by the friends and admirers of Duff Cooper, 1st Viscount Norwich (1890–1954) after his death.

## The Rose Mary Crawshay Prizes

The British Academy, 10 Carlton House Terrace, London SW1Y 5AH
*tel* 020-7969 5200 *fax* 020-7969 5300
*email* secretary@britac.ac.uk

*website* www.britac.ac.uk

One or more prizes are awarded each year to women of any nationality who, in the judgement of the Council of the British Academy, have written or published within the 3 calendar years immediately preceding the date of the award an historical or critical work of sufficient value on any subject connected with English literature, preference being given to a work regarding Byron, Shelley or Keats. Founded 1888.

## The John D. Criticos Prize

*Coordinator* Michael Moschos, The London Hellenic Society, 11 Stormont Road, London N6 4NS
*tel* 020-7626 0006 *fax* 020-7626 0601

A prize of £10,000 will be awarded to an artist, writer or researcher for an original work on Hellenic culture. Areas of particular interest are archaeology, art, art history, history and literature. No application necessary: send 2 copies of book plus covering letter. Closing date: 31 January. Founded 1996.

## CWA Awards

*email* secretary@thecwa.co.uk
*website* www.thecwa.co.uk

Awards for crime writing: the Cartier Diamond Dagger; the Creasey Dagger; the Gold Dagger and Silver Dagger for Fiction; the Gold Dagger for Non-Fiction; the Short Story Dagger; the CWA Ellis Peters Historical Dagger; the Debut Dagger; the Ian Fleming Steel Dagger, the Dagger in the Library. See website for details.

## The Rhys Davies Trust

*Details* Prof Meic Stephens, The Secretary, The Rhys Davies Trust, 10 Heol Don, Whitchurch, Cardiff CF14 2AU
*tel* 029-2062 3359 *fax* 029-2052 9202

The Trust aims to foster Welsh writing in English and offers financial assistance to English-language literary projects in Wales, directly or in association with other bodies.

## The Dundee Book Prize

*Details* Deborah Kennedy, Dundee City Council, Economic Development, 3 City Square, Dundee DD1 3BA
*tel* (01382) 434275 *fax* (01382) 434096
*email* deborah.kennedy@dundeecity.gov.uk
*website* www.dundeecity.gov.uk

A biennial prize (£6000 and the chance of publication by Polygon) awarded for an unpublished novel. Next award: 2006. Founded 1996.

## EAC Art Awards for the Over 60s

*Details* 11 Westrow, Westleigh Avenue, London SW15 6RH
*tel* 020-8789 6185 *fax* 020-8789 6185

An annual competition for people over the age of 60 for works in the 2 dimensional medium of their choice in 4 categories – portrait, still life, flora/fauna, land/seascape. The judges look for original and creative ideas in preference to copies of other artists' work. Prizes of £1000 are awarded in each category. Closing date: April. Founded 1995.

## The T.S. Eliot Prize

*Applications* Poetry Book Society, Book House, 45 East Hill, London SW18 2QZ
*tel* 020-8870 8403
*email* info@poetrybooks.co.uk
*website* www.poetrybooks.co.uk

An annual prize of £10,000 is awarded to the best collection of new poetry published in the UK or the Republic of Ireland during the year. Submissions are invited from publishers in the summer. Donated by Valerie Eliot. Founded 1993.

## Encore Award

*Details* Awards Secretary, The Society of Authors, 84 Drayton Gardens, London SW10 9SB
*tel* 020-7373 6642
*email* info@societyofauthors.org
*website* www.societyofauthors.org

This annual award of £10,000 is for the best second novel of the year. The work submitted must be: a novel by one author who has had one (and only one) novel published previously, and in the English language, first published in the UK. Entries should be submitted by the publisher. Closing date: 30 November.

## European Jewish Publication Society Grants

*Details* Dr Colin Shindler, Editorial Director, European Jewish Publication Society, PO Box 19948, London N3 3ZJ
*tel* 020-8346 1776
*email* cs@ejps.org.uk
*website* www.ejps.org.uk

Awards of up to £3000 are given to publishers to assist in the publication of books of Jewish interest, including fiction, non-fiction and poetry. Translations from other languages are considered eligible. Founded 1995.

## European Publishers Award for Photography

*Details* Dewi Lewis Publishing, 8 Broomfield Road, Heaton Moor, Stockport SK4 4ND
*tel* 0161-442 9450 *fax* 0161-442 9450
*email* mail@dewilewispublishing.com
*website* www.dewilewispublishing.com

Annual competition for the best set of photographs suitable for publication as a book. All photographic material must be completed and unpublished in book form and be original. Projects conceived as anthologies are not acceptable. Copyright must belong to the photographer. Closing date: 31 January. Founded 1994.

## Christopher Ewart-Biggs Memorial Prize

*Details* The Secretary, Memorial Prize, Flat 3, 149 Hamilton Terrace, London NW8 9QS
*fax* 020-7328 0699

This prize of £5000 is awarded once every 2 years to the writer, of any nationality, whose work is judged to contribute most to:
• peace and understanding in Ireland;
• to closer ties between the peoples of Britain and Ireland;
• or to cooperation between the partners of the EU.

Eligible works must be published during the 2 years to 31 December 2004. Closing date: 31 December 2005.

## The Geoffrey Faber Memorial Prize

An annual prize of £1000 is awarded in alternate years for a volume of verse and for a volume of prose fiction, first published originally in the UK during the 2 years preceding the year in which the award is given which is, in the opinion of the judges, of the greatest literary merit. Eligible writers must be not more than 40 years old at the date of publication of the book and a citizen of the UK and Colonies, of any other Commonwealth state or of the Republic of Ireland. The 3 judges are reviewers of poetry or fiction who are nominated each year by the literary editors of newspapers and magazines which regularly publish such reviews. Faber and Faber invite nominations from reviewers and literary editors. No submissions for the prize are to be made. Established in 1963 by Faber and Faber Ltd, as a memorial to the founder and first Chairman of the firm.

## The Alfred Fagon Award

*tel* 020-7251 4052
*email* info@alfredfagonaward.co.uk
*website* www.alfredfagonaward.co.uk
*Submissions* The Alfred Fagon Award,
The Royal Court Theatre, Sloane Square,
London SW1W 8AS

An annual award of £3500 for the best new play (which need not have been produced) for the theatre in English. TV and radio plays and film scripts will not be considered. Writers from the Caribbean or with Caribbean antecedents are eligible. Applicants should submit 2 copies of their play plus sae for return of their script and a CV which includes details of the writer's Caribbean connection. Closing date: end August. Founded 1997.

## Fallen Leaves Short Story Competition

*Details* Cork Campus Radio, Level 3, Áras na Mac Léinn, University College Cork, Cork City, Republic of Ireland
*tel* (021) 4902170 *fax* (021) 4903108
*email* radio@ucc.ie
*Contact* Sinéad O'Donnell, Station Manager

Fallen Leaves is a short story radio series devised to provide new and innovative Irish short story writers with an opportunity to write for radio. Stories should be 1800–2000 words long and unpublished. Fee: £4 for the first story and £2 for each subseqent story. Founded 1996.

## The Eleanor Farjeon Award

An annual prize of (minimum) £750 may be given to a librarian, teacher, author, artist, publisher, reviewer, TV producer or any other person working with or for children through books. Instituted in 1965 by the Children's Book Circle for distinguished services to children's books and named after the much-loved children's writer.

## The Fish Short Story Prize

Durrus, Bantry, Co. Cork,
Republic of Ireland
*tel* (353) 27 61246
*email* info@fishpublishing.com
*website* www.fishpublishing.com
*Contact* Clem Cairns

An annual international award which aims to discover, encourage and publish exciting new literary talent. Previously unpublished stories of up to 5000 words are eligible. 1st prize: £1000 (€1500); 2nd prize: one week residence at Anam Cara Writers' and Artists' Retreat, West Cork. The best 15–20 stories are published in an anthology. Entry fee: £11 (€15) for the first, £8 (€10) for subsequent entries. Concession rate: £8 (€10). Closing date: 30 November. Critiques available all year for £35 (€45). Founded 1994.

## E.M. Forster Award

The distinguished English author, E.M. Forster, bequeathed the American publication rights and royalties of his posthumous novel *Maurice* to Christopher Isherwood, who transferred them to the American Academy of Arts and Letters (633 West 155th Street, New York, NY 10032, USA), for the establishment of an E.M. Forster Award, currently $15,000, to be given annually to a British or Irish writer for a stay in the USA. Applications for this award are not accepted.

## Forward Poetry Prizes

*Details* Forward Poetry Prize Administrator, Colman Getty PR, Middlesex House, 34–42 Cleveland Street, London W1T 5JE
*tel* 020-7631 2666 *fax* 020-7631 2699
*email* pr@colmangettypr.co.uk

Three prizes are awarded annually:
• The Forward Prize for best collection of poetry published between 1 October and 30 September (£10,000);
• The Prize for best first collection of poetry published between 1 October and 30 September (£5000); and
• The Tolman Cunard Prize for best individual poem, published but not as part of a collection between 1 May and 30 April (£1000).

All poems entered are also considered for inclusion in the *Forward Book of Poetry*, an annual anthology. Entries must be submitted by book publishers and editors of newspapers, periodicals and magazines in the UK and Eire. Entries from poets will not be accepted. Established 1992.

## Miles Franklin Literary Award
*email* linda.ingalelo@permanentgroup.com.au

This annual award of $28,000 is for a novel or play first published in the preceding year, which presents Australian life in any of its phases. More than one entry may be submitted by each author, and collaborations between 2 or more authors are eligible. Biographies, collections of short stories or children's books are not eligible. Closing date: approx. 15 December. Founded 1957.

## The Lionel Gelber Prize
*Details* Prize Manager, The Lionel Gelber Prize, c/o Munk Centre for International Studies, 1 Devonshire Place, Toronto, Ontario M5S 3K7, Canada
*tel* 416-946 8900 *fax* 416-946 8915
*email* meisner@interlog.com
*website* www.utoronto.ca/mcis/gelber

This international prize is awarded annually in Canada to the author of the year's most outstanding work of non-fiction in the field of international relations. Submissions must be published in English or in English translation. Books must be submitted by the publisher. Full eligibility details are on website. Established 1989.

## The Gilchrist-Fisher Award
*Contact* Maria Morrow, Rebecca Hossack Gallery, 35 Windmill Street, London W1T 2JS

Biennial prize (1st £3500, 2nd prize £1000) awarded to a young artist (aged under 30) for landscape painting. Award exhibition for finalists held at Rebecca Hossack Gallery, London W1. Founded 1987.

## Gladstone History Book Prize
*Submissions* Executive Secretary, Royal Historical Society, University College London, Gower Street, London WC1E 6BT
*email* royalhistsoc@ucl.ac.uk

An annual award (value £1000) for a history book. The book must:
• be on any historical subject which is not primarily related to British history;
• be its author's first solely written history book;
• have been published in English during the calendar year of 2004 by a scholar normally resident in the UK;
• be an original and scholarly work of historical research.

Three non-returnable copies of an eligible book should be submitted before 31 December.

## Glenfiddich Food & Drink Awards
*Details* William Grant & Sons, The Glenfiddich Awards, Independent House, 84 Lower Moatlake Road, Richmond, Surrey TW9 2HS
*tel* 020-8332 1188 *fax* 020-8332 1695
*website* www.glenfiddich.com/foodanddrink

Awards are given annually to recognise excellence in writing, publishing and broadcasting relating to the subjects of food and drink. £1000 is given to each of 12 categories, together with a special bottling of Glenfiddich Single Malt Scotch whisky and an award. The overall winner receives the Glenfiddich Trophy and an additional £3000. Founded 1970.

## Kate Greenaway Medal – see The CILIP
### Carnegie and Kate Greenaway Awards

## E.C. Gregory Trust Fund
*Details* Awards Secretary, The Society of Authors, 84 Drayton Gardens, London SW10 9SB
*tel* 020-7373 6642
*email* info@societyofauthors.org
*website* www.societyofauthors.org

A number of substantial awards are made annually for the encouragement of young poets who can show that they are likely to benefit from an opportunity to give more time to writing. An eligible candidate must:
• be a British subject by birth but not a national of Eire or any of the British dominions or colonies and be ordinarily resident in the UK or Northern Ireland;
• be under the age of 30 on 31 March in the year of the Award (i.e. the year following submission). Send sae for entry form. Closing date: 31 October.

## Griffin Poetry Prize
*Details* The Griffin Trust for Excellence in Poetry, 6610 Edwards Boulevard, Mississauga, Ontario L5T 2V6, Canada
*tel* 905-565-5993 *fax* 905-564 3645
*website* www.griffinpoetryprize.com

Two annual prizes of Can.$40,000 will be awarded for collections of poetry published in English during the preceding year. One prize will go to a living Canadian poet, the other to a living poet from any country. Collections of poetry translated into English from other languages are also eligible and will be assessed for their literary quality in English. Submissions only from publishers. Closing date: 31 December. Founded 2000.

### The Guardian Children's Fiction Prize
*tel* 020-7239 9694
*email* books@guardian.co.uk
*The Guardian's* annual prize of £1500 is for a work of children's fiction for children over 8 (no picture books) published by a British or Commonwealth writer. The winning book is chosen by the Children's Book Editor together with a team of 3–4 other authors of children's books.

### The Guardian First Book Award
*Contact* Claire Armitstead
*tel* 020-7239 9694 *fax* 020-7713 4366
*email* books@guardian.co.uk
*Submissions* Literary Editor, The Guardian, 119 Farringdon Road, London EC1R 3ER

Open to first-time authors published in English in the UK across all genres of writing, the award will recognise and reward new writing by honouring an author's first book. The winner will receive £10,000 plus an advertising package within *The Guardian* and *The Observer*. Publishers may submit up to 3 titles per imprint with publication dates between January and December 2005. Closing date: late July.

### The Guardian Research Fellowship
*Details* Guardian Research Fellowship, College Secretary, Nuffield College, Oxford OX1 1NF
*tel* (01865) 278542 *fax* (01865) 278666
*email* college.secretary@nuffield.oxford.ac.uk
A biennial Fellowship to be held for one year at Nuffield College, Oxford, to research or study any project related to the experience of working in the media. It is hoped that the Fellow will produce a book or substantial piece of written work. The Fellow will be asked to give the *Guardian* lecture following the end of their Fellowship. The Fellowship is open to people working in newspapers, TV, the internet or other media. Closing date: 9 January. Founded 1987.

### The Paul Hamlyn Foundation Awards to Artists
*Details* The Administrator, 18 Queen Anne's Gate, London SW1H 9AA
*tel* 020-7227 3500 *fax* 020-7222 0601
*email* information@phf.org.uk
Five awards of £30,000 spread over 3 years will be made to visual artists in 2005 to support the creative process. Strength of talent, promise and need, as well as achievement, are all assessed.

Nominations are made by a nationwide panel of 20 artists and others. The scheme is not open to application. Founded 1993.

### The Hawthornden Prize
*Details* The Administrator, 42A Hays Mews, Berkeley Square, London W1J 5QA
This prize is awarded annually to the author of what, in the opinion of the Committee, is the best work of imaginative literature published during the preceding calendar year by a British author. Books do not have to be specially submitted.

### Hawthornden Writers' Fellowships
The Administrator, Hawthornden Castle International Retreat for Writers, Hawthornden Castle, Lasswade, Midlothian EH18 1EG
*tel* 0131-440 2180
Applications are invited from novelists, poets, dramatists and other creative writers whose work has already been published. Four-week fellowships are offered to those working on a current project.

### Francis Head Bequest
*Details* Awards Secretary, The Society of Authors, 84 Drayton Gardens, London SW10 9SB
*tel* 020-7373 6642 *tel fax* 020-7373 5768
*email* info@societyofauthors.org
*website* www.societyofauthors.org
This fund provides grants to published British authors over the age of 35 who need financial help during a period of illness, disablement or temporary financial crisis. Apply for an information sheet and application form.

### The Felicia Hemans Prize for Lyrical Poetry
*Submissions* The Sub-Dean, Faculty of Arts, The University of Liverpool, PO Box 147, Liverpool L69 3BX
*tel* 0151-794 2458 *fax* 0151-794 3765
*email* wilderc@liv.ac.uk
This annual prize of books or money, open to past and present members and students of the University of Liverpool only, is awarded for a lyrical poem, the subject of which may be chosen by the competitor. Only one poem, either published or unpublished, may be submitted. Poems, endorsed 'Hemans Prize', must be submitted by 1 May.

### Heywood Hill Literary Prize
*Administration* Heywood Hill Booksellers, 10 Curzon Street, London W1J 5HH
An award of £15,000 is given annually to a person chosen for their lifetime's contribution to the enjoyment of books. No applications. Established 1995.

## William Hill Sports Book of the Year Award

*Details* Graham Sharpe, William Hill Organisation, Greenside House, 50 Station Road, London N22 4TP
*tel* 020-8918 3731

This award is given annually in November for a book with a sporting theme (record books and listings excluded). The title must be in the English language, and published for the first time in the UK during the relevant calendar year. Total value of prize is £15,000, including £12,500 in cash. An award for the best cover design has total value of £1000. Founded 1989.

## The Calvin and Rose G. Hoffman Memorial Prize for Distinguished Publication on Christopher Marlowe

*Applications* The Headmaster, The King's School, Canterbury, Kent CT1 2ES
*tel* (01227) 595501 *fax* (01227) 595595

This annual prize of around £5000 is awarded to the best unpublished work that examines the life and works of Christopher Marlowe and the relationship between the works of Marlowe and Shakespeare. Closing date: 1 September.

## L. Ron Hubbard's Writers and Illustrators of the Future Contests

*Administrator* Andrea Grant-Webb, PO Box 218, East Grinstead, West Sussex RH19 4GH

Aims to encourage new and aspiring writers and illustrators of science fiction, fantasy and horror. In addition to the quarterly prizes there is an annual prize of £2500 for each contest. All 24 winners are invited to the annual L. Ron Hubbard Achievement Awards, which include a series of writers' and illustrators' workshops, and their work is published in an anthology. Write for an entry form.

### Writers of the Future Contest

Entrants should submit a short story of up to 10,000 words or a novelette of less than 17,000 words. Prizes of £640 (1st), £480 (2nd) and £320 (3rd) are awarded each quarter. Founded 1984.

### Illustrators of the Future Contest

Entrants should submit 3 b&w illustrations on different themes. Three prizes of £320 are awarded each quarter. Founded 1988.

## Hunting Art Prizes

*Details* Parker Harris Partnership, PO Box 279, Esher, Surrey KT10 8YZ
*tel* (01372) 462190 *fax* (01372) 460032
*email* hap@parkerharris.co.uk
*website* www.parkerharris.co.uk

An annual national art competition open to all artists resident in the UK. Total prize monies:

£24,000. Entry fee is £10 (£4 students) per work and artists may submit up to 3 works. Closing date: November 2004. An exhibition will be held at the Royal College of Art in early 2005. Established 1980.

## Images – The Best of British Illustration

*Details* Association of Illustrators, 81 Leonard Street, London EC2A 4QS
*tel* 020-7613 4328 *fax* 020-7613 4417
*email* info@a-o-illustrators.demon.co.uk
*website* www.theaoi.com
*Contact* Images Co-ordinator

Illustrators are invited to submit work for possible inclusion in the *Images Annual*, a jury-selected showcase of the best of contemporary British illustration. Selected work forms the Images exhibition, which tours the UK. UK illustrators or illustrators working for UK clients are all eligible. Send sae for entry form in the Spring. Founded 1976.

## The Richard Imison Memorial Award

*Details/entry form* The Secretary, The Broadcasting Committee, The Society of Authors, 84 Drayton Gardens, London SW10 9SB
*tel* 020-7373 6642
*email* info@societyofauthors.org
*website* www.societyofauthors.org

This annual prize of £1500 is awarded to any new writer of radio drama first transmitted within the UK during the previous year by a writer new to radio. Founded 1993.

## Independent Foreign Fiction Prize

*Details* The Literature Dept, Arts Council England, 14 Great Peter Street, London SW1P 3NQ
*tel* 020-7973 6442
*website* www.artscouncil.org.uk

In collaboration with *The Independent* newspaper and Champagne Taittinger, Arts Council England awards the £10,000 prize to honour a great work of fiction by a living author which has been translated into English from any other language and published in the UK. The prize is shared equally between the author and the translator.

## Insight Guides Travel Photography Prize

*Details* APA Publications (UK) Ltd, 58 Borough High Street, London SE1 1XF
*tel* 020-7403 0284 *fax* 020-7403 0290
*website* www.insightguides.com

An annual competition open to amateur and professional photographers resident in the UK (theme to be announced). First prize is a commission to photograph for an *Insight Guide* worth £3000. Closing date: to be confirmed but is likely to be August/September 2005. Founded 2000.

## International IMPAC Dublin Literary Award

*Details* International IMPAC Dublin Literary Award, Dublin City Library & Archive, 138–144 Pearse Street, Dublin 2, Republic of Ireland
*tel* (01) 674 4802 *fax* (01) 674 4879
*email* dubaward@iol.ie
*website* www.impacdublinaward.ie

An annual award of €100,000 is presented to the author of a work of fiction, written and published in the English language or written in a language other than English and published in English translation, which in the opinion of the judges is of high literary merit and constitutes a lasting contribution to world literature. Nominations are accepted from library systems of major cities from all over the world, regardless of national origin of the author or the place of publication. Founded 1995.

## International Playwriting Festival

*Details/entry form* Festival Administrator, Warehouse Theatre, Dingwall Road, Croydon CRO 2NF
*tel* 020-8681 1257 *fax* 020-8688 6699
*email* info@warehousetheatre.co.uk
*website* www.warehousetheatre.co.uk

An annual competition for full-length unperformed plays. Selected plays are showcased during the festival weekend in November. Plays are also presented in Italy at the leading Italian playwriting festival Premio Candoni Arta Terme. Entries are welcome from all parts of the world. Send sae for further details or visit the website. Deadline for entries: 30 June. Founded 1985.

## Jerwood Painting Prize

PO Box 279, Esher, Surrey KT10 8YZ
*tel* (01372) 462190 *fax* (01372) 460032
*email* jpp@parkerharris.co.uk
*website* www.parkerharris.co.uk

An annual single prize of £30,000 is awarded to celebrate excellence and originality in contemporary painting in the UK. All professional artists are eligible. Closing date: February 2005. Founded 1993.

## Jewish Quarterly Literary Prizes

*Details* The Administrator, Jewish Quarterly, PO Box 37645, London NW7 1WB
*tel* 020-7284 1117

Prizes are awarded annually for a work of fiction (£4000) and non-fiction (£4000) which best stimulate an interest in and awareness of themes of Jewish concern among a wider reading public. Founded 1977.

## The Petra Kenney Poetry Competition

*Details* Morgan Kenney, Danny, Hurstpierpoint, East Sussex BN6 9BB
*fax* (01273) 831889
*email* morgan@petrapoetrycompetition.co.uk
*website* www.petrapoetrycompetition.co.uk

This annual competition is for unpublished poems on any theme and in any style, and is open to everyone. Poems should be no more than 80 lines. Prizes: £1000 (1st), £500 (2nd), £250 (3rd), 3 at £125; also an inscribed Royal Brierley crystal vase to each winner and publication in *Writers' Forum* magazine. Entry fee: £3 per poem. Closing date: 1 December each year. Founded 1995.

## Kent and Sussex Poetry Society Open Poetry Competition

*Submissions* The Organiser, 13 Ruscombe Close, Southborough, Tunbridge Wells, Kent TN4 0SG

This competition is open to all unpublished poems, no longer than 40 lines in length. Prizes: 1st £500, 2nd £200, 3rd £100, 4th 4 at £50. Closing date: 31 January. Entries should include an entry fee of £3 per poem, the author's name and address and a list of poems submitted. Founded 1985.

## Kerry Group Irish Fiction Award

*Details* Writers' Week, 24 The Square, Listowel, Co. Kerry, Republic of Ireland
*tel* (353) 6821074 *fax* (353) 6822893
*email* writersweek@eircom.net
*website* www.writersweek.ie

An annual award of €10,000 for a published work of fiction by an Irish author. No entry fee. Closing date: 1 March.

## Killie Writing Competition

*Details* Killie Writing Competition, Kilmarnock College KA3 7AT
*tel* (01355) 302160
*email* editor@killie.co.uk
*website* www.killie.co.uk

Annual competition usually with 4 categories: 5–7 year-olds, 8–11 year-olds, 12–16 year-olds, adults. Free expessive writing (poetry or fiction) with no limit on subject, word count, style or format. See website for guidelines. Work submitted must have been previously unpublished. Various prizes with the overall best entry receiving £1000 and a trophy. Closing date: April. Founded 2000.

## The Kiriyama Prize

*Details* Pacific Rim Voices, 650 Delancey Street, Suite 101, San Francisco, CA 94107, USA
*tel* 415-777-1628 *fax* 415-777-1646
*email* manager@kiriyamaprize.org
*website* www.kiriyamaprize.org

An international book prize to recognise outstanding books about the Pacific Rim and South Asia that encourage greater mutual understanding and foster peace among the peoples of this vast and diverse region. The prize of $30,000 is divided equally between the winning fiction author and winning non-fiction author. Closing date: late October. Founded 1996.

## The John Kobal Foundation Photographic Portrait Grants

*Details* The John Kobal Foundation, Mount Pleasant Studios, 51–53 Mount Pleasant, London WC1X 0AE
*tel* 020-7278 8482 *fax* 020-7278 8482
*email* admin@johnkobal.org
*website* www.johnkobal.org

Portrait photography is defined here as 'photography concerned with portraying people with the emphasis on their identity as individuals' and applications for grants towards portrait photographic projects are accepted throughout the year.

## Kraszna-Krausz Awards

*Details* Andrea Livingstone, Administrator, Kraszna-Krausz Foundation, 122 Fawnbrake Avenue, London SE24 0BZ
*tel* 020-7738 6701 *fax* 020-7738 6701
*email* awards@k-k.org.uk
*website* www.k-k.org.uk

Awards totalling over £10,000 are made each year, alternating annually between the best books on:
• moving image (film, TV and video): culture and history; business, techniques and technology (2005);
• still photography: art, culture and history; craft, technology and scientific (2006).

The prize in each category will be awarded to the best book published in the preceding 2 years. Closing date: 1 July. The Foundation is also open to applications for grants (UK only) concerned with the literature of photography and the moving image. Instituted in 1985.

## The Lady Short Story Competition

The Lady, 39–40 Bedford Street, London WC2E 9ER

Open to anyone, details are published in an October/November issue of *The Lady*. First prize is £1000. No entry fee. Further information in the relevant issue.

## Leverhulme Research Fellowships

The Leverhulme Trust, 1 Pemberton Row, London EC4A 3BG
*tel* 020-7822 6477 *fax* 020-7822 5084
*email* jcater@leverhulme.org.uk
*website* www.leverhulme.org.uk

The Leverhulme Trustees offer annually approximately 110 Fellowships to individuals in aid of original research – not for study of any sort. These awards are not available as replacement for past support from other sources. Applications will be considered in all subject areas. Total Fellowship monies for 2004 was £21,000. Completed

application forms must be received by mid November 2004 for 2005 awards. Founded 1933.

## John Llewellyn Rhys Prize

*Details* Booktrust, Book House, 45 East Hill, London SW18 2QZ
*tel* 020-8516 2973/2972 *fax* 020-8516 2978
*email* kate@booktrust.org.uk
*Contact* Kate Mervyn-Jones, Tarryn McKay

This annual prize of £5000 (plus £500 to each shortlisted author) is made to an author aged 35 or under for a work of literature (fiction, poetry, drama, non-fiction, etc) which has been published during the calendar year prior to the presentation. The author must be a citizen of the UK or the Commonwealth. Closing date: August. Inaugurated in memory of the writer John Llewellyn Rhys by his widow Jane Oliver. Established 1942.

## London Press Club Awards

*Details* Dr Mark Bryant, Hon. Secretary, London Press Club, St Bride Institute, 14 Bride Lane, Fleet Street, London EC4Y 8EQ
*tel* 020-7353 7086/7 *fax* 020-7353 7087
*email* lpressclub@aol.com

Business Journalist of the Year, Consumer Affairs Journalist of the Year, Broadsheet Newspaper of the Year, Tabloid Newspaper of the Year and Broadcasting Journalist of the Year.

### Scoop of the Year Award

Chosen by a panel of senior editors, this annual award of a bronze statuette is given for the reporting scoop of the year, appearing in either a newspaper or electronic media. Founded 1990.

### Edgar Wallace Award

Chosen by a panel of senior editors, this annual award of a silver inkstand is given for outstanding writing or reporting by a journalist. Founded 1990.

## London Writers Competition

*Details* Arts Office, Room 224A, Wandsworth Town Hall, High Street, London SW18 2PU
*tel* 020-8871 8711
*email* arts@wandsworth.gov.uk
*website* www.wandsworth.gov.uk

Open to writers who live, work or study in the Greater London Area. Awards are made annually in 4 classes (Poetry, Short Story, Fiction for Children and Play) and prizes total £1000 in each class. Entries must be previously unpublished work. Judging is under the chairmanship of Francine Stock.

## The Elizabeth Longford Grants

*Details* Awards Secretary, The Society of Authors, 84 Drayton Gardens, London SW10 9SB
*tel* 020-7373 6642 *fax* 020-7373 5768
*email* info@societyofauthors.org
*website* www.societyofauthors.org

A grant of £2500 is made payable to a historical biographer whose publisher's advance is insufficient to cover the costs of research involved. Flora Fraser and Peter Soros are kindly sponsoring a grant every 6 months. Final entry dates: 30 April and 31 October.

## The Elizabeth Longford Prize for Historical Biography

*Details* Awards Secretary, The Society of Authors, 84 Drayton Gardens, London SW10 9SB
*tel* 020-7373 6642  *tel fax* 020-7373 5768
*email* info@societyofauthors.org
*website* www.societyofauthors.org

A prize of £3000 is awarded annually for a historical biography published in the year preceding the prize. No unsolicited submissions. Established in 2003 in affectionate memory of Elizabeth Longford, the acclaimed biographer, and sponsored by Flora Fraser and Peter Soros.

## The Sir William Lyons Award

*Details* General Secretary, 30 The Cravens, Smallfield, Surrey RH6 9QS
*tel* (01342) 843294 *fax* (01342) 844093
*email* sharon@scott-fairweather.freeserve.co.uk
*website* www.newspress.co.uk/guild

This annual award (trophy, £1000 and 2 years' probationary membership of the Guild of Motoring Writers) was set up to encourage young people in automotive journalism, including broadcasting, and to foster interest in motoring and the motor industry through these media. Open to any person of British nationality resident in the UK aged 17–23, it consists of writing 2 essays and an interview with the Award Committee.

## The McKitterick Prize

*Details* Awards Secretary, The Society of Authors, 84 Drayton Gardens, London SW10 9SB
*tel* 020-7373 6642
*email* info@societyofauthors.org
*website* www.societyofauthors.org

This annual award of £4000 is open to first published novels and unpublished typescripts by authors over the age of 40. Closing date: 20 December. Endowed by the late Tom McKitterick. Send sae for entry form.

## The Enid McLeod Literary Prize

*Details* Executive Secretary, Franco-British Society, Room 227, Linen Hall, 162–168 Regent Street, London W1R 5TB
*tel* 020-7734 0815 *fax* 020-7734 0815
*email* execsec@francobritishsociety.org.uk
*website* www.francobritishsociety.org.uk

This annual prize of £250 is given for a full-length work of literature which contributes most to

Franco–British understanding. It must be first published in the UK between 1 January and 31 December, and written in English by a citizen of the UK, British Commonwealth, the Republic of Ireland, Pakistan, Bangladesh or South Africa. Closing date: 31 December.

## Bryan MacMahon Short Story Award

Writers' Week, 24 The Square, Listowel, Co. Kerry, Republic of Ireland
*tel* (353) 6821074 *fax* (353) 6822893
*email* writersweek@eircom.net
*website* www.writersweek.ie

An annual award for the best short story (up to 3000 words) on any subject. Prize: €2000. Entry fee: €8. Closing date: 1 March. Founded 1971.

## The Macmillan Prize for Children's Picture Book Illustration

*Applications* Imogen Blundell, Macmillan Children's Books, 20 New Wharf Road, London N1 9RR
*tel* 020-7014 6124
*email* i.blundell@macmillan.co.uk

Three prizes are awarded annually for unpublished children's book illustrations by art students in higher education establishments in the UK. Prizes: £1000 (1st), £500 (2nd) and £250 (3rd).

## The Mail on Sunday/John Llewellyn Rhys Prize – see John Llewellyn Rhys Prize

## Marsh Award for Children's Literature in Translation

*Administered by* National Centre for Research in Children's Literature, Digby Stuart College, University of Surrey Roehampton, Roehampton Lane, London SW15 5PU
*tel* 020-8392 3008
*Contact* Dr Gillian Lathey

This biennial award of £1000 is given to the translator of a book for children (aged 4–16) from a foreign language into English and published in the UK by a British publisher. Electronic books, and encyclopedias and other reference books, are not eligible. Next award: January 2005.

## Marsh Biography Award

*Administered by* The English-Speaking Union, Dartmouth House, 37 Charles Street, London W1J 5ED
*tel* 020-7529 1550 *fax* 020-7495 6108
*email* tim_rolph@esu.org

This major national biography prize of £4000 plus a trophy is presented every 2 years. Entries must be serious biographies written by British authors and published in the UK. Next award: October 2005. Founded 1985–6.

## The John Masefield Memorial Trust

*Details* Awards Secretary, The Society of Authors,
84 Drayton Gardens, London SW10 9SB
*tel* 020-7373 6642  *tel fax* 020-7373 5768
*email* info@societyofauthors.org
*website* www.societyofauthors.org

This trust makes occasional grants to professional
poets who find themselves with sudden financial
problems. Apply for an information sheet and
application form.

## The Somerset Maugham Awards

*Details* Awards Secretary, The Society of Authors,
84 Drayton Gardens, London SW10 9SB
*tel* 020-7373 6642
*email* info@societyofauthors.org
*website* www.societyofauthors.org

These annual awards, totalling about £12,000, are for
writers under the age of 35. Candidates must be
British subjects by birth, and ordinarily resident in
the UK or Northern Ireland. Poetry, fiction, non-
fiction, belles-lettres or philosophy, but not dramatic
works, are eligible. Entries should be submitted by
the publisher. Closing date: 20 December.

## Meyer-Whitworth Award

*Details* Charles Hart, Literature Dept, Arts Council
England, 14 Great Peter Street, London SW1P 3NQ
*tel* 020-7973 6431
*email* charles.hart@artscouncil.org.uk
*website* www.artscouncil.org.uk

This award of £8000 is to help further the careers of
UK playwrights who are not yet established.

## Millfield Arts Projects

Atkinson Gallery, Millfield, Butleigh Road, Street,
Somerset BA16 0YD
*tel* (01458) 442291 *fax* (01458) 447276
*email* lag@millfield.somerset.sch.uk
*website* www.millfield.somerset.sch.uk
*Director of Art* Len Green

'The mandate of the Millfield Arts Project
programme is to search for, promote and support,
primarily but not exclusively, young aspiring artists
at local, regional, national and international levels.'
In a professional art context MAP offers:
• Sculpture Commission. Artists work on campus
for 8 weeks (£7500). Deadline for entries: mid
January.
• Summer Show. An open exhibition. Application
forms available: March.
• Six Gallery exhibitions selected by the Director of
Art. Interested artists should send slides and CV to
the Director of Art.

## Mind Book of the Year

*Details* Anny Brackx, Information Department,
Granta House, 15–19 Broadway, London E15 4BQ

*tel* 020-8519 2122 *fax* 020-8522 1725

This £1500 award is given to the author of any book
(fiction or non-fiction) published in the UK in the
current year which outstandingly furthers public
understanding of the prevention, causes, treatment
or experience of mental health problems. Entries by
31 December. Administered by Mind, the National
Association for Mental Health. Inaugurated in
memory of Sir Allen Lane in 1981.

## Kathleen Mitchell Award

35 Clarence Street, Sydney, NSW 2000, Australia
*postal address* GPO Box 4270, Sydney, NSW 2001,
Australia
*tel* (02) 8295 8191 *fax* (02) 8295 8693
*email* linda.ingaldo@permamentgroup.com.au
*website* www.permamentgroup.com.au

A biennial literary award ($5000) for authors under
the age of 30 for the advancement and
improvement of Australian literature. Eligible
authors must be born in or resident in Australia,
either British born or naturalised Australian.
Founded 2002.

## Montana Zew Zealand Book Awards

*Details* c/o Booksellers New Zealand, PO Box 13248,
Johnsonville, Wellington, New Zealand
*tel* (04) 478-5577 *fax* (04) 478-5519
*email* jayne.wasmuth@booksellers.conz
*website* www.booksellers.co.nz

Annual awards to celebrate excellence in, and
provide recognition for, the best books written and
illustrated by New Zealanders each year. Awards are
presented in 8 categories. The winner of the fiction
category is awarded the Dentz Medal for Fiction
and $15,000. One of the 7 non-fiction categories is
awarded the Montana Medal for Non-Fiction and
$15,000. Eligible authors' and illustrators' books
must have been published in New Zealand in the
calendar year preceding the awards year. Closing
date: December. Founded 1996.

## The Oscar Moore Screenwriting Prize

*Details* The Oscar Moore Foundation,
33–39 Bowling Green Lane, London EC1R 0DA
*tel* 020-7505 8080 *fax* 020-7505 8087
*email* annmarie.oconnor@media.emap.com
*website* www.screendaily.com

The Foundation works to build for a Europe-wide
culture of screenwriting excellence and to this end
makes this annual award (£10,000) to finance the
first draft of a promising screenplay. A different
genre is chosen for each year.

## John Moores 23 exhibition of contemporary painting

The Walker, William Brown Street, Liverpool L3 8EL
*tel* 0151-478 4199 *fax* 0151-478 4190

*email* stephen.guy@liverpoolmuseums.org.uk
*websites* www.liverpoolmuseums.org.uk,
www.thewalker.org.uk/johnmoores23
*Contact* Stephen Guy

Biennial painting exhibition open to any artist living or working in the UK. First prize of £25,000, 4 prizes of £2500 each and a £1000 'visitor's choice' prize. Next exhibition: 18 September–28 November 2004. Next registration deadline: March 2006 – forms can be obtained from the Walker or via its website. Founded 1957.

### Shiva Naipaul Memorial Prize

*Details* The Spectator, 56 Doughty Street, London WC1N 2LL

This annual prize of £3000 is given to an English language writer of any nationality under the age of 35 for an essay of not more than 4000 words giving the most acute and profound observation of a culture alien to the writer. Founded 1985.

### National Poetry Competition

*Contact* Competition Organiser, The Poetry Society, 22 Betterton Street, London WC2H 9BX
*tel* 020-7420 9880 *fax* 020-7240 4818
*email* info@poetrysociety.org.uk
*website* www.poetrysociety.org.uk

One of Britain's major annual open poetry competitions. Poems on any theme, up to 40 lines. Prizes: 1st £5000, 2nd £1000, 3rd £500, plus 10 commendations of £50. All poems will be read by a team of poetry specialists before the final judging process. For rules and entry form send an sae. Entries also accepted via the website. Closing date: 31 October each year.

### The Natural World Book Prize

*Details/entry form* Booktrust, Book House, 45 East Hill, London SW18 2QZ
*tel* 020-8516 2973/2972 *fax* 020-8516 2978
*email* kate@booktrust.org.uk
*Contacts* Kate Mervyn-Jones, Tarryn McKay

Awards of £5000 to the winner and £1000 to the runner up for an adult book which most imaginatively promotes the conservation of the natural environment and all its animals and plants. Books must have been published between 1 June and the following 31 May. An amalgamation of the BP Conservation Book Prize and the Natural World Book of the Year Award. Sponsored by BP and Subbuteo Books.

### The Nestlé Smarties Book Prize

*Details* Booktrust, Book House, 45 East Hill, London SW18 2QZ
*tel* 020-8516 2973/2972 *fax* 020-8516 2978
*email* kate@booktrust.org.uk,
tarryn@booktrust.org.uk

*Contact* Kate Mervyn-Jones, Tarryn McKay

Three prizes (Gold, Silver and Bronze) are awarded to the 3 shortlisted books in each category (5 and under, 6–8 and 9–11 years). The Gold Award winners each receive £2500, the Silver Award winners receive £1500, and the Bronze Award winners receive £500. Eligible books must be published in the UK in the 12 months ending 30 September of the year of presentation and be a work of fiction or poetry for children written in English by a citizen or resident of the UK. Closing date for entries: contact Administrator. Sponsored by Nestlé Smarties.

### New Millennial Science Essay Competition

*Details* The Wellcome Trust, 210 Euston Road, London NW1 2BE
*tel* 020-7611 7221 *fax* 020-7611 8269
*email* r.birse@wellcome.ac.uk
*website* www.wellcome.ac.uk/ScienceEssay

Postgraduate students (in science, engineering or technology) currently writing up their theses are invited to write an entertaining essay on the possible impact of their research on society of no more than 700 words. The aim is to make the research topic interesting and accessible to a wider non-specialist audience. Applicants must be registered at an internationally recognised institution. The competition is open from mid March to mid May each year. A collaboration between the Wellcome Trust and *New Scientist* magazine. Prizes: £1500 and publication in *New Scientist* (1st), £750 (2nd), 2 prizes of £375 (3rd). All winners, including the next 10 best essays, receive a one-year subscription to *New Scientist*. Founded 1993.

### The New Writer Prose and Poetry Prizes

*Details* The New Writer Poetry Prizes, PO Box 60, Cranbrook, Kent TN17 2ZR
*tel* (01580) 212626 *fax* (01580) 212041
*email* editor@thenewwriter.com
*website* www.thenewwriter.com

Short stories up to 5000 words, novellas, essays and articles; poets may submit either one or a collection of 6–10 previously unpublished poems. Total prize money £2500 as well as publication for the prize-winners in the *New Writer* magazine. Entry fees: £3 per poem; £10 for a collection of 6–10 poems. Send for an entry form or visit the website for information about the short fiction and non-fiction sections. Closing date: 31 October each year. Founded 1997.

### New Zealand Post Book Awards for Children and Young Adults

*Details* c/o Booksellers New Zealand, PO Box 13248, Johnsonville, Wellington, New Zealand
*tel* (04) 478-5577 *fax* (04) 478-5519

*email* jayne.wasmuth@booksellers.conz
*website* www.booksellers.co.nz

Annual awards to celebrate excellence in, and provide recognition for, the best books for children and young adults published annually in New Zealand. Awards are presented in 4 categories: non-fiction, picture book, junior fiction and young adult fiction. The winner of each category wins $5000. One category winner is chosen as the *New Zealand Post* Book of the Year and receives an additional $5000. Eligible authors' and illustrators' books must have been published in New Zealand in the calendar year preceding the awards year. Closing date: December. Founded 1990.

## Nielsen Gold and Platinum Book Awards

*tel* (01252) 742555 *fax* (01252) 742556
*email* gold&platinumawards@whitaker.co.uk

The awards are a recognition of sales purchases of a book by the general public. Eligible books are those priced at £4.99 or above that reach 500,000 unit sales (Gold) or 1,000,000 unit sales (Platinum) as measured by Nielsen BookScan within a 5-year period. All qualifying titles receive an award, funded for the author by their publisher. Founded 2001.

## The Nobel Prize in Literature

*Awarding authority* Swedish Academy, Box 2118, S–10313 Stockholm, Sweden
*tel* (08) 10-65-24 *fax* (08) 24-42-25
*email* sekretariat@svenskaakademien.se
*website* www.svenskaakademien.se

This is one of the awards stipulated in the will of the late Alfred Nobel, the Swedish scientist who invented dynamite. No direct application for a prize will be taken into consideration. For authors writing in English it was bestowed upon Rudyard Kipling in 1907, W.B. Yeats in 1923, George Bernard Shaw in 1925, Sinclair Lewis in 1930, John Galsworthy in 1932, Eugene O'Neill in 1936, Pearl Buck in 1938, T.S. Eliot in 1948, William Faulkner in 1949, Bertrand Russell in 1950, Sir Winston Churchill in 1953, Ernest Hemingway in 1954, John Steinbeck in 1962, Samuel Beckett in 1969, Patrick White in 1973, Saul Bellow in 1976, William Golding in 1983, Wole Soyinka in 1986, Joseph Brodsky in 1987, Nadine Gordimer in 1991, Derek Walcott in 1992, Toni Morrison in 1993, Seamus Heaney in 1995 and V.S. Naipaul in 2001.

## Northern Rock Foundation Writer's Award

*Details* New Writing North, 2 School Lane, Whickham, Newcastle Upon Tyne NE16 4SL
*tel* 0191-488 8580 *fax* 0191-488 8576
*email* mail@newwritingnorth.com
*website* www.newwritingnorth.com
*Contact* Silvana Michelini

An annual award of £20,000 p.a. for a 3-year period (i.e. £60,000) designed to release a writer from commitments such as teaching to devote time to a major work. Eligible are writers of poetry, prose, children's books and biography with at least 2 books published by a recognised publisher. Writers must reside in Northumberland, Tyne & Wear, County Durham, Cumbria or Tees Valley. Closing date: early January. Founded 2002.

## Northern Writers' Awards

*Administered by* New Writing North, 2 School Lane, Whickham, Newcastle Upon Tyne NE16 4SL
*tel* 0191-488 8580 *fax* 0191-488 8576
*email* mail@newwritingnorth.com
*website* www.newwritingnorth.com
*Contact* Silvana Michelini

Awards (from £1000 to £5000) are aimed at developing writers at different stages in their careers. A panel of professional writers shortlists and makes awards once a year. Applicants must be resident in the Arts Council England North East region (Northumberland, Tyne & Wear, Durham, Tees Valley). See website for details. Deadline for applications: early January

## The Observer Hodge Award/Exhibition

*Details* The Observer Hodge Award, The Observer, 119 Farringdon Road, London EC1R 3ER
*tel* 020-7713 4091
*email* hodge.award@observer.co.uk
*website* www.observer.co.uk/hodgeaward
*Contact* Catherine Stokes

Set up in memory of David Hodge who died aged 29, this annual award is given to student and professional photographers under 30. First prize: £3000 plus an expenses-paid assignment for *The Observer*; best student prize: £1500. Closing date: June 2005. Founded 1986.

## Orange Award for New Writers

*Details* Booktrust, Book House, 45 East Hill, London SW18 2QZ
*tel* 020-8516 2972 *fax* 020-8516 2978
*email* tarryn@booktrust.org.uk
*Contact* Tarryn MacKay

A new prize of £10,000 will be awarded annually to recognise emerging female fiction-writing talent in the UK. The prize will be awarded to a woman for her first work of fiction – a novel, novella or short story collection. Applications are welcome from women of any age or nationality whose first work of fiction is published in book form between 1 April 2004 and 31 March 2005. The emphasis of the award will be on emerging talent and the evidence of future potential.

## Orange Prize for Fiction

*Details* Booktrust, Book House, 45 East Hill,
London SW18 2QZ
*tel* 020-8516 2973/2972 *fax* 020-8516 2978
*email* kate@booktrust.org.uk,
tarryn@booktrust.org.uk
*Contact* Kate Mervyn-Jones, Tarryn McKay

This award of £30,000, and a statuette known as
'The Bessie', is for a full-length novel written in
English by a woman of any nationality and first
published in the UK between 1 April and 31 March.
Sponsored by Orange PCS. Established 1996.

## George Orwell Memorial Prize

*Details* Alive Events, Fulton House, Fulton Road,
Wembley Park, Middlesex HA9 0TF
*tel* 020-8584 0444 *fax* 020-8584 0443
*email* orwell@aliveevents.co.uk
*website* www.aliveevents.co.uk
*Contact* Sue Dowsett

Two prizes of £1000 each are awarded in April each
year – one for the best political book, and one for
best political journalism, either fiction or non-
fiction – of the previous year, giving equal merit to
content and good style accessible to the general
public. Founded 1993.

## Catherine Pakenham Award

*Entry form* Emma Gilbert-Harris, Corporate Affairs
Dept, The Sunday Telegraph, 1 Canada Square,
Canary Wharf, London E14 5DT
*email* emma.gilbert-harris@telegraph.co.uk

This award is open to young women journalists
aged 18–25 who may submit a non-fiction
750–2000-word article by 30 May 2005. The winner
will receive £1000 and the chance to write for a
*Telegraph* publication. Three runners-up each
receive £200. Entry forms are available from
February 2005. Founded in 1970 in memory of
Catherine Pakenham, who died in a car crash whilst
working for the *Telegraph Magazine*.

## The Parker Romantic Novel of the Year Award

*Details* Mary de Laszlo, 57 Coniger Road,
London SW6 3TB
*tel* 020-7736 4968
*website* www.rna-uk.org

This annual award of £10,000 for the best romantic
novel of the year is open to both members and
non-members of the Romantic Novelists'
Association, provided non-members are domiciled
in the UK. Novels must be published between the
previous 1 December and 30 November of the year
of entry. Three copies of the novel are required.
Send sae for entry form and details, available from
July onwards.

## New Writers' Award

*Details* Nicola Cornick, North End Cottage,
Kingston, Winslow, Swindon SN6 8NG
*email* ncornick@madasafish.com
For writers previously unpublished in the adult
novel field and who are probationary members of
the Association. MSS can be submitted until the end
of September under the New Writers' Scheme. All
receive a critique. Any MSS which have passed
through the Scheme and which are subsequently
accepted for publication become eligible for the
Award.

## Pendleton May First Novel Award

c/o Tourist Information Centre, Tunsgate,
Guildford GU1 3QT
*tel* (01483) 444334
*email* assistant@guildfordbookfestival.co.uk
*website* www.guildfordbookfestival.co.uk

The award of £2500 is made for a first novel in any
genre published in between the Guildford Book
Festivals, i.e. November–October. Applications
should be made through a publisher or literary
agent. Eligible authors must live in the area covered
by London and the South East. Closing date: 31
July. Founded 1997.

## The Samuel Pepys Award

*Details* Jolyon Dromgoole, Chairman, Montreal
House, Winson, Cirencester, Glos. GL7 5EL

A biennial prize is given to a published book that
makes the greatest contribution to the
understanding of Samuel Pepys, his times, or his
contemporaries. The winner receives £2000 and the
Robert Latham Medal. Founded by the Samuel
Pepys Award Trust in 2003 on the tercentenary of
the death of Pepys. Closing date: May 2005.

## Peterloo Poets Open Poetry Competition

*Details* Peterloo Poets, The Old Chapel, Sand Lane,
Calstock, Cornwall PL18 9QX

This annual competition offers a first prize of £2000
and 14 other prizes totalling £2100. There is also a
15–19 age group section with 5 prizes each of £100.
Closing date: 1 March 2005. Founded 1986.

## Charles Pick Writing Fellowship

School of English & American Studies,
University of East Anglia, Norwich NR4 7TJ
*tel* (01603) 592810 *fax* (01603) 507728
*email* v.striker@uea.ac.uk
*website* www.uea.ac.uk/eas/pcik/shtml

An annual fellowship to assist and support the work
of a new and unpublished writer of fiction or non-
fiction and to give the writer time to devote to the
development of his/her talent. All writers of any age
or nationality are eligible to apply. The award is
£10,000 plus free accommodation. Founded 2002.

## The Poetry Business Book & Pamphlet Competition

*Competition Administrator* The Poetry Business,
The Studio, Byram Arcade, Westgate,
Huddersfield HD1 1ND
*tel* (01484) 434840 *fax* (01484) 426566
*email* edit@poetrybusiness.co.uk
*website* www.poetrybusiness.co.uk
*Directors* Peter Sansom, Janet Fisher

An annual award is made for a poetry collection.
The judges select up to 5 short collections for
publication as pamphlets; on further submission of
more poems, one of these will be selected for a full-
length collection to be published under the Poetry
Business's Smith/Doorstop imprint. All winners
share a cash prize of £1000. Poets over the age of 18
writing in English from anywhere in the world are
eligible. Closing date: 31 October. Founded 1986.

## Poetry Life Open Poetry Competition

*Details* 1 Blue Ball Corner, Water Lane, Winchester,
Hants SO23 0ER
*website* www.freespace.virgin.net/poetry.life/

Competitions are held 3 times a year with a first
prize of £3000. Any style is acceptable with an
80-line limit on each poem. Poems must be
previously unpublished (in book form) and must
not have won a prize in another competition. All
winning poems are published in *Poetry Life*
magazine and on its website. Send sae for further
details. Founded 1994.

## The Portico Prize

*Details* Miss Emma Marigliano, Librarian,
Portico Library, 57 Mosley Street,
Manchester M2 3HY
*tel* 0161-236 6785 *fax* 0161-236 6803

This biennial prize of £3000 is awarded for a
published work of fiction or non-fiction, of general
interest and literary merit set wholly or mainly in
the North West of England (Lancashire,
Manchester, Liverpool, High Peak of Derbyshire,
Cheshire and Cumbria). Next award: 2006. Founded
1985.

## Dennis Potter Screenwriting Award

*Details* Jeremy Howe, BBC Broadcasting House,
Whiteladies Road, Bristol BS8 2LR

Information about this award is obtainable from the
above office. Founded 1994.

## The Mathew Prichard Award for Short Story Writing

*Details* The Competition Secretary, The Mathew
Prichard Award, 2 Rhododendron Close, Cyncoed,
Cardiff CF23 7HS
*website* www.samwaw.org.uk

Total prize money of £2000 is awarded annually in
this open competition for original short stories in
English of not more than 2500 words. Adjudication
is organised in May each year by the South and Mid
Wales Association of Writers. Send sae for entry
form or download from website. Closing date for
entry: February 2005.

## The V.S. Pritchett Memorial Prize

*Details* The Royal Society of Literature,
Somerset House, Strand, London WC2R 1LA
*tel* 020-7845 4676 *fax* 020-7845 4679
*email* info@rslit.org
*website* www.rslit.org

An annual prize of £1000 is awarded for a
previously unpublished short story of up to 5000
words. Entry fee: £5 per story. For entry forms
contact the Secretary. Founded 1999.

## The Peggy Ramsay Foundation

G. Laurence Harbottle, Hanover House,
14 Hanover Square, London W1J 1HP
*tel* 020-7667 5000 *fax* 020-7667 5100
*email* laurence.harbottle@harbottle.com
*website* www.peggyramsayfoundation.org

Grants are made to writers of stage plays, to
theatrical organisations to facilitate new writing for
the stage and to established writers of stage plays in
need. Awards are made at intervals during each year
and a single project award to an organisation is
made annually. A total of approx. £160,000 is
expended annually. Founded 1992.

## Real Writers Short Story Awards

PO Box 170, Chesterfield, Derbyshire S40 1FE
*tel* (01246) 238492 *fax* (01246) 238492
*email* info@real-writers.com
*website* www.real-writers.com

First prize: £2500 plus 10 regional awards. Send sae
for entry form. Optional critiques. Entry fee: £5.
Closing date: 30 November. Founded 1994.

## The Red House Children's Book Award

*Details* Marianne Adey, The Old Malt House,
Aldbourne, Marlborough, Wilts. SN8 2DW
*tel* (01672) 540629 *fax* (01672) 541280
*email* marianneadey@aol.com

This award is given annually to authors of works of
fiction for children published in the UK. Children
participate in the judging of the award. 'Pick of the
Year' booklist is published in conjunction with the
award. Founded in 1980 by the Federation of
Children's Book Groups.

## Trevor Reese Memorial Prize

*Details* Events and Publicity Officer, Institute of
Commonwealth Studies, 28 Russell Square,
London WC1B 5DS

*tel* 020-7862 8829 *fax* 020-7862 8813
*email* robert.holland@sas.ac.uk
*website* www.sas.ac.uk/commonwealthstudies

This prize of £1000 is awarded biennially, usually for a scholarly work by a single author in the field of Imperial and Commonwealth history. Next award: 2005 for a book published in 2002 or 2003.

## The Rooney Prize for Irish Literature

*Details* J.A. Sherwin, Strathin, Templecarrig, Delgany, Co. Wicklow, Republic of Ireland
*tel* (01) 287 4769 *fax* (01) 287 2595
*email* rooneyprize@ireland.com

An annual prize of €8000 is awarded to encourage young Irish writing talent. To be eligible individuals must be Irish, published and under 40 years of age. The prize is non-competitive and there is no application procedure or entry form. Founded in 1976 by Daniel M. Rooney, Pittsburgh, Pennsylvania.

## The Royal Society of Literature Award under the W.H. Heinemann Bequest

*Details/Submissions* Julia Abel Smith, Royal Society of Literature, Somerset House, Strand, London WC2R 1LA
*tel* 020-7845 4676 *fax* 020-7845 4679
*email* info@rslit.org

Serious works of non-fiction – biography, poetry, history, criticism – may be submitted by publishers for this award of £5000. Books must be written in the English language and have been published in the previous year. Translations are not eligible for consideration, nor are single poems, nor collections of pieces by more than one author, nor may individuals put forward their own work. Entries published during the current year should be submitted between 1 October and 15 December.

## The Royal Society of Literature/Jerwood Awards

*Submissions* Paula Johnson, The Royal Society of Literature, Somerset House, Strand, London WC2R 1LA
*tel* 020-7845 4676 *fax* 020-7845 4679
*email* rsl&jerwood@billingplace.co.uk
*website* www.rslit.org

New awards offering financial assistance to authors engaged in writing their first major commissioned works of non-fiction. Three awards – one of £10,000 and 2 of £5000 – will be offered annually in 2004, 2005 and 2006 to writers working on substantial non-fiction projects. The awards are open to UK and Irish writers and writers who have been resident in the UK for at least 3 years. Applications for the first awards should be submitted by the end of August 2005. See website for further details.

## The Royal Society of Literature Ondaatje Prize

*Submissions* Paula Johnson, The Royal Society of Literature, Somerset House, Strand, London WC2R 1LA
*tel* 020-7845 4676 *fax* 020-7845 4679
*email* paulaj@rsl.org
*website* www.rslit.org

Newly established prize (£10,000), administered by the Royal Society of Literature and endowed by Sir Christopher Ondaatje. The prize, which replaces the Winifred Holtby Memorial Prize, will be awarded annually to a book of literary merit, fiction or non-fiction, best evoking the spirit of a place. All entries must be published within the calendar year 2004 and should be submitted between 1 September and 1 December 2004. The writer must be a citizen of the UK, Commonwealth or Ireland. See website for further details.

## RSPCA Young Photographer Awards

*Details* Publications Department, RSPCA, Wilberforce Way, Southwater, Horsham, West Sussex RH13 9RS
*tel* (0870) 7540455 *fax* (0870) 7530455
*email* publications@rspca.org.uk
*website* www.rspca.org.ukyp

Annual awards are made for animal photographs taken by young people in 2 age categories: under 12 and 12–18. Prizes: overall winner (£250 cash, digital camera), age group winners (£100 cash, camera). Four runners-up in each age group receive a camera and £50 cash. Closing date for entries: 17 September 2004. Sponsored by Olympus and Truprint. Founded 1990.

## RTE New Playwrights Awards

RTE Radio Drama, Donnybrook, Dublin 4, Republic of Ireland
*tel* (01) 2083111 *fax* (01) 2083248
*Producer in Charge* Michael Campion

An annual competition for a 30-minute original radio play, open to unproduced writers born in or living in Ireland. Prizes: €3000 (1st), €2000 (2nd), €1000 (3rd). Closing date: tbc.

## Runciman Award

*Details* The Administrator, The Anglo-Hellenic League, 16–18 Paddington Street, London W1U 5AS
*tel* 020-7486 9410 *fax* 020-7486 4254 (mark FAO The Anglo-Hellenic League)

An annual prize of not less than £5000 sponsored by the National Bank of Greece and named after the late Sir Steven Runciman, former Chairman of the Anglo-Hellenic League, for a work wholly or mainly about some aspect of Greece or the world of

Hellenism, which has been published in its first English edition in the United Kingdom during the previous year and listed in *Whitaker's Books in Print*, or in Greece, during 2004. The Award may be given for a work of fiction, poetry, drama or non-fiction; concerned academically or non-academically with the history of any period; biography or autobiography; travel and topography; the arts, architecture, archaeology and the environment; the social and political sciences and current affairs; a guidebook or a translation from the Greek of any period. Final entry date: 31 January; award presented in May/June. Established 1985.

## Sainsbury's Baby Book Award – see
Booktrust Early Years Awards

## The David St John Thomas Charitable Trust Competitions & Awards
The David St John Thomas Charitable Trust, PO Box 6055, Nairn IV12 4YB
*tel* (01667) 453351
*email* dsjtcharitynairn@fsmail.ne
*Contact* Lorna Edwardson

Programme of writing competitions and awards totalling £20,000–£30,000. Regular competitions are the annual ghost story and annual love story (each 1600–1800 words with £1000 1st prize) and the open poetry competition (up to 32 lines, total prize money £1000). Publication of winning entries is guaranteed, usually in *Writers' News/Writing Magazine* and/or an annual anthology.

The Self-Publishing Awards are open to anyone who has self-published a book during the preceding calendar year, with 4 categories each with £250 prize. The overall winner is declared Self-Publisher of the Year with a total award of £1000. For full details of these and other awards, including an annual writers' groups anthology and letter-writer of the year send a large sae.

## The Saltire Society Awards
*Details* The Saltire Society, 9 Fountain Close, 22 High Street, Edinburgh EH1 1TF
*tel* 0131-556 1836 *fax* 0131-557 1675
*email* saltire@saltiresociety.org.uk
*website* www.saltiresociety.org.uk

### Scottish Book of the Year
An annual award of £5000 open to authors of Scottish descent or living in Scotland, or for a book by anyone which deals with a Scottish topic. Books published between 1 September and 31 August are eligible. Established 1982.

### Scottish First Book of the Year
An annual award of £1500 open to any author who has not previously published a book. Authors of Scottish descent or living in Scotland, or for any book which deals with the work or life of a Scot or with a Scottish problem, event or situation are eligible. Established 1988.

### Scottish Research Book Award
An annual award of £1500 is open to the authors of books which represent a significant body of research; offer new insight or dimension to the subject; and add knowledge and understanding of Scotland and the Scots. Established 1998.

## Alastair Salvesen Art Scholarship
Admin Secretary, The Royal Scottish Academy, The Mound, Edinburgh EH2 2EL
*tel* 0131-225 6671 *fax* 0131-220 6016

The Scholarship consists of 2 parts:
• A 3–6 months travel scholarship of up to £10,000 depending on the plan submitted; and
• An exhibition in Nov/Dec organised by the Royal Scottish Academy.

Applicants must be painters aged 25–35 who have been trained at one of the 4 Scottish colleges of art; are currently living and working in Scotland; have worked for a minimum of 3 years outside a college or student environment; and have during 2004 had work accepted for an exhibition in the Annual Exhibition organised by certain Scottish institutes or, in a recognised gallery, have held a one-artist exhibition or participated in a group exhibition. Application forms available in December. Founded 1989.

## Scottish Arts Council
*Contact* Gavin Wallace, Head of Literature, Scottish Arts Council, 12 Manor Place, Edinburgh EH3 7DD
*tel* 0131-226 6051
*email* gavin.wallace@scottisharts.org.uk

A limited number of writers' bursaries – up to £15,000 each – are offered to enable professional writers based in Scotland, including writers for children, to devote more time to writing. Priority is given to writers of fiction and verse and playwrights, but writers of literary non-fiction are also considered. Applications may be discussed with Gavin Wallace.

### Scottish Book Awards
Up to 7 awards ranging from £2000 to £10,000 are made in the spring to new and established authors of published books in recognition of high standards of writing, for both adults and children. Preference is given to literary fiction and poetry, but literary non-fiction is also considered. Authors should be Scottish, resident in Scotland or have published books of Scottish interest. Entries from publishers only. Guidelines available on request.

## Scottish Book of the Year – see The
Saltire Society Awards

## Scottish First Book of the Year – see The
Saltire Society Awards

## Scottish Research Book Award – see The
Saltire Society Awards

## The Kim Scott Walwyn Prize
*Details* Booktrust, Book House, 45 East Hill,
London SW18 2QZ
*tel* 020-8516 2972 *fax* 020-8516 2978
*email* tarryn@booktrust.org.uk
*Contact* Tarryn MacKay

A new prize of £3000 will be awarded bi-anuually to
a woman who has made an outstanding
contribution in any area of UK book publishing. It
commemorates the life and career of Kim Scott
Walwyn, publishing director at Oxford University
Press until her death in 2002. Applications are
welcome from women of any age working in any
area of book publishing in the UK. Applicants
should submit a written description of a particular
achievement for which they wish to be recognised,
or an aspect of their publishing career which merits
recognition. Full details, and the judges' guidelines,
can be obtained from Booktrust. Applications must
be received by 1 September 2004 and the first prize
will be awarded in December 2004. The prize is
being funded by donations from Kim's family,
colleagues, authors and friends.

## The André Simon Memorial Fund Book Awards
*Details* Tessa Hayward, 5 Sion Hill Place,
Bath BA1 5SJ
*tel* (01225) 336305 *fax* (01225) 421862
*email* tessa@tantraweb.co.uk

Two awards (£2000 each) are given annually, one
each for the best new book on food and on drink,
plus one Special Commendation of £1000 in either
category. Closing date: November each year.
Founded 1978.

## Singer & Friedlander/Sunday Times Watercolour Competition
*Details* Parker Harris Partnership, PO Box 279,
Esher, Surrey KT10 8YZ
*tel* (01372) 462190 *fax* (01372) 460032
*email* sf@parkerharris.co.uk
*website* www.parkerharris.co.uk

An annual competition 'to promote the continuance
of the British tradition of fine watercolour painting'.
Total prize money: £30,000. Open to artists born or
resident in the UK. Closing date: July 2005.

Winning entries will be exhibited in London and
Manchester. Exhibition: 7–18 September 2004.
Launched 1987.

## WHSmith 'People's Choice' Awards
*Details* WHSmith plc, Nations House,
103 Wigmore Street, London W1U 1WH
*tel* 020-7514 9623 *fax* 020-7514 9635
*email* elizabeth.walker@WHsmith.co.uk
*website* www.WHSmithbookawards.co.uk
*Contact* Elizabeth Walker, Group Events Marketing
Manager

Now in their fourth year, WHSmith were the first
UK book awards to have the winners voted for
entirely by the public. Teams of celebrity and public
judges choose the shortlists but any book published
during the calendar year can be voted for. There are
9 Award categories in total, and 8 are voted for by
the public: Fiction; Debut Novel; Lifestyle;
Autobiography/Biography, Travel Writing; Business;
Factual and Teen Choice. The public can vote in
WHSmith stores, in libraries, by text, by Freepost or
via the website. Voting starts in January and lasts 6
weeks, and the winners are announced in March.

The 9th category is the long-standing WHSmith
Literary Award, the prize for good writing. This is
not put out to public vote but is decided by a panel
led by the Professor of English Literature at Merton
College, Oxford and Chief Book Reviewer for *The
Sunday Times*, John Carey. Three members of the
public join at the shortlist stage to help decide the
winner. Each winning author receives a trophy and
£5000.

## WHSmith Thumping Good Read Award
*Details* Award Administrator, WHSmith,
Greenbridge Road, Swindon,
Wilts. SN3 3LD
*tel* (01793) 616161 *fax* (01793) 562590

An annual award of £5000 is presented to the best
popular fiction author of the year. The award is
judged by a panel of WHS customers. Founded 1992.

## The Jill Smythies Award
The Linnean Society of London, Burlington House,
Piccadilly, London W1J 0BF
*tel* 020-7434 4479 *fax* 020-7287 9364
*email* john@linnean.org
*website* www.linnean.org

Established in honour of Jill Smythies whose career
as a botanical artist was cut short by an accident to
her right hand. The rubic states that 'the Award, to
be made by Council usually annually consisting of a
silver medal and a purse (currently £1000) … is for
published illustrations, such as drawings and
paintings, in aid of plant identification, with the
emphasis on botanical accuracy and the accurate
portrayal of diagnostic characteristics. Illustrations

of cultivars of garden origin are not eligible'. Closing date for nominations: 30 September. Founded 1988.

## Society for Theatre Research Book Prize

*Details* The Society for Theatre Research,
c/o The Theatre Museum, 1E Tavistock Street,
London WC2E 7PR
*email* e.cottis@btinternet.com
*website* www.str.org.uk

An annual award (£400) is given to the author whose book, in the opinion of the judges, is the best original research into any aspect of the history and technique of the British theatre. Books must have been published in English in the preceding calendar year. Founded 1997.

## The Society of Authors and The Royal Society of Medicine Medical Book Awards

*Details* The Secretary, MWG,
The Society of Authors, 84 Drayton Gardens,
London SW10 9SB
*tel* 020-7373 6642
*email* info@societyofauthors.org
*website* www.societyofauthors.org

Entries should be submitted by the publisher. Closing date for submissions of medical text books: 20 April. The Medical Writers Group of the Society of Authors administers the prizes sponsored by the Royal Society of Medicine.

## Sony Radio Academy Awards

*Details* Sony Radio Academy Awards Secretariat,
Zafer Associates, 47–48 Chagford Street,
London NW1 6EB
*tel* 020-7723 0106 *fax* 020-7724 6163
*email* secretariat@radioawards.org
*website* www.radioawards.org

'The Sony Radio Academy Awards celebrate excellence in broadcast work. They reward creative achievement through imagination, originality, wit and integrity. The Awards offer an opportunity to enter work in a range of categories which reflect today's local, regional and national radio. The Awards are for everyone regardless of resources – for stations big and small, for a team or for one person with a microphone.' See website for further information. Founded 1982.

## The Spoken Word Awards

*Contact* The Spoken Word Publishing Association,
c/o Zoe Howes, Macmillan Publishers Ltd,
20 New Wharf Road, London N1 9RR
*tel* 020-7014 6041 *fax* 020-7014 6141
*email* z.howes@macmillan.co.uk
*website* www.swpa.co.uk

Annual awards are made for excellence in the spoken word industry. There are over 40 judges from all areas of the industry including audiobook reviewers, radio broadcasters, producers, abridgers, etc. Closing date: April.

## The Sunday Times Young Writer of the Year Award

*Details* The Society of Authors, 84 Drayton Gardens,
London SW10 9SB
*tel* 020-7373 6642
*email* info@societyofauthors.org
*website* www.societyofauthors.org

Annual award to published fiction and non-fiction writers under the age of 35. The panel consists of *Sunday Times* journalists and critics. Entry by publishers. Closing date: 31 October. Established 1991.

## The James Tait Black Memorial Prizes

*Submissions* Department of English Literature,
David Hume Tower, George Square,
Edinburgh EH8 9JX
*tel* 0131-650 3619 *fax* 0131-650 6898
*website* www.englit.ed.ac.uk/jtbinf.htm

Two prizes of £3000 are awarded annually: one for the best biography or work of that nature, the other for the best novel, published during the calendar year. The adjudicator is the Professor of English Literature in the University of Edinburgh. Eligible novels and biographies are those written in English and first published or co-published in Britain in the year of the award. Both prizes may go to the same author, but neither to the same author a second time.

Publishers should submit a copy of any appropriate biography, or work of fiction, as early as possible with a note of the date of publication, marked 'James Tait Black Prize'. Closing date for submissions: 30 September. Founded in memory of a partner in the publishing house of A & C Black, these prizes were instituted in 1918.

## TAPS (Television Arts Performance Showcase)

*Details* Shepperton Studios, Studios Road,
Shepperton, Middlesex TW17 0QD
*tel* (01932) 592151 *fax* (01932) 592233
*email* taps@tvarts.demon.co.uk

A national scheme to train and promote new writers for film and TV. TAPS workshop training courses are open to any British scriptwriter with less than 2 hours work broadcast on network TV. Full-length drama (min. 60 mins), comedy (30 mins) or shorts (10 mins) will be accepted as qualifying script submissions for the appropriate course. Scripts selected from each course are showcased by professional actors, taped and screened to industry executives culminating in the annual Writer of the Year Awards.

## Reginald Taylor and Lord Fletcher Essay Competition

*Submissions* Dr Martin Henig, Hon. Editor, British Archaeological Association, Institute of Archaeology, 36 Beaumont Street, Oxford OX1 2PG

A prize of a medal and £300 is awarded biennially for the best unpublished essay of high scholarly standard, not exceeding 7500 words, which shows original research on a subject of archaeological, art-historical or antiquarian interest within the period from the Roman era to AD1830. The successful competitor will be invited to read the essay before the Association and the essay may be published in the Association's *Journal*. Competitors should notify the Hon. Editor in advance of the intended subject of their work. Next award: autumn 2006. The essay should be submitted not later than 1 June 2006, enclosing an sae. Founded in memory of E. Reginald Taylor FSA and Lord Fletcher FSA.

## Tir Na N-og Awards

*Details* Welsh Books Council, Castell Brychan, Aberystwyth, Ceredigion SY23 2JB
*tel* (01970) 624151 *fax* (01970) 625385
*email* menna.lloydwilliams@cllc.org.uk
*website* www.cllc.org.uk

There are 3 annual awards to children's authors and illustrators: best original Welsh-language fiction, including short stories and picture books; best original Welsh-language non-fiction book of the year; best English book with an authentic Welsh background. Total prize value: £3000. Founded 1976.

## The Tom-Gallon Trust Award and the Olive Cook Prize

*Details* Awards Secretary, The Society of Authors, 84 Drayton Gardens, London SW10 9SB
*tel* 020-7373 6642
*email* info@societyofauthors.org
*website* www.societyofauthors.org

An award of £1000 is made on the basis of a submitted short story to fiction writers of limited means who have had at least one short story accepted for publication. Both awards are biennial and are awarded in alternate years. Send sae for entry form. Closing date: 20 September each year.

## The Translators Association Awards

*Details* Dorothy Sym, The Translators Association, 84 Drayton Gardens, London SW10 9SB
*tel* 020-7373 6642
*email* info@societyofauthors.org
*website* www.societyofauthors.org

The Translators Association of the Society of Authors administers a number of prizes for published translations into English. They include prizes for translations of Dutch and Flemish, French, German, Greek, Italian, Portuguese, Spanish and Swedish works. Entries should be submitted by the publisher.

## The Betty Trask Awards

*Details* Awards Secretary, The Society of Authors, 84 Drayton Gardens, London SW10 9SB
*tel* 020-7373 6642
*email* info@societyofauthors.org
*website* www.societyofauthors.org

These awards are for the benefit of young authors under the age of 35 and are given on the strength of a first novel (published or unpublished) of a romantic or traditional nature. It is expected that prizes totalling at least £25,000 will be presented each year. The winners are required to use the money for a period or periods of foreign travel. Send sae for entry form. Closing date: 31 January. Made possible through a generous bequest from Miss Betty Trask.

## The Travelling Scholarships

*Administered by* The Society of Authors, 84 Drayton Gardens, London SW10 9SB

These are honorary awards established in 1944 by an anonymous benefactor. Submissions are not accepted.

## John Tripp Award for Spoken Poetry

Academi, Mount Stuart House, Mount Stuart Square, Cardiff CF10 5FQ
*tel* 029-2047 2266 029-2049 2930
*email* competition@academi.org
*website* www.academi.org

A competition for any form of spoken poetry in the English language. There are 5 regional heats around Wales, with the winners from each heat going forward to the Grand Final in Cardiff. Performers have 5 minutes to read their work at each stage of the competition and are judged on the content of their poetry and their performance skills. Anyone either born or currently living in Wales is eligible to enter and all works must be unpublished. Founded 1990.

## The V&A Illustration Awards

*Enquiries* The Word & Image Department, Victoria and Albert Museum, London SW7 2RL
*tel* 020-7942 2414
*website* www.nal.vam.ac.uk
*Contact* Annemarie Riding *tel/fax* 020-7942 2381
*email* a.riding@vam.ac.uk

These annual awards are given to practising book and magazine illustrators, for work first published in Great Britain in the 12 months preceding the judging of the awards. There are 6 awards, including for the first time in 2004, a new prize for book covers. A first and second prize winner will be chosen from the 3 following award categories: book illustration, book cover and jacket illustration, and editorial illustration. Of the 3 category winners, one will be selected to receive the Premier Award of £2500 as the best overall illustration. The other 2 winners will each receive £1000; and the 3 second prize winners will each be awarded £500. Closing date for submissions: mid July.

## 'Charles Veillon' European Essay Prize

*Details* The Secretary, Charles Veillon Foundation, CH Y–1030 Bussigny-prés-Lausanne, Switzerland *tel* (021) 706 9029

A prize of 30,000 Swiss francs is awarded annually to a European writer or essayist for essays offering a critical look at modern society's way of life and ideology. Founded 1975.

## Ver Poets Open Competition

*Organiser* May Badman, Ver Poets, 61–63 Chiswell Green Lane, St Albans, Herts. AL2 3AL *tel* (01727) 867005 *email* may.badman@virgin.net

A competition open to all for poems of up to 30 lines of any genre or subject matter, which must be unpublished work in English. Prizes: £500 (1st), £300 (2nd), £100 (2 x 3rd). Entry fee: £3 per poem with 2 copies of each poem (each year a gift to charity is made); send sae for entry form. Closing date 30 April each year.

### Young Ver Poets Competition

A new competition for younger poets, aged 15–19. Organised as above. Prizes total £500, together with a copy of an anthology of winning and selected poems to poets. Poems must be unpublished, in English, and no longer than 30 lines. Entry fee: £1 per poem (3 for £2, 4 for £3, etc). Send sae for entry form.

## The Walford Award – see The CILIP/Whitaker Reference Awards

## David Watt Prize

*tel* 020-7753 2316 *email* davidwattprize@riotinto.com *website* www.riotinto.com

An annual award (£7500) initiated to commemorate the life and work of David Watt. Open to writers currently engaged in writing for English language newspapers and journals on international and national affairs. The winners are judged as having made 'outstanding contributions towards the greater understanding of national, international or global issues'. Entries must have been published during the year preceding the award. Final entry date: 31 March.

## The Welsh National Literature Promotion Agency and Society for Writers

Mount Stuart House, Mount Stuart Square, Cardiff CF10 5FQ

*tel* 029-2047 2266 *fax* 029-2049 2930 *email* post@academi.org *website* www.academi.org *Ceo* Peter Finch

### Book of the Year Award

A £5000 prize is awarded to winners, in Welsh and English, and £1000 to 4 other short-listed authors for works of exceptional merit by Welsh authors (by birth, subject matter or residence) published during the previous calendar year in the categories of poetry, fiction and creative non-fiction.

### Bursaries

Bursaries totalling about £100,000 are awarded annually to authors writing in both Welsh and English. Application forms are available or visit the website.

## The Wheatley Medal – see The CILIP/Whitaker Reference Awards

## Whitbread Book Awards

*Details* Anna O'Kane, The Booksellers Association, Minster House, 272 Vauxhall Bridge Road, London SW1V 1BA *tel* 020-7802 0802 *fax* 020-7802 0803 *email* anna.okane@booksellers.co.uk *website* www.whitbreadbookawards.co.uk

The awards celebrate and promote the most enjoyable contemporary British writing. Judged in 2 stages and offering a total of £50,000 prize money, the awards are open to 5 categories: Novel, First Novel, Biography, Poetry and Children's. They are judged by a panel of 3 judges and the winner in each category receives an award of £5000. Nine final judges then choose the Whitbread Book of the Year from the winners of all categories. The winner receives a cheque for £25,000. Writers must have lived in Great Britain or Ireland for 3 or more years. Submissions must be received from publishers. Closing date: early July.

## The Whitfield Prize

*Submissions* Executive Secretary, Royal Historical Society, University College London, Gower Street, London WC1E 6BT *tel* 020-7387 7532 *fax* 020-7387 7532 *email* royalhistsoc@ucl.ac.uk *website* www.rhs.ac.uk

The Prize (value £1000) is announced in July each year for the best work on a subject within a field of British history. It must be its author's first solely written history book, an original and scholarly work of historical research and have been published in the UK in the preceding calendar year. Three copies of an eligible book should be submitted before 31 December to the Executive Secretary.

## John Whiting Award

*Details* Charles Hart, Literature Dept, Arts Council England, 14 Great Peter Street, London SW1P 3NQ
*tel* 020-7973 6431
*email* charles.hart@artscouncil.org.uk
*website* www.artscouncil.org.uk

This prize of £6000 is to help further the careers and enhance the reputations of British playwrights. The play does not have to have been staged but must have been written during 2003 or 2004.

## Wildlife Photographer of the Year

*Details* Wildlife Photographer of the Year, The Natural History Museum, Cromwell Road, London SW7 5BD
*tel* 020-7942 5015 *fax* 020-7942 5084
*email* wildphoto@nhm.ac.uk
*website* www.nhm.ac.uk/wildphoto

An annual award given to the photographer whose individual image is judged to be the most striking and memorable. The overall adult winner receives £2000. The Young Wildlife Photographer of the Year receives £500, plus a day out with a photographer. Open to all ages. Closing date: April 2005.

## The Raymond Williams Community Publishing Prizes

*Details* The Literature Dept, Arts Council England, 14 Great Peter Street, London SW1P 3NQ
*tel* 020-7973 6442
*website* www.artscouncil.org.uk

This award commends published works of outstanding creative and imaginative quality that reflect the life, voices and experiences of the people of particular communities. The winning entry will be awarded £3000 and the runner-up £2000.

## The Wolfson Foundation

*Details* The Prize Administrator, The Wolfson Foundation, 8 Queen Anne Street, London W1G 9LD
*tel* 020-7323 5730 ext. 213  *fax* 020-7323 3241

Annual awards are made to encourage and recognise books by British historians that can be enjoyed by a general readership and will stimulate public interest in history. The awards total £25,000. Authors must be British citizens and normally resident in the UK. The book must be published in the calendar year of the prize. Closing date varies: contact the office. Founded 1972.

## David T.K. Wong Fellowship

*Details* David T.K. Wong Fellowship, School of English & American Studies, University of East Anglia, Norwich NR4 7TJ
*tel* (01603) 592810 *fax* (01603) 507728
*email* v.striker@uea.ac.uk
*website* www.uea.ac.uk/eas/fellowships/wong/wong.shtml

Founded by David Wong, retired senior civil servant, journalist and businessman, the annual Fellowship (worth £25,000) at the University of East Anglia will give writers of exceptional talent the chance to produce a work of fiction in English which deals seriously with some aspect of life in the Far East. Residential: Oct–June. Write for full details. Closing date: 31 October each year. Founded 1997.

## The David T.K. Wong Prize for Short Fiction

*Details* International PEN, 9–10 Charterhouse Buildings, Goswell Road, London EC1M 7AT
*tel* 020-7253 4308 *fax* 020-7253 5711
*email* gvincent@dircon.co.uk
*website* www.internatpen.org

This biennial international prize is presented to promote literary excellence in the form of the short story written in English. Unpublished stories of between 2500 words and 6000 words are welcome from writers worldwide but entries must incorporate one or more of International PEN's ideals as set out in its Charter. Entries should be submitted via the entrant's local PEN Centre, not sent to International PEN. The closing date for entries for 2006/7 is likely to be the end of September 2006 but details should be obtained from individual Centres. In those few countries without a PEN Centre, entrants can be directed to the nearest appropriate Centre by International PEN. First prize: £7500. Copies of PEN's Charter in English, French and Spanish and addresses of PEN Centres can be found on the website. Established 2000.

## Write A Story for Children Competition

*Entry forms* The Academy of Children's Writers, PO Box 95, Huntingdon, Cambs. PE28 5RL
*tel* (01487) 832752
*email* per_ardua@lycos.co.uk

Three prizes (1st £1000, 2nd £200, 3rd £100) are awarded annually for a short story for children, maximum 1000 words, by an unpublished writer of children's fiction. Send sae for details. Founded 1984.

## Writers' Forum Short Story Competition

*tel* (01202) 589828 *fax* (01202) 587758
*email* editorial@writers-form.com
*website* www.writers-form.com

*Writers' Forum* (12 p.a.) is an anthology of short stories from the winners of its competitions. Prizes range from £150 to £250 in each issue with an annual trophy and a cheque for £1000 for the best story of the year. Entry fee: £10 to non-subscribers of *Writers' Forum*; £6 to subscribers.

## Writers' Week Poetry Competition

*Details* Writers' Week, 24 The Square, Listowel,
Co. Kerry, Republic of Ireland
*tel* (353) 6821074 *fax* (353) 6822893
*email* writersweek@eircom.net
*website* www.writersweek.ie

Annual awards for a single poem (prize: €850; entry
fee: €8.50) and for a collection of 6–12 poems
(prize: €850 plus financial support towards
publication of a slim volume; entry fee: €25).

## Yorkshire Post Book of the Year

*Submissions* Margaret Brown, Yorkshire Post
Literary Awards, Yorkshire Post Newspapers Ltd,
PO Box 168, Wellington Street, Leeds LS1 1RF
*tel* (01423) 772217 *fax* (01423) 772217

An annual prize of £1200 for the Best Book, either
fiction or non-fiction. Submissions are accepted
only from publishers, and authors should be British
or resident in the UK. Next closing date: 31
December.

## Young Writers' Programme

*Details* Young Writers' Programme, Royal Court
Young Writers' Programme, Sloane Square,
London SW1W 8AS
*tel* 020-7565 5034 *fax* 020-7565 5001

Anyone aged 13–25 can submit a play on any
subject. A selection of plays are professionally
presented by the Royal Court Theatre with the
writers fully involved in rehearsal and production.
Pre-Festival Development Workshops are run by
professional theatre practitioners and designed to
help everyone attending to write a play. Playwriting
projects run all year round

# Literature festivals

There are hundreds of arts festivals held in the UK each year – too many to mention in this
*Yearbook* and many of which are not applicable specifically to writers. We give here a
selection of literature festivals and general arts festivals which include literature events.
Space constraints and the nature of an annual publication together determine that only
brief details are given; contact festival organisers for a full programme of events. The
British Council will supply a list of forthcoming literature festivals on receipt of a large sae.

## The Academi Ty Newydd Festival

3rd Floor, Mount Stuart House, Mount Stuart
Square, Cardiff CF10 5FQ
*tel* (02920) 472266 *fax* (02920) 492930
*email* post@academi.org
*website* www.academi.org
*Contact* Peter Finch, Chief Executive
*Takes place* April 2005 (biennial)

Events are centred on the writing centre at
Llanystumdwy in Gwynedd and feature a mix of
Welsh and English events including Poetry Stomps
and guest readers. The Academi, the Welsh National
Literature Promotion Agency and Ty Newydd work
together to create this festival.

## Aldeburgh Poetry Festival

Aldeburgh Poetry Trust, Goldings, Goldings Lane,
Leiston, Suffolk IP16 4EB
*tel* (01379) 668345
*email* info@aldeburghpoetryfestival.org
*website* www.aldeburghpoetryfestival.org
*Festival Director* Naomi Jaffa
*Takes place* First weekend in Nov

An annual contemporary poetry festival: readings,
workshops, a public masterclass, a lecture and a
children's event. Includes a substantial line-up of
international and national poets as well as fringe
events and a writer-in-residence. Aldeburgh Festival
Prize is awarded for the year's best first collection.

## Aspects Festival

North Down Heritage Centre, The Castle, Bangor,
Co. Down BT20 4BT
*tel* (028) 91 271200 *fax* (028) 91 271370
*Contact* Gail Prentice, Arts Officer/Festival
Co-ordinator
*Takes place* last week of September

An annual celebration of contemporary Irish
writing with novelists, poets, playwrights and non-
fiction writers. Includes readings, discussions,
workshops and a children's day.

## Ballymena Arts Festival

Ballymena Borough Council, Ardeevin, 80 Galgorm
Road, Ballymena, Co. Antrim BT42 1AB
*tel* (01266) 660300 *fax* (01266) 660400
*Takes place* Oct

## Bath Literature Festival

Bath Festivals Trust, 5 Broad Street, Bath BA1 5LJ
*tel* (01225) 462231, (01225) 463362 (box office)
*fax* (01225) 445551
*email* info@bathfestivals.org.uk
*website* www.bathlitfest.org.uk

*Director* Sarah LeFanu
*Takes place* 26 Feb–6 March 2005

An annual 9-day festival with leading guest writers. Includes readings, debates, discussions and workshops, and events for children and young people. Programme available from box office in December.

## Bay Lit

Academi, Mount Stuart House, Mount Stuart Square, Cardiff CF10 5FQ
*tel* 029-2047 2266 *fax* 029-2049 2930
*email* post@academi.org
*website* www.academi.org
*Contact* Peter Finch, Chief Executive
*Takes place* Spring/early summer

A bilingual (Welsh and English) literature festival, held in Cardiff Bay. It is organised by Academi, the Welsh National Literature Promotion Agency and Society for Writers, and features an array of writers from Wales and beyond.

## Belfast Festival at Queen's

Festival House, 25 College Gardens, Belfast BT9 6BS
*tel* 028-9097 2600 *fax* 028-9097 2630
*email* festival@qub.ac.uk
*website* www.belfastfestival.com
*Director* Stella Hall
*Takes place* 22 Oct–7 Nov 2004

The largest annual arts event in Ireland. Includes literature events. Programme available mid September.

## Birmingham Book Festival

Unit 116, The Custard Factory, Gibb Street, Birmingham B9 4AA
*tel* 0121-246 2770 *fax* 0121-246 2771
*email* jonathan@bookcommunications.co.uk
*website* www.lit-net.org/bbf
*Programmer* Jonathan Davidson
*Takes place* 7–22 Oct 2004

An annual festival which presents a range of events with all types of writers of both fiction and non-fiction.

## Book Now!

Education, Arts & Leisure Department, Orleans House Gallery, Riverside, Twickenham TW1 3DJ
*tel* 020-8831 6000 *fax* 020-8744 0507
*website* www.richmond.gov.uk
*Takes place* Throughout Nov

An annual literature festival covering a broad range of subjects. Leading British and overseas guest writers and poets hold discussions, talks, debates and workshops and give readings. There are also exhibitions, storytelling sessions and a schools programme.

## Brighton Festival

12A Pavilion Buildings, Castle Square, Brighton BN1 1EE
*tel* (01273) 700747 *fax* (01273) 707505
*email* info@brighton-festival.org.uk
*website* www.brighton-festival.org.uk
*Takes place* May

An annual general arts festival with a large literature programme. Leading guest writers cover a broad range of subjects in a diverse programme of events. Programme published end of February.

## Buxton Festival

5 The Square, Buxton SK17 6AZ
*tel* (01298) 70395
*email* info@buxtonfestival.co.uk
*website* www.buxtonfestival.co.uk
*Artistic Director* Aidan Long, *General Manager* Glyn Foley
*Takes place* July

The main festival has a growing literary strand with featuring distinguished authors.

## Cambridge Conference of Contemporary Poetry

Kevin Nolan, 2 Bells Close, West Road, Saffron Walden, Essex CB11 3DU
*email* k.nolan@virgin.net
*website* www.cccp-online.org
*Takes place* April

An annual weekend of poetry readings, discussion and performance of international poetry in the modernist tradition.

## Canterbury Festival

Festival Office, Christ Church Gate, The Precincts, Canterbury, Kent CT1 2EE
*tel* (01227) 452853 *fax* (01227) 781830
*email* info@canterburyfestival.co.uk
*website* www.canterburyfestival.co.uk
*Takes place* 9–24 Oct 2004

An annual general arts festival with a literature programme. Programme published in July.

## Chaucer Festival

Chaucer Heritage Trust, Chaucer Centre, 22 St Peter's Street, Canterbury, Kent CT1 2BQ
*tel* 020-7229 0635 *fax* (01227) 761416
*Director* Martin Starkie,
*Events Organiser* Zoran Tesic *tel* (01227) 470379
*Takes place* Spring, Summer and Autumn

An annual festival which includes commemoration services, theatre productions, exhibitions, readings, recitals, Chaucer site visits, medieval fairs, costumed cavalcades, educational programmes for schools. Takes place in London, Canterbury and the County of Kent in the Spring (Easter Chaucer Pilgrimage), Summer (June–July), and Autumn (Oct).

## Cheltenham Festival of Literature

Town Hall, Imperial Square, Cheltenham,
Glos. GL50 1QA
*tel* (01242) 227979 (box office), 237377 (brochure),
263494 (festival office) *fax* (01242) 256457
*email* adam.pushkin@cheltenham.gov.uk
*website* www.cheltenhamfestivals.co.uk
*Artistic Director* Christopher Cook
*Takes place* October and April each year

This annual festival is the largest of its kind in
Europe. Events include talks and lectures, poetry
readings, novelists in conversation, exhibitions,
discussions, workshops and a large bookshop. *Book
It!* is a festival for children within the main festival
with an extensive programme of events and a
multimedia room. Brochures are available in August.

## Chester Festivals – Literature

8 Abbey Square, Chester CH1 2HU
*tel* (01244) 319985 *fax* (01244) 341200
*email* freda@chesterfestivals.co.uk
*Festival Administrator* Freda Hadwen
*Takes place* 2–29 2004, 8–29 Oct 2005

An annual festival commencing the first weekend in
October. Events featuring international, national
and local writers and poets are part of the
programme, as well as a literary lunch and festival
dinner. There is a poetry competition for school
children, events for children and workshops for
adults. A Cheshire Prize for Literature is awarded
each year, only residents in Cheshire are eligible.

## Chichester Festivities

Canon Gate House, South Street, Chichester,
West Sussex PO19 1PU
*tel* (01243) 785718 *fax* (01243) 528356
*email* info@chifest.org.uk
*website* www.chifest.org.uk
*Takes place* June/July

## City of London Festival

Bishopsgate Hall, 230 Bishopsgate,
London EC2M 4HW
*tel* 020-7377 0540 *fax* 020-7377 1972
*email* admin@colf.org
*website* www.colf.org
*Takes place* Last week of June and first two weeks of
July, 2005

An annual multi-arts festival with a programme of
literary events. Programme published in April.

## City Voice

Central Library, Calverley Street, Leeds LS1 3AB
*tel* 0113-247 8421
*website* www.leeds.gov.uk/wordarena
*Contact* Festival Organiser
*Takes place* May/June

An annual 2-week celebration of the voices of the
city – provides a platform for Leeds writers
alongside established names.

## The Cúirt International Festival of Literature

Galway Arts Centre, 47 Dominick Street, Galway,
Republic of Ireland
*tel* (091) 565886 *fax* (091) 568642
*email* gac@indigo.ie
*website* www.galwayartscentre.ie
*Managing Director* Tomás Hardiman, *Progammer
Director* Maura Kennedy
*Takes place* April

An annual week-long festival to celebrate writing,
bringing together national and international writers
to promote literary discussion. Events include
readings, performances, workshops, seminars,
lectures, poetry slams and talks. The festival is
renowned for its convivial atmosphere ('cúirt'
means a 'bardic court or gathering').

## Dublin Writers' Festival

c/o Dublin City Council, Arts Office,
10 Cornmarket, Dublin 8, Republic of Ireland
*tel* (01) 8722816 *fax* (01) 6773887
*email* dublinwritersfestival@eircom.net
*website* www.dublinwritersfestival.com
*Programme Director* Pat Boran
*Takes place* June

An annual festival with readings by major Irish and
international poets and writers to celebrate the best
in contemporary literature.

## Durham Literature Festival 2004

c/o Durham City Arts Ltd, Byland Lodge, Hawthorn
Terrace, Durham DH1 4TD
*tel* 0191-301 8830 *fax* 0191-301 8821
*email* alison@durhamcityarts.demon.co.uk
*Festival Coordinator* Alison Lister
*Takes place* Sept–Oct

## Edinburgh International Book Festival

Scottish Book Centre, 137 Dundee Street,
Fountainbridge, Edinburgh EH11 1BG
*tel* 0131-228 5444 *fax* 0131-228 4333
*email* admin@edbookfest.co.uk
*website* www.edbookfest.co.uk
*Director* Catherine Lockerbie
*Takes place* 13–29 Aug 2005

Now established as Europe's largest book event for
the public. In addition to a unique independent
bookselling operation, over 600 writers contribute
to the programme of events. Programme details
available in June.

## Everybody's Reading

Leicester City Council, 12th Floor, Block A,
New Walk Centre, Welford Place, Leicester LE1 6ZG

*email* libraries@leicester.gov.uk
*Contact* Damien Walter
*Takes place* October

## Exeter Festival

Festival Office, Civic Centre, Exeter EX1 1JJ
*tel* (01392) 265200 *fax* (01392) 265265
*website* www.exeter.gov.uk
*Festival Manager* Lesley Waters
*Takes place* July

An annual general arts festival which includes a
programme of literary activities. Programme of
events available in May.

## Federation of Worker Writers and Community Publishers Festival of Writing

Burslem School of Art, Queen Street,
Stoke-on-Trent ST6 3EJ
*tel* (01782) 822327 *fax* (01782) 822327
*email* thefwwcp@tiscali.co.uk
*website* www.thefwwcp.org.uk
*Takes place* April

## Festival at the Edge Storytelling Festival

c/o Rose Cottage, Church Road, Welshpool,
Powys SY21 7LN
*tel* (01939) 236626
*email* info@festivalattheedge.org
*website* www.festivalattheedge.org
*Contact* Ali Quarrell
*Takes place* Third full weekend of July in Much
Wenlock, Shrops.

## The Guardian Hay Festival

Festival Office, The Drill Hall, 25 Lion Street,
Hay-on-Wye HR3 5AD
*tel* (01497) 821217, (01497) 821299 (box office)
*fax* (01497) 821066
*email* admin@hayfestival.co.uk
*website* www.hayfestival.com
*Takes place* May/June

This annual festival aims to celebrate the best in
writing and performance from around the world, to
commission new work, and to promote and
encourage young writers of excellence and
potential. Over 200 events in 10 days with leading
guest writers. Programme published April.

## Guildford Book Festival

c/o Tourist Information Office, 14 Tunsgate,
Guildford GU1 3QT
*tel* (01483) 225388
*email* book-festival-director@surrey.ac.uk
*websites* www.guildford.org.uk,
www.guildfordbookfestival.co.uk
*Festival Director* Glenis Pycraft
*Takes place* 17–31 Oct 2004

An annual festival with a varied programme of over
60 events held at different venues in Guildford,
including readings, discussions, literary lunches and
teas, performance poetry, workshops, competitions.
High-profile authors and many children's events. Its
aim is to involve, instruct and entertain all who care
about literature and to encourage in children a love
of reading. Founded 1990.

## Harrogate International Festival

1 Victoria Avenue, Harrogate,
North Yorkshire HG1 1EQ
*tel* (01423) 562303 *fax* (01423) 521264
*email* info@harrogate-festival.org.uk,
crime@harrogate-festival.org.uk
*website* www.harrogate-festival.org.uk
*Takes place* July/Aug

An annual international multi-arts festival.
Programme available in May.

**Harrogate Crime Writing Festival** (July): A
weekend of events featuring the best of British and
American crime writers.

## Hastings International Poetry First of All

c/o The Snoring Cat, 16 Marianne Park, Dudley
Road, Hastings, East Sussex TN35 5PU
*tel* (01424) 428855 *fax* (01424) 428855
*email* josephine-poetry@btopenworld
*website* www.josephineaustin.co.uk
*Organiser and Editor of First Time* Josephine Austin
*Takes place* 6–7 Nov 2004

Started in 1968, this national festival is now held in
the Yelton Hotel. Includes the prize-giving of the
*Hastings National Poetry Competition*. Poems are
invited for consideration for the bi-annual *First
Time* poetry magazine. Please include sae.

## Ilkley Literature Festival

The Manor House, Ilkley LS29 9DT
*tel* (01943) 601210 *fax* (01943) 817079
*email* admin@ilkleyliteraturefestival.org.uk
*website* www.ilkleyliteraturefestival.org.uk
*Festival Director* Rachel Feldberg
*Takes place* Oct

The north of England's oldest and largest literature
festival organises a full programme of writing and
reading events.

## International Playwriting Festival

Warehouse Theatre, Dingwall Road,
Croydon CR0 2NF
*tel* 020-8681 1257 *fax* 020-8688 6699
*email* info@warehousetheatre.co.uk
*website* www.warehousetheatre.co.uk
*Takes place* Nov

The weekend festival features: a showcase of the
best selected work from the IPF competition (see
page 558), and selected plays from the festival's

international partners – the leading Italian playwriting festival, the Premio Candoni Arta Terme, and Theatro Ena, Cyprus.

## King's Lynn Festival
5 Thoresby College, Queen Street, King's Lynn, Norfolk PE30 1HX
*tel* (01553) 767557 *fax* (01553) 767688
*website* www.kl-festival.freeserve.co.uk
*Administrator* Joanne Rutterford
*Takes place* 17–30 July 2005

An annual general arts festival with literature events featuring leading guest writers.

## King's Lynn Literature Festivals
19 Tuesday Market Place, King's Lynn, Norfolk PE30 1JW
*tel* (01553) 691661 *fax* (01553) 691779
*Chairman* Tony Ellis
*Takes place* Sept/March

**Poetry Festival** (24–26 Sept 2004): An annual festival which brings 8 published poets to King's Lynn for the weekend for readings and discussions.

**Fiction Festival** (13–15 March 2005): An annual festival which brings 12 published novelists to King's Lynn for the weekend for readings and discussions.

## Ledbury Poetry Festival
Town Council Offices, Church Street, Ledbury HR8 1DH
*tel* (0845) 458 1743
*email* prog@poetry-festival.com
*website* www.poetry-festival.com
*Festival Director* Charles Bennett
*Takes place* 1–10 July 2005

An annual festival featuring top poets from around the world, together with a poet-in-residence programme, competitions (send sae for entry form), workshops and exhibitions. Full programme available in May.

## Lincolnshire Literature Festival
Education and Cultural Services Directorate, Lincolnshire County Council, County Offices, Lincoln LN1 1YL
*tel* (01522) 552831 *fax* (01522) 552811
*email* david.lambert@lincolnshire.gov.uk
*County Literature Development Officer* David Lambert
*Takes place* Throughout the year

A monthly series of varied literary events. Occasional festivals, tours, publications in Lincolnshire.

## Litfest
26 Castle Park, Lancaster, Lancs. LA1 1YQ
*tel* (01524) 62166
*email* all@litfest.org

*website* www.litfest.org
*Contact* Andrew Darby
*Takes place* mid Nov

Annual festival featuring readings, performances and workshops by contemporary writers for adults; includes performance of several new commissioned works each year. Litfest also acts as a year-round literature development agency in Lancashire.

## Lit Up!
The Plough Arts Centre, 9–11 Fore Street, Torrington, Devon EX38 8HQ
*tel* (01805) 622552 *fax* (01805) 622113
*Contact* Richard Wolfenden-Brown
*Takes place* Throughout the year

An occasional literature programme including workshops, readings, performances and exhibitions, as part of a larger programme of arts work, including community and educational workshops, projects, residencies and performances.

## Lowdham Book Festival
4th Floor, Arts, County Hall, West Bridgford, Nottingham NG2 7QP
*tel* 0115-977 4435
*email* ross.bradshaw@nottscc.gov.uk
*website* www.lowdhambookfestival.co.uk
*Contact* Ross Bradshaw, Literature Officer
*Takes place* June

An annual 10-day festival of literature events for adults and children with a daily programme of high-profile national writers. There is a writer-in-residence and a book fair on the last Saturday.

## Manchester Poetry Festival
3rd Floor, 24 Lever Street, Manchester M1 1DZ
*tel* 0161-236 5725 *fax* 0161-236 5719
*email* info@manchesterpoetryfestival.co.uk
*website* www.manchesterpoetry.co.uk
*Contact* Rachel Lewis
*Takes place* 9–13 Oct 2004

An annual festival catering for all ages, including readings, slams, workshops and live events. See website for details. Recent Regional Lottery Arts Programme funding now enables the Festival to take events out of the city centre and into districts of Greater Manchester and the Northwest for a year-round programme of events over 2005.

## Arthur Miller Centre International Literary Festival
School of English & American Studies, University of East Anglia, Norwich NR4 7TJ
*tel* (01603) 592810 *fax* (01603) 507728
*email* v.striker@uea.ac.uk
*website* www.uea.ac.uk/eas/events/intro.shtml
*Contact* Val Striker, Administrative Officer
*Takes place* Late Sept–early Dec

An annual festival of weekly events to bring well-established international writers of fiction, biography, poetry, etc to a public audience in the Eastern region.

## National Eisteddfod of Wales
40 Parc Ty Glas, Llanisien, Cardiff CF14 5WU
*tel* 029-2076 3777 *fax* 029-2076-3737
*email* elfedateisteddfod.org.uk
*website* www.eisteddfod.org.uk
*Director* Elfed Roberts
*Takes place* 30 July–6 Aug 2005

An annual festival attracting 160,000 visitors and over 6000 competitors. It is the largest popular festival of competitive music making and poetry writing in Europe.

## Norfolk and Norwich Festival
42–58 St George's Street, Norwich NR3 1AB
*tel* (01603) 614921 *fax* (01603) 632303
*email* info@n-joy.org.uk
*website* www.n-joy.org.uk
*Artistic Director/Chief Executive* Peter Bolton
*Takes place* May

## North East Lincolnshire Annual Literature Festival
Arts Development, Regeneration & Community Learning, King Edward Street, Grimsby, North East Lincolnshire DN31 3LU
*tel* (01472) 323007 *fax* (01472) 323377
*email* liz.bennet@nelincs.gov.uk
*Contact* Arts Development Unit
*Takes place* Oct/Nov

Reflecting the heritage and culture of the area, this annual festival aims to make literature accessible to all ages and abilities through a varied and unusual programme. Write or telephone for details.

## Northern Children's Book Festival
22 Highbury, Jesmond,
Newcastle Upon Tyne NE2 3DY
*tel* 0191-2813289
*email* annkey@waitrose.com
*website* www.ncbf.org.uk
*Chairperson* Ann Key
*Takes place* 8–20 Nov 2004

An annual festival to bring authors, illustrators, poets and performers to children in schools, libraries and community centres across the North East of England. About 36 authors visit the North East over the 2-week period for 2–8 days, organised by the 12 local authorities. The climax of the festival is a huge public event in a different part of the North East each year when over 4000 children and their families visit to take part in author seminars, drama workshops, and to enjoy a variety of book-related activities. The Gala Day will be on 20 Nov 2004.

## Off the Shelf Literature Festival
Central Library, Surrey Street,
Sheffield S201 1XZ
*tel* 0114-273 4716 *fax* 0114-273 5009
*email* offtheshelf@sheffield.gov.uk
*website* www.offtheshelf.org.uk
*Contacts* Maria de Souza, Su Walker
*Takes place* 16–30 Oct 2004

The festival comprises a wide range of events for adults and children, including author visits, writing workshops, storytelling, competitions, theatre performances and exhibitions. Programme available in September.

## Oxford Literary Festival – see The Sunday Times Oxford Literary Festival

## Poetry International
Literature Section, Royal Festival Hall,
South Bank Centre, London SE1 8XX
*tel* 020-7921 0906 *fax* 020-7928 2049
*email* awhitehead@rfh.org.uk
*website* www.rfh.org.uk
*Contact* Angela Whitehead
*Takes place* Oct 2004, 2006 (biennial)

The biggest poetry festival in the British Isles, bringing together a wide range of poets from around the world. Includes readings, workshops, discussions and events for children. The Literature Section also runs a year-round programme of readings, talks and debates.

## proudWORDS
PO Box 181, Newcastle upon Tyne NE6 5XG
*tel* (07973) 894912
*email* pwcwf@hotmail.com
*website* www.proudwords.org.uk
*Coordinator* Mary Lowe
*Takes place* Autumn

An annual festival to promote the best lesbian and gay writing within the North. The focus is participation and self expression, and the atmosphere is informal. The festival consists of workshops, performances, readings, competitions and discussions, culminating in a festival party.

## Royal Court Young Writers' Festival
The Royal Court Young Writers' Programme,
Sloane Square, London SW1W 8AS
*tel* 020-7565 5050
*Contact* The Administrator
*Takes place* Biennially

A national festival which anyone aged 13–25 can enter. Promising plays which arise from the workshops are then developed and performed at the Royal Court's Theatre Upstairs (see page 573).

## Royal National Eisteddfod of Wales

40 Parc Ty Glas, Llanishen,
Cardiff CF14 5WU
*tel* 029-2076 3777
*email* info@eisteddfod.org.uk
*website* www.eisteddfod.org.uk
*Marketing Officer* Betsan Williams
*Takes place* 30 July–6 Aug 2005

Wales' largest cultural festival, based on 800 years of tradition. Activities include competitions in all aspects of the arts, fringe performances and majestic ceremonies. In addition to activities held in the main pavilion, it houses over 300 trade stands along with a literary pavilion, a music studio, a movement and dance theatre, a rock pavilion and a purpose-built theatre. The event is set in a different location each year, and is set to take place on the Faenol Estate near Caernarfon in August 2005.

## Rye Festival

PO Box 33, Rye, East Sussex TN31 7YB
*tel* (01797) 224982 *fax* (01797) 224226
*email* hilary.brooke@virgin.net
*website* www.ryefestival.co.uk
*Literary Events Manager* Mrs Hilary Brooke
*Takes place* First 2 weeks of Sept (15 days); Winter Series held last weekend Jan and first weekend Feb (4 days)

An annual festival of 15 literary events featuring novelists, biographers, and political and scientific writers, with book signings and discussions. Runs concurrently with the Rye festival of music and visual arts.

## Salisbury Festival

75 New Street, Salisbury, Wilts. SP1 2PH
*tel* (01722) 332241 *fax* (01722) 410552
*Director* Trevor Davies
*Takes place* May/June

An annual general multi-arts festival with a literature programme of events. Programme published in April.

## Stratford-upon-Avon Poetry Festival

Shakespeare Centre, Henley Street,
Stratford-upon-Avon CV37 6QW
*tel* (01789) 204016 *fax* (01789) 296083
*email* info@shakespeare.org.uk
*website* www.shakespeare.org.uk
*Director* Roger Pringle
*Takes place* Nine Sunday evenings throughout July and Aug

An annual festival which aims to present poetry of many different ages and to provide opportunities for readings by established contemporary poets. Sponsored by the Shakespeare Birthplace Trust. Founded 1954.

## The Sunday Times Oxford Literary Festival

301 Woodstock Road, Oxford OX2 7NY
*tel* (01865) 514149 *fax* (01865) 514804
*email* oxford.literary.festival@ntlworld.com
*website* www.sundaytimes-oxfordliteraryfestival.co.uk
*Festival Directors* Angela Prysor-Jones, Sally Dunsmore
*Takes place* 2 weeks prior to Easter

An annual 6-day festival for both adults and children. Presents topical debates, fiction and non-fiction discussion panels, and adult and children's authors who have recently published books. Topics range from contemporary fiction to discussions on politics, history, science, gardening, food, poetry, philosophy, art and crime fiction.

## Swindon Festival of Literature

Lower Shaw Farm, Shaw, Swindon, Wilts. SN5 5PJ
*tel* (01793) 771080 *fax* (01793) 771080
*email* swindonlitfest@lowershawfarm.co.uk
*website* www.swindonfestivalofliterature.co.uk
*Festival Director* Matt Holland
*Takes place* Starts at dawn on 1 May for 15 days

An annual celebration of literature – prose, poetry, drama and storytelling – by readings, discussions, performances, talks, etc, indoors and out.

## Tales & Trails

Mythstories Museum, The Morgan Library,
Aston Street, Wem, Shrops. SY4 5AU
*tel* (01939) 235500
*email* tandt@mythstories.com
*website* www.mythstories.com
*Contact* Del Quarréll, Curator/Storyteller
*Takes place* Three times a year: March, May, Sept

A strolling festival of storytelling with morning storywalks and evening story concerts featuring Britain's top storytellers and the cream of Border storytellers.

## Dylan Thomas – The Celebration

The Dylan Thomas Centre, Somerset Place,
Swansea SA1 1RR
*tel* (01792) 463980 *fax* (01792) 463993
*email* dylanthomas.lit@swansea.gov.uk
*website* www.dylanthomas.org
*Events Manager* David Woolley
*Takes place* 27 Oct–9 Nov 2004

An annual festival celebrating the life and work of Swansea's most famous son: performances, lectures, debates, poetry, music and film. Also, regular events throughout the summer including guided tours.

## Warwick Festival

Warwick Arts Society, Pageant House, 2 Jury Street,
Warwick CV34 4EW

tel (01926) 410747 *fax* (01926) 409050
*email* admin@warwickarts.org.uk
*website* www.warwickarts.org.uk
*Festival Director* Richard Phillips
*Takes place* 30 June–10 July 2005

A music festival which includes some literature and poetry events: readings, performances and workshops.

## Ways With Words Literature Festival

Droridge Farm, Dartington, Totnes, Devon TQ9 6JQ
tel (01803) 867373 *fax* (01803) 863688
*email* admin@wayswithwords.co.uk
*website* www.wayswithwords.co.uk
*Contact* Kay Dunbar
*Takes place* 10 days in middle of July each year

200 speakers give readings, talks, interviews, discussions, seminars, workshops with leading guest writers. Also organises Words by the Water: a Cumbrian literature festival (March) and Sole Bay Literature Festival, Southwold (Nov), as well as writing courses and writing and painting holidays in Italy.

## Wells Festival of Literature

25 Chamberlain Street, Wells, Somerset BA5 2PQ
tel (01749) 670929
*website* www.somersite.co.uk/wellsfest.htm
*Takes place* Late Oct

An annual festival which features leading guest writers and poets. It also includes writing workshops as well as short story and poetry competitions. The main venue is the historic Bishop's Palace, Wells.

## Wigtown Book Town Literary Festival

County Buildings, Wigtown, Dumfries, Galloway DG8 9JH
tel (01988) 402036 *fax* (01988) 402506
*email* booktown-wigit@btinternet.com
*website* www.wigtown-booktown.co.uk
*Project Manager* John Robertson, *Book Town Assistant* Jenny Bradley
*Takes place* Last 2 weekends in Sept

An annual festival taking place in Scotland's national book town which boasts 23 bookshops. Readings and talks take place in bookshops, Wigtown's County Buildings or at the nearby Bladnoch Distillery.

## Winter's Edge Storytelling Festival

c/o Rose Cottage, Church Road, Welshpool, Powys SY21 7LN
tel (01939) 236626
*email* info@festivalattheedge.org
*website* www.festivalattheedge.org
*Contact* Ali Quarrell
*Takes place* 31 Jan–6 Feb 2005 in Much Wenlock, Shrops.

## Wonderful Words Book Festival

Bude Library, The Wharf, Bude, Cornwall EX23 8LG
tel (01288) 359242 *fax* (01288) 355176
*email* rrowland@cornwall.gov.uk
*website* www.cornwall.gov.uk/library
*Festival Organiser* Rebecca Rowland
*Takes place* Sept/Oct 2006

A biennial festival organised by the Cornwall Library Service. Events take place throughout the county, including talks, discussions, workshops, poetry and storytelling. The festival attracts high-profile authors.

## World Book Day

World Book Day, 66 Burlington Lane, London W4 2RR
tel 020-7631 2666 *fax* 020-7631 2699
*email* pr@colmangettypr.co.uk
*website* www.worldbookday.com
*Contact* Cathy Schofield
*Takes place* Early March

An annual celebration of books and reading aimed at promoting their value and creating the readers of the future. Every schoolchild in full-time education receives a £1 book token. Events take place all over the UK in schools, bookshops, libraries and arts centres.

## Writers' Week

24 The Square, Listowel, Co. Kerry, Republic of Ireland
tel (068) 21074 *fax* (068) 22893
*email* writersweek@eircom.net
*website* www.writersweek.ie
*Administrator* Maria O'Connor
*Takes place* 1–5 June 2005

Aims to promote the work of Irish writers in both the English and Irish language, and to provide a platform for new and established writers to discuss their works. Events include readings, seminars, lectures and book launches.

## Young Readers Birmingham

Children's Office, Central Library, Chamberlain Square, Birmingham B3 3HQ
tel 0121-303 3368 *fax* 0121-464 1004
*email* patsy.heap@birmingham.gov.uk
*website* www.birmingham.gov.uk/youngreaders
*Contact* Patsy Heap
*Takes place* 21 May–4 June 2005

An annual festival targeted at young people aged 0–19 and adults who care for or work with them. It aims to motivate them to enjoy reading and through this to encourage literacy; to provide imaginative access to books, writers and storytellers; to encourage families to share reading for pleasure; to provide a national focus for the celebration of books and reading for children and young people and help raise the media profile of children's books and writing. Approximately 150 events.

# Writers and artists online

## E-publishing

E-publishers offer a variety of services to authors and have no set standards of quality or provision. Jane Dorner looks at the electronic minefield facing authors.

All major UK publishers have websites on which they promote their books. Some are publishing electronic versions downloadable directly from the web. Some, like Random House, are sharing the revenue from e-titles 50–50 with their authors. This is still basically traditional publishing, and all the brand name expectations apply.

There's another, new, set of e-publishers which do not have an established track record – there has been no time for the investment in a brand (high standards, quality provision, peer review, integrity). Some are genuine publishers operating in the new environment and some come perilously close to vanity publishers eager to make money out of the unwary. Others offer useful services to self-publishers. And some call themselves publishers, but are effectively book showrooms. The boundaries can sometimes be so vague that it is difficult to be dogmatic about what value they provide.

For example, one e-publisher offers a core free service, but that is only if you throw a completely finished, edited file into a standard template; anything individual or quality-vetted costs £200 and upwards. Another charges £40 to act as an e-agent, showcasing a synopsis and first chapter and targeting agents and publishers with an email alerter. A third requires £99 to turn your book into an electronic format, plus minimal marketing, and charges a flat rate of nearly £5 a book of which £2 goes to the author. Some take anything they are offered (within the bounds of censorship) and others have strict filtering systems. Not many provide editing, design or quality control.

Until new reputations form, writers will have to look closely at the new e-publisher's websites, read carefully through submission statements, look for an online contract or terms and conditions and judge for themselves. Enter into an email dialogue and get as much information as you can before you submit anything.

The most obvious appeal is to writers who have unpublished works, out-of-print works whose rights have reverted to them, or previously published materials that could have a renewed life in a new format.

### E-formats

The choice of formats is diverse, including:

- book-a-likes – book-sized electronic devices designed for reading continuous texts – the texts displayed on them are e-books (not popular in the UK);
- personal digital organisers (pocket PDAs) which can carry e-books;

- any platform using Adobe Portable Document Format (PDF), which is a universal standard for preserving the original appearance (fonts, formatting, colours and graphics) of any source document, regardless of the application and platform used to create it;
- notebook PCs using Microsoft Reader format – electronic reading software designed for easy screen reading;
- coded web pages (in HTML or XML, the coding used by software browsers);
- plain vanilla text (ASCII);
- tablet PCs – textbooks and notebooks rolled into one;
- new generation mobile phones.

All content can be downloaded into the reading devices from a website and can be paid for at that time. These formats are relatively cheap for a publisher to produce – but only assuming they do nothing to add to the editorial value. None of the electronic formats are secure from plagiarists, though some make a better attempt at security than others. At present, PDF files are the most secure (though hackable), with options ranging from preventing text selection (so users cannot cut and paste), disabling reading onscreen (so only one print copy can be made), or, conversely, disabling printing, to password-protection. However, accessibility to those with disabilities is also important and may mean compromising on full security.

The question here is whether yours is the sort of book that people will want to read from screens – small or large.

### Print on Demand

E-publishers are also offering Print on Demand (POD) services for good quality paper copies in runs of 1 to 250. This has a double appeal to authors: for self-publishing and for bringing an out-of-print book back into circulation.

The self-publishing route is attractive. There's a set-up cost and a per title cost, but they're generally lower than the self-publishing options that have been available up to now. This option may well be of interest to authors who don't mind doing their own promotion. POD offers a potentially viable digital production model to the publishing industry as a whole. If the technology settles and origination costs come down a little lower than they are now, we could see certain types of book being ordered on the internet for collection an hour later at the local bookshop where it is bound and printed. Authors in some genres may be able to bypass publishers.

Out-of-print publishing is more complex. It is unlikely that the author will have a digital copy of a former work. Corrections, design and late changes to the latest version of either the author's or the editor's file is not the final version. This means a published copy must be scanned in and converted. To do this at reasonable cost and with acceptable accuracy requires a sophisticated scanner and two copies of the book with cut spines, merged and assembled in book order. There are two problems. With older books, the author may only have one precious copy and may not be willing to cut it up. With newer books, the chances are the rights have reverted, but the typographical right still belongs to the publisher for 25 years after publication. It's arguable that scanning violates that right.

## Marketing

The listing below offers just some of the new e-publishers which are offering services to authors who would like to sell or resell their works in one of the formats described. Some market in the same way as traditional publishers. Many new e-publishers double as online booksellers, so they are not publishers in the sense we have been used to – although they also promote their best-selling authors more aggressively than the ones no one has heard of. The difference is that they can offer showcase capacity to any author, well known or not. Most guarantee visitors against pornography and real rubbish, but it's fairly rudimentary quality control. Showcasing is generally just that – a space on the bookshelf. And in this environment bookshelving is infinitely expandable. Most are sited in the US, but that doesn't matter since this is global exposure anyway.

## Websites

Note, this is a fast-moving area and more online publishers will spring up and some of these will disappear. In all cases, authors should check all details of the contracts.

The *Writers' & Artists' Yearbook* cannot be held responsible for any content on any of these sites. It came to our attention that in a previous edition one site led to a pornography page. This was because the original owner of the domain had not yet paid for a renewal and another party had instantly acquired it. They posted an offensive page and they effectively blackmailed the e-publisher to pay a large sum to get it back. Be aware that this can happen.

### Artemis Press
www.artemispress.com/

Women's fiction, 40% royalty; contract and submission details online; exclusive rights requested.

### Atlantic Bridge
www.atlanticbridge.net/

Seeks science fiction, horror, romance and mystery writers; non-exclusive contract and submission details online; 30–45% royalty.

### Author House
www.authorhouse.com/

Committed to quality self publishing.

### Author's Studio
www.theauthorsstudio.org/

Community of small presses owned and operated by commercial authors.

### Book4Publishing
www.book4publishing.com/

Shropshire-based e-agent which showcases synopsis and first chapter and then auto-targets publishers and agents; £49.95 fee.

### BookLocker
www.booklocker.com/

E-book publisher offering 35–70% royalties to authors only requesting non-exclusive rights. Authors are free to list and sell their books elsewhere.

### Books on Line
www.books-on-line.com/

Public domain titles as well as opportunities to offer your own work.

### BookSurge
www.booksurge.com/

A POD self-publishing concern with useful affiliates but read all the small print before committing to them.

### Boson Books
www.cmonline.com/boson/

Electronic book imprint of C&M Online Media Inc.; eclectic list.

## Centre House Press
www.centrehousepress.co.uk/

Publishes excerpts of literary works of all types, where the respective authors intend later full production in book form.

## Crowsnest Books
www.computercrowsnest.com/

Science fiction, fantasy, horror, adventure, war, crime and thriller novels; some non-fiction.

## Diskus Publishing
www.diskuspublishing.com/

Indiana-based romantic fiction niche publisher. Books for several e-reader formats can be downloaded for about £6.30 a book. Said to publish about 5% of submissions.

## Domhan Books
www.domhanbooks.com/

Multicategory genre listing for publications in a variety of formats.

## Eastgate
www.eastgate.com/

New hypertext technologies; publication of serious hypertext, fiction and non-fiction: serious, interactive writing. Good reputation.

## eBook Palace
www.ebookpalace.com/

Visitor-submitted directory of e-books; authors can list their own.

## eBooks.com
www.ebooks.com/

Internet Digital Bookstore. Invites authors to let publisher or agent know about it; authors should check rights deals with their publishers.

## EBooks on the Net
www.ebooksonthe.net/

Non-mainstream genres. Closes periodically to new submissions.

## FictionWise
www.fictionwise.com/

Independent eBook publisher and distributor. Work must be previously published fiction works from established authors. Does not accept unsolicited material or work from new writers.

## Fiction Works
www.fictionworks.com/

E-books and audio book opportunities; submissions in certain genres only.

## iUniverse
www.iuniverse.com/

A service for redeploying out-of-print books; check the author contract carefully.

## KnowBetterCom
www.knowbetter.com/

Resource of information on the e-publishing scene, including the latest information on technology, industry news, tips, advice and reviews. Useful overview and discussion forums.

## MediaVast
www.mediavast.com/

Digital everything marketplace and portal; opportunities for authors to sell directly.

## Microsoft Reader
www.microsoft.com/reader/authors

The page about the Reader (e-books designed to be read on pocket PCs and mobile phones) aimed at authors; keep your eye on this one.

## netLibrary
www.netlibrary.com/

Free and purchasable titles using the Knowledge Station software; expanding into hand-held computers; check the licensing agreements before signing up titles.

## New Concepts Publishing
www.newconceptspublishing.com/

Specialises in romance writers seeking publication; inexpensive for buyers; not obvious what the advantages to sellers are.

## No Spine
www.nospine.com/

A UK self-publishing facilitator that takes 20% of whatever an author charges to cover e-commerce and web overheads. Quotes *Writers & Artists'* *Yearbook* profusely. Track record unknown.

## Online Originals
www.onlineoriginals.com/
One of the higher-profile venues for new writers wanting to get published; UK based.

## Open eBook initiative
www.openebook.org/

Format specifications, sponsored by the National Institute of Standards and Technology.

## Palm Digital Media
www.palmdigitalmedia.com

E-books for hand-held computers; has e-books by well-known authors.

## Paperbackwriters
www.paperbackwriters.co.uk/

Showcase focusing exclusively on aspiring novelists in any genre looking for a publisher.

## Replica Books
www.replicabooks.com/

Would you like to see an out-of-print book back on the shelf? See what their terms are.

## Rosetta Books
www.rosettabooks.com/

Sells and distributes books in various e-formats (Microsoft Reader and Adobe Acrobat).

## UK Children's Books
www.ukchildrensbooks.co.uk/

Listings of authors, illustrators and publishers.

## Unlimited Publishing
www.unlimitedpublishing.com/

A POD system for new and out-of-print titles; will cost authors a minimum of $800 as long as they use Word or similar.

## Virtual Bookworm
www.virtualbookworm.com/

POD and e-book supplier.

## Writers Co-operative
www.books-4u-online.com, www.rabbitbooks.com/

Mixed collection of UK self-publishing writers' work and its authors publishing venue.

## Writers World
www.writersworld.co.uk/

A self-publishing resource for writers to publish their books by POD or e-books in both the USA and the UK. Huge resource database. Free newsletter and chatroom.

## Xlibris
www.xlibris.com/

Self-publishing centre; says it exists solely to serve and empower authors – at a price.

## Zoetrope Stories
www.all-story.com

Authors submit and critique each others' stories; seemingly no remuneration.

## Critical comment

## BeeHive
http://beehive.temporalimage.com/

A hypertext and hypermedia online literary journal in several volumes.

## The Book and the Computer
www.honco.net/

Quarterly journal; views from book people around the world.

## Dichtung-Digital
www.dichtung-digital.de/english.htm

Contributions on digital aesthetics.

## Digital Art Museum
www.dam.org/

Cultural centre for artists and theorists.

## eBookWeb
http://12.108.175.91/ebookweb/

Central source for news and information on all aspects of electronic publishing.

## Electronic Literature Organization
www.eliterature.org/

Promotes new media art and literature.

## El Pub Weekly
www.elpub.org/

Electronic publishing R&D and resources. El Pub has been giving analyses of the market and technical aspects of electronic publishing since 1996.

## JoDI Journal of Digital Information
http://jodi.ecs.soton.ac.uk/

Peer-reviewed with extensive academic editorial board from the University of Southampton.

## Rhizome
www.rhizome.org/

Centre of information on internet art and text that supports a global new media art community.

## trAce
http://trace.ntu.ac.uk/Review/

News and reviews of new media writing, art and events.

## Turbulence
www.turbulence.org/

Supports and commissions net art (radio and performance).

# Setting up a website

Computer users who have email almost certainly have web space available to them.
Jane Dorner explains the points for writers and artists to consider when setting up a
personal website and how to best make it work for them.

This article assumes that readers are familiar with websites and have used the
internet for research. To set up your own website the main investment you need
to make is in time, perhaps more than you initially think. The process may have
its frustrating moments, but it is ultimately creative.

## Personal websites

A website can be a useful self-publicity medium for writers. It can be especially
useful if you self-publish, but equally worthwhile for showing the world a
portfolio of your artistic achievements and accomplishments. Many writers and
artists are polymaths and the web shows up such diversity to advantage.

A personal website can be set up to demonstrate your writing or illustration
style(s) and areas of interest with examples of work so that commissioning
editors can see if they are choosing the right writer or artist for the job. You can
include an outline of your skills and achievements, and list your publications –
or you could even offer a personal syndication service for stories, articles,
photographs or illustrations (if first or resale rights are yours).

You need to let people know that your website exists – there is no point
having a wonderful site if no one visits it – for which old-fashioned marketing
techniques are necessary. Posting your site on the web and registering hopefully
with a few (or even a hundred) search engines is no substitute for careful
targeting. You will probably be easily found on Google, but only if people know
about you. Refer potential clients to your website, and make sure it attracts them
sufficiently to explore it.

## Skills required

In order to create the website yourself, you will need to have:
- a capacity for logical thinking;
- secure language expertise;
- some technical understanding;
- good visual sense;
- patience; and
- familiarity with applicable law.

If you don't have (or can't acquire) these skills then it is worth thinking about
asking someone else to build the site for you. Expect to pay for at least one day
of a professional designer's time (between £300 and £500) to create a modest
suite of individually tailored pages with some attention to what you want and
need. Bear in mind that the less you pay, the more likely it is that your material
is simply being poured into a standard template, as is the case with sites that
offer five pages for £50.

## Planning a website

Whether you get involved with the technological side or not, you will still have to plan and write the copy yourself. Writing for the web is a new art form that uses writerly skills: it is genuinely creative; requires writers, not programmers; and needs editors with an understanding of traditional editorial values.

Writing the text for a website is like any other writing project. The more effort that goes into the planning stage, the better the result. You need to identify who you are targeting and be clear about the purpose of the website. For instance, is it your calling card; a PR brochure; a sales outlet; an information resource; a literary club or part of a network; a designer's showcase; or a medium of self-expression? The website needs to be planned and created accordingly. For example, if you just want a simple calling card, then a single screen – called a splash page – might suffice. It would have your name, perhaps a photograph of you, a few lines about your specialist skills and interests, possibly some work you have had published, and your contact details. You can then be found by anyone who uses the internet; your personal front cover is on the world bookshelf.

## Writing for screen reading

If you write for radio, you will have an advantage over other writers. Writing for the web is a bit like writing for broadcasting: the style has to compensate for the loss of the visual impact of words. It's a common mistake to cut and paste from documents created for print because the text will not read as well on a website.

The average adult spends eight hours a week reading as opposed to 27 hours watching television. And that's reading from paper – reading from a screen has so far proved less efficient than paper.

When writing the introductory text for a website, aim for the reluctant reader with a less than three-minute attention span and use easy words and short sentences. As readers delve deeper into a site, their acceptance of more discursive reading matter increases. Once they are committed to the subject material, you can write in your normal style and assume they will print out the text and read from paper. Take writing for radio or television as the paradigm and then make it even simpler. Here are a few pointers:

- **Use the tadpole or pyramid structure**. Present the main points at the top of the page (people are reluctant to scroll) and use interior pages to unfold details.
- **Be concise.** The overall length of a radio or television piece is about a third of a print article; a web page should be even shorter. Cut every word that doesn't contribute. A good web page length is under 200 words – it is better to divide anything longer than that into sub-topics.
- **Write short paragraphs**. Paragraph breaks refresh the eye: between two and five sentences is enough.
- **Write simple sentences**. Ideas are easier to digest in a simple subject-verb-object progression. Make subclauses into separate sentences. Use one idea per sentence. Make them under the 17-word print average.
- **Use the present or present perfect tense**. The web is here and now. Keep passives away.

- **Be consistent**. Use the same font, type size, alignment and background colour throughout your site. Or use different colour bands to denote different 'areas' (novels, poetry, teaching and so on). Remember that capital letters onscreen look like SHOUTING.
- **Consider navigation**. If a visitor makes Choice A here, what are the ramifications for Choice B there? Web writing is not static, but writing dynamically is something that most writers have not learned. It is, perhaps, something we will all have to discover as we progress into the web publishing age.
- **Links**. Don't link every prompt phrase that leads somewhere else. If you want readers to stay with you to absorb your point, put the link outside the main text area. Don't link just because you can.
- **Define the main areas of your site**. Consider synonyms for your top level labels (the four to six main areas of your site). How often have you got lost in a website simply because the way in which your mind works isn't the same as the mindset of the person who created it? Try to second guess what visitors to your site will want to see when they come to each page then find a single word that most unambiguously describes it.

## Useful websites

### Amazon Bookshop Associates Scheme
www.amazon.co.uk/associates/
For linking to sales of your own (or recommended) books.

### Alert Box
www.useit.com/alertbox/
Web usability and readability analysis. Opinionated but pertinent.

### Bobby
http://bobby.watchfire.com/bobby/
Free tool to analyse web pages for their accessibility to people with disabilities.

### The CGI Resource Index
www.cgi-resources.com/
Scripts that you can buy (some are free), e.g. automatic forms and page counters.

### 1st Site Free
www.1stsitefree.com/
Create a website in 7 easy steps. A good starting point; links to useful tools.

### FTP Explorer
www.ftpx.com/
File transfer software for PCs.

### Netfinder
www.ozemail.com.au/~pli/netfinder/
File transfer software for Macs.

## Designing for screens

The first thing to remember about designing for screens is that you cannot control how the screen page will look as there are so many variables, such as screen resolution and type of web browser. You should therefore test your design on several platforms. Design depends on purpose, but here are a few good practice points:

- **Colour**. Have a white or pale cream background and black or very dark type (studies show that sharp contrasts aid readability). Use 'web-safe' colours (see box). There are 216 of them based on RGB, which simply stands for Red, Green, Blue – nature's three primary colours. Monitors and television sets transmit RGB – after all colour is light – so the only colours available are the ones that standard monitors can transmit.
- **Fonts**. How typefaces appear onscreen depends on which ones are on that particular system, not what you specify on yours. The ones you can rely on to look good on screens – and are universally available – are known as 'web-safe' fonts (see box).

**Useful websites (cont.)**

### Pedalo
www.pedalo.co.uk/
Website design and promotion services to writers.

### Site Aid
www.siteaid.com/
Freeware HTML editor. Looks similar to Microsoft's FrontPage.

### UK2.Net
http://uk2.net/
Inexpensive domain registration and web forwarding.

### Validator
http://validator.w3.org/
Free online validation of HTML code.

### Web Style Guide
www.webstyleguide.com/
Excellent guide to aspects of web writing. Used to be the Yale Style Manual.

### Xenu
http://home.snafu.de/tilman/xenulink.html
Free software to check your site for broken links.

- **Line length**. Put the text in invisible tables so that the line length is limited to about 10 words in standard browsers – this is an optimum reading line length. If you do not set a limit, the chances are that at high screen resolutions readers might get a line length of 25 words on the default reading typeface. This leads to what is known as 'regression pauses' while the reader struggles to make sense of the text.

- **Page size**. A reasonable rule of thumb is to make each page a maximum of 35K. People don't like watching a blank screen and research suggests that 10 seconds is as long as most people will wait for the screen to be filled. Standard dialup connections download at around 4–5K a second, so that means the first 20K or so need to be interesting enough to grab the viewer's attention. A short text page with three or four thumbnail-sized graphics will generally load quickly.

- **Graphics**. Every graphic must speak: make sure its iconography is clear and unambiguous. Remember that when you insert a picture you must give an explanatory note in the ALT (Alternative) command so that software that reads to the partially sighted or blind can tell the user what the pictures are. It also pops up as a little yellow box hovering over the image area and presents an opportunity to preview in words what the picture illustrates.

- **Artist's portfolio**. A gallery of small thumbnail illustrations is useful for showcasing an artist's range of work, with a click-link to larger pictures. Take care not to offer high-quality graphics that could be plagiarised: most internet graphics are in JPEG format, which is 72 dpi and not suitable for print reproduction. It's advisable to watermark all artwork.

- **Animation**. Bullet points or graphic elements help pick out key words but animations should be avoided. Studies show that the message is lost when television images fail to reinforce spoken words. The same is true of the web.

- **Frames**. Using frames can be an elegant solution to navigation problems but for the user it's not ideal, especially for anyone with accessibility problems. Because the page name on the URL never varies, the visitor never knows where they are. They cannot bookmark a particular page, or find it again on a second visit and that can be very frustrating.

## Going online

Once you have the planning, writing and graphics of your website organised, you need a little basic technical understanding to get it online. Your service provider will have a starter kit of instructions – although whether they make sense is another matter. You may well have to turn to other sources for instruction.

The internet is chock-a-block with instructional material. Try 1st Site Free (see page 588), which outlines and expands on seven easy steps – plan, design, code, upload, test, promote and maintain.

An alternative is to use software that 'talks you through' setting up a small site with what are called 'wizards'. Wizards come in software

### Websites for design

#### Art and the Zen of Web Sites
www.tlc-systems.com/webtips.shtml
Why the web is not a place to show off artistic skills.

#### Creating Graphics for the Web
www.widearea.co.uk/designer/
Information on GIFs, JPEGs, anti-aliasing and other design matters.

#### Killer Sites
www.killersites.com/
Website of *Creating Killer Web Sites* by David Siegal. Both book and site are full of information for designers.

#### VisiBone
www.visibone.com/
Web-safe colours, style sheets and other resources

#### Web-safe fonts
www.microsoft.com/truetype/fontpack/

programs such as FrontPage (part of later versions of Microsoft Office) and its free look-a-like Site Aid. Both resemble word processors and keep the coding hidden from view. Hard core web designers will sneer at these programs, because programmers like to control the way the code works themselves. What they do not realise is that writers want to concentrate on the words, not the coding, and as long as it functions, the refinements of the underlying structure are of less importance. For artists who are more concerned with design, the best package is Dreamweaver (which is expensive and not easy to learn).

Once the pages are ready, the next step is to transmit them to the service provider's machines. The mechanics of this are frequently opaque even when you are offered a handy button that says 'Publish'. The chances are that your service provider will not have the extensions that make the 'Publish' button work and you will have to acquire a (free) File Transfer Protocol (ftp) program. If you are technophobe, this may seem frightening at first. However, it is really very simple and once you have successfully transferred (or uploaded) the pages from your computer to the web space on the remote server, you will wonder what the problem was. For this transfer process you will need to know the host name, your user ID and your password, information available from your provider.

## HTML

If you want to learn HTML (HyperText Markup Language) – the code that tags elements such as text, links and graphics so that browser software will know how to display a document – then you need only a plain text program, like Notepad, and an HTML primer (there are plenty online as well as in printed form). Find some website pages which you like and look at their source code to see how they have been constructed (click the subsidiary button of the mouse, usually the right button, and select View Source). If the originators have used JavaScript or Cascading Style Sheets, this may well be more code than you want to know about so look at simple pages first.

### Going a step further

You may wish to have a web address or URL that is short or memorable so that it is easier for people to find your website. You can choose this domain name yourself, and is now relatively cheap (see boxes on pages 588–9).

It is probably best to leave e-commerce (having a secure site that can handle credit card sales) till later. In the meantime, however, a simple way to boost your income is to become an Amazon Associate. If your book titles are linked to Amazon, you'll make 15% on a direct sale made from your site.

# Websites for writers

*The Internet: A Writer's Guide* by Jane Dorner (www.internetwriter.co.uk) is published by A & C Black and has the full listing of over 1000 resources for writers from which the sites below have been selected.

## New to the internet

### BBC Web Wise
www.bbc.co.uk/education/webwise/
How to get started on the internet.

### FAQ
www.faqs.org/
Frequently Asked Questions on just about anything to do with the internet.

### Google
www.google.co.uk/
The current favourite amongst search engines.

### How Stuff Works
www.howstuffworks.com/
Fairly technical explanations about how the internet works, and much more.

### New to the Web
http://home.netscape.com/netcenter/newnet
A basic tutorial with a good glossary.

## Fact finding online

### Ananova (UK Press Association)
www.ananova.com/
Latest stories from the UK's top news and information websites; useful free daily round-up of news, sport and information by email.

### Ask Oxford
www.askoxford.com/
Various bits from the language dictionaries; changing word news and word-based interest.

### Bartlett's Familiar Quotations
www.bartleby.com/

### Bibliomania
www.bibliomania.com/
Excellent full text with a good word or phrase retrieval; includes the wonderful Brewer's *Dictionary of Phrase & Fable* (which no author can do without).

### British Library
http://portico.bl.uk/
Free search for material held in the major Reference and Document Supply collections of the British Library.

### CIA World Factbook
www.cia.gov/cia/publications/factbook/
Statistical data about countries and other useful data.

## Crossref
www.crossref.org/

A collaborative reference linking service for researchers.

## Encyclopaedia Britannica
www.britannica.com/

Full text and searching, together with a huge resource of information, grammar and reference links. Some free; premium subscription.

## Free Pint
www.freepint.com/

Free bi-monthly email newsletter with tips and articles on finding reliable sites and searching more effectively. Written by information professionals.

## Internet Public Library
www.ipl.org

Reference section containing subject overviews, biography, etc.

## Response Source
http://sourcewire.com/

UK journalists can request business information in a single step from over 300 organisations.

## Roget's Thesaurus
www.bartleby.com/62/

Third edition (1995).

## WATCH – Writers, Artists and their Copyright Holders
http://tyler.hrc.utexas.edu/

Database of information on whom to contact for permission to publish in copyright text and images. Not fully comprehensive. A joint project of the University of Texas and the University of Reading.

## WISDOM: Knowledge & Literature Search
http://thinkers.net/

Links to writing and literature sites under the headings Creativity, Literature, Authors, Thoughts, Publishing, Words, Languages.

## Interactivity

## Alt-X
www.altx.com/

Online publishing network – 'where the digerati meet the literati'.

## Digital Arts
www.da2.org.uk

## Eastgate Systems
www.eastgate.com

Many interesting works of serious hypertext offered for sale.

## Electronic Poetry Center
http://wings.buffalo.edu/epc/

## E-Zone
http://ezone.org

Literary site that includes an e-zine 'entryzone'; some permanent hypertext works.

# Writing communities

## Agent Research
www.agentresearch.com/

For professional writers and agents in the UK, USA and Canada.

## Ask About Writing
www.askaboutwriting.net/

Reviews writing websites from a writer's point of view. Also shows Swanwick news.

## Author Zone
www.authorzone.com

Interactive author and writer community with free self-promotion opportunities and webspace.

## Axis
www.axisartists.org

Some writing installations.

## BBC WritersRoom
www.bbc.co.uk/writersroom/ *and*
http://www.bbc.co.uk/commissioning/

How to submit ideas and scripts to the BBC.

## Bloomsbury Magazine
www.bloomsburymagazine.com/writersarea/

Writers' area; advice and resources for authors.

## Digital Literature Institute
www.digitallit.org/

## E-Writers
http://e-writers.net

Community, competitions and advice – weekly online publishing newsletter.

## Fiction Writer's Connection
www.fictionwriters.com

Provides help with novel writing and information on finding agents and editors and getting published; has a mailing list of 3000+.

## For writers
www.forwriters.com
Self-help; links and professional markets.

## HackWriters
www.hackwriters.com/
UK-based free internet magazine devoted to good writing on any subject. No fees; forum of exchange.

## Hyperizons
www.duke.edu/~mshumate/hyperfic.html
Literary texts and criticism.

## Literature North East
www.literaturenortheast.co.uk/
Events taking place in North East England.

## Littoral
www.littoral.org.uk
Arts trust which aims to develop new arts projects.

## Live Literature Network
www.liveliterature.net/
Database of writers offering live events in the UK.

## National Association for Literature Development
www.literaturedevelopment.com/development/

## Online Writing Community
http://trace.ntu.ac.uk
Centre of experimental writing in the UK; also has courses.

## Pier Playwrights
www.pierplaywrights.co.uk/
Organisation for playwrights run by playwrights.

## Publishers' Lunch
www.caderbooks.com
Free daily e-zine of news and events in US publishing. Authors can advertise their services for $15 a month in a database searchable by publishers and agents.

## Reactive Writing
www.reactivewriting.co.uk/
Exploring writing on the Web.

## Word Circuits
www.wordcircuits.com/
A community as well as a gallery of new fiction and poetry.

## The Word Hoard
www.wordhoard.co.uk/
A cooperative of writers, visual artists, performers

and musicians sited in Huddersfield. Has a text factory.

## Writernet
www.writernet.org.uk/
British community, mostly for writers working in theatre, TV, radio, film, live art and performance poetry; a professional network.

## Writer's Market
www.writersmarket.com/
Subscriber-based access ($29.99 a year) to market information on book and magazine publishers, agents, script buyers and general advice.

## Writers Net
www.writers.net
US-based forum for writers, editors, agents and publishers. Participants exchange ideas about the writing life and the business of writing.

## Writelink
www.writelink.co.uk/
Resource site linking to paying markets, competitions, reference sites, software and so on.

## Writers on the Net
www.writers.com
Busy community offering online (paid for) classes.

## WritersServices.com
www.writersservices.com/
Offers editorial services and advice from well-known writers; pitched largely at unpublished authors.

# New media writing prizes

## Electronic Literature Awards
www.eliterature.org/
One for fiction and one for poetry.

## Eppie Awards for E-books
www.epicauthors.org/
21 fiction and non-fiction categories.

## Gutenberg-e
www.historians.org/prizes/gutenberg/
A prize competition for history dissertations

## Java Museum Online Awards
www.javamuseum.org/
For innovative art and new media installations.

## Media Arts Plaza Awards
http://plaza.bunka.go.jp/english/

## Nesta Awards for Art and Science
www.nesta.org.uk/

Up to £40,000 to spend a year developing a new creative idea; very competitive.

## The Oscar Moore Screenwriting Prize
www.screendaily.com/

An annual prize of £10,000 is awarded to the best first draft screenplay in a specified genre, which changes each year. Application form on website.

## SunOasis
www.sunoasis.com/

A site for writers, editors and copywriters with some international job opportunities.

## trAce
http://trace.ntu.ac.uk/

Competitions and bursaries – go to main site and search or look at news pages. Major new prize in new media writing launches in 2005.

## Miscellany

### Dying Words
www.corsinet.com/braincandy/dying.html

For the historical novelist.

### Famous Birthdays
www.famousbirthdays.com/

Month-by-month and day-by-day listing of birth dates, historical and in the media.

### Famous Firsts
www.corsinet.com/trivia/1-triv.html

People-who-did-something-first arranged in ascending date order.

### iTools
www.itools.com/research-it

Little battery of dictionaries and acronym converters.

### Literary Calendar: An Almanac of Literary Information
http://english.yasuda-u.ac.jp/lc

Significant literary events.

### Lives
http://amillionlives.com/

Links to biographies, autobiographies, memoirs, diaries, letters, narratives and oral histories.

### Perpetual Virtual Calendars
www.vpcalendar.net/

A historical or science fiction novelist's dream: verify any date or day of the week in the 20th and 21st centuries.

### Rhyming dictionary
www.rhymezone.com

### Time Zone Converter
www.timezoneconverter.com/

What time it is or will be anywhere in the world.

### What's on when
http://www.whatsonwhen.com/

Useful for newspaper and magazine writers (or for planning holidays).

### Who is or Was
www.biography.com/

Good for checking people's dates; incorporates the *Cambridge Dictionary of American Biography*.

### World Wide Words
www.quinion.com/words/

Verbal cornucopia for anyone interested in words; circulates a newsletter.

## Texts online

### Bible Gateway
http://bible.gospelcom.net/bible

### Electronic Text Center
http://etext.lib.virginia.edu/english.html

Collection of online English language texts; links to other texts online by subject or by author.

### The English Server
http://eserver.org/

Large collection of interesting resources.

### Etext Archives
www.etext.org

Archives of religious, political, legal and fanzine text.

### Oxford Text Archive
www.ota.ahds.ac.uk/

Distributes more than 2500 resources in over 25 different languages for study purposes only.

### Project Gutenberg
www.gutenberg.net/

The official sites (many mirrors all over the world); vast library of e-texts, mostly public domain; all in plain text format.

## Shakespeare Resources
www.shakespeare.com/

Links to many other sites.

## Writing tools
## Screenwriting

### Dramatica
www.dramatica.com/

Screenplay software; not free – compare it with ScreenForge below.

### Final Draft
www.finaldraft.com/

Apparently the bees knees of scripting software – expensive (about £150), high functionality and cross-platform compatibility.

### ScreenForge
www.apotheosispictures.com/

Almost free Hollywood scriptwriting format bolt-on for Word.

## Storyware

### Alice
http://alice.cs.cmu.edu/

Software program for storyboard modelling; quite technical but interesting.

### Blogger
www.blogger.com/

Free web-based tool for instantly publishing 'blogs' (web diaries).

## Creativity Unleashed
www.cul.co.uk/

Software to stimulate creative thinking, originally intended for business.

### KidPad
www.kidpad.org/

Collaborative story-writing tool for children being developed at the University of Maryland.

### StoryBoard Quick
www.powerproduction.com/

Storyboard software for films, animation, games, etc.

### Web Store for Writers and Creative Pros
www.masterfreelancer.com/

Plots Unlimited, Writer's Software Companion and other software aids.

## Word-processing aids

### Tricks and Trinkets
www.tricksandtrinkets.com/pk/

To make word processing easier, e.g. autotext for often-used phrases.

### WordTips
www.VitalNews.com/wordtips/

How to get the best out of Microsoft Word; useful tips, many a real boon for writers.

**Jane Dorner** is the author of 22 books and represents authors' interests on the Boards of ALCS and CLA. She is author of *The Internet: A Writer's Guide* (A & C Black) (www.internetwriter.co.uk) which has the full listing of over 1000 resources for writers. The following genre areas have substantial listings: academic writing; business writing; children's writing; crime writing and mystery; fantasy; fiction; health writers; historical research; horror; interactive fiction and experimental forms; journalism; literature festivals; literature resources; mystery; poetry; prizes; residencies; romance; science fiction, fantasy and horror; specialist subjects; screen, TV and playwriting; translation; travel writing; STM writers; technical writing; women's and gender issues; writing courses and many other themes.

### See also...
- *Setting up a website*, page 586
- *E-Publishing*, page 581

# Websites for artists

Several of the regional arts offices sites provide useful information for artists, as do some of the government sites, and many artist organisation sites provide links to other sites. Alison Baverstock introduces some web addresses which will be useful as a starting point.

## Information for artists

### AN The Artists Information Company
www.a-n.co.uk

*Sister sites* www.workingwithartists.co.uk *and* www.artistscareers.co.uk

A very broad site, covering all aspects of being an artist from current events to developing and maintaining good business practice. Initial section headings are:

- Forum – an interactive space for artists to seek and exchange advice on practice, career, project and business issues
- Practice – practical information and examples on showing, selling, commissions, residencies, production and collaboration
- Career – information on developing a career as an artist: first steps, looking at yourself, skills, developing a career, portfolio careers
- Business – valuable know-how and tips on becoming and being self employed, accounts, tax, contracts, promotion and insurance
- Contacts – over 1000 links to visual arts organisations in the UK and internationally which offer email and web links
- Artists – artists tell the real story of practice: their approaches, achievements and setbacks
- Research – introducing research on visual arts and artists' practice.

AN publishes *AN Magazine*, which specifically caters for the needs of visual and applied artists.

### Art Quest
www.artquest.com

This site directly connects buyers and sellers of art, helping artists and collectors eliminate the commissions and fees usually found in the process.

### Art Train
www.arttrain.org.uk

A sign-posting and information website of business and professional skills and support for visual and applied artists in Scotland.

### Artifact
www.artifact.ie

An online register representing work by over 1000 contemporary professional artists based in the Republic of Ireland and Northern Ireland.

### The Art Net Directory
www.artnetdirectory.co.uk

A wide range of information for professional and amateur artists.

### Arts Council England
www.artscouncil.org.uk

The national development agency for the arts in England, distributing public money to fund a range of activities. The website offers useful information on public policy towards the arts and current funding (such as which areas of the arts each organisation handles). The 'news and information' section offers useful statistics on the arts in England as well as links to other sites.

### The Arts Council of Northern Ireland
www.artscouncil-ni.org

Information on arts policy, funding schemes and contacts in Northern Ireland and the Republic.

### The Arts Council of Wales
www.ccc-acw.org.uk

Information on arts policy, funding schemes and contacts in Wales.

### Birkbeck College, University of London
www.bbk.ac.uk/lib/artlibgu/html

Offers details of art libraries in London.

### Center for Safety in the Arts
http://artswire.org:70/1/csa

Based in the USA but includes excellent information on health and safety in the visual arts.

### The Crafts Council
www.craftscouncil.org.uk

Offers services for both makers and members of the public interested in craft practice and purchase.

### Cultural Enterprise – Menter Diwylliannol
www.cultural-enterprise.com

Information on business support for creative industries in Wales.

### CX – Creative Export
www.creativexport.co.uk

Provides UK creative businesses with a portal to information that will support their development of export strategies.

## Cywaith Cymru – Artworks Wales
www.cywaithcymru.org

Listings of public art and residency projects in Wales.

## Department for Culture, Media and Sport
www.culture.gov.uk

Holds the latest research reports on the creative industries.

## Design and Artists Copyright Society
www.dacs.co.uk

Information on copyright and intellectual property.

## The Gallery Channel UK
www.thegallerychannel.co.uk

An excellent and almost comprehensive exhibition listings website.

## Inland Revenue
www.inlandrevenue.gov.uk

Useful information on tax, national insurance and self-assessment – particularly helpful if you are new to being self employed.

## Institute of International Visual Arts (inIVA)
www.iniva.org

A contemporary visual arts organisation with a special interest in new technologies, commissioning site-specific artworks and international collaborations.

## Intellectual Property
www.intellectual-property.gov.uk

The Government's information site on copyright and other intellectual property rights.

## International Association of Residential Arts Centres
www.resartis.org

An online directory of residency centres worldwide.

## International Cultural Desk
www.icd.org.uk

Offers international opportunities for Scottish artists.

## Live Art Magazine
www.liveartmagazine.com

News, reviews and listings.

## The London Association of Art and Design Education
www.laade.org

Promotes contact between artists and schools; includes a database of artist-in-residence opportunities.

## Metier
www.metier.org.uk

The national training organisation for the arts and entertainment industries, representing 500,000 people involved in the arts (including visual arts and all aspects of arts management).

## National Disability Arts Forum
www.ndaf.org

Offers disability arts news and information on opportunities and contacts.

## National Statistics: the official UK statistics site
www.statistics.gov.uk

Publishes a range of general and specific statistics on the arts.

## Public Art South West
www.publicartonline.org.uk

Offers information on contacts, opportunities and practical advice on public art.

## The Scottish Arts Council
www.sac.org.uk

Information on arts policy, funding schemes and contacts in Scotland.

## Trans Artists
www.transartists.nl

Netherlands-based site providing information on international artists-in-residence and exchange programmes, finances, cultural institutes (with links to their websites).

## Your Creative Future
www.yourcreativefuture.org

A career-planning site for those involved in the arts.

## Selling art online

Selling art online is becoming big business and is a popular and convenient method for viewing, commissioning and buying works of art. For the artist, online galleries are a very cost-effective, and occasionally free, method of trying out new pieces of work or bringing new custom to your own linked web pages. Some of the larger sites allow you to exhibit for nothing; on the other hand, payment for inclusion may mean there is less competition to distract potential buyers from your work.

### www.arthaus.co.uk

Artists exhibiting on this site are offered guidance on marketing. You either pay a standard fee for exhibiting (£35/10 works), or pay commission on work sold.

### www.aarti.co.uk

A strong exhibition site for artists. You either pay 35% commission and display for nothing, or pay a fee (£30/10 works) and reduce the commission to 20%.

### www.artcommunity.co.uk

An exhibition site. One year's website hosting costs £69.95 but there is no commission on what is sold.

### www.artshole.co.uk

A website dedicated to promoting the work of student and contemporary artists, as well as providing information on exhibitions throughout the UK. No charge for artists to register.

### www.axisartists.org

The largest interactive database of contemporary British art on the internet, currently features the work of more than 4000 professional and student artists. Registration fee £70/£35 for recent graduates.

### www.bigart.co.uk

£19.50 buys you the chance to display 5–15 works and commission is also taken on what is sold.

### www.blinkred.com

A well thought out site offering buyers the chance to specify what they are looking for, e.g. original oils or watercolours.

### www.britart.com

Exhibits and promotes the work of emerging British artists. You can submit information (CV and personal statement) in support of your work.

### www.illustratorsagents.com

A highly visited site used by at least 10,000 art/creative buyers who get email newsletters every second month. £437+VAT to display a 12-image portfolio for a year.

### www.laade.org

The London Association of Art and Design Education promotes contact between artists and schools; includes a database of artist-in-residence opportunities.

### www.larts.co.uk

Displays the work of 60 contemporary artists. A page costs £25+VAT.

### www.newartportfolio.com

Various types of membership, the most common offers the chance to display a wide range of artworks for £85+VAT/12 works, plus 20% commission.

### www.numasters.com

Exhibits professional work free of charge but takes a commission when works are sold/loaned/made copyright. Also includes information on maintaining and developing an art collection.

### www.panicnot.com

A database of freelance artists and illustrators. Charges £75/5 samples for a year.

### www.saa.co.uk

The Society for All Artists allows artists to compete to show work in the Members' Gallery. Themes vary and artists can link to their own sites. Various membership packages and associated benefits.

### www.theartshopper.com

Claims to be the world's largest online gallery for original art. There is no joining fee but commission is added to the price you set for your work (and deducted when paid).

### www.wwar.com

US-based site where you can exhibit free and no commission is charged. Huge with supporting chat room, opportunities for advertising, etc.

After 10 years in publishing **Alison Baverstock** set up her own marketing consultancy, specialising in running campaigns for the book trade and training publishers to market more effectively. She is a well-established speaker on the book business and has written widely on how to market books. Her most recent title is *Marketing Your Book: An Author's Guide* (A & C Black 2001). She may be contacted at baverstockjam@cwcom.net

# Resources for writers

## The writer's toolkit

Sooner or later, whatever the nature of their work, all writers must do some research. When they confront the sheer volume of information currently available in printed and manuscript form, as well as on the internet, this can seem a daunting task. Ann Hoffmann looks at the skills involved and recommends a number of standard sources.

Throughout the centuries writers have relied for their research on their own curiosity and observation skills. They have also fed voraciously on the knowledge and output of others. The earliest storytellers gathered their material through a combination of oral enquiry and attentive listening, each one in turn 'embroidering' in varying degrees what they had learnt. These tales later came to be written down and laboriously copied again and again in manuscript form, with little or no regard for accuracy or spelling. A new dimension was added in the wake of Caxton: the newspaper and the printed book, so that by the mid-18th century Samuel Johnson would speak of a writer turning over 'half a library' to make one book. Clearly the great Doctor had in mind a private collection of a few hundred books – nothing like the vast libraries and databases available to us today.

We live in an age of 'information overload'. Books galore, websites, and internet 'newsgroups' are on offer on every subject under the sun. The skill no longer lies in *finding* the information, but in *finding it quickly* and, most importantly, *sorting out the authoritative from the inaccurate*. At the same time, because so few of us today maintain proper diaries, and most choose to telephone rather than write a personal letter, there is already a serious dearth of information at the disposal of biographers, social historians and writers of historical fiction, from the mid-20th century onwards. Thus the traditional skills of looking and listening have come back into their own. Today's researchers cannot safely rely only on books and manuscripts, or even on the web, but must look closely at video and film and – the novelist and the dramatist especially – listen to tape recordings and to the spoken word. They must also master the art of the interview.

Photocopying and microfilming techniques have relieved us of the laborious chore of copying by hand – with all the risks of error that that involved. Information technology (IT) enables us to obtain instantly, in the comfort of our own study, the most up-to-the-minute factual information on record, from anywhere in the world. Another bonus is that we can keep abreast of current research – new discoveries and theories which so often shed a different, if controversial, light on historical events and people, and which will be reflected in our creative work.

That said, writers should not regard the internet as a substitute for the library or archive centre, or original sources, but think of it rather as a springboard or first port of call. They should also be wary of using any material that does not come from an authoritative source.

## Using the internet as a research tool

The internet is a global network of computers. Its most useful component for research is the World Wide Web (usually referred to as the 'web' or 'WWW'). This is the world's fastest-growing information research source. It is open 24 hours a day, 365 days a year.

To access the web, you must go online. Basic requirements are a personal computer, a telephone line and a modem. You then sign up with an Internet Service Provider (ISP), who supplies software to connect your computer with their own, through which you can access the worldwide network. If you are not yet online, you can gain access through your local library, university or college, or at one of the growing number of cybercafés.

The choice of ISP is wide open, and it is best to take the recommendation of a fellow writer. Some providers offer a 'free' service, in which case you incur telephone charges for every minute you spend online. Others quote a range of subscription rates, from the flat rate 'anytime' to 'off-peak', and/or a fixed number of hours online per month, with no additional charge for telephone calls. A 'broadband' subscription allows you to make and receive calls while online. The speed of connection and the time it takes for data to reach you are important factors, as is the facility of a 24-hour technical support service at a local call rate. Basically you get what you pay for, i.e. the fee-paying ISPs are usually the least complicated to use and may offer additional services. There is no difficulty about changing your ISP, should you wish to do so later.

The amount of information online is huge. It is accessed with the aid of 'web browser' software, such as Microsoft Internet Explorer or Netscape Navigator. When a web page address, known as a URL (Uniform Resource Locator) and starting usually with http://www., or simply www., is typed in, the required page appears on the screen. Most pages displayed contain useful 'links' and 'hyperlinks' (cross-references) to other web pages.

If you do not know the URL, or you are conducting a search by subject, you can use one or more of the 'search engines' on the web: when you type in a keyword or topic, all relevant sites found are displayed. As each search engine is different, a knowledge of how they operate is essential if you wish to speed up your research.

The secret of successful, economic researching on the web is to *be specific*. Refining searches down to the *precise* information required saves time and money, and also avoids the chore of having to wade through a mass of superfluous, irrelevant material. It is very important to keep a record of the path to your information, by using the 'Bookmark' or 'Favourite' facilities on the browser program. The maintenance of a personal website address book is also recommended.

There are two other internet resources of immense value to the writer: the 'Usenet' discussion or newsgroups, and email. Thousands of groups are listed on the Google Groups site. Messages 'posted' will be read by all members of the group,

## Major UK sources

### The British Library
96 Euston Road, London NW1 2DB
*tel* 020-7412 7676 (enquiries)  *fax* 020-7412 7609
*email* reader-services-enquiries@bl.uk
reader-admissions@bl.uk
*website* www.bl.uk

### The British Library Public Catalogue (BLPC)
*website* www.blpc.bl.uk

### The British Library National Sound Archive
96 Euston Road, London NW1 2DB
*tel* 020-7412 7440  *fax* 020-7412 7441
*email* sound-archive@bl.uk
*website* www.bl.uk/collections/sound-archive

### The British Library Newspaper Library
Colindale Avenue, London NW9 5HE
*tel* 020-7412 7353  *fax* 020-7412 7379
*email* newspaper@bl.uk
*website* www.bl.uk/collections/newspapers

### Family Records Centre
1 Myddleton Street, London EC1R 1UW
*tel* 020-8392 5300 (enquiries)  *fax* 020-8392 5307
*email* frc@nationalarchives.gov.uk
*website* www.familyrecords.gov.uk

### The National Archives: Public Record Office (PRO) and Historical Manuscripts Commission (HMC)
Ruskin Avenue, Kew, Richmond, Surrey TW9 4DU
*tel* 020-8876 3444  *fax* 020-8878 8905
*email* enquiry@nationalarchives.gov.uk
*website* www.nationalarchives.gov.uk

### National Register of Archives
At the National Archives: Historical Manuscripts Commission (see above).

and much information not available elsewhere may be forthcoming. Most groups produce a useful 'Frequently Asked Questions' (FAQ) information list. Email scarcely needs any recommendation here. It is fast, it is cheap, and it is indispensable.

Useful manuals include: *The Internet: A Writer's Guide* by Jane Dorner (A & C Black, London, 2nd edn, 2001); *A Writer's Guide to the Internet* by Trevor Lockwood and Karen Scott (Allison & Busby, London, 2000; new edition in preparation); and *Research Using IT* by Hilary Coombes (Palgrave Macmillan, London, 2001).

### Using libraries and archive centres

Although much preparatory catalogue searching can be done online, the bulk of a writer's research is carried out in a library or archive centre. Nearly every country in the world has its national library and its national archives collection. Their catalogues – nowadays online – are among the most valuable of all research tools.

In the United Kingdom we have the British Library and the National Archives, a merger since April 2003 of the Public Record Office (PRO) and the Royal Commission on Historical Manuscripts (HMC). There are also six copyright libraries (The British Library, London; The Bodleian Library, Oxford; Cambridge University Library, Cambridge; The National Library of Wales, Aberystwyth; The National Library of Scotland, Edinburgh; Trinity College Library, Dublin), each of which has received one free copy of every book published here since the early 18th century. Among other major collections are the British Library Newspaper Library and the British Library National Sound Archive. We also have an excellent public library lending system which, if unable to meet a user's needs from its local stock, will obtain books on loan from other libraries or through the British Library Document Supply Service.

The advantage of using the local library, especially if it has a reference section, is that you have access to the stacks and can browse at will, whereas at the British

Library and copyright libraries a limited number of books are on the open shelves: the rest have to be ordered, which means either entering author, title or keyword on the computer terminal or filling in a docket and waiting for the book to be delivered to the counter or to your desk.

To search official or genealogical records you may need to visit the National Archives at Kew, the Family Records Centre in London, or a local county record office or archives centre. The whereabouts of private papers can be ascertained by consulting the indexes at the National Register of Archives or its online directory of repositories at www.hmc.gov.uk (click on 'ARCHON').

Admission to the British Library and most of the sources mentioned above is free, with some exceptions, i.e. the Bodleian and Cambridge University Library, which currently make a modest charge, but you will need a reader's ticket (ask for details in advance). If you are a graduate you can use any university library. Professional bodies with specialist collections will usually grant bona fide researchers access on application. There are also a small number of private subscription libraries in London and the major cities.

There are few formalities at the Family Records Centre or county record offices, but you must book in advance to secure a seat, especially if you wish to use a computer or microfilm reader. Laptops are permitted in most libraries and archive centres, but you will almost certainly be restricted to note-taking in pencil and, if handling fragile documents, you may be issued with gloves.

The golden rule of research is *accuracy*. When transcribing or taking notes, you should check carefully all dates, figures and unusual names, and *keep a meticulous record of all sources*. Take full advantage of photocopying and filming facilities: the rule of thumb is that if copying by hand is likely to take more than 10 minutes, it is worth the expense. (A photocopy is an accurate copy!)

## Selected titles for the bookshelf

*Brewer's Dictionary of Phrase & Fable*
*The Cassell Dictionary of Slang* (Jonathan Green)
*Chambers Biographical Dictionary*
*The Encyclopedia of World History* (W.L. Langer)
*Fowler's Modern English Usage*
*Mind the Gaffe: The Penguin Guide to Modern Errors in English* (R.L. Trask)
*The New Shell Book of Firsts* (ed. P. Robertson)
*The Oxford Companion to British History* (ed. J. Cannon)
*The Oxford Companion to English Literature* (ed. M. Drabble)
*Oxford Style Manual* (ed. R.M. Ritter)
*Pears Cyclopedia*
*Roget's Thesaurus* (ed. B. Kirkpatrick)
*The Statesman's Yearbook*
*The Times Atlas of the World* (concise edition)
*UK 2005* (TSO official handbook)
*Whitaker's Almanack*
*Who's Who*
*The Writers' & Artists' Yearbook*
*The Writer's Handbook*

### On CD-Rom

*Encyclopedia Britannica*
*The Oxford Pop-up English Language Reference Shelf*
*Who Was Who 1897–2000*

If you are very rich you may subscribe to *The Oxford English Dictionary* online; otherwise make do with the *New Shorter OED* or the *Concise OED* and consult the main version at the library. A third edition of the *OED* is due in 2010. The *Oxford Dictionary of National Biography, 2004* (60 vols and online) replaces the former *DNB*.

*The Aslib Directory of Information Sources in the United Kingdom,* published biennially, should be available in every reference library. *The New Walford: Guide to Reference Sources* is a major revision of a standard work (Vol 1, 2004; Vols 2 and 3 in preparation).

## Indexes and bibliographies

A well-constructed index should lead the researcher directly to the subject matter required. A good bibliography suggests avenues of further search.

As well as indexes to individual books, the various indexes to newspapers and periodicals are useful tools. Outstanding among these are *The Times Index* (from 1906, with an unofficial earlier version from 1790) and *The British Humanities Index,* formerly the *Subject Index to Periodicals,* from 1915. There are of course subject indexes in many fields, too numerous to list here.

*The British National Bibliography,* known as the *BNB,* published since 1950, is also available online and on CD-Rom. The best international source is the *World Bibliographies on CD-Rom* series (K.G. Saur, Munich).

## The writer's bookshelf

Much reference material is now published in electronic as well as in printed form. Shelf space (and possibly also money!) may be saved by buying, say, your main encyclopedia, thesaurus and dictionary on CD-Rom; but it is wise to keep a concise edition at your elbow for quick reference. From time to time the book clubs come up with excellent offers. Buying online (i.e. at www.amazon.co.uk) may also carry worthwhile discounts. Your minimum needs are:

- an up-to-date English dictionary;
- a thesaurus;
- a guide to English usage;
- an up-to-date atlas (also a historical atlas if you write about the past);
- a dictionary of quotations;
- a dictionary of dates;
- a concise world history and/or chronology;
- a biographical dictionary; and
- a current *Yearbook.*

Add to these according to your field of writing and your pocket: for the modern novelist perhaps a dictionary of slang; the historical novelist something on costume, the history of food, the cost of living in centuries past; and so on.

The easiest way to acquire an out-of-print title is to contact your local secondhand bookdealer or a major bookseller, i.e. Waterstone's, who operate a book-search service. Or you can try online at www.bibliofind.com, or use an independent searcher. Now that most bookfinders use the internet, obtaining out-of-print books is much faster – and cheaper – than it used to be.

**Ann Hoffmann** is a professional writer researcher of many years' standing and the author of five non-fiction books. Her *Research for Writers* (A & C Black, 7th edn 2003) includes chapters on research methods, online research, basic sources, research for modern and historical fiction writers, biographers, local and family historians, as well as an up-to-date listing by subject of major sources.

# The writer's ultimate workspace

Arranging for a space to write in a domestic environment can be a mammoth challenge for some people. Rib Davis gives the benefit of his experience of writing from home.

This is a work of fiction. It is based on fact – as much of the best fiction is – but there is certainly more of the wish than the accomplishment in what follows. I have been asked to write an article giving advice to the prospective writer about some of the day-to-day material conditions and habits of mind that one should attempt to establish in order to be able to work happily and efficiently. I assume that I was chosen on the basis that I have, over 25 years, failed to do these so spectacularly that I am now considered an expert in the field. I may not have learned much from my mistakes but at least I can list some of them, and let the reader do the learning.

## Finding the ideal workspace

Where should the workspace be located? When we have to, we can write anywhere. At my most desperate I have written parts of scripts on trains, in crowded offices, in pubs and even leaning on a car steering wheel while waiting for the AA to rescue me. Such is the power of the deadline. Sometimes, strangely, I have produced some rather good work while battling with the distractions and other limitations of the immediate environment; I would hesitate, however, to recommend the practice too highly.

So what would be the ideal workspace location? It seems to be generally agreed that a writer (or writers, if you are working collaboratively) should work in a place where distractions are minimal. Some highly successful writers have taken this to the extreme of working in a shed or a caravan at the bottom of the garden, with only elves for company. I have never owned a caravan, and unless I learn to write seated on a bicycle I will always have trouble squashing into our slowly rotting shed, so that has never been an option. But where possible a degree of isolation – and particularly isolation from family activities and domestic duties – does seem desirable. Sustained concentration is extremely important for any sort of creative work, and such a location helps to facilitate it. In my own case, when I am actually scripting (as opposed to researching or planning) I usually find that I have to read my notes and then the latest part of the script for about an hour before I can even begin to put new words onto the page, so anything that breaks the concentration is unwelcome.

At the same time, though, we are only as strong as our will-power. Many of us could stick ourselves in an arctic igloo to write and yet still manage to find distractions (examining snowflakes can be so fascinating). For about a year I did my writing in a room at the back of a bookshop in Milton Keynes, well away from my home. It seemed to offer the ideal combination of relative isolation along with a congenial, supportive and vaguely arty environment. But the lure of the books and the customers ultimately proved too much; I soon found myself helping out at the till rather then tapping away at my *magnum opus*.

Perhaps my need to write was not sufficiently urgent. Certainly it is true that in those days I was driven by blind hope rather than deadlines, but I don't think that was the problem. The problem was (and is) fear: fear of writing badly, of not living up to one's own – and others' – expectations. For me, at least, it is this fear above all that gets in the way of creativity. First I fear the blank page (of course), then the writing, and then the finishing. This is why those awful distractions can seem, in fact, very welcome indeed. And it is part of the reason why we should try to avoid them as far as possible.

For a few years, remarkably, I did work in a suitable location. Quite simply, this was a room in the house that I was able to turn into my study. It was not totally cut off from the rest of Life, but it was sufficiently separate to allow generally uninterrupted concentration. My small son had difficulty understanding why, if I was behind the door, I refused to open it, but apart from that it worked well. I am shortly to return to that blissful state of having a personal study, but for years now I have done most of my writing on the living room table. My laptop and notes are moved away at meal times; people traipse through the living room to get to the kitchen (why didn't we think of this when we bought the house?); the television is in the same room. In short, my workplace is set in the teeming hub of the house. Big mistake. Even with a family that has been whipped into acknowledging the needs of a writer, it is still a big mistake.

## Cordial domestic relations

A word on educating one's family. A writer's partner and/or children will generally recognise and respect the writer's need to focus on the work in hand, but there is at least one point which needs clarifying. When I write, I take breaks. These breaks can occur for a variety of reasons. Perhaps I have reached an interim target, or I have become stuck, or I am thirsty, or just tired. So I might stop and play the piano, or make a cup of coffee, or – exceptionally – even do some washing up, and then return to the writing with a clearer head. No problem, except that this might be observed, and the observing partner/child may think, 'Ah, so he doesn't mind his concentration being broken after all.' This can be a problem. You have to be selfish. You have to make clear that you can break your own concentration as and when you feel the need – you can wrong-note your way through a whole Beethoven sonata if you feel like it – but that does not give others the green light to break your concentration as and when they feel the need. Be unreasonable.

So much for location. Now, what should the workspace look like? My answer would simply be: pleasant. It should be a welcoming place, where you will feel comfortable and not oppressed. For me, this means well decorated in soft colours, with the desk facing out to a window, preferably with a view, and a temperature that's warm but not sleep-inducing. For others, windows may present yet another distraction, colours should be severe, the radiator should be off and the whole place should be tatty. The point is that you should feel comfortable in it – it should feel like *your* space.

Where I have been able to, I have turned my space into an almost self-sufficient world. This requires at the very least coffee (stimulation), Scotch (counter the extreme effects of coffee) and a variety of non-laxative snacks (counter the other effects of coffee). Ideally I suppose an en-suite bathroom would be a good idea, but we should keep to the feasible. When I am really rich and famous I will also have an extra piano in my study, but for now I make do with a stereo. I find music (at least, some music) can create a less intense atmosphere when I am researching or planning, but when I am actually scripting I tend to turn it off, as otherwise I find the writing being influenced moment-to-moment by every passing mood of the music, which does not tend to improve the quality of my literary product at all.

## Working efficiently

Writing is of course more than simply tapping words onto a page. It is also thinking, researching, planning and finally doing all the administrative work connected to the sale and then either publication or production of the work, whether through an agent or otherwise. So your workspace must be able to accommodate all this too. Give yourself as much work surface as possible, so that you can refer to as many materials as you need simultaneously, and you can even have materials left out for more than one project at a time. And set up an efficient filing system from the start. Or if, as in my case, this is certainly not the start, do it now anyway. Do not simply put every new publisher's letter, piece of research and pizza takeaway leaflet together in an in-tray. The in-tray eventually overflows; you get a second one; that overflows too. You will eventually be surrounded by in-trays. File everything as it comes along, and don't hesitate to open a new file for even the germ of a new project.

This filing particularly applies to emails. One can make the mistake of thinking that because something is there on the computer it has been filed. It hasn't. Electronic documents – and emails most of all – can be just as much of a mess as a physical desktop. When you receive an email, save it in the relevant project file elsewhere in the computer. If you are feeling super-efficient, you could also print it off and keep it in that same project's hard-copy file.

Mention of emails leads me on to phones. Both can take over your whole existence if you allow them to; they will certainly try. Deal with emails when you are at your least productive as a writer. If you think of yourself as a 'morning person' then that is when you should be writing; do the emails in the evening. Or if mornings tend to be barren periods of grogginess and haze, those are the times for doing emails. And try to deal with all the day's emails in one sitting; certainly don't let them interrupt you whenever they feel like it. Set up your computer in such a way that it does not let you know when emails have arrived; instead, just check them once or twice per day.

Similarly, don't simply answer the phone whenever it rings. The phone can of course be very useful for your writing, particularly for research, but in general – put the answerphone on. Better still, put it on and set it to silent. If the caller doesn't leave a message, it can't be very important.

A great deal of research is now done on the web, but I still like having books around. One of them is Jane Dorner's *The Internet: A Writer's Guide* (see page 595). Obviously a writer should have a really good dictionary (some of the larger ones give a date for each word usage, which is particularly helpful for period writing), and I also find a large thesaurus very useful (the original format, not the alphabetical kind; the latter is simpler to use but as it is necessarily so repetitive it contains far fewer options). Then there are always the books needed for the particular project in hand, alongside Ann Hoffmann's excellent *Research for Writers* (see page 603).

Most writers actually fit their research and other writing activities in with other work, whether writing-related or not. This means that time becomes a very precious commodity. I have always worked best when I have been able to arrange my writing time in large chunks, preferably whole days. An hour here or there really is hardly any use. And whenever possible I have tried to establish routines. The truth is that I have been particularly bad at this, perhaps because I have often had too many projects at different stages simultaneously, but I would still recommend adopting a daily routine as far as possible. It means there is just one less decision to have to make: your writing times have been decided and that's it.

## Writer's block

So now you are all set. You have bought yourself Final Draft software (or something similar) and you have the workspace, the materials, the books, the filing – the lot. You write and write. You pin the best rejection slips onto the wall (we've all had them). You write and write. And then you don't. You get writer's block. I have had this. It is a particularly nasty affliction as in almost everyone else's eyes 'writer's block' translates as 'laziness'. This is not the place for a full discussion, but I can pass on a couple of pieces of advice I received, which worked for me. Firstly, don't always try to see the whole piece of work, as that may be overwhelming to you. Try to focus on a particular section of it and nothing more. Secondly, when you have writer's block a whole day of writing ahead of you looks interminable. So don't do it. Strictly limit yourself to writing for two hours and no more. You may well find yourself writing with real urgency, trying to cram all that you can into those two allotted hours. Only much later can you gradually increase the limit back to a normal day.

Well, it worked for me. But then there are all sorts of writers. My old friend Jack Trevor Story had a writer's solution for insomnia: he wrote right through the night. Every night. It worked for him.

Now, as usual, I am going to try to learn from what I've written.

**Rib Davis** has been writing professionally for 25 years. He has over 60 credits, including scripts for radio, television and stage, as well as two books on the art of writing scripts. He is close to sorting out his domestic writing arrangements.

# Writers' retreats

Some writers find that spending some time at a writers' retreat proves bountiful. An author who has twice benefited from this experience is Maggie Gee.

Writers' retreats are not for everyone. They aren't, for example, for the poet who once said to me, *a propos* of Hawthornden Castle International Writers' Retreat, 'But it's so quiet. And Edinburgh is *half an hour away* by bus.' For him, to be half an hour from the metropolis was a penance.

Before going into the desert, think long and hard. Are you quarrelsome, or oversensitive, or both? The other writers will, for the most part, be busy and quiet, but mealtimes are generally communal. People are more vulnerable when they are off their own territory and away from loved ones. Do not always eat the last piece of cake (food gains an emotional significance when other props are missing) or be competitive about how much you have written, or how much you get paid. Actual numbers of words and pounds should never be quoted. Do not give a reading from your new work unless asked.

Ask yourself hard questions before you go. Do you mind very much being away from your loved ones, your cat, your garden? Will you be wracked by guilt? Are you addicted to *The Bill*? Do you feel anxious if you can't pick up emails or vary the monotony of your work with half-hourly binges on Google? Most retreats have no televisions and no internet facilities.

But if you are a writer who can never get enough time uninterrupted by phone calls, plumbers, pets, children, and the washing-machine, writers' retreats are absolute heaven. For me personally, two widely spaced four-week stays at Hawthornden Castle produced the first drafts of two novels, *Where are the Snows* (1991) and my most recent novel, *The Flood*. When I am away from all the things I ought to do at home, 200–300 words a day swells into 2000–3000.

Prose writers have to come to terms with the leaden truth that you cannot write a book without hours of immobility. I personally prefer concentrating those hours into a smaller number of weeks and months. I speak as one whose penultimate novel (*The White Family*), took seven years to write and rewrite (no retreats), whereas the most recent one, after 18 months of mulling over, took just a month to dream up and write (at a retreat) and six months to rewrite. Poets like retreats too. I was at Hawthornden Castle last time with, among others, the poet Jean Sprackland, and while she was there she wrote most of her new book *Hard Water*, since shortlisted for the T.S. Eliot Prize.

In the USA there is a wider choice of retreats. Google will present you with a bewildering variety of American retreats, many of them luxurious and long established. But although most of them are free, you have to find the air fare. In the UK there are fewer choices and only one retreat is free. The Arvon Foundation, which specialises in tutored retreats, also offers one week for plain untutored retreats at each of its four centres. Ireland has scenic, remote, beautiful Anam Cara, on the coast of Western Cork. Hawthornden Castle in

Scotland is free, but unfortunately writers can only go there once every five years. You must make a formal application to the trustees and if you are accepted you can look forward to a stay in a beautiful castle in dramatic wooded grounds. The rooms are warm and attractive, the food is good, the staff are kind and the five or six writers who are in residence at any one time pay only for their pre-prandial sherry.

There are alternatives. When I struck a complete log jam in my work this year, I tried a few days at St Cuthman's in Culham, near Billingshurst. A former Anglican retreat of long standing, this beautiful, peaceful place has been completely revivified by the Catholics who have now taken it over. As before, it is open to those of any or no faith who need rest. The rooms are simple, comfortable and elegant, with views over a lake and swans, fresh vegetables and home baking. There are prayers night and morning but you don't have to attend, though they seemed to work wonders for my novel.

There again, there are bargain weekly deals at out-of-season seaside hotels, or if you once went to a college or university, you could try ringing up to see if they let former *alumni* stay there cheaply in empty rooms. Many do, and they should have decent desks and chairs. Once the washing-machine, the telephone and the pets have fallen silent, the dream of the book can begin.

**Maggie Gee** is the author of nine novels, the most recent of which is *The Flood* (Saqi 2004). *The White Family* (2002) was shortlisted for the Orange Prize for Fiction and the International Impac Prize for Fiction. She is the first female Chairman of the Royal Society of Literature.

## Contact details

### Anam Cara
*website* www.ugr.com/anamcararetreat

### The Arvon Foundation
See below.

### Hawthornden Castle
*tel* 0131-44 02180
See below.

### St Cuthman's
Culham, near Billingshurst
*website* www.dabnet.org/stcuth2.htm
*tel* (01403) 741220

### Craetive Cauldron
www.creativecauldron.com/retreats
A useful encyclopedic web page of retreats in the USA.

## The Arvon Foundation
42A Buckingham Palace Road, London SW1W 0RE
*website* www.arvonfoundation.org
*National Director* Stephanie Anderson

See individual entries for the Foundation's 4 centres: The Hurst – The John Osborne Arvon Centre, Lumb Bank – The Ted Hughes Arvon Centre, Moniack Mhor and Totleigh Barton. As well as facilitating writers' retreats, the centres run many creative writing courses.

## Hawthornden Castle
The International Retreat for Writers, Lasswade, Midlothian EH18 1EG
*tel* 0131-440 2180 *fax* 0131-440 1989
*Contact* The Administrator

Exists to provide a peaceful setting where published writers can work without disturbance. The Retreat houses 5 writers at a time, who are known as Hawthornden Fellows. Writers from any part of the world may apply for the fellowships. No monetary assistance is given, nor any contribution to travelling expenses, but once arrived at Hawthornden, the writer is the guest of the Retreat. Application forms provided must be made by the end of September for the following calendar year. Previous occupants include Les Murray, Alasdair Gray, Helen Vendler, Olive Senior, Hilary Spurling and Maggie Gee.

## The Hurst – The John Osborne Arvon Centre
The Arvon Foundation, The Hurst, Clunton, Craven Arms, Shrops. SY7 0JA
*tel* (01588) 640658
*email* hurst@arvonfoundation.org

*website* www.arvonfoundation.org
*Centre Directors* Edmund Collier, Paul Warwick

Offers a one-week writing retreat in August. The Hurst is situated in the beautiful Clun Valley in South Shropshire, 12 miles from Ludlow, and is set in 30 acres of woodland, with gardens and a lake.

## Irish Writers' Centre
19 Parnell Square, Dublin 1
*tel* (353) 1 8721302 *fax* (353) 1 8726282
*email* info@writerscentre.ie
*Contact* Bernadette Larkin

Studio available for rent by a writer for a period of 3 months or less. Recent occupants include Talaya Delaney while she was working on a piece for the Abbey Theatre, 2 comedy scriptwriters to write a new 6-part TV series for RTE and Mary Dorcey to finish writing her latest novel.

## Lumb Bank – The Ted Hughes Arvon Centre
The Arvon Foundation, Lumb Bank, Heptonstall, Hebden Bridge, West Yorkshire HX7 6DF
*tel* (01422) 843714 *fax* (01422) 843714
*email* l-bank@arvonfoundation.org
*website* www.arvonfoundation.org
*Centre Directors* Stephen May, Caron May

Offers a one-week writing retreat in September. Lumb Bank is an 18th-century former mill-owner's house set in 20 acres of steep pasture land.

## Moniack Mohr
The Arvon Foundation, Moniack Mhor, Teavarran, Kiltarlity, Beauly, Inverness-shire IV4 7HT
*tel* (01463) 741675 *fax* (01463) 741733

*email* m-mohr@arvonfoundation.org
*website* www.arvonfoundation.org
*Centre Directors* Margaret West, Nicky Guthrie

Offers a one-week writing retreat in October. Moniack Mhor is a traditional croft house commanding panoramic views over Highland landscapes with forest walks nearby.

## Totleigh Barton
The Arvon Foundation, Totleigh Barton, Sheepwash, Beaworthy, Devon EX21 5NS
*tel* (01409) 231338 *fax* (01409) 231144
*email* t-barton@arvonfoundation.org
*website* www.arvonfoundation.org
*Centre Directors* Monique Roffey, Ian Marchant

Offers a writing retreat in August. Totleigh Barton is a thatched, pre-Domesday manor house, surrounded by farmland in Devon, 2 miles from the village of Sheepwash.

## Ty Newydd
Ty Newydd Writers' Centre, Llanystumdwy, Cricieth, Gwynedd LL52 0LW
*tel* (01766) 522811 *fax* (01766) 523095
*email* tynewydd@dial.pipex.com
*website* www.tynewydd.org

Writers' retreats are organised at different times during the year to give writers the opportunity to find a week's peace and quiet in Ty Newydd's stimulating environment. Everyone has a single room and stays on a self-catering basis with a shared meal in the evening.

# Digital imaging for writers

The way in which images are presented can sway an editor's decision to use an article. David Askham explains how to transfer images to a computer and suggests ways to arrange them for best effect.

An editor, who regularly commissioned me to produce profiles of small gardens, telephoned me as soon as he received one of my proposals. He said, "When I first read your letter, I was convinced that it would not be suitable for our British readers. Then I turned the page and said 'WOW!' Please go ahead with the feature." So what tipped the scales? Admittedly the subject was a rather unusual one, in fact a so-called 'shade garden'. Furthermore, it was located far away in Australia! Because of this, I suspected that the proposal would fail if I sent words alone. I could have sent accompanying small colour prints to illustrate the potential of the article, but they would have lacked impact and risked becoming separated from my proposal. So I tried an experiment. I scanned a selection of photographs and compiled a simple but bold and colourful composite A4 sheet which formed part of my brief proposal. It worked and I have used variants of this idea with success ever since.

But the advantages of digital photography outlined above do not end there because once pictures are filed on a writer's personal computer they are available for a variety of useful purposes. They can serve as inspiration, providing quick recall of a scene or a person's facial features or attire. It is like revisiting a location or experiencing an unexpected reunion with an old friend. Digital images are quick visual references; they can jog a writer's memory and inspire. Let us look at the subject in a little more detail.

### Technical aspects
Most writers will be familiar with cameras which use conventional film, either black and white or colour. These films produce negatives from which prints are produced; or transparencies which can be projected (for lecture purposes) or used by publishers to provide illustrations in print. In contrast, a new generation of cameras has arrived which do not use film, but instead record and store images digitally on special reusable memory. These digitally stored images must then be transferred to a personal computer so that they may be cropped, modified and integrated into the desired documents, such as a proposal. If the source is a digital camera it is relatively straightforward to transfer images using the computer software which came with the camera. Using the connecting cables supplied, images are 'downloaded' into the computer or the memory cards are inserted into memory card readers. The whole chain is digital which makes it so easy.

However, you do not necessarily need a digital camera to transfer images to your computer. You can work with prints which you already have – or could produce at will in the future. Or you can digitise your existing colour (or black and white) slides or negatives. For the latter operation your pictures need to be scanned and recorded on a CD, a process which has become increasingly available at most processing laboratories. Alternatively, with the right equipment, you can do the whole process yourself. Possibly the easier and cheaper method is to buy a flatbed scanner which will produce digital files from your original colour or black and white prints. Flatbed scanners have tumbled in price over the past few years and are now often bundled with new computers. Alternatively, they can be bought for well under £100 although, like most consumer goods, it does not pay to buy the cheapest available. Take advice from a knowledgeable friend or trusted dealer.

If you wish to work from negatives or colour slides, you will need to buy a film scanner. These are more expensive (from £150 up to £1000 or more), but they give superior results particularly if you want to produce photo-realistic prints from a colour printer, say for promotional or exhibition purposes.

Initially, you can achieve commendable results by using your existing camera and having selected images scanned onto a CD by a processing laboratory. Then you can extract copies of the desired pictures from the CD and place them in your chosen document file. When you feel more confident and can justify the expense, you can then shop around for a suitable scanner to use at home.

Before moving on, I think a word is needed on the relative merits of using conventional film or digital cameras. The latter have developed rapidly over recent years. However, except for the top-priced models (£2000–£5000), results of consumer digital cameras are only just beginning to compare favourably with film and fall well short if big enlargements are needed in print. Like-for-like, they are also more expensive. However, the gap is already closing. There is also another factor. If you think it is likely that your pictures merit long-term archiving, film still has the edge. Why? Because computer systems evolve rapidly and yesterday's computer technology soon becomes obsolete. In a few years it may not be possible to read old digital files.

## Using visual references

In addition to using photographs in a book or article proposal, digital pictures are also a valuable aid to many forms of research and writing. For example, the value of tape-recorded research or interview notes is significantly enhanced if you add thumbnail pictures to enrich and augment the narrative information. Words and pictures which are integrated in this way have to be more reliable than unaided human memory when writing begins, particularly if there is a significant time interval between research and writing. But it is in the production of proposals, those all important selling documents, where digital imaging comes into its own.

However, I do not advocate using any old pictures. They have to be directly relevant to the subject being proposed and they must be of good quality. Therefore, it is worthwhile budgeting for your photography and providing high quality pictures using conventional cameras and films at the outset. You will then have confidence in being able to deliver high quality images to the editor.

## Computing and software

Unless you are a computer buff, eyes can easily glaze when faced with yet more software to master. Unfortunately, some knowledge is essential but I will keep it simple. Most modern computers can handle graphics which includes digital photographs and drawings. Indeed most modern word processing software, such as WordPerfect, can integrate pictures directly into documents. Provided you know the filename of the required picture, or can find it by exploring the file listing hierarchy, you merely have to point to INSERT ... GRAPHICS ... FROM FILE and select the appropriate file. (The commands may be slightly different in other word processing programs.) The photograph then appears and you can adjust both its size and position within the document.

Ideally you will have made any cropping or other adjustments using the picture management software which may have been delivered with your digital camera or scanner. If the pictures supplied by your film processor were delivered on a CD, you may find a simple program included on the disk. Alternatively, you may choose to buy a picture processing program, such as Paint Shop Pro or Photoshop, which possess enormous capabilities for enhancing and transforming digital images, way beyond what you require initially. Photoshop is expensive, although a simpler version or comparable software of the program is bundled with some scanners and is perfectly adequate for first-time users. Alternatively, Adobe Photoshop Elements is an extremely popular and effective lower cost option. Consider buying one or two magazines which specialise in digital photography to study reviews and tables of available digital hardware and software. A study of analytical reports can be very helpful in short-listing potential solutions.

One last word on specialist software. Be prepared to invest plenty of time if you wish to explore digital image processing capabilities beyond basic cropping of your photographs. It can be very rewarding, but it takes time to learn and is beyond the scope of this article.

### Adding visual elements

A simple example was given earlier of how you can add photographs to a text document. Sometimes it is better to devote an A4 page exclusively to the visual side of your proposals. Although this can be done using a word processor, a publishing program such as Microsoft Home Publishing or Serif PagePlus is more adept and flexible for designing layout and adding captions. However, you will soon find that you are straying into the realms of graphic design which appears to be much easier than it really is.

Working out the relative sizes of your pictures on the page and their positions can be extremely time consuming. It requires patience and discipline. My advice is to keep things as simple as possible before tackling more ambitious layouts. Avoid trying to include too many pictures on a page; six should be a maximum. Try to vary their individual sizes so that there is variety. Your aim should be to present just sufficient visual information to whet an editor's appetite with the whole effect being easy on the eye. There is no doubt that in a highly competitive world digital imaging can endow a writer with a competitive edge. Take heart and inspiration from my experience and see if your success rate improves.

**David Askham** is author of *Photo Libraries and Agencies* (BFP Books) and has been illustrating his written work for over 35 years. His photographs have been published worldwide in books, brochures, magazines and newspapers, many through international agencies.

# Indexing

A good index is a joy to the user of a non-fiction book; a bad index will downgrade an otherwise good book. The function of indexes, together with the skills needed to compile them, are examined here.

An index is a detailed key to the contents of a document, in contrast to a contents list, which gives only the titles of the parts into which the document is divided (e.g. chapters). Precisely, an index is 'A systematic arrangement of entries designed to enable users to locate information in a document'. The document may be a book, a series of books, an issue of a periodical, a run of several volumes of a periodical, an audiotape, a map, a film, a picture, a CD-Rom, a website, a database, an object, or any other information source in print or non-print form.

The objective of an index is to guide enquirers to information on given subjects in a document by providing the terms of their choice (single words, phrases, abbreviations, acronyms, dates, names, and so on) in an appropriately organised list which refers them to specific locations using page, column, section, frame, figure, table, paragraph, line or other appropriate numbers or hyperlinks.

An index differs from a catalogue, which is a record of the documents held in a particular collection, such as a library; though a catalogue may require an index, for example to guide searchers from subject words to class numbers.

A document may have separate indexes for different classes of heading, so that personal names are distinguished from subjects, for example, or a single index in which all classes of heading are interfiled.

## The Society of Indexers

The Society of Indexers is a non-profit organisation founded in 1957 and is the only autonomous professional body for indexers in the UK. It is affiliated with the American Society of Indexers, the Australian Society of Indexers, the China Society of Indexers, the Indexing and Abstracting Society of Canada, and the Association of Southern African Indexers and Bibliographers, and has close ties with the Chartered Institute of Library and Information Professionals (CILIP) and the Society for Editors and Proofreaders (SfEP).

The main objectives of the Society are to promote all types of indexing standards and techniques and the role of indexers in the organisation of knowledge; to provide, promote and recognise facilities for both the initial and the further training of indexers; to establish criteria for assessing conformity to indexing standards; and to conduct research and publish guidance, ideas and information about indexing. It seeks to establish good relationships between indexers, librarians, publishers and authors, both to advance good indexing and to improve the role and wellbeing of indexers.

### Services to indexers

The Society publishes a learned journal *The Indexer* (2 p.a.), a newsletter and *Occasional Papers in Indexing*. Local and special interest groups provide the chance for members to meet to discuss common interests, while email discussion lists have encouraged the development of a virtual community of indexers. A two-day conference is held every year. All levels of training are supported by regular workshops held at venues throughout the country.

Professional competence is recognised in two stages by the Society. Accredited Indexers who have completed the open-learning course qualification (see below) have shown theoretical competence in indexing, while Registered Indexers have proved their experience and competence in practical indexing through a rigorous assessment procedure and admission to the Register of Indexers. The services of Registered Indexers are actively promoted by the Society while all trained and experienced members have the opportunity of an annual entry in *Indexers Available*, a directory published by the Society and distributed without charge to over 1000 publishers to help them find an indexer.

The Society sets annually recommended minimum rates for indexing (£16–£30 per hour; £1.20–£5 per page in 2004) and provides advice on the business side of indexing to its members.

## Further information

### Society of Indexers

Blades Enterprise Centre, John Street, Sheffield S2 4SU
*tel* 0114-292 2350 *fax* 0114-292 2351
*email* admin@indexers.org.uk
*website* www.indexers.org.uk
*Administrator* Wendy Burrow
*Registrar* Elizabeth Wallis *tel* 020-8940 4771
*Membership* £60 p.a. UK/Europe, £75 overseas; £120 corporate

Visit the website or contact the Administrator for further information. Publishers and authors seeking to commission an indexer should consult *Indexers Available* on the website or contact the Registrar.

### Services to publishers and authors

Anyone who commissions indexes needs to be certain of engaging a professional indexer working to the highest standards and able to meet deadlines.

*Indexers Available*, now searchable on the Society's website, lists only qualified and experienced members of the Society and gives basic contact details, subject specialisms and indexing experience. Advice on the selection of indexers is available from the Registrar, who may also be able to suggest names of professionals able to undertake related tasks such as thesaurus construction, terminology control or database indexing. The Registrar will also advise on relations with indexers.

The Society co-operates with CILIP in the award of the Wheatley Medal for an outstanding index.

### Training in indexing

The Society's course (in electronic format with accompanying printed books) is based on the principle of open learning with units, tutorial support and formal tests all available separately so that individuals can learn in their own way and at their own pace. The units cover four core subjects and contain practical exercises and self-administered tests. After completing the four assessed units, trainees undertake a practical indexing assignment to prepare them for work in the commercial world. Members of the Society receive a substantial discount on the cost of the course, although anyone can purchase the units. Only members of the Society can apply for the formal tests.

**Further reading**

Booth, P.F., *Indexing: the manual of good practice*, K.G. Saur, 2001

British Standards Institution, *British Standard recommendations for examining documents, determining their subjects and selecting indexing terms*, (BS6529:1984)

International Standards Organisation, *Information and documentation – guidelines for the content, organization and presentation of indexes* (ISO 999:1996)

# Correcting proofs

The following notes and table are extracted from BS 5261 Part 2: 1976 (1995) and are reproduced by permission of the British Standards Institution.

## 4 Marks for copy preparation and proof correction

**4.1** The marks to be used for marking up copy for composition and for the correction of printers' proofs shall be as shown in Table 1 (see pages 617–626).

**4.2** The marks in Table 1 are classified in three groups as follows:

(a) Group A: general.

(b) Group B: deletion, insertion and substitution.

(c) Group C: positioning and spacing.

**4.3** Each item in Table 1 is given a simple alpha-numeric serial number denoting the classification group to which it belongs and its position within the group.

## Further information

### British Standards Institution (BSI)
Technical Information Group,
389 Chiswick High Road, London W4 4AL
*tel* 020-8996 7111 *fax* 020-8996 7048
*Customer Services tel* 020-8996 9001
*fax* 020-8996 7001
*email* info@bsi.org.uk
*website* www.bsi.org.uk/

BSI is the independent national body responsible for preparing British Standards. It presents the UK view on standards in Europe and at the international level. It is incorporated by Royal Charter.

For a complete standard, contact Customer Services.

**4.4** The marks have been drawn keeping the shapes as simple as possible and using sizes which relate to normal practice. The shapes of the marks should be followed exactly by all who make use of them.

**4.5** For each marking-up or proof correction instruction a distinct mark is to be made:

(a) in the text: to indicate the exact place to which the instruction refers;

(b) in the margin: to signify or amplify the meaning of the instruction.

It should be noted that some instructions have a combined textual and marginal mark.

**4.6** Where a number of instructions occur in one line, the marginal marks are to be divided between the left and right margins where possible, the order being from left to right in both margins.

**4.7** Specification details, comments and instructions may be written on the copy or proof to complement the textual and marginal marks. Such written matter is to be clearly distinguishable from the copy and from any corrections made to the proof. Normally this is done by encircling the matter and/or by the appropriate use of colour (see below).

**4.8** Proof corrections shall be made in coloured ink thus:

(a) printer's literal errors marked by the printer for correction: green;

(b) printer's literal errors marked by the customer and his agents for correction: red;

(c) alterations and instructions made by the customer and his agents: black or dark blue.

## Table 1. Classified list of marks

NOTE. The letters M and P in the notes column indicate marks for marking-up copy and for correcting proofs respectively.

### Group A  General

| Number | Instruction | Textual mark | Marginal mark | Notes |
|--------|-------------|--------------|---------------|-------|
| A1 | Correction is concluded | None | / | P<br>Make after each correction |
| A2 | Leave unchanged | – – – – – –<br>under characters to remain | (✓) | M P |
| A3 | Remove extraneous marks | Encircle marks to be removed | ✕ | P<br>e.g. film or paper edges visible between lines on bromide or diazo proofs |
| A3.1 | Push down risen spacing material | Encircle blemish | ⊥ | P |
| A4 | Refer to appropriate authority anything of doubtful accuracy | Encircle word(s) affected | (?) | P |

### Group B  Deletion, insertion and substitution

| Number | Instruction | Textual mark | Marginal mark | Notes |
|--------|-------------|--------------|---------------|-------|
| B1 | Insert in text the matter indicated in the margin | ⋏ | New matter followed by ⋏ | M P<br>Indentical to B2 |
| B2 | Insert additional matter identified by a letter in a diamond | ⋏ | ⋏<br>Followed by for example ⟨A⟩ | M P<br>The relevant section of the copy should be supplied with the corresponding letter marked on it in a diamond e.g. ⟨A⟩ |
| B3 | Delete | / through character(s)<br>or<br>⊢——⊣ through words to be deleted | ∂ | M P |
| B4 | Delete and close up | ⌢/⌣ through character<br>or<br>⊢——⊣ through characters<br>e.g. charac͡ter<br>chara͡cter | ⌢∂ | M P |

**Table 1** *(continued)*

| Number | Instruction | Textual mark | Marginal mark | Notes |
|---|---|---|---|---|
| B5 | Substitute character or substitute part of one or more word(s) | / through character<br>or<br>├────────┤<br>through word(s) | New character<br>or<br>new word(s) | M P |
| B6 | Wrong fount. Replace by character(s) of correct fount | Encircle character(s) to be changed | ⊗ | P |
| B6.1 | Change damaged character(s) | Encircle character(s) to be changed | ✕ | P<br>This mark is identical to A3 |
| B7 | Set in or change to italic | ───────<br>under character(s) to be set or changed | ⊔ | M P<br>Where space does not permit textual marks encircle the affected area instead |
| B8 | Set in or change to capital letters | ═══════<br>under character(s) to be set or changed | ≡ | |
| B9 | Set in or change to small capital letters | ═══════<br>under character(s) to be set or changed | ═ | |
| B9.1 | Set in or change to capital letters for initial letters and small capital letters for the rest of the words | ═══<br>under initial letters<br>and<br>═══════<br>under rest of the word(s) | ≝ | |
| B10 | Set in or change to bold type | ∿∿∿∿∿∿<br>under character(s) to be set or changed | ∿ | |
| B11 | Set in or change to bold italic type | ∿∿∿∿∿∿<br>under character(s) to be set or changed | ⊔<br>∿ | |
| B12 | Change capital letters to lower case letters | Encircle character(s) to be changed | ≢ | P<br>For use when B5 is inappropriate |

**Table 1** *(continued)*

| Number | Instruction | Textual mark | Marginal mark | Notes |
|---|---|---|---|---|
| B12.1 | Change small capital letters to lower case letters | Encircle character(s) to be changed | ⧧ | P<br>For use when B5 is inappropriate |
| B13 | Change italic to upright type | Encircle character(s) to be changed | ⊔ | P |
| B14 | Invert type | Encircle character to be inverted | ↺ | P |
| B15 | Substitute or insert character in 'superior' position | / through character<br><br>or<br><br>⅄ where required | ⌐ under character<br><br>e.g. ⌐2 | P |
| B16 | Substitute or insert character in 'inferior' position | / through character<br><br>or<br><br>⅄ where required | L over character<br><br>e.g. L2 | P |
| B17 | Substitute ligature e.g. ffi for separate letters | ⊢———⊣ through characters affected | ⌣ e.g. ffi | P |
| B17.1 | Substitute separate letters for ligature | ⊢———⊣ | Write out separate letters | P |
| B18 | Substitute or insert full stop or decimal point | / through character<br><br>or<br><br>⅄ where required | (·) | M P |
| B18.1 | Substitute or insert colon | / through character<br><br>or<br><br>⅄ where required | (⁝) | M P |
| B18.2 | Substitute or insert semi-colon | / through character<br><br>or<br><br>⅄ where required | ⁏ | M P |

**Table 1** *(continued)*

| Number | Instruction | Textual mark | Marginal mark | Notes |
|---|---|---|---|---|
| B18.3 | Substitute or insert comma | / through character<br><br>or<br><br>⋀ where required | , | M P |
| B18.4 | Substitute or insert apostrophe | / through character<br><br>or<br><br>⋀ where required | ⁊ | M P |
| B18.5 | Substitute or insert single quotation marks | / through character<br><br>or<br><br>⋀ where required | ⁊ and/or ⁊ | M P |
| B18.6 | Substitute or insert double quotation marks | / through character<br><br>or<br><br>⋀ where required | ⁊ and/or ⁊ | M P |
| B19 | Substitute or insert ellipsis | / through character<br><br>or<br><br>⋀ where required | • • • | M P |
| B20 | Substitute or insert leader dots | / through character<br><br>or<br><br>⋀ where required | ⊙•• | M P<br>Give the measure of the leader when necessary |
| B21 | Substitute or insert hyphen | / through character<br><br>or<br><br>⋀ where required | ⊢⊣ | M P |
| B22 | Substitute or insert rule | / through character<br><br>⋀ where required | ⊢ | M P<br>Give the size of the rule in the marginal mark e.g.<br>⊢1 em⊣  ⊢4 mm⊣ |

**Table 1** *(continued)*

| Number | Instruction | Textual mark | Marginal mark | Notes |
|---|---|---|---|---|
| B23 | Substitute or insert oblique | / through character  or  ⋀ where required | (/) | M P |

**Group C   Positioning and spacing**

| Number | Instruction | Textual mark | Marginal mark | Notes |
|---|---|---|---|---|
| C1 | Start new paragraph | | | M P |
| C2 | Run on (no new paragraph) | | | M P |
| C3 | Transpose characters or words | between characters or words, numbered when necessary | | M P |
| C4 | Transpose a number of characters or words | 3   2   1 | 1 2 3 | M P To be used when the sequence cannot be clearly indicated by the use of C3. The vertical strokes are made through the characters or words to be transposed and numbered in the correct sequence |
| C5 | Transpose lines | | | M P |
| C6 | Transpose a number of lines | | ——— 3 ——— 2 ——— 1 | P To be used when the sequence cannot be clearly indicated by C5. Rules extend from the margin into the text with each line to be transposed numbered in the correct sequence |
| C7 | Centre | ⌐enclosing matter to be centred⌐ | [ ] | M P |
| C8 | Indent | | | P Give the amount of the indent in the marginal mark |

**Table 1** *(continued)*

| Number | Instruction | Textual mark | Marginal mark | Notes |
|---|---|---|---|---|
| C9 | Cancel indent | | | P |
| C10 | Set line justified to specified measure | and/or | | P<br>Give the exact dimensions when necessary |
| C11 | Set column justified to specified measure | | | M P<br>Give the exact dimensions when necessary |
| C12 | Move matter specified distance to the right | enclosing matter to be moved to the right | | P<br>Give the exact dimensions when necessary |
| C13 | Move matter specified distance to the left | enclosing matter to be moved to the left | | P<br>Give the exact dimensions when necessary |
| C14 | Take over character(s), word(s) or line to next line, column or page | | | P<br>The textual mark surrounds the matter to be taken over and extends into the margin |
| C15 | Take back character(s), word(s), or line to previous line, column or page | | | P<br>The textual mark surrounds the matter to be taken back and extends into the margin |
| C16 | Raise matter | over matter to be raised<br>under matter to be raised | | P<br>Give the exact dimensions when necessary. (Use C28 for insertion of space between lines or paragraphs in text) |
| C17 | Lower matter | over matter to be lowered<br>under matter to be lowered | | P<br>Give the exact dimensions when necessary. (Use C29 for reduction of space between lines or paragraphs in text) |
| C18 | Move matter to position indicated | Enclose matter to be moved and indicate new position | | P<br>Give the exact dimensions when necessary |

**Table 1** *(continued)*

| Number | Instruction | Textual mark | Marginal mark | Notes |
|--------|-------------|--------------|---------------|-------|
| C19 | Correct vertical alignment | ‖ | ‖ | P |
| C20 | Correct horizontal alignment | Single line above and below misaligned matter<br><br>e.g.<br>mi₍s₎aligned | ▬<br>▬ | P<br>The marginal mark is placed level with the head and foot of the relevant line |
| C21 | Close up. Delete space between characters or words | linking ⌢ characters | ⌣⌢ | M P |
| C22 | Insert space between characters | │<br><br>between characters affected | Y | M P<br>Give the size of the space to be inserted when necessary |
| C23 | Insert space between words | Y<br><br>between words affected | Y | M P<br>Give the size of the space to be inserted when necessary |
| C24 | Reduce space between characters | │<br><br>between characters affected | ⋏ | M P<br>Give the amount by which the space is to be reduced when necessary |
| C25 | Reduce space between words | ⋏<br><br>between words affected | ⋏ | M P<br>Give amount by which the space is to be reduced when necessary |
| C26 | Make space appear equal between characters or words | │<br><br>between characters or words affected | Ⴤ | M P |
| C27 | Close up to normal interline spacing | ⌐( each side of column linking lines )⌐ | | M P<br>The textual marks extend into the margin |

**Marked galley proof of text**

(B9.1)

(B13)

(C7)

(C9)

## At the sign of the red pale

*The Life and Work of William Caxton, by H W Larken*

[An Extract]

(B12)

(B18.5)

(B18.5)

Few people, even in the field of printing, have any clear conception of what William Caxton did or, indeed, of what he was. Much of this lack of knowledge is due to the absence of information that can be counted as factual and the consequent tendency to vague generalisation.

Though it is well known that Caxton was born in the county of Kent, there is no information as to the precise place. In his prologue to the *History of Troy*, William Caxton wrote 'for in France I was never and was born and learned my English in Kent in the Weald where I doubt not is spoken as broad and rude English as in any place of England.' During the fifteenth century there were a great number of Flemish cloth weavers in Kent; most of them had come to England at the instigation of Edward III with the object of teaching their craft to the English. So successful was this venture that the English cloth trade flourished and the agents who sold the cloth (the mercers) became very wealthy people. There have been many speculations concerning the origin of the Caxton family and much research has been carried out. It is assumed often that Caxton's family must have been connected with the wool trade in order to have secured his apprenticeship to an influential merchant.

(B6)

(B17)

(C8)

(B14)

(A4)
(B7)

W. Blyth Crotch (*Prologues and Epilogues of William Caxton*) suggests that the origin of the name Caxton (of which there are several variations in spelling) may be traced to Cambridgeshire but notes that many writers have suggested that Caxton was connected with a family at Hadlow or alternatively a family in Canterbury.

Of the Canterbury connection a William Caxton became freeman of the City in 1431 and William Pratt, a mercer who was the printer's friend, was born there. H. R. Plomer suggests that Pratt and Caxton might possibly have been schoolboys together, perhaps at the school St. Alphege. In this parish there lived a John Caxton who used as his mark three cakes over a barrel (or l tun) and who is mentioned in an inscription on a monument in the church of St. Alphege.

In 1941, Alan Keen (an authority on manuscripts) secured some documents concerning Caxton; these are now in the British Museum. Discovered in the library of Earl Winterton at Shillinglee Park by Richard Holworthy, the documents cover the period 1420 to 1467. One of Winterton's ancestors purchased the manor of West Wratting from a family named Caxton, the property being situated in the Weald of Kent.

There is also record of a property mentioning Philip Caxton and his wife Dennis who had two sons, Philip (born in 1413) and William.

Particularly interesting in these documents is one recording that Philip Caxton junior sold the manor of Little Wratting to John Christemasse of London in 1436, the deed having been witnessed by two aldermen, one of whom was Robert Large, the printer's employer. Further, in 1439 the other son, William Caxton, conveyed to John Christemasse, and an indenture of 1457 concerning this property mentions one William Caxton veyed his rights in the manor Bluntes Hall at Little alias Causton. It is an interesting coincidence to note that the lord of the manor of Little Wratting was the father of Margaret, Duchess of Burgundy.

In 1420, a Thomas Caxton of Tenterden witnessed the will of a fellow townsman; he owned property in Kent and appears to have been a person of some importance.

¹ See 'William Caxton'.

(A3.1)
(B18.1)

(B15)

(C26)

(B8)
(B6)

(C27)

(B18)

(C27)

(B18.3)

(C21)

(C19)

(C22)

(B10)

(B9)

(B1)

(A2)
(B19)

(C23)
(C1)

(B5)

(B3)

(C3)

(B7)

(C20)

(B2)

(A3)

(B12.1)

(C2)
(B4)

(B22)
(C14)

(B21)

(C6)

(C25)
(C28)
(C29)

Ⓐ attached to Christchurch Monastery in the parish of

**Revised galley proof of text incorporating corrections**

## AT THE SIGN OF THE RED PALE

The Life and Work of William Caxton, *by H W Larken*

### An Extract

FEW PEOPLE, even in the field of printing, have any clear conception of what William Caxton did or, indeed, of what he was. Much of this lack of knowledge is due to the absence of information that can be counted as factual and the consequent tendency to vague generalisation.

Though it is well known that Caxton was born in the county of Kent, there is no information as to the precise place. In his prologue to the *History of Troy*, William Caxton wrote '. . . for in France I was never and was born and learned my English in Kent in the Weald where I doubt not is spoken as broad and rude English as in any place of England.'

During the fifteenth century there were a great number of Flemish cloth weavers in Kent; most of them had come to England at the instigation of Edward III with the object of teaching their craft to the English. So successful was this venture that the English cloth trade flourished and the agents who sold the cloth (the mercers) became very wealthy people.

There have been many speculations concerning the origin of the Caxton family and much research has been carried out. It is often assumed that Caxton's family must have been connected with the wool trade in order to have secured his apprenticeship to an influential merchant.

W. Blyth Crotch (*Prologues and Epilogues of William Caxton*) suggests that the origin of the name Caxton (of which there are several variations in spelling) may be traced to Cambridgeshire but notes that many writers have suggested that Caxton was connected with a family at Hadlow or alternatively a family in Canterbury.

Of the Canterbury connection: a William Caxton became freeman of the City in 1431 and William Pratt, a mercer who was the printer's friend, was born there. H. R. Plomer[1] suggests that Pratt and Caxton might possibly have been schoolboys together, perhaps at the school attached to Christchurch Monastery in the parish of St. Alphege. In this parish there lived a John Caxton who used as his mark three cakes over a barrel (or tun) and who is mentioned in an inscription on a monument in the church of St. Alphege.

In 1941, Alan Keen (an authority on manuscripts) secured some documents concerning Caxton; these are now in the British Museum. Discovered in the library of Earl Winterton at Shillinglee Park by Richard Holworthy, the documents cover the period 1420 to 1467. One of Winterton's ancestors purchased the manor of West Wratting from a family named Caxton, the property being situated in the Weald of Kent. There is also record of a property mentioning Philip Caxton and his wife Dennis who had two sons, Philip (born in 1413) and William.

Particularly interesting in these documents is one recording that Philip Caxton junior sold the manor of Little Wratting to John Christemasse of London in 1436—the deed having been witnessed by two aldermen, one of whom was Robert Large, the printer's employer. Further, in 1439, the other son, William Caxton, conveyed his rights in the manor Bluntes Hall at Little Wratting to John Christemasse, and an indenture of 1457 concerning this property mentions one William Caxton alias Causton. It is an interesting coincidence to note that the lord of the manor of Little Wratting was the father of Margaret, Duchess of Burgundy.

In 1420, a Thomas Caxton of Tenterden witnessed the will of a fellow townsman; he owned property in Kent and appears to have been a person of some importance.

[1] See 'William Caxton'.

**Table 1** *(continued)*

| Number | Instruction | Textual mark | Marginal mark | Notes |
|--------|-------------|--------------|---------------|-------|
| C28 | Insert space between lines or paragraphs | | or | M P<br>The marginal mark extends between the lines of text. Give the size of the space to be inserted when necessary |
| C29 | Reduce space between lines or paragraphs | | or | M P<br>The marginal mark extends between the lines of text. Give the amount by which the space is to be reduced when necessary |

# Libraries

Listed below are specialist, reference and general libraries. Contact individual libraries to find out about accessibility and opening hours.

## University of Aberdeen

Queen Mother Library, Meston Walk,
Aberdeen AB24 2UE
*tel* (01224) 272579 *fax* (01224) 487048
*email* library@abdn.ac.uk
*website* www.abdn.ac.uk/diss/library

## Aberdeen Central Library

Rosemount Viaduct, Aberdeen AB25 1GW
*tel* (01224) 652500
*email* centlib@arts-rec.aberdeen.net.uk
*website* www.aberdeencity.gov.uk

## Barbican Library

Barbican Centre, London EC2
*website* www.cityofLondon.gov.uk
*tel* 020-7628 9447 (Children's Library)

The largest of the City of London's lending libraries
with a strong arts and music section.

## Bath Central Library

19 The Podium, Northgate Street, Bath BA1 5AN
*tel* (01225) 787400 (Enquiry Desk), (01225) 787402
(Children's Library) *fax* (01225) 787426
*email* library@bathnes.gov.uk
*website* www.bathnes.gov.uk/libraries

## BBC Written Archives Centre

BBC Written Archives Centre, Reading RG4 8TZ
*tel* 0118-948 6281 *fax* 0118-946 1145
*email* heritage@bbc.co.uk
*website* www.bbc.co.uk/thenandnow

Home of the BBC's written records. Holds
thousands of files, scripts and working papers from
the BBC's formation in 1922 to the 1980s together
with information about past programmes and the
history of broadcasting. Does not have recordings
or information about current programmes.

## Bedford Central Library

Harpur Street, Bedford MK40 1PG
*tel* (01234) 350931 *fax* (01234) 342163
*website* www.galaxy.bedfordshire.gov.uk

## Belfast Public Library

Central Library, Royal Avenue, Belfast BT1 1EA
*tel* (01232) 243233 (01232) 332819

## BFI National Library

British Film Institute, 21 Stephen Street,
London W1T 1LN
*tel* 020-7255 1444 *fax* 020-7436 2338

*email* library@bfi.org.uk
*website* www.bfi.org.uk/nationallibrary

As a major national research collection, the main
priority is to provide comprehensive coverage of
British film and TV, but the collection itself is
international in scope.

## Birmingham Central Library

Chamberlain Square, Birmingham B3 3HQ
*tel* 0121-303 4511 *textphone* 0121-303 4547
*fax* 0121-233 4458
*email* central.library@birmingham.gov.uk
*website* www.birmingham.gov.uk

## Bodleian Library

Oxford OX1 3BG
*tel* (01865) 277034 *fax* (01865) 277029
*website* www.bodley.ox.ac.uk

The main research library of the University of
Oxford. It is also a legal deposit library.

## Booktrust

Book House, 45 East Hill, London SW18 2QZ
*tel* 020-8516 2977 *fax* 020-8516 2998
*email* info@booktrust.org.uk
*websites* www.booktrust.org.uk,
www.booktrusted.com

Holds the Children's Literature Collection, a unique
collection of all children's books published in the
last 2 years.

## Bristol Central Library

College Green, Bristol BS1 5TL
*tel* 0117-903 7200 (switchboard), 0117-903 7202
(Reference Library and art enquiries),
0117-903 7215 (Children's Library), 0117-903 7219
(drama enquries) *minicom* 0117-903 7437
*fax* 0117-922 1081
*email* refandinfo@bristol-city.gov.uk,
childrens_library@bristol-city.gov.uk,
music_collection@bristol-city.gov.uk

## The British Library

96 Euston Road, London NW1 2DB
*tel* 020-7412 7000 (switchboard), 020-7412 7676
(advance reservations, St Pancras reading rooms
and humanities enquiries), 020-7412 7702 (maps),
020-7412 7513 (manuscripts), 020-7412 7772
(music), 020-7412 7873 (Oriental and India Office)
*website* www.bl.uk

The national library of the UK and a legal deposit
library. The collection includes 150 million items, in

most known languages. Online catalogues. See also other British Library listings below.

## British Library Business Information Service (BIS)

96 Euston Road, London NW1 2DB
*tel* 020-7412 7977  *fax* 020-7412 7453
*email* business-information@bl.uk
*website* www.bl.uk/bis

Holds the most comprehensive collection of business information literature in the UK.

## British Library Document Supply Centre

Boston Spa, Wetherby, West Yorkshire LS23 7BQ
*tel* (01937) 546060  *fax* (01937) 546333

## British Library for Development Studies at IDS

Institute of Development Studies,
University of Sussex, Brighton BN1 9RE
*tel* (01273) 678263  *fax* (01273) 621202/691647
*email* blds@ids.ac.uk
*website* www.ids.ac.uk/blds

Europe's most comprehensive research collection on development issues.

## The British Library National Bibliographic Service

Boston Spa, Wetherby, West Yorkshire LS23 7BQ
*tel* (01937) 546585  *fax* (01937) 546586
*email* nbs-info@bl.uk
*website* www.bl.uk/services/bibliographic

Holds a record of the nation's publishing output.

## British Library Newspapers

Colindale Avenue, London NW9 5HE
*tel* 020-7412 7353  *fax* 020-7412 7379
*email* newspaper@bl.uk
*website* www.bl.uk/collections/newspapers

National archive collections in the UK of British and overseas newspapers, made available in hard copy, in microform, and on CD-Rom in the Newspaper Reading Rooms. Online catalogue.

## The British Library Sound Archive

The Recorded Sound Information Service, The British Library Sound Archive, 96 Euston Road, London NW1 2DB
*tel* 020-7412 7440  *fax* 020-7412 7441
*email* sound-archive@bl.uk
*website* www.bl.uk/collections/sound-archive

The collections come from all over the world and cover the entire range of recorded sound from music, drama and literature to oral history and wildlife sounds. Its online catalogue includes entries for almost 2.5 million recordings.

## Buckinghamshire County Reference Library

Walton Street, Aylesbury, Bucks. HP20 1UU
*tel* (01296) 383252  *fax* (01296) 382405
*email* countyreflib@buckscc.gov.uk
*website* www.buckscc.gov.uk/libraries

## Camberwell College of Arts Library

Peckham Road, London SE5 8UF
*tel* 020-7514 6349
*website* www.linst.ac.uk/library

Art history, ceramics, conservation, film, fine art, graphics, illustration, metalwork, photography, posters, printmaking, silversmithing and textiles.

## Cambridge University Library

West Road, Cambridge CB3 9DR
*tel* (01223) 333000 *fax* (01223) 333160
*email* library@lib.cam.ac.uk
*website* www.lib.cam.ac.uk

Collections are housed in the University Library and its 4 dependent libraries. It is also a legal deposit library.

## Cardiff Central Library

St David's Link, Frederick Street, Cardiff CF10 2DU
*tel* 029-2038 2116
*website* www.cardiff.gov.uk

The largest public library in Wales.

## Catholic Central Library

Lancing Street, London NW1 1ND
*tel* 020-7383 4333  *fax* 020-7388 6675
*email* librarian@catholic-library.org.uk
*website* www.catholic-library.org.uk

Holds 65,000 books and periodicals on theology, spirituality and related subjects, biography and history.

## Central St Martins College of Art & Design Library

Southampton Row, London WC1B 4AP
*tel* 020-7514 7037
*website* www.linst.ac.uk/library

## Chelsea College of Art & Design Library

Manresa Road, London SW3 6LS
*tel* 020-7514 7773
*website* www.linst.ac.uk/library

Modern and contemporary art (including women's art), Afro–American art, Afro–Carribean British art and Asian British art.

## City Business Library

1 Brewers' Hall Garden, off Aldermanbury Square, London EC2
*tel* 020-7332 1812

*website* www.cityofLondon.gov.uk/leisure_heritage/
One of the leading business information sources in
the UK.

## City of London Libraries – see City
Business Library, Guildhall Library, St Bride
Printing Library and Barbican Library

## Civil Aviation Authority Library and Information Centre (CAA)
Aviation House, Gatwick Airport South,
West Sussex RH6 0YR
*tel* (01293) 573725  *fax* (01293) 573181
*email* library-enquiries@srg.caa.co.uk
*website* www.caa.co.uk

Holds books, reports, directories, statistics, videos
and periodicals on most aspects of civil aviation
and related subjects.

## College of Psychic Studies Library
16 Queensberry Place, London SW7 2EB
*tel* 020-7589 3293
*website* www.psychic-studies.org.uk

## The Library of the Commonwealth Secretariat
Commonwealth Secretariat, Marlborough House,
Pall Mall, London SW1Y 5HX
*tel* 020-7747 6164  *fax* 020-7747 6168
*email* d.blake@commonwealth.int
*Librarian* David Blake

Collection covers politics and international
relations, economics, education, health, gender,
environment, science and technology, and
management.

## Cornwall Library Service
Reference and Information Library, Union Place,
Truro, Cornwall TR1 1EP
*tel* (01872) 272702, 0800 0322345 (Enquiry Express
Freephone)  *fax* (01872) 223772
*email* reference.library@cornwall.gov.uk,
enquiryexpress@cornwall.gov.uk
*website* www.db.cornwall.gov.uk/library

## Crafts Council Reference Library
The Crafts Council, 44A Pentonville Road,
London N1 9BY
*tel* 020-7278 7700  *fax* 020-7837 6891
*website* www.craftscouncil.org.uk

Holds over 3000 texts on various aspects of
contemporary crafts, together with current craft
magazines and periodicals from 18 countries. It is
also a resource which can be used for research into
specific crafts and to provide information on
specific UK craftspeople.

## Cranfield Information and Library Service
Cranfield University, Cranfield, Beds. MK43 0AL
*tel* (01234) 754444  *fax* (01234) 752391
*website* www.cranfield.ac.uk/cils/library

## Croydon Central Library
Croydon Clocktower, Katharine Street,
Croydon CR9 1ET
*tel* 020-8760 5400  *fax* 020-8253 1004
*email* controldesk@croydononline.org
*website* www.croydon.gov.uk/ledept/libraries

## Dartington College of Arts
Library & Learning Resources Centre (LLRC),
Dartington College of Arts, Totnes, Devon TQ9 6EJ
*tel* (01803) 862224  *fax* (01803) 861666
*email* registry@dartington.ac.uk
*website* www.dartington.ac.uk

Holds over 80,000 books, videos, CDs and sheet
music items reflecting the interests of the College.
Subscribes to over 150 journals and provides access
to a wide range of electronic information resources.

## Derby Central Library
The Wardwick, Derby DE1 1HS
*tel* (01332) 255398  *fax* (01332) 369570
*email* central.library@derby.gov.uk
*website* www.visitderby.com/libraries

## Douglas Public Library
10 Victoria Street, Douglas, Isle of Man
*tel* (01624)696453  *fax* (01624) 696400
*email* jbowring@douglas.org.im
*Librarian* John Bowring

## Durham University Library
Stockton Road, Durham DH1 3LY
*tel* 0191-3743018  *fax* 0191-3747481
*website* www.dur.ac.uk/library

## Edinburgh University Library
30–38 George Square, Edinburgh EH8 9LJ
*tel* 0131-650 3384, 0131-650 3374 (reference &
information services)  *fax* 0131-667 9780
*email* library@ed.ac.uk
*website* www.lib.ed.ac.uk

## University of Exeter Library
Stocker Road, Exeter EX4 4PT
*tel* (01392) 263869 *fax* (01392) 263871
*email* library@exeter.ac.uk
*website* www.ex.ac.uk/library

The website lists sites on the internet which are
especially useful resources maintained by libraries,
museums and centres of research, as well as
publishers.

## Foreign and Commonwealth Office Library
King Charles Street, London SW1A 2AH
*tel* 020-7008 1500
*website* www.fco.gov.uk

## University of Glasgow Library
Hillhead Street, Glasgow G12 8QE
*tel* 0141-330 6704  *fax* 0141-330 4952
*email* library@lib.gla.ac.uk
*website* www.lib.gla.ac.uk

## Glasgow Women's Library
109 Trongate, Glasgow G1 5HD
*tel* 0141-552 8345
*email* gwl@womens-library.org.uk
*website* www.womens-library.org.uk

Reference and lending library of information for and about women.

## Goethe-Institut London Library
50 Princes Gate, Exhibition Road, London SW7 2PH
*tel* 020-7596 4044  *fax* 020-7594 0230
*email* infoservice@london.goethe.org
*website* www.goethe.de

Specialises in German literature and books/audiovisual material on German culture and history.

## Guildhall Library
Aldermanbury, London EC2
*tel* 020-7332 1868/1870 (printed books), 020-7332 1862 (manuscripts), 020-7332 1839 (Print & Map Room)  *fax* 020-7600 3384
*email* manuscripts.guildhall@corpoflondon.gov.uk, print&maps@corpoflondon.gov.uk
*website* www.cityoflondon.gov.uk

Specialises in the history of London, especially the City, as well as holding other significant collections.

## High Wycombe Reference and Business Library
Queen Victoria Road, High Wycombe, Bucks. HP11 1BD
*tel* (01494) 510241  *fax* (01494) 533086
*email* lib-hiwref@buckscc.gov.uk
*website* www.buckscc.gov.uk/libraries

## Jersey Library
Place St Helier, Jersey JE2 4WH, Channel Islands
*tel* (01534) 759992  *fax* (01534) 769444
*email* library@jsylib.gov.je
*website* www.jsylib.gov.je

## Lambeth Palace Library
London SE1 7JU
*tel* 020-7898 1400  *fax* 020-7928 7932
*website* www.lambethpalacelibrary.org

The historic library of the archbishops of Canterbury and the principal library and record office for the Church of England.

## Leeds Central Library
Calverley Street, Leeds LS1 3AB
*tel* 0113-247 8274  *fax* 0113-247 8271
*website* www.leeds.gov.uk

Central lending library. The Art Library has approx. 25,000 books available for loan covering art and design, architecture, sculpture, ceramics, costumes, fashion and photography and another 20,000 items for use in the library.

## Leeds University Library
Leeds LS2 9JT
*tel* 0113-233 6388, 0113-233 5501  *fax* 0113-233 5561
*email* library@library.novell.leeds.ac.uk
*website* www.leeds.ac.uk/library

## University of Leicester Library
University Road, Leicester LE1 9QD
*Mailing address* PO Box 248, Leicester LE1 9QD
*tel* 0116-252 2043  *fax* 0116-252 2066
*email* libdesk@le.ac.uk
*website* www.le.ac.uk

## Leicester Reference and Information Library
Bishop Street, Leicester LE1 6AA
*tel* 0116-299 5401  *fax* 0116-299 5444
*email* central.reference@leicester.gov.uk
*website* www.leicester.gov.uk

## The Linen Hall Library
17 Donegall Square North, Belfast BT1 5GB
*tel* 028-9032 1707  *fax* 028-9043 8586
*email* info@linenhall.com
*website* www.linenhall.com
*Irish and Local Studies Librarian* Gerry Healey, *NIPC Librarian* Yvonne Murphy

Subscription library renowned for its Irish and Local Studies Collection, ranging from early Belfast and Ulster printed books to the 250,000 items in the Northern Ireland Political Collection (NIPC), with bestsellers and classics in the General Lending Collection.

## Liverpool Central Library
William Brown Street, Liverpool L3 8EW
*tel* 0151-233 5835  *fax* 0151-233 5886
*email* refbt.central.library@liverpool.gov.uk
*website* www.liverpool.gov.uk

## London College of Fashion Library
20 John Princes Street, London W1G 0BJ
*tel* 020-7514 7453, 020-7514 7455
*website* www.linst.ac.uk/library

## London College of Printing Libraries
Elephant & Castle, London SE1 6SB
*tel* 020-7514 6527
Back Hill, London EC1R 5LQ
*tel* 020-7514 6882
*website* www.linst.ac.uk/library

## London Institute Libraries – see
Camberwell College of Arts Library, Central St
Martins College of Art & Design, Chelsea College
of Art & Design Library, London College of
Fashion Library and London College of Printing
Libraries

## The London Library
14 St James's Square, London SW1Y 4LG
*tel* 020-7930 7705 *fax* 020-7766 4766
*email* membership@londonlibrary.co.uk
*website* www.londonlibrary.co.uk

Subscription lending library holding about a
million books in all European languages and a
subject range across the humanities, with particular
emphasis on literature, history and related subjects.

## University of London Library
Senate House, Malet Street, London WC1E 7HU
*tel* 020-7862 8500
*email* enquiries@ull.ac.uk
*website* www.ull.ac.uk

One of the major academic libraries of the UK.

## Library of the London School of Economics and Political Science
10 Portugal Street, London WC2A 2HD
*tel* 020-7955 7229 *fax* 020-7955 7454
*website* www.lse.ac.uk/library

## Manchester Central Library
St Peter's Square, Manchester M2 5PD
*tel* 0161-234 1900 *fax* 0161-234 1963
*email* mclib@libraries.manchester.gov.uk
*website* www.manchester.gov.uk/libraries

## The Mitchell Library
North Street, Glasgow G3 7DN
*tel* 0141-287 2999 *fax* 0141-287 2915
*website* www.glasgowlibraries.org/mitchell.html

One of Europe's largest public reference libraries
with almost 2 million volumes. Holds an unrivalled
collection of material relating to the City of
Glasgow.

## National Art Library
Victoria and Albert Museum, South Kensington,
London SW7 2RL
*website* www.nal.vam.ac.uk

A major reference library and the Victoria and
Albert Museum's curatorial department for the art,
craft and design of the book.

## National Library for the Blind (NLB)
Far Cromwell Road, Bredbury, Stockport SK6 2SG
*tel* 0161-355 2000 *minicom* 0161-355 2043
*fax* 0161-355 2098
*email* enquiries@nlbuk.org
*website* www.nlb-online.org

The website provides a gateway to library and
information services for visually impaired people.

## National Library of Ireland
Kildare Street, Dublin 2
*tel* (353) 1 603 02 00 *fax* (353) 1 676 66 90
*email* info@nli.ie
*website* www.nli.ie

The world's largest collection of Irish documentary
material.

## The National Library of Scotland
George IV Bridge, Edinburgh EH1 1EW
*tel* 0131-226 4531 (switchboard), 0131-466 2812
(manuscripts and archives enquiries),
0131-446 2806 (Rare Books Collections)
*fax* 0131-622 4803
*email* enquiries@scotbis.com (Scottish Business
Information Service), manuscripts@nls.uk
(manuscripts and archives enquiries),
rarebooks@nls.uk (Rare Books Collections)
*website* www.nls.uk

A legal deposit library and Scotland's largest library.

## The National Library of Wales
Aberystwyth, Ceredigion SY23 3BU
*tel* (01970) 632800 *fax* (01970) 615709
*email* holi@llgc.org.uk
*website* www.llgc.org.uk

A legal deposit library. Holds large collection of
works about Wales and other Celtic countries,
including manuscripts and archives.

## Natural History Museum Library and Information Services
Cromwell Road, London SW7 5BD
*tel* 020-7942 5507/5873 (archives), 020-7942 5685
(Botany Library), 020-7942 5476 (Earth Sciences
Library), 020-7942 5751 (Entomology Library),
020-7942 5460 (General Library and Zoology
Library), 020-7942 6156 (Ornithology Library)

Online catalogue contains all library material
acquired since 1989 and about 80% of earlier items.
The collections are of international importance
with extensive holdings of early works, periodicals
and current literature, including over 800,000
books, 20,000 periodical titles (about half of them

current) and original watercolour drawings, as well as maps, manuscripts and archives of the Museum.

### Newcastle upon Tyne City Library
Princess Square, Newcastle upon Tyne NE99 1DX
*tel* 0191-2774100 *fax* 0191-2774107
*website* www.newcastle.gov.uk

### Norfolk and Norwich Millennium Library
The Forum, Millennium Plain, Norwich NR2 1AW
*tel* (01603) 774774 *fax* (01603) 774775
*email* millennium.lib@norfolk.gov.uk
*website* www.nwia.tagish.co.uk

### The Northern Poetry Library – see
page 306

### Nottingham Central Library
Angel Row, Nottingham NG1 6HP
*tel* 0115-915 2828 *fax* 0115-915 2850
*email* business.library@nottinghamcity.gov.uk
*website* www.nottinghamcity.gov.uk

### Open Library
*website* www.library.open.ac.uk

The Open University's electronic library service.

### School of Oriental & African Studies Library (SOAS)
University of London, Thornhough Street,
Russell Square, London WC1H 0XG
*tel* 020-7323 6109 *fax* 020-7636 2834
*email* kw@soas.ac.uk
*website* www.soas.ac.uk

### Oxford Central Library
Westgate, Oxford OX1 1DJ
*tel* (01865) 815509 (general enquiries), (01865)
815549 (information desk), (01865) 815373
(children's library), (01865) 815388 (music library),
(01865) 815409 (periodicals room), (01865) 810182
(Business Information Point) *fax* (01865) 721694
*website* www.oxfordshire.gov.uk

### PA News Library
292 Vauxhall Bridge Road, London SW1V 1AE
*Northern Headquarters* Bridgegate, Howden, East
Yorkshire DN14 7AE
*tel* 020-7963 7000
*email* information@pa.press.net
*website* www.pa.press.net

Holds a bank of more than 14 million cuttings
which span events, sports, people and topics from
the start of the 19th century to the present day.

### The Poetry Library – see page 306

### The Portico
57 Mosley Street, Manchester M2 8HY
*tel* 0161-236 6785
*website* www.theportico.org.uk

Subscription library which stocks mainly 19th
century literature.

### University of Reading Library
Whiteknights, PO Box 223, Reading RG6 6AE
*tel* 0118-9318770 *fax* 0118-9316636
*email* library@reading.ac.uk
*website* www.library.rdg.ac.uk

### John Rylands University Library of Manchester
Oxford Road, Manchester M13 9PP
*tel* 0161-275 3738 *fax* 0161-273 7488

### St Albans Central Library
The Maltings, St Albans, Herts. AL1 3JQ
*tel* (01438) 737333 (enquiries)
*minicom* (01438) 737599
*website* www.hertsdirect.org/infoadvice/libraries

### St Bride Printing Library
Bride Lane, London EC4
*tel* 020-7353 4660 *textphone* 020-7332 3803
*fax* 020-7583 7073
*email* stbride@corpoflondon.gov.uk
*website* www.cityofLondon.gov.uk

Collections cover printing and allied subjects
including paper and binding, graphic design and
typography, typefaces and calligraphy, illustration
and printmaking, publishing and bookselling, and
the social and economic aspects of the printing,
book, newspaper and magazine trades generally.

### Salisbury Library
Market Place, Salisbury, Wilts. SP1 1BL
*tel* (01722) 324145
*website* www.wiltshire.gov.uk/lib

### Science Museum Library
Imperial College Road, London SW7 5NH
*tel* 020-7942 4242 *fax* 020-7942 4243
*email* smlinfo@nmsi.ac.uk
*website* www.sciencemuseum.org.uk/library

In recent years the Library has specialised in the
history of science and technology as its key role as
part of the National Museum of Science & Industry.

### The Scottish Poetry Library – see
page 306

### Sheffield Central Library
Surrey Street, Sheffield S1 1XZ
*tel* 0114-273 4761 *fax* 0114-273 4712
*website* www.sheffield.gov.uk

## University of Southampton Libraries

University Road, Highfield, Southampton SO17 1BJ
*tel* (01703) 592180 *fax* (01703) 593007
*website* www.library.soton.ac.uk

## The Society for Storytelling Library

PO Box 2344, Reading, Berks. RG6 7FG
*tel* 0118-935 1381
*email* sfs@fairbruk.demon.co.uk
*websites* www.sfs.org.uk,
www.mythstories.com/sfslibrary.html

Storybooks and folklore; also a collection of taped reminiscences, archive tellings and performances.

## The Tate Library

Millbank, London SW1P 4RG
*tel* 020-7887 8725 *fax* 020-7887 8729
*website* www.tate.org.uk/researchservices/
researchcentre/library.htm

Broadly covers those areas in which the Tate collects: British art from the Renaissance to the present day and international modern art.

## Trinity College Library

Cambridge CB2 1TQ
*tel* (01223) 338488 *fax* (01223) 338532
*website* www.rabbit.trin.cam.ac.uk/

## United Nations Reference Library

United Nations Information Centre, Millbank
Tower (21st Floor), 21–24 Millbank,
London SW1P 4QH
*tel* 020-7630 2703 *fax* 020-7976 6478
*email* library@uniclondon.org
*website* www.unitednations.org.uk/info

## Wellcome Library for the History and Understanding of Medicine

183 Euston Road, London NW1 2BE
*History of Medicine enquiries*
*tel* 020-7611 8582 *fax* 020-7611 8369
*email* library@wellcome.ac.uk
*website* www.library.wellcome.ac.uk
*Information Service*
*tel* 020-7611 8722 *fax* 020-7611 8726
*email* infoserv@wellcome.ac.uk
*website* www.library.wellcome.ac.uk
*Medical Photographic Library*
*tel* 020-7611 8348 *fax* 020-7611 8577
*email* medphoto.info@wellcome.ac.uk
*website* www.medphoto.wellcome.ac.uk/mpl
*Medical Film & Audio Collections*
*tel* 020-7611 8596/7 *fax* 020-7611 8765
*email* mfac@wellcome.ac.uk
*websites* www.library.wellcome.ac.uk/collections/
visual_mfac.shtml, www.library.wellcome.ac.uk/
collections/ vis_mfac_cat.shtml

## Westminster Music Library

Victoria Library, 160 Buckingham Palace Road,
London SW1W 9UD
*tel* 020-7641 4287 (Victoria Library),
020-7641 4292 (Westminster Music Library)
*minicom* 020-7641 4879 *fax* 020-7641 4281,
*email* victorialibrary@westminster.gov.uk
musiclibrary@westminster.gov.uk
*website* www.westminster.gov.uk/libraries/victoria

Holds a wide range of scores, orchestral sets, books on music and the GLASS collection of Mozart sound recordings.

## Westminster Reference Library

35 St Martin's Street, London WC2H 7HP
*tel* 020-7641 4636 (general reference & performing arts), 020-7641 4634 (business, official publications & EU), 020-7641 4638 (arts)
*minicom* 020-7641 4879 *fax* 020-7641 4606
*email* referencelibrarywc2@westminster.gov.uk
*website* www.westminster.gov.uk/libraries/westref

## Winchester Reference Library

81 North Walls, Winchester, Hants. SO23 8BY
*tel* (01962) 826666 *fax* (01962) 856615
*email* winchester.reference@hants.gov.uk
*website* www.hants.gov.uk

## The Women's Library

Old Castle Street, London E1 7NT
*tel* 020-7320 2222 *fax* 020-7320 2333
*email* moreinfo@the womenslibrary.ac.uk
*website* www.thewomenslibrary.ac.uk

Houses the most extensive collection of women's history in the UK.

## Working Class Movement Library

51 The Crescent, Salford M5 4WX
*tel* 0161-736 3601
*email* enquiries@wcml.org.uk
*website* www.wcml.org.uk
*Librarian* Alain Kahan

A collection of books, periodicals, pamphlets, archives and artefacts concerned with the activities, expression and enquiries of the labour movement, its allies and its enemies, since the late 18th century.

## York Central Reference Library

Museum Street, York YO1 7DS
*tel* (01904) 552824, 552828 *fax* (01904) 611025
*email* reference.library@york.gov.uk
*website* www.york.gov.uk/libraries

## The Zoological Society of London Library

Regent's Park, London NW1 4RY
*tel* 020-7449 6293
*email* library@zsl.org
*website* www.zsl.org/core/library.html

# Creative writing courses

Anyone wishing to participate in a writing course should first satisfy themselves as to its content and quality. For day and evening courses consult your local Adult Education Centre. Details of postgraduate writing courses follow on page 638.

## Alston Hall Residential College for Adult Education

Alston Lane, Longridge, Preston PR3 3BP
*tel* (01772) 784661 *fax* (01772) 785835
*email* alston.hall@ed.lancscc.gov.uk
*website* www.alstonhall.com

## Annual Writers' Conference

Chinook, Southdown Road, Shawford, Winchester, Hants SO21 2BY
*tel* (01962) 712307
*email* Writerconf@aol.com
*website* www.gmp.co.uk/writers/conference
*Conference Director* Barbara Large MBS, FRSA
*Venue* King Alfred's College, Winchester – 24–26 June 2005. One-week workshops 27 June–1 July.

Mini courses and workshops, lectures, seminars, one-to-one appointments with agents and commissioning editors, Bookfair, 15 writing competitions; followed by one-week workshops June–4 July. Pitstop Refuelling Writers' Weekend Workshops planned for 18–20 March 2005 and 21–23 October 2005, and How to Self Publish Your Book day courses in May and October 2005.

## Arista

11 Wells Mews, London W1P 3FL
*tel* 020-7323 1775 *fax* 020-7323 1772
*website* www.aristotle.co.uk
*Contact* Stephanie Faugier

A 7-day story-editing workshop held 3 times a year at different locations throughout Europe. Producers and writers apply as a team with a project.

## The Arvon Foundation

Lumb Bank, Heptonstall, Hebden Bridge, West Yorkshire HX7 6DF
*tel* (01422) 843714 *fax* (01422) 843714
*email* l-bank@arvonfoundation.org
*website* www.arvonfoundation.org
*Contact* Ann Anderton
Moniack Mhor, Teavarran, Kiltarlity, Beauly, Inverness-shire IV4 7HT
*tel* (01463) 741675 *fax* (01463) 741733
*email* m-mhor@arvonfoundation.org
*Contact* Chris Aldridge
The Arvon Foundation, Totleigh Barton, Sheepwash, Beaworthy, Devon EX21 5NS
*tel* (01409) 231338 *fax* (01409) 231144

*email* t-barton@arvonfoundation.org
*Contact* Julia Wheadon
The Hurst – The John Osborne Arvon Centre
Clunton, Craven Arms, Shropshire SY7 0JA
*tel* (01588) 640658 *fax* (01588) 640509
*email* hurst@arvonfoundation.org

## Belstead House Education & Conference Centre (Residential Courses)

Belstead, Ipswich, Suffolk IP8 3NA
*tel* (01473) 686321 *fax* (01473) 686664
*email* belstead.house@educ.suffolkcc.gov.uk

## Birkbeck College, University of London

Malet Street, London WC1E 7HX
*tel* 020-7580 6622 *fax* 020-7631 6255
*email* imcdonagh@bbk.ac.uk
*website* www.bbk.ac.uk
*Contact* Dr Jo McDonagh

Part-time accredited evening courses.

## Burton Manor

Burton, Neston, Cheshire CH64 5SJ
*tel* 0151-336 5172 *fax* 0151-336 6586
*email* enquiry@burtonmanor.com
*website* www.burtonmanor.com
*Principal* Keith Chandler

## University of Cambridge

Board of Continuing Education,
University of Cambridge, Madingley Hall,
Madingley, Cambridge CB3 8AQ
*tel* (01954) 280399 *fax* (01954) 280200
*email* residential@cont-ed.cam.ac.uk
*website* www.cont-ed.cam.ac.uk
*Contact* The Registrar

Accredited creative writing courses. Also one-week residential course: the Writer's Craft.

## Castle of Park

Cornhill, Aberdeenshire AB45 2AX
*tel* (01466) 751111 *fax* (01466) 751111
*email* booking@castleofpark.net
*website* www.castleofpark.net
*Proprietors* Bill and Lois Breckon

## Centerprise Literature Development Project

136 Kingsland High Street, London E8 2NS

tel 020-7249 6572 *fax* 020-7923 1951
*email* literature@centerprisetrust.org.uk
See also page 513.

## Central St Martins College of Art & Design

Southampton Row, London WC1B 4AP
tel 020-7514 7000  *fax* 020-7514 7024
*website* www.csm.linst.ac.uk
*Contact* Sean Geoghegan

Five-day (Saturday) course in screenwriting for
screenwriters with a basic foundation in
scriptwriting technique.

## Creative in Calvados

1 Ormelie Terrace, Joppa, Edinburgh EH15 2EX
tel 0131-669 4025
*email* steveharvey@creativeincalvados.co.uk
*website* www.creativeincalvados.co.uk
*Contact* Stephen Harvey

Midweek and long weekend courses in poetry,
songwriting/music, scriptwriting, drama and prose.
Courses take place in Normandy. Founded 2001.

## Dingle Writing Courses Ltd

Ballintlea, Ventry, Tralee, Co Kerry,
Republic of Ireland
tel 66 9159118 *fax* 66 9159118
*email* info@dinglewriting.com
*website* www.dinglewriting.com
*Directors* Abigail Joffe, Nicholas McLachlan

## The Earnley Concourse

Earnley Trust Ltd, Earnley, Chichester,
West Sussex PO20 7JL
tel (01243) 670392 *fax* (01243) 670832
*email* info@earnley.co.uk
*website* www.earnley.co.uk

## Emerson College

Emerson College, Forest Row, East Sussex RH18 5JX
tel (01342) 822238  *fax* (01342) 826055
*email* mail@emerson.co.uk
*website* www.emerson.org.uk
*Contact* Paul Matthews
*Takes place* August

*Poetry OtherWise*: a week of writing workshops,
readings by established poets, space for paticipants
to share their poetry, together with music, dancing,
conversation, talks and social events.

## University of Essex

Wivenhoe Park, Colchester CO4 3SQ
tel (01206) 872400
*email* proffice@essex.ac.uk
*website* www.essex.ac.uk/writingspace
*Contact* Public Relations Office

*Writingspace 2004* is a 4-day summer school to
write, learn new methods and be inspired by
experienced tutors and successful writers.

## Essex Literature Development

Cultural Services, Essex County Council,
PO Box 47, Chelmsford CM2 6WN
tel (01245) 436156 *fax* (01245) 436841
*email* kaveri.woodward@essexcc.gov.uk
*website* www.essexlivelit.org.uk
*Contact* Kaveri Woodward

One-day seminars covering fiction genres, writing
for children, biography, non-fiction, poetry,
scriptwriting and editing. Writers will include
Michael Holroyd, Martina Cole, Peter Forbes, Brian
Keaney and Julia Bell.

## University of Exeter, Department of Lifelong Learning

St Luke's Campus, Heavitree Road, Exeter EX1 2LU
tel (01392) 262828 *fax* (01392) 262829
*website* www.ex.ac.uk/dll

Offers distance learning and online creative writing
courses.

## Far West

23 Chapel Street, Penzance, Cornwall TR18 4AP
tel (01736) 363146
*email* farwest@waitrose.com
*website* www.writing-courses-cornwall.com
*Contact* Angela Stoner

## Federation of Worker Writers and Community Publishers Festival of Writing – see page 576

## The Indian King

Camelford, Cornwall PL32 9TP
*email* indianking@btconnect.com
*website* www.indianking.co.uk

Creative writing workshops all year.

## Irish Writers Centre

19 Parnell Square, Dublin 1
tel (01) 8721302 *fax* (01) 8726282
*email* info@writerscentre.ie
*website* www.writerscentre.ie

Runs an educational programme which offers
courses and workshops in writing.

## Knuston Hall

Irchester, Wellingborough, Northants. NN29 7EU
tel (01933) 312104 *fax* (01933) 357596
*email* enquiries@knustonhall.org.uk
*website* www.knustonhall.org.uk
*Contact* Daphne Brittin

## Lancaster University

Dept of Continuing Education, Lonsdale College,
Lancaster University LA1 4YN
*tel* (01524) 592623/4 *fax* (01524) 592448
*email* Conted@lancaster.ac.uk
*website* www.lancs.ac.uk/users/conted/index.htm

## University of Leeds

Springfield Mount, Leeds LS2 9JT
*tel* 0113-233 4732  *fax* 0113-233 4774
*email* chair@english.novell.leeds.ac.uk,
r.b.watson@leeds.ac.uk
*website* www.leeds.ac.uk
*Contact* Prof J. Hill or Rob Watson

Writing Drama: a part-time Continuing Education
course aimed at new or more experienced writers
who want to produce scripts for stage, radio and
screen.

## Liberato

9 Bishop's Avenue, Bishop's Stortford,
Herts. CM23 3EJ
*tel* (01279) 833690  *fax* (01279) 505513
*email* liberato@tesco.net
*website* www.liberato.co.uk
*Contact* Maureen Blundell, Tutor

## Marlborough College Summer School

Marlborough, Wilts. SN8 1PA
*tel* (01672) 892388 *fax* (01672 892476
*email* admin@mcsummerschool.org.uk
*website* www.mcsummerschool.org.uk
*Contact* Tracey Borthwick

A 3-week summer school where participants can
attend for 1, 2 or 3 weeks. There are a large variety
of courses, including creative writing, covering
many subjects with each course lasting half a day.

## Middlesex University Summer School

Summer School Office, Middlesex University,
Trent Park, Bramley Road, London N14 4YZ
*tel* 020-8411 5782
*email* a.mascarenhas@mdx.ac.uk
*Contact* Anita Mascarenhas

## Missenden Abbey

Great Missenden, Bucks HP16 0BD
*tel* (08450) 454040 *fax* (01753) 783756
*email* adultlearning@buckscc.gov.uk
*website* www.aredu.org.uk/missendenabbey

## Morley College

61 Westminster Bridge, London SE1 7HT
*tel* 020-7928 8501  *fax* 020-7928 8501
*email* enquiries@morleycollege.ac.uk
*website* www.morleycollege.ac.uk

Offers a number of one-day creative writing
courses.

## The National Academy of Writing

University of Central England, Margaret Street,
Birmingham B3 3BX
*tel* 0121-331 5963
*email* info@naw-uk.org, martin.eggleston@uce.ac.uk
*website* www.writingacademy.org
*Hon. President* Lord Bragg of Wigton, *Development
Manager* Martin Eggleston

A dedicated writing school set up by internationally
renowned writers offering a one-year full-time
vocational course. Teaching is by individual
tutorials and in small groups led by established
writers.

## University of Newcastle upon Tyne

School of English, Percy Building,
Newcastle upon Tyne NE1 7RU
*tel* 0191-222 7619 *fax* 0191-222 8708
*email* melanie.birch@ncl.ac.uk
*website* www.ncl.ac.uk/elll/cpd
*Contact* Melanie Birch

A number of 6-week courses in creative writing.

## North West Kent College

Oakfield Lane, Dartford DA1 2JT
*tel* (01322) 629400 *fax* (01322) 629468
*website* www.nwkent.ac.uk
*Contact* Neil Nixon, Pathway Leader, Professional
Writing

Offers full-time, part-time and one-off courses in
professional writing.

## University of Nottingham Study Tours

Centre for Continuing Education, University of
Nottingham, Jubilee Campus, Wollaton Road,
Nottingham NG8 1BB
*tel* 0115-951 6526 *fax* 0115-951 6556
*email* ce-studytours@nottingham.ac.uk
*Manager* Helen Frost

## Open Studies – Part-time Courses for Adults: Office of Lifelong Learning

University of Edinburgh, 11 Buccleuch Place,
Edinburgh EH8 9LW
*tel* 0131-650 4400 *fax* 0131-667 6097
*email* oll@ed.ac.uk
*website* www.lifelong.ed.ac.uk

## Oxford University Summer Schools for Adults

The Oxford Experience, Department for
Continuing Education, Oxford University, Rewley
House, 1 Wellington Square, Oxford OX1 2JA
*tel* (01865) 270396 *fax* (01865) 280761
*email* oussa@conted.ox.ac.uk
*website* www.conted.ox.ac.uk/oussa
*Contact* Programme Secretary

A 4-week summer school with a variety of courses on offer, including creative writing. Studends choose one course and follow it for a week.

## Scottish Universities International Summer School
21 Buccleuch Place, Edinburgh EH8 9LN
*tel* 0131-650 4369 *fax* 0161-662 0275
*email* suiss@ed.ac.uk
*website* www.arts.ed.ac.uk/suiss
*Directors* Dr Ance Ferrebe, Kathryn Napier Gray

A 3-week creative writing course for undergraduates, postgraduates and teachers, as well as published writers keen to widen their skills.

## South and Mid Wales Association of Writers
c/o IMC Consulting Group, Denham House, Lambourne Crescent, Cardiff CF14 5ZW
*tel* 029-2076 1170 *fax* 029-2076 1304
*Contact* Julian Rosser

## Southern Writers' Conference
Stable House, Home Farm, Coldharbour Lane, Dorking, Surrey RH4 3JG
*Contact* Lucia White
*Venue* The Earnley Concourse, Chichester

Caters for published and serious writers.

## Summer Academy, Keynes College
The University, Canterbury, Kent CT2 7NP
*tel* (01227) 470402/823473 *fax* (01227) 784338
*email* summeracademy@ukc.ac.uk
*website* www.ukc.ac.uk/sa/index.html
*Contact* Andrea McDonnell

## Surrey University
School of Educational Studies, University of Surrey, Guildford GU2 7XH
*tel* (01483) 300800 *fax* (01483) 300803
*email* edx029@surrey.ac.uk
*Contact* Averil Heaton, Marketing Assistant

Offers a summer programme of short courses, including creative writing.

## Swanwick, The Writers' Summer School
*Contact* Jean Sutton, The Secretary, 10 Stag Road, Lake, Sandown, Isle of Wight PO36 8PE
*website* www.wss.org.uk

## Tamar Writing Workshops
Roselle Angwin Retreats, PO Box 17, Yelverton, Devon PL20 6YF
*tel* (01822) 841081
*email* roselle.angwin@internet-today.co.uk
*website* www.roselleangwin.internet-today.co.uk
*Contact* Roselle Angwin

## Ty Newydd
Ty Newydd, National Creative Writing Centre of Wales, Llanystumdwy, Cricieth, Gwynedd LL52 0LW
*tel* (01766) 522811 *fax* (01766) 523095
*email* post@tynewydd.org
*website* www.tynewydd.org

## Urchfont Manor College
Urchfont, Devizes, Wilts. SN10 4RG
*tel* (01380) 840495 *fax* (01380) 840005
*email* urchfont@wccyouth.org.uk

## Wedgwood Memorial College
Station Road, Barlaston, Stoke-on-Trent ST12 9DG
*tel* (01782) 372105/373427 *fax* (01782) 372393

## Write Away
Arts Council England (East Midlands Arts), Mountfields House, Epinal Way, Loughborough, Leics. LE11 0QE
*tel* (01509) 218292 *fax* (01509) 262214
*email* info@em-arts.co.uk
*website* www.arts.org.uk/director/regions/east_mid/
*Contact* Assistant to Literature Officer

A short programme providing a different range of weekend courses annually, currently held at Leicester University.

## Writers' Holiday at Caerleon
School Bungalow, Church Road, Pontnewydd, Cwmbran, South Wales NP44 1AT
*tel* (01633) 489438 *fax* (01633) 489438
*email* writersholiday@lineone.net
*website* www.writersholiday.net
*Contact* Anne Hobbs

A 6-day annual conference for writers of all standards from absolute beginner to bestselling author. The event includes 12 courses.

## Wye Valley Arts Centre
The Coach House, Mork, St Briavel's, Lydney, Glos. GL15 6QH
*tel* (01594) 530214, (01291) 689463
*fax* (01594) 530321
*email* wyeart@cwcom.net
*website* www.wyeart.cwc.net

Offers a creative writing course with the focus on switching off the critic within and accessing the intuitive and imaginative side of the brain. Activities improve suppleness of style and help to identify and clarify the personal writing voice.

## Postgraduate courses

### Bath Spa University College
School of English and Creative Studies, Bath Spa
Universtiy College, Newton Park, Newton St Loe,
Bath BA2 9BN
*tel* (01225) 873701  *fax* (01225) 874123
*website* www.bathspa.ac.uk
MA in Creative Writing.

### Bolton Institute
Faculty of Arts, Science and Education, Bolton
Institute, Chadwick Street, Bolton BL2 1JW
*tel* (01204) 528851  *fax* (01204) 399074
*email* S.J.Johnson@bolton.ac.uk
*website* www.bolton.ac.uk
*Contact* Sam Johnson, Head of English
MA in Creative Writing.

### University of Bristol
Department of English, University of Bristol,
3–5 Woodland Road, Bristol BS8 1TB
*tel* 0117-928 8924  *fax* 0117-925 1424
*email* rowena.fowler@bristol.ac.uk
*website* www.bris.ac.uk
*Contact* Dr Rowena Fowler, Course Director
MA in Modern & Contemporary Poetry.

### Brunel University
English Department, Brunel University, Uxbridge,
Middlesex UB8 3PH
*tel* (01895) 274000  *fax* (01895) 232806
*email* Rose.Atfield@brunel.ac.uk
*website* www.brunel.ac.uk/faculty/arts/english
*Contact* Dr J.R. Atfield, Course Leader
MA in Creative/Transactional Writing.

### Cardiff University
Creative Writing, PO Box 94, Cardiff University,
Cardiff CF10 3XB
*tel* 029-2087 4241  *fax* 029-2087 4647
*email* creativewriting@cardiff.ac.uk
*website* www.cf.ac.uk/encap/creativewriting
MA in the Teaching and Practice of Creative
Writing, MPhil in Creative Writing, and PhD in
Creative and Critical Writing.

### Central School of Speech and Drama
Central School of Speech and Drama, Embassy
Theatre, Eton Avenue, London NW3 3HY
*tel* 020-7722 8183
*website* www.cssd.ac.uk
MA in Advanced Theatre Practice: Playwriting.

### University College Chichester
Chichester Institute of Higher Education,
Bishop Otter Campus, College Lane, Chichester,
West Sussex PO19 4PE
*tel* (01243) 816184  *fax* (01243) 816080
*email* marketing@ucc.ac.uk
*website* www.ucc.ac.uk
*Contact* Dr Duncan Salkeld, Research Coordinator;
Stephanie Northgate, MA in Creative Writing
Coordinator
MA/Postgraduate Diploma/Postgraduate Certificate
in Creative Writing.

### City College Manchester
Arden School of Theatre, City College Manchester,
Sale Road, Manchester M23 0DD
*tel* 0161-957 1712  *fax* 0161-957 1715
*email* ast@ccm.ac.uk
*website* www.ccm.ac.uk/ast
*Contact* The Course Coordinator
Postgraduate Diploma in Writing for the Stage.

### City University
Department of Journalism, City University,
Northampton Square, London EC1V 0HB
*tel* 020-7040 8221  *fax* 020-7040 8594
*email* journalism@city.ac.uk
*website* www.city.ac.uk
*Contact* The Course Officer (Creative Writing)
MA in Creative Writing (Plays and Scripts) and MA
in Creative Writing (Novels).

### Dartington College of Arts
Dartington College of Arts, Totnes, Devon TQ9 6EJ
*tel* (01803) 861620  *fax* (01803) 861666
*email* registry@dartington.ac.uk
*website* www.dartington.ac.uk
*Contact* The Registry
MA in Performance Writing.

### De Montfort University
Department of Media and Cultural Production,
De Montfort University, City Campus,
The Gateway, Leicester LE1 9BH
*tel* 0116-255 1551/0116-250 6179  *fax* 0116-255 0307
*email* murphy@dmu.ac.uk
*website* www.dmu.ac.uk
*Contact* Robert Murphy
MA in Television Screenwriting.

### University of Derby
University of Derby, Kedleston Road,
Derby DE22 1GB
*tel* (01332) 622222  *fax* (01332) 294861
*email* C.Tighe@derby.ac.uk
*website* www.derby.ac.uk
*Contact* Carl Tighe, Subject Leader, Creative Writing
MA in Narrative Writing.

### University of East Anglia
School of English and American Studies,
University of East Anglia, Norwich NR4 7TJ

tel (01603) 593820 fax (01603) 593799
email www.uea.ac.uk/eas/
Contact The Graduate Admissions Secretary
MA in Creative Writing and MA in Life Writing.

## Edge Hill University College

Edge Hill University College, St Helens Road,
Ormskirk L39 4QP
tel (01695) 584274 fax (01695) 579997
email sheppardr@edgehill.ac.uk
website www.ehche.ac.uk
Contact Dr Robert Sheppard, Head of Department
MA in Writing Studies.

## University of Edinburgh

Department of English Literature, University of
Edinburgh, David Hume Tower, George Square,
Edinburgh EH8 9JX
tel 0131-650 3612 fax 0131-650 6898
website www.ed.ac.uk/englit/
Contact The Graduate Secretary
MSc in Creative Writing.

## University of Exeter, Theatre Practice

University of Exeter, Theatre Practice, Northcote
House, The Queens Drive, Exeter EX4 4QJ
tel (01392) 264580 fax (01392) 264594
email PZarrilli@exeter.ac.uk
website www.exeter.ac.uk
Contact Phillip Zarrilli
MA in Theatre Practice: playwriting for stage and
radio, performance writing.

## Falmouth School of Arts

Falmouth School of Arts, Wood Lane, Falmouth,
Cornwall TR11 4RA
tel (01326) 211077
email admissions@falmouth.ac.uk
website www.falmouth.ac.uk/showpage.asp?
W=747&H=434
Contact Admissions Office
Postgraduate Diploma in Professional Writing.

## University of Glamorgan

School of Humanities and Social Sciences,
University of Glamorgan, Treforest,
Pontypridd CF37 1DL
tel (01443) 482570 fax (01443) 482138
email tcurtis@glam.ac.uk
website www.glam.ac.uk
Contact Prof Tony Curtis, Director of Studies
MA in Scriptwriting and M.Phil in Writing.

## University of Glasgow

Department of English Literature, University of
Glasgow, 12 University Gardens, Glasgow G12 8QQ
tel 0141-339 8855 ext. 4165 fax 0141-330 4601
website www.arts.gla.ac.uk/EngLang

Contact Head of Department
M.Litt in Creative Writing.

## University of Greenwich

School of Humanities, University of Greenwich,
Bexley Road, London SE9 2PQ
tel/fax 020-8331 8800
email J.Longmore@greenwich.ac.uk
website www.greenwich.ac.uk
Contact Jane Longmore, Head of Department
MA in Creative Writing.

## University of Huddersfield

Division of English, University of Huddersfield,
Room 3/05, St Peter's Building,
Huddersfield HD1 3DH
tel (01484) 473395 fax (01484) 478428
email l.jeffries@hud.ac.uk
website www.hud.ac.uk/schools
Contact Dr Lesley Jeffries, English Studies Pathway
Leader
MA in Poetry.

## University of Hull

Faculty of Arts, Department of English, University
of Hull, Cottingham Road, Hull HU6 7RX
tel (01482) 466188 fax (01482) 465641
email r.g.wymer@english.hull.ac.uk
website www.hull.ac.uk
Contact Rowland Wymer, Head of Department
MA in Creative Writing.

## King Alfred's College

School of Cultural Studies, King Alfred's College,
Winchester SO22 4NR
tel (01962) 827235 fax (01962) 827406
website www.kingalfreds.ac.uk
Contact The Admissions Office
MA in English: Writing for Children.

## Lancaster University

Department of Creative Writing, C Floor, Lonsdale
College, Lancaster University, Lancaster LA1 4YN
tel (01524) 594169
email l.anderson@lancaster.ac.uk
website www.lancs.ac.uk/users/cw/
Contact The Secretary
MA in Creative Writing.

## Leeds Metropolitan University

Northern Film School, Leeds Metropolitan
University, 2 Queens Square, Leeds LS2 8AF
tel 0113-283 1900 fax 0113-283 1901
email nfs@lmu.ac.uk
website www.lmu.ac.uk/hen/aad/nfs
Contact Alby James, Head of Screenwriting
MA/Postgraduate Diploma in Screenwriting
(Fiction).

## Liverpool John Moores University

School of Media, Critical and Creative Arts,
Liverpool John Moores University, Dean Walters
Building, St James Road, Liverpool L1 7BR
*tel* 0151-231 5052 *fax* 0151-231 5049
*website* www.livjm.ac.uk
*Contact* Research Coordinator

MA in Screenwriting and MA in Writing.

## University of London, Goldsmiths College

Department of Drama, Goldsmiths College,
University of London, London SE14 6NW
*tel* 020-7919 7414 *fax* 020-7919 7413
*email* drama@gold.ac.uk
*website* www.goldsmiths.ac.uk
*Contact* Drama Secretary

MA in Writing for Performance.

## University of London, Goldsmiths College

Department of English, Goldsmiths College,
University of London, London SE14 6NW
*tel* 020-7919 7436 *fax* 020-7919 7509
*email* english@gold.ac.uk
*website* www.goldsmiths.ac.uk
*Contact* Maria Macdonald, Secretary for
Postgraduate Enquiries

MA in Creative and Life Writing.

## University of London, King's College

University of London, King's College, Strand,
London WC2R 2LS
*tel* 020-7848 2184 *fax* 020-7848 2257
*email* louise.henderson@kcl.ac.uk
*website* www.kcl.ac.uk
*Contact* Louise Henderson

MA in Text and Performance Studies; scriptwriting
option supervised at RADA.

## University of London, Royal Holloway

Department of Media Arts, Royal Holloway,
University of London, Egham, Surrey TW20 0EX
*tel* (01784) 443734 *fax* (01784) 443832
*email* mediaarts@rhul.ac.uk
*website* www.media.dr.rhul.ac.uk

MA in Feature Film Screenwriting.

## University of London, Royal Holloway

Department of Drama and English, Royal
Holloway, University of London, Egham Hill,
Surrey TW20 0EX
*tel* (01784) 443922 *fax* (01784) 431018
*email* j.bratton@rhul.ac.uk
*website* www.rhul.ac.uk
*Contact* Prof Jacqueline Bratton

MA in Theatre (Playwriting).

## London College of Printing

School of Media, London College of Printing,
10 Back Hill, London EC1R 5EN
*tel* 020-7514 6853 *fax* 020-7514 6848
*website* www.lcp.linst.ac.uk
*Contact* School of Media Office

MA in Screenwriting.

## Loughborough University

Department of English and Drama, Loughborough
University, Loughborough, Leics. LE11 3TU
*tel* (01509) 222951 *fax* (01509) 610813
*website* www.lboro.ac.uk
*Contact* Dr S.J. Schad

MA in Modern and Contemporary Writing.

## University of Manchester

Department for English Language and Literature,
University of Manchester, Manchester M13 9PL
*tel* 0161-275 3144 *fax* 0161-275 3256
*website* www.art.man.ac.uk/english/hom.htm
*Contact* Prof J. Pearson

MA in Novel Writing.

## Manchester Metropolitan University

Department of English, Faculty of Humanities and
Social Science, Manchester Metropolitan University,
Geoffrey Manton Building, Rosamond Street West,
Off Oxford Road, Manchester M15 6LL
*tel* 0161-247 1730 *fax* 0161-247 6345
*email* m.beetham@mmu.ac.uk
*website* www.mmu.ac.uk
*Contact* Margaret Beetham

MA in Creative Writing.

## Manchester Metropolitan University

Department of English, Faculty of Humanities and
Social Science, Manchester Metropolitan University,
Geoffrey Manton Building, Rosamond Street West,
Off Oxford Road, Manchester M15 6LL
*tel* 0161-247 6760 *fax* 0161-247 6345
*email* m.schmidt@mmu.ac.uk
*website* www.mmu.ac.uk/h-ss/eng
*Contact* Prof Michael Schmidt, Editor, Carcanet Press

MA in Poetry.

## National Film and Television School

National Film and Television School, Beaconsfield
Studios, Station Road, Beaconsfield, Bucks. HP9 1LG
*tel* (01494) 671234 *fax* (01494) 674042
*email* admin@nftsfilm-tv.ac.uk
*website* www.nftsfilm-tv.ac.uk

MA in Film and Television Screenwriting.

## University of Newcastle

Department of English Literary and Linguistic
Studies, University of Newcastle, Newcastle upon
Tyne NE1 7RU

*tel* 0191-222 7761 *fax* 0191-222 8708
*website* www.ncl.ac.uk/english
*Contact* Postgraduate Admission Secretary

MA in Writing Poetry.

## University of North London

University of North London, 166–220 Holloway
Road, London N7 8DB
*tel* 020-7753 5111 *fax* 020-7753 3159
*email* b.wood@unl.ac.uk
*website* www.unl.ac.uk
*Contact* Dr Briar Wood, Subject Tutor, Creative
Writing

MA in Creative Writing.

## University of Northumbria at Newcastle

Postgraduate School of Humanities, University of
Northumbria at Newcastle, Lipman Building,
Sandyman Road, Newcastle upon Tyne NE1 8ST
*tel* 0191-227 3777 *fax* 0191-227 4630
*website* online.unn.ac.uk/faculties/art/humanities
*Contact* The Admissions Tutor

MA in Creative Writing.

## Nottingham Trent University

Department of English and Media Studies,
Nottingham Trent University, Clifton Lane,
Nottingham NG11 8NS
*tel* 0115-941 8418 ext. 3286 *fax* 0115-948 6632
*website* www.ntu.ac.uk
*Contact* Prof Sandra Harris

MA/Postgraduate Diploma/Postgraduate Certificate
in Writing.

## University of Plymouth

Faculty of Arts and Education, University of
Plymouth, Douglas Avenue, Exmouth,
Devon EX8 2AT
*tel* (01395) 255418 *fax* (01395) 264196
*email* t.lopez@plymouth.ac.uk
*website* www.plymouth.ac.uk
*Contact* Dr Tony Lopez, Prof of Poetry

MA/Postgraduate Diploma in Creative Writing.

## The Poets' House

The Poets' House, Clonbarra, Falcarrash,
Co. Donegal, Republic of Ireland
*tel* (353) 746 5470 *fax* (353) 746 5471
*Contact* John Fitzsimmons

MA in Creative Writing: Poetry.

## Queen Margaret University College

Gateway Theatre, Queen Margaret University
College, 42 Elm Row, Edinburgh EH7 4AB
*tel* 0131-317 3950 *fax* 0131-317 3902
*email* mkinloch@gmuc.ac.uk
*website* www.gmuc.ac.uk
*Contact* Maggie Kinloch, Head of Drama

MA in Creative Writing and MFA in Creative
Writing/Dramatic Writing.

## Queen's University, Belfast

School of English, Queen's University, Belfast,
Belfast BT7 1NN
*tel* 028-9024 5133 ext. 5103 *fax* 028-9031 4615
*website* www.qub.ac.uk/en/pg
*Contact* Prof Brian Caraher, Head of Graduate
Teaching and Reseach

MA/Postgraduate Diploma in Creative Writing.

## University of St Andrews

School of English, University of St Andrews,
St Andrews, Fife KY16 9AL
*tel* (01334) 462666 *fax* (01334) 462655
*email* jg9@st-andrews.ac.uk
*website* www.st-andrews.ac.uk/academic/english/
schoolofenglish.html
*Contact* Postgraduate Director

M.Litt/Graduate Diploma in Creative Writing.

## St Martin's College, Lancaster

St Martin's College, Lancaster, Bowerham Road,
Lancaster LA1 3JD
*tel* (01524) 384328 *fax* (01524) 384385
*email* k.flann@ucsm.ac.uk
*website* www.ucsm.ac.uk
*Contact* Kathy Flann, Course Leader, Creative Writing

MA in Writing Studies.

## University of Salford

University of Salford, Adelphi, Peru Street, Salford,
Greater Manchester M3 6EQ
*tel* 0161-295 6027 *fax* 0161-295 6023
*email* c.muir@media-perf.salford.ac.uk
*website* www.salford.ac.uk/media/courses/masw/masw
*Contact* Sue Horn

MA/Postgraduate Diploma in Television and Radio
Scriptwriting.

## University of Sheffield

School of Education, University of Sheffield,
388 Glossop Road, Sheffield S10 2JA
*tel* 0114-222 8177 *fax* 0114-279 6236
*email* f.inglis@sheffield.ac.uk
*website* www.sheffield.ac.uk
*Contact* Prof Fred Inglis, Course Director

MA in Creative Writing for Film and Television.

## Sheffield Hallam University

School of Cultural Studies, Sheffield Hallam
University, 32 Collegiate Crescent, Sheffield S10 2BP
*tel* 0114-225 4364
*email* p.t.cox@shu.ac.uk
*website* www.shu.ac.uk/schools/cs/teaching/
pc/index.htm
*Contact* Dr Phil Cox, Principal Lecturer in English

MA/Postgraduate Diploma/Postgraduate Certificate in Creative Writing.

## University of Strathclyde

Department of English Studies, University of Strathclyde, Glasgow G1 1XH
*tel* 0141-553 4150 *fax* 0141-552 3493
*email* margaret.philips@strath.ac.uk
*website* www.strath.ac.uk/departments/english
*Contact* Margaret Philips

M.Litt/Postgraduate Diploma/Postgraduate Certificate in Creative Writing.

## University of Sussex

Centre for Continuing Education, University of Sussex, Education Development Building, Falmer, Brighton BN1 9RG
*tel* (01273) 678040 *fax* (01273) 678848
*email* r.a.crane@sussex.ac.uk
*website* www.sussex.ac.uk
*Contact* Richard Crane

MA in Creative Writing and Personal Development.

## Trinity College, Carmarthen

School of English and Communication, Trinity College, Carmarthen, Dyfed SA31 3EP
*tel* (01267) 676617 *fax* (01267) 676766
*email* c.wigginton@trinity-cm.ac.uk
*website* www.trinity-cm.ac.uk
*Contact* Christopher Wigginton, Subject Head

MA in Creative Writing.

## University of Wales, Aberystwyth

Department of English, Hugh Owen Building, Penglais Campus, University of Wales, Aberystwyth, Aberystwyth, Ceredigion SY23 3DY
*tel* (01970) 622535
*email* www.aber.ac.uk/~engwww/
*Contact* The Secretary

MA in Writing: Process and Practice.

## University of Wales, Cardiff

School of English, Communication and Philosophy, University of Wales, Cardiff, PO Box 94, Cardiff CF10 3XB
*tel* 029-2087 6049 *fax* 029-2087 4502
*website* www.cf.ac.uk
*Contact* The Head of School

MA in the Teaching and Practice of Creative Writing.

## University of Warwick

Department of English and Comparative Literary Studies, University of Warwick, Senate House, Coventry CV4 7AL
*tel* 024-7652 4928 *fax* 024-7652 3323
*email* ensak@dredd.warwick.ac.uk
*website* www.warwick.ac.uk
*Contact* Prof Jeremy Treglown/Dr David Morley

MA in Creative Writing.

## University of York

Department of English and Related Literature, University of York, Heslington, York YO10 5DD
*tel* (01904) 433369 *fax* (01904) 433372
*email* engl13@york.ac.uk
*website* www.york.ac.uk/depts/engl/
*Contact* The Graduate Secretary

MA in Writing and Performance (Drama/Film/Television).

# Editorial, literary and production services

The specialists listed below offer a wide variety of services to writers publishers, journalists and others. Services include advice on manuscripts, editing and book production, indexing, translation, research and writing. See page 767 for a subject index.

## 'A Feature Factory' Editorial Services

4 St Andrews Court, Norwich NR7 0EW
*tel* (01603) 435229 *mobile* (07970) 368228
*fax* (01603) 435229
*email* editorial@fdsltd.com
*Editors* Dr Dennis Chaplin, Sara de Villeurbanne, Debbie Storey

Contract magazine/book publishing, editorial consultancy and troubleshooting, DTP (Quark/Photoshop), proofreading, sub-editing, legal copy checks, typesetting, advertisement design, book publishing, copywriting, features, broadcast backgrounders, news releases, autobiography ghostwriting, novel/script editing, brochures, leaflets, research projects, tourist guides, editorial/journalism training. Researchers often needed (send CV and samples).

## Aaron Editorial

19 Albemarle Road, Gorleston-on-Sea,
Norfolk NR31 7AR
*tel* (01493) 444556 *fax* (01493) 444556
*email* aared@onetel.net.uk
*website* www.aaroneditorial.com
*Contact* Eldo Barkhuizen

Project management, onscreen editing, copy-editing, web-editing, proofreading, Anglicising/Americanising. Psychology, philosophy, English literature, history, archaeology, Egyptology, business studies, theology, biblical studies, classical Hebrew, Hellenistic Greek, Jewish studies, self-help, diet/nutrition. Advanced Member of SfEP. Established 1997.

## Abbey Writing Services

Twitchen Cottage, Holcombe Rogus, Wellington,
Somerset TA21 0PT
*tel* (01823) 672762 *fax* (01823) 672762
*email* john.mcilwain@virgin.net
*Director* John McIlwain

Comprehensive non-fiction writing, project management and editorial service. Educational writing. Autobiographies. Lexicography. Founded 1989.

## Academic File

PO Box 13666, 27 Wallorton Gardens,
London SW14 8WF
*tel* 020-8392 1122 *fax* 020-8392 1422
*email* afis@eapgroup.com
*website* www.eapgroup.com
*Director* Sajid Rizvi

Research, advisory and consultancy services related to politics, economics and societies of the Near and Middle East, Asia and North Africa and related issues in Europe. Risk analysis, editorial assessment, editing, contract publishing, design and production. Founded 1985.

## Advice and Criticism Service

1 Beechwood Court, Syderstone, Norfolk PE31 8TR
*tel* (01485) 578594 *fax* (01485) 578138
*email* hilary@hilaryjohnson.demon.co.uk
*website* www.hilaryjohnson.demon.co.uk
*Contact* Hilary Johnson

Authors' consultant: detailed and constructive assessment of typescripts/practical advice regarding publication. Former organiser of RNA New Writers' Scheme, adjudicator of literary awards and publishers' reader. All fiction genres including science fiction/fantasy. Also children's books, TV/radio/film scripts, poetry and non-fiction. Close link with leading literary agent. Outstanding authors can be given a direct route to this agency.

## AESOP (All Editorial Services Online for Publishers & Authors)

Uplands, 28 Abberbury Road, Iffley,
Oxford OX4 4ES
*tel* (01865) 429563 *fax* (01865) 395758
*email* aesop@all-eds.com
*website* www.all-eds.com
*Contact* Martin Noble

Editing; copy-editing; rewriting, proofreading; indexing; editorial reports and reviews; advice to publishers, authors and literary agents; co-writing; ghostwriting; novelisation; research; fact-checking; bibliographical research; CRC (Word); text capture; scanning/OCR; e-book production on CD-Rom or online; keying in MSS; audio transcription; tagging. Specialises in fiction, literature, poetry, media, music, performing arts, humour biography, memoirs, education, psychology, alternative health, special needs, thesis and dissertation editing and printing; improving use of English of non-native

English writers of academic reports and books. Established 1979.

## Agent Research & Evaluation Inc
25 Barrow Street, New York, NY 10014, USA
*tel* 212-924-9942 *fax* 646-924-1864
*email* info@agentresearch.com
*website* www.agentresearch.uk.net
*President* Bill Martin

Provides authors, editors and other professionals with data on clients and sales made by literary agents in the USA, UK and Canada, i.e. who sells what to whom for how much. Information is culled from the trade and general press, and collection has been continuous since 1980. Individual reports on specific agents and various forms of MS–agent match-up services are available. See website for pricing or send an sae. Publishes *Talking Agents*, the AR&E newsletter (10 p.a.). The website offers a free service of agent verification: information on whether or not the database reflects that a given agent has created a public record of sales. Founded 1996.

## Amolibros
Loundshay Manor Cottage, Preston Bowyer, Milverton, Somerset TA4 1QF
*tel* (01823) 401527 *fax* (01823) 401527
*email* amolibros@aol.com
*website* www.amolibros.co.uk
*Managing Consultant* Jane Tatam

A self-publishing consultancy/packager. Also offers copy-editing, proofreading, typesetting, advice on marketing and sales. Established 1992.

## Anchor Editorial Services
Anchor House, 5 High Street, Dulverton, Somerset TA22 9HB
*tel* (01398) 324350 *fax* (01398) 324350
*Editorial Director* Leigh-Anne Perryman,
*Photographic Director* Martyn Collins

A complete editorial, research and photographic service for company brochures and magazines; guidebooks, publicity leaflets and tourism projects; press releases and newsletters. Established 1998.

## Angel Books
6 Lancaster Road, Harrogate, North Yorkshire HG2 0EZ
*tel* (01423) 566804
*Contact* Angela Sibson BA, AFBPsS

Professional author (21 titles) and tutor in creative writing offers comprehensive, sympathetic assessment of fiction MSS. Revision suggested with a view to getting into print. Special interests: crime, women's, teenage. Established 1994.

## Apple Pips Editing Services
18 Raglan Grove, Kenilworth, Warwickshire CV8 2NH
*tel* (01926) 858864

*email* primrosecroft@hotmail.com
*Contact* Ann Richards

Editing, copy-editing, proofreading, keying-in MSS (Word), research, book reviews. Special interests: history (especially Irish, social history of medicine, American – early colonial, Wild West, Tudor, Stuarts), educational books for schools, crime, fiction, biographies. Established 2001.

## Arioma Editorial Services
PO Box 53, Aberystwyth, Ceredigion SY24 5WG
*tel* (01970) 871296 *fax* (01970) 871733
*Proprietor* Moira W. Smith

Research, co-writing, ghostwriting, DTP, complete book production service. Specialities: non fiction, history and autobiography.

## Arkst Publishing
1 Lindsey House, Lloyds's Place, London SE3 0QF
*tel* 020-8297 9997 *fax* 020-8318 4359
*email* jim@arkst.demon.co.uk
*Director* James H. Willis MA, FRCP (Edin.)

Independent appraisal of MSS – fiction and non-fiction. Founded 1995.

## Asterisk Design & Editorial Solutions Ltd
8 Carnyorth Terrace, Carnyorth, Penzance, Cornwall TR19 7QE
*tel* (01736) 786470
*email* yvonnebristow@blue-earth.co.uk, rogerbristow@blue-earth.co.uk
*Directors* Roger Bristow, Yvonne Bristow (née McFarlane)

Full editorial and design service for books, brochures, catalogues, etc; project management; legal consultancy for publishing and creative contacts; commissioning authors, illustrators, photographers; research service; writing, journalism; restaurant/pub/other reviews. Specialises in integrated illustrated non-fiction books: practical art, cookery, gardening, natural history, general reference. Opportunities for freelances. Founded 2003.

## Authors' Advisory Service
24 Lyndale Avenue, Childs Hill, London NW2 2QA
*tel* 020-7794 3285

All typescripts professionally evaluated in depth by long-established publishers' reader specialising in constructive advice to new writers and with wide experience of current literary requirements. Founded 1972.

## Authors' Aid
11 Orchard Street, Fearnhead, Warrington, Cheshire WA2 0PL
*tel* (01925) 838431
*email* chris.sawyer@btinternet.com

*website* www.authorsaid.co.uk
*Partners* Chris Sawyer, Deborah Ramage

Appraisal and editorial services. Offers honest, constructive feedback and detailed guidance on style, presentation, characterisation, plot, construction, marketability, etc. A personalised service by a publishing professional with the clear aim of maximising the writer's chances of publication. Other services: rewriting, proofreading, ghostwriting, word processing, commissioned work. Write, phone or email before sending work. Established 1991.

## Authors Appraisal Service
12 Hadleigh Gardens, Boyatt Wood, Eastleigh, Hants SO50 4NP
*Literary consultant* J. Evans

Professional writer offers critical appraisal of MSS – fiction only. Specialises in romantic and historical fiction. Competitive rates. Preliminary letter essential and sae for reply. Founded 1988.

## AuthorsOnLine Ltd
40 Castle Street, Hertford SG14 1HR
*tel/fax* (0870) 7500544
*Submissions* Mrs W.A. Lake, Submissions Editor, Wayside, Downs Road, Eaast Studdal, Kent CT15 5BZ
*tel* (01304) 374762
*email* theeditor@authorsonline.co.uk
*website* www.authorsonline.co.uk
*Managing Director* Richard Ovenden, *Editor* Richard Fitt

Offers a service for authors wishing to self publish, including full publishing facilities on a print-on-demand basis, including distribution throughout the UK and North America. All genres considered. E-book formatting; all books made available on website. Authors retain intellectual property rights. New and established writers welcome.
  Prices (inc. VAT) – E-book only: £95 (automatically included with the POD service). Printed books: standard service £550; enhanced service, including cover design and full editing £1292.50. Reading only: £11.75 per 1000 words. Founded 1997.

## Authors' Research Services
32 Oak Village, London NW5 4QN
*tel* 020-7284 4316
*email* rmwindserv@aol.com
*Contact* Richard Wright

Offers comprehensive research service to writers, academics and business people worldwide, including fact checking, bibliographical references and document supply. Specialises in English history, social sciences, business. Founded 1966.

## Anne Barclay Enterprises
The Old Farmhouse, Hexworthy, Yelverton, Devon PL20 6SD

*mobile* (07885) 476 944  *fax* (01364) 631 112
*email* anne@theswiftgroup.co.uk

Typing MSS and audio transcription through to full editorial services – appraisal, editing, research, feature writing, co-writing and ghostwriting. Special interests: food, travel, crime, memoirs. Founded 1996.

## Richard M. Bennett
*email* RBMedia@supanet.com
*Senior Associate* Richard Bennett

Author, journalist, broadcaster, researcher. Expert and confidential worldwide coverage of: espionage, national security, defence, conflicts and current affairs.

## Beswick Writing Services
19 Haig Road, Stretford M32 0DS
*tel* 0161-865 1259
*Contact* Francis Beswick

Editing, research, information books. Special interests: religious, philosophical and educational. Expertise in correspondence courses and Open Learning materials. Founded 1988.

## Black Ace Book Production
PO Box 6557, Forfar DD8 2YS
*tel* (01307) 465096 *fax* (01307) 465494
*website* www.blackacebooks.com
*Directors* Hunter Steele, Boo Wood

Book production and text processing, including text capture (or scanning), editing, proofing to camera-ready/film, printing and binding, jacket artwork and design. Delivery of finished books; can sometimes help with distribution. Founded 1990.

## Blair Services
Blair Cottage, Aultgrishan, Melvaig, Gairloch, Wester Ross IV21 2DZ
*tel* (01445) 771228 *fax* (01445) 771228
*email* BlairServices@aultgrisham.freeserve.co.uk
*Director* Ian Mertling-Blake MA, DPhil

Editing and revision: fiction and non-fiction (such as prospectus for schools and other educational purposes). Also specialist academic revision for books/articles on archaeology and associated subjects. Founded 1992.

## Book Production Consultants plc
25–27 High Street, Chesterton, Cambridge CB4 1ND
*tel* (01223) 352790 *fax* (01223) 460718
*email* tl@bpccam.co.uk
*website* www.bpccam.co.uk
*Directors* A.P. Littlechild, C.S. Walsh

Complete publishing service: writing, editing, designing, illustrating, translating, indexing, photography; production management of printing and binding; specialised sales and distribution;

advertising sales. For books, journals, manuals, brochures, magazines, catalogues, electronic media. Founded 1973.

## Brackley Proofreading Services
PO Box 5920, Brackley, Northants. NN13 6YB
*tel* (01280) 703355 *fax* (01280) 703355
*email* brackleyproof@LineOne.net

Proofreading. Founded 2000.

## Mrs D. Buckmaster
51 Chatsworth Road, Torquay, Devon TQ1 3BJ
*tel* (01803) 294663 *fax* (01803) 294663

General editing of non-fiction, with particular attention to clarity of expression and meaning, grammar, punctuation and flow. Experience in editing architecture, photography, financial, religious, natural health and human potential MSS. Founded 1966.

## John Button – Editorial Services
Tower House, 6 Burnham Court, Martello Bay, Clacton on Sea, Essex CO15 1RE
*tel* (01255) 470405 *fax* (01225) 470405
*email* john.button@btconnect.com

Copy-editing and proofreading, specialising in government committee of enquiry reports, legal, financial, taxation, business education and corporate identity publications; Legal Reference Library series. Founded 1991.

## Causeway Resources
8 The Causeway, Teddington, Middlesex TW11 0HE
*tel* 020-8977 8797 *fax* 020-8977 8797
*email* kskinner@causeway-dagonet.fsnet.co.uk
*Director* Keith Skinner

Biographical and historical research, specialising in Metropolitan Police history and true crime research. Founded 1989.

## Chase Publishing Services
Mead, Fortescue, Sidmouth, Devon EX10 9QG
*tel* (01395) 514709 *fax* (01395) 514709
*email* r.addicott@btinternet.com
*Proprietor* Ray Addicott

Coordinates a network of specialists in academic bookwork taking raw MSS through to finished books. Services include copy-editing and proofreading, design, typesetting, indexing and a full production service. Founded 1989.

## Barbara Cheney
*tel* (01225) 316376
*email* barbara@cheney4402.freeserve.co.uk

Copy-editing, proofreading, layout and design. Books (up to 8328pp), directories, magazines, newsletters, annual reports, prospectuses, catalogues, leaflets. Clients include publishers,

institutes and government departments. Freelance since 1987.

## Karyn Claridge Book Production
244 Bromham Road, Biddenham,
Bedford MK40 4AA
*tel* (01234) 347909
*email* claridge@toppan.co.uk

Complete book production management service offered from MS to bound copies; graphic services available; sourcing service for interactive book projects. Founded 1989.

## Johnathon Clifford
27 Mill Road, Fareham, Hants PO16 0TH
*tel* (01329) 822218 *fax* (01329) 822218
*website* www.vanitypublishing.info

Offers a free, unbiased advice service for anyone looking for a publisher or who has experienced difficulties with a publishing house. Has extensive knowledge of vanity publishing and acted as adviser to the Advertising Standards Authority regarding the wording of the 'Advice Note Vanity Publishing July 1997'. See website for his report on the government White Paper against rogue traders and its effectiveness where authors are concerned. See also page 282. Established 1994.

## Combrógos
Prof Meic Stephens, 10 Heol Don, Whitchurch, Cardiff CF14 2AU
*tel* 029-2062 3359 *fax* 029-2052 9202

Specialises in books (including fiction and poetry) about Wales or by Welsh authors, providing a full editorial service and undertaking arts and media research. Founded 1990.

## Cornerstones & Kids' Corner Ltd
Milk Studios, 34 Southern Row, London W10 5AN
*tel* 020-8968 0777 *fax* 020-8969 8677
*email* helen@cornerstones.co.uk,
kidscorner@cornerstones.co.uk
*website* www.cornerstones.co.uk
*Proprietor* Helen Corner

Specialist team of readers (authors and editors) provides literary guidance and constructive assessment of MSS for published or unpublished authors. Scouts for agents and publishers. Established 1998.

**Kids' Corner** (children's division): All age ranges of children's fiction, from picture books to teenage.

## Ingrid Cranfield
16 Myddelton Gardens, London N21 2PA
*tel* 020-8360 2433 *fax* 020-8360 2433
*email* ingrid_cranfield@hotmail.com

Advisory and editorial services for authors, publishers and media, including critical assessment, rewriting, proofreading, copy-editing, indexing, research, interviews, transcripts. Special interests: geography, travel, exploration, adventure (own archives), language, education, youth training, art and architecture (including Japanese). Translations from German and French. Not an employer or agency. Founded 1972.

## Andrew Crofts
Westlands Grange, West Grinstead, Horsham, West Sussex RH13 8LZ
*tel* (01403) 864518
*email* croftsa@aol.com
*website* www.andrewcrofts.com

Ghostwriting.

## Dr David A. Cross
10 Red Gables, Chatsworth Square, Carlisle CA1 IHE
*tel* 01228 525964

Research and information service; editing texts, specialising in art history and biography; creative writing tutorials; lectures on artists and writers of the Lake District (especially George Romney and John Ruskin).

## Josephine Curtis Editorial
Heathfield House, Balloorclerhy, Kiltimagh, Co. Mayo, Republic of Ireland
*tel* (00 353) 9493 82883
*email* jcurtis002@aol.com

Editing – hard copy and onscreen, proofreading, legal tabling. Established 1990.

## D & N Publishing
Unit 3c, Lowesden Business Park, Lambourn Woodlands, Hungerford, Berks. RG17 7RU
*tel* (01488) 73657 *fax* (01488) 73657
*email* dandnpub@aol.com
*Partners* David and Namrita Price-Goodfellow

Complete project management including some or all of the following: commissioning, editing, picture research, illustration and design, page layout, proofreading, indexing, printing and repro. All stages managed in-house and produced on Apple Macs running the latest software. All subjects considered with Natural History a speciality. Founded 1991.

## David Wineman, Solicitors
Craven House, 121 Kingsway, London WC2B 6NX
*tel* 020-7400 7800 *fax* 020-7400 7890
*email* law@davidwineman.co.uk
*website* www.davidwineman.co.uk
*Contact* Irving David

A broadly based media law firm. Offers legal advice to authors, illustrators, photographers, composers, songwriters and their agents on all forms of publishing agreement, including negotiation and review of commercial terms, where required, with book and music publishers, film, TV and theatrical production companies, packagers and merchandisers. Founded 1981.

## Meg Davies
31 Egerton Road, Ashton, Preston, Lancs. PR2 1AJ
*tel* (01772) 725120 *mobile* (07789) 433254
*email* megindex@aol.com

Indexing at general and postgraduate level in the arts and humanities. Also proofreading and copy-editing. Registered Indexer with Society of Indexers since 1971.

## Rosemary Dooley
Crag House, Witherslack, Grange-over-Sands, Cumbria LA11 6RW
*tel* (015395) 52286 *fax* (015395) 52013
*email* rd@booksonmusic.co.uk
*website* www.booksonmusic.co.uk
*Proprietor* Rosemary Dooley

Collaborative publishers' exhibitions: music books. Founded 1985.

## Editorial Solutions
537 Antrim Road, Belfast BT15 3BU
*tel* 028-9077 2300 *fax* 028-9078 1356
*email* info@editorialsolutions.com
*website* www.editorialsolutions.com
*Partners* Sheelagh Hughes, Michael Johnston

Offers a comprehensive editorial and publications service, including news and feature writing, copywriting, editing and copy-editing, proofreading, publication design, page layout and complete publication management. Qualified journalists. Specialisms: business, public sector, education, web writing.

## Editorial/Visual Research
21 Leamington Road Villas, London W11 1HS
*tel* 020-7727 4920 *mobile* (07973) 820020
*Contact* Angela Murphy

Comprehensive research service including historical, literary, film and picture research for writers, publishers, film and TV companies. Services also include copy-writing, editing, and travel and feature writing. Founded 1973.

## Lewis Esson Publishing
45 Brewster Gardens, London W10 6AQ
*tel* 020-7854 0668 *fax* 020-8968 1623
*email* lewisesson@supanet.com

Project management of illustrated books in areas of food, art and interior design; editing and writing of food books; copywriting, especially in the area of food packaging and FMCGs. Founded 1989.

## Finers Stephens Innocent
179 Great Portland Street, London W1N 6LS
tel 020-7323 4000 fax 020-7344 5600
email nsolomon@fsilaw.co.uk
website www.fsilaw.co.uk
Contact Nicola Solomon, Partner

Services include: drafting and negotiating agency and publishing agreements; advice on copyright and moral rights, libel reading, defamation advice and insurance; breaches or termination of contract; errors in printing and failure or refusal to publish or delay in publishing; debt collection for payment of royalties, commission or fees, including suing or insolvency proceedings where necessary; injunctions; preparation of wills, administering artistic and literary estates; permissions, rights, copyright infringement and negligent misstatement; electronic rights and international sales. Solicitors to the Society of Authors, the Writers' Guild, the British Association of Picture Libraries and Agencies and the Association of Illustrators.

## First Edition Translations Ltd
6 Wellington Court, Wellington Street, Cambridge CB1 1HZ
tel (01223) 356733 fax (01223) 321488/316232
email info@firstedit.co.uk
website www.firstedit.co.uk
Directors Sheila Waller, Jeremy Waller

Translation, interpreting, voice-over recording, editing, proofreading, Americanisation, DTP; books, manuals, reports, journals and promotional material. Founded 1981.

## FJN Associates
Little Theobald, Sandy Cross, Heathfield, East Sussex TN21 8BT
tel (01435) 866653 fax (01435) 868998
email fred@nixonf.freeserve.co.uk
Partners Frederick J. Nixon, Brenda Mellen Nixon

Comprehensive DTP and editorial service including magazine and newsletter design and production; advice to authors, editing and preparation of MSS for submission to publishers/editors; proofreading. Founded 1990.

## Christine Foley Secretarial Services
Glyndedwydd, Login, Whitland, Carmarthenshire SA34 0TN
tel (01994) 448414 fax (01994) 448414
Partners Christine Foley, Michael Foley

Word processing service: preparation of MSS from handwritten/typed notes and audio-transcription. Complete secretarial support. Founded 1991.

## Freelance Market News
Sevendale House, 7 Dale Street, Manchester M1 1JB
tel 0161-228 2362 fax 0161-228 3533
email fmn@writersbureau.com
website www.writersbureau.com
Contact Angela Cox, Editor

A monthly market newsletter. A good rate of pay made for news of editorial requirements. Information on UK and overseas publications with editorial content, submission requirements and contact details. Founded 1968.

## Freelance Services
41A Newal Road, Ballymoney, Co. Antrim BT53 6HB
tel 028-2766 2953
website www.joanshannon.co.uk
Contact Joan Shannon

Publishing services, photography and postcards. Commercial, industrial, scenic, fine art and natural light photography. Founded 1991.

## Shelagh Furness
Hallgarth Farmhouse, The Hallgarth, Durham, Co. Durham DH1 3BJ
tel 0191-384 3840
email sfurness543@aol.com

Research, editorial and information services. Experienced book and journal editor; online and library research; specialises in current affairs, geopolitics, environment and information systems. Founded 1992.

## Geo Group & Associates
4 Christian Fields, London SW16 3JZ
tel 020-8764 6292 fax 0115-981 9418
email publishing@geo-group.co.uk
website www.geo-group.co.uk

Publishing services. From copy-editing and proofreading to complete package. Research and publishing consultancy. Low-cost, quality, short-run printing. Publishing imprint: Nyala Publishing. Two photo libraries (including aerial); photography commissioned. Special rates to author-publishers. Established 1968.

## Ghostwriter
21 Hindsleys Place, London SE23 2NF
tel 020-8244 5816
email parkerwrite@yahoo.co.uk
Contact John Parker

I will assist with your novel, autobiography, speech, report, thesis, essay etc by editing or writing it for you. Advice and tuition for 'struggling' new writers. Negotiable rates, student and OAP discounts. Published journalist and ghostwriter. Founded 1991.

## C.N. Gilmore
27 Salisbury Street, Bedford MK41 7RE
tel (01234) 346142
email Intel_Thug@compuserve.com

Sub-editing, slush-pile reading, reviewing. Will also collaborate. Undertakes work in all scholarly and academic fields as well as fiction and practical writing. Specialises in editing translated works. Founded 1987.

## Graham-Cameron Publishing

The Studio, 23 Holt Road, Sheringham, Norfolk NR26 8NB
*tel* (01263) 821333 *fax* (01263) 821334
*Partners* Helen Graham-Cameron, Mike Graham-Cameron

Complete editorial, including writing, editing, illustration and production services. Absolutely no unsolicited MSS. Founded 1984.

## Bernard Hawton

6 Merdon Court, Merdon Avenue, Chandler's Ford, Hants SO53 1FP
*tel* 023-8026 7400
*email* bernardhawton@hotmail.com
Proofreading, copy-editing. Also online.

## Antony Hemans

Maranatha, 1 Nettles Terrace, Guildford, Surrey GU1 4PA
*tel* (01483) 574511

Biographical and historical research, specialising in industrial archaeology – railways, canals and shipping, air, military and naval operations – genealogy and family history. Founded 1981.

## Rosemary Horstmann

122 Mayfield Court, 27 West Savile Terrace, Edinburgh EH9 3DR
*tel* 0131-667 5383

Broadcasting scripts evaluated; general consultancy on editorial and marketing matters.

## E.J. Hunter

6 Dorset Road, London N22 7SL
*tel* 020-8889 0370

Editing, copy-editing, appraisal of MSS. Special interests: novels, short stories, drama, children's stories; primary education, alternative lifestyles, complementary medicine

## Indexing Specialists (UK) Ltd

202 Church Road, Hove, East Sussex BN3 2DJ
*tel* (01273) 738299 *fax* (01273) 323309
*email* richardr@indexing.co.uk
*website* www.indexing.co.uk
*Director* Richard Raper BSc, DTA

Indexes for all types: books, journals and reference publications on professional, scientific and general subjects; copy-editing, proofreading services; consultancy on indexing and electronic indexing. Founded 1965.

## The Information Bureau

51 The Business Centre, 103 Lavender Hill, London SW11 5QL
*tel* 020-7924 4414 *fax* 020-7738 2513
*email* info@informationbureau.co.uk
*website* www.informationbureau.co.uk
*Contact* Jane Hall

Offers an on-demand research service on a variety of subjects including current affairs, business, marketing, history, the arts, media and politics. Resources include range of cuttings amassed by the bureau since 1948.

## Intype Libra Ltd

Units 3–4, Elm Grove Industrial Estate, Elm Grove, London SW19 4HE
*tel* 020-8947 7863, (07976) 223501
*fax* 020-8947 3652
*email* sales@intypelibra.co.uk
*website* www.intypelibra.co.uk
*Directors* Tony Chapman, John Raw, Alton Irby, David Greenwood, Graham Sherren

Digitally printed books, paperback and case bound, and typesetting and data manipulation. Offers 24-hour service. Founded 1974.

## Library Research Agency

Burberry, Devon Road, Salcombe, Devon TQ8 8HJ
*tel* (01548) 842769
*Directors* D.J. Langford MA, B. Langford

Research and information service for writers, journalists, artists, businessmen from libraries, archives, museums, record offices and newspapers in UK, USA and Europe. Sources may be in English, French, German, Russian, Serbo-Croat, Bulgarian, and translations made if required. Founded 1974.

## Dr Kenneth Lysons

Lathom, Scotchbarn Lane, Whiston, Nr Prescot, Merseyside L35 7JB
*tel* 0151-426 5513 *fax* 0151-430 6934
*email* lysons@literaryservices.co.uk
*Contact* Dr Kenneth Lysons MA, MEd, DPA, DMA, FCIS, FInstPS, FBIM

Company and institutional histories, support material for organisational management and supervisory training, house journals, research and reports service. Full secretarial support. Founded 1986.

## Duncan McAra

28 Beresford Gardens, Edinburgh EH5 3ES
*tel* 0131-552 1558 *fax* 0131-552 1558
*email* duncanmcara@hotmail.com

Consultancy on all aspects of general trade publishing; editing, re-writing, copy-editing and proof-correcting for publishers, financial companies, academic institutions and other organisations. Main subjects include art, architecture, archaeology, biography, military, Scottish and travel. See also page 412. Founded 1988.

## Janet McKerron

Apple Tree Cottage, Title Road, Middleton, Saxmundham, Suffolk IP17 3NF
*tel* (01728) 648973 *fax* (01728) 648973
*email* janet@janetmckerron.demon.co.uk

Indexing and proofreading books (up to 1000pp), loose-leaf publications and academic journals. Clients include publishers and NGOs. Specialist subjects: civil law in England and Wales, European law, the environment. Established 1996.

## McText

Denmill, Tough, By Alford, Aberdeenshire AB33 8EP
*tel* (019755) 62582 *fax* (019755) 62582
*email* d@mctext.com
*website* www.mctext.com
*Partners* Duncan and K. McArdle

Proofreading, copy-editing, website proofing. Specialist interests: archaeology, equestrian, oil-related commerce. Founded 1986.

## Manuscript Appraisals

Lanetrees, Simpson Cross, Haverfordwest, Pembs. SA62 6AE
*tel* (01437) 710534 *fax* (01437) 710534
*email* manuscript_app@hotmail.com
*Proprietor* Norman Price *Consultants* Ray Price, Mary Hunt

Independent appraisal of authors' MSS (fiction and non-fiction, but no poetry) with full editorial guidance and advice. In-house editing, copy-editing, rewriting and camera-ready copy if required. Staff expertise embraces thrillers, crime, adventure, travel, comedy, popular women's fiction. Will undertake editorial work in most areas of academic research and tertiary education. Overseas enquiries welcome. Interested in the work of new writers. Founded 1984.

## Marlinoak

22 Eve's Croft, Birmingham B32 3QL
*tel* 0121-475 6139 *fax* 0121-475 6139
*Proprietor* Hazel J. Billing JP, BA, DipEd

Preparation of scripts, plays, books, MSS service, proofreading; also audio-transcription, word processing. Founded 1984.

## Murder Files

Dommett Hill Farm, Hare Lane, Buckland St Mary, Chard, Somerset TA20 3JS
*tel* (01460) 234065
*email* enquiry@murderfiles.com
*website* www.murderfiles.com
*Director* Paul Williams

Crime writer and researcher specialising in British murders. Holds information on thousands of murders dating from 1400 to the present day. Copies of press cuttings available from 1920 to date. Details of executions, particularly at the Tyburn and Newgate. Information on British Hangmen. Specialist in British police murders since 1700. Service available to general enquirers, writers, leagal services, TV, radio, film, video, etc. Founded 1994.

## Elizabeth Murray

3 Gower Mews Mansions, Gower Mews, London WC1E 6HR
*tel* 020-7636 3761 *fax* 020-7636 3761
*email* MurraySearch@aol.com

Literary, biographical, historical, crime, military, cinema, genealogy research for authors, journalists, radio and TV from UK, European and USA sources. Founded 1975.

## My Word!

138 Railway Terrace, Rugby, Warks. CV21 3HN
*tel* (01788) 571294 *fax* (01788) 550957
*email* enquiries@myword.co.uk
*website* www.myword.co.uk
*Partners* Roddie Grant, Janet Grant

Specialises in typesetting and website solutions. Produces materials for printing and websites, e.g. magazines, newsletters, books, brochures, leaflets, conference and sales literature. Founded 1994.

## Paul Nash

Munday House, Aberdalgie, Perth PH2 0QB
*tel* (01738) 621584 *fax* (01738) 621584
*email* paulnash@zetnet.co.uk

Indexer specialising in sciences, engineering, technology, environmental science. Registered with the Society of Indexers. Winner of Library Association Wheatley Medal (1992) for outstanding index. Founded 1979.

## Peter Nickol

50 St Leonards Road, Exeter EX2 4LS
*tel* (01392) 255512 *fax* (01392) 255512
*email* pnickol@ninoakes.freeserve.co.uk

Editing and page layout; typesetting and music engraving; copyright licensing; project management including mixed media coordination, CD recording and production. Specialises in music and music education. Established 1987.

## Nidaba Publishing Services

68 Bramblebury Road, London SE18 7TG
*tel* 020-8317 3767
*email* ali.glen@virgin.net
*Contact* Ali Glenny PHd Eng. Lit.

Copy-editing, proofreading and onscreen text correction (Word, Quark). Established 1997.

## Paul H. Niekirk
40 Rectory Avenue, High Wycombe,
Bucks. HP13 6HW
*tel* (01494) 527200

Text editing for works of reference and professional and management publications, particularly texts on law; freelance writing. Founded 1976.

## Nielsen BookData
Globe House, 1 Chertsey Road,
Twickenham TW1 1LR
*tel* 0870 777 8710 *fax* 0870 777 8711
*email* sales@bookdata.co.uk
*websites* www.nielsenbookdata.com,
www.nielsenbooknet.com
*Contact* Sales Department

Nielsen BookData is the leading supplier of high-quality, content-rich book information and other published media to the book industry. Nielsen BookData takes information from publishers and creates a unique title record, which includes bibliographical details, text summaries, tables of contents, extensive subject-related information, market-rights details, jacket images and prize information. This bibliographic record is then available through a variety of Nielsen BookData sevices worldwide: as a direct feed, range of CD-Roms or online. The company also offers order routing, order tracking, EDI and web services.

## Northern Writers Advisory Services
77 Marford Crescent, Sale, Cheshire M33 4DN
*tel* 0161-969 1573
*email* grovesjill@aol.com
*Proprietor* Jill Groves

Offers typesetting to small publishers, societies and authors. Local history only. Founded 1986.

## Oriental Languages Bureau
Lakshmi Building, Sir P. Mehta Road, Fort,
Bombay 400001, India
*tel* 22661258/22665640 *fax* 22664598
*email* icsolb@vsnl.net
*website* orientallanguagesbureau.com
*Proprietor* Rajan K. Shah

Undertakes translations, phototypesetting-DTP, artwork and printing in all Indian languages and a few foreign languages.

## Ormrod Research Services
Weeping Birch, Burwash, East Sussex TN19 7HG
*tel* (01435) 882541

Comprehensive research service: literary, historical, academic, biographical, commercial. Critical reading with report (novels, theses, non-fiction), editing, indexing, proofreading, ghostwriting. Founded 1982.

## OTS
29 Edge Avenue, Grimsby,
North East Lincolnshire DN33 2DD
*tel* (01472) 237961 *fax* (01472) 237961
*email* pat.ots@virgin.net
*Owner* Pat Hewson

Video, audio and CD transcription, verbatim and edited; copy-edeiting (hard copy or on screen) and proofreading in all subjects; keying in MSS, word processing. Specialist areas are geographical, social and financial research, business management, finance, social care, crime (fiction and true) and ornithology; also general reference/fiction. Not an employer or agency. Founded 1995.

## Oxford Designers & Illustrators
Aristotle House, Aristotle Lane, Oxford OX2 6TR
*tel* (01865) 512331 *fax* (01865) 512408
*email* name@odi-illustration.co.uk
*website* www.o-d-i.com
*Directors* Peter Lawrence, Richard Corfield,
Andrew King

Over 30 years' experience in the design, typesetting and illustration of educational and general books. In-house artists for all subjects including scientific and technical, medical, natural history, cartoons, maps and diagrams. Full project management and repro service. Not an agency.

## Pages Editorial & Publishing Services
Ballencrieff Cottage, Ballencrieff Toll, Bathgate,
West Lothian EH48 4LD
*tel* (01506) 632728
*Director* Susan Coon

Editorial and production service of magazines/newspapers for companies or for commercial distribution. Founded 1995.

## Pagewise
2 Butlers Close, Amersham, Bucks. HP6 5PY
*tel* (01494) 729760 *fax* (01494) 729760
*email* info@pagewise.co.uk
*Director* Monica Bratt

Specialist service for self publishers: design, typesetting, editing and indexing, proofreading and production services. Founded 1999.

## Geoffrey D. Palmer
47 Burton Fields Road, Stamford Bridge,
York YO41 1JJ
*tel* (01759) 372874
*email* gdp@lineone.net
*website* www.geoffreydpalmer.co.uk

Editorial and production services, including STM and general copy-editing, on-screen editing, artwork editing, proofreading and indexing. Pre-press project management. Founded 1987.

## Roger Palmer Ltd

Antonia House, 262 Holloway Road, London N7 6NE
*tel* 020-7609 4828 *fax* 020-7609 4878
*email* contracts@rogerpalmerltd.co.uk
*Contact* Peter Palmer

Drafts, advises on and negotiates all media contracts for publishers, packagers, agents, authors and others; operates complete outsourced contracts department functions for publishers; undertakes contractual audits and devises contracts and permissions systems; provides advice on copyright and related issues; provides training and seminars. Special terms for members of the Society of Authors and the Writers' Guild of Great Britain. Founded 1993.

## Phoenix 2

Lantern House, Lodge Drove, Woodfalls, Salisbury, Wilts SP5 2NH
*tel* (01725) 512200 *fax* (01725) 511819
*email* enquiries@phoenix2.co.uk
*Partners* Bryan Walker, Amanda Walker

Writing, editing, sub-editing, typesetting and design of magazines, newsletters, journals, brochures and promotional literature. Specialist areas are business, tourism, social affairs and education. Founded 1994.

## Christopher Pick

41 Chestnut Road, London SE27 9EZ
*tel* 020-8761 2585 *fax* 020-8761 6388
*email* cpick@netcomuk.co.uk

Publications consultancy, project management, writing and editing for companies and public-sector and voluntary-sector agencies: e.g. annual reports, brochures and booklets, information materials, website text, strategy documents, research reports, books, organisational histories. Extensive expertise and experience in presenting information clearly and concisely for non-specialist readers. Specialist in writing and producing corporate and institutional histories.

## Picture Research Agency

Jasmine Cottage, Spring Grove Road, Richmond, Surrey TW10 6EH
*tel* 020-8940 5986 *fax* 020-8940 5986
*email* pat.hodgpix@virgin.net
*Contact* Pat Hodgson

Illustrations found for books, films and TV. Written research also undertaken particularly on historical subjects, including photographic and film history. Small picture library.

## Reginald Piggott

Decoy Lodge, Decoy Road, Potter Heigham, Norfolk NR29 5LX
*tel* (01692) 670384

Cartographer to the University Presses and academic publishers in Britain and overseas. Maps and diagrams for academic and educational books. Founded 1962.

## Plum Communications

11 Fleming Way, Wellingtonia Park, Exeter EX2 4SE
*tel* (01392) 421323 *fax* (01392) 421323
*email* stephanie.plum@btopenworld.com,
stephanie.plum@btinternet.com
*Contact* Stephanie Walshe

Appraisal of fiction and non-fiction MSS with report (write, phone or email first). Proofreading and copy-editing (hard copy and onscreen), copywriting, ghostwriting, rewriting, indexing, page layout, research, project management. Backlog reading. Website authoring. Complete marketing service and production of all promotional material, training manuals, strategy documents, research reports and company histories. Founded 1990.

## Keith Povey Editorial Services

Stoneleigh House, South Brentor, Tavistock, Devon PL19 0NW
*tel* (01822) 810190 *fax* (01822) 810191
*email* Povedservs@aol.com

Copy-editing, indexing, proofreading, publisher/author liaison. Partnership with T & A Typesetting Services (*tel* 01706 861662) – specialist book typesetting to final output of any kind, graphic design.

## David Price

Acupunctuation Ltd, 4 Harbidges Lane, Long Buckby, Northampton NN6 7QL
*tel* (01327) 844119 *fax* (01327) 844119
*email* waywithwords@fireflyuk.net
*website* www.waywithwords.co.uk

Copy-editing, proofreading, research, writing, rewriting. Special interests: fine art (particularly modern art), operetta and musicals, travel guides, modern European history (including the former Soviet Union), alternative health. Founded 1995.

## Victoria Ramsay

Abbots Rest, Chilbolton, Stockbridge, Hants SO20 6BE
*tel* (01264) 860251 *fax* (01264) 860026
*email* victoredit@supanet.com

Freelance editior, copy-editor and proofreader; non-fiction research and writing of promotional literature and pamphlets. Any non-scientific subject undertaken. Special interests: education, cookery, travel, Africa and Caribbean and works in translation. Established 1981.

## Reading and Righting (Robert Lambolle Services)

618B Finchley Road, London NW11 7RR
*tel* 020-8455 4564 *fax* 020-8455 4564
*email* ziph@macunlimited.net
*website* www.readingandrighting.netfirms.com

MSS/script advisory and evaluation service: fiction, non-fiction, stage plays and screenplays; editorial services; one-to-one tutorials, creative writing courses and lectures. Send sae for leaflet. Founded 1987.

## S. Ribeiro, Literary Services

42 West Heath Court, North End Road, London NW11 7RG
*tel* 020-8458 9082
*email* sribeiroeditor@aol.com
*Contact* S. Ribeiro

Literary consultant and editor. MSS reading and appraisal with detailed chapter-by-chapter analysis. Sensitive editing for publication on disk or printout. Writing, rewriting and ghostwriting. Copywriting, including synopses and reader's reports to send to agents and publishers, book reviews and jacket information. Americanisation. Guidance in submission to publishers and in self-publishing. Creative writing tutor. Special experience and interests: literary fiction; memoirs and biography; theses; poetry; e-books. Published and new writers, including overseas, and small presses, welcome. Send sae or telephone for leaflet.

## Anton Rippon Press Services

20 Chain Lane, Michleover, Derby DE3 9AJ
*tel* 01332 510604
General feature and sports writing for newspapers and magazines. Ghostwriting (preliminary letter essential). Radio and film documentary treatments and scripts. Complete book production service. Part of the Breedon Publishing Group.

## Sandhurst Editorial Consultants

36 Albion Road, Sandhurst, Berks. GU47 9BP
*tel* (01252) 877645 *fax* (01252) 890508
*email* mail@sand-con.demon.co.uk
*website* www.sand-con.demon.co.uk
*Partners* Lionel Browne, Janet Browne

Specialists in technical, professional and reference work. Project management, editorial development, writing, rewriting, copy-editing, proofreading, and general editorial consultancy. Founded 1991.

## Sandton Literary Agency

PO Box 785799, Sandton 2146, South Africa
*tel* (011) 442-8624
*Directors* J. Victoria Canning, M. Sutherland

Evaluating, editing and/or indexing book MSS. Preparing reports, company histories, house journals, etc. Critical but constructive advice to writers. Lecture agents. Please write or phone first. Founded 1982.

## SciText

18 Barton Close, Landrake, Saltash, Cornwall PL12 5BA

*tel* (01752) 851451 *fax* (01752) 851451
*email* bg@scitext.fsnet.co.uk
*Contact* Dr Brian Gee

Proofreading and editing in science, chemical and electrical engineering and the history of science and technology; IBM compatible PC. Founded 1988.

## SfEP (Society for Editors and Proofreaders) – see Society for Editors and Proofreaders (SfEP)

## Gill Shepherd

87 Elm Park Mansions, Park Walk, London SW10 0AP
*tel* 020-7352 1770
*email* rgbshepherd@msn.com

Research, fact checking, rewriting for authors. Specialises in history, politics, biography and genealogy. Established 1985.

## Small Print

The Old School House, 74 High Street, Swavesey, Cambridge CB4 5QU
*tel* (01954) 231713 *fax* (01954) 205061
*email* info@smallprint.co.uk
*website* www.smallprint.co.uk
*Proprietor* Naomi Laredo

Editorial, design, page layout, project management, and audio production services for conventional or electronic publishing. Textbooks, manuals, travel guides, websites, newsletters. Translation from/to and editing in many European and Asian languages. Photography and picture research. Founded 1986.

## Society of Indexers – see page 614

## Special Edition Pre-press Services

*Partners* Romilly Hambling, 17 Almorah Road, London N1 3ER
*and* Corinne Orde, 2 Caledonian Wharf, London E14 3EW
*tel* 020-7226 5339 *fax* 020-7226 5339
*email* mail@special-edition.co.uk
*website* www.special-edition.co.uk
*tel* 020-7987 9600 *fax* 020-7987 9600

Integrated editing and page make-up for publishers of general and STM titles. Design and project management undertaken. See website for downloadable brochure. Established 1993.

## Mrs Gene M. Spencer

63 Castle Street, Melbourne, Derbyshire DE73 1DY
*tel* (01332) 862133
*email* genespencer@supanet.com

Editing, copy-editing and proofreading; feature writing; theatrical profiles; book reviews; freelance writing. Founded 1970.

## SPREd (Society of Picture Researchers and Editors) – now The Picture Research Association, see page 530

## StorytrackS
PO Box 3155, Glastonbury, Somerset BA16 0EJ
*tel* (01395) 279659
*email* storytracks@aol.com
*website* www.storytracks.net
*Directors* Marina Oliver, Margaret James, Chris Dukes

A team of widely published writers offer honest appraisals of MSS and comment on content and structure. Constructive guidance is based on extensive experience and sound market awareness. Specialist consultants in children's and teenage fiction, and theatre, radio and screenplays. Fiction typescripts of publishable quality are guaranteed consideration by an appropriate editor or agent. Also offers ghostwriting services, advice on self-publishing and editorial assistance. Founded 2001.

## Strand Editorial Services
16 Mitchley View, South Croydon, Surrey CR2 9HQ
*tel* 020-8657 1247 *fax* 020-8651 3525
*Joint Principals* Derek and Irene Bradley

Provide a comprehensive service to publishers, editorial departments, and public relations and advertising agencies. Proofreading and copy-editing a speciality. Founded 1974.

## Success Writing Bureau
Thirsol House, Earby, Barnoldswick, Lancs BB18 6NE
*tel* (01282) 842495 *fax* (01282) 842495
*email* john@writers-aid-services.com
*website* www.john@writers-aid-services.com
*Contact* John O'Toole

MSS appraisal with agency links where applicable. Home study courses in journalism/article writing, short story, radio, TV and novel writing. Speedy turnaround. John O'Toole tutorials since 1965; bureau founded 1980.

## Hans Tasiemka Archives
80 Temple Fortune Lane, London NW11 7TU
*tel* 020-8455 2485 *fax* 020-8455 0231
*Proprietor* Mrs Edda Tasiemka

Comprehensive newspaper cuttings library from 1850s to the present day on all subjects for writers, publishers, picture researchers, film and TV companies. Founded 1950.

## Lyn M. Taylor
Anchorfield, 9 Gosford Road, Port Seton, East Lothian EH32 0HE
*tel* (01875) 812315 *fax* (01875) 814126
*email* eve.line@virgin.net

General comprehensive editorial service for publishers: copy-editing (hard copy or onscreen) and proofreading in all subjects. Specialises in scientific and medical books, journals and reports and wildlife publishing. Formatting, coding, author collation, template creation.

## Tecmedia Ltd
Bruce House, 258 Bromham Road, Biddenham, Beds. MK40 4AA
*tel* (01234) 325223 *fax* (01234) 353524
*email* jojobaxter@cs.com
*Managing Director* J.D. Baxter

Specialists in the design, development and production of information packages, newsletters and promotional material. Founded 1972.

## Teral Research Services
111 The Avenue, Bournemouth, Dorset BH9 2UX
*tel* (01202) 519220
45 Forest View Road, Bournemouth BH9 3BH
*tel* (01202) 516834 *fax* (01202) 516834
*Contact* Alan C. Wood, Terry C. Treadwell

Research and consultancy on military aviation, army, navy, defence, space, weapons (new and antique), police, intelligence, medals, uniforms and armour. Founded 1980.

## The Freelance Editorial Service
4 Cranston Drive, Cousland, Dalkeith, Midlothian EH22 2PP
*tel* 0131-663 1238
*email* williamhouston@amserve.com
*Contact* Bill Houston BSc, DipLib, MPhil

Editing, proofreading, indexing, abstracting, translations, bibliographies; particularly scientific and medical. Founded 1975.

## The Literary Consultancy (TLC)
Diorama Arts Centre, 34 Osnaburgh Street, London NW1 3ND
*tel* 020-7813 4330 *fax* 020-7813 4330
*email* swifttlc@dircon.co.uk
*website* www.literaryconsultancy.co.uk
*Director* Rebecca Swift, *Administrator* Rebecca de Saintonge

Offers a detailed assessment of fiction, non-fiction and autobiography from a team of professional editors and writers. Fees based on length. Quick turnaround. Personal links with agents and publishers. Approved by the Arts Council England. Established 1996.

## Thoughtbubble Ltd
58–60 Fitzroy Street, London W1T 5BU
*tel* 020-7387 8890 *fax* 020-7383 2220
*email* enquiries@thoughtbubble.com
*website* www.thoughtbubble.com
*Contact* James Maltby

Website design and development, database integration, Flash animation, audio/video editing and production, e-commerce, intranet design and development, software development, print design, CD-Rom design and production. Also presentation, training and website hosting. Founded 1997.

## Felicity Trotman
Downside, Chicklade, Salisbury, Wilts. SP3 5SU
*tel* (01747) 820503 *fax* (01747) 820503
*email* f.trotman@btinternet.com

For publishers only: editing, copy-editing, proofreading, writing, rewriting. Children's books only, fiction activity and non-fiction, all ages. Established 1982.

## John Vickers
27 Shorrolds Road, London SW6 7TR
*tel* 020-7385 5774

Archives of British Theatre photographs by John Vickers, from 1938–74.

## Gordon R. Wainwright
22 Hawes Court, Sunderland SR6 8NU
*tel* 0191-548 9342 *fax* 0191-548 9342
*email* gordon@gordonwainwright.co.uk
*website* www.gordonwainwright.co.uk

Criticism, advice and revision for non-fiction authors; training seminars in business writing, speed reading, freelance journalism and other subjects; non-fiction authors' publishing consultant. Established 1961.

## Susan Wallace
PO Box 95, Lark Lane, Liverpool L17 8WY
*tel* 0151-233 3689
*email* susanwallace@blueyonder.co.uk
*website* www.susanwallace.co.uk
*Contact* Susan Wallace BA(Hons), MA

Specialises in UK national feature writing and online journalism, especially for the women's market. Psychology graduate and expert writer with worldwide syndication of psychology quizzes, features and columns. Provides agency creative copywriting and editorial services at a senior level. Other special interests include exclusive true-life and reportage, relationships/sex, health, TV/showbiz, casino gambling (with industry experience), off-beat/lifestyle and travel. MA in Screenwriting. Established 1988.

## Caroline White
78 Howard Road, London E17 4SQ
*tel* 020-8521 579; 07890 800 465
*email* cwhite@bmjgroup.com

Journalist specialising in health and medicine. Press and public relations. Written and spoken Italian, Spanish and French. Founded 1985.

## Derek Wilde
59 Victoria Road, Woodbridge, Suffolk IP12 1EL
*tel* (01394) 384557 *fax* (01394) 384557
*email* jillderek@care4free.net

Copy-editing, proofreading, indexing, research. Particular expertise in directories and reference books. Special interests: higher education, performing arts, travel and transport. Languages: French and Latin plus some knowledge of German and Italian. Established 1991.

## David L. Williams
7 Buckbury Heights, Newport,
Isle of Wight PO30 2LX
*tel* (01983) 528729 *fax* (01983) 822116
*email* davidw@genpix.fsnet.co.uk

Complete research and information service (pictures and text) specialising in transport, particularly maritime and aviation; history and genealogy. Established 1982.

## David Winpenny
33 St Marygate, Ripon, North Yorkshire HG4 1LX
*tel* (01765) 608320 *fax* (01765) 607641
*email* david@dwpr.freeserve.co.uk

Writer and editor, including research and writing of features, news stories, brochures, speeches, advertising copy. Full public relations service. Special interest in country walks, architectural history, the arts, music, landscape, heritage, business and the North. Founded 1991.

## Rita Winter Editorial Services
'Kilrubie', Eddleston, Peeblesshire EH45 8QP
*tel* (01721) 730353 *fax* (01721) 730353
*email* rita@ednet.co.uk

Fiction (crime, literary, fantasy) and non-fiction (biography, travel, art/design, complementary medicine, New Age. Copy-editing and proofreading (English and Dutch). Founded 1988.

## WORDSmith
2 The Island, Thames Ditton, Surrey KT7 0SH
*tel* 020-8339 0945 *fax* 020-8339 0945
*email* mruswords@aol.com
*website* www.good-writing-matters.com
*Partners* Michael Russell, Elaine Russell

Copy-editing on paper and onscreen: all areas including film scripts. Specialises in new writer fiction, rewriting and abridging. Also short-run publishing for new writing, as Riverside Press. No poetry. Founded 1998.

## Wordwise
37 Elmthorpe Road, Wolvercote, Oxford OX2 8PA
*tel* (01865) 510098 *fax* (01865) 310556
*email* wordwise@mendes.demon.co.uk
*Director* Valerie Mendes

Specialises in creative writing projects for children and young adults. Author of *Girl in the Attic, Coming of Age, Lost and Found, Beyond the Waves.* Founded 1990.

## Richard M. Wright

32 Oak Village, London NW5 4QN
*tel* 020-7284 4316
*email* rmwindserv@aol.com

Indexing, copy-editing, specialising in politics, history, business, social sciences. Founded 1977.

## Write

3 Cedar Park, Caterham, Surrey CR3 5DZ
*tel* (07956) 352770 (01883) 370967
*email* mikedonald@dunelm.org.uk
*Director* Mike Donald

General copy-editing, proofreading and rewriting. Specialises in technical work: maths, science, technology and management studies; also sports and children's literature. Established 2003.

## The Write Coach

2 Rowan Close, Wokingham, Berks. RG41 4BH
*tel* 0118-978 4904
*email* info@thewritecoach.co.uk
*website* www.thewritecoach.co.uk
*Contact* Rebecca Hill

One-to-one coaching and workshops to develop the writer and their writing, build confidence, increase motivation, release blocks, increase creativity and assist both professional and aspiring writers to become more successful. Established 2002.

## Write on ...

62 Kiln Lane, Oxford OX3 8EY
*tel* (01865) 744336 *fax* (01865) 744336
*email* yn@writeon1989.co.uk
*Director* Yvonne Newman

Non-fiction book planning. Preparation of open-learning handbooks.Feature writing and photography. Subjects: UK property, family, history, consumer and retirement issues. Founded 1989.

## The Writers' Exchange

14 Old School Mews, Bacup, Lancs. OL13 0QN
*tel* (01706) 877480
*email* writers'exchange@j-m-wright.freeserve.co.uk
*website* www.world-wide-words.co.uk
*Secretary* Mike Wright

Copywriting, ghostwriting, internet publishing and editorial services, including appraisal service for amateur writers preparing to submit material to literary agents/publishers. Offers 'constructive, objective evaluation service, particularly for those who cannot get past the standard rejection slip barrier, or who have had work rejected by publishers and need an impartial view of why it did not sell'. Novels, short stories, film, TV, radio and stage plays. Send sae for details. Founded 1977.

## Martyn Yeo

66 Russell Road, Lee-on-the-Solent,
Hants PO13 9HP
*tel* 023-9235 9960 *fax* 0871 733 5554
*email* martyn@wordwise.co.uk
*Contact* Martyn Yeo

Typesetting and editorial servies offered to publishers only. Scope includes database publishing and project management, especially for directories and loose-leaf titles. Member of SfEP. Established 1984.

## Hans Zell, Publishing Consultant

Glais Bheinn, Lochcarron, Ross-shire IV54 8YB
*tel* (01520) 722951 *fax* (01520) 722953
*email* hanszell@hanszell.co.uk
*website* www.hanszell.co.uk/

Consultancies, project evaluations, market assessments, feasibility studies, research and surveys, funding proposals, freelance editorial work, commissioning, journals management, internet training. Specialises in services to publishers and the book community in Third World countries and provides specific expertise in these areas. Also mailing list services, and information resources (pint/online) on African publishing and African studies. Founded 1987.

# Government offices and public services

Enquiries to any of the following bodies should be accompanied by a sae. Details of many other public bodies can be found in *Whitaker's Almanack*.

## Advertising Standards Authority
2 Torrington Place, London WC1E 7HW
*tel* 020-7580 5555 *fax* 020-7631 3051
*email* enquiries@asa.org.uk
*website* www.asa.org.uk

## Advisory, Concilliation and Arbitration Service
Brandon House, 180 Borough High Street, London SE1 1LW
*tel* 020-7210 3613 *fax* 020-7210 3708
*website* www.acas.org.uk

## Ministry of Agriculture, Fisheries and Food – see DEFRA (Department for Environment, Food and Rural Affairs)

## American Embassy
24 Grosvenor Square, London W1A 1AE
*tel* 020-7499 9000
*website* www.usembassy.org.uk

## Ancient Monuments Board for Wales (CADW)
Crown Buildings, Cathays Park, Cardiff CF10 3NQ
*tel* 029-2050 0200 *fax* 029-2082 6375
*email* cadw@wales.gsi.gov.uk
*website* www.cadw.wales.gov.uk

## Apsley House, The Wellington Museum
Hyde Park Corner, London W1J 7NT
*tel* 020-7499 5676 *fax* 020-7493 6576
*website* www.apsleyhouse.org.uk
Open Tues–Sun, 11am–5pm.

## Arts Council England – see page 502

## Arts Council of Northern Ireland – see page 502

## Arts Council of Wales – see page 502

## Australian High Commission
Australia House, Strand, London WC2B 4LA
*tel* 020-7379 4334 *fax* 020-7240 5333
*website* www.australia.org.uk

## Austrian Embassy
18 Belgrave Mews West, London SW1X 8HU
*tel* 020-7235 3731 *fax* 020-7344 0292
*email* embassy@austria.org.uk
*website* www.austria.org.uk
Austrian Cultural Forum, 28 Rutland Gate, London SW7 1PQ
*tel* 020-7584 8653 *fax* 020-7225 0470
*email* culture@austria.org.uk

## The Bank of England
Threadneedle Street, London EC2R 8AH
*tel* 020-7601 4444 *fax* 020-7601 4771
*website* www.bankofengland.co.uk

## Belgian Embassy
103 Eaton Square, London SW1W 9AB
*tel* 020-7470 3700 *fax* 020-7470 3795
*email* info@belgium-embassy.co.uk
*website* www.diplobel.org/uk

## Bodleian Library
Oxford OX1 3BG
*tel* (01865) 277000 *fax* (01865) 277182
*email* enquiries@bodley.ox.ac.uk
*website* www.bodley.ox.ac.uk

## Embassy of Bosnia and Herzegovina
5–7 Lexham Gardens, London W8 5JJ
*tel* 020-7373 0867 *fax* 020-7373 0871

## British Board of Film Classification
3 Soho Square, London W1D 3HD
*tel* 020-7440 1570 *fax* 020-7287 0141
*email* webmaster@bbfc.co.uk
*website* www.bbfc.co.uk

## British Broadcasting Corporation
Broadcasting House, London W1A 1AA
*tel* 020-7580 4468
*website* www.bbc.co.uk

## The British Council – see page 509

## British Film Commission
10 Little Portland Street, London W1W 7JG
*tel* 020-7861 7860 *fax* 020-7861 7864
*email* info@bfc.co.uk
*website* www.bfc.co.uk

## British Film Institute – see page 509

## The British Library
96 Euston Road, London NW1 2DB
*tel* 020-7412 7332 *fax* 020-7412 7340
*website* www.bl.uk
See also page 627.

## British Library Document Supply
Boston Spa, Wetherby, West Yorkshire LS23 7BQ
*tel* (01937) 546060 *fax* (01937) 546333
*email* dsc-customer-services@bl.uk
*website* www.bl.uk

## British Library Newspaper Library
Colindale Avenue, London NW9 5HE
*tel* 020-7412 7353 *fax* 020-7412 7379
*email* newspaper@bl.uk
*website* www.bl.uk/collections/newspaper/

## British Museum
Great Russell Street, London WC1B 3DG
*tel* 020-7323 8000
*email* information@thebritishmuseum.ac.uk
*website* www.thebritishmuseum.ac.uk

## British Railways Board – see Strategic Rail
Authority

## British Standards Institution
Technical Information Group, 389 Chiswick High
Road, London W4 4AL
*tel* 020-8996 7111 *fax* 020-8996 7048
*email* the@bsi-global.com
*website* www.bsi-global.com

## VisitBritain
Thames Tower, Black's Road, London W6 9EL
*tel* 020-8846 9000 *fax* 020-8563 0302
*website* www.visitbritain.com/presscentre

## Broadcasting Standards Commission –
see The Office of Communications (Ofcom)

## Embassy of the Republic of Bulgaria
186–188 Queen's Gate, London SW7 5HL
*tel* 020-7584 9400/9433, 020-7581 3144 (5 lines)
*fax* 020-7584 4948
*email* bgembasy@globalnet.co.uk

## The Cabinet Office
70 Whitehall, London SW1A 2AS
*tel* 020-7276 1234
*website* www.cabinet-office.gov.uk

## Cadw: Welsh Historic Monuments
Crown Building, Cathays Park, Cardiff CF10 3NQ
*tel* 029-2050 0200 *fax* 029-2082 6375
*email* cadw@wales.gsi.gov.uk
*website* www.cadw.wales.gov.uk

## Canadian High Commission
Cultural Affairs Section, Canada House, Trafalgar
Square, London SW1Y 5BJ
*tel* 020-7258 6412 *fax* 020-7258 6434
*Contact* Literature Officer

## Central Office of Information – see COI
Communications

## CILT, The National Centre for Languages
20 Bedfordbury, London WC2N 4LB
*tel* 020-7379 5101 *fax* 020-7379 5082
*email* library@cilt.org.uk
*website* www.cilt.org.uk

## Charity Commission
Harmsworth House, 13–15 Bouverie Street,
London EC4Y 8DP
*tel* (0870) 3330123, *minicom* (0870) 3330125
*fax* 020-7674 2300
*email* enquiries@charitycommission.gsi.gov.uk
*website* www.charitycommission.gsi.gov.uk
2nd Floor, 20 King's Parade, Queen's Dock,
Liverpool L3 4DQ
*tel* (0870) 3330123 *fax* 0151-703 1555
Woodfield House, Tangier, Taunton,
Somerset TA1 4BL
*tel* (0870) 3330123 *fax* (01823) 345003

## Church Commissioners
1 Millbank, London SW1P 3JZ
*tel* 020-7898 1000  *fax* 020-7898 1131
*website* www.churchcommissioners.org

## Civil Aviation Authority
CAA House, 45–59 Kingsway, London WC2B 6TE
*tel* 020-7393 7311
*website* www.caa.co.uk

## The Coal Authority
200 Lichfield Lane, Mansfield, Notts. NG18 4RG
*tel* (01623) 427162 *fax* (01623) 622072
*email* thecoalauthority@coal.gov.uk
*website* www.coal.gov.uk

## COI Communications
Hercules House, Hercules Road, London SE1 7DU
*tel* 020-7928 2345

## College of Arms (or Heralds' College)
Queen Victoria Street, London EC4V 4BT
*tel* 020-7248 2762 *fax* 020-7248 6448
*email* enquiries@college-of-arms.gov.uk
*website* www.college-of-arms.gov.uk

## Commission for Architecture and the
## Built Environment (CABE)
The Tower Building, 11 York Road, London SE1 7NX
*tel* 020-7960 2400 *fax* 020-7960 2444
*email* enquiries@cabe.org.uk
*website* www.cabe.org.uk

## Commission for Integrated Transport
Romney House, 5th Floor, 43 Marsham Street,
London SW1P 3HW

*tel* 020-7944 4101 *fax* 020-7944 2919
*website* www.cfit.gov.uk

## Commission for Racial Equality
St Dunstan's House, 201 Borough High Street,
London SE1 1GZ
*tel* 020-7939 0000 *fax* 020-7939 0004
*website* www.cre.gov.uk

## Committee on Standards in Public Life
35 Great Smith Street, London SW1P 3BQ
*tel* 020-7276 2595 *fax* 020-7276 2585
*email* nigel.wicks@gtnet.gov.uk
*website* www.public-standards.gov.uk

## Commonwealth Secretariat
Marlborough House, Pall Mall, London SW1Y 5HX
*tel* 020-7747 6200 *fax* 020-7930 6128
*email* info@commonwealth.int
*website* www.thecommonwealth.org

## Community Fund
St Vincent House, 16 Suffolk Street,
London SW1Y 4NL
*tel* 020-7747 5300 *fax* 020-7747 5297
*website* www.community-fund.org.uk

## Competition Commission (CC)
Victoria House, Southampton Row,
London WC1B 4AD
*tel* 020-7271 0100 *fax* 020-7271 0367
*email* info@competition-commission.gsi.gov.uk
*website* www.competition-commission.gsi.org.gov

## Contributions Agency, International Services (InS) – see The Inland Revenue

## Copyright Enquiries – see Patent Office

## Copyright Tribunal
Room 1/8, Harmsworth House, 13–15 Bouverie
Street, London EC4Y 8DP
*tel* 020-7596 6510 *textphone* (08459) 222250
*fax* 020-7596 6526
*email* copyright.tribunal@patent.gov.uk
*website* www.patent.gov.uk/copy/tribunal/index.htm

## Corporation of London Records Office
c/o London Metropolitan Archives,
40 Northampton Road, London EC1R 0HB
*tel* 020-7332 1251 *fax* 020-7710 8682
*email* CLRO@corpoflondon.gov.uk
*website* www.cityoflondon.gov.uk/archives/clro

## Corporation of Trinity House
Tower Hill, London EC3N 4DH
*tel* 020-7481 6900 *fax* 020-7480 7662
*email* howard.cooper@thls.org
*website* www.trinityhouse.co.uk

## Countryside Agency
John Dower House, Crescent Place, Cheltenham,
Glos. GL50 3RA
*tel* (01242) 521381 *fax* (01242) 584270
*website* www.countryside.gov.uk

## Countryside Council for Wales/Cyngor Cefn Gwlad Cymru
Maes y Ffynnon Penrhosgarnedd, Bangor,
Gwynedd LL57 2DW
*tel* (01248) 385500 *fax* (01248) 355782

## Court of the Lord Lyon
HM New Register House, Edinburgh EH1 3YT
*tel* 0131-556 7255 *fax* 0131-557 2148

## Crafts Council
Resource Centre, 44A Pentonville Road,
London N1 9BY
*tel* 020-7806 2501 *fax* 020-7833 4479
*email* reference@craftscouncil.org.uk
*website* www.craftscouncil.org.uk

## Embassy of the Republic of Croatia
21 Conway Street, London W1T 6BN
*tel* 020-7387 1790 *fax* 020-7387 3289

## Department for Culture, Media and Sport
2–4 Cockspur Street, London SW1Y 5DH
*tel* 020-7211 6200
*email* enquiries@culture.gov.uk
*website* www.culture.gov.uk

## Cyprus High Commission
93 Park Street, London W1K 7ET
*tel* 020-7499 8272 *fax* 020-7491 0691
*email* cyphclondon@dial.pipex.com,
presscounsellor@chclondon.org.uk (press office)
*website* www.cyprus.gov.cy

## Embassy of the Czech Republic
26 Kensington Palace Gardens, London W8 4QY
*tel* 020-7243 1115 *fax* 020-7727 9654
*email* london@embassy.mzv.cz
*website* www.czechembassy.org.uk

## Ministry of Defence
Northumberland House, Northumberland Avenue,
London WC2N 5BP
*tel* 020-7218 9000
*website* www.mod.uk

## DEFRA (Department for Environment, Food and Rural Affairs)
3–8 Whitehall Place, London SW1A 2HH
*tel* 020-7270 8000 *Helpline* (0845) 9335577
*fax* 020-7270 8419
*website* www.defra.gov.uk

## Design Council
34 Bow Street, London WC2E 7DL
*tel* 020-7420 5200 *fax* 020-7420 5300
*email* info@designcouncil.org.uk
*website* www.designcouncil.org.uk

## DFID (Department for International Development)
1 Palace Street, London SW1E 5HE
*tel* 020-7023 0000
*email* enquiry@dfid.gov.uk
*website* www.dfid.gov.uk
Abercrombie House, Eaglesham Road,
East Kilbride, Glasgow G75 8EA
*tel* (01355) 844000
*Public Enquiry Point tel* (0845) 300 4100 (local rate)
*tel* (01355) 843132 (for enquiries from overseas)

## Disability Rights Commission
DRC, Stratford upon Avon CV37 9BR
*tel* (0845) 762 2633 (DRC Helpline)
*website* www.drc-gb.org

## DTI (Department of Trade and Industry)
1 Victoria Street, London SW1H 0ET
*tel* 020-7215 5000 (general enquiries)
*minicom/textphone* 020-7215 6740 *fax* 020-7215 0105
*website* www.dti.gov.uk

## DTLR (Department of Transport, Local Government and the Regions)
Eland House, Bressenden Place, London SW1E 5DU
Great Minster House, 76 Marsham Street,
London SW1P 4DR
Ashdown House, 123 Victoria Street,
London SW1E 6DE
*tel* 020-7944 3000
*website* www.dtlr.gov.uk

## DWP (Department for Work and Pensions)
Richmond House, 79 Whitehall, London SW1A 2NS
*tel* 020-7238 0800

## Economic and Social Research Council
Polaris House, North Star Avenue, Swindon,
Wilts. SN2 1UJ
*tel* (01793) 413000 *fax* (01793) 413130
*email* exrel@esrc.ac.uk
*website* www.esrc.ac.uk

## Department for Education and Skills
Sanctuary Buildings, Great Smith Street,
London SW1P 3BT
*tel* (0870) 000 2288 *minicom* (01928) 794274
*fax* (01928) 794248
*email* info@dfes.gsi.gov.uk
*website* www.dfes.gov.uk

## Engineering and Physical Sciences Research Council
Polaris House, North Star Avenue, Swindon,
Wilts. SN2 1ET
*tel* (01793) 444000
*email* infoline@epsrc.ac.uk
*website* www.epsrc.ac.uk
*Press Officer* Jane Reck *tel* (01793) 444312
*email* jane.reck@epsrc.ac.uk

## English Heritage
23 Savile Row, London W1S 2ET
*tel* 020-7973 3000 *fax* 020-7973 3001
*website* www.english-heritage.org.uk

## English Nature
Northminster House, Peterborough PE1 1UA
*tel* (01733) 455000 *fax* (01733) 568834
*email* www.english-nature.org.uk

## The Environment Agency
*Head Office* Rio House, Waterside Drive, Aztec West,
Almondsbury, Bristol BS32 4UD
*tel* (01454) 624400 *fax* (01454) 624409
*website* www.environment-agency.gov.uk

## Equality Commission for Northern Ireland
Equality House, 7–9 Shaftesbury Square,
Belfast BT2 7DP
*tel* 028-9050 0600  *fax* 028-9033 1544
*email* information@equalityni.org
*website* www.equalityni.org

## Equal Opportunities Commission
Arndale House, Arndale Centre, Manchester M4 3EQ
*tel* (0845) 601 5901 *fax* 0161-838 8303
*email* info@eoc.org.uk
*website* www.eoc.org.uk

## The European Commission
8 Storey's Gate, London SW1P 3AT
*tel* 020-7973 1992 *fax* 020-7973 1900
*email* eu-uk-press@cec.eu.int
*website* www.cec.org.uk

## European Parliament
*UK Office* 2 Queen Anne's Gate, London SW1H 9AA
*tel* 020-7227 4300 *fax* 020-7227 4302
*email* eplondon@europarl.eu.int
*website* www.europarl.org.uk

## European Parliament Office in Scotland
The Tun, 4 Jackson's Entry, Holyrood Road,
Edinburgh EH8 8PJ
*tel* 0131-557 7866 *fax* 0131-557 4977
*email* epedinburgh@europarl.eu.int
*website* www.europarl.org.uk

## Embassy of Finland
38 Chesham Place, London SW1X 8HW
*tel* 020-7838 6200 *fax* 020-7235 3680 (general)
020-7259 5602 (press and information office)
*website* www.finemb.org.uk

## Food Standards Agency Northern Ireland
10B and 10C Clarendon Road, Belfast BT1 3BG
*tel* 028-9041 7700 *fax* 028-9041 7726
*email* infosani@foodstandards.gsi.gov.uk
*website* www.food.gov.uk

## Food Standards Agency Scotland
St Magnus House, 25 Guild Street,
Aberdeen AB11 6NJ
*tel* (01224) 285100 *fax* (01224) 285167
*email* scotland@foodstandards.gsi.gov.uk
*website* www.food.gov.uk

## Food Standards Agency (UK)
Aviation House, 125 Kingsway, London WC2B 6NH
*tel* 020-7276 8000 *fax* 020-7276 8004
*website* www.food.gov.uk

## Food Standards Agency Wales
1st Floor, Southgate House, Wood Street,
Cardiff CF10 1EW
*tel* 029-2067 8999 *fax* 029-2067 8919
*email* wales@foodstandards.gsi.gov.uk
*website* www.food.gov.uk

## Foreign and Commonwealth Office
King Charles Street, London SW1A 2AH
*tel* 020-7270 3000
*website* www.fco.gov.uk

## Forestry Commission
Silvan House, 231 Corstorphine Road,
Edinburgh EH12 7AT
*tel* 0131-334 0303 *fax* 0131-334 4473
*email* info@forestry.gov.uk
*website* www.forestry.gov.uk

## French Embassy
58 Knightsbridge, London SW1X 7JT
*tel* 020-7073 1000
*email* box.office@ambafrance.org.uk
*website* www.institut-francais.org.uk
*Cultural Department* 23 Cromwell Road,
London SW7 2EL
*tel* 020-7073 1300

## German Embassy
23 Belgrave Square, London SW1X 8PZ
*tel* 020-7824 1300 *fax* 020-7824 1435
*email* mail@german-embassy.org.uk
*website* www.german-embassy.org.uk

## Government Communications Headquarters (GCHQ)
Priors Road, Cheltenham, Glos. GL52 5AJ
*tel* (01242) 221491 *fax* (01242) 574349
*website* www.gchq.gov.uk

## Embassy of Greece
Press and Communications Office, 1A Holland Park,
London W11 3TP
*tel* 020-7727 3071 *fax* 020-7727 8960
*email* pressoffice@greekembassy.org.uk

## Hayward Gallery
Belvedere Road, London SE1 8XZ
*tel* 020-7960 5226 *fax* 020-7401 2664
*website* www.hayward.org.uk

## Department of Health
Richmond House, 79 Whitehall, London SW1A 2NS
*tel* 020-7210 3000
*website* www.doh.gov.uk

## Health and Safety Executive Infoline
Caerphilly Business Park, Caerphilly CF83 3GG
*tel* (08701) 545500 *minicom* (02920) 808537
*fax* (02920) 859260
*email* hseinformationservices@natbrit.com
*website* www.hse.gov.uk

## Historical Manuscripts Commission –
### see The National Archives

## Historic Scotland
Longmore House, Salisbury Place,
Edinburgh EH9 1SH
*tel* 0131-668 8600 *fax* 0131-668 8699
*website* www.historic-scotland.gov.uk

## HM Customs and Excise
New King's Beam House, 5th Floor East,
22 Upper Ground, London SE1 9PJ
*tel* 020-7620 1313, (0845) 010900 (Advice Service)
*website* www.hmce.gov.uk

## HM Land Registry
Lincoln's Inn Fields, London WC2A 3PH
*tel* 020-7917 8894 *fax* 020-7917 5934
*email* michele.bennett@landreg.gsi.gov.uk
*website* www.landreg.gov.uk
*Head of Communications* Mrs M. Bennett

## HMSO Books – see The Stationery Office (TSO)

## HM Treasury
Parliament Street, London SW1P 3AG
*tel* 020-7270 5000 *Press Office tel* 020-7270 5238
*fax* 020-7270 5244
*website* www.hm-treasury.gov.uk

## Home Office
Queen Anne's Gate, London SW1H 9AT
*tel* 020-7273 3757
*Communication Director* B. Butler

## Housing Corporation
Maple House, 149 Tottenham Court Road,
London W1T 7BN
*tel* 020-7393 2000 *fax* 020-7393 2111
*email* enquiries@housingcorp.gsx.gov.uk
*website* www.housingcorp.gov.uk

## Human Fertilisation and Embryology Authority
Paxton House, 30 Artillery Lane, London E1 7LS
*tel* 020-7377 5077 *fax* 020-7377 1871
*website* www.hfea.gov.uk

## Human Genetics Commission
Area 652C, Skipton House, 80 London Road,
London SE1 6LH
*tel* 020-7972 1518 *fax* 020-7972 1717
*website* www.hgc.gov.uk

## Embassy of the Republic of Hungary
35 Eaton Place, London SW1X 8BY
*tel* 020-7235 5218 *fax* 020-7823 1348
*email* office@huemblon.org.uk
*website* www.huemblon.org.uk

## Imperial War Museum
Lambeth Road, London SW7 5BD
*tel* 020-7942 500
*website* www.iwm.org.uk

## The Independent Police Complaints Commission
90 High Holborn, London WC1V 6BH
*tel* 020-7166 3000
*website* www.ipcc.gov.uk

## Independent Television Commission –
see The Office of Communications (Ofcom)

## High Commission of India, Press & Information Wing
India House, Aldwych, London WC2B 4NA
*tel* 020-7836 8484 ext 147, 286, 327
*fax* 020-7836 2632
*email* 106167.1470@compuserve.com

## Information Commissioner's Office
Wycliffe House, Water Lane, Wilmslow,
Cheshire SK9 5AF
*tel* (01625) 545745(enquiries), (01625) 545700
(switchboard) *fax* (01625) 524510
*email* mail@ico.gsi.gov.uk
*website* www.informationcommissioner.gov.uk

## The Inland Revenue
Visitors Centre, Ground Floor, SW Wing,
Bush House, Strand, London WC2B 4RD
*tel* 020-7438 6420/5
*website* www.inlandrevenue.gov.uk
Inland Revenue, Centre for Non-Residents
(Newcastle), Benton Park View, Longbenton,
Newcastle upon Tyne NE98 1ZZ
*tel* 0191-225 4811 *fax* 0191-225 0067
*email* internationalservices.ir.sbg@ir.gsi.gov.uk

Contact Inland Revenue, Centre for Non-Residents
(Newcastle) for queries about working abroad and
paying National Insurance contributions.

## International Pension Centre
Tyneview Park, Whitley Road,
Newcastle upon Tyne NE98 1BA
*tel* 0191-218 7777
*email* TVP-IPC-customer-care@thepensionservice.
gsi.gov.uk

## Embassy of Ireland
17 Grosvenor Place, London SW1X 7HR
*tel* 020-7235 2171 *fax* 020-7245 6961
Passport and Visa Office Montpelier House,
106 Brompton Road, London SW3 1JJ
*tel* 020-7225 7700 *fax* 020-7225 7777/8

## Embassy of Israel
2 Palace Green, London W8 4QB
*tel* 020-7957 9500 *fax* 020-7957 9555
*email* info-assist@london.mfa.gov.il
*website* www.israel-embassy.org.uk

## Italian Embassy
14 Three Kings Yard, London W1K 4EH
*tel* 020-7312 2200 *fax* 020-7312 2230
*email* ambasciata.londra@esteri.it
*website* www.embitaly.org.uk

## Embassy of Japan
101–104 Piccadilly, London W1J 7JT
*tel* 020-7465 6500 *fax* 020-7491 9347 (information)
*fax* 020-7491 9328 (visa section)
*email* info@embjapan.org.uk
*website* www.uk.emb-japan.go.jp

## Law Commission
Conquest House, 37–38 John Street, Theobalds
Road, London WC1N 2BQ
*tel* 020-7453 1220 *fax* 020-7453 1297
*email* chief.executive@lawcommission.gsi.gov.uk
*website* www.lawcom.gov.uk

## Learning and Skills Council
Cheylesmore House, Quinton Road, Coventry,
West Midlands CV1 2WT
*tel* (0845) 019 4170 *fax* 024-7649 3600
*website* www.lsc.gov.uk

## The Legal Deposit Office
The British Library, Boston Spa, Wetherby,
West Yorkshire LS23 7BY
*tel* (01937) 546267/546268 *fax* (01937) 546176

## Legal Services Commission
85 Gray's Inn Road, London WC1X 8TX
*tel* 020-7759 0000
*website* www.legalservices.gov.uk

## Embassy of Luxembourg
27 Wilton Crescent, London SW1X 8SD
*tel* 020-7235 6961 *fax* 020-7235 9734

## Malta High Commission
Malta House, 36–38 Piccadilly, London W1J 0LE
*tel* 020-7292 4800 *fax* 020-7734 1831
*website* www.foreign.gov.mt/london

## Medical Research Council
20 Park Crescent, London W1B 1AL
*tel* 020-7636 5422 *fax* 020-7436 6179
*email* firstname.surname@headoffice.mrc.ac.uk
*website* www.mrc.ac.uk

## Millennium Commission
Portland House, Stag Place, London SW1E 5EZ
*tel* 020-7880 2001 *fax* 020-7880 2000
*email* info@millennium.gov.uk
*website* www.millennium.gov.uk

## Monopolies and Mergers Commission –
now Competition Commission (CC)

## Museum of London
London Wall, London EC2Y 5HN
*tel* 020-7600 3699 *fax* 020-7600 1058
*email* info@museumoflondon.org.uk
*website* www.museumoflondon.org.uk

## Museums, Libraries and Archives Council
16 Queen Anne's Gate, London SW1H 9AA
*tel* 020-7273 1444 *fax* 020-7273 1404
*website* www.mla.gov.uk

## The National Archives
Ruskin Avenue, Kew, Richmond,
Surrey TW9 4DU
*tel* 020-8876 3444 *fax* 020-8878 8905
*email* enquiry@nationalarchives.gov.uk
*website* www.nationalarchives.gov.uk

## The National Archives of Scotland
HM General Register House,
Edinburgh EH1 3YY
*tel* 0131-535 1314 *fax* 0131-535 1360
*email* enquiries@nas.gov.uk
*website* www.nas.gov.uk

## National Army Museum
Royal Hospital Road, London SW3 4HT
*tel* 020-7730 0717 *fax* 020-7823 6573
*website* www.national-army-museum.ac.uk

## National Assembly for Wales
Public Information and Education Services,
Cardiff Bay, Cardiff CF99 1NA
*tel* 029-2089 8200
*email* Assembly.Info@wales.gsi.gov.uk
*website* www.wales.gov.uk

## National Audit Office
157–197 Buckingham Palace Road,
London SW1W 9SP
*tel* 020-7798 7000 *fax* 020-7798 7070
*email* enquiries@nao.gsi.gov.uk
Audit House, 23-24 Park Place, Cardiff CF1 3BA
*tel* 029-2037 8661 *fax* 029-2067 8501

## National Consumer Council
20 Grosvenor Gardens, London SW1W 0DH
*tel* 020-7730 3469 *fax* 020-7730 0191
*email* info@ncc.org.uk
*website* www.ncc.org.uk

## National Galleries of Scotland
**National Gallery of Scotland**
The Mound, Edinburgh EH2 2EL
**Scottish National Portrait Gallery**
1 Queen Street, Edinburgh EH2 1JD
**Scottish National Gallery of Modern Art**
Belford Road, Edinburgh EH4 3DR
**The Dean Gallery**
Belford Road, Edinburgh EH4 3DS
*tel* 0131-624 6200, 0131-624 6332 (press office)
*fax* 0131-343 3250 (press office)
*email* pressinfo@nationalgalleries.org
*website* www.nationalgalleries.org

## National Gallery
Trafalgar Square, London WC2N 5DN
*tel* 020-7747 2885 *fax* 020-7747 2423
*email* information@ng-london.org.uk
*website* www.nationalgallery.org.uk

## National Library of Scotland
George IV Bridge, Edinburgh EH1 1EW
*tel* 0131-226 4531 *fax* 0131-622 4803
*email* enquiries@nls.uk
*website* www.nls.uk

## The National Library of Wales
Aberystwyth, Ceredigion SY23 3BU
*email* holi@llgc.org.uk
*website* www.llgc.org.uk

## National Lottery Commission
101 Wigmore Street, London W1U 1QU
*tel* 020-7016 3400 *fax* 020-7016 3464

*email* publicaffairs@natlotcomm.gov.uk
*website* www.natlotcomm.gov.uk

## National Maritime Museum
Greenwich, London SE10 9NF
*tel* 020-8858 4422 *fax* 020-8312 6632
*websites* www.nmm.ac.uk, www.port.nmm.ac.uk
(gateway site for maritime information),
www.rog.nmm.ac.uk (for astronomy information)

## The National Monuments Record
English Heritage, National Monuments Record
Centre, Kemble Drive, Swindon, Wilts. SN2 2GZ
*tel* (01793) 414600 *fax* (01793) 414606
*email* nmrinfo@english-heritage.org.uk
*website* www.english-heritage.org.uk

## National Museums and Galleries of Wales/Amgueddfeydd Ac Orielau Cenedlaethol Cymru
Cathays Park, Cardiff CF10 3NP
*tel* 029-2039 7951  *fax* 029-2037 3219
*website* www.nmgw.ac.uk

## National Museums Liverpool
PO Box 33, 127 Dale Street, Liverpool L69 3LA
*tel* 0151-207 0001  *fax* 0151-478 4790

## National Museums of Scotland
Chambers Street, Edinburgh EH1 1JF
*tel* 0131-225 7534  *fax* 0131-220 4819
*website* www.nms.ac.uk

## National Portrait Gallery
St Martin's Place, London WC2H 0HE
*tel* 020-7306 0055  *fax* 020-7306 0056
*website* www.npg.org.uk

## Natural Environment Research Council
Polaris House, North Star Avenue, Swindon,
Wilts. SN2 1EU
*tel* (01793) 411500 *fax* (01793) 411501
*email* requests@nerc.ac.uk
*website* www.nerc.ac.uk

## The Natural History Museum
Cromwell Road, London SW7 5BD
*tel* 020-7942 5000
*website* www.nhm.ac.uk

## NESTA (National Endowment for Science, Technology and the Arts
Fishmongers' Chambers, 110 Upper Thames Street,
London EC4R 3TW
*tel* 020-7645 9500  *fax* 020-7645 9501
*website* www.nesta.org.uk

## New Opportunities Fund
1 Plough Place, London EC4A 1DE

*tel* 020-7211 1800  *fax* 020-7211 1750
*website* www.nof.org.uk

## New Zealand High Commission
New Zealand House, Haymarket, London SW1Y 4TQ
*tel* 020-7930 8422 *fax* 020-7839 4580
*website* www.nzembassy.com/uk

## Northern Ireland Assembly
Parliament Buildings, Belfast BT4 3XX
*tel* 028-9052 1333

## Northern Ireland Authority for Energy Regulation
Brookmount Buildings, 42 Fountain Street,
Belfast BT1 5EE
*tel* 028-9031 1575 *fax* 028-9031 1740
*email* ofreg@nics.gov.uk
*website* www.ofreg.nics.gov.uk

## Northern Ireland Human Rights Commission
Temple Court, 39–41 North Street, Belfast BT1 1NA
*tel* 028-9024 3987  *fax* 028-9024 7844
*website* www.nihrc.org

## Northern Ireland Office
11 Millbank, London SW1P 4PN
*tel* 020-7210 3000
Castle Buildings, Belfast BT4 3ST
*tel* 028-9052 0700
*website* www.nio.gov.uk

## Northern Ireland Tourist Board
59 North Street, Belfast, Northern Ireland BT1 1NB
*tel* 028-9023 1221 *fax* 028-9024 0960
*email* info@nitb.com
*website* www.discovernorthernireland.com

## Office for National Statistics
1 Drummond Gate, London SW1V 2QQ
*tel* (0845) 601 3034
*website* www.statistics.gov.uk

## Office for Standards in Education (OFSTED)
Alexandra House, 33 Kingsway, London WC2B 6SE
*tel* 020-7421 6800 *fax* 020-7421 6707

## The Office of Communications (Ofcom)
Riverside House, 2A Southwark Bridge Road,
London SE1 9HA
*tel* 0845 456 3000 *fax* 0845 456 3333
*email* contact@ofcom.org.uk
*website* www.ofcom.org.uk

Established to regulate the communications sector
in the UK. It merges the 5 functions of the 5
regulatory bodies: the Independent Television

Commission (ITC), the Broadcasting Standards Commission (BSC), the Office of Telecommunications (Oftel), the Radio Authority (RAu) and the Radiocommunications Agency (RA). It aims to further the interest of consumers in relevant markets, secure the optimum use of the radio spectrum, ensure the availability throughout the UK of TV and radio services and to protect the public from any offensive or potentially harmful effects of broadcast media, as well as safeguarding people from being unfairly treated in TV and radio programmes. Established 2003.

### Office of Fair Trading

Fleetbank House, 2–6 Salisbury Square, London EC4Y 8JX
*tel* 020-7211 8000 *fax* 020-7211 8800
*email* enquiries@oft.gov.uk
*website* www.oft.gov.uk

### Office of Gas and Electricity Markets (OFGEM)

*Head Office* 9 Millbank, London SW1P 3GE
*tel* 020-7901 7000
*website* www.ofgem.gov.uk
*OFGEM Scotland* Regents Court, 70 West Regent Street, Glasgow G2 2QZ
*tel* 0141-331 2678

### Office of Telecommunications – see The Office of Communications (Ofcom)

### Office of the Data Protection Commissioner – see Information Commissioner's Office

### Office of the Legal Services Ombudsman

3rd Floor, Sunlight House, Quay Street, Manchester M3 3JZ
*tel* 0161-839 7262, *Lo call* (0845) 6010794 (charged at local rate) *fax* 0161-832 5446
*email* lso@olso.gsi.gov.uk
*website* www.olso.org

### Office of Water Services (OFWAT)

Centre City Tower, 7 Hill Street, Birmingham B5 4UA
*tel* 0121-625 1300 *fax* 0121-625 1400
*email* enquiries@ofwat.gsi.gov.uk
*website* www.ofwat.gov.uk

### Oftel (Office of Telecommunications) – see The Office of Communications (Ofcom)

### OFWAT – see Office of Water Services (OFWAT)

### Ordnance Survey

Romsey Road, Southampton SO16 4GU

*tel Press Office* 023-8079 2265, *Customer Contact Centre* (08456) 050505 *fax* 023-8079 2615
*email* enquiries@ordsvy.gov.uk
*website* www.ordnancesurvey.co.uk

### Particle Physics and Astronomy Research Council (PPARC)

Polaris House, North Star Avenue, Swindon, Wilts. SN2 1SZ
*tel* (01793) 442000 *fax* (01793) 442002
*email* pr.pus@pparc.ac.uk
*website* www.pparc.ac.uk

### Patent Office

*General enquiries* (designs, patents, trade marks), Concept House, Cardiff Road, Newport, South Wales NP10 8QQ
*tel* (0845) 9500505 *textphone* (0845) 9222250
*email* enquiries@patent.gov.uk
*website* www.patent.gov.uk
*Copyright enquiries* Copyright, The Patent Office, Room 1/10, Harmsworth House, 13–15 Bouverie Street, London EC4Y 8DP
*tel* 020-7596 6566 *textphone* (0845) 9222250
*fax* 020-7596 6526
*email* copyright@patent.gov.uk
*websites* www.patent.gov.uk, www.intellectual-property.gov.uk

### The Pensions Ombudsman

11 Belgrave Road, London SW1V 1RB
*tel* 020-7834 9144 *fax* 020-7821 0065
*email* enquiries@pensions-ombudsman.org.uk
*website* www.pensions-ombudsman.org.uk

### Pensions and Overseas Benefits Directorate (POD) – see DWP (Department for Work and Pensions)

### PLR Office – see page 296

### Embassy of the Republic of Poland

47 Portland Place, London W1B 1JH
*tel* (0870) 774 2700 *fax* 020-7291 3575
*email* polishembassy@polishembassy.org.uk
*tel* (0870) 7742 900 *fax* 020-7637 2190
Polish Cultural Institute, 34 Portland Place, London W1B 1HQ
*email* pci@polishculture.org.uk
*website* www.polishculture.org.uk

### Portuguese Embassy

11 Belgrave Square, London SW1X 8PP
*tel* 020-7235 5331 *fax* 020-7245 1287, 020-7235 0739
*email* Portembassy-London@dialin.net

### Postal Services Commission (Postcomm)

Hercules House, Hercules Road, London SE1 7DB
*tel* 020-7593 2100

*website* www.postcomm.gov.uk

## Post Office Headquarters – see Royal Mail
Headquarters

## Privy Council Office
2 Carlton Gardens, London SW1Y 5AA
*tel* 020-7210 1033 *fax* 020-7210 1071
*email* prosecretariat@pco-x.gsi.gov.uk
*website* www.privy-council.gov.uk

## Public Guardianship Office
Archway Tower, 2 Junction Road, London N19 5SZ
*tel* 020-7664 7000 *fax* 020-7664 7705
*website* www.guardianship.gov.uk

## Public Record Office – see The National
Archives

## Public Record Office of Northern Ireland
66 Balmoral Avenue, Belfast BT9 6NY
*tel* 028-9025 1318  *fax* 028-9025 5999

## Qualifications and Curriculum Authority (QCA)
83 Piccadilly, London W1J 8QA
*tel* 020-7509 5555 *fax* 020-7509 6666
*email* info@qca.org.uk
*website* www.qca.org.uk

## The Radio Authority – see The Office of
Communications (Ofcom)

## Rail Safety and Standards Board
Evergreen House, 160 Euston Road,
London NW1 2DX
*tel* 020-7904 7518  *fax* 020-7557 9072
*website* www.railwaysafety.org.uk

## Resource: The Council for Museums, Libraries and Archives – see Museums,
Libraries and Archives Council

## Embassy of Romania
4 Palace Green, London W8 4QD
*tel* 020-7937 9666 *fax* 020-7937 8069
*email* roemb@copperstream.co.uk

## Royal Airforce Museum
Grahame Park Way, London NW9 5LL
*tel* 020-8205 2266  *fax* 020-8200 1751
*website* www.rafmuseum.org.uk

## Royal Commission on the Ancient and Historical Monuments of Scotland
John Sinclair House, 16 Bernard Terrace,
Edinburgh EH8 9NX

*tel* 0131-662 1456 *fax* 0131-662 1477/1499
*email* postmaster@rcahms.gov.uk
*website* www.rcahms.gov.uk

## Royal Commission on the Ancient and Historical Monuments of Wales
Crown Building, Plas Crug, Aberystwyth,
Ceredigion SY23 1NJ
*tel* (01970) 621200 *fax* (01970) 627701
*email* nmr.wales@rcahmw.org.uk
*website* www.rcahmw.org.uk

## Royal Commission on the Historical Monuments of England – merged with
English Heritage

## Royal Danish Embassy
55 Sloane Street, London SW1X 9SR
*tel* 020-7333 0200 *fax* 020-7333 0270
*email* lonamb@um.dk
*website* www.denmark.org.uk

## Royal Fine Art Commission for Scotland
Bakehouse Close, 146 Canongate,
Edinburgh EH8 8DD
*tel* 0131-556 6699 *fax* 0131-556 6633
*email* plan@RoyfinartcomforSco.gov.uk
*website* www.RoyfinartcomforSco.gov.uk

## Royal Mail Headquarters
5th Floor, 148 Old Street, London EC1V 9HQ
*tel* 020-7490 2888
*websites* www.royalmail.com, www.postoffice.co.uk

## Royal Mint
Llantrisant, Pontyclun CF72 8YT
*tel* (01443) 222111
*email* judith.nicholas@royalmint.gov,uk
*website* www.royalmint.com

## Royal National Theatre Board
South Bank, London SE1 9PX
*tel* 020-7452 3333 *fax* 020-7452 3344
*website* www.nationaltheatre.org.uk
*Chairman* Sir Christopher Hogg, *Director* Nicholas Hytner

## Royal Netherlands Embassy
38 Hyde Park Gate, London SW7 5DP
*tel* 020-7590 3200 *fax* 020-7581 0053 (Press and cultural affairs)
*email* cultural@netherlands-embassy.org.uk
*website* www.netherlands-embassy.org.uk

## Royal Norwegian Embassy
25 Belgrave Square, London SW1X 8QD
*tel* 020-7591 5500 *fax* 020-7245 6993
*email* emb.london@mfa.no

*website* www.norway.org.uk

## Royal Observatory of Greenwich – see
National Maritime Museum

## Embassy of the Russian Federation
13 Kensington Palace Gardens, London W8 4QX
*tel* 020-7229 2666 *fax* 020-7727 8625
*email* office@rusemblon.org
*website* www.great-britain.mid.ru

## Science Museum
Exhibition Road, London SW7 2DD
*tel* (0870) 870 4868
*email* sciencemuseum@nmsi.ac.uk
*website* www.sciencemuseum.org.uk

## The Scotland Office
Dover House, Whitehall, London SW1A 2AU
*tel* 020-7270 6754
*website* www.scottishsecretary.gov.uk

## Scottish Arts Council – see page 536

## Scottish Environment Protection Agency
Erskine Court, The Castle Business Park,
Stirling FK9 4TR
*tel* (01786) 457700, (0800) 807060 (Hotline)
*website* www.sepa.org.uk

## The Scottish Executive
St Andrew's House, Regent Road,
Edinburgh EH1 1DG
*tel* 0131-556 8400
*website* www.scotland.gov.uk

## Scottish Law Commission
140 Causewayside, Edinburgh EH9 1PR
*tel* 0131-668 2131 *fax* 0131-662 4900
*email* info@scotlawcom.gov.uk
*website* www.scotlawcom.gov.uk

## Scottish Legal Aid Board
44 Drumsheugh Gardens, Edinburgh EH3 7SW
*tel* 0131-226 7061 *fax* 0131-220 4878
*website* www.slab.org.uk

## Scottish Natural Heritage
12 Hope Terrace, Edinburgh EH9 2AS
*tel* 0131-447 4784 *fax* 0131-446 2279 (press office)
*website* www.snh.org.uk

## The Scottish Office – see The Scottish
Executive

## The Scottish Parliament
Edinburgh EH99 1SP
*tel* 0131-348 5000 (public information service)
*fax* 0131-348 5601 *textphone* 0845 2700152

*email* sp.info@scottish.parliament.uk
*website* www.scottish parliament.uk

## Embassy of Serbia and Montenegro
28 Belgrave Square, London SW1X 8QB
*tel* 020-7235 9049 *fax* 020-7235 7092
*email* londre@jugisek.demon.co.uk
*website* www.yugoslavembassy.org.uk

## Serpentine Gallery
Kensington Gardens, London W2 3XA
*tel* 020-7402 6075, 020-7298 1501 (public
information) *fax* 020-7402 4103
*website* www.serpentinegallery.org

## Singapore High Commission
9 Wilton Crescent, London SW1X 8SP
*tel* 020-7235 8315 *fax* 020-7245 6583
*email* info@singaporehc.org.uk
*website* www.mfa.gov.sg/london

## Embassy of the Slovak Republic
25 Kensington Palace Gardens, London W8 4QY
*tel* 020-7313 6470 *fax* 020-7313 6481
*email* mail@slovakembassy.co.uk
*website* www.slovakembassy.co.uk

## Embassy of Slovenia
10 Little College Street, London SW1P 3SH
*tel* 020-7222 5400 *fax* 020-7222 5277
*email* vlo@mzz-dkp.gov.si

## Department of Social Security – see
DWP (Department for Work and Pensions)

## South Africa High Commission
South Africa House, Trafalgar Square,
London WC2N 5DP
*tel* 020-7451 7299 *fax* 020-7451 7283/7284
*email* general@southafricahouse.com
*website* www.southafricahouse.com

## Spanish Embassy
39 Chesham Place, London SW1X 8SB
*tel* 020-7235 5555 *fax* 020-7259 5392

## Sport England
3rd Floor, Victoria House, Bloomsbury Square,
London WC1B 4SE
*tel* 020-7273 1500 *fax* 020-7383 5740
*email* info@sportengland.org
*website* www.sportengland.org

## High Commission of the Democratic Socialist Republic of Sri Lanka
13 Hyde Park Gardens, London W2 2LU
*tel* 020-7262 1841 *fax* 020-7262 7970

## The Stationery Office (TSO)

PO Box 291, Norwich NR3 1GN
*tel* (0870) 600 5522
*website* www.clickkso.com

## Strategic Rail Authority
55 Victoria Street, London SW1H 0EU
*tel* 020-7654 6000 *fax* 020-7654 6046
*website* www.sra.gov.uk

## Embassy of Sweden
11 Montagu Place, London W1H 2AL
*tel* 020-7917 6400 *fax* 020-7917 6477
*email* ambassaden.london@foreign.ministry.se
*website* www.swedish-embassy.org.uk

## Swiss Embassy Cultural Section
16–18 Montagu Place, London W1H 2BQ
*tel* 020-7616 6000 *fax* 020-7723 6949
*email* swissembassy@lon.rep.admin.ch
*website* www.swissembassy.org.uk

## Tate
**Tate Britain, Millbank**
London SW1P 4RG
*tel* 020-7887 8008, 020-7887 8000 (admin)
**Tate Modern**
Bankside, London SE1 9TG
*tel* 020-7887 8008
**Tate Liverpool**
Albert Dock, Liverpool L3 4BB
*tel* 0151-702 7400
**Tate St Ives**
Porthmeor Beach, St Ives, Cornwall TR26 1TG
*tel* (01736) 796226
*email* information@tate.org.uk
*website* www.tate.org.uk

## Theatre Museum – see page 489

## Transport for London (TfL)
Windsor House, 42–50 Victoria Street,
London SW1H 0TL
*tel* 020-7941 4500
*website* www.tfl.gov.uk

## Turkish Embassy
43 Belgrave Square, London SW1X 8PA
*tel* 020-7393 0202 *fax* 020-7393 0066
*email* info@turkishembassy.co.uk

## UK Film Council
10 Little Portland Street, London W1W 7JG
*tel* 020-7861 7861 *fax* 020-7861 7862
*website* www.filmcouncil.org.uk

## United Kingdom Sports Council (UK Sport)
40 Bernard Street, London WC1N 1ST
*tel* 020-7211 5100 *fax* 020-7211 5246
*website* www.uksport.gov.uk

## Victoria and Albert Museum
South Kensington, London SW7 2RL
*tel* 020-7942 2000
*email* www.vanda@vam.ac.uk
*website* www.vam.ac.uk

## VisitBritain – see page 658

## Visiting Arts – see page 541

## VisitScotland
23 Ravelston Terrace, Edinburgh EH4 3TP
*tel* 0131-332 2433 *fax* 0131-343 1513
*email* info@visitscotland.com
*website* www.visitscotland.com

## The Wales Office
Gwydyr House, Whitehall, London SW1A 2ER
*tel* 020-7270 0549 *fax* 020-7270 0568
*website* www.walesoffice.gov.uk

## Wales Tourist Board
Production Services Dept., Brunel House,
2 Fitzalan Road, Cardiff CF24 0UY
*tel* 029-2047 5214 *fax* 029-2048 2436
*email* info@tourism.wales.gov.uk
*website* www.visitwales.com

## Wallace Collection
Hertford House, Manchester Square,
London W1M 3BN
*tel* 020-7563 9500  *fax* 020-7224 2155
*website* www.wallacecollection.org

## Women's National Commission
Cabinet Office, 1st Floor, 35 Great Smith Street,
London SW1P 3BQ
*tel* 020-7276 2555 *fax* 020-7276 2563
*website* www.thewnc.org.uk

# Copyright and libel
## Copyright questions

Copyright is a vital part of any writer's assets, and should never be assigned or sold without due consideration and the advice of a competent authority, such as the Society of Authors, the Writers' Guild of Great Britain, or the National Union of Journalists. Michael Legat answers some of the most commonly asked questions about copyright.

**Is there a period of time after which the copyright expires?**

Copyright in the European Union lasts for the lifetime of the author and for a further 70 years from the end of the year of death, or, if the work is first published posthumously, for 70 years from the end of the year of publication. In most other countries of the world copyright exists similarly for the lifetime and for either 50 years or 70 years after death or posthumous publication.

**If I want to include an extract from a book, poem or article, do I have to seek copyright? How much may be used without permission? What happens if I apply for copyright permission but do not get a reply?**

It is essential to seek permission to quote from another author's work, unless that author has been dead for 70 years or more, or 70 years or more has passed from the date of publication of a work published posthumously. Only if you are quoting for purposes of criticism or review are you allowed to do so without obtaining permission, and even then the Copyright, Designs and Patents Act of 1988 restricts you to 400 words of prose in a single extract from a copyright work, or a series of extracts of up to 300 words each, totalling no more than 800 words, or up to 40 lines of poetry, which must not be more than 25% of the poem. However, a quotation of no more than, say, half a dozen words may usually be used without permission since it will probably not extend beyond a brief and familiar reference, as, for example, Rider Haggard's well-known phrase, 'she who must be obeyed'. If in doubt, always check. If you do not get a reply when you ask for permission to quote, insert a notice in your work saying that you have tried without success to contact the copyright owner, and would be pleased to hear from him or her so that the matter could be cleared up – and keep a copy of all the relevant correspondence, in order to back up your claim of having tried to get in touch.

**If a newspaper pays for an article and I then want to sell the story to a magazine, am I free under the copyright law to do so?**

Yes, provided that you have not granted copyright or exclusive use to the newspaper. When selling your work to newspapers or magazines make it clear, in writing, that you are selling only First or Second Serial Rights, not your copyright.

**If I agree to have an article published for no payment do I retain any rights over how it appears?**

Whether or not you are paid for the work has no bearing on the legal situation. However, the Moral Rights which apply to books, plays, television and radio scripts, do not cover you against a failure to acknowledge you as the author of an article, nor against the mutilation of your text, when it is published in a newspaper or magazine.

**I want to publish a photograph that was taken in 1950. I am not sure how to contact the photographer or even if he is still alive. Am I allowed to go ahead and publish it?**

The Copyright, Designs and Patents Act of 1988 works retrospectively, so a photograph taken in 1950 is bound to be in copyright until at least 2020, and the copyright will be owned by the photographer, even though, when it was taken, the copyright would have belonged to the person who commissioned it, according to the laws then in place. You should therefore make every effort to contact the photographer, keeping copies of any relevant correspondence, and in case of failure take the same course of action as described above in relation to a textual extract the copyright owner of which you have been unable to trace.

**I recently read an article on the same subject as one I have written. It contained many identical facts. Did this writer breach my copyright? What if I send ideas for an article to a magazine editor and those ideas are used despite the fact that I was not commissioned? May I sue the magazine?**

Facts are normally in the public domain and may be used by anyone. However, if your article contains a fact which you have discovered and no one else has published, there could be an infringement of copyright if the author who uses it fails to attribute it to you. There is no copyright in ideas, so you cannot sue a writer or a journal for using ideas that you have put forward; in any case you would find it very difficult to prove that the idea belonged to you and to no one else. There is also no copyright in titles.

**Does being paid a kill fee affect my copyright in a given piece?**

No, provided that you have not sold the magazine or newspaper your copyright.

**Do I need to copyright a piece of writing physically – whether an essay or a novel – or is it copyrighted automatically? Does it have to carry the © symbol?**

Anything that you write is your copyright, assuming that it is not copied from the work of someone else, as soon as you have written it on paper or recorded it on the disk of a computer or on tape, or broadcast it. It is not essential for the work to carry the © symbol, although its inclusion may act as a warning and help to stop another writer from plagiarising it.

**Am I legally required to inform an interviewee that our conversation is being recorded?**

The interviewee owns the copyright of any words that he or she speaks as soon as they are recorded on your tape. Unless you have received permission to use those words in direct quotation, you could be liable to an action for infringement of copyright. You should therefore certainly inform the interviewee that the conversation is being recorded and seek permission to quote what is said directly.

**More and more newspapers and magazines have versions both in print and on the internet. How can I ensure that my work is not published on the internet without my permission?**

Make sure that any clause granting electronic rights to anyone in any agreement that you sign in respect of your work specifies not only the proportion of any fees received which you will get, but that your agreement must be sought before the rights are sold. Copyright extends to electronic rights, and therefore to publication on the internet, in just the same way as to other uses of the material.

**I commissioned a designer to design a business card for me, and I paid her well. Does the design belong to me or to her?**

Copyright would belong to the designer, and not to the person who commissioned it (as is also true in the case of a photograph, copyright in which belongs to the photographer). However, copyright in the business card might be transferred to you if a court considered you to have gained beneficially from the card.

Michael Legat became a full-time writer after a long and successful publishing career. He is the author of a number of highly regarded books on publishing and writing.

## See also...

- *UK copyright law*, page 672
- *US copyright law*, page 691
- *Authors' Licensing and Collecting Society*, page 686
- *Design and Artists Copyright Society*, page 689
- *The Copyright Licensing Agency Ltd*, page 684

# UK copyright law

Amanda Michaels describes the main types of work which may qualify for copyright protection, or related protection as a design, together with some of the main problems which may be faced by readers of this Yearbook in terms of protecting their own works or avoiding infringement of existing works in the UK. This is a technical area of the law, and one which is constantly developing; in an article of this length, it is not possible to deal fully with all the complexities of the law. It must also be emphasised that copyright is national in scope, and whilst works of UK authors will be protected in many other countries of the world, and works of foreign authors will generally be protected in the UK, foreign laws may deal differently with questions of subsistence, ownership and infringement.

Copyright is a creation of statute, now shaped and influenced significantly by EU harmonisation measures. On 1 August 1989, the Copyright, Designs & Patents Act 1988 ('the Act') replaced the Copyright Act 1956, which in turn replaced the Copyright Act 1911. All three Acts are still relevant to copyright today. Whilst the Act to a large degree restated the existing law, it was also innovative, in particular in the creation of a new 'design right' offering protection (generally speaking in lieu of copyright) for many industrial or commercial designs, and in the wider protection of moral rights.

The law has changed further since 1989, largely as a result of EU directives. An important change occurred on 1 January 1996, when the duration of copyright protection in respect of most works (see below) was extended from 'life of the author' plus 50 years to life plus 70 years. Further changes came into force on 1 January 1998, when a new 'database right' was created. New Community design rights were brought into effect in 2003 and numerous other amendments were made, in particular to the rules on fair dealing with copyright works, by the Copyright and Related Rights Regulations 2003 (see below).

## Continuing relevance of old law

In this article, I discuss the law as it currently stands, but where a work was created prior to 1 August 1989 it will always be necessary to consider the law in force at the time of creation (or possibly first publication) in order to assess the existence or scope of any rights. Particular difficulties may arise with foreign works, which may qualify for protection in the UK as a matter of international obligation. Each Act has contained transitional provisions and these, as well as the substantive provisions of any relevant earlier Act, will need to be considered where, for instance, you wish to use an earlier work and it is necessary to decide whether permission is needed and if so, who may grant it. Publishing or licence agreements designed for use under older Acts and prior to the development of modern technologies may be unsuitable for current use.

## Copyright protection of works

Copyright protects the particular form in which an author's idea has been expressed, not the idea itself. Generally speaking, plots or artistic ideas are not protected by copyright, but what is protected is the particular manner in which the idea is presented. See *Designers Guild Limited* v. *Russell Williams (Textiles) Limited* [2001] FSR 113 in which a fairly simple fabric design was found to be original and to have been copied. Of course, if someone has written an outline, script or screenplay for a television show, film, etc and that idea is confidential, then dual protection may arise in the confidential idea embodied in the documents and in the literary (and sometimes artistic) works in which the idea has taken material form. If the idea is used, but not the form, this might give rise to an action for breach of confidence, but not for infringement of copyright. Copyright prevents the copying of the *material form* in which the idea has been presented, or of a substantial part of it, measured in terms of quality, not quantity.

Section 1 of the Act sets out a number of different categories of works which can be the subject of copyright protection. These are:

- original literary, dramatic, musical or artistic works,
- sound recordings, films, broadcasts or cable programmes, and
- typographical arrangements of published editions.

These works are further defined in ss.3–8 (see box for examples).

However, no work of any description enjoys copyright protection until it has been reduced into or recorded in a tangible form, as s.3(2) provides that no copyright shall subsist in a literary, musical or artistic work until it has been recorded in writing or otherwise.

On the other hand, all that is required to achieve copyright protection is to record the original work in an appropriate medium. Once that has been done, copyright will subsist in the work (assuming that the qualifying features set out below are present) without any formality of registration or otherwise. There is, for instance, no need to publish a work to protect it. Please note, however, that the law of the United States does differ on this – see page 691.

Nonetheless, there can be a real benefit in keeping a proper record of the creation of a work. Drafts or preliminary sketches should be kept and dated, so as to be able to show the development of a work. It may also be beneficial (especially where works are to be submitted to potential publishers or purchasers) to take a complete copy of the documents and send them to oneself or lodge them with a responsible third party, sealed and dated, so as to be able to provide cogent evidence of the form or content of the work at that date. Such evidence may help prove one's independent title either as claimant or defendant in a copyright infringement (or indeed breach of confidence) action.

## Originality

In order to gain copyright protection, literary, dramatic, artistic and musical works must be original. Sound recordings or films which are copies of pre-existing sound recordings or films, broadcasts which infringe rights in another broadcast or cable programmes which consist of immediate retransmissions of broadcasts are not protected by copyright.

Just as the law protects the form, rather than the idea, originality relates to the 'expression of the thought', rather than to the thought itself. A work need not be original in the sense of showing innovative artistic, literary or cultural merit, but must have been the product of skill and labour on the part of the author. This can be seen for instance in the definition of certain artistic works, and in the fact that copyright protects works such as compilations (like football pools coupons or directories) and tables (including mathematical tables).

There may be considerable difficulty, at times, in deciding whether a work is of sufficient originality, or has original features, where there is a series of similar designs or amendments of existing works. See *L.A. Gear Inc.* [1992] FSR 121 and *Biotrading* [1998] FSR 109. A new edition or an adaptation of an existing work may obtain a new copyright depending upon the scope of the changes to the work; this will not affect the earlier copyright

> ### Definitions under the Act
>
> **Literary work** is defined as: 'any work, other than a dramatic or musical work, which is written, spoken or sung, and accordingly includes: (a) a table or compilation other than a database, (b) a computer program, (c) preparatory design material for a computer program and (d) a database.'
>
> **A musical work** means: 'a work consisting of music, exclusive of any words or action intended to be sung, spoken or performed with the music.'
>
> **An artistic work** means: '(a) a graphic work, photograph, sculpture or collage, irrespective of artistic quality, (b) a work of architecture being a building or model for a building, or (c) a work of artistic craftsmanship.'
>
> These categories of work are not mutually exclusive, e.g. a film may be protected both as a film and as a dramatic work. See *Norowzian* v. *Arks* [2000] FSR 363.

protection. See *Cala Homes* [1995] FSR 818. What is clear, though, is that merely making a 'slavish copy' of a work will not create an original work: see *Interlego AG* [1989] AC 217. On the other hand, if the work gives particular expression to a commonplace idea or an old tale, copyright may subsist in it (e.g. *Christoffer* v. *Poseidon Film Distributors Limited* (6/10/99) in which it was held that a script for an animated film of a story from Homer's *Odyssey* was an original literary work). Copyright protection will be limited to the original features of the work, or those features created or chosen by the author's input of skill and labour.

'Works' such as the titles of books or periodicals, or advertising slogans, which may have required a good deal of original thought, generally are not accorded copyright protection, because they are too short to be deemed literary works.

### Qualification

The Act is limited in its effects to the UK (and to colonies to which it may be extended by Order). It is aimed primarily at protecting the works of British citizens, or works which were first published here. However, in line with the requirements of various international conventions, copyright protection in the UK is also accorded to the works of nationals of many foreign states, as well as to works first published in those states, on a reciprocal basis.

As for works of nationals of other member states of the European Union, there is a principle of equal treatment, so that protection must be offered to such works here: see *Phil Collins* [1993] 3 CMLR 773.

The importance of these rules mainly arises when one is trying to find out whether a foreign work is protected by copyright here, for instance, if one wishes to make a film based upon a foreign novel.

## Ownership

The general rule is that the copyright in a work will first be owned by its author, the author being the creator of the work. In most cases this is self-explanatory, but the definition of 'author' in relation to films and sound recordings has changed over the years; currently, the author of a sound recording is its producer, and the authors of a film are the producer and principal director.

One important exception to the general rule is that the copyright in a work made by an employee in the course of his or her employment will belong to their employer, subject to any agreement to the contrary. However, this rule does not apply to freelance designers, journalists, etc, and not even to nominally self-employed company directors. This obviously may lead to problems if the question of copyright ownership is not dealt with when an agreement is made to create, purchase or use a work (see box, page 677).

Where a work is produced by several people who collaborate in such a way that each one's contribution is not distinct from that of the other(s), then they will be joint authors of the work. Where two people collaborate to write a song, one producing the lyrics and the other the music, there will be two separate copyright works, the copyright of which will be owned by each of the authors separately. But where two people write a play, each rewriting what the other produces, there will be a joint work.

The importance of knowing whether the work is joint or not arises:
- in working out the duration of the copyright, and
- from the fact that joint works can only be exploited with the agreement of all the joint authors, so that all of them have to join in any licence, although each of them can sue for infringement without joining the other(s) as a claimant in the proceedings.

## Duration of copyright

As a result of amendments brought into effect on 1 January 1996, copyright in literary, dramatic, musical or artistic works expires at the end of the period of 70 years from the end of the calendar year in which the author dies (s.12(1)). Where there are joint authors, then the 70 years runs from the death of the last of them to die. If the author is unknown, there will be 70 years protection from the date the work was first made or (where applicable) first made available to the public. Previously, the protection was for 'life plus 50'.

The extended 70-year term also applies to films, and runs from the end of the calendar year in which the death occurs of the last to die of the principal director, the author of the screenplay or the dialogue, or the composer of any music created for the film (s.13B). This obviously may be a nightmare to establish, and there are certain presumptions in s.66A which may help someone wishing to use material from an old film.

However, sound recordings are still protected by copyright only for 50 years from the year of making or release (s.13A); similarly, broadcasts, cable programmes and computer-generated works still get only 50 years protection.

The new longer term applies without difficulty to works created after 1 January 1996 and to works in copyright on 31 December 1995. The owner of that extended copyright will be the person who owned it on 31 December 1995, unless that person had only a limited term of ownership, in which case the extra 20 years will be added on to the reversionary term.

Where copyright had expired here,

## Licensing

A licence is granted to another to exploit the right whilst the licensor retains overall ownership.

Licences do not need to take any form in particular, and may indeed be granted orally. However, an exclusive licence (i.e. one which excludes even the copyright owner himself from exploiting the work) must be in writing, if the licensee is to enjoy rights in respect of infringements concurrent with those of the copyright owner.

but the author died between 50 and 70 years ago, the position is more complicated. EC Directive 93/98 provided that if a work was protected by copyright anywhere in the European Union on 1 July 1995, copyright would revive for it in any other state until the end of the same 70-year period. This may make it necessary to look at the position in the states offering a longer term of protection, namely Germany, France and Spain.

Ownership of the revived term of copyright will belong to the person who was the owner of the copyright when the initial term expired, save that if that person died (or a company, etc, ceased to exist) before 1 January 1996, then the revived term will vest in the author's personal representatives, and in the case of a film, in the principal director's personal representatives.

Any licence affecting a copyright work which subsisted on 31 December 1995 and was then for the full term of the copyright continues to have effect during any extended term of copyright, subject to any agreement to the contrary (paragraph 21 of the Regulations).

The increased term offered to works of other EU nationals as a result of the Term Directive is not offered automatically to the nationals of other states, but will only apply where an equally long term is offered in their state of origin.

Where acts are carried out in relation to such revived copyright works, pursuant to things done whilst they were in the public domain, protection from infringement is available. A licence as of right may also be available, on giving notice to the copyright owner and paying a royalty.

### Dealing with copyright works

Ownership of the copyright in a work confers upon the owner the exclusive right to deal with the work in a number of ways, and essentially stops all unauthorised exploitation of the work. Ownership of the copyright is capable of being separated from ownership of the material form in which the work is embodied, depending upon the terms of any agreement or the circumstances. Even buying an original piece of artwork will not in general carry with it the legal title to the copyright, as an effective assignment must be in writing signed by the assignor (although beneficial ownership might pass: see page 677).

## Assignments

In an assignment, rights in the work are sold, with the owner retaining no interest in it (except, possibly, for payment by way of royalties).

An assignment must be in writing, signed by or on behalf of the assignor, but no other formality is required. One can make an assignment of future copyright (under s.91). Where the author of a projected work agrees in writing that he will assign the rights in a future work to another, the copyright vests in the assignee immediately upon the creation of the work, without further formalities.

These rules do not affect the common law as to beneficial interests in copyright. One possibility may be that a court will, in the right circumstances, find or infer an agreement to assign the copyright in a work, e.g. where a sole trader who had title to the copyright used in his business later incorporated the business and allowed the company to exploit the software as if it were its own, an agreement to assign was inferred (see *Lakeview Computers plc* 26/11/99). Alternatively, if the court finds that a work was commissioned to be made, and that there was a common intention that the purchaser should own the copyright, the court may order the author to assign the copyright to him. 'Commission' in this context means only to order a particular piece of work to be done: see *Apple Corps Ltd* v. *Cooper* [1993] FSR 286 (a 1956 Act case).

Copyright works can be exploited by their owners in two ways:

● Assignment: rights in a work may be sold, with the owner retaining no interest in it (except, possibly, for payment by way of royalties or some reversionary rights in certain agreed circumstances) – see box; or

● Licensing: the owner may grant a licence to another to exploit the right, whilst retaining overall ownership (see box).

Agreements dealing with copyright should make it clear whether an assignment or a licence is being granted. There may be significant advantages for the author in granting a licence rather than an assignment, for where the assignee's rights pass to a third party, for instance on his insolvency, the author cannot normally enforce the original agreement to pay royalties, etc against the purchaser (*Barker* v. *Stickney* [1919] 1 KB 121). If the agreement is unclear, the Court is likely to find that the grantee took the minimum rights necessary for his intended use of the work, very probably an exclusive licence rather than an assignment (*Ray* v. *Classic FM plc* [1998] FSR 622). The question of moral rights (see below) will also have to be considered by the parties.

Assignments and licences often split up the various rights contained within the copyright. So, for instance, a licence might be granted to one person to publish a novel in book form, another person might be granted the film, television and video rights, and yet another the right to translate the novel into other languages.

Assignments and licences may also confer rights according to territory, dividing the USA from the EU or different EU countries one from the other. Any such agreement should take into account divergences between different national copyright laws. Furthermore, when seeking to divide rights between different territories of the EU there is a danger of infringing the competition rules of the EU. Professional advice should be taken, as breach of these rules may attract a fine and can render the agreement void in whole or in part.

Licences can, of course, be of varying lengths. There is no need for a licence to be granted for the whole term of copyright. Well-drafted licences will provide for termination on breach, including the failure of the licensee to exploit the work, and on the insolvency of the licensee and will specify whether the rights may be assigned or sub-licensed.

Copyright may be assigned by will. A bequest of an original document, etc embodying an unpublished copyright work will carry the copyright.

## Infringement

The main type of infringement is what is commonly thought of as plagiarism, that is, copying the work. In fact, copyright confers on the owner the exclusive right to do a number of specified acts, so that anyone doing those acts without his permission will infringe. It is important to note that it is not necessary to copy a work exactly or use all of it; it is sufficient if a substantial part is used. That question is to be judged on a qualitative not a quantitative basis, bearing in mind that it is the skill and labour of the author which is to be protected (see *Ravenscroft* v. *Herbert* [1980] RPC 193 and *Designers Guild*). It is important to note that primary infringement, such as copying, can be done innocently of any intention to infringe.

The form of infringement common to all forms of copyright works is that of copying. This means reproducing the work in any material form. Infringement may occur where an existing work provides the inspiration for a later one, if copying results, for example by including edited extracts from a history book in a novel (*Ravenscroft*), using a photograph as the inspiration for a painting (*Baumann* v. *Fussell* [1978] RPC 485), or words from a verse of one song in another (*Ludlow Music* v. *Williams* [2001] FSR 271). Infringement will not necessarily be prevented merely by the application of significant new skill and labour by the infringer, nor by a change of medium.

In the case of a two-dimensional artistic work, reproduction can mean making a copy in three dimensions, and vice versa. However, s.51 of the Act provides that in the case of a 'design document or model' (for definition, see page 681) for something which is not *itself* an artistic work, it is no infringement to make an article to that design. This means that whilst it would be an infringement of copyright to make an article from a design drawing for, say, a sculpture, it will not be an infringement of copyright to make a handbag from a copy of the design drawing for it, or from a handbag which one has purchased. Instead, such designs are generally protected by design right or as registered designs (for both see below).

Copying a film, broadcast or cable programme can include making a copy of the whole or a substantial part of any image from it (see s.17(4)). This means that copying one frame of the film will be an infringement. It is not an infringement of copyright in a film to reshoot the film (*Norowzian*) (though there would doubtless be an infringement of the copyright in underlying works such as the literary copyright in the screenplay).

Copying is generally proved by showing substantial similarities between the original and the alleged copy, plus an opportunity to copy. Surprisingly often, minor errors in the original are reproduced by an infringer.

## 'Secondary' infringements

Secondary infringements consist not of making infringing copies, but of dealing with existing infringing copies in some way. It is an infringement to import an infringing copy into the UK, and to possess in the course of business, or to sell, hire, offer for sale or hire, or distribute in the course of trade an infringing copy. However, none of these acts will be an infringement unless the alleged infringer knew or had reason to believe that the articles were infringing copies. What is sufficient knowledge will depend upon the facts of each case (see *LA Gear Inc.* [1992] FSR 121, *ZYX Records* v. *King* [1997] 2 All ER 132 and *Pensher Security* [2000] RPC 249). Merely putting someone on notice of a dispute as to ownership of copyright may not suffice to give him or her reason to believe in infringement for this purpose: *Hutchison* [1995] FSR 365.

Other secondary infringements consist of permitting a place to be used for a public performance in which copyright is infringed and supplying apparatus to be used for infringing public performance, again, in each case, with safeguards for innocent acts.

Copying need not be direct, so that, for instance, where the copyright is in a fabric design, copying the material without ever having seen the original drawing will still be an infringement, as will 'reverse engineering' of industrial designs, for example to make unlicensed spare parts (*British Leyland* [1986] AC 577; *Mars* v. *Teknowledge* [2000] FSR 138).

Issuing copies of a work to the public when they have not previously been put into circulation in the UK is also an infringement of all types of work.

Other acts which may amount to an infringement depend upon the nature of the work. It will be an infringement of the copyright in a literary, dramatic or musical work to perform it in public, whether by live performance or by playing recordings. Similarly, it is an infringement of the copyright in a sound recording, film, broadcast or cable programme to play or show it in public. Many copyright works will also be infringed by the rental or lending of copies of the work.

One rather different form of infringement is to make an adaptation of a literary, dramatic or musical work. An adaptation includes, in the case of a literary work, a translation, in the case of a non-dramatic work, making a dramatic work of it, and vice versa. A transcription or arrangement of a musical work is an adaptation of it.

There are also a number of 'secondary' infringements – see box.

### Exceptions to infringement

The Act provides a large number of exceptions to the rules on infringement which were extended and amended with effect from 31 October 2003 by the Copyright and Related Rights Regulations 2003. They are far too numerous to be dealt with here in full, but they include:

- fair dealing with literary, dramatic, musical or artistic works for the purpose of non-commercial research or private study (s.29);
- fair dealing for the purpose of criticism or review or reporting current events, as to which see e.g. *Pro Sieben Media* [1999] FSR 610; *Hyde Park* v. *Yelland* [2001] Ch. 143; *NLA* v. *Marks & Spencer Plc* [2002] RPC 4) (s.30);
- incidental inclusion of a work in an artistic work, sound recording, film, broadcast or cable programme (s.31);

- educational exceptions (ss.32–36A);
- exceptions for libraries (ss.37–44A) and public administration (ss.45–50);
- making transient copies as part of a technological process (s.28A) and backing-up, or converting a computer program or accessing a licensed database (s.50A–D);
- dealing with a work where the author cannot be identified and the work seems likely to be out of copyright (s.57);
- public recitation, if accompanied by a sufficient acknowledgement (s.59).

The effect of the Human Rights Act on copyright in relation to the right to free speech seems likely to be limited, as sufficient protection is to be found in the fair dealing provisions: *Ashdown* v. *Telegraph Group Limited* [2002] Ch. 149.

There is no defence of parody.

## Remedies for infringements

The copyright owner will usually want to prevent the repetition or continuation of the infringement and he will want compensation.

In almost all cases an injunction will be sought to stop the infringement. The Courts have useful powers to grant an injunction at an early stage, indeed even before any infringement takes place, if a real threat of damage can be shown. Such an interim injunction can be applied for on three days' notice (or without notice in appropriate cases), but will not be granted unless the claimant has a reasonably good case and can show that he would suffer 'unquantifiable' damage if the defendant's activities continued pending trial. Delay in bringing an interim application may be fatal to its success. An injunction may not be granted where the claimant clearly only wants financial compensation (*Ludlow Music*).

Financial compensation may be sought in one of two forms. Firstly, damages. These will usually be calculated upon evidence of the loss caused to the claimant, sometimes based upon loss of business, at others upon the basis of what would have been a proper licence fee for the defendant's acts. Additional damages may be awarded in rare cases for flagrant infringements. See for example *Notts. Healthcare* v. *News Group Newspapers* [2002] RPC 49.

Damages will not be awarded for infringement where the infringer did not know, and had no reason to believe, that copyright subsisted in the work. This exception is of limited use to a defendant, though, in the usual situation where the work was of such a nature that he should have known that copyright would subsist in it.

The alternative to damages is an account of profits, that is, the net profits made by the infringer by virtue of his illicit exploitation of the copyright. Where an account of profits is sought, no award of flagrant damages can be made.  See *Redrow Homes Limited* [1999] 1 AC 197.

A copyright owner may also apply for delivery up of infringing copies.

Finally, there are various criminal offences relating to the making, importation, possession, sale, hire, distribution, etc of infringing copies.

## Design right

Many industrial designs are excluded from copyright protection by s.51. Alternatively, the term of copyright protection is limited to 25 years from first industrial exploitation, by s.52. However, they may instead be protected by the 'design right' created by ss.213–64. Like copyright, design right does not depend upon registration, but upon the creation of a suitable design by a "qualifying person".

Design right is granted to original designs consisting of the shape or configuration (internal or external) of the whole or part of an article, not being merely 'surface decoration'. A design is not original if it was commonplace in the design field in question at the time of its creation. In *Farmers Build* [1999] RPC 461, 'commonplace' was defined as meaning a design of a type which would excite no 'peculiar attention' amongst those in the trade, or one which amounts to a run-of-the-mill combination of well-known features. Designs are not protected if they consist of a method or principle of construction, or are dictated by the shape, etc of an article to which the new article is to be connected or of which it is to form part, the so-called 'must-fit' and 'must-match' exclusions. In *Ocular Sciences* [1997] RPC 289, these exclusions had a devastating effect upon numerous design rights claimed for contact lens designs.

Design right subsists in designs made by or for qualifying persons (see, broadly, 'Qualification' on page 674) or first marketed in the UK or EU or any other country to which the provision may be extended by Order.

Design right lasts only 15 years from the end of the year in which it was first recorded or an article made to the design, or (if shorter) 10 years from the end of the year in which articles made according to the design were first sold or hired out. During the last five years of the term of protection, a licence to use the design can be obtained 'as of right' but against payment of a proper licence fee. Hence, design right may give only five years 'absolute' protection, as opposed to the 'life plus 70' of copyright.

The designer will be the owner of the right, unless it was commissioned, in which case the commissioner will be the first owner. An employee's designs made in the course of employment will belong to the employer.

The right given to the owner of a design right is the exclusive right to reproduce the design for commercial purposes. The rules as to assignments, licensing and infringement, both primary and secondary, are substantially similar to those described above in relation to copyright, as are the remedies available.

There have recently been significant changes to the law on registered designs, which coexist with the right given by the unregistered design right discussed above. The Registered Design Act 1949 has been amended (and expanded) in line with EU legislation, and now permits the registration of designs consisting of the appearance of the whole or any part of a product resulting from features of the product itself, such as shape, materials, etc or from the ornamentation of the product. It covers industrial or handicraft items, their packaging or get-up, etc. Designs must be novel and not solely dictated by function. The range of designs which may be registered is wider than under the old law, and designs need not necessarily have 'eye appeal'. Such designs provide a monopoly right renewable for up to 25 years. For further explanation see the useful guidance on the Patent Office website.

EU Regulation 6/2002 has created two new Community design regimes, one for registered and one for unregistered designs. It is not possible in the space available here to describe these new regimes in detail but the Regulation is available online at www.europa.ue.int/eur-lex. In brief, such designs (which are *very* broadly defined in Article 3) must be 'new' and have 'individual character'. The registered right, available from April 2003, may be enjoyed for up to 25 years in five-year tranches, but an unregistered Community design right lasts only three years. The unregistered right protects the design from copying, but the registered right gives 'absolute' exclusivity, in that it may be infringed without copying.

## Moral rights

The Act also provides for the protection of certain 'moral rights'.

The right of 'paternity' is for the author of a copyright literary, dramatic, musical or artistic work, or the director of a copyright film, to be identified as the author/ director, largely whenever the work is commercially exploited (s.77).

However, the right does not arise unless it has been 'asserted' by appropriate words in writing, or in the case of an artistic work by ensuring that the artist's name appears on the frame, etc (see end). There are exceptions to the right, in particular where first ownership of the copyright vested in the author's or director's employer.

The right of 'integrity' protects work from 'derogatory treatment', meaning an addition to, deletion from, alteration or adaptation of a work which amounts to distortion or mutilation of the work or is otherwise prejudicial to the honour or reputation of the author/director.

Again, infringement of the right takes place when the maltreated work is published commercially or performed or exhibited in public. There are various exceptions set out in s.81 of the Act, in particular where the publication is in a newspaper, etc, and the work was made for inclusion in it or made available with the author's consent.

Where the copyright in the work vested first in the author's or director's employer, he or she has no right to 'integrity' unless identified at the time of the relevant act or on published copies of the work.

These rights subsist for as long as the copyright in the work subsists.

A third moral right conferred by the Act is not to have a literary, dramatic, musical or artistic work falsely attributed to one as author, or to have a film falsely attributed to one as director, again where the work in question is published, etc. This right subsists until 20 years after a person's death.

None of these rights can be assigned during the person's lifetime, but all of them either pass on the person's death as directed by his or her will or fall into his residuary estate.

A fourth but rather different moral right is conferred by s.85. It gives a person who has commissioned the taking of photographs for private purposes a right to prevent copies of the work being issued to the public, etc.

The remedies for breach of these moral rights again include damages and an injunction, although s.103(2) specifically foresees the granting of an injunction qualified by a right to the defendant to do the acts complained of, if subject to a suitable disclaimer.

Moral rights are exercisable in relation to works in which the copyright has revived subject to any waiver or assertion of the right made before 1 January 1996 (see details as to who may exercise rights in paragraph 22 of the Regulations).

## Useful websites

**www.patent.gov.uk/index.htm**
Website of the Patent Office.

**www.intellectual-property.gov.uk**

**www.wipo.int**
Website of the World Intellectual Property Organisation.

**www.baillii.org**
A website containing judgements from UK courts and with links to equivalent foreign websites. Legislation on the site may be in an unamended form.

*NOTICE*
*AMANDA LOUISE MICHAELS hereby asserts and gives notice of her right under s.77 of the Copyright, Designs & Patents Act 1988 to be identified as the author of the foregoing article.*

*AMANDA MICHAELS*

**Amanda L. Michaels** is a barrister in private practice in London, and specialises in copyright, designs, trade marks, and similar intellectual property and 'media' work. She is author of *A Practical Guide to Trade Mark Law* (Sweet & Maxwell, 3rd edn 2002).

## Further reading

Garnett, Rayner James and Davies, *Copinger and Skone James on Copyright*, Sweet & Maxwell, 14th edn, 1999 and Supplement 2002

Laddie, Prescott and Vitoria, *The Modern Law of Copyright*, Butterworths, 3rd edn, 2000

Flint, *A User's Guide to Copyright*, Butterworths, 5th edn, 2000

Bainbridge, David, *Intellectual Property*, Pearson Education, 5th edn, 2002

## Copyright Acts

Copyright, Designs and Patents Act 1998 (but it is vital to use an up-to-date amended version)

The Duration of Copyright and Rights in Performances Regulations 1995 (SI 1995 No 3297)

The Copyright and Related Rights Regulations 2003 (SI 2003 No 2498)

*see also* Numerous Orders in Council

# The Copyright Licensing Agency Ltd

The Copyright Licensing Agency (CLA) collects and distributes money on behalf of artists, writers and publishers for the copying, scanning and emailing of their work. CLA operates on a non-profit basis, and issues licences to schools, further and higher education, business and government bodies so that such organisations can access the copyright material in books, journals, law reports, magazines and periodicals.

### Why was CLA established?

CLA was established in 1982 by its members, the Authors' Licensing and Collecting Society (ALCS) and the Publishers Licensing Society (PLS) to promote and enforce the intellectual property rights of British rightsholders both at home and abroad. CLA also has an agency agreement with the Design and Artists Copyright Society (DACS), which represents artists and illustrators.

ALCS has two corporate members – the Society of Authors and the Writers' Guild of Great Britain. It also has a large number of individual authors as members and affiliations with the National Union of Journalists and the Chartered Institute of Journalists. PLS members are the Publishers Association, the Periodical Publishers Association and the Association of Learned and Professional Society Publishers.

### How CLA helps artists and writers

CLA allows licensed users access to over 16 million titles worldwide. In return CLA ensures artists and writers, along with publishers, are fairly recompensed by the licence fees, which CLA collects and forwards to its members for onward distribution to artists, writers and publishers.

The collective management of licensing schemes means that CLA can provide users with the simplest and most cost-effective means of obtaining authorisation for photocopying, while copy limits ensure fair recompense is maintained for rightsholders.

CLA is has developed licences which enable digitisation of existing print material. The licence enables users to scan and electronically send extracts from copyright works. Scanning and email distribution is only available for UK works at present.

### Licence to copy

CLA's licensees fall into three main categories:
- education (schools, further and higher education);
- government (central, local, public bodies); and
- business (business, industry, professionals).

CLA develops licences to meet the specific needs of each sector and groupings within each sector. Depending on the requirement, there are both blanket and transactional licences available. Every licence allows the photocopying of most books, journals, magazines and periodicals published in the UK.

## An international dimension

Many countries have established equivalents to CLA and the number of such agencies is set to grow. Nearly all these agencies, including CLA, are members of the International Federation of Reproduction Rights Organisations (IFRRO).

Through reciprocal arrangements with these organisations, any CLA licence also allows copying from an expanding list of publications in other countries. Currently these countries are: Australia, Canada (including Quebec), Denmark, Finland, France, Germany, Greece, Iceland, Ireland, The Netherlands, New Zealand, Norway, South Africa, Spain, Sweden, Switzerland and the USA.

CLA receives monies from these organisations for the copying of UK material abroad and forwards it to rightsholders.

## Further information

**The Copyright Licensing Agency Ltd**
90 Tottenham Court Road, London W1T 4LP
*tel* 020-7631 5555 *fax* 020-7631 5500
*email* cla@cla.co.uk
*website* www.cla.co.uk
CBC House, 24 Canning Street,
Edinburgh EH3 8E9
*tel* 0131-272 2711 *fax* 0131-272 2811
*email* clascotland@cla.co.uk

## Distribution

The fees collected from licensees are forwarded to artists, authors and publishers via ALCS, DACS and PLS respectively, and are based on statistical surveys and records of copying activity. For the year ending 31 March 2003 in excess of £36 million was returned to rightsholders.

## Respecting copyright

CLA also believes it is important to raise awareness of the copyright in published material and the need to protect the creativity of artists, authors and publishers. To this end, CLA organises a range of activities such as copyright workshops in schools, seminars for businesses and institutions and an extensive exhibition programme. A comprehensive website is regularly updated and a bi-annual newsletter, *Clarion*, is posted to all licensees and to those individuals and groups concerned with copyright.

## Protecting creativity

CLA believes in working together with all sectors to take into account their differing needs, meaning legal action is rare. However, organisations – especially in the business sector – need to be made aware that copyright is a legally enforceable right enshrined in statute law, not a voluntary option. CLA's recently restructured compliance division aims to continue the education programme. However, as a last resort it has the power to take legal proceedings on behalf of rightsholders.

# Authors' Licensing and Collecting Society

The Authors' Licensing and Collecting Society (ALCS) is the rights management society for all UK writers.

The Authors' Licensing and Collecting Society (ALCS) is the UK collective rights management society for writers. Established in 1977, the Society represents the interests of all UK writers and aims to ensure that they are fairly compensated for any works that are copied, broadcast or recorded.

A non-profit company, ALCS was set up in the wake of the campaign to establish a Public Lending Right to help writers protect and exploit their collective rights. Today, it is the largest writers' organisation in the UK with a membership of over 44,000 and an annual distribution of over £12 million in royalties to writers.

The Society is committed to ensuring that the rights of writers, both intellectual property and moral, are fully respected and fairly rewarded. It represents all types of writers and includes educational, research and academic authors drawn from the professions; scriptwriters, adaptors, playwrights, poets, editors and freelance journalists, across the print and broadcast media.

Internationally recognised as a leading authority on copyright matters and authors' interests, ALCS is committed to fostering an awareness of intellectual property issues among the writing community. It maintains a close watching brief on all matters affecting copyright both in the UK and internationally and makes regular representations to the UK government and the European Union.

ALCS works closely with the Writers' Guild of Great Britain, the Society of Authors and by reciprocal agreement with over 50 collecting societies overseas. Owned and controlled by writers, it is governed by a non-executive board of 12 directors, all of whom are working writers. Four of these directors are nominated by the Writers' Guild of Great Britain and four by the Society of Authors. The other four independent members are elected directly by ALCS Ordinary Members.

The Society collects fees that are difficult, time-consuming or legally impossible for writers and their representatives to claim on an individual basis, money that is nonetheless due to them. To date, it has distributed over £80 million in secondary royalties to writers.

Over the years, ALCS has developed highly specialised knowledge and sophisticated systems that can track writers and their works against any secondary use for which they are due payment. A network of international contacts and reciprocal agreements with foreign collecting societies also ensures that British writers are compensated for any similar use overseas.

The primary sources of fees due to writers are secondary royalties from the following:

## Photocopying

The single largest source of income, this is administered by the Copyright Licensing Agency (CLA – see page 684). Created in 1982 by ALCS and the Publishers Licensing Society (PLS), the CLA grants licences to users for the copying of books, periodicals and journals. This includes schools, colleges, universities, central and local government departments as well as the British Library, businesses and other institutions. Licence fees are based on the number of people who benefit and the number of copies made. The revenue from this is then split between the rightsholders: authors, publishers and artists. Money due to authors is transferred to ALCS for distribution. ALCS also receives photocopying payments from foreign sources.

## Digitisation

In 1999, the CLA launched its licensing scheme for the digitisation of printed texts. It offers licences to organisations for storing and using digital versions of authors' printed works, which have been scanned into a computer. Again, the fees are split between authors and publishers.

## Foreign Public Lending Right

The Public Lending Right (PLR) system pays authors whose books are borrowed from public libraries. Through reciprocal agreements with VG Wort (the German collecting society) and Stichting Leenrecht (the Dutch collecting Society), ALCS members receive payment whenever their books are borrowed from German and Dutch libraries. (Please note that ALCS does not administer the UK Public Lending Right, this is managed directly by the UK PLR Office; see page 296.)

ALCS also receives other payments from Germany. These cover the loan of academic, scientific and technical titles from academic libraries; extracts of authors' works in textbooks and the press, together with other one-off fees.

## Simultaneous cable retransmission

This involves the simultaneous showing of one country's television signals in another country, via a cable network. Cable companies pay a central collecting organisation a percentage of their subscription fees, which must be collectively administered. This sum is then divided by the rightsholders. ALCS receives the writers' share for British programmes containing literary and dramatic material and distributes this to them.

## The BBC

ALCS licenses BBC Worldwide Ltd for the inclusion of material within the ALCS repertoire. The licence covers the direct reception and cable retransmission of BBC Prime, a satellite entertainment channel, in Europe and Africa and other countries.

## Educational recording

ALCS, together with the main broadcasters and rightsholders, set up the Educational Recording Agency (ERA) in 1989 to offer licences to educational establishments. ERA collects fees from the licensees and pays ALCS the amount due to writers for their literary works.

Other sources of income include a blank tape levy and small, miscellaneous literary rights.

## Tracing authors

ALCS is dedicated to protecting and promoting authors' rights and enabling writers to maximise their income. It is committed to ensuring that royalties due to writers are efficiently collected and speedily distributed to them. One of its greatest challenges is finding some of the writers for whom it holds funds and ensuring that they claim their money.

Any published author or broadcast writer could have some funds held by ALCS for them. It may be a nominal sum or it could run in to several thousand pounds. Either call or visit the ALCS website – see box for further details.

## Membership

### Authors' Licensing and Collecting Society Ltd

14-18 Holborn, London EC1N 2LE
*tel* 020-7395 0600 *fax* 020-7395 0660
*email* alcs@alcs.co.uk
*website* www.alcs.co.uk
*Chief Executive* Jane Carr

ALCS membership is open to all writers and successors to their estates at a current annual subscription fee of £10 for Ordinary members. Members of the Society of Authors and the Writers' Guild of Great Britain have free Ordinary membership of ALCS. In addition, members of the National Union of Journalists, Chartered Institute of Journalists, British Association of Journalists and the British Comedy Writers' Association have free Associate membership of ALCS. You may also register direct with ALCS for free Associate membership.

ALCS operations are primarily funded through a commission levied on distributions and membership fees. The commission on funds generated for Ordinary members is currently 11%. Writers do not have to become Ordinary members of ALCS to receive funds due to them for the reproduction of their works; however, for Associate members such funds are subject to a levy of 14%. Most writers will find that this, together with a number of other membership benefits, provides excellent value to membership.

# Design and Artists Copyright Society

The Design and Artists Copyright Society (DACS) is a not-for-profit membership organisation which exists to protect and promote the copyright of visual creators in the UK and worldwide.

## About DACS

DACS was established in 1984 and is the UK's copyright licensing and collecting society for visual creators. It acts as an agent for its members, offering a Primary Licensing service for copyright consumers wishing to license artistic works. It negotiates a share of revenue from Collective Licensing schemes on behalf of all visual creators and distributes this through the its Payback scheme.

DACS membership represents over 36,000 international fine artists as well as 16,000 commercial visual creators for collective licensing only. It is a not-for-profit organisation and retains only 25% of licensing revenue to cover costs, so 75% goes to visual creators.

## DACS Licensing Services

Copyright in artistic works is governed in the UK by the Copyright, Designs & Patents Act 1988 (as amended).

### What is Primary Licensing?

A primary licence is a one-off use, for example when a publisher wants to reproduce an artistic work in a book. DACS offers licences for many uses and charges fees according to the type, purpose and extent of the reproduction. Its fees are set on a rate card, or by negotiation for merchandising or advertising uses.

### What is collective licensing of secondary uses?

Secondary uses of artistic works are often collectively administered under blanket licences, for example when a business needs to photocopy pages of books or magazines. Primary licences may not be practical so DACS offers collective licences, either directly or through appointed agents. It negotiates a share of the revenue from these schemes on behalf of visual creators and pays it out via Payback.

## Membership

Membership of DACS is open to all visual creators, their heirs and beneficiaries working in any medium. It manages their copyright by negotiating terms and collecting fees on their behalf. Its experienced licensing staff work closely with both artists and consumers to ensure the best balance of interests is achieved when licensing works. DACS provides licences for a wide range of primary uses, both commercial and non-commercial, in academic and business environments.

## Other benefits

DACS belongs to an international network of collecting societies in 27 countries. Visual creators' rights are administered on the same basis in all these countries and they will receive royalties when their work has been reproduced overseas.

DACS is committed to protecting copyright. In some circumstances, it may be able to investigate infringement of an artist's copyright.

Because DACS is an authoritative voice for visual creators' rights in the UK, new members who join will be strengthening the presence of visual creators and their rights in the copyright community as a whole. DACS also gives its members access to a range of services.

**Contact details**

**Design and Artists Copyright Society (DACS)**
Parchment House, 13 Northburgh Street, London EC1V 0JP
*tel* 020-7336 8811  *fax* 020-7336 8822
*email* info@dacs.org.uk
*website* www.dacs.org.uk

## Copyright

- Copyright is a right granted to creators under law.
- Copyright in all artistic works is established from the moment of creation – the only qualification is that the work must be original.
- There is no registration system in the UK; copyright comes into operation automatically and lasts the lifetime of the visual creator plus a period of 70 years after their death.
- After death, copyright is usually transferred to the visual creator's heirs or beneficiaries. When the 70-year period has expired, the work then enters the public domain and no longer benefits from copyright protection.
- The copyright owner has the exclusive right to authorise the reproduction (or copy) of a work in any medium by any other party.
- Any reproduction can only take place with the copyright owner's consent. Permission is usually granted in return for a fee, which enables the visual creator to derive some income from other people using his or her work.
- If a visual creator is commissioned to produce a work, he or she will usually retain the copyright unless an agreement is signed which specifically assigns the copyright. When visual creators are employees and create work during the course of their employment, the employer retains the copyright in those works.

## See also...
- *Copyright questions*, page 669
- *UK copyright law*, page 672
- *Freelancing for beginners*, page 433

# US copyright law

Gavin McFarlane, barrister, introduces US copyright law and points out the differences, and similarities, of British copyright law.

## International copyright
## International copyright conventions

No general principle of international copyright provides a uniform code for the protection of right owners throughout the world. There are, however, two major international copyright conventions which lay down certain minimum standards for member states, in particular requiring member states to accord to right owners of other member states the same protection which is granted to their own nationals. One is the higher standard Berne Convention of 1886, the most recent revision of which was signed in Paris in 1971. The other is the Universal Copyright Convention signed in 1952 with lower minimum standards, and sponsored by Unesco. This also was most recently revised in Paris in 1971, jointly with the Berne Convention. To this latter Convention the United States has belonged since 1955. On 16 November 1988, the Government of the United States deposited its instrument of accession to the Paris Revision of the Berne Convention. The Convention entered into force as regards the United States on 1 March 1989. Together with certain new statutory provisions made in consequence of accession to Berne, this advances substantially the process of overhaul and modernisation of US copyright law which was begun in the 1970s.

## Effect on British copyright owners

The copyright statute of the United States having been brought into line with the requirements of the Berne Convention, compliance with the formalities required by American law has been largely removed. The Berne Convention Implementation Act of 1988 makes statutory amendments to the way foreign works are now treated in US law. These are now inserted in the US codified law as Title 17 – The Copyright Act. 'Foreign works' are works having a country of origin other than the United States. The formalities which were for so long a considerable handicap for foreign copyright owners in the American system have now become optional, though not removed altogether. The new system provides incentives to encourage foreign right owners to continue to comply with formalities on a voluntary basis, in particular notice, renewal and registration.

## US copyright law – summary
## Introduction of new law

The Copyright Statute of the United States was passed on 19 October 1976. The greater part of its relevant provisions came into force on 1 January 1978. It has extended the range of copyright protection, and further eased the requirements whereby British authors can obtain copyright protection in America. New Public Law 100–568 of 31 October 1988 has made further amendments to the

Copyright Statute which were necessary to enable ratification of the Berne Convention to take place. The Universal Copyright Convention is now for all practical purposes moribund. The problems which derived from the old system of common law copyright no longer exist.

### The rights of a copyright owner

(1) To reproduce the copyrighted work in copies or phonorecords.

(2) To prepare derivative works based upon the copyrighted work.

(3) To distribute copies or phonorecords of the copyrighted work to the public by sale or other transfer of ownership, or by rental, lease or lending.

(4) In the case of literary, musical, dramatic and choreographic works, pantomimes, and motion pictures and other audiovisual works, but not sound recordings, to perform the copyrighted work publicly. However, in 1995 Congress granted a limited performance right to sound recordings in digital format in an interactive medium.

(5) In the case of literary, musical,

### Works protected in American law

Works of authorship include:
- Literary works. Note: Computer programs are classified as literary works for the purposes of United States copyright. In *Whelan Associates Inc.* v. *Jaslow Dental Laboratory Inc.* (1987) FSR1, it was held that the copyright of a computer program could be infringed even in the absence of copying of the literal code if the structure was part of the expression of the idea behind a program rather than the idea itself.
- Musical works, including any accompanying words.
- Dramatic works, including any accompanying music.
- Pantomimes and choreographic works.
- Pictorial, graphic and sculptural works.
- Motion pictures and other audiovisual works. Note: copyright in certain motion pictures has been extended by the North American Free Trade Agreement Information Act 1993.
- Sound recordings, but copyright in sound recordings is not to include a right of public performance.
- Architectural works: the design of a building as embodied in any tangible medium of expression, including a building, architectural plans or drawings. The Architectural Works Copyright Protections Act applies this protection to works created on or after 1 December 1990.

dramatic, and choreographic works, pantomimes, and pictorial, graphic, or sculptural works, including the individual images of a motion picture or other audiovisual work, to display the copyrighted work publicly.

(6) By the Record Rental Amendment Act 1984, s.109 of the Copyright Statute is amended. Now, unless authorised by the owners of copyright in the sound recording and the musical works thereon, the owner of a phonorecord may not, for direct or indirect commercial advantage, rent, lease or lend the phonorecord. A compulsory licence under s.115(c) includes the right of a maker of a phonorecord of non-dramatic musical work to distribute or authorise the distribution of the phonorecord by rental, lease, or lending, and an additional royalty is payable in respect of that. This modifies the 'first sale doctrine', which otherwise permits someone buying a copyright work to hire or sell a lawfully purchased copy to third parties without compensating the copyright owners, and without his or her consent.

(7) A further exception to the 'first sale doctrine' and s.109 of the Copyright Act is made by the Computer Software Rental Amendments Act. A similar restriction has been placed on the unauthorised rental, lease or lending of software, subject to certain limited exceptions. Both the phonorecord and software exceptions to the first sale doctrine terminated, and were extended by Congress on 1 October 1997.

(8) The Semiconductor Chip Protection Act 1984 adds to the Copyright Statute a new chapter on the protection of semiconductor chip products.

(9) The Visual Artists Rights Act 1990 has added moral rights to the various economic rights listed above. These moral rights are the right of integrity, and the right of attribution or paternity. A new category of 'work of visual art' is defined broadly as paintings, drawings, prints and sculptures, with an upper limit of 200 copies. Works generally exploited in mass market copies such as books, newspapers, motion pictures and electronic information services are specifically excluded from these moral rights provisions. Where they apply, they do so only in respect of works created on or after 1 June 1991, and to certain works previously created where title has not already been transferred by the author.

## Manufacturing requirements
With effect from 1 July 1986, these ceased to have effect. Prior to 1 July 1986, the importation into or public distribution in the United States of a work consisting preponderantly of non-dramatic literary material in the English language and protected under American law was prohibited unless the portions consisting of such material had been manufactured in the United States or Canada. This provision did not apply where, on the date when importation was sought or public distribution in the United States was made, the author of any substantial part of such material was not a national of the United States or, if a national, had been domiciled outside the United States for a continuous period of at least one year immediately preceding that date.

Since 1 July 1986, there is no manufacturing requirement in respect of works of British authors. With American ratification of the Berne Convention, the formalities previously required in relation to copyright notice, deposit and registration have been greatly modified.

## Formalities
**Notice of copyright**. Whenever a work protected by the American Copyright Statute is published in the United States or elsewhere by authority of the copyright owner, a notice of copyright should be placed on all publicly distributed copies. This should consist of:
- either the symbol © or the word 'Copyright' or the abbreviation 'Copr.' plus
- the year of first publication of the work, plus
- the name of the copyright owner.

Since the Berne Amendments, both US and works of foreign origin which were first published in the US after 1 March 1989 without having notice of copyright placed on them will no longer be unprotected. In general, authors are advised to place copyright notices on their works, as this is a considerable deterrent to plagiarism. Damages may well be lower in a case where no notice of copyright was placed on the work.

**Deposit.** The owner of copyright or the exclusive right of publication in a work published with notice of copyright in the United States must within three months of such publication deposit in the Copyright Office for the use or disposition of the Library of Congress two complete copies of the best edition of the work (or two records, if the work is a sound recording). Failure to comply with the deposit requirements does not result in the loss of copyright, but a court could assess fines and issue an injunction.

**Registration.** Registration for copyright in the United States is optional. However, any owner of copyright in a work first published outside the United States may register a work by making application to the Copyright Office with the appropriate fee, and by depositing one complete copy of the work. This requirement of deposit may be satisfied by using copies deposited for the Library of Congress. Whilst registration is still a requirement for works of US origin and from non-Berne countries as a precondition to filing an infringement action, it is no longer necessary for foreign works from Berne countries. But as a matter of practice there are procedural advantages in any litigation where there has been registration. The United States has interpreted the Berne Convention as allowing formalities which are not in themselves conditions for obtaining copyright protection, but which lead to improved protection. The law allows statutory damages and attorneys' fees only if the work was registered prior to the infringement.

## Restoration of copyright

Works by non-US authors which lost copyright protection in the United States because of failure to comply with any of these formalities may have had protection automatically restored in certain circumstances. Works claiming restoration must still be in copyright in their country of origin. If a work succeeds in having copyright restored, it will last for the remainder of the period to which it would originally have been entitled in the United States.

## Duration of copyright

Copyright in a work created on or after 1 January 1978 endures for a term of the life of the author, and a period of 70 years after the author's death. The Supreme Court has ruled this extension by Congress is not unconstitutional. The further amendments made by Public Law 100–568 of 31 October 1988 have enabled the government to ratify the higher standard Berne Convention. Copyright in a work created before 1 January 1978, but not published or copyrighted before then, subsists from 1 January 1978, and lasts for the life of the author and a post-mortem period of 70 years.

Any copyright, the first term of which under the previous law was still subsisting on 1 January 1978, shall endure for 28 years from the date when it was originally secured, and the copyright proprietor or his or her representative may apply for a further term of 47 years within one year prior to the expiry of the original term. Until 1992, application for renewal and extension was required.

## Copyright: criminal proceedings

- Anyone who infringes a copyright wilfully and for purposes of commercial advantage and private financial gain shall be fined not more than $10,000 or imprisoned for not more than 3 years, or both. However, if the infringement relates to copyright in a sound recording or a film, the infringer is liable to a fine of not more than $250,000 or imprisonment for not more than 5 years or both on a first offence, which can be increased to a fine of up to $250,000 or imprisonment for not more than 10 years or both for a subsequent offence.
- Following a conviction for criminal infringement a court may in addition to these penalties order the forfeiture and destruction of all infringing copies and records, together with implements and equipment used in their manufacture.
- It is an offence knowingly and with fraudulent intent to place on any article a notice of copyright or words of the same purport, or to import or distribute such copies. A fine is provided for this offence of not more than $2500. The fraudulent removal of a copyright notice attracts the same maximum fine, as does the false representation of a material particular on an application for copyright representation.

Failure to do so produced disastrous results with some material of great merit passing into the public domain in error. By Public Law 102–307 enacted on 26 June 1992, there is no longer necessity to make a renewal registration in order to obtain the longer period of protection. Now renewal copyright vests automatically in the person entitled to renewal at the end of the 28th year of the original term of copyright.

The duration of any copyright, the renewal term of which was subsisting at any time between 31 December 1976 and 31 December 1977, or for which renewal registration was made between those dates, is extended to endure for a term of 75 years from the date copyright was originally secured.

All terms of copyright provided for by the sections referred to above run to the end of the calendar year in which they would otherwise expire.

### Public performance

Under the previous American law provisions relating to performance in public were less generous to right owners than those existing in United Kingdom copyright law. In particular, performance of a musical work was formerly only an infringement if it was 'for profit'. Moreover, the considerable American coin-operated record-playing machine industry (juke boxes) had obtained an exemption from being regarded as instruments of profit, and accordingly their owners did not have to pay royalties for the use of copyright musical works.

Now by the new law one of the exclusive rights of the copyright owner is, in the case of literary, musical, dramatic and choreographic works, pantomimes, and motion pictures and other audiovisual works, to perform the work publicly, without any requirement of such performance being 'for profit'. By s.114 however, the exclusive rights of the owner of copyright in a sound recording are specifically stated not to include any right of public performance, although this provision was modified in 1995.

The position of coin-operated record players (juke boxes) is governed by the new s.116A, inserted by Public Law 100–568 of 31 October 1988. It covers the position of negotiated licences. Limitations are placed on the exclusive right if licences are not negotiated.

## Mechanical right

Where sound recordings of a non-dramatic musical work have been distributed to the public in the United States with the authority of the copyright owner, any other person may obtain a compulsory licence to make and distribute sound recordings of the work. This right is known in the United Kingdom as 'the mechanical right'. Notice must be served on the copyright owner, who is entitled to a royalty in respect of each of his or her works recorded of either two and three fourths cents or one half of one cent per minute of playing time or fraction thereof, whichever amount is the larger. These rates are adjusted periodically by the Copyright Arbitration Royalty Panels (CARP). Failure to serve or file the required notice forecloses the possibility of a compulsory licence and, in the absence of a negotiated licence, renders the making and distribution of such records actionable as acts of infringement.

## Transfer of copyright

Under the previous American law copyright was regarded as indivisible, which meant that on the transfer of copyright, where it was intended that only film rights or some other such limited right be transferred, the entire copyright nevertheless had to be passed. This led to a cumbersome procedure whereby the author would assign the whole copyright to his or her publisher, who would return to the author by means of an exclusive licence those rights which it was not meant to transfer.

Now it is provided by s.201(d) of the Copyright Statute that (1) the ownership of a copyright may be transferred in whole or in part by any means of conveyance or by operation of law, and may be bequeathed by will or pass as personal property by the applicable laws of intestate succession, and (2) any of the exclusive rights comprised in a copyright (including any subdivision of any of the rights set out in 'The rights of a copyright owner' above) may be transferred as provided in (1) above and owned separately. The owner of any particular exclusive right is entitled, to the extent of that right, to all the protection and remedies accorded to the copyright owner by that Statute. This removes the difficulties which existed under the previous law, and brings the position much closer to that existing in the copyright law of the United Kingdom. All transfers and assignments of copyright must be recorded in the US Copyright Office to have legal effect.

## Copyright Arbitration Royalty Panels

In 1993, the Copyright Royalty Tribunal which had been established by the Copyright Act was eliminated by Congress. In its place a new administrative mechanism was established in the Copyright Office with the purpose of making adjustments of reasonable copyright royalty rates in respect of the exercise of certain rights, mainly affecting the musical interests. The Copyright Arbitration Royalty Panels are constituted on an ad hoc basis and perform in the United States a function similar to the Copyright Tribunal in the United Kingdom.

The American law spells out the economic objectives which the CARP is to apply in calculating the relevant rates. These are:
- to maximise the availability of creative works to the public;

- to afford the copyright owner a fair return for his or her creative work and the copyright user a fair income under existing economic conditions;
- to reflect the relative roles of the copyright owner and the copyright user in the product made available to the public with respect to relative creative contribution, technological contribution, capital investment, cost, risk, and contribution to the opening of new markets for creative expression and media for their communication;
- to minimise any disruptive impact on the structure of the industries involved and on generally prevailing industry practices.

Every final determination of the CARP shall be published in the Federal Register. It shall state in detail the criteria that the CARP determined to be applicable to the particular proceeding, the facts that it found relevant to its determination in that proceeding, and the reasons for its determination. Any final decision of the CARP may be appealed to the United States Court of Appeals within 30 days after its publication in the Federal Register.

## Fair use

One of the most controversial factors which held up the revision of the American copyright law for at least a decade was the extent to which a balance should be struck between the desire of copyright owners to benefit from their works by extending copyright protection as far as possible, and the pressure from users of copyright to obtain access to copyright material as cheaply as possible – if not completely freely.

The new law provides by s.107 that the fair use of a copyright work, including such use by reproduction of excerpts, for purposes such as criticism, comment, news reporting, teaching (including multiple copies for classroom use), scholarship or research is not an infringement of copyright. In determining whether the use made of a work is a fair use, the factors to be considered include:
- the purpose and character of the use, including whether such use is of a commercial nature or is for non-profit educational purposes;
- the nature of the copyrighted work;
- the amount and substantiality of the portion used in relation to the copyrighted work as a whole; and
- the effect of the use upon the potential market for or value of the copyrighted work.

It is not an infringement of copyright for a library or archive, or any of its employees acting within the scope of their employment, to reproduce or distribute no more than one copy of a work, if:
- the reproduction or distribution is made without any purpose of direct or indirect commercial advantage;
- the collections of the library or archive are either open to the public or available not only to researchers affiliated with the library or archive or with the institution of which it is a part, but also to other persons doing research in a specialised field; and
- the reproduction or distribution of the work includes a notice of copyright.

It is not generally an infringement of copyright if a performance or display of a work is given by instructors or pupils in the course of face-to-face teaching activities of a non-profit educational institution, in a classroom or similar place devoted to instruction.

Nor is it an infringement of copyright to give a performance of a non-dramatic literary or musical work or a dramatico-musical work of a religious nature in the course of services at a place of worship or other religious assembly.

It is also not an infringement of copyright to give a performance of a non-dramatic literary or musical work other than in a transmission to the public, without any purpose of direct or indirect commercial advantage and without payment of any fee for the performance to any of the performing artists, promoters or organisers if either:

● there is no direct or indirect admission charge; or
● the proceeds, after deducting the reasonable costs of producing the performance, are used exclusively for educational, religious or charitable purposes and not for private financial gain.

In this case the copyright owner has the right to serve notice of objection to the performance in a prescribed form.

Note the important decision of the Supreme Court in *Sony Corporation of America* v. *Universal City Studios* (No. 81–1687, 52 USLW 4090). This decided that the sale of video recorders to the public for the purpose of recording a copyrighted programme from a broadcast signal for private use for time-switching purposes alone (not for archiving or 'librarying') does not amount to contributory infringement of the rights in films which are copied as a result of television broadcasts of them. In 2001 the World Trade Organisation upheld a complaint by the EU that s.110(5)(B) of the US Copyright Act infringes WTO agreements. The US must now abolish its present exemption from public performance royalties for bars, shops and restaurants.

## Remedies for copyright owners
### Infringement of copyright

Copyright is infringed by anyone who violates any of the exclusive rights referred to in 'The rights of a copyright owner' (page 692), or who imports copies or records into the United States in violation of the law. The owner of copyright is entitled to institute an action for infringement so long as that infringement is committed while he or she is the owner of the right infringed. Previously, no action for infringement of copyright could be instituted until registration of the copyright claim had been made, but this requirement has been modified now that the United States has ratified the Berne Convention. Under the new provision, US authors must register, or attempt to register, but non-US Berne authors are exempt from this requirement.

### Injunctions

Any court having civil jurisdiction under the copyright law may grant interim and final injunctions on such terms as it may deem reasonable to prevent or restrain infringement of copyright. Such injunction may be served anywhere in the United States on the person named. An injunction is operative throughout the whole of the United States, and can be enforced by proceedings in contempt or otherwise by any American court which has jurisdiction over the infringer.

## Impounding and disposition

While a copyright action under American law is pending, the court may order the impounding on such terms as it considers reasonable of all copies or records claimed to have been made or used in violation of the copyright owner's exclusive rights; it may also order the impounding of all VCRs, tape recorders, plates, moulds, matrices, masters, tapes, film negatives or other articles by means of which infringing copies or records may be reproduced. A court may order as part of a final judgement or decree the destruction or other disposition of all copies or records found to have been made or used in violation of the copyright owner's exclusive rights. It also has the power to order the destruction of all articles by means of which infringing copies or records were reproduced.

## Damages and profits

An infringer of copyright is generally liable either for the copyright owner's actual damage and any additional profits made by the infringer, or for statutory damages.

• The copyright owner is entitled to recover the actual damages suffered by him or her as a result of the infringement, and in addition any profits of the infringer which are attributed to the infringement and are not taken into account in computing the actual damages. In establishing the infringer's profits, the copyright owner is only required to present proof of the infringer's gross revenue; it is for the infringer to prove his or her deductible expenses and the elements of profit attributable to factors other than the copyright work.

• Except where the copyright owner has persuaded the court that the infringement was committed wilfully, the copyright owner may elect, at any time before final judgement is given, to recover, instead of actual damages and profits, an award of statutory damages for all infringements involved in the action in respect of any one work, which may be between $750 and $30,000 according to what the court considers justified.

• Where the copyright owner satisfies the court that the infringement was committed wilfully, the court has the discretion to increase the award of statutory damages to not more than $150,000. Where the infringer succeeds in proving that he or she was not aware and had no reason to believe that his or her acts constituted an infringement of copyright, the court has the discretion to reduce the award of statutory damages to not less than $200.

## Costs: time limits

In any civil proceedings under American copyright law, the court may allow the recovery of full costs by or against any party except the Government of the United States. It may also award a reasonable sum in respect of an attorney's fee. No civil or criminal proceedings in respect of copyright law shall be permitted unless begun within three years after the claim or cause of action arose.

## Counterfeiting

By the Piracy and Counterfeiting Amendment Act 1982, pirates and counterfeiters of sound recordings and of motion pictures now face maximum penalties of up to five years imprisonment or fines of up to $250,000.

## Colouring films

The United States Copyright Office has decided that adding colour to a black and white film may qualify for copyright protection whenever it amounts to more than a trivial change.

## Satellite home viewers

The position of satellite home viewers is controlled by the Satellite Home Viewer Act of 1988. (Title II of Public Law 100– 667 of 16 November 1988.) The Copyright Remedy Clarification Act has created s.511 of the Copyright Act, in order to rectify a situation which had developed in case law. By this, the component States of the Union, their agencies and employees are placed in the same position as private individuals and entities in relation to their liability for copyright infringement.

## Digital Millennium Copyright Act

The US Congress in 1998 passed new legislation to make clear that copyright law applies to all works transmitted, or simply made available to, users over the internet.

This measure is unique in that for the first time it gives its copyright owner the right to control access to the digital work, which is so crucial to security on the internet. To allow the United States to ratify two new WIPO (World Intellectual Property Organisation) treaties – the WIPO Copyright Treaty and the WIPO Performance and Phonograms Treaty, negotiated in 1996 – the Digital Millennium Copyright Act (DMCA) makes two changes in US law. First, it outlaws, with substantial criminal and civil penalties, any tampering with copyright management information – the invisible digital coding embedded on sound recordings, software, motion pictures, and databases that identify the owner of the work and stipulate the price and conditions of use. This encoding will help promote e-commerce and curtail internet piracy.

Second, the DMCA prohibits anyone from disabling anti-copying circuitry in a machine or signal. It also bans the manufacture, sale, and importation of electronic devices that would permit the disabling of that circuitry. The DMCA specifies stiff civil and criminal penalties for acts of circumvention and for the manufacture or sale of the devices.

With the DMCA passed, the United States quickly joined the two new WIPO treaties in the hope that its action would serve as an example to other countries.

## General observations

The copyright law of the United States was improved as a result of the statute passed by Congress on 19 October 1976. (Title 17, United States Code.) Apart from lifting the general standards of protection for copyright owners to a higher level than that which previously existed, it has on the whole shifted the

## Further information

### US Copyright Office

*website* www.loc.gov/copyright

Forms for registration, etc can be obtained online.

balance of copyright protection in favour of the copyright owner and away from the copyright user in many of the areas where controversy existed. But most important for British and other non-American authors and publishers, it has gone a long way towards bringing American copyright law up to the same standards of international protection for non-national copyright proprietors which have long been offered by the United Kingdom and the other major countries, both in Europe and elsewhere in the English-speaking world. The ratification by the United States of the Berne Convention with effect from 1 March 1989 was an action which at that time put American copyright law on par with the protection offered by other major countries.

**Gavin McFarlane** LLM, PhD is a barrister at Temple Chambers, Cardiff. He specialises in international trade law, and is particularly interested in the involvement of the World Trade Organisation in intellectual property matters.

# Libel

Any writer should be aware of the law of libel. Antony Whitaker gives an outline of the main principles, concentrating on points which are most frequently misunderstood. However, specific legal advice should be taken when practical problems arise.

The law discussed is the law of England and Wales. Scotland has its own, albeit somewhat similar, rules. A summary of the main differences between the two systems appears in the box (below). The Defamation Act 1996, designed mainly to streamline and simplify libel litigation, became fully effective in February 2000.

## Libel: liability to pay damages

English law draws a distinction between defamation published in permanent form and that which is not. The former is libel, the latter slander. 'Permanent form' includes writing, printing, drawings and photographs and radio and television broadcasts. It follows that it is the law of libel rather than slander which most concerns writers and artists professionally, and the slightly differing rules applicable to slander will not be mentioned in this article.

Publication of a libel can result in a civil action for damages, an injunction to prevent repetition and/or in certain cases a criminal prosecution against those responsible, who include the author (or artist or photographer), the publishers and the editor, if any, of the publication in which the libel appeared. 'Innocent disseminators', such as printers, distributors, broadcasters, internet service providers and retailers, who can show they took reasonable care and had no reason to believe what they were handling contained a libel, are protected under the 1996 Act. Prosecutions are rare. Certain special rules apply to them and these will be explained below after a discussion of the question of civil liability, which in practice arises much more frequently.

Libel claims do not qualify for legal aid, although the closely analogous remedy of malicious falsehood does. Most libel cases are usually heard by a judge and jury, and it is the jury which decides the amount of any award, which is tax-free. It is not necessary for the plaintiff to prove that he or she has actually suffered any loss, because the law presumes damage. While the main purpose of a libel claim is to compensate the plaintiff for the injury to his or her reputation, a jury may give additional sums either as 'aggravated' damages, if it appears a defendant has behaved malevolently or spitefully, or as 'exemplary', or 'punitive', damages where a defendant hopes the economic advantages of publication will outweigh any sum awarded. Damages can also be 'nominal' if the libel complained of is trivial. It is generally very difficult to forecast the amounts juries are likely to award, though awards against newspapers disclose a tendency towards considerable generosity. The Court of Appeal has power to reduce excessive awards of damages.

In an action for damages for libel, it is for the plaintiff to establish that the matter he or she complains of has been published by the defendant; refers to the plaintiff; is defamatory. If this is done, the plaintiff establishes a prima facie case. However, the defendant will escape liability if he or she can show he has a good defence. There are five defences to a libel action. They are: Justification; Fair Comment; Privilege; Offer of Amends: ss.2–4 of the Defamation Act, 1996; Apology, etc, under the Libel Acts, 1843 and 1845. A libel claim can also become barred under the Limitation Acts, as explained below. These matters must now be examined in detail.

## The plaintiff's case
### The meaning of 'published'

'Published' in the legal sense means communicated to a person other than the plaintiff. Thus the legal sense is wider than the lay sense but includes it. It follows that the content of a book is published in the legal sense when the manuscript is first sent to the publishing firm just as much as it is when the book is later placed on sale to the public. Subject to the 'innocent dissemination' defence referred to above, both types of publication are sufficient for the purpose of establishing liability for libel, but the law differentiates between them, since the scope of publication can properly be taken into account by the jury in considering the actual amount of damages to award. Material placed on the internet is unquestionably 'published' there, and the extent of publication can be judged by the number of visits made to the relevant website. If challenged as defamatory, it is generally wise to remove such material, in order to block potential claims of continuing publication. It should be noted that Internet Service Providers can compel website operators to identify the authors of defamatory material anonymously posted to their discussion boards.

## Establishing identity

The plaintiff must also establish that the matter complained of refers to him or her. It is of course by no means necessary to mention a person's name before it is clear that he or she is referred to. Nicknames by which he or she is known or corruptions of his name are just two ways in which his or her identity can be indicated. There are more subtle methods. The sole question is whether the plaintiff is indicated to those who read the matter complained of. In some cases he or she will not be unless it is read in the light of facts known to the reader from other sources, but this is sufficient for the plaintiff's purpose. The test is purely objective and does not depend at all on whether the writer intended to refer to the plaintiff.

It is because it is impossible to establish reference to any individual that generalisations, broadly speaking,

### English and Scottish law

Much of the terminology of the Scots law of defamation differs from that of English law, and in certain minor respects the law itself is different. North of the border, libel and slander are virtually indistinguishable, both as to the nature of the wrongs and their consequences; and Scots law does not recognise the offence of criminal libel. Where individual English litigants enjoy absolute privilege for what they say in court, their Scottish counterparts have only qualified privilege. 'Exemplary', or 'punitive', damages are not awarded by the Scottish courts. Until recently, libel cases in Scotland were for the most part heard by judges sitting alone, but there is now a marked trend towards trial by jury, which has been accompanied by a significant increase in the levels of damages awarded.

are not successfully actionable. To say boldly 'All lawyers are crooks' does not give any single lawyer a cause of action, because the statement does not point a finger at any individual. However, if anyone is named in conjunction with a generalisation, then it may lose its general character and become particular from the context. Again, if one says 'One of the X Committee has been convicted of murder' and the X Committee consists of, say, four persons, it cannot be said that the statement is not actionable because no individual is indicated and it could be referring to any of the committee. This is precisely why it is actionable at the suit of each of them as suspicion has been cast on all.

## Determining what is defamatory

It is for the plaintiff to show that the matter complained of is defamatory. What is defamatory is decided by the jury except in the extreme cases where the judge rules that the words cannot bear a defamatory meaning. Various tests have been laid down for determining this. It is sufficient that any one test is satisfied. The basic tests are:

● Does the matter complained of tend to lower the plaintiff in the estimation of society?
● Does it tend to bring him or her into hatred, ridicule, contempt, dislike or disesteem with society?
● Does it tend to make him shunned or avoided or cut off from society? The mere fact that what is published is inaccurate is not enough to involve liability; it is the adverse impact on the plaintiff's reputation that matters. For example, merely to overstate a person's income is not defamatory; but it will be if the context implies he has not fully declared it to the tax authorities.

'Society' means right-thinking members of society generally. It is by reference to such people that the above tests must be applied. A libel action against a newspaper which had stated that the police had taken a statement from the plaintiff failed, notwithstanding that the plaintiff gave evidence that his apparent assistance to the police (which he denied) had brought him into grave disrepute with the underworld. It was not by their wrongheaded standards that the matter fell to be judged.

Further, it is not necessary to imply that the plaintiff is at fault in some way in order to defame him. To say of a woman that she has been raped or of someone that he is insane imputes to them no degree of blame, but nonetheless both statements are defamatory. Lawyers disagree over whether the claim that an individual is 'ugly' is, or could be, defamatory.

Sometimes a defamatory meaning is conveyed by words which on the face of them have no such meaning. 'But Brutus is an honourable man' is an example. If a jury finds that words are meant ironically they will consider this ironical sense when determining whether the words are defamatory. In deciding, therefore, whether or not the words are defamatory, the jury seeks to discover what, without straining the words or putting a perverse construction on them, they will be understood to mean. In some cases this may differ substantially from their literal meaning.

Matter may also be defamatory by innuendo. Strictly so called, an innuendo is a meaning that words acquire by virtue of facts known to the reader but not stated in the passage complained of. Words, quite innocent on the face of them, may acquire a defamatory meaning when read in the light of these facts. For example, where a newspaper published a photograph of a man and a woman, with the caption that they had just announced their engagement, it was held to be defamatory of the man's wife since those who knew that she had cohabited with him were led to the belief that she had done so only as his mistress. The newspaper was unaware that the man was already married, but some of its readers were not. In general, however, imputations of unchastity against members of either sex would today be regarded as far less defamatory than they were in 1929 when this case was decided.

## Defences to a libel action

Quite apart from the provisions concerning statutory apologies mentioned below, a swift and well publicised apology will always go some way towards assuaging injured feelings and help reduce an award of damages.

## Justification

English law does not protect the reputation that a person either does not or should not possess. Stating the truth therefore does not incur liability, and the plea of justification – namely, that what is complained of is true in substance and in fact – is a complete answer to an action for damages. However, this defence is by no means to be undertaken lightly. For instance, to prove one instance of using bad language will be insufficient to justify the allegation that a person is 'foulmouthed'. It would be necessary to prove several instances, and the defendant is obliged in most cases to particularise in his pleadings giving details, dates and places. However, the requirement that the truth of every allegation must be proved is not absolute, and is qualified by the 'multiple charge – no worse off' defence. This applies where two or more distinct charges are levelled against a plaintiff, and some of what is said turns out to be inaccurate. If his or her reputation in the light of what is shown to be true is made no worse by the unprovable defamatory allegations – for example, mistaken accusations that a convicted pickpocket and car thief is also a shoplifter – the publisher will be safe. This is the extent of the law's recognition that some individuals are so disreputable as to be beyond redemption by awards of damages regardless of what is said about them. Subject to this, however, it is for the defendant to prove that what he or she has published is true, not for the plaintiff to disprove it, though if he can do so, so much the better for him.

One point requires special mention. It is insufficient for the defendant to prove that he or she has accurately repeated what a third person has written or said or that such statements have gone uncontradicted when made on occasions in the past. If X writes 'Y told me that Z is a liar', it is no defence to an action against X merely to prove that Y did say that. X has given currency to a defamatory statement concerning Z and has so made it his own. His only defence is to prove that Z is a liar by establishing a number of instances of Z's untruthfulness. Nor does it help a defence of justification to prove that the defendant genuinely believed what he or she published to be true. This may, however, form part of a qualified privilege defence (see below), and might well be a complete answer in an action, other than a libel action, based on a false but non-defamatory statement. For such statements do not incur liability in the absence of fraud or malice which, in this context, means a dishonest or otherwise improper motive. Bona fide belief, however, may be relevant to the assessment of damages, even in a libel action.

Special care should be taken in relation to references to a person's convictions, however accurately described. Since the Rehabilitation of Offenders Act, 1974, a person's less serious convictions may become 'spent' and thereafter it may involve liability to refer to them. Reference to the Act and orders thereunder must be made in order to determine the position in any particular case.

## Fair comment

It is a defence to prove that what is complained of is fair comment made in good faith and without malice on a matter of public interest. 'Fair' in this context means 'honest'. 'Fair comment' means therefore the expression of the writer's genuinely held opinion. It does not necessarily mean opinion with which the jury agree. Comment may therefore be quite extreme and still be 'fair' in the legal sense. However, if it is utterly perverse the jury may be led to think that no one could have genuinely held such views. In such a case the defence would fail, for the comment could not be honest. 'Malice' here covers any dishonest or improper motive but, in contrast to its application in the context of qualified privilege (see below), it does not include actuation by spite or animosity, even if this is the dominant or sole motive. Care should, however, be taken since evidence of such motivation could also be seen as a lack of genuine belief in the view expressed.

The defence only applies when what is complained of is comment as distinct from a statement of fact. The line between comment and fact is notoriously difficult to draw in some cases. Comment means a statement of opinion. The facts on which comment is made must be stated together with the comment or be sufficiently indicated with it. This is merely another way of saying that it must be clear that the defamatory statement is one of opinion and not of fact, for which the only defence would be the onerous one of justification. The exact extent to which the facts commented on must be stated or referred to is a difficult question, but some help may be derived in answering it by considering the purpose of the rule, which is to enable the reader to exercise his own judgement and to agree or disagree with the comment. It is quite plain that it is not necessary to state every single detail of the facts. In one case it was sufficient merely to mention the name of one of the Press lords in an article about a newspaper though not one owned by him. He was so well known that to mention his name indicated the substratum of fact commented upon, namely his control of his group of newspapers. No universal rule can be laid down, except that, in general, the fuller the facts set out or referred to with the comment, the better. All these facts must be proved to be true subject, however, to the flexibility of the 'proportionate truth' rule. This means that the defence remains available even if, for example, only three out of five factual claims can be proved true, provided that these three are by themselves sufficient to sustain, and are proportionate to, the fairness of the comment. The impact of the two unproven claims would probably fall to be assessed in accordance with the 'multiple charge – no worse off' rule in justification, set out above.

The defence only applies where the matters commented on are of public interest, i.e. of legitimate concern to the public or a substantial section of it. Thus the conduct of national and local government, international affairs, the administration of justice, etc, are all matters of public interest, whereas other people's private affairs may very well not be, although they undoubtedly interest the public, or provoke curiosity.

In addition, matters of which criticism has been expressly or impliedly invited, such as publicly performed plays and published books, are a legitimate subject of comment. Criticism need not be confined merely to their artistic merit but equally may deal with the attitudes to life and the opinions therein expressed.

It is sometimes said that a man's moral character is never a proper subject of comment for the purpose of this defence. This is certainly true where it is a private individual who is concerned, and some authorities say it is the same in the case of a public figure even though his or her character may be relevant to his or her public life. Again, it may in some cases be exceeding the bounds of fair comment to impute a dishonourable motive to a person, as is frequently done by way of inference from facts. In general, the imputation is a dangerous and potentially expensive practice.

## Privilege

Privilege in the law of libel is either 'absolute' or 'qualified', and denotes the two levels of protection from liability afforded, in the public interest, to defamatory statements made on certain occasions. Absolute privilege – where the individual defamed has no remedy whatever – has applied to Parliamentary papers published by the direction of either House, or full republications thereof, since early in the 19th century. Following the implementation of section 14 of the 1996 Defamation Act, this privilege also applies to fair, accurate and contemporaneous reports of public judicial proceedings in the United Kingdom, the European Courts of Justice and Human Rights, and any international criminal tribunal established by the Security Council.

Qualified privilege confers protection provided publication is made only for the reason that the privilege is given and not for some wrongful or indirect motive. In October 1999 the House of Lords extended the defence to protect publications where a defamatory mistake on a matter of public concern has been made by a writer who can show he did his best to uncover the truth. He must show he acted responsibly both in checking his sources and, where appropriate, seeking the potential plaintiff's comments. The precise limits of this defence are not clear, and will only become so as other cases are decided in the future.

The defence also applies, under section 15 of the Act, to fair and accurate reports of public proceedings before a legislature, a court, a government inquiry and an international organisation or conference anywhere in the world, and of certain documents, or extracts from such documents, issued by those bodies. While there is no requirement to correct or publish explanations concerning these reports, such an obligation does arise under section 15 in respect of a separate category of reports of notices issued by various bodies within the European Community and of proceedings of certain bodies or organisations within the United Kingdom. Apart from the Act, such privilege also attaches to extracts from Parliamentary papers and fair and accurate reports of Parliamentary proceedings.

This list of privileged occasions is by no means exhaustive, and the second category may now be expanded by an order of the Lord Chancellor. The privilege defence is extended to the media generally, rather than being restricted, as it was hitherto, simply to newspapers.

### Offers of Amends under the 1996 Act
Sections 2, 3 and 4 of the 1996 Act offer a flexible method of nipping in the bud potential libel actions by those who have been unintentionally defamed. The range of libel meanings for which this defence caters is much wider than that previously available. It envisages the payment of damages as well as costs, together with the offer of a correction and apology, and the damages figure will be fixed by a judge if the parties cannot agree. He or she will do this bearing in mind the generosity of the correction and apology, and the extent of its publication. While recourse to this defence excludes reliance on the defences of justification, privilege and fair comment, it offers a considerable incentive to settle complaints and will save substantially on costs.

### Apology under 1843 and 1845 Acts
This defence is rarely utilised, since if any condition of it is not fulfilled, the plaintiff must succeed and the only question is the actual amount of damages. It only applies to actions in respect of libels in newspapers and periodicals. The defendant pleads that the libel was inserted without actual malice and without gross negligence and that before the action commenced or as soon afterwards as possible he inserted a full apology in the same newspaper, etc, or had offered to publish it in a newspaper, etc, of the plaintiff's choice, where the original newspaper is published at intervals greater than a week. Further a sum must be paid into court with this defence to compensate the plaintiff.

### 'Fast-track disposal' procedure
In its recognition of the generally cumbersome nature of libel litigation, the 1996 Act provides a simplified mechanism for dealing with less serious complaints. Sections 8, 9 and 10 enable a judge alone to dismiss unrealistic claims at the outset; and he will also be able to dispose 'summarily' of relatively minor, but well-founded, claims, on the basis of an award of up to £10,000, a declaration that the publication was libellous, an order for an apology and an order forbidding repetition.

## Limitation and death

The 1996 Act has reduced from three years to one the period within which a libel action must generally be started if it is not to become 'statute-barred' through lapse of time. But successive and subsequent publications, such as the issue of later editions of the same book, or the sale of surplus copies of an old newspaper, or the failure to remove libellous material from the internet, can give rise to fresh claims.

Civil claims for libel cannot be brought on behalf of the dead. If an individual living plaintiff or defendant in a libel case dies before the jury gives their verdict, the action 'abates', i.e. comes to an end, so far as their involvement is concerned, and no rights arising out of it survive either for or against their personal representatives.

## Insurance

For an author, the importance of at least an awareness of this branch of law lies first, in the fact that most book contracts contain a clause enabling the publisher to look to him should any libel claims result; and second, in the increasingly large awards of damages. It is therefore advisable to check what libel insurance a publisher carries, and whether it also covers the author who, if he or she is to have the benefit of it, should always alert the publisher to any potential risk. This insurance for authors can now only be obtained through an insurance broker registered with the General Insurance Standards Council, and one such company is Royal Sun Alliance, Professional and Financial Risks, 4th Floor, Leadenhall Court, Leadenhall Street, London EC3V 1PP (*tel* 020-7283 9000). Premiums start at £1000, and can be substantially higher if the book is tendentious or likely to be controversial. The company generally insists on the author obtaining, and paying for, a legal opinion first. Indemnity limits vary between £250,000 and £1 million, and the author is required to bear at least the first £5000 of any loss. It is worth remembering that 'losses' include legal costs as well as damages, which they can often exceed.

## Criminal liability in libel

Whereas the object of a civil action is to obtain compensation for the wrong done or to prevent repetition, the object of criminal proceedings is to punish the wrongdoer by fine or imprisonment or both. There are four main types of writing which may provoke a prosecution: defamatory libel; obscene publications; sedition and incitement to racial hatred; blasphemous libel.

## Defamatory libel

The publication of defamatory matter is in certain circumstances a crime as well as a civil wrong. But whereas the principal object of civil proceedings will normally be to obtain compensation, the principal object of a criminal prosecution will be to secure punishment of the accused, for example by way of a fine. Prosecutions are not frequent, but there have been signs of late of a revival of interest. There are important differences between the rules applicable to criminal libel and its civil counterpart. For example, a criminal libel may be 'published' even though only communicated to the person defamed and may be found to have occurred even where the person defamed is dead, or where only a group of persons but no particular individual has been maligned. During election campaigns, it is an 'illegal practice' to publish false statements about the personal character or conduct of a candidate irrespective of whether they are also defamatory.

## Obscene publications

It is an offence to publish obscene matter. By the Obscene Publications Act, 1959, matter is obscene if its effect is such as to tend to deprave and corrupt persons who are likely, having regard to all relevant circumstances, to read, see or hear it. 'To deprave and corrupt' is to be distinguished from 'to shock and disgust'. It is a defence to a prosecution to prove that publication of the matter in question is justified as being for the public good, on the ground that it is in the interests of science, literature, art or learning, or of other objects of general concern. Expert evidence may be given as to its literary, artistic, scientific or other merits. Playwrights, directors and producers should note that the Theatres Act, 1968, though designed to afford similar protection to stage productions, does not necessarily prevent prosecutions for indecency under other statutes.

## Sedition/incitement to racial hatred

Writings which tend to destroy the peace of the realm may be prosecuted as being seditious or as amounting to incitement to racial hatred. Seditious writings include those which advocate reform by unconstitutional or violent means or incite contempt or hatred for the monarch or Parliament. These institutions may be criticised stringently, but not in a manner which is likely to lead to insurrection or civil commotion or indeed any physical force. Prosecutions are a rarity, but it should be remembered that writers of matter contemptuous of the House of Commons, though not prosecuted for seditious libel are, from time to time, punished by that House for breach of its privileges, although, if a full apology is made, it is often an end of the matter. The Public Order Act 1986 makes it an offence, irrespective of the author's or publisher's intention, to publish, or put on plays containing, threatening, abusive or insulting matter if hatred is likely to be stirred up against any racial group in Great Britain.

## Blasphemous libel

Blasphemous libel consists in the vilification of the Christian religion or its ceremonies. Other religions are not protected. The offence lies essentially in the impact of what is said concerning, for instance, God, Christ, the Bible, the Book of Common Prayer, etc; it is irrelevant that the publisher does not intend to shock or arouse resentment. While temperate and sober writings on religious topics however anti-Christian in sentiment will not involve liability, if the discussion is 'so scurrilous and offensive as to pass the limit of decent controversy and to outrage any Christian feeling', it will.

**Antony Whitaker** OBE is a barrister and an independent media legal adviser; *email* blairwhitaker@lineone.net

# Finance for writers and artists

## FAQs for writers

Peter Vaines, a chartered accountant and barrister, addresses some questions
frequently asked by writers.

### What can a working writer claim against tax?

A working writer is carrying on a business and can therefore claim all the expenses which are incurred wholly and exclusively for the purposes of that business. A list showing most of the usual expenses is contained on page 717 of this *Yearbook* but there will be other expenses which can be allowed in special circumstances.

Strictly, only expenses which are incurred for the sole purpose of the business can be claimed; there must be no 'duality of purpose' so an item of expenditure cannot be divided into private and business parts. However, the Inland Revenue is usually quite flexible and is prepared to allow all reasonable expenses (including apportioned sums) where the amounts can be commercially justified.

Allowances can also be claimed for the cost of business assets such as a motor car, personal computers, fax, copying machines and all other equipment (including books) which may be used by the writer. An allowance of 25% of the cost can be claimed on the reducing balance each year and for most assets (except cars) an allowance of 40% can be claimed in the first year of purchase. This is increased to 50% for the year ending 5 April 2005. Some expenditure on information technology now benefits from a special 100% allowance. See page 719 for further details of the deductions available in respect of capital expenditure.

### Can I request interest on fees owed to me beyond 30 days of my invoice?

Yes. A writer is like any other person carrying on a business and is entitled to charge interest at a rate of 8% over bank base rate on any debt outstanding for more than 30 days – although the period of credit can be varied by agreement between the parties. It is not compulsory to claim the interest; it is up to you to decide whether to enforce the right.

### What can I do about bad debts?

A writer is in exactly the same position as anybody else carrying on a business over the payment of his or her invoices. It is generally not commercially sensible to insist on payment in advance but where the work involved is substantial (which will normally be the case with a book), it is usual to receive one third of the fee on signature, one third of the fee on delivery of the manuscript and the remaining one third on publication. On other assignments, perhaps not as substantial as a book, it could be worthwhile seeking 50% of the fee on signature and the other 50% on delivery. This would provide a degree of protection in case of cancellation of the assignment because of changes of policy or personnel at the publisher.

### What financial disputes can I take to the Small Claims Court?

If somebody owes you money you can take them to the Small Claims Section of your local County Court, which deals with financial disputes up to £5000. The procedure is much less formal than normal court proceedings and involves little expense. It is not necessary to have a solicitor. You fill in a number of forms, turn up on the day and explain the background to why you are owed the money. Full details of the procedure can be found on: www.courtservice.gov.uk.

### If I receive an advance, can I divide it between two tax years?

Yes. There used to be a system known as 'spreading' but in 2001 a new system called 'averaging' was introduced. This enables writers (and others engaged in the creation of literary, dramatic works or designs) to average the profits of two or more consecutive years if the profits for one year are less than 75% of the profits for the highest year. This relief can apply even if the work takes less than 12 months to create. Both the spreading relief and the averaging relief allow the writer to avoid the higher rates of tax which might arise if the income in respect of a number of years' work were all to be concentrated in a single year.

### How do I make sure I am taxed as a self-employed person so that tax and National Insurance Contributions are not deducted at source?

To be taxed as a self-employed person under Schedule D you have to make sure that the contract for the writing cannot be regarded as a contract of employment. This is unlikely to be the case with a professional author. The subject is highly complex but one of the most important features is that the publisher must not be in a position to direct or control the author's work. Where any doubt exists, the author might find the publisher deducting tax and National Insurance Contributions as a precaution and that would clearly be highly disadvantageous. The author would be well advised to discuss the position with the publisher before the contract is signed to agree that he or she should be treated as self employed and that no tax or National Insurance Contributions will be deducted from any payments. If such agreement cannot be reached, professional advice should immediately be sought so that the detailed technical position can be explained to the publisher.

### Is it a good idea to operate through a limited company?

It can be a good idea for a self-employed writer to operate through a company but generally only where the income is quite large. The costs of operating a company can outweigh any benefit if the writer is paying tax only at the basic rate. Where the writer is paying tax at the higher rate of 40%, being able to retain some of the income in a company at a tax rate of only 19% is obviously attractive. However, this will be entirely ineffective if the writer's contract with the publisher would otherwise be an employment. The whole subject of operating through a company is complex and professional advice is essential.

### When does it become necessary to register for VAT?

Where the writer's self-employed income (from all sources, not only writing) exceeds £58,000 in the previous 12 months or is expected to do so in the next 30 days, he or she must register for VAT and add VAT to all his/her fees. The publisher will pay the VAT to the writer, who must pay the VAT over to the Customs and Excise each quarter. Any VAT the writer has paid on business expenses and on the purchase of business assets can be deducted. It will be possible for some authors to take advantage of the simplified system for VAT payments which applies to small businesses. This involves a flat rate payment of VAT without any need to keep records of VAT on expenses.

### If I make a loss from my writing can I get any tax back?

Where a writer makes a loss, the Inland Revenue may suggest that the writing is only a hobby and not a professional activity thereby denying any relief or tax deduction for the loss. However, providing the writing is carried out on a sensible commercial basis with an expectation of profits, any resulting loss can be offset against any other income the writer may have for the same or the previous year.

# Income tax

Despite attempts by successive Governments to simplify our taxation system, the subject has become increasingly complicated. Peter Vaines, a chartered accountant and barrister, gives a broad outline of taxation from the point of view of writers and other creative professionals. The proposals in the April 2004 Budget are broadly reflected in this article.

## How income is taxed
### Generally

Authors are usually treated for tax purposes as carrying on a profession and are taxed in a similar fashion to other professionals, i.e. as self-employed persons taxed under Schedule D. This article is directed to self-employed persons only, because if a writer is employed he or she will be subject to the much less advantageous rules which apply to employment income.

Attempts are often made by employed persons to shake off the status of 'employee' and to attain 'freelance' status so as to qualify for the advantages of Schedule D, such attempts meeting with varying degrees of success. The problems involved in making this transition are considerable and space does not permit a detailed explanation to be made here – individual advice is necessary if difficulties are to be avoided.

Particular attention has been paid by the Inland Revenue to journalists and to those engaged in the entertainment industry with a view to reclassifying them as employees so that PAYE is deducted from their earnings. This blanket treatment has been extended to other areas and, although it is obviously open to challenge by individual taxpayers, it is always difficult to persuade the Inland Revenue to change its views.

There is no reason why employed people cannot carry on a freelance business in their spare time. Indeed, aspiring authors, painters, musicians, etc, often derive so little income from their craft that the financial security of an employment, perhaps in a different sphere of activity, is necessary. The existence of the employment is irrelevant to the taxation of the freelance earnings although it is most important not to confuse the income or expenditure of the employment with the income or expenditure of the self-employed activity. The Inland Revenue is aware of the advantages which can be derived by an individual having 'freelance' income from an organisation

## Arts Council category A awards

- Direct or indirect musical, design or choreographic commissions and direct or indirect commission of sculpture and paintings for public sites.
- The Royalty Supplement Guarantee Scheme.
- The contract writers' scheme.
- Jazz bursaries.
- Translators' grants.
- Photographic awards and bursaries.
- Film and video awards and bursaries.
- Performance Art Awards.
- Art Publishing Grants.
- Grants to assist with a specific project or projects (such as the writing of a book) or to meet specific professional expenses such as a contribution towards copying expenses made to a composer or to an artist's studio expenses.

of which he or she is also an employee, and where such circumstances are contrived, it can be extremely difficult to convince an Inspector of Taxes that a genuine freelance activity is being carried on. Where the individual operates through a company or partnership providing services personally to a particular client, and would be regarded as an employee if the services were supplied directly by the individual, additional problems arise from the notorious IR35 legislation and professional advice is essential.

For those starting in business or commencing work on a freelance basis the Inland Revenue produces a very useful booklet, *Starting in Business (IR28)*, which is available from any tax office.

## Income

For income to be taxable it need not be substantial, nor even the author's only source of income; earnings from casual writing are also taxable but this can be an advantage, because occasional writers do not often make a profit from their writing. The expenses incurred in connection with writing may well exceed any income receivable and the resultant loss may then be used to reclaim tax paid on other income. There may be deducted from the income certain allowable expenses and capital allowances which are set out in more detail below. The possibility of a loss being used as a basis for a tax repayment is fully appreciated by the Inland Revenue, which sometimes attempts to treat casual writing as a hobby so that any losses incurred cannot be used to reclaim tax; of course by the same token any income receivable would not be chargeable to tax. This treatment may sound attractive but it should be resisted vigorously because the Inland Revenue does not hesitate to change its mind when profits begin to arise. In the case of exceptional or non-recurring writing, such as the autobiography of a sports personality or the memoirs of a politician, it could be better to be treated as pursuing a hobby and not as a professional author. Sales of copyright cannot be charged to income tax unless the recipient is a professional author. However, the proceeds of sale of copyright may be charged to capital gains tax, even by an individual who is not a professional author.

### Arts Council category B awards

- Bursaries to trainee directors.
- Bursaries for associate directors.
- Bursaries to people attending full-time courses in arts administration (the practical training course).
- In-service bursaries to theatre designers and bursaries to trainees on the theatre designers' scheme.
- In-service bursaries for administrators.
- Bursaries for actors and actresses.
- Bursaries for technicians and stage managers.
- Bursaries made to students attending the City University Arts Administration courses.
- Awards, known as the Buying Time Awards, made not to assist with a specific project or professional expenses but to maintain the recipient to enable him or her to take time off to develop his personal talents. These at present include the awards and bursaries known as the Theatre Writing Bursaries, awards and bursaries to composers, awards and bursaries to painters, sculptures and print makers, literature awards and bursaries.

### Royalties

Where the recipient is a professional author, a series of cases has laid down a clear principle that sales of copyright are taxable as income and not as capital receipts. Similarly, lump sums on account of, or in advance of royalties are also taxable as income in the year of receipt, subject to a claim for averaging relief (see below).

Copyright royalties are generally paid without deduction of income tax. However, if royalties are paid to a person who normally lives abroad, tax must be deducted by the payer or his agent at the time the payment is made unless arrangements are made with the Inland Revenue for payments to be made gross under the terms of a Double Taxation Agreement with the other country.

## Arts Council grants

Persons in receipt of grants from the Arts Council or similar bodies will be concerned whether or not such grants are liable to income tax. The Inland Revenue has issued a Statement of Practice after detailed discussions with the Arts Council regarding the tax treatment of the awards. Grants and other receipts of a similar nature have now been divided into two categories (see boxes) – those which are to be treated by the Inland Revenue as chargeable to tax and those which are not. Category A awards are considered to be taxable; awards made under category B are not chargeable to tax.

This Statement of Practice has no legal force and is used merely to ease the administration of the tax system. It is open to anyone in receipt of a grant or award to disregard the agreed statement and challenge the Inland Revenue view on the merits of their particular case. However, it must be recognised that the Inland Revenue does not issue such statements lightly and any challenge to their view would almost certainly involve a lengthy and expensive action through the Courts.

The tax position of persons in receipt of literary prizes will generally follow a decision by the Special Commissioners in connection with the Whitbread Literary Award. In that case it was decided that the prize was not part of the author's professional income and accordingly not chargeable to tax. The precise details are not available because decisions of the Special Commissioners were not, at that time, reported unless an appeal was made to the High Court; the Inland Revenue chose not to appeal against this decision. Details of the many literary awards which are given each year start on page 546, and this decision is of considerable significance to the winners of each of these prizes. It would be unwise to assume that all such awards will be free of tax as the precise facts which were present in the case of the Whitbread award may not be repeated in another case; however it is clear that an author winning a prize has some very powerful arguments in his or her favour, should the Inland Revenue seek to charge tax on the award.

## Allowable expenses

To qualify as an allowable business expense, expenditure has to be laid out wholly and exclusively for business purposes. Strictly there must be no 'duality of purpose', which means that expenditure cannot be apportioned to reflect the private and business usage, e.g. food, clothing, telephone, travelling expenses, etc. However, the Inland Revenue does not usually interpret this principle strictly and is prepared to allow all reasonable expenses (including apportioned sums) where the amounts can be commercially justified.

It should be noted carefully that the expenditure does not have to be 'necessary', it merely has to be incurred 'wholly and exclusively' for business purposes. Naturally, however, expenditure of an outrageous and wholly unnecessary character might well give rise to a presumption that it was not really for business purposes. As with all things, some expenses are unquestionably allowable and some expenses are equally unquestionably not allowable – it is the grey area in between which gives rise to all the difficulties and the outcome invariably depends on negotiation with the Inland Revenue.

Great care should be taken when claiming a deduction for items where there may be a 'duality of purpose' and negotiations should be conducted with more than usual care and courtesy – if provoked the Inspector of Taxes may well choose to allow nothing. An appeal is always possible although unlikely to succeed as a string of cases in the Courts has clearly demonstrated. An example is the case of *Caillebotte* v. *Quinn* where the taxpayer (who normally had lunch at home) sought to claim the excess cost of meals incurred because he was working a long way from his home. The taxpayer's arguments failed because he did not eat only in order to work, one of the reasons for his eating was in order to sustain his life; a duality of purpose therefore existed and no tax relief was due.

Other cases have shown that expenditure on clothing can also be disallowed if it is the kind of clothing which is in everyday use, because clothing is worn not only to assist the pursuit of one's profession but also to accord with public decency. This duality of purpose may be sufficient to deny relief – even where the particular type of clothing is of a kind not otherwise worn by the taxpayer. In the case of *Mallalieu* v. *Drummond* a barrister failed to obtain a tax deduction for items of sombre clothing that she purchased specifically for wearing in Court. The House of Lords decided that a duality of purpose existed because clothing represented part of her needs as a human being.

## Allowances
Despite the above, Inspectors of Taxes are not usually inflexible and the following list of expenses are among those generally allowed.
(a) Cost of all materials used up in the course of preparation of the work.
(b) Cost of typewriting and secretarial assistance, etc; if this or other help is obtained from one's spouse then it is entirely proper for a deduction to be claimed for the amounts paid for the work. The amounts claimed must actually be paid to the spouse and should be at the market rate although some uplift can be made for unsocial hours, etc. Payments to a wife (or husband) are of course taxable in her (or his) hands and should therefore be most carefully considered. The wife's earnings may also be liable for National Insurance contributions and it is important to take care because otherwise you may find that these contributions may outweigh the tax savings. The impact of the National Minimum Wage should also be considered.
(c) All expenditure on normal business items such as postage, stationery, telephone, email, fax and answering machines, agent's fees, accountancy charges, photography, subscriptions, periodicals, magazines, etc, may be claimed. The

cost of daily papers should not be overlooked if these form part of research material. Visits to theatres, cinemas, etc, for research purposes may also be permissible (but not the cost relating to guests). Unfortunately, expenditure on all types of business entertaining is specifically denied tax relief.

(d) If work is conducted at home, a deduction for 'use of home' is usually allowed providing the amount claimed is reasonable. If the claim is based on an appropriate proportion of the total costs of rent, light and heat, cleaning and maintenance, insurance, etc (but not the Council Tax), care should be taken to ensure that no single room is used 'exclusively' for business purposes, because this may result in the Capital Gains Tax exemption on the house as the only or main residence being partially forfeited. However, it would be a strange household where one room was in fact used exclusively for business purposes and for no other purpose whatsoever (e.g. storing personal bank statements and other private papers); the usual formula is to claim a deduction on the basis that most or all of the rooms in the house are used at one time or another for business purposes, thereby avoiding any suggestion that any part was used exclusively for business purposes.

(e) The appropriate business proportion of motor running expenses may also be claimed although what is the appropriate proportion will naturally depend on the particular circumstances of each case; it should be appreciated that the well-known scale benefits, whereby one is taxed according to the size and cost of the car, do not apply to self-employed persons.

(f) It has been long established that the cost of travelling from home to work (whether employed or self-employed) is not an allowable expense. However, if home is one's place of work then no expenditure under this heading is likely to be incurred and difficulties are unlikely to arise.

(g) Travelling and hotel expenses incurred for business purposes will normally be allowed but if any part could be construed as disguised holiday or pleasure expenditure, considerable thought would need to be given to the commercial reasons for the journey in order to justify the claim. The principle of 'duality of purpose' will always be a difficult hurdle in this connection – although not insurmountable.

(h) If a separate business bank account is maintained, any overdraft interest thereon will be an allowable expense. This is the only circumstance in which overdraft interest is allowed for tax purposes and care should be taken to avoid overdrafts in all other circumstances.

(i) Where capital allowances (see below) are claimed for a personal computer, fax, modem, television, video, CD or tape player, etc, used for business purposes the costs of maintenance and repair of the equipment may also be claimed.

Clearly many other allowable items may be claimed in addition to those listed. Wherever there is any reasonable business motive for some expenditure it should be claimed as a deduction although it is necessary to preserve all records relating to the expense. It is sensible to avoid an excess of imagination as this would naturally cause the Inspector of Taxes to doubt the genuineness of other expenses claimed.

The question is often raised whether the whole amount of an expense may be deducted or whether the VAT content must be excluded. Where VAT is reclaimed from the Customs and Excise by someone who is registered for VAT, the VAT element of the expense cannot be treated as an allowable deduction. Where the VAT is not reclaimed, the whole expense (inclusive of VAT) is allowable for income tax purposes.

## Capital allowances
### Allowances
Where expenditure of a capital nature is incurred, it cannot be deducted from income as an expense – a separate and sometimes more valuable capital allowance being available instead. Capital allowances are given for many different types of expenditure, but authors and similar professional people are likely to claim only for 'plant and machinery'; this is a very wide expression which may include motor cars, personal computers, fax and photocopying machines, modems, televisions, CD, video and cassette players used for business purposes. Plant and machinery generally qualify for a 40% allowance in the year of purchase (which has been increased to 50% for the year 2004/05) and 25% of the reducing balance in subsequent years. Expenditure on information technology for the purposes of the business now benefits from a special 100% allowance in the year of purchase. Where the useful life of an asset is expected to be short, it is possible to claim special treatment as a 'short life asset' enabling the allowances to be accelerated.

The reason these allowances can be more valuable than allowable expenses is that they may be wholly or partly disclaimed in any year that full benefit cannot be obtained – ordinary business expenses cannot be similarly disclaimed. Where, for example, the income of an author does not exceed his personal allowances, he would not be liable to tax and a claim for capital allowances would be wasted. If the capital allowances were to be disclaimed their benefit would be carried forward for use in subsequent years. Careful planning with claims for capital allowances is therefore essential if maximum benefit is to be obtained.

As an alternative to capital allowances, claims can be made on the 'renewals' basis whereby all renewals are treated as allowable deductions in the year; no allowance is obtained for the initial purchase, but the cost of replacement (excluding any improvement element) is allowed in full. This basis is no longer widely used, as it is considerably less advantageous than claiming capital allowances as described above.

Leasing is a popular method of acquiring fixed assets, and where cash is not available to enable an outright purchase to be made, assets may be leased over a period of time. Whilst leasing may have financial benefits in certain circumstances, in normal cases there is likely to be no tax advantage in leasing an asset where the alternative of outright purchase is available. Indeed, leasing can be a positive disadvantage in the case of motor cars with a new retail price of more than £12,000. If such a car is leased, only a proportion of the leasing charges will be tax deductible.

## Books

The question of whether the cost of books is eligible for tax relief has long been a source of difficulty. The annual cost of replacing books used for the purposes of one's professional activities (e.g. the cost of a new *Writers' & Artists' Yearbook* each year) has always been an allowable expense; the difficulty arose because the initial cost of reference books, etc (e.g. when commencing one's profession) was treated as capital expenditure but no allowances were due as the books were not considered to be 'plant'. However, the matter was clarified by the case of *Munby* v. *Furlong* in which the Court of Appeal decided that the initial cost of law books purchased by a barrister was expenditure on 'plant' and eligible for capital allowances. This is clearly a most important decision, particularly relevant to any person who uses expensive books in the course of exercising his or her profession.

## Pension contributions
### Personal pensions

Where a self-employed person pays annual premiums under an approved personal pension policy, tax relief may now be obtained each year for the following amounts:

| Age at 6/4/2003 | Maximum % |
| --- | --- |
| 35 and under | 17.5% (max) £17,850 |
| 36 – 45 | 20% (max) £20,400 |
| 46 – 50 | 25% (max) £25,500 |
| 51 – 55 | 30% (max) £30,600 |
| 56 – 60 | 35% (max) £35,700 |
| 61 – 74 | 40% (max) £40,800 |

These figures do not apply to existing retirement annuity policies; these remain subject to the old limits which are unchanged.

These arrangements can be extremely advantageous in providing for a pension as premiums are usually paid when the income is high (and the tax relief is also high) and the pension (taxed as earned income when received) usually arises when the income is low and little tax is payable. There is also the opportunity to take part of the pension entitlement as a tax-free lump sum. It is necessary to take into account the possibility that the tax advantages could go into reverse. When the pension is paid it could, if rates rise again, be taxed at a higher rate than the rate of tax relief at the moment. One would be deferring income in order to pay more tax on it later. However, this involves a large element of guesswork, and many people will be content simply with the long-term pension benefits.

Since April 2001 it has been possible for up to £3600 to be paid into a Stakeholder pension without the need for any earnings.

## Class 4 National Insurance contributions

Allied to pensions is the payment of Class 4 National Insurance contributions, although no pension or other benefit is obtained by the contributions; the Class 4 contributions are designed solely to extract additional amounts from self-employed persons and are payable in addition to the normal Class 2 (self-employed) contributions. The rates are changed each year and for 2004/05 self-employed persons will be obliged to contribute 8% of their profits between the range £4745–£31,720 per annum. This amount is collected in conjunction with the Schedule D income tax liability.

From 6 April 2003 there is a further 1% charge on earnings above £31,720 limit to correspond with the increase in employees' contributions.

## Averaging relief
### Relief for copyright payments

For many years special provisions enabled authors and similar persons engaged on a literary, dramatic, musical or artistic work for a period of more than 12 months, to spread certain amounts received over two or three years depending on the time spent in preparing the work.

On 6 April 2001 a simpler system of averaging was introduced. Under these rules, professional authors and artists engaged in the creation of literary, dramatic works or designs may claim to average the profits of two or more consecutive years if the profits for one year are less than 75% of the profits for the highest year. This new relief can apply even if the work took less than 12 months to create and is available to people who create works in partnership with others.

The purpose of the relief is to enable the creative artist to utilise his allowances fully and to avoid the higher rates of tax which might apply if all the income were to arise in a single year.

## Collection of tax
### Self-assessment

In 1997, the system of sending in a tax return showing all your income and the Inland Revenue raising an assessment to collect the tax was abolished. So was the idea that you pay tax on your profits for the preceding year. Now, when you send in your tax return you have to work out your own tax liability and send a cheque; this is called 'self-assessment'. If you get it wrong, or if you are late with your tax return or the payment of tax, interest and penalties will be charged.

Under this system, the Inland Revenue rarely issue assessments; they are no longer necessary because the idea is that you assess yourself. A colour-coded tax return was created, designed to help individuals meet their tax obligations. This is a daunting task but the term 'self-assessment' is not intended to imply that individuals have to do it themselves; they can (and often will) engage professional help. The term is only intended to convey that it is the taxpayer, and not the Inland Revenue, who is responsible for getting the tax liability right and for it to be paid on time.

The deadline for sending in the tax return is 31 January following the end of the tax year; so for the tax year 2004/05, the tax return has to be submitted to the Inland Revenue by 31 January 2006. If for some reason you are unwilling or unable to calculate the tax payable, you can ask the Inland Revenue to do it for you, in which case it is necessary to send in your tax return by 30 September 2005.

Income tax on self-employed earnings remains payable in two instalments on 31 January and 31 July each year. Because the accurate figures may not necessarily be known, these payments in January and July will therefore be only payments on account based on the previous year's liability. The final balancing figure will be paid the following 31 January together with the first instalment of the liability for the following year.

When the Inland Revenue receives the self-assessment tax return, it is checked to see if there is anything obviously wrong; if there is, a letter will be sent to you immediately. Otherwise, the Inland Revenue has 12 months from the filing date of 31 January in which to make further enquiries; if it doesn't, it will have no further opportunity to do so and your tax liabilities are final – unless there is something seriously wrong such as the omission of income or capital gains. In that event, the Inland Revenue will raise an assessment later to collect any extra tax together with appropriate penalties. It is essential for the operation of the new system that all records relevant to your tax returns are retained for at least 12 months in case they are needed by the Inland Revenue. For the self-employed, the record-keeping requirement is much more onerous because the records need to be kept for nearly six years. One important change in the rules is that if you claim a tax deduction for an expense, it will be necessary to have a receipt or other document proving that the expenditure has been made. Because the existence of the underlying records is so important to the operation of self-assessment, the Inland Revenue treats them very seriously and there is a penalty of £3000 for any failure to keep adequate records.

### Interest

Interest is chargeable on overdue tax at a variable rate, which at the time of writing is 6.5% per annum. It does not rank for any tax relief, which can make the Inland Revenue an expensive source of credit.

However, the Inland Revenue can also be obliged to pay interest (known as repayment supplement) tax-free where repayments are delayed. The rules relating to repayment supplement are less beneficial and even more complicated than the rules for interest payable but they do exist and can be very welcome if a large repayment has been delayed for a long time. Unfortunately, the rate of repayment supplement is only 2.5%, much lower than the rate of interest on unpaid tax.

### Value added tax

The activities of writers, painters, composers, etc are all 'taxable supplies' within the scope of VAT and chargeable at the standard rate. (Zero rating which applies to publishers, booksellers, etc on the supply of books does not extend to the work performed by writers.) Accordingly, authors are obliged to register for VAT if their income for the past 12 months exceeds £58,000 or if their income for the coming month will exceed that figure.

Delay in registering can be a most serious matter because if registration is not effected at the proper time, the Customs and Excise can (and invariably do) claim VAT from all the income received since the date on which registration should have been made. As no VAT would have been included in the amounts received during this period the amount claimed by the Customs and Excise must inevitably come straight from the pocket of the author.

The author may be entitled to seek reimbursement of the VAT from those whom he or she ought to have charged VAT but this is obviously a matter of some difficulty and may indeed damage his commercial relationships. Apart from these disadvantages there is also a penalty for late registration. The rules are extremely harsh and are imposed automatically even in cases of innocent error. It is therefore extremely important to monitor the income very carefully because if in any period of 12 months the income exceeds the £58,000 limit, the Customs and Excise must be notified within 30 days of the end of the period. Failure to do so will give rise to an automatic penalty. It should be emphasised that this is a penalty for failing to submit a form and has nothing to do with any real or potential loss of tax. Furthermore, whether the failure was innocent or deliberate will not matter. Only the existence of a 'reasonable excuse' will be a defence to the penalty. However, a reasonable excuse does not include ignorance, error, a lack of funds or reliance on any third party.

However, it is possible to regard VAT registration as a privilege and not a penalty, because only VAT registered persons can reclaim VAT paid on their expenses such as stationery, telephone, professional fees, etc, and even typewriters and other plant and machinery (excluding cars). However, many find that the administrative inconvenience – the cost of maintaining the necessary records and completing the necessary forms – more than outweighs the benefits to be gained from registration and prefer to stay outside the scope of VAT for as long as possible.

## Overseas matters

The general observation may be made that self-employed persons resident and domiciled in the United Kingdom are not well treated with regard to their overseas work, being taxable on their worldwide income. It is important to emphasise that if fees are earned abroad, no tax saving can be achieved merely by keeping the money outside the country. Although exchange control regulations no longer exist to require repatriation of foreign earnings, such income remains taxable in the UK and must be disclosed to the Inland Revenue; the same applies to interest or other income arising on any investment of these earnings overseas. Accordingly, whenever foreign earnings are likely to become substantial, prompt and effective action is required to limit the impact of UK and foreign taxation. In the case of non-resident authors it is important that arrangements concerning writing for publication in the UK, e.g. in newspapers, are undertaken with great care. A case concerning the wife of one of the great train robbers who provided detailed information for a series of articles in a Sunday newspaper is most instructive. Although she was acknowledged to be resident in Canada for all the relevant years, the income from the articles was treated as arising in this country and fully chargeable to UK tax.

The United Kingdom has double taxation agreements with many other countries and these agreements are designed to ensure that income arising in a foreign country is taxed either in that country or in the UK. Where a withholding tax is deducted from payments received from another country (or where tax is paid in full in the absence of a double taxation agreement), the amount of foreign tax paid can usually be set off against the related UK tax liability. Many successful authors can be found living in Eire because of the complete exemption from tax which attaches to works of cultural or artistic merit by persons who are resident there. However, such a step should only be contemplated having careful regard to all the other domestic and commercial considerations and specialist advice is essential if the exemption is to be obtained and kept; a careless breach of the conditions could cause the exemption to be withdrawn with catastrophic consequences.

Further information concerning the precise conditions to be satisfied for exemption for tax in Eire can be obtained from the Revenue Commissioners, Blocks 3–10, Dublin Castle, Dublin 2, or from their website (www.revenue.ie).

## Companies

When an author becomes successful the prospect of paying tax at the higher rate may drive him or her to take hasty action such as the formation of companies, etc, which may not always be to his advantage. Indeed some authors seeing the exodus into tax exile of their more successful colleagues even form companies in low tax areas in the naive expectation of saving large amounts of tax. The Inland Revenue is fully aware of the opportunities and have extensive powers to charge tax and combat avoidance. Accordingly, such action is just as likely to increase tax liabilities and generate other costs and should never be contemplated without expert advice; some very expensive mistakes are often made in this area which are not always able to be remedied.

To conduct one's business through the medium of a company can be a most effective method of mitigating tax liabilities, and providing it is done at the right time and under the right circumstances very substantial advantages can be derived. However, if done without due care and attention the intended advantages will simply evaporate. At the very least it is essential to ensure that the company's business is genuine and conducted properly with regard to the realities of the situation. If the author continues his or her activities unchanged, simply paying all the receipts from his work into a company's bank account, he cannot expect to persuade the Inland Revenue that it is the company and not himself who is entitled to, and should be assessed to tax on, that income.

It must be strongly emphasised that many pitfalls exist which can easily eliminate all the tax benefits expected to arise by the formation of the company. For example, company directors are employees of the company and will be liable to pay much higher National Insurance contributions; the company must also pay the employer's proportion of the contribution and a total liability of over 23% of gross salary may arise. This compares most unfavourably with the position of a self-employed person. Moreover, on the commencement of the company's business the individual's profession will cease and the possibility of revisions being made by the Inland Revenue to earlier tax liabilities means that the timing of a change has to be considered very carefully.

## The tax return

No mention has been made above of personal reliefs and allowances; this is because these allowances and the rates of tax are subject to constant change and are always set out in detail in the explanatory notes which accompany the Tax Return. The annual Tax Return is an important document and should be completed promptly with extreme care, particularly since the introduction of self-assessment. If filling in the Return is a source of difficulty or anxiety, comfort may be found in the Consumer Association's publication *Money Which?* – *Tax Saving Guide*; this is published in March of each year and includes much which is likely to be of interest and assistance.

**Peter Vaines** FCA, ATII, barrister, is a partner in the international law firm of Haarmann Hemmelrath and writes and speaks widely on tax matters. He is Managing Editor of *Personal Tax Planning Review*, on the Editorial Board of *Taxation*, and tax columnist of the *New Law Journal* and author of a number of books on taxation.

# Social security contributions

In general, every individual who works in Great Britain either as an employee or as a self-employed person is liable to pay social security contributions. The law governing this subject is complicated and Peter Arrowsmith FCA gives here a summary of the position. This article should be regarded as a general guide only.

All contributions are payable in respect of years ending on 5 April. See box (below) for the classes of contributions.

### Employed or self-employed?

The question as to whether a person is employed under a contract *of* service and is thereby an employee liable to Class 1 contributions, or performs services (either solely or in partnership) under a contract for service and is thereby self-employed liable to Class 2 and Class 4 contributions, often has to be decided in practice. One of the best guides can be found in the case of *Market Investigations Ltd* v. *Minister of Social Security* (1969 2 WLR 1) when Cooke J. remarked:

'... the fundamental test to be applied is this: "Is the person who has engaged himself to perform these services performing them as a person in business on his own account?" If the answer to that question is "yes", then the contract is a contract for services. If the answer is "no", then the contract is a contract of service. No exhaustive list has been compiled and perhaps no exhaustive list can be compiled of the considerations which are relevant in determining that question, nor can strict rules be laid down as to the relative weight which the various considerations should carry in particular cases. The most that can be said is that control will no doubt always have to be considered, although it can no longer be regarded as the sole determining factor; and that factors which may be of importance are such matters as:

- whether the man performing the services provides his own equipment,
- whether he hires his own helpers,
- what degree of financial risk he takes,
- what degree of responsibility for investment and management he has, and
- whether and how far he has an opportunity of profiting from sound management in the performance of his task.'

## Classes of contributions

**Class 1** These are payable by employees (primary contributions) and their employers (secondary contributions) and are based on earnings.

**Class 1A** Payable only by employers in respect of all taxable benefits in kind (cars and fuel only prior to 6 April 2000).

**Class 1B** Payable only by employers in respect of PAYE Settlement Agreements entered into by them.

**Class 2** These are weekly flat rate contributions, payable by the self-employed.

**Class 3** These are weekly flat rate contributions, payable on a voluntary basis in order to provide, or make up entitlement to, certain social security benefits.

**Class 4** These are payable by the self-employed in respect of their trading or professional income and are based on earnings.

The above case has often been considered subsequently – notably in November 1993 by the Court of Appeal in the case of *Hall* v. *Lorimer*. In this case a vision mixer with around 20 clients and undertaking around 120–150 separate engagements per annum was held to be self-employed. This follows the, perhaps surprising, contention of the Inland Revenue that the taxpayer was an employee.

## Further guidance

There have been three cases dealing with musicians, in relatively recent times, which provide further guidance on the question as to whether an individual is employed or self-employed.

- *Midland Sinfonia Concert Society Ltd* v. *Secretary of State for Social Services* (1981 ICR 454). A musician, employed to play in an orchestra by separate invitation at irregular intervals and remunerated solely in respect of each occasion upon which he plays, is employed under a contract for services. He is therefore self-employed, not an employed earner, for the purposes of the Social Security Contributions and Benefits Act 1992, and the orchestra which engages him is not liable to pay National Insurance contributions in respect of his earnings.

- *Addison* v. *London Philharmonic Orchestra Ltd* (1981 ICR 261). This was an appeal to determine whether certain individuals were employees for the purposes of section 11(1) of the Employment Protection (Consolidation) Act 1978.

  The Employment Appeal Tribunal upheld the decision of an industrial tribunal that an associate player and three additional or extra players of the London Philharmonic Orchestra were not employees under a contract of service, but were essentially freelance musicians carrying on their own business. The facts found by the industrial tribunal showed that, when playing for the orchestra, each appellant remained essentially a freelance musician, pursuing his or her own profession as an instrumentalist, with an individual reputation, and carrying on his or her own business, and they contributed their own skills and interpretative powers to the orchestra's performances as independent contractors.

- *Winfield* v. *London Philharmonic Orchestra Ltd* (1979 ICR 726). This case dealt with the question as to whether an individual was an employee within the meaning of section 30 of the Trade Union and Labour Relations Act 1974. The following remarks by the appeal tribunal are of interest in relation to the status of musicians:

  "… making music is an art, and the co-operation required for a performance of Berlioz's *Requiem* is dissimilar to that required between the manufacturer of concrete and the truck driver who takes the concrete where it is needed … It took the view, as we think it was entitled on the material before it to do, that the company was simply machinery through which the members of the orchestra managed and controlled the orchestra's operation … In deciding whether you are in the presence of a contract of service or not, you look at the whole of the picture. This picture looks to us, as it looked to the industrial tribunal, like a co-operative of distinguished musicians running themselves with self and mutual discipline, and in no sense like a boss and his musician employees."

Other modern cases have concerned a professional dancer and holiday camp entertainers (all of whom were regarded as employees). In two other cases income from part-time lecturing was held to be from an employment.

Accordingly, if a person is regarded as an employee under the above rules, he or she will be liable to pay contributions even if his employment is casual, part-time or temporary. Furthermore, if a person is an employee and also carries on a trade or profession either solely or in partnership, there will be a liability to more than one class of contributions (subject to certain limits – see below).

### Exceptions

There are certain exceptions to the above rules, those most relevant to artists and writers being:

● The employment of a wife by her husband, or vice versa, is disregarded for social security purposes unless it is for the purposes of a trade or profession (e.g. the employment of his wife by an author would not be disregarded and would result in a liability for contributions if her salary reached the minimum levels).

● The employment of certain relatives in a private dwelling house in which both employee and employer reside is disregarded for social security purposes provided the employment is not for the purposes of a trade or business carried on at those premises by the employer. This would cover the employment of a relative (as defined) as a housekeeper in a private residence.

● In general, lecturers, teachers and instructors engaged by an educational establishment to teach on at least four days in three consecutive months are regarded as employees, although this rule does not apply to fees received by persons giving public lectures.

### Freelance film workers

There is a list of grades in the film industry in respect of which PAYE need not be deducted and who are regarded as self-employed for tax purposes.

Further information can be obtained from the 2003 edition of the Inland Revenue guidance notes on the application of PAYE to casual and freelance staff in the film industry. In view of the Inland Revenue announcement that the same status will apply for PAYE and National Insurance contributions purposes, no liability for employee's and employer's contributions should arise in the case of any of the grades mentioned above.

However, in the film and television industry this general rule was not always followed in practice. In December 1992, after a long review, the DSS agreed that individuals working behind the camera and who have jobs on the Inland Revenue Schedule D list are self-employed for social security purposes.

There are special rules for, *inter alia*, personnel appearing before the camera, short engagements, payments to limited companies and payments to overseas personalities.

### Artistes, performers/non-performers

The status of artistes and performers for tax purposes will depend on the individual circumstances but for social security new regulations which took effect on 17 July 1998 require most actors, musicians or similar performers to be treated as employees for social security purposes, whether or not this status applies under general and/or tax law. It also applies whether or not the individual is supplied through an agency.

## Personal service companies

From 6 April 2000, those who have control of their own 'one-man service companies' are subject to special rules. If the work that the owner of the company does for the company's customers would – but for the one-man company – fall to be considered as an employment of that individual (i.e. rather than self-employment), a deemed salary may arise. If it does, then some or all of the income of the company will be treated as salary liable to PAYE and National Insurance contributions. This will be the case whether or not such salary is actually paid by the company. The same situation may arise where the worker owns as little as 5% of a company's share capital.

The calculations required by the Inland Revenue are complicated and have to be done very quickly at the end of each tax year (even if the company's year-end is different). It is essential that affected businesses seek detailed professional advice about these rules which may also, in certain circumstances, apply to partnerships.

## Class 1 contributions

As mentioned above, these are related to earnings, the amount payable depending upon whether the employer has applied for his employees to be 'contracted-out' of the State earnings-related pension scheme; such application can be made where the employer's own pension scheme provides a requisite level of benefits for his or her employees and their dependants or, in the case of a money purchase scheme (COMPS) certain minimum safeguards are covered. Employers with employees contributing to 'stakeholder pension plans' continue to pay the full not contracted-out rate. Such employees have their contracting out arrangements handled separately by government authorities.

Contributions are payable by employees and employers on earnings that exceed the earnings threshold. Contributions are normally collected via the PAYE tax deduction machinery, and there are penalties for late submission of returns and for errors therein. From 19 April 1993, interest is charged automatically on unpaid PAYE and social security contributions.

## Employees liable to pay

Contributions are payable by any employee who is aged 16 years and over (even though they may still be at school) and who is paid an amount equal to, or exceeding, the earnings threshold. Nationality is irrelevant for contribution purposes and, subject to special rules covering employees not normally resident in Great Britain, Northern Ireland or the Isle of Man, or resident in EEA countries or those with which there are reciprocal agreements, contributions must be paid whether the employee concerned is a British subject or not provided he is gainfully employed in Great Britain.

## Employees exempt from liability to pay

Persons over pensionable age (65 for men; 60 – until 2010 – for women) are exempt from liability to pay primary contributions, even if they have not retired. However, the fact that an employee may be exempt from liability does not relieve an employer from liability to pay secondary contributions in respect of that employee.

## Employees' (primary) contributions

From 6 April 2003, the rate of employees' contributions on earnings from the earnings threshold to the upper earnings limit is 11% (9.4% for contracted-out employments). Certain married women who made appropriate elections before 12 May 1977 may be entitled to pay a reduced rate of 4.85%. However, they will have no entitlement to benefits in respect of these contributions.

From April 2003, earnings above the upper earnings limit attract an employee contribution liability of 1% – previously, there was no such liability.

## Employers' (secondary) contributions

All employers are liable to pay contributions on the gross earnings of employees. As mentioned above, an employer's liability is not reduced as a result of employees being exempted from contributions, or being liable to pay only the reduced rate (4.85%) of contributions.

For earnings paid on or after 6 April 2003 employers are liable at a rate of 12.8% on earnings paid above the earnings threshold (without any upper earnings limit), 9.3% where the employment is contracted out (salary related) or 11.8% (money purchase). In addition, special rebates apply in respect of earnings falling between the lower earnings limit and the earnings threshold. This provides, effectively, a negative rate of contribution in that small band of earnings. It should be noted that the contracted-out rates of 9.3% and 11.8% apply only up to the upper earnings limit. Thereafter, the not contracted-out rate of 12.8% is applicable.

The employer is responsible for the payment of both employees' and employer's contributions, but is entitled to deduct the employees' contributions from the earnings on which they are calculated. Effectively, therefore, the employee suffers a deduction in respect of his or her social security contributions in arriving at his weekly or monthly wage or salary. Special rules apply to company directors and persons employed through agencies.

### Rates of Class 1 contributions and earnings limits from 6 April 2004

| | Rates payable on earnings in each band | | | |
|---|---|---|---|---|
| Earnings per week | Not contracted-out | | Contracted-out | |
| | Employee | Employer | Employee | Employer |
| £ | % | % | % | % |
| Below 79.00 | — | — | — | — |
| 79.00 – 90.99 | — | — | — (*) | — (*) |
| 91.00 – 610.00 | 11 | 12.8 | 9.4 | 9.3 or 11.8 |
| Over £610.00 | 1 | 12.8 | 1 | 12.8 |

* Special rebates deductible in respect of this band of earnings.

## Items included in, or excluded from, earnings

Contributions are calculated on the basis of a person's gross earnings from their employment. This will normally be the figure shown on the deduction working sheet, except where the employee pays superannuation contributions and, from 6 April 1987, charitable gifts under payroll giving – these must be added back for the purposes of calculating Class 1 liability.

Earnings include salary, wages, overtime pay, commissions, bonuses, holiday pay, payments made while the employee is sick or absent from work, payments to cover travel between home and office, and payments under the statutory sick pay, statutory maternity pay, statutory paternity pay and statutory adoption pay schemes.

However, certain payments, some of which may be regarded as taxable income for income tax purposes, are ignored for Class 1 purposes. These include:

- certain gratuities paid other than by the employer,
- redundancy payments and some payments in lieu of notice,
- certain payments in kind,
- reimbursement of specific expenses incurred in the carrying out of the employment,
- benefits given on an individual basis for personal reasons (e.g. wedding and birthday presents),
- compensation for loss of office.

IR Booklet CWG 2 (2004 edition) gives a list of items to include in or exclude from earnings for Class 1 contribution purposes. Some such items may, however, be liable to Class 1A (employer only) contributions.

## Miscellaneous rules

There are detailed rules covering a person with two or more employments; where a person receives a bonus or commission in addition to a regular wage or salary; and where a person is in receipt of holiday pay. From 6 April 1991 employers' social security contributions arise under Class 1A in respect of the private use of a company car, and of fuel provided for private use therein. From 6 April 2000, this charge was extended to cover most benefits in kind. The rate is now 12.8%. From 6 April 1999, Class 1B contributions are payable by employers using PAYE Settlement Agreements in respect of small and/or irregular expense payments and benefits, etc. This rate is also currently 12.8%.

## Class 2 contributions

Class 2 contributions are payable at the weekly rate of £2.05 as from 6 April 2004. Exemptions from Class 2 liability are:

- A man over 65 or a woman over 60.
- A person who has not attained the age of 16.
- A married woman or, in certain cases, a widow who elected prior to 12 May 1977 not to pay Class 2 contributions.
- Persons with small earnings (see below).
- Persons not ordinarily self-employed (see below).

## Small earnings

Application for a certificate of exception from Class 2 contributions may be made by any person who can show that his or her net self-employed earnings per his profit and loss account (as opposed to taxable profits):

- for the year of application are expected to be less than a specified limit (£4215 in the 2004/05 tax year); or
- for the year preceding the application were less than the limit specified for that year (£4095 for 2003/04) and there has been no material change of circumstances.

Certificates of exception must be renewed in accordance with the instructions stated thereon. At the Inland Revenue's discretion the certificate may commence up to 13 weeks before the date on which the application is made. Despite a certificate of exception being in force, a person who is self-employed is still entitled to pay Class 2 contributions if they wish, in order to maintain entitlement to social security benefits.

## Persons not ordinarily self-employed

Part-time self-employed activities (including as a writer or artist) are disregarded for contribution purposes if the person concerned is not ordinarily employed in such activities and has a full-time job as an employee. There is no definition of 'ordinarily employed' for this purpose but a person who has a regular job and whose earnings from spare-time occupation are not expected to be more than £1300 per annum may fall within this category. Persons qualifying for this relief do not require certificates of exception but may be well advised to apply for one nonetheless.

## Method of payment

From April 1993, Class 2 contributions may be paid by monthly direct debit in arrears or, alternatively, by cheque, bank giro, etc following receipt of a quarterly (in arrears) bill.

## Overpaid contributions

If, following the payment of Class 2 contributions, it is found that the earnings are below the exception limit (e.g. the relevant accounts are prepared late), the Class 2 contributions that have been overpaid can be reclaimed, provided a claim is made between 6 April and 31 January immediately following the end of the tax year.

## Class 3 contributions

Class 3 contributions are payable voluntarily, at the weekly rate of £7.15 per week from 6 April 2004, by persons aged 16 or over with a view to enabling them to qualify for a limited range of benefits if their contribution record is not otherwise sufficient. In general, Class 3 contributions can be paid by employees, the self-employed and the non employed.

Broadly speaking, no more than 52 Class 3 contributions are payable for any one tax year, and contributions cannot be paid in respect of tax years after the one in which the individual concerned reaches the age of 64 (59 for women).

Class 3 contributions may be paid in the same manner as Class 2 (see above) or by annual cheque in arrears.

## Class 4 contributions

In addition to Class 2 contributions, self-employed persons are liable to pay Class 4 contributions. These are calculated at the rate of 8% on the amount of profits or gains chargeable to income tax under Schedule D Case I or II which exceed £4745 per annum but which do not exceed £31,720 per annum for 2004/05. Profits above the upper limit of £31,720 attract a Class 4 charge at the rate of 1%.

The income tax profit on which Class 4 contributions are calculated is after deducting capital allowances and losses, but before deducting personal tax allowances or retirement annuity or personal pension or stakeholder pension plan premiums.

Class 4 contributions produce no additional benefits, but were introduced to ensure that self-employed persons as a whole pay a fair share of the cost of pensions and other social security benefits yet without those who make only small profits having to pay excessively high flat rate contributions.

## Payment of contributions

In general, contributions are now self-assessed and paid to the Inland Revenue together with the income tax under Schedule D Case I or II, and accordingly the contributions are due and payable at the same time as the income tax liability on the relevant profits. Under self-assessment, interim payments of Class 4 contributions are payable at the same time as interim payments of tax.

## Class 4 exemptions

The following persons are exempt from Class 4 contributions:
- Men over 65 and women over 60 at the commencement of the year of assessment (i.e. on 6 April).
- An individual not resident in the United Kingdom for income tax purposes in the year of assessment.
- Persons whose earnings are not 'immediately derived' from carrying on a trade, profession or vocation (e.g. sleeping partners).
- A child under 16 on 6 April of the year of assessment.
- Persons not ordinarily self-employed.

## Married persons and partnerships

Under independent taxation of husband and wife from 1990/91 onwards, each spouse is responsible for his or her Class 4 liability.

In partnerships, each partner's liability is calculated separately. If a partner also carries on another trade or profession, the profits of all such businesses are aggregated for the purposes of calculating their Class 4 liability.

When an assessment has become final and conclusive for the purposes of income tax, it is also final and conclusive for the purposes of calculating Class 4 liability.

## Maximum contributions

There is a form of limit to the total liability for social security contributions payable by a person who is employed in more than one employment, or is also self-employed or a partner.

Where only not contracted-out Class 1 contributions, or not contracted-out Class 1 and Class 2 contributions, are payable, the maximum contribution payable at the main rates (11%, 9.4% or 4.85% as the case may be) is limited to 53 primary Class 1 contributions at the maximum weekly not contracted-out standard rate. For 2004/05 this 'maximum' will thus be £3025.77 (amounts paid at only 1% are to be excluded in making this comparison).

However, where contracted-out Class 1 contributions are payable, the maximum primary Class 1 contributions payable for 2004/05 where all employments are contracted out are £2575.48 (again excluding amounts paid at only 1%).

Where Class 4 contributions are payable in addition to Class 1 and/or Class 2 contributions, the Class 4 contributions payable at the full 8% rate are restricted so that they shall not exceed the excess of £2266.65 (i.e. 53 Class 2 contributions plus maximum Class 4 contributions) over the aggregate of the Class 1 and Class 2 contributions paid at the full (i.e. other than 1%) rates.

### Transfer to Inland Revenue

The administrative functions of the former Contributions Agency transferred to the Inland Revenue from 1 April 1999. Responsibility for National Insurance contribution policy matters was also transferred from DSS Ministers to the Inland Revenue and Treasury Ministers on the same date. The DSS is now known as the Department for Work and Pensions (DWP).

Peter Arrowsmith FCA is a sole practitioner specialising in National Insurance matters. He is chairman of the Employer Issues Committee of the Institute of Chartered Accountants in England and Wales, and Consulting Editor to *Tolley's National Insurance Contributions 2004/05*.

# Social security benefits

There are many leaflets produced by the Department for Work and Pensions. However, due to the nature of the subject social security benefits can be quite difficult to understand. In this article, K.D. Bartlett FCA has summarised some of the more usual benefits that are available under the Social Security Acts.

This article deliberately does not cover every aspect of the legislation but the references given should enable the relevant information to be easily traced. These references are to the leaflets issued by the Department for Work and Pensions.

It is usual for only one periodical benefit to be payable at any one time. If the contribution conditions are satisfied for more than one benefit it is the larger benefit that is payable. Benefit rates shown below were those payable from the week commencing 6 April 2004.

Self-employed persons (Class 2 and Class 4 contributors) are covered for all benefits except earnings-related supplements, unemployment benefit, widow's and invalidity pensions, widowed mother's allowance and industrial injury benefits. Most authors are self employed.

## Family benefits

Child benefit (Leaflet CH 1) is payable for all children who are either under 16 or under 19 and receiving full-time education at a recognised educational establishment. The rate is £16.50 for the first or eldest child and £11.05 a week for each subsequent child. It is payable to the person who is responsible for the child but excludes foster parents or people exempt from UK tax. Furthermore, one-parent families receive £17.55 per week for the eldest child.

Those with little money may apply for a maternity loan or grant from the social fund. Those claiming Working Families Tax Credit or Disabled Persons Tax Credit can apply for a Sure Start Maternity Grant of £500 for each baby expected, born, adopted or subject to a parental order. Any savings over £500 are taken into account. This grant will only be paid on the provision of a relevant certificate from a doctor, midwife or health visitor.

A guardian's allowance (Leaflet NI 14) is paid at the rate of £9.70 a week. For each subsequent child the rate of benefit is £11.85 a week to people who have taken orphans into their own family. Usually both of the child's parents must be dead and at least one of them must have satisfied a residence condition.

The allowance can only be paid to the person who is entitled to child benefit for the child (or to that person's spouse). It is not necessary to be the legal guardian. The claim should be made within three months of the date of entitlement.

## Disability living allowance

Disability living allowance has replaced attendance allowance for disabled people before they reach the age of 65. It has also replaced mobility allowance.

Those who are disabled after reaching 65 may be able to claim attendance allowance. The attendance allowance board decide whether, and for how long, a person is eligible for this allowance. Attendance allowance is not taxable. The care component is divided into three rates whereas the mobility allowance has two rates. The rate of benefit from 6 April 2004 is as follows:

|  | Per week |
|---|---|
| *Care component* | |
| Higher rate (day and night, or terminally ill) | £58.80 |
| Middle rate (day or night) | £39.35 |
| Lower rate (if need some help during day, or over 16 and need help preparing a meal) | £15.55 |
| *Mobility component* | |
| Higher rate (unable or virtually unable to walk) | £41.05 |
| Lower rate (can walk but needs help when outside) | £15.55 |

## Benefits for the ill

Incapacity benefit (Leaflet DS 700) replaced sickness benefit and invalidity benefit. The contribution conditions haven't changed but a new medical test has been brought in which includes a comprehensive questionnaire. The rates from 8 April 2004 are:

| | |
|---|---|
| Long-term incapacity benefit | £74.15 |
| Short-term incapacity benefit | £55.90 |
| Increase of long-term incapacity benefit for age: | |
| Higher rate | £15.15 |
| Lower rate | £7.80 |

Carers allowance, formerly invalid care allowance, is a taxable benefit paid to people of working age who cannot take a job because they have to stay at home to look after a severely disabled person. The basic allowance is £44.35 per week. An extra £9.70 is paid for the first dependent child and £11.35 for each subsequent child.

## Pensions and Widowed Parent's Allowance

The state pension (Leaflets NP 23, NP 35, NP 31) is divided into two parts – the basic pension, presently £79.60 per week for a single person or £127.25 per week for a married couple.

Women paying standard rate contributions into the scheme are eligible for the same amount of pension as men but five years earlier, from age 60. The Pensions Act 1995 incorporated the provision for an equal state pension age of 65 for men and women to be phased in over a 10-year period beginning 6 April 2010. If a woman stays at home to bring up her children or to look after a person receiving attendance allowance she can have her basic pension rights protected without paying contributions.

Pension Credit is a new entitlement for people aged 60 or over. It guarantees everyone aged 60 and over an income of at least:
- £105.45 a week if you are single; or
- £160.95 a week if you have a partner.

For the first time, people aged 65 and over will be rewarded for some of their savings and income they have for their retirement. In the past, those who had saved a little money were no better off than those who had not saved at all. Pension Credit will change this by giving new money to those who have saved – up to £15.51 if you are single, or £20.22 if you have a partner.

The person who applies for Pension Credit must be at least 60 but their partner can be under 60. Partner means a spouse or a person with whom one lives as if you were married to them.

## Widowed Parent's Allowance

This is a new system of bereavement benefits for men and women introduced in April 2001. Women who were receiving benefits under the previous scheme are unaffected as long as they still qualify under the rules. A Widowed Parent's Allowance is:

- based on the late husband's or wife's contributions;
- for widows or widowers bringing up children;
- a regular payment.

The main conditions for receiving this benefit are:

- You must be aged over 45 and must have a dependent child or children.
- If you were over the state pension age when you were widowed you may receive Retirement Pension based on the husband's or wife's NI contributions.
- If the spouse died as a result of their job, it is possible to receive bereavement benefits even if they did not pay sufficient NI contributions.
- You cannot receive bereavement benefits if you remarry or if you live with a partner as if you are married to them.
- Bereavement benefits are not affected if you work.

The allowance is £79.60 for those over 55 and varies between £23.88 and £74.03 for those aged between 45 and 54.

There are increases for dependent children. You receive £9.65 for the oldest child who qualifies for child benefit and £11.35 for each child who qualifies.

## Bereavement payment and benefits

From 9 April 2001 bereavement benefits are payable to both widows and widowers but the benefits are only paid to those without children. Benefits are based on the National Insurance contributions of the deceased. No benefit is payable if the couple were divorced at the date of death or if either of the survivors remarries or cohabits.

Widows and widowers bereaved on or after 9 April 2001 are entitled to a tax-free bereavement payment of £2000.

The death grant to cover funeral expenses was abolished from 6 April 1987. It has been replaced by a funeral payment from the social fund where the claimant is in receipt of income support, income-based Jobseekers' Allowance, Disabled Persons' Tax Credit, Working Families' Tax Credit or housing benefit. The full cost of a reasonable funeral is paid, reduced by any savings of over £600 held by the claimant.

## Child Tax Credits and Working Tax Credit

Child Tax Credits were introduced on 6 April 2003. To obtain them a claim form has to be submitted (Tax Credit Form TC600 is available by either telephoning 0845 300 3900 or applying online – see below). In April 2004 a renewal form was sent out to all claimants. The current deadline for returning that form to the Inland Revenue is 5 July 2004. Missing the deadline may result in a fine of up to £300. For the self employed this may mean estimating the income for the tax year 2003/04 if accounts are not available.

Child Tax Credit has replaced the Children's Tax Credit previously claimed through tax paid. It is paid directly to the person who is mainly responsible for caring for the child or children. A family unit earning up to £58,000 will be entitled to the Tax Credit (£66,000 if the family has a child under one year old). To ascertain which tax credits you could be entitled to, visit the Tax Credits website (www.taxcredits.inlandrevenue.gov.uk).

Child Tax Credits are especially complicated for those on variable income and the self employed. The tax credit for the tax year 2004/05 is initially based on the income earned in the tax year 2002/03. If the income is now lower in 2004/05 than in 2002/03 then potentially you should be receiving more tax credit or even be eligible for it when before you were earning too much. In this situation you should make a protective claim by completing and sending off a Tax Credit Form TC600.

## Working Tax Credit

Working Tax Credit is paid to support people in work and is administered by the Inland Revenue. It is not necessary to have paid National Insurance contributions to qualify. The following do qualify:

● Those over 16 who are responsible for a child or young person and work at least 16 hours a week.

People without children can claim if:

● they are over 25 and work at least 30 hours a week;
● they are aged 16 or over and work at least 16 hours a week and have a disability that puts them at a disadvantage in obtaining a job;
● a person or their partner are aged 50 or more and work at least 16 hours a week and are returning to work after time spent on obtaining a qualification.

Working Tax Credit is paid as well as any Child Tax Credit you are entitled to. The calculations on how much you receive are complicated but it will depend on how many hours you work and your income or joint income.

If you are employed then you will receive the payment via your employer and if self employed you will be paid direct. If you think you are eligible to receive Working Tax Credit, either telephone 0800-500 222 or visit the tax credits website (www.inlandrevenue.gov.uk/taxcredits).

## Disabled Persons Tax Credit

There is a tax credit to assist people with an illness or disability who are in work. It replaced Disability Working Allowance. It is for people who have an illness or a disability which puts them at a disadvantage in getting a job and who:

- work at least 16 hours per week;
- are resident in the UK and are entitled to work here;
- have one of a number of qualifying benefits for disability or were receiving one of them up to 182 days prior to the application;
- have savings of £16,000 or less.

**K.D. Bartlett** FCA qualified as a Chartered Accountant in 1969 and became a partner in a predecessor firm of Horwath Clark Whitehill in 1972.

# Subject indexes
## Magazines by subject area

These lists can be only a broad classification. They should be regarded as a guide to possible markets and be used with discrimination. Addresses for magazines start on page 31.

### Fiction (see also Literary)

Active Life
Ambit
Aquila
The Australian Women's Weekly
Bella
Best
Brownie
Cencrastus: Scottish & International Literature, Arts and Affairs
Chapman
Chat
Critical Quarterly
Cyphers
The Dalhousie Review
Day by Day
Descant
Diva
The Dublin Review
The Edge
The Erotic Review
The Fiddlehead
Fly-Fishing & Fly-Tying
For Women
Granta
Interzone
Ireland's Own
Irish Pages: A Journal of Contemporary Writing
The Jewish Quarterly
Junior Magazine
Kent Life
The Lady
The London Magazine: A Review of Literature and the Arts
Lothian Life
The Malahat Review
Mayfair
More
Mslexia
My Weekly
My Weekly Story Collection
Neo-opsis Science Fiction Magazine
New Impact
The New Writer
The Newspaper
New Zealand Woman's Day

New Zealand Woman's Weekly
ontheedge
Overland
Peninsular Magazine
People's Friend
People's Friend Story Collection
Planet
Pretext
Pride
Prospect
Quadrant
Queen's Quarterly
QWF
The Scots Magazine
Scuba Diver
SHERLOCK
Shoot Monthly
Springboard
Stand Magazine
Staple
Starburst
Takahe
Take a Break
that's life!
The Third Alternative
Time Out
The Times Literary Supplement
Walk
Wascana Review of Contemporary Poetry & Short Fiction
The Weekly News
Woman and Home
Woman's Day
Woman's Own
Woman's Value
Woman's Way
Woman's Weekly
Woman's Weekly Fiction Special
Writers' Forum
Young Writer
Your Cat Magazine
Yours

### Letters to the Editor

Architecture Today
The Australian Women's Weekly
Bella
Best
The Big Issue
Bizarre
Caravan Magazine
Chat
Choice
Classics
Dolly
The Economist
Electrical Times
Executive PA
Fairlady
Femina Magazine
FHM (For Him Magazine)
Flora International
The Furrow
H&E Naturist
Here's Health
Modern Painters
Moneywise
Mother & Baby
My Weekly
New Law Journal
New Zealand Woman's Day
Now
Nursery Education
NW Magazine
People's Friend
PN Review
Practical Householder
Practical Parenting
The Practising Midwife
Prima
Racing Post
Retail Week
Saga Magazine
Scuba World
Ski and Board
Television
that's life!
Third Way
TV Quick
The Weekly News
What's on TV
Woman's Day

Woman's Value
Woman's Way
Woman's Weekly
Yours

## Gossip paragraphs

Australian Bookseller & Publisher
The Big Issue
Broadcast
Buses
Campaign
Church of England Newspaper
Classical Music
Country Life
Dirt Bike Rider
Electrical Times
Fairlady
Femina Magazine
FHM (For Him Magazine)
Flora International
Garden News
Geographical
Golf Weekly
Golf World
Hampshire – The County
   Magazine
Irish Medical Times
Irish Printer
Junior Magazine
The Lawyer
Marketing Week
Men Only
Minor Monthly
Mojo
Motor Cycle News
Music Week
My Weekly
New Welsh Review
Nursing Times
Opera Now
The Pink Paper
Pride Magazine
Radio Times
Retail Week
Rugby World
Runner's World
Running Fitness
Satellite Times
Scuba World
Time Out
The Voice
World Soccer
Your Dog Magazine

## Brief filler paragraphs

Active Life
The Architects' Journal
Australian Bookseller & Publisher
The Big Issue
Broadcast
Cencrastus: Scottish &
   International Literature, Arts
   and Affairs
Communicate
Country Life
The Countryman
Decanter
Electrical Times
Fairlady
Flight International
Flora International
The Furrow
Garden News
Geographical
Gibbons Stamp Monthly
Golf Weekly
Golf World
Greetings Today
Hampshire – The County
   Magazine
H&E Naturist
Health & Fitness
Horticulture Week
Hotel and Catering Review
Insurance Age
Inuit Art Quarterly
Ireland of the Welcomes
Ireland's Own
Irish Medical Times
Irish Printer
Jane's Defence Weekly
The Lawyer
Marketing Week
Men Only
Motor Cycle News
My Weekly
New Welsh Review
Nursing Times
Opera Now
Overland
Peninsular Magazine
Picture Postcard Monthly
Pig Farming
The Pink Paper
Post Magazine & Insurance Week
Pride Magazine
Radio Times
Reader's Digest
Reader's Digest (Australia)
Retail Week
Runner's World
Running Fitness
Satellite Times

Snooker Scene
Southern Cross
Studio Sound
Technology Ireland
The Times Educational
   Supplement
Trucking
Weight Watchers Magazine
The Woodworker
World Airnews
World Fishing
World Soccer
Your Dog Magazine

## Puzzles and quizzes

*The following take puzzles and/or
quizzes on an occasional or, in
some cases, regular basis. Ideas
must be tailored to suit each
publication: approach in writing
in the first instance.*

Active Life
The Australian Women's Weekly
Best of British
The Big Issue in the North
Bird Watching
Bona
Brownie
The Bulletin
The Catholic Herald
(Christchurch) The Press
Country Life
The Dandy
Dirt Bike Rider
Electrical Times
Executive PA
Fairlady
Farmer's Weekly
Femina Magazine
Fire
Flora International
FRANCE Magazine
Garden and Home
Hotel and Catering Review
Irish Medical Times
Kids Alive! (The Young Soldier)
Living and Loving
(Melbourne) Herald Sun
More
The Newspaper
Nursing Times
ontheedge
Opera Now
Performing Arts & Entertainment
   in Canada (PA&E)
Picture Postcard Monthly
Runner's World

Running Fitness
Satellite Times
Scottish Home and Country
Snooker Scene
Southern Cross
The Spectator
Take a Break
Take a Break's Take a Puzzle
The Times Literary Supplement
TV Quick
The Universe
The War Cry
Woman's Way
The Woodworker
The Word
World Soccer
Your Dog Magazine
Your Family

## UK ethnic weekly newspapers

Asian Times
Caribbean Times
Eastern Eye
The Voice

## Women's interest magazines

The Australian Women's Weekly
B
Bella
Best
Black Beauty & Hair
Bliss
Bona
Chat
Chatelaine
Company
Cosmopolitan
Diva
Elle (UK)
Essentials
Executive PA
Executive Woman
Fairlady
Femina Magazine
For Women
Girl About Town Magazine
Glamour
Good Housekeeping
Hairflair
Harpers & Queen
Harper's Bazaar
Heat
Hello!
Hiya!
Home
HQ Magazine

InStyle
Irish Tatler
Junior Magazine
The Lady
Living and Loving
Marie Claire
Modern Woman Nationwide
More
Mother & Baby
Ms London
Mslexia
My Weekly
My Weekly Story Collection
New Woman
New Woman
New Zealand Woman's Day
New Zealand Woman's Weekly
Now
Nursery World
Office Secretary (OS Magazine)
OK!
People's Friend
The Pink Paper
Pregnancy
Pride
Prima
Prima Baby
Real
Red
She
She
Take a Break
Tatler
that's life!
U magazine
Vanity Fair
Vive
Vogue
Vogue Australia
Wedding and Home
WI Home and Country
Woman
Woman Alive
Woman and Home
Woman's Day
Woman's Own
Woman's Value
Woman's Way
Woman's Weekly
Woman's Weekly Fiction Special
Women's Health
World's Children
You & Your Wedding
Your Family

## Men's interest magazines

Arena
Attitude
Country
Esquire
FHM (For Him Magazine)
Gay Times
GQ
Jack
Loaded
Maxim
Mayfair
Men Only
Men's Health
The Pink Paper

## Children's and young adult magazines

Animals and You
Aquila
The Beano
Brownie
Commando
Cosmogirl
The Dandy
Dolly
Hot Press
i-D Magazine
Mizz
The Newspaper
Pony Magazine
Scouting Magazine
Shout
Smash Hits
Young Writer

## Subject articles

### Advertising, design, printing and publishing
Arena
Australian Bookseller & Publisher
British Journalism Review
Campaign
Freelance Market News
Greetings Today
Irish Printer
Media Week
PR Week
Press Gazette
Printing World
Publishing News

### Agriculture, farming and horticulture
Country Life
The Countryman
Country Smallholding
Dairy Farmer
Farmer's Weekly
Farmers Weekly
The Field
The Grower
Horticulture Week
Irish Farmers Journal
Pig Farming
Poultry World
The Scottish Farmer
Smallholder
Straight Furrow

### Architecture and building
The Architects' Journal
Architectural Design
The Architectural Review
Architecture Today
Blueprint
Building
Building Design
Built Environment
Country Homes and Interiors
Country Life
Education Journal
Homes and Gardens
Housebuilder
Self Build & Design

### Art and collecting
AN Magazine
Antiques & Art Independent
Antiques and Collectables
Apollo
Art Business Today
Art Monthly
Art Monthly Australia

The Art Newspaper
Art Review
The Artist
Artists and Illustrators
The Book Collector
Book and Magazine Collector
The Burlington Magazine
C international contemporary art
Coin News
Contemporary
Country Life
Craftsman Magazine
Eastern Art Report
Embroidery
Gibbons Stamp Monthly
The Illustrated London News
Inuit Art Quarterly
Leisure Painter
Medal News
Modern Painters
RA Magazine
Stamp Lover
Stamp Magazine
TATE

### Aviation
Aeroplane Monthly
Aircraft & Aerospace Asia Pacific
Air International
Australian Flying
Aviation News
Flight International
Pilot
Today's Pilot
World Airnews

### Business, industry and management
Business Life
Business Scotland
Chartered Secretary
Communicate
Director
European Chemical News
Executive PA
Executive Woman
Fasttrack
Fire
Fishing News
Land & Liberty
Management Magazine
Management Today
New Impact
Office Secretary (OS Magazine)
People Management
Restaurant Magazine
SA Jewellery News
Ulster Business
The Woodworker

### Cinema and films
Campaign
The Edge
Empire
Film Review
Hotdog
Screen International
Sight and Sound
Studio Sound
Total DVD
Total Film

### Computers
Computer Weekly
Computing
MacUser
Macworld
.net The Internet Magazine
PC Advisor
PC Answers
Personal Computer World
Scientific Computing World
Total DVD
What Laptop & Handheld PC

### Economics, accountancy and finance
Accountancy
Accountancy Age
Accounting & Business
Active Life
Africa Confidential
African Business
The Australian Financial Review
The Banker
Business Scotland
Contemporary Review
Economica
The Economist
Financial Adviser
The Grower
Insurance Age
Insurance Brokers' Monthly
Investors Chronicle
Land & Liberty
MoneyMarketing
Moneywise
Pensions World
Personal Finance
Post Magazine & Insurance Week
Taxation

### Education
Aquila
Carousel – The Guide to
    Children's Books
Child Education
Education Journal

Infant Projects
Junior Education
Junior Focus
The Linguist
Modern Language Review
Music Teacher
New Impact
Nursery Education
Nursery World
Practical Parenting
Reality
Report
Right Start
Safety Education
The School Librarian
The Teacher
TES Cymru
The Times Educational
    Supplement
Times Educational Supplement
    Scotland
Times Higher Education
    Supplement
Under Five Contact
World's Children
Young People Now

## Engineering and mechanics

Car Mechanics
EA Today Magazine
EE Times
Electrical Review
Electrical Times
The Engineer
Engineering
Everyday Practical Electronics
Fire
Model Engineer
Practical Woodworking
Rail
Railway Gazette International
Railway Magazine

## Gardening

Country
Country Life
The Field
Garden and Home
Garden News
Homestyle
House & Garden
NZ House & Garden
Organic Gardening

## Health and home

Active Life
Australian Home Beautiful

Australian House and Garden
Black Beauty & Hair
British Deaf News
Choice
Classic Stitches
Country Homes and Interiors
Country Living
Garden and Home
H&E Naturist
Health & Fitness
Here's Health
Home
Homes and Gardens
Homestyle
House & Garden
House Beautiful
Ideal Home
In Balance Health & Lifestyle
    Magazine
Inspirations For Your Home
Junior Magazine
NZ House & Garden
Perfect Home
Period Living & Traditional
    Homes
Practical Householder
Practical Parenting
Prediction
Prima Baby
Running Fitness
Safety Education
Saga Magazine
Sainsbury's Magazine
Scottish Home and Country
Slimmer, Healthier, Fitter
Slimming Magazine
The Vegan
Weight Watchers Magazine
Woman's Value
Women's Health
The World of Interiors
Your Family
Your Home and Garden
Yours
Zest

## History and archaeology

Best of British
Coin News
Geographical
History Today
The Illustrated London News
In Britain
The National Trust Magazine
Picture Postcard Monthly
Scottish Memories

## Hotel, catering and leisure

Caterer & Hotelkeeper
Health Club Management
Hotel and Catering Review
The Leisure Manager

## Humour and satire

Private Eye
Viz

## Inflight magazines

Business Life

## Legal and police

Family Law
Justice of the Peace
The Lawyer
Legal Week
New Law Journal
Police Journal
Police Review
Solicitors Journal

## Leisure interests, pets

Astronomy Now
Bird Watching
Birdwatch
British Philatelic Bulletin
Camping Magazine
Canal & Riverboat
Caravan Magazine
Classic Stitches
Classics
Climber
Country Walking
Decanter
Dogs Today
Family Tree Magazine
The Field
Flora International
Folio
Gibbons Stamp Monthly
Guiding Magazine
Koi, Ponds & Gardens
The List
Military Modelling
Mixmag
Model Boats
Motor Caravan Magazine
Motorcaravan Motorhome
    Monthly (MMM)
Needlecraft
Our Dogs
Park Home & Holiday Caravan
Popular Crafts
Practical Caravan
Practical Fishkeeping

Radio Control Models and
Electronics
Scottish Field
Scouting Magazine
Scuba World
Sewing World
The Spark Magazine
Stamp Lover
Stamp Magazine
Swimming Magazine
TGO (The Great Outdoors)
Magazine
Time Out
Traditional Woodworking
Venue
Wine
The Woodworker
Workbox Magazine
Your Cat Magazine
Your Dog Magazine
Your Horse

## Literary (see also Poetry)
American Markets Newsletter
Australian Bookseller & Publisher
The Author
The Book Collector
The Bookseller
Books Ireland
British Journalism Review
Canadian Literature
Canadian Writer's Journal
Carousel – The Guide to
Children's Books
Cencrastus: Scottish &
International Literature, Arts
and Affairs
Chapman
Contemporary Review
Critical Quarterly
The Dalhousie Review
Descant
The Dickensian
The Dublin Review
The Edge
Edinburgh Review
The Fiddlehead
The Fix
Granta
Index on Censorship
International Affairs
Irish Pages: A Journal of
Contemporary Writing
Journal of Canadian Studies
The Literary Review
LOGOS
The London Magazine: A Review
of Literature and the Arts
London Review of Books

The Malahat Review
Market Newsletter
Meanjin
Modern Language Review
Mslexia
Neo-opsis Science Fiction
Magazine
New Welsh Review
The New Writer
The Oldie
Orbis
Outposts Poetry Quarterly
Overland
Peninsular Magazine
Planet
Pretext
Prospect
Publishing News
Quadrant
Queen's Quarterly
Quill & Quire
QWF
Reality
Scottish Book Collector
SHERLOCK
The Spectator
Springboard
Stand Magazine
Starburst
Studies, An Irish quarterly review
Takahe
The Third Alternative
The Times Literary Supplement
Tribune
Wascana Review of
Contemporary Poetry & Short
Fiction
The Woman Writer
Writers' Forum
Writers' News
Writing Magazine
Young Writer

## Local government and civil service
Community Care
Justice of the Peace
LGC (Local Government Chronicle)
PCS View

## Marketing and retailing
Drapers
Greetings Today
The Grocer
Marketing Week
Retail Week
Ulster Grocer

## Medicine and nursing
Balance
BMA News
British Medical Journal
Disability Now
Hospital Doctor
Irish Journal of Medical Science
Irish Medical Times
Journal of Alternative and
Complementary Medicine
Lancet
Nursery World
Nursing Times
The Practising Midwife
The Practitioner
Professional Nurse
Pulse
Therapy Weekly
This Caring Business
Veterinary Review
Young People Now

## Military
Jane's Defence Weekly
RUSI Journal

## Motor transport and cycling
Auto Express
Autocar
Back Street Heroes
Bike
Buses
Car
Car
Car Mechanics
Cars and Car Conversions
Classic & Sports Car
Classic Cars
Classics
Commercial Motor
Custom Car
Cycling Weekly
Dirt Bike Rider
Minor Monthly
Motor Cycle News
Truck & Driver
Trucking
What Car?

## Music and recording
Arena
Brass Bandworld Magazine
Classical Music
Early Music
Hi-Fi News
i-D Magazine
Jazz Journal International

Kerrang!
Making Music
Mojo
Musical Opinion
Musical Times
Music Teacher
Music Week
New Musical Express (NME)
Opera
Opera Now
Q Magazine
Record Collector
Smash Hits
The Songwriter
Songwriting and Composing
The Strad
Studio Sound
Tempo

## Natural history
Birding World
Birdwatch
Bird Watching
British Birds
Cat World
The Ecologist
Equinox
Geo Australasia
Geographical
The National Trust Magazine
Naturalist
Natural World
Nature
Our Dogs
Today's Fishkeeper

## Nautical and marine
Australian Powerboat
Canal & Riverboat
Classic Boat & The Boatman
Diver
Motor Boat and Yachting
Motor Boats Monthly
Nautical Magazine
Practical Boat Owner
Sea Breezes
Ships Monthly
Waterways World
Yachting Monthly
Yachting World
Yachts and Yachting

## Photography
Amateur Photographer
Australian Photography
The British Journal of
    Photography
Camcorder User
Camera

Freelance Photographer
Market Newsletter
Photo Life
Practical Photography
Professional Photographer
What Camcorder

## Poetry
*Some magazines only take the
occasional poem. Check with the
Editor before submitting.*

Acumen
Agenda
Ambit
Cencrastus: Scottish &
    International Literature, Arts
    and Affairs
Chapman
Cordite Poetry Review
Critical Quarterly
Cumbria and Lake District
    Magazine
Cyphers
The Dalhousie Review
Descant
Edinburgh Review
Envoi
The Fiddlehead
HQ Poetry Magazine
Irish Pages: A Journal of
    Contemporary Writing
The Literary Review
The London Magazine: A Review
    of Literature and the Arts
London Review of Books
The Malahat Review
Meanjin
New Welsh Review
Orbis
Other Poetry
Outposts Poetry Quarterly
Overland
Oxford Poetry
Peninsular Magazine
Planet
PN Review
Poetry Ireland Review/Éigse
    Éireann
Poetry Life
Poetry London
Poetry Nottingham
Poetry Review
Poetry Wales
Pretext
Pride Magazine
Quadrant
Queen's Quarterly
The Rialto

The Shop: A Magazine of Poetry
Springboard
Stand Magazine
Staple
Takahe
Wascana Review of
    Contemporary Poetry & Short
    Fiction
Young Writer

## Politics
Africa Confidential
Australian Journal of
    International Affairs
Australian Journal of Politics and
    History
The Bulletin
The China Quarterly
Christian Herald
Contemporary Review
Fortnight – An Independent
    Review of Politics and the Arts
Green Futures
The Illustrated London News
International Affairs
Justice of the Peace
New Internationalist
New Statesman
Peace News
The Political Quarterly
Prospect
Red Pepper
Studies, An Irish quarterly review
Tribune
The World Today

## Radio, TV and video
Broadcast
Cable Guide
Campaign
EA Today Magazine
Empire
Film Review
Hi-Fi News
InterMedia
Opera Now
Practical Wireless
Radio Times
Satellite Times
The Short Wave Magazine
The Stage
Studio Sound
Television
Total DVD
TV Quick
TVTimes Magazine
What's on TV

## Religion, philosophy and New Age

Africa: St Patrick's Missions
Baptist Times
The Catholic Herald
Catholic Pictorial
Catholic Times
Christian Herald
Church of England Newspaper
Church Times
Contemporary Review
Day by Day
Fortean Times
The Friend
The Furrow
Home and Family
Home Words
Jewish Chronicle
The Jewish Quarterly
Jewish Telegraph
Kids Alive! (The Young Soldier)
Life & Work
Methodist Recorder
New Humanist
Priests & People
Reality
Reform
The Sign
Southern Cross
Studies, An Irish quarterly review
The Tablet
Third Way
The Universe
The War Cry
Woman Alive
The Word

## Rural life and country

Buckinghamshire Countryside
Cambridgeshire Journal
Country
Country Life
Country Quest
The Countryman
Cumbria and Lake District
    Magazine
Dalesman
Derbyshire Life and Countryside
Dorset Life – The Dorset
    Magazine
East Lothian Life
Essex Life & Countryside
Essex Magazine and East Anglian
    Life
Evergreen
The Field
Hampshire – The County
    Magazine
Hertfordshire Countryside

In Britain
Kent Life
Lancashire Magazine
Lincolnshire Life
Lothian Life
The National Trust Magazine
The Scots Magazine
Scottish Field
Scottish Home and Country
Shooting Times and Country
    Magazine
The Shropshire Magazine
Staffordshire Life Magazine
This England
Yorkshire Ridings Magazine

## Sciences

Equinox
Focus
Geological Magazine
Nature
New Scientist
Science Progress
Scientific Computing World
Technology Ireland

## Sports and games

Ace Tennis Magazine
Angler's Mail
Angling Times
Athletics Weekly
Australian Powerboat
Boards
Bowls International
Cycle Sport
Darts World
Descent
Eventing
The Field
Fly-Fishing & Fly-Tying
FourFourTwo
Golf Monthly
Golf Weekly
Golf World
Horse & Hound
Horse and Rider
ontheedge
Our Dogs
Racing Post
Rock
Rugby World
Runner's World
Running Fitness
Scuba Diver
Scuba World
Sea Angler
Shooting Times and Country
    Magazine
Ski and Board

The Skier and The Snowboarder
    Magazine
Snooker Scene
Sport First
The Squash Player
Swimming Magazine
Tennis World
TGO (The Great Outdoors)
    Magazine
Today's Golfer
Total Off Road
Trail
Trout and Salmon
The Wisden Cricketer
The Word
World Fishing
World Soccer

## Theatre, drama and dancing (see also Cinema and films, Music and recording)

Amateur Stage
Canadian Theatre Review (CTR)
Dance Australia
Dance Today!
Dancing Times
The Illustrated London News
In Britain
New Theatre Quarterly
Performing Arts & Entertainment
    in Canada (PA&E)
Radio Times
The Stage
Tribune
TVTimes Magazine

## Travel and geography

Australian Geographic
Caravan Magazine
The China Quarterly
Condé Nast Traveller
Equinox
FRANCE Magazine
Geo Australasia
Geographical
Geographical Journal
Global
The Illustrated London News
In Britain
Ireland of the Welcomes
Traveller
Traveltalk West Coast
Wanderlust
Wild
The Witness

# Publishers of fiction

Addresses for *Book publishers UK and Ireland* start on page 135.

## Publishers of fiction
### Adventure/thrillers

Bantam
Bantam Press
Black Ace Books
Blackstaff Press Ltd
Black Swan
Bloomsbury Publishing Plc
Chatto & Windus
Constable & Robinson Ltd
Faber & Faber Ltd
Fourth Estate
Gairm Publications
The Gay Men's Press
Robert Hale Ltd
Harlequin Mills & Boon Ltd
HarperCollins
Headline Book Publishing Ltd
Hodder Headline Ltd
Honno Ltd (Welsh Women's Press)
Hutchinson
William Heinemann
Macmillan Publishers Ltd
Mentor Books
Michael Joseph
John Murray (Publishers) Ltd
The Orion Publishing Group Ltd
Penguin Group (UK)
Piatkus Books
Random House Group Ltd
Time Warner Books UK
TownHouse, Dublin
Transworld Publishers
Vintage
Virago
Warner
The X Press

### Crime/mystery/suspense

Allison & Busby Ltd
Arcadia Books Ltd
Arrow Books Ltd
Bantam
Bantam Press
Black Ace Books
Black Swan
BlackAmber Books Ltd
Blackstaff Press Ltd
Bloomsbury Publishing Plc
Breese Books Ltd
Collins Crime
Constable & Robinson Ltd
Corgi

Coronet
Everyman's Library
Faber & Faber Ltd
Flambard Press
Fourth Estate
Gairm Publications
The Gay Men's Press
Robert Hale Ltd
Hamish Hamilton
HarperCollins Publishers
Headline Book Publishing Ltd
William Heinemann
Hodder & Stoughton
Hodder Headline Ltd
Honno Ltd (Welsh Women's Press)
Hutchinson
Michael Joseph
William Heinemann
Macmillan Publishers Ltd
Mentor Books
New English Library
Oldcastle Books Ltd
Michael O'Mara Books Ltd
The Orion Publishing Group Ltd
Penguin Group (UK)
Piatkus Books
Polygon
Random House Group Ltd
Sceptre
Seren
Serpent's Tail
Severn House Publishers
Time Warner Books UK
TownHouse, Dublin
Transworld Publishers
Viking
Vintage
Virago
The Women's Press
The X Press

### Gay/lesbian

Arcadia Books Ltd
Bantam
Black Swan
Marion Boyars Publishers Ltd
Chapman Publishing
Corgi
Fourth Estate
The Gay Men's Press
Hamish Hamilton
HarperCollins Publishers
Hodder & Stoughton General

Honno Ltd (Welsh Women's Press)
Libris Ltd
Macmillan Publishers Ltd
MQ Publications Ltd
Michael O'Mara Books Ltd
Onlywomen Press Ltd
Penguin Group (UK)
Polygon
Sceptre
Serpent's Tail
Time Warner Books UK
Vintage
Virago
The Women's Press

### General

Abacus
Allison & Busby Ltd
Arcadia Books Ltd
Bantam
Bantam Press
Black Ace Books
Black Swan
BlackAmber Books Ltd
Blackstaff Press Ltd
Bloomsbury Publishing Plc
Marion Boyars Publishers Ltd
Calder Publications Ltd
Canongate Books Ltd
Jonathan Cape
Century
Chapman Publishing
Chatto & Windus
Cló Iar-Chonnachta Teo.
Corgi
Crescent Moon Publishing
Doubleday (UK)
11:9
Faber & Faber Ltd
Fourth Estate
Gairm Publications
The Gallery Press
Garnet Publishing Ltd
Victor Gollancz Ltd
Peter Halban Publishers Ltd
Robert Hale Ltd
Hamish Hamilton
Harlequin Mills & Boon Ltd
HarperCollins Publishers
Headline Book Publishing Ltd
William Heinemann
Hodder & Stoughton
Honno Ltd (Welsh Women's Press)

Hutchinson
Michael Joseph
Karnak House
Libris Ltd
Macmillan Publishers Ltd
Mentor Books
The Mercat Press
Methuen Publishing Ltd
MQ Publications Ltd
New English Library
New Island Books
The Oleander Press
Michael O'Mara Books Ltd
Onlywomen Press Ltd
The Orion Publishing Group Ltd
Paternoster
Penguin Group (UK)
Piatkus Books
Pipers' Ash Ltd
Pocket Books
Poolbeg Group Services Ltd
Random House Group Ltd
Route
Sceptre
SCP Publishers Ltd
Secker and Warburg
Seren
Serpent's Tail
Severn House Publishers
Simon & Schuster
Time Warner Books UK
Tivoli
TownHouse, Dublin
Transworld Publishers
Viking
Vintage
Virago
Warner
The Women's Press
Y Lolfa Cyf.

## Historical

Allison & Busby Ltd
Bantam
Bantam Press
Birlinn Ltd
Black Ace Books
BlackAmber Books Ltd
Blackstaff Press Ltd
Jonathan Cape
Chapman Publishing
Constable & Robinson Ltd
Doubleday (UK)
Everyman's Library
Flambard Press
Fourth Estate
The Gay Men's Press
Gollancz
Robert Hale Ltd

Harlequin Mills & Boon Ltd
HarperCollins Publishers
Headline Book Publishing Ltd
William Heinemann
Hodder & Stoughton
Honno Ltd (Welsh Women's Press)
John Hunt Publishing Ltd
Hutchinson
Michael Joseph
Karnak House
The Lilliput Press Ltd
Macmillan Publishers Ltd
Mentor Books
MQ Publications Ltd
The Oleander Press
Onlywomen Press Ltd
Penguin Group (UK)
Piatkus Books
Random House Group Ltd
Sceptre
SCP Publishers Ltd
Severn House Publishers
Time Warner Books UK
Transworld Publishers
Vintage
Virago
Warner
The Women's Press

## Literary

Abacus
Allison & Busby Ltd
Arcadia Books Ltd
Atlantic Books
Bantam
Bantam Press
Black Ace Books
Black Swan
BlackAmber Books Ltd
Blackstaff Press Ltd
Bloomsbury Publishing Plc
Marion Boyars Publishers Ltd
Calder Publications Ltd
Canongate Books Ltd
Jonathan Cape
Cassell Reference
Chapman Publishing
Chatto & Windus
Constable & Robinson Ltd
Corgi
Crescent Moon Publishing
Dedalus Ltd
Doubleday (UK)
Enitharmon Press
Everyman's Library
Faber & Faber Ltd
Flambard Press
Fourth Estate
The Gay Men's Press

Victor Gollancz Ltd
Gomer Press
Granta Publications
Peter Halban Publishers Ltd
Robert Hale Ltd
Hamish Hamilton
HarperCollins Publishers
Harvill Secker Press
Headline Book Publishing Ltd
William Heinemann
Hodder & Stoughton
Honno Ltd (Welsh Women's Press)
Hutchinson
Karnak House
Libris Ltd
The Lilliput Press Ltd
Macmillan Publishers Ltd
Mentor Books
The Mercier Press
Methuen Publishing Ltd
John Murray (Publishers) Ltd
New Beacon Books
The Oleander Press
Onlywomen Press Ltd
Peter Owen Ltd
Paternoster
Penguin Group (UK)
Piatkus Books
Picador
Polygon
Quartet Books Ltd
Random House Group Ltd
Sceptre
SCP Publishers Ltd
Scribner
Secker and Warburg
Seren
Serpent's Tail
Simon & Schuster
Skoob Russell Square
Time Warner Books UK
TownHouse, Dublin
Transworld Publishers
Viking
Vintage
Virago
The Women's Press
The X Press

## Romantic

Bantam
Bantam Press
Black Swan
Blackstaff Press Ltd
Corgi
Coronet
Doubleday (UK)
Gill & Macmillan Ltd
Harlequin Mills & Boon Ltd

Headline Book Publishing Ltd
William Heinemann
Historical™
Hodder & Stoughton
Hodder Headline Ltd
Honno Ltd (Welsh Women's Press)
Macmillan Publishers Ltd
Medical™
Mentor Books
Monarch Books
Piatkus Books
Random House Group Ltd
Red Dress Ink™
Severn House Publishers
Silhouette®
Time Warner Books UK
Transworld Publishers
Warner

## Short stories

Jonathan Cape
Chapman Publishing
Chatto & Windus
Cló Iar-Chonnachta Teo.
Everyman's Library
Faber & Faber Ltd
Flambard Press
Fourth Estate
Gairm Publications
Granta Publications
Hamish Hamilton
William Heinemann
Hodder & Stoughton
Honno Ltd (Welsh Women's Press)
Karnak House
The Lilliput Press Ltd
Macmillan Publishers Ltd
Methuen Publishing Ltd
The Octagon Press Ltd
Penguin Group (UK)
Pipers' Ash Ltd
Polygon
Random House Group Ltd
SCP Publishers Ltd
Secker and Warburg
Seren
TownHouse, Dublin
Transworld Publishers
The Women's Press
Y Lolfa Cyf.

## Other
### Ethnic
Allison & Busby Ltd
Arcadia Books Ltd
Chapman Publishing
Honno Ltd (Welsh Women's Press)

MQ Publications Ltd
Skoob Russell Square
The Women's Press
The X Press

## Erotic
Black Lace
Honno Ltd (Welsh Women's Press)
William Heinemann
Nexus
The Women's Press
X Libris

## Graphic
Knockabout Comics
Titan Books

## Horror
Black Ace Books
Gold Eagle Books
Mentor Books
Titan Books
Warner

## Humour
Allison & Busby Ltd
Black Swan
Breese Books Ltd
Corgi
Everyman's Library
Victor Gollancz Ltd
Methuen Publishing Ltd
The Oleander Press
Michael O'Mara Books Ltd
The Orion Publishing Group Ltd
Paternoster
Piccadilly Press
Time Warner Books UK
Transworld Publishers
Warner
The Women's Press

## New/experimental
Calder Publications Ltd
Canongate Books Ltd
Chapman Publishing
Crescent Moon Publishing
Faber & Faber Ltd
Flambard Press
Honno Ltd (Welsh Women's Press)
William Heinemann
Polygon
Quartet Books Ltd
Seren
Serpent's Tail
Stride Publications

## Teenage
Andersen Press Ltd
Blackwater Press
The Chicken House
Dref Wen
Egmont Books
Faber & Faber Ltd
David Fickling Books
Floris Books
HarperCollins Children's
Hodder Children's Books
Mantra
Mentor Books
Orion Children's Books
Piccadilly Press
Poolbeg Group Services Ltd
Puffin
Walker Books Ltd
The Watts Publishing Group Ltd

## Translations
Arcadia Books Ltd
Calder Publications Ltd
Canongate Books Ltd
Chapman Publishing
Cló Iar-Chonnachta Teo.
Dedalus Ltd
Enitharmon Press
Everyman's Library
Faber & Faber Ltd
Flambard Press
Gomer Press
Peter Halban Publishers Ltd
Harvill Secker Press
Honno Ltd (Welsh Women's Press)
Libris Ltd
The Oleander Press
The Orion Publishing Group Ltd
Pipers' Ash Ltd
Pushkin Press
Seren
Serpent's Tail
Skoob Russell Square
The Women's Press

## War
Calder Publications Ltd
Libris Ltd
The Orion Publishing Group Ltd
Pipers' Ash Ltd
Severn House Publishers
Time Warner Books UK
Transworld Publishers
Ulric Publishing

## Westerns
Robert Hale Ltd

# Children's book publishers and packagers

Listings for *Book publishers UK and Ireland* start on page 135 and listings for *Book packagers* start on page 225.

## Teenage fiction
### Book publishers
Andersen Press Ltd
Blackwater Press
The Chicken House
Dref Wen
Egmont Books
Faber & Faber Ltd
David Fickling Books
Floris Books
HarperCollins Children's
Hodder Children's Books
Mantra
Mentor Books
Orion Children's Books
Piccadilly Press
Poolbeg Group Services Ltd
Puffin
Walker Books Ltd
The Watts Publishing Group Ltd

## Children's fiction
### Book publishers
Andersen Press Ltd
Anvil Books/The Children's Press
Barefoot Books Ltd
Barrington Stoke
A & C Black Publishers Ltd
Bloomsbury Publishing Plc
Bodley Head Children's Books
Jonathan Cape Children's Books
Child's Play (International) Ltd
James Clarke & Co. Ltd
Cló Iar-Chonnachta Teo.
Dref Wen
Egmont Books
Evans Brothers Ltd
Everyman's Library
Faber & Faber Ltd
Floris Books
Gairm Publications
Gomer Press
Patrick Hardy Books
HarperCollins Publishers
Hippo
Hodder Children's Books
Honno Ltd (Welsh Women's Press)
House of Lochar
Hutchinson Children's Books

Kingfisher Publications plc
Ladybird
Frances Lincoln Ltd
Lion Hudson plc
Lutterworth Press
Macmillan Children's Books Ltd
Mammoth
Mantra
Kevin Mayhew Ltd
Mentor Books
The Mercier Press
Methuen Children's Books
The O'Brien Press Ltd
Orchard Books
The Orion Publishing Group Ltd
Oxford University Press
Piccadilly Press
Pipers' Ash Ltd
Point
Mathew Price Ltd
Puffin
Ragged Bears Publishing Ltd
Ransom Publishing Ltd
Red Fox Children's Books
Robinson
Saint Andrew Press
Scholastic Fiction
Scholastic Press
Scottish Children's Press
Scripture Union
Simon & Schuster
Tamarind Ltd
D.C. Thomson & Co. Ltd
Usborne Publishing Ltd
Walker Books Ltd
The Watts Publishing Group Ltd
The Women's Press
Y Lolfa Cyf.
Zero to Ten Ltd

### Book packagers
Graham-Cameron Publishing &
    Illustration
Mathew Price Ltd
Quarto Children's Books Ltd
Working Partners Ltd

## Children's non-fiction
### Book publishers
Aladdin/Watts
Anness Publishing
Apple Press
Atlantic Europe Publishing Co. Ltd
Award Publications Ltd
A & C Black Publishers Ltd
Child's Play (International) Ltd
Chrysalis Children's Books
Dref Wen
Egmont Books
Encyclopaedia Britannica (UK) Ltd
Evans Brothers Ltd
Faber & Faber Ltd
First and Best in Education Ltd
Folens Publishers
Geddes & Grosset
Gomer Press
HarperCollins Publishers
Hippo
Hodder Children's Books
Hodder Wayland
Hopscotch Educational
    Publishing Ltd
John Hunt Publishing Ltd
Kingfisher Publications plc
Ladybird
Frances Lincoln Ltd
Lion Hudson plc
Lutterworth Press
Macmillan Children's Books Ltd
Mantra
Mentor Books
The National Trust
Neate Publishing
nferNelson Publishing Co. Ltd
NMSI
The O'Brien Press Ltd
Michael O'Mara Books Ltd
The Orion Publishing Group Ltd
Oxford University Press
Paternoster
Piccadilly Press
Pipers' Ash Ltd
Portland Press Ltd
Mathew Price Ltd
Puffin
Ransom Publishing Ltd

Saint Andrew Press
Salariya Book Company Ltd
Schofield & Sims Ltd
Scholastic Children's Books
Scholastic Non-fiction
Scottish Children's Press
Scripture Union
Simon & Schuster
Tamarind Ltd
Ulric Publishing
Usborne Publishing Ltd
Walker Books Ltd
Warne
The Watts Publishing Group Ltd
The Women's Press
Y Lolfa Cyf.
Zero to Ten Ltd
Zoë Books Ltd

**Book packagers**
Aladdin Books Ltd
Andromeda Oxford Ltd
Bender Richardson White
BLA Publishing Ltd
Breslich & Foss Ltd
John Brown Junior
The Brown Reference Group Plc
Brown Wells & Jacobs Ltd
Cambridge Publishing
    Management Ltd
Design Eye Ltd
Graham-Cameron Publishing &
    Illustration
Hart McLeod Ltd
Marshall Editions Ltd
Monkey Puzzle Media Ltd
Orpheus Books Ltd
Mathew Price Ltd
Quarto Children's Books Ltd
Toucan Books Ltd
Tucker Slingsby Ltd
Wordwright Books

**Picture books**
**Book publishers**
Andersen Press Ltd
Award Publications Ltd
Barefoot Books Ltd
Bloomsbury Publishing Plc
Bodley Head Children's Books
Jonathan Cape Children's Books
Child's Play (International) Ltd
Chrysalis Children's Books
Cló Iar-Chonnachta Teo.
Dref Wen
Egmont Books
Evans Brothers Ltd
Everyman's Library
Faber & Faber Ltd

Floris Books
Gairm Publications
Geddes & Grosset
Gomer Press
HarperCollins Publishers
Hippo
Hodder Children's Books
John Hunt Publishing Ltd
Hutchinson Children's Books
Kingfisher Publications plc
Ladybird
Frances Lincoln Ltd
Lion Hudson plc
Lutterworth Press
Macmillan Children's Books Ltd
Magi Publications
Mammoth
Mantra
Methuen Children's Books
The O'Brien Press Ltd
Michael O'Mara Books Ltd
Orchard Books
The Orion Publishing Group Ltd
Oxford University Press
Paternoster
Piccadilly Press
Mathew Price Ltd
Puffin
Ragged Bears Publishing Ltd
Red Fox Children's Books
Scholastic Children's Books
Scottish Children's Press
Scripture Union
Tamarind Ltd
Usborne Publishing Ltd
Walker Books Ltd
Warne
The Watts Publishing Group Ltd
Zero to Ten Ltd

**Book packagers**
Aladdin Books Ltd
The Albion Press Ltd
Breslich & Foss Ltd
John Brown Junior
Brown Wells & Jacobs Ltd
Graham-Cameron Publishing &
    Illustration
Lion Hudson International
    Co-Editions
Marshall Editions Ltd
Mathew Price Ltd
Tangerine Designs Ltd
The Templar Company plc
Tucker Slingsby Ltd
Ventura Publishing Ltd

**Other**
**Activity and novelty**
**Book publishers**
Apple Press
Award Publications Ltd
A & C Black Publishers Ltd
Bloomsbury Publishing Plc
Child's Play (International) Ltd
Chrysalis Children's Books
Dref Wen
Egmont Books
First and Best in Education Ltd
Floris Books
Geddes & Grosset
Hippo
Hodder & Stoughton
Hodder Children's Books
Kingfisher Publications plc
Ladybird
Frances Lincoln Ltd
Lion Hudson plc
Lutterworth Press
Macmillan Children's Books Ltd
Magi Publications
Mammoth
Kevin Mayhew Ltd
Mentor Books
Methuen Children's Books
Michael O'Mara Books Ltd
Orchard Books
Oxford University Press
Pinwheel Ltd
Mathew Price Ltd
Puffin
Ransom Publishing Ltd
Robinson
Scholastic Children's Books
Scottish Children's Press
Scripture Union
Tango Books Ltd
Tarquin Publications
Treehouse Children's Books
Usborne Publishing Ltd
Walker Books Ltd
Warne
The Watts Publishing Group Ltd

**Book packagers**
Aladdin Books Ltd
Andromeda Oxford Ltd
Breslich & Foss Ltd
John Brown Junior
Brown Wells & Jacobs Ltd
Cowley Robinson Publishing Ltd
Design Eye Ltd
Lion Hudson International
    Co-Editions
Marshall Cavendish Partworks Ltd
Playne Books Ltd

Mathew Price Ltd
Quarto Children's Books Ltd
Tangerine Designs Ltd
The Templar Company plc
Emma Treehouse Ltd
Tucker Slingsby Ltd

## Audiobooks
**Book publishers**
Barefoot Books Ltd
BBC Audiobooks Ltd
Child's Play (International) Ltd
Dref Wen
HarperCollins Publishers
Hodder Children's Books
Ladybird
Mantra
The Orion Publishing Group Ltd
Random House Group Ltd
St Pauls
Scholastic Children's Books
Scripture Union
The Watts Publishing Group Ltd

## Multimedia
**Book publishers**
Atlantic Europe Publishing Co. Ltd
Ginn & Co.
HarperCollins Publishers
Heinemann Educational
Macmillan Children's Books Ltd
Mantra
Nelson Thornes Ltd
nferNelson Publishing Co. Ltd
Oxford University Press
Paternoster
Puffin
Random House Group Ltd
Ransom Publishing Ltd
St Pauls
Warne

**Book packagers**
Andromeda Oxford Ltd
John Brown Junior

## Poetry
**Book publishers**
Anvil Press Poetry
A & C Black Publishers Ltd
Bloomsbury Publishing Plc
Bodley Head Children's Books
Jonathan Cape Children's Books
Dref Wen
Evans Brothers Ltd
Everyman's Library
Faber & Faber Ltd
Gairm Publications
Gomer Press
HarperCollins Publishers
Hodder & Stoughton
Hutchinson Children's Books
Kingfisher Publications plc
Frances Lincoln Ltd
Lutterworth Press
Macmillan Children's Books Ltd
Mammoth
Methuen Children's Books
Orchard Books
Oxford University Press
Paternoster
Puffin
Red Fox Children's Books
Saint Andrew Press
Scholastic Children's Books
Scottish Children's Press
Walker Books Ltd
The Watts Publishing Group Ltd

## Religion
**Book publishers**
Atlantic Europe Publishing Co. Ltd
A & C Black Publishers Ltd
Canterbury Press Norwich
Catholic Truth Society
Christian Education
Dref Wen
Gresham Books Ltd
HarperCollins Publishers
Hodder & Stoughton

John Hunt Publishing Ltd
The Islamic Foundation
Kingfisher Publications plc
Frances Lincoln Ltd
Lion Hudson plc
Lutterworth Press
Mantra
Marshall Pickering
Kevin Mayhew Ltd
Oxford University Press
Paternoster
George Ronald
Saint Andrew Press
St Pauls
Scripture Union
Society for Promoting Christian
    Knowledge
Stacey International
Usborne Publishing Ltd
Veritas Publications
The Watts Publishing Group Ltd

**Book packagers**
The Albion Press Ltd
Lion Hudson International
    Co-Editions
Tucker Slingsby Ltd

# Publishers of plays

Playwrights are reminded that it is unusual for a publisher of trade editions of plays to publish plays which have not had at least reasonably successful, usually professional, productions on stage first. See listings beginning on page 135 for addresses.

Amber Lane Press Ltd
Brown, Son & Ferguson, Ltd
Calder Publications Ltd
Chapman Publishing
Cló Iar-Chonnachta Teo.
Colin Smythe Ltd
Cressrelles Publishing Co. Ltd
Dublar Scripts
Everyman's Library
Faber & Faber Ltd
The Gallery Press

J. Garnet Miller
Josef Weinberger Plays Ltd
Kenyon-Deane
Kevin Mayhew Ltd
The Lilliput Press Ltd
Methuen Publishing Ltd
New Playwrights' Network
New Theatre Publications/The
    Playwright Co-operative
Nick Hern Books Ltd
Oberon Books

The Oleander Press
Pipers' Ash Ltd
The Playwrights Publishing
    Company
Samuel French Ltd
SCP Publishers Ltd
Seren
Skoob Russell Square
Ward Lock Educational Co. Ltd

# Publishers of poetry

Addresses for *Book publishers UK and Ireland* start on page 135.

Anvil Press Poetry
Arc Publications
Blackstaff Press Ltd
Bloodaxe Books Ltd
Calder Publications Ltd
Carcanet Press Ltd
Chapman Publishing
Chatto & Windus
Cló Iar-Chonnachta Teo.
Crescent Moon Publishing
diehard
Enitharmon Press
Everyman Publishers plc
Faber & Faber Ltd
Flambard Press

Gairm Publications
The Gallery Press
The Goldsmith Press
Gomer Press
Headland Publications
Hippopotamus Press
Honno Ltd (Welsh Women's Press)
Jonathan Cape
Libris Ltd
The Lilliput Press Ltd
Liverpool University Press
MQ Publications Ltd
New Beacon Books
New Island Books
The Oleander Press

Onlywomen Press Ltd
Payback Press
Penguin Group (UK)
Peterloo Poets
Pipers' Ash Ltd
Polygon
Random House Group Ltd
Rivelin Grapheme Press
Saint Andrew Press
SCP Publishers Ltd
Seren
Skoob Russell Square
Stride Publications
TownHouse, Dublin

# Literary agents for children's books

The following literary agents will consider work suitable for children's books, from both authors and illustrators. Listings start on page 400. See also *Writing and the children's book market* on page 247 and *Art agents and commercial art studios* on page 440.

The Agency (London) Ltd
Darley Anderson Literary, TV
    and Film Agency
Celia Catchpole
Curtis Brown Group Ltd
Eddison Pearson Ltd
Fraser Ross Associates
Marianne Gunn O'Connor
    Literary Agency
A.M. Heath & Co. Ltd
David Higham Associates Ltd
The Inspira Group

Juvenilia
LAW Ltd
The Christopher Little Literary
    Agency
Eunice McMullen Children's
    Literary Agent Ltd
Andrew Mann Ltd
Sarah Manson Literary Agent
Martinez Literary Agency
Maggie Noach Literary Agency
PFD
Pollinger Ltd

The Lisa Richards Agency
Rogers, Coleridge & White Ltd
Elizabeth Roy Literary Agency
Rosemary Sandberg Ltd
Caroline Sheldon Literary Agency
United Authors Ltd
Ed Victor Ltd
A.P. Watt Ltd

# Literary agents for television, film, radio and theatre

Listings for these and other literary agents start on page 400.

A & B Personal Management Ltd
American Play Company Inc.
Author Literary Agents
Berman, Boals & Flynn Inc.
Blake Friedmann Literary, TV &
    Film Agency Ltd
Alan Brodie Representation Ltd
Capel & Land Ltd
Casarotto Ramsay & Associates Ltd
Jonathan Clowes Ltd
Elspeth Cochrane Personal
    Management
Rosica Colin Ltd
Jane Conway-Gordon Ltd
Richard Curtis Associates Inc.
Curtis Brown Group Ltd
Curtis Brown Ltd
Judy Daish Associates Ltd
Felix De Wolfe
Bryan Drew Ltd
Robert Dudley Agency
Ann Elmo Agency Inc.
Janet Fillingham Associates
Film Rights Ltd
The Firm
Laurence Fitch Ltd

Jill Foster Ltd
Robert A. Freedman Dramatic
    Agency Inc.
French's
Samuel French Inc.
Futerman, Rose & Associates
Juri Gabriel
Eric Glass Ltd
Antony Harwood Ltd
Richard Hatton Ltd
David Higham Associates Ltd
Valerie Hoskins Associates
Juvenilia
Michelle Kass Associates
The Lazear Agency Inc./Talkback
LBLA (Lorella Belli Literary
    Agency)
Limelight Management
Sterling Lord Literistic Inc.
Andrew Mann Ltd
Martinez Literary Agency
The Marton Agency Inc.
Blanche Marvin
MBA Literary Agents Ltd
Helen Merrill Ltd
William Morris Agency Inc.

William Morris Agency (UK) Ltd
Multimedia Product
    Development Inc.
Fifi Oscard Agency Inc.
PFD
PMA Literary and Film
    Management Inc.
PVA Management Ltd
Rosenstone/Wender
Sayle Screen Ltd
Susan Schulman Literary &
    Dramatic Agents Inc.
The Sharland Organisation Ltd
Sheil Land Associates Ltd
The Shukat Company Ltd
Micheline Steinberg Associates
Rochelle Stevens & Co.
Talent Media Group t/a ICM
The Tennyson Agency
J.M. Thurley Management
Trident Media Group
Watkins/Loomis Agency Inc.
A.P. Watt Ltd
Josef Weinberger Plays Ltd

# Newspapers and magazines which accept cartoons

Listed below are newspapers and magazines which take cartoons – either occasionally, or on a regular basis. Approach in writing in the first instance (see listings starting on pages 7, 15 and 31 for addresses) to ascertain the Editor's requirements.

## Newspapers and colour supplements

(Adelaide) Advertiser
(Brisbane) The Sunday Mail
(Christchurch) The Press
Daily Dispatch
Independent Newspapers Gauteng
Independent Newspapers
   Kwa-Zulu Natal Ltd
Independent Newspapers (South
   Africa) Ltd
(Invercargill) The Southland Times
(Melbourne) Herald Sun
(New Plymouth) The Daily News
(Sydney) The Sunday Telegraph
(Wellington) The Dominion Post

## Consumer and special interest magazines

Active Life
Aeroplane Monthly
African Business
Aquila
Art Business Today
The Author
Back Street Heroes
Bella
Best of British
The Big Issue Australia
Boards
Bowls International
British Philatelic Bulletin
Canal & Riverboat
Car
The Catholic Herald
Chapman
Christian Herald
Church of England Newspaper
Classic Cars
Computer Weekly
Computing
The Countryman
Cycle Sport
Cycling Weekly
Dance Australia
The Dandy
Dirt Bike Rider
Disability Now
Dogs Today

Dolly
East Lothian Life
EA Today Magazine
The Erotic Review
Flora International
Fortean Times
Garden News
Gay Times
Golf Monthly
Golf World
GQ
H&E Naturist
Index on Censorship
Ireland of the Welcomes
Ireland's Own
Jewish Telegraph
Kids Alive! (The Young Soldier)
Life & Work
Lothian Life
Mayfair
Men Only
Modern Woman Nationwide
More
Motor Caravan Magazine
Mslexia
New Internationalist
New Musical Express (NME)
New Scientist
New Statesman
The Oldie
Opera Now
Organic Gardening
Overland
Park Home & Holiday Caravan
Picture Postcard Monthly
Planet
Poetry Review
Pony Magazine
Pregnancy
Pride
Private Eye
Red Pepper
Reform
Rugby World
Running Fitness
Scottish Home and Country
Scouting Magazine
Sight and Sound
Ski and Board
Smallholder

The Spectator
The Squash Player
Staple
The Strad
Suffolk Norfolk Life
The Tablet
that's life!
Time Out
Tribune
Trout and Salmon
The Universe
The Vegan
Viz
The Voice
The War Cry
The Weekly News
Weight Watchers Magazine
What's on TV
WI Home and Country
The Word
Writers' Forum
Yachting Monthly
Yachting World
Young Writer
Yours

## Business and professional magazines

Accountancy
BMA News
Broadcast
Education Journal
EE Times
Electrical Review
Electrical Times
Hospital Doctor
Hotel and Catering Review
Housebuilder
Irish Medical Times
LGC (Local Government
   Chronicle)
Nursing Times
PCS View
Pilot
Police Review
Post Magazine & Insurance Week
Printing World
Therapy Weekly
Truck & Driver

# Picture agencies and libraries by subject area

This index gives the major subject area(s) only of each entry in the main listing which begins on page 463, and should be used with discrimination.

## Aerial photography
Aerofilms
Aviation Picture Library (Austin J. Brown)
Sue Cunningham Photographic
Geo Aerial Photography
Jason Hawkes Library
Sealand Aerial Photography Ltd
Skyscan Photolibrary

## Africa
Academic File News Photos
AMIS
Ancient Egypt Picture Library
Andes Press Agency
Animal Photography
Sue Cunningham Photographic
C.M. Dixon
Geoslides
Images of Africa Photobank
Link Picture Library
Tibet Pictures
Yemen Pictures

## Agriculture and farming
Stephen Benson Slide Bureau
The Anthony Blake Photo Library
Dennis Davis Photography
Ecoscene
Heritage & Natural History Photography
Holt Studios
Frank Lane Picture Agency Ltd
Sutcliffe Gallery

## Aircraft and aviation
Air Photo Supply
Aviation Picture Library (Austin J. Brown)
Dr Alan Beaumont
Photo Link
The Picture Company
Skyscan Photolibrary
TRH Pictures

## Archaeology, antiquities, ancient monuments and heritage
A.A. & A. Ancient Art & Architecture Collection
Lesley and Roy Adkins Picture Library
akg-images
Ancient Egypt Picture Library
Stephen Benson Slide Bureau
Sarah Boait Photography and Picture Library
Rev. J. Catling Allen
C.M. Dixon
English Heritage Photo Library
Werner Forman Archive
Fortean Picture Library
John Glover Photography
Heritage & Natural History Photography
Kilmartin House Trust
Photo Resources
Ritmeyer Archaeological Design
Mick Sharp Photography
Sites, Sights and Cities
Travel Photo International
York Archaeological Trust Picture Library

## Architecture, houses and interiors
A.A. & A. Ancient Art & Architecture Collection
Abode Interiors Picture Library Ltd
Arcaid Architectural Photography and Picture Library
Stephen Benson Slide Bureau
BookArt & Architecture Picture Library
Rev. J. Catling Allen
Sylvia Cordaiy Photo Library
Country Life Picture Library
Dennis Davis Photography
Edifice
English Heritage Photo Library
Werner Forman Archive
Historical Features & Photos
Houses & Interiors Photographic Features Agency

Mick Sharp Photography
Venice Picture Library

## Art, sculpture and crafts
akg-images
Allied Artists
Bodleian Library
BookArt & Architecture Picture Library
The Bridgeman Art Library
Christie's Images
Country Life Picture Library
Crafts Council Photostore®
Fine Art Photographic Library
Werner Forman Archive
National Galleries of Scotland Picture Library
National Portrait Gallery Picture Library
Ann and Bury Peerless
Photo Resources
Retrograph Nostalgia Archive
Royal Collection Enterprises
Sotheby's Picture Library
V&A Images
Venice Picture Library

## Asia
Academic File News Photos
Andes Press Agency
Australia Pictures
Das Photo
Douglas Dickins Photo Library
C.M. Dixon
Andrew N. Gagg's Photo Flora
Geoslides
Imagefinder Pte Ltd
Japan Archive
Link Picture Library
Ann and Bury Peerless
The Royal Society for Asian Affairs
Society for Anglo-Chinese Understanding
Tibet Pictures
Travel Ink Photo & Feature Library
World Religions Photo Library
Yemen Pictures

## Australia and New Zealand

Australia Pictures
George A. Dey
Geoslides
Yemen Pictures

## Britain (see also Ireland, Scotland, Wales)

Air Photo Supply
John Birdsall Social Issues Photo
  Library
Sarah Boait Photography and
  Picture Library
Britain on View
David Broadbent Birds
Rev. J. Catling Allen
COI Photo Library
Collections
English Heritage Photo Library
Jason Hawkes Library
Isle of Wight Pictures
Lakeland Life Picture Library
S. & O. Mathews
Bill Meadows Picture Library
Merseyside Photo Library
Photofusion
Skyscan Photolibrary
True North Picture Source
Simon Warner
Westcountry Pictures
Roy J. Westlake
Tim Woodcock
York Archaeological Trust Picture
  Library
Yorkshire Now!

## Business, industry and commerce

acestock.com
Financial Times Pictures
Fotoccompli – The Picture Library
Horizon International
Photolibrary.com
Christopher Ware Photography

## Children and people (see also Social issues)

Barnardo's Photographic Archive
Das Photo
Barry Davies
Angela Hampton – Family Life
  Picture Library

## Cities and towns (see also London)

Lesley and Roy Adkins Picture
  Library
Financial Times Pictures
Bill Meadows Picture Library
Sites, Sights and Cities
Skyscan Photolibrary

## Civilisations, cultures and way of life

A.A. & A. Ancient Art &
  Architecture Collection
Bryan and Cherry Alexander
  Photography
Andalucía Slide Library
Australia Pictures
Dee Conway Ballet & Dance
  Picture Library
Werner Forman Archive
Angela Hampton – Family Life
  Picture Library
The Irish Image Collection
Photo Resources
Royal Geographical Society
  Picture Library
Peter Sanders Photography Ltd
STILL PICTURES The Whole
  Earth Photo Library
Tibet Pictures
World Religions Photo Library

## Countryside and rural life (see also Landscapes)

Andalucía Slide Library
Dr Alan Beaumont
Country Life Picture Library
Forest Life Picture Library
National Museums & Galleries of
  Northern Ireland, Ulster Folk
  & Transport Museum
Wildlife Matters Photographic
  Library

## Developing countries

Exile Images
Geoslides
Nature Picture Library
Panos Pictures
STILL PICTURES The Whole
  Earth Photo Library
Tropix Photo Library
World Religions Photo Library

## Environment, conservation, ecology and habitats

Heather Angel/Natural Visions
Arctic Camera
Sylvia Cordaiy Photo Library
Ecoscene
Environmental Investigation
  Agency
Fogden Wildlife Photographs
Forest Life Picture Library
Brian Gadsby Picture Library
GeoScience Features
Martin and Dorothy Grace
Harper Horticultural Slide Library
Holt Studios
Horizon International
Frank Lane Picture Agency Ltd
Chris Mattison
Natural Image
Nature Picture Library
NHPA Ltd
OSF Ltd, Photo Library
Panos Pictures
Premaphotos Wildlife
STILL PICTURES The Whole
  Earth Photo Library
Tropix Photo Library
Colin Varndell Natural History
  Photography
Wildlife Matters Photographic
  Library

## Europe and Eastern Europe (excluding UK and Ireland)

Andalucía Slide Library
Andes Press Agency
John Birdsall Social Issues Photo
  Library
Sue Cunningham Photographic
Das Photo
C.M. Dixon
Just Europe
John Massey Stewart Picture
  Library
Medimage
Panos Pictures
Russia and Eastern Images
Skishoot – Offshoot
Charles Tait Photo Library
Venice Picture Library
Vidocq Photo Library
The Weimar Archive
David Williams Picture Library

## Fashion and lifestyle
Art Sense
V&A Images

## Food and drink
The Anthony Blake Photo Library
Cephas Picture Library
Retrograph Nostalgia Archive

## Gardens, gardening and horticulture (see also Plant life)
A–Z Botanical Collection Ltd
Arcaid Architectural Photography and Picture Library
Country Life Picture Library
Forest Life Picture Library
Garden and Wildlife Matters Photographic Library
Garden World Images
John Glover Photography
Harper Horticultural Slide Library
Hortipix/PSP Image Library
Houses & Interiors Photographic Features Agency
S. & O. Mathews
Natural Image
Tim Woodcock

## General and stock libraries
acestock.com
Alamy.com
Art Sense
Stephen Benson Slide Bureau
Chrysalis Images
Bruce Coleman Inc.
Corbis
Barry Davies
C.M. Dixon
Greg Evans International Photo Library
Fotocompli – The Picture Library
Freelance Focus
GeoScience Features
Geoslides
Getty Images
Robert Harding World Imagery
Horizon International
Huntley Film Archive
Hutchison Picture Library
Image Diggers
Imagefinder Pte Ltd
ImageState Pictor Ltd
The MacQuitty International Collection
Chandra S. Perera Cinetra
Photofusion

Photolibrary.com
Popperfoto (Paul Popper Ltd)
Raleigh International Picture Library
Retna Pictures Ltd
Dawn Runnals Photographic Library
S & G Press Agency Ltd
Topham Picturepoint
Universal Pictorial Press & Agency (UPPA)

## Geography, biogeography and topography
Arctic Camera
B. & B. Photographs
GeoScience Features
Geoslides
John Massey Stewart Picture Library
Royal Geographical Society Picture Library
Mick Sharp Photography

## Glamour, moods and nudes
Scope Features
Trevillion Picture Library
Murray Wren

## Health and medicine
Education Photos
Angela Hampton – Family Life Picture Library
Science Photo Library
Science & Society Picture Library
Shout Picture Library
Wellcome Photo Library

## High-tech, high-speed, macro/micro, special effects and step-by-step
Earth Images Picture Library
GeoScience Features
Houses & Interiors Photographic Features Agency
Microscopix
The Nature and Landscape File
NHPA Ltd
OSF Ltd, Photo Library

## History
akg-images
American History Picture Library
The Associated Press Ltd
Barnaby's Picture Library

Bodleian Library
British Library Imaging Services
Chrysalis Images
Mary Evans Picture Library
John Frost Newspapers
Heritage & Natural History Photography
Historical Features & Photos
Pat Hodgson Library & Picture Research Agency
Katz Pictures Ltd
Dave Lewis Nostalgia Collection
Elizabeth Linley Collection
London Metropolitan Archives
The Billie Love Historical Collection
Museum of London
The National Archives Image Library
National Museums & Galleries of Northern Ireland, Ulster Folk & Transport Museum
Peter Newark Picture Library
Sylvia Pitcher Photo Library
Pixfeatures
Retrograph Nostalgia Archive
Rex Features Ltd
Ann Ronan Picture Library
The Royal Society for Asian Affairs
Royal Society of Chemistry Library and Information Centre
SCR Photo Library
The Tank Museum Archive & Reference Library
Topham Picturepoint
The Weimar Archive

## Illustrations, prints, engravings, lithographs and cartoons
Allied Artists
American History Picture Library
Barnaby's Picture Library
Bodleian Library
British Library Imaging Services
CartoonStock
Mary Evans Picture Library
Fotomas Index
Pat Hodgson Library & Picture Research Agency
The Illustrated London News Picture Library
Katz Pictures Ltd
Elizabeth Linley Collection
The Billie Love Historical Collection
The National Archives Image Library

National Portrait Gallery Picture
  Library
Peter Newark Picture Library
Punch Cartoon Library
Retrograph Nostalgia Archive
Ann Ronan Picture Library
Royal Society of Chemistry
  Library and Information
  Centre
V&A Images
Western Americana Picture
  Library
Zoological Society of London

## Ireland
Collections
Heritage & Natural History
  Photography
The Irish Image Collection
National Museums & Galleries of
  Northern Ireland, Ulster Folk
  & Transport Museum
The Weimar Archive

## Landscapes and scenics
Lesley and Roy Adkins Picture
  Library
Andalucía Slide Library
Ardea Wildlife Pets Environment
BookArt & Architecture Picture
  Library
Bruce Coleman The Natural
  World
Barry Davies
George A. Dey
John Glover Photography
Hortipix/PSP Image Library
Isle of Wight Pictures
S. & O. Mathews
Bill Meadows Picture Library
Medimage
The Nature and Landscape File
The Photolibrary Wales
Railways – Milepost 92½
Raleigh International Picture
  Library
Charles Tait Photo Library
Simon Warner
Richard Welsby Photography
Roy J. Westlake
Windrush Photos
The Allan Wright Photo Library

## Latin America
Andes Press Agency
Sue Cunningham Photographic
Das Photo

## London
Jason Hawkes Library
The Illustrated London News
  Picture Library
London Metropolitan Archives
Museum of London

## Middle East
Academic File News Photos
Ancient Egypt Picture Library
Australia Pictures
Stephen Benson Slide Bureau
Das Photo
Barry Davies
Link Picture Library
Ann and Bury Peerless
World Religions Photo Library
Yemen Pictures

## Military and armed forces
Air Photo Supply
Chrysalis Images
Imperial War Museum
Military History Picture Library
The National Archives Image
  Library
The Tank Museum Archive &
  Reference Library

## Mountains
AMIS
Chris Bonington Picture Library
Hamish Brown, Scottish
  Photographic
Mountain Dynamics
Mountain Visions and Faces
Royal Geographical Society
  Picture Library
Wilderness Photographic Library

## Natural history (see also
**Environment, Plant life)**
A–Z Botanical Collection Ltd
Heather Angel/Natural Visions
Animal Photography
Ardea Wildlife Pets Environment
B. & B. Photographs
Dr Alan Beaumont
Bird Images
David Broadbent Birds
Bruce Coleman Inc.
Bruce Coleman The Natural World
Sylvia Cordaiy Photo Library
Barry Davies
Ecoscene
Environmental Investigation
  Agency
Fogden Wildlife Photographs

Christine Foord
Forest Life Picture Library
Brian Gadsby Picture Library
GeoScience Features
Martin and Dorothy Grace
Robert Harding World Imagery
Heritage & Natural History
  Photography
Hortipix/PSP Image Library
David Hosking
Image Diggers
Frank Lane Picture Agency Ltd
Michael Leach
Chris Mattison
Natural Image
The Nature and Landscape File
Nature Picture Library
NHPA Ltd
OSF Ltd, Photo Library
Papilio Natural History & Travel
  Library
Photo Resources
Premaphotos Wildlife
Roundhouse Ornithology
  Collection
RSPCA Photolibrary
Scotland in Focus Picture Library
Steffi Schubert, Wildlife
  Conservation Collection
  Photographic Library
STILL PICTURES The Whole
  Earth Photo Library
Colin Varndell Natural History
  Photography
Richard Welsby Photography
Wildlife Matters Photographic
  Library
Windrush Photos
Zoological Society of London

## Nautical and marine
Peter Cumberlidge Photo Library
National Maritime Museum
  Picture Library
National Museums & Galleries of
  Northern Ireland, Ulster Folk
  & Transport Museum

## News, features and photo features
Academic File News Photos
The Associated Press Ltd
Bandphoto Agency
Corbis
Financial Times Pictures
John Frost Newspapers
Getty Images
International Press Agency (Pty)
  Ltd

## Social issues and social history
Barnardo's Photographic Archive
BBC Photo Library
John Birdsall Social Issues Photo Library
COI Photo Library
Education Photos
Mary Evans Picture Library
Exile Images
FirePix International
Getty Images
The Illustrated London News Picture Library
Imperial War Museum
Elizabeth Linley Collection
London Metropolitan Archives
Photofusion
Ann Ronan Picture Library
RSPCA Photolibrary
Science & Society Picture Library
Shout Picture Library
Stockwave
Welfare History Picture Library
Wellcome Photo Library

## South America
Animal Photography
Australia Pictures
Stephen Benson Slide Bureau
Das Photo
David Hosking

## Space and astronomy
Bruce Coleman The Natural World
Earth Images Picture Library
Galaxy Picture Library
Genesis Space Photo Library
National Maritime Museum Picture Library
OSF Ltd, Photo Library
Science Photo Library
TRH Pictures

## Sport and leisure
Action Plus
The Associated Press Ltd
Boxing Picture Library
Michael Cole Camerawork
Sylvia Cordaiy Photo Library
Peter Dazeley

George A. Dey
Eyeline Photography
Fotosports International
Getty Images
Isle of Wight Pictures
Ludvigsen Library
Mirrorpix
Mountain Visions and Faces
PA Photos
Popperfoto (Paul Popper Ltd)
Skishoot – Offshoot
Skyscan Photolibrary
Snookerimages (Eric Whitehead Photography)
Sporting Pictures (UK) Ltd
The Still Moving Picture Company
B.M. Totterdell Photography
Universal Pictorial Press & Agency (UPPA)
Visions in Golf
Waterways Photo Library
Tim Woodcock
World Pictures

## Strange phenomena, occult and mystical
Fortean Picture Library
Image Diggers
Sites, Sights and Cities

## Transport (cars and motoring, railways)
Das Photo
George A. Dey
Ludvigsen Library
Motorcycles Unlimited
Motoring Picture Library
National Museums & Galleries of Northern Ireland, Ulster Folk & Transport Museum
Railways – Milepost 92½
Science & Society Picture Library
TRH Pictures
Christopher Ware Photography

## Travel and tourism
AA World Travel Library
acestock.com
Arcaid Architectural Photography and Picture Library

Aviation Picture Library (Austin J. Brown)
Sarah Boait Photography and Picture Library
Britain on View
Bruce Coleman Inc.
Thomas Cook Archives
Sylvia Cordaiy Photo Library
Peter Cumberlidge Photo Library
James Davis Travel Photography
Douglas Dickins Photo Library
C.M. Dixon
Ecoscene
Greg Evans International Photo Library
Brian Gadsby Picture Library
Andrew N. Gagg's Photo Flora
Getty Images
Robert Harding World Imagery
Hutchison Picture Library
The Illustrated London News Picture Library
J.S. Library International
Just Europe
Lonely Planet Images
Mountain Visions and Faces
Papilio Natural History & Travel Library
Photolibrary.com
The Picture Company
Raleigh International Picture Library
Royal Geographical Society Picture Library
Charles Tait Photo Library
Travel Ink Photo & Feature Library
Travel Photo International
Wilderness Photographic Library
World Pictures

## Wales
The Photolibrary Wales
Travel Ink Photo & Feature Library
Christopher Ware Photography
Simon Warner

## Waterways
Peter Cumberlidge Photo Library
Waterways Photo Library
Roy J. Westlake

# Prizes and awards by subject area

This index gives the major subject area(s) only of each entry in the main listing which begins on page 546, and should be used with discrimination.

The Rhys Davies Trust
European Jewish Publication
Society Grants
E.M. Forster Award
E.C. Gregory Trust Fund
Hawthornden Writers' Fellowships
Francis Head Bequest
Leverhulme Research Fellowships
The Elizabeth Longford Grants
The John Masefield Memorial
Trust
Northern Writers' Awards
Charles Pick Writing Fellowship
The Peggy Ramsay Foundation
Scottish Arts Council
The Travelling Scholarships
The Welsh National Literature
Promotion Agency and Society
for Writers
David T.K. Wong Fellowship

## Illustration

The Hans Christian Andersen
Awards
The Bisto Book of the Year Awards
Booktrust Early Years Awards
British Fantasy Awards
The Eleanor Farjeon Award
L. Ron Hubbard's Writers and
Illustrators of the Future
Contests
Images – The Best of British
Illustration
The Macmillan Prize for
Children's Picture Book
Illustration
The Jill Smythies Award
Tir Na N-og Awards
The V&A Illustration Awards

## Journalism

ABSW Science Writers Awards
British Press Awards
London Press Club Awards
George Orwell Memorial Prize
Catherine Pakenham Award

## Non-fiction

The Alexander Prize
The Australian/Vogel Literary
Award
Authors' Club Awards
The Aventis Prizes for Science
Books
The David Berry Prize
The British Academy Book Prize
British Academy Medals and Prizes
The CILIP/Whitaker Reference
Awards

The Thomas Cook Travel Book
Award
The Duff Cooper Prize
The Rose Mary Crawshay Prizes
The John D. Criticos Prize
CWA Awards
Christopher Ewart-Biggs
Memorial Prize
Gladstone History Book Prize
Glenfiddich Food & Drink
Awards
The Calvin and Rose G. Hoffman
Memorial Prize for
Distinguished Publication on
Christopher Marlowe
Jewish Quarterly Literary Prizes
The Kiriyama Prize
Kraszna-Krausz Awards
John Llewellyn Rhys Prize
The Enid McLeod Literary Prize
The Somerset Maugham Awards
Mind Book of the Year
Montana Zew Zealand Book
Awards
The Natural World Book Prize
Northern Rock Foundation
Writer's Award
The Portico Prize
Trevor Reese Memorial Prize
The Royal Society of Literature
Award under the W.H.
Heinemann Bequest
The Royal Society of
Literature/Jerwood Awards
The Royal Society of Literature
Ondaatje Prize
Runciman Award
The Saltire Society Awards
Scottish Arts Council
The André Simon Memorial
Fund Book Awards
WHSmith 'People's Choice'
Awards
Society for Theatre Research
Book Prize
The Society of Authors and The
Royal Society of Medicine
Medical Book Awards
The Sunday Times Young Writer
of the Year Award
David Watt Prize
The Whitfield Prize
The Wolfson Foundation
Yorkshire Post Book of the Year

## Photography – see Visual art

## Poetry

The Arts Council/An Chomhairle
Ealaíon, Ireland
Arts Council England
Arts Council England, London
Arvon Foundation International
Poetry Competition
Biscuit International Poetry and
Fiction Prizes
The Bridport Prize
Cardiff International Poetry
Competition
Cholmondeley Awards
The David Cohen British
Literature Prize
The T.S. Eliot Prize
The Geoffrey Faber Memorial
Prize
Forward Poetry Prizes
The Felicia Hemans Prize for
Lyrical Poetry
The Petra Kenney Poetry
Competition
Kent and Sussex Poetry Society
Open Poetry Competition
Killie Writing Competition
London Writers Competition
The Somerset Maugham Awards
National Poetry Competition
The Nestlé Smarties Book Prize
The New Writer Prose and Poetry
Prizes
Northern Rock Foundation
Writer's Award
Peterloo Poets Open Poetry
Competition
The Poetry Business Book &
Pamphlet Competition
Poetry Life Open Poetry
Competition
The Royal Society of Literature
Award under the W.H.
Heinemann Bequest
Runciman Award
The David St John Thomas
Charitable Trust Competitions
& Awards
Scottish Arts Council
John Tripp Award for Spoken
Poetry
Ver Poets Open Competition
The Welsh National Literature
Promotion Agency and Society
for Writers
Whitbread Book Awards
Writers' Week Poetry Competition

## Short stories

The Bridport Prize
The David Cohen British
  Literature Prize
CWA Awards
The Fish Short Story Prize
L. Ron Hubbard's Writers and
  Illustrators of the Future
  Contests
The Lady Short Story Competition
London Writers Competition
Bryan MacMahon Short Story
  Award
The Mathew Prichard Award for
  Short Story Writing
Real Writers Short Story Awards
The David St John Thomas
  Charitable Trust Competitions
  & Awards
The Tom-Gallon Trust Award
  and the Olive Cook Prize
Write A Story for Children
  Competition
Writers' Forum Short Story
  Competition

## Translation

Marsh Award for Children's
  Literature in Translation
The Translators Association
  Awards

## Specialist

BA/Book Data Author of the Year
The Boardman Tasker Prize
British Academy Medals and Prizes
British Book Awards
British Fantasy Awards
The CILIP/Whitaker Reference
  Awards
The Lionel Gelber Prize
The Guardian Research Fellowship
Heywood Hill Literary Prize
William Hill Sports Book of the
  Year Award
The Enid McLeod Literary Prize
The Somerset Maugham Awards
Nielsen Gold and Platinum Book
  Awards
The Nobel Prize in Literature
The Portico Prize
The Rooney Prize for Irish
  Literature
Runciman Award
The David St John Thomas
  Charitable Trust Competitions
  & Awards
The Saltire Society Awards
Scottish Arts Council
The Kim Scott Walwyn Prize
Sony Radio Academy Awards
The Spoken Word Awards

## Visual art

Artists' Residencies in Tuscany
BP Portrait Award
British Council Grants to Artists
  Scheme
Citigroup Photography Prize
The John D. Criticos Prize
EAC Art Awards for the Over 60s
The Gilchrist-Fisher Award
The Paul Hamlyn Foundation
  Awards to Artists
Hunting Art Prizes
Images – The Best of British
  Illustration
Jerwood Painting Prize
The John Kobal Foundation
  Photographic Portrait Grants
Millfield Arts Projects
John Moores 23 exhibition of
  contemporary painting
The Observer Hodge
  Award/Exhibition
RSPCA Young Photographer
  Awards
Alastair Salvesen Art Scholarship
Singer & Friedlander/Sunday
  Times Watercolour
  Competition
Wildlife Photographer of the Year

# Editorial, literary and production services by specialisation

Addresses for editorial, literary and production services start on page 643.

## Complete editorial, literary and book production services

'A Feature Factory' Editorial Services
Academic File
Anchor Editorial Services
Asterisk Design & Editorial Solutions Ltd
Book Production Consultants plc
Chase Publishing Services
Karyn Claridge Book Production
D & N Publishing
Editorial Solutions
Geo Group & Associates
Graham-Cameron Publishing
Oxford Designers & Illustrators
Pages Editorial & Publishing Services
Pagewise
Keith Povey Editorial Services
Anton Rippon Press Services
Martyn Yeo

## Advisory and consultancy services, critical assessments, reports

Academic File
Advice and Criticism Service
AESOP
Amolibros
Angel Books
Arkst Publishing
Asterisk Design & Editorial Solutions Ltd
Authors' Advisory Service
Authors' Aid
Authors Appraisal Service
Johnathon Clifford
Cornerstones & Kids' Corner Ltd
Ingrid Cranfield
FJN Associates
Geo Group & Associates
C.N. Gilmore
Rosemary Horstmann
E.J. Hunter
Indexing Specialists (UK) Ltd
Duncan McAra
Manuscript Appraisals
Ormrod Research Services

Christopher Pick
Reading and Righting (Robert Lambolle Services)
S. Ribeiro, Literary Services
Sandhurst Editorial Consultants
Sandton Literary Agency
StorytrackS
Success Writing Bureau
Teral Research Services
The Literary Consultancy (TLC)
Felicity Trotman
Gordon R. Wainwright
Wordwise
The Write Coach
Write on …
The Writers' Exchange
Hans Zell, Publishing Consultant

## Editing, copy-editing, proofreading

Aaron Editorial
Abbey Writing Services
AESOP
Amolibros
Apple Pips Editing Services
Arkst Publishing
Asterisk Design & Editorial Solutions Ltd
Authors' Aid
Beswick Writing Services
Black Ace Book Production
Blair Services
Mrs D. Buckmaster
John Button – Editorial Services
Barbara Cheney
Combrógos
Ingrid Cranfield
Dr David A. Cross
Josephine Curtis Editorial
Meg Davies
Editorial Solutions
Editorial/Visual Research
Lewis Esson Publishing
First Edition Translations Ltd
FJN Associates
Freelance Services
C.N. Gilmore
Bernard Hawton
E.J. Hunter
Indexing Specialists (UK) Ltd
Duncan McAra

McText
Manuscript Appraisals
Marlinoak
My Word!
Peter Nickol
Nidaba Publishing Services
Paul H. Niekirk
Northern Writers Advisory Services
Ormrod Research Services
OTS
Geoffrey D. Palmer
Phoenix 2
Christopher Pick
Plum Communications
Keith Povey Editorial Services
David Price
Victoria Ramsay
Reading and Righting (Robert Lambolle Services)
S. Ribeiro, Literary Services
Sandhurst Editorial Consultants
Sandton Literary Agency
SciText
Small Print
Mrs Gene M. Spencer
Strand Editorial Services
Lyn M. Taylor
The Freelance Editorial Service
Felicity Trotman
Derek Wilde
David Winpenny
Rita Winter Editorial Services
Richard M. Wright
The Writers' Exchange
Hans Zell, Publishing Consultant

## Design, typing, word processing, DTP, book production

'A Feature Factory' Editorial Services
AESOP
Arioma Editorial Services
Asterisk Design & Editorial Solutions Ltd
Authors' Aid
Black Ace Book Production
Barbara Cheney
Editorial Solutions
First Edition Translations Ltd

FJN Associates
Christine Foley Secretarial Services
Freelance Services
Shelagh Furness
Intype Libra Ltd
Marlinoak
My Word!
Peter Nickol
Nidaba Publishing Services
Northern Writers Advisory
  Services
Oriental Languages Bureau
Phoenix 2
Small Print
Special Edition Pre-press Services
Tecmedia Ltd
The Writers' Exchange

## Research and/or writing, rewriting, picture research

'A Feature Factory' Editorial
  Services
Aaron Editorial
Abbey Writing Services
Academic File
AESOP
Arioma Editorial Services
Asterisk Design & Editorial
  Solutions Ltd
Authors' Research Services
Richard M. Bennett
Beswick Writing Services
Blair Services
Causeway Resources
Combrógos
Ingrid Cranfield
Dr David A. Cross
Editorial Solutions
Editorial/Visual Research
Lewis Esson Publishing
Freelance Services
Shelagh Furness
Geo Group & Associates
Ghostwriter
Antony Hemans
The Information Bureau
Library Research Agency
Dr Kenneth Lysons
Manuscript Appraisals
Murder Files
Elizabeth Murray

Paul H. Niekirk
Ormrod Research Services
Phoenix 2
Christopher Pick
Picture Research Agency
Plum Communications
David Price
Victoria Ramsay
S. Ribeiro, Literary Services
Anton Rippon Press Services
Sandhurst Editorial Consultants
Sandton Literary Agency
Gill Shepherd
Small Print
Mrs Gene M. Spencer
Teral Research Services
Felicity Trotman
Gordon R. Wainwright
Susan Wallace
Caroline White
David L. Williams
David Winpenny
Wordwise
The Writers' Exchange
Hans Zell, Publishing Consultant

## Indexing

AESOP
Ingrid Cranfield
Meg Davies
Indexing Specialists (UK) Ltd
Janet McKerron
Paul Nash
Ormrod Research Services
Geoffrey D. Palmer
Keith Povey Editorial Services
Sandton Literary Agency
Society of Indexers
The Freelance Editorial Service
David L. Williams
Richard M. Wright
Martyn Yeo

## Translations

Ingrid Cranfield
First Edition Translations Ltd
Oriental Languages Bureau
Small Print
The Freelance Editorial Service

## Specialist services

### Archives

The Information Bureau
Murder Files
Nielsen BookData
Hans Tasiemka Archives
John Vickers

### Cartography

Reginald Piggott

### Cassettes, visual aids

Ghostwriter
OTS
Small Print

### Contracts and copyright services

Peter Nickol
Geoffrey D. Palmer

### Interpreting

First Edition Translations Ltd

### Legal services

David Wineman, Solicitors
Finers Stephens Innocent

### Media and publicity services

Agent Research & Evaluation Inc
Rosemary Dooley
Freelance Market News
Nielsen BookData
Plum Communications

### Multimedia/websites/ internet/database services

AESOP
AuthorsOnLine Ltd
Editorial Solutions
McText
My Word!
Peter Nickol
Nielsen BookData
Thoughtbubble Ltd
Martyn Yeo
Hans Zell, Publishing Consultant

# Index